Teacher's Manual

Today's Teen

Fifth Edition

GLENCOE

McGraw-Hill

New York, New York   Columbus, Ohio   Mission Hills, California   Peoria, Illinois

Contributors

Gwen Bagaas
Family and Consumer Sciences Writer
Jamestown, New York

Linda Glosson, Ph.D.
Consumer Homemaking Instructor
Wylie High School
Wylie, Texas

Barbara Smith
Family and Consumer Sciences Instructor
Biddeford Middle School
Biddeford, Maine

Glencoe/McGraw-Hill

A Division of The ***McGraw-Hill*** *Companies*

Send all inquiries to:
Glencoe/McGraw-Hill
3008 W. Willow Knolls Drive
Peoria, Illinois 61614-1083

ISBN 0-02-642784-2 (Teacher's Wraparound Edition)
ISBN 0-02-642783-4 (Student Edition)

Printed in the United States of America

1 2 3 4 5 6 7 8 9 10 RRDW 01 00 99 98 97 96

Teacher's Manual Contents

Credits

Mark Romine, TM–4
Dana White, TM–5, TM–7, TM–10, TM–23
Nancy Wood, TM–11, TM–12

Teaching with Today's Teen

The Fifth Edition of *Today's Teen* continues to retain its practical, hands-on emphasis. This comprehensive text has been strengthened and updated to reflect new information and trends in education. The upbeat tone, relevant information, and visual program make learning a positive experience for students.

Why Use Today's Teen?

With a rapidly changing world and the necessity for more and more parents or guardians to work outside the home, young teens are often faced with the responsibility of making many life management decisions. For example, many teens are responsible for choosing nutritious meals, using resources wisely, and making healthful value-based decisions. The information and concepts emphasized in the *Today's Teen* program take on an immediate application based on these needs. The revised edition combines the strengths of previous editions with improvements such as:

- Content that encourages character development.
- Special emphasis on developing leadership, management, volunteerism, cooperation, decision making, and higher-level thinking skills.
- Suggestions for using technology and computers effectively at home, at school, and within the workplace.

To meet the needs of students and teachers alike, the Fifth Edition of *Today's Teen* provides a completely integrated program of components.

- ***Student Text.*** Student oriented information and features along with colorful cartoons and photos are found in the expanded 640 pages of text.
- ***Teacher's Wraparound Edition.*** The teacher's materials include lesson plans, teaching suggestions, learning activities, and much more surrounding every page of the student text.
- ***Teacher's Classroom Resources.*** This file box of booklets provides a wealth of reproducible materials.
- ***ABCNews InterActive™ Videodiscs.*** This edition has been correlated to the ABCNews InterActive™ Videodisc series *Understanding Ourselves,* which is distributed by Glencoe/McGraw–Hill.
- ***Student Workbook.*** This booklet contains 224 pages of study guides and activities for the student that reinforce the chapter content.

> We welcome comments from teachers and students on *Today's Teen* and other Glencoe/McGraw-Hill family and consumer sciences publications.
>
> Address your letters to:
Director of Family and Consumer Sciences
Glencoe/McGraw-Hill
3008 W. Willow Knolls Drive
Peoria, Illinois 61614-1083

Using the Student Text

At the heart of the Fifth Edition of the *Today's Teen* teaching and learning program is the student text. It contains logically organized information that is visually reinforced with cartoons, drawings, and photographs.

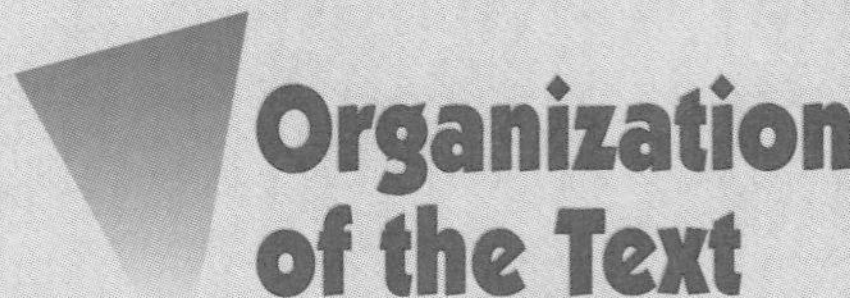

Organization of the Text

The *Today's Teen* text is divided into six units. Each unit contains chapters that deal with a major content strand.

- **Unit 1 — Self-Discovery.** Explores the changes in growth and development and answers many of the questions teens have about growing up in the world today. Special emphasis is placed on building character and self-esteem and growing toward maturity.
- **Unit 2 — Relationships.** Examines teen relationships with friends, family, and children. Special emphasis is placed on communication and building strong families.
- **Unit 3 — Resources to Manage.** Encourages teens to become good managers of personal resources as well as environmental resources. Emphasizes the role technology plays in managing resources.

- **Unit 4 — Housing.** Explores decisions about choosing housing, introduces basic design concepts and how to use design in creating a comfortable atmosphere, and emphasizes maintaining a clean, safe, and well-maintained home environment.
- **Unit 5 — Clothing.** Emphasizes clothing selection and care, maintaining and repairing clothing, and basic sewing skills. Introduces students to sewing technology that speeds up the sewing process and provides a ready-to-wear look.
- **Unit 6 — Foods.** Provides students with updated guidelines for good health, wellness, and nutrition. Special emphasis is placed on using the *Dietary Guidelines* and *Food Guide Pyramid* in meal planning in addition to buying, storing, and preparing food.

Key Chapter Elements

Each chapter of the text includes a variety of carefully planned and designed elements that enhance student interest and learning.

▼ Chapter Opener Page ▼

The first page of every chapter provides a motivational emphasis for students. It includes:

- ***A full-color photograph*** that illustrates the essence or theme of each chapter.
- ***Student Objectives*** that are written in behavioral terms. The objectives set the stage for learning and establish goals for students to work toward. You might also find these objectives helpful in planning lessons and documenting learning outcomes.

- ***Terms to Learn*** are vocabulary terms that also appear on the opening page. The terms have been chosen carefully to assist students in learning content. You will find the terms listed in order of appearance within the chapters. Each term is clearly highlighted and defined the first time it appears in the chapter. For difficult terms, pronunciation guidelines are included.

Text and Features

The text is written in an informal, enjoyable manner that provides warm examples to help students relate the text materials to everyday life. A carefully controlled reading level, the use of frequent headings to organize concepts, and a positive tone increase the text effectiveness and appeal.

The special features found in *Today's Teen* are an integral part of the program. Each feature is designed to capture student interest and extend learning. The features found in Today's Teen are as follows:

How to ...

- ***How to ...*** provides hands-on instructions that are designed to encourage the development of life skills. The "How to ..." features are directly related to chapter content.

- ***Around the World*** is a multicultural feature that exposes students to the characteristics of a culturally diverse world population. These features are informative and factual, and encourage students to understand the richness of tradition and custom found in all cultures.

- ***Career Connections*** is a two-page feature found at the end of each unit. The feature introduces students to volunteering as a way to explore career interests and gain career skills. The first-person narratives include a student volunteer talking about his or her volunteer job and two adults who decided on their chosen careers after successful volunteer experiences.

TAKING ACTION

- ***Taking Action*** is a half-page feature that encourages students to be resourceful. Each feature draws upon a chapter-related concept in which students must use decision-making and critical thinking skills. You will find this feature located at the end of every chapter just before the chapter review.

- ***Meeting Special Needs*** offers students an opportunity to gain understanding and think about ways they can help meet the needs of individuals with special needs.

- ***Safety Check*** provides students with safety tips related to chapter content.

- ***Tips*** features are short features that are sprinkled throughout the text. They extend the text information in a high-interest format.

- ***Investigate!*** features are short, single-concept labs that are related to chapter material and can be completed in a short amount of time. These features are found in Units 4, 5, and 6 and often have a science connection.

SUCCESSFUL SERGING

- ***Successful Serging*** are short features which instruct students with simple serger (overlock) sewing techniques. These features are found only in Unit 5.
- ***Recipes*** are included in the food preparation chapters of Unit 6. The recipes reflect the nutrition concepts emphasized in the *Dietary Guidelines* and the *Food Guide Pyramid*.
- ***Boxes, Charts, and Tables*** are used throughout the text to enhance and extend chapter content.

▼ Illustrations and Captions ▼

Full-color photographs, cartoons, and illustrations are used generously throughout the text. The photographs, cartoons, and illustrations are used to instruct, reinforce, and extend the text. The captions encourage discussion and the use of critical thinking skills.

▼ Chapter Review Page ▼

Every chapter ends with a full-page review. This comprehensive review section includes:

- ***Summary.*** Each summary draws out the key concepts students learn from every chapter.
- ***Facts to Recall.*** A list of factual recall questions assists students in identifying information to be learned from each chapter.
- ***Ideas to Explore.*** These discussion oriented questions and statements encourage students to utilize critical thinking skills.
- ***Activities to Try.*** Several activities accompany every chapter to provide students with an opportunity to apply

the information they have learned in the chapter. These activities promote thought and action.

LINK TO *Math*

▶ ***Link To.*** These cross-curricular features appear on every chapter review page. Each feature focuses on a different curricular connection related to the chapter material. This feature is activity oriented and encourages students to use higher-level thinking skills.

▼ Glossary and Index ▼

The glossary provides a complete listing of all of the vocabulary terms and their definitions found in the text. The number of the chapter in which each term appears is found in parentheses following each term for easy reference.

The expanded index provides a complete alphabetical listing of concepts found within the text.

The Student Workbook

The Student Workbook provides creative and varied activities that enhance student learning. For each chapter, a study guide utilizing short-answer questions is provided to guide students as they read and review the chapter material. In addition, activity sheets that extend and strengthen student learning through the use of basic skills of reading, writing, math, and critical thinking are included. The pages are perforated for easy removal.

Please note that the Student Workbook is a consumable product designed for use by one student. ***Reproduction of worksheets for classroom use is a violation of copyright***.

Using the Teacher's Wraparound Edition

As you are reading through this Teacher's Manual, you are looking at one of the most exciting new components of the *Today's Teen* program. It has been carefully constructed to provide you, the classroom teacher, with as much support and information as possible.

The Teacher's Wraparound Edition (TWE) is written in an easy-to-use format that allows you to follow along with every page of the student text. Lesson material is found with every two-page spread of text. Reduced reproductions of the student pages allow room for teaching materials along the side and bottom margins. The lesson materials fall into the following categories:

- ***Lesson Plans.*** This material provides you with motivational suggestions for each unit and chapter, comprehension questions, learning activities, and follow-up activities in the form of reteaching and enrichment activities. A number of materials that provide extension information and activities are also included within the lesson plan.
- ***Supplemental Information.*** In addition to feature boxes found in the bottom margins, you will find special "More About" boxes that provide additional information about topics covered in the student text.

Unit Opener Pages

In the Teacher's Wraparound Edition, you will find the following information to assist you in planning the unit:

- ***Planning the Unit*** provides you with a brief synopsis of the content in each chapter which will help you decide how much time to spend on each chapter.
- ***Introducing the Unit*** offers an overview of the purpose of the unit. In addition, you will find *Unit Motivators* — activities to help you capture student interest in the unit.
- ***Completing the Unit*** offers review activities and ideas for evaluation.

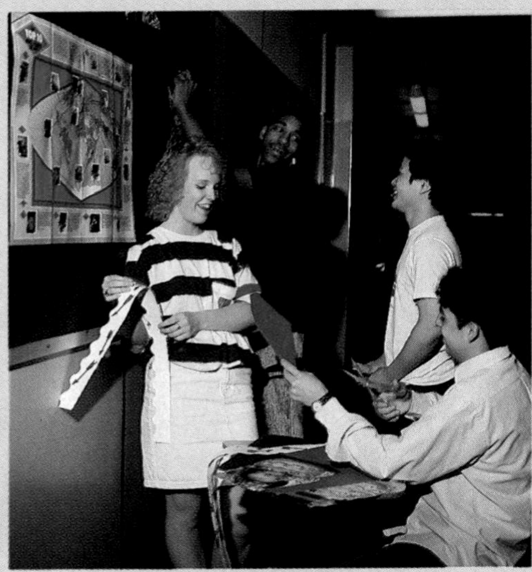

- ***Cooperative Learning*** boxes appear in the bottom margin of the unit opener pages. The left box, *Cooperative Learning Tips*, offers information on organizing cooperative learning in your classroom. The right box, *Implementing Cooperative Learning*, provides a teaching method that encourages students to work cooperatively. Both boxes coordinate with the *Cooperative Learning Activities* booklet in the Teacher's Classroom Resources file box.

Chapter Opener Pages

The side columns surrounding the chapter opener pages include the following information. (You might want to follow along on page 18 of the text as you read this description.)

- ***Chapter Outline.*** As a convenience in planning, the chapter outline includes a listing of the major headings with page numbers that indicate on which page the topics are located.
- ***Chapter Resources.*** This provides you with a listing of resource materials for the chapter that can be found in the Teacher's Classroom Resources file box. It also lists titles from the ABCNews InterActive™ Videodisc series that are relevant to the chapter.
- ***Introducing the Chapter.*** This lesson plan material helps you lay the foundation for studying the chapter. It includes the following material:
  Motivators — The motivators are helpful in creating student interest in the chapter content. The motivators may center on a discussion topic or provide a practical, hands-on activity to capture student interest.
  Chapter Objectives and Vocabulary — Effective learning takes place when students understand the purposes and goals that support what they are studying.
  Guided Reading — The study guides found in the Student Workbook are designed to help students read through the chapters in a logical, organized way.

Teaching the Chapter Content

For every chapter of the Teacher's Wraparound Edition, you will find a number of consistent elements arranged in a logical order to assist you in teaching the content on each set of facing pages. As you continue this "walk through" the Teacher's Wraparound Edition, you might want to refer to page 22 in Chapter 1.

▼ The Basic Lesson ▼

The lesson plan materials appear in the left and right side columns of every chapter. In the upper left corner of every two-page spread, you will find the header *"Teaching ..."* followed by a listing of concepts and page numbers on which the concepts are covered. For example, on page 22 you will find the header *"Teaching ... Building Self-Esteem (pp. 22-23)."* In most cases, the teaching materials relate to both pages of a two-page spread. The elements that compose the basic lesson plan are as follows:

- ***Comprehension Check*** provides you with a number of factual recall questions related to the content followed by the answers which are written in italic type.
- ***Learning Activities*** offers a number of activities to reinforce learning and meet a variety of student learning styles. You will find that each activity is identified with a boldface label and brief description of the activity. The wide range of activities includes discussion, small and large group activities, individual research, surveys, guest speakers, lab projects, and many more.
- ***Follow Up*** provides you with two special types of activities. *Reteaching* offers another way to teach the content for students that may need some additional practice or guidance in grasping concepts. *Enrichment* benefits students who need more challenge.
- ***"Theme" Boxes*** provide you with supplemental information and activities in such areas as technology, family, wellness, citizenship, and ecology.
- ***Feature Boxes.*** Every time a feature appears on a student page, you will find a related box on the same page of the TWE. This box will contain teaching suggestions, questions, and possibly answers to questions and problems found within the feature. The *How to ...*, *Investigate!*, and *Taking Action* feature boxes can always be found at the bottom of the teaching page. All other feature boxes can be found in the side margins.
- ***"More About"*** boxes provide you with information to extend student learning beyond the text. They offer another way to capture student interest.

The wide range of activities offered in every two-page spread provides you with enough material to meet student and classroom needs.

Chapter Review Pages

Every chapter lesson plan ends with *Completing the Chapter*. For your convenience, reteaching, enrichment, and evaluation materials from the Teacher's Classroom Resources are referenced here.

Career Feature Pages

In addition to providing students information about careers from a volunteer viewpoint, the Teacher's Wraparound Edition offers some additional information. The left margin of the TWE lists some possible volunteer jobs that students might work at as young teens in addition to addresses of organizations that run volunteer programs. The right margin lists a number of related careers ranging from those that require little education to those requiring a four-year (or more) degree. Related occupational organizations and their addresses are also listed. The bottom margin provides discussion ideas for the career feature along with answers to the review questions listed in the feature.

Using the Teacher's Classroom Resources (TCR)

One of the exciting new features of the *Today's Teen* program is the Teacher's Classroom Resources (TCR), a file box filled with a multitude of supplemental resources and teaching materials to meet your needs and a variety of student ability levels. Each type of material is bound in its own booklet. You may either file like materials together or file all the materials for each chapter together using the chapter divider tabs supplied in the TCR. A description of all the materials included in the TCR follows.

Reproducible Lesson Plans

These reproducible checklist style lesson plans contain a listing of all the resource materials with page references you might use in planning lessons for each chapter. All you need to do is check off the items you will be using in your lessons. They require little planning time and are easily filed.

Reteaching and Practical Skills

This booklet contains 60 activities that provide extra guidance for those students who may need a little more help grasping chapter concepts. The activities take a practical approach and tend to focus on life skills necessary to carry out a responsible and productive life. Where applicable, the activities utilize basic skills.

Extending the Lesson

These reproducible masters provide you with supplementary handouts and transparency masters. The handout masters expand chapter concepts beyond the text for in-depth learning.

The transparency masters help you introduce chapter concepts, summarize key concepts, offer discussion ideas, or help you review the chapter concepts. The transparency masters have large type for easier reading and are illustrated. They might also be used as reproducible handouts for students.

Enrichment Activities

This 80-page booklet provides you with higher level activities to challenge the more academically-able students. Some activities may provide additional information (often at a higher reading level) such as readings, charts, or simulations. Although many activities can be done in class, the activities are not limited to the classroom. Some may require students to do research outside of the classroom.

The students will be required to use one or more critical thinking skills as they work on the activities. Some of the critical thinking skills included are:

- Identifying cause and effect
- Recognizing bias

- Drawing conclusions
- Predicting consequences
- Recognizing stereotypes
- Comparing facts

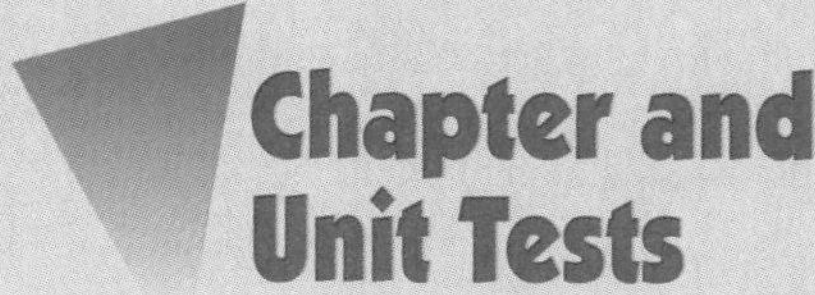

Chapter and Unit Tests

The chapter and unit tests offer you an effective way to evaluate student learning. The tests utilize two to three types of test questions per test including matching, cluster true or false, multiple choice, completion, and short answer.

In addition, two optional essay questions will be listed at the end of each test. Simply delete these questions if you do not wish to use them. The answer key is found in the back of the testing booklet.

Cooperative Learning

The cooperative learning activities found in this booklet offer students an opportunity to learn academic material and interpersonal skills at the same time.

In this booklet, you will find teacher-directed information to assist you with strategies for establishing cooperative learning in the classroom. A look at cooperative learning from an historical perspective along with methods for creating a cooperative learning environment is provided as a resource. A reproducible lesson plan is also included for your convenience. You will find an activity related to each chapter which will encourage the development of one or more cooperative skills.

Personal Safety

The activities in this booklet focus on safe behavior and awareness of possible dangers—in the home, on the street, at school, even on the Internet. Students explore ways of resolving conflicts, of being aware of their surroundings, and of protecting themselves in a variety of situations.

Technology and Computers

This booklet takes a unit-by-unit look at how technology and computers impact everyday life. Each unit contains at least one activity, handout, transparency master, and computer program to enhance student learning. The computer programs have a two-fold purpose. First, they provide students with exposure to computer programming as students are required to correctly enter the program onto either IBM (or compatible) or APPLE computers. Secondly, each program has a practical application to each unit. For example, in Unit 6 students will enter and use a program for figuring their basal metabolic rate.

Meeting the Special Needs of Students

Professional Development Series

Within today's classrooms, teachers are confronted with a great variety of educational challenges. As teachers aspire to meet the learning needs of all of their students, additional knowledge and methods of teaching may be necessary to reach this goal. *Meeting the Special Needs of Students* provides teachers with background information concerning physical, learning, and behavior disabilities that may interfere with students' ability to learn in addition to methods for meeting the needs of gifted youth.

Linking Home, School, and Community

Professional Development Series

Family and consumer sciences teachers who reach out to parents and community members can help them develop an understanding of life–management programs. Students benefit when family and community members appreciate the value of family and consumer sciences programs. This booklet provides you with ideas and steps to communicate effectively and to develop partnerships in the community.

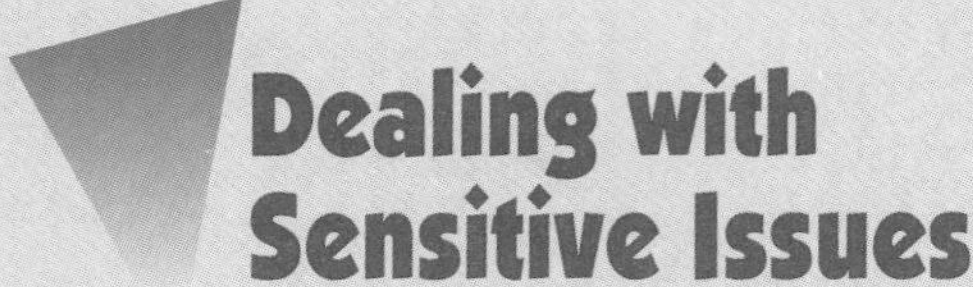

Dealing with Sensitive Issues

Professional Development Series

Family and consumer sciences programs cover many topics that are generally considered sensitive. This booklet provides background material and teaching strategies designed especially for sharing and discussing sensitive material with your students.

Leadership and Citizenship

Professional Development Series

Leadership and Citizenship offers a variety of materials to assist students in becoming effective leaders and citizens. You will find the following types of information included in this booklet:

- Suggestions for integrating leadership and citizenship in the classroom through FHA/HERO.
- An introduction to Parliamentary procedure and *Robert's Rules of Order*. Activities and worksheets that allow students to practice these leadership skills are an integral part of the booklet.
- Methods to encourage students to use leadership skills at home and at school. Activities center around making presentations and working as a team.
- Suggestions for starting school and community citizenship projects. Along with ideas on how to get organized, a number of citizenship projects and resources are included in this booklet.

Sewing and Serging Handbook

This 96-page booklet includes reproducible handouts for every sewing technique discussed in the text and many more. A special section on serger or overlock sewing has been included to assist you in teaching the students about using some of the latest of sewing technology. All handouts may be reproduced for easy use in the sewing lab.

Foods Lab Management and Recipes

The *Foods Lab Management and Recipes* booklet offers additional tips for organizing foods lab experiences. In addition to reproducible recipe sheets, ideas for menu planning, student work plans, teacher work plans, evaluation forms, and ideas for managing the lab are also included.

The reproducible recipe sheets include a recipe evaluation along with several "Think About It!" questions for student review. This helps make the foods lab a well-rounded experience. When appropriate, microwave directions are included with the recipes.

Color Transparency Package

This package offers over 50 ready-to-use full color transparencies that include photographs, charts, and other graphic forms. Specific teaching suggestions accompany each transparency to help you make effective use of every transparency. You will find them to be advantageous for introducing concepts, initiating discussion, reviewing and reinforcing concepts, and encouraging the use of critical thinking skills.

ABCNews InterActive™ Videodiscs

The ABCNews InterActive™ Videodisc series, *Understanding Ourselves,* offers programs which explore the following issues: Violence Prevention; Teenage Sexuality; Drugs and Substance Abuse; Alcohol; Tobacco; AIDS; and Food and Nutrition. For each topic, the program includes a videodisc accompanied by a guidebook with barcoded lesson plans, and a print directory. ABC News Anchor Ted Koppel provides the on–screen editorial structure. A booklet in the Teacher's Classroom Resources box correlates the programs to relevant chapters of the *Today's Teen* text.

Student Workbook Teacher's Edition

This annotated edition of the Student Workbook provides you with study guides and creative activity sheets that reinforce the concepts presented in the chapters. Answers for all study guides and activities are printed right on the activity page for your convenience.

Testmaker Software

The *Today's Teen Testmaker* is a computer software package of test items developed specifically for this text. The program allows you to personalize tests quickly and easily. You might also use the testmaker for developing pop quizzes, constructing your own study guides and review sheets, and other homework assignments. It is especially useful in constructing study materials for students who have been absent. In addition to a complete set of operating instructions, you will find this software is completely "user friendly." Testmaker software is available for Apple II, Macintosh, and IBM computers.

Teaching Effectively

Effective teaching is difficult to define, but is a joy to experience. The following information discusses some of the important areas that make up effective teaching.

Basic Skills

How is teaching basic skills relevant to *Today's Teen*? The *Today's Teen* text and supplemental program was written with the philosophy that teaching basic skills can be integrated into the six curricular strands of comprehensive family and consumer sciences. The materials presented can be used to reinforce and enhance skills that students have learned in other subject areas. By helping students to transfer these skills more effectively, the classroom teacher promotes self-confidence and success along with knowledge.

The following is an overview of how basic skills, critical thinking skills, and study skills might be taught and reinforced through the use of *Today's Teen*. Before introducing basic skills techniques in the classroom, assess the current skill levels of your students. You might consult standardized test scores, guidance counselors, and student records in this process.

▼ Reading ▼

Reading skills are essential using any textbook. The reading level of *Today's Teen* has been carefully controlled to meet student needs. Reading skills are reinforced throughout the text and its supplemental program.

The materials do not require the teacher to have special training in reading. An awareness that reading problems exist and a willingness to help students learn better by reading better are necessary. Because the needs of every class and every subject are different, it is important to reinforce reading skills in every class.

The first step is to identify students with reading problems. You might also try the simple technique of having students read aloud during the first days of class. You will be able to easily identify students who may be poor readers. There is no need to single these students out. Most of the techniques used here to improve reading are suitable for all students, but do provide poor readers with extra help and reinforcement.

Here are some practical suggestions:

- Try reading some chapters aloud (as a class or in small groups). This offers poor readers a chance to hear and see what is in the text. Hearing a passage read with expression is more helpful to a student than stumbling along from word to word alone. Vary the pace of oral reading by asking questions about sections or having students summarize what they have read or heard.

- Consider forming a volunteer reading group for assignments to be read aloud. Give students the assignment ahead of time so that they have the opportunity to practice reading unfamiliar words and phrases.
- Use the study guides in the *Student Workbook* to provide a focus for reading assignments. The student knows what to look for while reading because the questions ask for specific information. Many students cannot separate important facts from less important details. Poor readers are likely to be poor notetakers. The study guides assist students in reading more completely. They also provide a guide for reviewing the chapter information for tests.
- For students with learning disabilities, you may wish to include the text pages on which students can find the answers to questions on the study guide.
- Make sure students understand the purpose of the *Terms to Learn, Summary,* and *Facts to Recall* sections in the text. These are all reading aids and can increase learning when used consistently.
- Teach students to use all the parts of the textbook, from the table of contents to the glossary and index. This enables students to use their textbooks to clarify reading problems that may occur.
- Every curricular area has technical vocabulary that must be learned. *Today's Teen* attempts to limit the number of unfamiliar terms in each chapter to important terms. These terms are identified at the beginning of the chapter in the *Terms to Learn* section. In addition, each of the terms is shown in bold type when first used in the chapter along with a definition. Pronunciation guides are included for difficult terms.
- To give importance to learning vocabulary, give vocabulary quizzes separate from regular exams.
- Use the *Facts to Recall* section of the text for students to check their comprehension of the chapter.
- Make sure all reading assignments have an identifiable purpose or objective. Purposes might include: identifying specific details; answering questions; gaining understanding of concepts or ideas; gathering information on a topic or a question; or distinguishing fact and opinion.
- The chapter opener pages of the TWE offer several suggestions for vocabulary development. Many students have not acquired skills needed for independent vocabulary development, such as word analysis (prefixes, root words, suffixes, etc.), finding context clues to meaning, and dictionary use. By spending a few minutes on vocabulary before beginning each chapter, you can help students improve these skills.
- If your school has a reading specialist, ask for his or her help. He or she can aid in determining the reading problems most common in the class and suggest ways to overcome them.

▼ Writing ▼

Students often have little opportunity to practice writing skills outside of English classes. Writing encourages self-expression, reasoning, and organization of thoughts, as well as practice in grammar. *Today's Teen* offers a variety of writing assignments to assist students in developing these skills.

Here are some tips for encouraging good writing skills:

- Use written activities often as class or homework assignments. These assignments require more time to grade, but offer students an opportunity to practice their skills. They also give you a better idea about student understanding than objective exercises.

- Mark incorrect spelling, grammar, and punctuation whenever possible on written assignments. This makes students aware that you expect good writing and points out their mistakes.
- Insist on correct spelling of vocabulary terms.
- Have students exchange papers in groups and allow group members to assist in editing rough drafts before final copies of assignments are turned in. Make sure each group is made up of students of all skill levels.
- Provide samples of good written assignments for students to use for reference. These might include letter forms, journal entries, etc.
- Make written assignments real to students whenever possible. A letter or note written to a friend or relative describing some aspect of relationships or nutrition or perhaps an article for the school paper are examples of *real* assignments.
- Teach and encourage the use of dictionaries, periodicals, newspapers, and reference materials. These will assist the student with poor writing skills.
- Use the essay questions included at the end of the "Chapter Tests." You may wish to include additional essay or short answer questions of your own. Whenever possible, give students a choice on essay and short answer questions, such as "Answer three out of five ..."

▼ Math ▼

Math skills are easily incorporated into a family and consumer sciences class. Topics such as developing a budget, balancing a checkbook, cost comparisons, figuring basal metabolic rate, and altering the yield of a recipe provide good opportunities for students to use math skills.

If you are a little fuzzy on math skills, obtain a refresher math book for reference. This will help you to outline steps for solving various math problems and to answer questions that may arise.

Other hints for reinforcing math skills include:

- Before beginning a math-related assignment, find out the level of current student mastery. Follow this with step-by-step instructions and practice problems at the appropriate level before giving actual assignments.
- Work examples for and with students on the board or on a transparency. Have students then complete sample problems. Check the samples to make sure each student is following procedures correctly. Reteach the steps when necessary.
- Have sample problems prepared on a flip chart or in a folder for students to refer to throughout the course. These should be available for students to use as they need them.
- Check with the math teachers in your school to make sure methods of solving math problems in your course are consistent with those being taught in math courses.
- Be creative in thinking of ways to include math skills in class. Using geometry skills to create a three-dimensional model of a room for interior decorating may be just the challenge an advanced student needs to transfer skills from math to a comprehensive family and consumer sciences course.

▼ Science ▼

Science has recently been added to the basic skills category with reading, writing, and math. With a little thought, it becomes obvious that basic science skills are transferable to other subject areas. Experimentation, problem solving, and scientific methods of research can be used in many areas of family and consumer sciences. A more scientific approach to teaching may also lend additional credibility to course content and teaching methods.

Some ways to enhance student use of scientific methods include:

- Encourage students to read and think through directions on items that range from tests to managing resources to preparing a recipe. Have them follow through the steps given in directions just as they might when conducting an experiment in science class. Point out to students the importance of doing things in sequence.
- Science requires thoughtful and deliberate reading in order to ascertain facts. Encourage students to employ this type of reading when given reading for homework.
- Use a variety of graphs, charts, diagrams, and formulas when presenting information to students. This will help students to transfer their ability to use these items.
- Use scientific methods of research to solve problems. Students might use experimental and control groups to test solutions.
- Encourage students to draw conclusions and make judgments about observations they make. This is often done in science when a hypothesis is being tested.
- Help students to question how and why things work or behave as they do, rather than accepting everything they see or hear as fact.
- Make use of the computer and scientific skills required to use it when possible.
- Use the *Investigate!* features in Units 4, 5, and 6 whenever possible to help students apply scientific methods.
- Encourage the use of structured checklists, rating sheets, and surveys for gathering information in science.

Critical Thinking Skills

Critical thinking skills differ from other types of thinking in that they involve reasoning through concepts rather than simply recalling facts and ideas. Often educators are criticized for failing to teach students to think through problems in order to come up with answers. Comprehensive family and consumer sciences courses, which involve real-life problem situations, are excellent courses for encouraging students to develop critical thinking skills.

Here are some ideas for encouraging students to use critical thinking skills:

- Use problem-solving and decision-making techniques to work through a variety of real-life situations. The *Ideas to Explore* and *Activities to Try* sections of the chapter review offer students a variety of ways to utilize critical thinking skills. The *Taking Action* feature found in every chapter encourages students to develop their resourcefulness through the use of critical thinking skills.
- Encourage students to ask *who, what, when, where,* and *why* about the topics they are studying.
- Ask students thought-provoking questions and allow them some "think time" before they give an answer.
- Build on students' answers to questions by asking higher-level questions.
- Ask students to elaborate on or extend the answers they give to questions.
- Conduct activities that require students to generalize, draw relationships, evaluate, or form opinions.
- Allow students to create new ideas and products and to use creative means for expressing ideas.
- Make sure that all classroom activities, questions, and discussions have an

identifiable purpose and, on occasion, ask students to identify that purpose.

Class Discussions

In using some portions of the *Today's Teen* program, you are likely to use classroom discussion as a teaching technique. Effective, stimulating discussions rarely happen without careful planning and skilled leadership.

Before you can have a beneficial discussion, you need to consider several factors:

1. ***Climate.*** Trust is an essential component of effective classroom discussion. If students do not know each other well, they may be reluctant to participate in classroom discussions. You may want to use ice breaker activities to help students get used to expressing their opinions and feelings. For example, have students write several things about themselves that their classmates probably don't know on an index card. Collect the cards in a basket, draw out and read the cards. Students must then link a classmate to the descriptions on each card. This results in students that know each other better.
2. ***Consideration.*** An attitude of respect is absolutely essential for good discussions. Students must understand that each person is entitled to his or her opinion. It is acceptable to disagree, but it is not acceptable to make personal attacks on classmates. Allow for humor as long as it does not lead to disrespect toward any person.
3. ***Content.*** Discussion topics must be valuable and relevant to students in their current situations. An interesting discussion is not likely to happen if students have no interest in, or understanding of, the subject. Be sure to provide the background information necessary for good discussion.

If your discussion topic is controversial, exercise some caution. You may want to talk with your principal first for suggestions on how to handle this situation. In some cases, you might want to send a letter home to parents or invite parents to preview materials before you present them to the class.

Discussion Format

A common discussion format involves the classroom teacher standing before the class and leading the discussion. Here are a few other formats you may want to try:

- Sit down with the students so that you are not as much of an authority figure. You may find that students talk more easily and freely with each other rather than just with you.
- Arrange chairs in a circle so students face each other. This encourages student exchange of ideas.
- Use small discussion groups. This is often less intimidating for students. Make sure that students are accountable for their discussions. Perhaps appoint someone to take notes on the discussion.
- Divide students into teams to debate an issue or have two students present opposing views to the class. Follow this up by having the class critique the presentations.

Managing Class Discussions

What techniques are helpful in facilitating an effective discussion? This is often the most challenging part of classroom discussions. Here are a few helpful suggestions:

- Be enthusiastic! If students sense your interest, they are more likely to participate.
- Allow time for students to respond. It takes some students longer than others to process ideas.
- Try to involve everyone. Often the quietest students have wonderful ideas

to share. They just need to be sensitively and carefully drawn out.

- Avoid using *yes* and *no* questions. Formulating your questions ahead of time helps foster good discussions.
- Encourage the use of critical thinking skills such as making inferences, drawing conclusions, identifying cause and effect, recognizing bias, etc.
- Evaluate the results of discussions. Some discussions are more successful than others. Take time for reflection and make notes on what worked and what didn't work in your class.

Journal Writing

W. H. Auden has been quoted as saying "How do I know what I think until I see what I've written?" This question summarizes the value in keeping a journal. Keeping a journal offers students an opportunity to write down their thoughts, feelings, and reflections. It provides a less-threatening way for students to process information. It also provides you with an effective tool for evaluating student understanding.

Because journals are personal, it is essential to recognize student privacy and reinforce this with the class.

There are a number of ways to approach journal writing with students. One method involves having students daily reflect on what they have learned. What are their thoughts, feelings, and reactions? Many "beginning journal writers," however, need some guidance. You might try offering students hypothetical situations to respond to. Another effective way to help students get started is to provide open-ended sentences for students to respond to. For example, when studying values you might ask students to respond to: "The most important value I hold is ..."

Journal writing is a valuable and effective learning tool when used with sensitivity and consistency.

Resource List

Unit 1 — Self-Discovery

References

Succeeding in the World of Work by Grady Kimbrell and Dr. Ben Vineyard. Columbus, OH: Glencoe, 1992.

Teen Guide by Dr. Valerie Chamberlain. Columbus, OH: Glencoe, 1990.

Young Living by Nanalee Clayton. Columbus, OH: Glencoe, 1990.

Audiovisual Materials

Leadership Skills. (2 filmstrips, 2 cassettes, guide.)
Glencoe
936 Eastwind Drive
Westerville, OH 43081-3374
(614-890-1111)

Understanding Decisions. (Video, guide.) Learning Tree.

Unit 2 — Relationships

References

Coping with Teen Parenting by Kay Beyer. New York: Rosen Group, 1990.

Parenting: Rewards and Responsibilities by Dr. Verna Hildebrand. Columbus, OH: Glencoe, 1997.

Small Group Decision Making: Communication and the Group Process by B. Aubrey Fisher. New York: McGraw-Hill, 1990.

Young Living by Nanalee Clayton. Columbus, OH: Glencoe, 1997.

Audiovisual Materials

Child Development: Ages and Stages. (Filmstrip, cassettes, guide.)
Glencoe
936 Eastwind Drive
Westerville, OH 43081-3374
(614-890-1111)

Dating: Coping with the Pressures. (3 filmstrips with cassettes, guide.)
Source: Sunburst Communications
101 Castelton Street
Pleasantville, NY 10570

Parent-Child Relationships. (4 filmstrips with cassettes, guide.) (Video, guide.)
Glencoe
936 Eastwind Drive
Westerville, OH 43081-3374
(614-890-1111)

Organizations

Educational Resources Information Center (ERIC)

Early Childhood Education, 805 W. Pennsylvania Ave., Urbana, IL 61801

Unit 3 — Resources to Manage

References

Consumer Education and Economics by Ross Lowe, Charles Malouf, Annette Jacobson, and James Niss. Columbus, OH: Glencoe, 1997.

Save Our Planet by Diane MacEachern. New York: Dell Publishing, 1990.

Teen Guide by Dr. Valerie Chamberlain. Columbus, OH: Glencoe, 1990.

Organizations

Consumer Information Center, Pueblo, CO 81009

U. S. Consumer Product Safety Commission, Washington, DC 20207

Underwriters Laboratories, Inc., 333 Pfingsten Road, Northbrook, IL 60062 (708-272-8800)

Audiovisual Materials

Handling Your Money. (Video, guide.) Educational Design.

Just in Time (ideas and technology). (Video.) West Glen Communications.

Unit 4 — Housing

References

Decor-Aide Space Planner. (Room planning kit that includes hundreds of easy-to-use templates and tips for furniture arrangement.)
Source: Decor-Aide
P.O. Box 2873
Alameda, CA 94501

Homes Today and Tomorrow by Ruth Sherwood. Columbus, OH: Glencoe, 1997.

The Room Planning Guide. (Kit designed to help plan a room and arrange furniture. Free.)
Source: Furniture Information Council
P.O. Box HP7
High Point, NC 27261

Audiovisual Materials

One Month's Rent in Advance (Housing: Renting and Buying). (Video, reproductable activities.)
Source: C. W. Publications
Box 744
Sterling, IL 61081

Making the Right Move: The Apartment Rental Game. (Video, guide.)
Source: Cambridge Video
P.O. Box 2153
Charleston, WV 25328

Simple Household Repairs. (3 filmstrips and cassettes, discussion guide. Purchase.)
Source: Franklin Clay Films
P.O. Box CDE-2036
Costa Mesa, CA 92638-1036

Unit 5 — Clothing

References

10-20-30 Minutes to Sew by Nancy Zieman, 1992.
Source: Book Division of Southern Progress Corporation
P.O. Box 2463
Birmingham, AL 35201

Clothing: Fashion, Fabrics, and Construction by Jeanette Weber. Columbus, OH: Glencoe, 1997.

Creative Serging Illustrated by Palmer, Brown, and Green, 1987.

Modern Textiles, 3rd ed. by Lyle and Kness, 1990.
Source: Macmillan Publishing Company
866 Third Avenue
New York, NY 10022

Sew News. PJS Publications, Inc., News Plaza, P.O. Box 1790, Peoria, IL 61656

Audiovisual Materials

Laundry Care Means Longer Wear. (2 filmstrips, 2 cassettes, teacher's guide. VHS. BETA videocassette. Purchase.)

Your Clothes Are Showing: Line and Design. (2 filmstrips, 2 cassettes, teacher's guide. VHS. BETA videocassette. Purchase.)
Source: Franklin Clay Films
P.O. Box KX-2808
Costa Mesa, CA 92628-2808

Unit 6 — Foods

References

Discovering Food by Helen Kowtaluk. Columbus, OH: Glencoe, 1997.

Food for Today by Helen Kowtaluk and Alice O. Kopan. Columbus, OH: Glencoe, 1997.

Modern Meals by Roberta Duyff, Doris Hasler, and Suzanne Stickler Ohl. Columbus, OH: Glencoe, 1990.

Your Food — Chance or Choice?
Source: National Dairy Council
6300 North River Road
Rosemont, IL 60018-4233

Organizations

The American Dietetic Association, 216 West Jackson Blvd., Chicago, IL 60606-6995

Human Nutrition Information Service, The United States Department of Agriculture, 6505 Belcrest Road, Hyattsville, MD 20782

Kansas Wheat Commission, 2630 Claflin Road, Manhattan, KS 66502

Kraft General Foods, Inc., Technology Center, 801 Waukegan Road, Glenview, IL 60025

National Dairy Council, 6300 North River Road, Rosemont, IL 60018

United States Department of Agriculture. *Dietary Guidelines for Americans.* Washington, DC: U.S. Government Printing Office, 1990

Audiovisual Materials

Kitchen Measurements. (Filmstrip with cassette, guide.)
Source: Guidance Associates
Communications Park
Box 3000
Mount Kisco, NY 10549

Label Literacy: How to Read Food Packaging. (2 filmstrips with cassettes, guide.)
Source: Sunburst Communications
101 Castelton Street
Pleasantville, NY 10570-9971

Nutrition on the Run: Snacks and Fast Foods. (3 filmstrips, 3 cassettes, student activity booklets, teacher's guide.) Sunburst Communications.

Supermarket Shopping: A Guide to Grocery Store Services. (Filmstrip with cassette, guide.)
Source: Glencoe
936 Eastwind Drive
Westerville, OH 43081-3374
(614-890-1111)

General Audiovisual Materials

Cambridge Educational, P.O. Box 2153, Dept. FN1, Charleston, WV 25328-2153 (800-486-4227)

Coronet/MTI Film and Video, 108 Wilmont Road, Deerfield, IL 60015-9925 (800-621-2131)

Glencoe, 936 Eastwind Drive, Westerville, OH 43081-3374 (614-890-1111)

The Learning Seed, 330 Telser Road, Lake Zurich, IL 60047 (800-634-4941)

Nasco, 901 Hanesville Avenue, P.O. Box 901, Fort Atkinson, WI 53538-0901 (800-558-9595)

National Audiovisual Center, National Archives and Records Administration, 8700 Edgeworth Drive, Capitol Heights, MD 20743-3701 (301-763-1891)

The Polished Apple, 3742 Seahorn Drive, Malibu, CA 90265-5699 (213-459-2630)

Sunburst Communications, 39 Washington Avenue, P.O. Box 40, Pleasantville, NY 10570-3498 (800-431-1934)

Scope and Sequence

Unit 1 — Self-Discovery

Self-Esteem	Ch. 1: Making the Most of Yourself Ch. 2: Your Values and Goals Ch. 3: Citizenship and Leadership
Relationship Skills	Ch. 2: Your Values and Goals Ch. 3: Making Decisions and Managing Your Life Ch. 5: Moving Toward Maturity Ch. 7: Exploring Careers
Wellness	Ch. 3: Making Decisions and Managing Your Life Ch. 4: Coping with Change and Stress Ch. 5: Moving Toward Maturity
Decision Making	Ch. 3: Making Decisions and Managing Your Life Ch. 4: Coping with Change and Stress Ch. 5: Moving Toward Maturity Ch. 6: Citizenship and Leadership Ch. 7: Exploring Careers
Resources and Management	Ch. 1: Making the Most of Yourself Ch. 2: Your Values and Goals Ch. 3: Making Decisions and Managing Your Life Ch. 4: Coping with Change and Stress Ch. 6: Citizenship and Leadership Ch. 7: Exploring Careers
Communication	Ch. 1: Making the Most of Yourself Ch. 4: Coping with Change and Stress Ch. 6: Citizenship and Leadership Ch. 7: Exploring Careers
Skill Development	Ch. 3: Making Decisions and Managing Your Life Ch. 4: Coping with Change and Stress Ch. 5: Moving Toward Maturity Ch. 7: Exploring Careers

Unit 2 — Relationships

Self-Esteem	Ch. 9: Improving Relationship Skills Ch. 10: Friends and You Ch. 11: Dating Ch. 13: Building a Strong Family Ch. 14: Handling Challenges Ch. 15: Understanding How Children Grow Ch. 17: A Look at Parenting
Relationship Skills	Ch. 8: Communicating Effectively Ch. 9: Improving Relationship Skills Ch. 10: Friends and You Ch. 11: Dating Ch. 12: A Look at Families Ch. 13: Building a Strong Family Ch. 14: Handling Challenges Ch. 15: Understanding How Children Grow Ch. 16: Taking Care of Children Ch. 17: A Look at Parenting
Wellness	Ch. 10: Friends and You Ch. 13: Building a Strong Family Ch. 14: Handling Challenges Ch. 15: Understanding How Children Grow Ch. 16: Taking Care of Children
Decision Making	Ch. 9: Improving Relationship Skills Ch. 11: Dating Ch. 14: Handling Challenges Ch. 17: A Look at Parenting
Resources and Management	Ch. 9: Improving Relationship Skills Ch. 10: Friends and You Ch. 12: A Look at Families Ch. 13: Building a Strong Family Ch. 14: Handling Challenges Ch. 17: A Look at Parenting
Communication	Ch. 8: Communicating Effectively Ch. 9: Improving Relationship Skills Ch. 12: A Look at Families Ch. 14: Handling Challenges Ch. 16: Caring for Children Ch. 17: A Look at Parenting

Unit 2 (Continued)

Skill Development	Ch. 8: Communicating Effectively Ch. 9: Improving Relationship Skills Ch. 12: A Look at Families Ch. 14: Handling Challenges Ch. 16: Caring for Children Ch. 17: A Look at Parenting

Unit 3 — Resources to Manage

Self-Esteem	Ch. 18: Managing Time and Energy
Relationship Skills	Ch. 18: Managing Time and Energy Ch. 21: Technology as a Resource
Wellness	Ch. 18: Managing Time and Energy Ch. 21: Technology as a Resource Ch. 22: Natural Resources
Decision Making	Ch. 18: Managing Time and Energy Ch. 19: Managing Money Ch. 20: Consumer Challenges Ch. 22: Natural Resources
Resources and Management	Ch. 18: Managing Time and Energy Ch. 19: Managing Money Ch. 20: Consumer Challenges Ch. 21: Technology as a Resource Ch. 22: Natural Resources
Communication	Ch. 20: Consumer Challenges Ch. 21: Technology as a Resource
Skill Development	Ch. 18: Managing Time and Energy Ch. 19: Managing Money Ch. 22: Natural Resources

Unit 4 — Housing

Self-Esteem	Ch. 23: Looking at Housing Choices
Relationship Skills	Ch. 23: Looking at Housing Choices Ch. 25: Making Design Work for You Ch. 26: Keeping Your Home Clean and Safe
Wellness	Ch. 23: Looking at Housing Choices Ch. 26: Keeping Your Home Clean and Safe
Decision Making	Ch. 23: Looking at Housing Choices Ch. 24: Making Design Work for You Ch. 25: Keeping Your Home Clean and Safe
Resources and Management	Ch. 23: Looking at Housing Choices Ch. 24: Understanding the Art of Design Ch. 25: Making Design Work for You
Communication	Ch. 24: Understanding the Art of Design Ch. 25: Making Design Work for You Ch. 26: Keeping Your Home Clean and Safe
Skill Development	Ch. 25: Making Design Work for You Ch. 26: Keeping Your Home Clean and Safe

Unit 5 — Clothing

Self-Esteem	Ch. 27: Looking Your Best
Relationship Skills	Ch. 27: Looking Your Best Ch. 28: Selecting Clothing
Wellness	Ch. 27: Looking Your Best Ch. 30: Caring for Clothing
Decision Making	Ch. 28: Selecting Clothing Ch. 29: Fibers to Fabrics Ch. 31: Selecting a Pattern Ch. 32: Fabrics and Notions Ch. 34: Preparing to Sew
Resources to Manage	Ch. 28: Selecting Clothing Ch. 29: Fibers to Fabrics Ch. 31: Selecting a Pattern Ch. 32: Fabric and Notions Ch. 33: Sewing Equipment

Unit 5 (Continued)

Communication	Ch. 27: Selecting Clothing Ch. 30: Caring for Clothing
Skill Development	Ch. 28: Selecting Clothing Ch. 30: Caring for Clothing Ch. 32: Fabric and Notions Ch. 33: Sewing Equipment Ch. 34: Preparing to Sew Ch. 35: Basic Sewing Essentials Ch. 36: Challenging Sewing Essentials

Unit 6 — Foods

Self-Esteem	Ch. 40: Managing Your Weight
Relationship Skills	Ch. 37: Staying Healthy Ch. 47: Working in the Kitchen Ch. 52: Etiquette and Eating Out
Wellness	Ch. 37: Staying Healthy Ch. 38: Nutrients and Their Functions Ch. 39: Guidelines for Healthful Eating Ch. 40: Managing Your Weight Ch. 41: Facts for Food Choices Ch. 42: Planning Meals and Snacks Ch. 43: Buying and Storing Food Ch. 47: Working in the Kitchen Ch. 48: Milk and Milk Products Ch. 49: Fruits and Vegetables Ch. 50: Protein Foods Ch. 51: Grain Products
Decision Making	Ch. 39: Guidelines for Healthful Eating Ch. 40: Managing Your Weight Ch. 41: Facts for Food Choices Ch. 42: Planning Meals and Snacks Ch. 43: Buying and Storing Food Ch. 45: Recipes and Measuring

Unit 6 (Continued)

Resources and Management	Ch. 37: Staying Healthy Ch. 38: Nutrients and Their Functions Ch. 40: Managing Your Weight Ch. 42: Planning Meals and Snacks Ch. 43: Buying and Storing Food Ch. 44: Kitchen Equipment
Communication	Ch. 37: Staying Healthy Ch. 41: Facts for Food Choices Ch. 45: Recipes and Measuring Ch. 46: Preparation Terms and Techniques
Skill Development	Ch. 37: Staying Healthy Ch. 38: Nutrients and Their Functions Ch. 40: Managing Your Weight Ch. 41: Facts for Food Choices Ch. 42: Planning Meals and Snacks Ch. 43: Buying and Storing Food Ch. 46: Preparation Terms and Techniques Ch. 47: Working in the Kitchen Ch. 48: Milk and Milk Products Ch. 49: Fruits and Vegetables Ch. 50: Protein Foods Ch. 51: Grain Products Ch. 52: Etiquette and Eating Out

Today's Teen

Fifth Edition

Teacher's Wraparound Edition

Joan Kelly-Plate, Ed.D.
Former Associate Professor
Department of Home Economics Education
Texas Tech University

Eddye Eubanks, Ph.D.
Education Specialist
Formerly of the Texas Education Agency

Today's Teen

Fifth Edition

GLENCOE
McGraw-Hill
New York, New York Columbus, Ohio Mission Hills, California Peoria, Illinois

Glencoe/McGraw-Hill 

A Division of The ***McGraw-Hill*** *Companies*

Send all inquiries to:
Glencoe/McGraw-Hill
3008 W. Willow Knolls Drive
Peoria, Illinois 61614-1083

ISBN 0-02-642783-4 (Student Edition)
ISBN 0-02-642784-2 (Teacher's Wraparound Edition)

Printed in the United States of America

1 2 3 4 5 6 7 8 9 10 RRDW 00 99 98 97 96

Contributors

Linda Glosson, Ph.D.
Consumer Homemaking Instructor
Wylie High School
Wylie, Texas

Mark Bregman

Christine Venzon

Reviewers

Catherine Gay
Home Economics Instructor
Pinellas County Schools
St. Petersburg, Florida

Linda Glosson, Ph.D.
Consumer Homemaking Instructor
Wylie High School
Wylie, Texas

Ann Price Gosch
Clothing and Textiles Writer
Tacoma, Washington

Chris Moore
Home Economics Instructor
Salt Lake City, Utah

Joanne Reid
Supervisor of Special Vocational Populations
and Occupational Home Economics
Evansville-Vanderburgh School Corporation
Evansville, Indiana

Contents

Unit 1 — Self-Discovery 16

Unit 2 — Relationships 98

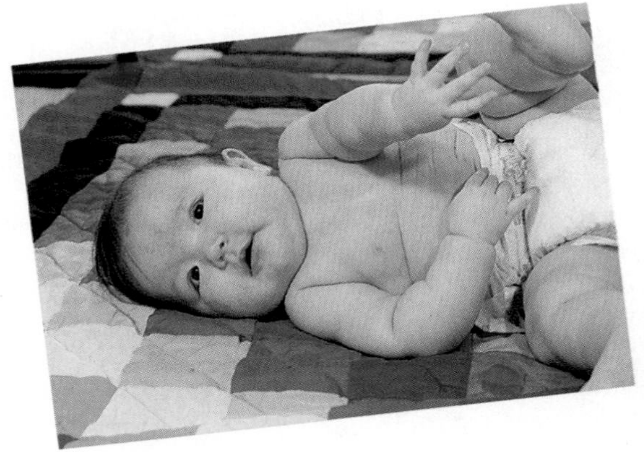

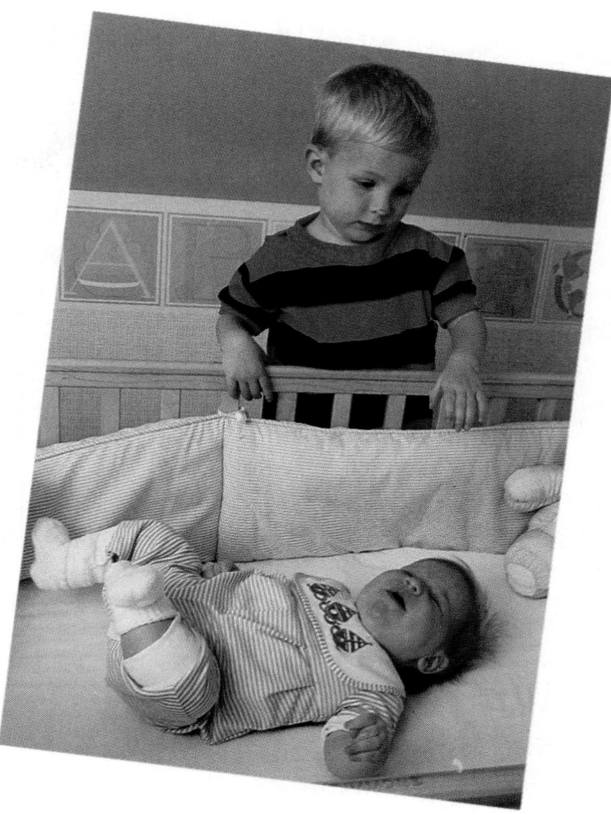

Unit 3 — Resources to Manage 192

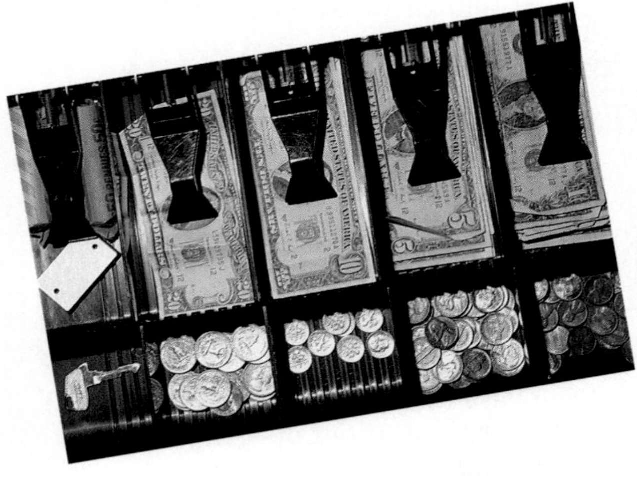

Unit 4 — Housing 248

Unit 5 — Clothing 298

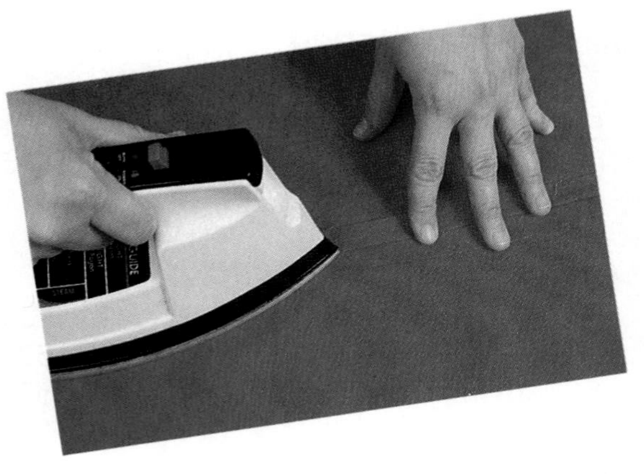

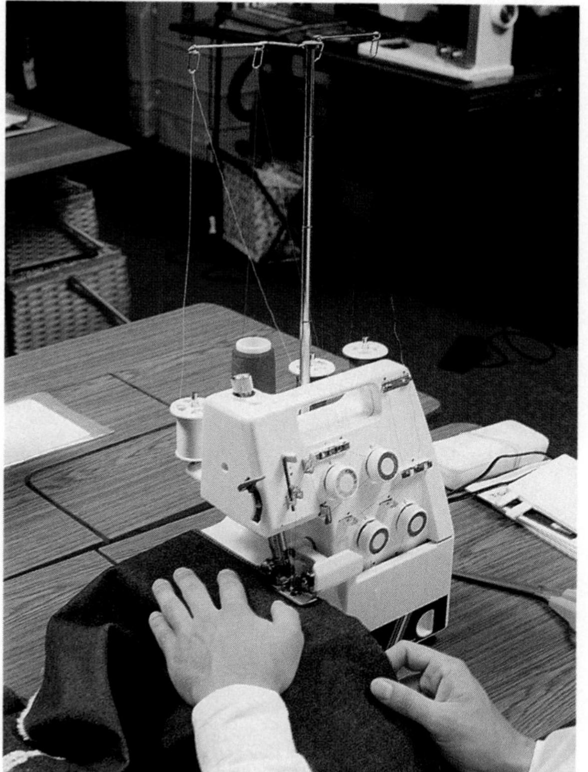

Unit 6 — Foods 426

Planning the Unit

Ch. 1: Making the Most of Yourself — Discusses ways in which self-esteem, heredity, environment, and personality influence reaching potential.

Ch. 2: Your Values and Goals — Examines how values are acquired and how they influence setting and working toward goals.

Ch. 3: Making Decisions and Managing Your Life — Discusses ways in which values and goals influence decision making. Integrates decision making and problem solving into the management process.

Ch. 4: Coping with Change and Stress — Addresses types of change and stress typical to adolescence along with coping strategies.

Ch. 5: Moving Toward Maturity — Emphasizes signs and examples of maturity in reaching full development as a person.

Ch. 6: Citizenship and Leadership — Discusses qualities and characteristics of citizens and leaders along with suggestions for practicing citizenship and leadership.

Ch. 7: Exploring Careers — Examines ways in which aptitudes, interests, and skills influence career choices. Addresses ways to gain work skills, apply and interview for a job.

UNIT 1 Self-Discovery

CHAPTERS

1. *Making the Most of Yourself*
2. *Your Values and Goals*
3. *Making Decisions and Managing Your Life*
4. *Coping with Change and Stress*
5. *Moving Toward Maturity*
6. *Citizenship and Leadership*
7. *Exploring Careers*

Cooperative Learning Tips

Recent research indicates that when students work cooperatively in groups, they develop stronger feelings of self-worth, are positive toward other people, and have a higher level of academic achievement.

Effective cooperative group learning involves the following elements:

- Heterogeneous groups of 3 to 4 students.
- Development of group goals and interdependence.
- Individual accountability for learning.
- Cooperative learning skill instruction.
- Time for processing, reviewing, and sharing information.

See the *Cooperative Learning* booklet in the TCR for more information.

Introducing the Unit

Unit 1 Overview

Unit 1 offers students an opportunity to explore and understand their own development. It emphasizes developing healthy self-esteem, identifying values and goals, and developing decision making and management skills. Emphasis is also placed on citizenship and thinking about future careers.

Unit Motivators

1. **Setting Goals.** Have students make a list of ten items that they would like to accomplish. Ask them to prioritize these items in the order in which they would like to achieve them. (Key Skill: *Decision Making*)
2. **Career Decisions.** Ask each student to write a one-page paper about their ideal choice of career. Encourage students to identify what the career might be like. What did they base this career decision on? Have students review their papers again at the end of the unit. How have their ideas about careers changed? (Key Skill: *Critical Thinking*)

Completing the Unit

Review

1. **Mobiles.** At the end of the unit, have each student create a mobile about themselves. Students may include awards or ribbons they have won, items that show hobbies that they enjoy, or values and goals that they have. Encourage students to include anything that helps them feel good about themselves. Display the mobiles in the classroom. (Key Skills: *Critical Thinking, Creativity*)

Evaluation

1. **Unit Test.** Have students complete the unit test on pp. 109-111 of the *Chapter and Unit Tests* booklet in the TCR.
2. **Testmaker Software.** Use the *Testmaker* software program to design your own unit test.

Implementing Cooperative Learning

One way to help students build cooperative skills is to use the *Heads Together* structure. Use the following steps:

- Identify a topic for the students. Self-esteem is a good choice for Unit 1.
- Have students put their *heads together* to brainstorm a list of information related to the topic (ways to build self-esteem for Unit 1).
- Set a specific time limit. You can always add more time if needed.
- Process information in the large group.
- Encourage students to continue their discussion outside the classroom (or think beyond the classroom).

See the *Cooperative Learning* booklet in the TCR for more information.

Preparing to Teach

Chapter Outline

Chapter Resources

The following booklet materials may be found in the *Teacher's Classroom Resources* box:

- Lesson Plans, p. 5
- Student Workbook, *Study Guide,* pp. 11-12; *Roses Are Red, Violets Are Blue,* p. 13; *Let Me Help,* p. 14
- Color Transparencies, *Looking at You,* CT-1
- Personal Safety, *High Self-Esteem Can Keep You Safe,* pp. 5-6
- Technology and Computers, pp. 7, 10, 11, 12
- Cooperative Learning, p. 13
- Extending the Text, *Building Skills, Self-Concept, and Self-Esteem,* p. 5
- Reteaching and Practical Skills, *Celebrate Yourself,* p. 5
- Enrichment Activities, *Enjoying Being Alone,* pp. 5-6
- Chapter and Unit Tests, pp. 5-6
- Testmaker Software

Also see:

- Leadership and Citizenship
- Meeting the Special Needs of Students
- Linking Home, School, and Community
- Dealing with Sensitive Issues

ABCNews InterActive™ Videodiscs

- *Food and Nutrition*
- *Drugs and Substance Abuse*
- *Teenage Sexuality*
- *Tobacco*
- *Alcohol*

See the ABCNews InterActive™ Bar Code Correlation booklet for applicable segments.

CHAPTER 1

Making the Most of Yourself

OBJECTIVES

- *Define self-concept and identify ways to boost self-esteem.*
- *Discuss how heredity and environment influence personality.*
- *Identify strategies for reaching your potential and using your resources.*

TERMS TO LEARN

- ***self-concept***
- ***self-esteem***
- ***personality***
- ***heredity***
- ***environment***
- ***potential***
- ***resource***
- ***human resources***
- ***material resources***
- ***resourceful***

"I did it!" Sean thought to himself with satisfaction. What a good feeling it was. To anyone else it might not have seemed like much, but, to him, this success in track meant a great deal. Now he felt confident. Now he felt good about himself. All of a sudden, it occurred to him that there was so much else he could do if he worked at it. He was ready and eager to try.

Getting Ready for Success

Did you ever wonder why some people succeed and others don't? The answer is not a simple one.

For one thing, success means different things to different people. Mr. Salazar felt successful when the business he built from the ground up brought him a good income. Maribeth O'Sullivan, a Peace Corps volunteer in Nepal, felt successful when she showed a group of women how to prepare healthy meals for their families. Sam Yoo knew success when he won the spelling bee at his school. For Andrea, passing her biology test was an achievement. What does success mean to you?

All of these people were successful in different ways. Something had to be working for them, however, in order to find their own successes. What worked for them can work for you too. You're in charge — if you decide to be.

Taking a Look at You

"They are able because they think they are able." In this quote, the Roman poet Virgil is stating that it is very important to believe in yourself. Nate had trouble with this. Because of a few mistakes, he no longer wanted to try anything. He branded himself as a failure. The image that Nate had of himself was affected by his past experiences.

▼ Your Self-Concept ▼

The picture you have of yourself and the way you believe others see you is your **self-concept**. Your self-concept is shaped by the experiences you have throughout your lifetime. Your self-concept can change, depending upon experiences you have along life's path. The way people are treated by family and friends from the time they are babies until they are senior citizens contributes to the images they have of themselves.

More About *The Self-Concept*

Toddlers are at a crucial age in the development of a positive self-concept. Parental reactions to children who try out personal ideas at this age give children a cue as to whether they are "good" or "bad" and whether their ideas have worth. Children are more likely to become self-confident if their parents show warmth and involvement while setting limitations and standards.

Introducing the Chapter

Motivators

1. **Personal Analysis.** Ask students to list some of their past accomplishments. Have them circle one accomplishment they feel the best about. Ask for volunteers to discuss what it took to reach some of the accomplishments. (Key Skills: *Communication, Critical Thinking*)
2. **Writing.** Ask students to choose someone they admire. The person may be an athlete, celebrity, family member, friend, religious leader, teacher, etc. Have students list five reasons why they admire that individual. (Key Skill: *Critical Thinking*)
3. **Writing.** Ask students to write a "You are special" note, letter, or poem to give to someone they know. Encourage students to make an "affirmation" file to save positive comments they receive about themselves. Talk about how the comments can be re-read and enjoyed on days when students do not feel good about themselves. (Key Skill: *Communication, Creativity*)

Chapter Objectives and Vocabulary

1. Have students read the chapter objectives. Ask them to rephrase the objectives as questions.
2. Ask students to state, in their own words, the purpose of studying this chapter.
3. Pronounce the vocabulary terms listed on the previous page. Ask students whether they are familiar with any of these. Explain that the terms will be defined in the chapter.

Guided Reading

1. Have students read the chapter and use the Study Guide on pp. 11-12 of the *Student Workbook*.

Teaching. . .
Taking a Look at You; Self-Concept; Self-Esteem; Personality
(pp. 19-21)

Comprehension Check

1. Give an example of how a person's self-concept is shaped. *(By experiences such as how he or she was treated by family and friends from an early age.)*
2. Name two things that can happen if a person's self-esteem is high. *(Confidence goes up; more willing to try or to take risks; more likely to be successful in accomplishing goals.)*
3. What are three common behaviors of a person with low self-esteem? *(Does not try to do well in school; does not try to be part of a group; feels that other people do not like him or her; shows anger at friends when actually angry at self.)*
4. Describe a person with a high self-esteem. *(Happy and pleasant to be around; smiles; has good sense of humor; doesn't take self too seriously; takes pride in his or her accomplishments; not afraid to try new things; not bothered by mistakes; gets pleasure from making other people feel good about themselves.)*
5. What three factors make up a person's personality? *(Feelings, attitudes, and habits.)*
6. What is the difference between heredity and environment? *(Heredity includes physical traits and abilities inherited from parents. Environment consists of everything around you, including people, places, and events.)*

Learning Activities

1. **Bulletin Board.** Have students locate magazine and newspaper articles about individuals (children, teens, adults, and older adults) who have achieved success in some way. Display and discuss the articles. Talk about factors, including a positive self-concept, that may have contributed to each individual's success. (Key Skill: *Critical Thinking*)
2. **Personal Analysis.** Ask a few volunteers to look in a hand

Can you put your own self-concept into words? Try it. Think about the kind of person you are. Don't label yourself as "good" or "bad"; just try to describe yourself realistically.

▼ Your Self-Esteem ▼

Your **self-esteem** is the way you feel about yourself — the confidence and happiness you have in yourself. If you like who you are and believe in yourself and your abilities, you have high self-esteem. If you do not like who you are very much and do not believe in yourself, you have low self-esteem. When your self-esteem is on the high side, you are self-confident. Your confidence makes you willing to try more, to take risks. You are more likely to accomplish things and be successful. Keep in mind, however, that everyone will have a low day now and then — a day when self-esteem may not be as high as usual. This is normal. Keeping a positive attitude through the low days and getting support from family and friends will help you maintain high self-esteem.

Ann never tries to do well in school or be part of a group. Often, she feels that other people do not like her. Sometimes she shows a dislike for herself by the way she treats others. When she is angry with herself, she often directs this anger at other people. How would you describe Ann's self-esteem?

In contrast, Gabriela takes pride in her accomplishments and is not afraid to try new things. She doesn't worry about making mistakes. Gabriela is happy and pleasant to be around. She smiles, has a good sense of humor, and isn't too hard on herself when she makes a mistake. She gets pleasure from making other people feel good about themselves. Even on her low days, Gabriela tries to keep her spirits up and brighten someone else's day. How do Ann and Gabriela differ in self-esteem?

AROUND THE WORLD

Getting involved in worthy causes is a great way to improve self-esteem. Many programs allow young people to offer their skills and services to people in other countries. Through *Amigos de las Americas*, for example, volunteers travel to South America and the Caribbean to help with health programs. In the *Earthwatch Research Corps*, volunteers help others study and protect natural resources. How does helping others benefit the volunteers as well as those they serve?

More About *Self-Concepts*

Self-concepts can be changed in either direction over a period of time. People with good self-concepts can have enough negative experiences to lower their self-concepts. People with poor self-concepts can find enough positive experiences to improve their self-concepts. One important way to improve self-concepts is to recognize messages that people give themselves. Students should be reminded to catch themselves when the message is negative, and restate it immediately in a positive way. Another important step is for teens to ask people who are close to them for assistance and support. This is critical because what those close to teens think and say about them affects their self-concept. A third step is for

Your own personality influences how you see others.

▼ Your Personality ▼

Your self-esteem and self-concept are often apparent to others. They show in your personality. Your **personality** is the combination of feelings, character traits, attitudes, and habits that you display to others. This combination of characteristics makes you unique, or one-of-a-kind.

The stage was first set for your personality before you were born. You are probably already aware that you received genes from each of your parents that determined your physical traits, such as and your height and your eye and hair color. The traits and characteristics passed along from parents to children is called **heredity** (huh-RED-uh-tee). Heredity also influences your personal characteristics, such as your intelligence, abilities, and your emotional responses.

Although your personality began with your heredity, it has been shaped much further by your environment. Your **environment** (in-VY-run-munt) is everything around you, including people, places, and events. The family is usually the most important environmental influence on a person.

students to concentrate on what they do well. They need to be encouraged to learn from their successes. Success builds confidence, and positive reinforcement from within and from others helps to build a person's self-concept. At the opposite extreme, negative comments break down one's self-concept.

Learning Activities (continued)

mirror, and give a short description of what they see. Discuss what their descriptions tell about their self-concepts. (Key Skill: *Critical Thinking*)

3. **Journal Writing.** Ask for volunteers to keep a daily journal describing events of the day, including their feelings about what happened and how they felt about themselves. Encourage them to find at least one positive thing to say about their day and about themselves. (Key Skill: *Communication*)
4. **Name Tags.** Assign students to make a "nameless name tag" using adjectives, symbols, or other illustrations expressing qualities that they like about themselves. Display the tags and have students try to identify the owner of each one. (Key Skills: *Critical Thinking, Creativity*)

Follow Up

1. **Reteaching.** Give each student an unlabeled, empty can. Instruct them to create designs on the outside that include their name as well as something positive about themselves. Next, provide plenty of strips of paper for students to write positive adjectives describing themselves. Encourage students to fill their cans with as many strips as possible. (Key Skills: *Critical Thinking, Creativity*)
2. **Enrichment.** Assign students to locate and read books, magazine, or newspaper articles about people who have overcome limits of heredity and environment. Discuss their findings in class. (Key Skill: *Communication*)

AROUND THE WORLD

After reading the feature, assign students to find articles about teens and adults who have served as volunteers in other countries. Survey the school and community to find individuals who have been volunteers in foreign locales. Ask them to speak to the class about their experiences. Have students write the Peace Corps and other groups to learn about service opportunities and qualifications required. Discuss and display the information that is received.

Teaching. . .
Building Self-Esteem
(pp. 22-23)

Comprehension Check

1. Why is it important to focus on your strengths rather than your weaknesses? *(So you can discover what you do well and work on those skills.)*
2. Give three questions or statements people sometimes make to themselves that may lower their self-concept. *(Examples include: "How could I be so stupid?" "What's the matter with me anyway?" "I can't do anything right.")*
3. What does it mean to "reach your potential?" *(To become all that you can be.)*
4. Give three suggestions for channeling your efforts. *(Don't get distracted; stay focused on goals; remember what is best for you and your future and stay on that path.)*

Learning Activities

1. **Discussion.** Divide the class into two groups. Have one group develop a list of statements people might hear as they grow up that would enhance self-esteem. Have the other group make a list of statements that would not enhance the development of self-esteem. Compare the lists. Discuss the impact of negative statements on a person's self-esteem, creativity, willingness to volunteer, and relationships. (Key Skills: *Communication, Critical Thinking*)

Making a Difference

Everyone has a self-concept. Sometimes it is positive; sometimes it is not. Encourage students to develop an awareness of things they say and do that might help family members, friends, and acquaintances improve their self-concepts. Have students practice skits in which they compliment a family member for a tasty dish or entire meal. Ask them to practice giving compliments when someone looks nice or does something well.

How might the development of self-esteem be encouraged in this family?

Within the family, the seeds of self-concept and self-esteem are sown. For example, children who live in an environment filled with love and encouragement are much more likely to feel good about themselves. This, in turn, contributes to a pleasing personality.

Building Self-Esteem

Felipe's life has not been easy. His father left the family several years ago. His mother has struggled to raise four children in the best way she can. Felipe remembers little of his father except the harsh words he always had for Felipe. Now Felipe believes he is not as smart or as strong as his older brothers. Felipe fears he will never be good enough to succeed at anything, so he acts as though he doesn't care about his future.

Felipe feels defeated. Can he turn his life around? What do you think? Felipe needs a big boost in his self-esteem to help him become successful. Examine your own self-esteem. If it needs a boost, here are some ideas to explore:

- ***Accept yourself.*** Differences make people interesting. Learn to value the qualities that make you a unique person. Remember that your true worth comes from inside, not outside.
- ***Dare to dream.*** Set your sights high. Plan to take little steps in order to get there. Working toward a dream can be helpful in itself. If the dream is too lofty, you will still profit from what you learn along the way. Who knows? You might even achieve the dream.

- ▶ ***Be realistic.*** Some things can be changed; others cannot. Time and energy wasted on unrealistic wishes is self-defeating and interferes with accomplishing other more realistic goals. Lora Lee spends much of her time worrying about her appearance. She wishes she had a smaller nose, straighter hair, and more height. Everyone thinks Lora Lee looks fine — everyone, that is, except Lora Lee.
- ▶ ***Don't settle for what is.*** In other words, know that some things can be changed. Just because Ray is shy doesn't mean he can't take some steps to turn that around a bit. You, too, can make changes in yourself and in your life, if you need and want to.
- ▶ ***Focus on your strengths.*** Everyone has strengths and weaknesses. Strengths, or the things you do well, help you work effectively toward your goals. Avoid worrying about your weaknesses. However, if a weakness is interfering with your goals, think about ways that you can overcome or compensate for that weakness. You may discover some new strengths.
- ▶ ***Turn to others for help.*** Ideas and assistance from others may help you affirm your strengths and find new ways to deal with your weaknesses.
- ▶ ***Get involved.*** Becoming involved in worthwhile activities, such as volunteer work or belonging to an interesting club, can really boost your self-esteem. Looking for ways to help or work with others can enable you to see new strengths and understand ways that you can assist others with their needs.
- ▶ ***Be proud of your accomplishments.*** Even small accomplishments are worthy. Often they are the stepping stones to bigger and better things.
- ▶ ***Believe in yourself.*** Remove statements like these from your thinking: "How could I be so stupid?" "What's the matter with me anyway?" "I can't do anything right." Instead, learn to forgive yourself for your mistakes and try again. People seldom succeed without some failure along the way. Only by trying can you become what you want to be.

What steps can you take to work toward your dreams?

Overcoming Barriers

Someone once said, "The control center of your life is attitude." Every person can point to reasons why he or she cannot succeed. One says, "I am female." Another says, "It's my race." Another explains, "I have no opportunity." Still another says, "I have lost my sight." Should these factors

More About *Making Changes*

People's emotions can affect their self-concept and self-esteem. Emotions can help people achieve goals, or they can cause them to fail. During the teen years, changes in the body cause people's emotions to shift suddenly. One minute they may feel happy, and the next minute they may feel down in the dumps. These shifts are quite normal during adolescence and are related to the body's production of hormones. Teens need to become aware of their emotions and to learn to express them in healthy, responsible ways. By doing so, they can focus their efforts and work toward reaching their potential.

Learning Activities (continued)

2. **Awareness Exercise.** Assign students to keep a tally of negative comments they hear or make in the course of a day. Challenge them to turn at least two negative statements around, making them positive, and observe the reaction they get. Ask them to share their experiences with the class. (Key Skills: *Communication, Problem Solving*)
3. **Questioning.** Ask and discuss the following questions: What are some reasons why people make negative comments about themselves and others? How do you feel when you hear a negative comment about yourself? What are some steps that people can take to deal positively with negative comments about themselves? (Key Skills: *Communication, Critical Thinking*)
4. **Writing.** Ask students to think about the people who have had positive influences on their self-concepts. Have them choose one of these people and write a thank-you note to him or her, mentioning how this person helped them. (Key Skills: *Communication, Critical Thinking*)
5. **Debate.** Have students debate the statement: A person's self-esteem improves with age. (Key Skills: *Communication, Critical Thinking*)

Follow Up

1. **Reteaching.** Have students print their name and identify a personal characteristic starting with each letter of their name. Encourage them to choose positive characteristics. (Key Skill: *Critical Thinking*)
2. **Enrichment.** Assign students to write public service announcements directed to teens with low self-esteem who may be thinking of suicide. Note: Use this activity with caution. (Key Skills: *Communication, Critical Thinking*)

Teaching. . .
Overcoming Barriers; Reaching Your Potential
(pp. 24-25)

Comprehension Check

1. What helps you overcome barriers? *(Determination and the right attitude.)*
2. What is one of the scariest parts of taking charge of your life? *(Facing risk.)*
3. Why is it important to take care of yourself when trying to develop your potential? *(So you can stay well and full of energy.)*

Learning Activities

1. **Skits.** Assign students to write and present skits about teens and other people who have taken positive risks when taking charge of their life. Discuss the skits, and talk about why taking risks to reach their potential can be frightening. Ask for volunteers to give personal examples of taking risks while trying to reach their potential. (Key Skills: *Communication, Critical Thinking*)
2. **Discussion.** Ask students to give examples of television characters who portray people that have overcome barriers. What personal characteristics helps these people successfully overcome barriers? (Key Skill: *Critical Thinking*)
3. **Reading.** Have students read books or magazine articles about teens or adults who have taken risks and overcome barriers. Discuss the stories in class, asking students to give examples showing ways that these individuals felt good about themselves and others and were able to meet the demands of life. (Key Skill: *Communication*)
4. **Collage:** Have students create a collage using words and pictures to show how they are working toward their potential. (Key Skill: *Creativity*)

How to . . .
Feel Good about Yourself

Sometimes this is easier said than done. You may have a bad day. You think you don't look right or act right. You want to feel good, but it just isn't happening. How can you turn things around? Read what these teens have to say.

- ***Brittany***. "Talking always saves me. Whenever I need to feel better, I find someone I can talk to. My stepfather is super. He listens and just seems to know what to say to help me have confidence in myself again."
- ***Dominick.*** "Some people I know like to put others down. They've done it to me. I believed what they said for a long time. Finally, it hit me. They were just saying those things to make themselves look better. Now I either avoid them or don't listen. That has made a big difference in how I feel about myself."
- ***Heidi.*** "Boredom is my worst enemy. When I don't have anything to do, I start feeling sorry for myself. I think of more things that are wrong with me. Now that I realize this, I try to get involved in activities that are interesting. Joining a club at school has helped. We have projects to work on and leaders with plenty of good ideas."

Determination and the right attitude help people succeed regardless of their limitations.

hold people back? In an imperfect world, any of these factors can get in the way.

The truth is people are not limited by their heredity, their environment, or even physical disabilities — if they have determination and the right attitude. Think about it. A pitcher makes it into the big leagues, even though he has only one arm. A young woman who cannot see learns to travel by herself. A young man graduates from college with honors after growing up in poverty. All of these are true examples of people who have succeeded because they have determination and positive attitudes. They believed in themselves. They did not let the attitudes of others hinder them. Their own positive attitudes helped them take charge and overcome the barriers to their successes.

How to ... Feel Good about Yourself

After reading the feature, have students identify how Brittany, Dominick, and Heidi find ways to feel better about themselves. Then have students find articles about people whose early experiences affected how they feel about themselves at the present time. Find magazine and newspaper pictures of infants and young children in situations that foster good self-concepts (babies being cuddled, parents playing with children, etc.). Have students survey the community for opportunities in which teens could be of service. What are the qualifications? Hours required?

The hurdles you have to jump may not be as high as those just described, or they may be higher. Whatever the case, you can move toward success. As society tries to solve the problems that hold people back, you have a choice to make. Do you wait for the solutions, hoping that someone else will make it easier for you, or do you take charge of your own life? Most people would agree that you can't sit back and wait. You must take charge and show others the skills and talents that you have to share.

▼ Taking Risks ▼

One of the scariest parts of taking charge is facing risk. It often feels safer to do nothing. A couple of Victor's friends scorned him when he worked to improve his grades. People in Noreen's community laughed when she decided to try out for the school's soccer team, since it had always been an all-male team. These individuals could have given up and chosen comfort and safety over risk. They would have also sacrificed the possibility for success.

Reaching Your Potential

All people have **potential** (puh-TEN-chul), or the possibility of becoming more than they are right now. Reaching your potential means becoming all that you can be. Because Kwang has good math and science skills, he has the potential to be an engineer if he wants to and if he works at it. Monica has the potential to be a competitive gymnast if she spends more time and effort in training.

Your potential is within your reach. Here are some suggestions for identifying and reaching it:

- ***Examine your interests and abilities.*** Make a list of each, asking others for input. Match interests and abilities. For example, Cassie loves children and gets along well with others. Because of this combined interest and ability, she plans to coach a T-ball team in the summer. This will allow her to develop a skill, explore an interest, and decide what steps she might take next.
- ***Keep your efforts focused.*** Many people do not reach their potential because they allow themselves to get distracted along the way. When you decide to accomplish something, stay focused. Remember what is best for you and your future and stay on that path.

It takes real effort and persistance to become the best you can be.

More About *Using Potential in Positive Ways*

Teens who send positive messages are more likely to feel good about themselves and to achieve their goals than those who project a negative frame of mind. One way to make messages come across in a positive manner is to give others a chance to talk without interrupting. Another way is to prevent misunderstandings by asking questions if they are unsure of what was said or intended. Also, concentrating on what other people are saying, rather than trying to do something and listen at the same time, tells individuals they are important and that their contribution is valued.

Follow Up

1. **Reteaching.** Have students brainstorm a list of positive ways to overcome barriers. (Key Skill: *Communication*)
2. **Enrichment.** Divide students into small groups. Have each group create a skit depicting one of the following: overcoming a barrier(s); taking a positive risk; reaching one's potential. (Key Skills: *Communication, Creativity*)

Wellness

Point out that high self-esteem tends to lead to good health—and vice versa. People with high self-esteem are generally willing to make an effort to be healthy. Likewise, people who enjoy good health feel good about themselves. Of course, the reverse tends to be true also: people suffering from low self-esteem are less likely to pay attention to their health. Have students brainstorm ways to help people improve their health and their self-esteem. Ask them to complete the following phrase as many times as they can: "You'll feel better about yourself if...." What practical suggestions can students offer for helping people overcome low self-esteem?

Teaching...
Using Your Resources
(pp. 26-27)

Comprehension Check

1. In what ways did Travis show he knew how to use resources? *(Kept good grades/ talked to counselor and teachers about college/ read pamphlets and flyers about scholarships; used the library to locate books about colleges, scholarships, and financial aid; filled out a scholarship application available through his father's job.)*
2. What are six community resources? *(Libraries, schools, churches, hospitals, clinics, and parks.)*
3. Name three human resources who may be available for counseling or enrichment opportunities. *(Educators, religious leaders, and artists.)*
4. Name six personal qualities that are classified as human resources. *(Energy, health, time, interests, skills, knowledge, abilities, attitudes, and personality.)*
5. Give an example of how sharpening a resource may increase another resource. *(Getting education and training can result in a higher salary; getting good nutrition and sufficient exercise to become fit enough to be chosen for an athletic team, and later receive an athletic scholarship.)*
6. How can you help others succeed? *(Treating others the way you want to be treated.)*

Learning Activities

1. **Classroom Survey.** Divide students into small groups, and have them list as many material resources as possible that are in the classroom. Compile the lists, and write them on the chalkboard. (Key Skill: *Critical Thinking*)

This Will Make You Feel Better

If you sometimes get discouraged, consider this fellow: He dropped out of grade school. Ran a country store. Went broke. Took 15 years to pay off his bills. Took a wife. Unhappy marriage. Ran for House. Lost twice. Ran for Senate. Lost twice. Delivered speech that became a classic. Audience indifferent. Attacked daily by the press and despised by half the country. Despite all this, imagine how many people all over the world have been inspired by this awkward, rumpled, brooding man who signed his name simply, A. Lincoln.

Learning to use the resources available to you can lead to future successes.

- ***Take care of yourself.*** You are more likely to develop your potential if you are healthy and full of energy. Eat foods that promote good health. (You will learn about healthful foods and eating habits in Unit 6.) Get enough sleep. Exercise and stay fit. Reject what is harmful to you, such as tobacco and drugs, including alcohol.
- ***Use your potential in positive ways.*** Luis is a talker. He is charming, convincing, and has a way of making others feel good about themselves. Some people might use such a skill in negative ways, persuading people to do what is harmful. Luis is not like this, however. He wants to find a way to use his skills, such as working with the homeless or elderly, to help himself and others.

Using Your Resources

Michael's older brother, Travis, wanted to go to college, but he did not have the money. Michael thought he might like to go too in a few years, so he watched closely as Travis made his plans. First, Travis kept his grades high. He talked to his counselor and a few teachers at school. The counselor gave him pamphlets and flyers about many scholarships for which he could apply. Travis applied for all of these. He found books about colleges, scholarships, and financial aid at the library. His father brought home an application for a scholarship that was offered through his place of employment. By the time Travis was ready, he had several offers for financial assistance. College became a reality for him. Travis knew how to use his resources.

Identifying Resources

Anything you use to help you accomplish something is a **resource**. Resources can be either human or material. Resources that have to do with people are called **human resources**. All other resources are material resources. **Material resources** are often objects. They include money, property, supplies, and tools. Material resources also include community resources, such as libraries, schools, churches, hospitals, clinics, and parks.

Like Travis, you might use family members and teachers as resources. Friends, neighbors, employers, and community contacts are other possibilities. For counseling, you might go to educators or religious leaders. For enrichment, you might go to a local artist, writer, or musician. Physicians, police officers, firefighters, and emergency service personnel are also resources. What might cause you to turn to these people

More About Identifying Resources

Teens sometimes say that a person has a lot "going for him," meaning that the person may have money, reputation, stable family background, intellect, athletic ability, or other attributes that help him get what he wants. Many teens need assistance in recognizing that they, too, have "things" going for them. Some of these "things," or resources, vary from student to student. However, all students can learn to identify resources that they previously may have overlooked.

as resources? A fee may be attached to using some of these resources, but many are available at little or no cost to you.

Personal qualities are also human resources. These include health, interests, skills, knowledge, abilities, and attitudes. Even your personality may be counted as a resource.

▼ Making the Most of Resources ▼

Once you identify your resources, you need to make them work for you. This can be done in several ways.

First, strive to increase your resources. People you meet may be able to help you, now or later. Read newspapers, bulletin boards, and pamphlets that are displayed in public places to learn what is going on. Discover what you can learn and with whom you can make useful contact. Develop your own knowledge and abilities. These resources are yours to keep. Sharpening them may increase other resources. For example, education and training can result in a higher salary when you have a career. Money can be an important resource.

Second, conserve your resources. Spending all your money on arcade games brings pleasure at the moment. Putting some money in a savings account brings more money later. Taking care of your possessions means they last longer. You won't have to spend time and money replacing them as often. Can you think of other ways to conserve resources?

Third, learn to substitute resources. For example, substitute the resource of personal energy for the resource of money by making a birthday gift. Instead of buying books and tapes, use the library. Instead of keeping the temperature high during the winter, put on warmer clothes.

Finally, share resources. Work together in a study group for a difficult class or assignment. Repair something for a friend who in return will teach you a new skill. Trade books, tapes, CDs, or clothes as long as both parties agree to take good care of the items. Sharing can be useful.

Resources are all around you. They are shared among people, communities, states, and countries. You only have to find them and learn how to use them to help you accomplish your goals and the goals of groups you are involved with. When you do this, you can be described as **resourceful**. Resourceful people can solve problems, an important skill for anyone who wants to succeed.

How would the costs of in-line skating compare to those of other sports and recreational activities?

Learning Activities (continued)

2. **Classified Advertisement.** Assign students to write three advertisements. (1) Have them specify the resources that they have that they could use as a good friend. (2) Ask them to spotlight the resources they have available to be a good family member. (3) Spotlight the resources they have to be a good student. Collect the advertisements, and without using names, share some of them with the class. (Key Skills: *Communication, Critical Thinking*)
3. **Community Survey.** Select students to survey the community to learn about human and material resources that are available to teens and their families. Have them develop a brochure that lists and describes some of the resources. (Key Skills: *Communication, Cooperation*)
4. **Writing.** Assign students to write a short story about someone who made the most of his or her resources. Have them share their stories with the class. (Key Skills: *Communication, Creativity*)

Follow Up

1. **Reteaching.** Have students make a mobile illustrating human and material resources. Display and discuss the completed projects. (Key Skills: *Communication, Creativity*)
2. **Extension.** Have the students read and discuss the handout on p. 5 of the *Extending the Lesson* booklet in the TCR.
3. **Enrichment.** Assign students to write and illustrate a children's story book about human and material resources. Have them base the story on ways that children and their families can use resources in positive ways. (Key Skills: *Communication, Creativity*)

More About Resources

Sometimes personal qualities can help overcome a lack in other resources. Courage can help overcome illness, injury, physical and emotional handicaps, frustration, loneliness, and hardship. Faith and belief in themselves can help people continue when trying to achieve their potential. A positive attitude, emotional stability, and sensitivity to the needs and wishes of other people can help open up opportunities in all areas of life.

Completing the Chapter

For Review

1. Emphasize the main concepts using the summary.
2. Have students complete the "Facts to Recall." (Answers below.)

For Reteaching

1. **Reteaching.** Use the activity on p. 5 of the *Reteaching and Practical Skills* booklet in the TCR.

For Enrichment

1. **Enrichment.** Use the activity on p. 7 of the *Enrichment Activities* booklet in the TCR.

For Evaluation

1. Choose items from "Ideas to Explore" and "Activities to Try."
2. Use the chapter test on pp. 5-6 of the testing booklet in the TCR or use the testmaker software.

Facts to Recall Answers

1. People with high self-esteem are more confident about themselves. This makes them more willing to take risks, which gives them more chances to succeed.
2. People with high self-esteem: are happy with themselves; pleasant to be around; not afraid to try new things; make others feel good about themselves. People with low self-esteem: do not like themselves; feel others do not like them; take out the anger they feel toward themselves on other people.
3. Heredity and environment.
4. **Any five:** accept yourself; dare to dream; be realistic; don't settle for what is; focus on your strengths; turn to others for help; get involved; be proud of yourself; believe in yourself.
5. It makes you focus on the needs of others instead of on your own concerns.
6. It means taking responsibility for your own success or failure; sacrificing feelings of comfort and safety and taking risks; facing ridicule from others.

How might helping others succeed benefit you as well?

Helping Others Succeed

"I know you can do it."
"I'd like to help you."
"I'm glad you're my friend."

How often do you say things like these to family and friends? Sometimes people become so caught up in their own concerns that they forget about others. Your life is closely intertwined with many people. *What you are depends on them, and what they are depends on you.* As you become older, remember that the positive way you treat others returns to you. In what ways may an attitude like this help make society stronger?

Ramona takes time to listen to her friends. She wants them to know that she enjoys being with them. She doesn't put them down or gossip about them to others. She is genuinely warm and gives trust whenever she can. All of this helps build self-esteem in Ramona's friends. They are better equipped to reach their own potential. In turn, they feel good about Ramona and support her, too. The same thing can happen to you. This, in itself, is a success like no other.

TAKING ACTION

Peer Tutoring

Reggie has a strong self-concept, makes good grades, and has a positive attitude. He is president of the student council and is well liked by most students. Mr. Armato, the school's guidance counselor, recently asked Reggie if he would be interested in helping set up a peer tutoring program. Students needing academic help would be paired with student tutors.

Mr. Armato plans to recruit students who do well in various subjects to act as peer tutors. Each peer tutor would need to commit to working with his or her partner for at least one grading period, or until the student's grades improve. The tutors would receive training from Mr. Armato on structuring tutoring time and establishing positive working relationships. Teachers of the various subject areas have already committed to helping the tutors. Reggie asks you to consider becoming a peer tutor.

Using Your Resourcefulness

- Would you be interested in becoming a peer tutor? Why or why not?
- Do you think that everyone who is having difficulty with classes would or could benefit from a peer tutor? Explain your answer.
- Does your school have a peer tutoring program? How does it compare to Mr. Armato's plan?
- Identify some changes you might make in Mr. Armato's plan to make it work effectively in your school.
- What resources might help you learn more about peer tutoring programs?

TAKING ACTION

Have students read the feature. Invite the school guidance counselor to talk about peer tutoring at school and in the community. Ask teens who currently serve as peer tutors to speak to the class about their experiences.

Have students research the topic and then write and present two skits about peer tutoring. Have one skit focus on personal qualities needed by the peer tutor. Have another skit represent a student who wants to serve as a peer tutor offering his services to the school guidance counselor.

Chapter 1 Review

Summary

In this chapter, you have read about:

- Factors that affect self-concept and self-esteem.
- How to move toward success by raising your self-esteem.
- Taking charge of your life and sometimes dealing with risks when you take charge.
- How to identify and reach your potential.
- Identifying, using, and conserving your resources.

Facts to Recall

1. Explain the relationship between self-esteem, confidence, and success.
2. How does a person's self-esteem affect his or her behavior?
3. What are two important factors that help shape your personality?
4. List five things you can do to boost your self-esteem.
5. How can getting involved help raise self-esteem?
6. Explain why it can be difficult to take charge of your own life.
7. What is potential? What are four ways of identifying and reaching it?
8. Define resource. Give five examples of human resources and five examples of material resources.
9. Identify four ways to make the most of your resources.
10. How can helping others build self-esteem also help you succeed?

Ideas to Explore

1. Identify specific factors that affect your own self-esteem.
2. Discuss specific ways in which your heredity and your environment have influenced your personality — your likes and dislikes, your interests, your attitudes.
3. Use the list of suggestions for boosting self-esteem found in this chapter and explain one way that you can apply each point to your life.

Activities to Try

1. As a class, develop a list of as many things as you can think of that you can do every day to raise other people's self-esteem.
2. On a sheet of paper, list all your resources — human and material. On a separate sheet of paper, list your goals and interests. Exchange your list of goals and interests with a group of two or three other classmates. List ways in which each of you can use your resources to help the others in the group succeed.

LINK TO *Communication*

IDENTIFYING QUALITIES FOR SUCCESS

Read a magazine article or book about a successful person whom you admire. Write a two-page summary about the factors that contributed to this person's success. In your summary, answer the following questions:

- How did this person get ready for success?
- What helped to develop this person's self-concept and self-esteem?
- How did others influence this person's success?
- How were barriers to his or her success eliminated?
- How did this person work to reach his or her potential?
- How did this person use resources to achieve success?
- In what ways has this person helped others succeed?

Facts to Recall Answers (continued)

7. The possibility of becoming more than you are now. Examine your interests and abilities; channel your efforts; take care of yourself; use your potential in positive ways.
8. Anything you use to help accomplish something. **Any five:** friends; neighbors; employers; physicians; police officers; fire fighters; emergency service personnel; educators; religious leaders; artists; energy; health, time; interests; skills; knowledge; abilities; attitudes; personality. **Any five:** money; property; supplies; tools; libraries; schools; churches; hospitals; clinics; parks.
9. Increase, conserve, substitute and share resources.
10. When you help others build their self-esteem, you help them reach their potential and succeed. This can make them better able to help you succeed as well.

Ideas to Explore

1. Answers will vary, but may include affirming the things people do and say, showing genuine concern for others, sincere praise, etc.
2. Answers will vary.
3. Answers will vary.

Using Your Resourcefulness Answers

- Answers will vary.
- Answers will vary, but may include: *yes* — anyone who is having difficulty with a subject would benefit from extra tuition; *no* — people who are not learning from their teacher are even less likely to learn from an untrained tutor.
- Answers will vary.
- Answers will vary.
- Answers will vary, but may include school guidance counselors, principals, and teachers.

LINK TO *Communication*

Answers will vary depending on the content of the magazine article or book.

Preparing to Teach

Chapter Outline

Chapter Resources

The following booklet materials may be found in the *Teacher's Classroom Resources* box:
- Lesson Plans, p. 6
- Student Workbook, *Study Guide,* pp. 15-16; *Your Values Are Showing,* p. 17; *Stepping Up to Your Goals,* p. 18
- Color Transparencies, *Values and Goals,* CT-2
- Technology and Computers, pp. 7, 10
- Cooperative Learning, p. 14
- Extending the Text, *Setting Standards,* p. 6
- Reteaching and Practical Skills, *Autobiographical Values,* p. 6
- Enrichment Activities, *Going for the Goal,* pp. 7-8
- Chapter and Unit Tests, pp. 7-8
- Testmaker Software

Also see:
- Meeting the Special Needs of Students
- Linking Home, School, and Community
- Dealing with Sensitive Issues

ABCNews InterActive™ Videodiscs
- *Violence Prevention*
- *Drugs and Substance Abuse*

See the ABCNews InterActive™ Bar Code Correlation booklet for applicable segments.

CHAPTER 2 Your Values and Goals

OBJECTIVES

- *Explain what values are and how they are learned.*
- *Explain the benefits of setting and working toward goals.*

TERMS TO LEARN

- ***values***
- ***goal***

If he made the team, basketball shoes would be expensive. Andre knew that. He also knew that his mother didn't have the money, nor did he. As he thought about tryouts, Andre wondered what to do. If he said something to his mother, he knew she would struggle to find a way to get the shoes. She might even make sacrifices to buy them. She would be very sad if there was no way that she could provide the shoes. For several long minutes, Andre stared at the sign-up sheet for tryouts. Then he turned and walked slowly away.

What's Important to You?

Making decisions is not always easy. What will you choose? Which way will you go? More importantly, what will influence your decision?

Values

Every day you use values to help you make decisions. Your **values** are the beliefs, ideas, and feelings about what is important to you. Deciding to have healthy lunches every day rather than having a soft drink and a candy bar shows that you value good health. Deciding to read a story to a younger brother shows that you value family relationships. Your values serve as guidelines by which to make decisions. Without values to guide you, these decisions might not be easily made.

Your values are always showing. For example, they are reflected in how you act. A person who values honesty believes it is wrong to cheat on tests. This value will guide this person's actions, even when exams are tough. Values also show in what you say. A person who cares about the feelings of others will speak kindly to them. In addition, values can be seen in how you spend your resources. Giving to a charity instead of buying new clothes shows you value the health or well-being of others over material things. Finally, values show in what you are willing to stand up for. A person who risks the opinions of others — and sometimes even his or her own personal safety — to stand up for a principle gives a clear message about values.

The directions people take in life are influenced by the values they hold as important. You may never have thought about the values that are important to you. By thinking about your values now, you can learn more about yourself. You may even discover something you'd like to change.

By returning a missing billfold, this teen is showing he values honesty.

Introducing the Chapter

Motivators

1. **Agree or Disagree.** Divide students into two groups. Ask students in one group to take the position that Andre should have signed up to try out for the basketball team. (See p. 31.) Have the other group represent the belief that Andre took the right step by choosing not to sign up for tryouts. Ask each group to discuss its position. Afterwards, bring the two groups together to debate what Andre should have done. (Key Skills: *Communication, Critical Thinking*)
2. **Brainstorming.** Lead students in brainstorming ways that Andre or his mother might have been able to get the money for his shoes. Talk about the advantages and disadvantages of each. (Key Skills: *Communication, Critical Thinking*)
3. **Discussion.** Have students list the names of people they admire. Discuss ways in which the individuals have influenced what is important to the students. (Key Skills: *Communication, Critical Thinking*)

Chapter Objectives and Vocabulary

1. Have students read the chapter objectives. Ask them to rephrase the objectives as questions.
2. Ask students to state, in their own words, the purpose of studying this chapter.
3. Pronounce the vocabulary terms listed on the previous page. Ask students whether they are familiar with any of these. Explain that the terms will be defined in the chapter.

Guided Reading

1. Have students read the chapter and use the Study Guide on pp. 15-16 of the *Student Workbook*.

More About *What's Important*

When people spend their time, energy, and money on someone or something, they are acting out their values. Values determine the times people take risks and when they make sacrifices. People also act out their values in their attitudes and by their lifestyles. Benjamin Franklin valued time as shown by his quote, "Do not squander time, for that is the stuff life is made of."

Teaching. . .
What's Important to You?; Values
(pp. 31-33)

Comprehension Check

1. Give two examples of how values help you make choices. *(You value good health and choose to eat nutritious lunches rather than skip midday meals; you value family relationships and choose to spend time reading to a younger sibling.)*
2. Give an example of how your values are reflected in the way you act. *(You value honesty and refuse to cheat on tests.)*
3. How do family members pass on their values to younger members? *(Through examples and teaching.)*
4. Besides the home, what are five other sources of values? *(Religion, school, friends, television, books, and magazines.)*
5. Name three ways that positive values are different from negative ones. *(Positive values do not cause harm; they tend to make your life and the lives of others better; they are lawful; they are more universally accepted.)*
6. Give an example of people with different values. *(Sarah values independence; Paul values security. Sarah moved away from her hometown to get a job; Paul found a job close to home.)*

After reading the feature, ask students what their reaction would be to being pushed into giving up the values and traditions they have been taught at home. How might this be similar to the way that Native Americans feel? If possible, invite one or more representatives of a Native American tribe in your area to speak to the class.

Basic values are generally acquired at home. However, values may also be acquired through friends, religious teachings, books, and magazines. Think about the ways you have acquired your values.

How Are Values Acquired?

Most people acquire basic values in the home. Family members pass on their beliefs and feelings to younger members through examples and teaching. Many of the values acquired at home last a lifetime. They provide a constant means for guiding action. They can become a source of strength. As you can see, teaching values is an important responsibility. When children learn values that can help them in life, they are more likely to be successful and happy.

Values are also acquired in other places. Religion teaches values. Some values are acquired in school. Still others come from friends, television, books, and magazines. What values might a person acquire from each of these sources? Could a person learn to value something that is harmful?

Types of Values

Some people value things that can hurt themselves as well as others. These are called negative values. Think about the people who value only their own needs, comforts, and desires and have no regard for the needs, feelings, rights, or property of others. They may not take care of what they borrow. They may destroy property, causing financial troubles and pain for people. They may even steal, never giving a thought to the anguish they cause.

Not all negative values are as obvious. What do you think about the following situations? Earl doesn't speak to the new student in school because he doesn't like the way Corbin looks. Because Marla spends all her time with her friends, she often forgets to feed her dog. Her pet goes hungry on some days. How do these examples show negative values?

Identifying values and goals is difficult for all young people. For young Native Americans who live on a reservation but go away to school, it is even harder. At home, they learn values that are traditional to their culture. They learn ways to express these values through such experiences as prayers, dancing, and other ceremonies. The lifestyles of young Native Americans at boarding school, however, are usually much different.

Some Native American parents feel their children are being pushed into giving up the values and traditions they have been taught at home and forced to accept the attitudes and culture of the rest of society. This confuses the young people, who feel caught between two different, and sometimes opposing, sets of values.

More About Values

Clarifying values helps people understand the "why" of what they are doing. Rational choices reflect the values of the person or group making them. People can begin to clarify their values by asking what and how much of anything they would be willing to give up for a thing, a relationship, a service, or an idea. People sometimes say, "I'd give anything to have that car," but they would not steal it. They value honesty more than the car. Others might say, "I'd do anything to be on the team," but they refuse to spend the time or the energy to work for it. They value other things more than being on the team.

Negative values need to be changed. However, first you must identify the fact that they are negative. How can this be done? When you want to test a value, ask yourself: "Will my actions hurt me or anyone else, either now or later? Could this cause others to lose respect for me?" A "yes" answer to either question means that you are acting on a negative value. Rethink your behavior and look for a more positive approach.

Positive values are just the opposite of negative ones. They do not cause harm — to you or to anyone or anything else. Often they make your life and the lives of others better. What are some ways you've chosen to use positive values in your life?

Look around and you'll see that people's values often vary. Some values, such as truth and honesty, are valued worldwide, by all people of all cultures. However, in many cases, what's important to one person or culture may not be equally important to another. This does not mean that some values are right and others are wrong. Sarah prizes independence. Paul feels a need for security. When Sarah looked for a job, she moved away from the town where she had been raised. Paul looked for and found a job close to home. Values entered into the decision that each made. They each made the decision that was right for them.

These teens are sharing their positive values by painting over some graffiti on a wall in their community. What are some ways that you can share your positive values?

Learning Activities

1. **Interviews.** Ask for volunteers to interview older adults in their family, neighborhood, or place of worship. Have students ask the following questions: • What are the values that have guided you in your life? • What was the source of these values? • What would you do differently if you could live life over again? (Key Skill: *Communication*)
2. **Discussion.** Divide the class into small groups, with one student in each group serving as reporter. Give each group one of the following situations: • Tom's friends want him to cut several classes with them. What should Tom do? • Julius is buying some things at the store, and the cashier gives him too much money back. What should Julius do? • Between classes, Yolanda finds a $10 bill on the floor of the classroom. What should she do? Ask each group to read the example, discuss it, decide on a solution, and list values related to their solution. Have each reporter read the situation to the class and briefly explain the group's solution. On the chalkboard, list the values identified by each group. (Key Skills: *Communication, Problem Solving*)

Follow Up

1. **Reteaching.** Have students identify and discuss some of the apparent values of public figures who have been featured in the media. Talk about whether the values are positive or negative. (Key Skills: *Communication, Critical Thinking*)
2. **Enrichment.** Talk about ways that advertisements in various media influence people's values. Have students locate newspaper and magazine advertisements that can be used as examples. Do these media examples communicate positive or negative values? If negative, offer some suggestions for changing media influences. (Key Skills: *Communication, Critical Thinking*)

Teaching. . .
What Are Goals?; Types of Goals; Group Goals (pp. 34-35)

Comprehension Check

2. What are four short-term goals? *(Reading a book, cleaning your room, writing a letter, learning more about a subject.)*
3. Give an example of a long-term goal? *(Buying a computer; going to summer camp)*
4. Give three examples of group goals. *(A family wants to have a family reunion; a church's youth group wants to buy gifts for residents in a nursing home; a volleyball team sets a goal to win a state championship; neighbors want to clean up a vacant lot to make a children's playground.)*

Learning Activities

1. **Bookmarks.** Provide basic art supplies for students to create bookmarks illustrating personal goals. Have students feature some of the short-term goals on one side of each bookmark and the related long-term goals on the other side. Ask for volunteers to display and discuss their bookmarks. (Key Skills: *Critical Thinking, Creativity*)
2. **Discussion.** Divide students into small groups, and ask for volunteers to discuss a goal they achieved recently and the steps they took to reach it. Ask them to talk about how they felt when the goal was achieved. (Key Skill: *Communication*)
3. **Writing.** Assign students to write a one-page paper about a goal they set but failed to achieve. Ask them to include reasons why they did not achieve their goal. Have them describe how they felt when they failed to meet the goal. (Key Skills: *Communication, Critical Thinking*)

Setting short-term and long-term goals helps you gain a sense of accomplishment when you achieve them. What short-term and long-term goals are you setting for yourself?

What Are Goals?

Your values have a strong impact on the goals you set for yourself. A **goal** is something you plan to be, do, or have and for which you are willing to work. Any time you set a goal, you are placing value on the objective. The goals you choose and the actions you take to reach them show what is important to you — your values.

▼ Types of Goals ▼

Some goals are as simple as getting a homework assignment done. This is a *short-term* goal. It can be achieved in the near future. Other goals are more broad. A plan to earn enough money to visit the country where your ancestors grew up is a *long-term* goal. It takes time to achieve goals of this type.

Both short- and long-term goals are important. Short-term goals, such as reading a book, cleaning your room, writing a letter, are easier to reach than long-term goals. By setting short-term goals, you gain a sense of accomplishment when you reach them.

Long-term goals may be more easily met if short-term goals are set first. Cicely wanted to go to a summer computer camp recommended by her teacher. She thought she could pay for it by babysitting. She set a goal of earning a specific amount of money each week. The smaller amounts were easier to deal with than the total cost of the camp.

More About Goals

People set goals to gain something of importance, something that has value, for them. When a goal is achieved, they have realized something of value in their life. Their actions have produced satisfying results. While values are the inner guides that shape people's choices, goals are the aims they wish to reach. As people mature, values remain fairly constant over time. Goals, on the other hand, shift and change as wants and needs are satisfied. When short-term goals are achieved, new ones may become important. When a long-term goal is met, different short- and long-term goals may come to mind.

▼ Group Goals ▼

People often share goals, with all members of a group working for the same goal. For example, families have common goals. The Chungs planned a family reunion last year — a goal they set together. As a group, they decided where to hold the reunion, what food to serve, who would prepare it, and what entertainment and games to provide. Working together to achieve their goal was rewarding, as was the end result. At times, working for group goals means that some individual goals will not be met. What examples can you think of?

You probably belong to a number of groups besides your family. These other groups also have goals that you share. Bart's youth group at church wanted to buy gifts for residents at a nursing home. They met this goal by holding a car wash to raise money. When Sonia's volleyball team won their conference championship, they felt they had a chance to go to state. Going to the state tournament became their goal, and they worked hard to move toward it. When people work together on common goals, much can be accomplished.

Many people prefer to work for goals that they help set. If you feel this way, keep that fact in mind when you join other groups. In some groups you will be able to help set goals, and in others the goals will already be in place. You will be expected to help work for the goals of any group you join.

Aim So High You'll Never Be Bored

The greatest waste of our natural resources is the number of people who never achieve their potential. Get out of that slow lane. Shift into that fast lane. If you think you can't, you won't. If you think you can, there's a good chance you will. Even making the effort will make you feel like a new person. Reputations are made by searching for things that can't be done and doing them. Aim low: boring. Aim high: soaring.

© United Technologies Corporation

How are these teens working together toward a common goal? How will they benefit from working together cooperatively?

Learning Activities (continued)

4. **Guest Speaker.** Invite the mayor or another community leader to speak to the class about some of the community's goals. Have students prepare a list of questions to ask the speaker. (Key Skills: *Communication, Critical Thinking*)

Follow Up

1. **Reteaching.** Discuss how people's true values guide their everyday living and influence their goals. Have students list some of their most important personal values in their journals. Next, ask them to keep a record of their actions for three days to see if those actions reflect the values they listed. (Key Skill: *Critical Thinking*)
2. **Enrichment.** Assign students to create a poem, song, or dance about achieving goals. Ask for volunteers to share their project with the class. (Key Skills: *Communication, Creativity*)

Life Management Skills

Achieving Goals

Ask students to choose a short-term or long-term goal they wish to achieve. Have them write down the goal and as many reasons as possible why they want to achieve it. Next, ask them to write and sign a contract with themselves detailing specific ways they plan to reach their goal. Have them include a starting date, suggested rewards for achieving sub-goals, and the date they plan to achieve the goal.

Photo Focus

Have students examine the photo on page 35. Ask students to identify some group goals these students are working toward. *(Answers may include: memorizing lines for the play by a specific date; putting on a quality production; helping and encouraging each other, etc.)*

More About *Values and Goals*

Talking to others is a good way for teens to learn more about values and goals. Through the give-and-take of discussion, not only do they get to know themselves better, but they also understand others better. They learn to identify differences in values and the goals that people set. They learn to understand why people behave as they do and why they make certain decisions.

Teaching. . .
Choosing Goals; Achieving Goals
(pp. 36-37)

Comprehension Check

1. Name three benefits of setting goals. *(Give you direction; force you to think about what you want and take action; success and satisfaction in life.)*
2. What is one danger of having lofty dreams? *(Possible disappointment.)*
3. List three guidelines for achieving your goals. *(Keep goals in mind; actively pursue goals; be determined.)*

Learning Activities

1. **Comic Books.** Assign students to create comic books contrasting dreams and realities in goal setting. Ask students to share their completed projects with the class. (Key Skills: *Communication, Creativity*)
2. **Writing.** Have students choose an individual to write about whose dreams influenced him or her to set goals that he or she later achieved. Discuss some of the individuals in class. (Key Skill: *Communication*)
3. **Sentence Completion.** Ask students to complete the following sentences: "One of my dreams is to cause. . .," and "I can help make my dream come true by . . ." (Key Skills: *Communication, Critical Thinking*)
4. **Skits.** In small groups, ask students to write and present skits about dreams and realities in setting goals. Afterwards, lead a discussion about the skits and the need to examine goals to make sure they are attainable. (Key Skills: *Communication, Creativity*)
5. **Interviews.** Ask for volunteers to interview individuals in the community who have achieved goals that are of interest to teens. (Key Skills: *Communication, Critical Thinking*)

Why Set Goals?

Think for a moment about what you accomplished yesterday. Can you list specific achievements? Do the same thing for the last month. When people look back in time, they often discover that they did not accomplish nearly what they had wanted to accomplish. The missed opportunities may cause regrets. Goals can give you direction. They force you to think about what you want and to take the necessary steps to meet your goals. By setting goals and working to achieve them, you are more likely to find success and satisfaction in life.

Choosing Goals

When choosing goals, you must reflect on your own values — to determine what is important to you. Parents, friends, and relatives may influence your goals. However, you must be sure that the goals you set reflect what *you* want, not what others want for you. To achieve any goal, you must be committed to it so you will work hard to achieve it.

Dreams vs. Reality

Deciding what goals to set is not always easy. You may need to draw the line between dreams and reality.

The chances of becoming a professional basketball player are very limited, yet millions of teens share this same dream. Lofty dreams are considered impractical by many people, yet often they are the motivators for success. The highest hopes will never be reached if you don't strive for them. Moreover, much can be gained along the way to a lofty dream.

Playing in the NBA was Victor's dream. The thought sparked him to work hard at basketball. He learned much, including teamwork, dedication, and discipline. He made good friends and stayed out of trouble. Eventually Victor realized that the NBA was far out of his reach, but he set a new goal for himself — playing junior college basketball.

The risk with dreaming is the possibility of disappointment. It can't hurt to try for something grand if you understand that it might not work out. Still, you may need to examine the goal carefully. Aiming to cut a record in Nashville is probably not a good idea if you sing off key. A goal that is totally unrealistic may not be worth spending time on, especially if you may be hurt by the outcome.

More About *Changing Goals*

Goals are sometimes dropped because the cost in time and effort required to reach them is unreasonable. Many goals gradually change as individuals mature or families pass through various stages of the life cycle. For example, parents whose children have left home may turn from a goal of home ownership to that of renting an apartment or condominium. A serious accident of illness, death, divorce, unemployment, or economic recession may bring sudden changes in an individual or family's life. Any one of these may shatter or change their goals.

When setting goals, you may have to choose between your dreams and reality. Do you have the skills and resources necessary to achieve your goals? Is your goal realistic and worthy of spending time on?

Achieving Goals

Once you have set meaningful, realistic goals, use the following guidelines as you work to achieve them:

- ***Keep goals in mind.*** Have you ever made a New Year's resolution and later forgotten it? The same thing can happen with any goal you set if you are not careful. Maintain a mental picture of your goal. Also, write it down on paper. Whatever your goal, read it aloud every morning and every night.
- ***Actively pursue goals.*** Just wanting to participate in a 5-kilometer (about 3 miles) run isn't enough. Even though it is a fine goal, it won't get you anywhere without action. To meet his running goal, Kevin made a commitment to follow a safe training program in which he gradually increased how far he ran. He set goals for the distance he wanted to achieve by the end of each week. With each new distance that he achieved, Kevin gave himself a positive reward — an incentive to reach his final goal.
- ***Be determined.*** Even though you have a goal and the will to succeed, stumbling blocks may come along. Like roads, most goals have a few bumps, detours, or other obstacles that can get in the way. Tackle these with confidence and enthusiasm. You often benefit as much from working toward a goal as you do from eventually meeting it.

6. **Writing.** Select volunteers to write "thank you" notes to individuals who have helped them set and/or achieve goals. (Key Skill: *Communication*)
7. **Agree or Disagree.** Ask students to agree or disagree with the following statement: "What you are is not necessarily what you'll always be." Have them give examples of people whose goals change as they mature. (Key Skills: *Communication, Critical Thinking*)
8. **Discussion.** Have students identify and discuss some realities that public figures have had to face before setting and achieving goals. (Key Skills: *Communication, Critical Thinking*)
9. **Mural.** Have students create a mural illustrating some of the community's or school's goals. Display and discuss the completed mural. (Key Skills: *Cooperation, Creativity*)

Follow Up

1. **Reteaching.** Ask students to complete the sentence, "Before I am 30 years old, I want ..." Have them list all the things they want to achieve. Next, have students rank them in order of what they want to do the most to what they want to do the least. Ask them to put an "R" beside each goal that they feel is realistic and worth spending time on. (Key Skill: *Critical Thinking*)
2. **Extension.** Have students read the extension handout on page 6 of *Extending the Lesson.*
3. **Enrichment.** Have students write, present, and videotape a public service announcement about setting and achieving goals. (Key Skills: *Cooperation, Creativity*)

Completing the Chapter

For Review

1. Emphasize the main concepts using the summary.
2. Have students complete the "Facts to Recall." (Answers below.)

For Reteaching

1. **Reteaching.** Use the activity on p. 6 of the *Reteaching and Practical Skills* booklet in the TCR.

For Enrichment

1. **Enrichment.** Use the activity on pp. 9-10 of the *Enrichment Activities* booklet in the TCR.

For Evaluation

1. Choose items from "Ideas to Explore" and "Activities to Try."
2. Use the chapter test on pp. 7-8 of the testing booklet in the TCR or use the testmaker software.

Facts to Recall Answers

1. Beliefs and feelings about what is important to you. They serve as guidelines by which to make decisions.
2. How you act; what you say; how you spend your resources; what you are willing to stand up for.
3. The values children learn will affect them throughout their lives; will guide their decisions and actions; can help them be successful and happy.
4. One that can hurt you as well as others. Ask yourself: Will my actions hurt me or anyone else, either now or later? Could it cause others to lose respect for me? A "yes" answer means you are acting on a negative value.
5. Something you plan to be, do, or have.
6. It gives you a feeling of accomplishment as you work toward your long-term goal. Long-term goals are easier to achieve when broken down into smaller short-term goals.
7. Goals give you direction. They force you to think about what you want and how to achieve it.

If you are not careful, it is very easy to forget your goals — much like this teen girl has forgotten about her New Year's resolution to cut back on sweets.

TAKING ACTION

Learning Through Volunteering

Your teacher has explained to the class that volunteer work — work without pay — is one very rewarding way to develop self-esteem and to learn how to get along and work with others. Volunteering gives you a chance to show that you're a responsible worker and it can provide experience that may help you get a paying job in the future. It's also a great way to find out about yourself. You can learn what kind of work you like and don't like, such as whether you prefer working indoors or outdoors.

Your teacher will divide you into groups. Each group must identify at least one volunteer opportunity that would best suit each team member's abilities and qualities. To do so, you'll also have to research a variety of volunteer services in your community.

Using Your Resourcefulness

- What resources would you use to find out about volunteer programs in your area?
- Evaluate each person and suggest volunteer work that would suit that person's abilities and qualities.
- What volunteer job would suit your own personality? Would you be willing to do volunteer work? Why or why not?

TAKING ACTION

Have students read the feature and answer the questions within the feature. Invite community volunteers to class to talk about volunteer opportunities available to teens. Have the volunteers talk about some of the satisfactions they receive from the service performed. Have students collect brochures and other materials from community groups and agencies that rely on volunteers. Ask the students to display and discuss some of the information in the materials. Select students to carry out a school survey of students who currently serve as community volunteers.

Chapter 2 Review

Summary

In this chapter, you have read about:

- How values affect your decisions.
- The ways in which you show your values.
- How and where values are learned.
- Positive and negative values.
- Different types of goals and why it is important to set them.
- The need to set meaningful goals and to balance your goals with reality.
- How to achieve goals.

Facts to Recall

1. What are values? How do they help you make decisions?
2. List four ways in which your values show.
3. Why is teaching values to children an important responsibility?
4. What is a negative value? How can you discover whether you are acting on a negative value?
5. What is a goal?
6. Explain how reaching short-term goals can help you achieve a long-term goal.
7. Why is setting goals important?
8. Identify two benefits of striving for dreams.
9. List three guidelines that will help you achieve your goals.

Ideas to Explore

1. Do you think it is possible to live without any values or goals? Explain.
2. Give a specific example of how your values have affected a decision you have made or an action you have taken.

Activities to Try

1. On a sheet of paper, write down a long-term goal. Then list five short-term goals that could be helpful in achieving it.
2. Write down a long-term goal on a sheet of paper. Exchange your paper with a classmate. Read your classmate's goal. Then write down below it an obstacle that would make achieving the goal more difficult. Return the paper. Read the obstacle your classmate has written on your paper. Write a paragraph explaining how you would overcome this obstacle. How might you change your goal to make it reachable in light of this obstacle?
3. Select two of your favorite songs. Examine the lyrics (words of the song) carefully to determine what values are expressed. Write several sentences about the underlying values in the lyrics of each song. Do the lyrics reflect positive or negative values? Discuss your findings with the class.

LINK TO *Social Studies*

EVALUATING THE EFFECTS OF VALUES

Values show the importance of people and things in your life. They affect your life in many ways including what you say and do, how you use money, and how you treat others. Think about the values you hold and then write your response to the following:

- Choose one value that you feel has had a great impact on your life.
- How does this value affect the way that you treat others?

(**Note:** Your answers are private and for your personal use only. Share them only if you want to.)

Facts to Recall Answers (continued)

8. It can be a motivator for success; you can learn much by working toward a dream.
9. Keep goals in mind; actively pursue goals; be determined.

Ideas to Explore

1. Answers will vary.
2. Answers will vary.
3. Answers will vary. **Advantages:** goals easier to reach when many work for them; group has more resources than individual. **Disadvantages:** individual may have limited input in choosing goal; may not like way group workers toward goal.

Using Your Resourcefulness Answers

- Answers will vary, but may include: community food banks, homeless shelters, "Big Brother" or "Big Sister" programs, meals on wheels programs, etc.
- Answers will vary.
- Answers will vary.

LINK TO *Social Studies*

Answers will vary. Encourage students to share *only* if they want to.

Preparing to Teach

Chapter Outline

Chapter Resources

The following booklet materials may be found in the *Teacher's Classroom Resources* box:

- Lesson Plans, pp. 7-8
- Student Workbook, *Study Guide,* pp. 19-20; *Thinking About Your Decisions,* p. 21; *Christina's Decision,* p. 22
- Color Transparencies, *Influences on Decisions,* CT–3
- Technology and Computers, pp. 7, 8
- Cooperative Learning, p. 15
- Extending the Text, *A Focus on Risky Decisions,* p. 7
- Reteaching and Practical Skills, *Focus on Decisions,* p. 7
- Enrichment Activities, *What's to Decide?,* pp. 9-10
- Chapter and Unit Tests, pp. 9-10
- Testmaker Software

Also see:

- Leadership and Citizenship
- Meeting the Special Needs of Students
- Linking Home, School, and Community
- Dealing with Sensitive Issues

ABCNews InterActive™ Videodiscs

- *Tobacco*
- *Teenage Sexuality*
- *Alcohol*
- *Drugs and Substance Abuse*

See the ABCNews InterActive™ Bar Code Correlation booklet for applicable segments.

CHAPTER 3

Making Decisions and Managing Your Life

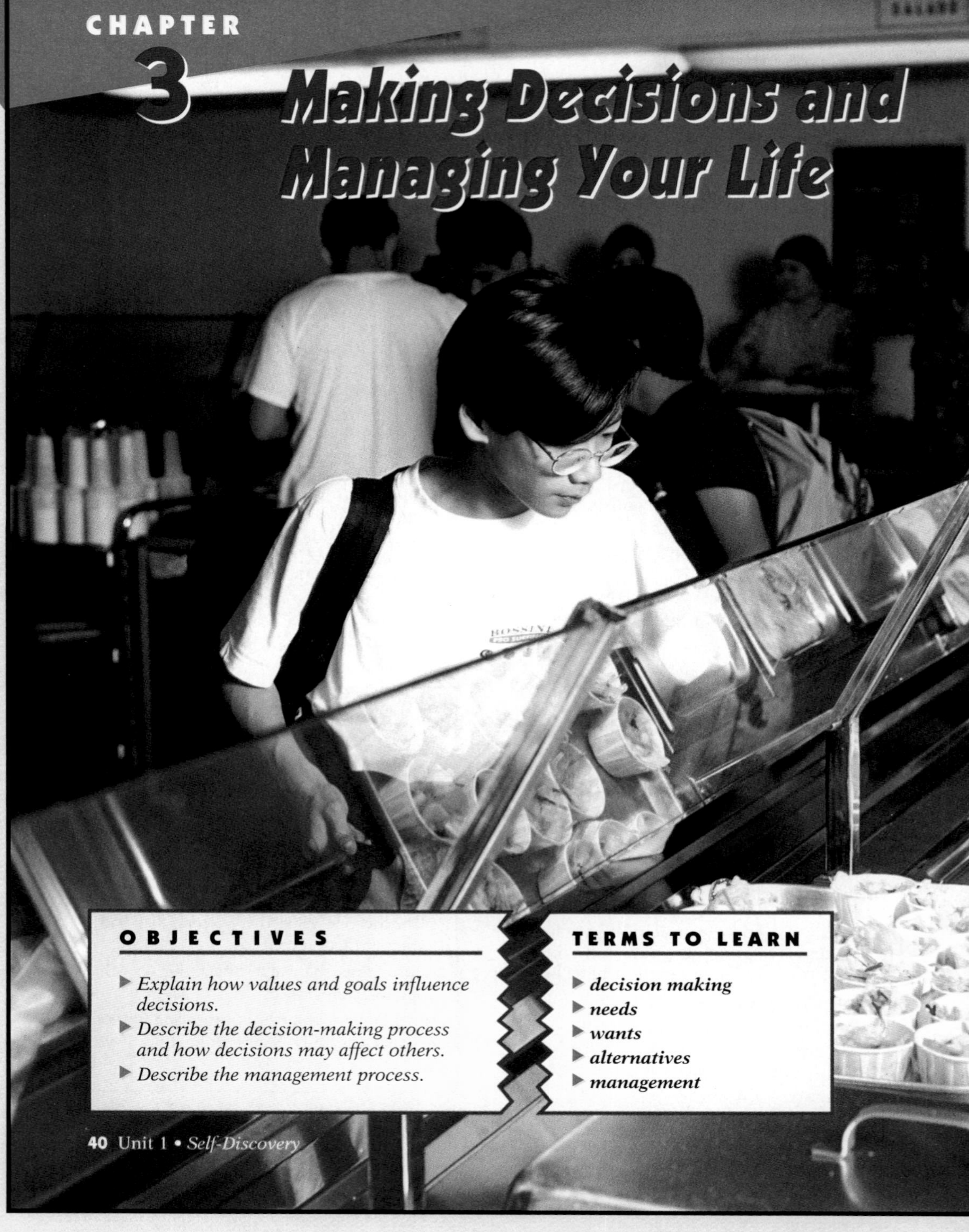

OBJECTIVES

- *Explain how values and goals influence decisions.*
- *Describe the decision-making process and how decisions may affect others.*
- *Describe the management process.*

TERMS TO LEARN

- ***decision making***
- ***needs***
- ***wants***
- ***alternatives***
- ***management***

It was a decision that Christa didn't think she could make. How could she choose? It would be like taking sides, and she didn't want to hurt anyone.

"Who do you want to live with," her grandfather had asked, "your mother or your father?"

Now that the divorce was certain, Christa wondered if her parents would ask her the same thing. She thought about what she would say if the question arose.

Making Decisions

Every day you make decisions. Some are easy; others are not. **Decision making** is the act of making a choice. It might involve something as simple as deciding what to eat or as complicated as picking a college.

Simple decisions are usually made almost without your noticing. When a decision has little effect on your life, it can be made this way. The route you take to school, for example, may not be important. If taking the long route will make you late, however, some thought should go into the decision. Which of the following decisions do you think could be made without much consideration?

- Which socks to put on in the morning.
- What classes to take next year.
- Which movie to see on Friday night.
- Who will be your closest friend.

Making some decisions may not be easy. You may need to do a lot of thinking before making a choice.

What Influences Decisions?

The decisions you make are influenced by many factors. Some are external and some are internal. That is, some come from people and things around you, and others come from the knowledge and attitudes within you.

Family

"I'm not going to tell you what to do, but . . ." Has anyone ever said this to you? Comments like this one are typical in families. As a small child, you could make few decisions on your own. During the teen years, however, more and more decisions become your responsibility. You need to learn decision-making skills in order to be able to do a good job of taking care of yourself both today and in the future.

Family members are usually willing and eager to help teens learn to make good decisions. To do this, they may offer advice and information to help the young person make

Introducing the Chapter

Motivators

1. **Brainstorming.** Have students read the opening paragraphs on page 41 and brainstorm a list of decisions that Christa might have to make in regard to her parents' divorce. Write the decisions on the chalkboard. (Key Skill: *Critical Thinking*)
2. **Discussion.** Refer students to the list of decisions on the chalkboard. (See Motivator #1). Draw lines to connect decisions that are related to each other. Talk about how one decision affects or leads to another. (Key Skill: *Communication*)
3. **Journal Writing.** Ask students to write in their journal three things they want most in life. Have them list some of the decisions they must make in order for these things to occur. (Key Skill: *Critical Thinking*)
4. **Bulletin Board.** Title a bulletin board "Your Life: It's Your Decision!" Display college and technical school catalogs and brochures; pictures of infants and families, people at work, and classroom scenes; travel brochures and posters, etc. Call attention to the display, and lead a discussion about how today's decisions affect tomorrow's choices and opportunities. (Key Skill: *Communication*)

Chapter Objectives and Vocabulary

1. Have students read the chapter objectives. Ask them to rephrase the objectives as questions.
2. Ask students to state, in their own words, the purpose of studying this chapter.
3. Pronounce the vocabulary terms listed on the previous page. Ask students whether they are familiar with any of these. Explain that the terms will be defined in the chapter.

Guided Reading

1. Have students read the chapter and use the Study Guide on pp. 19-20 of the *Student Workbook.*

More About Decision Making

In the United States, there are nearly 300 long distance telephone companies, hundreds of brands of dog and cat food, and thousands of different cosmetics and hair care products. Across the country, consumers and consumer advocates question if there are too many choices requiring too many decisions. Fortunately, as the choices and confusion increase, sources of information to answer consumer questions seem to be increasing as well. Copies of consumer publications, such as *Consumer Reports* magazine and information from government agencies and the Better Business Bureau, can be valuable resources in the classroom.

Teaching...
Making Decisions; What Influences Decisions?
(pp. 41-43)

Comprehension Check

1. What are three simple decisions that teens often make? *(Which socks to put on in the morning, which movie to see on Friday night, what cereal to have for breakfast today.)*
2. What is the difference between internal and external decisions? *(Internal decisions come from the knowledge and attitudes within you; external decisions come from people and things around you.)*
3. Name two ways that family members try to help teens learn to make good decisions. *(They offer advice and information; they make the decision for the teen.)*
4. Give an example of how a family's resources may affect a teen's decisions. *(If the family wage earner is out of work, the teen may decide to look for a part-time job, to delay buying new clothes, or to stay home on weekends in order to save gas.)*
5. What are two problems that can happen with values and decisions? *(Decisions may be based on a negative value; some people, if influenced by others or if their values are not clearly and carefully defined, go against their values when making a decision.)*
6. What are three basic physical needs? *(Food, clothing, shelter.)*
7. What are five basic emotional needs? *(Affection, security and safety, independence, belonging or acceptance, and achievement.)*
8. Explain the difference between needs and wants. *(Needs are essential for health and well-being; wants are things desired but not essential for health and well-being.)*

Learning Activities

1. **Skits.** Assign students to write and present skits about the influence of the family on a teen's decision. Afterwards, ask questions such as: How realistic was the skit? How was the family's influence helpful and harmful to the teen? Was the teen ready to make the decision alone? Would

Decisions, Decisions

Sometimes the decision to do nothing is wise. But you can't make a career of doing nothing. Freddie Fulcrum weighed everything too carefully. He would say, "On the one hand. . . but then, on the other," and his arguments weighed out so evenly he never did anything. When Freddie died, they carved a big zero on his tombstone. If you decide to fish — fine. Or, if you decide to cut bait — fine. But if you decide to do nothing, you're not going to have fish for dinner.

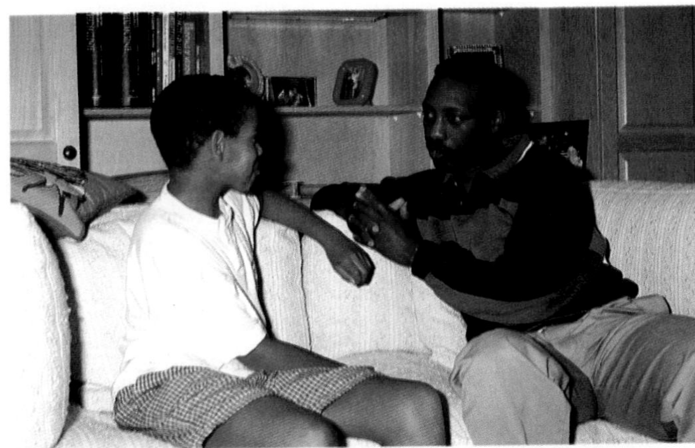

Talking through serious decisions with a trusted adult can help you make responsible choices.

his or her own decision. Sometimes they may make the decision for the teen. When might this be necessary? The adults in a family do not want to see teens make serious mistakes. They may even feel that the teen is not ready or able to make the decision alone. Although they know that young people learn by some mistakes, adults have a responsibility to protect and teach.

Families have a very strong influence on decisions. Even when family members are not providing direct input into a decision, the effect of the family is there. Everything you have experienced and learned within the family will come to bear upon the decisions you make and your ability to make them.

Friends

As you grow older, do you find yourself turning more often to friends for help with decisions? This is often the case. Friends have a strong influence on each other. Remember a couple points, however. Your friends often have no more experience or knowledge than you do. Some may even want to influence you for their own reasons. Be smart about seeking their help. You can always listen and learn, but, in the end, you must make your own decisions.

Resources

Decisions are often affected by resources including time, knowledge, money, and skills. Money, for example, is a common influence. While his stepfather was on strike for several months, Brett made some decisions related to the situation.

More About Resources

Many social institutions, including marriage and the family, are resources for reaching goals. Beyond the family, social resources exist in the neighborhood and community. Many institutions offer important services to individuals and families. Hospitals, clinics, and various agencies offer medical, dental, and mental health services along with treatment for drug and alcohol addiction. Schools, libraries, museums, art galleries, and training institutes are resources, as are banks, day care centers, police departments, and employment agencies.

He decided to look for a part-time job. He also decided to wear his track shoes for another season. In addition, he decided to stay home more on weekends in order to save gas. All of these decisions were directly linked to his family's reduced income during the strike.

Values

Should you get a job or play a team sport at school? Should you study or watch television? Should you buy a new sweater or save the money? The decisions you make are nearly always based on what you feel is important. As you read in the last chapter, these are your values. The decisions you make are a showcase for your values.

Sometimes problems arise when people base decisions on a negative value. If you don't have your values in order, you may pay the price of living with the consequences of a bad decision. Some people make decisions that go against their values because they give in to other outside influences. Believing in honesty and then letting someone talk you into doing something dishonest can cause real feelings of conflict, not to mention other problems.

Good decisions are much more likely to result when your values are clearly and carefully defined and carefully followed.

Decisions involve choosing one thing over another. Clearly defined values help you make good decisions.

Needs and Wants

As you make decisions, your needs and wants will be a strong influence. All human beings have certain needs. **Needs** are things that are essential for your health and well-being. You have physical, emotional, mental, and social needs.

You have three basic physical needs: food, clothing, and shelter. Your basic emotional needs include affection, security and safety, independence, belonging or acceptance, and achievement. Your desire to learn and experience the world around you is an intellectual need. Socially, you need to establish positive relationships with other people, including family, friends, and acquaintances.

Wants are those things you desire even though they are not essential for your health and well-being. Sometimes wants are viewed as needs even though they really aren't. Sometimes the line between the two is hard to see. Does Leila *want* a new dress for the prom or does she *need* one? What do you think?

More About *The Cost of Decisions*

No decision, or choice, is really *free*. Every choice has a cost. The cost is measured in resources used to reach a goal. The very act of making a choice limits a person's other choices. When one goal is chosen, the door may be closed on other goals. However, people who do not make choices allow things to happen to them by default. They fail to act in ways that will bring them satisfaction and freedom for future choices.

Learning Activities (continued)

the teen's decision have been difficult without the family's influence? If so, how? (Key Skills: *Communication, Critical Thinking*)

2. **Personal Analysis.** Have students divide a sheet of paper into two columns headed *needs* and *wants*. Next, ask them to imagine that a relative sent them $500. Have them think about how they would spend (or save) the $500. Ask them to list each expenditure in the appropriate column. Select volunteers to discuss their lists. (Key Skill: *Critical Thinking*)

Follow Up

1. **Reteaching.** Assign students to create mobiles, windsocks, or murals featuring six factors that influence people's decisions. Display and discuss the completed projects. (Key Skills: *Communication, Creativity*)
2. **Enrichment.** Assign small groups of students to develop two different commercials for products of interest to teens. Have them aim one commercial toward needs and the other toward wants. Have groups present their commercials to the class. (Key Skills: *Cooperation, Creativity*)

Life Management Skills

Human Relationships = Valuable Resources

Human relationships are important resources because of the help and support they offer. From family members, for example, teens can gain self-confidence. From friendships, their self-image can be strengthened. From relationships with teachers and counselors, teens can receive sound advice and constructive criticism. All of these relationships can provide the kind of support needed to reach goals.

Teaching. . .
Steps in Decision Making (pp. 44-45)

Comprehension Check

1. Why is it helpful to work a decision through on paper? *(Keeps attention focused on the decision to be made and on the process itself.)*
2. What is the advantage of identifying as many alternative ways to deal with a situation as possible? *(The more alternatives you think of, the more likely you are to find one that works.)*
3. What is one reason that people sometimes fail to act on their decision? *(Lack confidence in their decision to see it through.)*
4. What are three advantages of taking time to evaluate and learn from your decision? *(You can be proud of a good decision; discover what may work for you again; learn from a mistake and avoid making the same errors again.)*

Learning Activities

1. **Discussion.** Ask students to discuss reasons why the last step in the decision-making process tends to be difficult for some people. (Key Skills: *Communication, Critical Thinking*)
2. **Debate.** Select students to debate the statement: "The only way that people learn is by making mistakes." (Key Skills: *Critical Thinking, Communication*)
3. **Writing.** Assign students to write short stories about people who failed to list and examine alternatives before making a decision. What were the consequences? Ask for volunteers to share their stories with the class. Talk about how the stories might be different if these two steps had been taken. (Key Skills: *Critical Thinking, Creativity*)

The decision-making process can be used for all types of decisions, but is especially critical for major decisions. How is the teen in this drawing using the decision-making process?

▼ Steps in Decision Making ▼

One of the tricks to making good decisions is in knowing when to make them quickly and when to think them through. Read Emil's description of Wes:

"Wes never seems afraid to make a decision. You can see him thinking, and then he just says it. When no one else can decide what to do or how to handle something, Wes is willing to take a stand. It makes him look confident, and everybody admires that. Of course, I've seen him hold back, too. He might say something like, 'Well, I'll have to think about that.' When this happens, you know it's more complicated. Wes can stop and take a close look when he needs to, and I like that."

The process that Wes uses to make decisions is basically a simple one. It can be used for all types of decisions, although it becomes more critical for major decisions. If you are making a major decision, you may find it helpful to write down your ideas for each step as you work through the process. This will help you keep your attention focused on the decision to be made. Follow these steps in making decisions:

- ***Step 1: Identify the Decision to Be Made.*** Clearly defining the situation or problem that requires a decision helps you know exactly what must be decided upon. Thinking about your goal or desired outcome can help you make a more effective decision. For example, your goal might be to buy a new camera for a family trip. You need to decide what type of camera and which features will meet your needs, wants, and budget.

More About *Making Decisions*

Infants and young children live in the immediate present. They want things *now*. As they grow older, they begin to understand the concepts of *yesterday* and *tomorrow*. Past events can be recalled and future events can be anticipated. They begin to look forward to an event. As persons begin to mature, they learn to postpone the gratification of one need to satisfy another. For example, they can put off seeing a movie to study for a test. They learn that many goals worth reaching are worth working and waiting for. This can help them make decisions that lead to success throughout their life.

- **Step 2: Analyze Your Resources.** What do you need and what do you have that will help you resolve the situation, reach the goal, or solve the problem? Are time and energy all you need? If money is needed, how much can you spend? Do you have skills that would help? Where can you get more information?
- **Step 3: List the Alternatives.** Several ways of dealing with a situation are usually possible. Think about the different **alternatives** (ahl-TUR-nuh-tivs), or choices you have, and make a list. The more alternatives you think of, the more likely you are to find one that works.
- **Step 4: Examine the Alternatives.** Think through the decision in your mind. Consider the possible results of each alternative — listing the advantages and disadvantages of each. You may need to learn more about each alternative to do this. Here's where some of the resources you identified in step 2 can be helpful. You may find more information from family members and teachers. Books, magazines, and newspapers can also be helpful. An informed decision is more likely to be a good decision. Some people skip this step and make a quick decision at the wrong time. Such decisions may not lead to the results they want or expect.
- **Step 5: Choose the Best Alternative.** Think about your values, goals, wants, and/or needs. Make a choice that best fits them.
- **Step 6: Act on Your Decision.** Carry it out to the best of your ability. You may need to make a plan of action for carrying it through. Sometimes people willingly go through the process of reaching a decision, but they stop short of taking action. Have enough confidence in your decision to see it through.
- **Step 7: Evaluate Your Decision.** When you evaluate a decision, you judge its quality or how well it worked for you. If the outcome of a decision is not what you expected or hoped for, you may have to make a new decision. By analyzing your decision and determining what went wrong, you can avoid making the same error another time.

Listing and examining the alternatives are important to making an informed decision.

Learning from Your Decisions

A good decision is something to be proud of — you may even discover things that will work for you in the future. However, not all decisions will work out right for you. When your decisions don't work out, keep your chin up. No one makes the right decision all the time. Sometimes you have to live with the consequences of a wrong decision. You have to say, "Okay, this was my decision, and it didn't turn out the

Learning Activities (continued)

4. **Decision Simulations.** Divide students into small groups. Assign each group one of the situations below. Ask them to use the steps in the decision-making process to find a possible solution to the problem. Discuss the solutions with the class. • You are invited to a dance by someone really popular after accepting an invitation from someone else. • On the way to school you come across a puppy that has been hit by a car. It is still alive, but badly injured. • Your friends want to come over while you are babysitting. • Your dad wants you to help clean the garage. You have already made plans with friends. (Key Skills: *Problem Solving, Cooperation*)

Follow Up

1. **Reteaching.** Have students make posters illustrating steps in decision making. (Key Skills: *Communication, Creativity*)
2. **Enrichment.** Have students interview an adult about the best and worst decisions the adult ever made. Ask students to develop a list of questions to use. They should include questions about the alternatives that were available, what was learned from the decision, and what were the consequences of the decision. Without using names, have students share their findings with the class. (Key Skills: *Communication, Critical Thinking*)

Life Management Skills

Economic Decisions

Economic decision making is required when people have more than one use for a resource. For example, a young man may want to improve his personal appearance but has only so much time, money, energy, and skill to use in reaching his goal. He is making economic decisions when he chooses among such alternatives as spending money to buy a new pair of slacks instead of a CD.

Teaching. . .
The Impact of Decisions; Solving Problems
(pp. 46-47)

Comprehension Check

1. Who, besides Marla's friend, may have been affected when Marla changed her mind at the last minute (p. 46)? *(Her friend's parents and siblings.)*
2. What are two reasons for considering the consequences when making decisions? *(To protect the feelings and well-being of others; to avoid having regrets about your decisions.)*
3. How is problem solving different from decision making? *(Problem solving involves breaking down a problem into parts; it involves making more than one decision.)*

Learning Activities

1. **Empathy Experience.** Assign students to imagine they are the friend (p. 46) who invited Marla to spend the night at her house. Have them write a personal account of the friend's thoughts and feelings after learning that Marla had changed her mind. (Key Skill: *Critical Thinking*)
2. **Skits.** Select students to write and present skits about Roland's situation (p. 46) while his parents were gone. Have them portray how his parents, neighbors, and the police officers were affected by his actions and those of his friends. (Key Skills: *Communication, Critical Thinking*)
3. **Guest Speakers.** Invite a panel of individuals whose lives have been negatively affected by the driving decisions of others. Ask them to share their experiences with the class. (Key Skill: *Communication*)

Photo Focus

Have the students carefully examine the photo at the bottom of page 46. Ask students to discuss the consequences of disobeying driving laws. Who is affected when someone disregards the rules of the road?

way I had hoped. I'll just accept my error and try to do better the next time. Since everyone makes mistakes, I won't let this stop me from making decisions with confidence in the future."

▼ The Impact of Decisions ▼

In one afternoon, Jon changed the direction of his life. At sixteen he decided to quit school. The decisions he would make from that point on would be quite different. This is the way it is with many decisions. It's like a chain reaction. You make one decision that sets you on a certain course. If the decision is a big one, everything else from that point on may be different. Do you see why making the right decision can be very important?

How Others Are Affected

Sometimes the decisions you make affect only you. Many, however, affect others as well. The effects can range from minor to very serious. Think about the decisions made in the following situations. Who, in addition to the decision maker, was affected?

- One of Marla's friends invited her to spend the night at her house. Marla accepted but changed her mind at the last minute when something came up that she wanted to do more.
- Roland, age fifteen, invited friends to his apartment for a party while his parents were gone. The party got out of hand with loud music, too many people, and a mess in the apartment. The police responded to complaint calls from other people in the building.

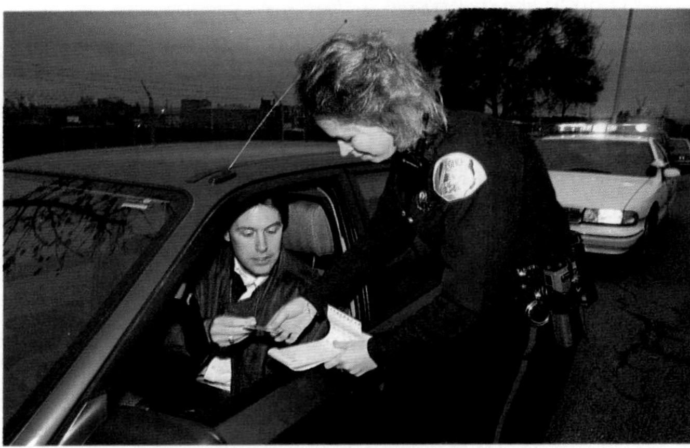

Think through the possible consequences of each decision. Who will your decision affect? This young man made the decision to disobey a traffic law. How might his decision affect others negatively?

More About *Decisions*

One of the decisions people make in life concerns career choices. In the past, people often thought that making a decision about a career was a once-in-a-lifetime event. All the experiences that happened before a career decision was made were thought to have had some effect on that decision. Actually, people usually do not make a single lifelong decision about a career. Throughout life they will make many decisions to reach their career goals. Even their goals and values may change as they change and as conditions change. Career development is a continuous process. It goes through stages as people grow and mature. The first stage involves *initial decisions* which are daydreams that people have about what

In 1987, some school children in Sweden set themselves a giant goal — saving the world's rain forests. They began small, with a bake sale that raised enough money to protect ten acres of rain forest. Soon, children and adults across Sweden were involved in raising funds and educating people about the importance of rain forests. The effort has spread among young people in over a dozen countries, including Great Britain, Australia, Costa Rica, and the United States. Tens of thousands of acres of rain forest have been purchased and protected. How have the decisions and actions of a small group of students affected — and continue to affect — the lives of many other people?

It's far too easy to make decisions without regard for the consequences to yourself and others. Choosing an alternative that protects another person's feelings and well-being, but does not produce the result you really wanted is more difficult. It may not be what is the most pleasing to you at the time. However, the self-centered alternative — one with no regard to its effects on others — can backfire on you. Think about all the consequences as you enter into the decision-making process. It can save many regrets.

Making decisions in a group is similar to making individual decisions. One big difference, however, is that the majority or all group members must agree upon the decision. What difficulties might there be in making group decisions? Read more about group decision making and improving relationship skills in Chapter 9.

Solving Problems

Sometimes the situations you face are more involved and require more than just making a single decision. For example, Aleesha was very lonely when her family moved to Chicago. It didn't seem like home to her. Aleesha's problem couldn't be solved by making a single decision. What she needed to do was break the problem down into parts she could better handle. Actually, several decisions needed to be made.

When Aleesha tackled her problem from several angles, she was able to solve it. Some of the decisions concerned how to find new friends, how to get to know her neighborhood and community, and in what types of activities she could get involved. Her problem was not as overwhelming when she took this approach.

TIPS: *Problem Solving*

Here are some helpful tips for solving problems:

- **Prepare yourself.** Gather the information you need to solve the problem.
- **Give yourself some "think" time.** Allow enough time to sort through the information you gathered. Spend time reflecting on all ideas and alternatives.
- **Take time to test the solution.** Apply the solution to the problem. Ask yourself, "Does the solution give me the results that I want?"

they want to do. *Exploratory decisions* are made when they find out more about careers that interest them and start to discover their own interests and work values. *Tentative decisions* help them define their work values and to experiment with various jobs. *Realistic decisions* are made when people make a choice and begin to work in a particular field. Encourage students to think about ways that initial, exploratory, tentative, and realistic decisions are used in other areas of life.

Follow Up

1. **Reteaching.** Print each of the following problems on separate strips of paper: a teen needs to get a job to help pay for school and recreation expenses; a teen finds it difficult to study while being a member of an athletic team; a teen is 25 pounds overweight; and a teen has no privacy in a room shared with a younger sibling. Give each student an empty can labeled with one of the printed strips of paper. Ask them to write the decisions that the teen must make to solve the specific problem on separate strips. Have students share their problem and decisions with the class. (Key Skill: *Problem Solving*)
2. **Enrichment.** Assign students to list, on separate sheets of paper, five major decisions that most parents must make; five major decisions that most elderly adults must make; and five major decisions that most teens must make. Ask them to identify people who might be affected by each of the decisions on their lists. Discuss the similarities and differences in the decisions and people affected. (Key Skill: *Critical Thinking*)

AROUND THE WORLD

Have students read the feature. Ask students to contact the library about international volunteer efforts of children and teens including the goals of the groups, successes and failures, and requirements for participation. Ask for volunteers to become pen pals with students of other countries. Request that they ask their pen pals to share information about work that teens are doing in their home country to improve the environment.

TIPS:

Problem Solving
Have students read the feature and use the suggested tips in solving a problem. How effective were the suggested tips?

Teaching. . .
Learning to Manage; The Management Process
(pp. 48-50)

Comprehension Check

1. What is management? *(Using what you have, to get what you need or want.)*
2. When making a management plan, what are four ways to put your plan in writing? *(In the form of a checklist, a schedule, a calendar, or reminder notes to yourself.)*
3. What does it mean to "control the plan?" *(To check progress and make any needed changes along the way.)*
4. What should you think about when evaluating the results of your plan? *(Was the goal reached? What worked well? What went wrong? Does a new goal need to get set?)*

Learning Activities

1. **Brainstorming.** Brainstorm a list of goals that many teens wish to achieve. Talk about how to set specific goals when following the management process. (Key Skills: *Communication, Critical Thinking*)
2. **Student Survey.** Assign students to design and carry out a survey of classmates to determine the number of hours they study each week. Ask them to report their findings to the class. (Key Skills: *Communication, Critical Thinking*)
3. **Bulletin Board.** Title a board "Get Hooked on Good Management." Display a fishing rod, along with newspaper and magazine articles featuring tips on managing one's life. Read and discuss some of the articles. (Key Skill: *Communication*)
4. **Self-Analysis.** Assign students to keep a record of everything they do and the time spent on each activity during the next 24 hours. Have them total the time in each type of activity, such as sleeping, eating, sitting in class, studying, visiting with friends, working, etc. Ask them to look at the results and discuss whether they are getting all they want from their 24 hours. Have them iden-

Learning to Manage

Camille never seemed to get much done. Even though she was able to do enough to get by, she had many things she wanted to accomplish. "What am I doing wrong?" she wondered.

The Management Process

A lesson in management could help Camille. **Management** means wisely using resources to achieve goals. In other words, management involves using what you have to get what you need or want. A good manager will use her or his decision-making, problem-solving, organizing, and planning skills. What other skills do you think might be helpful for a good manager?

Management may occur in many situations — from simple to complex. For example, using resources to manage a study schedule may be more easily accomplished than managing a small business.

When Camille learned a few basic steps in the management process, she found that she had much better control over her life. These steps are found in **Fig. 3-1**.

Figure 3-1 How to Manage in 5 Easy Steps

Following this management process can be helpful in many situations.

Set a Goal. Nothing will be accomplished until you decide what you want or need to do. Write your goal down in specific terms. Include a time frame. Instead of saying, "I want to do better in school," say "I plan to raise my language grade to a B by the end of the semester." This way you can see exactly what the expected result is and how long you have to achieve your goal. A time frame helps you pace yourself in working toward your goal.

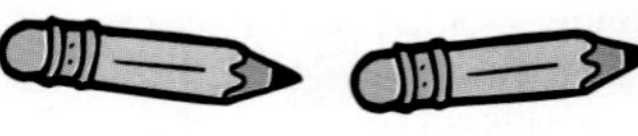

Make a Plan.

Now use your decision-making and problem-solving skills to determine what must be done to reach your goal. What steps must be taken? When, where, and how will you proceed? What resources can be used? Put your plan in writing. It may take the form of a checklist, a schedule, a calendar, or reminder notes to yourself. Whatever you use, keep it handy for regular reference.

Act on the Plan.

Putting the plan into action is an easy step for some people but a hard one for others. Remember that a plan without action won't get you anywhere.

Control the Plan.

This helps you keep the plan working. It involves checking the progress of your plan and making decisions about any needed changes along the way. For instance, you might say something like, "Because I didn't do well on my English test, I will ask the teacher for help with what I don't understand."

Evaluate the Results.

Was the goal reached? If so, remember what worked well for you. If not, determine what went wrong and think about revising your plan. You may need to set a different goal. Becoming a goal-oriented person can put an "A" for accomplishment in your life.

More About *Management*

After reading "Luisa's Attempt to Manage" on the next page, ask students if they have ever experienced a situation similar to Luisa's. Have them talk about what happened and what they might have done differently. Brainstorm appropriate responses Luisa might have given her best friend, Esther, when she called. Choose students to select and demonstrate some of the most suitable responses Luisa could have used to end the telephone conversation graciously so she could return to the task at hand.

tify the weak spots and ways in which they could be better time managers. (Key Skills: *Problem Solving, Management*)

5. **Guest Speaker.** Invite the school counselor to discuss ways to avoid procrastination by putting plans into action. (Key Skill: *Communication*)

Follow Up

1. **Reteaching.** Have students imagine they are to give a talk on the management process. Ask them to write a detailed outline for the presentation. (Key Skills: *Communication, Critical Thinking*)
2. **Extension.** Have students read the handout from p. 7 from the *Extending the Lesson* booklet of the TCR.
3. **Enrichment.** Ask students to discuss the relationship between the decision-making process and the management process. Have them identify ways the two processes are similar and ways they are different. (Key Skills: *Communication, Critical Thinking*)

Life Management Skills

Setting Goals and Priorities

Remind students that one way to set priorities is to think about specific goals. Some specific goals may be *fixed* and some may be *flexible*. A student might set a fixed goal of visiting his or her grandparents each week. The amount of time to spend on a shopping trip, however, is an example of a flexible goal. Some goals, such as how much time to spend on a social studies project, that are flexible to start with may become fixed if the student procrastinates.

Completing the Chapter

For Review

1. Emphasize the main concepts using the summary.
2. Have students complete the "Facts to Recall." (Answers below.)

For Reteaching

1. **Reteaching.** Use the activity on p. 7 of the *Reteaching and Practical Skills* booklet in the TCR.

For Enrichment

1. **Enrichment.** Use the activity on pp. 11-12 of the *Enrichment Activities* booklet in the TCR.

For Evaluation

1. Choose items from "Ideas to Explore" and "Activities to Try."
2. Use the chapter test on pp. 9-10 of the testing booklet in the TCR or use the testmaker software.

Facts to Recall Answers

1. The act of making a choice. Family, friends, resources, values, needs, and wants.
2. When a teen is not ready or able to make the decision alone, the adult is responsible for protecting the teen from making a serious mistake.
3. Often friends have no more experience or knowledge; to influence you for their own reasons.
4. It can cause feelings of conflict and other problems.
5. The four types of needs are physical, emotional, mental, and social. **Physical:** (any one) food, clothing, shelter. **Emotional:** (any one) affection, security and safety, independence, belonging or acceptance, achievement. **Mental:** desire to learn and experience your world. **Social:** need to relate to other people.
6. Identify the decision to be made; analyze your resources; list the alternatives; examine the alternatives; choose the best alternative; act on your decision; evaluate your decision.

Luisa's Attempt to Manage

4:00 p.m. — Luisa rushes into the house. She should have been home an hour ago.
4:15 p.m. — Luisa gets out all the ingredients to make hamburgers, french fries, and tossed salad. She also sets out the salad dressing and milk.
4:20 p.m. — Luisa peels and slices the potatoes.
4:35 p.m. — She finds that the hamburger patties are still frozen, so she begins to cook them anyway at a low temperature so they can defrost.
4:40 p.m. — Luisa's best friend, Esther, calls and they talk for 10 minutes.
4:50 p.m. — Luisa's mother comes home from work. Luisa had promised that dinner would be ready at 5 p.m. because her mother has plans for the evening.
4:55 p.m. — Luisa begins heating up the oil to fry the potatoes.
5:00 p.m. — She begins tearing up the lettuce but finds that it has gotten warm from sitting by the range. She puts it into the freezer to cool quickly. Luisa finally puts the potatoes into the hot oil.
5:10 p.m. — Luisa cuts up the tomatoes. She calls to her little brother, asking him to set the table.
5:15 p.m. — The hamburgers are sticking to the pan from cooking too long on one side. Luisa flips them over.
5:20 p.m. — Mother helps Luisa finish the salad, although Luisa promised to do everything by herself. Most of the lettuce has frozen and cannot be used.
5:25 p.m. — The hamburgers are done — well done. The french fries still have 10 more minutes to go. They must be eaten last. The salad dressing and the milk are too warm. Luisa blames everything on her friend's telephone call. She decides to serve peanut butter sandwiches the next time.

What specific problems can you identify in Luisa's management plan? What could she have changed to bring about better results?

Good management skills take practice. Developing your decision-making and problem-solving skills is part of learning to manage effectively. Management skills may be used in any number of situations throughout life. As you read through other chapters in this book, you will learn more ways to use your management skills.

TAKING ACTION
Solving a Dilemma

"Help me figure out what to do!" Trish nearly cries when she calls you on the phone. She had planned to work after school tomorrow at her part-time job at Henderson's Sporting Goods. Trish had also promised her mother, who works full-time, that she'd shop for food on the way home tomorrow since Aunt Sue is coming for dinner and Trish's mom plans to cook a special meal. After tomorrow's dinner, Trish had intended to study for a big test the next day.

Now Trish's friend Libby has called with a last-minute surprise. On a call-in radio program, Libby had won two tickets for the concert event of the year — tomorrow night. Trish has wanted to go for ages, but the concert was sold out before she could buy tickets. Now Libby has asked her to go, and Trish is torn over what to do. She needs your advice, especially since you sometimes fill in for her at her part-time job.

Using Your Resourcefulness

- After considering the choices and decisions that Trish needs to make, explain what course of action you would suggest.
- Could Trish manage her time in such a way as to fulfill all responsibilities and still attend the concert? If so, draw up a schedule for Trish.
- Suppose you have the same test as Trish. Would you be willing to fill in for her at work? Why or why not?

TAKING ACTION

After having the students read the feature, have them list all of Trish's obligations on the chalkboard. By student vote, rank the importance of each of the obligations. If the ranking was not unanimous, discuss reasons for the differences. Ask students to brainstorm a list of obligations that Trish's mother probably has. Have them vote on the ranking of each of her obligations. Contrast the mother's obligations with Trish's. Select several students to play the parts of Trish and her mother. Have the mother offer solutions to her daughter.

Chapter 3 Review

Summary

In this chapter, you have read about:
- Things that influence the decisions you make.
- The seven steps of the decision-making process.
- How the decisions you make can affect others.
- The five steps of the management process.

Facts to Recall

1. What is decision making? Identify six things that may influence your decisions.
2. Why is it sometimes necessary for an adult in a family to make a decision for a teen?
3. What are two problems with turning to friends for help with decisions?
4. What happens if you make a decision that goes against your values?
5. Identify the four types of needs and give an example of each.
6. List the seven steps in the decision-making process.
7. Briefly explain how you choose the best alternative when making a decision.
8. How can decision making have a "chain reaction" effect?
9. List the five steps of the management process.
10. How is it helpful to give yourself a time frame in which to accomplish a goal?

Ideas to Explore

1. Who do you think has more influence on a teen's decision making, family or friends? Explain.
2. Discuss how it can be difficult to tell the difference between needs and wants.
3. There is often conflict between teens and adults in a family as teens begin to want to make their own decisions. How might this conflict be avoided?

Activities to Try

1. Make a list of ten decisions you have made in the last week. For each one, write down what things influenced your decision and what effects your decision had on you and others.
2. Write a short essay explaining how you would use the seven-step decision-making process to help make one of the following decisions: where to go to college; what type of summer job you should look for; how to best use your allowance.

LINK TO *Communication*

MAKING AN EFFECTIVE DECISION

Create a skit in which someone needs to make a major decision. Write two versions of the skit. The question or course of action that needs to be decided upon will be the same for both versions; how the decision is made will be different. The first version should show the person taking a shortcut in decision making. The second version should show the same person using the seven-step decision-making process. Share the skit with the class. Discuss the following:
- How did the results of each method of decision making compare?
- Which method of decision making was the most effective?
- What are the benefits of using the decision-making process for major decisions?

Facts to Recall Answers (continued)

7. Make the choice that best fits your values, goals, wants, and/or needs.
8. The decisions you make now will affect the decisions you will have to make in the future. They can change the entire direction of your life.
9. Set a goal; make a plan; act on the plan; control the plan; evaluate the results.
10. It helps you pace yourself in working toward your goal.

Ideas to Explore

1. Answers will vary.
2. Answers will vary.
3. Answers will vary, but should include keeping the lines of communication open.

Using Your Resourcefulness Answers
- Answers will vary.
- Answers will vary, but may include *yes* if she finds someone to fill in for her at her job.
- Answers will vary.

LINK TO *Communication*

The skits will vary according to content of the skits.
- Answers will vary.
- Students should find the second version of decision making to be more effective.
- Answers will vary, but may include: better decisions are made, a more informed decision is made, less mistakes will be made with major decision, etc.

Preparing to Teach

Chapter Outline

Chapter Resources

The following booklet materials may be found in the *Teacher's Classroom Resources* box:
- Lesson Plans, p. 9
- Student Workbook, *Study Guide,* pp. 23-24; *Going Through Change,* p. 25; *Are You Burning Out?,* p. 26
- Color Transparencies, *Stress Busters,* CT-4
- Personal Safety, *Stress and Safety,* pp. 7-8
- Technology and Computers, pp. 8, 11
- Cooperative Learning, p. 16
- Extending the Text, *Stress Survival Tips,* p. 8
- Reteaching and Practical Skills, *Change On!,* p. 8
- Enrichment Activities, *Keeping a Record of Stress,* pp. 11-12
- Chapter and Unit Tests, pp. 11-12
- Testmaker Software

Also see:
- Meeting the Special Needs of Students
- Linking Home, School, and Community
- Dealing with Sensitive Issues

ABCNews InterActive™ Videodiscs
- *Food and Nutrition*
- *Teenage Sexuality*
- *Drugs and Substance Abuse*
- *Alcohol*
- *Violence Prevention*
- *Tobacco*

See the ABCNews InterActive™ Bar Code Correlation booklet for applicable segments.

CHAPTER 4

Coping with Change and Stress

OBJECTIVES

- *Discuss the types of changes typical during adolescence and ways to cope with them.*
- *Identify signs of stress and ways to manage stress positively.*

TERMS TO LEARN

- ***adolescence***
- ***puberty***
- ***growth spurt***
- ***hormones***
- ***character***
- ***ethics***
- ***stress***

Looking at old family photo albums was always fun. It had been a few years since anyone had dug them out at Ben and Joy's house. One rainy Sunday afternoon, they decided to browse through them. Seeing Uncle Bill and Grandma Lacey as teens was always cause for a chuckle. Not only had styles changed, but they both looked so different. Everyone had changed, from childhood through the teen years to adulthood, including Ben and Joy. They wondered what changes were yet ahead for them. Someday the family album would tell.

Understanding Change

Adolescence (ad-uh-LESS-unts), or the stage of growth between childhood and adulthood, is a time of many changes. During these years, teens change faster than they ever will again. Like Ben and Joy, you have changed since you were younger, and the process is continuing.

During adolescence, teens often experience a rapid growth spurt.

Physical Changes

Right now your body is probably changing rapidly. These rapid changes affect the way you feel, behave, and think about yourself.

It is helpful to know some facts about adolescence. The beginning of adolescence is marked by puberty. **Puberty** (PYOO-burt-ee) is the time when boys and girls start to develop the physical characteristics of adult women and men. For girls, the beginning of menstruation — a monthly discharge of blood from the uterus — is an early sign that puberty has begun. For boys, the reproductive system begins producing sperm. Both girls and boys usually experience a rapid increase in height, a **growth spurt**. Girls may notice their body shape changes. Boys often notice facial hair growth and their voices deepening. Both boys and girls may notice strong surges of physical energy.

During puberty, your **hormones**, or chemical substances in your body, are at a very high level. They help stimulate body changes and the development of the male and female reproductive systems.

Puberty lasts an average of three years, but it can start at different ages. Boys usually begin puberty around age thirteen, but it can come as early as eleven or as late as fifteen, or even older. Girls usually begin puberty around age eleven,

Introducing the Chapter

Motivators

1. **Question Box.** Invite students to write down questions they would like to have discussed during the study of this chapter. Ask them to place their unsigned questions in a closed box with a slot cut in the top. Select some of the questions to answer each day. (Key Skills: *Communication, Critical Thinking*)
2. **Class Discussion.** Discuss some of the changes in the lives of Uncle Bill and Grandma Lacey since they were teens (p. 53). Have students list on the chalkboard personal changes that the two individuals may have experienced as they grew older. Next, ask them to list changes that the two observed throughout the world. Ask students to predict what changes may be ahead for them from now until their old age. (Key Skills: *Communication, Critical Thinking*)
3. **Creative Project.** Have students write poems, songs, and jingles about change. Ask for volunteers to share their completed projects. (Key Skills: *Communication, Creativity*)
4. **Historical Analysis.** Display and discuss pictures showing changes in areas such as clothing, hairstyles, housing, appliances, children's toys, electronics, and automobiles. Talk about reasons for some of the changes. (Key Skill: *Communication*)

Chapter Objectives and Vocabulary

1. Have students read the chapter objectives. Ask them to rephrase the objectives as questions.
2. Ask students to state, in their own words, the purpose of studying this chapter.
3. Pronounce the vocabulary terms listed on the previous page. Ask students whether they are familiar with any of these. Explain that the terms will be defined in the chapter.

Guided Reading

1. Have students read the chapter and use the Study Guide on pp. 23-24 of the *Student Workbook.*

More About Exercising to Cope with Change and Stress

An appropriate exercise program can help relieve the anxiety and tension that are common among people in today's fast-paced world. It also can help individuals in difficult life circumstances cope with change and stress that they may experience. Exercise helps promote a sense of well-being by enhancing self-esteem and self-confidence, dissipating anger and hostility, relieving boredom, and resolving frustration.

Teaching. . .
Understanding Change; Physical, Emotional, Social and Intellectual Change; Moral Development
(pp. 53-55)

Comprehension Check

1. What is puberty and how long does it usually last? *(Puberty is the time when you develop adult characteristics; it lasts an average of three years.)*
2. Why do teens often feel awkward during puberty? *(Because of rapid changes in height and build.)*
3. Give two examples of how teens develop physically at different rates. *(A girl may look much older than her peers; one boy may not need to shave while another boy of the same age can grow a beard.)*
4. Why is knowledge about puberty helpful to teens? *(Knowing what is happening to their body and emotions can help teens understand reasons for their spurts of energy and changing emotions and feelings.)*
5. Name four ways to deal with strong emotions and the extra energy of the teen years. *(Getting involved with intramural sports, joining the pep squad, taking part in other forms of exercise, helping other people.)*
6. Describe people who have developed morally. *(They base their decisions on a set of ethics that work positively in their lives; they develop character and act according to a set of high moral principles; they gain respect from others and get along better in life.)*

Learning Activities

1. **Photo Analysis.** Ask students to look at pictures of themselves, family members, or friends that were taken in infancy, childhood, and adolescence. Have them discuss the physical differences they observed from one state to the next. (Key Skills: *Communication, Critical Thinking*)

Teens go through rapid changes during puberty as they grow to adulthood. What are some changes that you've experienced?

but it is normal for it to start any time between nine and thirteen. Some begin even later. For example, one fifteen-year-old girl may have completed her development. Another may be just beginning puberty at the same age.

Teens sometimes feel awkward with rapid changes in height and build. Eventually, the awkward feelings disappear, as teens adjust to the new growth and development.

It is common to worry that you are changing too slowly or too quickly. Teresa is thirteen but looks like seventeen. She feels out of place among her friends. Rob is seventeen and doesn't need to shave. His younger brother Drake, however, is already shaving. Teens develop at different rates. If you are not growing and changing as quickly as your friends, don't worry. Every healthy human being grows up. Whether you start early or late has no effect upon the end product — the adult you.

Emotional Changes

Do you sometimes feel on top of the world one day and down in the dumps the next? Along with spurts of physical growth and energy come surges of strong emotions. Emotions and feelings can change rapidly during puberty. They can make you feel restless and irritable or happy and full of life.

These surges of emotion are also affected by the changing hormones in your body. They can cause emotions to be very intense and swing rapidly — part of the "growing pains" of adolescence.

Knowledge is a special ally during this stage of your life. When you know what is happening to your body and causing your emotional ups and downs, you can understand some things better. Some teens tend to think that if they feel down about something, that feeling will never go away. This is not true. You need to know that the strong emotions you sometimes feel will probably last just a short time. The emotional swings you experience in adolescence eventually settle down as you enter adulthood.

There are many positive ways to deal with strong emotions and use the extra energy of the teen years. Get involved in physical activities, such as intramural sports, pep squad, or an exercise program that you enjoy. Try helping other people. You will feel better and worry less about yourself.

Social and Intellectual Changes

Although physical and emotional development are most apparent, you are also developing socially and intellectually. All of these areas of development are related.

More About *Physical Development*

Physical growth in adolescence is triggered by hormones which are released primarily from the pituitary gland. Besides hormones, the health habits of teens, particularly diet and exercise, strongly influence their physical development. Personal health habits affect their weight, posture, complexion, hair, and energy level.

As physical and emotional changes occur, teens are growing socially and intellectually, too. Developing good social skills as a teen will serve you well in relationships with others throughout your life.

You have many opportunities for learning how to get along with others — family, friends, and acquaintances. This is social development. Your relationships change throughout your life. As you change and grow, your interests may change, leading to new friendships. Developing good social skills will serve you well throughout life.

At the same time that you are growing socially, you are gaining both knowledge and experience. This is your intellectual development. The education you receive, and the school and community activities in which you participate, give you new insights and ways of looking at things.

▼ Moral Development ▼

At times you will face decisions that deal with issues of right and wrong. In a complex situation, these decisions can be difficult. Although you want to do what's right, sometimes it's not clear which course of action is right and which is wrong. Your choices may also be more difficult if you feel pressure from others.

The challenge is to learn to base important decisions on a set of **ethics** or moral principles — generally accepted guidelines for right and wrong behavior. For example, telling the truth and treating people fairly are commonly accepted as standards of right behavior. Strong ethics, based on positive

The Snake That Poisons Everybody

It topples governments, wrecks marriages, ruins careers, busts reputations, causes heartaches, nightmares, indigestion, spawns suspicion, generates grief, and dispatches innocent people to cry in their pillows. Even its name hisses. It's called gossip. Office gossip. Shop gossip. Party gossip. It makes headlines and headaches. Before you repeat a story, ask yourself: Is it true? Is it fair? Is it necessary? If not, shut up.

Learning Activities (continued)

2. **Discussion.** Lead the class in a discussion of whether students receive adequate information about puberty before entering adolescence. Identify sources of information that have been, or would be, helpful. (Key Skills: *Communication, Critical Thinking*)
3. **Research Project.** Assign students to research some of the physical changes that occur during puberty. Have them present their findings to the class. (Key Skills: *Communication, Critical Thinking*)
4. **Writing.** Have students write a paragraph about one or more teenagers whose moral development took place due to various influences in their lives. These might include parental example, school activities, volunteer work, friendships, work experiences, crises, etc. (Key Skills: *Communication, Critical Thinking*)
5. **Research.** Select students to investigate the relationship of hormones and emotions, such as anger and moodiness, during puberty. Discuss their research findings with the class. (Key Skills: *Communication, Critical Thinking*)

Follow Up

1. **Reteaching.** Divide students into groups, and have them write and present skits about a typical teen going through puberty. Ask them to feature some of the physical and emotional changes that take place. (Key Skills: *Cooperation, Creativity*)
2. **Enrichment.** Assign students to use library resources to prepare illustrated reports contrasting the growth spurt that occurs during the first year of life with the growth spurt that happens during puberty. Have them present their reports to the class. (Key Skills: *Critical Thinking, Communication*)

More About Emotional Growth

Emotional growth develops at a different rate among adolescents — perhaps more so than physical and intellectual development. Changes in the body may make young people very happy one minute and moody the next. These body changes may also arouse interest in the opposite sex and promote a desire for closeness. Emotional growth helps teens to understand others' needs and feelings and, at times, to put another person's needs ahead of theirs.

Teaching. . .
Managing Stress
(pp. 56-57)

Comprehension Check

1. Define stress. *(Physical or emotional strain or tension that is caused by pressures, fears, worries, and changes in life.)*
2. In what ways can some degree of stress be helpful? *(Keeps you on your toes by pushing you to do better and to work harder.)*
3. Explain how stress can be compared to the tightness of a violin string. *(Enough tension is needed to make music, but not so much that the string snaps.)*
4. How are signs of stress like warning lights? *(They could be warning you of serious problems or illnesses.)*

Learning Activities

1. **Brainstorming.** Have students brainstorm a list of situations and changes in teen lives that can cause stress. Next, ask them to brainstorm a list of situations and changes in parental lives that can also cause stress. Point out that people can never be completely free of stress. (Key Skills: *Communication, Critical Thinking*)
2. **Discussion.** Ask students to share and discuss times in which some degree of stress has been helpful to them. Also, discuss instances in which stress has been harmful to students, their friends, or their families. (Key Skills: *Communication, Critical Thinking*)
3. **Reading.** Assign students to locate and read magazine and newspaper articles about stress. Ask them to discuss the key points in what they read with the class. (Key Skill: *Communication*)

TIPS:

Character Development
Have students read the feature on page 56. Ask them to write down an example showing how they are developing a positive character for each item listed in the feature.

TIPS: *Character Development*

Here are some tips that may indicate your progress in developing a positive character:

- Your willingness to act without rewards or acknowledgement.
- Your ability to control strong emotions and find ways to express them constructively.
- Developing patience in delaying personal pleasure or reward when needed.
- Showing your dependability by keeping promises.
- Showing your ability to admit mistakes rather than making excuses for yourself.
- Developing your ability to look at problems and situations from all angles.

values, can guide you through difficult times. When making difficult choices, it is also helpful to seek guidance from parents, teachers, religious leaders, or counselors. When you act according to a set of high ethical principles, you are said to be a person of good **character**. People of good character gain respect and trust from others.

Managing Stress

While change goes on within you, it goes on around you as well. All of these changes can cause pressures, fears, self-doubt, feelings of self-consciousness, and emotional highs and lows. Sometimes the combination can be challenging to handle and lead to a great deal of stress.

▼What Is Stress?▼

Stress is the physical or emotional strain or tension that is caused by pressures, fears, worries, and changes in your life. During adolescence, you may find that you have increased responsibilities and others expect more of you. This may add even more pressure and stress.

Everyone has stress. Anyone who moves to a new city, job, or school experiences stress. Divorce or remarriage can cause stress for everyone involved — children, parents, grandparents, and close friends. Trying to meet a deadline for school or work can also cause stress. You can never be completely free of it. You can, however, learn how to manage it.

Everyone experiences stress. Some learn to manage that stress better than others. What are some healthful ways to manage your stress?

More About *Stress*

Poor health is a major cause of stress. The fear of injury, surgery, or a serious illness can also cause great stress. In addition, people feel stress if they are afraid for the health of family members and friends. Fear of becoming disabled or handicapped, especially of going blind, is common. An actual handicap creates even more stress. Learning to use a wheelchair or a guide dog is not easy. Accepting the fact that the wheelchair or the dog will always be needed may be even more difficult.

▼ What Can You Do? ▼

How you react to the stress you face every day is important. Some stress is helpful because it keeps you on your toes. It pushes you to do better and work harder. Too much stress, however, can cause emotional strain and may even lead to physical problems. Think of stress as the tension, or tightness, of a violin string. You need enough to make music, but not so much that the string snaps. In the section that follows, you will learn ways to identify and manage stress — to keep yourself well tuned, just like that violin.

Identify Signs of Stress

How do you know if you are suffering from stress? Your body will give you physical signs of stress. It will also give you emotional signs. For example, a pounding heart when you are scared and sweating hands when you are nervous are physical signs of stress. You may find it hard to go to sleep when you are worrying about something. These are some ways in which your body reacts to stress. Other physical signs of stress include:

- Headaches and backaches
- Upset stomach or other digestive problems
- Tight muscles or pain in the shoulders or neck
- Dizziness
- Eating too much or too little
- Feeling tired much of the time

Symptoms of stress may be physical or emotional and are common to people of all ages.

These physical symptoms could be caused by problems other than stress. There might be some other reason for a headache or sleeplessness. Stress, however, is a very common problem among people of all ages. When you suffer physical symptoms such as those just listed, stress may be the cause.

Emotional signs of stress are often more difficult to detect than physical signs. Matt has learned that when he starts getting too critical of himself and his friends, it is a sign that he has too much stress. Midori becomes depressed when she is stressed. Other emotional signs of stress include:

- Restlessness
- Boredom with school or work
- Irritability and difficulty in getting along with others
- Anger at self and others
- Carelessness about mistakes

Signs of stress are like warning lights. They could be warning you of serious problems. Stress can sometimes

More About Causes of Stress

Stress resulting from divorce is similar to the stress caused by the death of a loved one. Divorce, like death, involves a loss. An important person is gone. Stress also comes about from fights and arguments that sometimes go along with divorce. This is especially true regarding custody of the children. The children, as well as their parents, can suffer stress. Children often feel guilty and think they may have caused the problems leading to divorce. Divorce may bring about other changes, such as moving to another home and school. It also may mean leaving favorite friends and relatives.

Learning Activities (continued)

4. **Advice Column.** Have students write an advice column, offering suggestions for recognizing signs of stress. (Key Skills: *Communication, Creativity*)
5. **Sentence Completion.** Have students complete and discuss the following sentences: "Some of the things that cause me to feel stressed are ...," "When I am really stressed, my body begins to ...," "Sometimes stress is helpful to me because ...," and "The most common sign of stress that I experience is ..." (Key Skills: *Communication, Critical Thinking*)

Follow Up

1. **Reteaching.** Assign students to write one-page stories about teens or adults who are suffering from stress. Have them identify some of the signs of stress that the characters are experiencing. (Key Skills: *Critical Thinking, Creativity*)
2. **Enrichment.** Select students to write public service announcements about stress. Have them include information about the advantages and disadvantages of stress and the physical and emotional signs of stress. Assist them in videotaping their completed announcements to share with other classes. (Key Skills: *Communication, Creativity*)

Wellness

Many people thrive on stress. They find working under pressure or against deadlines highly stimulating, providing the motivation to do their best. Others are just the opposite and do not find stress a helpful motivation to get work done. Have students assign themselves to one of two groups: "Stress, Oh Yes!" and "Stamp Out Stress." Ask each group to discuss their feelings about stress. Have them identify some of their physical and emotional reactions to stress. Bring the two groups together to contrast their reactions to stress.

Teaching. . .
Look at Your Attitude; Relax; Exercise (pp. 58-59)

Comprehension Check

1. Name at least three ways the right attitude helps reduce stress. *(Think about the positive side; be choosy about problems to meet head on; time to examine your attitude; be more accepting; be open to other points of view.)*
2. How can relaxing help you deal with stress? *(Relaxing helps you loosen up and become less tense and more at ease.)*
3. What are two ways to relax? *(Daydream or read a good book.)*
4. How can exercise help you manage stress? *(Hard workouts won't leave you much energy for worrying.)*

Learning Activities

1. **Discussion.** Ask students to give examples of how their attitudes affect the way they deal with stressful situations. Talk about healthy ways to change attitudes. (Key Skills: *Communication, Critical Thinking*)
2. **Personal Analysis.** Ask students to list stressors in their lives that they consider positive and stressors that they consider negative. Have them underline the negative stressors that cannot be changed and circle the negative stressors that can be changed, lessened, or overcome. Ask them to make a written plan for overcoming or lessening one or more

Around the World

Have students read the feature. Select students to research entrance requirements for high schools and universities in various countries. Invite foreign students to speak to the class and contrast various stressors in their home country and in the United States. Have them discuss the types of sports, music, and youth organizations enjoyed by teens in their country.

Education is very important in Japan. Young people are expected to study hard to get into good schools and find high-paying jobs after graduating. Students must pass entrance exams to get into high school and universities — the best schools have the toughest exams. Therefore, many students, some as young as age seven, take extra classes to improve their studying and test-taking skills. Like American youths, Japanese young people deal with stress through sports such as baseball and judo, or by joining youth clubs or listening to music.

cause illnesses, such as high blood pressure and heart disease. These diseases often afflict young people as well as adults. To protect your health, you need to be alert for signs of stress. When you see signs of stress in yourself, you need to find healthful ways to reduce stress in your life. Consider the tips that follow.

Look at Your Attitude

Much of the time, it's your attitude about an event, not the event itself, that results in stress. For example, if you have to stand in a long line, your attitude about waiting will determine how stressful the situation will be. You can become frustrated and angry about the delay. On the other hand, you can choose not to be upset. Instead, you can use the time to plan your day's activities or just relax and watch the people around you. Which attitude would create stress? Here are some tips for reducing or avoiding stress by having the right attitude:

- ***Think about the positive side of a situation.*** If you are moving to another city, think about the opportunities and the new friendships the move will bring.
- ***Be choosy about the problems you decide to meet head on.*** Don't let small irritations become large problems. If something is important to you, by all means stand up for your beliefs. However, learn to keep your reaction in proportion to the situation. Adding frustration — your own and everyone else's — only increases the stress.
- ***Give yourself time to examine your attitude.*** Sometimes you can change your attitude by backing off and leaving the room, taking a walk, jogging, or watching a favorite television show. Taking a little break gives you time to get control of your emotions and will help you see the situation more clearly.

More About Stress

Dr. Hans Selye, an international authority on stress, called stress "the very salt and spice of life." Without any stress, life would be dull. Too much stress, on the other hand, can be dangerous both to people's physical and mental health. Extended periods of stress can make a person feel exhausted and depressed, and can wear down the body's natural immune system, often causing illness. Many of the mechanisms individuals use to reduce stress, such as smoking, drinking alcohol, and using other drugs, only increase the likelihood of health problems.

Giving yourself time to examine your attitude is a helpful way to manage your stress. Backing off from a situation and taking time to play a family game or go for a walk can help you control your emotions and lessen the stress in your life.

- ***Learn to be more accepting.*** Some things just can't be changed. You will be much happier if you say something like, "Well, since I can't change this situation, I may as well make the best of it."
- ***Be open to other points of view.*** Looking at stressful situations from the viewpoint of others, and not just your own, can help you understand all angles of the situation. This can help you change your attitude.

Relax

Learn how to relax. When you relax, you loosen up. You become less tense and are more at ease. When you feel tension building up, try to get away from the cause of your stress for a while.

Sometimes it helps to occasionally sit in a chair and daydream. Keep your thoughts positive, or think about a beautiful beach you saw in a magazine. Try reading a good book to take your mind off your troubles.

Exercise

Physical exercise can help too. If you are upset, work off your stress with physical activity. Get a hard workout by playing something you enjoy, such as basketball or tennis.

Learning Activities (continued)

of the circled stressors. Have volunteers share some of their plans with the class. (Key Skills: *Problem Solving, Management*)

3. **Interviews.** Select students to interview a family that has moved from one city to another within the year. Have students ask questions such as: What stress did the family experience? Was the stress different for different family members? How did they manage the stress? Lead a classroom discussion of the interview findings. (Key Skills: *Communication, Critical Thinking*)
4. **Time Lines.** Ask for volunteers to draw individual time lines, for their analysis only. Have them identify times of stress that they recall from birth until the present. (Key Skill: *Critical Thinking*)
5. **Commercials.** Have students create radio or television commercials for one or more ways to manage stress, such as relaxation, physical exercise, goal setting, list making, developing healthy habits, and volunteer service. Ask them to present their commercials to the class. (Key Skills: *Communication, Creativity*)

Follow Up

1. **Reteaching.** Have students write a summary identifying the main points concerning how attitude, relaxation, and exercise affect stress. (Key Skill: *Critical Thinking*)
2. **Enrichment.** Select students to research various service opportunities for teens in the community. Ask for volunteers to choose one area of service and to spend one or two hours each week helping others. Have them keep a journal about their experiences. Later, ask them to share some of the experiences with the class. (Key Skills: *Citizenship, Cooperation*)

More About *Stress Management*

In stressful situations, many people tend to restrict their breathing. It becomes short and shallow, and centered primarily in the chest area. This cuts down on the amount of oxygen that reaches the brain, and creates added tension in the stomach and lower back. Since the rhythm and regularity of breathing can have a calming effect on the nervous system, deep breathing can help reduce the stress a person feels. It is done by sitting quietly for several minutes with eyes closed and attention focused on breathing through the nose easily and naturally, letting shoulder and neck muscles relax.

Photo Focus

Have students examine the photo at the top of page 59. Ask them to identify ways that spending time relaxing with family and friends benefits stress reduction.

Teaching... *Realistic Goals; Plan Your Days; Healthy Habits; and Help Others* *(pp. 60-62)*

Comprehension Check

1. Why is it important to be realistic when setting goals? *(If too many goals are beyond your reach, stress may be added to life by working too long and worrying too much about failure.)*
2. Name four healthy habits that can help you manage stress. *(Eat a balanced diet, get plenty of sleep and rest, do some form of exercise daily, avoid alcohol and other drugs.)*
3. How can helping others assist you in managing stress? *(It helps you get your mind off yourself and your own stress.)*
4. In what way might your family doctor or the school nurse be especially helpful in dealing with stress? *(They can put you in touch with social agencies and professionals who can provide additional help.)*
5. Name three community organizations that may help you find ways to cope with change and stress. *(The YMCA, YWCA, and the Red Cross.)*
6. Why is it sometimes helpful to talk over problems with a trusted friend or religious leaders? *(Saying something out loud may help you put a problem in perspective.)*

Learning Activities

1. **Discussion.** Ask students to answer and discuss the following questions: What kind of problem would make you want to talk to someone about your stress? To whom would you talk? Why would you choose this person? (Key Skills: *Communication, Critical Thinking*)
2. **Bulletin Board.** Assign students to collect comic strips and cartoons showing supportive friendships. Display some of these on a bulletin board titled "Special Friends in Times of Stress." (Key Skill: *Cooperation*)

Participating in a physical activity that you enjoy can help you work off your stress and leave little time for worrying.

Try running or jogging. The energy it takes won't leave you much energy for worrying. Let off steam by doing household tasks, such as cleaning out a closet or doing yard work. This will help you do two things at once — get some work done and work off your stress.

Set Realistic Goals

Setting goals may help you reduce or manage stress. If you have a goal to work toward, extra tasks and responsibilities will be more meaningful. A goal will also help you measure your work. You'll be able to see how much you have accomplished and how much more there is to do.

Remember to be realistic about your goals. You can challenge yourself and dare to dream, but setting too many goals that are beyond your reach may add stress to your life. You must be realistic about the number of goals you set for yourself, too. Don't expect to be able to do everything at once; take one thing at a time. If you set unrealistic goals, you'll end up working too long and worrying too much about failure.

Plan Your Days

Many people find it helpful to do their planning on paper by making lists. Try making daily and weekly activity lists and crossing off items as you finish them. This will let you see what you've accomplished. At the end of each day, and at the end of each week, you can check your progress. You will learn more about managing your time in Chapter 18.

Develop Healthy Habits

Eat a balanced diet, including a variety of healthful foods. Get plenty of sleep, rest, and exercise. Lack of sleep reduces your ability to manage stress. It can also make you tired and irritable.

Do not use alcohol and other drugs. These present legal as well as health problems. The ability to manage stress comes from within you. Pills, alcohol, and other drugs reduce your ability to manage stress and add new problems. If you try to cope this way, you will never learn how to manage stress. Instead, you will have more stress.

Help Others

Sometimes when you feel stressed, you may be thinking too much about yourself. You might be all wrapped up in your own problems and too close to the situation to see a positive solution.

When managing stress, it often helps to get your mind off yourself. By doing something for others, you forget your own stress for awhile. Doing something extra around the house, helping a younger brother or sister with school work, running an errand for an elderly neighbor, and visiting someone in the hospital are just a few examples of ways you can help others and deal with stress at the same time.

Developing healthy habits shows you care about yourself and can help you manage stress.

Learning Activities (continued)

3. **Discussion.** Have students name and describe several television programs that feature characters helping each other deal with stress. Talk about ways that students help each other and their family members deal with stress. (Key Skills: *Social Studies, Critical Thinking*)
4. **Discussion.** Ask students to discuss ways they can be a supportive person for their friends and family members. (Key Skill: *Critical Thinking*)

Follow Up

1. **Reteaching.** Distribute several 3-inch by 5-inch notecards to students. Ask them to write on each card the name and telephone number of people they could go to in times of stress or change. Have them write a sentence on each card about the individual reason(s) why this person could be of help. Encourage students to fill out several notecards and keep them in a safe place for future use, if needed. (Key Skills: *Problem Solving, Management*)
2. **Extension.** Have students review the extension handout on p. 8 of *Extending the Lesson* in the TCR.
3. **Enrichment.** Have students research community "hot lines" used for individuals in need of help. Ask them to find out about services provided, training, and requirements for listener volunteers, types of clientele served, and types of follow-up, if any. (Key Skill: *Problem Solving*)

More About *Managing Stress*

Planning is a major key to effective stress management. People who handle stress well usually are good planners. To show a variety of ways for students to plan each day, set up a display of attractive calendars, personal planners, and simple notepads for making lists of things to do. Remind students, however, that even with the best of plans, other things can happen to change those plans. By recognizing that changes can and often do occur, especially when other people are involved, teens will be better able to deal with the changes, disappointments, frustrations, and delays that might take place.

Completing the Chapter

For Review

1. Emphasize the main concepts using the summary.
2. Have students complete the "Facts to Recall." (Answers below.)

For Reteaching

1. **Reteaching.** Use the activity on p. 8 of the *Reteaching and Practical Skills* booklet in the TCR.

For Enrichment

1. **Enrichment.** Use the activity on p. 13-14 of the *Enrichment Activities* booklet in the TCR.

For Evaluation

1. Choose items from "Ideas to Explore" and "Activities to Try."
2. Use the chapter test on pp. 11-12 of the testing booklet in the TCR or use the testmaker software.

Facts to Recall Answers

1. The stage of growth between childhood and adulthood. Physically, emotionally, socially, intellectually, and morally.
2. **Any three:** growth spurt, change in body shape, facial hair growth, deepening voices, strong surges of physical energy.
3. Chemical substances in your body. They can cause intense emotions and rapid mood swings.
4. Opportunities for learning how to get along with others; develop new interests and make new friends; gain knowledge and experience through education and school and community activities.
5. Act according to a high set of standards; gain respect and trust from others.
6. Physical or emotional strain or tension caused by pressures and change in home, job, or school; divorce or remarriage; meeting school or work deadlines.

Talking with a youth worker or a trusted friend can help you find constructive ways to cope with change and stress.

▼ Sources of Help ▼

Don't hesitate to ask for help when you feel stressed. For example, your family — including grandparents, aunts, and uncles — may be able to help you understand and deal with a problem. Adults at school, such as a counselor or trusted teacher, can also help. Choose someone you are comfortable talking with.

Your family doctor or the school nurse may be especially helpful in dealing with stress. Like family members and other school personnel, they can put you in touch with social agencies and professionals who can provide additional help when needed.

Community organizations, such as the YMCA, YWCA, recreation centers, or the Red Cross, may have a youth worker. This person's job is to work with young people as individuals and in groups. A youth worker can help you find ways to cope with change and stress.

Sometimes talking over difficult problems with a trusted friend or religious leader is just the help you need. You may find that just talking about a problem out loud helps your outlook toward the problem.

Never be hesitant to ask for help. Think about it. If someone came to you with a problem, how would you feel? Chances are, you would feel good about giving help. The same is true in reverse. People are willing to be there for you too.

TAKING ACTION

Taming Stress

"Since my dad died, I've had a lot more responsibility at home, and it gets tough sometimes," Garrett explained. "My mom depends on me to do most chores and watch over my sister and two brothers. One brother doesn't do his share at all. We argue all the time, and it's stressful."

Garrett doesn't have much time to see friends except on weekends. Lately as he heads out the door on a Friday or Saturday night, his mother will ask him to stay home and spend time with her. Garrett enjoys spending time with his mother but wants to see more of his friends too. Between school, the track team, homework, and chores at home, he sometimes feels "burned out."

Using Your Resourcefulness

- What options does Garrett have to deal with and relieve stress?
- How should he communicate his needs to his mother, brother, and friends so that they help him out?
- How do you deal with personal and family stress?
- What resources are available to you for coping with stress?

TAKING ACTION

After reading the feature, have students brainstorm ideas to help Garrett deal with his stress. Ask the class to identify some of Garrett's values and goals, and to rank them in the order they think he feels are important. Talk about how an awareness of his values and goals could help him manage his time — and stress — better. Have students write short skits, presenting suggestions for equalizing the sharing of chores among Garrett and his siblings.

Using Your Resourcefulness Answers

- Answers will vary, but may include: talking with his mother, setting a schedule, and perhaps letting go of some activities.

Chapter 4 Review

Summary

In this chapter, you have read about:

- How you change physically, emotionally, intellectually, socially, and morally during adolescence.
- How change in your life can cause stress.
- How stress can cause physical and emotional problems.
- What you can do to cope with stress.
- Where you can turn for help in dealing with stress.

Facts to Recall

1. What is adolescence? In what five ways do you change during this period?
2. List three changes in physical development that occur during adolescence.
3. What are hormones? How can they cause difficulties during adolescence?
4. Explain how adolescence can be an opportunity for social and intellectual growth.
5. Name two qualities that identify a person of strong character.
6. What is stress? What changes during adolescence can cause stress?
7. List five physical signs and three emotional signs of stress.
8. Explain how your attitude can make a situation less stressful.
9. How can setting reasonable goals and planning your day reduce stress?
10. Identify four sources of help in dealing with stress.

Ideas to Explore

1. Do you think teens today face more stress than their parents did as young people? What pressures or concerns might they have faced that you do not?
2. Discuss the relationship between feeling in control of a situation and stress. What can you do to feel more in control of a situation when stressful change occurs?

Activities to Try

1. With one or two classmates, write and perform two skits. In the first, show a teen reacting to a specific change in life with a negative attitude. In the second, show the person dealing with the situation positively.
2. Using newspapers and magazines, find articles about different resources available to help people cope with change and stress. Write down the name, address, and/or phone number of each resource. Share these with the class.

LINK TO *Health*

IDENTIFYING STRESS IN YOUR LIFE

In itself, stress is neither good nor bad, harmful nor beneficial. Too little stress may be just as bad as too much stress. Because people react differently to the same events, the best amount of stress for you is very personal. The sources of your stress may be yourself, your family, school, or work. Sometimes stress in one area of your life causes stress in another area. For example, your work schedule allows you less time for family and school work. On a sheet of paper:

1. Identify the things in your life which are stressful to you.
2. Indicate whether each stress is positive or negative.
3. Identify the source(s) of each stress.
4. Describe ways to manage the stress in your life.

(**Note:** Your answers are private and for your personal use only. Share them only if you want to.)

Facts to Recall Answers (continued)

7. **Any five:** headaches and backaches; digestive problems; tight muscles or pain in shoulders or neck; dizziness; eating too much or too little; feeling tired much of the time. **Any three:** restlessness; boredom; irritability; anger, carelessness.
8. Choose not to become upset; to try to make the best of a stressful situation; by deciding which problems to confront and which to deal with later.
9. Makes tasks more meaningful; gives feeling of accomplishment. Helps you manage your time.
10. **Any four:** family members; adults at school; family doctor or school nurse; community organizations; trusted friend; religious leader.

Ideas to Explore

1. Answers will vary. Encourage teens to talk about differences with their parents or guardians.
2. Answers will vary.

LINK TO *Health*

Answers

1. Answers will vary, but may include school, family life, work, and friends.
2. Answers will vary.
3. Answers will vary.
4. Answers will vary, but may include: changing attitude, rest and relaxation, exercise, setting realistic goals, planning, developing healthy habits, helping others, and talking to others.

- Answers will vary. Garrett should positively communicate his concerns to those involved in a mature way.
- Answers will vary.
- Answers will vary, but may include: family, friends, counselors, religious leaders, youth workers, etc.

Preparing to Teach

Chapter Outline

Chapter Resources

The following booklet materials may be found in the *Teacher's Classroom Resources* box:

- Lesson Plans, p. 10
- Student Workbook, *Study Guide,* pp. 27-28; *Identifying Signs of Maturity,* p. 29; *Reading About a Role Model,* p. 30
- Color Transparencies, *Expressing Emotions,* CT-5
- Personal Safety, *Your Safety Attitude,* pp. 9-10
- Technology and Computers, pp. 8, 10
- Cooperative Learning, p. 17
- Extending the Text, *Identifying the Physical Changes of Puberty,* p. 9; *Values and Maturity,* p. 10
- Reteaching and Practical Skills, *Showing Maturity in the Family,* pp. 9-10
- Enrichment Activities, *Accepting Differences,* pp. 13-14
- Chapter and Unit Tests, pp. 13-14
- Testmaker Software

Also see:

- Leadership and Citizenship
- Meeting the Special Needs of Students
- Linking Home, School, and Community
- Dealing with Sensitive Issues

ABCNews InterActive™ Videodiscs

- *Violence Prevention*
- *Drugs and Substance Abuse*
- *Teenage Sexuality*

See the ABCNews InterActive™ Bar Code Correlation booklet for applicable segments.

CHAPTER 5

Moving Toward Maturity

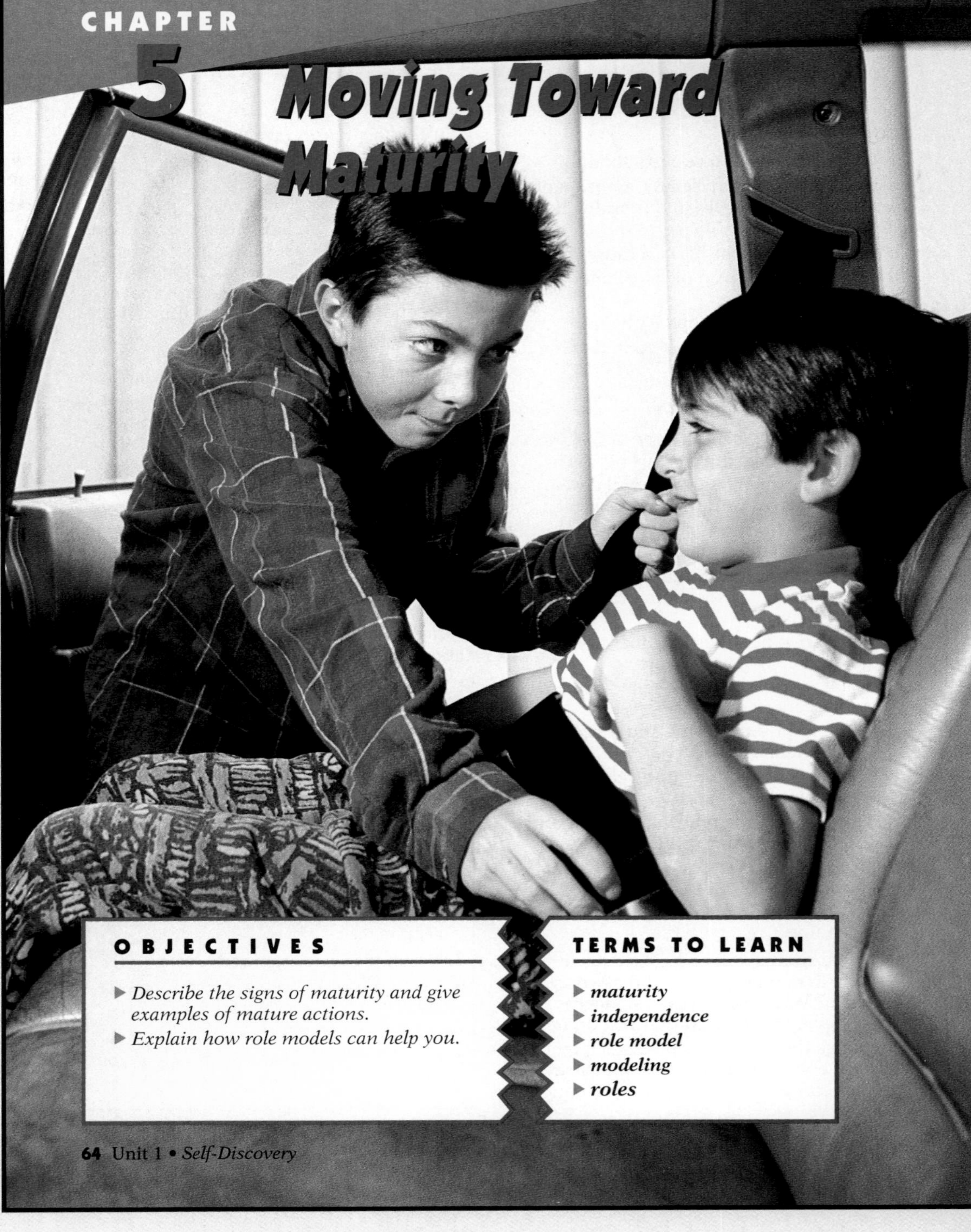

OBJECTIVES

- *Describe the signs of maturity and give examples of mature actions.*
- *Explain how role models can help you.*

TERMS TO LEARN

- ***maturity***
- ***independence***
- ***role model***
- ***modeling***
- ***roles***

"Sometimes it's hard to figure. I'm too young to vote, too young to drive, too young to stay out late, and too young to go camping alone with my friends. On the other hand, I'm old enough to take care of my brothers, work on the farm, and help with my aunt's campaign for a seat on the county board.

"It's frustrating to have people expect things from you one minute and hold you back the next. My sister says she remembers feeling the same way a few years ago. She says to be patient and enjoy my 'carefree' years. Well, I'm trying."

Seeking Maturity

Can you identify in some way with the speaker in the previous paragraphs? Most teens can. The desire to become an adult is normal and necessary. This is what gives teens the incentive to learn what they need to know and to test their wings as they move toward adulthood.

Simply becoming an adult is not the real goal, however. Becoming mature is. There is a difference. **Maturity** (muh-TUR-uht-ee) means reaching full development. People mature in all the areas of development — physical, emotional, social, intellectual, and moral. That is, they gradually move toward full development in each area. However, not everyone matures at the same rate. In addition, some people mature rapidly in one area, but lag behind in other areas. As a matter of fact, some people never reach maturity in some areas of development. What characteristics do you think go along with the development of maturity?

Age is a commonly used indicator of maturity. This is the basis for laws that require you to be a certain age before you can get a work permit, a driver's license, or a marriage license. The right to vote also depends on your age. Different states may set different ages for these rights, but age is a legal measure of maturity almost everywhere. It is not a complete one, however.

At age twenty-one, Justin is legally an adult. His temper and his lack of ability to manage his money, however, show some immaturity. As you can see, age alone does not determine maturity.

Age is used as a legal measure of maturity, as in determining when you can drive or vote.

More About Maturity

Mature people avoid playing games of one-upmanship. They do not try to prove their importance. Instead, they value others and show this in their actions. One simple way of making others feel important is to know and use their names correctly. Another way of making people feel valued is giving them your sincere, undivided attention. Asking them questions and concentrating on what they say tells them that what they think is important.

Introducing the Chapter

Motivators

1. **Discussion.** Ask each student to write down their definition of *maturity.* Have students compare and discuss their definitions with the class. (Key Skills: *Communication, Critical Thinking*)
2. **Classified Ads.** Assign students to write a one-paragraph advertisement describing a person who is mature. (Key Skills: *Communication, Critical Thinking*)
3. **Incomplete Sentences.** Ask students to complete and discuss the following sentences: "I think I am mature because ...," "When I become mature, I plan to ...," "You can tell that people are becoming mature when they ...," "Mature people are ...," and "Some of the signs of immaturity are ...". (Key Skills: *Communication, Critical Thinking*)
4. **Writing.** Assign students to write a one-paragraph description of someone they know or have heard about who seems to be mature. Ask for volunteers to read their descriptions to the class. (Key Skills: *Communication, Critical Thinking*)

Chapter Objectives and Vocabulary

1. Have students read the chapter objectives. Ask them to rephrase the objectives as questions.
2. Ask students to state, in their own words, the purpose of studying this chapter.
3. Pronounce the vocabulary terms listed on the previous page. Ask students whether they are familiar with any of these. Explain that the terms will be defined in the chapter.

Guided Reading

1. Have students read the chapter and use the Study Guide on pp. 27-28 of the *Student Workbook.*

Teaching. . .

Seeking Maturity; Signs of Maturity

(pp. 65-67)

Comprehension Check

1. What is maturity? *(Reaching full development in all areas — physical, social, emotional, intellectual, and moral.)*
2. What are some actions that Lenny could take to control his emotions? *(Let little things go without getting angry; when he got angry, think before reacting; count to ten or walk away; learn to talk about a problem; get involved in things to take his mind off a problem.)*

Learning Activities

1. **Brainstorming.** Have students brainstorm and write on the chalkboard a list of phrases and statements describing people who are mature. Next, ask them to list phrases and statements that describe people who are immature. For their own use, have them divide a sheet of paper into two columns labeled "Mature" and "Immature." Ask them to write, in the appropriate column, some of the words on the board that describe themselves most of the time. Talk about steps that people can take to become more mature. (Key Skill: *Critical Thinking*)

MEETING SPECIAL NEEDS

Through Understanding

Have students read the feature on pp. 66-67. Ask students if they have ever known someone like Devon. How did they respond to this person? Ask students to write brief responses to the questions within the feature (in their journals, if you are having them keep journals). What suggestions do students have for changing people's attitudes about those who are disabled?

MEETING SPECIAL NEEDS

Through Understanding

Think about someone you know who has a disability. How do you view this person? Often, the first reaction is to focus on a person's disability. However, people with disabilities are people first. They have the same feelings, problems, and the need for friends that you have.

Devon, a teen with a learning disability, shared what life was like for him. "Sometimes people ignore me or make fun of me because they think I'm different. That hurts! Whenever I can, I try to find ways to let people know that I'm no different from other kids — they just need to understand more about me. I like to do the same things that everybody does — listen to music, talk, eat pizza, watch movies, and go to football games."

Ask yourself the following questions in thinking about people with disabilities:

- Do you see the person's abilities or disabilities first?
- How might you feel if people only looked at you in terms of a disability?

(Continued on next page)

Signs of Maturity

- "What a mature child she is!"
- "Oh, I would never go out with him. He's too immature."
- "Why don't you just grow up?"

Have you ever heard people make comments like these? They are evaluations of maturity. What makes some people more mature than others? You can probably list some qualities. See how your list compares with the ideas that follow.

Dealing with Emotions

Happy, sad, fearful, glad, jealous, lonely, peaceful, and loved. What do all these terms have in common? If you identified them as emotions, you are absolutely correct. How many other emotions can you name? You may wonder what emotions have to do with maturity — the fact is they have a lot to do with maturity.

Learning to label your emotions and express them in a healthful way is an important part of maturing. Everyone has emotions. However, the way you choose to act on your emotions can be appropriate or inappropriate. How can you tell if you are choosing a healthful, or right, response to your emotions? Try asking yourself the following questions:

- Do I respond to my emotions in a way that is harmful to myself or others?
- Do I respond to my emotions in ways that are appropriate for the time and place?

The way you choose to act on your emotions can be appropriate or inappropriate. In what ways is this teen acting on his emotions inappropriately?

More About *Accepting Differences*

Racial prejudice is prejudice against people because of their race, or the color of their skin. It also is a refusal to accept people because of their nationality. Racial prejudice is unkind and unfair, and it keeps people from becoming all that they can be. History is full of sad examples of actions against people just because of their skin color or accent. Many people have been killed or tortured because others refused to accept their differences.

Mature people learn to be in charge of their emotions, rather than letting their emotions be in charge of them. They show their feelings in constructive ways, and they don't go to pieces whenever something goes wrong. They know that everyone has difficulty dealing with emotions at one time or another.

Lenny was twenty-three years old when he lost his third job. He quit the first one in a moment of anger. On the other two jobs, he was fired after too many arguments with bosses and employees. Unfortunately, Lenny had never learned to control his emotions. Even little things made him lash out in anger.

Most people respond in a positive, healthful way to emotions such as love and hopefulness. However, learning to control emotions such as anger in a positive, healthful way is easier for some than for others. Here are some ways to help control difficult feelings:

- ***Think about the way you feel before reacting.*** If necessary, count to ten or walk away from the situation for a short time.
- ***Avoid letting small irritations upset you.*** You may find your attitude improving if you can let go of the little things.
- ***Talk about the way you feel.*** Naming your emotions as you talk with someone you trust can help you put a positive perspective on your feelings.

Allowing yourself to feel your emotions and deal with them in an appropriate, healthful way shows you are well on your way to emotional maturity.

Through Understanding (Continued)

- How can you appreciate and affirm the abilities in someone who has a disability?
- How can you encourage others to look beyond the disabilities and focus on the abilities that people have?

Try getting to know someone with a disability a little better. You will gain maturity and build your self-esteem as well as the self-esteem of the disabled person. Who knows — you might just find a good friend.

▼ Acceptance ▼

Another sign of maturity is the ability to be accepting. This comes in two ways.

In the first place, a mature person is accepting of others. Can you imagine your classroom filled with people who all look and act just alike? What if people were all the same everywhere you went? How boring the world would be if this were true! Differences make people interesting; they do not make people wrong or unacceptable. Anyone who judges people or hurts them according to their differences — whether the differences are in appearance, attitude, ability, custom, or any other way — shows a lack of maturity. This doesn't mean that you have to like everyone you meet. It does mean that you should be tolerant and not view their differences as wrong.

More About Accepting People with Handicaps

Some people refuse to give people with handicaps a fair chance. In spite of federal and state laws making prejudice illegal, blind people often have difficulties getting a job. So do people in wheelchairs, people with hearing aids, and people with physical and mental diseases. People with handicaps can do many kinds of jobs. They can work, can succeed, and can enjoy life. However, they often are not given the chance to work simply because they are different.

Learning Activities (continued)

2. **Skits.** Select students to write and present a skit about Lenny and his problem with anger on the job. Choose several other students to write and present a skit about Lenny after he found some better ways to handle his feelings. Afterwards, have students contrast the two skits; and discuss ways that teens can deal with anger at home, school, and at work. (Key Skills: *Critical Thinking, Creativity*)
3. **Guest Speaker.** Invite the school counselor or a local mental health professional to discuss ways of handling emotions in appropriate ways. Have students prepare a list of questions to ask the speaker. (Key Skills: *Communication, Critical Thinking*)
4. **Creative Projects.** Provide an assortment of basic art supplies. Assign students to create a variety of projects encouraging people to accept and appreciate others' differences. Possible projects might include banners, bookmarks, bumper stickers, buttons, placemats, or T-shirts. Display and discuss the completed projects. (Key Skills: *Critical Thinking, Creativity*)

Follow Up

1. **Reteaching.** Provide art supplies for students to make banners portraying signs of maturity. Display the finished projects, and discuss some of the signs of maturity that they see in people each day. (Key Skills: *Communication, Creativity)*
2. **Enrichment.** Assign students to research the legal age of maturity in various states. Have them make a chart showing the state, age at which people can get a driver's license, marriage license, and work permit. Ask them to share their findings with the class. Discuss reasons for differences among the states. (Key Skills: *Communication, Problem Solving*)

Teaching. . .
Willingness to Work Hard; Patience; Dependability
(pp. 68-69)

Comprehension Check

1. Why is it not a good idea to follow Ellie's example as a volunteer? *(Jobs won't get done; you might become like Ellie.)*
2. What does patience shown by a person say about what this individual thinks of others? *(The person thinks the needs of others are important, also; and is willing to wait his or her turn.)*
3. What does it mean to be dependable? *(Others can count on you.)*

Learning Activities

1. **Puppet Show.** Ask for volunteers to create and present a puppet show, depicting characters similar to Ellie who avoid doing their part. Afterwards, talk about how it feels to be on committees, teams, or job crews with people who do not get anything done. (Key Skills: *Cooperation, Creativity*)
2. **Comics.** Assign students to locate comics and cartoon strips showing examples of people's impatience and self-interest. Have the class share and discuss their examples. (Key Skills: *Communication, Critical Thinking*)
3. **Sentence Completion.** Have students complete the following sentences: "When I have to wait in line, I ...," "Long lines or heavy traffic makes me ...," and "When I have to wait my turn, I feel ..." (Key Skills: *Communication, Critical Thinking*)

Photo Focus

Have students examine the photo on the top of p. 68. Ask students to discuss the benefits of working together to achieve a goal.

Working together cooperatively can be fun and rewarding for all those involved.

Don't Be Afraid to Fail

You've failed many times, although you may not remember. You fell down the first time you tried to walk. You almost drowned the first time you tried to swim, didn't you? Did you hit the ball the first time you swung a bat? Heavy hitters, the ones who hit the most home runs, also strike out a lot. R.H. Macy failed seven times before his store in New York caught on. English novelist John Creasey got 753 rejection slips before he published 564 books. Babe Ruth struck out 1,330 times, but he also hit 714 home runs. Don't worry about failure. Worry about the chances you miss when you don't even try.

Another form of acceptance involves circumstances. When things cannot be changed, a person needs to understand and accept that fact. After an auto accident, Beth went through some difficult times. It wasn't until she accepted her resulting disability that she was able to get on with her life.

Remember there is another side to this coin, however. In some situations, acceptance is the wrong approach. This is true when positive change is possible. Kent knew his family could not finance his college education, but did he simply accept this and let go of his dream? No! Instead, Kent looked for ways to get help and worked for what he wanted. In this case, acceptance would have been a mistake.

▼ Willingness to Work Hard ▼

The decorating committee was hard at work getting ready for the homecoming dance. Ellie was up to her usual tricks. She loved to volunteer so she could be in the middle of all the activity. When it came down to work, however, she drew the line. Instead Ellie would flit around, talking to people, joking with them, and not getting anything done. Her immaturity was showing.

Very little is accomplished without work. Good grades come with effort. Winning teams develop with practice. Successful employees are rewarded for giving their all. People admire those who do their part. These are the people you want on your committee, team, or staff.

May 5 is celebrated as *Children's Day* in Japan. It expresses the love and respect the Japanese feel for their children. It also sends a message to young people about growing up. On *Children's Day,* large kites shaped like carp are flown from the rooftops. The carp, a fish that swims against the current, symbolizes the difficulties to be overcome in life.

When the "Ellies" of the world are around, what do you do? Some people respond by stating: "Well, if she's not going to do anything, I'm not either." Following Ellie's example is not a good idea. First, the job does not get done. Second, you become just like Ellie. Others will see you in the same light. A more mature attitude is to do your part — and more, if necessary. There is satisfaction — and often eventual reward — in knowing that you put forth your best effort to get a job done.

Good grades come with effort. How do you think this teen feels about her efforts?

▼ Patience ▼

Long lines, heavy traffic, slow service — all of these and more can bring out the impatient nature of some people. What other examples can you think of that cause people to become impatient?

Impatience indicates self-interest. It says, "My wants and needs come first and now." Patience, on the other hand, says, "I can wait to have what I want or need, because the wants and needs of others are important too."

You have no doubt seen children hovering around a teacher, all trying to get attention at once. A few may be willing to wait, realizing that their turn will come. They know that patience is in order and that they must sometimes delay satisfying their own needs. This shows they are developing maturity.

▼ Dependability ▼

One quality most people like to find in their friends is dependability. It's nice to know that you can count on someone. This is one more characteristic of a mature person.

How would you rate the dependability of the following people?

- In over a year on the job, Tina has never been late for work.
- Chelsie takes phone calls for others in her family but doesn't write down or remember to pass along the messages.

Learning Activities (continued)

4. **Debate.** Select students to debate the statement: "Only the weak are patient." (Key Skills: *Communication, Critical Thinking*)
5. **Short Stories.** Assign half of the students in class to write short stories about teens whose friends and family can depend on them. Have the other half write stories about teens whose friends and family cannot depend on them. Ask each group to discuss their stories. Talk about the differences between the two types of teens in the stories. Brainstorm a list of ways that teens can show they are dependable. (Key Skills: *Critical Thinking, Creativity*)

Follow Up

1. **Reteaching.** Provide a variety of newspapers and magazines. Assign students to locate articles about individuals who have exhibited some of the signs of maturity. Ask students to identify the signs of maturity and to summarize their articles for the class. (Key Skill: *Critical Thinking*)
2. **Enrichment.** Assign students to use library resources to research the behavior patterns of Type A and Type B personalities. Have them contrast the degree of patience, or impatience, these personality types tend to have. Ask them to identify which personality type they tend to exhibit. (Key Skill: *Critical Thinking*)

Around the World

Have students read the feature. Assign students to research rites or rituals of maturity carried out in various parts of the world. Have them investigate the differences in the rituals for females and for males. Ask them to write a report of their findings and to discuss them with the class. Invite a representative from the local Jewish community to speak to the class about celebrations of maturation for Jewish young people and their families.

More About *Being Dependable*

Dependability on the job is an important trait. All employers expect their employees to be dependable. For example, if an employee promises that a particular job will be done by a certain time, it will be expected at that time. Employers also count on their workers to be dependable in coming to work on time and in being honest and loyal. They expect employees to not let them down by being absent or late or by stealing something from the company.

Teaching. . .
Independence, Good Judgment; Responsibility; Using Role Models
(pp. 70-72)

Comprehension Check

1. Name three sources of information you need to become an independent person. *(Family, friends, education.)*
2. What does it mean to have a "broader vision?" *(To see all sides of an issue.)*
3. What does it mean to take responsibility for yourself? *(Accountability for actions; admit mistakes; take responsibility for others; help others; put needs of others first at times; show respect for property, the environment.)*
4. What is a role model? *(A person who sets an example for others.)*
5. Name five typical role models for many teens. *(Parents, siblings, other relatives, teachers, athletes.)*

Learning Activities

1. **Media Survey.** Have students name and describe television shows depicting people with good judgment. Discuss how the characters demonstrated good judgment and what the results might have been if they had failed to use good judgment. (Key Skills: *Communication, Critical Thinking*)
2. **Empathy Experience.** Select students to play the part of Callie's parents. Have them talk about how they feel as parents when Callie fails to be responsible and does not show any concern for them. (Key Skills: *Communication, Critical Thinking*)

Family Perspective

Keeping promises made to others is part of being dependable. Ask students to make a list of the promises they've made in the past and check the ones they kept. Ask them to circle the promises that they failed to keep. Discuss how it feels to break a promise. Talk about how it feels when others fail to keep promises.

Do your actions show that you are mature and responsible?

- Even though Arlo doesn't get much actual playing time in the basketball games, he never misses a practice.
- Once a week, Joe picks up groceries for his grandmother and delivers them to her.

Independence

Independence, or the ability to take care of one's self, is perhaps what every teen is striving for. A mature person learns the skills that make this possible. Just think about what you need to know and be able to do in order to be independent. You must be able to make good decisions. You will need money-making and management abilities. You will also need knowledge about taking care of housing and health needs. Self-confidence is a necessary quality for those learning how to be independent.

Without such skills as these, a person remains dependent on others. As a teen, you are steadily gathering the information you need to become an independent person. This comes through your family, friends, and education.

Good Judgment

Why is it that some people get themselves in trouble all the time and others don't? It may be a matter of judgment.

Some people have developed the ability to see all sides of an issue. They have what might be called a broader vision. They are able to look at a situation and see the positive and negative effects — on themselves or on others. This helps them make decisions about what is good, right, or practical.

You can see real-life examples of this all around you. Think about people you know who get themselves into tough situations. Is bad judgment a factor? Chances are, it is. Developing good judgment takes time, effort, and learning from your past experiences and the experiences of others. Once acquired, it can make your life move along much more smoothly.

Responsibility

Few qualities of mature people are more valued than responsibility. Responsibility involves knowing what is expected of you and following through with the appropriate behavior. It involves knowing that you are accountable for your actions. Admitting your mistakes, rather than blaming someone else, shows you can be trusted. This is one quality that families often look for in their growing children. A teen who shows a sense of responsibility earns trust and, therefore, the privileges that go along with that trust. Too often, teens want to be trusted before they have proven their ability to be responsible.

Callie was seldom home on time. She often missed dinners and arrived home after curfew. Because she didn't call, her family worried about what might have happened to her. When Callie was invited to go with a group of friends on a weekend trip to an amusement park, her parents said no. Callie was upset and couldn't understand why they were doing this. Do you?

Mature people often take responsibility for more than themselves — for family, friends, and community. They are willing to help others and even put the needs of others before their own needs at times. For example, if Callie had acted responsibly, she would have had some concern for her parents' feelings as well as her own. A sense of responsibility toward community shows in such ways as having respect for property and concern for the environment. When a group of teens work together to clean up a vacant lot, they are showing community responsibility.

You demonstrate your maturity when you are willing to put the needs of others before your own.

Using Role Models

Patterning yourself after role models can help as you seek maturity. **Role models** are people who, through their behavior and attitude, serve as an example for others. Who are some of your role models?

Even when you are not aware of it, you model people. **Modeling**, or watching and imitating the behavior of others, gives you a chance to act like them and see if their behavior works for you. You try out their **roles**, or the parts they play in life. For example, a person may play the part of a football player, president of the student body, or a teacher. Within the family, a person may be a mother, father, sister, brother, or grandparent, to name a few. When you follow the actions of role models, you may dress like them, talk the way they talk, and do the things they do. People may fulfill several roles at one time. For example, you may be a brother or sister, soccer player, and student all at the same time.

How do role models help you as you grow in maturity?

More About *Independence*

For most individuals, independence means separating from parents and accepting the responsibility to govern oneself. Few parents want to hold back the growing independence of their adolescent children, but many are concerned about the time table. Parents usually prefer a slow, more gradual schedule. Most teens want freedoms more quickly. Some sons and daughters ask for more independence than they really want. In other cases, parents hold them back too much.

Learning Activities (continued)

3. **Personal Analysis.** Ask students to think about whether they are someone's role model. Have them list personal characteristics that others might choose to model. (Key Skill: *Critical Thinking*)
4. **Writing.** Divide students into two groups to write an advice column. Have one group write letters from imaginary teens who are in trouble because they used bad judgment in various situations. Have the second group answer the letters, giving advice in resolving the situations. (Key Skills: *Communication, Problem Solving*)

Follow Up

1. **Reteaching.** On a sheet of paper, ask students to list the names of some of their role models. Have them write a description of each role model and one or two sentences explaining why the student models and admires each individual. (Key Skill: *Critical Thinking*)
2. **Extension.** Use the extension information on p. 9 of the *Extending the Lesson* booklet in the TCR.
3. **Enrichment.** Have students write one or two paragraphs, explaining the difference between being dependable and in being responsible. Have them list behaviors for each of these two signs of maturity. (Key Skill: *Critical Thinking*)

The World Around You

Environmental Responsibility

Responsibility involves taking care of the environment. With administrative approval, work with the class in organizing and carrying out a clean-up day for the whole school or for the community. Ask volunteers to start a recycling campaign at school and to take the collections to community recycling centers. Assign students to find items that would normally be thrown away and to create art projects with the materials. Display and discuss the completed projects.

Completing the Chapter

For Review

1. Emphasize the main concepts using the summary.
2. Have students complete the "Facts to Recall." (Answers below.)

For Reteaching

1. **Reteaching.** Use the activity on pp. 9-10 of the *Reteaching and Practical Skills* booklet in the TCR.

For Enrichment

1. **Enrichment.** Use the activity on pp. 15-16 of the *Enrichment Activities* booklet in the TCR.

For Evaluation

1. Choose items from "Ideas to Explore" and "Activities to Try."
2. Use the chapter test on pp. 13-14 of the testing booklet in the TCR or use the testmaker software.

Facts to Recall Answers

1. Reaching full development; process that applies to all areas of development. Causes confusion — teens may be considered mature enough for some responsibilities, but not for others.
2. No — age is common legal indicator; maturity is attitude and actions that show full development.
3. Think about feelings before reacting; avoid letting small irritations upset them; talk about feelings.
4. Acceptance of others; of things that cannot be changed. When positive change is possible.
5. Don't follow their example; do your part, and more if necessary.
6. They show they believe their needs should be met before others'.
7. **Any three:** decision making; money management; knowledge of housing and health care needs; self-confidence.

Sometimes people choose the wrong role models. In trying to be like another person, you may find yourself acting in ways that cause problems. You may go against your own values and goals. This is an example of using poor judgment and shows a lack of maturity.

It is true that you can learn a great deal from someone you admire, but you need to ask yourself if your role model will send you in the right direction. Are there signs of maturity? Are the values shown positive ones? Only if these answers are "yes" will the role model be helpful to you.

Your Level of Maturity

By now you should have a pretty good idea of what it means to be mature. You may even have additional ideas about what maturity is. Now take a look at yourself. Where are you on the maturity scale?

At this stage of your life, the important thing is to be moving in the right direction. You should be able to identify ways you have changed since childhood. You should also see ways in which you can move closer to maturity in the future. Why not make this your goal?

TAKING ACTION

Standing Up to Peer Pressure

You're going out with a new group of acquaintances, some of whom are older than you are. They are all part of the most popular crowd in school and you feel flattered to be included.

Mike has a car and is driving the group to a movie. On the way, Anthony produces a six-pack of beer his brother bought for him. He offers everyone a can. As Mike drinks and speeds along the highway, he and Anthony keep everybody laughing with their jokes. When they finish their beers, they toss their cans out the window. After Mike parks the car, Anthony starts to spray paint the wall of a building. The rest of the group encourages him and seems to be having a good time.

Using Your Resourcefulness

- What are the possible consequences of this situation?
- If you were a passenger in the car, how would you react to the situation? In all honesty, what would you say and do?
- Do you think it's hard to resist negative pressure from friends? Why or why not?
- What is the connection between going against the crowd and maturity? Why do you think some teens act more responsibly and use better judgment than others? How can one change to become more responsible?

TAKING ACTION

After reading the feature, ask students to write or discuss times when they had other teens put pressure on them to do something they didn't want to do. Have them evaluate their responses to this pressure. Talk about reasons why some of the responses were successful and why others were unsuccessful. Have students brainstorm a list of things people have said to try to pressure them. Afterwards, select some of the things that were said, and have students suggest and practice responses to resist the pressure.

Using Your Resourcefulness Answers

- Answers will vary. Possible consequences

Chapter 5 Review

Summary

In this chapter, you have read about:
- The difference between age and maturity.
- Types of mature behavior.
- The function of role models.
- Rating your own development in maturity.

Facts to Recall

1. What is maturity? How can it be a source of confusion and frustration for teens?
2. Is age the same as maturity? Explain.
3. List three ways mature people deal with emotions.
4. In what two situations is acceptance a sign of maturity? When is it the wrong approach?
5. What is a mature response to someone who shows an immature attitude toward hard work?
6. How do people show self-interest by impatience?
7. Identify three skills or characteristics needed for independence.
8. What abilities are involved in good judgment?
9. How do mature people show responsibility toward others?
10. How can role models help you?

Ideas to Explore

1. In what ways or situations are teens encouraged or required to show maturity? When are they not?
2. Can a person be mature in some ways — physically, emotionally, socially — but immature in others? Explain.
3. How can you tell when a situation should be accepted as something you cannot change, and when you should work to try to make it better?
4. Debate the following statement: "Teens are given too much (or not enough) responsibility in our society."

Activities to Try

1. Make a list of five situations in which you have trouble controlling your emotions. Beside each one, write down something you can do to deal with your emotions maturely.
2. Make a maturity timeline. Begin with your birth and mark off each year. Write down major events or significant points on your road to maturity — physical, emotional, social, intellectual, and moral. Project the timeline five years into the future, showing the ways you hope to develop in that time span.
3. Describe an incident or tell a short story in which you made a conscious effort to behave maturely. Explain how this was a step forward in your physical, emotional, social, intellectual, or moral development.

LINK TO *Communication*

CHOOSING A MENTOR

Mentor was the elderly friend and adviser of Odysseus (oh-dis-ee-us), the hero of the *Odyssey* — an ancient Greek play. Today, the word "mentor" means a wise and faithful counselor. Young adults are often advised to find a mentor in their career field to guide and advise them. Identify an adult you might choose as a mentor. Write a one-page paper describing the qualities that would make this person a good choice for your personal mentor. How could this person help you as you move toward maturity?

Facts to Recall Answers (continued)

8. Ability to see all sides of an issue; to see positive and negative effects; to learn from experiences.
9. Willing to help others; put others' needs before their own; have respect for property and concern for the environment.
10. Can help you find maturity if you choose those who do not cause you to go against your own values and goals.

Ideas to Explore

1. Answers will vary, but may include: responsibilities at home and school, caring for others and the environment, etc. Teens may not be expected to take total responsibility for their well-being.
2. Answers will vary, but may include answers such as a person may look physically mature, but may not be emotionally ready to handle the responsibilities that go along with physical maturity (i.e. becoming sexually active before emotionally ready for the experience — use this answer at your discretion).
3. Answers will vary.
4. Answers will vary.

include arrest of all group members for damaging property; an accident if Mike continues to drive after drinking; trouble with the police for underage drinking; possible loss of driver's license and suspension from driving.

- Answers will vary. Encourage students to think of suitable ways of getting out of the situation.
- Answers will vary.
- Answers will vary. Going against the crowd shows you are willing to stand up for your own values.

LINK TO *Communication*

Answers

Answers will vary.

Preparing to Teach

Chapter Outline

Chapter Resources

The following booklet materials may be found in the *Teacher's Classroom Resources* box:
- Lesson Plans, p. 11
- Student Workbook, *Study Guide,* pp. 31-32; *Celebrating Citizenship,* p. 33; *Who's the Leader?,* p. 34
- Color Transparencies, *Citizenship Opportunities,* CT-6
- Personal Safety, *Be Aware of Your Surroundings,* p. 11
- Technology and Computers, p. 8
- Cooperative Learning, p. 18
- Extending the Text, *Learning More About Leadership,* p. 11
- Reteaching and Practical Skills, *You and Your Community,* p. 11
- Enrichment Activities, *What If?,* p. 15
- Chapter and Unit Tests, pp. 15-16
- Testmaker Software

Also see:
- Leadership and Citizenship
- Meeting the Special Needs of Students
- Linking Home, School, and Community
- Dealing with Sensitive Issues

ABCNews InterActive™ Videodiscs
- *Violence Prevention*
- *Alcohol*
- *Drugs and Substance Abuse*
- *Tobacco*

See the ABCNews InterActive™ Bar Code Correlation booklet for applicable segments.

CHAPTER

6 Citizenship and Leadership

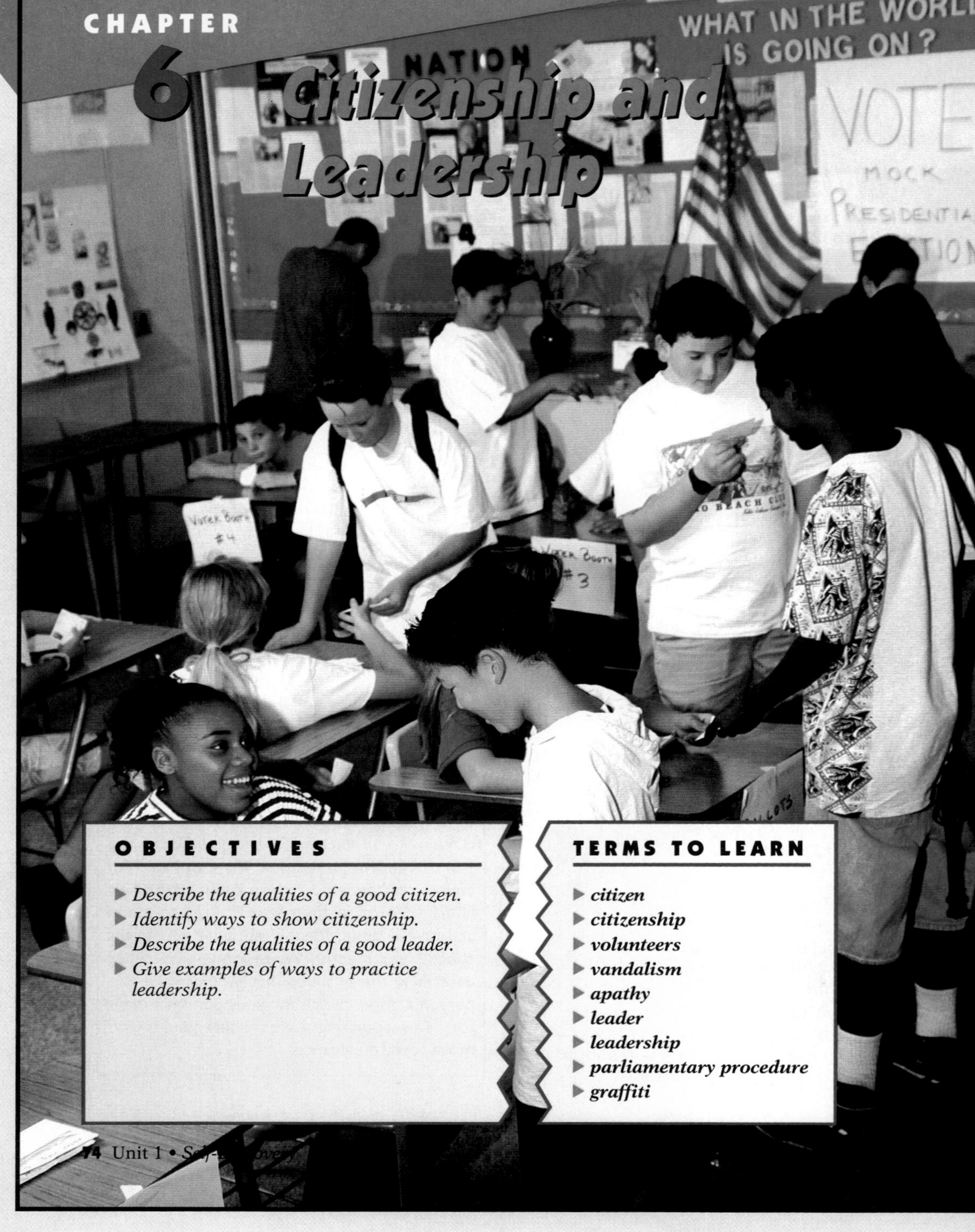

OBJECTIVES

- *Describe the qualities of a good citizen.*
- *Identify ways to show citizenship.*
- *Describe the qualities of a good leader.*
- *Give examples of ways to practice leadership.*

TERMS TO LEARN

- ***citizen***
- ***citizenship***
- ***volunteers***
- ***vandalism***
- ***apathy***
- ***leader***
- ***leadership***
- ***parliamentary procedure***
- ***graffiti***

The doors in the front-hall restroom were a mess. Kimi was tired of looking at them. The scribbled names and senseless messages were everywhere, a lasting reminder of the ignorance of some people. It was then that Kimi decided to do something.

"We need more pride," she thought. "We need to find ways to make people want to take care of school property. I think a school-pride campaign might work. Then we need some volunteers to repaint the restroom doors."

With these thoughts, Kimi began her first organized effort at active citizenship. Along the way she would learn some new leadership skills as well.

What Is Citizenship?

A **citizen** (SIT-uh-zen) is someone who is a member of a community, such as a city or town, state, or country. The fact that you are a citizen doesn't automatically make you a good one. The way that you handle your responsibilities as a citizen is known as **citizenship**. Some people do this well; others do not.

Citizens are entitled to the rights and privileges that come with being a member of a certain community. In return, they have duties and responsibilities that must be returned to the community. This allows the community to survive and function well. A community that thrives has many good citizens. In one that does not, too many people place no value on good citizenship.

In a community that thrives, people take the duties and responsibilities that come with citizenship seriously. What duties and responsibilities do you think come with being a citizen?

More About *Citizenship*

Many teens think they have to be old enough to vote or to be out of school before making a contribution to their community. However, this is not true. They can begin to make an important contribution by becoming well-informed. By learning about what is going on in the community, teens can identify areas of service in which they wish to become involved. Sources of information include the local newspaper, local television and radio news, public meetings, community bulletin boards, public service announcements, and individuals in the community.

Introducing the Chapter

Motivators

1. **Conversation in the Round.** Arrange chairs so that students sit in a circle. Ask students to think about how their school campus appears to others. Is it treated as a source of pride or as property to vandalize or deface? Talk about reasons why the campus is valued or not valued. Brainstorm ideas for developing school pride. List ways that students and faculty can work together to improve the campus. (Key Skills: *Critical Thinking, Citizenship*)
2. **Writing.** Divide the class in half. Have each student in one group write a definition of *citizen*. Ask students in the other group to write a definition of *leader*. Have the groups share their definitions and develop one single definition for each term. Ask students to divide a sheet of paper into two columns. Title the left-hand column "Citizens" and the right-hand column "Leaders." Give them two minutes to write the names of as many citizens and as many leaders as they can. Talk about the similarities and differences between the two groups. What does it take to be a citizen? A leader? How would you rank yourself as a citizen? As a leader? (Key Skills: *Communication, Critical Thinking*)

Chapter Objectives and Vocabulary

1. Have students read the chapter objectives. Ask them to rephrase the objectives as questions.
2. Ask students to state, in their own words, the purpose of studying this chapter.
3. Pronounce the vocabulary terms listed on the previous page. Ask students whether they are familiar with any of these. Explain that the terms will be defined in the chapter.

Guided Reading

1. Have students read the chapter and use the Study Guide on pp. 31-32 of the *Student Workbook*.

Teaching. . . What Is Citizenship?; Becoming a Good Citizen (pp. 75-77)

Comprehension Check

1. Where are the first two places that most people learn and practice citizenship? *(Home and school.)*
2. What are two basic criteria to be a good citizen? *(You must care; you must act on your concerns.)*
3. What is one way to show concern for others in the home? *(By willingly doing your part.)*
4. Give two examples of how Leroy was a good citizen. *(He showed respect for property by returning the art teacher's supplies in good condition; he showed he cared about children who use the community center by helping repair the fence.)*
5. What does it mean to be a "volunteer?" *(To offer your services for free; to put caring into action.)*
6. What are three reasons why good citizens live by the rules and laws of their communities? *(They care about the welfare of all people; they want order in the community; they want to live where people feel safe, secure, and happy.)*

Learning Activities

1. **Discussion.** Ask students to share ways in which they, or their families and friends, have been good citizens in the past month. Talk about how it feels to help others. (Key Skills: *Critical Thinking, Citizenship*)
2. **Article Analysis.** Have students collect, analyze, and discuss articles about people who are good citizens. (Key Skills: *Communication, Critical Thinking*)
3. **Writing.** Assign each student to write an article about an individual who is a good citizen in the community. The article can be about a real or a fictitious person. Ask for volunteers to read their articles to the class. (Key Skills: *Critical Thinking, Citizenship*)

You're The Finest

In just 200 years, your country, through freedom and hard work, has changed the world. In agriculture, industry, education, medicine, law, transportation, and on and on. No country can match America's record in religious freedom, civil freedom, human rights, the importance and dignity of the individual. We do have our differences. But when we join together in times of crisis, our strength is awesome. Among all the world's nations, America still stands out front. You're an American. You're the finest ever — and don't you ever, ever forget it.

Becoming a Good Citizen

You first learn and practice citizenship in your home and school. If you can make them better places in which to live and learn, then you can do the same in your community. No matter what the setting is, good citizenship involves using many of the same skills and qualities.

Qualities of Good Citizenship

To be a good citizen, you must meet two basic requirements. First, you must care. Second, you must act on your concerns.

In the home, you show a concern for others when you willingly do your part to help family members. A person who cares enough to do this at home will transfer the same attitude into the community. This is also true with such attitudes as respect, honesty, and courtesy.

The members of Leroy's family have respect for each other's property. When one member borrows something, it is returned in good condition. They also take care of their home. Although it is small, it is clean and neat.

This is the attitude that Leroy carries with him — to school and to other places in the community. When he borrowed some supplies from the art teacher for a committee he was on, Leroy made sure everything was returned in good condition. He cared enough to show respect for the teacher's property. When a group of neighbors decided to repair the fence around the community center, Leroy was there to help. He cared about the children who use the center and wanted to make it a better place for them.

There are many ways that people can practice good citizenship. For example, citizens can work together to improve their surroundings.

Leroy learned about caring at home. Now this attitude is helping him become a good citizen. Just caring is not enough, however. To be a good citizen, you must act on your feelings, just as Leroy did at the community center. There are many ways for people to take an active part in practicing good citizenship.

Volunteering

Every community has needs that often go unmet. Through volunteers, much can be done. **Volunteers,** people who offer their services free of charge, help meet these needs. They put caring into action.

People who volunteer are not motivated by money. They have discovered rewards that mean much more. The good feeling that comes from helping others is the first reward. In addition, it is a good way to make new friends. Getting to know people who have similar interests is often one of the aims of volunteers. For many teens, volunteer work offers an opportunity to learn new job skills and gain valuable work experience. They may even make contacts that may later result in employment.

In almost any community, you can find ways to become involved. Look in the yellow pages of your telephone directory under volunteer services or social service organizations. You may find opportunities there. School counselors may also be able to direct you to organizations that need help in your community. There may even be service clubs in your school that you can join.

Being part of the Future Homemakers of America (FHA) is one way to get started in volunteer work. This organization offers a variety of ways to contribute to your home, school, and community. By becoming a member of FHA, you can also make new friends and get involved in activities that will help you grow as a person.

Stopping Crime

Crime hurts people. It ruins neighborhoods. It creates fear and anger.

Most people learn to live by rules as children. These rules are learned at home and in school. Rules, in the form of laws, also exist in communities. Good citizens follow the laws because they care about the welfare of all people. They want order in the community, and they want to live where people feel safe, secure, and happy.

Unfortunately, some people have never learned to live by rules. They have no respect for them. They care only about themselves, never facing or understanding how their actions affect others.

TIPS: *Volunteer Activities*

- Form a group that will clean up **graffiti** (gruh-FEE-tee), unwanted drawings and writing on walls and other property.
- Tutor students who need help with a particular subject.
- Run for student government. Then you can help set rules and policies to make your school a better place.
- Start a community service program if your school does not already have one.
- Join or start a group that is interested in cleaning up the environment.
- Become a hospital volunteer.
- Participate in a charity walk-a-thon.
- Visit shut-ins and run errands for them.
- Visit nursing home residents.
- Organize games for children in your neighborhood.
- Beautify your neighborhood by planting trees and flowers.
- Participate in a food drive for those in need.
- Collect recyclable materials.

Learning Activities (continued)

4. **Campus Survey.** Divide students into small groups. Assign each group to survey various parts of the school. Have them note specific examples of graffiti, broken glass, trash, etc. that represent a lack of school pride. Also, ask them to note specific examples of school pride and concern for school property. Select students to use the surveys to take photographs of the school. Ask them to select examples that show pride and lack of pride. With administrative approval, display the photographs throughout the school. Suggested titles for the displays include: "School Pride: What's Your Role In It?" "School Pride: Let's Get It Back!" and "School Pride: We Have It!" (Key Skills: *Problem Solving, Citizenship*)

Follow Up

1. **Reteaching.** Ask each student to write a thank-you note to someone who is a good citizen in the local community. Have each student write about some of the specific actions of the individual that have made the community a better place to live. Encourage students to send their notes to each individual. (Key Skills: *Communication, Critical Thinking*)
2. **Enrichment.** Select a small group of students to design and carry out a survey of the number of teen volunteers at school. Ask them to include questions about where students volunteer and how many hours they spend each week. Have the group summarize the results of its survey in the form of an article to submit to the school newspaper. (Key Skills: *Communication, Cooperation*)

More About *Volunteering*

Being a volunteer provides rewards that money cannot buy. For example, volunteering helps people feel good about themselves. Their self-respect and self-confidence grow. Volunteering offers special opportunities to find new friends. When people volunteer, they become involved with others who have similar interests. Some develop life-long friendships because of their volunteer work. Also, many young people learn job skills while volunteering. Others discover vocational interests they did not know they had.

TIPS:

Volunteer Activities
Have the students read the feature. Ask students to respond to each of the ideas. Would any of these ideas be feasible for their school? What other volunteer ideas can students think of?

Teaching. . . Stopping Crime; Staying Informed (pp. 78-79)

Comprehension Check

1. How do stores make up for their losses due to shoplifting? *(They have to charge higher prices.)*
2. How long does a person's criminal record last? *(A lifetime.)*
3. What are two ways to stay informed of community issues? *(Read the newspaper and listen to radio and television news programs.)*

Learning Activities

1. **Book Survey.** Assign students to check each of their textbooks for any signs of vandalism. Ask them to show some of the examples. Afterwards, invite a school administrator in charge of textbooks to speak to the class about the costs of textbooks (initial purchase as well as repair and replacement costs. Talk about how these costs are borne by taxpayers (who include students' families) and how the money spent for repair and replacement could be used in more productive ways, such as student services. (Key Skills: *Critical Thinking, Citizenship*)
2. **Guest Speakers.** Invite several local business owners to speak to the class about the problems and costs of shoplifting. (Key Skill: *Communication*)

AROUND THE WORLD

Have students read and discuss the feature. Select class members to interview foreign students about volunteerism in their home countries. Have the interviewers find out if actual rewards are earned because of the volunteer work. In class, have students brainstorm a list of nonmaterial rewards local volunteers may earn for their hours of service. Select students to look up the definition of the term *psychic income*. Talk about how this form of income relates to volunteerism.

AROUND THE WORLD

In Cuba, volunteerism is strongly encouraged and supported by the government through its state-owned businesses, farms, and factories. Volunteers earn points for every hour of service. Everyone's points are posted in their workplace. At year's end, their fellow workers vote for whom they think is most deserving. A yearly reward may be a large appliance at a low price or a vacation at a beach resort. Over many years, a volunteer may accumulate enough points for a car or an apartment.

Gathering food for hungry people is one way these teens are being good citizens.

Crime affects everyone — the criminal and the victims. Good citizens obey laws.

Crime occurs at many levels. It may begin as **vandalism**, the deliberate destruction of property, and move on to stealing and acts of violence. Every criminal act has consequences that affect the victims of a crime, the criminal, and all citizens. Think about these consequences:

- ***Someone pays for the criminal acts of others.*** Shoplifting, for example, occurs when people steal items from stores. In order to make up for lost goods, stores have to charge higher prices. Everyone must pay these higher costs. Vandalism is expensive, too. Every time property is destroyed, someone has to pay the cost of repairs. When the property is public, everyone pays through tax dollars, leaving less money for other needs. If vandalism gets out of hand in a neighborhood and repairs cannot be made, the consequence may be a ruined community. In the saddest of cases, some people pay the ultimate cost of crime — their lives.
- ***Crime has long-lasting effects on its victims.*** After Mrs. Carrera's purse was yanked from her arm by a youth on a bicycle, she was never the same. She was elderly and lived in fear from that point on in her life. The few dollars she lost were nothing compared to what the incident did to her emotionally.
- ***A criminal record lasts a lifetime.*** It can affect a person's ability to get a job. It definitely affects the attitudes others have toward the person.

These are only a few of the consequences of crime. There are many others. Indeed, the more serious the crime, the greater the consequences to everyone involved.

What can good citizens do to stop crime? The first line of defense is to follow the law yourself. Avoid people who are already mixed up in the wrong kinds of activity. Choose friends who want to make your community a better place,

More About Good Citizenship at Home

Most teens and adults practice courtesy every day. They say "please" and "thank you" to total strangers. Unfortunately, many people fail to do the same to those closest to them — their family. Usually, people simply forget to practice good manners and common courtesy around family members. Those who are good citizens at home are good listeners and do not interrupt when others are talking. They respect the property of others and do not borrow things without the owner's permission. They also show respect for privacy by knocking before entering someone's room and by not listening to other people's telephone conversations.

How to ...

Be a Good Citizen

You have learned that a good citizen cares about others and acts on his or her concerns. Here are some specific ways to do this, now and in the future:

- Take care of public property, as well as your own.
- Don't litter. Pick up litter when you see it.
- Follow rules and laws.
- Respect the rights of all people. Public places are shared by all. Your conduct should reflect this.
- Stay informed.
- Vote in all elections.
- Find ways to make your community a better place for everyone.

not a worse one. If people scorn you for trying to do what is right, reject their reasoning. They are likely to pay a price for their attitude, a price that you will not want to pay too.

Second, be willing to take action. Report any criminal activity you see. Many communities have *Crime Watch* programs that enable you to do this easily. You might even become involved in setting up a neighborhood program that encourages people to look out for each other.

Over the years, crime has become a more serious problem. As a good citizen, you need to be part of the solution, not part of the problem. If you treat others in a positive way — showing care, respect, and courtesy — you send them a clear message that you expect to be treated in the same manner. If your actions don't show this, then making a change is in order.

Good citizens look out for one another.

Staying Informed

Good citizenship involves staying informed. Your ability to contribute to your community hinges on what you know.

How to ... Be a Good Citizen

Have students read the feature. What other qualities do students feel show good citizenship? Assign students to design bumper stickers, T-shirts, or public service announcements about the problem of litter and the need to take care of public property. Arrange for volunteers to visit a local landfill site and to report on some of the solid waste they observed that could be reused or recycled. Ask a representative from the local sanitation collection department to speak to the class about solid waste disposal, what it costs, who pays for it, and what teens and their families can do to reduce the amount of waste.

Learning Activities (continued)

3. **Personal Analysis.** Ask each student to think about one person for whom he or she could make a difference. Without using names, have them write a description of the person. Next, ask them to write down ways they could make a difference to that individual by being a good citizen. (Key Skill: *Critical Thinking*)
4. **Radio or Television Project.** Assign students to follow daily radio or television news for one week. Have them keep a list of national, state, and local issues. Discuss some of the information that was presented. (Key Skills: *Communication, Social Studies*)

Follow Up

1. **Reteaching.** Have students make a bulletin board display of various community newspapers, bulletins, and brochures that help local citizens stay informed of various issues. Ask them to title the display: "Keep Up With What's Going On!" (Key Skills: *Communication, Cooperation*)
2. **Enrichment.** Assign students to visit several different places where volunteers are at work in the community. Have them take photographs or videotapes of volunteers in action. Ask them to share and discuss their photographs or videotapes with the class. (Key Skills: *Communication, Cooperation*)

Family Perspective

It is easy to spot good citizens at home. They do their share of work, and sometimes more. Ask students to think about what kind of citizens they are at home. Have them keep a record of each time they do the dishes, cook a meal, mop the floor, take out the trash, care for a younger brother or sister, or perform some other task. Ask them to put a check mark beside each task they complete without complaining. Also, have them put a star beside each task they perform without being asked.

Teaching. . . Avoiding Apathy; What Is Leadership? (pp. 80-82)

Comprehension Check

1. Define apathy. *(Lack of feeling or interest.)*
2. What is leadership? *(The ability to lead.)*
3. Why is it important for a leader to listen to the ideas, problems, and concerns of group members? *(Encourages a positive attitude and commitment within a group.)*
4. What is the purpose of parliamentary procedure? *(Allows leaders to keep order while group members voice opinions and make majority decisions.)*
5. How can a leader help individual members feel special and wanted? *(By showing appreciation.)*
6. Give five examples of leadership other than an elected position. *(Deciding where to go and what to do in a group of friends; sparking class discussion and influencing others by what they say; older siblings setting an example and giving encouragement to younger siblings; senior athlete showing a freshman what it means to win or lose with class; veteran employee showing new employees how to work well with others.)*

Learning Activities

1. **Skits.** Assign students to small groups to create and present skits about people who have apathy. Discuss ways that people can help combat apathy. (Key Skills: *Cooperation, Creativity*)
2. **Discussion.** Lead a discussion about experiences and problems students have had as members of various groups. Establish discussion rules so that specific names of individuals and groups will not be mentioned. (Key Skills: *Communication, Critical Thinking*)

Eventually as a voter, you can help choose leaders. The more you know, the better equipped you will be to make such decisions.

By reading the newspaper and listening to radio and television broadcasts, you can keep up with what is going on within your community and the world. You will have informed opinions that may even enable you to influence others. When you know what is going on in your world, you will know who needs help and when.

Avoiding the Problem of Apathy

The headline reads: "Crowd Watches While Elderly Man Is Assaulted." This sad story smacks of a problem that is seen all too often in society — **apathy**. This is just the opposite of caring and taking action. It is a lack of feeling or interest. People who have apathy see what's going on around them as someone else's problem or responsibility. They don't care enough to get involved.

Apathy occurs for a variety of complex reasons. It's more important to focus on curing apathy than to worry about why people are apathetic. You need to know that you can make a difference in the world. Even though ten people around you are doing nothing, you can step forward and help. You can take on that responsibility. It will bring you respect and admiration plus a good feeling inside. Even when ten people around you are doing a lot, you can make a contribution. There is room for everyone when it comes to caring.

A good leader provides positive guidance to a group.

What Is Leadership?

Anyone can be a citizen, but not everyone is a leader. A **leader** is a person who has influence over and guides a group. **Leadership** is not just holding an office, such as student body president, it is the ability to lead. In fact, a good deal of leadership comes from people with no title at all. It is influencing people in other, more informal, ways too. Leadership can be learned and practiced — just like skating, skiing, or making speeches.

What Makes a Good Leader?

Leaders have two main functions. One, they get the job done. Two, they keep the group together. The "job" is whatever the group is organized to do. It might be a game, a contest, or a committee project.

More About Volunteering

Encourage students to make volunteering a family affair. Provide fact sheets about various volunteer opportunities in the community for students to take home to their families. In class, distribute an oversized blank check to each student. Ask each of them to fill in the check. On the "Pay to the order of" line, have them write one specific population which they would like to help, such as the homeless, the elderly, the mentally retarded, etc. Next to the dollar sign and on the line beneath, ask them to write the resources they are willing to share, such as time to visit an elderly adult. Display the signed checks.

Good leaders share certain qualities. Think about which of the following qualities you have already and which ones you might work to develop. Good leaders:

- ***Listen to the ideas, problems, and concerns of group members.*** Good leaders listen to the feelings behind what is said as well as to the words. This brings about a positive attitude within the group and encourages commitment to the project.
- ***Build a team from the members of the group.*** Good leaders must build a team, not just expect it to fall into place. A way to do this is to recognize the worth of each member and his or her ideas. The group can then build on those ideas to make them more workable. As a result, members can see that their ideas play a role in the group's decision. They will be more enthusiastic about carrying out the decision.
- ***Think creatively to aid the goals of the group.*** They aren't afraid to try new ways to achieve goals, to look for new solutions to old problems, or to risk failure.
- ***Clearly identify group goals.*** They provide each member with information and direction about the goals. As a result, group members don't lose focus of what they are trying to accomplish.
- ***Organize activities, projects, and tasks of the group.*** Good leaders must have a clear picture of what needs to be done and of the steps necessary to carry out the task. They make sure each member understands his or her specific role in accomplishing group activities, projects, and tasks.
- ***Solve conflicts within the group.*** Conflicts may occur when members try to influence the leader or other members. Personality clashes and unpleasant past experiences can also cause differences that leaders must handle.
- ***Direct group decision making.*** They make sure the group doesn't get sidetracked. Good leaders know and follow rules, known as **parliamentary procedure** (PAR-luh-MENT-uh-ree), established years ago by the English Parliament. These rules, listed in a book called *Robert's Rules of Order*, allow leaders to keep order while group members voice their opinions and reach a majority decision.
- ***Participate with group members.*** They do not consider themselves to be more important than the rest of the group. They are willing to pitch in and do the work, too.
- ***Show appreciation for group members.*** They are aware that a group becomes strong when individual members feel special and wanted.

Good leaders help the team work effectively. What leadership skills do you have?

TIPS: *Working with Leaders*

Responsible group members show the following characteristics:

- Work cooperatively with leaders and other group members toward common goals.
- Show that they are trustworthy.
- Speak positively about leaders and other group members.
- Promote unity among group members.

Learning Activities (continued)

3. **Brainstorming.** Lead students in brainstorming a list of leaders in the local community, in the state, and in the nation. Have them identify some of the qualities these people have in common. (Key Skills: *Social Studies, Critical Thinking*)
4. **Questioning.** Ask students to answer and discuss the following questions: Who is the leader in your family? Does the person in leadership vary depending on the activity? Are you ever in a leadership role at home? (Key Skills: *Communication, Critical Thinking*)

Follow Up

1. **Reteaching.** Have students make entries in their journals each time they assume a formal or informal leadership role. (Key Skills: *Critical Thinking, Leadership*)
2. **Extension.** Use the extension information from p. 11 of the *Extending the Lesson* booklet.
3. **Enrichment.** Assign students to read and study *Robert's Rules of Order*. Have them practice leading various classroom groups. (Key Skill: *Leadership*)
4. **Enrichment.** Have students use library and other community resources to research ways to get involved in the legislative process. Examples include voting, writing letters, demonstrating, volunteering in a campaign, using legislative hot lines, etc. Ask for volunteers to make a decision, based on their values, to become proactive in at least one way. (Key Skills: *Social Studies, Citizenship*)

More About *Good Citizenship*

People are citizens of many groups and places. One of these is their neighborhood. Regardless of the kind of neighborhood, good citizens are needed there. Good neighbors and good citizens look out for one another. They get to know each other's names and how they can be of help. Good neighbors try to offer their help to those in need. They also respect other's privacy and their right to have a quiet place to live. Keeping the volume of stereos down, as well as other noise, is one of the ways to be a good citizen in the neighborhood. Barking dogs, loud cars and motorcycles, and other disturbances can ruin a good neighborhood fast.

TIPS:

Working with Leaders
Have students read the feature. Ask students to identify other characteristics that show how groups members should be supportive and take responsibility. What might happen if there were too many leaders in a group?

Completing the Chapter

For Review

1. Emphasize the main concepts using the summary.
2. Have students complete the "Facts to Recall." (Answers below.)

For Reteaching

1. **Reteaching.** Use the activity on p. 11 of the *Reteaching and Practical Skills* booklet in the TCR.

For Enrichment

1. **Enrichment.** Use the activity on p. 17 of the *Enrichment Activities* booklet in the TCR.

For Evaluation

1. Choose items from "Ideas to Explore" and "Activities to Try."
2. Use the chapter test on pp. 15-16 of the testing booklet in the TCR or use the testmaker software.

Facts to Recall Answers

1. Show you care; concern for others; develop attitudes such as respect, honesty, and courtesy.
2. You must act on your feelings; take an active part in good citizenship.
3. **Any three:** good feeling from helping others; making new friends; meeting people with similar interests; learning job skills.
4. Stores raise prices; tax money is spent repairing vandalized property instead of on other needs.
5. Follow the law; report criminal activity.
6. Ability to contribute and choose good leaders hinges on what you know.
7. Lack of interest or feeling; step forward and help, whether or not others do.
8. **Any four:** take care of public property and your own; don't litter; follow rules and laws; respect rights of all people; stay informed; vote; find ways to improve community.
9. Get the job done; to keep the group together.

Setting examples for good behavior and giving encouragement are ways that you can practice leadership with those around you. How is the teen in this photo demonstrating his leadership capabilities?

- ***Manage time, money, and other resources for the group.*** They make sure all members share the workload equally. They schedule what must be done and when it must be done in order to meet the group goal. Also, good leaders are honest and are able to account for money and other resources that belong to the group.

▼ Practicing Leadership ▼

You don't need to be appointed or win an election to be a leader. Opportunities for leadership are all around you. In a group of friends, someone leads the rest in deciding where to go and what to do. In school, some students spark the class discussion and influence others by what they say.

With younger family members, an older brother or sister sets an example for behavior and gives encouragement. Just as you may look up to someone for guidance and behavior worth imitating, young people may do the same with you. This is providing a role model instead of using one. A senior on the track team can show a freshman what it means to win or lose with a positive attitude. A veteran employee at the fast-food restaurant can show the new person how to work well with others.

All of these are examples of leadership. Making the effort to practice leadership today can get you ready for even bigger opportunities in the future.

TAKING ACTION

Organizing a Fund-Raising Event

Marianne, your student council president, has asked several students for their help. She hopes to raise money for projects through activities that highlight different areas of the school.

Marianne asks you to represent the family and consumer sciences department. She wants you to generate ideas, such as a recycled clothing sale, that create both positive public relations for the department and help raise money for the class treasury. Marianne expects you to offer several ideas that are fun yet practical. She also wants you to organize specific groups and appoint leaders from your class to carry out the ideas.

Using Your Resourcefulness

- Think of three ideas that would promote family and consumer sciences and raise money in your school.
- Decide how you would divide members of your class into three groups to carry out your ideas. Who would you appoint as the three group leaders?
- What would influence your choice of leaders? What leadership qualities do they have?

TAKING ACTION

Have the class read the feature and respond to the questions. Lead the class in brainstorming a list of major subjects that are studied in family and consumer sciences. Write the subjects on the chalkboard. Divide the class into groups, and assign each group several of the subjects. Ask them to think of fund-raising ideas that would promote one or more of the subject areas. Also, have them identify students in the class who could serve as leaders for the project. Bring the entire class together to compile, discuss, and vote on their ideas.

Chapter 6 Review

Summary

In this chapter, you have read about:

- Ways in which good citizens show they care about their community.
- Ideas for volunteering.
- How a good leader helps a group achieve its goals.

Facts to Recall

1. Name three qualities of a good citizen learned in the home.
2. Why is "just caring" about your community not enough to make you a good citizen?
3. Identify three rewards of volunteering.
4. Explain how shoplifting and vandalism hurt the whole community.
5. What are two ways good citizens can help stop crime?
6. How is staying informed important to good citizenship?
7. What is apathy? How can you fight it?
8. List four specific ways you can act as a good citizen.
9. What are two main functions of a good leader?
10. List seven characteristics of good leaders.

Ideas to Explore

1. You have read about a leader's responsibilities to the group. What are the group's responsibilities to its leader?
2. Discuss the conflict that arises when citizens of a group cannot follow certain rules that they believe are wrong. Suggest ways of resolving this problem.
3. What action would you take, individually or within a group, if you felt your leader was a poor one or had made a poor decision for the group?

Activities to Try

1. Make a collage of pictures, photographs, and headlines illustrating good citizenship.
2. As a class, brainstorm a list of things you can do today to make your home, school, and community better places in which to live and work.
3. On a sheet of paper, write the term "citizen," "volunteer," or "leader" down the left-hand margin. Next to each letter, write a word beginning with that letter that relates to the term you've chosen.

LINK TO *Social Studies*

IDENTIFYING LEADERSHIP CHARACTERISTICS

Some people believe that leadership ability is inherited. However, many people who are not "born" leaders can and do learn to be good leaders. Many people believe that authority makes a leader. Today, however, authority is a much less effective basis for leadership than in the past. Today's leaders *guide* groups rather than *rule* them. Certain personal qualities are also associated with good leaders. At the same time, the characteristics of great leaders are as varied as the leaders themselves. Using your knowledge of history:

- Identify three great leaders.
- List at least five of each individual's personal qualities that made him or her an outstanding leader.

Facts to Recall Answers (continued)

10. **Any seven:** listen to group members; build team from group members; think creatively to aid in group's goals; solve conflicts in group; identify group goals; organize group activities; direct group decision making; participate with group members; give service and time to group; manage group resources.

Ideas to Explore

1. Answers will vary. Also see "Tips" feature on p. 81.
2. Answers will vary. Citizens might contact government officials and work to resolve problems.
3. Answers will vary.

Using Your Resourcefulness Answers

- Answers will vary, but may include offering a child care service, recycled clothing shop, etc.
- Answers will vary.
- Answers will vary.

LINK TO *Social Studies*

Answers

- Leaders will vary.
- Characteristics of leaders will vary but should represent characteristics discussed within the text.

Preparing to Teach

Chapter Outline

Chapter Resources

The following booklet materials may be found in the *Teacher's Classroom Resources* box:

- Lesson Plans, p. 12
- Student Workbook, *Study Guide,* pp. 35-36; *Let's Work,* p. 37; *Career Consultation,* p. 38
- Color Transparencies, *Considering Careers,* CT-7
- Personal Safety, *Know Your Interview Rights,* pp. 12-13
- Technology and Computers, pp. 9, 10, 12
- Cooperative Learning, p. 19
- Extending the Text, *Education and Training,* p. 12
- Reteaching and Practical Skills, *Career Interest Survey,* pp. 12-13
- Enrichment Activities, *Help Wanted,* pp. 16-17
- Chapter and Unit Tests, pp. 17-18; pp. 109-111
- Testmaker Software

Also see:

- Leadership and Citizenship
- Meeting the Special Needs of Students
- Linking Home, School, and Community
- Dealing with Sensitive Issues

ABCNews InterActive™ Videodiscs

- *Drugs and Substance Abuse*
- *Food and Nutrition*

See the ABCNews InterActive™ Bar Code Correlation booklet for applicable segments.

CHAPTER 7 Exploring Careers

OBJECTIVES

- *Explain how interests, aptitudes, and skills influence career choices.*
- *Identify ways to gain work skills.*
- *Discuss sources for finding jobs.*
- *Give strategies for applying and interviewing for a job.*

TERMS TO LEARN

- ***career***
- ***interests***
- ***aptitudes***
- ***skills***
- ***paraprofessionals***
- ***apprenticeship***
- ***entrepreneur***
- ***interview***

Have you ever wondered where the future will lead you? One of the most important decisions you'll make in the next few years about your future concerns the type of **career**, or chosen occupation, you want. With thousands of jobs to choose from, it's never too early to begin thinking about your future career.

Adrienne, an active teen, has been thinking a lot about her future. After a conversation with the guidance counselor at her school, she discovered that she can expect to work at least 35 years with several job changes along the way. The counselor said that changes in the world will affect the jobs available. "The best advice I can give you," said the counselor, "is to get a good education and some training that will allow you to branch out into other career areas during your work life."

Your Future Career

To find a career that you'll enjoy, you need to look at more than just the type of work involved. How does your career choice relate to your family and way of life? How much stress are you willing to work under? What are your interests, aptitudes, and skills? What kind of education do you want? The answers to these questions will have a big influence on your career decision.

Work and Family

A job that sounds interesting may have other qualities that might not fit your needs or way of living. Many times people forget to consider how personal and family life relates to their careers. For example, a person who values time with his or her family, but chooses a job that requires a lot of overtime, will not be happy. Someone who likes independence and flexible work hours — often to help meet the needs of children in a family — won't like a highly structured nine-to-five job. If a family depends on a steady income, then work that is seasonal — or only available part of the year — might not be the answer. Take time to consider the schedule, the number of hours, and income to achieve happiness in your chosen job.

What type of job might fit your needs now? How might this affect the career you choose in the future?

More About *Careers*

People who work full-time spend most of each working day on the job. Their work often determines their lifestyles and influences their choice of friends. Besides the need to earn a living, people work for many reasons. One reason is to satisfy values. Many people value work that is interesting to them. They enjoy new ideas and the opportunity to learn new things. Many people also work because they value satisfying relationships with other people. Some enjoy belonging to a group, and work can provide this opportunity.

Introducing the Chapter

Motivators

1. **Writing.** Assign students to write a one-page paper, answering the question: What would you plan for your future if you had no limits on time, money, and other resources? Next, ask students to write several paragraphs about the kinds of careers they would need to provide the future they described. Have them discuss the education and training they would need for each of the careers. (Key Skills: *Communication, Critical Thinking*)
2. **Brainstorming.** Lead students in brainstorming a list of as many occupations as they can. Write the occupations on the chalkboard. Ask students to circle the occupations that require a college education. Have them put a check mark beside those that require technical training and a star beside those that require post-graduate college education. (Key Skills: *Communication, Critical Thinking*)
3. **Personal Analysis.** Ask students to list occupations that interest them. Have them circle the ones that they might consider as future careers. Write the occupations on the chalkboard, and discuss some of the requirements for each one. (Key Skills: *Communication, Critical Thinking*)

Chapter Objectives and Vocabulary

1. Have students read the chapter objectives. Ask them to rephrase the objectives as questions.
2. Ask students to state, in their own words, the purpose of studying this chapter.
3. Pronounce the vocabulary terms listed on the previous page. Ask students whether they are familiar with any of these. Explain that the terms will be defined in the chapter.

Guided Reading

1. Have students read the chapter and use the Study Guide on pp. 35-36 of the *Student Workbook*.

Teaching. . .

Your Future Career: Work and Family, Stress; Interests; Aptitudes and Skills

(pp. 85-87)

Comprehension Check

1. What are four job qualities to consider when thinking about a career? *(Schedule, hours, income stability, job stress.)*
2. Name two ways to minimize the problems caused by job stress. *(Find a satisfying career; learn ways to manage stress.)*
3. What are two clues that tell about your interests? *(Hobbies; the way free time is spent.)*
4. What are four questions to ask yourself when identifying your aptitudes? *(In what school subjects do you make the highest grades? What are your talents or natural abilities? What do you think you could learn to do well? What do other people think you could do?)*
5. What is the difference between aptitudes and skills? *(Aptitudes are natural abilities or talents that make it easy to learn certain things; skills are what you know how to do well.)*

Learning Activities

1. **Guest Speaker.** Invite the school guidance counselor to speak to the class about his or her role in helping students select careers.

AROUND THE WORLD

Have students read the feature and discuss the differences and similarities in the ways that German and American students choose careers. Assign classroom members to interview students who attended area vocational and technical schools. Have them develop a list of interview questions about courses taken; kind and quality of training received; and costs such as tuition, supplies, books, and student fees. Select some of the class to research job opportunities available to graduates of the area vocational and technical schools.

The amount of stress on the job varies from job to job. How much stress do you think this man faces daily on the job?

▼ Stress on the Job ▼

Stress on the job is another important factor to consider. All jobs have stress — some have more than others. In many jobs, stress is a positive, motivating factor that encourages creativity and accomplishment. In others, stress is a negative factor that keeps employees from meeting goals.

Remember that job stress can carry over to your personal life. The opposite is also true. Personal problems can make people less productive at work. Finding a career that is satisfying is one way to decrease the problems caused by stress. Learning ways to manage stress is another. (See pages 56-62 in Chapter 4 for ways to manage stress.)

AROUND THE WORLD

In the German educational system, identifying a career choice comes earlier than in American schools. After the tenth grade, some students begin preparing for university entrance exams. However, about two thirds of all German young people attend vocational/technical schools instead of the university after the tenth grade. They take courses in their chosen profession or trade, such as restaurant management, engineering, or metalworking. In addition, they work for pay at a firm or business in their chosen field to gain hands-on experience. After graduation from vocational/technical school at age 19, many students are fully prepared for work in their chosen career.

More About *Exploring Careers*

To know and understand themselves, teens need to be aware of their interests. What do they enjoy doing the most? How do they like to spend their time? What are their hobbies? What do they like most in school? Their lists of answers can help them identify careers that will be interesting to them. Sometimes teens find it difficult to determine their interests. This is because their interests tend to change as they mature, meet new people, and participate in new activities. Interests are learned, and teens are likely to develop new interests as they experience new activities.

▼ Your Interests ▼

Considering your **interests**, or what you like to do, is one factor to think about when looking at career options. Hobbies and the other ways you spend your free time tell about your interests. You may enjoy working with people or working with your hands. Perhaps you like reading, using words, and writing. On the other hand, numbers and solving problems may hold a special appeal to you. Whatever your interests, consider careers that will make those interests part of your working life.

▼ Your Aptitudes and Skills ▼

Everyone has **aptitudes**, or natural abilities or talents for learning certain skills. A **skill** on the other hand, is the ability to do something that comes from training and practice. A skill that comes to you easily is often something you have an aptitude for. Even when you have an aptitude for a certain skill, it still requires hard work, training, and practice to be developed.

How can you find out what your aptitudes and skills are? One way is to ask yourself these questions:

- In what school subjects do I make the highest grades?
- What do I think I could learn to do well?
- What skills do I have?
- Which of these skills were easiest for me to learn?
- What aptitudes or skills do other people see in me?

Hey, Kids

Just before you go to sleep tonight, check this list: Did you get up on time? Did you make your bed? Did you eat a good breakfast? Did you read something interesting? Did you learn something? Were you polite? Did you help a friend? Did you do some work around the house? Did you try to earn some money to help pay for your clothes? Did you think about your future? Did you read a newspaper or watch a newscast? Did you brush your teeth? Twice? Did you tell your parents how much you appreciate them? Imagine how good you'll feel about yourself if you can say "yes" to these questions, today, and every day.

This teen is developing her aptitude toward art. She might consider a career as a commercial artist or an illustrator of children's books. What are your aptitudes?

Learning Activities (continued)

Ask the counselor to share information about self-assessment tests that are available to students. (Key Skill: *Communication*)

2. **Questioning.** Ask students to discuss the following questions: What skills do you have? What skills would you like to improve or develop? What can you do to learn new skills? (Key Skills: *Communication, Critical Thinking*)
3. **Interviews.** Have students interview people who have a variety of job schedules including: an individual with a nine to five job; another with flexible work hours; and an individual with seasonal or freelance work. Interview questions should concern the relationship of the job schedule to personal and family life and the way stress is minimized by the workers. (Key Skill: *Critical Thinking*)

Follow Up

1. **Reteaching.** Have students collect pictures showing people at work in a variety of occupations. Ask them to identify each occupation and some of the interests, aptitudes, and skills related to it. (Key Skills: *Communication, Critical Thinking*)
2. **Enrichment.** Assign students to create an illustrated, color advertisement about themselves. Have them feature their interests, aptitudes, and skills. Display and discuss the completed advertisements. Ask the class to identify some occupations that are related to the students' qualities featured in the ads. (Key Skills: *Critical Thinking, Creativity*)

Wellness

Signs of stress are like warning lights telling people to slow down. They may be saying that people need to change jobs or that they should not work so hard. The signs of stress may also be telling people to get some recreation or to find someone to help with their problems. Ask students to list some things that cause, or have caused, stress in their lives. Discuss healthy practices they can follow to help their bodies become better able to handle stress.

More About Aptitudes

Aptitudes are seemingly natural tendencies to do well in some areas. An aptitude is not a skill or an ability. An aptitude only makes it a little easier for an individual to acquire a skill or an ability. Although the person may have an aptitude in some particular area, the individual will not be able to develop a skill or ability in that area without work and practice. The same is true of all careers. If people want to be good at what they do, they have to find something for which they have an aptitude and then work hard to acquire the necessary skills and background for their chosen career.

Teaching. . .
Careers: Education; Your Opportunities Now (pp. 88-89)

Comprehension Check

1. Where are four places people can get specialized job training? *(Vocational high school courses, junior and community colleges, vocational-technical schools, through on-the-job training, four-year colleges.)*
2. What are two advantages of volunteering? *(Develop interests, test aptitudes, develop skills, workplace references.)*
3. What are three advantages of part-time jobs? *(You can learn about a career field of interest to you; observe various jobs; compare a variety of jobs; build confidence and self-esteem.)*
4. What is an entrepreneur? *(One who starts and manages a business.)*

Learning Activities

1. **Classified Ads.** Assign students to locate classified advertisements for various part-time jobs. Ask each student to select one listing and to research the job. Have them find out the prerequisites for the job, its duties, hours, and wages. Afterwards, have students share their research with the class. (Key Skills: *Communication, Problem Solving*)
2. **Discussion.** Have students make a list of abbreviations and terms used in help wanted ads that they do not understand. Answer their questions in a group discussion. (Key Skills: *Communication, Critical Thinking*)
3. **Bulletin Board.** Select students to locate help wanted ads for part-time workers. Have them post the ads on a bulletin board titled "Looking for a Part-time Job?" (Key Skill: *Cooperation*)
4. **Guest Speaker.** Invite a representative from an employment office to speak to the class about part-time job opportunities and requirements for teens. (Key Skill: *Communication*)

Aptitude tests provide another way to find out about your natural abilities and skills. Some tests predict how easy or difficult it would be for you to develop the skills needed for a certain career. Check with your school counselor or the state employment office about aptitude tests that you could take.

▼ Education ▼

Where do you see education fitting into career choices? The less education and training a worker has, the less chance there is for obtaining a steady job. Lack of education and training also make it more difficult to change to other jobs in the future. A high school graduate has a better chance than a dropout does for finding a job that provides interesting work, good wages, and steady employment.

The type and level of training you need varies with the type of job you want. Some jobs require little or no training, while others require four years of college plus an advanced degree. The following outlines the various levels of jobs:

- ***Entry-level jobs.*** Entry-level jobs require little or no training. The training that is needed is usually provided on the job. Types of jobs in this category include a maintenance worker, a counter person at a fast food restaurant, a dishwasher at a hospital or restaurant, a sales clerk, or a child care aide.
- ***Paraprofessional jobs.*** **Paraprofessionals** are trained to assist professional people. These jobs require a high school diploma and some additional education at a vocational/technical school or a 2-year college. Some states require a special license for some paraprofessional jobs. Emergency medical technicians (EMTs), child care workers, and dietary assistants are examples of paraprofessionals. Skilled-trade jobs, such as carpentry and plumbing, are also included in the paraprofessional category. Some skilled-trade jobs offer **apprenticeships**, or on-the-job training with pay. An apprentice works under the guidance of a skilled tradesperson to learn a trade.
- **Professional jobs.** Jobs at the professional level require four years of college and often an advanced degree from a graduate school. Teachers, doctors, counselors, architects, and social workers are examples of professional workers.

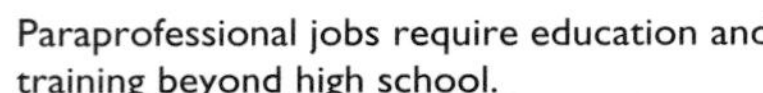
Paraprofessional jobs require education and training beyond high school.

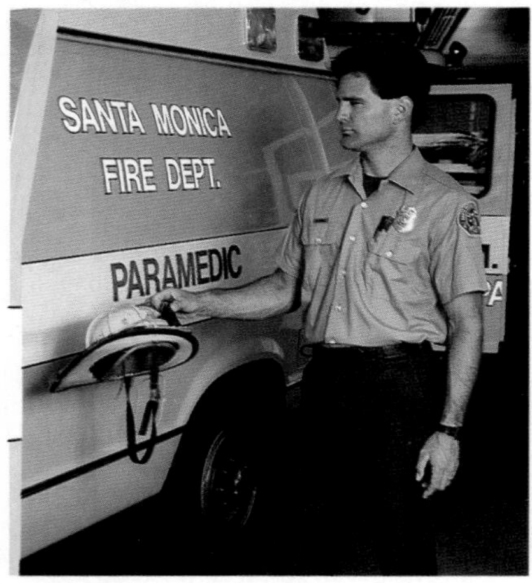

Your Opportunities Now

There are always jobs to be done. Most of these jobs are for adults who have completed the necessary education or training. However, there are many jobs that you could do right now. Most are part-time and offer paid wages. Others are volunteer jobs that provide pay in the form of skills learned and personal satisfaction.

▼ Volunteer Opportunities ▼

Before you get a part-time job, you may want to try volunteer work. Volunteering gives you an opportunity to develop new interests, test your aptitudes, and develop skills. Volunteer experiences may also offer valuable workplace references when you look for paid employment. Volunteer opportunities are often available at hospitals, schools, the American Red Cross, and humane societies. See page 77 for more ideas about volunteering. How else might you find opportunities for volunteering?

Volunteer jobs provide a wealth of experience. This teen volunteers at a community center for the elderly. How might this experience help him as he decides on a career?

▼ Part-time Work Opportunities ▼

One of the best ways to learn about a career is by working at a part-time job in a field that interests you. Most part-time jobs offer work during the summer, after school, or on the weekends.

A good part-time job is one that you can do well and that you find interesting. Most importantly, it should give you an opportunity to observe various jobs in the career of your choice.

Working at a variety of part-time jobs over a period of time can be helpful. It gives you a chance to compare the characteristics and duties of different jobs in a variety of areas. In addition, knowing that you can adjust to different work situations and job demands can help build your confidence and self-esteem.

▼ Opportunities for Entrepreneurs ▼

Are you a goal-oriented, self-disciplined person who has good decision-making skills? Perhaps you have what it takes to be an **entrepreneur** (AHN-truh-pruh-NUR) — a person who starts and manages his or her own business.

Many teens have found creative ways to start a business and make money on their own. For example, Jason started his own lawn-mowing and gardening service when he was 13 years old. He enjoyed the outdoors and found that he had a

Learning Activities (continued)

5. **Guest Speaker.** Invite a person who owns and manages his or her own business to discuss the advantages and disadvantages of entrepreneurship. Have students prepare questions regarding being an entrepreneur. (Key Skill: *Critical Thinking*)

Follow Up

1. **Reteaching.** Assign students to survey the classified ads and the yellow pages to find various local employers who hire part-time workers. Have the students make a list of as many of the employers as they can find. Compile the lists and post the single list of information in the classroom. (Key Skills: *Communication, Critical Thinking*)
2. **Enrichment.** Assign students to go to a library and review trade or professional journals that relate to their career interests. Have them note the latest developments or trends in the trade or profession. Also, ask them to check to see if the journals list job ads. Have them summarize their findings in a short paper. (Key Skills: *Communication, Problem Solving*)

More About *The Perfect Career*

What is it that allows some people to be invigorated by their work, while others are tired or burned out? Is it the amount of physical energy expended? Then why might a file clerk, who burns few calories at work, feel tired at the end of the day, while a construction worker, who burns a great deal of calories, feels energized at day's end? Is it the hours spent on the job? The key ingredient in work that will be invigorating is a keen interest and involvement in the job to be done. A joy in working comes from the matchup of a person's talents and skills with a sense of commitment to and interest in the job.

Life Management Skills

Getting a Job

In many communities, there are social service organizations that help young people locate part-time work. The YMCA and YWCA, Urban League, and other local community groups have helped many teens find jobs by sponsoring a free employment service. Assign students to survey the community for free job placement services available for young people. Sources of information may include the school guidance counselor, the coordinators of the various cooperative education programs at school, the yellow pages, the state employment agency, the local Chamber of Commerce, and local religious leaders.

Teaching. . . Getting a Job (pp. 90-91)

Comprehension Check

1. Why does job hunting take work? *(Jobs will not come to you, you have to go to the jobs; you have to find employers who are looking for a worker with your qualifications.)*
2. What are five sources to use when looking for a job? *(Friends, relatives, school or vocational counselors, employers, newspaper ads.)*
3. Why is it important not to depend on your school as your only source of job leads? *(Competition may be tough; you may be one of many selected to interview for a job.)*
4. Name three people in a company who often have the authority to hire employees. *(Personnel director, department manager, and the owner.)*
5. Name three things newspaper ads can teach you about the job market. *(What types of jobs are most available, what skills are needed for certain jobs, and what salaries are being paid.)*
6. Why is it important to answer want ads as soon as possible? *(The longer you wait to apply, the more likely the jobs will be filled by other applicants.)*

Photo Focus

Have students examine the photo at the top of page 90. How is this teen using his interests, skills, and abilities as an entrepreneur? Ask students to brainstorm a list of business ideas for teens as entrepreneurs? Some teens may wish to investigate articles about teens who have started entrepreneurial adventures and turned them into successful careers.

As an entrepreneur, you can manage your own business. What skills do you have that might lead to owning and managing your own business?

real aptitude for working with lawns and outdoor plants. Kristin, on the other hand, had developed bicycle repair skills while working beside her father as a child. At age 14, she put these skills to good use by starting her own bicycle repair service.

Special operating permits are required for all businesses. In addition to operating permits, a tax number is assigned to all businesses. Check with your local government offices about the requirements for running your own business.

Getting a Job

Finding a job that you can do well and that you will enjoy takes some careful thought and planning.

▼ Looking for a Job ▼

Have you ever thought about how to get a job? Ann wants a job to earn money for her post-high school education. Her big problem right now is where to start looking for a job. She is aware of her skills and knows she would be a reliable, courteous employee. However, she first has to find a job.

Job hunting takes a lot of hard work. Jobs won't come to you; you have to go to the jobs. When looking for job openings, it helps to have a plan of action to find employers who are looking for a worker with your qualifications.

How do you find these employers? There are a variety of sources you can use, including personal contacts, school counselors, direct contact with employers, newspaper ads, and employment agencies. The more sources you use, the more job openings you're likely to find. You will have a better chance of finding a job you really like instead of taking the first job that comes along.

More About *Getting a Job Through Direct Calls*

In addition to following up job leads from counselors, friends, and family, students may want to make some direct calls on their own. Making direct calls means either telephoning or visiting potential employers. Students will not be responding to an ad or following up a referral. Teens who make direct calls will probably make many phone calls and visits before they succeed. However, if they contact enough businesses directly, they will probably find some that are looking for workers with their skills.

Talk with Friends and Relatives

Friends and relatives can be one of your best sources of job leads. They may know of employers who need someone with your skills. In addition, they may know people who do the kind of work that interests you.

Although you should not be timid about asking friends and relatives for job leads, do not expect them to find you a job. It is your responsibility to follow up on job leads, set up interviews, and make a good impression with potential employers.

Check with Your School Counselor

Many schools have a school or vocational counselor to help students find jobs in the community. Other schools may have placement offices where students may register for jobs.

Although your school may be a good source for job information, remember you may be one of many selected to interview for available jobs. Don't depend on your school as your only source of job leads. Investigate and use other sources available to you.

School counselors and job placement offices are often good resources for locating jobs. However, you will want to investigate as many sources as possible.

Contact Employers Directly

One of the best ways to find job openings is to contact employers directly. About half of all people who use this method of looking for a job are successful in finding one.

Before talking to employers, do some research to locate employers that need people with your skills. Look through the telephone book and make a list of possible employers. You can also check with the Chamber of Commerce or public library for potential employers.

Once you have a list of employers, contact the person in each company who has hiring authority. This may be the personnel director, the department manager, or the owner. If you do not know the name of this person, call the company and ask the receptionist. When you find out the name of the person to contact, write him or her a letter, make a phone call, visit the company, or use a combination of these methods.

Read Newspaper Ads

Newspaper ads are another place to look for a job. Jobs are listed in newspapers under the section called the "Classified Ads" or the "Want Ads." You can learn what types of jobs are most available, what skills are needed for certain jobs, and what salaries are being paid.

Sunday is one of the best days to find job leads in the paper. Circle the ads that match your job interests and skills. Respond to the ads as quickly as possible. The longer you wait to apply, the more likely it is that the jobs will be filled by other applicants.

Follow up on job leads as quickly as possible.

Learning Activities

1. **Class Survey.** Take a survey of class members to find out who has had a job or has one at the present time. Ask how they got their jobs and what job hunting tips worked for them. (Key Skill: *Communication*)
2. **Newspaper Analysis.** Provide a number of daily and Sunday editions of the want ads. Have students compare and contrast the number of want ads each day. (Key Skill: *Critical Thinking*)
3. **Skits.** Have small groups of students develop skits concerning how to contact potential employers about job openings by telephone. Students should include whom to talk to, how to ask about job openings, how to thank the receptionist, etc. Have students perform the skits for the class. The class might critique the effectiveness of the skits. (Key Skills: *Critical Thinking, Creativity*)

Follow Up

1. **Reteaching.** Have students practice writing inquiry letters to potential employers about possible job openings. Students should include some biographical information about themselves and their skills and abilities. (Key Skills: *Critical Thinking, Decision Making*)
2. **Enrichment.** Ask students to select an ad from a newspaper for a job that interests them. Have them compose a letter of application for a job advertised. (Key Skill: *Communication*)

More About *Letters of Application*

Many job-hunters write a letter of application to employers to apply for a job. The purpose of the letter is to interest employers in the applicants' qualifications so that they are asked to come in for an interview. Letters of application should be short and to the point. Three carefully worded paragraphs should be enough. In the opening paragraph, applicants should mention the job or type of work for which they are applying. In the middle paragraph, personal qualifications should be explained briefly to show that the applicant is right for the job. In the last paragraph, a request for an interview is made.

Teaching. . .

Getting a Job: Employment Agencies; Applying for a Job (pp. 92-94)

Comprehension Check

1. What information might an employment agency ask you for? *(Information about skills and interests.)*
2. How can you get a Social Security number? *(Obtain one free of charge from your local Social Security office.)*
3. Name three things to remember when filling out a job application. *(Read application carefully; ask questions about things you don't understand; print; use ink, not pencil; keep it neat; put N/A in spaces that do not apply to you.)*
4. What two things should you say to an employer when a job interview is over? *(Thank the employer for seeing you; tell him or her you would like the job.)*
5. What is one way to remind an employer of how much you want a job? *(Write a short thank-you note after the interview.)*
6. If you do not receive any news after several weeks about a job opening for which you were interviewed, what should you do? *(Call and ask if a decision on hiring has been made.)*

Learning Activities

1. **Class Project.** Call the local Social Security office and request application forms for a Social Security card. Have students make sure they have a Social Security card. Discuss how to obtain a duplicate when the original cannot be found. (Key Skills: *Communication, Critical Thinking*)
2. **Writing.** Obtain job application forms from local employers. Make additional copies, and have students practice filling them in. Discuss the importance of a neat and properly completed application. Ask students why the questions on the forms have been included. (Key Skills: *Communication, Critical Thinking*)

How to ...
Be a Responsible Employee

It's an exciting moment when you hear the magic words, "The job is yours." However, what's next? The next step is to show that you are a responsible employee. Here are some guidelines for showing that you are responsible:

- Arrive at work on time.
- Avoid long breaks. Take only the amount of time given for breaks.
- Follow safety rules and business procedures.
- Be honest and loyal to your employer.
- Be pleasant, friendly, and cooperative.
- Do your share of the work.
- Be willing to learn new things at work.
- Give two weeks' notice if you decide to leave a job.

Fill out job applications carefully to avoid making any errors.

Check with Employment Agencies

Government and private employment agencies help people find jobs. Government agencies provide free services. You may be asked to fill out a personal information sheet that identifies your skills and interests. A counselor will then tell you about jobs available that match some or all of your skills.

Private employment agencies charge a fee for helping people find jobs. Depending on the situation, either the employer or the person looking for work will pay the agency fee. Private agencies generally require that you sign a contract. Be sure that you understand everything in the contract before you sign it. *Do not sign anything that you do not understand.* You may want to have a knowledgeable person that you trust read through the contract before you sign it.

How to ... Be a Responsible Employee

Have students read and discuss the characteristics of a responsible employee. Ask students to describe the benefits of being a responsible employee. What might be the consequences of being irresponsible on the job? What other suggestions do students have for showing responsibility on the job? What implications does showing responsibility at home and at school have for future employment? Ask each student to write a paragraph explaining what personal qualities they have that might show a future employer they would be a responsible employee.

▼ Applying for a Job ▼

Before applying for a job, there are a few facts that you should know. First, you must have a Social Security card. If you do not have one, you can get one free of charge from the Social Security office in your community. Second, the United States Department of Labor has guidelines for employing young people. Check with your local Labor Department office to find out the minimum age guidelines that affect teens.

When you apply for a job, you'll be competing with others. Be prepared to give an employer complete information. Prepare a list of personal information to carry with you that includes:

- Full name, address, and telephone number.
- Social Security number.
- Work experience including dates when you began and left each job and a description of your job duties.
- Schools you have attended including when you attended them and any certificate, diploma, or degree you received.
- Special training you've received including when and where you received it.
- Skills or aptitudes you may have.
- Personal interests, hobbies, and activities.
- References. List the full names, addresses, and telephone numbers of at least three people. Do not use relatives as references. Be sure to contact your references and ask for permission to give their names to possible employers.
- Telephone numbers of persons to contact in case of emergency.

Some employers request a letter of application for employment. A good letter takes time and thought to write. It will tell the employer about your interest in the job, your skills, your education and training, and your work experience. It will also show your ability to express ideas. Be sure to use correct grammar, spelling, and punctuation. It's a good idea to have someone proofread your letter for any errors.

When applying for a job, fill out job applications carefully. Read through any application before filling it out. Ask questions about anything you do not understand. These forms will ask for the information you have prepared for the personal information list discussed on this page.

Keep the application form neat. Use ink instead of pencil. Print rather than write. Correctly spell each word you use and fill in all blanks on the application. If you have nothing to write, put "does not apply" or "N/A" (not applicable) in the appropriate blank. This way, the employer will know you did not overlook a question.

TIPS: *Interview Know-How*

The following tips may help you make a good impression and come out of an interview with a smile:

- Know where to go for the interview. If you do not know the location of the business, call and ask for directions.
- Arrive five to ten minutes early. Tell the receptionist who you are and with whom you have an appointment.
- Go to the interview alone.
- Wear simple, clean, and neatly pressed clothes. Try to look your very best so you'll make a good impression. Go light on makeup and jewelry. Avoid wearing jeans, T-shirts, and tennis shoes.
- Greet the interviewer with a firm handshake and a friendly smile. Wait to be offered a seat, and then sit up straight. Look alert and interested.
- Avoid distractions such as chewing gum and cracking your knuckles. Try to look relaxed even if you're not.
- Listen carefully to what the interviewer says. Keep good eye contact with the interviewer.

More About *Interview Communication*

Employers always try to hire workers who can communicate effectively on the job. When employers read an application form, they see if the applicant can write and spell words properly. During interviews, employers listen carefully to the way applicants speak to make sure their vocabulary and grammar are acceptable. Job-hunters need to avoid using casual expressions such as "you know," "like," and "okay" repeatedly. They can be irritating to the listener, or prospective employer.

Learning Activities (continued)

3. **Brainstorming.** Have students brainstorm a list of common interview questions. Assign several students to write down the questions on separate index cards. (Key Skill: *Communication*)
4. **Simulations.** Divide students into pairs. Have one student play the part of a job applicant and the other the part of an employer. Distribute the interview questions written on index cards during the previous activity and have students practice answering several questions. Afterwards, have students reverse the parts so each has a chance to answer several questions. (Key Skill: *Critical Thinking*)

Follow Up

1. **Reteaching.** Assign students to make a list of references they might use when applying for a job. Encourage students to ask the people's permission to serve as references. (Key Skills: *Communication, Management*)
2. **Reteaching.** Assign each student to write a thank-you note, expressing appreciation for a job interview. (Key Skill: *Communication*)
3. **Extension.** Have students read the extension handout on p. 12 of the *Extending the Lesson* booklet of the TCR.
4. **Enrichment.** Select students to play the parts of a job applicant and an employer. Videotape their job interviews, and have the class evaluate the experience. (Key Skills: *Critical Thinking, Cooperation*)

TIPS:

Interview Know How
Have students read the feature. Ask students to identify the implications of not following the tips suggested in the feature. Ask students to assume they are job applicants. Have them practice shaking hands with an employer, using a firm grip and direct eye contact. Ask them to evaluate each other's performance.

Completing the Chapter

For Review

1. Emphasize the main concepts using the summary.
2. Have students complete the "Facts to Recall." (Answers below.)

For Reteaching

1. **Reteaching.** Use the activity on pp. 12-13 of the *Reteaching and Practical Skills* booklet in the TCR.

For Enrichment

1. **Enrichment.** Use the activity on p. 18 of the *Enrichment Activities* booklet in the TCR.

For Evaluation

1. Choose items from "Ideas to Explore" and "Activities to Try."
2. Use the chapter test on pp. 17-18 of the testing booklet in the TCR or use the testmaker software.
3. Use the unit test on pp. 109-111 of the testing booklet in the TCR or use the testmaker software.

Chapter 7 Review

Facts to Recall Answers

1. Person who values time with family will not like a job requiring much overtime; someone who needs flexibility for family needs will not like structured job; family that needs steady income cannot rely on seasonal work.
2. **Any three:** In what subjects do I make the highest grades? What do I think I could learn to do well? What skills do I have? Which skill was easiest to learn? What aptitudes do others see in me?
3. Education increases chances of finding steady jobs at good wages; makes it easier to change jobs in the future.
4. Opportunity to develop new interests, test aptitudes, develop skills.
5. Person who starts and manages his or her own business.
6. First check Yellow Pages or Chamber of Commerce for list of potential employers; write, call, or visit person with hiring authority in each company.

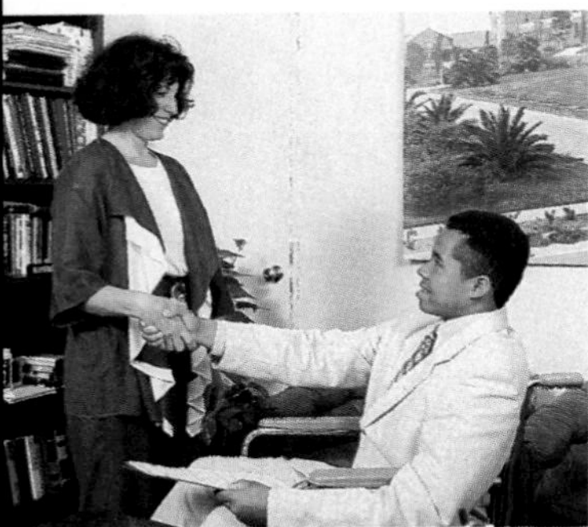

When applying for a job, first impressions are important. Many employers know within the first few minutes of an interview if they want to hire a person.

▼ Interviewing for a Job ▼

A job **interview**, or a meeting between a potential employer and a job-seeker, is part of the process in applying for most jobs. The interviewer will explain the job and ask you questions. An interview also gives you a chance to ask questions about both the job and the company.

When interviewers finish talking, they will ask if you have any questions. Be sure to ask about any points you do not understand. After your questions are answered, the interview is just about over. At this time, thank the interviewer for seeing you. Tell him or her you would like the job.

People rarely are offered a job at the end of the interview. Employers usually interview several people before making a decision. If no mention is made of what is to happen next, ask when a decision to hire will be reached.

After the interview, write a short thank-you note to the employer. Simply state that you enjoyed the meeting and appreciated the chance to interview for the position. Such a note shows that you are interested in the job. It will also show you are a thoughtful person.

If you do not receive any news after several weeks, call and ask if a decision has been made. If you are not hired, you may wish to politely ask why. In this way, you can find out the points you need to work on to be more successful in future interviews.

TAKING ACTION

Matching Skills and Careers

The students in Mrs. Dawson's family and consumer sciences class have been thinking about their future careers. Nick is skilled at using his hands and enjoys building models and making household repairs. Many of Sarah's friends talk to her when they have personal problems because she's a good listener and offers helpful advice. Tony has already made a small profit by investing the earnings he has saved from his two paper routes. Carlene enjoys taking care of young children and volunteers after school at a local nursery school. Robert has won an award for a short story in a literary magazine. Janell is a math whiz and helps her mother balance the household budget.

Using Your Resourcefulness

- For each of Mrs. Dawson's students, offer four possible career choices that would suit their interests and skills.
- Choose one career goal for one of the students and then research the education, training, and experience needed to achieve that goal.
- What resource materials can help you learn more about future career opportunities?
- How can you learn which are the fastest growing and fastest declining jobs of the near future?

TAKING ACTION

Have students read the feature and respond to the questions and statements.

Talk with students about grouping jobs for easier career exploration by organizing them by career interest areas. Each interest area is a category of jobs that are similar in terms of the interests they involve. By learning about the general interest areas, students may get a better idea of the kinds of jobs they would enjoy.

Assign students to use classroom and library resources to explore each of the interest areas. Ask the business education teacher to speak to the class about the interest areas and other ways teens can explore possible career choices.

Chapter 7 Review

Summary

In this chapter, you have read about:

- ▶ Factors to consider when choosing a career.
- ▶ Job and volunteer opportunities for teens.
- ▶ Sources for locating job possibilities.
- ▶ Helpful guidelines for applying for a job.
- ▶ Tips on interviewing for a job.

Facts to Recall

1. Name three ways attitude toward family life influence your choice of a career.
2. List three questions you can ask yourself to identify your aptitudes and skills.
3. Explain the importance of education and training in career choices.
4. What are three benefits of volunteer jobs?
5. What is an entrepreneur?
6. Explain how to go about making contact with possible employers.
7. Give five ways of showing that you are a responsible employee.
8. List four guidelines to follow when applying for a job.
9. Give six tips for interviewing for a job.

Ideas to Explore

1. What can businesses do to reduce conflicts between family and work obligations? How does reducing these conflicts benefit both employers and families?
2. What types of jobs are available to most teens? What can you learn from these jobs?
3. Why might an employer ask you about your personal interests during an interview?

Activities to Try

1. Bring job applications from different employers to class. Practice filling them out.
2. Find articles about the job market in magazines and newspapers. How is the job market expected to change in the future? What types of skills will be in demand? Report your findings to the class.
3. Research the history of child labor laws in the United States and elsewhere. Also, research the current child labor laws in your state. Prepare a short report for the class.
4. Find articles about teens involved in volunteer work or unusual jobs in magazines and newspapers. Share them with the class.

LINK TO Health

WORK, HEALTH, AND WELL-BEING

Your ability to get and keep a job is directly related to your health. Being healthy means more than not being sick. It means having energy and a feeling of well-being. In other words, health involves both your mind and your body. Without good health, you may be unable to work to support yourself. Think about your health as an employee and complete the following:

- ▶ Make a list of ways health can affect your work. What signs of illness should workers watch for?
- ▶ Develop a list of guidelines for maintaining good health as an employee. (Refer to Chapter 37 if necessary.)

Using Your Resourcefulness Answers

- Answers will vary.
- Answers will vary.
- Answers will vary, but may include the *DOT* (Dictionary of Occupational Titles) and career magazines.
- Answers will vary, but may include: job counselors, employment agencies, government publications, newspapers, and magazines.

Facts to Recall Answers (continued)

7. **Any five:** arrive at work on time; avoid long breaks; follow safety rules and business procedures; be honest and loyal to employer; be pleasant and cooperative; do your share of work; be willing to learn new things; give two weeks notice before quitting.
8. Have Social Security card; have well-organized personal information; write good letter of application; fill out job application carefully.
9. **Any six:** know where to go for interview; arrive five to ten minutes early; go to the interview alone; wear simple, clean clothes; greet interviewer with firm handshake and friendly smile; avoid distractions such as chewing gum; listen to interviewer; tell about your good qualities; learn more about job during interview.

Ideas to Explore

1. Answers will vary and may include: sponsor family social activities; offer flexible work schedules. Employees will be happier and under less stress. Happy employees are more productive.
2. Answers will vary, but may include: newspaper delivery, child care, fast food workers, etc.
3. Answers will vary, but may include: to learn more about your personality; to find work most suitable to personality.

LINK TO Health

Answers

- Answers will vary, but may include: health problems might make you less productive, cause you to miss work, and may interfere with working relationships. Workers should be concerned about fatigue, sore throats, etc.
- Answers will vary, but may include: get proper rest and exercise, eat right, reduce stress, etc.

Career Connections

Volunteer Options

- Girl Scouts of the U. S. A.
- Boy Scouts of America.
- 4-H.
- Future Homemakers of America (FHA-Hero).
- FFA.
- Talking Books (reading books onto tape).
- Nursing home visitations.
- Animal Shelter volunteers.
- Hotline volunteers.

Volunteer Organizations

Volunteers in Service to America (VISTA)
1100 Vermont Ave., Suite 8100
Washington, DC 20525

FOUR-ONE-ONE (Volunteerism)
7304 Beverly St.
Annandale, VA 22003

Girl Scouts of the U.S.A.
830 Third Ave. and 51st St.
New York, NY 10022

Boy Scouts of America
1325 Walnut Hill Lane
Irving, TX 75038

CAREER *Connections*

Get Ready for Your Future Through Volunteering

Janell

"I think I always knew I liked helping people, but it wasn't until I began volunteering at Brandis Nursing Home that I realized how much it meant to me.

"The first time I even knew Brandis existed was when Ms. Applegate, the director, spoke to our family and consumer sciences class. She explained how the home was operated and described how the elderly residents craved special attention. She said that many of the residents' families live far away and aren't able to visit often. They need people to talk to, and Ms. Applegate wondered if any of us would like to help.

"Although I was a little nervous about going, I went anyway. I wasn't sure what I would say to the elderly people. My first few visits were awkward. I guess it was more me than them. It was like any new situation, though; it just takes a little while to feel comfortable.

"Now I have many friends at Brandis. Annie is like a grandmother to me, but many of the other residents are special too. I have learned what they need and how to meet those needs. This may mean reading letters for one, threading a needle for another, pouring a glass of water, or just listening. I feel very useful to my new friends, and I guess the director thinks that I am too. She asked me to become a part-time employee this spring. That means I'll get paid for what I already enjoy doing. I'm not sure what kind of job I want in my future, but I have discovered one thing for certain. I want to work where I can help people."

Katrina

"As a nursing student, I was headed for a career that would allow me to care for people. That was always important to me. After working with the elderly during my training, I decided to become a geriatric nurse. I suppose my close relationship with my grandfather pushed me in this direction.

"Every year our population grows a little older. People are living longer, making the needs of the elderly

Discussing Career Connections

Have students read the *Career Connections* feature. Ask students:

- What personal qualities are important for people to have in service oriented (nursing, teaching, recreation, etc.) volunteer or career jobs?
- What qualities do you have that would be helpful or beneficial in a service oriented career? List at least five qualities.
- What types of volunteer opportunities might you enjoy most at this point in your life?

If possible, have students investigate the types of volunteer opportunities available for teens in your community.

an increasing concern. I work in a nursing home where my duties cover a wide range of activities. I monitor the condition of patients and keep the physicians who visit our facility up-to-date. I keep track of medications and make sure residents take what they are supposed to in the correct dosages. I have also become very knowledgeable about Alzheimer's disease and how to deal with it. Sometimes I have to work with families to help them understand the needs and problems of their loved ones. Every day I know that I make a difference in people's lives, and that feels good."

Eldon

"I love working with people, especially the elderly. That's why I decided to become a recreation director in a nursing home. I don't think any group of people anywhere could be more grateful for the small pleasures I create for them. We sing, dance, play games, exercise, and have parties for every special occasion. I plan activities that help them stay in touch—with life and good health.

"My first interest in the recreation field came when I was a volunteer for the Park District in my home town. I worked with youth. Young or old, it doesn't matter. I find a real reward in enriching the lives of others."

MAKING THE CONNECTION

- What qualities do the individuals above have in common?
- Describe how Janell has benefitted from her volunteer work.
- Explain why Janell might be happy in either of the careers described above. What other jobs might she consider?
- Why is working with older people a good job possibility for the future?
- Describe any experiences you have had that involved relating to older adults.

Making the Connection

Answers

- They all enjoy helping people; they all enjoy working with elderly people; they all have a desire to enrich the lives of others.
- Janell has developed friendships, learned how to meet the needs of elderly people, and she gained job skills which lead to part-time work.
- Answers will vary. Janell might also enjoy nursing, social work, psychology, etc.
- The elderly population is growing. There will be more job opportunities.
- Answers will vary.

Occupational Outlook

Listed below are some possible occupations. Some require little training while others require a 4-year degree.

- Animal Shelter Clerk
- Sheltered Workshop Employee
- Election Clerk
- Police Officer
- Firefighter
- Recreation Leader
- Braille Proofreader
- Fundraising Director
- Elementary School Teacher
- Secondary School Teacher
- FBI Agent
- Employee Welfare Manager
- District Executive for Girl or Boy Scouts of America
- Priest
- Rabbi
- Minister
- Imam
- Academic Advisor
- School Social Worker
- Mental Health Counselor
- School Psychologist
- Pediatrition
- Geneticist
- Nurse
- Home Health Care Provider
- Dentist

Organizations

American School Counselor Association
5999 Stevenson Ave.
Alexandria, VA 22304

National Federation of the Blind
1800 Johnson Street
Baltimore, MD 21230

National Education Association
1201 Sixteenth St., N. W.
Washington, DC 20036

American Medical Association
535 N. Dearborn St.
Chicago, IL 60610

National Association of Healthcare Recruiters
P.O. Box 93851
Cleveland, OH 44101

Planning the Unit

Ch. 8: Communicating Effectively — Emphasizes developing good communication skills in building and maintaining relationships.

Ch. 9: Improving Relationship Skills — Examines ways in which students can develop qualities that strengthen relationships and resolve conflicts.

Ch. 10: Friends and You — Addresses the benefits of friendship, how to make and keep friends, and ending a friendship when necessary.

Ch. 11: Dating — Emphasizes ways in which group dating and single dating differ, the challenges that go along with dating and how to handle them, and being patient in finding real love.

Ch. 12: A Look at Families — Examines various family forms, the family life cycle, and how roles vary and affect families.

Ch. 13: Building a Strong Family — Addresses ways to build and improve strong relationships with family members.

Ch. 14: Handling Challenges — Discusses ways in which families can handle life's challenges (unemployment, drug addiction, death, etc.) in healthful ways.

Ch. 15: Understanding How Children Grow — Examines the stages of development and the influences heredity and environment have on development.

Ch. 16: Taking Care of Children — Emphasizes ways to care for children of various ages, safety guidelines, and how to handle emergencies.

Ch. 17: A Look at Parenting — Explores the factors to consider when making the decision to become a parent, identifies the responsibilities of parenthood, and resources available to parents.

UNIT 2 Relationships

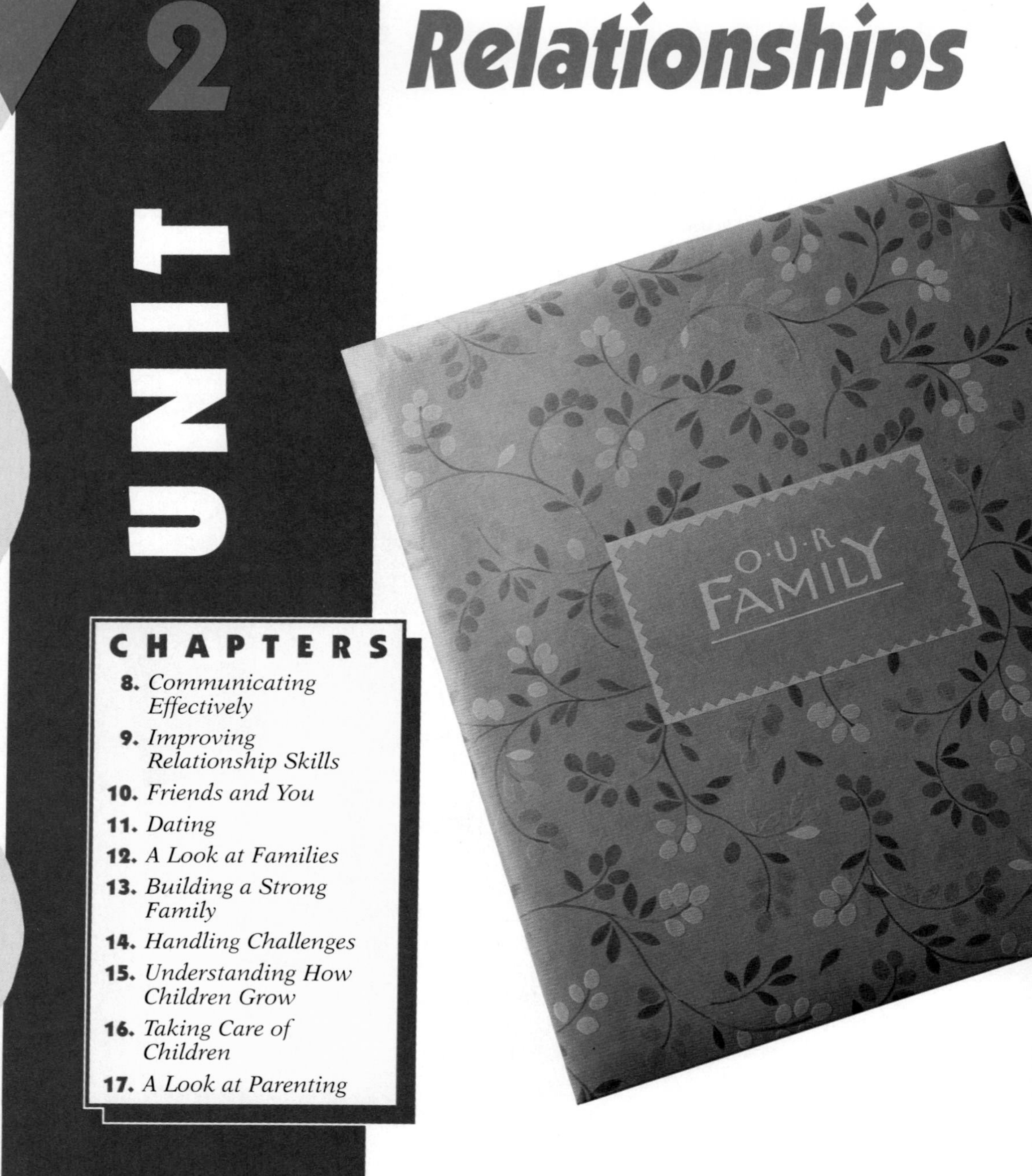

CHAPTERS

Cooperative Learning Tips

One of the elements of cooperative learning is to help students develop positive interdependence. Students learn to depend on each other for information, materials, ideas, energy, and motivation. Positive interdependence is encouraged by using specific roles and responsibilities.

- **Recorder** — writes down actions and ideas of the team.
- **Reporter** — gives the team report to the large group.
- **Leader** — keeps the team focused on the task.
- **Encourager** — provides affirmations and praises appropriate social skills and ideas.

See the *Cooperative Learning* booklet in the TCR for more information.

Introducing the Unit

Unit 2 Overview

Unit 2 helps students explore the various types of relationships they have with friends and family. The unit provides students with an opportunity to develop communication and relationship skills that will enhance their relationships with friends, dating partners, and family members. Special emphasis is placed on building strong families and caring for children.

Unit Motivators

1. **Brainstorming.** Display photographs showing different families (include photos of parent(s) with young children and with teens). Have small groups of students brainstorm a list of ways the parent(s) are providing for the needs of the children and teens. Use these lists as a springboard to discuss the responsibilities parents have to children and to building strong families. What responsibilities do teens have toward keeping a family strong? (Key Skill: *Critical Thinking*)

Completing the Unit

Review

1. **Resource Directory.** Have students develop a directory of resources or places teens and families could go for help. Students might try to identify the needs and problems affecting people in the community and identify agencies that offer help. Students could make the directories available to all students. (Key Skills: *Problem Solving, Critical Thinking*)

Evaluation

1. **Unit Test.** Have students complete the unit test on pp. 112-114 of the *Chapter and Unit Tests* booklet in the TCR.
2. **Testmaker Software.** Use the *Testmaker* software program to design your own unit test.

Implementing Cooperative Learning

A variety of methods can be used to build cooperation skills among students. One useful method is called *Around the Table.* Provide each student with a sheet of paper. Then, give students a concept or incomplete sentence to write about and have them begin writing. For example, as you introduce Unit 2, you might have students respond to the incomplete sentence "A family is ..." After 60 to 90 seconds, have each student pass their paper to the right and continue writing on the new sheet. Repeat this process until every student has written on every paper. Have volunteers share the information on their papers.

See the *Cooperative Learning* booklet in the TCR for more information.

Preparing to Teach

Chapter Outline

Chapter Resources

The following booklet materials may be found in the *Teacher's Classroom Resources* box:

- Lesson Plans, p. 13
- Student Workbook, *Study Guide,* pp. 39-40; *Clues to Communication,* p. 41; *Who Communicates?,* p. 42
- Color Transparencies, *Overcoming Communication Obstacles,* CT-8
- Personal Safety, *No Thanks,* p. 14
- Technology and Computers, pp. 11, 13, 15
- Cooperative Learning, p. 20
- Extending the Text, *Speak Up for Success,* p. 13; *Communicating with People with Disabilities,* p. 14
- Reteaching and Practical Skills, *How Well Do You Know Your Parents?,* pp. 14-15
- Enrichment Activities, *Communicating Creatively,* pp. 18-19
- Chapter and Unit Tests, pp. 19-20
- Testmaker Software

Also see:

- Leadership and Citizenship
- Meeting the Special Needs of Students
- Linking Home, School, and Community
- Dealing with Sensitive Issues

ABCNews InterActive™ Videodiscs

- *Tobacco*
- *Violence Prevention*
- *Alcohol*
- *Drugs and Substance Abuse*
- *Teenage Sexuality*

See the ABCNews InterActive™ Bar Code Correlation booklet for applicable segments.

CHAPTER 8

Communicating Effectively

OBJECTIVES

- *Explain how good communication helps build relationships.*
- *Distinguish between verbal and nonverbal messages.*
- *Explain the listening process.*
- *Identify barriers to communication and describe assertive communication.*

TERMS TO LEARN

- ***relationship***
- ***communication***
- ***verbal communication***
- ***nonverbal communication***
- ***body language***
- ***rapport***
- ***interpreting***
- ***responding***
- ***assertive***

Kaitlin and Tessa are two very different people. Kaitlin gets along well with others. People seem to like her; not just her friends and classmates, but others as well. Tessa, on the other hand, often finds herself in difficult situations. Friendships come and go quickly. There are very few adults she likes, and her family life is stormy. Which of these two girls do you think is more likely to be happy in life?

Relationships Count

Every day you come in touch with all kinds of people. Besides family and friends, your list might include a school bus driver, teachers, store clerks, and your friends' families.

Everyone needs to feel connected to others. How do your friends meet your needs?

When you connect with another person, a relationship of some type forms. A **relationship** is a bond between people. The people may be friends, family members, or people you know but are not close to. The bond may include shared interests, an exchange of information, or shared feelings. Some relationships never grow much beyond a casual conversation whenever you happen to see that person. Others become deep and lasting. Most deep relationships develop over time.

Quality relationships can make a difference in your life. Most people enjoy life more when they have people with whom to share thoughts, feelings, experiences, and interests. In sharing, you are able to get support when you need it and help others when they are in need. When people have good relationships at home, at school, and on the job, they function better in life.

Making Relationships Work

Tessa knows that she doesn't get along well with others. Figuring out how to improve her relationships is the challenge she faces. Most people find that sharpening communication skills makes relationships work better.

Introducing the Chapter

Motivators

1. **Bulletin Board.** Display a variety of colorful pictures showing communication among friends. Include pictures of young children, teens, adults, and older adults. Label it "Communication: A Great Way to Make and Keep Friends." (Key Skill: *Communication*)
2. **Sentence Completion.** Ask students to complete the following sentences: "Communication is ...," "Some people are easy to communicate with because they ...," "One of my strengths in communicating with others is ...," "One of my weaknesses in communicating with others is ...," "Some of the things I can do to improve my communication skills are ..." Ask for volunteers to share their sentences. (Key Skills: *Communication, Critical Thinking*)
3. **Brainstorming.** Lead the class in listing ways students and teachers can work together to improve communication in the classroom. Stress that improving communication at home, at school, and in the community can improve relationships and reduce stress. (Key Skills: *Critical Thinking, Cooperation*)

Chapter Objectives and Vocabulary

1. Have students read the chapter objectives. Ask them to rephrase the objectives as questions.
2. Ask students to state, in their own words, the purpose of studying this chapter.
3. Pronounce the vocabulary terms listed on the previous page. Ask students whether they are familiar with any of these. Explain that the terms will be defined in the chapter.

Guided Reading

1. Have students read the chapter and use the Study Guide on pp. 39-40 of the *Student Workbook*.

More About Words

Words have different meanings to people who live and work in various communities and occupations. For example, doctors, lawyers, and other professionals often use technical terms, or jargon, with each other. Sometimes they exchange special jokes and puns that have little meaning to outsiders. In other instances, jargon serves mainly to confuse an issue. Ask students to find examples of such jargon, such as human resource redundancy, operational parameters, operationization, prioritize, and accountability formula, in government documents and public notices.

Teaching. . .
Relationships Count; What Is Communication? (pp. 101-103)

Comprehension Check

1. What is a relationship? *(A bond between people.)*
2. What are some factors that may cause a bond to be formed between two or more people? *(Shared interests, exchange of information, shared feelings.)*
3. What is the difference between verbal and nonverbal communication? *(Verbal communication uses words; nonverbal communication is sent without words.)*
4. What are some ways to use words effectively? *(Think about your audience, be clear and specific, think before you talk, speak clearly.)*
5. Name three suggestions to make body language work for you. *(Smile, use direct eye contact, make sure your nonverbal messages are accurate.)*
6. How can you identify mixed messages? *(When people use words that do not match their nonverbal messages.)*

Learning Activities

1. **Questioning.** Ask students to list reasons why communication is difficult for some people and easy for others. (Key Skills: *Communication, Critical Thinking*)
2. **Discussion.** Open a discussion on ways that teens and their families can improve communication with each other. (Key Skills: *Critical Thinking, Cooperation*)
3. **Skits.** Select students to create skits demonstrating various kinds of nonverbal communication. (Key Skills: *Communication, Creativity*)
4. **Guest Speaker.** Invite a speech or drama teacher to talk to the class about ways to use verbal and nonverbal communication effectively. (Key Skill: *Communication*)

What Is Communication?

Communication is the exchange of information — facts, opinions, and feelings. Exchanging information means sending and receiving messages. You send others these messages through what you say and how you say it. You receive messages when you listen carefully. Each day, most people spend 60 to 80 percent of their time speaking and listening.

When you speak, you send verbal messages. This is called **verbal communication**. Other messages that you send make up **nonverbal communication**; they are sent without words. Instead you use facial expressions and body movements to communicate. You may give a smile, a frown, a hug, a nod, a wave, or a handshake. Sometimes nonverbal communication is called **body language**.

Communication is usually a mixture of verbal and nonverbal messages. How well you send and receive messages will influence your school, work, and personal life.

▼ Verbal Messages ▼

Although communication is more than just talk, you must use words effectively to communicate a message well. The tips in **Fig. 8-1** may help.

Figure 8-1 **Sending Effective Verbal Messages**

More About *Mixed Messages*

Researchers have found that when people communicate their feelings, only about ten percent of the communication is through words. Much of the message comes through the way the words are said — through the speaker's tone of voice. More than half of the message is passed along through movements of the body, or body language. Problems in communication arise when one's words send one message and the body language or tone of voice sends a different message. These mixed messages can be a source of confusion, and can lead to poor relationships.

The centuries-old Hawaiian hula dance is a beautiful example of both verbal and nonverbal communication. Dancers, both women and men, chant a story while a drummer beats to the rhythm of their poetry. The dancers, in turn, move their hips and feet in time to the drum beat, while their gestures and facial expressions emphasize the words of their story. The dancers' words, faces, and bodies combine to relate a story in a uniquely expressive way.

▼ Nonverbal Messages ▼

With tear-filled eyes, eighteen-month-old Ben reached out to his father. Without a word, the child had sent a message — he was tired and needed comforting. The nonverbal message was easily received and understood by Mr. Defabio.

Body language is a powerful communicator. It often says more than your words. Your facial expressions show enthusiasm, thoughtfulness, or sadness. Your hand and arm gestures and your body posture can reflect your true inner feelings.

People send mixed messages when their words don't match their nonverbal messages. What they say is different from what they feel or think. The difference shows in their actions and facial expressions. See **Fig. 8-2** for examples.

Figure 8-2
Communicating Nonverbally

Learning Activities (continued)

5. **Cartoons.** Have students draw cartoons illustrating the use of nonverbal communication. Share the cartoons with the class, having students identify the types of nonverbal communication and messages sent in each illustration. (Key Skills: *Communication, Creativity*)
6. **Demonstration.** Have students demonstrate examples of mixed messages. Afterwards, discuss reasons why people sometimes send mixed messages. (They may be shy, may be telling a lie, or unwilling to share feelings.) (Key Skills: *Communication, Critical Thinking*)

Follow Up

1. **Reteaching.** Have students make a list of some of the relationships they have formed during their lifetime. Ask for volunteers to share some of the rewards they have experienced as a result of quality relationships. (Key Skills: *Communication, Critical Thinking*)
2. **Enrichment.** Ask for volunteers to take photographs of people using various types of nonverbal communication. (Provide a standard permission sheet to use for the pictures.) Have them design and put up a photo display of their work. (Key Skills: *Problem Solving, Creativity*)

Around the World

After reading the feature, assign students to research ways that nonverbal communication can be misinterpreted among people of different cultural backgrounds. For example, a pat on the head of an American child may show affection. In Japan it shows disrespect. Contrast how some cultures value direct eye contact among all individuals, including children, while other cultures may teach their children to avoid eye contact with an adult as a sign of respect.

More About *Communicating at Home*

Good communication skills begin at home. Teens can develop these skills by taking time to communicate with younger brothers and sisters. Encourage students to listen as much as they talk. After speaking for half a minute or so, they can stop and let their siblings have a chance. While youngsters share their thoughts, teens can focus on the words, using both their eyes and ears. By doing so, they will learn to understand some of the actions and reactions of others. Also, their attention will help younger family members improve self-esteem and confidence.

Teaching. . .
Delivering Your Message; Listening Skills; Barriers; Assertive Communication
(pp. 104-106)

Comprehension Check

1. Why is the way you speak often as important as what you say? *(Tone of voice shows your emotions; when emotions are in control, messages are more easily understood; tone of voice affects how message is received.)*
2. What is the difference between communication and rapport? *(Communication is the exchange of information; rapport — harmony or understanding between people.)*
3. Which one of the four areas of listening show a speaker that you understand what is being said? *(Responding.)*
4. What are some barriers to communication? *(Gossip, lies, insults, blaming and accusing others, threatening or controlling language, messages that nag or preach, complaining, a know-it-all attitude, not allowing others' ideas, sarcasm, interrupting others.)*
5. How can you identify people who communicate assertively? *(Express their opinions and also listen to those of others; stand up for themselves, but do not bully others with words and actions; when there is a difference in opinion, they try to reach an agreement by each giving in part way to the other.)*

Learning Activities

1. **Discussion.** Ask students to describe what emotions are expressed through a hug. *(Affection, caring, concern, warmth.)* Have them identify other gestures that communicate positive feelings as strongly, or more strongly, than words. (Key Skill: *Communication*)
2. **Skits.** Assign students to small groups to write and present skits about building rapport with others. (Key Skills: *Cooperation, Creativity*)

Delivering Your Message

Repeat the sentence "I would be glad to do that for you." out loud four times, emphasizing a different word (*I, glad, that,* and *you*) each time. How does the meaning of the sentence change each time?

The way you speak is often as important as what you say. Your tone of voice shows whether you are happy or sad, relieved, or upset. When you keep your emotions in control, it is easier for people to understand your message. Your tone of voice affects how well your message is received.

For good communication, choose a time when the listener is interested in communicating with you. When people are tired, hungry, or busy, they may not be willing to give you their full attention.

Even if you're speaking in a clear, organized manner, successful communication will not take place unless you have rapport with your listener. **Rapport** (rah-POHR) is harmony or understanding between people. It is the feeling of being listened to and accepted.

This speaker wants to be understood by her listeners. Are there indications that she is being successful?

One way to establish rapport is to put other people at ease. Show interest in them. Make them feel comfortable. Call them by name, and get them involved in the conversation. Ask them questions for their opinions on a topic. Give listeners time to respond to your questions. Also, be yourself. If you are relaxed and comfortable, others will be too.

Developing Listening Skills

About 60 percent of communication time is spent listening, not talking. In fact, your role as a listener is as important to communication as your role as a speaker.

Have you ever noticed a person in a group trying to say something when others are not paying any attention? How do you think that individual felt? A caring person in the group can "rescue" the speaker by quickly becoming a good listener. Eye contact and a nodding head are appreciated by the speaker. Sometimes listening is more than just looking for messages you want to hear. It involves showing respect for other people.

More About Communicating Without Words

How far people stand from each other can determine how their message comes across. For example, close friends usually feel comfortable talking at distances of 6 to 8 inches (15 to 20 centimeters) from one another. When people stand uncomfortably close, or if they stand too straight or lean too far forward, they may be seen as being overly aggressive. However, people who stand too far away are sometimes considered too passive and unsure of their message. Also, people who stand with their head down and shoulders rounded may seem too passive. The best way to stand is in a natural and relaxed manner.

You can be a good listener if you sharpen your skills in each of these four areas:

Hearing
Tune in to what people are saying. Give the speaker your full attention.

Interpreting
Understanding what the speaker actually says and means is called interpreting the message. Be alert for nonverbal messages.

Evaluating
Weigh the information and decide how you will use it. Evaluate the words, not the person speaking. Avoid letting preformed ideas or feelings get in the way of your evaluation.

Responding
Responding is your reaction (in words and actions) to what is being communicated. Your response shows the speaker whether you understand the message. You might nod your head, for example, to indicate understanding. If you do not understand the message, ask for an example. Try rephrasing in your own words what you think has been said.

Success at school or on the job often depends on hearing and understanding directions or instructions. Misunderstandings are less likely when you take time to hear, interpret, evaluate, and respond.

Barriers to Communication

Gossip, lies, insults, threats, and accusations are barriers to communication. They close lines of communication and show little concern for others. Talk that hurts may even destroy relationships.

Nagging and preaching turn listeners off. "You should have called last night" and "You should exercise more" are some examples. Messages that focus more on "I" rather than "you" are usually more effective.

A "know-it-all" stops communication because he or she is not open to other people's thoughts, ideas, or opinions. There are usually many ways to look at any situation.

Sometimes people use a tone that shows they mean the opposite of what they are saying. This is called *sarcasm*. For example, one might say, "Julian is really something," but the tone of voice says just the opposite. Sarcasm can hurt as well as prevent good communication.

How should you respond to someone who interrupts before you are finished speaking? Because the receiver responds to only part of the message, his or her response may not be right. Continue your message in a patient, yet determined, way. You may need to say something like, "Excuse me. I didn't get to finish what I wanted to say."

More About *Breaking Down Barriers to Communication*

Verbal communication is difficult for some teens. They often find it uncomfortable expressing themselves face to face with another person. They may avoid looking someone straight in the eye and saying what they really think. Telling a friend they like them or that they are sorry about something they said may seem almost impossible. In such cases, teens may find it helpful to write letters to each other. Suggest that they write as if they have not seen the other person for several months. They can make the letters as long as they wish. This approach can help them learn to express their thoughts and feelings to one another.

3. **Telephone.** Whisper a brief message to a student in the front of the room. Have the students pass the message around the room until the last student receives the message. Have this student repeat the message out loud. Was the message the same as stated to the first student? Discuss the implications of not listening carefully to messages. (Key Skills: *Communication, Cooperation*)
4. **Class Practice.** Have students work in small groups to practice assertive telephone responses when friends call during family mealtime. (Key Skills: *Cooperation, Creativity*)

Follow Up

1. **Reteaching.** Write the words *hear* and *listen* on the chalkboard. Lead students in a discussion of the difference in meaning between the two words. Ask students what this suggests about the *art* of listening. (That this does not come naturally, that it requires work.) (Key Skills: *Communication, Critical Thinking*)
2. **Extension.** Have the students read the extension material on p. 13 of the *Extending the Lesson* booklet of the TCR.
3. **Enrichment.** Divide students into small groups. Assign them to write and present short lessons to elementary students on being assertive rather than passive or aggressive. Have them write one-page summaries of their experience. (Key Skills: *Communication, Cooperation*)

Life Management Skills

Improving Communication

Encourage students to make sure that facial expressions match the words they say. For instance, an angry face can make even the nicest verbal message seem negative, while a smile can make a serious message seem like a joke. Stress the need to make eye contact during the most important parts of a message.

Completing the Chapter

For Review

1. Emphasize the main concepts using the summary.
2. Have students complete the "Facts to Recall." (Answers below.)

For Reteaching

1. **Reteaching.** Use the activity on p. 14 of the *Reteaching and Practical Skills* booklet in the TCR.

For Enrichment

1. **Enrichment.** Use the activity on pp. 19-20 of the *Enrichment Activities* booklet in the TCR.

For Evaluation

1. Choose items from "Ideas to Explore" and "Activities to Try."
2. Use the chapter test on pp. 19-20 of the testing booklet in the TCR or use the testmaker software.

Facts to Recall Answers

1. You enjoy life more, get and give needed support.
2. The exchange of information. Verbal: messages made of spoken words; nonverbal: messages sent without words, through facial expressions and body movements.
3. Think about your audience; be clear and specific; think before you talk; speak clearly.
4. Smile as you speak; use direct eye contact; make sure messages are accurate.
5. Control tone of voice and emotions; choose time when listener is interested in communicating; develop rapport with listener.
6. Hearing: giving speaker full attention; interpreting: understanding message; evaluating: weighing information and deciding how to use it; responding: reaction to message.
7. Success at school, success at work; avoiding misunderstandings.
8. **Any five:** gossip; lies; threats; insults; accusations; nagging and preaching; "know-it-all"; sarcasm. They are hurtful, turn off listeners, show closed mind.

Assertive people express their opinions in a positive way without hurting others. How are you assertive in your communication?

Assertive Communication

Many people are afraid to express their own feelings. They feel uncomfortable saying what they think or pressing for what they want. They are passive. *Passive* people do not stand up for themselves. They are afraid to say anything that might make others angry.

Other people are *aggressive* when communicating. They are often thought of as pushy and rude, concerned mostly with their own needs and wants. They want to be in control. They may try to get their way by bullying others.

People who communicate assertively are neither passive nor aggressive. **Assertive** (uh-SURT-iv) people stand up for themselves in a determined or confident manner, but they do not bully others with their words and actions. They not only express their opinions, but they also listen to the opinions of others. When opinions differ, they try to reach an agreement acceptable to all involved.

Your opinion and your wishes are worthwhile. You have the right to express them, even though others may disagree at times. Everyone has to learn to accept give-and-take as part of the communication process. When you strive for confidence and you practice the skills you have learned, you will be well on the way to becoming a good communicator.

TAKING ACTION

Overcoming Shyness

"A lot of people think I'm not friendly, but I'm really just shy," Tina says to you. Tina is new at your school and the students don't know her well. You have been asked to show Tina around, so you have gotten to know her a little in the past few days.

One thing you've noticed is that Tina has a habit of not looking people in the eye. If she passes someone in the halls, she looks away nervously. She never speaks first to anyone. Instead, she waits for others to take the first step.

You have learned that Tina has very definite interests. Her music collection is large and varied. She loves to swim. She also enjoys reading, especially about American history. You find her interesting and fun to be with as you get to know her.

Tina wants to make new friends but doesn't know where to start. For one thing, she cannot walk up to people she doesn't know well and start a conversation. It isn't her personal style. As a result, she feels lost and unsure of herself.

Using Your Resourcefulness

- Are Tina's feelings typical ones? Describe any similar feelings you may have had.
- What are some possible reasons for Tina's feelings?
- What action can you take to help Tina in this situation?
- What might Tina do to help herself?

TAKING ACTION

Have students read the feature. Have they ever met others like Tina? What suggestions do students have for helping shy people make friends? Have students brainstorm a list of *conversation starters* that may be useful for anyone who wants to meet new people.

Using Your Resourcefulness Answers

- Tina's feelings are often typical of very shy people. Answers will vary.
- Answers will vary, but may include: moving and not knowing anyone, lack of confidence, possible low self-esteem.
- Answers will vary, but may include: taking the first step and introducing yourself. Find

Chapter 8 Review

Summary

In this chapter, you have read about:

- The importance of good communication skills to strong, rewarding relationships.
- Using verbal and nonverbal communication to express yourself clearly.
- Establishing rapport with others to encourage them to listen to your message.
- How to be a good listener.
- Types of messages and behavior that are destructive to communication.
- The role of assertiveness in successful communication.

Facts to Recall

1. Why are good relationships important in life?
2. What is communication? Explain the difference between verbal and nonverbal communication.
3. Identify four ways to improve your verbal communication skills.
4. Give three suggestions for making body language work for you.
5. Give three suggestions for delivering messages successfully.
6. Name and describe the four areas you should work on to become a good listener.
7. List three benefits of being a good listener.
8. Describe five barriers to good communication.
9. What is the difference between being aggressive and being assertive in communication?

Ideas to Explore

1. Evaluate your own communication skills, both as a speaker and a listener. How do you send messages? How are your listening skills? How could you improve?
2. When might it be appropriate to interrupt a speaker? If people interrupt Jay all the time, who is at fault, Jay or the interrupters? Explain your answer.
3. How can body language both help and hurt communication between two persons from different cultures?
4. Explain what you think this quotation by Carlo Goldoni means: "He who talks much cannot talk well."

Activities to Try

1. Use body language to pantomime different emotions. Have the rest of the class try to identify the emotion you are expressing.
2. With a partner, perform two short skits. In one, portray a poor speaker or listener. In the other, show a good speaker and/or listener. Have the rest of the class identify the good or bad habits of each character.

LINK TO *Social Studies*

SOLVING MISCOMMUNICATION

Embarrassing miscommunications are often the result when words are not pronounced or interpreted correctly. Communication errors may also result from a lack of awareness about foreign cultures. Some people believe that a single, international written and spoken language would solve many of our world communication problems. Do you agree or disagree? What might be some advantages and disadvantages of such a language? How might this affect communication problems related to the lack of understanding about cultural differences?

Facts to Recall Answers (continued)

9. Aggressive: pushy, bullying, concerned mostly with own needs. Assertive: stand up for themselves but also listen to others' opinions.

Ideas to Explore

1. Answers will vary.
2. Answers will vary, but may include to ask an appropriate question for clarification.
3. Answers will vary. Various cultures often attach different meanings to the same nonverbal action.
4. Answers will vary.

ways to encourage Tina and make her feel comfortable.

- Answers will vary.

LINK TO *Social Studies*

Answer

Answers will vary, but may include: (advantages) less miscommunication because everyone would understand the same language, easier to conduct business; (disadvantages) may take away from cultural diversity, may discourage learning other languages.

Preparing to Teach

Chapter Outline

Chapter Resources

The following booklet materials may be found in the *Teacher's Classroom Resources* box:

- Lesson Plans, p. 14
- Student Workbook, *Study Guide,* pp. 43-44; *How Do You Relate to Others?,* p. 45; *A Recipe for Overcoming Prejudice,* p. 46
- Color Transparencies, *Formula for Successful Relationships,* CT-9
- Personal Safety, *How Do You Handle Anger?,* pp. 15-16
- Technology and Computers, p. 11
- Cooperative Learning, p. 21
- Extending the Text, *Facing Conflicts in a Family,* pp. 15-16
- Reteaching and Practical Skills, *Family Responsibility Inventory,* p. 16
- Enrichment Activities, *Recognizing Stereotypes,* pp. 20-21
- Chapter and Unit Tests, pp. 21-22
- Testmaker Software

Also see:

- Leadership and Citizenship
- Meeting the Special Needs of Students
- Linking Home, School, and Community
- Dealing with Sensitive Issues

ABCNews InterActive™ Videodiscs

- *Violence Prevention*

See the ABCNews InterActive™ Bar Code Correlation booklet for applicable segments.

CHAPTER 9

Improving Relationship Skills

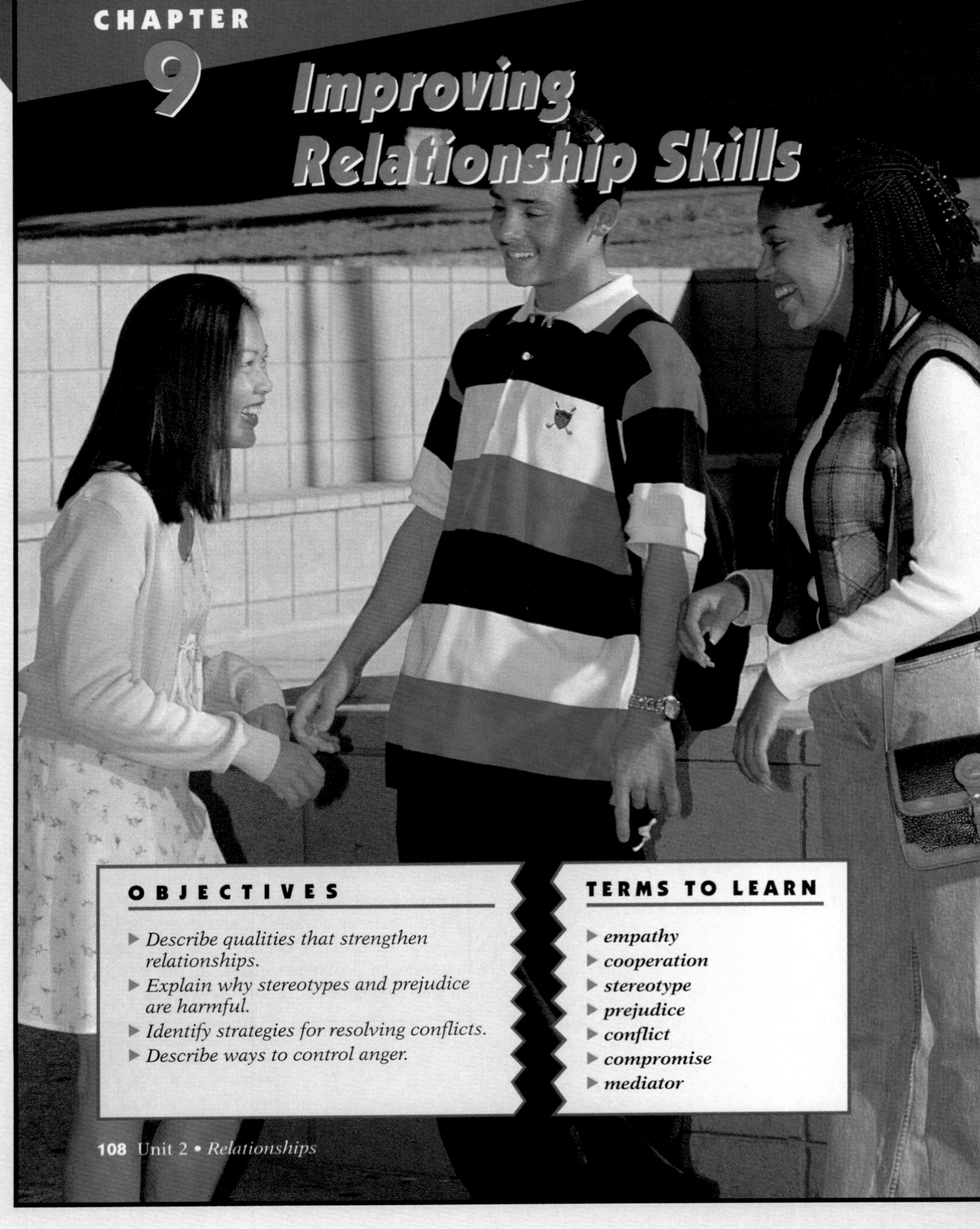

OBJECTIVES

- *Describe qualities that strengthen relationships.*
- *Explain why stereotypes and prejudice are harmful.*
- *Identify strategies for resolving conflicts.*
- *Describe ways to control anger.*

TERMS TO LEARN

- ***empathy***
- ***cooperation***
- ***stereotype***
- ***prejudice***
- ***conflict***
- ***compromise***
- ***mediator***

Marcus is someone everybody likes. One day Shana was trying to pinpoint just what it is that makes Marcus so successful with people.

One quality that immediately came to Shana's mind was Marcus's skill in communication. He can speak his mind with confidence and yet still be sensitive to other viewpoints. When he listens to people, he stands silent and thoughtful, giving them his full attention. His responses are directly related to what they have said.

Communication, however, is not the only skill Marcus possesses. He gets along well because of other qualities too. Recognizing this, Shana decided to pay attention to how Marcus deals with people. She wanted to learn something from him.

Qualities That Count

Today, relationships are challenged in many ways. Busy schedules and a changing world can make good relationships difficult to maintain. You can make them work, however, just as Marcus has. By showing you care, empathizing with others, cooperating, being accepting, and keeping your sense of humor, you will have the qualities that are key to maintaining good relationships.

Show You Care

First you must learn to care about others. Then you must show it. When people become too focused on themselves, they are viewed as self-centered. What do you think would happen in a society where most people thought only of themselves?

When you reach out to others and show that you care, it gives people a good impression of you. Reaching out to others also gives you a good feeling about yourself.

See if you can add to the following list of ways to show people that you care.

- Point out their special qualities with sincerity.
- Give sincere praise whenever you can.
- Use peoples' names when you talk to them.
- Encourage people to talk about themselves by asking questions and listening. Include subjects that are of interest to others in your conversations.
- Do a favor when possible.

Lending a helping hand to someone is a positive way to show that you care.

More About *Relationships*

Relationships among peers provide the testing ground for teens to try out emerging adult identities. These relationships are a bridge between childhood dependence and adult independence. With the help of peers, teens learn how to develop relationships, including friendships with the opposite sex. They learn about trust, compromise, and the value of friendship. Teens use each other to develop and practice social skills that will serve them throughout their adult lives. Being accepted by the crowd (the club, team, band, or "just friends") eases self-doubt and builds confidence.

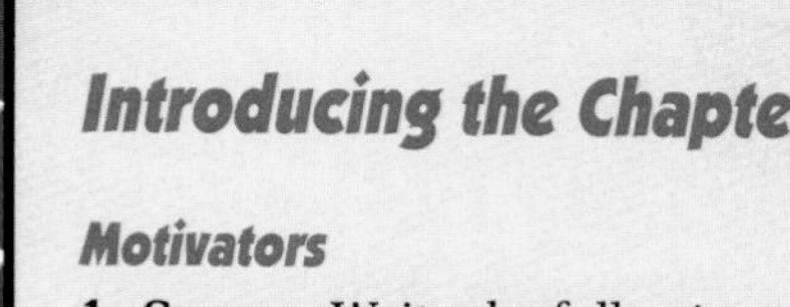

Introducing the Chapter

Motivators

1. **Survey.** Write the following on the chalkboard for students to answer: "List five qualities you value in a friend." Survey students' responses, and write on the board the qualities most frequently listed. (Key Skills: *Communication, Critical Thinking*)
2. **Discussion.** Ask students to choose a television character they would like to have for a friend. Have them give reasons for choosing each character. (Key Skills: *Communication, Decision Making*)
3. **List.** Have students list on a sheet of paper the different groups to which they belong. Suggest they start by listing their family and their classification group at school. Ask them to add as many groups, including classes, clubs, religious groups, sports teams, and any others, that they can recall. Conclude by stressing the importance of good relationship skills in all groups. (Key Skills: *Communication, Social Studies*)

Chapter Objectives and Vocabulary

1. Have students read the chapter objectives. Ask them to rephrase the objectives as questions.
2. Ask students to state, in their own words, the purpose of studying this chapter.
3. Pronounce the vocabulary terms listed on the previous page. Ask students whether they are familiar with any of these. Explain that the terms will be defined in the chapter.

Guided Reading

1. Have students read the chapter and use the Study Guide on pp. 43-44 of the *Student Workbook*.

Teaching. . .
Qualities That Count: Care; Empathy; Cooperate; Accepting
(pp. 109-111)

Comprehension Check

1. What are five ways to show people you care about them? *(Point out special qualities, give sincere praise, use people's names when talking to them, encourage people to talk about themselves and their interests, do favors when possible.)*
2. What is the difference between empathy and cooperation? *(Empathy: the ability to understand what someone else is experiencing. Cooperation: working together for the good of all.)*
3. In what ways does empathy help in forming good relationships? *(Prevents misunderstandings; allows people to be sensitive to each other's needs.)*
4. How can you improve your cooperation skills? *(Focus on the goal and participate in reaching it; do your share; be agreeable; be willing to use another's ideas or plan.)*
5. In what ways are stereotypes and prejudice harmful? *(Stereotypes often are used to justify the way all people in a particular group are treated; stereotypes may lead to prejudice; people may use differences to dislike or hurt others; prejudice causes people to hate without just cause.)*

Learning Activities

1. **Brainstorm.** Lead students in brainstorming a list of ways to show caring to their peers, their families, and to people in the community. (Key Skills: *Communication, Cooperation*)

AROUND THE WORLD

Have students read the feature. Ask one student to read the definition of humility to the class. Have students compare and contrast humility in Japan and the United States. Ask students how all people might benefit from developing true humility.

AROUND THE WORLD

In Japanese society, one of the most important traits for building strong personal and professional relationships is humility. Everyone, from the youngest student to the most powerful business executive, is expected to show some degree of humility. This means accepting praise graciously, admitting mistakes honestly, and respecting the ideas and needs of others. Humility is based not on feelings of low self-esteem, but on a desire for the social harmony that comes from placing others before one's self.

Have Empathy

Empathy (EM-puh-thee) is the ability to understand what someone else is experiencing. You empathize by putting yourself in another's place and trying to see things from their point of view. Empathy has been accurately described in this well-known Native American prayer: "Great Spirit, grant that I may not criticize my neighbor until I have walked a mile in his moccasins."

Empathy helps form good relationships because it prevents many misunderstandings. When Dorita had very little to say to Frank, he could have easily been offended. Instead he thought about how she was feeling after her parents' divorce and understood her actions. Empathy allowed him to be sensitive to her needs.

Cooperate

Cooperation is working together with others for the good of all. Another name for cooperation is teamwork. A group of junior high students were asked to make a video that showed a scene from the book they were studying. Two of the six students forgot props, failed to learn their lines, and constantly distracted the group from the project. As a result, the video was not what the rest had hoped it would be. By not cooperating, the two troublesome students damaged their relationship with the others.

To improve your cooperation skills, try these ideas:

- Do your share. Focus on the goal and participate in reaching it.
- Be agreeable. Some tasks are not fun but they must be done.
- Be willing to use another's ideas or plan. Express your own ideas, but realize that yours won't always be selected.

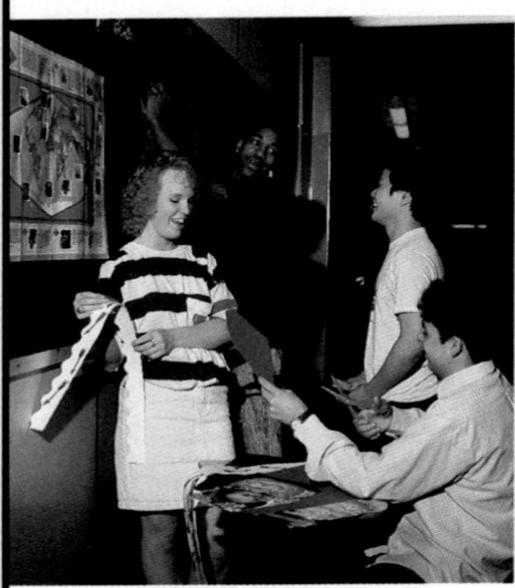

Working together can be fun and accomplish great things, too!

More About *The History of Caring*

History is full of human people who cared for one another. There are many examples of commitments and sacrifices people made for each other out of conviction and caring. Documents, such as the *Mayflower Compact*, the *Declaration of Independence*, the *United States Constitution*, and the *Emancipation Proclamation*, provide opportunities for class discussions on caring, empathy, cooperation, and acceptance. Political movements, such as the abolition of slavery, civil rights, women's rights, and the war on poverty, can be tied to a study of current events that are affected by stereotypes and prejudice.

▼ Be Accepting ▼

No matter where you go in life you will find many people who are different from you. In fact, most people in the world are different from you in one way or another. That does not make them inferior or wrong. As you read in an earlier chapter, differences are refreshing. You can also learn from them. Differences should be a reason for appreciating others, not rejecting them.

Stereotypes

Until recently, Chuck believed that all homeless people were lazy. He felt that they were homeless simply because they refused to get a job. Chuck had stereotyped the homeless. A **stereotype** is a belief that an entire group of people fit a fixed, common pattern — that they are all alike in certain ways. When Chuck stereotyped all homeless people, he didn't see them as individuals; he saw them as a group who all shared the same characteristic of being lazy and not wanting to work.

After joining a volunteer program that provided help for the homeless, Chuck's stereotype of the homeless began to change. He met a homeless family whose small house had burned to the ground. The single mother had a part-time job, but it didn't pay enough for housing. There was no low-income housing in the community that she could afford. As he heard about this family's situation and other similar situations, Chuck began to question his thinking. He was learning to look at people as individuals rather than using stereotypes.

Prejudice

Stereotypes often lead to prejudice. When people use differences to dislike or hurt others, they are showing prejudice. **Prejudice** (PREJ-ud-us) is an unfair or biased opinion. Often it is a judgment against a person or a group formed without knowing the facts or by ignoring the facts. For example, prejudice may be directed against people because of their race, religion, or gender (male or female). Age and disabilities are also sometimes used as a basis for prejudice.

The sad thing about prejudice is that it causes people to distrust and hate without just cause. Some people even act on that hate. How do you want to be treated? No doubt, you want others to look beyond what they see and discover who you are inside as an individual person. That is exactly what you must do when you relate to others.

TIPS: *Avoiding Gossip*

Gossip communicates hurtful messages or rumors that are not to be believed. Many friendships and families have often been hurt or destroyed by careless gossip passed from one person to the next.

How can you tell the difference between what is truth and what is gossip? Here are some tips to help you uncover the truth in messages:

- ▶ Reject messages that are not based in fact.
- ▶ Consider the source of the message. Is this person trustworthy and reliable?
- ▶ Talk with the person who is the subject of the message before you believe what is said.
- ▶ Use direct questions of those involved to uncover the truth.

Differences in people are refreshing.

Learning Activities (continued)

2. **Coupons.** Assign students to make and give coupons to their friends and family that are attractive and entitle the recipient to an act of caring. (Key Skills: *Communication, Creativity*)
3. **Guest Panel.** Invite several people of different races, cultures, or from various countries to share examples of stereotyping and prejudice they have witnessed or experienced. Have students prepare questions for the speakers. (Key Skills: *Communication, Social Studies*)
4. **Quilt Making.** Have students make a "Cooperation Quilt." Give each student a sheet of construction paper to use as the background for a quilt square. Provide scissors, glue, colored markers, old magazines, newspapers, and colored yarn. Encourage students to express their feelings about cooperation among people in their quilt squares. They may use words, pictures, drawings or designs on their squares. Afterwards, have the class tape the squares together into a big paper "quilt." Display it on the wall of the classroom or on a hallway bulletin board. (Key Skills: *Cooperation, Creativity*)

Follow Up

1. **Reteaching.** Provide newspapers and magazines for students to locate examples of caring, empathy, cooperation, acceptance, stereotypes, and prejudice. (Key Skills: *Social Studies, Critical Thinking*)
2. **Enrichment.** Assign students to write a poem or song illustrating the harm that can be done by prejudice or stereotyping. (Key Skills: *Communication, Creativity*)

More About *Stereotypes*

Stereotypes and prejudice sometimes keep people from achieving their potential. Incorrect beliefs and attitudes about old age may hinder healthy and able older adults from participating in certain activities or jobs. In the past, stereotypes have kept many females from choosing to become pilots, physicians, or engineers. Likewise, few males chose to become kindergarten teachers, nurses, or librarians. To dispel various stereotypes and prejudices, role models in the community, including teachers, administrators, and parents, can be invited to the classroom as guest speakers, panelists, lunch guests, etc.

TIPS:

Avoiding Gossip
Have students read the feature. Ask students to share experiences they know of in which gossip destroyed relationships (students should not use names of those involved). What suggestions do students have for avoiding gossip?

Teaching. . .

Sense of Humor; Resolving Conflicts; Dealing with Anger (pp. 112-114)

Comprehension Check

1. What is a healthy alternative to anger? *(A sense of humor.)*
2. What other qualities are useful in building and keeping good relationships? *(Showing respect and courtesy for others, patience, positive attitude.)*
3. What is a conflict, and what are some of its characteristics? *(A disagreement or struggle between two people or groups with opposing points of view; it may be short and personal; it may be a long, continuous struggle; it may be either positive or negative.)*
4. What is a mediator, and when is one needed? *(Someone who is not involved, who assists in solving a conflict.)*
5. What are some appropriate ways to deal with anger? *(Physical activities; letting annoyances go; allowing cool off time before reacting; talking about feelings.)*

Learning Activities

1. **Skits.** Divide students into small groups to write and present short skits about keeping a sense of humor in a friendship. Discuss the skits and the importance of keeping a sense of humor. (Key Skills: *Communication, Creativity*)
2. **Cartoons.** Assign students to create cartoons based on keeping a sense of humor in relationships to share with others. (Key Skills: *Communication, Creativity*)
3. **Videotape.** Select a group of students to make a short videotape about resolving conflicts among teens. Choose another group to make a video about conflict resolution among teens and their families. Use these presentations to stimulate discussions about resolving conflicts. (Key Skills: *Communication, Critical Thinking*)

Keep a Sense of Humor

Relationships are more likely to thrive when people find humor around them. Sometimes you may have to make an effort to find it.

When Tamica accidentally dropped Danette's purse through a sidewalk grate, the two spent an hour retrieving it. Instead of feeling angry, Danette laughed about how the purse got there in the first place and about the things they had to do to get it back. Danette had an amusing story to tell others, and her relationship with Tamica stayed as strong as ever.

Look for More

The list of qualities that are useful in building and keeping good relationships goes on. Showing respect and courtesy for others is important. Being patient also helps keep relationships on track. Having a positive attitude can help, too. All of these are tools to use and improve. They can make your life and your relationships happier.

Resolving Conflicts

One of the greatest threats to relationships is conflict. A **conflict** is a disagreement or struggle between two or more people or groups who have opposing points of view. A conflict may be short and personal, as in a brief argument with a friend; or it may be a long, continuous struggle, as within a family or between countries. Without the ability to settle problems, your relationships with others will suffer.

Conflict can be either positive or negative. It is positive when problems are brought out into the open and settled in a satisfying manner. It is negative when people use destructive tactics in trying to solve the problem.

Most conflicts grow out of disagreements over territory (or space), property, values and beliefs, power and authority, and who gets rewards or privileges. You can't avoid conflicts, but you can work to resolve them. Read "How To Resolve Conflicts" on page 113 for some ideas.

Conflict can threaten relationships. How might these teens resolve their conflict without destroying their relationship?

Mediators

Sometimes you may find it impossible to work through a problem, even with cooperation and communication. Deadlocks, in which no one will budge, occur when people can't agree on a solution.

More About Positive Conflict

A conflict can have a number of positive results, depending on how a person or group handles it. For example, a conflict can encourage change by keeping people from getting into ruts and from maintaining old habits which they need to review and change. Conflicts can make life more interesting by causing people to look more deeply into an issue, particularly from a new perspective. A conflict can even help to deepen and improve a relationship by strengthening each person's belief that the bond between the individuals is stronger than any issue causing conflict.

How to ...
Resolve Conflicts

Settling differences is easier if you follow some basic suggestions:

- ***Confront the problem.*** Some people find conflicts so difficult or frightening that they run away from them. They may pretend they don't exist or make excuses for not dealing with them. Avoid conflict only if your safety is at stake or the problem is not worth worrying about.
- ***If possible, choose the right time and location to discuss the issue.*** When people are in the right frame of mind, it is easier to discuss sensitive topics.
- ***Identify the problem.*** Make sure that both sides agree on what it is. Ask questions of each other to find out.
- ***Don't get sidetracked by other issues.*** Save them for another time.
- ***Discuss the issue, not the people involved.*** Hurtful statements directed at people will not be helpful.
- ***Use good communication skills.*** State your position clearly so that it can be fully understood. Listen carefully to the other person's position so that you will understand.
- ***Avoid jumping to conclusions.*** Determine the facts and look for options.
- ***Stay calm and objective.*** Being objective involves sticking to the facts and not being influenced by stereotypes and prejudices. You need to see both sides of the issue clearly.
- ***Cooperate with each other.*** Conflict is not a competitive sport. You will both win when the problem is solved.
- ***Learn to compromise.*** Through **compromise**, each person gives up something in order to reach a satisfactory solution. Compromise is also known as give-and-take.

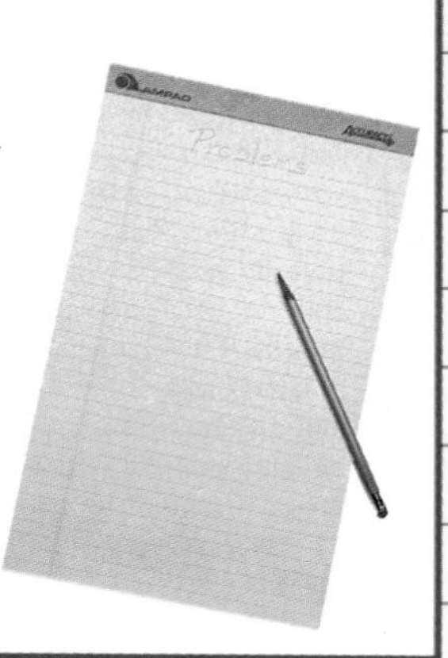

Learning Activities (continued)

4. **Guest Speaker.** Invite the school counselor or psychologist to speak to the class about resolving conflicts. Ask students to write questions about conflict to submit to the speaker(s). (Key Skill: *Communication*)
5. **Writing.** Assign students to write a paper, describing a positive conflict that has helped them grow in some way. (Key Skills: *Communication, Critical Thinking*)
6. **Discussion.** Talk about ways anger is dealt with on television and in the movies. Identify which of these were constructive and which were destructive. (Key Skill: *Critical Thinking*)

Follow Up

1. **Reteaching.** Assign students to summarize in writing what they learned in this chapter. Ask for volunteers to share their summaries with the class. (Key Skills: *Communication, Critical Thinking*)
2. **Extension.** Have the students read the extension material on pp. 15-16 from the *Extending the Lesson* booklet of the TCR.
3. **Enrichment.** Ask for volunteers to choreograph two dances with two dancers. The first dance should symbolize negative conflict. The second dance should symbolize positive conflict. Arrange for the dancers to perform the two dances for the class. (Key Skills: *Communication, Creativity*)

Making a Difference

Write the following sentence on the board: "Prejudice is a learned behavior." Ask students to list as many sources of prejudice as they can (media, community, school, and family). Talk about ways to overcome prejudicial beliefs. Stress that learning facts about others helps people to begin to identify their own prejudices. In so doing, they often begin to look for positive ways to get to know people against whom stereotypes are held and prejudice is directed.

How to ... Resolve Conflicts

Ask students to list and describe common conflicts among teens and between teens and their families. Discuss which of the conflicts tend to be the most difficult to resolve. Which tend to be the easiest to resolve? Talk about reasons why this is so. Have them identify movies and television programs in which conflicts were resolved in appropriate ways.

Conclude by reviewing the basic suggestions for resolving conflicts. Ask students to suggest ways that this information will help them solve conflicts in the future.

Completing the Chapter

For Review

1. Emphasize the main concepts using the summary.
2. Have students complete the "Facts to Recall." (Answers below.)

For Reteaching

1. **Reteaching.** Use the activity on p. 15 of the *Reteaching and Practical Skills* booklet in the TCR.

For Enrichment

1. **Enrichment.** Use the activity on pp. 21-22 of the *Enrichment Activities* booklet in the TCR.

For Evaluation

1. Choose items from "Ideas to Explore" and "Activities to Try."
2. Use the chapter test on pp. 21-22 of the testing booklet in the TCR or use the testmaker software.

Facts to Recall Answers

1. **Any three:** point out special qualities; give sincere praise; use peoples' names; encourage people to talk about themselves; do a favor.
2. The ability to understand what someone else is experiencing. Prevents misunderstandings, allows sensitivity to needs.
3. Do your share; be agreeable; be open to others' ideas.
4. Stereotypes encourage people to treat all members of a group in same way, rather than as individuals; prejudice encourages hate and distrust without just cause.
5. Helps you deal with angry feelings, focus on positive side.
6. Disagreement or struggle between two or more people or groups who have opposing points of view.
7. Positive when problems are brought out into the open, settled in a satisfying manner. Negative when people use destructive tactics in trying to solve problem.

Sometimes a person not directly involved in a conflict can help people identify the problem and work toward a positive solution.

A **mediator** (MEED-ee-ATE-ur), or someone who is not directly involved in a conflict, can help people look at a problem and work toward a solution. In some schools, mediators are used when students experience conflict with others. School counselors, teachers, social workers, members of the clergy, and mature students may serve as mediators. They are trained to evaluate a situation. As careful observers and listeners, they ask questions and respond to both parties. Mediators try to resolve the conflict by determining the problem and suggesting acceptable solutions.

Dealing with Anger

Everyone feels anger. Not everyone knows how to handle it. Evan used to react physically when he was angry. Because fist fights were common for him, many people began to avoid him.

When Evan learned that violence does not solve problems, his life began to change. He learned to let little annoyances go and allowed himself time to cool off before reacting at all. He doesn't keep his feelings locked inside now, but he does control himself. When the feelings are very strong, he does something physically active, such as playing basketball. Now people like to be around Evan. His relationships have improved, just as yours can when you look for better ways to get along.

TAKING ACTION
Accepting Differences

"I don't understand teamwork," Jared thinks to himself. Maybe it's because he's an only child. Jared isn't used to sharing possessions or playing with a sister or brother. He likes to work on his own, rather than in a group. He enjoys spending time by himself drawing. For a project on family conflict, he created a comic book that surprised and impressed everyone.

Jared has a few friends, most of whom are quiet and different from most teens. Sometimes he feels he's missing out on what others call "being part of the crowd," but he isn't sure he wants to change. Mostly, he thinks of himself as content and doesn't feel lonely.

Using Your Resourcefulness

- How would you explain the concept and value of teamwork, so Jared might consider it more often? Identify resource materials, such as movies, novels, or magazine articles, that illustrate the meaning of teamwork.
- Do you have a friend who seems unusual or different? If so, how do you let that friend know you care?
- Do you think Jared is someone you might want to know? Why or why not? What steps might you take to get to know him?

TAKING ACTION

Have students brainstorm a list of the pros and cons of teamwork. Discuss ways in which teamwork might be difficult for someone who spends a great deal of time alone. What ways can students think of to encourage others to become part of a team? Have students read the feature and respond to the questions.

Using Your Resourcefulness Answers

- Answers will vary.
- Answers will vary based on student experiences. Answers may include: by listening, showing encouragement, empathy, etc.
- Answers will vary.

Chapter 9 Review

Summary

In this chapter, you have read about:

- ▶ Personal qualities that help you build good relationships with others.
- ▶ How stereotypes and prejudice discourage the development of strong personal relationships.
- ▶ Ways of resolving conflict.
- ▶ How to deal with anger constructively.

Facts to Recall

1. Name three ways of showing people that you care about them.
2. What is empathy? Why is it important in a relationship?
3. List three suggestions for improving cooperation skills.
4. How do stereotypes and prejudice hurt relationships?
5. How can a sense of humor help with relationships?
6. What is a conflict?
7. How can conflict be positive? When is it negative?
8. List six suggestions for resolving conflicts.
9. What purpose does a mediator serve in resolving conflict?
10. How might a person handle angry feelings in a positive manner?

Ideas to Explore

1. Can people learn personal traits — caring, empathy, respect for others — that enable them to relate successfully to others, or must they feel them instinctively?
2. What conflicts have you experienced? How did you solve them? Were all the parties involved satisfied with the solution? If not, how could the conflict have been resolved more acceptably?
3. Discuss the importance of relationship-building qualities — such as empathy, cooperation, and humor — in resolving conflicts.
4. Is anger always negative? Discuss ways in which it can be turned into a positive reaction.

Activities to Try

1. With two other students, perform a skit in which one student acts as a mediator in solving a conflict between the other two. Have the rest of the class identify the qualities of the mediator that enabled him or her to help reach a resolution.
2. In current newspapers and magazines, find examples of how conflicts between opposing groups were resolved.

LINK TO *Social Studies*

Eliminating Stereotypes and Prejudice

Everyone has some trait or characteristic that has served as the basis for stereotyping and prejudice. Males, females, teens, redheads, senior citizens, blondes, people who are overweight or underweight, as well as persons of various ethnic origins, races, religions, or regions of the country have all been unfairly judged by others. Choose a group that has been the target of stereotyping and prejudice. Identify some common stereotypes about the group. Then do some research about ways to help correct these false ideas. Perhaps get involved in some volunteer work with this group. Write a one- or two-page report summarizing what you have learned.

Facts to Recall Answers (continued)

8. **Any six:** confront problem; choose right time and location to discuss issue; identify problem; don't get sidetracked; discuss issue, not people; use good communication skills; avoid jumping to conclusions; stay calm; cooperate; compromise.
9. Tries to resolve conflict by determining problem and suggesting acceptable solutions.
10. Let little annoyances gò; take time to cool off; do something physically active.

Ideas to Explore

1. Answers will vary.
2. Answers will vary.
3. Answers will vary and may include: empathy helps you see others' side; humor helps avoid angry feelings.
4. Answers will vary and may include: it can motivate person to improve unfair situation; can tell others their behavior is hurtful.

LINK TO *Social Studies*

Answer

Answers will vary depending on information studied.

Preparing to Teach

Chapter Outline

Chapter Resources

The following booklet materials may be found in the *Teacher's Classroom Resources* box:

- Lesson Plans, p. 15
- Student Workbook, *Study Guide,* pp. 47-48; *Tell Me Who-oo-oo,* p. 49; *Friendly Faces,* p. 50
- Color Transparencies, *Circle of Friends,* CT-10
- Personal Safety, *What Do You Know About Gangs?,* p. 17; *Safety Around Town,* pp. 18-19
- Cooperative Learning, p. 22
- Extending the Text, *Understanding Aging,* p. 17
- Reteaching and Practical Skills, *Human Relationship Scale,* p. 17
- Enrichment Activities, *Friends of All Types,* pp. 22-23
- Chapter and Unit Tests, pp. 23-24
- Testmaker Software

Also see:

- Leadership and Citizenship
- Meeting the Special Needs of Students
- Linking Home, School, and Community
- Dealing with Sensitive Issues

ABCNews InterActive™ Videodiscs

- *Tobacco*
- *Violence Prevention*
- *Alcohol*
- *Teenage Sexuality*
- *Drugs and Substance Abuse*

See the ABCNews InterActive™ Bar Code Correlation booklet for applicable segments.

CHAPTER

10 Friends and You

OBJECTIVES

- *Describe the benefits of various kinds of friendship.*
- *Discuss how you can make and keep friends.*
- *Explain how to end a friendship when necessary.*

TERMS TO LEARN

- ***acquaintances***
- ***peers***
- ***peer pressure***
- ***clique***

Anna is one of fourteen-year-old Ming's best friends. As far as Ming is concerned, there is no one like Anna. When Ming is troubled, he goes to Anna for advice or just a willing ear. Anna listens to him and gives him support. Sometimes she even confides in Ming, sharing her concerns with him. They enjoy their time together even though it is limited. Anna lives next door to Ming. She is eighty years old.

Regardless of age, friendship is important to nearly everyone. Most people enjoy the companionship that comes with friendship. They like having someone to share with. The benefits of friendship are many. Friends can broaden your life. They provide advice and show understanding. They make you feel accepted and give support when you need it.

Making Friends

Because most people find pleasure in friendship, they are often looking for ways to begin new ones. Here are some ideas:

- ***Smile.*** A friendly face is the first signal that you are willing to begin a friendship.
- ***Start a conversation.*** Ask a question that doesn't require a simple "yes" or "no" answer. Then listen and respond to the answer. Look for common interests. Great friendships can begin with a simple conversation.
- ***Practice relationship skills.*** Make a real effort to improve your relationship skills. This will make you a person that others want to be around.
- ***Go where there are people.*** Schools, religious organizations, and communities all offer clubs and programs.
- ***Invite someone to do something.*** Don't wait to be asked. That's what the other person may be doing. If you are turned down, don't worry about it. This happens to everyone. Just try later on with someone else.
- ***Give it some time.*** Friendships take time and effort to build. The more time you spend together, the easier the relationship will be to handle.

More About Special Friendships

Are there individuals with physical handicaps in your school? If so, your students have a special opportunity for friendship. People with handicapping conditions sometimes are isolated, and anxious to make new friends. There are a number of ways students can make them feel wanted. First, encourage students to go out of their way to be friendly. Stress the need to ask others about themselves and what they like to do. Suggest that students introduce their new-found friends to people they know. By sharing their circle of acquaintances and friends, they will help others make new friends while finding friends of their own.

Introducing the Chapter

Motivators

1. **Writing.** Ask students to write a paragraph describing the kind of friend they are. Next, have them write a second paragraph describing someone they would like to have as a friend. Collect the papers; and without revealing names, read some of the paragraphs to the class. Discuss the similarities and differences between the two paragraphs. (Key Skills: *Communication, Critical Thinking*)
2. **Discussions.** Have students identify movies and television programs that focus on friendships. Discuss ways these friendships are similar and different from real-life friendships. (Key Skills: *Communication, Critical Thinking*)
3. **Sentence Completion.** Have students complete the following sentences: "Friends are important to me because ...," "To be a friend, I should ...," "It's hard to make new friends because ...," "Some ways to make new friends are ..." (Key Skills: *Communication, Critical Thinking*)

Chapter Objectives and Vocabulary

1. Have students read the chapter objectives. Ask them to rephrase the objectives as questions.
2. Ask students to state, in their own words, the purpose of studying this chapter.
3. Pronounce the vocabulary terms listed on the previous page. Ask students whether they are familiar with any of these. Explain that the terms will be defined in the chapter.

Guided Reading

1. Have students read the chapter and use the Study Guide on pp. 47-48 of the *Student Workbook*.

Teaching. . .
Making Friends; Keeping Friends; Kinds of Friends
(pp. 117-119)

Comprehension Check

1. What are some basic ways to make new friends? *(Smile; start a conversation; practice relationship skills; go where there are people; invite someone to do something; give it some time.)*
2. What is the difference between an acquaintance and a peer? *(An acquaintance is someone you know but who is not a friend; a peer is someone you associate with who is about your age.)*
3. What is a clique? How do cliques hurt others? *(A group that excludes others. Hurt is caused by rejection, usually based on external qualities.)*
4. When is peer pressure harmful? *(When it causes you to go against your own values and standards.)*

Learning Activities

1. **Guest Speakers.** Invite representatives from Big Brothers and Big Sisters to speak to the class about the importance of friendship. Ask the speakers to focus on ways that students can volunteer or help younger children to form lasting friendships. (Key Skill: *Communication*)
2. **Debate.** Select students to debate the following: "A real friend would not pressure you into doing something you do not want to do." (Key Skills: *Critical Thinking, Communication*)
3. **Discussion.** Ask students to give some examples of peer pressure during adolescence. Discuss healthy ways to deal with peer pressure. (Key Skills: *Communication, Critical Thinking*)

Keeping Friends

Friendship carries responsibilities with it. If you want a friendship to last, you must give as well as take. How do you think friendship will be affected in the following situations?

- ▶ When Shawna tells Jessica something private, Jessica passes the information along to others.
- ▶ Drake listens to all Marty's complaints, but Marty will never take time to listen to him.
- ▶ Tonya doesn't want Stacey to have any other friends but her.

Good friendships are very valuable. Effort must be made to make them and to *keep* them.

All Kinds of Friends

Friendship comes in all degrees. People you may know, but who are not personal friends, are called **acquaintances** (uh-KWAINT-uhnt-sehs). For example, a cashier at the supermarket or a neighbor down the street might be an acquaintance. A friendship generally goes through stages on the way to becoming a close relationship.

Unfortunately, some people use differences, such as age, race, and nationality, to limit their opportunities for friendship. Even differences in income level may be used to prevent friendship at times. People need to realize that satisfying friendships are based on something other than what you see. True friendship goes much deeper than this.

▼ Peers ▼

Your **peers** are the people you associate with who are about your age. During the teen years, peer friendships are usually the most important kind.

When Shelette thought about friendship, she was often discouraged. She had one close friend and a few others who were not so close. Often she found herself wishing she were like Joy or Amelia, who both had many friends and who always seemed to be included in everything.

It wasn't until Shelette had a heart-to-heart talk with her sister-in-law, Yolanda, that she began to put things in perspective. Yolanda pointed out that Shelette always had a good time with her best friend. Wasn't that of value to her? Yolanda also explained that sometimes "popular" people are not as happy as people think. They may have many friends, but not someone who is very special to them. They may

More About *Cliques*

Cliques are exclusive friendship groups, usually bringing together friends with common interests or backgrounds. Since members of a clique are so similar in dress, behavior, values, and backgrounds, they often are completely unaccepting of others who are different. In some ways, gangs are similar to cliques. They are made up of people with many similarities, such as interests, looks, dress, values, and expectations. Like cliques, gangs usually are unaccepting of anyone who is different.

struggle to be popular or even do things they shouldn't in order to be accepted. Yolanda told Shelette that people who like themselves don't always need others around them to boost their self-esteem.

Cliques

In any setting where people gather, they tend to move into groups where they feel comfortable. There is nothing wrong with that. Many teens, as well as adults, form groups to have a sense of belonging.

Unfortunately, some groups go too far by excluding people from their circle. A group that does this is called a **clique** (klick). In some way or another, the members of a clique reject those who are on the outside. Only by the group's approval can someone join in. The basis for acceptance is often superficial, based on external qualities such as appearance, clothing, income, or status. When rejection occurs, it hurts people.

How do you fulfill a need for belonging without rejecting others? **Fig. 10-1** gives some suggestions.

Figure 10-1
Peer Friendships, Not Peer Cliques

Here are some suggestions for keeping friends and avoiding cliques:

- Avoid groups that treat others unfairly.
- Try forming your own circle of friends who do not exclude or judge people.
- If the "clique" mentality arises in your group, challenge it. Strive to include, rather than reject, others.

Peer Pressure

Because teens look to others for approval, they sometimes give in to pressure to do something they do not want to do. The pressure or stress you feel to do what others your age are doing is called **peer pressure**. Peer pressure can be good if it encourages you to do something positive, but it's bad if it causes you to go against your own values.

How do you react when people want you to do something wrong? First, think carefully about what they are pressuring you to do. Then ask yourself these questions: Will this hurt anyone? Will it be harmful to me? Are there risks involved? Could there be negative effects, either now or in the future? If any of the answers are "yes," then you must respond with a clear "no." If you feel you need to, offer a simple reason for not going along with what they want. Then change the subject or walk away. Finally, realize that you don't need friends who don't care about your well-being or their own. Look around you to find someone who does.

Learning Activities (continued)

4. **Panel Discussion.** Have a panel discussion on positive and negative ways of dealing with friends; requests to borrow personal items, etc. (Key Skills: *Communication, Problem Solving*)
5. **Journals.** Ask for volunteers to make journal entries about specific friendships they would like to change. Ask them to include all the things they might do to make the friendship better. (Key Skill: *Problem Solving*)
6. **Agree or Disagree.** Ask students to agree or disagree with the following statements, justifying their responses. • A friend is honest with you even if it hurts your feelings. • A friend will stand by you no matter what. • A friend must sometimes go against your wishes to do what is best for you. (Key Skills: *Critical Thinking, Communication*)

Follow Up

1. **Reteaching.** Have students list ways that peer pressure can be positive and ways that it can be negative. (Key Skill: *Critical Thinking*)
2. **Enrichment.** Choose volunteers to make a "Friendship Kit" by writing down birthdays of good friends. Ask them to make or collect an assortment of cards, small gifts, etc. to send or present on these special days. (Key Skill: *Creativity*)

More About *Peer Pressure*

One way that people exert pressure over others is through manipulation. Manipulation is an indirect and often dishonest means of attempting to control someone else's attitudes or behavior. People who manipulate others do so to get what they want without respect for the individuals being manipulated. One method of manipulation includes making threats or some other negative means to get their way. Another method is by using flattery or praise to influence people. Additional methods used to manipulate include mocking or teasing in hurtful ways and using guilt trips to get desired results.

Teaching. . . Adults; Older Adults; Children; Ending a Friendship (pp. 120-122)

Comprehension Check

1. What are some of the concerns of most adults? *(Responsibilities of a job; setting and enforcing rules for children and young people.)*
2. What are some of the concerns of many older adults? *(Health problems; difficulty moving; loneliness.)*
3. What are some advantages of forming friendships with children? *(Your attention is special to them; you may feel more relaxed and appreciated than with peers or adults; you can use what you learn about children in your own future.)*
4. If necessary, how should you end a friendship? *(Be sensitive; be direct, but kind; explain why the friendship needs to be ended; focus on personal feelings, not the other person; be honest about the reasons.)*

Learning Activities

1. **Interview.** Ask students to interview an older adult and a child about what they look for in a friend. Discuss student findings

Around the World

Have students read the feature. Assign students to find examples in history of actions against people simply because of their skin color or accent. Have them find instances when people have been killed or tortured because of their race or nationality. Talk about the fact that this still occurs in some parts of the world. Invite adults or older students of different races and cultures to talk to the class about accomplishments of heroes, leaders, and other prominent persons of their race or culture.

Friendships with adults can provide you a valuable source of support and fun.

▼ Adults ▼

Many adults have authority over teens. This means the adults are in charge. They set the rules to be followed. When a teen is learning and striving for independence, this is not always easy to handle.

Mr. Pratt, a math teacher, cares about his students. Blake is always causing disturbances in class. He doesn't care whether or not classmates learn anything because *he* doesn't want to. Mr. Pratt knows that it is his responsibility to keep order in the classroom. If his students don't perform well on the district proficiency exams, his teaching will be questioned. If students do not learn the math, they will have a harder time in future math classes — and in life. He sees that Blake, in particular, is headed down a destructive path.

For adults like Mr. Pratt, setting and enforcing rules is part of their responsibility to young people. Enforcing rules is not fun, nor is it always easy. Rules are made to provide guidance for appropriate behavior — a necessary part of functioning in an orderly world.

Most adults, even when they have authority over you, want to be your friend, too. They, too, have many personal problems and concerns. Respect and offer friendship to adults. When you do, they will return these to you.

Like you, adults can make mistakes. When you do not understand why an adult does something, you may want to talk about it with that person. The best approach is to use all the relationship skills you read about in the previous chapters.

For many years, apartheid (uh-PAR-tide) was the law of the land in South Africa. This meant that people were limited by their skin color in where they could live and work and with whom they could socialize. Legal reforms, however, now allow people of all racial backgrounds to work, attend schools, and enjoy leisure activities together. Some South Africans, though, still oppose sharing public places with people of different races. Why do you suppose this is? How can this prejudice be changed?

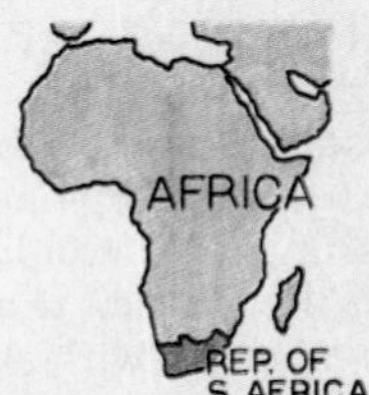

More About *Friendships with Older Adults*

Friendship is excellent medicine for the older person, although it is not an easy prescription to fill. For example, retired workers tend to drop away from former business associates. Old friends may have died. New opportunities for making friends their own age can be limited. Encourage students and their families to help an older person strike up new friendships by drawing the individual into various kinds of social and family activities. Paying attention to the older adult and showing the person that someone cares can be just what the doctor ordered.

▼ Older Adults ▼

You live in a country that has an increasing number of older citizens. This is because people are living longer today than ever before. Because of this, you probably have opportunities to relate to older adults.

As a teen, the concerns of older adults may seem very different from your own. If you are close to aging family members, however, you may understand some of their concerns. Elderly people often have health problems. Difficulty moving around may contribute to loneliness and make it difficult for them to take care of routine tasks.

Friendship with older adults can provide mutually-rewarding relationships. You can provide them with companionship and lend them a helping hand occasionally. They can give you the benefit of all the wisdom and understanding they have gained from years of living. Older adults can be a valuable source of advice and support.

▼ Children ▼

Although most of your friends are probably other teens, children make good friends, too. Because you're older, your attention is very special to them. You may feel more relaxed and appreciated with children than you do with others.

In today's world, there are children who could use your friendship. Many children need good role models. The quality of their lives could improve greatly if you could give them some time. You might teach them a skill you have, or just sit on the step and talk. What you learn about children can be carried over to your own future, perhaps as a parent someday.

Younger children often need and enjoy the friendship of teens. How can you be a friend to younger children?

Learning Activities (continued)

in class. Compare the similarities and differences in the answers. (Key Skills: *Communication, Critical Thinking*)

2. **Writing.** Assign students to write case studies contrasting the concerns of adolescents, adults, and older adults. Select some of the case studies to share with the class. (Key Skills: *Communication, Critical Thinking*)
3. **Incomplete Sentences.** Ask students to complete the following sentences in writing: "An advantage of growing old is ...," "A disadvantage of growing old is ..." Discuss the sentences with the class. Point out that growing older is not all negative, while assisting students in brainstorming a list of positive aspects of aging. (Key Skills: *Communication, Critical Thinking*)
4. **Advertisement.** Have students create an advertisement for an imaginary children's magazine, advertising themselves as a friend. (Key Skills: *Communication, Creativity*)
5. **Discussion.** Talk about the positive and negative sides of breaking friendships. (Key Skill: *Critical Thinking*)

Follow Up

1. **Reteaching.** Work with students in preparing a chalk talk on the concerns of adults and older adults. (Key Skills: *Communication, Critical Thinking*)
2. **Extension.** Have the students read the extension material on p. 17 from the *Extending the Lesson* booklet of the TCR.
3. **Enrichment.** Select students to interview older adults about the effect of friends on their life. Assign them to summarize their findings in a short paper. (Key Skill: *Communication*)

More About Older Friends

Part of growing older often involves the death of a spouse and close friends. Sometimes it includes adult children who move a distance away. Having a pet, such as a dog, cat, bird, or tropical fish, can help older adults who are lonely and miss human companionship. *Pet Facilitated Therapy*, which is used in many nursing and retirement homes, can ease the stress of loneliness and can help people feel needed and useful. Also, many animals offer affection and enjoyment, as well as opportunities for moderate exercise, such as walking.

Photo Focus

Have students examine the photo on p. 121. Ask students to brainstorm a list of activities that they might do with younger children. How might children and teens benefit from such experiences?

Completing the Chapter

For Review

1. Emphasize the main concepts using the summary.
2. Have students complete the "Facts to Recall." (Answers below.)

For Reteaching

1. **Reteaching.** Use the activity on p. 16 of the *Reteaching and Practical Skills* booklet in the TCR.

For Enrichment

1. **Enrichment.** Use the activity on pp. 23-24 of the *Enrichment Activities* booklet in the TCR.

For Evaluation

1. Choose items from "Ideas to Explore" and "Activities to Try."
2. Use the chapter test on pp. 23-24 of the testing booklet in the TCR or use the testmaker software.

Chapter 10 Review

Facts to Recall Answers

1. Friends can broaden life; provide advice and understanding; give acceptance and support.
2. They may have friends, but no one special; may do things they shouldn't to be popular.
3. A group of people who exclude others from their circle. Can cause conflict between need for belonging and rejecting others.
4. Avoid groups that treat others unfairly; form own group that does not exclude others; join existing group that does not exclude teens.
5. Pressure to do what others your age are doing. Helpful if it encourages you to do something positive; hurtful when it causes you to go against own values and standards.
6. Offer reason for not going along; change subject or walk away; realize you don't need friends who don't care about your well-being.
7. Setting and enforcing rules is adults' responsibility; adults want to be friends, but have many other concerns; adults can make mistakes.

Ending a friendship can be difficult, but sensitivity and kindness go a long way in easing the pain of loss. What suggestions do you have for these two teens who are struggling in ending a friendship?

Ending a Friendship

Because people change, not all friendships last forever. New interests, goals, and experiences can cause you to drift away from some people and link with new ones. In some cases, you may discover that the relationship is destructive. If someone causes problems or is unpleasant to be around, the friendship won't be worthwhile. Sometimes outside circumstances interrupt friendships. For example, a friend may move away, causing the relationship to end. A very strong friendship might survive if the two individuals are committed to keeping in touch through the mail and telephone.

If you must deliberately end a friendship, do so with sensitivity. Be direct, but kind. Explain why you need to end the friendship. Focus on how you feel, not on the other person, and be honest about the reasons.

If a friendship ends against your wishes, understand that this just happens sometimes. The good times you had will be remembered. As you move on to other friendships, you can take what you have learned with you.

TAKING ACTION

Broken Friendships

Rachel just doesn't understand. Two weeks ago she and Joelle were practically inseparable, going everywhere together and talking on the phone at night. Now Joelle seems distant at school. She looks away or lowers her head when she passes Rachel in the halls. If Rachel calls Joelle at home, Joelle's sister tells her Joelle is out, and Joelle doesn't call back.

What happened? Rachel wants to know. How can close friends turn into strangers so quickly? What should she do? Should she try to talk to Joelle or let it go and concentrate on other friends? Rachel feels sad and confused.

Using Your Resourcefulness

- What do you think Rachel should do? How should she communicate her feelings? What should or shouldn't she say? Why?
- What does Joelle's body language tell you? What kind of person does Joelle seem to be?
- Is ending a friendship difficult for you? Why or why not? What personal resources can help you get over losing a friendship?

TAKING ACTION

Without sharing names, ask volunteers to share an experience in which a friendship ended. Was it handled in a positive way? How did the student feel after the friendship ended? Ask students why they think it might be important to have some kind of closure when ending a friendship? Have students read the feature and respond to the questions.

Using Your Resourcefulness Answers

- Answers will vary, but may include: Rachel might confront Joelle at a time when they are alone and ask what happened to cause distance in their friendship.
- Answers will vary. Joelle's body language may indicate low self-esteem, insecurity.
- Answers will vary.

Chapter 10 Review

Summary

In this chapter, you have read about:

- How having friends helps your emotional well-being.
- Having friends of all types, including adults and children.
- How to handle peer pressure and cliques.
- The responsibilities of being a friend.
- How friendships can begin and why they sometimes end.

Facts to Recall

1. Name three benefits of friendship.
2. Why may "popular" people be less happy than others think?
3. What are cliques? How can cliques be a problem?
4. Name three ways you can fulfill the need for acceptance without rejecting others.
5. What is peer pressure? How can it be both helpful and hurtful?
6. Give three suggestions for handling negative peer pressure.
7. What do you need to understand about adults in order to get along with them?
8. How can teens benefit from friendships with children and older adults? How do children and older adults benefit from friendships with teens?
9. List four ways to begin a new friendship.
10. List three things to remember when ending a friendship.

Ideas to Explore

1. You have probably heard the expression, "Opposites attract." Can this be true in friendships? How can having friends whose tastes or personalities differ from your own be rewarding?
2. Suppose you saw a good friend doing something that you felt was harmful, even dangerous. How would you persuade your friend to stop without ending the friendship?
3. Sometimes a person can be friends with two people who do not like each other. How can this situation be resolved without ending one of the relationships?
4. Do you think it is easier for small children to make and keep friends than it is for teens? Why or why not?

Activities to Try

1. List the five most important qualities you want in a friend. Compare lists in the class and see if you can agree on a group list.
2. Create a collage entitled, "Friendship is..." Use pictures and words from magazines and newspapers showing the different aspects of friendship.

LINK TO *Geography*

PEN PAL EXCHANGE

One way to learn about other parts of the United States or even another country is from a pen pal. A pen pal is someone you may never meet in person, but, instead, get to know through writing letters. Pen pals share information about their daily lives — interests, activities, and goals. Pen pals often exchange pictures. These long-distance friendships sometimes last for years and may even result in exchange visits. The sharing that takes place through letters can lead to a better understanding of people in another region or country. Ask your teacher or librarian for assistance in finding a pen pal. Write a letter to your new pen pal describing yourself, your home, the area in which you live, and your lifestyle.

Facts to Recall Answers (continued)

8. Teens feel more relaxed and appreciated with children; get wisdom, understanding, support from older adults. Children benefit from attention given, skills taught by teens; older adults get companionship, help with physical tasks.
9. **Any four:** smile; start conversation; overcome shyness; practice relationship skill; go where there are people; invite someone to do something; give it time.
10. **Any three:** be direct, but kind; explain why you need to end friendship; focus on your feelings, not other person.

Ideas to Explore

1. Answers will vary.
2. Answers will vary.
3. Answers will vary.
4. Answers will vary.

LINK TO *Geography*

Answer

Answers and letters will vary.

Preparing to Teach

Chapter Outline

Chapter Resources

The following booklet materials may be found in the *Teacher's Classroom Resources* box:

- Lesson Plans, p. 16
- Student Workbook, *Study Guide,* pp. 51-52; *Thinking About Things to Do,* p. 53; *What Do You Suggest?,* p. 54
- Color Transparencies, *The Dating Scene,* CT-11
- Cooperative Learning, p. 23
- Extending the Text, *It's Okay to Say 'No',* p. 18
- Reteaching and Practical Skills, *What Kind of Love Are You Looking For?,* p. 18
- Enrichment Activities, *What's Your Advice?,* p. 24
- Chapter and Unit Tests, pp. 25-26
- Testmaker Software

Also see:

- Meeting the Special Needs of Students
- Linking Home, School, and Community
- Dealing with Sensitive Issues

ABCNews InterActive™ Videodiscs

- *Teenage Sexuality*

See the ABCNews InterActive™ Bar Code Correlation booklet for applicable segments.

CHAPTER

11 Dating

OBJECTIVES

- *Explain how group and single dating differ.*
- *Discuss challenges of dating and how to handle them.*
- *Explain the importance of time and patience in finding real love.*

TERMS TO LEARN

- ***group dating***
- ***crush***

When Carrie looked around the classroom, it occurred to her that they were a very mixed group. Ages ranged probably from thirteen to fifteen, but you couldn't tell by looking. Some of her friends looked very mature. They acted that way too. Others had not matured yet and seemed to have a long way to go. As far as dating was concerned, some were interested and some weren't. Carrie wasn't sure how she felt — and how her parents felt about it. It would happen sometime, but maybe not yet.

Everyone Is Different

Your class may be very much like Carrie's. Teens mature at different rates. This is especially noticeable during the early teen years. Although some may be ready for dating relationships with others, many are not. This is normal and should not be cause for concern.

Enrico likes girls as friends, but he's not interested in dating. For him, spending time with the guys is first priority. If he's anything like his older brother, he might not even start dating until after high school.

Meg is just the opposite. She began dating at an early age. Although she sometimes goes places with boys her age, she more typically dates those who are a year or two older.

Danita thinks she would like to date, but the opportunities are not there. She has decided to be patient. She will enjoy her girlfriends and her active life and not worry about the rest.

Friendship Groups

One of the first steps that many teens take toward dating is getting together in groups that include both males and females. Many teens think of this as a form of **group dating**. They have a chance to go out in a mixed group without having an actual date. Getting together this way helps build understanding the easy way. The feelings, thoughts, and actions of male and female friends can be examined and compared. The pressures that can come in a dating situation are not as likely to be present.

Friendship groups allow you to get to know a variety of people without the pressures of dating. What do you think about friendship groups or group dating?

More About Dating

Adolescence can be a period of rapid social growth and a step toward independence. During these years, teens increasingly look for close friendships outside of the family. Many teens begin relationships with the opposite sex, thus sharing friendship, affection, and even love. Although people start to date mainly to have fun, dating gives them a chance to meet and get to know others and to learn what they like, and do not like, in other people.

Introducing the Chapter

Motivators

1. **Definitions.** Ask each student to give his or her definition of dating. Collect the definitions, and write some of them on the chalkboard. (Key Skill: *Communication*)
2. **Brainstorming.** Brainstorm some of the purposes of friendship groups and dating. (Key Skill: *Communication*)
3. **Comics.** Collect an assortment of comic strips/cartoons about friendship groups and single dating. Divide students into small groups, and share some of the comics with each group. Ask students to discuss whether the comics are relevant to their present situations. (Key Skills: *Communication, Critical Thinking*)
4. **Suggestion Box.** Invite students to write down questions or concerns they would like to have discussed during the study of this chapter. Ask them to place unsigned questions or concerns in a suggestion box. (Key Skills: *Communication, Critical Thinking*)
5. **Bulletin Board.** Display a variety of pictures of young people to illustrate group dating and single dating. Title the display "Dating — Different Kinds of Friendships." (Key Skills: *Creativity, Communication*)

Chapter Objectives and Vocabulary

1. Have students read the chapter objectives. Ask them to rephrase the objectives as questions.
2. Ask students to state, in their own words, the purpose of studying this chapter.
3. Pronounce the vocabulary terms listed on the previous page. Ask students whether they are familiar with any of these. Explain that the terms will be defined in the chapter.

Guided Reading

1. Have students read the chapter and use the Study Guide on pp. 51-52 of the *Student Workbook*.

Teaching...
Everyone Is Different; Friendship Groups; Single Dating
(pp. 125-127)

Comprehension Check

1. What is one of the first steps teens take toward dating? *(Taking part in group dating.)*
2. What are some of the advantages of group dating? *(Enjoy a mixed group without having actual date; learn to understand and compare the feelings, thoughts, and actions of male and female friends; may not be as many pressures as in a dating situation.)*
3. What are some of the purposes of single dating? *(Explore how a male-female relationship works; examine feelings of attraction and affection; begin to discover what they might like in a marriage partner.)*
4. What are four ways to help you deal with feelings of insecurity when going on first dates? *(Focus on putting the other person at ease; practice and plan what to say; plan dates that are activity oriented; think positively about yourself.)*
5. Why is it not necessarily a good idea to focus only on appearances when choosing a date? *(You may miss others' more important qualities.)*

Learning Activities

1. **Community Analysis.** Ask students to list as many activities as they can think of that are available for friendship groups, group dating, and single dating. Discuss the cost of activities and the kinds

AROUND THE WORLD

After reading the feature, ask students to make a list of qualities they would look for in a marriage partner and check each quality they believe they possess. Collect the papers and make a single list on the chalkboard. Ask students to rank the five qualities they feel are the most important. Discuss reasons for their choices.

AROUND THE WORLD

Love Park in China's capital city of Beijing is a popular meeting place for single persons interested in marriage. Marriage is highly valued in Chinese society; married people have a better chance at finding jobs, finding housing, and getting an education. What do young Chinese people look for in a possible partner? According to China's marriage law, it should be "character" and "compatibility." According to a Beijing University study, however, it is appearance, education, and social standing. How do you think this compares with American attitudes toward marriage?

When teens gather in groups, they are often looking for something to do. Some communities offer a wide variety of fun places to go and things to do. Other communities offer a very limited choice. In such cases, some creative thinking can help provide ideas. What kinds of group activities can you think of?

Cost and transportation can restrict what many teens are able to do. If this is true for you and your friends, look for inexpensive and simple ways to spend time. Planning activities to do at home may be a good alternative. An afternoon or evening spent watching a video, playing games, listening to music, or having a pizza party can be fun.

When you spend time with others in a group, remember that you have some responsibilities. Often the places where teens go are used by other people as well. Businesses must make money to survive. People who own property want to preserve its value. Teens who gather in community places need to think about how their actions affect others. For example, what might happen to a restaurant if a large group of people routinely take up booth space by ordering only soft drinks? If you were the owner, how would you react?

Although dating may be fun, it is a challenge, too.

Single Dating

Eventually many young people turn to single dating as another stage in their relationships with others. Single dating allows two people to explore how a male-female relationship works. New feelings of attraction and affection are examined. Close friendships can turn to romantic interests. As people date, they begin to discover what they might like in a partner if they decide to marry someday.

More About Male-Female Friendships

Platonic friendships offer an opportunity for both males and females to learn to understand and feel comfortable with the opposite gender without the pressures of dating. These relationships, in which there is affection but it is not romantic, can be very special during adolescence. In fact, it is common for platonic friendships to last for many years. On the other hand, romantic relationships among teens may be very short-lived.

Dating can be a challenge for people at any age, but during the early teen years this may be especially true. Without experience as a guide, concerns may arise. Some teens have had questions like these: How do I ask someone out? How do I talk to someone as more than a friend? How do I turn down an invitation? The answers are not always simple.

▼ Gaining Confidence ▼

Few people get through their first dates without some discomfort. Trying to work up the courage to ask someone out; asking someone out; what to do or say on the date itself — any or all of these can be a source of discomfort. Keep a few things in mind if you need to boost your confidence.

Feelings of insecurity are common. Many people have them and overcome them. Chances are, when you feel uncomfortable, so does the other person. Focus on putting the other person at ease instead of thinking about yourself.

Practice and plan what to say. Doing this will help give you confidence conversing. It also helps to plan dates that are activity oriented. Having something to do reduces the need for continual conversation.

Think positively about yourself and about your strengths rather than your weaknesses. A positive attitude makes you more attractive to others, both as a friend and a date.

▼ Choosing a Date ▼

"Your problem, Taylor, is that you only want to go out with the cutest girl in school." Jim's comment to his friend points to an attitude that prevents many good relationships from happening. When you stop to notice, you will see that many of the finest people are not necessarily the best looking. People who focus only on appearances often miss the more important qualities in others. As you look at others with the thought of dating in mind, who would you pick? How often do you let your friends influence your opinions about others? Take a second look around and see if you are eliminating some people for the wrong reasons.

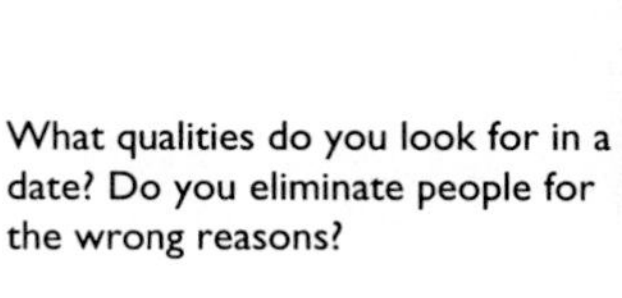

What qualities do you look for in a date? Do you eliminate people for the wrong reasons?

Learning Activities (continued)

of transportation that are available. (Key Skill: *Critical Thinking*)

2. **Questioning.** Have students form a circle and answer the following questions. How does dating help people grow? What are some ways to get involved in group dating? What are some of the most popular activities for group dating? Single dating? What are some appropriate verbal responses you might give others if you are not yet ready to date? What are some of the financial costs involved in group dating and single dating? (Key Skills: *Communication, Critical Thinking*)
3. **Advertisements.** Assign each student to write a classified ad for a dating partner they would enjoy. Next, have them write an ad for someone they would choose to marry as a life partner. Ask for volunteers to share their ads, and talk about the similarities and differences between their two ads. (Key Skills: *Communication, Critical Thinking*)

Follow Up

1. **Reteaching.** Have students list all of the activities they would enjoy and places they would like to go on a group date. Have them put a dollar sign to the left of each activity that requires an expenditure of more than $5.00. (Key Skill: *Critical Thinking*)
2. **Enrichment.** Select students to create and present a short play about a couple going out on a first date. Have them feature appropriate ways each person might deal with feelings of insecurity. (Key Skills: *Critical Thinking, Creativity*)

Making a Difference

Some students are very shy around others, especially those of the opposite gender. They lack the assertiveness to initiate a group date. Encourage one or more class leaders to plan and carry out an informal friendship group activity that will include some of the previously excluded students.

More About *Dating — A Time of Exploration*

The teen years are a time of trying out a variety of relationships and roles. Some teens stay in a relationship because they do not know how to get out of it gracefully. Others cling to a relationship when the partner wants to end it. In these two common but very painful situations, honesty and open communication are necessary. So is the realization that all individuals have control only over their own actions and emotions. They cannot control the behavior or feelings of others.

Teaching. . .

Single Dating: Handling Rejection; Responsibility; Thinking about Love

(pp. 128-130)

Comprehension Check

1. Why is rejection a normal part of the dating process? *(People may not always share the same feelings for each other.)*
2. What are three main responsibilities you have when you begin to date? *(To make personal decisions about your conduct based on your own standards of behavior; to treat your date in the same way that you would want to be treated; to abide by family rules in regard to dating, such as curfew times, destinations, and transportation.)*
3. How does a crush differ from love? *(A crush is usually one-sided; it may be felt for someone you do not know personally; it usually ends quickly.)*
4. What are three descriptions used to identify real love? *(It is a two-way street of give and take; sharing and trusting; having mutual respect for one another; wanting what is best for the other person; long lasting.)*

Learning Activities

1. **Skits.** Choose students to write and present short skits about the importance of affection from family and friends when dealing with rejection by the opposite gender. Have them demonstrate healthy ways to show affection, such as smiles, hugs, and pats on the back. Afterwards, talk about

TIPS:

Handling Rejection or Rejecting a Date
Have students read and discuss the tips listed in the feature. What do they find most helpful? Least helpful? Have students brainstorm a list of possible statements to use when turning down a date. How might they affirm a person when turning down a date?

TIPS: *Handling Rejection or Rejecting a Date*

Here are some helpful tips for handling rejection or rejecting a date:

- Don't be afraid of rejection; you can learn from it.
- To deal with disappointment, think positively. There are others to date even if one person turns you down.
- Recognize that you are a good person and remind yourself of that when facing rejection.
- Try again. Asking others for a date may not be easy, but it's worth the effort.
- If you are rejecting a date, do it with kindness in an honest, gentle, supportive way. You might want to say: "It was nice of you to ask me, but I just don't think we have a lot in common. I hope we can still be friends even if we don't date."
- Remember that rejection can hurt if not handled in a positive way. You may want to think about ways that you might gently reject (or accept) a date.

Handling Rejection

Rejection is part of the dating process. It only stands to reason that sometimes two people may not always share the same feelings for each other. Sometimes one person knows this immediately and turns down the invitation for a first date. Sometimes it takes several dates or even a long relationship before the discovery is made. Whatever the case, one party may have to experience rejection.

Responsibility

Along with dating come several responsibilities. The first is to yourself. As you begin to date, you must make decisions about your conduct. Setting your standards of behavior ahead of time can help you if any difficult situations arise.

You also have a responsibility to your date. The person you go out with deserves your respect. Treat your date the same way that you would want to be treated. Think about how you would handle each of the following when on a date: choosing a time to leave and to return; picking up your date; deciding what to do; handling expenses; showing consideration and appreciation; and ending the date.

Still another responsibility is to your family. Young teens need to talk over the rules with responsible family members when they are ready to date. Some families have a particular age in mind to begin dating. Other families look for signs of readiness in the young person. Family rules may involve curfew times, transportation, and where teens may and may not go. A teen who disagrees with the family rules may need to discuss them and show a willingness to listen. This is much more likely to lead to cooperation and perhaps compromise than arguing will.

Showing consideration and appreciation are two of your responsibilities to your date. What are some ways that you can show appreciation to someone you care about?

More About *Rejection*

Teens who experience rejection by others may begin to display various symptoms of adolescent depression. Some of the signs, or risk factors, include difficulty in concentrating; sadness; withdrawal and isolation; poor self-esteem; changes in eating, sleeping, or hygiene; unexplained decline in quality of schoolwork and athletics; inappropriate guilt; personality changes; outbursts of violent behavior; and substance abuse. If teens display one or more of these symptoms for several weeks, encourage them to seek help from their parents, family physician, school counselor, or school nurse.

Once the rules are set, abiding by them is important. Families make rules because they are responsible for your safety and well-being. Breaking rules causes family members to worry and lose trust. Any teen who cares about family members would not want to let this happen.

Thinking about Love

For Kathleen it was her science teacher. For Mike it was a movie star. For Jamal it was the high school girl next door. Each of these teens was experiencing what is known as a crush. A **crush** is a strong attraction to someone. Usually a crush is one-sided. In fact, a crush may be felt for someone you don't even know, such as Mike's crush on a movie star.

Although a crush may be mistaken for love, it really isn't. Crushes seldom last long. Once over, you may even wonder why you felt the way you did.

Crushes are common, especially for teens. The emotions may be powerful. Most teens simply let such feelings run their course. Talking can help, perhaps to friends. If the feelings are difficult to handle, a trusted adult may be able to help.

Sometimes a crush is mistaken for love, but it really isn't. The emotions may be powerful, but crushes seldom last long. Talking with someone you trust can help you cope with the feelings.

Real Love

Becca says she is in love. Her relationship with Ryan is close and special, but is it really love? Defining love is not easy to do. Frank may use the word to talk about his family, a pet, his favorite food, a movie, friends, and a special person in his life. His feelings for a hamburger, however, can hardly be the same as those he has for his beloved dog, Frisky.

Real love is what many people try to identify when they pair up with someone special. Having many experiences with friendships and close relationships can make real love easier to have and to identify. This takes time. It takes most people until at least their late teens or early twenties to be able to identify true love. For others, it may take even longer.

Most people feel that love is a two-way street of give-and-take. It is sharing and trusting and having mutual respect for one another. When you are together, it feels right. Even more important, it is wanting what's best for the other person. Furthermore, it lasts. Whenever there is doubt, a wait-and-see attitude is best.

The road to real love begins within you. Loving and respecting yourself makes you capable of loving and respecting others. It helps prepare you for real love later on.

Learning Activities (continued)

how it feels to receive affection. (Key Skills: *Communication, Creativity*)

2. **Discussion.** Talk about reasons why a person might be turned down for a date. List and discuss the feelings the person might experience. (Key Skills: *Communication, Critical Thinking*)
3. **Creative Expression.** Have students write poems or short stories about the experience of rejection. Ask volunteers to share their work. (Key Skills: *Communication, Creativity*)
4. **Public Service Announcements.** Have students write and present one-minute PSAs about the responsibilities of dating. (Key Skill: *Creativity*)
5. **Debate.** Select students to debate the following: "Teens who break family rules are not mature enough to date." (Key Skills: *Communication, Critical Thinking*)
6. **Creative Writing.** Assign students to write short stories about teen infatuation and crushes. Select some of the stories to share with the class, followed by a discussion of healthy ways to deal with these emotions. (Key Skills: *Critical Thinking, Creativity*)

Follow Up

1. **Reteaching.** Assign students to write a short paper titled "The Write Stuff." Ask them to discuss three responsibilities of dating. (Key Skill: *Communication*)
2. **Extension.** Have the students read the extension material on p. 18 from the *Extending the Lesson* booklet of the TCR.
3. **Enrichment.** Select students to develop a checklist for defining real love. Duplicate the checklist for the entire class. (Key Skills: *Critical Thinking, Communication*)

More About Emotions

The teen years are at a time when emotions play a major role in many behaviors. It is important for students to realize that emotions are natural and that all people, young and old, experience them. Emotions can be very positive by helping people accomplish tasks and reach goals. They also can protect individuals from danger. Encourage students to learn to identify their feelings so they can express their emotions and deal with them in healthy ways. Also, remind them that no one else can know for certain how others feel if they do not define and talk about their feelings.

Photo Focus

Have students examine the photo on p. 129. Ask students to describe the feelings this teen may be experiencing. How might a friend or trusted adult provide encouragement and hope for future real love?

Completing the Chapter

For Review

1. Emphasize the main concepts using the summary.
2. Have students complete the "Facts to Recall." (Answers below.)

For Reteaching

1. **Reteaching.** Use the activity on p. 17 of the *Reteaching and Practical Skills* booklet in the TCR.

For Enrichment

1. **Enrichment.** Use the activity on pp. 25-26 of the *Enrichment Activities* booklet in the TCR.

For Evaluation

1. Choose items from "Ideas to Explore" and "Activities to Try."
2. Use the chapter test on pp. 25-26 of the testing booklet in the TCR or use the testmaker software.

Facts to Recall Answers

1. Teens naturally mature at different rates.
2. Builds understanding easily; feelings and actions of males and females can be compared.
3. Teens need to think about how actions will affect others; others use, earn living from, want to preserve value of places teens go.
4. Allows examination of male-female relationships, new feelings of attraction; allows people to discover what they might like in a partner.
5. Feelings of insecurity are common; plan and practice what to say; think positively about yourself.
6. Be honest in gentle, supportive way; know that rejection can hurt.
7. To yourself: making decisions about conduct, knowing standards of behavior. To date: respect in choosing length, activities, finances of date. To family: obey family rules.

Later in life, some people choose to marry. As you date different people, think about the qualities that you might want in a mate.

▼ Looking Ahead ▼

When people find real love, marriage is often the next step. The decision to marry cannot be taken lightly. It means looking closely at each other before making a commitment. Dating different people as you mature will help you understand yourself and others better and can help you decide what qualities you value.

As you think about the kind of mate you might want in the future, ask yourself these questions: What kind of person do I want for a mate? What kind of person do I need to be in order to attract the kind of person I want? What changes do I need to make? Am I willing to make those changes?

Marriage, of course, is not for everyone. It's quite common to stay single — or to marry later in life. Many people remain single because they value their independence and the opportunity to pursue their own goals.

Whatever you choose to do with your life, it's too early right now to consider such a major decision. Instead, take the time to prepare yourself for the future. Look at how you relate to others and strive for improvement. What you learn during your teen years can help you develop and maintain a long-term relationship in the future.

TAKING ACTION

The Dating Game

"It's really common at my school to date in groups," Emily explains. "Four or six friends go to the movies or ice skating together instead of dating separately. There are couples, but we don't really date. We're not old enough to drive," she says.

Emily has known Ken a few months, and likes spending time with him. Sometimes she feels Ken pressures her to be closer emotionally. He would like to start single dating, but Emily doesn't feel ready yet. "I've thought a lot about it. I've made the decision to wait until I'm a little older. I'd like to get to know a lot of different people rather than limiting myself to just one right now," says Emily. Still, Ken's pressure makes her anxious sometimes. She wishes she could handle the issue better.

Using Your Resourcefulness

- How should Emily communicate her feelings to Ken? What options does she have to make the relationship work and grow slowly?
- What resources are available to help you better understand dating and developing relationships?
- Would the idea of "group dating" appeal to you? Why or why not?

TAKING ACTION

Ask student volunteers to share experiences in which they or persons they know have felt pressure to date just one person rather than getting to know a variety of people. How did they handle the situations? Have students read the feature and respond to the questions.

Using Your Resourcefulness Answers

- Answers will vary. Emily should share her feelings openly and honestly with Ken, but should also be considerate of his feelings. Emily might consider setting limits on how often she spends time with Ken.
- Answers will vary, but may include parents and other trusted adults, school counselors, teachers, etc.
- Answers will vary.

Chapter 11 Review

Summary

In this chapter, you have read about:

- How individual teens differ from one another in maturity and dating relationships.
- How group dating can pave the way to single dating.
- Challenges that go along with single dating.
- Responsibilities of dating.
- The differences between a crush and real love.

Facts to Recall

1. Explain why some teens begin to date at an earlier age than others.
2. Explain how group dating can help prepare teens for single dating.
3. What responsibilities do teens have when they go places in groups?
4. How can single dating better equip a person for selecting a marriage partner?
5. What are three things to remember if you need to build confidence for dating?
6. If someone asks you for a date, how can you say no in a positive way?
7. Describe the responsibilities you have to yourself, your date, and your family when dating.
8. Explain the difference between a crush and real love.
9. Explain why "the road to real love begins within you."
10. What four questions should you ask yourself as you think about selecting a mate for the future?

Ideas to Explore

1. What qualities do you, or would you, look for in a date? Are these the same qualities that you might look for in a marriage partner? Explain.
2. Which do you think would be better, going out with someone you're not really interested in or risking hurt feelings by turning the person down? Explain your answer.
3. Why is it important to know and understand yourself before trying to begin a serious relationship with another person? What might happen if you do not have this self-understanding?

Activities to Try

1. Make a list of activity ideas for teens who are dating, either in groups or on single dates. Think about the resources available in your community. Work in groups or individually and share your lists with the class.
2. Work in pairs to plan a date, focusing on the costs involved. Determine how the costs could be met.
3. Write a paragraph explaining what this quotation from John Donne means to you: "Love built on beauty, soon as beauty, dies."

LINK TO *Geography*

DATING AND MARRIAGE CUSTOMS

Dating and marriage customs vary from one culture to another. In India and many other countries, most marriages are arranged by parents. In some cultures, marriage involves a gift — called a dowry — from the family of the bride or groom to the other family. Research the dating and marriage customs of another culture that interests you. How are these customs similar to and different from those in the United States? Share your findings with the class.

Facts to Recall Answers (continued)

8. Crush: short; powerful emotions; usually one-sided. Love: sharing and trusting; mutual respect and concern for other; lasting.
9. Loving and respecting yourself makes you able to love and respect others.
10. What kind of person do I want for a mate? What kind of person must I be to attract this kind of person? What changes must I make? Am I willing to make them?

Ideas to Explore

1. Answers will vary.
2. Answers will vary.
3. Answers will vary, but may include understanding yourself allows you to look for characteristics of compatibility. Without knowing self, one may set unrealistic expectations in relationships.

LINK TO *Geography*

Answer

Answers will vary depending on culture studied.

Preparing to Teach

Chapter Outline

Chapter Resources

The following booklet materials may be found in the *Teacher's Classroom Resources* box:

- Lesson Plans, p. 17
- Student Workbook, *Study Guide,* pp. 55-56; *Family Circle,* p. 57; *Assigning Responsibility,* p. 58
- Color Transparencies, *A Family Photo,* CT-12
- Technology and Computers, p. 14
- Cooperative Learning, p. 24
- Extending the Text, *Getting Along with Stepparents,* pp. 19-20
- Reteaching and Practical Skills, *That's Me!,* p. 19
- Enrichment Activities, *Considering the Options,* pp. 25-26
- Chapter and Unit Tests, pp. 27-28
- Testmaker Software

Also see:

- Meeting the Special Needs of Students
- Linking Home, School, and Community
- Dealing with Sensitive Issues

ABCNews InterActive™ Videodiscs

- *Teenage Sexuality*

See the ABCNews InterActive™ Bar Code Correlation booklet for applicable segments.

CHAPTER 12 A Look at Families

OBJECTIVES

- *Identify various family forms.*
- *Explain the family life cycle and how roles affect families.*
- *Describe factors that make families unique.*

TERMS TO LEARN

- ***nuclear families***
- ***single-parent family***
- ***custody***
- ***blended families***
- ***extended family***

In thinking about her family, Paula realized just how fortunate she was. Of course the ache of her mother's death was still there. However, she knew that she was probably closer to her dad and younger brother because of it. Their laughter and support could be counted on to help her through the rough spots. She knew they counted on her, too. In what ways do you count on your family for support?

Families Are Important

Most people live their lives as part of a family. Although families today may differ from those in the past, their importance to individual members and to society remains the same.

What Families Provide

Families still serve the basic functions that they have throughout history. The first function of the family is to satisfy the basic physical needs of all members — young and old. These needs include food, clothing, and shelter. Health and safety are other important needs. The safety needs of a young child are quite different from those of a teen.

Families not only provide for physical needs, they also help members grow socially, intellectually, and emotionally. Social growth is promoted when adult family members teach younger ones how to behave in different situations and how to get along with others. Intellectual growth comes through education. Families must see that children learn both at school and at home, so that the children can eventually become independent. Emotional growth develops in a loving, caring environment. Children learn how to express feelings and give, as well as receive, support. They also learn respect and responsibility.

Families have a very strong influence on their members. Within the family, you learn values and attitudes that are carried with you throughout life. If you have children someday, many of these will be passed on to them. As you can see, a positive environment is very important.

Having fun together is one way that families supply social and emotional support. What other ways can you think of?

Types of Families

Even though families serve the same functions that they always have, their forms may not be the same. A look around your neighborhood or school will show you that not all families are alike. What families can you think of that fit the forms described in the following paragraphs?

More About ***Families***

Family unity requires ongoing effort. Some of the ways that families can strengthen the bonds among each other are good communication, commitment to each other, and appreciation and support of one another. Quality time spent both one-on-one and in a group can be a fun way to keep the family together. Also, the ability to laugh together, even through rough times, is important. Remind students that even the strongest family is unlikely to demonstrate every one of these characteristics all of the time. However, families do not get strong by themselves. They need work, rather than leaving family strength to chance.

Introducing the Chapter

Motivators

1. **Sentence Completion.** Ask students to complete the following sentences: "In the past, a family ...," "Today's families are ...," "My family in the future ...," "When I have my own family I ..." (Key Skills: *Communication, Critical Thinking*)
2. **Discussion.** Have students name television programs and movies that portray different types of families. Talk about whether the portrayals are realistic and why or why not. (Key Skills: *Communication, Critical Thinking*)
3. **Discussion.** Lead a discussion on ways in which television has affected family life. (Key Skill: *Critical Thinking*)
4. **Bulletin Board.** Display an assortment of current family photographs as well as family photographs from the past. Title the display "Looking at Families: Past and Present." Refer to the board, and lead a discussion about ways families have stayed the same and ways they have changed over the years. (Key Skills: *Communication, Critical Thinking*)

Chapter Objectives and Vocabulary

1. Have students read the chapter objectives. Ask them to rephrase the objectives as questions.
2. Ask students to state, in their own words, the purpose of studying this chapter.
3. Pronounce the vocabulary terms listed on the previous page. Ask students whether they are familiar with any of these. Explain that the terms will be defined in the chapter.

Guided Reading

1. Have students read the chapter and use the Study Guide on pp. 55-56 of the *Student Workbook*.

Teaching. . .
Families Are Important; What Families Provide; Types of Families
(pp. 133-135)

Comprehension Check

1. What are five functions of families? *(Satisfy the basic needs of all members; keep its members safe; help members grow socially, mentally, and emotionally; teach values and influence attitudes; to provide a positive environment.)*
2. How does a nuclear family differ from a single-parent family? *(Nuclear family consists of two parents living with their children; a single-parent family has one parent living in the household.)*
3. What family members often make up an extended family? *(Grandparents, aunts, uncles, cousins, etc.)*
4. When might a blended family also be an adoptive family? *(When one or more children become part of a family through adoption by the other parent.)*
5. What kinds of families may also be foster families? *(Nuclear, single-parent, extended, blended families.)*

Learning Activities

1. **Writing.** Have students write a paragraph describing how they think families have changed over the past fifty years. Select volunteers to read their descriptions to the class. (Key Skills: *Social Studies, Critical Thinking*)

AROUND THE WORLD

Ask for volunteers to survey the community for businesses that are run by various members of the same family. Help them create a list of questions to ask in interviewing the individuals involved. Focus on the advantages and disadvantages of the business arrangement, including how working hours and tasks are divided. Have students summarize their findings and share them with the class.

Nuclear Families

Families in which two parents share a household with their children are called **nuclear families** (NOO-klee-ur). The family may consist of two parents and one child or perhaps a dozen children. The children may be adopted, born into the family, or both.

Spending time together relaxing and enjoying each other is especially important in single-parent families.

Single-Parent Families

A family that has only one parent living in the household is called a **single-parent family**. Most often the parent is the mother, especially after divorce or separation. This is because the court generally awards the care, or **custody** (CUS-tud-ee) of the children to the mother. A growing number of fathers, however, are seeking and receiving custody of their children. Another type of single-parent family is a single adult who has adopted one or more children.

About 19 million children — more than one out of every four under the age of eighteen — live in a single-parent home today. This is largely the result of an increasing divorce rate. The parent in these families often faces extra challenges. With no other adult to share the responsibilities, it can be difficult. Many children in single-parent homes take on extra responsibilities to help the parent. They often learn independence earlier than they otherwise might.

Blended Families

Families that include a stepparent and stepchildren are called **blended families**. These families are a type of nuclear family in which one or both adults have been married before and one or both may already have children.

Blended families are very common today. When blended families first form, an adjustment period may be needed. The family may feel very different for awhile. Members must learn to share space, manage schedules, and relate in all new

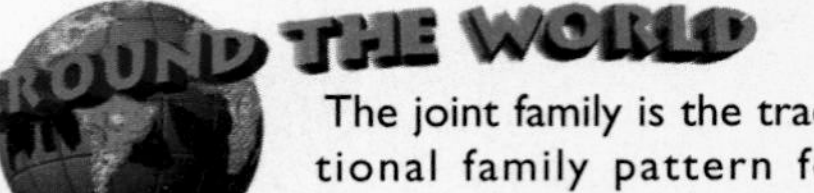

The joint family is the traditional family pattern for many in India. This type of extended family includes the husband and wife; the sons, their wives, and children; and unmarried daughters. There are several advantages to this arrangement. It is convenient for family members who work together in the same business. There are more people to help with household tasks. Young children almost always have others to play with and adults to look after them.

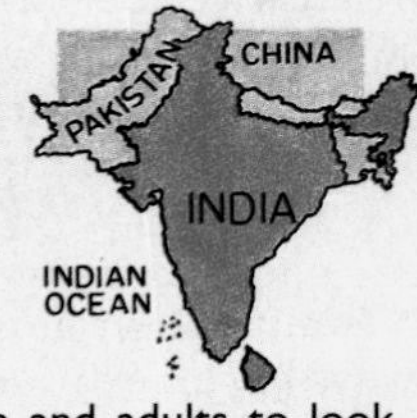

More About *Single Parenting*

Guilt on the part of the parent is a major problem that often interferes with single parenting. This may take the form of guilt for not being able to accomplish more, for not providing another parent in the home, for lack of adequate funds, for having needs, and for taking time for self-care. Inappropriate or excessive guilt may lead parents to overindulge children and to have difficulty setting limits. Also, it may cause feelings of stress and lowered self-esteem, which may result in parents becoming overly impatient and harsh with their family.

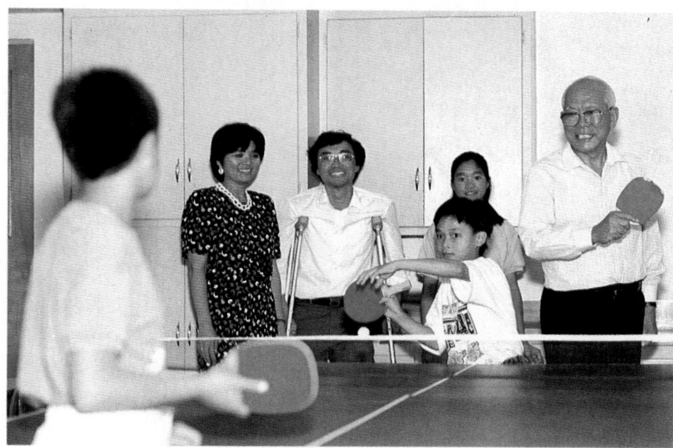

Members of an extended family share good times together as well as household responsibilities.

ways. Feelings of friendship and love may take awhile in coming. With patience, understanding, and a sense of humor, most blended families make the adjustment well.

Extended Families

An **extended family** includes one or more relatives in addition to the basic family unit. Melissa's grandfather, for example, lives with her family. Todd's aunt shares a home with his family. Extended family members — grandparents, aunts, uncles, and cousins — can serve as an extra support system for the family.

Adoptive Families

These families may be nuclear, single-parent, blended, or extended families. The adopted children are not related by birth to one or both parents. Through a legal adoption process, one or more children can become part of a family. The parent or parents are responsible for the care of the children they have adopted as though they were their children by birth.

Foster Families

A foster family can also be a nuclear, single-parent, blended, or extended family. One or more of its children are not the birth or adopted children of the parents. Instead, government agencies or other organizations make arrangements for a particular family to care for children from another family or families. Sometimes the children stay for extended periods of time; in other cases, they stay only for a short time. In some circumstances, the children are adopted later by the foster family.

TIPS:
Making Blended Families Work

To help make life go more smoothly in a blended family, try the following tips:

- Keep your sense of humor. Things will not go smoothly all the time. It helps to be able to laugh during the difficult times.
- Set aside some time to spend with each new family member. Taking genuine interest in another person makes him or her feel good and helps you to get to know that person.
- Keep the lines of communication open. Talk about problems openly and work to find positive solutions.
- Look for the little things that can help break down barriers. For example, does your new stepsister or stepbrother like chocolate chip cookies? Try baking a batch together. Working on a simple task together can help break the ice.

Learning Activities (continued)

2. **Collages.** Ask students to use newspaper and magazine pictures to make collages illustrating some of the functions that families have served throughout history. Display the collages, and use them to summarize the functions of the family. (Key Skills: *Social Studies, Critical Thinking*)
3. **Guest Speakers.** Invite several parents to speak to the class about the joys and challenges of step-parenting and blended families. Afterward, ask students to write and present skits about stepchildren and stepparents adjusting to a new family situation. (Key Skills: *Critical Thinking, Creativity*)
4. **Interview.** Select students to interview a representative from an adoption agency about the requirements and procedures of adoption. Ask students to share their findings with the class. (Key Skills: *Communication, Critical Thinking*)

Follow Up

1. **Reteaching.** Divide students into pairs. Assign each pair one of the family types. Ask them to write a short paper describing their family type. Have students share their papers with the class. (Key Skills: *Communication, Cooperation*)
2. **Enrichment.** Divide students into three groups: one to depict the family in the early 1900s; the second to depict the contemporary family; and the third to depict the family in the mid 2000s. Using library resources and interviews with older adults, have students present reports on how family life was, is, and may be in the future. (Key Skills: *Social Studies, Critical Thinking*)

More About Adoptive Families

About 100,000 children are adopted each year in the United States. Many of these adoptions are closed adoptions, or adoptions in which records are sealed. The names, addresses, and telephone numbers of the birth parents remain unavailable to either the adoptive parents or the children. However, a growing number of adoptions are open, and information is made available to both sides in an adoption. Adoptive parents may meet natural parents. Sometimes they may even be with the birth mother during delivery of the infant.

TIPS:

Making Blended Families Work Have students read the tips in the feature. Which suggestions do students feel would be most helpful? Least helpful? What do students see as the most difficult challenges facing blended families?

Teaching. . .
Family Life Cycle; Family Roles; Families Are Unique
(pp. 136-138)

Comprehension Check

1. Give two circumstances in which the family life cycle is not the same for all families. *(Couple may remain childless; adult children may return home to live; divorce; death.)*
2. What are three concerns of a couple when there are young children in the family? *(Income, expenses, time, children's needs.)*
3. In what ways have the roles of men and women changed in recent years? *(Many women have work or career roles; many men have more active roles in parenting and in sharing household responsibilities.)*
4. Describe three ways families are unique. *(Families vary in how feelings are expressed; interests or traditions; unique in using material or personal resources; unique in how they work together at home.)*

Learning Activities

1. **Bulletin Board.** Have students find magazine pictures of people to depict various stages in the family life cycle. Title the board "Ages and Stages in the Family Life Cycle." (Key Skills: *Critical Thinking, Creativity*)
2. **Case Studies.** Assign students to write case studies about concerns of families at different stages of the family life cycle. Use some of the case studies during a discussion of the cycle. (Key Skill: *Communication*)
3. **Writing.** Assign students to write articles for submission to the school newspaper about some of the recent changes in men's and women's roles in the family. (Key Skills: *Communication, Creativity*)
4. **Pictures.** Assign students to locate newspaper and magazine pictures depicting changes in men's and women's roles at home and in the workplace. Post and discuss pictures. (Key Skill: *Critical Thinking*)

Some families include adopted children. There are many reasons why some people adopt children. However, the most important reason is that they want to provide a loving home for children that are already in the world.

Other Kinds of Families

Many couples do not have children but are considered to be a family because of the way they fulfill needs. In some situations, people have few or no family members. They may band together to take care of each other. For example, Mrs. Collins, an elderly widow, likes to think of her friends as "family." Mrs. Collins and her friends care about and support each other just as family members do.

The Family Life Cycle

Social scientists have identified a series of stages families typically go through called the family life cycle. In this cycle, a couple marries, adjusts to the new relationship, and eventually has children. Over the next several years, the children are raised and then launched from the family home. The couple must then adjust to the *empty nest* — a home with children no longer present. They go through the middle years and, in time, experience the retirement and aging stage of the cycle.

Not all families follow the typical life cycle. If a couple remains childless, the pattern will not be the same for them. When grown children return home after they have left, the characteristics of the empty nest stage are different. Can you think of other situations that alter the family life cycle?

Families have different concerns at different stages of the cycle. As Fred and Alma Perry looked at their photo albums one day, they reminisced about what their lives had been like. They recalled starting out as a young married couple with a low income and few responsibilities. When the children came along, things changed. They had many expenses and less time for each other. Once the children were raised, they had some time and money to spend on themselves. They

More About *Employed Wives and Mothers*

Many of today's wives and mothers are employed. This is true even in families consisting of both parents. The increase in the number of women entering the labor force is due mainly from the fact that many of today's households need two incomes to support a family. The increasing divorce rate is another major reason for the growing numbers of women who are employed. Other women work outside the home because of a desire to use their talents and training.

bought a camper so that they could see more of the country. At retirement, their income decreased. Now they enjoy their grandchildren and travel when they can. They are planning for their aging years. Although health has not been a problem thus far, they know that it is likely to be in the future.

Family Roles

Whatever the stage, living in a family means fulfilling one or more roles. Tom's mother has a number of roles. She's a wife, mother, daughter, and sister. Outside the home she is also an employee and friend. What roles do you have in life?

Problems can come when people do not agree on what a role should be. Who will be the breadwinner in a family? Who will handle household duties? Who will care for the children? What responsibilities do teens have to the family? Reaching agreement on these role-related questions requires effort, understanding, and compromise.

One of the trends seen in recent years has been the changes in women's and men's roles. Today more than 50 million women are employed outside the home. For many, the income is needed. Others choose careers for fulfillment.

More than half of the nation's preschoolers have working mothers. Concern has been raised about how these children fare in child care situations. Some studies have shown that, with quality care, the children can do just fine. Some families still feel that young children thrive best at home with a parent present. Not everyone can choose this option, however.

The family role of men has changed, too. Many men are now taking a more active role in parenting and in sharing household responsibilities. Both fathers and children benefit by the closer bond that results.

Family roles and responsibilities change from time to time. What's routine in one family may be a role reversal in another. How do you think roles have changed for this family?

Families Are Unique

Think about the families you have seen on television. Some seem to be perfect. They are attractive people with fashionable clothes, new cars, and beautiful places to live. Others are just the opposite. Most of them can solve almost any problem, large or small, in a half hour. Did you ever wonder if any families like these fictional families exist in the real world? Chances are, they don't. Although the families you know may share some characteristics with those you see on television, most real-life families are not the same at all.

Learning Activities (continued)

5. **Idea Exchange.** Encourage students to post written thoughts and ideas about handling household duties. Discuss some of the ideas posted on the board. (Key Skills: *Critical Thinking, Cooperation*)
6. **Incomplete Sentences.** Ask students to complete the following sentences: "My family is unique because …," "Some of the personal resources that my family has are …" (Key Skills: *Critical Thinking, Communication*)

Follow Up

1. **Reteaching.** Have students list as many roles as possible that they hold in their family, at school, and in the community. Next, ask them to list the roles of their parents or guardians. Have them circle the roles that they share with their parents. (Key Skill: *Critical Thinking*)
2. **Extension.** Have students read the extension material on pp. 19-20 from the *Extending the Lesson* booklet of the TCR.
3. **Enrichment.** Assign students to write a one-page paper titled "Maintaining a Strong Family in a Changing World." Their ideas should reflect positive steps families can take to address the stressers of change. (Key Skill: *Critical Thinking*)

More About Family Roles

Children's concepts of family roles are learned from personal experiences at home; at school; in the community; and from books, movies, and television. In some situations, concepts of family roles are very idealistic and romanticized. The result is that few family members, including parents, children, grandparents, or siblings, can hope to live up to the expectations of other family members. Few parents, for example, can approach the concept of the "ideal" parent presented by the media. Likewise, it is unrealistic for spouses to try to fill the role of ideal husband or ideal wife.

The World Around You

Families of the World

There are many different types of families in today's world. They vary in size, in relationships, and in the way they meet the needs of family members. Select volunteers to interview foreign students or use library resources to learn about families in various countries. Have them find out about changes in family functions and lifestyles that may have occurred in the past fifty years.

Completing the Chapter

For Review

1. Emphasize the main concepts using the summary.
2. Have students complete the "Facts to Recall." (Answers below.)

For Reteaching

1. **Reteaching.** Use the activity on p. 18 of the *Reteaching and Practical Skills* booklet in the TCR.

For Enrichment

1. **Enrichment.** Use the activity on pp. 27-28 of the *Enrichment Activities* booklet in the TCR.

For Evaluation

1. Choose items from "Ideas to Explore" and "Activities to Try."
2. Use the chapter test on pp. 27-28 of the testing booklet in the TCR or use the testmaker software.

Facts to Recall Answers

1. To satisfy the basic physical needs of all members.
2. Socially: adults teach younger ones how to behave in different situations and how to get along with others. Intellectually: seeing that children learn at home and at school. Emotionally: teaching children to express feelings, give and receive support.
3. Nuclear families consist of parent and children in the home. Extended families include grandparents, aunts, uncles, cousins, etc.
4. Parent must assume all adult responsibilities; children often take on extra responsibilities and learn independence earlier.
5. Type of nuclear family in which one or both adults have been married before and one or both have children from previous marriage.

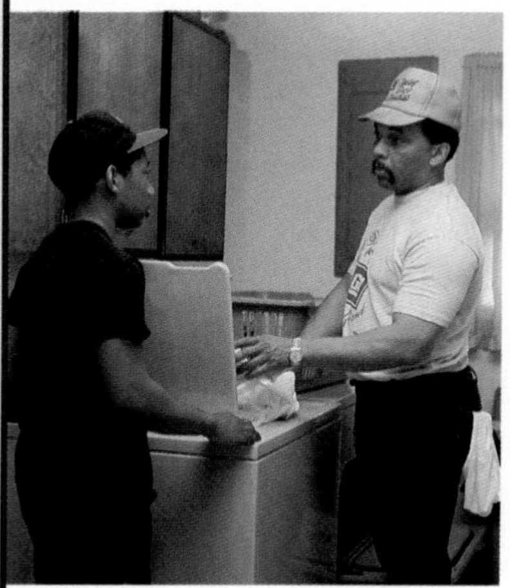

Working together as a family encourages communication and strengthens families.

Families are unique, or unlike other families, in many ways. Some families are different in the way they show feelings. In Webb's house, for example, people express their emotions freely. Hugs are common among family members. Dean's family is the opposite. They love each other just as much as Webb's family, but they are very private people. They find it hard to show their feelings openly with each other.

Families are also unique in their interests and traditions. For instance, the Wongs and the Garcias have very special traditions they have passed on to their children. Their traditions are a unique part of their culture and their family life. Shared family interests may involve music, sports, religious activities, or hobbies. Sharing these interests can help create bonds in a family.

Families are also unique in the ways they use resources to reach their goals. They may use material resources, such as money, housing, equipment, and transportation. They may also use personal resources, such as energy, interests, skills, and knowledge.

A family's uniqueness also depends on how its members work together at home. When all family members commit to making a good life together, it doesn't matter that one family is different from another. Strong families can be happy families regardless of their form, expression of affection, traditions, interests, and resources.

TAKING ACTION

Understanding Family Changes

Gavin and his sister, Toni, were spending part of the summer with their grandparents on Lake Waramug. Toni's best friend, Claire, and Gavin's friend, Tom, were coming to spend a few days with them. Claire's parents are divorced. Tom lives in a blended family that includes his two sisters and two stepbrothers. Their situations led to a conversation about changes in family life.

"In my day, parents usually stayed together for the sake of the children despite any personal problems," their grandmother said.

"Growing up, I never knew anybody who was divorced, but I don't think parents who are unhappy together should stay married for the sake of their children," their grandfather replied.

Using Your Resourcefulness

- How would you respond to the statements made by Gavin and Toni's grandparents? Why do you agree or disagree with the statements?
- What different types of family groups do your friends have? Which families seem positive and supportive? Which seem negative and unsupportive?
- What are some reasons for the change in family groups today? What resources can help you learn more about family life and various family groups?

TAKING ACTION

Have students make a list of ten families that they know. Ask them to list the people (mother, father, children, etc.) that make up each family. Do not use names. Survey the class to determine how many families are made up of both the mother and father, one parent only, a stepparent, one or more stepchildren, only the couple with no children, or a parent and older relatives. How have attitudes toward different types of families changed in recent years? What goals do students have for families of their own in the future? Have students read the feature and respond to the questions.

Using Your Resourcefulness Answers

• Answers will vary.

Chapter 12 Review

Summary

In this chapter, you have read about:

- How families meet the physical, social, mental, and emotional needs of their members.
- The variety of forms a family may take.
- How families experience the family life cycle.
- The roles that people have within families.
- The uniqueness of each family in interests, resources, and lifestyles.

Facts to Recall

1. What is the first function of a family?
2. Describe how families help people grow socially, intellectually, and emotionally.
3. How do nuclear and extended families differ?
4. What extra challenges face both children and parents of single-parent families?
5. What is a blended family?
6. How are adoptive and foster families similar? How do they differ?
7. Briefly describe the typical family life cycle.
8. How do roles affect families?
9. Identify three ways that families can be unique.

Ideas to Explore

1. What is the form of your family? How has its form changed over time?
2. What suggestions can you offer to the members of a recently-formed blended family?
3. What roles do you have in your family? How may the different roles you have now conflict with one another? Explain which of your roles you think is most important.
4. Briefly describe what you believe the roles of a husband and a wife should be in a marriage. What might happen if a couple does not agree on these roles? When should a couple make decisions about role responsibilities?

Activities to Try

1. Write a short television commercial for any product you choose. Include characters, dialogue, and settings that you believe reflect real family life today.
2. Work with a group of class members to list challenges that families face at each stage of the family life cycle. What are some possible solutions for these family challenges?
3. As a class, debate the following statement: "Children who are raised in a family in which one parent stays at home are happier, better cared for, and more emotionally secure than children raised by parents who both work outside the home."

LINK TO Social Studies

TRACING FAMILY ROLES

The roles of family members have changed over time. Trace the development of the family from its origins among prehistoric people more than 300,000 years ago to today. Note how the roles played by men, women, and children within the family changed over time. How did the family itself and its roles in society change? Using the information you've gathered, make a time line tracing the history of the family up to the present time. Develop a creative way to present your time line to the class.

Facts to Recall Answers (continued)

6. Similarities: created through legal process; children not related to one or both parents; can be nuclear, single-parent, blended, or extended. Differences: adoption is permanent, foster family is temporary.
7. Couple marries, has children; children are raised and launched; couple adjusts to empty nest, goes through middle years, retirement, and aging.
8. Can cause problems if not agreed on within family; affects concerns of family; affects bonds between family members.
9. **Any three:** in way they show feelings; interests and traditions; ways they use resources; how members work together at home.

Ideas to Explore

1. Answers will vary based on student experience.
2. Answers will vary.
3. Answers will vary based on student experience.
4. Answers will vary.

- Answers will vary. Remind students not to use names of families.
- Answers will vary, but may include divorce, death, abuse, family mobility, etc. Resources may include teachers, counselors, religious leaders, magazines, and books, etc.

LINK TO Social Studies

Answer

Student answers will vary based on information studied.

Preparing to Teach

Chapter Outline

Your Role in a Strong Family (p. 141)

Getting Along in a Family (p. 141)
- Relating to Parents and Guardians (p. 143)
- Relating to Siblings (p. 146)
- Relating to Other Family Members (p. 148)

Chapter Resources

The following booklet materials may be found in the *Teacher's Classroom Resources* box:
- Lesson Plans, p. 18
- Student Workbook, *Study Guide,* pp. 59-60; *How Well Do You Know Your Family?,* p. 61; *How Responsible Are You?,* p. 62
- Color Transparencies, *Growing a Strong Family Tree,* CT-13
- Personal Safety, *Assert Yourself,* pp. 20-21
- Technology and Computers, p. 14
- Cooperative Learning, p. 25
- Extending the Text, *Thinking of Ways to Show You Care,* p. 21
- Reteaching and Practical Skills, *Promoting Family Strength—M.V.P. Award,* p. 20
- Enrichment Activities, *Looking at the Funny Side,* pp. 27-28
- Chapter and Unit Tests, pp. 29-30
- Testmaker Software

Also see:
- Meeting the Special Needs of Students
- Linking Home, School, and Community
- Dealing with Sensitive Issues

ABCNews InterActive™ Videodiscs
- *Teenage Sexuality*
- *Violence Prevention*

See the ABCNews InterActive™ Bar Code Correlation booklet for applicable segments.

CHAPTER 13 Building a Strong Family

OBJECTIVES

- *Explain why it takes effort to build a strong family.*
- *Describe ways to improve relationships with other family members.*

TERMS TO LEARN

- ***siblings***
- ***age span***
- ***sibling rivalry***

Sometimes it takes a near tragedy to wake people up. That's what happened to Alejandro. A heart attack put his father in the hospital and left him near death for several weeks. Alejandro, caught up in his own problems, had been spending as much time as possible away from home. He and his father had not been getting along. When death loomed, however, Alejandro did some soul searching. So much of what had seemed important to him before suddenly seemed unimportant. He began to see that he wanted a second chance with his father. He was willing, even eager, to take the first steps to make things better. That's just what he did.

Your Role in a Strong Family

Strong families don't just happen; it takes time and effort from every family member to keep a family strong. Alejandro realized how important his father is to him and also realized it would take time and effort to build a strong relationship with his father. Family members build stronger bonds when attitudes and actions are constructive rather than destructive. Read "How to Build a Strong Family" on page 142 for more ideas on strengthening families.

Getting Along in a Family

Think of all the ways that family members can be different. Age, gender, and life experiences all set them apart right away. By the time you add interests, obligations, and abilities, you can have a set of very different individuals, all living under the same roof. Effort must be made to bridge the differences. A strong family can be created when attitudes and actions are constructive, not destructive.

If friendships seem easier to maintain than family relationships at times, think about why this may be true. You can choose supportive friends and drop those who are disagreeable. You can base friendship on shared interests and attitudes. Moreover, you can easily decide how much time to spend with friends. You have far less control over family situations. What you do control, however, are your attitude and actions within the family.

Individuals in families can be very different from one another. It takes effort to bridge the differences and get along.

More About *Family Councils*

A family council is a family meeting in which all members have a right to express their thoughts and feelings. Some families hold a family council at a regular time each week. Others get together only when there are special requests or problems that need attention. Family councils are a good way to include children in the family's plans. Also, they help children identify family values and make appropriate decisions based on those values.

Introducing the Chapter

Motivators

1. **Discussion.** Bring a pair of hand weights to class. Ask a student to pick them up and demonstrate several ways to use the weights to build body strength. Have students list other factors that are necessary for a strong body such as good nutrition, adequate rest, aerobic exercise, etc. Talk about how the family is like the human body in that it, too, needs regular attention and care in order to be strong. (Key Skill: *Communication*)
2. **Brainstorming.** Have students brainstorm a list of factors that can weaken a family, such as little time to be together, irresponsibility, etc. (Key Skill: *Critical Thinking*)
3. **Exhibit.** Set up a table with four cans of food. Remove or cover each of the labels with paper, and write one of the following words on each can: understanding, respect, appreciation, and responsibility. Title the exhibit "Four Factors for Family Strength." (Key Skill: *Communication*)
4. **Writing.** Assign students to write a paragraph describing a family that is strong. Ask for volunteers to read their paragraphs. Discuss similarities and differences in the paragraphs. (Key Skills: *Communication, Critical Thinking*)

Chapter Objectives and Vocabulary

1. Have students read the chapter objectives. Ask them to rephrase the objectives as questions.
2. Ask students to state, in their own words, the purpose of studying this chapter.
3. Pronounce the vocabulary terms listed on the previous page. Ask students whether they are familiar with any of these. Explain that the terms will be defined in the chapter.

Guided Reading

1. Have students read the chapter and use the Study Guide on pp. 59-60 of the *Student Workbook*.

Teaching. . .

Your Role in a Strong Family; Getting Along; Parents and Guardians

(pp. 141-143)

Comprehension Check

1. Why are friendships sometimes easier to maintain than good family relationships? *(More control over friendships, you can choose friends and drop those who are disagreeable; you can base friendships on shared interests and attitudes; you can decide how much time to spend with friends.)*
2. Name three questions that may help you better understand your parents. *(What has life been like for them over the years? What responsibilities do they have? What are some of their problems?)*
3. Give a situation in which parents' past experiences affect the decisions they make now. *(Try to protect children from problems; they act in ways that reflect how they grew up.)*

Learning Activities

1. **Suggestion Box.** Invite students to write down questions or concerns they would like to have discussed during the study of this chapter. Provide a box for students to place their unsigned questions or concerns. (Key Skills: *Communication, Critical Thinking*)
2. **Guest Speaker.** Invite a counselor or member of the clergy to speak to the class about personal qualities and other factors that are conducive to strong family relationships. (Key Skill: *Communication*)
3. **Brainstorming.** Help students brainstorm a list of recreational activities family members can share with each other. Write the list on the chalkboard, and place a check mark to the left of each activity that can be done at home. Place an asterisk to the left of each activity that costs less than $5.00 for the entire family. (Key Skills: *Critical Thinking, Cooperation*)

How to ...
Build a Strong Family

Families can become stronger by:

- ***Spending time together.*** Join each other regularly at certain meals. Play games. Go on an outing. Attend events that concern individual family members such as a music recital, a play, a debate, or a team sport.
- ***Observing traditions***. These may relate to holidays, religion, or routine activities — such as picking apples at an orchard — that the family decides to turn into tradition.
- ***Communicating.*** Share your ideas and thoughts with others and listen to theirs.
- ***Working together to solve problems.*** Discuss problems when they arise. Consider holding family council meetings.
- ***Sharing the work load.*** Set up a schedule and do your part willingly. Be ready to help others when they need it.
- ***Respecting the privacy of others.*** Learn to knock on closed doors and listen only to conversations that concern you.
- ***Showing consideration.*** Think about how you use the phone, treat others' belongings, and use family space.
- ***Putting family needs first.*** Remember that a "me-first" attitude is not constructive. Friends are important, but families are too.
- ***Sharing beliefs.*** These may be religious, political, or community concerns. Act on these beliefs together.
- ***Showing appreciation and love for each other.*** Remember birthdays and anniversaries. Give a hug. Learn to say, "I love you."
- ***Being tolerant.*** Forgive and forget when family members do something you don't like. Most incidents are not worth making an issue of.
- ***Having a positive attitude.*** You'll be pleasant to be around.

How to ... Build a Strong Family

Provide classroom and individual opportunities for students to help strengthen their families. Encourage them to plan and carry out family outings or activities. If ideas are limited, lead the class in brainstorming a list of things families can do together at home and in the community. Help students learn to appreciate family traditions by having them read about their culture or interview local leaders who observe the same or similar traditions.

When you work out ways to relate well to your parents, brothers and sisters, and other family members, you are doing your share to promote family strength. Sometimes you must be willing to take the first step.

▼ Relating to Parents and Guardians ▼

Learning to get along with people begins at home. The way you act and react will set life-long patterns of behavior.

Understanding

The first step toward a good relationship is understanding. How well do you know your parents? Answers to these questions may help you see more clearly: What has life been like for them over the years? Can you list all the responsibilities they have? What problems must they deal with?

Understanding your parents means trying to walk in their shoes some of the time. You may discover that they have their own reasons for what they do. Recognizing this is very helpful. In addition, allow room for them to be human — parents make mistakes just like everyone else.

Keep in mind that parents' past experiences affect the decisions they make now. For instance, they may try to protect you from problems they had when they were your age. They may also act in ways that reflect how they grew up. Tara's mother was raised in a home where money was scarce. As a child, Mrs. Holmes never had more than the basics. She learned what it was like to scrimp in order to survive. Tara has not had to live like that, so she is often frustrated by her mother's efforts to economize. After a little thought and conversation about her mother's childhood, Tara saw her mother's point of view more clearly.

Discussing your differences and feelings with your parents openly and honestly is a step toward building a strong family. You might try asking your parents what life was like for them as teens.

Learning Activities (continued)

4. **Discussion.** Talk about reasons why it is important for teens to learn to get along with their parents. (Key Skills: *Communication, Critical Thinking*)
5. **Bulletin Board.** Title a board "Walk a Mile in their Shoes." Near the top, display pictures of men's and women's shoes. Underneath, display pictures or actual items to depict some of the responsibilities and tasks of parents. At the bottom of the board, write the question, "How well do you understand the responsibilities of your parents?" (Key Skill: *Critical Thinking*)

Follow Up

1. **Reteaching.** Assign students to give specific examples of ways that teens can show understanding of their family members. (Key Skill: *Critical Thinking*)
2. **Enrichment.** Select students to write and illustrate a comic book for younger children featuring ways to show appreciation to family members. Share the completed project with the class. (Key Skills: *Cooperation, Creativity*)

Family Perspective

Students' households sometimes include a grandparent or older aunt or uncle. Ask for volunteers to design a piece of clothing for an elderly person's special needs, preferences, safety, and comfort.

Wellness

Family relationships are a very important factor in helping people successfully adjust to aging. Teens living in households with older adults may find it helpful to review the physical changes that take place as the body ages. Some teens may want to develop a physical activity program for older adults, keeping in mind the needs of older family members.

More About *Strong Families*

Members of strong families tend to spend a great deal of time together — working, playing, eating meals, and attending religious services together. What they do is not as important as *doing* it. Strong families realize the time they spend together needs to be quality time. It also needs to be sufficient; quality interaction is not likely to develop in a few seconds together. Encourage students to think of ways they can spend more time with their families, even if it means working rather than playing together. Washing dishes, folding clothes, and making beds can be a time for family members to talk and laugh with one another.

Teaching. . . Relating to Parents or Guardians: Respect; Appreciation; Responsibility (pp. 144-145)

Comprehension Check

1. What are two ways to show respect to your parents? *(Understand why they act as they do; use words and tones of voices that do not turn parents off; listen to parents.)*
2. Name four ways to show appreciation to family members. *(Smiles or hugs; sincere compliments; ask for advice; say "thank you;" notes of appreciation; offer help before it's asked for; show concern.)*
3. What are five ways to show you are responsible? *(Do tasks without being reminded; be honest and admit mistakes; let parents know where you are when away from home; watch out for younger siblings; make grades the best they can be; use study time wisely.)*

Learning Activities

1. **Skits.** Assign students to write and present skits contrasting situations in which one teen lets her parents know where she is going and another who does not let her parents know where she is going with her friends. Have students write their skits from the perspective of the parents. (Key Skills: *Critical Thinking, Creativity*)

AROUND THE WORLD

After reading the feature, have students volunteer to visit a nursing home to observe points of interest such as the physical layout of the home, dining areas, places for informal recreation, and residents' rooms. Is the home clean and attractive? Does it seem inviting to residents and visitors? Do other older Americans have the same concern about respect as those Italian-Americans mentioned in the feature?

Understanding is a two-way street. You want your parents to understand you, too. Even though teens want this, many of them hide their thoughts and feelings. This just blocks understanding. Your friends understand you because you talk to them. The same can be true with your parents.

Respect

Respect follows understanding. When you know why people act as they do, it is easier to give them respect. Respect is shown in what you say as well as how you say it. When people talk to you, what words and tones of voice turn you off? Listen to them and then to yourself. Practice the kinds of things you like to hear and then try them out. You may be surprised to discover that you receive more respect when you learn to give it more often.

Appreciation

People who respect others find ways to show appreciation. Sometimes friends do this without even thinking. Showing appreciation is just as important in families, but sometimes is overlooked. Family members have a tendency to take each other for granted. Can you add to the following list of ways to show appreciation for your parents?

- Give a hug or a smile.
- Give a sincere compliment.
- Ask for their help or advice. You may be surprised at how much they have to offer and how willing they are to support you.
- Say "thank you."
- Buy or make a card and include a note of appreciation.
- Offer your help without being asked.
- Show concern. When problems arise, listen and offer to help find a solution.

THE WORLD

For many Italian-American families, the decision to place an aged family member in a nursing home is especially hard. Italian tradition places high value on family loyalty and respect to elderly family members. Some older Italian-Americans were born in Italy and feel misunderstood in American nursing homes. The respect shown to elderly people is not the same as they feel it should be. One solution to this problem has been the creation of nursing homes run by Italian-Americans for Italian-Americans. These retirement communities provide their residents not only with health care, but with understanding of their history, their culture, and their traditions.

ITALY

More About *Understanding Your Family*

Strong families are not without problems. However, good communication among family members eases frustrations and helps to create a sense of belonging. It also helps prevent some full-blown crises. Strong families know that good communication does not necessarily happen; it usually takes time and practice. Time spent in casual conversations can be very special. Important issues, feelings, or values can be expressed; and misunderstandings can be cleared up.

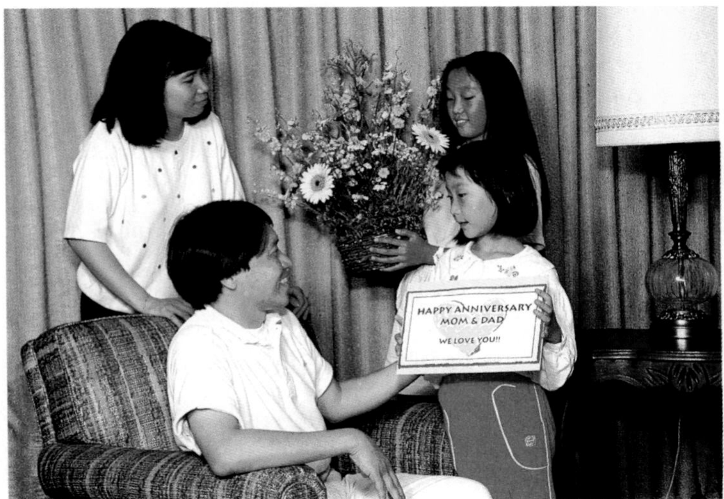

How do you feel when someone shows appreciation to you? How might you strengthen your relationship with your parents by showing your appreciation to them?

Responsibility

Good relationships with parents depend on one more thing — a sense of responsibility. For many years, children rely on parents and guardians to provide for their needs. This is the responsibility of parenthood. Eventually children grow, and it's their turn to begin taking on responsibilities. This is part of growing toward maturity and independence. Teens who are willing to be responsible usually get along better and are often given more privileges. Responsible teens are more likely to be trusted.

What does it mean to be responsible? Here are some examples:

- Justine has certain jobs to do at home. She carries them out without reminders. Sometimes she does extra tasks, especially when she notices that someone in the family is overburdened.
- Carlton is honest with his parents. He admits his mistakes. His parents appreciate this and reward him with trust.
- Shelly lets her parents know where she is going to be when she will be away from home. This is important information for her parents. It gives them peace of mind to know that she is safe. It is important for other reasons, too. When Shelly's older brother had a car accident several months ago, her stepfather needed to reach her quickly. This was easy to do because Shelly had just called home to tell them where she and her friends were going for pizza.

Learning Activities (continued)

2. **Mural.** Have students create a mural depicting ways that teens can show responsibility. (Key Skill: *Critical Thinking*)
3. **Questioning.** Ask for volunteers to answer the following questions: What jobs do you do at home on a regular basis without being reminded to do them? When was the last time you did an extra task for someone in your family, and what was that task? Why is it hard sometimes to be honest with your parents? How does it feel to be the youngest sibling in the family? How does it feel to be the oldest sibling? (Key Skill: *Communication*)
4. **Sentence Completion.** Ask students to complete the following sentences: "I showed a sense of responsibility when I ...," "When I am honest with my parents I feel ...," "My parents like to know where I am going because I have ..." (Key Skills: *Communication, Critical Thinking*)

Follow Up

1. **Reteaching.** Help students make a daily schedule for study time. Have them explain why this is one way to show they have a sense of responsibility. (Key Skills: *Critical Thinking, Management*)
2. **Enrichment.** Ask students to record in their journals instances in which they show respect, appreciation, or a sense of responsibility to family members. How do these instances relate to the students' contribution to family strength? (Key Skill: *Critical Thinking*)

More About *Strengthening the Family*

One way to make a family strong is to build on its history and traditions. Some families collect and assemble family information. They record family legends, fill out family trees, identify family photos, and visit places where their ancestors once lived. Participants get a history lesson and learn the values of family records while interacting with family members. Interviewing older relatives and recording their experiences and memories so they can be enjoyed in the future helps build an understanding of oneself and people of all ages.

Family Perspective

Select students to locate and study examples of various contracts used in the world of business. Next, have students design and write a contract specifying actions they will take to be a responsible family member. Encourage them to share their contract with their parents.

Teaching. . .
Relating to Siblings; Relating to Other Family Members
(pp. 146-148)

Comprehension Check

1. How does age span affect sibling relationships? *(It affects how well siblings get along; if close in age, they may share interests; young children tend to idolize older siblings and do what they do.)*
2. What is another name for sibling rivalry? *(Competition.)*
3. Why is it important to maintain a good relationship with your siblings? *(At some point in your life, you probably will need the support and friendship of your siblings. If you want them to be there for you when you need them someday, you must work to keep a good relationship.)*
4. Name three advantages of good relationships with relatives. *(Learn about family history; expand your horizons to the communities where they live; may be good friends; may be a support system during tough times.)*

Learning Activities

1. **Discussion.** Have students compare age spans between siblings, and discuss advantages and disadvantages of short and long age spans. (Key Skills: *Communication, Critical Thinking*)
2. **Guest Speakers.** Invite teachers, counselors, administrators, or other school personnel to speak to the class about their childhood and adolescent experiences with siblings. Ask them to share ways in which these experiences helped them grow as individuals. (Key Skill: *Communication*)

- Tony watches out for his younger brother. Sometimes this is his job. Other times he just sees that Steven needs him, so he helps out.
- Billy Jo works to keep her grades as high as possible. She includes study time in her daily schedule and uses this time wisely. Billy Jo knows that her future depends on what she does now. Her foster parents never have to prod her to get her work done.

All of these teens are showing responsibility. Even though their families don't always say so, they do notice. What's more, these teens get along well in their families. That's the best part.

▼ Relating to Siblings ▼

The same skills that you use in getting along with parents or guardians are useful when relating to **siblings**, or brothers and sisters. Trying to understand them will help you give them respect. Showing that you appreciate them will make them feel good, and they are likely to return the positive feelings to you in some way.

The **age span**, or number of years between children, affects sibling relationships. Sixteen-year-old Tim likes to rebuild car engines, but his ten-year-old brother Michael hangs around and asks endless questions while Tim is working. How would you handle this if you were Tim?

It is easy to think of younger siblings as bothersome. Put yourself in their place, though, and you may think differently. Young children in a family often idolize older siblings. They may want to be like them and do what they do. They are anxious to be older, too. Rejecting them or becoming angry with them just frustrates them and may even turn them into pests. A far better approach is to give them some attention, include them when you can, and distract them some of the time. One day Tim gave Michael some whitewall cleaner and let him work on making the car tires look like new. Michael was happy to be included while Tim went about his work.

Spending time with your siblings, even if it's working at a task together, is a way to build positive feelings. If you have them, what can you do to help strengthen your relationship with your siblings?

Photo Focus

Have students examine the photo on p. 146. Ask them to brainstorm a list of activities or chores they might do with their siblings to strengthen their relationship.

More About *Getting Along with Siblings*

Conflict among siblings is a normal part of family life. In a strong family, brothers and sisters are encouraged to express their feelings to each other and to work at resolving disagreements. Also, they are taught to show appreciation for each other. Saying more about the positive things and less about negative ones is practiced and rewarded. Praise, smiles, and hugs are often freely given.

What might be some ways to eliminate sibling rivalry in this family?

TIPS: *Getting Along with Siblings*

Here are some tips for getting along with siblings:

- Ask permission before borrowing possessions. Return what you borrow on time and in good condition.
- Don't expect to be included every time an older sibling has friends over for a visit.
- Talk out your disagreements. Be ready to compromise. Then stick to your agreement.
- Be supportive of your siblings.
- Find similar interests you can talk about or do together.
- Teach each other new skills.
- Do household jobs together. They will be easier and more fun to do.
- Compliment your siblings on what they do well.
- Talk to them. Share your feelings, and let them get to know you.

Here's one last thought to remember about siblings. At some point in their lives, most people need the support and friendship of their siblings. Friends can drift apart, but siblings have a bond like no other. If you want them to be there for you when you need them someday, then you must work to keep the relationship in good shape.

Competition

Competition for parents' and other family members' love and attention is a common problem between siblings. This is called **sibling rivalry**. Sibling rivalry can cause people to feel down about themselves. Rebecca feels that her sister gets more privileges than she does. Taylor wishes he could play basketball the way his older brother did in high school. Maria gets tired of listening to people talk about her sister's good grades.

If you ever feel that fairness is a problem in your family, remember this. Parents have a great deal to think about. It is almost impossible for them to keep track of everything said to, bought for, or rewarded to each child. Children have a remarkable ability to tally up all these things — from their own viewpoint. Try not to fall into this trap. Everyone and every situation is different. Some children are more responsible at an earlier age than others. Rewards and discipline that work for one child may not work for another. Making things perfectly even among siblings is practically impossible, and it can even work against you. As one mother put it: "Denise doesn't even see what she would have lost if we had tried to make everything the same for her and her sister. She has gotten to do many things at a younger age than her sister did. She doesn't even think about that when she complains about equal treatment."

Learning Activities (continued)

3. **Debate.** Have students debate the following: "Good parents can eliminate sibling rivalry." (Key Skills: *Communication, Critical Thinking*)
4. **Cartoons.** Assign students to draw cartoons about sibling rivalry. Display and discuss some of the finished cartoons. Talk about how it feels to experience sibling rivalry. (Key Skills: *Communication, Creativity*)

Follow Up

1. **Reteaching.** Provide art supplies for students to use to illustrate a page of tips for getting along with siblings. Ask them to list as many tips as possible. Display their completed pages. (Key Skills: *Communication, Creativity*)
2. **Extension.** Have the students read the extension material on p. 21 from the *Extending the Lesson* booklet of the TCR.
3. **Enrichment.** Ask for volunteers to take their younger siblings or other young relatives to the park, zoo, concert, museum, or other exhibit. Have them take responsibility for planning and carrying out the excursion. Assign them to write a summary and evaluation of the experience. (Key Skills: *Leadership, Management*)

TIPS:

Getting Along with Siblings
Ask students to read the list of suggestions in the feature. What other suggestions do students have for ways to improve sibling relationships? Can students expect sibling relationships to improve immediately or should they anticipate change over time? Discuss the benefits of developing patience with siblings.

More About *Sibling Rivalry*

Jealousy of brothers and sisters is common during childhood and adolescence. Some parents increase such problems, often subconsciously, by showing favoritism to one child. Another common error is trying to improve behavior by comparing one child to another. Such comparisons rarely improve behavior, but they can harm a child's self-concept and his or her relationship to the family. Normally, sibling rivalry fades as a child matures and develops interests outside the family. However, some children never seem to outgrow it and are jealous even as adults.

Completing the Chapter

For Review

1. Emphasize the main concepts using the summary.
2. Have students complete the "Facts to Recall." (Answers below.)

For Reteaching

1. **Reteaching.** Use the activity on p. 19 of the *Reteaching and Practical Skills* booklet in the TCR.

For Enrichment

1. **Enrichment.** Use the activity on pp. 29-30 of the *Enrichment Activities* booklet in the TCR.

For Evaluation

1. Choose items from "Ideas to Explore" and "Activities to Try."
2. Use the chapter test on pp. 29-30 of the testing booklet in the TCR or use the testmaker software.

Facts to Recall Answers

1. You can control choice of friends, include only those with shared interests, agreeable personalities. Family members differ greatly, family situations cannot always be controlled.
2. **Any five:** spend time together; observe tradition; communicate; work together to solve problems; share work load; respect others' privacy; show consideration; put family needs first; share beliefs; show appreciation and love; be tolerant; have positive attitude.
3. You discover reasons for their actions; realize they are human; understand how past experiences affect their decisions.
4. **Any five:** hug or smile; give sincere compliment; ask for help and advice; say, "thank you;" give card and note of appreciation; offer help unasked; show concern.

When competitive feelings strike, it also helps to remember that you have your own special qualities and abilities. They may not be the same as those of your siblings, but that doesn't matter. Discover what you do well, and develop those skills.

▼ Relating to Other Family Members ▼

Relatives are family members, including those outside the immediate household. They are related by birth, adoption, or marriage. Some families have many relatives who get together for birthdays, graduations, and holidays. Other families have few relatives, or they may live too far away to see them often.

By learning to get along with — and enjoy — your relatives, you will have a fuller life. You can learn about family history from them. Often relatives turn out to be good friends and a tremendous support system in tough situations. These relationships are well worth nurturing through visits and through correspondence when separated by distance.

TAKING ACTION

Solving Family Conflicts

Family life has been a difficult issue for Adam for a long time. His parents used to argue a lot. Eventually they divorced and he lived with his mother. It took Adam a while to make the adjustment, especially since he'd felt closer to his father. He was extremely distressed when his father moved to another city. It seemed like he and his mom were fighting every day. Over time, they worked out differences and developed a smoother relationship.

Six months ago, Adam's mother remarried. Now he and his stepfather don't get along. To complicate things, Renee, a stepsister one year younger than Adam, is at odds with her own mother and has come to stay with them for a while. She seems to get all the attention and Adam gets the blame when things go wrong. He knows he needs help quickly, but doesn't know what to do.

Using Your Resourcefulness

- What options does Adam have in changing and improving his family conflicts? What would happen if he did nothing to change the situation
- If he decides to talk to any or all family members, how should he communicate his feelings? What should he say? What shouldn't he say?
- What resources in your community could help Adam and his family? What kind of services do counselors and support groups offer? How does one contact such resources?

TAKING ACTION

Have students read the feature and respond to the questions. How might students show empathy for Adam or someone they know in a similar situation to Adam's? What value is there in working toward strengthening the family bond even through adversity?

Using Your Resourcefulness Answers

- Answers will vary. Adam might consider keeping the lines of communication open with his mother, father, and stepfather.
- Answers will vary. He should avoid blaming and just state the way he feels. He might offer suggestions for improving family life.

Chapter 13 Review

Summary

In this chapter, you have read about:

- Why it sometimes takes a greater effort to get along with family members than with friends.
- How understanding, respect, and appreciation affect relationships with parents and guardians.
- Ways of showing responsibility within the family.
- Things you can do to strengthen your relationships with siblings.
- The contributions of other relatives to your life.

Facts to Recall

1. Explain why it can sometimes be more challenging to get along with family members than with friends.
2. List five ways to help make a family stronger.
3. Why is it easier to respect parents and guardians when you understand them?
4. List five ways to show appreciation for parents.
5. How can responsible behavior lead to greater independence for teens?
6. What is helpful to remember when someone feels that fairness is a problem in the family?
7. List five tips for getting along with siblings.
8. How can relatives outside your immediate household make your life more full?

Ideas to Explore

1. Discuss two ways in which the experiences of your parents or guardians as teens were different from your experiences as a teen. How has that made their attitudes and opinions different from yours?
2. Why do you think some teens have trouble talking with their parents? What suggestions do you have for improving the lines of communication?
3. How can asking a family member for advice show appreciation?

Activities to Try

1. Develop a questionnaire that could be used to help you better understand a parent or guardian.
2. Imagine you are the parent or guardian of a child who is your age. Write a letter explaining your reasons for making a decision or taking an action that the child thinks is unfair.
3. Imagine that you are your own eight-year-old brother or sister. Write a short essay describing your daily activities as your younger sibling might see them.

LINK TO *Geography*

FAMILY LIFE AROUND THE WORLD

Throughout the world, a variety of family patterns exist. People may live in nuclear or extended families. The amount of respect given to women and the elderly depends largely on the culture. The way families trace their ancestry also differs — some trace the mother's family line, others the father's family line. A variety of family customs exist in different parts of the world. Examine family life in another country by completing the following:

- Choose a country.
- Read about families and their ways of life in this country.
- Write a skit describing family life in the country you chose.
- Work with several classmates to present your skit to the class.

Facts to Recall Answers (continued)

5. Responsible teens are more likely to be trusted and given more privileges.
6. Parents cannot make things perfectly even among siblings because each person and situation is different.
7. **Any five:** ask permission before borrowing; don't expect to be included in all activities; talk out disagreements; be supportive; find similar interests; teach other new skills; share household jobs; compliment siblings on skills; talk to them.
8. They can teach you family history, give friendship and support.

Ideas to Explore

1. Answers will vary.
2. Answers will vary. To improve communication, teens might talk more openly to parents, listen more carefully to parents, show parents they are trustworthy, etc.
3. It shows repect for the person and their insight, experience, and wisdom.

- Answers will vary, but may include school counselors, doctors, nurses, members of the clergy, social workers, etc.

LINK TO *Geography*

Answer
Answers and skits will vary depending on country or culture choices.

Preparing to Teach

Chapter Outline

Chapter Resources

The following booklet materials may be found in the *Teacher's Classroom Resources* box:
- Lesson Plans, p. 19
- Student Workbook, *Study Guide,* pp. 63-64; *Keeping the Family Afloat,* p. 65; *Facing Up to Family Challenges,* p. 66
- Color Transparencies, *Personal Safety Check,* CT-14
- Personal Safety, *Protect Yourself,* pp. 22-23
- Cooperative Learning, p. 26
- Extending the Text, *Preventing Child Abuse,* p. 22
- Reteaching and Practical Skills, *Family Financial Struggles,* p. 21
- Enrichment Activities, *Rebecca's Story,* p. 29
- Chapter and Unit Tests, pp. 31-32
- Testmaker Software

Also see:
- Meeting the Special Needs of Students
- Linking Home, School, and Community
- Dealing with Sensitive Issues

ABCNews InterActive™ Videodiscs
- *Drugs and Substance Abuse*
- *Alcohol*
- *Violence Prevention*
- *Tobacco*
- *Health: AIDS*

See the ABCNews InterActive™ Bar Code Correlation booklet for applicable segments.

CHAPTER 14 Handling Challenges

OBJECTIVES

- *Describe ways families can handle life's challenges.*
- *List resources available to families who need help.*

TERMS TO LEARN

- ***financial***
- ***credit rating***
- ***addicted***
- ***alcoholism***
- ***alcoholics***
- ***spouse***

If there was one thing that Dorita learned through her ordeal, it was that a crisis should not be faced alone. First she had tried to deny that anything was wrong. Even when she accepted the reality of what was happening, she locked so much inside. Everything stayed there until Dorita couldn't handle it anymore. Confiding in her best friend's mother made all the difference in the world. Once it was out, Dorita began to deal with it, looking for other sources of help. She hoped that she would never have to face anything like this again, but if she did, she knew that she would never choose to go it alone.

The Challenges People Face

Life is not without its ups and downs. Many people find themselves somewhere in the middle most of the time, with day-to-day challenges to meet. Sometimes, however, challenges have high impact. When this happens, people must know how to cope. All problems can be handled; the question is *how*.

▼ New Family Members ▼

When new members are added to a family, some adjustments may be needed. Adding members to a family can upset routines. Space and possessions must be shared. Feelings like resentment and insecurity may surface. This is the negative, or down side — if you choose to see it that way.

A healthier approach is to look at the positive side. A baby is entertaining and loving. A new sibling means one more lifelong source of support. A grandmother who moves in may have interesting stories and information to share. A grandparent may be a source of support when a parent is not available or doesn't seem to understand. You can, no doubt, think of other reasons to value the addition of a new family member. Such thoughts make it easier to accept change, and acceptance is essential.

Many times facing personal and family challenges can be difficult. Reaching out to others and finding ways to cope enables you to work through difficult times.

▼ Moving ▼

Have you ever moved to a new community? If so, you know that it can be difficult. Adults and children in a family have many adjustments to make. They will have to adjust to new schools, a new neighborhood, and new people. The feeling of strangeness about a new place is normal, and it goes away after awhile.

More About *Family Challenges*

In many countries around the world, families face challenges that are brought about by war, political upheaval, and social turmoil. In some situations, children become weapons of war as they are forced to become soldiers and fight in long-term battles. Likewise, children become victims of war, and are maimed or killed as a result of terrorism or civil unrest.

Class members who are interested in geography, history, and social studies may choose to read about these global situations and predict the kind of family members the survivors of these wars will become.

Introducing the Chapter

Motivators

1. **Discussion.** Ask students to name and describe movies and television programs about families facing challenges. Were the challenges faced realistically or unrealistically? (Key Skills: *Communication, Critical Thinking*)
2. **Search and Find.** Have students search through the yellow pages to find names of agencies and other sources that might be of help to families who are facing challenges. Ask them to list all of the sources they find. Compile the sources, and write them on the chalkboard. (Key Skills: *Communication, Cooperation*)
3. **Word Association.** Divide students into small groups, and have them list as many words as they can think of to define and describe challenges. Ask each group to share their list with the entire class. (Key Skills: *Critical Thinking, Cooperation*)
4. **Book Search.** Select students to locate children's books that deal with family challenges and crises. Ask them to read and evaluate them, and to select some to share with the class. (Key Skills: *Communication, Critical Thinking*)

Chapter Objectives and Vocabulary

1. Have students read the chapter objectives. Ask them to rephrase the objectives as questions.
2. Ask students to state, in their own words, the purpose of studying this chapter.
3. Pronounce the vocabulary terms listed on the previous page. Ask students whether they are familiar with any of these. Explain that the terms will be defined in the chapter.

Guided Reading

1. Have students read the chapter and use the Study Guide on pp. 63-64 of the *Student Workbook*.

Teaching. . .
Challenges: New Family Members; Moving; Unemployment; Financial; Homelessness; Illness
(pp. 151-153)

Comprehension Check

1. What are two advantages and two disadvantages a family must face when there is a new family member? *(Advantages: a new baby is entertaining and loving; a grandparent may have interesting stories to share. Disadvantages: routines may be upset; space and possessions must be shared; feelings of resentment and insecurity may surface.)*
2. What are two ways you can make moving to a new school a positive experience? *(Sign up for an activity of interest; be friendly and show interest in others.)*
3. Name five causes of financial problems in the family. *(Lack of a job, overdue credit bills, serious illness, a natural disaster, death in the family.)*
4. What are two positive outcomes that may occur when people learn to manage with very little money? *(People often become better money managers; may be more appreciative of what they have.)*

Learning Activities

1. **Discussion.** Ask students to describe a challenge experienced by a family they know and how the family dealt with the challenge. (Key Skill: *Communication*)
2. **Small Group Discussion.** Divide students into small groups, and have them locate newspaper and magazine articles about families overcoming problems. Ask each group to identify what qualities these families have in common that

Photo Focus

Ask students to examine the photo on p. 152. Have them list the advantages and disadvantages of moving. What might students do to help new students feel welcome?

Moving can be an adventure and a challenge, too! What are some ways that people can make the transition to a new neighborhood or community easier?

When you begin classes at a new school, sign up for an activity or sport that interests you. This will make it easier for you to meet other students with similar interests. Finding classmates who share your interests is the first step in making new friends. Be friendly and show your interest in others. New friendships come in time.

▼ Unemployment ▼

Unemployment complicated Youseff's life. Both of his parents were laid off for several months. This kind of temporary unemployment is a fact of life for many families. As Youseff found out, it was very stressful for the entire family. In addition to surviving on a reduced income, Youseff found his family members having to cope with feelings of low self-esteem, anger, and frustration.

Youseff tried to keep a positive attitude for his parents' sake. He didn't want to make them feel guilty about what they couldn't provide. Youseff found extra ways to help at home and even got a part-time job to pay for school supplies and other expenses. Youseff's parents were proud of the efforts he made.

▼ Financial Problems ▼

Financial, or money-related, problems can be very stressful. They may be caused by the lack of a job, serious illness, a natural disaster, or even death. Some families routinely struggle with financial problems because their income doesn't stretch far enough.

When bills are overdue, creditors welcome a talk to make new arrangements for payment. This can protect a person's **credit rating** — a record that shows a person's ability and willingness to pay his or her debts. Usually for a fee, consumer credit counseling services offer ideas to people who need to control their spending. They also suggest methods for getting out of debt. These services are listed in the yellow pages of the phone book under "Credit."

Understanding helps when this kind of problem exists. Money for clothes and entertainment may be scarce. Altering clothing (see "How to Alter and Recycle Clothing" in Chapter 36) and finding free sources of entertainment can be helpful. A young person's ability to handle financial difficulties in a positive way can take some of the pressure off parents. Although it may seem difficult at the time, learning to manage with very little often makes people better money managers throughout life. They may also be more appreciative of what they have.

▼ Homelessness ▼

This problem has become more common in recent years. When people lose their homes, financial troubles or job loss is usually the reason. Poor economic conditions in a country can cause this to happen to large numbers of people, often through no fault of their own. Natural disasters such as major flooding, hurricanes, and tornadoes also lead to homelessness, although this is more often temporary. Fires can also lead to homelessness. Most communities try to provide a safety net for those who find themselves with nowhere to go. The Red Cross, Salvation Army, and other agencies are usually able to place people in shelters until they can get on their feet again.

▼ Illness and Disabilities ▼

When illness or disability strikes a family, stress comes to all members. Families who pull together manage best. Learning all you can about the illness or disability is a good idea. Libraries and physicians have information. Others who have gone through similar difficulties have firsthand experience. They can offer valuable information, advice, and support. Attitudes of understanding, compassion, sacrifice, and a willingness to help are useful.

The cost of child care outside the home can cause financial difficulties for many people. This family solved this problem by having one parent work out of the home and provide child care at the same time. What other solutions do you see for this challenge?

More About *Illness and Disability*

Serious illness or injury of a child is a difficult challenge for most families to face. Families often experience severe financial hardship, along with a disrupted home life. Ronald McDonald Houses offer a low-cost temporary home for parents and families of children being treated in out-of-town hospitals and clinics. They are a welcome substitute for sleeping on hospital sofas, chairs, and cots or renting hotel rooms in order for families to be near their children. Over 125 Ronald McDonald Houses worldwide allow families to re-establish some sort of normal routine with kitchen and laundry facilities and a room of their own.

helped them deal with challenges. (Key Skills: *Communication, Critical Thinking*)

3. **Skits.** Assign students to write and present a skit about a family facing a challenge. Afterwards, discuss with the class steps that the family could take to get help. Make a list of some of the sources of help in the community. (Key Skills: *Communication, Critical Thinking*)
4. **Brainstorming.** Ask students to imagine that their family is experiencing financial problems. Help them brainstorm a list of skills they have that could be used to earn extra money. (Key Skills: *Critical Thinking, Creativity*)
5. **Guest Speaker.** Have a representative from a human services agency speak to the class about homelessness in the community. Assign students to prepare a list of questions to ask the speaker, such as what people are homeless, reasons for homelessness, what is being done to help the homeless, and what teens and their families can do to help. (Key Skills: *Communication, Critical Thinking*)
6. **Writing.** Assign students to write a short paper, beginning with the following words: "If one of my parents became seriously ill or disabled, some ways I could be of help are ..." Before writing, have students make an outline of the points they want to include. Later, ask for volunteers to share their compositions. (Key Skills: *Communication, Critical Thinking*)

Follow Up

1. **Reteaching.** Assign students to list seven challenges that families sometimes face. Under each challenge, have them write down ways that teens might do their part to help the family deal with the situation. (Key Skill: *Communication*)
2. **Enrichment.** Have students research opportunities for service to the homeless in the community. Ask for volunteers to participate in some of the opportunities and to share their experiences with the class. (Key Skills: *Citizenship, Cooperation*)

Teaching. . .
Challenges: Separation and Divorce; Substance Abuse
(pp. 154-155)

Comprehension Check

1. What are three mistakes made by some parents during an emotional divorce? *(Saying negative things about each other to the children; wanting children to take sides; trying to take the children illegally.)*
2. Name three sources of help for teens whose parents are going through a divorce. *(Parents; a trusted adult such as a teacher, a school counselor, or a religious leader; a friend.)*
3. What does it mean to be addicted to a drug? *(Physical or psychological dependence on the substance.)*

Learning Activities

1. **Panel Discussion.** Select a panel of divorced adults (with children) to talk to the class about the effect of divorce on the family, custody and visitation arrangements, adjustments required on the part of family members, whether professional counseling was received, suggestions for teens whose parents are going through divorce (or are divorced), etc. Have students write a summary of the discussion. (Key Skills: *Communication, Critical Thinking*)

AROUND THE WORLD

After reading the feature, have students investigate the effects of hunger in various countries around the world including the United States. Are problems associated with hunger similar or different among the countries? What solutions do students have to offer?

AROUND THE WORLD

In recent years, many countries in Africa were affected by severe droughts. Without water, farmers were not able to grow crops to supply food in these countries. Food surpluses were used up quickly and many Africans died from hunger. Many Western countries sent food and millions of dollars of aid to African countries. However, much of the food did not reach needy Africans in time. The challenge that many researchers feel is to find better means of monitoring weather, developing better agricultural methods, and monitoring the health of people (especially children) in high-risk areas to help solve the devastating effects of the hunger problem.

▼ Separation and Divorce ▼

Children of parents who are separated or getting a divorce go through a difficult period of emotional adjustment. When separation or divorce occurs, children sometimes feel they are the cause of the problems. They need reassurance that this is not true and loving support from both parents.

Some parents make mistakes when the separation or divorce process is emotional. They say negative things about each other to the children. They may want the children to take sides. One parent may even try to take the children illegally. This is not good for children, but it does happen. Children have the right to say how this makes them feel.

Coping after a divorce requires special effort. Children may have increased responsibilities in the home and may spend less time with both parents — not just the absent one.

Children sometimes feel torn between their parents during a divorce or separation. It's important for children to spend time with both parents and talk about their feelings.

More About *Teen Alcoholics*

It is estimated that more than 1.3 million teenagers are problem drinkers. Of this group, more than half are alcoholics. Usually the physical problems that develop with older alcoholics are not present in young alcoholics, mainly because young people have not had as many years of drinking. During adolescence, problem drinkers have difficulties with family, school, and police. This becomes a vicious circle. If teens have problems at home in the first place and then start drinking, the drinking often leads to more family problems. This points to the futility of drinking as a solution to personal and family problems.

Ricky lives with his mother and sees his father on certain weekends. Handling the schedule was awkward at first, especially since he missed having his father around. The weekend visits with his father are packed with fun activities, no strong rules, and no limits on watching television or listening to music. This makes it important for Ricky to be careful about how he views each of his parents. It would be easy to see his mother as the tough parent and his father as the fun one.

Even though many of the effects of divorce are unpleasant, most people make adjustments and accept their new way of life. Talking with parents can help a young person understand the parents' decision. A trusted adult — perhaps a teacher, school counselor, or religious leader — may also be able to help.

Substance abuse affects more people than just the abuser. It's important to keep the lines of communication open and get help with coping when you need it.

▼ Substance Abuse ▼

When people use substances that cause them harm, the effects are far-reaching. Substance abuse occurs when medications are misused. It also occurs when other drugs, such as alcohol, inhalants (substances that are breathed in), tobacco, and illegal drugs are used. Often people become **addicted** (uhd-IK-ted) to a drug. That is, they have a physical or psychological dependence on the substance — their body tells them they need it; their brain tells them they need it. They cannot give it up. They will do almost anything to get it. Serious health problems and even death result from substance abuse.

Alcoholism is one type of drug problem. Those who are addicted to alcohol, in the form of beer, wine, or other liquor, have this disease. They are called **alcoholics**.

More About *Alcoholism*

Alcoholism is recognized as a disease by the American Medical Association, American Psychiatric Association, American Psychological Association, and the American Bar Association. It is a progressive disease that may have a genetic predisposition. Alcoholism involves increased tolerance to the chemical, impairment of interpersonal and often occupational functioning, and withdrawal symptoms when its use is discontinued. Deaths due to alcoholism are third only to heart disease and cancer, although alcohol's involvement in many other deaths often goes unrecorded.

Learning Activities (continued)

2. **Reading.** Have students read magazine articles about individuals or families who have been affected by substance abuse. Ask them to summarize their conclusions about the impact of the substance abuse on family members. (Key Skills: *Communication Critical Thinking*)
3. **Bulletin Board.** Cover a bulletin board with butcher paper. Title the board "Speaking Out About Substance Abuse." Provide felt marking pens, and encourage students to write their thoughts on the board about substance abuse and the family. (Key Skill: *Communication*)
4. **Guest Speaker.** Invite a medical representative or mental health worker to speak to the class about alcoholism and other forms of substance abuse. (Key Skill: *Communication*)
5. **Writing.** Assign students to write a one-minute public service announcement for families facing challenges. Have them tape record their PSAs, and share them with the class. (Key Skills: *Communication, Creativity*)

Follow Up

1. **Reteaching.** Assign students to write a short paper about how divorce and substance abuse may affect families and individual family members. (Key Skill: *Communication*)
2. **Enrichment.** Have students research and debate the following: "All divorced parents should have joint custody of their children." (Key Skills: *Communication, Critical Thinking*)

Family Perspective

Alcoholism is a physical and psychological dependence on alcohol. It has three clearly defined stages that happen over a period of time (1. Social drinking; 2. Gradually reaches the point when person can't stop drinking; 3. Final stage — uncontrolled drinking). Have students read about the stages of alcoholism, and discuss how families may be affected in each of the stages.

Teaching. . .
Challenges: Effects; Solutions
(pp. 156-157)

Comprehension Check

1. What are some signs that teens may have a drug or alcohol problem? *(They do poorly in school or on the job; frequently fight with parents; may have a "don't care" attitude; may turn to additional drugs; may attempt suicide; may have legal troubles.)*
2. Why is it recommended that family members not assume responsibilities for an alcoholic in the family? *(To avoid enabling the person to continue drinking.)*
3. Name two self-help groups that may be helpful to friends and family members of alcoholics. *(Alateen and Al-Anon.)*
4. What can friends and family members of an alcoholic learn from Alateen and Al-Anon? *(How to deal with the alcoholic in order to promote possible recovery.)*

Learning Activities

1. **Debate.** Select students to debate the statement: "You have to drink to be popular." (Key Skills: *Communication, Critical Thinking*)
2. **Discussion.** Talk about reasons why it is difficult for people to admit they have a drinking problem. (Key Skills: *Critical Thinking, Communication*)
3. **Guest Speaker.** Ask a representative from Mothers Against Drunk Driving (MADD) to talk about problems of drinking and driving and the work MADD is doing to prevent drunk driving. (Key Skill: *Communication*)
4. **School and Community Service.** Some schools have chapters of SADD (Students Against Drunk Driving). If there is no chapter in your school, ask for volunteers to work to establish one. (Key Skills: *Problem Solving, Citizenship*)

The Effects

Young or old, people with any drug problem can make life very difficult for their families. Their behavior often becomes troublesome. Out of touch with themselves and reality, they may say what they normally would not. Often they deny that they have a problem. Their actions may be abusive, endangering themselves and others. They often neglect their responsibilities. Financial problems may occur due to the cost of the drug or perhaps the loss of a job. They may even turn to crime to pay for a drug habit.

When teens use alcohol and other drugs, they face serious consequences that can affect them for life. Long-lasting physical, psychological, and emotional effects, can interfere with how well teens do in school or on the job. They frequently fight with their parents and have a "don't care" attitude. Sometimes they even turn to additional drugs. Also, since their use of alcohol and many other drugs is against the law, they may face serious legal troubles.

Loved ones are saddened, frustrated, and angered when a family member has a subtance abuse problem. The result is often hurt and broken families. As you can see, this is a problem for society, too. A society with many troubled families cannot be strong. Obviously, the way to break the cycle is to stop substance abuse at its base — with the individual.

Looking for Solutions

The best solution to the substance abuse problem is prevention. If you don't start — with alcohol or any other kind of drug — you won't have a problem.

Unfortunately for some people, it is too late for prevention. They already have the problem and they need somewhere to turn. If you need help for yourself, a friend, or a family member, look in the yellow pages of area phone books

For people who need help with substance abuse, there are many counseling centers and programs that provide treatment.

More About *MADD*

Mothers Against Drunk Driving (MADD) is a non-profit organization made up of mothers, fathers, grandparents, high school and college students and other citizens who are concerned about driving while impaired. MADD assists victims of drunk driving by offering emotional support, criminal justice assistance, and referrals to other community resources.

Members of MADD also work to educate the public about the serious consequences involved in impaired driving. In addition, they strive to achieve stricter legislation against impaired drivers.

How to ...
Get Help for Alcoholism

The following organizations provide help for alcoholics and their families. Look for locations for the first three in the telephone directory.

- ***Alcoholics Anonymous (AA)***. All members are recovering alcoholics. The members provide support to others who are trying to remain sober. This is done through regular meetings.
- ***Alateen.*** Children and teens who have an alcoholic parent(s) are helped in Alateen.
- ***Al-Anon.*** This group helps the friends, husbands, wives, and other relatives of alcoholics.
- ***National Council on Alcoholism and Drug Dependence.*** The council provides information and a list of organizations that can help. The address is 12 W. 21st St., 8th Floor, New York, NY, 10010.

under "Drug Abuse" or "Alcoholism." You will find lists of counselors and programs that provide help with every kind of drug problem.

If you are concerned about someone close to you who is an alcoholic, some specific guidelines may be useful.

- Let the person know you are concerned and willing to help.
- Discuss the problem calmly and specifically. Call the problem by its name, alcoholism, and tell the person what is happening to the family and the alcoholic because of the addiction.
- Don't assume responsibilities for the drinker. This just enables the person to continue drinking.
- Never argue with someone who has been drinking. The person is not able to think clearly and may react in a violent way.

Learning Activities (continued)

5. **Reading.** Ask students to read and collect newspaper and magazine articles about accidents and deaths caused by people who had been drinking alcohol or using drugs. Have them share some of the stories with the class. (Key Skill: *Communication*)
6. **Guest Speaker.** Invite a police officer to speak to the class about the relationship alcohol has to accidents and deaths in the community. (Key Skill: *Communication*)
7. **Booklets.** Select a small group of students to design and create a booklet that lists and describes alcohol and drug treatment services available in the community. Duplicate the booklet, and share it with the class. (Key Skills: *Problem Solving, Cooperation*)

Follow Up

1. **Reteaching.** Have students brainstorm a list of ways to refuse alcohol and drugs. (Key Skills: *Communication, Critical Thinking*)
2. **Enrichment.** Ask students to locate answers to the following questions: What are some of the behaviors of alcoholics? In what ways does each of the behaviors affect the other? Why is it dangerous for alcoholics to drink in social situations? Why is hospitalization sometimes necessary during the detoxification of an alcoholic? (Key Skills: *Communication, Critical Thinking*)

How to ... Get Help for Alcoholism

After reading the feature, select students to set up an *All You Need to Know About Alcoholism* table at school. Have them provide information about local resources for alcoholics and their families and friends. Assign other students to research two local support groups for alcoholics and their families. Ask them to interview a facilitator from each group to learn about the program. If no group presently exists, have students interview counselors, religious leaders, and other members of the community about the need for such a group in the area.

Teaching. . .

Challenges: Violence; Crime; Death; Getting Help

(pp. 158-160)

Comprehension Check

1. Who are potential victims of abuse in a violent home? *(A spouse, child, disabled person, or an older adult.)*
2. Name four forms of abuse. *(Emotional, physical, neglect of a child or disabled person, and sexual abuse.)*
3. What are two immediate needs of an abused person? *(Someone who will listen, possible shelter.)*
4. What is the best defense against crime? *(Following safety rules.)*
5. What are four helpful ways to handle grief? *(Talking, crying, thinking about the good memories you have of the deceased, time to recover.)*
6. What are support groups? *(Groups made up of people who have personal experience with specific problems.)*
7. Name three sources of outside help for family challenges. *(Libraries, police and fire departments, medical services, support groups, welfare assistance, religious and community organizations, social workers, school counselors, and teachers.)*

Learning Activities

1. **Crisis Intervention.** Ask a crisis counselor to speak with the class about why violence occurs, the effects of violence on the family and society, help that is available to victims, and how families can recover from violence. What might students do if they or someone they know is in a violent situation? (Key Skills: *Critical Thinking, Problem Solving*)
2. **Preventing Crime.** Have students develop a plan of action to keep themselves and their families as safe as possible against crime. (Key Skill: *Problem Solving*)
3. **Interview.** Have students talk with individuals who have been members of a grief support group. Ask students to find out how these people coped with grief. Have students write a brief summary about what they learned. (Key Skill: *Communication*)

Let the alcoholic know that help is available. Talk about the agencies listed in the chart on page 157. Realize, however, that the alcoholic must be ready to seek assistance. You cannot do this for the person. Even when the alcoholic is unwilling to find help, friends and family members can. They can learn how to deal with an alcoholic in order to promote possible recovery. Alateen and Al-Anon, described in the chart, have suggestions. With help, many alcoholics and their families have succeeded in finding the road to recovery.

Violence is destructive to families and is never acceptable. Help is available for individuals and families dealing with domestic violence. Many times, the victims of abuse need to seek help before the abuser gets help.

▼ Violence in the Home ▼

Another kind of abuse occurs when someone harms or threatens another's physical or mental health. Abuse can be aimed at a **spouse** (one's husband or wife), a child, a disabled person, or an older adult.

Abuse comes in several forms. Emil grew up feeling that he was worthless. Constant put-downs from his father caused this *emotional abuse*. Mr. Brown *physically abused* his wife by hitting her when he was angry. *Neglect* was cited when two small children were found in an apartment without food or adult supervision. *Sexual abuse* happened when Tracy was subjected to sexual activity by an adult.

Every one of these types of abuse is wrong. No excuse can make them right for anyone. People who are abused need help. The risk of serious physical and emotional damage cannot be ignored. An abused person must find someone who will listen and provide shelter if needed. Some teens try to run away from abusive situations. The result can be more trouble from strangers who take advantage of them. Many communities have safe places for abused people to go. You can locate them by calling 911 (or the emergency number in your area) or asking for a referral at a hospital emergency room or from a religious organization.

Violence is destructive to families. A person who is abusive in any way needs to learn self-control. This may not happen unless the victims seek help first.

More About Family Violence

Issues of power and control are at the core of violence in the family. There are many ways an abuser will attempt to gain control over the victim. These may include: physical violence such as hitting; controlling the money available to the family; or threatening to take the children if the victim reports the abuse. The victims of abuse, often women and children, feel powerless. They may not seek the help they need because of low self-esteem.

▼ Crime ▼

The fear of becoming a victim of crime can be very stressful. Anyone can become a victim of crime. Those who live alone or are elderly or disabled feel especially at risk. Following safety rules is the best defense. What safety rules do you and your family follow to prevent crime?

Victims of crime can be deeply scarred. Family and friends need to rally around to give support. Crimes, as well as any suspicious activity, should be reported to the police immediately.

When a family member commits a crime, the rest of the family suffers. The best approach is to seek legal help and work to get the person's life back on track.

▼ Death ▼

No family can escape death. When it happens, a grieving process follows. People go through grief in very different ways. Family members need to allow each other to mourn in their own ways.

In handling grief, talking and crying are useful. It is important to release the strong feelings that are inside. Try to think about the good memories you have of the deceased, and give yourself some time to recover.

If you know someone who is grieving, reach out in some way. Simple acts are usually most appreciated — a card, a phone call, or a short visit, for example. Simple words are

SAFETY CHECK ✔

Here are some safety rules to follow to help prevent crime:

- Keep doors and windows locked on the inside.
- Never give your address and telephone number to people you do not know well.
- Keep emergency telephone numbers next to the telephone especially if your area does not have 9-1-1 service.
- Let someone know where you are when you are away from home.
- Carry a whistle when you walk alone or find others to walk with you.
- Always carry identification and telephone numbers of people to contact in case of emergency.

Talking with a trusted adult or qualified counselor can help you cope with many different types of problems. Where could you turn for help if you needed it?

More About *Accepting Death in the Family*

In their grief and mourning, family members and friends of a dying person usually go through a series of stages. The first stage is one of denial or disbelief. The stage of anger follows, and may be directed toward the dying person. If there is forewarning of the death, the grieving person may bargain to prolong the dying person's life. As the grieving person realizes the futility of this, depression may set in. With time, survivors pass to a stage of acceptance as they understand that the death of the person is a reality.

Learning Activities (continued)

4. **Discussion.** Discuss with students what they might say when talking with someone who has recently experienced the death of a loved one. Talk about ways that students might help the family cope with their grief. (Key Skill: *Critical Thinking*)

Follow Up

1. **Reteaching.** Have students use newspapers and telephone books to compile a list of local support groups. Post the list in the classroom. (Key Skill: *Communication*)
2. **Extension.** Have the students read the extension material on p. 22 from the *Extending the Lesson* booklet of the TCR.
3. **Enrichment.** Select volunteers (with parental permission) to visit a hospice and talk with employees and with those who receive its services. Ask students to keep a journal of the experience and, afterwards, evaluate how their views of illness and death have been changed by the experience. (Key Skills: *Communication, Problem Solving*)

Wellness

One of the top three causes of death among teens is suicide. Remind students that most people who attempt suicide really do not want to die, but are looking for help. Suggest to students that they may be of help in preventing suicide. Being aware of warning signs, such as depression, change in sleep and eating patterns, a change in grades, giving away possessions, and increased risk-taking, is a key to providing help. (Note: Some research indicates that the number of suicide attempts often rises when suicide is addressed through the media or discussion.)

SAFETY CHECK ✔

After reading the feature, have students prepare an emergency identification card to carry with them when they are away from home.

Completing the Chapter

For Review

1. Emphasize the main concepts using the summary.
2. Have students complete the "Facts to Recall." (Answers below.)

For Reteaching

1. **Reteaching.** Use the activity on p. 20 of the *Reteaching and Practical Skills* booklet in the TCR.

For Enrichment

1. **Enrichment.** Use the activity on p. 31 of the *Enrichment Activities* booklet in the TCR.

For Evaluation

1. Choose items from "Ideas to Explore" and "Activities to Try."
2. Use the chapter test on pp. 31-32 of the testing booklet in the TCR or use the testmaker software.

Facts to Recall Answers

1. Can hurt if you look only at negative side, think of what must be given up. Can help when you see what you have to gain from situation.
2. Keep positive attitude; don't make parents feel guilty; help more at home; get part-time job.
3. Libraries; physician; others who have gone through similar difficulties.
4. They may feel they are cause of divorce; parents may try to make them take sides; children may have more responsibilities, less time with parents; children must be careful about how they view parents.
5. Individuals may become abusive, endanger selves and others, neglect responsibilities, do themselves long-lasting harm. Family members are saddened and frustrated; families can be broken.

helpful, too. Be a good listener both now and later, when the grieving person may feel that everyone has forgotten about the person who died.

As with any other serious problem that people face, counseling is available. Counseling can be especially useful to people who have been through a loss.

Getting Help

People need not face challenges alone. Relatives, neighbors, and friends can help in times of need. Many willing people stand ready to give emotional and financial support.

Communities have many services for families. Libraries are a good source of information. Police and fire departments provide assistance in emergencies. Medical services and support groups are available in most communities. Support groups are made up of people who have personal experience with similar problems. Welfare assistance is available to families who cannot meet their basic physical needs. Religious and community organizations provide families with many services, such as crisis centers and hot lines. Professionals, including social workers, religious leaders, school counselors and trusted teachers, also give aid. Help is just around the corner if people will only ask.

TAKING ACTION

Consoling a Grieving Friend

Your friends have gathered to watch a video together. No one is really focused on the movie, though. Although Carter never missed get-togethers before, he is not with you tonight. His father died last month after a long bout with cancer, and Carter is home with his family.

Since the funeral, Carter has seemed distanced from all of you. He hasn't shown up for lunch in the cafeteria since returning to school. You've all seen him in the halls and in classes, but he hasn't really had anything to say. "I don't know what to say to him anyway," Devon says.

Without saying so, you silently agree with Devon, but you know that avoiding Carter is not the answer. Aaron wants to just leave Carter alone, thinking he'll come around when he wants to. You are not so sure.

Using Your Resourcefulness

- Why do you think Carter is acting so distant?
- Evaluate the responses of Carter's friends.
- What suggestions do you have for Carter and the others?

TAKING ACTION

Invite a funeral home director or hospice worker to talk with students about the grieving process and how to help someone who has experienced a loss.

Then have students read the feature and respond to the questions.

Using Your Resourcefulness Answers

- Answers will vary. Carter is feeling the loss of his father and may not know how to express those feelings to his friends.
- Answers will vary.
- Answers will vary.

Chapter 14 Review

Summary

In this chapter, you have read about:

- Challenges that families must handle.
- How a positive attitude can help you cope with different situations.
- How you can help others in their hard times.
- Outside resources that can help you cope with challenges.

Facts to Recall

1. How can your attitude hurt or help the situation when a new member is added to the family?
2. How can a teen help parents if one or both become unemployed?
3. Identify three sources of information about illnesses and disabilities.
4. Explain the special difficulties that children face during and after a divorce.
5. Describe how substance abuse affects individuals and families.
6. List six guidelines for confronting an alcoholic about his or her problem.
7. Is abuse always physical? Explain.
8. Why is it important for abused people to seek help?
9. What people are especially at risk of crime?
10. What are some simple but effective ways of reaching out to a grieving person?
11. Name four community resources available to families in times of difficulty.

Ideas to Explore

1. What would you do to support a friend whose family was having problems?
2. Why do you think many people have trouble asking for help in times of crisis?
3. Why do you think some people stay in abusive situations?
4. Why do you think some people have difficulty reaching out to a grieving person?
5. What time do you think is worse for a person who is grieving over the death of a loved one — the time of the funeral or the days that follow? Defend your answer.

Activities to Try

1. Working together as a class, try to rank all the challenges described in the chapter in order of difficulty. Start with the least difficult to handle and end with the most. Why is it hard to agree on the ranking?
2. List ways you could help your family through tough financial times or unemployment.
3. Investigate the resources available in your community for families who need help with different problems.

LINK TO *Communication*

CRISIS ASSISTANCE

Teens may feel overwhelmed, helpless, and alone when confronted by one of the challenges that families may face. Friends may not know how to help. Work with your classmates to develop a student assistance program for your school. Your efforts might include the following:

1. Develop a crisis handbook that provides facts about a variety of crises that families may face. In the handbook, include tips on ways teens can help their families and each other during times of crisis. In addition, create a directory of sources of information and organizations that provide help to families with problems.
2. Work with a faculty sponsor (such as a guidance counselor) to develop a student counseling program for your school.

Facts to Recall Answers (continued)

6. Let person know you are concerned; discuss problem calmly; don't assume responsibilities for drinker; never argue with someone who has been drinking; let alcoholic know help is available.
7. No. It can be emotional when person is made to feel worthless; neglect when children are deprived basic needs; sexual when person is subjected to unwanted sexual activity.
8. They must save selves from physical or emotional damage; abusive person needs to learn self-control.
9. Those who live alone, those who are elderly or disabled.
10. Send a card; call on the phone; pay a short visit; be a good listener.
11. **Any four:** libraries; police and fire departments; medical services; support groups; welfare assistance; religious and community organizations; other professionals trained to give support.

Ideas to Explore

1. Answers will vary.
2. Answers will vary. Low self-esteem may keep them from asking. May not want to be a burden to others.
3. Answers will vary.
4. Answers will vary. May feel awkward, not knowing what to say.
5. Answers will vary.

LINK TO *Communication*

Answers

1. Crisis handbooks will vary according to available community resources.
2. Student counseling programs will vary depending on student needs. Student must work closely with the guidance counselor in addition to receiving some specific crisis intervention training.

Preparing to Teach

Chapter Outline

Chapter Resources

The following booklet materials may be found in the *Teacher's Classroom Resources* box:

- Lesson Plans, p. 20
- Student Workbook, *Study Guide,* pp. 67-68; *Children's Stages of Development,* p. 69; *Children's Growth and Development,* p. 70; *Child Development Word Puzzle,* p. 71; *Clues to Development,* p. 72
- Color Transparencies, *Developmental Stages,* CT-15
- Technology and Computers, p. 16
- Cooperative Learning, p. 27
- Extending the Text, *Helping Children Learn,* pp. 23-24
- Reteaching and Practical Skills, *A Babysitter's Bag of Tricks,* p. 22
- Enrichment Activities, *Observing Development,* p. 30
- Chapter and Unit Tests, pp. 33-34
- Testmaker Software

Also see:

- Leadership and Citizenship
- Meeting the Special Needs of Students
- Linking Home, School, and Community
- Dealing with Sensitive Issues

ABCNews InterActive™ Videodiscs

- *Teenage Sexuality*
- *Alcohol*
- *Tobacco*
- *Drugs and Substance Abuse*

See the ABCNews InterActive™ Bar Code Correlation booklet for applicable segments.

CHAPTER 15

Understanding How Children Grow

OBJECTIVES

- *Describe the four main stages of development.*
- *Explain how children develop physically, intellectually, emotionally, socially, and morally.*
- *Discuss influences on development.*

TERMS TO LEARN

- ***fetus***
- ***infancy***
- ***toddler***
- ***preschooler***
- ***conscience***

When Valerie took her first steps at eight months of age, her parents were delighted. They placed a chair close to the sofa and encouraged her to let go of one and toddle in the direction of the other. By twelve months, she was walking well. A few years later Valerie's little brother, Dylan, was still scooting along the floor at the age of thirteen months. Mr. Davis began to worry about his son. After all, Valerie had walked so much earlier. Then, one day his mind was put at ease. All of a sudden, Dylan just stood up and walked with very little trouble. Both children, the Davis family realized, were quite normal. They had just developed at different rates.

Stages of Development

Even though children develop at different rates, they still go through four main stages of development, or growth:

- ***Prenatal stage.*** This stage usually lasts about nine months as the **fetus** (FEE-tus), or unborn child, develops inside the mother's body. During this time, a single cell develops into a baby capable of surviving in the outside world.
- ***Infancy.*** The stage called **infancy** begins at birth and lasts about one year. Physical development occurs more quickly during infancy than any other stage of life.
- ***Childhood.*** This period begins at about one year of age. It lasts until the beginning of adolescence — at about eleven or twelve years. During childhood, a number of changes take place as the child grows and develops. To make it easier to understand this age group, many people break it into three smaller groups. A **toddler** is a child one to three years of age. A **preschooler** is three to five years old. Children enter the *school-age* category at age five and leave it when they enter adolescence.
- ***Adolescence.*** Next to infancy, the second fastest period of growth is adolescence. As you read in an earlier chapter, adolescence is the time of life between childhood and adulthood. Adolescence continues until the young person is able to assume adult responsibilities, usually between ages eighteen and twenty-two.

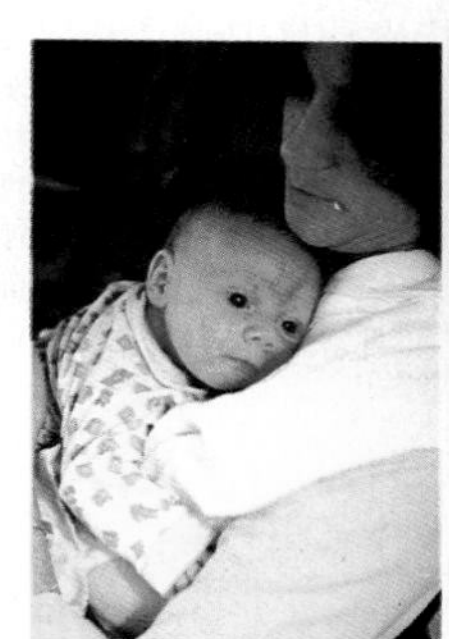

Children grow and develop in four main stages, but may grow at different rates.

More About *Prenatal Development*

The human body is made up of trillions of cells. Each has the ability to divide, reproduce, and repair itself, with the exception of cells that make up the nervous system. The human body begins as one cell, so tiny that it can be seen only with a powerful microscope. The first cell is formed by the union of an egg cell from the mother and a sperm cell from the father in a process called *fertilization*. The union of the egg cell and the sperm cell forms a fertilized egg cell that begins a complicated process of cell division. Over a nine month period, this fertilized egg cell develops and grows into a complex, fully formed individual.

Introducing the Chapter

Motivators

1. **Class Survey.** Take a class survey to find out how many students have younger siblings, have baby-sat, have changed a diaper, have visited a day care center, and have played with an infant or a younger child. (Key Skill: *Communication*)
2. **Bulletin Board.** Ask for volunteers (students and school personnel) to bring photographs of themselves when they were infants and young children. Display and label the photographs. Title the display "My, How We've Grown!" (Key Skill: *Creativity*)
3. **Writing.** Assign students to write a paper about the kind of family they hope to have in the future. Have them be as specific as possible, including the number of children, if any, they want to have. (Key Skills: *Communication, Critical Thinking*)
4. **Self-Quiz.** Ask students to make three vertical columns with the headings: prenatal stage, infancy, and childhood. Have them write as much as they can about each stage. Afterwards, ask students to share what they wrote under each heading. (Key Skills: *Communication, Critical Thinking*)

Chapter Objectives and Vocabulary

1. Have students read the chapter objectives. Ask them to rephrase the objectives as questions.
2. Ask students to state, in their own words, the purpose of studying this chapter.
3. Pronounce the vocabulary terms listed on the previous page. Ask students whether they are familiar with any of these. Explain that the terms will be defined in the chapter.

Guided Reading

1. Have students read the chapter and use the Study Guide on pp. 67-68 of the *Student Workbook*.

Teaching. . .

Stages of Development; How Children Grow and Develop; Physical; Intellectual

(pp. 163-165)

Comprehension Check

1. Describe the fetus' growth during the prenatal stage. (*It develops inside the mother's body, growing from a single cell to a baby capable of surviving in the world.*)
2. What is the difference between infancy and childhood? (*Infancy begins at birth and lasts about one year. Childhood begins at about one year of age and lasts until the beginning of adolescence.*)
3. Name the three small groups the period of childhood is often broken down into. (*Toddler, preschooler, school-age.*)
4. When does adolescence normally end? (*When the adolescent is able to assume adult responsibilities, usually between the ages 18-22.*)
5. What is the difference between intellectual and emotional development? (*Intellectual — involves the ability to learn, think, and judge. Emotional — means learning to control emotions and express them in acceptable ways.*)
6. What are three skills that require control of smaller muscles? (*Writing; throwing and catching balls; using tools.*)
7. Name four parts of the body that an infant uses to learn about his or her environment. (*Eyes, ears, mouth, and hands.*)

Learning Activities

1. **Guest Speaker.** Invite the science teacher or school nurse to speak to the class about the development of the fetus during the prenatal period. (Key Skill: *Communication*)
2. **Classroom Guests.** Invite several parents (and their infants) to come to class. Ask the parents to relate experiences about prenatal and infancy stages. Have students prepare questions beforehand to ask the parents. (Key Skills: *Communication, Critical Thinking*)

Except for infancy, adolescence is the second fastest period of growth. How have you noticed growth changes in yourself?

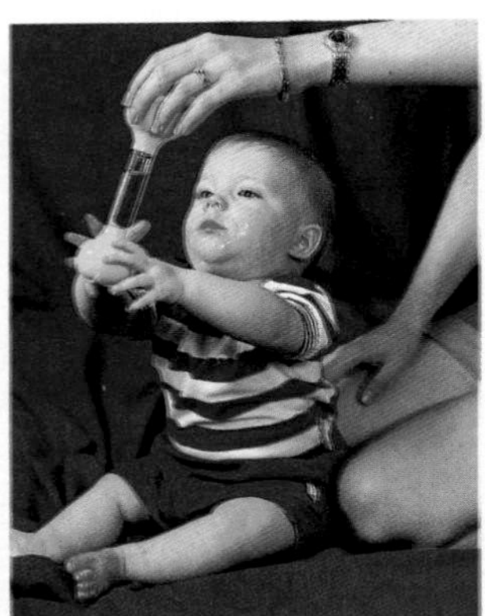

Gaining control over motor skills is an important part of infancy. During this time, infants learn to use their large muscles for walking and running. Control of smaller muscles is used for grasping objects, catching balls, and writing.

How Children Grow and Develop

Children grow and develop in several different ways. They grow in size and in muscle strength and coordination. This is called *physical development*. They grow in their ability to learn, think, and judge. This is *intellectual (mental) development*. *Emotional development* means learning to control emotions and to express them in acceptable ways. Through *social development*, children learn to interact with people in various situations. They must also learn to tell right from wrong. This is known as *moral development*.

Children grow in all of these areas at the same time. They don't develop physically one month and intellectually the next. In addition, children may be advanced in one area of development, but lag behind in another. They are learning right from wrong at the same time that they are learning to relate to people.

Physical Development

When Tyler was born, he had wrinkled skin and an oddly-shaped head. Because infants grow quickly, Tyler's parents knew that he would be very different in a short time. Not only would his appearance change, but his abilities would, too.

Gaining control over body muscles is one part of physical development. The skills needed for this control are called *motor skills*. During the first five years of life, children learn to master control of the large muscles needed for activities such as walking and running. They also start gaining better control of smaller muscles. These are needed for such skills as writing, throwing and catching balls, and using tools.

Infants learn to control their body movements beginning with their head and gradually working toward other parts of the body. At one month, an infant can briefly lift its chin when lying on its stomach. From three to four months, many infants can hold their heads steady, roll from side to back, and reach for objects such as toys. At five to six months, many infants can usually roll over completely, sit with support, and reach and grasp objects successfully. By seven months, most infants can sit alone and feed themselves some finger foods.

Babies must learn to use their eyes, arms, and hands together. Learning to grasp an object means that the baby knows exactly where the object is and can touch it. This takes time. By the ninth month, most babies can reach for an object and grasp it.

More About Learning to Walk

Learning to walk is an important accomplishment because it gives the child a feeling of independence. It also provides much more mobility for exploring the surrounding environment. At first, the toddler walks by holding on to furniture or other objects. The first steps alone are wobbly, with toes pointed outward and arms held out for balance. After a few shaky steps, the child collapses into a sitting position. Constant practice brings about improvement in balance and body control.

Walking movements begin at birth or perhaps even before. Newborn infants make kicking movements that look like walking. By stretching and kicking, babies strengthen and learn to control muscles of the legs and trunk. With increased strength and muscle control, babies can get up on their knees and crawl. The next step is to stand while holding onto furniture or a person. This helps develop balance, which is necessary before babies can walk alone. Some babies start to walk almost as soon as they can stand. Others take a month or more to try their first step. Many babies will walk with support by one year of age. Others take a little longer.

AROUND THE WORLD

The importance of protecting children against disease is demonstrated by the success of the United Nations World Health Organization's (WHO) vaccination program. When it was begun in 1974, less than 5% of children in developing nations were protected against childhood diseases, and over 3 million children died of diseases such as measles, polio, and whooping cough. Today, WHO workers vaccinate 80% of the world's children against these and other life-threatening diseases. WHO hopes to increase that number to 90% by the year 2000. The organization also hopes to reduce death from measles by 95% and to wipe out polio completely by the turn of the century.

▼ Intellectual Development ▼

As children grow intellectually, they develop the ability to learn, think, and judge. How will you see evidence of this growth? For one thing, children gradually understand more words and ideas. They can also pay attention for a longer time.

Infants learn with their eyes, ears, mouth, and hands. Colorful toys, trips to the store, reading books, and simple songs all provide learning experiences.

The main intellectual skill young children learn is language. Most children begin to talk around the middle of their second year. First, they speak individual words and phrases. By the third year, they speak full sentences. They can connect two thoughts, such as "The stove is hot and can burn me!" or "I'll hurt my brother if I hit him."

By their fourth year, most children seem to ask questions continually. They may ask questions like: "Why does Daddy have hair on his face?" "Why does my hair stay on my head?"

Children need to hear words in order to learn to speak. They must also have someone to talk with. All family members are important in helping children grow intellectually.

Spending time talking with children encourages intellectual development.

More About *Learning to Use Hands and Fingers*

Most children learn to feed themselves and to drink from a cup between the ages of one and two. Eye-hand coordination is poor at first, and there may be many spills. However, neatness improves with practice. Two- and three-year-olds grow increasingly skillful in using their hands and fingers. They learn to turn the pages of a book one at a time, turn on faucets, and use crayons. Around the age of three, children spend a great deal of time taking things apart and putting them back together again. Taking lids off jars and screwing them on again is a favorite activity for many children around this age.

3. **Observation.** Have students observe small children of similar ages at school, at home, or in the community. Ask them to note differences in the children's patterns of growth. Discuss their findings with the class. (Key Skills: *Communication, Critical Thinking*)
4. **Poetry Writing.** Assign students to write poems from the viewpoint of a preschooler looking back over the physical development that made him or her less like an infant. (Key Skills: *Communication, Creativity*)
5. **Discussion.** Talk about some of the changes a family must make after a baby starts to walk. (Key Skills: *Critical Thinking, Communication*)

Follow Up

1. **Reteaching.** Have students write six true statements about the four main stages of human development and six true statements about physical and intellectual development. Discuss in class. (Key Skills: *Communication, Critical Thinking*)
2. **Enrichment.** Ask for volunteers to study pictures of themselves between infancy and school-age. Have them write a paper analyzing changes they see in the size of their head, trunk, arms, and legs. (Key Skills: *Critical Thinking, Communication*)

AROUND THE WORLD

Have students read the feature and discuss the following information. Some immunizations, such as those for measles and mumps, require only one inoculation for lifelong immunity. Others, such as tetanus, need boosters every ten years throughout life. Because smallpox has been eliminated in the United States, there is no longer a requirement for the smallpox vaccination. However, people traveling to certain foreign countries still have to be vaccinated. Free polio vaccines are provided to children in various countries through the efforts of *Rotary International.*

Teaching. . . Emotional, Social, and Moral Development; What Influences Development? (pp. 167-168)

Comprehension Check

1. What are three ways that infants show emotions? *(Body movements, facial expressions, crying.)*
2. Name six specific emotions that are shown by children as they grow older. *(Joy, anger, fear, curiosity, jealousy, affection.)*
3. What are the three steps in social development? *(Learning to trust others, learning independence, learning acceptable behavior.)*
4. What is the difference between morals and a conscience? *(Morals — learned rules of behavior. Conscience — an inner sense of right or wrong that helps people monitor their own behavior.)*
5. What is the difference between heredity and environment? *(Heredity — traits inherited from parents. Environment — everything that surrounds and affects development and behavior.)*

Learning Activities

1. **Discussion.** Ask students to discuss ways that parents can help infants and young children develop intellectual skills. (Key Skills: *Communication, Critical Thinking*)
2. **Discussion.** Have students collect pictures of babies and young children showing various emotions. Discuss what emotions seem to be expressed in each instance. (Key Skills: *Communication, Critical Thinking*)
3. **Observation.** Assign students to plan and give a party for a small group of young children. Ask students to observe examples of social and emotional development. Afterwards, discuss their observations with the class. (Key Skills: *Problem Solving, Cooperation*)
4. **Questioning.** Have students discuss the following questions: What are some ways parents can help children become more independent? In what ways do parents and other adults help

Children show their emotions easily. What emotion is this young girl displaying?

▼ Emotional Development ▼

At first, infants can show emotions only by making body movements and facial expressions. They show they're unhappy by crying, kicking, and squirming. Infants respond in a happy way when sucking milk, when being rocked, or when someone speaks soothingly to them.

As children grow older, their emotions become more specific. They show joy, anger, fear, curiosity, jealousy, and affection. Children develop some of their emotional reactions by imitating, or copying, other people.

Children's emotions change rapidly. They may cry one moment and laugh the next. As children grow older, they learn to control their emotions.

▼ Social Development ▼

Social growth involves learning to interact with people in socially acceptable ways. Social development is closely linked to emotional development. Trusting others is the first step in developing socially. Children learn to trust when their caregivers feed them, answer their cries, and give them love and affection.

A second step in social development is to learn independence. Parents can help their children become independent. For instance, children's clothes should be easy to put on so that they can learn to dress themselves.

A third step is to learn acceptable behavior. At age two Michael threw his toys and screamed, "No, no!" when he was told to share them with another child. At age three, he clutched a toy tightly and refused to share it. By the time Michael was five, through consistent interaction with his parents and other children, he had learned to share his toys. He discovered that not only would his toys be returned, but he would also get to play with someone else's toys.

Learning to share is a challenging part of social development for a toddler.

▼ Moral Development ▼

Morals are generally accepted guidelines for right and wrong behavior. Children learn morals mainly in the home, in their place of worship, and in school.

At first, young children really don't understand the difference between right and wrong. They only know that some behavior makes adults upset or angry. Other behavior makes them happy. Gradually, they learn why certain actions are good or bad. With help from parents and caregivers, they develop a **conscience** (KAHN-chunts), an inner sense of right or wrong. This helps children monitor their own behavior.

More About *Child's Play*

Play is an important part of children's social development. As they grow, children go from playing alone to playing beside one another. Parallel play or playing beside, rather than actually with, other children varies from child to child. Some watch another child play with a toy while others will grab the toy away. Other children may seem to ignore the children nearby. In time, most learn to get along with their peers, take turns, and share. Parents can encourage development by letting children have the time, space, and materials to play alone, with other children, and with caregivers.

What Influences Development?

Two factors work together to shape a child into a unique — or special — individual. These are heredity and environment.

Heredity and Environment

In an earlier chapter, you learned that heredity refers to the traits that you inherit from your parents. It includes such characteristics as eye color, hair color and texture, height, and even some abilities. Environment is everything that surrounds you and affects your development and behavior. The way a family treats a child and the opportunities the child has to grow and develop are environmental influences.

Which do you think affects children more, heredity or environment? In truth, both heredity and environment are responsible for how children grow and develop. Children need both the ability to learn (heredity) and the opportunity to learn (environment). What if a child's diet is poor? With poor physical health, children may not have the energy to devote to learning new things. Without a good educational environment at home and at school, children may not develop their intellectual abilities. As you can see, both heredity and environment are important.

Heredity plays a part in who you are and what you look like. What hereditary traits do these young girls have?

Schools

School has high impact on children. Through this environmental influence, children gain knowledge and skills that prepare them for life. Schools teach reading, writing, and mathematics, which are all basic tools in today's world. Schools also teach important ideas about morality and social behavior. In school, children learn to relate to those outside the family. School is a testing ground for finding out what is socially accepted.

At school, children further develop their personality and self-concept. As Karin studies different subjects and meets

The first day of school is often an exciting day for young children. Schools provide an environmental influence in the development of children.

children learn morals? How else can children be taught an inner sense of right or wrong? (Key Skill: *Critical Thinking*)

5. **Research.** Have students investigate recent findings about the role of heredity and environment on children's growth and development. Ask them to share what they learn with the class. (Key Skills: *Science, Critical Thinking*)
6. **Round-Table Discussion.** Discuss the characteristics of home life that provide a good environment for children. (Key Skill: *Critical Thinking*)

Follow Up

1. **Reteaching.** Have students list and describe three steps in social development. Ask them to find pictures to illustrate each step. (Key Skills: *Critical Thinking, Communication*)
2. **Extension.** Have the students read the extension material on pp. 23-24 from the *Extending the Lesson* booklet of the TCR.
3. **Enrichment.** Assign students to observe infants, toddlers, and preschoolers playing with children of the same age. Have them record their observations, and compare and contrast the social development of each group. (Key Skills: *Critical Thinking, Communication*)

Family Perspective

The family is the place most infants and young children begin to develop socially. Family members are their first and closest relationships. As children grow, they need to learn about the outside world. Trips to the playground and opportunities to be with children and adults are important in developing socially. Lead students in discussing their early memories of family events and outings. Afterwards, brainstorm places to go for family outings. Categorize them as appropriate for infants, toddlers, or preschoolers.

More About *Moral Development*

Very young children only understand right and wrong in terms of being scolded or praised. With time, guidance on the part of parents and other adults helps children begin to understand why certain action are right or wrong. This is an important part of children's moral development. Guidance helps children develop a conscience, or an inner sense of what is the right thing to do. Children who have developed the ability to direct their own behavior in a responsible way have acquired self-discipline. In the process, they learn to make decisions and to take responsibility for their actions.

Completing the Chapter

For Review

1. Emphasize the main concepts using the summary.
2. Have students complete the "Facts to Recall." (Answers below.)

For Reteaching

1. Reteaching. Use the activity on p. 21 of the *Reteaching and Practical Skills* booklet in the TCR.

For Enrichment

1. Enrichment. Use the activity on p. 32 of the *Enrichment Activities* booklet in the TCR.

For Evaluation

1. Choose items from "Ideas to Explore" and "Activities to Try."
2. Use the chapter test on pp. 33-34 of the testing booklet in the TCR or use the testmaker software.

Facts to Recall Answers

1. **Prenatal:** lasts nine months, single cell grows into baby inside mother's body; **infancy:** birth to one year most rapid physical development; **childhood:** from one year of age to adolescence, changes take place as child grows and develops; **adolescence:** between childhood and adulthood, second fastest period of growth, continues until young person can assume adult responsibilities.
2. Infancy and adolescence.
3. Skills needed for control over the body's muscles. Turning the body from side to back; sitting alone; reaching for an object and grasping it; walking.

new people, she learns more about her own likes and dislikes and her strengths and weaknesses. As she relates to older children and adults, she begins to think about the future. "What will I be like as an adult? What will I do?" she wonders. The world is opening up to her through education. If she seizes the opportunities, success will surely follow.

Family

Even though schools have a great impact on children, nothing quite compares to the effects that families have. To do well in school and in life, children need to feel good about themselves. Praise, encouragement, and support from family members are important to developing self-esteem. Children who feel good about themselves are better able to work and complete tasks. On the other hand, children who are not encouraged may not be sure about what they can do and may not make the effort to try new things.

In addition to encouraging the development of self-esteem, families can help children develop their learning ability in a variety of ways. Family field trips to museums, dance classes, working on projects at home such as building models, and playing games together are all ways that families encourage learning.

TAKING ACTION

Understanding Children

Ron will get credit toward a family and consumer sciences class project when he volunteers after school at the Kaiser Child Care Center. His job is to assist in caring for a group of two-year-olds.

On his first day, he approaches and picks up a girl who is chewing on a block. She starts to wail loudly. Ron quickly puts her down and goes over to a boy who is crawling on all fours. Ron tries to talk to him, but the boy merely points at Ron's shoes and replies, "Ga-ga." Then the boy sits on Ron's foot and tries to untie his shoelaces. "Don't do that!" Ron orders. A third child walks over holding a toybox. She proceeds to drop the box and spill toys all over the floor. Ron tries to get her to pick them up, but she doesn't understand what he's saying.

Using Your Resourcefulness

- Evaluate Ron's behavior with each child. What other options of behavior does he have?
- Is each child's behavior appropriate for the physical and mental development of a two-year-old? Why or why not? What resource materials can teach you more about child development?
- What topics would you include if you were developing an orientation program for the teens who will be volunteering at the child care center?
- Are there volunteer services that work with small children in your area? How would one find them?

TAKING ACTION

Have students read the feature and respond to the questions.

Ask students to make a list of places where they usually see children during a normal day. Have them place a check mark on the list beside each place that could be a possible observation site. Encourage them to take time each week to observe some of the children. Ask for volunteers to make a video of several children at play. Show the video to the class, and have students write a short description of what they observed. Have students read some of their observations.

Chapter 15 Review

Summary

In this chapter you have read about:

- The stages of a child's development.
- How children develop physically, intellectually, emotionally, socially, and morally.
- How heredity and environment work together to affect a child's development.
- What children learn about themselves and their world in school.

Facts to Recall

1. Name and briefly describe the four main stages of child development.
2. During which two stages is growth the greatest?
3. What are motor skills? Put the following motor skills in order as they are learned by infants: reaching for an object and grasping it; turning the body from side to back; walking; sitting alone.
4. What is the main intellectual skill young children learn?
5. What is the first step in a child's social development? How can caregivers help children learn this?
6. How can parents help children become independent?
7. A five-year-old who shares her toys with her brother is displaying what type of growth?
8. How do heredity and environment work together to affect learning?
9. Besides skills like reading and mathematics, what do children learn in school?

Ideas to Explore

1. What do you think is the most important thing you can teach children to help them become happy, successful adults?
2. Discuss the conflict between teaching a child obedience, yet also encouraging independence. How can this problem be resolved?
3. After reading about the high impact of education on children, what qualities do you think a good teacher should have, besides knowledge of the subject taught?

Activities to Try

1. Choose one talent that you have. In a short paragraph, explain how it was developed through both heredity and environment.
2. List ten ways in which you can help a young child grow intellectually.
3. Discuss ten ways of helping children feel good about themselves when starting school.

LINK TO *Health*

GROWTH AND DEVELOPMENT CHART

A child's development progresses through different stages. The events of normal development do not always occur at the same age for all children. However, they usually occur in the same order. Develop a chart showing the events of normal development during infancy, the toddler stage, the preschool years, the early school years, and the adolescent years. You may need to check the library for additional resources. In the chart include physical, intellectual, emotional, social, and moral development at each stage.

Facts to Recall Answers (continued)

4. Language.
5. Trusting others; by feeding children, answering their cries, and giving them love and affection.
6. By making it easier for them to do things on their own.
7. Social growth.
8. Heredity provides abilities for learning, environment provides opportunities for learning.
9. Important ideas about morality and social behavior; to relate to those outside the family; their own personalities.

Ideas to Explore

1. Answers will vary.
2. Answers will vary. Reinforcing obedience to rules with praise and encouragement.
3. Answers will vary, but may include empathy, compassion, love of children, etc.

Using Your Resourcefulness Answers

- Answers will vary. Ron attempts to intervene in each situation; however, he appears to lack understanding about what to expect from children of this age. Ron might try modeling expected behaviors, speaking on the children's level, and possibly asking for assistance.
- Answers will vary. Students might suggest training about appropriate toys and activities for different ages and stages.
- Behavior is somewhat typical of children this age. Answers will vary.
- Answers will vary.

LINK TO *Health*

Answer

Individual charts will vary. Information should follow the general patterns for growth and development discussed in the chapter.

Preparing to Teach

Chapter Outline

Chapter Resources

The following booklet materials may be found in the *Teacher's Classroom Resources* box:

- Lesson Plans, p. 21
- Student Workbook, *Study Guide,* pp. 73-74; *Reporting on Children's Play,* p. 75; *Keeping Children Safe,* p. 76
- Color Transparencies, *Play It Safe,* CT-16; *Bathing a Baby,* CT-17
- Personal Safety, *Babysitting Safety,* p. 24
- Technology and Computers, p. 16
- Cooperative Learning, p. 28
- Extending the Text, *Turning "Treasures" into Toys,* p. 25
- Reteaching and Practical Skills, *Babysitting Dilemmas,* pp. 23-24
- Enrichment Activities, *Emergency Encounters,* p. 31
- Chapter and Unit Tests, pp. 35-36
- Testmaker Software

Also see:

- Leadership and Citizenship
- Meeting the Special Needs of Students
- Linking Home, School, and Community
- Dealing with Sensitive Issues

ABCNews InterActive™ Videodiscs

- *Food and Nutrition*
- *Tobacco*

See the ABCNews InterActive™ Bar Code Correlation booklet for applicable segments.

CHAPTER

16 Taking Care of Children

OBJECTIVES

- *Describe appropriate care for children of various ages.*
- *Identify special safety guidelines for children.*
- *Describe what to do in an emergency.*

TERMS TO LEARN

- ***poison control centers***
- ***first aid course***

Jason didn't know much about taking care of children until his sister and her son and daughter moved back home. Jason had to help out, and that meant doing everything from changing diapers to singing nursery rhymes. For the year that they were there, Jason learned so much. Sometimes it wasn't easy, but by the time they left, he knew more about children than he ever had before. He figured it all might come in handy someday.

Caring for Children

Children enter most people's lives at some point or another. Even if you never have any of your own, you may have to care for the children of friends and relatives sometime. Knowing what to expect will help you do a better job.

▼ Playtime ▼

Children need to play in order to grow and learn. In fact, play is sometimes called children's work.

Playing with Infants

Until he began looking after his eight-month-old niece Lara, Jason thought that babies must have a boring life. Like other infants around six to twelve months of age, Lara constantly tried to touch, taste, smell, and feel everything within reach. She was learning about the world through her senses.

Lara loved the games that Jason played with her. When he handed her a soft ball, she dropped it on the floor and watched him pick it up — again and again. Games like "pat-a-cake" and "peek-a-boo" delighted her. Lara's favorite toys were brightly colored ones. She had a variety of toys, including small blocks, big wooden beads, and rubber and plastic rings and balls. Jason even entertained her with plastic measuring cups and puppets he made from an old pair of socks. He talked to her as they played, which helped her with language skills.

Playing with Toddlers

A toddler's play is more active than an infant's. Toddlers can also concentrate on an activity longer. They like to play with simple toys that can be taken apart and put together again. Blocks and boxes of different sizes make ideal toys. Toddlers ages two to three also enjoy simple puzzles, storybooks, coloring books, large crayons, and paper.

Laticia's caregiver, Mrs. Odell, makes sure Laticia has room for walking and running during playtime. When two-year-old Laticia gets bored or frustrated, Mrs. Odell helps her

Introducing the Chapter

Motivators

1. **Class Survey.** Survey the class to find out how many students have babysat an infant or young child. Ask how many regularly serve as caregivers of young siblings or other young relatives. (Key Skill: *Communication*)
2. **Agree or Disagree.** Take a class poll to determine the age students think most people are responsible enough to babysit. Discuss reasons for their answers. (Key Skill: *Critical Thinking*)
3. **Brainstorming.** Have students brainstorm a list of things to know when caring for infants and young children. Talk about available resources to help teens learn about children (textbook, library resources, parents, relatives, etc.) (Key Skills: *Critical Thinking, Communication*)
4. **Discussion.** Ask for volunteers to share caregiving or babysitting experiences. Talk about ways the experiences could have been improved. (Key Skill: *Critical Thinking*)
5. **Questioning.** Ask and discuss the following questions: Why is "babysitting" not a very accurate term? What are the qualities of a good babysitter or caregiver? (Key Skill: *Critical Thinking*)

Chapter Objectives and Vocabulary

1. Have students read the chapter objectives. Ask them to rephrase the objectives as questions.
2. Ask students to state, in their own words, the purpose of studying this chapter.
3. Pronounce the vocabulary terms listed on the previous page. Ask students whether they are familiar with any of these. Explain that the terms will be defined in the chapter.

Guided Reading

1. Have students read the chapter and use the Study Guide on pp. 73-74 of the *Student Workbook*.

More About *Infants*

Newborn infants sleep about ninety percent of the time. Half of this time is spent in quiet sleep, the other half in active sleep. These two states alternate about every thirty minutes. In quiet sleep, a baby's face is relaxed, and the eyelids are closed and still. There are no body movements except rare startles and slight mouth movements. The infant is at full rest, and breathing is very regular. In active sleep, a baby's eyes are usually closed, but occasionally they will flutter from closed to open. While they remain asleep, infants in this state often make faces, and may display chewing or sucking movements.

Teaching. . .
Caring for Children: Playtime; Mealtime
(pp. 171-173)

Comprehension Check

1. Why is play sometimes called "children's work?" *(It helps children grow and learn.)*
2. How do babies learn about the world? *(Through touch, taste, smell, and feel.)*
3. Why is it helpful to talk to infants during any activity? *(To help them with beginning language skills.)*
4. What are two ways to keep toddlers from becoming bored or frustrated? *(Variety in activities; alternate active play with quiet play.)*
5. What are two statements by preschoolers that indicate they are proud of new abilities? *("Watch me!" "I'm the best!")*

Learning Activities

1. **Discussion.** Display toys or pictures of toys for students to examine. Ask students to choose appropriate toys for children of various ages. Discuss the reasons for their choices. Talk about types of toys that can help infants and small children learn. (Key Skills: *Problem Solving, Critical Thinking*)
2. **Guest Speakers.** Invite a preschool or kindergarten teacher to talk to the class about toys and games that children enjoy. Ask the speaker(s) to demonstrate how to teach a game to young children. (Key Skill: *Communication*)

TIPS:

Babysitting Basics
Have students read the feature. Discuss the importance of each suggestion. Ask students to prepare a "babysitting bag" that includes a notepad to write down necessary information along with age-appropriate games, activities, and books for children the students often care for.

TIPS: *Babysitting Basics*

Some teens earn money by taking care of children. Here are some tips that can help:

- Write down the name, address, and telephone number of the people you work for. Have this available for your family while you are gone.
- Find out about the job before you go: time and date (write this down); names and ages of children; transportation.
- Agree on your fee and duties.
- Be prompt.
- Ask the parents where they can be reached.
- Be sure that emergency phone numbers — doctor, police, fire department, ambulance, poison control center — are available. Keep these and the phone number of a nearby neighbor by the phone. Also write down the address of the home you are in and put this by the phone. It must be accurate for emergency personnel to find you quickly.
- Ask parents for any special instructions about medication for children, meals or snacks, bathing and bedtime routines and times, and television viewing.

(Continued on next page)

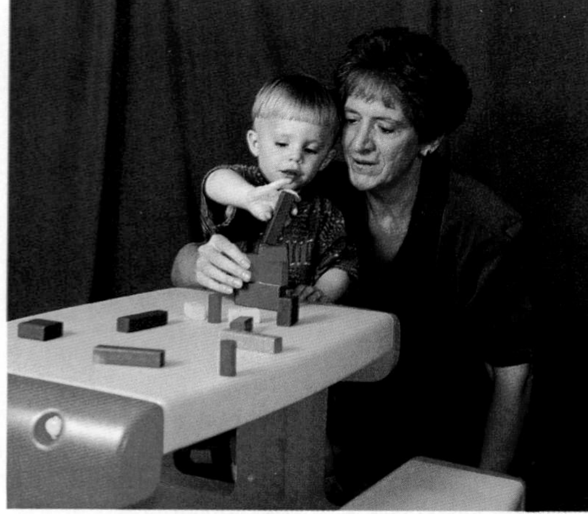

Playing with toddlers can require a lot of patience. When you care for toddlers, be sure to plan a variety of active and quiet play experiences.

find a different activity. She often alternates active play, such as running or throwing a ball, with quiet play. Mrs. Odell talks to Laticia often, describing what she is doing and what she sees.

Playing with Preschoolers

As a preschooler, Charlie is very proud of his new abilities. Often he says something like, "Watch me!" or "I'm the best!" He also has many questions. He is very curious, trying to understand so many new things. Charlie's parents and older sister try to answer his questions as patiently and clearly as they can.

Preschoolers like both active and quiet play. Many can ride a tricycle with ease. They may like to throw and catch balls. For quiet play, they enjoy books, finger paints, clay, crayons, and coloring books. They can also learn to cut with blunt scissors. When you care for preschoolers, take time to read them stories, making sure they see books as fun. Ask them to tell you stories of their own.

Preschoolers love exploration. For example, try turning over a rock to see what you find. On a tour through the neighborhood, a park, or a store, talk about what you see. Even the simplest occasions are opportunities for discovery.

Preschoolers love to pretend. Dressing up and acting like other people is fun. A box of old clothes and accessories can be a treasure to a child of this age.

Learning to play with others is important to preschoolers. Encourage them to join with others and share their toys.

More About *Infant Senses*

The skin is the largest sense organ of the human body. The sense of touch is especially developed in infants; and this can be observed in their enjoyment of closeness, warmth, and tactile comforting. Infants generally like to be cuddled, and will often nestle and mold to a caregiver's body. Parents and caregivers all over the world naturally lift, hold, stroke, rock, and walk with their infant, as well as use other comforting touching motions to soothe the baby.

Playing with School-Age Children

Older children are better at playing on their own but will still want your attention. School-age children like to take part in running games, such as tag and hide-and-seek. When they are with others, you can be sure there will be plenty of activity and noise.

▼ Mealtime ▼

As a caregiver, you are responsible for a child's meals. This includes not only preparing healthy meals and snacks, but also serving them safely and making mealtime relaxing and refreshing. Here are some tips for feeding children:

▶ ***Infants.*** When you care for an infant, you may need to give a bottle. Many caregivers will warm the milk by setting the bottle in a bowl of warm tap water for a couple of minutes. Check the temperature by shaking the bottle upside down over your wrist. The milk should feel warm, not hot. Do you know why the bottle should not be heated in the microwave? The liquid heats unevenly and may be too hot in places.

If feeding the infant baby food that is to be served warm, make sure the food is no warmer than body temperature. It is not necessary to warm baby food. Give small spoonfuls. Be prepared for messiness. For a baby, eating is a new skill to learn as well as an opportunity for fun by sputtering and playing with the food.

Feeding infants can provide a real challenge to the caregiver. Be sure to ask the parents for specific instructions about what to feed infants and when to feed them.

Babysitting Basics (Continued)

- ▶ Ask parents for instructions about answering the phone and the door. Do not give information about where you are or about parents being gone to anyone on the phone. The safest approach to a knock at the door is to not answer it.
- ▶ Before the parents leave, locate the children's rooms and bathroom, first aid supplies, fire extinguishers, fire exits, and flashlights.
- ▶ Distract children with a game or toy if they are unhappy when parents leave.
- ▶ Be attentive to children at all times. Stay awake and keep the television volume low while children are sleeping so that you can hear any cries.
- ▶ Don't talk on the phone to your friends. It distracts you from caring for the children. The phone should be free for a call from the parents.
- ▶ Respect the family's property. This means cleaning up after yourself, eating only what you have permission to, and leaving closets, drawers, and mail alone.

Learning Activities (continued)

3. **Classroom Search.** Divide students into pairs to find at least one object in the classroom that could serve as an appropriate toy for an infant, toddler, or preschooler. Display the objects and discuss why each object makes an appropriate toy. (Key Skill: *Critical Thinking*)
4. **Collection Box.** Ask for volunteers to collect articles of clothing, etc. for dress-up games and activities. Help students plan and carry out a "Let's Pretend" party for preschoolers. Afterwards, discuss the party and the observations that were made. (Key Skills: *Problem Solving, Cooperation*)
5. **Discussion.** Discuss problems students have experienced with small children while playing and at mealtime. Talk about ways to handle problems effectively. (Key Skill: *Problem Solving*)

Follow Up

1. **Reteaching.** Assign students to collect recipes of simple, nutritious foods for children. Have them prepare recipes to share with the class. (Key Skill: *Critical Thinking*)
2. **Enrichment.** Select students to visit a supermarket or drug store and list the different brands of formula sold. For one brand, have them list the forms (concentrate, liquid, powder, etc.) in which the formula is sold and the unit price. Ask the students to contrast the advantages and disadvantages of using each form. (Key Skills: *Math, Critical Thinking*)

Family Perspective

Family life can provide an informal child development lab for many teens. Encourage students to talk with infant siblings and note how responsive they are to human voices. Have students note what happens when they talk to a baby a short distance from one ear in a gentle, high-pitched voice. *(Baby's eyes and head will turn toward teen's voice; face brightens, and eyes open wider.)*

More About *Preschoolers*

Most preschoolers speak clearly, use a good deal of expressive language, and are fairly advanced in all language skills. Around the third year, children move from understanding around three hundred words to around 1,000 words. Their intellectual skills grow, and stories become increasingly interesting to them. Invite a children's librarian to come to class and discuss appropriate and popular books for preschoolers. Encourage students to observe story time for children in the school or community library.

Teaching. . .
Mealtime; Bedtime; Changing a Diaper
(pp. 174-175)

Comprehension Check

1. What are three foods to avoid serving small children? *(Hard candy, nuts, popcorn, and any other food that might cause choking.)*
2. Name five foods that are popular as well as nutritious for preschoolers. *(Milk, cheese, crackers, peanut butter, fresh and dried fruit, vegetable sticks.)*
3. Name two techniques that are helpful when putting children to bed. *(Keep to a routine so children know what to expect; telling a story makes children more comfortable.)*
4. What are two ways to make changing a diaper a pleasant experience? *(Talk or sing to the baby; make up a game.)*

Learning Activities

1. **Panel Discussion.** Have a panel of teenagers who babysit share some of their experiences on the job. Discuss the differences involved in caring for and feeding infants, toddlers, and preschoolers. (Key Skills: *Communication, Critical Thinking*)

MEETING SPECIAL NEEDS

Caring for Children with Disabilities

Have students read the feature. Ask students to list reasons why people are sometimes uncomfortable around children and others with disabilities. What are some ways to become more comfortable? Have students investigate the support services available for children with special needs in your community.

MEETING SPECIAL NEEDS

Caring for Children with Disabilities

In many ways, children with physical and mental disabilities are like all others. They need love, attention, friendship, and family. Caregivers may need to provide special education, special exercises, and equipment. Patience and encouragement are important qualities for a caregiver.

Shawn first met Damon when Shawn's family living class put on a puppet show for severely disabled children. At first, Shawn was uncomfortable and afraid he would accidentally hurt Damon. Mrs. Davis, Damon's primary teacher, assured Shawn that Damon just needed love and attention like other children.

After several visits, Shawn was an expert at feeding Damon, playing with him, and entertaining Damon with books and stories. Although he could not speak, Damon's affection for Shawn sparkled in his eyes when his friend Shawn entered the room.

When the challenges are met, children with special needs can develop to their fullest potential. Many communities have support groups and services that help special needs children and their families succeed.

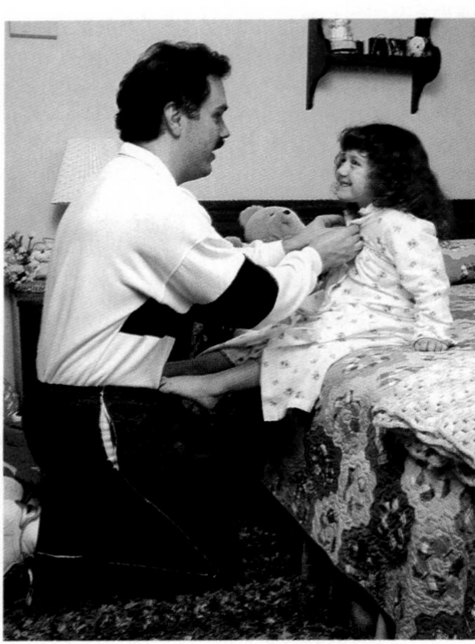

Following a regular bedtime routine helps make bedtime a comfortable and enjoyable experience for children and parents or caregivers.

- ▶ ***Toddlers.*** A toddler's first solid food is usually simple finger foods. Cut foods into bite-sized pieces to prevent choking. If a high chair is used, place it in a safe, easy-to-clean location. A bib can help protect the child's clothes.
- ▶ ***Preschoolers.*** Simple foods, such as milk, cheese, crackers, peanut butter, fresh and dried fruit, and vegetable sticks are popular as well as healthful foods for preschoolers. Even though they may lack neatness and good manners, they are somewhat skillful at eating. Keep mealtimes pleasant, without too many directions. Avoid giving foods that are high in fat and sugar. Never give small children hard candy, nuts, popcorn, or any other food that might cause them to choke.

▼ Bedtime ▼

Shawna leads her son in a quiet activity like coloring before bedtime to help settle him down. She lets Corey know about fifteen minutes early that bedtime is coming. Her attitude is kind but firm.

By following a bedtime routine every evening, Corey knows what to expect and is usually cooperative. A story and his special stuffed bear make bedtime comfortable and enjoyable for him. These techniques are helpful for most young children at bedtime.

How to ...

Change a Diaper

When changing a baby's diaper, try to make the experience a pleasant one. Talk or sing to the baby while you are diapering. Make up a game, such as patting the feet rhythmically, to associate with the process. The task will be easier if the child is willing. Here are the steps to follow:

1. Place everything you need within easy reach.
2. Place the child face up on a clean, flat surface. You might use a changing table, the crib, or a towel on the floor.
3. Remove the old diaper with the soiled part folded in. Keep one hand on the baby at all times.
4. Clean the baby with disposable wipes or a clean, damp, warm washcloth. It is important to wipe from front to back on female babies.
5. Lift the baby's legs with one hand, and slip a clean diaper underneath.
6. Secure disposable diapers with the tapes attached. Pin a cloth diaper with diaper pins. Always put your finger inside the diaper to protect the baby from being stuck as you pin.
7. Place the baby in the crib while you dispose of the old diaper. If it is disposable, put it in the garbage. If it is a cloth diaper, hold it firmly in a flushing toilet to rinse. Then place it in a diaper pail. Be sure to wash your hands thoroughly after diapering a baby.

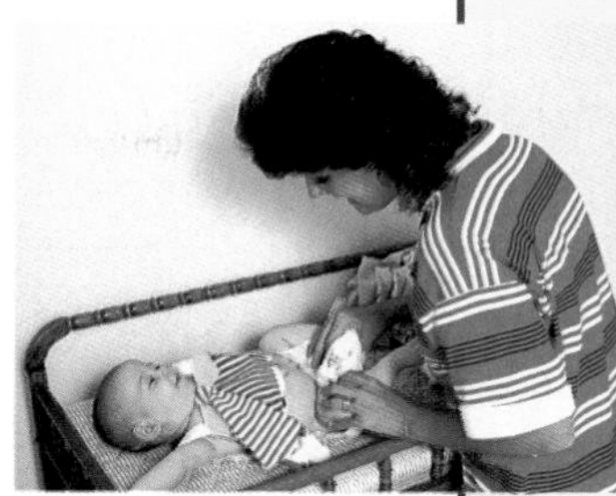

Steps 1, 2, and 3

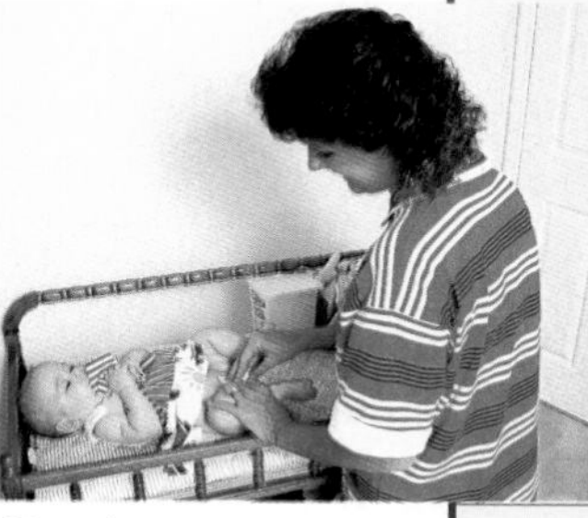

Step 4

Step 5

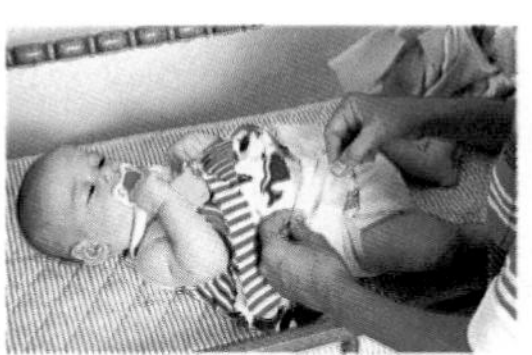

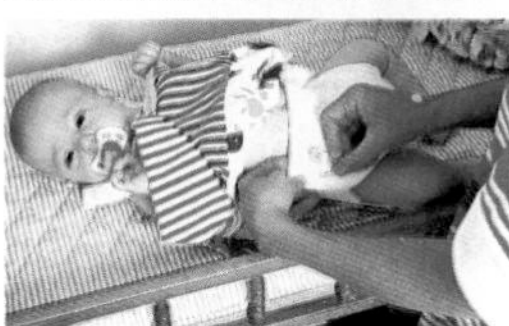

Step 6

Step 7

How to ... Change a Diaper

Have students read about and discuss the advantages and disadvantages of using cloth diapers, disposable diapers, or diaper services. What are the pros and cons of each choice? Ask students to demonstrate methods for folding cloth diapers. Talk about how the fold might differ based on the baby's gender.

Have several students investigate the variety of products available that are used when diapering a baby. Products may include such items as disposable wipes, baby lotion, ointments for diaper rash, etc. What are the costs of each? What might be some less costly alternatives?

Learning Activities (continued)

2. **Literature Evaluation.** Have students visit the children's section of a library and search for books that would be appropriate for bedtime stories. Ask each student to select and critique a children's book explaining why they think the book is a good choice for bedtime reading. (Key Skill: *Critical Thinking*)
3. **Demonstration.** Ask for volunteers to prepare a demonstration on diapering a baby. Have them share the demonstration with the class. (Note: Have students use a life-size baby doll for the demonstration.) (Key Skill: *Cooperation*)

Follow Up

1. **Reteaching.** After reviewing pp. 174-175, have students write a brief summary on feeding toddlers and preschoolers, bedtime for children, and diapering a baby. (Key Skill: *Communication*)
2. **Enrichment.** Have students investigate the effects of using disposable or cloth diapers on the environment. What are the long-term effects of using each? What factors should parents consider when choosing diapers? (Key Skills: *Critical Thinking; Communication*)

Wellness

Most babies and young children have a special method of comforting they like best especially at bedtime. Some like to be held and rocked. Other are comforted by sucking on a thumb, fist, or pacifier. Many children have a special stuffed toy or blanket that they like to hold. When you are caring for infants and children, it helps to know how best to comfort them. In what ways might building a sense of trust through providing comfort benefit a child's self esteem?

Teaching. . .
Keeping Children Safe: Indoors
(pp. 176-177)

Comprehension Check

1. What is one way you can be safety-minded and think about how small children see things? *(Get down on the floor to check for anything that could hurt a crawling baby.)*
2. Why is it unsafe to allow young children to stay in the bathroom alone? *(They may lock themselves in the room or get dangerous items from the medicine cabinet.)*
3. What are two reasons to lock all windows and outside doors when small children are around? *(To keep intruders out and children safely inside.)*
4. Where should poisonous products be stored? *(In a locked place.)*
5. What is a poison control center? *(A place with staff to advise and treat poison victims.)*

Learning Activities

1. **Exhibit.** Set up an exhibit of plants and trees that are poisonous to young children. Have students label and identify each example. (Key Skill: *Critical Thinking*)
2. **Brainstorming.** Lead students in brainstorming a list of household items that are hazardous to young children. (Key Skills: *Communication, Critical Thinking*)
3. **Reading.** Assign students to collect and read newspaper and magazine articles about accidents involving children. Discuss how each of the accidents might have been avoided. (Key Skills: *Critical Thinking, Communication*)

AROUND THE WORLD

Have students read the feature. Discuss with students the similarities of preschools in the United States to those of Reggio Emilia, Italy. What other types of activities and learning centers can students think of that would stimulate the creativity of young children? If possible, visit a nearby preschool for observation.

AROUND THE WORLD

The preschools of the Italian city of Reggio Emilia (REJ-joe ay-MEE-lee-ah) are designed to encourage creativity and love of learning and exploration. Children paint pictures on the classroom windows. They send letters to one another through the classroom "communication center." Classrooms even have dressing rooms with costumes for children who wish to "disguise" themselves for the day.

FRANCE
YUGOSLAVIA
ITALY

Keeping Children Safe

Part of being a good caregiver involves watching both the children and their surroundings. Your job is to make sure those under your care are safe, both inside and outside the home.

▼ Indoors ▼

When you're caring for small children, think about how *they* see things. Try getting down on the floor to check for anything that could hurt a crawling baby. Look for any small items a young child might put in his or her mouth. (Young children explore *everything* with their mouths.) Electrical outlets are less tempting to a child if they are covered. If this hasn't been done, put a chair or another large object in front of the outlet to keep the child away. Avoid placing items on the edge of a table where a crawling infant or toddler might pull them off.

The most important step you can take to keep children safe is to stay with them all the time. Until children are about five, don't let them stay in the bathroom alone. They may lock themselves in the room or get into the medicine cabinet where dangerous items like medicines and razor blades are stored.

Safety is very important when you bathe a child. Make sure you never leave young children alone in a bathtub. Even a minute away to answer the phone or get clean clothes can be tragic.

Stairways can be dangerous to children of all ages. Infants and younger toddlers can fall down stairs very easily. Keep them away from stairs and fasten any gates at stairways. Older toddlers and preschoolers need to be taught to hold onto the handrail to prevent falls.

More About *Taking Care of Children*

Sometimes children develop nosebleeds, and they usually occur without warning. Nosebleeds can be caused by an injury, by being in a very dry place for a period of time, or by a cold. Nosebleeds generally are not serious, but they should be stopped. When children have a nosebleed, they should be kept quiet and instructed not to blow their nose. Have them sit down and lean slightly forward with their head low. The nose should be pinched firmly for about five minutes or a cold cloth can be held to the nose. Remind students that if these measures do not stop the bleeding, they should get medical help.

Never leave a young child alone in the bathtub. If you must answer the telephone, take the child with you.

Doors and Windows

Make sure that all windows and outside doors are locked when small children are around. This will keep intruders out and the child safely inside. Falls from windows are more common than you might think. Safety is especially important in high-rise apartment buildings where windows can be many stories above the ground.

Poisons, Matches, and Lighters

Many ordinary products can be dangerous for children. Some are poisonous if swallowed. Others cause damage if breathed into the lungs or if they touch the skin or eyes. Common household poisons include insecticides, cleaning fluids and powders, furniture polish, and drugs, such as baby aspirin and vitamin pills. Even many houseplants are poisonous. Store poisonous products in a locked place.

How can you tell if a child has been poisoned? Here are some symptoms that can give you a clue:

- Choking, coughing, nausea, or dizziness.
- Unconsciousness or difficulty breathing.
- Vomiting from swallowing poisons or chemicals (may cause some burns around the mouth).
- Skin rashes or burns.

If you suspect that a child has been poisoned, immediately call the poison control center. **Poison control centers** have a special staff of people who advise and treat poison

MEETING SPECIAL NEEDS

Encouraging Gifted Children

Children who have an especially high level of ability in one or more areas, such as reading, math, music, or art, are known as gifted children. They often learn to read before starting school and enjoy adult company. Gifted children may constantly ask questions that show surprisingly advanced thought.

Gifted children need to be challenged without making them feel superior to, or different from, other children. Many schools and communities have programs that provide stimulating activities for gifted children.

More About *Child Safety*

Many household substances, such as cleaning fluids and detergents, should never be taken into the body. However, sometimes they are, especially by infants and young children. To help someone who has swallowed a poison, a 24-hour poison control center, the 911 emergency telephone number, or a physician should be called. The caller should be prepared to give the victim's age and weight, what was swallowed, how much was swallowed, and when. The caller should ask for instructions and follow them. The container of the poisonous substance that was swallowed should be saved to show to the medical workers.

Learning Activities (continued)

4. **Small Group Discussion.** Divide students into small groups, and have them discuss ways that families can make homes safer for children. Ask the groups to develop a checklist for home safety and share them with the entire class. (Key Skill: *Critical Thinking*)

Follow Up

1. **Reteaching.** Assign students to write public service announcements on ways to keep children safe indoors. Have them share their announcements with the class. (Key Skills: *Communication, Creativity*)
2. **Enrichment.** Select students to make a fire safety video giving tips on how to plan an escape during a home fire. Show the completed video in class. (Key Skills: *Critical Thinking, Creativity*)

Wellness

Knowing fire safety is a must for all caregivers of young children. Students should know that if they are caught in a fire, acting quickly and remaining calm could save lives. Ask the fire department to demonstrate the use of home fire extinguishers. Also, allow students to have "hands on" practice in using an extinguisher. Talk about the importance of regularly checking fire extinguishers and smoke detectors.

MEETING SPECIAL NEEDS

Encouraging Gifted Children

Have students read the feature and discuss the importance of challenging gifted children. Have students investigate programs available in your community that encourage and challenge gifted children. (Note: See *Meeting the Special Needs of Students* booklet in the TCR for more information.)

Teaching. . .
Keeping Children Safe: Toys; Outdoors; Handling Emergencies
(pp. 178-180)

Comprehension Check

1. Name four items, excluding poisons, to keep out of the reach of children. *(Ranges, stoves, heaters, hot water faucets, and hot drinks.)*
2. Why is it important to keep toys that make very loud sounds out of the hands of children? *(To prevent hearing damage.)*
3. Name two things children should be taught about streets and roads. *(Never play in the street or road; never chase balls that roll into the street or road; cross streets safely.)*

Learning Activities

1. **Display.** Select students to set up a display of toys that may be unsafe or safe for infants and young children. Discuss reasons for the selection of each toy for the display. (Key Skills: *Critical Thinking, Cooperation*)
2. **Research.** Have students read about swimming programs for infants and toddlers. Ask them to find answers to questions such as: What drowning prevention methods are taught? How successful are the programs? Where are they offered, and what are their costs? Have students summarize their findings and share them with the class. (Key Skills: *Communication, Critical Thinking*)
3. **Form Design.** Have students make a form for writing down emergency numbers that might be needed while caring for children. (Key Skill: *Critical Thinking*)

SAFETY CHECK ✓

Ask students to read the feature. Discuss with students different ways to distract children from chewing on paint and plaster. If possible, have students contact a local Poison Control Center for more information on lead poisoning.

SAFETY CHECK ✓

Lead poisoning can cause anemia and permanent brain damage. Sources of lead include painted surfaces (often found in older homes), magazines, some pottery, lead water pipes, and some insecticides. Here are some ways to prevent lead poisoning:

- Keep children busy and away from possible sources of lead poisoning.
- Do not let children eat anything but food.
- Keep children from chewing on paint, plaster, or wood surfaces such as window sills.
- Cover walls with paneling or vinyl wallpaper to cover up possible sources of lead if you own a home.
- If you rent a home, have your landlord fix the walls and ceilings — it's the law in most states.

When choosing toys for children, be sure that they are unbreakable, too large to swallow, and free of sharp edges and small parts. Be sure to keep toys clean, too!

victims. They are often located in hospitals. People at the center will tell you exactly what to do. If your community doesn't have a poison control center, call a hospital emergency room or a doctor right away.

Matches and lighters can be deadly in little hands, so keep them out of reach. Also, keep children away from ranges, wood-burning stoves, heaters, hot water faucets, and hot drinks.

Toys

Some toys can be highly dangerous to infants and small children. When you give a toy to a baby, sooner or later it will go into the baby's mouth. Be sure that each toy you give a baby is unbreakable, too large to swallow, free of sharp edges that can cut, and free of small parts that can come off and be swallowed. Also, be sure the toy is clean, since it may eventually go into the baby's mouth.

Beware of noise-making guns and other toys that make very loud sounds. Some can damage hearing. Toys with long strings or cords may also be dangerous. The cords can become wrapped around an infant's neck and cause choking. Never hang toys with long strings, cords, loops, or ribbons in cribs or playpens where children can get tangled in them.

You need to consider the safety of toys for older children, too. Be certain toys are in good working condition. Don't let children play with broken toys or use them as they were not

More About Keeping Children Safe from Falls

Each year many small children fall from high chairs. To help prevent falls, most high chairs have a waist strap to prevent children from standing up in the chair. Most also have a strap that runs between the legs to prevent children from slipping under the tray. Have students practice restraining a child (or a doll) by these straps. Demonstrate how easy it would be for an unrestrained child to topple from the chair when standing, climbing, or reaching. Stress that the tray should not be used as a restraining device in place of the strap. Without the strap, children can slip beneath the tray and strangle if the head becomes stuck between the tray and seat of the chair.

intended. Five-year-old Kelvin wanted to give his two-year-old sister a ride in his plastic wheelbarrow. His father explained that the wheelbarrow can only carry plastic tools and toys. It is not strong enough to hold Alicia — and neither is Kelvin.

▼ Outdoors ▼

The world gets bigger for children as they begin to play outdoors. Caregivers must supervise young children at all times wherever they go.

- ***Streets and Roads.*** Never let children play in the street or road, and teach them not to chase balls that roll into the street. Fasten gates if the yard is fenced in. When children are old enough, show them the proper way to cross streets and help them cross safely. Most children are active and want to be independent. If you're not careful, they can dart away from you and into the street without thinking. Point out rules for bicycle safety for older children.
- ***Wading and Swimming Pools.*** Another place to keep a sharp eye on children is a wading pool or swimming pool. Never leave children alone in a pool of any kind.
- ***Playgrounds.*** Most neighborhood playgrounds can provide wonderful entertainment for the children in your care. Check the condition of the play equipment to see if it looks safe. Don't let children play on broken or damaged equipment.

Children need supervision as they play outside. Sometimes children are so caught up in their play that they don't realize when situations are dangerous. Keep a close watch on children at all times.

4. **Skits.** Have small groups present skits showing a teen accepting an offer to care for a child with special needs. Discuss ways in which the teen can be an effective caregiver in this situation. (Key Skill: *Critical Thinking*)

Follow Up

1. **Reteaching.** Have students work in groups to discuss and demonstrate several first aid techniques such as stopping a nosebleed or keeping an injured child calm. (Key Skills: *Communication, Cooperation*)
2. **Extension.** Have the students read the extension material on p. 25 from the *Extending the Lesson* booklet of the TCR.
3. **Enrichment.** Have students develop a puzzle, toy, or game that could be used with a preschool child. Games, toys, or puzzles should be durable, colorful, and fun. (Key Skill: *Creativity*)

Wellness

The majority of today's toys are designed and tested to be safe. However, accident-free play is likely only when toys are properly matched to a child's age and ability level. For that reason, be selective in the purchase of toys. Before offering a new toy to a child, inspect the toy's packaging for play-use and safety messages.

Photo Focus

Ask students to examine the photo on page 179. Discuss the safety conditions of outdoor play equipment. What should students look for? *(Durability, smooth surfaces — no splintering, securely fastened together and to the ground, etc.)* If students had an opportunity to choose outdoor play equipment for children, what would they choose and why?

Completing the Chapter

For Review

1. Emphasize the main concepts using the summary.
2. Have students complete the "Facts to Recall." (Answers below.)

For Reteaching

1. **Reteaching.** Use the activity on pp. 22-23 of the *Reteaching and Practical Skills* booklet in the TCR.

For Enrichment

1. **Enrichment.** Use the activity on p. 33 of the *Enrichment Activities* booklet in the TCR.

For Evaluation

1. Choose items from "Ideas to Explore" and "Activities to Try."
2. Use the chapter test on pp. 35-36 of the testing booklet in the TCR or use the testmaker software.

Facts to Recall Answers

1. Stimulate child's senses with brightly colored toys in a variety of shapes and textures; play repetitious games; talk to child as you play.
2. More active play, longer activities. Simple puzzles, storybooks, coloring books, large crayons, paper.
3. **Any four:** books; finger paints; clay; crayons; coloring books; cutting with blunt scissors; storytelling.
4. The liquid heats unevenly and may be too hot in places. Set the bottle in a bowl of warm tap water for a couple of minutes.
5. It lets children know what to expect, helps make them cooperative.
6. Stay with them all the time.
7. **Any four:** insecticides; cleaning fluids and powders; furniture polish; drugs; some house plants. Immediately call a poison control center.

Handling Emergencies

Suppose you were walking through the park where children were playing on the equipment. Would you know what to do if a child fell? When Kyle saw this happen, he remained calm. His quiet, soothing approach was reassuring to the injured child.

While evaluating the situation, Kyle decided that there might be serious injury. The angle of the little boy's arm just didn't look right. Kyle would not let anyone move the boy because that might worsen the injury. He kept the child warm by covering him with his own jacket. He then told the boy's friend to go to the nearest house to get help.

It was this incident that prompted Kyle to take a first aid course. He wanted to know more about handling emergencies in the future. **First aid courses** are available in schools and through the Red Cross and other community agencies. They provide instruction in basic emergency care for injuries of all types.

TAKING ACTION

Starting a Babysitting Service

Gwen is considered an entrepreneur by most people who know her. (As you learned in Chapter 7, an entrepreneur is someone who owns and manages his or her own business.) Among other projects, she is organizing a babysitting pool in your neighborhood. Gwen has checked around and discovered many families in need of babysitters. She plans to maintain contact with each family, coordinate their needs and schedules, and suggest responsible babysitters. She will collect a small portion of each babysitting fee in order to run her service and earn a profit.

She needs to recruit six teens who will make excellent babysitters. All will take a babysitting course offered by the Red Cross. The ages of the children to be cared for range from one to five. She asks you if you're interested and to suggest friends who would be right for the job.

Using Your Resourcefulness

- Name and evaluate six personal qualities or skills that make someone a good babysitter.
- Would you be interested in such a job? Why or why not? Do you have friends who would be right for the job? Who? Why?
- What qualities and skills does Gwen need to be a successful entrepreneur?

TAKING ACTION

Ask students to read the feature and respond to the questions and statements. Then, have students design a list of questions to use while interviewing students who babysit regularly. Include questions about the days of the week students usually babysit, the number of children they baby-sit on average, common responsibilities while babysitting, how they get babysitting jobs, what they feed the children they baby-sit, advantages and disadvantages of babysitting, and what they charge for babysitting. Ask students to compile and discuss their findings.

Chapter 16 Review

Summary

In this chapter, you have read about:

- ▶ Helping children learn about their world through play.
- ▶ Making children's mealtime safe and enjoyable.
- ▶ Keeping children safe in the home.
- ▶ Identifying unsafe toys.
- ▶ Supervising children outdoors.
- ▶ Babysitting for children.

Facts to Recall

1. Explain how to play with infants.
2. How is a toddler's play different from an infant's? What kinds of toys do they like?
3. List four "quiet play" activities that preschoolers enjoy.
4. Why shouldn't you heat an infant's bottle in a microwave? How should you heat the bottle?
5. How is following a routine helpful to young children at bedtime?
6. What is the most important step you can take to keep children safe?
7. Name four common household poisons. What should you do if you suspect a child has been poisoned?
8. List four characteristics of a toy that is safe for a baby.
9. Identify six things a good babysitter remembers to do.

Ideas to Explore

1. Of the four stages of childhood discussed here — infancy, toddler, preschooler, and school-age — which do you think is the most exciting for the child? Explain your answer.
2. How are the needs of children with physical and mental disabilities and the needs of gifted children similar? What challenges do both face?

Activities to Try

1. Imagine yourself as an infant, a toddler, or a preschooler. Write a short story about an everyday event, such as a meal or a trip to a grocery store, as you experience it.
2. Plan a day's schedule for an infant, toddler, or preschooler. Include such things as: what toys you will give the child to play with; what activities you will do with him or her; what you will feed the child, and if and when the child will nap.
3. Get down on a child's eye level and find anything that might be a safety hazard for a child. Identify ways of eliminating the potential hazards.

LINK TO Art

ART MATERIALS AND EQUIPMENT

Children use all of their senses in learning. One way to encourage learning and creative expression in children is through art. Put together a variety of materials and equipment — such as tempera paint, finger paint, paper, crayons, clay, paste, felt and scraps of lace and trims, and safety scissors — you think would be helpful to have in a "babysitter's bag." Remember to keep safety in mind as you gather materials. Never include any materials that could be harmful or dangerous.

Facts to Recall Answers (continued)

8. **Any four:** unbreakable; too large to swallow; no sharp edges; no small parts; clean.
9. **Any six:** write down client's name, address, and phone number; find out about job beforehand; agree on fee and duties; be prompt; ask parents where they can be reached; keep emergency numbers near phone; ask for any special instructions; ask for instructions about answering phone and door; locate rooms, emergency supplies and exits before parents leave; distract children if unhappy when parents leave; be attentive to children at all times; don't talk on phone to friends; respect family's property.

Ideas to Explore

1. Answers will vary.
2. Answers will vary and may include: same physical and emotional needs; same challenges of developing selves to their fullest.

Using Your Resourcefulness Answers

- Answers should include those items listed on pp. 172-173 of this chapter.
- Answers will vary.
- Answers will vary, but may include: she must be a good organizer and manager, have good "people" skills, etc.

LINK TO Art

Answer

Answers will vary. Students should keep the safety of children in mind when planning what materials to gather.

Preparing to Teach

Chapter Outline

Chapter Resources

The following booklet materials may be found in the *Teacher's Classroom Resources* box:

- Lesson Plans, p. 22
- Student Workbook, *Study Guide,* pp. 77-78; *Weighing the Responsibilities,* p. 79; *Parent Wanted,* p. 80
- Color Transparencies, *Children Need...,* CT-18
- Technology and Computers, p. 16
- Cooperative Learning, p. 29
- Extending the Text, *Teaching Children About Tasks,* p. 26
- Reteaching and Practical Skills, *Parents Are People,* p. 25
- Enrichment Activities, *Guiding Children,* p. 32
- Chapter and Unit Tests, pp. 37-38; pp. 112-114
- Testmaker Software

Also see:

- Leadership and Citizenship
- Meeting the Special Needs of Students
- Linking Home, School, and Community
- Dealing with Sensitive Issues

ABCNews InterActive™ Videodiscs

- *Teenage Sexuality*

See the ABCNews InterActive™ Bar Code Correlation booklet for applicable segments.

CHAPTER

17 A Look at Parenting

OBJECTIVES

- *Discuss important considerations in the decision to become a parent.*
- *Describe the problems that result when teens become parents.*
- *Identify and explain the responsibilities of parenthood.*
- *Identify resources available to parents.*

TERMS TO LEARN

- ***parenting***
- ***nurturing***
- ***discipline***
- ***time out***

"Let's have a show of hands. How many of you plan to get a degree in parenting someday?"

Virgil thought Mr. Antoine's question was an attempt at humor. In fact, the whole class reacted the same way — until they gave it some thought. As Mr. Antoine pointed out, hardly a job in society is tackled without some kind of training, yet every day people become parents without any formal preparation. There is no aptitude test. There is no supervisor. There are no evaluations. When mistakes are made, however, a price is paid — by parents and children.

The Parenting Question

People have children for different reasons. Not all reasons are good ones. They may feel pressure from family or friends. They may want to pass on the family name and heredity. They may simply have children because it is the thing to do. The decision to have children should be taken more seriously than this.

Deciding to Be a Parent

A decision about becoming a parent should be made carefully with a great deal of thought. People must first ask themselves, "Do we want to have children?" For many people, having children because they want them is the right decision. Having children just because "everyone does" or because of pressure from others, may not be the best reason for having children. Remaining childless may be the right decision for some.

People who are committed to loving and caring for children may deal with a second question — when to have children. They are ready to ask:

- "Do we have enough money to support ourselves and the baby on our own?"
- "Have we finished our schooling?"
- "How will a baby affect our relationship at this time? What about our social life?"
- "Can we make the personal sacrifices needed to care for another person?"
- "What do we know about babies, children, and the responsibilities of parenthood?"

Making the decision to become a parent requires a great deal of communication and thought.

More About Parenting

Becoming a parent requires a tremendous adjustment on the part of a married couple. Rearing a family probably is the most difficult job people can have, and couples usually have little preparation for the responsibilities involved. A couple should give a great deal of thought to this decision, because it will have a significant impact on each of them as well as on their relationship. Children are a full-time responsibility. If there were marital problems before a child, these problems are likely to increase with the birth of a baby.

Introducing the Chapter

Motivators

1. **Incomplete Sentences.** Ask students to complete the following sentences: "A parent is ...," "Being a parent means ...," "I want to be a parent because ...," "I don't want to be a parent because ..." (Key Skills: *Communication, Critical Thinking*)
2. **Writing.** Ask students to imagine that they will be a parent someday. Have them write a paragraph describing what kind of parent they would like to be. (Key Skills: *Communication, Critical Thinking*)
3. **Brainstorming.** Lead students in brainstorming a list of television programs that feature one or more parents. Ask students to identify the programs that feature positive parenting roles. (Key Skills: *Communication, Critical Thinking*)
4. **Writing Questions.** Divide students into pairs. Have them write a list of questions they would like to ask teen parents about the roles and responsibilities of parents. Collect and compile the questions to be used in future interviews. (Key Skills: *Communication, Critical Thinking*)

Chapter Objectives and Vocabulary

1. Have students read the chapter objectives. Ask them to rephrase the objectives as questions.
2. Ask students to state, in their own words, the purpose of studying this chapter.
3. Pronounce the vocabulary terms listed on the previous page. Ask students whether they are familiar with any of these. Explain that the terms will be defined in the chapter.

Guided Reading

1. Have students read the chapter and use the Study Guide on pp. 77-78 of the *Student Workbook*.

Teaching. . .
The Parenting Questions: Deciding; The Responsibilities of Parenthood: Physical Needs; Teaching
(pp. 183-185)

Comprehension Check

1. What are three reasons why some people have children? *(Pressure from family or friends; desire to pass on the family name and heredity; a feeling it is the thing to do.)*
2. What factors should a couple consider about when to have a child? *(Money; finished education; affect of baby on relationship; personal sacrifices needed; parenting knowledge and responsibilities.)*
3. Name three groups of people, besides parents, who find parenting skills useful. *(Relatives, friends, and professional child care workers.)*
4. What physical needs of children must parents meet? *(Food, clothing, shelter, health care.)*
5. How do parents and caregivers provide for intellectual development? *(Provide tools and opportunities.)*

Learning Activities

1. **Classroom Survey.** Have students indicate anonymously if they wish to have children someday or prefer to remain childless. Collect the responses and record

Around the World

After reading the feature, have students read and report about parenting and child care in several other countries. Invite parents from other countries to speak to the class about factors that influence couples to have children or remain childless. Discuss average age at marriage, average family size, responsibilities of the husband and wife, and housing arrangements. Request that they talk about child care options and costs.

Social and economic conditions in Germany make it more difficult for people to decide to become parents. The cost of living in Germany is very high, often requiring that both a husband and a wife work. However, day care is hard to find, so if a couple decides to have children, one parent must stay home to care for them. About half of all German couples have no children. The government is trying to help. It offers child support payments to couples who otherwise could not afford to have children. It also uses advertisements to promote parenthood.

The answers to these questions can help a couple decide when to have children. Waiting can give them a better start in life and make it easier and more enjoyable to raise children later.

Teen parents face many difficult challenges.

Teens as Parents

Parenthood too soon is tough in many ways. That's why there is so much concern about the increase in the number of teen parents. Parenthood disrupts the lives of teens and pushes them down a difficult road they are not ready to handle. It can hurt the children, too. Many are raised by parents without the resources, knowledge, and readiness needed to be *good* parents.

Often the responsibility for the child falls mainly on the mother. Some teen fathers take an active role in parenting. Many, however, don't live up to their legal and moral responsibilities to their child. If either teen parent drops out of school, the lack of a diploma becomes a lifelong barrier to a good job.

Do you think most teens are emotionally, socially, and financially ready for parenthood? Are they ready to make the personal sacrifices needed to provide total care for another person? What can you personally do to help solve this problem?

The Responsibilities of Parenthood

Have you ever watched or played a team sport at school? Imagine what it would be like for a team to go out on the field or court with very little idea of what they were supposed to do. They would probably lose the game.

You can lose at anything in life, or at least have a tough time, when you don't know what you are doing. Parenting is no exception. **Parenting** is the process of caring for children

More About *Decisions to Become a Parent*

In the past, it was assumed that when people got married they would have children. In today's world that is not always the case. Changing attitudes, economics, education and career priorities, and new advances in medical technology have made it possible for people to delay parenthood or choose not to have children at all. Delayed parenthood, employed mothers, fathers involved in childrearing, and single parenting are more common these days than in previous years.

and helping them grow and develop. Many parenting skills are learned by trial and error. There are better ways. Reading, talking, and thinking about these skills early can help.

Remember that parenting skills are useful to many people. Parents are not the only ones who care for children. Relatives, friends, and professional child care workers all do, too. These people need these skills as much as parents do. Knowing what the responsibilities of parenting are and how to carry them out can make for success when caring for children in any situation.

▼ Meeting Physical Needs ▼

Try making a list of the physical needs that children have. The first things that come to mind are probably food, clothing, and shelter. Did you think to include health needs? The foods children eat must be healthy and contain everything they need to grow and develop properly. They need adequate rest and exercise too. Medical care and protection against common childhood diseases, such as diptheria, polio, and measles, must also be provided. A knowledgeable parent is better able to take care of all this.

▼ Teaching Children ▼

Can you imagine knowing nothing? That's the way an infant begins life. Immediately, caregivers begin the infant's learning process. Parents must provide the tools and opportunities for intellectual development of their children.

Reading to children and looking at pictures is a special time for families. It not only encourages intellectual development, but also provides some time to enjoy each other as a family.

More About *Choosing When to Become a Parent*

Many couples wait to have children until their marriage, careers, or economic situation has been established. Other couples find themselves facing unplanned pregnancies. Though many babies who are unplanned, or conceived by accident, are later accepted and loved, other babies may not be so fortunate. Couples who are not ready to have children may resent new additions to the family. Weak marriages may be weakened even more by unwanted pregnancies. Marriages that take place because of pregnancy are more likely to fail than other marriages. A pregnancy that is planned has the best chance of success for both the parents and the child.

Learning Activities (continued)

the numbers on the chalkboard. Ask for volunteers to share reasons for their responses. (Key Skill: *Critical Thinking*)

2. **Guest Speakers.** Invite teen parents (several in school and several who dropped out) to speak to the class about being a parent. Ask them to discuss ways in which parenting has affected their schooling, family relationships, and social life. Were they ready to face the responsibilities of parenthood? (Key Skill: *Communication*)
3. **Journal Writing.** Have students write in their journals about how they feel about having children, their readiness for parenthood, and what kind of parent they think they might be someday. (Key Skill: *Critical Thinking*)
4. **Debate.** Divide students into three groups, and have them debate the following statements: Parenting never ends; parenting is the mother's responsibility. (Key Skills: *Communication, Critical Thinking*)

Follow Up

1. **Reteaching.** Have students create posters encouraging teens to postpone parenting until they are older. Students should think about parenting responsibilities as they create their posters. (Key Skills: *Communication, Creativity*)
2. **Enrichment.** Divide students into small groups. Have students investigate the costs of meeting the physical needs of children from birth to age eighteen. What implications does this information have for being financially ready for children? Ask them to be as specific as possible and to present their illustrated findings to the class. (Key Skills: *Communication, Problem Solving*)

Photo Focus

Ask students to examine the photo on p. 185. Discuss the responsibilities of parents to the intellectual development of their children. Have students brainstorm a list of activities and materials that parents might provide for their children that promote intellectual development.

Teaching. . .
The Responsibilities of Parenthood: Nurturing; Guiding
(pp. 186-188)

Comprehension Check

1. What can parents and other caregivers do to help children develop intellectually? *(Talk, read, and listen to children; avoid baby talk; provide opportunities to play and learn; library story hours for children.)*
2. What is nurturing? *(Giving love, affection, attention, and encouragement.)*
3. Why is effective guidance of children important? *(It influences their behavior; helps them learn to get along with others; helps them deal with feelings in acceptable ways; teaches self-discipline.)*
4. Why is it important to set limits for children? *(Limits help them know what is acceptable, appropriate, and safe for them to do.)*
5. What is discipline? *(A response that helps children learn appropriate behavior.)*
6. What is time out? *(A discipline technique in which a child who is misbehaving is removed from an activity for a short period of time.)*

Learning Activities

1. **Writing.** Assign students to write a short essay titled "A Parent Is a Child's First Teacher," describing the effects parents have on their children's intellectual development. Have them share essays with other class members and list ways that parents can encourage a child's intellectual development. (Key Skill: *Critical Thinking*)
2. **Skits.** Assign students to write and present skits demonstrating ways that parents and other caregivers can nurture children. Discuss the skits, and talk about the importance of nurturing to a child's physical, intellectual, and emotional development. (Key Skills: *Communication, Creativity*)

As a parent or other caregiver, what can you do? Talk, read, and listen to children from the time they are born. Avoid baby talk so that children learn correct language skills. Provide opportunities for children to play and learn. Most communities have a number of resources, such as library story hours, that can help satisfy children's intellectual needs.

▼ Nurturing Children ▼

Children need a great deal of **nurturing** (NUR-chur-ing). This means giving love, affection, attention, and encouragement. Without nurturing, they may not develop right physically, intellectually, socially, or emotionally. Nurturing makes children feel secure and accepted as they are. It gives them a sense of worth and adequacy. It also helps them relate well to others. Children who are comfortable with themselves and secure in the family can reach out to others more easily.

▼ Guiding Children ▼

Through guidance, parents and caregivers encourage appropriate behaviors in children. How is this dad providing guidance?

Through effective guidance or **discipline**, parents and other caregivers provide the training that helps children become responsible and cooperative. Many people think of guidance and discipline only in terms of punishment, however, it is much more. Effective discipline helps children learn to get along with others and deal with their own feelings in acceptable ways. Gradually, children begin to see why certain actions are right or wrong. They learn to control their own behavior and take responsibility for their actions.

One way that parents provide guidance is by example. Children imitate what adults say and do. Setting a good example often works better than telling children what to do.

Another way of providing guidance is to explain what behavior is inappropriate and why it is inappropriate. Children need to know what they're doing wrong, why it's wrong, and what should be done instead. When Craig grabbed a book from another child in the doctor's waiting room, his mother said to him, "She chose that book first, Craig. Which one of these would you like to read?"

Messages must be suited to a child's age and level of understanding. At first, you do not need to explain the reasons behind what is expected. Saying, "Pat the kitty," along with a demonstration of gentle handling, is sufficient. Later, simple reasoning may be added: "It hurts the cat when you pull her tail. If you want to play with her, you will have to be gentle."

Praise is an important part of guiding children. Children feel good about themselves when given praise. They are also more likely to continue the desired behavior.

More About *Teaching Children*

Parents and other caregivers can teach children and stimulate their senses, beginning at a very young age. Bright colors help stimulate eyes, soft music encourages talking and singing, and interesting noises stimulate hearing. Objects with a variety of textures help develop a sense of touch, as does being held and cuddled. Storytelling encourages imagination and creativity. Toys such as building blocks not only help the imagination grow but also enhance motor control and body coordination.

Setting simple and clear limits of behavior is another way to guide children. Children both want and need limits. They don't have the maturity to make good judgments in all areas of their life. Limits help them know what is acceptable, appropriate, and safe for them to do.

Handling Misbehavior

When children break limits, discipline takes on another role. Parents need to respond to misbehavior in some way. The aim is to help children learn appropriate behavior.

Knowing when to punish can be tricky. A mistake is not misbehavior. Andrew dropped a glass of milk because he lacked coordination. He needed encouragement and help in cleaning up the spill, not angry words. When three-year-old Sheri pulled up the tulips by the roots, she was only trying to find out what makes them grow. She needed some explanation, not punishment.

Deliberate misbehavior, on the other hand, needs a stronger response and should be appropriate to the child's level of understanding. Discipline can be handled in several ways. Taking away privileges is one method used. For misbehaving, Mattie was not allowed to go outdoors to play with a friend for the afternoon. Enforcing this was hard for Mattie's grandmother, since she had to keep Mattie inside and deal with her mood for the afternoon. It was worth the effort, though, because Mattie learned something that would affect her future behavior.

Ignoring misbehavior is another discipline technique. Devon always whined when he wanted his father to buy him something at the store. When Mr. Talbott gave in, Devon learned that whining worked. Finally Mr. Talbott decided to ignore Devon's whining after giving him a simple "no." Before long Devon gave up whining because it no longer produced results.

Removing a child from the activity for a short period of time can also be helpful. This is called **time out**. A parent might say, "I know you're angry, but you still can't hit people. When you can play without hitting, you may go back with the others." This helps reinforce the idea that the child must learn to control behavior.

Handling discipline correctly takes thought, practice, and dedication. Here are some tips to keep in mind:

- Be consistent in your actions and words. If you laugh at Raoul's action one day and punish him for the same thing the next, you will confuse him.
- Let children know you mean what you say. If you tell Tanisha that it is bedtime and then allow her to stay up longer, she learns that you didn't really mean it.

A mistake or accident is not misbehavior.

"Time out" is often helpful in handling misbehavior.

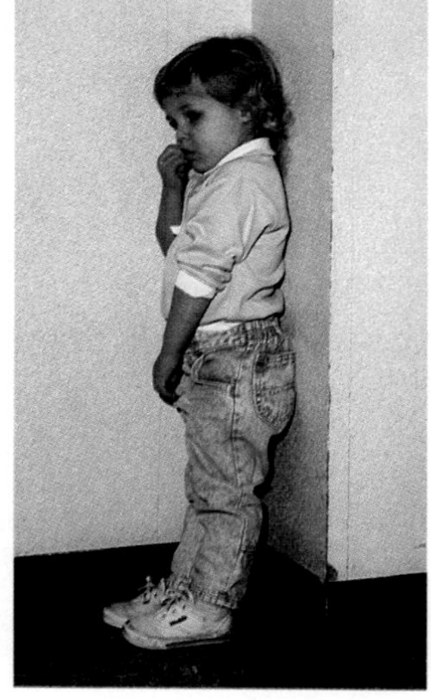

Learning Activities (continued)

3. **Discussion.** Ask students to describe situations in which young children exhibit anger. Talk about reasons why the anger occurs, what the outbursts are like from a child's point of view, and ways parents can guide the child. (Key Skills: *Communication, Problem Solving*)
4. **Skits.** Select students to act out situations involving a teen parent who is in danger of physically abusing his or her child. Have them practice encouraging the parent to seek help. Follow up by discussing local sources of help. (Key Skill: *Critical Thinking*)
5. **Guest Speaker.** Invite a social worker, counselor, or member of Parents Anonymous to speak to the class about families at risk of hurting their children. (Key Skills: *Communication, Critical Thinking*)

Follow Up

1. **Reteaching.** Assign students to write an advice column, telling parents about time out and two other discipline techniques. (Key Skill: *Critical Thinking*)
2. **Extension.** Have the students read the extension material on p. 26 from the *Extending the Lesson* booklet of the TCR.
3. **Enrichment.** Ask students to observe children's television programs. Have them note instances in which children misbehave and whether they were disciplined. Afterwards, assign students to write a short story about a child who misbehaves and is disciplined in a positive way. (Key Skill: *Critical Thinking*)

Making a Difference

Teen parents, overwhelmed with the responsibilities of parenthood, school, work, and relationships, may become frustrated and angry at their children. Have students learn more about crisis intervention hotlines and organizations such as Parents Anonymous. Assign them to create posters, write short stories, or public service notices featuring sources of help for teen parents.

More About *Guidance*

Effective guidance makes a distinction between actions or behavior and the person. Caregivers can disapprove of the behavior, but still love the child. Sometimes this is difficult for children to understand. However, if adults do not make the distinction, children may develop negative feelings of self-worth. Children should be allowed to express their feelings, and parents and other caregivers should help children learn to express those feelings in an appropriate manner. Adults should praise children for their efforts. Children want to please, and it is important that their efforts be recognized.

Completing the Chapter

For Review

1. Emphasize the main concepts using the summary.
2. Have students complete the "Facts to Recall." (Answers below.)

For Reteaching

1. **Reteaching.** Use the activity on p. 24 of the *Reteaching and Practical Skills* booklet in the TCR.

For Enrichment

1. **Enrichment.** Use the activity on p. 34 of the *Enrichment Activities* booklet in the TCR.

For Evaluation

1. Choose items from "Ideas to Explore" and "Activities to Try."
2. Use the chapter test on pp. 37-38 of the testing booklet in the TCR or use the testmaker software.
3. Use the unit test on pp. 112-114 of the testing booklet in the TCR or use the testmaker software.

Chapter 17 Review

Facts to Recall Answers

1. **Any three:** Do we have enough money to support ourselves and the baby on our own? Have we finished our schooling? How will a baby affect our relationship at this time? What about our social life? Can we make the personal sacrifices needed to care for another person? What do we know about babies, children, and the responsibilities of parenthood?
2. It disrupts parents' lives, possibly interrupts education, leading to poverty; children are raised by parents who lack resources, knowledge, and readiness.
3. The process of caring for children and helping them grow and develop.
4. Health needs; rest and exercise; medical care; protection against childhood diseases.

- Discipline should not be an outlet for the caregiver's anger or frustration. Instead it should be carried out with thought and control.
- Make sure children understand that you still love them even when you disapprove of their behavior.

Resources for Parents

As any parent can tell you, caring for children can be demanding. Physical and emotional fatigue are common. Anyone who cares for children needs some time to get away on a regular basis. Even two or three hours a week is refreshing. Many couples share child care so that all the burden is not on one parent.

Parents need some time to themselves, too. If a paid babysitter is not possible, family members and friends may offer to help out. Taking turns giving each other some time off works well for many people.

TAKING ACTION

Planning for the Future

Van and Meegan, both 18, are planning their futures. They've been dating for two years, and they want to get married soon and have a child. They think of themselves as caring and responsible young adults, but Meegan's family is extremely upset by her plans. They want her to go to college and wait several years to marry Van.

The young couple hopes to live with Van's parents until they can afford an apartment of their own. So far, the only jobs Van has been able to find pay minimum wage, so Meegan is looking for work, too. They know they're going to face a lot of obstacles, but they believe their relationship is strong enough to last. They want to know your opinion about their plans.

Using Your Resourcefulness

- What do you think of Meegan and Van's plans? Are they ready to become parents? Why or why not?
- What resource materials can help them determine the costs of raising a baby? How much will it cost them to raise a child for the first three years?
- In your opinion, what are the three most important personal qualities or skills that make a successful parent?

TAKING ACTION

Have students read the feature. Parenting skills will be very important to Van and Meegan. Have students develop a resource list of agencies, organizations, and programs in the community that can help teens learn (and improve) parenting skills. Duplicate copies of the list for the class. Select several students to design an outline for a parenting course and for a child care course. Distribute the outlines, and ask the class to evaluate them and make changes, if necessary. Ask the class to answer and discuss the questions, "Do most teens view parenthood realistically? Why or why not?"

Chapter 17 Review

Summary

In this chapter, you have read about:

- How people decide if and when to have children.
- The problems facing teen parents.
- Parents' responsibilities for meeting children's physical, intellectual, and emotional needs.
- How parents and other caregivers provide guidance and discipline for children.
- When and how to take action when children misbehave.
- The resources that are available to parents.

Facts to Recall

1. What are three questions that people should ask themselves in deciding when to have children?
2. How can becoming a parent too soon hurt the parents, their children, and society?
3. What is parenting?
4. Besides food, clothing, and shelter, what physical needs do children have?
5. What is nurturing? How does it benefit children?
6. Identify three ways in which parents provide positive discipline and guidance.
7. Name three ways that parents can deal with misbehavior.
8. Identify two ways in which parents can prevent physical and emotional fatigue, that might result in their hurting their children.

Ideas to Explore

1. Do you think most teens have a realistic view of parenting? If not, in what ways is it unrealistic?
2. In your own words, define discipline and punishment. Are they the same thing? If not, how do they differ?
3. Do you think schools should offer teens more classes on parenting? Where else might people of all ages learn about parenting before having or caring for children?

Activities to Try

1. With a classmate, act out a situation showing a child's misbehavior and the parent's response. Have the rest of the class evaluate the effectiveness of the discipline technique used.
2. As a class, brainstorm ideas and images associated with the word "baby." Evaluate the list. Which ideas or images are positive? Which are negative? Which reflect the responsibilities of raising a child?

LINK TO Health

COPING WITH CHILDHOOD PROBLEMS

During childhood, children may experience physical or emotional problems that require special attention. Some children develop unrealistic fears as a result of a frightening experience. Some exhibit aggressive behavior (a tendency to start frequent fights and quarrels) or have temper tantrums. Other special problems of childhood may include hyperactivity (inability to control one's activity or concentrate for a normal length of time), poor performance in school, extreme shyness, or bedwetting.

- Read more about one of these problems and make a brief report to the class.
- Identify the symptoms of the problem, possible causes, and actions parents and caregivers should take to help the child.

Facts to Recall Answers (continued)

5. Giving love, affection, attention, and encouragement. It makes them feel secure and accepted as they are, helps them relate well to others.
6. **Any three:** by example; by explaining appropriate and inappropriate behavior; by praise; by setting limits of behavior.
7. Taking away privileges; ignoring misbehavior; removing child from activity for short time (time out).
8. Get away on a regular basis (spend time on themselves); share child care with partner.

Ideas to Explore

1. Answers will vary. Teens often underestimate the emotional and financial costs of parenting.
2. Answers will vary. Discipline is positive and guides children toward appropriate behavior. Punishment tends to be viewed negatively and may or may not lead to appropriate behavior.
3. Answers will vary.

Using Your Resourcefulness Answers

- Answers will vary. They may be emotionally and physically mature, but are not financially ready for children.
- Answers will vary.
- Answers will vary.

LINK TO Health

Answers

- Reports will vary depending on problems read about.
- Answers will vary.

Career Connections

Volunteer Options

- Big Brother or Big Sister.
- Crisis hotline worker.
- Pen pal.
- Crisis nursery worker.
- Abuse shelter worker.
- After school daycare volunteer.
- Tutoring.
- Hospital volunteers.
- Camp counselors.

Volunteer Organizations

Big Brothers/Big Sisters of America
230 N. 13th St.
Philadelphia, PA 19107-1510

UNICEF
331 E. 38th St., 6th Floor
New York, NY 10016

United Way of America
701 N. Fairfax St.
Alexandria, VA 22314-2045

CARE (Relief)
660 First Avenue
New York, NY 10016

Association of Junior Leagues
660 First Avenue
New York, NY 10016

Junior Optimist Clubs
4494 Lindell Boulevard
St Louis, MO 63108

Lions Clubs International
300 22nd Street
Oak Brook, IL 60570

Rotary International
1560 Sherman Avenue
Evanston, IL 60201

CAREER *Connections*

Get Ready for Your Future Through Volunteering

Yvonne

"A friend and I recently volunteered to become summer interns at Camp Palms — a camp for physically disabled teens. We worked for Ramon Aldonza, our supervisor. Ramon trained us to make sure newcomers are comfortable and help them adjust to their surroundings. For some teens who come here for the first time, the experience is stressful. We act like 'buddies' and end up making all kinds of friends.

"I've also volunteered at the Beverly Child Center in my town. There I played with small children. Some days I taught a new song or game, or helped the children fingerpaint. I felt good about myself because I think it's important to take care of another human being.

"My goal is to be a licensed child care teacher. The child care field is growing due to the number of families with both parents working. These families need proper day care for their children. That means there should be many job opportunities no matter where I want to live. I believe volunteer work paves the road for the future and offers a world of experience right now."

Ramon

"I've always enjoyed being around kids. During high school, I worked at Camp Palms for physically disabled teens. In college, I majored in physical education. I planned to coach sports at a middle school. However, while counseling at a summer camp for teenagers, I became friends with the camp director. He asked me to assist him full-time and after graduation I agreed. I learned how to run a camp and supervise the staff. Two years later when the director left the job, I replaced him.

"I enjoy introducing teens to nature and all kinds of outdoor activities and sports. However, that's only part of what I like about the job. I don't have to commute to work; I live right on the grounds. I like working with my hands. Off-season my biggest responsibility is maintaining the facilities. I fix roofs, deal with plumbing and electrical problems, and paint cabins.

Discussing Career Connections

Have students read the *Career Connections* feature. Ask students:

- What personal qualities and skills should people have for working with families and children?
- What special qualities and skills might be necessary for working with disabled children and adults?
- What skills and abilities do you have that may benefit you in a career in working with children and families?

Have students interview a person who works with families or children to find out more about careers in this area.

"Still another part of the job is scheduling the campers and informal fundraising. I talk to interested organizations about the camp and its needs. I hire all summer camp counselors, cooks, maintenance crew members, and lifeguards. The staff works and plays together, and becomes just like a family. I certainly don't expect to make a lot of money at this job, but do I love the work and living in the country."

Cindy

"Teacher, public-relations expert, business person — like Ramon, I'm all these things. I received a bachelor's degree in early childhood education and taught for several years. Now I am the director of the Beverly Children's Center. Companies in the area set up the center for their employees and the community. Every day I'm responsible for the education and care of up to one hundred infants and young children.

"I spend part of the morning in eight classrooms where I oversee teachers, pitch in to help, or just play with kids. However, most of the time I make sure the nonprofit center operates smoothly. This includes hiring a staff of 15 to 20 teachers and aides, paying bills, and interacting with parents.

"At weekly staff meetings we discuss curriculum development and the problems and progress of each child. If it sounds like a juggling act — it is. I'm also the mother of two children who need care and attention at home, too. This job requires a love of small children, infinite patience, and a strong sense of humor. I can't imagine doing anything else."

MAKING THE CONNECTION

- Do you think working with young children or teenagers might interest you as a career? Why or why not?
- What related career options do Yvonne, Ramon, and Cindy have with their training? What resource materials can help you learn more about child care careers?
- How might you go about learning business and public relations skills?

Occupational Outlook

Listed below are some possible occupations. Some require little training while others require a 4-year degree.

- Cashier
- Babysitter
- Children's tutor
- Child care center director
- Customer service representative
- Shop steward
- Residence counselor
- Lobbyist
- Recruiter
- Teacher
- Reporter or correspondent
- Guidance counselor
- Job analyst
- Psychologist
- Marriage counselor
- Public relations specialist
- Human resources specialist
- Family caseworker
- Adoption agency caseworker
- Mental health counselor
- Child welfare worker
- Occupational therapist

Related Organizations

American Association for Counseling and Development
5999 Stevenson Avenue
Alexandria, VA 22304

National Association of Social Workers
750 First Street N. E., Suite 700
Washington, DC

National Recreation and Park Association
2775 S. Quincy Street, Suite 300
Alexandria, VA 22206

Making the Connection

Answers

- Answers will vary depending on student interest.
- Yvonne, Ramon, and Cindy might choose careers in teaching, social work, health care, psychology, physical therapy, etc.
- On the job, business schools, working with people, etc.

Planning the Unit

Ch. 18: Managing Time and Energy — Addresses ways to manage time and energy effectively in addition to providing ideas for work simplification.

Ch. 19: Managing Money — Explores how to use records of income and expenses in developing a budget. Provides guidelines for using checking and savings accounts and credit.

Ch. 20: Consumer Challenges — Examines factors that influence consumer choices in addition to identifying wise steps to take when making purchases.

Ch. 21: Technology as a Resource — Explores the use of technology at home, at school, and in the workplace. Addresses ways in which technology might be used in the future.

Ch. 22: Natural Resources — Discusses renewable and nonrenewable resources, resource management, and identifying conservation measures.

UNIT 3 Resources to Manage

CHAPTERS

Cooperative Learning Tips

Collaborative social skills play an important role in cooperative learning. Each new social skill that is taught should be clearly defined for the students. Students need to understand why a skill is important and how they can benefit from learning the skill.

Collaborative social skills to be focused on at this age level are:

- Paraphrasing.
- Direct eye contact.
- Sharing feelings.
- Listening to other people's opinions.
- Agreeing to disagree.
- Checking for understanding.

See the *Cooperative Learning* booklet in the TCR for more information.

Introducing the Unit

Unit 3 Overview

In Unit 3, students explore ways to use resources wisely. Time, personal energy, the benefits of using money wisely, saving money, and how to establish credit and maintain a good credit rating are covered in practical detail. Students develop an understanding about the influences on consumers and ways to make wise purchases. In addition, this unit explores ways to effectively use technology and manage natural resources.

Unit Motivators

1. **Analyzing Advertising.** Display advertisements from magazines aimed at teens. Have students identify the kinds of products that are advertised most often and list techniques commonly used to create interest in a product. Ask students to identify misleading claims. Have students identify ways to become wise consumers. (Key Skill: *Critical Thinking*)
2. **Creative Writing.** Have students write to an inhabitant of another planet about the condition of the environment on Earth. Students should address issues and propose some solutions. (Key Skills: *Critical Thinking, Creativity*)

Completing the Unit

Review

1. **Planning Purchases.** Have students look through a catalog and choose an item they might like to buy. Ask them to compare the price, quality, and warranty to a similar item in a store. Ask them to evaluate the advantages and disadvantages of buying through a catalog or a store. How does this purchase fit into each student's budget? (Key Skill: *Critical Thinking*)

Evaluation

1. **Unit Test.** Have students complete the unit test on pp. 115-117 of the *Chapter and Unit Tests* booklet in the TCR.
2. **Testmaker Software.** Use the *Testmaker* software program to design your own unit test.

Implementing Cooperative Learning

A technique which encourages students to think about a concept and then articulate a response is called *Think-Pair-Share*. Announce a concept, idea, or question that you want answered and ask students to think about it (about 30 seconds). Have students turn to a partner and share their answers with each other. Students develop communication skills and receive an affirmation about their thinking at the same time. To take this one step further, have each pair team up with another pair and share their answers again. Process the group information by having one person from each team share the responses of their group.

See the *Cooperative Learning* booklet in the TCR for more information.

Preparing to Teach

Chapter Outline

Chapter Resources

The following booklet materials may be found in the *Teacher's Classroom Resources* box:

- Lesson Plans, p. 23
- Student Workbook, *Study Guide,* pp. 81-82; *Making the Most of Time,* p. 83; *Managing Time,* p. 84
- Color Transparencies, *Space Management,* CT-19
- Technology and Computers, pp. 14, 23, 24, 25
- Cooperative Learning, p. 30
- Extending the Text, *Is Your Motor an Early Bird or a Night Owl?,* p. 27
- Reteaching and Practical Skills, *Why Does Time Fly?,* p. 26
- Enrichment Activities, *Taking Control of Time,* p. 33
- Chapter and Unit Tests, pp. 39-40
- Testmaker Software

Also see:

- Leadership and Citizenship
- Meeting the Special Needs of Students
- Linking Home, School, and Community
- Dealing with Sensitive Issues

ABCNews InterActive™ Videodiscs

- *Food and Nutrition*
- *Drugs and Substance Abuse*

See the ABCNews InterActive™ Bar Code Correlation booklet for applicable segments.

CHAPTER

18 Managing Time and Energy

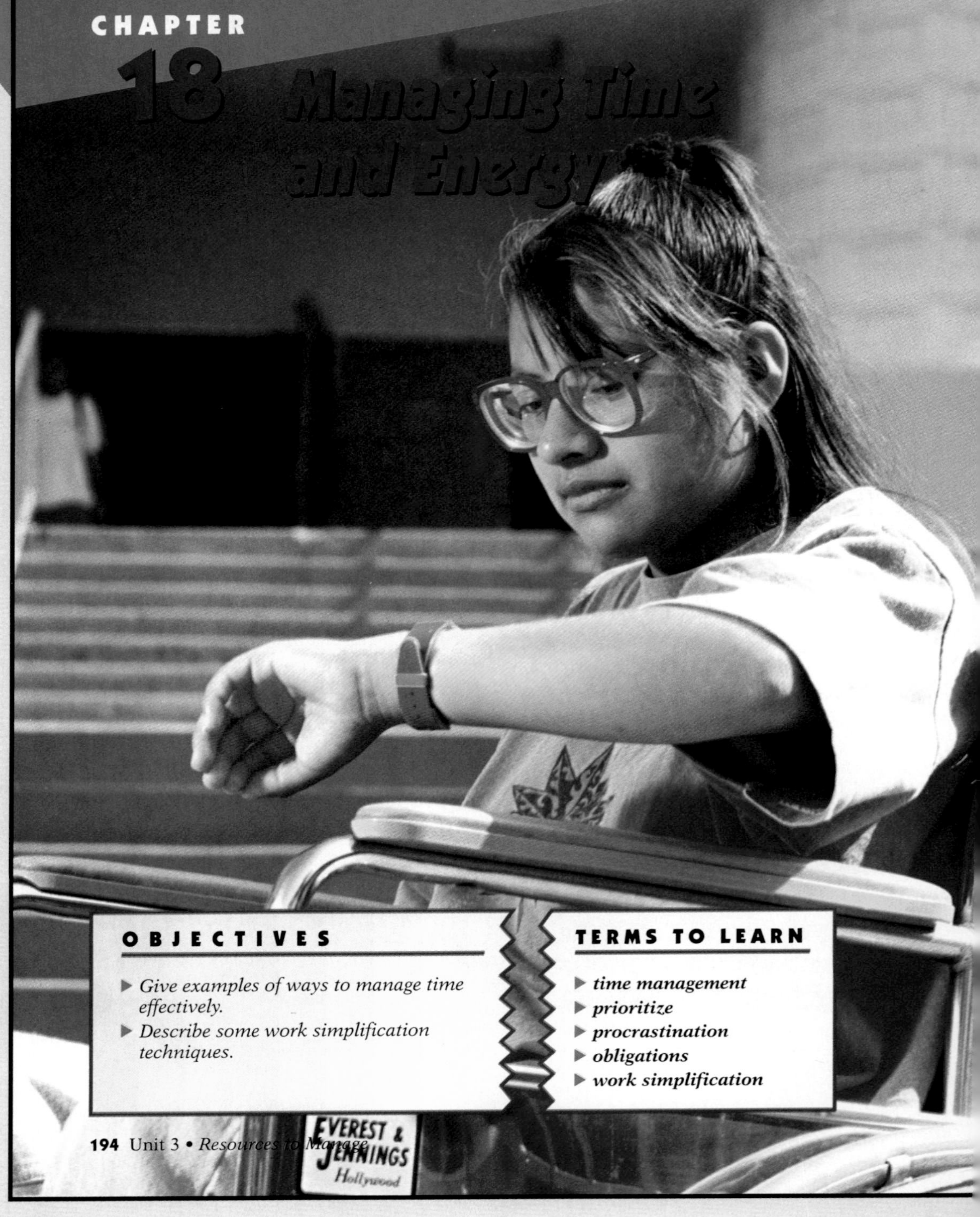

OBJECTIVES

- *Give examples of ways to manage time effectively.*
- *Describe some work simplification techniques.*

TERMS TO LEARN

- ***time management***
- ***prioritize***
- ***procrastination***
- ***obligations***
- ***work simplification***

Mona is an active, full-time student who has a part-time job after school. In addition to classes, homework, and her job, she develops photographs for her school's yearbook. Mona enjoys photography. In fact, she plans on a career as a newspaper photographer. She wishes she had more time to give to photography now, but somehow she always feels rushed. There's just so much to do!

Mona would like to have more time to spend with family and friends and more energy to use for all her activities. "Everyone has the same amount of time each day," she protests. "How do some people accomplish so much and still have time to relax, while my days are a race with the clock — a race that leaves me exhausted?"

Does Mona's complaint sound familiar to you? Do you often find yourself short of time and energy? You can stretch your time and energy resources by learning to manage them more efficiently.

Managing Your Time

Everything that you do requires a certain amount of time. Do you ever say "yes" to a number of activities and then wonder how you will find the time to do them all? When you agree to participate in an activity, you are agreeing to spend some time on it. You can accomplish much more if you take charge of your time and manage it. **Time management** involves planning your use of time so that you can get the most out of the time you have. Taking charge of your time allows you to do what needs to be done and still have time left for doing those things that you like best.

Becoming an Effective Time Manager

To begin managing your time, look at how you use your time now. Keep a record of your activities in a small notebook for a single day. Include such categories as sleeping, eating, bathing, going to school, studying, working, helping out at home, visiting with friends, participating in sports, etc. As you complete each activity, write down the amount of time you spent on that activity. Total up the time that you have spent on each category to see where your time goes. See **Fig. 18-1** for tips on managing your time.

Is this something you've done? To improve your time management skills, first review how you currently use time.

More About *Managing Time and Energy*

Everyone has three hundred sixty-five days, five hours, forty-eight minutes, and forty-six seconds of time each year. One way that people can get the maximum use of their time and energy is to plan their activities according to their peak levels of energy. This involves doing the most important work during their peak hours, and the less important things when their energy level is low.

Introducing the Chapter

Motivators

1. **Discussion.** Ask students to discuss the need for teens and families to manage time and energy. How do lifestyles and time demands differ from those of previous generations? (Key Skill: *Communication*)
2. **Brainstorming.** Have students list well-known phrases using the word time. ("Time out," "On time," "Time flies when you're having fun," etc.) (Key Skill: *Communication*)
3. **Class Survey.** Take a class survey on the number of hours students sleep, study, watch television, visit with their families, talk on the phone, work, etc. (Key Skill: *Critical Thinking*)
4. **Question Box.** Invite students to write questions they would like discussed about time and energy management and place them in a box with a slot in the top. Select some to answer each day. (Key Skill: *Communication*)
5. **Personal Analysis.** Have students make a list of their activities during an average weekday. List activities from the moment they get up until they go to sleep. Afterwards, divide students into small groups to contrast their lists. (Key Skill: *Communication*)

Chapter Objectives and Vocabulary

1. Have students read the chapter objectives. Ask them to rephrase the objectives as questions.
2. Ask students to state, in their own words, the purpose of studying this chapter.
3. Pronounce the vocabulary terms listed on the previous page. Ask students whether they are familiar with any of these. Explain that the terms will be defined in the chapter.

Guided Reading

1. Have students read the chapter and use the Study Guide on pp. 81-82 of the *Student Workbook*.

Teaching. . .
Managing Your Time and Becoming an Effective Time Manager
(pp. 195-197)

Comprehension Check

1. What are two advantages of taking charge of your time? *(You have time to do what needs to be done and to do things you like best.)*
2. What are three ways to prevent interruptions? *(Announce your wish not to be interrupted; tell people when you'll be able to call them back; avoid places where you can be interrupted.)*
3. What is an important reference to use when you prepare your "To Do" list? *(Your monthly calendar.)*

Learning Activities

1. **Time Analysis.** Have students make and follow a "To Do" list for several days, assigning priorities to each item, and crossing them off when completed. Or, have students record everything they do for 24 hours. Total the time spent in each activity. Ask: Are you getting all you want from your 24 hours? Where are the weak spots? How could you improve? (Key Skills: *Problem Solving, Management*)
2. **Calendar Work.** Provide students with calendar pages for the coming month. Have them write in their present commitments. Ask how a calendar helps if they have a part-time job or if their family schedules a special

Figure 18-1 Knowing Where the Time Goes

The following techniques will help you take charge of your time.

More About *Managing Time*

Teens and their families can work together to save time by streamlining various household maintenance tasks. One way is to simplify the inside environment by using fewer accessories and pieces of furniture. Another way is to decorate with practicality in mind. This may include choosing upholstery fabrics which show soil the least and using simple window treatments that do not require frequent care. A third way is to discard items that are unneeded or unused. Cleaning out closets, medicine cabinets, and outdated piles of paperwork can help change a too-busy household into a time conscious one.

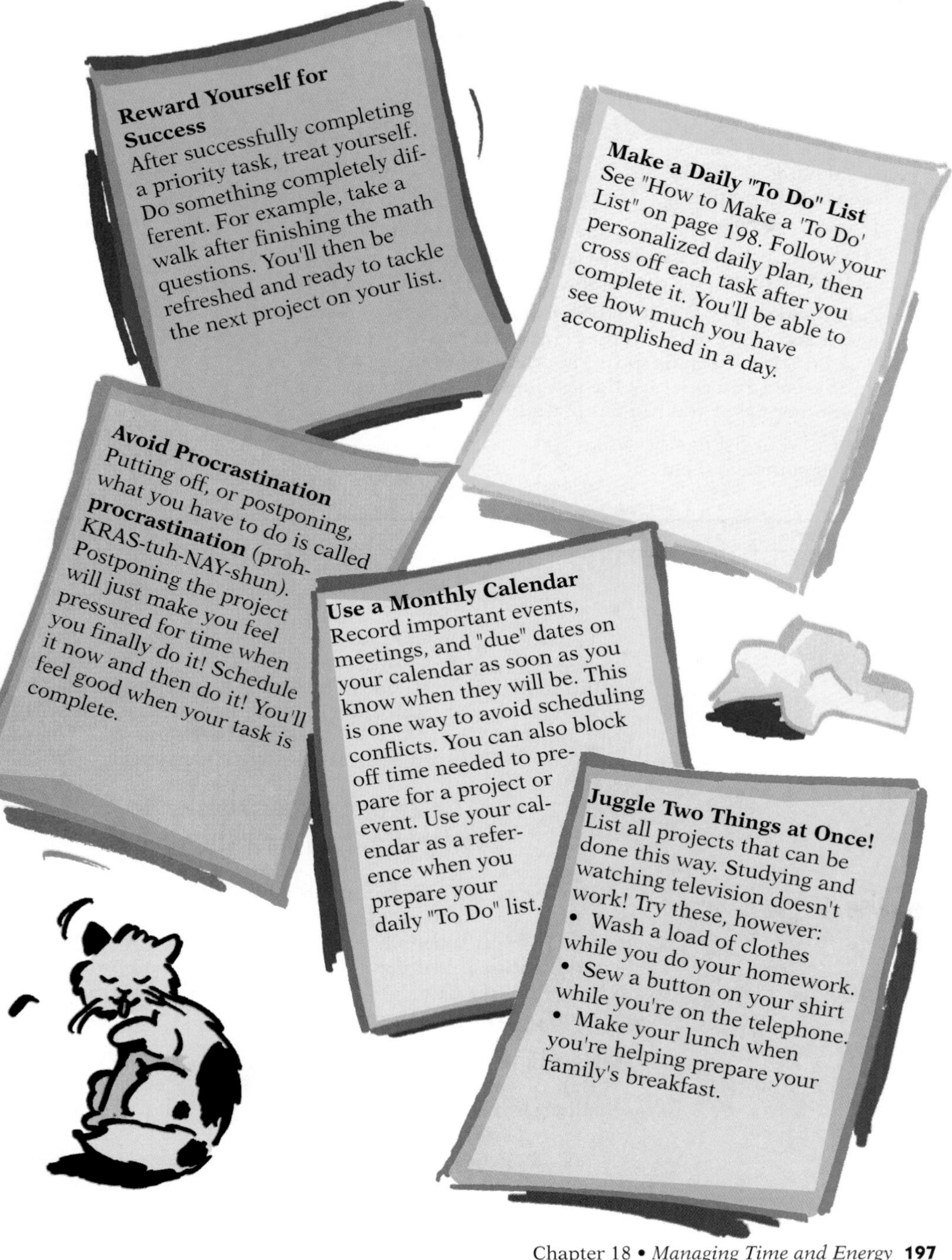

Learning Activities (continued)

celebration. How else do calendars help manage time? (Key Skills: *Communication, Management*)

3. **Skits.** Select students to write and present skits about an efficiency expert who is advising clients on ways to use time more effectively. Have students share time saving tips they use. (Key Skills: *Management, Creativity*)
4. **Response Practice.** Divide students into two groups. Have groups demonstrate tactful responses when friends call and interrupt: 1.) study time and 2.) family mealtimes. (Key Skill: *Communication*)

Follow Up

1. **Reteaching.** Assign students to make "To Do" lists of tasks and other activities to be done for one day. Rank items in priority order and discuss reasons for the rankings. (Key Skills: *Decision Making, Management*)
2. **Enrichment.** Ask volunteers to create activity kits to use when they have short segments of time. (Examples: a writing kit with stationery and letters to answer; a sewing kit by the phone with sewing supplies and garments to mend; reading kits with books and crossword puzzles.) Display the kits that students made and descriptions of when to use them. (Key Skills: *Management, Creativity*)

Life Management Skills

Use Short Segments of Time

If people could save ten minutes each day, every day, their time bank account would increase by more than sixty-hours each year — more than an average work week. Ask small groups to list mini-tasks to do in odd moments, such as during television commercials, or when waiting for someone. What tasks can be combined with others to save time?

More About Procrastination

A true crisis cannot be avoided. Poor planning and procrastination, however, can easily turn a simple task into a major crisis. It is unwise for people to wait until the zero hour to complete a task when they know a week or two in advance that the assignment is due. Procrastination can lead to mental and physical fatigue. Rarely is it worth the pain or the pressure. Instead, doing tasks when a person's energy and time are at their peak can get jobs done and reduce unnecessary pressure.

Teaching. . .
Balancing Schoolwork, Family Life, and Activities
(pp. 198-199)

Comprehension Check

1. What are obligations? *(Things that you must do.)*
2. Why is it helpful to review notes soon after class? *(To clarify them if needed.)*
3. What physical conditions will help you study more effectively outside of class? *(You need a well-lighted, quiet place that is not stuffy and where you can sit at a desk or table.)*

Learning Activities

1. **Personal Analysis.** Ask students: Are you always rushing? Do you have enough time for rest or for personal relationships in your life? Do you regularly miss deadlines? Discuss the difficulty of balancing schoolwork, family life, and other activities. (Key Skill: *Communication*)
2. **Discussion.** Ask students: Which do you put the most thought into — spending time on Saturday or Sunday or spending your allowance? Discuss the answers. (Key Skill: *Critical Thinking*)
3. **Small Groups.** Ask groups to discuss ways teens could reward themselves for successfully completing school projects, home tasks, and other activities. Have each group share some ideas. (Key Skill: *Critical Thinking*)
4. **Note Taking.** Tell students you will collect their notes on today's class. Evaluate and discuss the completed notes. Ask students to share tips on note taking. (Key Skill: *Communication*)
5. **Guest Speakers.** Invite favorite teachers to give tips on note taking, studying, and test taking. Have students take notes and write a summary of the suggestions. (Key Skill: *Communication*)

How to . . .
Make a "To Do" List

Making a "To Do" list helps you to get the most out of each day. In preparing a "To Do" list, use the following steps:

1. Write down all the tasks and activities that you intend to accomplish that day. Be as realistic as possible. Don't include more on your list than you will be able to do.
2. **Prioritize** (pry-OR-uh-TIES), or rank the items on your list according to their importance. After each item, place a 1, 2, or 3, with the most important items rating a 1. This way, you can save the less important items for another day if you run out of time.
3. Keep your list handy so that you can cross off items as you complete them.

Periodically, evaluate how your time management skills are serving you. If you find your "To Do" lists include too much, make the next ones shorter. If you forget to check your monthly calendar, put it in a place where you will remember it. The object is to learn what works and what doesn't so that you can become a better time manager.

▼ Balancing Schoolwork, Family Life, and Activities ▼

Having enough time for schoolwork, your family, and your friends isn't easy. It means keeping your goals and values in mind as you schedule your use of time. You most likely have **obligations**, or things that you must do or have promised to do. After you finish those, you can spend what time you have left on other activities.

Making Time for Learning

Half of your waking hours are spent at school or doing schoolwork. Thus it is important that you learn to manage your school-related hours well.

You can get more out of class time if you have done your homework and know what the day's subject is about. Then, by listening closely and paying attention, you can better

How to ... Make a "To Do" List

Assign students to debate the relationship of people's values and goals to their ranking of items on their "To Do" List. Encourage students to think of number 1 items as "absolutely essential," number 2 items as "something they should do,"and number 3s as "something that would be nice to do if they had the time." Remind them to carry uncompleted priority items to their next day's list. Talk about how some number 3 items may never get done or carried over to a new list. The important point is to concentrate on number 1 items.

understand what your teacher is talking about. You will also learn the subject matter better and more easily. Take notes on the important points that are presented and discussed in class. Good notes will help jog your memory when you study after class. Also write down assignments, instructions for doing them, and the dates when they are due.

As soon after class as possible, find a few minutes to review your notes. Going over your notes while they are fresh in your mind allows you to clarify the information. You may also find it helpful to rewrite your class notes in a more organized way. The tips shown below will help you to improve your study skills outside of class.

TIPS: *Taking Notes*

To take effective notes, try these tips:

- Take notes in outline form, focusing on main ideas.
- Use a few words to write down the main ideas and supporting details. It's impossible to write down every word your teacher says.
- Abbreviate words when you can. For example, use "w/" instead of "with."
- Double or triple space your notes. You can fill in more details later if needed.
- Review your notes frequently.
- Use different colored highlighter markers to emphasize main ideas and supporting details.

More About *Managing Time and Space*

Good time managers avoid the crowded desk syndrome. Desk tops should be a work area rather than an open file cabinet. When people clutter their desk with numerous papers and files, they give the impression of being disorganized. Also, they place themselves in a position of being easily distracted from their task at hand. People tend to be more efficient with their time if they keep only those materials on their desk that pertain to the current task. Other materials should be placed out of sight. This will help people give the task at hand the priority it deserves.

Follow Up

1. **Reteaching.** Have students list the kinds of interruptions they experience while studying at home. Assign them to small groups to discuss ways to minimize or avoid the interruptions. Ask groups to share suggestions. (Key Skills: *Critical Thinking, Management*)
2. **Enrichment.** Select students to create and present a puppet show for younger students featuring specific study tips that students can use in the classroom, in study hall, and at home. (Key Skills: *Creativity, Management*)

Life Management Skills

Managing Study Space

Making *time* for learning is one of the most effective ways of reducing study stress. Another way to reduce study stress is by making *room* for learning. In class, talk about how to choose a place to study that instantly means "get to work." Have students make a portable desk from a large, sturdy cardboard box and decorate the box to display in the classroom. Collect a supply of pens, pencils, erasers, paper clips, scrap paper, and file folders. Include a stapler, scissors, ruler, and dictionary. Brainstorm other ways to make study places pleasant and efficient.

TIPS:

Taking Notes
After students read the feature, ask them to take notes on all or part of this chapter and compare note-taking techniques and shortcuts.

Teaching. . .
Making Time for Family, Friends, and Activities; Managing Your Energy
(pp. 200-202)

Comprehension Check

1. What does it mean to "manage your time"? *(To make choices that make the most of time.)*
2. Why does it help to be aware of your regular energy cycle? *(So you can schedule jobs that require alertness and energy when you are at your peak.)*
3. What are four health habits that can help increase your energy level? *(Eating healthful foods, getting adequate rest, exercising regularly, and avoiding harmful substances.)*
4. What are four work simplification techniques? *(Analyzing each job, thinking about what it involves; using the best tool or utensil for the job; conserving your energy by conserving motion; organizing storage areas now to save energy later.)*
5. What is one way to conserve energy by conserving motion? *(Using a tray, basket, or cart to carry several items in one trip instead of several.)*

Learning Activities

1. **Class Survey.** Survey the class to see who are morning persons and who are night persons. Ask them to think about daily times when they have high energy or when they seem droopy. Contrast their energy cycles. (Key Skill: *Communication*)

AROUND THE WORLD

Have students with foreign pen pals find out about time spent in school and on homework and share the responses. Invite foreign students to your class to talk about school experiences in their home countries, contrasting them with your school. Ask them to describe their school systems and required courses for high school students.

AROUND THE WORLD

A recent survey of how people in Japan and the United States spend their time produced some interesting results. Adults in both countries spend about the same amount of time working, eating, and sleeping, and on leisure activities. However, Japanese children spend a vastly different amount of time on school work than American children. Japanese school children spend about 55% more hours in class than American children and about five times as many hours on homework. What factors might be responsible for this great difference?

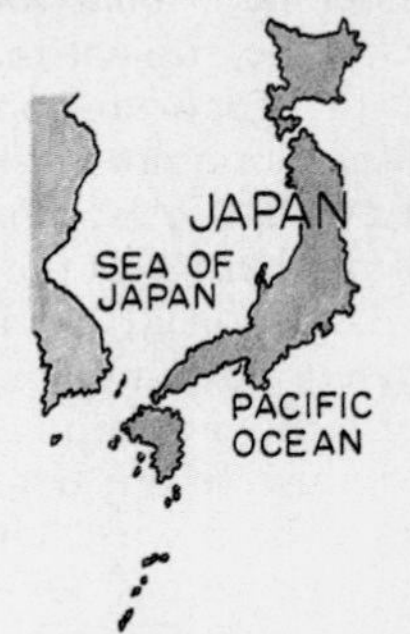

Making Time for Family, Friends, and Activities

When you aren't involved in school activities, there are still many things that you may want or need to do. It takes time to be a good family member and to be a good friend. In addition, you need time for yourself to pursue your interests and relax. Careful time management is required to have plenty of time for everything.

One way to avoid time shortages in your out-of-school life is planning. Decide ahead of time what you will do, and set aside the time for it. Make plans with your parents or your brothers and sisters. Record those plans on your monthly calendar. Plan to share a favorite activity with a friend or friends. Find out when everyone is free, and commit to that time.

Planning ahead keeps you from wasting time. You won't suddenly find yourself with nothing to do. It also helps you to focus on what is important to you. People tend to spend

Getting your studying done early gives you more time to spend with friends and family.

More About *Making Time to Exercise and Relax*

No effective time management plan is complete unless people have time to exercise and relax. The body and mind are like a well-run machine controlled by a very complex computer. Both the body and the mind need to be nourished, exercised, and allowed to rest and relax. For this reason, each day needs to include physical activity. People are better able to work effectively with the time they have if they are in good physical condition. Likewise, people need to schedule time for activities that they find restful and relaxing more time on the things that they value. If you value time with your brother, you might plan to talk with him, play catch, or go fishing. If you and your friend share an interest in art, you might skip watching television to go to the museum. To manage your time well, you need to make choices — often based on the things that you value — about how to get the most out of it. This might mean limiting telephone time in order to exercise. It could also mean giving some of your time to help others.

Managing Your Energy

Do you operate in high gear in the morning and slow down in the afternoon? Perhaps, instead, you get off to a slow start but become so energetic at night that it's hard to go to sleep. Whether you are a morning person or a night person, you — like all people — have a regular energy cycle. It helps to remember this and schedule jobs that require alertness and energy when you are at your peak.

You can increase your energy level in general by improving your health habits. Eat healthful foods. Get adequate rest. Exercise regularly and avoid harmful substances. Chapter 37 will give you more specifics about health habits and good health.

Another important aspect of energy management is saving energy through **work simplification**. This means finding the easiest and quickest way to do each job well. Here are some ideas that will help you conserve your energy as you work:

Day people rise early, do their best work in the morning, slow down in the afternoon, and fade in the evening. Night people are slow starters in the morning, pick up in the afternoon, and are at their best during the evening.

Learning Activities (continued)

2. **Display Case.** Assist students in setting up a display of time- and energy-saving tools, trays, utensils, and other supplies in the classroom or in a showcase in the hallway. Title the display "Hour Power — Tools to Save You Time and Energy." Have students first make a list of items in groups and then have them demonstrate some of the tools they have included. (Key Skills: *Communication, Management*)

Follow Up

1. **Reteaching.** Present a case study about Tom, a teen who has trouble managing his energy. Have each student write him a letter suggesting ways to save energy. Also, ask them to give Tom some hints on increasing his energy level by following good health habits. Ask for volunteers to read their letters to the class. (Key Skills: *Communication, Critical Thinking*)
2. **Extension.** Use the activity on p. 27 of the *Extending the Lesson* booklet in the TCR.
3. **Enrichment.** Assign students to redesign storage areas in the classroom to make maximum use of energy and time. Have them take before and after photographs of each storage area. Display and discuss the photos. (Key Skills: *Problem Solving, Decision Making*)

Family Perspective

Some teens never seem to have time to do their share of household tasks. They may put off cleaning their room, mowing the grass, or straightening closets. Introduce the game, "Time Roulette," for getting started on unpleasant tasks. Have students write three to five jobs they have been putting off on slips of paper. Have each put the slips in an envelope; on a day when they have extra time, draw a slip and do the job. Even if they draw a much-disliked job, they are on their honor to get it done.

Completing the Chapter

For Review

1. Emphasize the main concepts using the summary.
2. Have students complete the "Facts to Recall." (Answers below.)

For Reteaching

1. **Reteaching.** Use the activity on p. 25 of the *Reteaching and Practical Skills* booklet in the TCR.

For Enrichment

1. **Enrichment.** Use the activity on pp. 35-36 of the *Enrichment Activities* booklet in the TCR.

For Evaluation

1. Choose items from "Ideas to Explore" and "Activities to Try."
2. Use the chapter test on pp. 39-40 in the testing booklet of the TCR or use the testmaker software.

Facts to Recall Answers

1. Planning your use of time to get the most out of it.
2. It gives you a good idea of where your time goes and if you are wasting it.
3. Deciding what you want to accomplish in a certain time period; writing down necessary tasks and time needed to complete each one. It helps you focus on what you need and want to do.
4. They help you plan ahead, so you can use your time instead of stopping to think about what you need to do next.
5. Interruptions cause time loss because you must recover your train of thought. Procrastination causes you to feel pressured for time.
6. When you are prepared for class, you understand the topic more easily. You can thus take better notes, helping you do your assignment quickly and well, which prepares you for the next day's class.
7. They help determine which activities you choose.

- ***Analyze each job, thinking about what it involves.*** Can any steps in the process be omitted or combined? For example, when you wash dishes by hand, you may also be drying them. If you skip this step and let the dishes air dry, you can do something else with the time you would have spent drying dishes.
- ***Always use the best tool or utensil for the job.*** If you choose the wrong tool just because it is easily found, you will waste time and possibly energy, too.
- ***Conserve your energy by conserving motion.*** For example, you might use a tray, basket, or cart to carry several items at once so you only have to make one trip instead of several trips.
- ***Organize your storage areas.*** Store articles where they are used most often. Place the items that you use frequently where you can easily see and reach them. Make use of free or inexpensive containers to separate articles in drawers and on shelves. That way, you won't waste your energy hunting for things when you need them.

You can probably think of many other ways to save yourself time and energy. Give your own ideas a try, along with the suggestions in this chapter. Do whatever works best for you in managing your time and energy. The important point is for you to take charge of your time and energy resources.

TAKING ACTION

Managing a Busy Schedule

Nicole clears tables and washes dishes at Dino's restaurant four times a week. Her work shift starts at 5 p.m. Sometimes she doesn't get home until after midnight.

Trying to juggle schoolwork, swim team practice, her job, and a social life puts Nicole under strain. If she has a test, she ends up studying after work and misses out on a good night's sleep. Nicole gets sick more often since she started her job. Her grades have also suffered. She breaks dates on weekends simply because she's too tired to go out. However, Nicole insists that she needs her job for extra spending money and to help save for college. She comes to you for some help with her schedule.

Using Your Resourcefulness

- What options does Nicole have to manage her time and energy more effectively?
- How would you suggest that she change or eliminate activities to reduce her stress?
- List two or three activities that you would like to add to your life. How would you manage your time and energy to get the most out of these?
- Make a monthly schedule of your own. Indicate how you will use your time each day.

TAKING ACTION

Ask for volunteers to interview schoolmates who are employed in part-time jobs. Have them make a list of questions to ask about school and work schedules, other activities, work's effect on grades, time- and energy-saving tips, health, level of stress, etc. Share the results of the interviews with the class. Have students identify the goals and values of the workers. Contrast their schedules and obligations with those of Nicole (p. 15).

Using Your Resourcefulness Answers

- Answers will vary. Nicole needs to prioritize her activities and possibly think about eliminating one from her schedule.

Chapter 18 Review

Summary

In this chapter, you have read about:

- Tips on getting the most out of your time to accomplish what you want.
- Tactics for using study time more efficiently.
- Finding time for out-of-school interests through planning and making choices.
- Managing your energy through work simplification.

Facts to Recall

1. What is time management?
2. How can recording your activities for one day help you begin to manage your time?
3. What does setting goals involve? How does goal setting help you manage your time?
4. Explain how making a daily "To Do" list and using a monthly calendar can help you use your time well.
5. What time management problems are caused by interruptions? By procrastination?
6. Explain how being prepared for class and taking good notes can help you get the most out of class time.
7. How do the things you value affect the way you plan your time?
8. Explain how to organize storage areas to save your energy.

Ideas to Explore

1. What do you find is the biggest obstacle to managing your time? How can it be overcome?
2. Describe an incident in which your values helped you solve a time or energy management problem when one or both were limited.
3. Theresa and Anton have promised to fix a pasta dinner for their family. They must warm the tomato sauce, cook the noodles, prepare a tossed salad, set the table, and clean up the kitchen before serving dinner. Give an example of two tasks that they can do at the same time to save time.
4. Why do you think people procrastinate? How can this habit be corrected?

Activities to Try

1. Make a "To Do" list for one day. Prioritize your tasks. See how many you have accomplished when your class meets again.
2. Write a short paragraph identifying three times during the past week when your schedule has been interrupted. Suggest ways of avoiding those situations in the future.

LINK TO *Science*

IMPROVING EFFICIENCY

The study of *human engineering*, or *ergonomics*, applies scientific knowledge about the human body and behavior to designing and building better tools and equipment. Today, this knowledge is applied to office equipment, farm and industrial machines, and other mechanical devices. The object is to reduce fatigue and health-related problems and to increase speed and accuracy. Human engineering also takes into account the lighting, spacing, ventilation (circulation of fresh air), noise level, and location of equipment. Try to think of ways that a work area or piece of equipment you use at home could be improved to make it easier to use. Draw a sketch of your improved version. Write down the details that support the changes you have made in your improved version.

Facts to Recall Answers (continued)

8. Store articles where they are most often used, where you can easily see and reach them.

Ideas to Explore

1. Answers will vary.
2. Answers will vary.
3. Answers will vary and may include: warming sauce while heating water for noodles; preparing salad while noodles cook.
4. Answers will vary.

- Answers will vary. Evaluate her time schedule to find small amounts of time she might use for studying and other tasks.
- Answers will vary.
- Schedules will vary.

LINK TO *Science*

Answer

Direct students to read the feature. Find a badly-arranged or used room (or a task that is being done clumsily) or a spot in the school building that needs a new plan and ask students to use it as the subject for the activity in the feature, or simply use your kitchen or sewing labs. Encourage them to be creative. Hang drawings and rationale and allow time for students to compare their ideas. Vote on the best and submit them to the principal or school newspaper.

Preparing to Teach

Chapter Outline

Chapter Resources

The following booklet materials may be found in the *Teacher's Classroom Resources* box:

- Lesson Plans, p. 24
- Student Workbook, *Study Guide,* pp. 85-86; *Write It Down,* p. 87; *What Kind of Money Manager Are You?,* p. 88
- Color Transparencies, *Paying for Purchases,* CT-20
- Personal Safety, *Keep Your Possessions Safe,* pp. 25-26
- Technology and Computers, pp. 17, 18, 22, 26
- Cooperative Learning, p. 31
- Extending the Text, *Special Checks and Money Orders,* pp. 28-29
- Reteaching and Practical Skills, *Money as a Resource Word Search,* p. 27
- Enrichment Activities, *Money Issues and Concerns,* p. 34
- Chapter and Unit Tests, pp. 41-42
- Testmaker Software

Also see:

- Meeting the Special Needs of Students
- Linking Home, School, and Community
- Dealing with Sensitive Issues

CHAPTER 19 Managing Money

OBJECTIVES

- *Use records of your income and expenses to make a budget.*
- *Give guidelines for using checking and savings accounts and credit.*

TERMS TO LEARN

- ***income***
- ***expenses***
- ***budget***
- ***endorse***
- ***deposit slip***
- ***check register***
- ***balance***
- ***interest***
- ***credit***

Managing your money effectively is a skill you will need throughout life. Whether you have little money or a great deal, money management skills are still important. People who manage their money well will achieve a balance between money going out and money coming in. They get what they need and want without wasting money on things they don't really need or want. Good money managers are careful not to spend more than they can actually afford. They also plan ahead for future spending. This allows them to meet the costs of their future goals.

Looking at Your Current Financial Picture

Before you can begin managing money better, it helps to know how you're managing money now. You may not even think about where your money goes or about how much money you have for spending and saving. One way to clarify your current financial (money-related) picture is to keep simple financial records. You might keep a weekly record for several weeks and then study and compare these records to learn from them.

To start a weekly record, first write down your **income**. That's the amount of money that you have coming in. It may be the pay you receive from babysitting or from a part-time job. Your income might also come from an allowance that your parents give you. Figure out the total of your weekly income by adding together all money received from various sources. Getting a clear idea of your income will allow you to see how much money you have available for use.

Next, keep track of your **expenses**. These are the things on which you spend money. Common teen expenses include snacks and meals, clothing, and entertainment such as movies.

Learning to manage your money as a teen will be a benefit in adulthood.

More About *Learning to Manage Money*

Personal money management is a skill that can be learned, developed with practice, and enjoyed like other skills. It is an important skill, because the job of managing money is a lifetime one. Some people do it well and live smoothly and pleasantly. Others seem to stumble from one financial disaster to the next. They never seem to solve their personal financial problems. However, most individuals and families work hard for their money and try to see that it is managed and used wisely.

Introducing the Chapter

Motivators

1. **Personal Analysis.** Ask students to divide a sheet of paper into two columns: "Needed" and "Wanted." Under the "Needed" column list items they have purchased within the last year that they really needed (winter coat or new shoes to replace a worn-out pair). Under the "Wanted" column list items that they wanted rather than needed (costume jewelry, cosmetics, CD). Check each wise purchase and circle each poor selection. Why do they consider the purchase an unwise one? (Key Skill: *Critical Thinking*)
2. **Bulletin Board.** Display play money by pictures of items purchased by teens. Title the board: "Dollars and Sense — How Wise Are Your Purchases?" (Key Skill: *Creativity*)
3. **Discussion.** Ask students to discuss how self-concepts, values, and goals influence people's purchases. (Key Skill: *Critical Thinking*)
4. **Advertisements.** Have students find ads directed to teens. Display and discuss them, talking about future goals vs. wasting money. (Key Skill: *Communication*)

Chapter Objectives and Vocabulary

1. Have students read the chapter objectives. Ask them to rephrase the objectives as questions.
2. Ask students to state, in their own words, the purpose of studying this chapter.
3. Pronounce the vocabulary terms listed on the previous page. Ask students whether they are familiar with any of these. Explain that the terms will be defined in the chapter.

Guided Reading

1. Have students read the chapter and use the Study Guide on pp. 85-86 of the *Student Workbook*.

Teaching. . .

Looking at Your Current Financial Picture; Planning for Better Money Management

(pp. 205-207)

Comprehension Check

1. What is one way to clarify your current financial picture? *(Keep simple financial records, such as a weekly record, for several weeks.)*
2. What is the difference between income and expenses? *(Income is the amount of money that you have coming in; expenses are the things on which you spend your money.)*
3. Give four examples of fixed expenses. *(Lunch, transportation, savings, and school activity fees.)*
4. What is a budget? *(A plan for how you want and intend to use your money.)*

Learning Activities

1. **Brainstorming.** Compile a list of ways that teens can earn extra income. (Key Skill: *Communication*)
2. **Discussion.** Ask students to list and discuss some of the daily, weekly, and monthly expenses of most families. (Key Skill: *Communication*)
3. **Personal Spending Analysis.** Have students keep an accurate record of all the money they receive for two weeks, including earnings from jobs and allowance. Ask them to record in a notebook every cent they spend during the same time. At the end of the two weeks, have them classify their expenses into these categories: food, school supplies, entertainment, transportation, grooming, savings, and miscellaneous. Next, have them total each category and analyze their data. Are there categories where they spend more than they thought? How might they improve their spending habits to make their money go farther? (Key Skills: *Problem Solving, Management*)

Transportation to school is a fixed expense for many teens. What are some of your fixed expenses?

Some expenses come about regularly. They are the same, or about the same, all the time. These are called *fixed expenses*. Many fixed expenses are costs for items and services that you need. Your fixed expenses might include such things as lunch, transportation, savings, and school activity fees. Divide your fixed expenses into categories. Then record how much you spend in each category.

After your fixed expenses, record the flexible ones. *Flexible expenses* vary from time to time. They are often expenses for items and services that you want rather than need. You might decide to buy a concert ticket or spend money on a hobby. In your financial record, write down these costs by category. You will probably find that your categories change each week.

As you study your weekly records, compare the totals of your income and your expenses. Do you spend all the money that you get, or do you have some left over? Look closely at your expenses. Are you spending too much in a particular category? Are you wasting money on things you don't really need? Are you satisfied with your spending habits?

Planning for Better Money Management

After identifying how you are managing money now, you can plan to manage your money better. You can change spending habits that don't please you by making different choices about how you will use your money. For example,

More About Automated Teller Machines

If you use automated teller machines (ATMs), there are several safety tips to keep in mind. First, use ATMs that are located in well-lighted areas with good general visibility. Consider having someone accompany you to the machine, especially at night. Do not use an ATM if you notice questionable activities occurring in the area. If the ATM is a walk-up, do not leave the car running or keys in the ignition. If the ATM is a drive-up, keep the engine running and the doors locked. Cancel your transaction at the first sign of suspicious activity. If you make a withdrawal from an ATM, put your cash away immediately.

Ben decided to spend less on snacks after school — something he didn't need — and save money for more important things in the future. If you want to save money for future use, you can choose to cut back your spending now.

A good way to accomplish managing your money is to create a **budget**. A budget is a plan for using the money you have available. When you make a budget for yourself, you are setting up financial guidelines. By following these guidelines, you will be able to reach your personal money management goals and live within your income. Here are some tips for creating a budget:

- First, record the income that you plan to have during the period of your budget. Base your income figure on what you learned from keeping weekly records.
- Next, write down what you plan to spend on fixed and flexible expenses. This information should reflect the choices you have made. Be sure to categorize your expenses. On what will you spend your money? How much will you spend? Be as realistic as you can. This will help you make a budget that you can live within.
- Review your budget periodically to see how it is working. If you have allowed too much or too little for some items, adjust your plan accordingly. If you have forgotten one or more expenses, include these as you update your budget.

In working with your budget, you learn to manage your money through practice. As time passes, your money management skills will improve.

AROUND THE WORLD

The price of goods and services is not always the best indicator of the cost of living in a country. A more accurate measure is *purchasing power,* or the amount of goods and services your money can buy. For example, a recent survey by the United Bank of Switzerland shows that Zurich, Switzerland is one of the most expensive cities in the world in which to live, based on expenses such as housing, clothing, and food. However, the study also shows that workers there are among the highest-paid in the world, and that their purchasing power is 75% higher than the worldwide average. Workers in Mexico City are among the world's lowest-paid, and their purchasing power is only 21% of the average. In more concrete terms, the average consumer in Zurich has to work 20 minutes to earn enough to buy a hamburger; in Mexico City, it takes almost four hours of work — half a day — to buy a hamburger.

Learning Activities (continued)

4. **Questioning.** Ask and discuss the following questions: Where are automated teller machines located in the community? How are they alike? How do they differ? Why do some people use them more than others? What are some of the costs of using ATMs? What safety precautions should people follow when using ATMs? (Key Skill: *Critical Thinking*)
5. **Class Comparison.** Collect check registers from several different financial institutions. Reproduce them, and ask students to compare the forms. Discuss the advantages and disadvantages of each. (Key Skill: *Critical Thinking*)

Follow Up

1. **Reteaching.** Make copies of a blank check that students can use to practice writing checks. Ask them to list precautions to keep in mind when writing checks. (Key Skill: *Critical Thinking*)
2. **Enrichment.** Select students to visit financial institutions and ask about opening up checking and savings accounts. Have them find out the minimum amount of money needed to open each account, cost of services and percentage of interest paid. (Key Skill: *Communication*)

AROUND THE WORLD

After reading the feature, have students locate and display advertisements of various goods and services frequently purchased by teens and their families. Next, ask the class to compute how many hours a minimum wage earner would have to work to purchase each of the items and services. Write the total number of hours on the chalkboard. Afterwards, discuss the term, *purchasing power* and its relationship to the class activity.

More About Checking Accounts

When people are given a check, they should cash or deposit it as soon as possible. A check usually is a valid obligation of the check writer until barred by the "statute of limitations" — generally after six years. However, it becomes "stale" if not presented to the bank within a reasonable period of time. This time varies under different state laws, but usually is six months. Staleness indicates to the bank that there may be some reason why the check should not be paid, and the bank may require the writer's consent before paying it.

Teaching. . .
Understanding and Using Financial Services; Checking Accounts
(pp. 208-209)

Comprehension Check

1. What does it mean to make a deposit? *(To put money into your account.)*
2. What does it mean to endorse a check? *(To sign your name on the back — transferring the right to the check to someone else or the bank.)*
3. What information goes on a deposit slip? *(Amount of cash or check being deposited; total of cash and checks; any cash desired back; final total.)*

Learning Activities

1. **Display.** Set up a display of various checks, check registers, check stubs, and deposit and withdrawal slips. Title the display: "Comparing the Components of Checking Accounts." Discuss the display, and talk about the importance of keeping careful records of checks, deposits, and withdrawals. (Key Skill: *Communication*)
2. **Questioning.** Assign students to use classroom and library resources to answer and discuss these questions: What is a bounced check? What happens to the person who wrote the check? What happens to the person or business to whom the check was written? What does a bank charge for bounced checks? What do businesses do to avoid

Photo Focus

Direct the students to the photos on p. 208. Have them imagine that they are standing in front of these buildings, ready to open the door, go in and open a savings account. Why might they feel intimidated? *(Banks are serious places that usually deal with adults; they may think teens aren't serious.)* How should teens act in a bank?

There are several types of financial institutions including banks and credit unions.

Understanding and Using Financial Services

Financial institutions, such as banks and credit unions, can help you manage your money. These businesses offer services to assist you, both as you spend and as you save. You may use some of these services now. Others will be part of your future. By learning how the main financial services work, you will be better equipped to use them when you need to.

▼ Checking Accounts ▼

You've probably seen your parents writing checks as they make purchases and pay bills. You may also have received checks as payment for work or, perhaps, as gifts. Checks represent money that has been placed in a checking account by the person who writes the checks. A check is a written order to a financial institution to pay a specific amount to the person or business named on the check.

Having a checking account is a convenience. It means that you can use checks instead of always carrying money to pay in cash. You can send checks through the mail instead of paying bills in person. Never send cash through the mail — it can be easily stolen.

When you open a checking account, you will be agreeing to certain terms, or conditions. One term is that you will not write checks for more than the amount of money in your

When writing a check, you need to include the date the check was written, the person or business to be paid, and the amount of money to be paid written in numerals and words. You also need to endorse or sign your check.

JANE SMITH
12235 LAKE FOREST DR.
PEORIA, IL 61525

111

19

70-4
711

PAY TO THE ORDER OF $

DOLLARS

Commercial National Bank
OF PEORIA
Member Midwest Financial Group, Inc.
PEORIA, ILINOIS 61631

MEMO

⑆071100099⑆ ⑈099⑉5600⑈ 0111

More About Financial Services

In addition to checking and savings accounts, some financial institutions rent safe deposit boxes in their vaults. Safe deposit boxes are small metal containers that people rent to protect their valuables from fire and theft. Jewelry, birth certificates, wills, deeds, stocks and bonds, insurance policies, and other important items are often kept in the boxes.

It takes two keys to open a safe deposit box; one belonging to the renter and one held by the bank. No one else can open the safe deposit box without the renter's written permission and key.

DEPOSIT TICKET

JANE SMITH
12235 LAKE FOREST DR.
PEORIA, IL 61525

DATE *Sept. 12* 19*98*

CASH	CURRENCY	15	00
	COIN		
LIST CHECKS SINGLY	70-8/711	27	63
TOTAL FROM OTHER SIDE		—	
TOTAL		42	63
LESS CASH RECEIVED			
NET DEPOSIT		42	63

70-4
711

USE OTHER SIDE FOR ADDITIONAL LISTING

BE SURE EACH ITEM IS PROPERLY ENDORSED

Commercial National Bank
OF PEORIA
Member Midwest Financial Group, Inc.
PEORIA, ILLINOIS 61631

⑈0994⑉5600⑈

CHECKS AND OTHER ITEMS ARE RECEIVED FOR DEPOSIT SUBJECT TO THE PROVISIONS OF THE UNIFORM COMMERCIAL CODE OR ANY APPLICABLE COLLECTION AGREEMENT.

You must fill out a deposit slip to deposit money into your checking account.

account. Another common term is that you will pay fees for the handling of your account by the bank. There may be a service charge every month. Some financial institutions may charge a fee for each check you write. Fees on checking accounts vary greatly depending on where you have your account and how much you keep in it. Compare the terms on accounts at different financial institutions. Before you select your account, be sure you understand the terms.

To begin using your checking account, you must first make a deposit, or put money into your account. You will deposit money periodically, as it is needed, to cover checks you will be writing. You may deposit cash or checks written to you by other people or businesses. Before depositing a check, you have to **endorse** it, or sign your name on the back. (This transfers your right to the check over to someone else — in this case, the bank.) Each time you make a deposit, you will need to fill out a **deposit slip**. This slip must have your checking account number on it. If the number is not preprinted, you will have to write the number on the slip. On the deposit slip, you write in the amount of cash being deposited (if any) and also individually list the amount of each check (if any) you want to deposit. You then total the amounts of all checks and the cash. If you want any cash back, you enter the amount desired and subtract it from the total. Your final total will be the amount you will be depositing in your account.

Your checkbook has two important parts. The first is the checks, which you will fill out as needed by writing the date, the name of the person or business you are paying, an amount written first in figures then in words, and your signature.

Learning Activities (continued)

bad checks? What safeguards do banks provide customers? (Key Skill: *Communication*)

3. **Discussion.** Ask students to imagine that they have opened a joint checking account with their spouse. Discuss these questions as a class or in small groups: Who is in charge of the checking account? Is the responsibility evenly shared? Who makes the deposits? The withdrawals? Who writes the checks? Who balances the checkbook? What can they do to prevent overdrawing? (Key Skills: *Communication, Management*)

Follow Up

1. **Reteaching.** Have students collect and display advertisements of checking accounts and their fees (and interest rates, if any) at different financial institutions. (Key Skill: *Critical Thinking*)
2. **Enrichment.** Ask for volunteers to interview a bank teller and other bank employees about their careers along with other career choices in banking. Discuss the interview findings with the class. (Key Skill: *Communication*)

Life Management Skills

Stopping Payment on a Check

Present a short case study to the class about a teen who lost a check he had written to buy tickets to a special event. Write the word "stop payment" on the chalkboard, and have volunteers ask a local financial institution for information. Have them report back to the class:

- What does "stop payment" mean?
- What are some instances when people stop payment on a check?
- What happens if a check is deposited before payment is stopped?

Teaching. . .
Checking and Savings Accounts
(pp. 210-211)

Comprehension Check

1. What is a check register? *(A record of deposits and withdrawals from your checking account.)*
2. Why does it pay to compare interest rates before opening a savings account? *(Because different financial institutions have different interest rates.)*
3. What is interest for a savings account? *(Money a financial institution pays you at regular intervals for using your money.)*

Learning Activities

1. **Brainstorming.** Have students brainstorm a list of advantages and disadvantages of using a checking account. (Key Skill: *Critical Thinking*)
2. **Math.** Have students compute the simple interest from the following savings accounts: $200 principal at 5% interest yearly; $185 principal at 4% interest yearly; $120 principal at 5.5% interest yearly. *($10.00; $7.40; $6.60)* (Key Skills: *Math, Problem Solving*)

Life Management Skills

Compound Interest

Interest paid annually on savings accounts is called simple interest. Today, most finanacial institutions pay interest quarterly, monthly, or daily. The interest is added to the savings before calculating the new interest — called *compounding*. Compounded interest will pay more than simple interest over a period of time.

How to . . .
Reconcile Your Bank Account Statement with Your Checkbook Balance

Follow these simple steps to reconcile your bank account statement with the balance in your check register:

1. Write the last balance shown on your bank account statement.

   $__________

2. Total any deposits you have made that do not appear on this statement or any previous statements. **Add** this amount to the one that appears on your statement.

   New Total: $__________

3. Write down all the checks that you have written that do not appear on this or any previous statement. Then total all the amounts.

Check Number	Amount of Check
______	______
______	______
______	______
______	______
______	______
______	______

   Total of checks still out: $__________

4. After you have added the amounts for the checks that are still out, *subtract* this total from the total in Step 2. This amount should agree with the balance in your check register.

   Final Balance: $__________

How to . . . Reconcile Your Bank Account Statement with Your Checkbook Balance

Give students a list of 20 or more checking account transactions, an opening balance, and blank check register pages. Assign them to calculate the present balance in the imaginary account. Point out the need to reconcile a bank account statement soon after receiving it. Give each student a bank statement to go with this imaginary account to practice reconciling the statement and checkbook register. Explain that this allows the account holder to catch quickly any personal errors or mistakes made by the financial institution.

The second part of your checkbook is for keeping a record of your account as you go along. It is called a **check register**. Each time you make a deposit or write a check, you record this information in your check register. When you make a deposit, you record the amount deposited and the day's date and then add this amount to the amount you already have in your account. When you write a check, you record the check number, the date the check was written, the party paid, and the amount. Then you subtract the amount of the check from the total you have in your account. The new total is called your **balance**, or the total amount of money remaining in your account.

It's as easy as that. Addition and subtraction are the only math skills required for using a checkbook. Careful record keeping is essential, however, if you want to manage your checkbook well.

Your financial institution will also keep records on your account and send them to you. These records, called statements, will tell you which checks have been paid, what deposits have been made, and what fees you have been charged. Go over each statement to be sure that your own records are correct. Subtract any fees you haven't already subtracted. Be certain your balance agrees with that on the statement. You may also receive your cancelled, or paid, checks back when you receive your statements. If you do, keep these as proof of bills you have paid and money you have spent.

▼ Savings Accounts ▼

Unlike checking accounts, savings accounts don't help you manage the money that you spend. Instead, their purpose is to assist you in managing your efforts to save. You might save money toward an expensive purchase. You might also put money away to pay for college. Families often save up for future vacations, new cars, new homes, and unplanned expenses, such as emergencies.

One advantage of savings accounts is that they keep your money safe until later. They also help you increase the amount you put away by paying you something called interest. **Interest** is the money a financial institution pays you at regular intervals for allowing it to use your money. The interest will be a certain percentage of the amount in your savings. Different financial institutions pay different percentages, or interest rates. It pays to compare interest rates before opening your account.

Many people open savings accounts to save for large expenditures such as a college education or an automobile.

More About *Saving Money*

If people have money to save for a certain period of time, they may choose to buy a certificate of deposit. A certificate of deposit (CD) usually pays a higher rate of interest than a savings account. This is because a CD requires people to commit their money for a specified period of time such as six months, two and a half years, or five years. In most cases the longer people agree to hold a CD, the higher the rate of interest they earn. If the certificate is cashed before the time period is up, a penalty may be charged.

Learning Activities (continued)

3. **Writing.** Write the following topic sentence on the board: "If you plan to manage your money wisely, you must protect your best interests." Then list the following terms: *savings account, checking account, interest*. Ask students to write an essay of two or more paragraphs that begins with the topic sentence and uses all the terms in appropriate contexts. (Key Skills: *Critical Thinking, Communication*)
4. **Guest Speaker.** Invite speakers from different banking institutions to speak to the class about the benefits of their institutions, the type and variety of accounts, hours, locations, bank services, etc. Encourage students to prepare questions for the speakers prior to the presentation. (Key Skills: *Cooperation, Critical Thinking*)
5. **Software Analysis.** Ask volunteers to visit a computer store to try out a checking account software package. Have them draw comparisons between the software and manually recording a checking account. Have them share their observations with the class. (Key Skills: *Communication, Management*)

Follow Up

1. **Reteaching.** Ask students to list the factors they should consider when deciding to open a savings account. (Key Skill: *Critical Thinking*)
2. **Enrichment.** Have students use the school library to find material dealing with the history of banking. Ask each student to report on one aspect of banking that is of particular interest to him or her. (Key Skills: *Social Studies, Critical Thinking*)

Teaching. . . Credit (pp. 212-214)

Comprehension Check

1. What is the difference between cash and credit? *(Cash is money; credit is an arrangement by which you purchase now and pay later.)*
2. How does credit help you buy time? *(You do not have to wait until you have all the money to make purchases.)*
3. What is a credit rating? *(A record of paying debts.)*
4. What is the purpose of the Truth-in-Lending Act? *(To guarantee information about what credit really costs.)*
5. In what ways does the Truth-in-Lending Act help compare credit costs? *(It requires all credit companies to state interest the same way.)*
6. How does the Truth-in-Lending Act protect people whose credit cards are stolen or lost? *(When credit card holders promptly report the loss of their cards, the Act limits their responsibility for charges they did not make.)*

Learning Activities

1. **Writing.** Select students to write their state and federal congress persons, requesting information about current legislation dealing with consumer credit. Read and discuss their responses. (Key Skill: *Communication*)
2. **Contract Analysis.** Have students read and discuss various credit contracts. Ask them to determine the responsibilities of the consumer and the true annual percentage rate. (Key Skill: *Problem Solving*)
3. **Interview.** Select students to interview a local retailer or representative from a financial institution about factors they consider when granting credit to consumers. Have students prepare a written summary of their interview. (Key Skill: *Communication*)

You can often start a savings account with a deposit of as little as $25. As with checking accounts, you may deposit cash or checks. At many financial institutions, you need to fill out a deposit slip.

When you are ready to use money from your savings, you can take out, or withdraw, part or all of your balance. (You may need to leave a certain amount in to keep your account open.) The procedure for this is to complete a withdrawal slip with your name, account number, signature, and the amount.

You will receive a record of your savings account showing deposits, withdrawals, and your current balance. This record is usually a printed statement sent at regular intervals.

▼ Credit ▼

Credit cards are convenient to use. However, you must discipline yourself to purchase only what you can afford.

Right now, you have limited income, and your expenses are relatively low. You probably pay cash for the items and services that you buy. In the future, you will have more income, but also more expenses, and many more responsibilities. At that time, you may decide to use credit as a tool to help you manage your money. **Credit** is an arrangement by which you purchase things now and are allowed to pay for them later.

One type of credit is loans. With loans, you borrow money from banks, credit unions, or loan companies. You use the money you borrow to pay for your purchases, and you pay back your loan little by little to the lending institution.

Another type of credit is sales credit, which is another name for charge accounts. With this type of credit, you receive your purchase now and pay a store or credit card company later for what you owe.

Both of these types of credit are helpful because, in a sense, they buy time. You don't have to wait until you have all the money you need to make your purchases. Even when you have no shortage of money resources, you may choose to use sales credit. Some people use it all the time because it is convenient not to always have to carry cash. They then pay for their purchases once a month when they receive their statements. Before you decide to use credit, think carefully about the convenience it offers. Also remember that credit is seldom free. It is a service that usually costs.

What Does Credit Cost?

In most instances, using credit costs money. In addition to the money you owe, you must also pay the lender a certain percentage of **interest**. This is the fee you must pay for the privilege of using someone else's money when you use credit, just as a financial institution pays you interest when

More About Credit

Credit has both good and bad points. For instance, it can be compared to fire. Used wisely, fire can warm a house and cook a family's meals, but if fire gets out of hand, it can destroy a house. Credit, like fire, must be used carefully. People should use it with caution, not charging more than they will be able to pay. This way, credit can be a convenient and helpful tool or resource.

it uses your money. When you take out a loan, for example, you agree to pay back the amount you borrow — plus interest. Each monthly payment on your loan will include an interest charge. If you use credit cards, you will pay interest unless you pay the total of your bill every month. The interest will be a percentage of the unpaid balance on your credit card account.

Many credit card companies charge 1½ percent a month, which doesn't seem like very much. However, if it takes you a year of 12 monthly payments to pay off your bill, you will be paying 1½ times 12, or 18 percent! This amount adds greatly to the total cost of the items or services you purchase. Since interest rates vary, shop around for credit. You can save money by taking the time to find the lowest rate.

When making purchases with a credit card, be sure to carefully consider the cost of credit.

What Does It Take to Get Credit?

Just as credit users want a good interest rate, businesses that give credit want good customers. Stores, banks, credit unions, and credit card companies prefer to give credit to dependable people.

When you apply for credit, you will be asked to provide information about yourself. Credit businesses will check your information and consider the following:

- ***Your credit rating.*** This is your record of paying debts in the past. Credit businesses look for good credit ratings — ones that reflect prompt, responsible payment.
- ***Your income and your money resources in general.*** Credit businesses want to know if you will have enough money to make payments on your sales credit or loan.
- ***Your property.*** Credit businesses often ask if you own a home, stocks, bonds, or automobiles. The reason for this question is that your property could be sold to get money if you fail to make payments.

Credit businesses do what they can to protect themselves against loss. After all, they are in business, and they want to stay in business.

What Are Your Credit Rights?

Laws have been passed to protect credit users as well as credit businesses. The 1968 Truth-in-Lending Act, for example, guarantees information about what credit really costs.

More About Credit Cards

In spite of what some ads imply, charging items often costs money. Someone has to pay for credit, and usually it is the consumer. To keep personal credit costs low, it is important that credit users keep a copy of all credit card transactions that they make. They should treat each purchase as if it were made with a check. The date of the purchase, its amount, and place of business need to be recorded. An extra checkbook ledger is a simple way to keep track of all credit purchases made. The idea simply is to keep an up-to-date record of what has been charged and what is owed.

4. **Guest Speaker.** Invite an attorney or a representative from a consumer counseling agency to speak to the class about the Truth-in-Lending Act and the Equal Credit Opportunity Act. Ask students to prepare a list of questions for the speaker. (Key Skill: *Communication*)
5. **Bulletin Board.** Have students locate and display ads for charge accounts and consumer loans. Ask them to evaluate the ads. Do they follow the legal guidelines? (Key Skill: *Critical Thinking*)

Follow Up

1. **Reteaching.** Have students list the two federal laws discussed in the chapter that apply to credit and summarize the laws and the protection offered in each one. (Key Skill: *Critical Thinking*)
2. **Reteaching.** Have students discuss the pros and cons of using credit. Is credit worth the cost? (Key Skill: *Critical Thinking*)
3. **Extension.** Use the activity on pp. 28-29 of the *Extending the Lesson* booklet in the TCR.
4. **Enrichment.** Assign students to use library or community resources to research the Truth-in-Lending Act and the Equal Credit Opportunity Act. Why was each act introduced? When was it introduced, and by whom? Discuss their findings with the class. (Key Skill: *Problem Solving*)

Family Perspective

Many individuals and families overextend themselves on credit. As a result, they may be late or fail to make payments. Nonprofit consumer counseling agencies can help when people find themselves willing but unable to pay their debts. Have students survey the community for services available to those who have lost control of credit buying.

Completing the Chapter

For Review

1. Emphasize the main concepts using the summary.
2. Have students complete the "Facts to Recall." (Answers below.)

For Reteaching

1. **Reteaching.** Use the activity on p. 26 of the *Reteaching and Practical Skills* booklet in the TCR.

For Enrichment

1. **Enrichment.** Use the activity on p. 37 of the *Enrichment Activities* booklet in the TCR.

For Evaluation

1. Choose items from "Ideas to Explore" and "Activities to Try."
2. Use the chapter test on pp. 41-42 in the testing booklet of the TCR or use the testmaker software.

Chapter 19 Review

Facts to Recall Answers

1. You can get what you need and want now without wasting money, and plan ahead to meet the costs of future goals.
2. Your spending and saving habits, and whether you are satisfied with them; whether you are spending more than you'd like or wasting money.
3. Record the income you plan to have; write down what you plan to spend; review your budget occasionally, adjusting it if necessary.
4. When making a deposit, record amount deposited and date; add amount to that in account. When writing a check, record check number, date, party paid, and amount; subtract amount from total in account.
5. **Savings interest:** money a financial institution pays you for allowing it to use your money. **Loan interest:** fee paid for the privilege of using someone else's money.

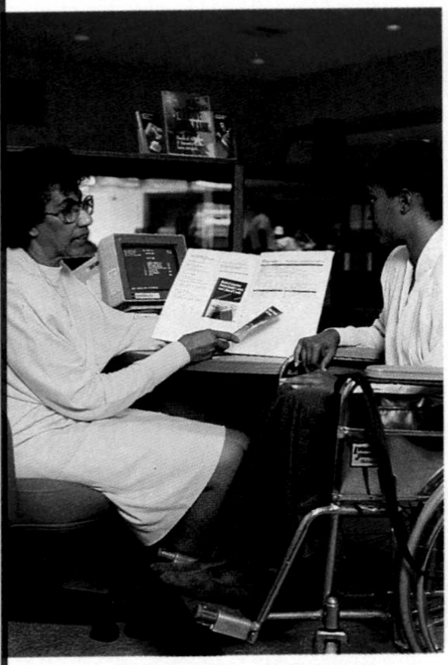

Lenders must tell you the total amount of interest on loans in dollars and cents.

According to this law, lenders must state what the *total* amount of interest on loans will be in dollars and cents. The law also provides that interest for any kind of credit must be stated as yearly costs, or annual percentage rates. With all credit companies stating interest the same way, people can compare credit costs. This allows people to make better decisions about the credit they will use.

The Truth-in-Lending Act also protects people whose credit cards are stolen or lost. According to this law, credit card holders must report the loss of their credit cards promptly. When they do, their responsibility for charges made without their permission is limited.

The advertising of credit is also controlled by law to prevent credit users from being misled. If one credit condition is mentioned in advertising, all other important conditions must also be stated. For example, an advertisement might say that you can purchase a sofa for $10 down. In such a case, the advertisement must also explain that you will pay $10 a week for the next two years.

In 1975, another important law, the Equal Credit Opportunity Act, went into effect. This act makes it illegal to refuse credit to people because of their sex, race, religion, or marital status. The purpose of this law is to prevent discrimination in the awarding of credit privileges.

TAKING ACTION
Cutting Expenses

"I'm a spendaholic," Brad admits, "and I need your help. By Sunday, any money I've tried to save is long gone. In fact, I'm $15 to $30 short. I was hoping to save for a used car. But, the way I spend money, there's no chance. I asked my mom for a car loan, but she turned me down."

"My weekly allowance is $10, and I earn $60 per week from my part-time job at the car wash. I spend $15 a week or more on fast-food dinners when my mom works late. Going out on weekends costs at least $20, and I spend about $50 a week on everything else. That includes things like basketball tickets, a baseball cap, a shirt, or a CD. It's not like I just throw my money away, but somehow it always disappears."

Using Your Resourcefulness

- Identify some of the reasons that Brad is always short of money.
- Identify some ways that Brad could save money on his meals.
- List several activities that would allow Brad to spend less on weekends and still have fun.
- Prepare a weekly income and expense record that will show Brad his current financial picture.
- Make a budget for Brad to help him manage his money better and save $10 a week.

TAKING ACTION

Have students read the feature. Ask students to keep a weekly income and expense record. Afterwards, have them contrast their records with Brad's income and expenses. Select several volunteers to bring to class menus from various fast food places in the community. Duplicate them for the class, and ask students to select three meals they might have during the week. Total the costs of the meals. Choose several students to visit a local supermarket and select three frozen food dinners that Brad could prepare rather than go to a fast food restaurant. Have them compare the differences in cost and discuss their findings with the class.

Chapter 19 Review

Summary

In this chapter, you have read about:

- The importance of good money management skills.
- Identifying your spending habits by recording your income and expenses.
- Establishing and following a budget.
- How to use a checking account.
- How savings accounts function.
- The advantages and costs of buying with credit.
- Laws governing how lenders do business.

Facts to Recall

1. Explain the benefits of managing your money well.
2. What can you learn from studying a record of your weekly income and expenses?
3. Explain how to make and follow a budget.
4. Explain how to balance a checking account using a check register.
5. What is the difference between interest paid on savings and interest paid on loans?
6. How does a loan differ from charge accounts?
7. Identify two advantages and one disadvantage of using credit.
8. Identify three factors that businesses consider when deciding whether to give credit to an individual.
9. According to the Truth-in-Lending Act, how must interest be stated? What is the reason for this?
10. What action is forbidden by the Equal Credit Opportunity Act? What is the purpose of this law?

Ideas to Explore

1. Do you think most teens handle money responsibly? Explain your answer.
2. Do you think it is a good idea to give children a regular, set allowance? Discuss reasons for and against this practice.
3. What responsibilities are involved in having a checking account?
4. Many people spend more than they can afford when using credit. Why do you think this occurs?

Activities to Try

1. Gather pamphlets from different financial institutions that explain the services each one offers. As a class, compare them on such points as interest rates on checking and savings accounts, terms of checking accounts, and credit requirements. What other services do these institutions provide?
2. Do research and then write a short report on different types of financial institutions, such as banks, credit unions, and savings and loans. Explain how they vary in purpose, in services, and in where they get their funds.

LINK TO *Math*

Figuring Simple Interest

Many financial institutions pay *simple interest* — interest paid only on the money you place in your savings account. The interest earned on the account does not earn interest. The following formula is used to figure simple interest: $i = prt$ (interest = principle × rate of interest × time in years). Use this formula to figure the interest earned on the following amounts of money:

- $300 invested at 6% for 6 months
- $275 invested at 4½% for 2 years
- $464 invested at 7% for 1½ years

Facts to Recall Answers (continued)

6. Loan: money borrowed from lending institution is used to pay for purchases, then paid back to lender. Charge accounts: receive purchases now and pay store or credit card company what you owe later.
7. **Advantages:** you don't have to wait until you have enough money for purchases; convenience. **Disadvantage:** cost.
8. Credit rating; income and money resources; property.
9. Total amount of interest in dollars and cents, and yearly costs (annual percentage rate). So people can compare credit costs.
10. Outlaws the refusal of credit because of sex, race, religion, or marital status. To prevent discrimination in the awarding of credit privileges.

Ideas to Explore

1. Answers will vary.
2. Answers will vary. Reasons for may include: gives children feeling of control and responsibility; teaches them to make value-based decisions. Reasons against may include: children become dependent; don't learn to associate money with work.
3. Answers will vary and may include: understanding terms of account; balancing checkbook.
4. Answers will vary and may include: most stores accept payment by credit; money is more easily spent when it is not seen changing hands.

Using Your Resourcefulness Answers

- Answers will vary, but may include: eating out more than he may need to, choosing more expensive weekend outings, etc.
- Answers will vary, but may include preparing meals at home.
- Answers will vary, but may include: renting videos instead of going to the movies, make use of community resources that cost little or no money (recreation facilities, etc.), or attending school events.
- Answers will vary.
- Answers will vary.

LINK TO *Math*

Direct students to read the feature and solve the problems in pairs.

Answers:

- $9.00
- $24.75
- $48.72

Preparing to Teach

Chapter Outline

Chapter Resources

The following booklet materials may be found in the *Teacher's Classroom Resources* box:

- Lesson Plans, p. 25
- Student Workbook, *Study Guide,* pp. 89-90; *Magic Shopping Square,* p. 91; *Consumer Clues,* p. 92
- Color Transparencies, *Accepting the Consumer Challenge,* CT-21
- Technology and Computers, pp. 13, 17, 18, 19, 22, 23
- Cooperative Learning, p. 32
- Extending the Text, *Fakes, Frauds, and False Promises in the Marketplace,* p. 30
- Reteaching and Practical Skills, *Investigating Return Policies,* p. 28
- Enrichment Activities, *Making Successful Consumer Complaints,* p. 35
- Chapter and Unit Tests, pp. 43-44
- Testmaker Software

Also see:

- Meeting the Special Needs of Students
- Linking Home, School, and Community

ABCNews InterActive™ Videodiscs

- *Food and Nutrition*

See the ABCNews InterActive™ Bar Code Correlation booklet for applicable segments.

CHAPTER 20 Consumer Challenges

OBJECTIVES

- *Identify factors that influence consumer choices.*
- *Describe steps wise consumers take when making purchases.*

TERMS TO LEARN

- ***consumer***
- ***impulse buying***
- ***comparison shopping***
- ***warranty***
- ***Better Business Bureau***

Every time you pay for a pizza or a haircut, you are acting as a **consumer**. Consumers are people who purchase and use goods and services. What kind of consumer are you? Do you get the most for your money? Are you satisfied with your purchases, or do you wish you had shopped more wisely? You can learn to improve your consumer skills. This chapter will show you how.

Understanding Influences on Consumers

A good way to start becoming a better consumer is to realize that each purchase involves a choice. You, as the consumer, are the one making the choices. However, many factors influence your choices.

- ***Your income affects your spending.*** You can't spend more than you earn — at least not for long.
- ***The job you have affects what you buy.*** For example, you buy clothing suitable for your job. If you work in outdoor construction, you will need a very different kind of wardrobe than if you worked indoors in a mall or an office.
- ***The environment in which you live makes certain purchases necessary.*** In a cold climate, you might need to buy snow tires. In a hot one, you might want and need air conditioning.

With careful management, you can make your money go farther — to purchase the items you need and the top priorities of things that you want.

More About Better Business Bureaus

In the United States there are approximately 200 Better Business Bureaus (BBBs). These bureaus are nonprofit organizations that are sponsored by local private businesses. They offer a variety of services to the consumer, such as general information on products or services, reliability reports, background information on local businesses and organizations, and records of a company's complaint-handling performance. The Council of Better Business Bureaus, sponsored by national companies, offers consumer education programs and reports on charitable organizations.

Introducing the Chapter

Motivators

1. **Discussion.** Ask students to list and discuss reasons why some people are not wise consumers. Which of these reasons seem most widespread: lack of knowledge, laziness, inconvenience, fear, or misleading advertising? (Key Skill: *Critical Thinking*)
2. **Advertising Analysis.** Collect advertisements that provide helpful information about various products. Display them. Ask students to identify information that is helpful and not helpful to consumers. (Key Skill: *Critical Thinking*)
3. **Brainstorming.** Brainstorm a list of advertising slogans that students have heard or read. What does each fail to say to the consumer? (Key Skill: *Critical Thinking*)
4. **Personal Analysis.** Ask students to think about the last time they decided not to purchase a product and to list some of the reasons for their decision. (Key Skill: *Critical Thinking*)
5. **Bulletin Board.** Display advertisements of products that are of interest to teens. Title the board "How Choosy a Consumer Are You?" (Key Skill: *Communication*)

Chapter Objectives and Vocabulary

1. Have students read the chapter objectives. Ask them to rephrase the objectives as questions.
2. Ask students to state, in their own words, the purpose of studying this chapter.
3. Pronounce the vocabulary terms listed on the previous page. Ask students whether they are familiar with any of these. Explain that the terms will be defined in the chapter.

Guided Reading

1. Have students read the chapter and use the Study Guide on pp. 89-90 of the *Student Workbook*.

Teaching. . .
Understanding Influences on Consumer; Taking Charge of Your Purchasing
(pp. 217-219)

Comprehension Check

1. What influences consumer choices? *(Income, job, environment, personal interests, advertising, peer pressure.)*
2. What is the first step toward effective purchasing? *(Identify what you will buy, based on your needs and wants.)*
3. How can your values guide you in making a purchase? *(They can help you determine your needs and wants and what is important to you.)*
4. What are four sources of information you can use to become well informed about products you want to buy? *(People who already own the product, manufacturer's literature, consumer magazines, and product advertising.)*

Learning Activities

1. **Small Group Discussion.** Assign each of six groups one occupation: automobile mechanic, bank vice-president, computer programmer, high school teacher, hairdresser, and dentist. Ask each group to brainstorm a list of ways their work would affect what they buy. Then have groups compare lists. (Key Skill: *Communication*)
2. **Student Survey.** Assign students to survey students, teachers, family members, and other adults who have lived in climates quite different from the local one. Have them find out how various environments made certain purchases necessary, such as snow tires or air conditioning. Discuss their findings with the class. (Key Skill: *Critical Thinking*)
3. **Skits.** Select students to write and present skits depicting ways in which peer pressure influences people's buying decisions. Discuss the skits, and brainstorm ways to deal with peer pressure. (Key Skills: *Communication, Creativity*)

- ***Your personal interests tend to direct your buying.*** You choose to spend money on those things that interest you most. It might be books. It might be music. It could be software for your computer.
- ***Advertising is designed to influence and increase your purchasing.*** It makes you want to buy all kinds of things. As a consumer, you must remember that you *do* have a choice over what to buy. You do not have to let advertisers influence your decisions about purchases.
- ***Peer pressure may cause you to buy things in order to feel like part of a group.*** It may be hard to make your own buying decisions at times. However, only you know what you need, want, and can afford.

Taking Charge of Your Purchasing

By keeping in mind the influences on your consumer choices, you can decide to make better choices from now on. One way to do this is to follow a plan for taking charge of your purchasing.

▼ Identify What You Will Buy ▼

This is an essential first step toward effective purchasing. You have to decide what you're going to buy and what you're *not* going to buy. Make your decisions based on your needs and wants, letting your values guide you. What is important to you? Can you afford to buy it and still have money left for other things you want and need?

Another way of taking charge of your buying is to resist **impulse buying**, or making unplanned purchases on the spur of the moment. For example, Blake saw a shirt he liked in a store and bought it. When he got the shirt home, he wasn't very happy with his unplanned purchase — it was the wrong color and didn't fit well. The money Blake spent on the shirt was really needed for new shoes.

▼ Gather Information ▼

Become well informed about the products you decide you want or need to buy. One source of information is people you know who own a product that you are thinking about buying. They can tell you if they like the product and if it has given them problems.

More About Advertising

The main goal of advertising is to persuade rather than inform. While advertisements may contain many facts or only a few facts, they are chosen to put a product in the best possible light. However, there are certain facts that sellers are required by law to disclose. These include changes in the nature or composition of a product, such as the substitution of a new ingredient for one that had been used for years. Sellers must also provide information on a product's composition when its appearance is deceptive. For example, a belt made of plastic that could be mistaken for leather must be labeled "imitation leather."

Literature put out by manufacturers is good for technical information. You can use it to compare the features of various brands — an important task before you choose which brand to buy.

Consumer magazines, such as *Consumer Reports*, are also helpful for comparing products. These publications test and rate different brands for quality, safety, and price.

Product advertising can be useful, and it is plentiful. You will find advertisements in newspapers and magazines, as well as on radio and television. Ads have their place in information gathering. For one thing, they can alert you to sales that may help you save money. However, beware. You can't always count on advertising to provide all of the facts about a product. Because ads are designed to appeal to emotions, they sound and look good. However, they may be misleading. They don't give all the facts; they may even misrepresent the facts. Sometimes if you really think about what an ad says, you may find out it really tells you nothing worthwhile about the product — it just offers a tune with a great beat or an attractive picture. Protect yourself by evaluating ads carefully. Never rely on them as your only information source.

When making purchases, it is a real benefit to be informed about the products you are buying. There is much literature available to help you make informed decisions.

▼ Decide When You Will Buy ▼

Knowing when to purchase something can be as important as deciding what to buy. Timing your purchases means planning to make them when it is best for you to do so. It may also save you money. For example, Shelly was able to buy the sweater she wanted at an end-of-season sale for less money than she would have at the beginning of the season. She was able to save credit costs by paying for the sweater with the cash she had set aside for the sweater.

Smart shoppers become aware of typical sale times, and they plan their purchases accordingly. For example, a preseason coat sale often occurs in July or August. One way to

AROUND THE WORLD

Consumers in India have a new decision to make — whether or not to buy an automatic dishwasher and, if so, which brand. Several manufacturers are now producing dishwashers that vary in price and features. These companies have been very successful in introducing other major electric appliances, such as clothes washing machines and food processors, to Indian households. They believe families will be eager to acquire this latest appliance, also. What factors might consumers in India consider before buying an automatic dishwasher?

PAK. CHINA INDIA INDIAN OCEAN

4. **Discussion.** Ask students if they can remember making their first major purchase. Where were they and what did they buy? Did they inspect the quality and compare prices before buying? (Key Skill: *Critical Thinking*)
5. **Personal Analysis.** Assign students to list their purchases for a week, designating each item a "planned" or an "impulse" purchase. Then, discuss some of their purchases. List ways to resist impulse buying. (Key Skills: *Critical Thinking, Management*)

Follow Up

1. **Reteaching.** Have each student design an ad that provides facts about a product. Display and discuss the ads. (Key Skills: *Communication, Creativity*)
2. **Enrichment.** Divide students into two groups. Assign one to research state bankruptcy laws, and the other to research the number of local bankruptcy filings during each of the past ten years. After discussing their findings, have them list as many reasons as they can for bankruptcies. (Key Skill: *Critical Thinking*)

Assign class members to read current consumer magazine articles that discuss and evaluate automatic dishwashers, write a short summary of their research, and discuss their findings with the class. Ask volunteers to survey adults about the kinds of dishwashers they have, what features they like and dislike, and problems they have had. Have students share the result with the class. Display dishwasher advertising brochures (and their prices) for sale locally.

More About *Gathering Information*

Various agencies of the federal government issue a wide variety of consumer information publications. The *Consumer Information Catalog* lists approximately 200 free or low-cost booklets covering various topics such as cars, child care, the environment, financial planning, food and nutrition, health, housing, and more. The catalog is free and is published quarterly by the Consumer Information Center of the U.S. General Services Administration. Individuals may order single copies of the catalog by sending their name and address to: Catalog, Consumer Information Center, Pueblo, CO 81009.

Teaching. . .
Taking Charge: Choose Where You Will Buy; Examine Before You Buy
(pp. 220-221)

Comprehension Check

1. What are three reasons why discount stores can offer low prices? *(They buy in large quantities and limit their number of clerks and customer services.)*
2. Name four advantages that neighborhood stores often have over discount stores. *(They are conveniently located; they may carry merchandise not found in larger stores; they have clerks available to help customers; they may offer services, such as free delivery.)*
3. When comparing prices, what charge should you add to a mail-order item? *(Shipping.)*

Learning Activities

1. **Shopping Project.** Ask students to select one item (e.g., sneakers, CD player) and comparison shop to determine where they would purchase it and why. Have them discuss their decision with the class. Ask them why some make different decisions with the same data. (Key Skill: *Problem Solving*)
2. **Community Survey.** Assign students to survey prices of nationally-advertised products in department, discount, and neighborhood stores. Have them determine the differences in prices and services offered at each of the stores. Ask them to share their findings with the class. (Key Skill: *Problem Solving*)
3. **Television Analysis.** Select volunteers to watch several home shopping television programs or "infomercials." Have them write down the items for sale and information given about each item. Afterwards, ask them to discuss their observations with the class. Talk about reasons why these kinds of marketing are effective. Stress the importance of comparison shopping and avoiding impulse buying. (Key Skills: *Communication, Critical Thinking*)

Impulse buying can cause you to run out of money before you purchase the items you really need.

find out when sales are going to occur is to refer to local advertising. Then you can get more for your money by buying what you've decided to buy when its price is reduced.

▼ Choose Where You Will Buy ▼

Comparison shopping — or taking the time to shop around and compare products, prices, and services — is a good strategy to use when choosing a place to buy a product. One place may have the product you want at a low price. However, it may not offer the services that you need or want.

As an example, assume you're purchasing a CD player. You may want the convenience of repair service in case anything goes wrong. One place may offer free repair right in the store. Another store may require you to go elsewhere for service. Still another may charge you for repair by selling you a service contract. By comparison shopping, you can find the place that offers the best balance of price and services that you want and need.

Before you decide where to buy, remember to consider these possibilities.

- ***Department stores.*** These stores sell a variety of goods such as clothing, jewelry, shoes, housewares, appliances, and furniture. Department stores also provide various services for their customers. These might include free delivery and special credit terms.
- ***Discount stores.*** Low prices are the main attraction of these stores. They can offer low prices because they buy in large quantities and limit the number of clerks and customer services.
- ***Neighborhood stores.*** These small businesses usually can't compete with the prices of discount stores. However, they are conveniently located and may carry merchandise not found in larger stores. Neighborhood businesses have clerks available to help their customers. They may also offer certain services, such as free delivery.

More About *Price and Quality*

The price of an item is not always a good guide to its quality. Sometimes a less expensive product is equally as good as a costlier one. One reason why items of the same quality have different prices is because of supply and demand. If one item is in demand when another is not, the item in demand will cost more regardless of its quality. Different prices for equal quality also result from different quantities that companies buy. Large companies that buy in large amounts can buy and sell at a lower price than a small company that buys in smaller amounts.

- ▶ ***Mail-order firms.*** These businesses have catalogs from which you can order products to be sent to you. Catalogs often include at least some items that are not available in stores near your home. Mail-order shopping can save you time. Sometimes it saves you money. However, often there is a charge for shipping your order. When you are comparing prices, remember to add in this charge.

- ▶ ***Door-to-door sales.*** These involve salespeople who come to your home to sell products. Products sold door-to-door include cosmetics, magazine subscriptions, cooking utensils, and other goods. Some buyers find it convenient to look at merchandise and test it in their own home. Before buying this way, however, it's still a good idea to compare prices and quality.
- ▶ ***Garage sales, yard sales, and flea markets.*** These are a source of merchandise at very low prices. Such sales are not businesses that operate all the time. Instead, they are ways for families and individuals to sell possessions. Garage sales, yard sales, and flea markets offer no customer services. Items are frequently used and must be purchased as they are. Such sales are often a source of unique or unusual items. Remember that you cannot return anything that is defective or otherwise unsatisfactory.

▼ Examine Before You Buy ▼

Learn as much as you can about a product before you actually purchase it. As discussed earlier, information gathering will get you started on this. Once you've narrowed down your choices, investigate some more.

- ▶ ***Inspect a product's quality.*** See how well or how poorly the item was made. For example, check clothing to see if seams are durable and buttons are attached securely. Remember, a high price is not necessarily a reliable sign of good quality.
- ▶ ***Look at the price tag.*** Can you afford this purchase? Is the product worth what it costs? Can you find a better buy?
- ▶ ***Consider the brand.*** Is it one you're familiar with and have had good luck with in the past? Is it a name brand or a store brand? Remember that name brands usually cost more than store brands. Manufacturers of name brands advertise more and this cost is passed on to the customer. Store brands generally are not advertised. You may find that the quality of store brands equals that of name brands while the price is much lower.
- ▶ ***Read product labels.*** Labels and packages give useful facts that may affect your buying decisions. For example,

Compare prices between name brands and store brands to get the best value for your dollar.

Learning Activities (continued)

4. **Interviews.** Select volunteers to interview people who have held several garage or yard sales. Have students ask the interviewees for suggestions for holding sales. Afterwards, have the interviewers compile their lists of suggestions to distribute to the class. (Key Skills: *Communication, Critical Thinking*)

Follow Up

1. **Reteaching.** Using catalog and local newspaper ads, ask students to compare the cost of buying an identical item locally or from a mail-order catalog. Be sure to calculate the cost of shipping. (Key Skills: *Math, Critical Thinking*)
2. **Enrichment.** Select volunteers to survey ads of local garage sales and flea markets. Have them visit some, and make a list of items and prices. Ask students to discuss their observations with the class. (Key Skill: *Management*)
3. **Enrichment.** Have students survey their wardrobe and other possessions for never- or seldom-used items to place in a garage sale or consignment store. Have them research the percentage charged by local stores for selling articles on consignment. (Key Skill: *Management*)

More About *Advertising*

Consumers can learn about new and better products through advertising. They also can save time and money by comparing products, prices, and services advertised in local newspapers, mail-order catalogs, and other media. However, consumers often pay for advertising in the form of higher prices. Advertising companies spend billions of dollars to study human behavior and to hire talented writers, artists, and salespeople to persuade consumers to buy certain products. Advertisers often rely on snob appeal, group appeal, or association with well-known individuals to sell goods and services.

Photo Focus

Ask the students to examine the photo and illustrations on pp. 220-221. What do they have in common *(shopping to save money)*? What other examples might you "picture?" How many of these options are available where you live?

Teaching. . .
Taking Charge: Your Consumer Responsibilities; Consumer Complaints (pp.222-224)

Comprehension Check

1. What is a warranty? *(A manufacturer's guarantee that a product will work properly for a certain length of time.)*
2. What are three instances in which you have the right to complain about a product you purchased? *(When the product was damaged, a service was not performed correctly, or a product was sold for more than the advertised price.)*
3. What are two reasons why it is important to check your warranty when dealing with a consumer problem? *(To see if the problem is covered; to follow warranty instructions.)*
4. In a warranty, what does the seller or manufacturer agree to do if a product fails to work a certain length of time? *(To repair or replace the product or refund the buyer's money.)*

Learning Activities

1. **Cartoons.** Ask volunteers to create cartoons featuring the consequences of failing to read care labels. Display and discuss the cartoons. (Key Skills: *Communication, Creativity*)
2. **Writing.** Provide a variety of warranties for students to read. Assign them to put in their own words what each warranty promises. Display and discuss their versions. (Key Skills: *Communication, Critical Thinking*)

TIPS:

Know Your Consumer Rights
After students have read the feature divide them into small groups and have each do an impromptu skit illustrating one right of a consumer.

TIPS: *Know Your Consumer Rights*

The "Consumer Bill of Rights" was introduced by President John F. Kennedy in 1962. Presidents Nixon and Ford added to the bill. It now includes the following:

- ***The right to safety.*** Consumers are protected against the sale of dangerous products.
- ***The right to be informed.*** Consumers have the right to ask for all the facts needed to make good choices. They are also protected against advertising that is dishonest or misleading.
- ***The right to be heard.*** Consumers have a voice in making laws that affect consumers.
- ***The right to choose.*** Consumers are assured of the right to choose from a variety of goods at competitive prices.
- ***The right to redress.*** This is the right to have problems quickly and fairly corrected.
- ***The right to consumer education.*** All consumers and students are entitled to information about consumer issues.

a clothing label gives you information about the fabric from which a garment is made. It also tells you how to care for the garment. Perhaps it needs to be washed by hand or dry-cleaned. In addition, the information on clothing and food labels is regulated by the federal government. Manufacturers decide what facts to include on labels for most other items. Carefully consider all label information before you decide which product is best for you.

- ***Inquire about a warranty.*** A **warranty** guarantees that a product will work as it should for a certain length of time unless it has been misused or mishandled by the customer. If the product fails to work properly during the specific time period due to any defects in parts, materials, or workmanship, the seller or manufacturer agrees to repair or replace the product or refund your money. Getting a warranty on merchandise is a little bit like getting insurance. In the event that the product has serious defects within the time period of the warranty, you won't have to pay for the repair or replacement. Some warranties cover an entire product for a specific period of time; other warranties are limited and may exclude some parts of a product. Read the warranty carefully to fully understand its conditions.

▼ Your Consumer Responsibilities ▼

Along with understanding your rights as a consumer comes consumer responsibility — the two go hand in hand. For example, if you are guaranteed the right to information about a product and product safety, then your responsibility is to learn as much as you can about the product and use it safely, according to the manufacturer's directions. The same holds true for making wise choices, speaking up when change is needed, and seeking redress when goods and services do not measure up to specified standards.

What other responsibilities do you have as a consumer? First, be as fair and honest with stores and businesses as you expect them to be with you. The biggest responsibility you have as a consumer is to pay for your purchases. If you don't pay, you're stealing. This is not only unfair, but it is also a crime for which you can be put in jail. In the long run, stealing raises prices on goods and services for everyone. Business owners have to cover the cost of their losses. They do this by passing on those costs to customers.

Another responsibility of all consumers is to take care of merchandise they handle or try on. Do your best not to get merchandise dirty or to damage it in any way. You owe it to the store owners and other customers to keep all products in good condition.

More About *Warranties*

A warranty is an assurance of the soundness of a product. A warranty is the same as a guarantee, and it tells what the seller or manufacturer will do if the product purchased is defective or needs repair. The Magnuson-Moss Warranty Act, a federal law, requires sellers to have any written warranties available for the consumer to read before making a purchase. This law applies only when a product sells for more than $15. The act does not require sellers or manufacturers to offer warranties. If there is a written warranty, the act requires it to be complete, written in ordinary language, and available before purchase.

When you make a purchase, watch closely while the sales transaction is being completed. Make sure the price is registered correctly and you get any change that is due you. However, if you get too much change, be honest. Give it back.

▼ Learn How to Handle Consumer Complaints ▼

Have you ever purchased a product only to find that it didn't work as it should a short time after purchase? You have the right to complain when a product you purchased was damaged or when a service you paid for wasn't performed correctly. You also have the right to complain when a product was sold to you for more than the advertised price.

The following steps may prove helpful in dealing with consumer problems.

1. Check your warranty. If the problem you have is covered, follow the instructions on the warranty.
2. If you have no warranty, or if your problem isn't covered, go to the store or business where you made the purchase. Politely and firmly explain your problem, and propose a fair solution. Go to the store's customer service department first. If your complaint is not satisfactorily resolved there, ask to speak to the manager. Expect to be treated fairly. Most stores and businesses want to keep their customers.
3. Clearly state to the customer service representative what the problem is and how you would like it to be corrected. Do you want a damaged item fixed or replaced? Do you want a poorly done service performed again?
4. If your trip to a store or business doesn't bring satisfaction, put your complaint in writing. A librarian can help you find out the correct address and to whom to write. Write a letter briefly stating the problem and the solution that you think would be fair. Be sure to include the date; your name, address, and telephone number; the place and date of your purchase; and the model number of the product. In addition, enclose copies of your receipt and your warranty. (Do not send original receipts and warranties.) Keep a copy of your letter for your files, along with the originals of your receipt and warranty.
5. If your letter doesn't bring results, you may choose to take your complaint to the **Better Business Bureau**. This is a private agency that works to improve local business practices and settle consumer complaints.
6. Another option is to take your problem to small claims court to be resolved. In this type of court, you present your complaint before a judge, and the store or business involved must respond.

More About *Full and Limited Warranties*

There are two kinds of written warranties defined in the Magnuson-Moss Warranty Act: full and limited. If a consumer buys a product that is under full warranty, and it needs repair before the expiration of the warranty, the consumer is entitled to have the item repaired without charge for parts or labor. If the product cannot be repaired, the buyer must be given a new one free or a refund of money. A full warranty may cover only specified parts of an item; it does not have to cover the entire product. A limited warranty often requires the buyer to pay labor charges or handling fees. Most manufacturers give limited warranties.

Learning Activities (continued)

3. **Research Project.** Select students to locate news articles about unsafe products or products being recalled by manufacturers. Have them present a short report to the class. Key Skills: *Critical Thinking, Communication*)
4. **Skits.** Ask students to write and present skits about a consumer returning a faulty product to a store. Then, have small groups practice responses likely to receive favorable action by store personnel. (Key Skills: *Problem Solving, Creativity*)
5. **Writing.** In pairs, ask students to write an ineffective complaint letter to an imaginary manufacturer about a defective product. Read a few to the class and talk about reasons why the letters would be unsuccessful. (Key Skills: *Communication, Critical Thinking*)
6. **Discussion.** Ask students if they have had any experience with contracts. Ask: Did they read the contract before signing it? Did they understand the contract? Did a parent or guardian also sign it? (Key Skills: *Communication, Critical Thinking*)

Follow Up

1. **Reteaching.** Have students write short public service announcements about how buyers may deal effectively with consumer problems. Videotape or record the announcements. (Key Skills: *Communication, Creativity*)
2. **Extension.** Use the activity on p. 30 of the *Extending the Lesson* booklet in the TCR.
3. **Enrichment.** Provide consumer care booklets for various products and appliances in the classroom and laboratory. Have students read and discuss the information in the booklets. Assign them to write a summary of important facts within each booklet. (Key Skills: *Communication, Critical Thinking*)

Completing the Chapter

For Review

1. Emphasize the main concepts using the summary.
2. Have students complete the "Facts to Recall." (Answers below.)

For Reteaching

1. **Reteaching.** Use the activity on p. 27 of the *Reteaching and Practical Skills* booklet in the TCR.

For Enrichment

1. **Enrichment.** Use the activity on p. 38 of the *Enrichment Activities* booklet in the TCR.

For Evaluation

1. Choose items from "Ideas to Explore" and "Activities to Try."
2. Use the chapter test on pp. 43-44 in the testing booklet of the TCR or use the testmaker software.

Facts to Recall Answers

1. Both influence you to buy things you may not need, want, or be able to afford; make it hard to make own buying decisions.
2. **Advantage:** they can alert you to sales. **Disadvantage:** they may not give you facts about the product.
3. Save credit costs by waiting until you can pay cash; spend less by waiting for sales.
4. Products, prices, services.
5. **Advantage:** low prices. **Disadvantage:** limited number of clerks and customer services.
6. **Advantages:** very low prices; unique or unusual items. **Disadvantages:** no customer services; items frequently used and must be purchased as is; items cannot be returned.
7. Can you afford purchase? Is item worth costs? Can you find better buy?
8. Name brands usually cost more. The quality is often equal.

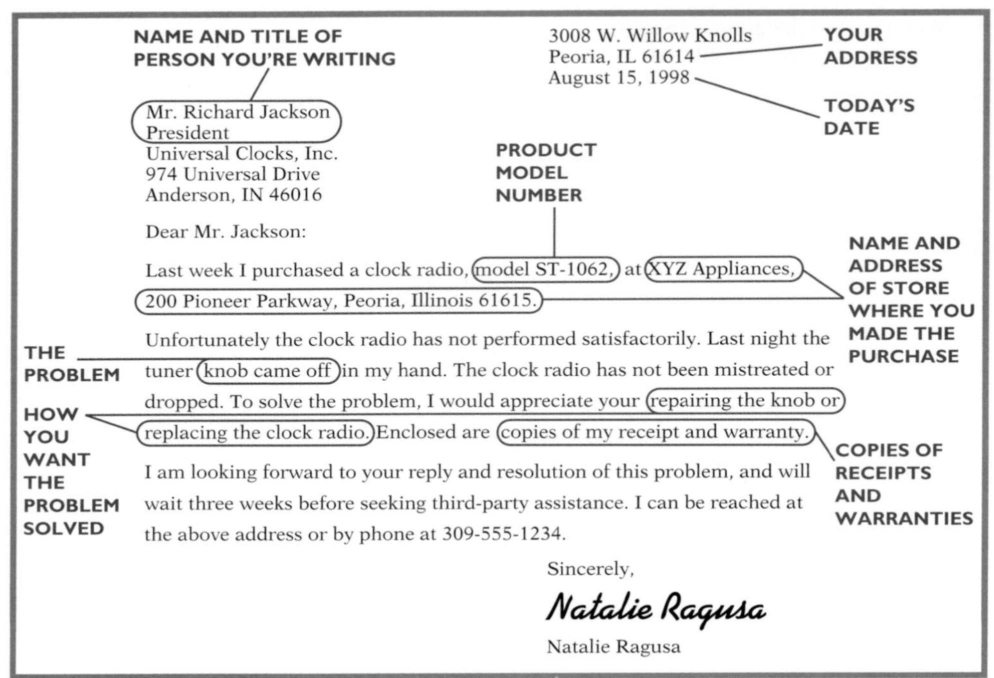

3008 W. Willow Knolls
Peoria, IL 61614
August 15, 1998

Mr. Richard Jackson
President
Universal Clocks, Inc.
974 Universal Drive
Anderson, IN 46016

Dear Mr. Jackson:

Last week I purchased a clock radio, model ST-1062, at XYZ Appliances, 200 Pioneer Parkway, Peoria, Illinois 61615.

Unfortunately the clock radio has not performed satisfactorily. Last night the tuner knob came off in my hand. The clock radio has not been mistreated or dropped. To solve the problem, I would appreciate your repairing the knob or replacing the clock radio. Enclosed are copies of my receipt and warranty.

I am looking forward to your reply and resolution of this problem, and will wait three weeks before seeking third-party assistance. I can be reached at the above address or by phone at 309-555-1234.

Sincerely,

Natalie Ragusa

Natalie Ragusa

TAKING ACTION

Shopping Savvy

"It was love at first sight when I saw these pants," exclaimed Brooke. "I absolutely had to have them, but I've only worn them once. This aqua blouse looked wonderful under the store's lights, but, once I got it home, it looked awful. I'll have to admit these new jeans don't really fit right. I bought them because of the designer label. I got this skirt because Mindy bought one, and she said we should have skirts alike. The skirt looks great on Mindy, but it looks terrible on me. See this sweater? I really loved it, and it fit perfectly when I bought it. But, the first time I washed it, it shrank. I didn't see the instruction label …"

Using Your Resourcefulness

- Identify the mistakes that Brooke made with her clothing purchases. In each case, what could she do in the future to become a better consumer?
- Have you made consumer mistakes similar to Brooke's? Offer an example from your own experience.
- Describe your general pattern as a clothes-buying consumer. Where and how do you shop? Are there ways you could get more clothing value for your money? Explain your answer.

TAKING ACTION

Have students read the feature and respond to the questions. Ask for volunteers to bring an item of clothing or other product they purchased that was a consumer mistake. Display the items, and ask students to discuss the reasons for their purchases and why they feel the purchases were a mistake. Invite a clothing buyer from a local department store to speak to the class about ways to avoid consumer mistakes when selecting clothing. Ask the speaker to demonstrate styles of clothing, types of fabrics, and care labels that tend to be successful purchases for teens.

Chapter 20 Review

Summary

In this chapter, you have read about:
- Factors that affect how you spend your money.
- Making decisions about what you will buy, and when and where you will buy it.
- Points to consider when selecting a product.
- Consumers' rights and responsibilities.
- Effective ways of getting consumer problems corrected.

Facts to Recall

1. How do advertising and peer pressure influence your purchasing? How can this create problems?
2. Identify one advantage and one disadvantage to using advertisements as an information source when choosing a product to buy.
3. Explain two ways timing and planning your purchases saves you money.
4. What three points should you consider when comparison shopping?
5. Identify one advantage and one disadvantage of buying from discount stores.
6. Identify two advantages and three disadvantages of buying items at garage and yard sales and flea markets.
7. What three questions should you ask yourself when examining an item's price tag?
8. Explain how brand names and store brands compare in price and quality.
9. Briefly explain the six steps in resolving consumer complaints.
10. Identify three consumer responsibilities.

Ideas to Explore

1. Which of the six influences on spending affects you the most? Explain your answer.
2. Using your most recent purchase as an example, identify which factors affected your decision and explain how they did so.
3. In general, do you believe advertisements are truthful? Defend your answer. Describe ways that they can be misleading.

Activities to Try

1. Choose one item you would like to purchase. Using a consumer magazine such as *Consumer Reports*, see how different brands of the item compare in quality, safety, price, and other categories. Write a short summary of the findings. Identify which of the tested brands you would buy, and why.
2. Practice writing a letter of complaint. Be sure to: explain your problem clearly and briefly; include all the necessary information as discussed in the chapter; and to state how you would like to have the problem corrected.

LINK TO *Communication*

MAKING A COMPLAINT

Toys for children are often found to have some unsafe features. Some may have trim or other small features that fall off and can be easily swallowed by an infant or young child. Bring a toy from home (or a picture of a toy from a catalog) that you think might be dangerous for young children. Respond to the following:
- Explain why you think this toy is dangerous.
- If you had purchased this toy, explain what course of action you could take as a consumer to complain to the manufacturer or place of purchase.
- What might you do if you get no response from the place of purchase or the manufacturer?

Using Your Resourcefulness Answers
- Impulse buying, hurrying—not trying on or looking at a color in natural light, peer pressure, not reading the label.
- Answers will vary.
- Answers will vary.

Facts to Recall Answers (continued)

9. Check warranty and follow instructions; go to store, explain problem, and propose solution; tell customer service representative what problem is and how you want it corrected; put complaint in writing; take complaint to Better Business Bureau; take problem to small claims court.
10. **Any three:** learn about product and use it safely; make wise choices; speak up for change; seek redress; be fair and honest; pay for purchases; handle merchandise carefully; watch sales transactions.

Ideas to Explore

1. Answers will vary.
2. Answers will vary.
3. Answers will vary.

LINK TO *Communication*

Answer

Before students read this feature show them examples of unsafe toys or recall stories of children playing with unsafe toys. After they read the feature and answer the questions *(Answers will vary.)*, ask them to think of other examples when consumers can and should make a difference.

Preparing to Teach

Chapter Outline

Chapter Resources

The following booklet materials may be found in the *Teacher's Classroom Resources* box:

- Lesson Plans, p. 26
- Student Workbook, *Study Guide,* pp. 93-94; *Thinking About Technology,* p. 95; *Technology Match-Up,* p. 96
- Personal Safety, *Safety on the Internet,* p. 27
- Technology and Computers, pp. 17, 18, 19, 20, 21, 22, 24, 25, 26
- Cooperative Learning, p. 33
- Extending the Text, *Setting Up Your Computer for Word Processing,* p. 31
- Reteaching and Practical Skills, *Computer Technology Concept Map,* p. 29
- Enrichment Activities, *Thinking About Technology,* p. 36
- Chapter and Unit Tests, pp. 45-46
- Testmaker Software

Also see:

- Meeting the Special Needs of Students
- Linking Home, School, and Community

CHAPTER 21 Technology as a Resource

OBJECTIVES

- *Give examples of technology at home, at school, and in the workplace.*
- *Describe ways technology might be used in the near future.*

TERMS TO LEARN

- ***technology***
- ***modem***
- ***ATMs (automatic teller machines)***
- ***UPC (universal product code)***

We live in a "high tech" age, one in which technology is abundant. **Technology** is the way in which science and inventions are put to practical use in everyday life. Technology includes time-saving and labor-saving devices, such as computers, appliances, and other machines. It also includes new materials for making things safer and stronger and improved methods for doing things faster and more efficiently.

Technology is a resource that people can use for various purposes in different areas of their lives. Today, technology can be found everywhere — at home, at school, and in the workplace.

Technology at Home

Have you ever thought about how technology touches your life at home? Many people take for granted the day-to-day ways in which technology touches their lives — saving time and energy.

Computers at Home

The number of families who have computers at home continues to increase. Those who do find them useful for everything from schoolwork and financial planning to entertainment and communicating with others. Computers' word processing capabilities allow you to write and revise papers with ease. If a computer has CD-ROM capability, you might even be able to look up information on an encyclopedia that fits on one CD. Computers are excellent tools for financial planning because they can calculate figures so quickly and accurately. If you use schedules to manage your time effectively, a computer can incorporate changes in seconds. Children enjoy interactive computer books and games, but much more challenging games and information are available for older users.

If you have a modem, your home computer can be used for even more functions. A **modem** is a piece of equipment that connects a computer to a telephone line. This allows a computer to communicate directly with other computers. For example, many people use it to check their bank balances or make travel reservations.

Many families use home computers for money and time management as well as entertainment.

More About Computers

The work of the human brain is similar to a combination of a computer and a chemical factory. Brain cells produce electrical signals and send them from cell to cell along pathways called circuits. These circuits receive, process, store, and retrieve information much like a computer. Unlike a computer, however, the brain creates its electrical signals by chemical means. Proper functioning of the brain depends on many chemical substances produced by brain cells.

Introducing the Chapter

Motivators

1. **Sentence Completion.** Ask students to complete the following sentences: "My favorite technology is ...," "Some of the ways that technology has improved my life are ...," and "In the future I think technology will ..." (Key Skill: *Critical Thinking*)
2. **Definitions.** Have students look up definitions of "Yankee ingenuity." Talk about how the term is sometimes used in place of "technology." (Key Skill: *Communication*)
3. **Writing.** Assign students to write short stories about ways that computers may be used in the future. (Key Skills: *Communication, Creativity*)
4. **Media Analysis.** Assign students to collect newspaper and magazine articles about technology. Ask them to talk about their articles with the class. (Key Skill: *Communication*)
5. **Mail Analysis.** Collect an assortment of electronic mail to share with the class. Have students compare and discuss some of the examples. (Key Skills: *Communication, Critical Thinking*)

Chapter Objectives and Vocabulary

1. Have students read the chapter objectives. Ask them to rephrase the objectives as questions.
2. Ask students to state, in their own words, the purpose of studying this chapter.
3. Pronounce the vocabulary terms listed on the previous page. Ask students whether they are familiar with any of these. Explain that the terms will be defined in the chapter.

Guided Reading

1. Have students read the chapter and use the Study Guide on pp. 93-94 of the *Student Workbook*.

Teaching. . .
Technology at Home; Computers; Home Appliances; Technology at School
(pp. 227-229)

Comprehension Check

1. Why are computers excellent tools for financial planning? *(Because they calculate figures quickly and accurately.)*
2. What is a modem, and what is its purpose? *(A piece of equipment that connects a computer to other computers.)*
3. What are three typical uses for a modem at home? *(Banking; reservations; connect to the Internet.)*
4. Give three examples of how students can use computers in family and consumer sciences. *(To calculate calories and nutrients, to determine differences of nutrients when planning a diet, to rearrange furniture.)*

Learning Activities

1. **Discussion.** Lead a discussion of some of the advantages of understanding and knowing how to use computers. Survey the class to find out the number of students who use computers regularly. (Key Skills: *Communication, Critical Thinking*)

AROUND THE WORLD

Ask for volunteers to research the geography and history of Costa Rica and create a bulletin board or display case presenting their findings. Assign students to investigate the effect of technology on various Native American groups. Have them share their findings with the class. Invite the Industrial Arts instructor to demonstrate simple projects that students can carry out at school or at home to save resources such as water, electricity, and/or other fuel.

AROUND THE WORLD

Technology is often accused of weakening ties between people. However, in Costa Rica, it is bringing them together. Since 1988, a group of American scientists and teachers have been showing people in rural Costa Rican communities how to build simple solar-powered ovens. After learning about this design, community members construct their own ovens from locally-produced materials — glass, wood, and cardboard. The teachers believe that this community involvement, which was missing from similar projects in the past, is helping to make this project a success.

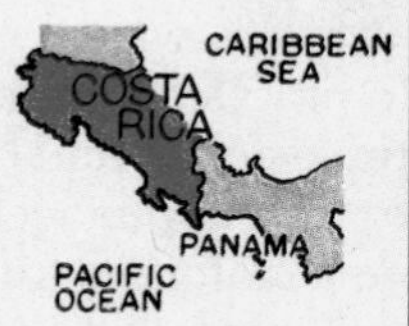

With a modem, it is also possible to connect to the Internet, an international network of computers. When you subscribe to an Internet service, you can "chat" with others about particular topics, find information, or leave electronic messages — E-mail — for friends or relatives who are also connected to the Internet.

Hidden Computer Technology

Computer technology is often present in homes even when there is no home computer. Many appliances contain hidden computers that help them perform some kind of special function. Electronic home sewing machines contain a microcomputer which allows for the creation and storage of hundreds of new designs and makes sewing faster and easier. There are irons that shut themselves off when they are not in use. A microchip — which acts like a minicomputer — inside these irons is responsible for the shut-off. Microwave ovens include computers that must be programmed in order to cook your food just right. Some coffee makers are equipped with microcomputers that can be programmed at night before you go to bed. This programming turns your coffee maker on in the morning, and your coffee is ready when you wake up.

Technology and Home Appliances

What technology do you have in your home? Does your family own a VCR? Video technology is popular for homes because it offers such convenience. You can watch movies at home on your VCR instead of spending money at a theater. You can see what movie you want when you want to, instead of adjusting to the theater's programming and schedule. You can also use your VCR to tape TV shows while you are away or busy. This allows you to do what you need to do and watch your favorite shows later, at the time that suits you best.

More About Computers at Home

Increasing numbers of homes are equipped with computer software programs that provide up-to-the minute news and weather, financial information, and shopping bargains. Also, many home computers are used as tutors for studying academic subjects and learning foreign languages.

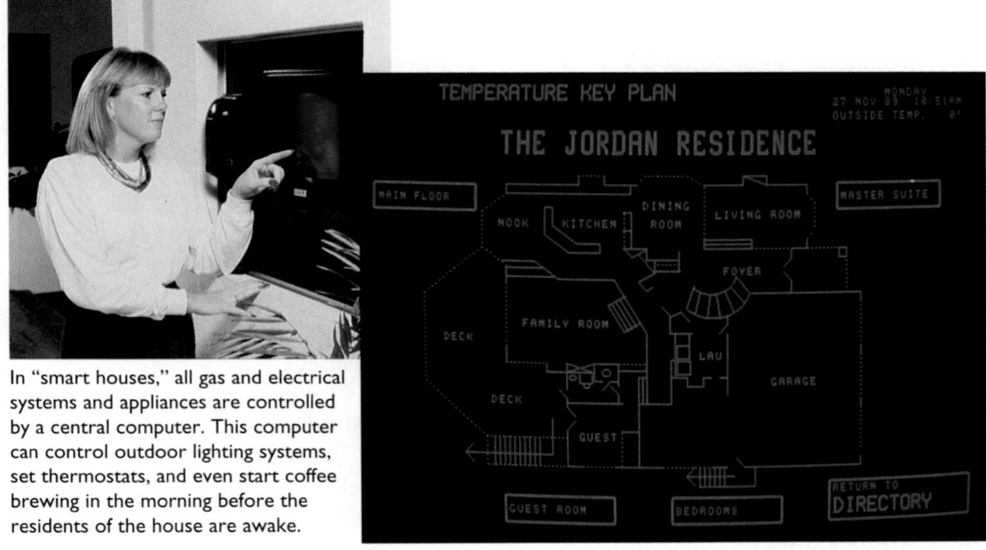

In "smart houses," all gas and electrical systems and appliances are controlled by a central computer. This computer can control outdoor lighting systems, set thermostats, and even start coffee brewing in the morning before the residents of the house are awake.

Much home technology aims at convenience, as in the case of computers and VCRs. Other technology makes your home more comfortable. Central heating and air conditioning are examples. Still other technology is directed at keeping your home safe, such as sensors that sound an alarm when doors or windows are opened. Motion-sensing and solar-powered lights are safety devices that turn on automatically, giving you light where you need it and when you need it most. Automatic garage door openers are technology that provides both safety and convenience. In addition, fully-automated home systems are available. These control many home functions, such as heating, cooling, and lighting, through one computerized panel.

Technology at School

Computer technology is a vital part of education in many schools today. Teachers depend on computers for creating tests and other materials that students use for class work or homework. Such materials are written on computers, printed out, and stored by computer for possible future use.

Students may also work directly with computers as a learning tool. For example, in foods class, you might use a computer when you are studying nutrition and wellness. Computers can be utilized to calculate the calories and healthful ingredients in the foods you eat.

Learning Activities (continued)

2. **Discussion.** Discuss the advantages of computers and word processors over typewriters. (Key Skills: *Communication, Critical Thinking*)
3. **Writing.** Set up a VCR in the classroom. Select several students to study the manual, practice using the VCR, and then write their own manual in easy-to-understand language. Ask for volunteers to learn to use the VCR by following the student-designed manual. Have them evaluate its effectiveness. (Key Skills: *Communication, Problem Solving*)
4. **Product Analysis.** Have students research home security systems. (Key Skill: *Problem Solving*)
5. **Guest Speaker.** Invite the computer science teacher to discuss different kinds of word processing and spreadsheet programs that students and their families might find helpful. (Key Skill: *Communication*)

Follow Up

1. **Reteaching.** Have each student make a collage of newspaper and magazine pictures showing technology at home and school. Display the completed project. (Key Skill: *Communication*)
2. **Enrichment.** Assign students to use computers to create newsletter articles, crossword puzzles, posters, and other graphics. Display their completed projects. (Key Skill: *Creativity*)
3. **Enrichment.** Select students to investigate various printers and modems. Have them contrast their features and prices, and present their findings to the class. (Key Skills: *Communication, Critical Thinking*)

More About Computers as a Source of Entertainment

For people who enjoy using computers for entertainment, the variety of computer game software is almost endless. Some examples are arcade-style games; war and space simulation; board games; and sports, puzzle, and strategy games. Other software programs are available for people to develop their horoscope, study biorhythms, compose music, or to "draw" computer graphics in color. Game software outsells any other type of software available for personal computers.

Teaching. . . Technology at School; Technology in the Workplace; Banking; and Retail Stores (pp. 230-231)

Comprehension Check

1. Name two ways computers are used in schools. *(In home design classrooms, library records of the entire collection, software programs for choosing a career, school offices.)*
2. What are three main advantages of technology in the workplace? *(It saves time, saves effort, helps to reduce the number of human errors.)*
3. In what ways do banks use technology to perform various tasks? *(They use computers to complete transactions, they provide ATMs, they use computers to read check codes and subtract the amount of each from your balance.)*

Learning Activities

1. **Guest Speaker.** Invite one or more school administrators to talk to the class about kinds of technology used in the local school district. (Key Skill: *Communication*)
2. **Discussion.** Ask students who use computers on the job: How often do they use computers? How does a computer make their job easier or harder? What type of training they were given. (Key Skill: *Communication*)
3. **Debate.** Select students to debate the pros and cons of electronic banking for businesses and individuals. (Key Skills: *Communication, Critical Thinking*)
4. **Research Project.** Assign students to research changes in computer technology in the past thirty years and present an oral report. (Key Skills: *Communication, Critical Thinking*)

How to . . .
Coordinate Family Needs and Technology

Technology is a positive thing. However, if it isn't managed well, it can cause problems in the family. For each situation below, suggest how family values could be put to work to solve the problem of meeting family needs and effectively using technology:

- The Klopner family rarely talks anymore. Their leisure time is spent watching television and videotaped movies.
- Sixteen-year-old Chad and his older brother argue over using the family's second car.
- The Blonski family has a very full schedule. They eat frozen dinners almost every night, and they're getting tired of them.
- Fourteen-year-old Ellen talks on the telephone every chance she gets. She complains when other family members ask her to let them use the phone.
- Fifteen-year-old Devon spends all his allowance on computer games. Then he asks his sister to lend him money for his other expenses.

Library computers help you find information.

When you are studying home design, you might take advantage of a computer program for trying out furniture arrangements. Moving furniture around by computer is easy. All you have to do is push a few buttons. You can see the results of each arrangement immediately on the computer screen. You can also print out copies of different arrangements to compare and see which you like best.

Your school library probably has a computer that stores a list of its entire collection. This means that you can use the computer to see if the library has a book or other publication you want. You can find out what materials are available on a certain subject or by a particular author. You can also locate your choice on the library's shelves by using information from the computer.

How to ... Coordinate Family Needs and Technology

Select several volunteers to interview grandparents and other older family members and adults. Work with the students in developing a list of questions to use during the interviews. Include questions such as: What values have guided you and your family throughout your life? What technological changes have you observed during your life? How have you and your family dealt with these changes? In what ways have they affected your family life? Afterwards, have students share and discuss the results of their interviews with the class.

Some school libraries have special software programs for assisting students in choosing a career. (At your school, this material may be in the counselor's office instead of the library.) One purpose of this software is to inventory your interests and supply you with a list of appropriate careers. Another purpose is to research available college programs and other training for certain careers. Some of these software programs are good resources for the most up-to-date information about specific careers. You can use them to learn the duties of a particular job as well as its usual salary range and its future outlook.

School offices make use of computers for various administrative tasks. Computers are often used for alphabetizing class lists and filing away other assorted information. Computers calculate, print, and store students' academic and attendance records. Some schools even depend on computers for making phone calls to parents of students who are absent.

Technology in the Workplace

Wherever you see people working today, you will probably see technology working, too. Technology saves time and human effort at work. It also helps to reduce the number of human errors. Various workplaces use different kinds of technology in different ways and amounts.

Banking

Banks count heavily on technology for help in performing various tasks. When you go to a teller to make a deposit or a withdrawal, the teller uses a computer to complete the transaction. Most banks also provide **ATMs**, or **automatic teller machines**. ATMs are computers that bank customers can use to make their transactions when tellers are busy or when the bank is closed.

Banks also rely on technology when they service your checking account. Computers read the code numbers on your checks and subtract the amount of each check from your balance.

Retail Stores

Technology is employed extensively by retail businesses today. Most large stores use computers for such functions as ordering, stocking, and keeping track of inventory (the amount of merchandise on hand). Many stores also have scanners connected to computers at the checkout stand. These

SAFETY CHECK ✓

Here are some guidelines for safely using your ATM card:

- Never tell anyone your personal identification number (PIN number).
- Only use an ATM in a well-lighted public place.
- Avoid using an ATM late at night.
- Check your bank statements as soon as you receive them to make sure that only the transactions you made are recorded. If there are ATM transactions listed that you did not make, this might indicate an error on the bank's part or that someone has used your pin number to access your account.

More About *Technology in the Workplace*

A facsimile, or FAX, machine makes it possible to transmit written documents over long distances in a matter of minutes. The machine resembles a small copier. However, instead of copying the page to a sheet of paper, information is sent over a telephone line and printed on a sheet of paper at its destination. Thousands of businesses depend on this ability to transmit written documents quickly over long distances.

Learning Activities (continued)

5. **Field Trip.** Arrange a trip to a bank. Ask a representative to explain how computers and other technology are used in the bank and how they benefit the bank and its customers. What was banking like before these developments? (Key Skill: *Communication*)

Follow Up

1. **Reteaching.** Have students collect and display universal product codes from a variety of items. Have them write a short paper explaining UPC functions. (Key Skills: *Communication, Critical Thinking*)
2. **Enrichment.** Ask volunteers to develop a data bank of community resources. Donate the results to the school counselor, local groups, or religious institutions that may be able to use them. (Key Skill: *Communication*)

SAFETY CHECK ✓

After students have read the feature, have them make posters, write a skit, or act out the importance of following these rules.

Teaching. . .
Retail Stores; Design; Transportation; Law Enforcement; Health Care; Future Technology
(pp. 232-234)

Comprehension Check

1. What information does a universal product code provide? *(What a product is, and its price.)*
2. How does CAD affect the work of designers? *(Makes it possible to experiment with changes in design.)*
3. Name three transportation professionals who depend on technology. *(Pilots, ship captains, railway workers.)*
4. What are three examples of technology used in law enforcement? *(Computer terminals in vehicles, computers in crime labs, and bulletproof and flame-resistant clothing.)*
5. What is the purpose of a CT scan? *(To diagnose a patient's condition by allowing doctors to see inside a patient's body.)*

Learning Activities

1. **Student Research.** Select students to investigate and report on computer products that are available to help disabled persons. (Key Skill: *Communication*)
2. **Library Research.** Assign students to investigate the use of robots in medicine. Discuss their findings with the class. (Key Skill: *Critical Thinking*)
3. **Interview.** Arrange for a small group of students to interview a police officer and/or fire fighter about some of the latest developments in protective technology. Have students ask about bulletproof and flame-resistant clothing. Ask what they learned. (Key Skills: *Communication, Critical Thinking*)

Photo Focus

Ask students to look at the photos throughout the chapter. Go around the room quickly, asking each student to tell one use for computers.

Scanners read the UPC labels on products and send this information to a central computer. The computer sends price information to the cash register which prints your receipt. What are some other ways that bar codes are used?

scanners are designed to read **universal product codes**, or **UPCs**, printed on each product or price ticket. A UPC is a bar code — or pattern of stripes that identifies a product. Each product has its own UPC. The checker passes each item across a scanner that "reads" the code and sends it to the computer. The computer sends information about the product's price back to the cash register, which then prints an itemized receipt. The computer also sends the product's code number to an inventory file which helps employees know when supplies of a product are getting low and must be reordered. Bar coding saves time in completing sales transactions and can reduce the number of errors.

Credit card purchases also involve computers. Computers permit store clerks to check a credit card before the purchase process is completed. The clerk can easily tell if the credit card has been reported as stolen and make sure that the current purchase won't exceed the customer's credit limit.

Computers can help customers in other ways, too. You may be able to see how you would look in a different hairstyle or another color shirt at the touch of a few keys.

Many stores utilize video technology. You might see a videotape that demonstrates the application of cosmetic products. In a supermarket, tapes may show how to use food products in delicious recipes. Video cameras are also used for security.

▼ Design ▼

Technology has vastly changed the way that design work is done. Drafters, architects, engineers, and interior designers now use computers. Computer-aided design (CAD) makes it possible to draw houses, bridges, cars, and airplanes quickly and easily. CAD also makes it possible to experiment with a variety of changes in the design of these items in order to determine the best design. In addition, CAD offers the option of working in three dimensions at a computer terminal. This allows architects and interior designers to plan the space in a room quite easily. By using CAD, they can visually "walk" through the space and decide how to use it.

Law enforcement officials use computers to help solve crime.

▼ Transportation ▼

People who work in transportation depend on the latest technology to assist them. For example, both pilots and ships' captains rely on computers to help them navigate, or remain on course. Some new jets have computers that are capable of landing the plane without the pilot's help. Workers on high-speed trains use computers for mapping out routes and for keeping track of railroad traffic.

More About Medicine and Technology

A computerized cardiac defibrillator is a device used to evaluate and sometimes revive patients suffering from cardiac arrest by restoring their heart rhythms. The device analyzes a patient's medical situation and determines whether an electric shock to jolt the heart is needed. Computerized defibrillators, now available in many ambulances, help paramedics and emergency medical technicians avoid the need for guesswork in determining what kind of emergency care should be given. If the computer decides that the patient needs the defibrillator, the emergency worker pushes a button and the machine delivers the shock.

▼ Law Enforcement ▼

Computer technology serves law enforcement agencies in many ways. One example is that many officers' vehicles are now equipped with computer terminals. Officers count on these computers as an information source. When they need to learn more about a suspect or a stolen car, they turn to their computers for quick answers.

Technicians in crime labs also use computers in the course of their work. National data banks (central computers that store information from all over the nation) help technicians identify fingerprints of suspects. Computers are also used to analyze such things as fibers found on a suspect's clothing. Careful computer analysis helps technicians determine whether a suspect was present at the scene of the crime.

Protective technology also plays an essential role in law enforcement work. This involves the latest developments in things such as bulletproof and flame-resistant clothing. Protective technology is important because it helps keep officers and firefighters safe.

▼ Health Care ▼

Health care is a field in which scientific knowledge advances very rapidly. Physicians and other health care workers need to keep up with the latest information. Computer technology is used to gather data about various illnesses and treatments.

Computers are also used today in diagnosing patients' conditions. With a CT scan, the patient's body is scanned by several X-ray machines. The information that is collected is then used to reconstruct an image on a computer screen, so the doctor can "see" graphic images of what is inside the patient's body. An MRI teams powerful magnets with computers.

Future Technology

Right now, technology provides tools that can make life better for individuals and families. Homes, schools, and workplaces are using technology to solve problems and perform tasks quickly and easily. While you are reading this book, new discoveries are being made, and technology is advancing even farther. In the near future, you are likely to see some of these uses of

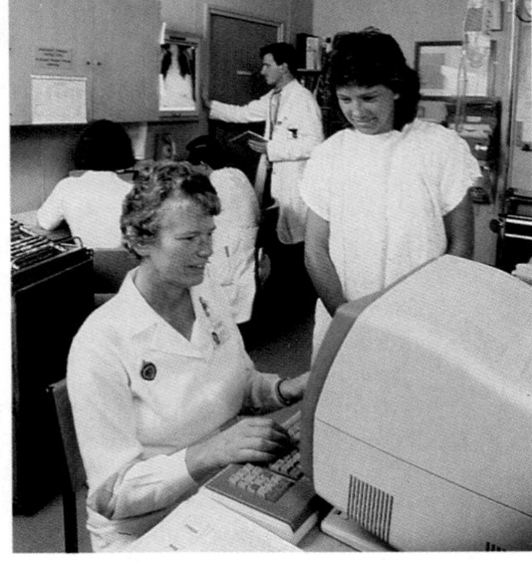

Physicians and hospitals use computers to identify illnesses and treatments.

MEETING SPECIAL NEEDS

Helping the Hearing and Visually Impaired

Special technology has also been designed to help people with disabilities. One example is the TDD, or Telecommunications Device for the Deaf. This technology uses a keyboard connected to a telephone. The hearing-impaired person communicates by sending and receiving printed conversations. Other technology is available for people with visual disabilities. Some computers read aloud from printed books or tell the user what appears on the computer screen.

More About *Medical Technology*

Magnetic resonance imaging, or MRI, allows medical professionals to evaluate neck, knee, shoulder, and other injuries in a painless way using a strong magnetic field. MRI even allows physicians to see through organs and bones. The patient lies on a table inside a giant magnet; and instead of using X-rays or contrast dyes, the MRI uses radio waves and magnetism to make images. A computer analyzes the pattern of magnetic energy, and turns the pattern into a three-dimensional image of inside the body that is used by radiologists to interpret and diagnose medical problems.

Learning Activities (continued)

4. **Guest Speaker.** Invite a police officer to talk about technology in law enforcement and to answer questions such as: What are the advantages and disadvantages of such use? What does technology cost? How has current technology changed law enforcement? What kinds of technology might be used in the future? (Key Skill: *Communication*)
5. **Guest Speaker.** Invite a medical representative to discuss technology used in the local medical community. (Key Skill: *Communication*)
6. **Field Trip.** Arrange a field trip to the office of an architect, engineer, or designer who uses computer assisted design (CAD) for a demonstration. Ask what work was like prior to the computer. (Key Skill: *Communication*)

Follow Up

1. **Reteaching.** Ask students to construct crossword puzzles featuring technology used in transportation, law enforcement, or medicine. Ask them to exchange and complete each other's puzzles. (Key Skill: *Creativity*)
2. **Extension.** Use the activity on p. 31 of the *Extending the Lesson* booklet in the TCR.
3. **Enrichment.** Have students use their imaginations to develop an idea for a useful form of technology in the future. Have them share and discuss their completed projects with the class. (Key Skill: *Science*)

MEETING SPECIAL NEEDS

Helping the Hearing and Visually Impaired

Select several students to interview people with disabilities who use special technology for daily life or in the workplace. Have students photograph or videotape the technology in use to share with the class. Have them submit their reports to the school newspaper. Assign other students to research the Americans with Disabilities Act of 1990.

Completing the Chapter

For Review

1. Emphasize the main concepts using the summary.
2. Have students complete the "Facts to Recall." (Answers below.)

For Reteaching

1. **Reteaching.** Use the activity on p. 28 of the *Reteaching and Practical Skills* booklet in the TCR.

For Enrichment

1. **Enrichment.** Use the activity on p. 39 of the *Enrichment Activities* booklet in the TCR.

For Evaluation

1. Choose items from "Ideas to Explore" and "Activities to Try."
2. Use the chapter test on pp. 45-46 in the testing booklet of the TCR or use the testmaker software.

Facts to Recall Answers

1. **Any five:** financial planning; making schedules; writing letters; entertainment; banking; making reservations; paying taxes.
2. **Any three:** sewing machines; irons; microwave ovens; coffee makers.
3. Sensors in window and door alarms; automatic lights; automatic garage door openers.
4. Inventory interests and give list of appropriate careers; research college programs and other training; give up-to-date information about careers.
5. Saves time; reduces errors; keeps track of inventory.
6. Computer-aided design. Helps drafters, architects, engineers, and interior designers to draw houses, bridges, cars, and airplanes quickly and easily, and to experiment with changes.
7. Help navigate airplanes and ships; land airplanes; map out routes and keep track of high-speed trains.

Technology can help people with special needs in a variety of ways. How many can you identify?

technology. Some things you may well see in the near future include:

- Even more people earning a living by doing their job at home from a computer and transmitting information electronically.
- Robots being used in the home for household tasks.
- Closed-circuit TV in the home for monitoring children.
- Home computers that will automatically contact supermarkets to place orders for food and household supplies.
- Increased use of computerized devices for medical patients that allow doctors to monitor health from a distance.
- Tiny implanted computers that will automatically measure the number of calories eaten and used by a person's body.

Managing Technology

Now, and in the future, it will be up to you to make the best possible use of technology in your life. Remember that technology is a resource that you can learn to manage well. Making good use of technology means choosing the equipment, materials, and methods that will work best for you. This will save you time, energy, and money that you can then devote to those things you value most.

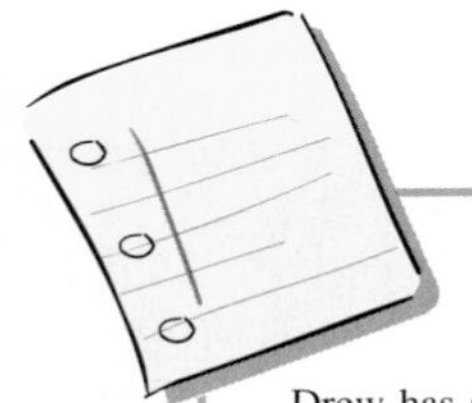

TAKING ACTION

Better Business with Computers

Drew has an idea. He hopes to start a neighborhood shopping service. The purpose of Drew's service will be to help elderly residents and working parents who have a hard time getting out to shop.

Drew already has quite a few names and addresses of neighbors who might be interested. He plans to write a letter explaining his idea and inviting these neighbors to try his service.

Once he gets customers, Drew will collect their shopping lists once a week. To help people make up their lists, Drew will comparison shop and circulate a list of available bargains. Customers will pay an estimated amount for their groceries, plus a reasonable fee for Drew's time and effort. This will allow Drew's service to make a profit. He plans to keep accurate records of all aspects of his business. Drew wonders how he can best use technology in operating his new business.

Using Your Resourcefulness

- In what ways would a computer be helpful for Drew's business? Offer some specific advantages of using a computer.
- How could a computer help you manage your own life more efficiently?
- What are some ways that you could learn more about the uses and programs of different computer systems?

TAKING ACTION

Invite a computer science instructor to discuss some of the latest developments in computer software. Identify developments that Drew might use to run his shopping service. Afterwards, divide the class into pairs, and assign several of the pairs to select a profession in which computer use is increasing. Have them interview people in the profession about their job-related use of computers. Select other student pairs to research prices and features of today's computers and popular software programs. Display and discuss advertisements of computers, software programs, and local computer classes.

Chapter 21 Review

Summary

In this chapter, you have read about:

- How technology can make home life more convenient, efficient, and enjoyable.
- How technology at school can help in learning, creativity, and choosing a career.
- How technology is used in various jobs to increase efficiency and reduce mistakes.
- Possible uses for technology in the future.

Facts to Recall

1. List five tasks performed with home computers that make life more convenient or enjoyable.
2. Give three examples of how microcomputers are used in home appliances.
3. Identify three ways in which technology is used to help keep your home safe.
4. Explain three ways in which specially designed software programs can help you choose a career or a college.
5. What are three advantages to using a UPC to check out items at a store?
6. What is CAD? Who uses it, and how it is helpful?
7. Identify three uses for computers in the field of transportation.
8. Describe two examples of technology that helps people with disabilities.
9. List two ways technology is used in health care.
10. Name two ways in which computers may someday help you prepare meals.

Ideas to Explore

1. How do you think the increasing use of technology will affect the job market in the future?
2. Technology has done much to improve the quality of life. What problems might arise from our growing use of technology?
3. Name three technological advances or inventions that you feel have had the greatest impact on your life, and explain how they have affected you. How would your life be different without them?

Activities to Try

1. On a sheet of paper, write down all the ways you depend on technology every day. What does your list tell you about the importance of technology in your life?
2. With a partner, make two lists: one, of the technological advances made in your lifetime; the other, of advances made in the first 12 to 15 years of your parents' generation. Draw conclusions about which time period brought more influential advances in technology.

LINK TO Science

PREDICTING TECHNOLOGICAL CHANGE

Technology is rapidly changing the world in which we live. It is affecting every aspect of our lives, making the unthinkable commonplace in only a short period of time. Locate and read an article describing ways technology is helping scientists in their work.

- What new research efforts are possible as a result of new technology?
- What recent discoveries have been made using new technology?
- Make five predictions of scientific advances that might result from technological development in the future. Your predictions may sound like science fiction today, but tomorrow — who knows?

Facts to Recall Answers (continued)

8. Telecommunications Device for the Deaf (TDD): keyboard connected to a telephone that allows hearing-impaired person to send and receive printed conversations; computers that help visually disabled people by reading aloud from books or telling user what appears on computer screen.
9. Gathering data about illnesses and treatments; diagnosing patients' conditions.
10. Home computers will automatically place orders from supermarkets; kitchen computers will count calories and analyze foods' nutritional content.

Ideas to Explore

1. Answers will vary and may include: increase demand for computer-related skills; decrease number of low-skilled jobs.
2. Answers will vary and may include: raise ethical or moral questions; depersonalize life; weaken relationship skills.
3. Answers will vary.

Using Your Resourcefulness Answers

- Answers will vary, but may include using a computer to tabulate bargains and shopping lists.
- Answers will vary.
- Answers will vary, but may include school courses, courses offered at computer centers and stores, newspapers and magazines.

LINK TO Science

Answer

To assist students in doing the research in the feature, have students check the *Reader's Guide to Periodical Literature* in your library. Have students report on their research in small groups, or assign one question to each group. Student answers will vary.

Preparing to Teach

Chapter Outline

Chapter Resources

The following booklet materials may be found in the *Teacher's Classroom Resources* box:

- Lesson Plans, p. 27
- Student Workbook, *Study Guide,* pp. 97-98; *Conservation Savvy,* pp. 99-100
- Color Transparencies, *Conserving Energy at Home,* CT-22
- Technology and Computers, p. 21
- Cooperative Learning, p. 34
- Extending the Text, *How Long Will Litter Last?,* p. 32
- Reteaching and Practical Skills, *Doing Your Part,* p. 30
- Enrichment Activities, *A Look at Your Environment,* p. 37
- Chapter and Unit Tests, pp. 47-48; pp. 115-117
- Testmaker Software

Also see:

- Leadership and Citizenship
- Meeting the Special Needs of Students
- Linking Home, School, and Community

CHAPTER 22 Natural Resources

OBJECTIVES

- *Give examples of renewable and nonrenewable resources.*
- *Explain the importance of resource management and identify conservation measures.*

TERMS TO LEARN

- ***natural resources***
- ***renewable resources***
- ***nonrenewable resources***
- ***conservation***
- ***recycling***

What do a glass of water, a chunk of coal, a clump of dirt, and a tree have in common? Water, coal, soil, and trees are **natural resources**. These are resources that occur in nature.

Some natural resources keep human beings alive and healthy. The air we breathe and the water we drink are two examples. Other natural resources, including coal and natural gas, are fuels that we use to provide heat and light and to power machines. Some natural resources, such as minerals and trees, are made into products that we use in our everyday lives. Many natural resources add quality to life. What would life be without forests, rivers, lakes, and blue skies to enjoy?

The Supply of Natural Resources

Technology, which you read about in Chapter 21, is a man-made resource. People create technology and control its availability. In contrast, natural resources can't be made by people. Only nature creates these resources and controls the amounts of them available to us.

Some resources renew, or replace, themselves over time. These are called **renewable resources**. Plants renew themselves by producing seeds, which, in turn, produce new plants. Air, water, and soil are also replaced, not by reproduction but through natural cycles. Supplies of air, water, and soil are always being produced unless something interferes with their natural cycles.

Other natural resources do not replace themselves. These are known as **nonrenewable resources**. The supply of these resources is limited. No more is available than what is on the planet right now. Oil is a nonrenewable resource. So are minerals, such as zinc, copper, and iron. Supplies of these resources could last a long time or run out — what happens will depend on how quickly existing supplies are used up.

Planting trees is one way that people can help our environment.

Natural Resources Today

One only needs to look at a newspaper or news broadcast to learn about the condition of natural resources today. Forests have been destroyed. Oil is in short supply. Air, water, and soil have been poisoned by pollution. The whole environment is threatened because resources have been misused

Introducing the Chapter

Motivators

1. **Brainstorming.** Compile a list of natural resources, and have students tell which resources they use each day. (Key Skill: *Critical Thinking*)
2. **Discussion.** Ask students to list environmental threats in your area. Discuss local problems that have received media coverage (landfills, air and water pollution). (Key Skill: *Critical Thinking*)
3. **Class Survey.** Ask the class how many students and families recycle items, buy recycled products, conserve water and fuel, and avoid polluting air and water. (Key Skill: *Critical Thinking*)
4. **Sentence Completion.** Ask students to complete: "I could improve my conservation of resources by ..." and "Some of the ways I waste resources are ..." (Key Skill: *Critical Thinking*)
5. **Classroom and Laboratory Survey.** Ask small groups to survey the classroom and laboratory for recycled items and items made of recycled resources. (Key Skill: *Problem Solving*)
6. **Journal Writing.** Ask students to record conservation efforts. (Key Skill: *Communication*)

Chapter Objectives and Vocabulary

1. Have students read the chapter objectives. Ask them to rephrase the objectives as questions.
2. Ask students to state, in their own words, the purpose of studying this chapter.
3. Pronounce the vocabulary terms listed on the previous page. Ask students whether they are familiar with any of these. Explain that the terms will be defined in the chapter.

Guided Reading

1. Have students read the chapter and use the Study Guide on pp. 97-98 of the *Student Workbook*.

More About *Environmentalists*

Henry David Thoreau was an early American environmentalist. He spent several years living in a small hut on the shore of an isolated pond. Thoreau's book, *Walden*, is about his experience. In his book, he recommended that people learn to live more simply and to respect the environment. In the years that followed, a man named John Muir helped launch the first major conservation movement. He urged that Americans set aside some parts of the country that would never be logged or farmed. His great love, California's Yosemite Valley, became one of America's first national parks.

Teaching. . .

The Supply of Natural Resources; Natural Resources Today; Your Role in Resource Management

(pp. 237-239)

Comprehension Check

1. What are four nonrenewable resources? *(Oil, zinc, copper, and iron.)*
2. What is the purpose of an aerator on a faucet or shower head? *(To mix air with water, causing less water to be used.)*
3. Why is it important to conserve electricity? *(Because it is often produced by burning a nonrenewable fuel.)*

Learning Activities

1. **Discussion.** Discuss ways in which renewable and nonrenewable resources can be conserved at school. (Key Skill: *Critical Thinking*)
2. **Discussion.** Ask students to collect articles about environmental issues. Discuss why the information in the articles is important to students and their families. (Key Skill: *Critical Thinking*)

Around the World

Select students to read articles about the global problem of deforestation. Have them locate on a world map places where this is occurring. Ask them to create a bulletin board about this problem titled: "What in the World is Happening to the Forests?" Have students come to the board and identify parts of the world where deforestation is taking place. Assign other students to make posters on the declining number of trees in the world. Ask volunteers to interview people who are originally from other countries about the environmental concerns of those countries.

Around the World

The rain forests of South America and Africa are very important to the worldwide environment. They clean the air and are home to many types of plants and animals. However, farmers in that region need the land to plant crops and graze animals. They also need the wood for building and for fuel. Environmental groups like the World Wildlife Fund are trying to teach farmers new techniques to help save the rain forests. However, many problems remain. Where else are there conflicts between protecting the environment and preserving a people's way of life?

and natural cycles have been disturbed. Good resource management is needed to avoid the misuse of resources and ensure the availability of resources now and in the future.

Your Role in Resource Management

The natural resources of planet Earth are shared by everyone on the planet. Therefore, it is the responsibility of everyone to help manage these resources effectively. You have already learned to take charge of your personal resources, such as time, energy, and money. Now you will discover what you can do to participate actively in managing natural resources.

Natural resource management involves **conservation**, which is protecting resources against waste and harm. The following sections describe conservation measures that you and your family can take on a regular basis.

Water

Have you ever wondered what your life would be like without the availability of fresh water? Water shortages exist in some areas today, and water supplies are polluted and unusable in other areas. Water conservation measures involve managing water use so that available water isn't wasted. Here are some ways that you can conserve water:

- Turn faucets all the way off each time you use them, and repair all plumbing leaks. A faucet leaking one drop of water per second can waste 650 gallons of water a year.
- Install aerators on your faucets and your shower heads. These inexpensive devices mix air with water. The result is that the water pressure remains the same, but less water is used.

More About *Rain Forests*

Rain forests are complex tropical ecosystems that provide much of the world's oxygen. They also help prevent flooding and droughts; help regulate the earth's temperature; and provide a home to at least fifty percent of the world's plant, animal, and insect species. Every year, new food strains and important medicines are derived from rain forest plants. According to the National Cancer Institute, about seventy percent of the plants found to be useful in cancer treatment have come from rain forests.

- Take quick showers instead of baths. You will use as little as one-fifth the amount of water. Wet yourself. Turn off the water while you lather. Then turn the water back on to rinse yourself off.
- Run full loads in your washing machine or dishwasher. Wait until you have a full load to make better use of the water.
- Fill the sink with water instead of leaving the water running wastefully down the drain when washing dishes by hand.
- Use only as much water as you need for brushing your teeth, shaving, or scrubbing fruits and vegetables. Don't let water run needlessly throughout the entire process.
- Sweep driveways and walkways outside your home rather than using water to hose them down.
- Use food scraps as compost for plants or a garden instead of using a garbage disposal, which requires the use of running water.

Heating and Cooling

It is essential to be aware of natural resources when you heat and cool your home. Some heating requires the use of fuels that are nonrenewable resources. Other kinds of heating and air conditioning depend on electricity. However, remember that electricity is often produced by burning a nonrenewable fuel. If we want fuel supplies to last, we must do our best to reduce fuel use now. Here are some ideas for conserving energy when heating or cooling your home:

- Set your heater no higher than 68°F (20°C) during the day to save fuel. At night, turn the temperature down even farther to 55-60° F (13-16°C).
- Keep your heat inside by using weather stripping and caulking to prevent heat from escaping around windows and doors.
- Install storm doors and windows in winter if your climate is cold. This will help you keep the heat in and keep out cold drafts. You will use less fuel.
- Close shades and draperies at night in cold weather to keep in the heat and keep out the cold. If the days are sunny, open shades and draperies in the daytime. This will allow you to heat your home using the sun's energy.
- Set your air conditioner no lower than 78°F (26°C) during the summer months. Have your air conditioner checked yearly to avoid coolant leaks, which can damage the Earth's atmosphere.
- Use a fan instead of an air conditioner. Fans use less electricity and, therefore, less fuel.

Learning Activities (continued)

3. **Comics.** Ask students to create comic strips focusing on conserving natural resources. Distribute and discuss them with the class. Publish a collection of the best to distribute. (Key Skills: *Communication, Creativity*)
4. **Brochures.** Have students design a brochure encouraging children to conserve and recycle. Exhibit and discuss the designs. With permission, distribute to elementary school classes. (Key Skill: *Creativity*)
5. **Design Projects.** Have students create designs for T-shirts, grocery sacks, bumper stickers, or baseball caps, promoting conservation. Display designs. Send photos to submit to school and local newspapers. (Key Skill: *Creativity*)
6. **Small Group Research.** Select several students to use library resources to find out which parts of the world are facing water shortage problem and what steps, if any, are being taken to deal with the situation. Ask them to share what they learn with the class. (Key Skills: *Social Studies, Communication*)
7. **Guest Speakers.** Invite representatives from organizations involved with global environmental issues to speak to the class. Select several students to summarize the presentation into an article to submit to the school newspaper. (Key Skills: *Communication, Social Studies*)

Follow Up

1. **Reteaching.** Ask students to write a public service announcement about ways to save natural resources. Videotape or record the announcements. (Key Skills: *Communication, Creativity*)
2. **Enrichment.** Have students find volunteer opportunities for environmental concerns. Ask them to summarize their findings in a one-page flyer to distribute to the class. (Key Skills: *Social Studies, Creativity*)

More About *Protecting the Rain Forests*

Despite the work of environmentalists and governments around the globe, the earth's rain forests are in trouble. The World Resources Institute reports that about forty million acres of rain forests, an area about the size of Washington state, are chopped down every year. When rain forests are destroyed, they fail to grow back. Without its protective forest canopy, the soil quickly turns to dust and blows away. It is estimated that, at present rates, eighty percent of the world's rain forests will be gone by the year 2000.

Teaching. . .
Lighting and Appliances; Transportation
(pp. 240-241)

Comprehension Check

1. What are two advantages of defrosting foods in a refrigerator instead of an oven or microwave? *(Saves energy; as frozen foods thaw, they keep the refrigerator cool.)*
2. Name six ways to cut fuel use and still meet your transportation needs. *(Bike or walk; join a carpool; keep your car well maintained; plan car trips; eliminate unnecessary trips; use public transportation.)*

Learning Activities

1. **Discussion.** Have students list everything in a house that requires energy. In what ways is energy commonly wasted? How can it be conserved? Why is energy often taken for granted? (Key Skill: *Critical Thinking*)
2. **Discussion.** Have students name and explain some of the advantages of carpooling. Talk about reasons why carpooling is not used in every community. (Key Skill: *Critical Thinking*)
3. **Demonstration.** Show how to use incandescent, halogen, and fluorescent lamps. Have students compare purchase price, light output, and energy usage. (Key Skills: *Math, Science*)
4. **Design Project.** Assign students to create designs for a postage stamp expressing the need to cut fuel used for transportation. Provide basic art supplies, and have students enlarge their designs on poster board. Exhibit completed projects. (Key Skills: *Problem Solving, Creativity*)

- Keep windows covered during the day in hot weather. This will keep heat out, and you will have to cool less.
- Close outside doors promptly when you enter or leave your home. This will keep out heat or cold that will change your home's temperature.
- Avoid heating or cooling rooms that no one is using. Doing so is a waste of fuel.
- Look into using solar energy for heating. The supply of sunlight is unlimited — and free.

Lighting and Appliances

Like heating and cooling, lighting and appliances draw on the Earth's reserves of fuel. Gas ranges and some other appliances use fuels directly, while lighting and electrical appliances make indirect use of fuels. You can help stretch the planet's fuel resources by carefully managing lighting and appliance use in your home.

- Clean lamps and lighting fixtures regularly so that as much light as possible can come through them.
- Replace high-wattage light bulbs with lower-wattage ones or with fluorescent lights, which use less electricity.
- Turn off lights, television sets, radios, and appliances when you leave the room for more than just a few minutes. It doesn't make sense to leave them on when they are not in use, and it takes electricity to run them.
- Choose the appliance that takes the smallest amount of energy for whatever task you do. For example, use an electric skillet to cook food rather than a regular skillet on a burner of an electric range. The electric skillet uses less energy.
- Use your oven to cook several items at once. Don't open the oven door unnecessarily while you are cooking. This allows heat to escape, which means that additional fuel must be used to bring the oven temperature back up to the correct temperature.
- Defrost foods in your refrigerator instead of in your microwave. This takes planning, but it saves energy. As frozen foods defrost, they will help to keep your refrigerator cool.
- Limit the number of times you open your refrigerator and the length of time you leave it open. When cool air escapes and warm air gets inside, your refrigerator has to run longer to stay cool.

More About *Taking Care of Natural Resources*

The root word for *ecology* is the Greek term, *oikos*, meaning house. The inference is that the earth is one house, the home for all life. The Student Conservation Corps (SCA), a 32-year-old non-profit organization, is one of many groups working to get the earth/house back in order. The organization is dedicated to providing education and information, as well as undertaking clean-up and recovery efforts. Participants can volunteer for long periods of time or for one-week programs in which they spend all or part of a vacation working for the environment.

- Run the dryer only as long as necessary to dry laundry. Drying laundry too long wastes fuel directly or indirectly, depending on the kind of dryer.
- Consider air-drying clothes instead of using a dryer. Take advantage of solar energy, which uses no nonrenewable fuels.

▼ Transportation ▼

Motor vehicles are powered either by gasoline or by diesel fuel. These products are made from crude oil, or petroleum, which is a nonrenewable resource. There are several ways to cut fuel use and still meet your transportation needs.

- Use transportation possibilities that don't require fuel, such as biking or walking.
- Use public transportation, such as buses and subways, if possible. It uses less fuel because it transports so many people at once.
- Join a carpool. Sharing rides is an efficient use of fuel.
- Maintain your car to insure that it makes the best possible use of gas. Change the oil, maintain the correct air pressure in tires, and have a tune-up regularly as recommended in your owner's manual.
- Plan car trips ahead to make good use of them. Accomplish as many tasks as you can during a single trip.
- Eliminate unnecessary trips in your car. For example, be sure that the store has what you want before you get into your car and drive there.

Using alternate sources of transportation helps save fuel — a nonrenewable resource.

Learning Activities (continued)

5. **Presentations.** Divide the class into small groups to design short presentations for elementary school children. Have them base their presentations on the conservation of the planet's fuel resources. Ask them to prepare illustrative material to use during their presentations. Have students practice by presenting their lessons to the class. Videotape their presentations, and ask them to critique what changes might be needed. If possible, request administrative approval for the students to present their lessons to elementary classes. (Key Skills: *Communication, Science*)
6. **Guest Speaker.** Ask a physics teacher to speak about nuclear power: its cost, safety, efficiency, environmental impact, and waste disposal. (Key Skill: *Critical Thinking*)

Follow Up

1. **Reteaching.** Assign students to keep a two-day tally of times they conserve lighting and appliance use at home. Ask them to share their results with the class. (Key Skill: *Critical Thinking*)
2. **Enrichment.** Ask volunteers to write to elected officials about the environmental concerns. Select some to read anonymously to the class. Display responses received. (Key Skill: *Communication*)

More About Natural Resources

Corn is a natural resource that people can eat, drink, and drive. One bushel of corn, weighing 56 pounds and containing 72,800 kernels, can yield 31.5 pounds of starch, 33 pounds of sweetener, 2.5 gallons of fuel ethanol, 12.4 pounds of 21 percent protein feed, 3 pounds of 60 percent gluten meal, or 1.5 pounds of corn oil. Corn, or some part of it, also is used in the production of cereal, ketchup, beer, ceiling tiles, firecrackers, crayons, and tires.

Photo Focus

Direct students to look at the photo on page 241. Ask what evidences of technology are present *(cars, helmet, bike)*. Ask why bicycle riding is not as common in the United States as it is in Europe and Asia *(cost, distance, weather, social acceptability)*.

Teaching... Consumer Goods and Pollution (pp. 242-244)

Comprehension Check

1. From what natural resource is paper made? *(Wood pulp.)*
2. What two natural resources are often required in manufacturing processes? *(Water and fuel.)*
3. What two natural resources are polluted in some manufacturing processes? *(Water and air.)*
4. What is recycling? *(Making used, discarded, or waste materials into new products.)*

Learning Activities

1. **Discussion.** Distribute copies of an EnergyGuide label. Ask students to identify some of the information provided on the label. Discuss ways in which it can help students and their families in comparison shopping. (Key Skill: *Critical Thinking*)
2. **Ranking.** Have students rank major appliances for their energy usage. Ask them to list first the one using the most energy. Ask them to rank small appliances the same way. Afterwards, have students draw conclusions about both lists. Discuss how this information might make people more efficient users of appliances. (Key Skills: *Communication, Critical Thinking*)
3. **Booklet Analysis.** Assign students to study use-and-care booklets for microwave ovens. Afterwards, discuss ways a microwave oven can substitute for an electric range. Point out the energy savings. (Key Skill: *Critical Thinking*)
4. **Student Analysis.** Have students investigate the use of carpools in the community, the MPG of their family car, or the amount of gasoline their family uses each week. Have students report to the class the relationship of these findings to energy conservation. (Key Skill: *Critical Thinking*)

▼ Consumer Goods ▼

The products that you buy are manufactured, using natural resources as raw materials. Paper, for example, is made from wood pulp, a substance that comes from the wood of trees. Manufacturing processes often involve using water, and they always require energy. Fuels are burned to produce energy directly or to produce electricity, which then runs machines. Some manufacturing processes result in pollution, particularly of water and air. Used consumer goods eventually become waste, which is usually buried and may pollute soil and ground water.

Making Wise Consumer Decisions

As a consumer, it is up to you to consider natural resources *before* you buy. By keeping resource conservation in mind when making consumer choices, you will be able to make decisions that are "resource-wise."

- Always ask yourself if you really need your purchase. If not, don't buy something that took a lot of resources to produce.
- When you do buy, avoid disposable items. They quickly become trash and aren't worth the use of resources.
- Choose items that last as long as possible. Examples include rechargeable batteries and long-lasting light bulbs.
- Select items with very little packaging. It takes resources to make wrappers and boxes. Since packaging is usually thrown away once the product is removed, the resources used to make the packaging are wasted.

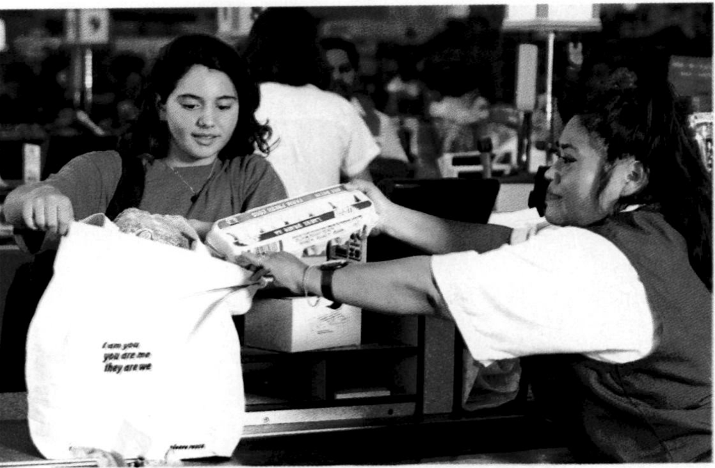

Keep conservation in mind as you make consumer purchases.

More About Trash

The average American produces more than 1,000 pounds of trash a year, or 3 to 4 pounds a day. As much as 84 percent of this trash is recyclable. However, Americans, on average, recycle only 10 percent of their trash. Buried in a landfill, even items that normally biodegrade quickly, such as paper, yard wastes, and food, have been known to last as long as 50 years. (Source: Texas A&M University, *Texas Energy*)

- Bring reusable bags to the supermarket, and use them to carry groceries home. This saves the resources needed to make paper and plastic bags, which tend to become trash very rapidly.
- When buying appliances, consider carefully how much electricity or gas they will use. EnergyGuide labels, such as the one on page 519, will help you choose appliances that make good use of fuels.
- When purchasing a car or other motor vehicle, find out how many miles per gallon various models get. Select a model that gets excellent mileage and, therefore, uses as little fuel as possible.

Cars vary in fuel efficiency. When you or your family are shopping for a car, compare fuel consumption estimates before making your purchase.

Making the Best Use of Consumer Goods

Existing supplies of natural resources will last longer if good use is made of products after they are purchased. Here are some ways that you can stretch a product's usable lifetime:

- Keep items longer. Don't throw them away because you are tired of them or because styles change.
- If you don't want a product anymore, give it to someone else who will use it. Charity organizations clean and repair used items so that they can be used further. Adding to product life in this way means that fewer resources are needed to manufacture new products.
- Contribute to recycling efforts. **Recycling** is using used, discarded products or scrap and waste materials to make new products. Glass, paper, tin, aluminum, iron, steel, and plastics are collected for recycling. In your community, there may be curbside pick-up of materials for recycling. If not, you can take your materials to official recycling centers.

Learning Activities (continued)

5. **Student Experiment.** Ask several students to conduct a classroom experiment involving a battery-powered radio or flashlight to contrast the life of disposable batteries with rechargeable ones. Then compare the actual operating costs. Talk about the effect of discarded batteries on landfills and water. (Key Skills: *Science, Problem Solving*)
6. **Bulletin Board.** Title a bulletin board: "Speaking Out About Natural Resources." Cover the board with large sheets of paper; and provide wide-tipped felt pens for students to write their thoughts about conservation, the environment, recycling, and reducing waste. (Key Skill: *Communication*)
7. **Guest Speaker.** Invite a community representative to speak about local recycling. Have students report on the presentation for the school newspaper. (Key Skill: *Communication*)

Follow Up

1. **Reteaching.** Give each student a month-long calendar. Entitle it: "A Month's Worth of Ways to Make Wise Consumer Decisions." Have students write in each square one idea for conserving resources or reducing waste. Encourage them to illustrate and display them in the classroom. (Key Skills: *Critical Thinking, Creativity*)
2. **Extension.** Use the activity on p. 32 of the *Extending the Lesson* booklet in the TCR.
3. **Enrichment.** Assist students in setting up an exhibit of disposable products. Discuss their effect on natural resources. Talk about why disposable products are popular. Select students to write an article for the school newspaper. (Key Skills: *Critical Thinking, Creativity*)

More About Recycling

Recycling makes economic sense because whatever a community recycles, it does not have to pay to bury or burn. Recycling also can save tax dollars by providing income from bottles, cans, newspapers, and other materials that are separated from trash and sold to industry. Approximately $1 of every $10 spent by consumers on food pays for packaging, most of which is not recycled. Instead, it goes straight from the store shelf to the customer's wastebasket. For example, Americans go through 2.5 million plastic bottles every hour. Only a small percentage of these are now recycled. (Source: *Environmental Defense Fund*)

Completing the Chapter

For Review

1. Emphasize the main concepts using the summary.
2. Have students complete the "Facts to Recall." (Answers below.)

For Reteaching

1. **Reteaching.** Use the activity on p. 29 of the *Reteaching and Practical Skills* booklet in the TCR.

For Enrichment

1. **Enrichment.** Use the activity on p. 40 of the *Enrichment Activities* booklet in the TCR.

For Evaluation

1. Choose items from "Ideas to Explore" and "Activities to Try."
2. Use the chapter test on pp. 47-48 in the testing booklet of the TCR or use the testmaker software.
3. Use the unit test on pp. 115-117 in the testing booklet of the TCR or use the testmaker software.

Facts to Recall Answers

1. To stay alive and healthy; to provide heat and light and to power machines; in everyday products; for quality of life.
2. Renewable resources: those that replace themselves over time. **Any two:** air; water; soil. Nonrenewable: those that can't be replaced and are limited in supply. Oil and minerals.
3. **Any four:** turn faucets off completely; install aerators; take quick showers instead of baths; run full loads in washing machine or dishwasher; fill sink with water when handwashing dishes; use only water needed for brushing teeth, shaving, or scrubbing foods; sweep driveways instead of hosing them down; compost food scraps instead of using garbage disposal.

Recycling saves new resources and cuts down on the amount of materials that end up in sanitary landfills.

Recycling old materials saves new resources. It also reduces the number of items that end up in the trash. In addition, producing products with recycled materials may save fuel because it uses less energy.

▼ Fighting Pollution ▼

Pollution makes resources such as air, water, and soil unusable or unhealthy. You and your family can do much to combat the harm that pollution does to our natural environment.

- Become informed about pollution in your community, the nation, and the world. Find out exactly what is happening, where it is happening, and what is being done to solve problems.
- Learn what laws are presently in effect to control pollution. Encourage leaders to get new laws passed as needed to stop pollution.
- Join with others who are interested in improving environmental conditions. For example, you might start a recycling drive at school so that materials won't become waste that pollutes the environment. A group might pick up roadside litter or help clean up a polluted waterway. Think about what you can do — and do it! Fighting pollution requires responsible action.

TAKING ACTION
Making a Difference in Your World

Mrs. Arnold, your family and consumer sciences teacher, asks your class to enter a national competition. Your goal is to identify an environmental problem or hazard in your community and develop a plan to improve or solve it. The problem might be as simple as a recycling drive or as complex as dealing with pollution or waste.

First brainstorm to identify the problem. Then you need to research a variety of resources to write a step-by-step plan that is both practical and effective. Mrs. Arnold will submit the best ideas to the competition, which offers college scholarships to winning students.

Using Your Resourcefulness

- Either singly or in groups, identify an environmental problem or hazard in your community.
- What resources will you need to use to learn more about the problem?
- How will you determine if these solutions are practical for your community?

TAKING ACTION

Ask students to read the feature and respond to the questions or statements in the feature. Have students explore alternative means of transportation such as carpools and vanpools, mass transit, and bicycling. Invite speakers from local businesses that encourage or provide car and vanpools for their employees to talk to the class about their transportation programs. Lead a discussion of the role that alternative means of transportation play in conserving fuel and reducing pollution.

Using Your Resourcefulness Answers

- Answers will vary.

Chapter 22 Review

Summary

In this chapter, you have read about:

- ▶ How people depend on natural resources in daily life.
- ▶ The supply and condition of natural resources today.
- ▶ Things you and your family can do to conserve natural resources.
- ▶ Ways to fight pollution.

Facts to Recall

1. Explain four ways in which people use natural resources.
2. Explain the difference between renewable and nonrenewable resources. Give two examples of each.
3. List four things you and your family can do to conserve water.
4. Name five ways in which you and your family can conserve energy when heating and cooling your home.
5. Identify four ways of conserving natural resources through managing lighting and appliance use.
6. List four ways of cutting fuel use in transportation.
7. Identify four ways in which natural resources are involved in the production of consumer goods.
8. Tell four "resource-wise" things you can do when buying products.
9. Name three ways in which recycling helps conserve existing supplies of natural resources.

Ideas to Explore

1. Give examples of laws designed to promote the conservation of natural resources or to fight pollution.
2. Would you and your family be willing to pay a higher price for products that created less pollution or used fewer natural resources to make? Why or why not?
3. Discuss how conserving natural resources affects your family's financial resources.
4. Identify four types of workers whose jobs depend directly on the continued availability of natural resources. What statement can you make about the relationship between wise use of natural resources and a region's or a nation's economy?

Activities to Try

1. In newspapers or magazines, find articles about natural resources. Make a report about their conservation, their destruction, or controversy about their use.
2. Find out about groups or companies that collect materials for recycling in your community. Learn where they are located, what materials they accept, and how much — if anything — they pay for the materials. Report your findings to the class.

LINK TO *Health*

HEALTH AND WATER

Many health problems have been linked to polluted water. Investigate what types of diseases and illnesses can be caused by polluted water. Respond to the following items as you complete your investigation:

- ▶ What are the most common water-related illnesses around the world?
- ▶ Describe the symptoms and treatments for these illnesses.
- ▶ What are some ways that we can take an active part in protecting our water supply?

Facts to Recall Answers (continued)

4. **Any five:** set heater no higher than 68°F (20°C) during day, 55-60°F (13-16°C) at night; weather-stripping and caulking; close shades at night, open on sunny days; set air condition no lower than 78°F (26°C); use fan instead of air conditioner; cover windows on hot days; close outside door promptly; don't heat or cool unused rooms; solar energy.
5. **Any four:** clean light fixtures regularly; use low-wattage bulbs; turn off appliances; choose appliance that uses least energy; use oven for several items at once; defrost foods in refrigerator; air-dry clothes.
6. **Any four:** use transportation that doesn't use fuel; carpool; maintain car; plan car trips; eliminate unnecessary trips.
7. As raw materials; in manufacturing; to produce energy; polluted by process or used goods.
8. **Any four:** do you need it; avoid disposable items; choose long-lasting items; select items with little packaging; reuse grocery bags; consider energy use; find out MPG of vehicles.
9. Saves new resources; reduces trash; saves fuel.

Ideas to Explore

1. Answers may include: water rationing; emissions standards.
2. Answers will vary.
3. Conserving natural resources usually saves financial resources.
4. Answers may include: farmers; tourism workers.

- Answers will vary, but may include library resources, governmental agencies, newspaper and magazine articles, etc.
- Answers will vary.

LINK TO *Health*

Answers

Direct students to read the feature.

- Answers will vary.
- Answers will vary.
- Answers will vary, but may include: avoid using harmful chemicals; use environmentally safe cleaning products, etc.

Career Connections

Volunteer Options

- Volunteer for environmental organizations.
- Volunteer for wildlife preservation.
- Public library volunteer (story hour programs, etc.).
- Public and private school volunteer.
- Collecting recyclables (newspapers, aluminum cans, etc.).
- Personal shopper for the elderly or disabled.

Volunteer Organizations

Sierra Club
730 Polk Street
San Francisco, CA 94109

Greenpeace
1436 U. Street N. W.
Washington, DC 10009

CAREER *Connections*

Get Ready for Your Future Through Volunteering

Lorenzo

"Last year all the schools in our rural community organized a fundraising drive to launch a county-wide recycling program. The organizers asked for student and adult volunteers with computer experience to help record the names of donors, the amount of each donation, and input other important information.

"I'd learned how to use computers at school, so I volunteered to enter this information on the computer. I enjoyed working with computers so much I started to research job possibilities to pursue after high school. After all, I was already doing what many data-entry operators are paid to do — enter and verify data on the computer. I found out word processing operators organize data, list logical steps for the computer to follow, and solve computer program problems. Computer sales personnel use their knowledge of hardware and software capabilities to sell and match systems and programs to their customers.

"I'm still not sure which direction I'll follow, but at least I know that the growing use of computers increases the need for employees with computer knowledge and training. The career opportunities seem limitless."

"Along with Lorenzo I volunteered as a computer operator for our county recycling program. I work full-time as a bank teller. Even though I enjoyed math classes in school, I never thought about working in a bank. I took a business class in which I learned calculator skills on a computer. The class took a tour of the local bank which gave me new insight into career opportunities.

"During the summer, I worked as a cashier at a pharmacy. I quickly learned I liked working with the public. After high school, I took classes for an associate's degree in business at a junior college. I also kept applying for a job at the bank, which I finally got!

"My daily activities involve counting money quickly and accurately, processing withdrawals and deposits on

Discussing Career Connections

Have students read the *Career Connections* feature. Ask students:

- What skills and abilities are necessary for working with computers and other types of technology?
- What personal skills and abilities do you have that might be beneficial to a career working with computers or finances?

If possible, have students tour a financial institution or business that relies on computer technology.

the computer, cashing checks, selling money orders, and taking utility payments. At the end of each day, I make sure that my cash drawer is in balance with the deposits and withdrawals I handled that day. Then I assist my supervisor with any additional work that needs to be done. I'm now being considered for a promotion and hope to be a bank officer one day. I'm so glad I found and pursued the right career for me."

"As a job placement counselor, I see many people like Naomi. They are young, skilled, and looking for a good job. Though my business and counseling courses in college helped prepare me for this position, hands-on experience has been my best training.

"The first thing I check carefully is a person's application form. I look at grammar and how well this person expresses himself or herself in writing. When I meet the person, I listen carefully to how the person communicates during the initial interview. Appearance, courtesy, and enthusiasm are just as important as a person's resumé.

"People who come to see me are often inexperienced in the job marketplace. I need to consider their personal resources such as interests, skills, and classes they've taken in high school and college. I believe in giving young people like Naomi a chance to prove themselves, especially when they've worked hard to make the most of themselves."

MAKING THE CONNECTION

- Do you think working with computers might interest you as a career? Why or why not? How might you use a computer in the career field of your choice? Explain your answer.
- Do you think working with money might interest you as a career? Why or why not? Besides banking, what other money-related careers can you name?
- What resource materials might help you choose the right career for you? Would you think about talking with a career counselor or job placement counselor to find work? Why or why not?

Occupational Outlook

Listed below are some possible resource-related occupations. Some require little training while others require a 4-year degree.

- Bank teller
- Charge account clerk
- Petroleum prospecting driller
- Field supervisor
- Office manager
- Park ranger
- Fish and game warden
- Soil conservationist
- Range manager
- Treasurer
- Securities sales representative
- Computer programmer
- Industrial engineer
- Nuclear medical technologist
- Credit counselor
- Consumer safety inspector
- Environmental health inspector
- Market research analyst
- Credit analyst
- Economist

Resource-Related Organizations

American Financial Services Association
1101 14th Street N. W.
Washington, DC 20005

Bureau of Land Management
U.S. Department of the Interior
Room 3619
Washington, DC 20240

Environmental Defense Fund
257 Park Avenue South
New York, NY 10010

Making the Connection

Answers

- Answers will vary.
- Answers will vary.
- Answers will vary. Remind students that talking with a career counselor might help them clarify what types of careers or jobs may be best for their skills and abilities.

Planning the Unit

Ch. 23: Looking at Housing Choices — Discusses factors that influence housing choices, the advantages and disadvantages of different types of housing, and reasons for purchasing or renting a home.

Ch. 24: Understanding the Art of Design — Explores the elements and principles of design and how they are used.

Ch. 25: Making Design Work for You — Describes ways to utilize living space, select and arrange furniture and accessories, and share living space.

Ch. 26: Keeping Your Home Clean and Safe — Examines home sanitation, safety, and security in addition to identifying repairs best made by professionals.

UNIT 4 Housing

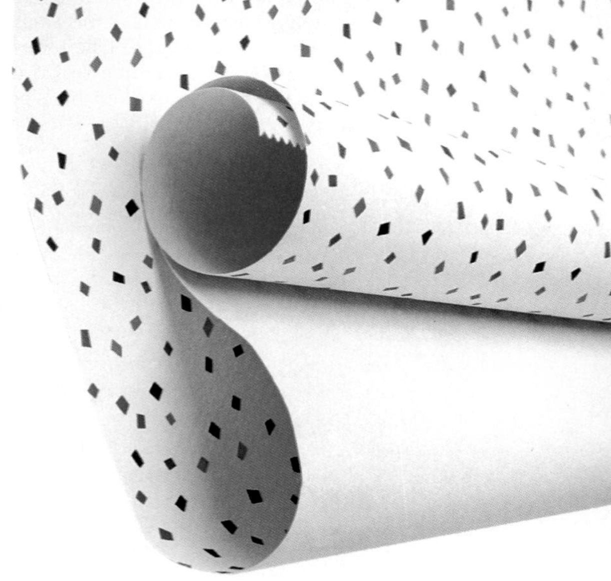

CHAPTERS

Cooperative Learning Tips

Teachers can use several methods to divide students into cooperative groups. Heterogeneous grouping can teach students that diversity broadens their information base and enhances learning. *Random grouping* (counting off by numbers, etc.) takes less time, but allows little control over elements such as reading ability and personality clashes. *Teacher-selected groups* require more time from the teacher, but may better meet objectives. Group synergy is often high with *student-selected* groups. However, they should be avoided to reduce the possibility of rejection until the cooperative process is firmly established.

See the *Cooperative Learning* booklet in the TCR for more information.

Introducing the Unit

Unit 4 Overview

Unit 4 introduces students to housing decisions including types of housing, influences on housing decisions, and ways to obtain housing. They are also introduced to the elements and principles of design as a way to organize space and create a personalized appearance. Students also will learn how to share space along with proper home sanitation, safety, and maintenance.

Unit Motivators

1. **Brainstorming.** Have students brainstorm a list of different types of housing in the community and write each type on the chalkboard. Ask students to draw conclusions about what factors they think influence the types of housing people choose and the types of housing available. (Key Skill: *Critical Thinking*)
2. **Choosing Accessories.** Have students choose a room in their home and list all of the accessories. Ask them to decide which accessories might be changed to create a different mood or feeling in the room. What might be the least costly way of making these changes? (Key Skill: *Decision Making*)

Completing the Unit

Review

1. **Evaluating Design.** Show students several household objects such as dinnerware, lamps, or furniture. Have them choose one object and evaluate the design using the following: Is the design overdone? Is the design part of the construction? Is the design suitable for the material and function of the item? (Key Skill: *Critical Thinking*)

Evaluation

1. **Unit Test.** Have students complete the unit test on pp. 118-120 of the *Chapter and Unit Tests* booklet in the TCR.
2. **Testmaker Software.** Use the *Testmaker* software program to design your own unit test.

Implementing Cooperative Learning

Jigsaw is an effective method for having students cover a large amount of reading material in a short amount of time. Each team member becomes an expert on a subject and then teaches that information to the rest of their team. For example, the teacher might assign each team member a different chapter (all teams covering the same chapters) to review and take notes on. After completing the assignment, each team member reports back to the team. For evaluation, each team member might take a short quiz or write a paragraph listing two key ideas from each chapter.

See the *Cooperative Learning* booklet in the TCR for more information.

Preparing to Teach

Chapter Outline

Chapter Resources

The following booklet materials may be found in the *Teacher's Classroom Resources* box:

- Lesson Plans, p. 28
- Student Workbook, *Study Guide,* pp. 101-102; *Housing Opinionaire,* p. 103; *Dollars and Sense,* p. 104
- Technology and Computers, pp. 28, 29, 34, 35
- Cooperative Learning, p. 35
- Extending the Text, *More About Manufactured Homes,* pp. 33-34
- Reteaching and Practical Skills, *A Place to Live,* p. 31
- Enrichment Activities, *Choosing a Place to Live,* p. 38
- Chapter and Unit Tests, pp. 49-50
- Testmaker Software

Also see:

- Meeting the Special Needs of Students
- Linking Home, School, and Community

CHAPTER

23 Looking at Housing Choices

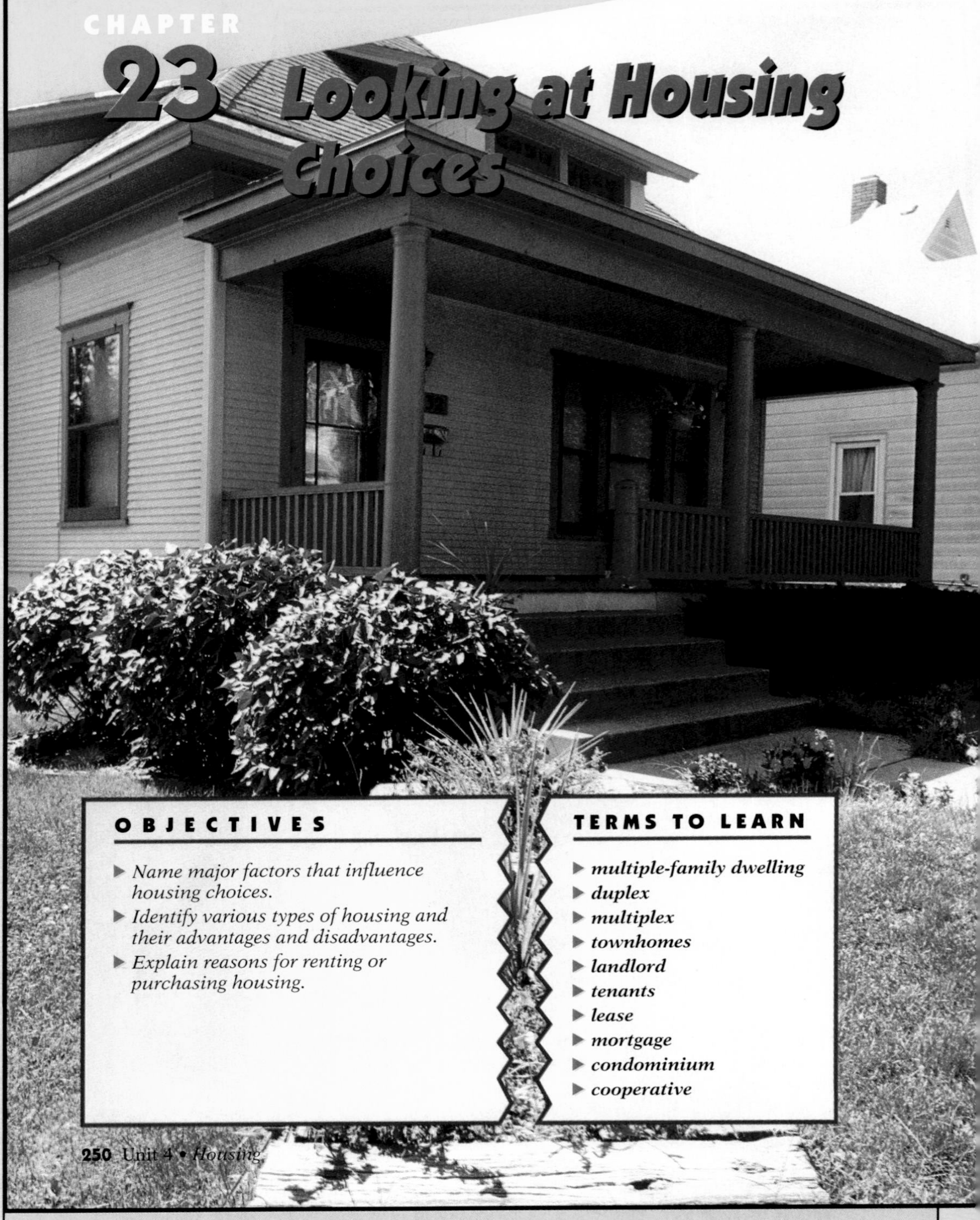

OBJECTIVES

- *Name major factors that influence housing choices.*
- *Identify various types of housing and their advantages and disadvantages.*
- *Explain reasons for renting or purchasing housing.*

TERMS TO LEARN

- ***multiple-family dwelling***
- ***duplex***
- ***multiplex***
- ***townhomes***
- ***landlord***
- ***tenants***
- ***lease***
- ***mortgage***
- ***condominium***
- ***cooperative***

More About Space

People need three types of space. Individuals need *private space* for sleeping, dressing, and relaxing. Family members need group or *social space* for recreation, conversation, dining, and entertaining. Support or *service space* is needed for preparing food and doing laundry and other work. Ask students to describe ways their housing meets or fails to meet each of these needs. How can flexible use of space help families meet more of their needs? How is flexible space use related to solving our long-term environmental concerns?

Lori and her sister live in an apartment with their mom. Mike and Carlos live in a duplex with their parents. Kim and her family share a house with her grandparents. It's easy to see why housing needs and decisions vary.

In most towns and cities, you don't have to go far to see several kinds of housing. This chapter will help you learn how individuals and families can make good housing choices.

The Meaning of Housing

Housing includes the many different types of shelter in which people live. Suppose you could look at all the housing that ever existed, everywhere in the world. Imagine the variety! Yet each was influenced by the same factors: society, culture, climate, available materials, and technology, to name just a few.

Housing can fulfill important needs of individuals and families. Everyone has certain basic needs in common.

- ***Physical needs.*** Physical needs are those necessary for survival, such as shelter, air, sunlight, sleep, and food. Housing should offer safety for you and your family.
- ***Emotional needs.*** Emotional needs can also be met by housing. A home can provide privacy, comfort, and a place for fun and relaxation. You can make your home reflect your personal taste.
- ***Social needs.*** These needs include the need for love and belonging. The home can serve as a gathering place for family and friends.

Housing that offers opportunities to meet emotional and social needs is more than just a structure. It becomes a home.

Influences on Housing Decisions

Although people share basic human needs, they are also individuals. When you and your family are choosing a place to live, think about your specific needs and wants. Then try to find a way to balance those needs and wants with available resources.

More About *Homes of the Future*

In the year 2010, will your dream home be futuristic or similar to the home you live in now? It will probably be some of each. You'll have push-button gadgets as well as features that foster family togetherness. Tomorrow's house is likely to have fewer walls and more windows. A central core will provide space for most family activities. When family members need to be alone, they can retreat to smaller multi-purpose rooms for hobbies or other activities. Outdoors you'll find both secluded retreats and public spaces.

Introducing the Chapter

Motivators

1. **Survey.** Survey students regarding their families' housing choices. Ask: "How many of you have lived in an apartment? A duplex? A house? A mobile home? Some other type of housing? How many of you have lived in more than one type of housing during your life?" Discuss reasons families choose different types of housing. (Key Skills: *Communication, Decision Making*)
2. **Discussion.** Ask students to identify the types of housing available in their community. Discuss factors that influence the type of housing people choose. (Key Skill: *Critical Thinking*)
3. **Discussion.** Have students draw slips of paper listing housing choices. Have the students work in groups to discuss who might choose that type of housing and why. Have a spokesperson for each group summarize the discussion for the class. (Key Skill: *Cooperation*)
4. **Bulletin Board.** Display a variety of colorful pictures of different types of housing choices. Label the bulletin board "Housing Choices with Appeal." (Key Skill: *Communication*)

Chapter Objectives and Vocabulary

1. Have students read the chapter objectives and rephrase the objectives as questions.
2. Ask students to state, in their own words, the purpose of studying this chapter.
3. Pronounce the vocabulary terms listed on the previous page. Ask students whether they are familiar with any of these. Explain that the terms will be defined in the chapter.

Guided Reading

1. Have students read the chapter and use the Study Guide on pp. 101-102 of the *Student Workbook*.

Teaching. . .
The Meaning of Housing and Housing Decisions
(pp. 251-253)

Comprehension Check

1. What important needs can housing fulfill? *(Housing fulfills physical needs including shelter, air, sunlight, sleep, and food; emotional needs such as privacy, comfort, and a place for fun and relaxation; and social needs including love, belonging, and socializing with family and friends.)*
2. What factors influence a family's housing needs and wants? *(A family's housing needs are influenced by family size, family life cycle, special needs of family members, location, and lifestyle.)*
3. What are some ways you can adapt a home to improve the independence of a person who has physical limitations? *(Choose smooth flooring or level-loop type carpeting without padding. Avoid throw rugs. Provide railings on both sides of stairs and hallways. Replace outside stairs with ramps. Provide adequate lighting. Adapt kitchen to meet specific needs. Add grab bars, safety seats and nonslip strips in bathroom.)*

Learning Activities

1. **Writing.** Have students write three paragraphs describing how well their own housing fulfills their family's physical, emotional, and social needs. (Key Skills: *Communication, Critical Thinking*)

MEETING SPECIAL NEEDS

. . . Aiding Independent Living

After reading the feature, have students discuss other ways in which a home could be adapted for the elderly or for people with disabilities. *(Answers will vary.)*

MEETING SPECIAL NEEDS

Aiding Independent Living

Everyone wants to live as independently as possible. The elderly and people with disabilities are no exception. If someone in your family has physical limitations, there are many ways you can improve the person's independence at home.

- ***Floors.*** Many people have problems walking or must use wheelchairs. Smooth flooring such as vinyl or wood is a good, safe choice. If carpeting is used, choose a level-loop type without padding. Avoid throw rugs. They cause many falls.
- ***Stairs.*** Railings on both sides of stairs and in hallways are helpful. For those in wheelchairs, stairs are a barrier. Outside the home, ramps can replace stairs. Inside, stairs may limit the person to one part of the house. If so, arrange a room for privacy.
- ***Lighting.*** Adequate lighting is especially important for those with poor vision. Check the number, placement, and brightness of lights. In each room, there should be a light that can be turned on near the entrance.

(Continued on next page)

What types of needs and wants might this family have for housing?

Needs and Wants

Needs and wants differ because families differ. What one family considers essential might be unnecessary or even a drawback to another family. Here are some factors to consider.

- ***Family size.*** An-Sook lives with his foster parents and five other children. His family's needs are quite different from Tanya's. Her family includes only herself and her father.
- ***Family life cycle.*** As explained in Chapter 12, every family goes through a life cycle. Changes during the life cycle can affect housing needs and wants. Rona and Jared just had their first baby. Soon they will start looking for a larger place to live with an outdoor play area nearby. Meanwhile, Rona's grandfather Carl is also planning ahead. Now that he lives alone, he would prefer a smaller place that requires little upkeep.
- ***Special needs of family members.*** Consider any special housing needs of family members. For example, someone with limited mobility may require a home that is all on one level. Existing housing can often be adapted to meet special needs. See the feature on pages 252-253 for suggestions.
- ***Location.*** Is it important to be close to a job or public transportation? Would the family prefer a quiet location or a neighborhood with lots of children?

More About Future Environments

Environmental changes are likely to influence housing in the future. If global warming and ozone depletion continue, future homes may exist inside giant greenhouses that will recycle air, water, wastes, and include space for growing food. The Biosphere II project in Arizona was designed to study the usefulness of closed environments in solving environmental problems on Earth and aid in the design of future space colonies. It was a miniature version of the Earth's biosphere. These studies may help us better understand why the Earth's biological system is self-sustaining.

- ***Lifestyle.*** The interests and activities of family members also influence housing decisions. Most people want a home that suits their way of life and sense of style.

These are just some of the factors that affect housing needs and wants.

▼ Considering Your Resources ▼

Resources play an important role in housing decisions. Available housing is one material resource. Only a limited number of housing units are on the market at any given time. If you cannot find what you are looking for, you may have to change some of your ideas about what you want.

The housing you choose must be not only available, but affordable. Most financial experts recommend that no more than about 28 percent of the family income be budgeted for housing. This includes not only monthly payments for the housing unit itself, but other costs such as insurance, repairs, and *utilities* (basic services such as electricity, gas or oil, and water).

Most people must make some compromises in order to find housing that fits their budget. Lori's mother wanted a larger place with a separate bedroom for Lori and her sister.

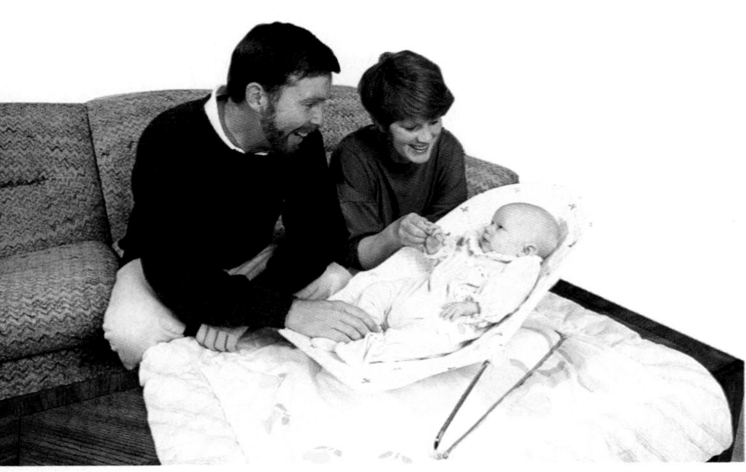

Changes in the family life cycle can affect housing needs. How might this family's needs be different from a family that includes several teens?

Aiding Independent Living (Continued)

- ***Kitchens.*** Kitchens present problems for people with disabilities. Cabinets may require too much bending or reaching. Open shelves are often better. People with wheelchairs need lower countertops. A sink without a cabinet beneath it allows a wheelchair to roll into position. Special faucets with longer spouts and handles are also available. Braille knobs, control panels, and appliance instruction books can be ordered for those who are blind.
- ***Bathrooms.*** Grab bars by the bathtub and toilet can increase safety. A seat added to the shower or tub and a hand-held shower make bathing easier for many. Also, add nonslip strips to the shower floor or tub bottom.

Few builders consider the needs of the elderly and those with disabilities. If someone in your family has a physical limitation, you can make a difference. Find out what tasks the person finds difficult. Then think of solutions that would increase independence. Check the library for books and pamphlets.

More About *Adaptable Space*

Homes of the future will be planned to make it easier for the family to add or subtract members. Flexible rooms with private baths can be outfitted as a private suite for Grandpa or a college-age child.

2. **Time Line.** Have students interview an elderly person to learn how a family's housing needs change throughout the life cycle. Using the information obtained, have students develop a time line depicting those changes. As a class, compare the time lines and discuss how changes during the family life cycle affect housing needs. (Key Skills: *Communication, Problem Solving*)
3. **Discussion.** Ask students to identify reasons their families chose to live in a particular location. Were decisions influenced by parents' jobs or public transportation? How did family preferences affect decisions? (Key Skills: *Communication, Critical Thinking*)

Follow Up

1. **Reteaching.** Have students make a list of questions to ask when choosing housing. The list should include questions related to basic needs, factors affecting family decisions, and family resources. (Key Skill: *Decision Making*)
2. **Enrichment.** Assist students in finding examples in magazines showing how housing could make life easier and more comfortable for elderly people. Include such things as arrangement of furniture, selection of furniture and accessories, floor coverings, ventilation, easy-care household fabrics, one-level housing, and views of the outdoors. (Key Skill: *Communication*)

Family Perspective

Adolescence is a time during which a young person may begin to look at housing in new ways. Some teenagers may feel that their homes are not as attractive as those of friends. Others may view their families' luxuries as status symbols. Lifestyle changes which cause changes in housing may be difficult to accept. These are normal feelings for teenagers. Knowing that many factors affect housing decisions and that changes in housing are not unusual may make feelings about family housing easier to accept.

Teaching... Types of Housing (pp. 254-255)

Comprehension Check

1. What are some advantages and disadvantages of single-family homes? *(Single-family homes come in all sizes from one room to many rooms and one story or multi-storied; provide privacy; and may have a lawn. However, they are often more expensive, require more land, and require upkeep and care by the owner.)*
2. Discuss reasons why people choose to live in mobile homes. *(Most mobile homes are less expensive than single-family homes. They may come with furniture and appliances.)*
3. Explain the difference between a duplex and a multiplex. *(A duplex is one building that contains two separate units. A multiplex is similar to a duplex, but three or more units share one building.)*
4. What are some advantages and disadvantages of multiple-family dwellings? *(They come in many sizes; may have a laundry area, swimming pool, and other special features. Upkeep is usually done by the owner or management. However, they may lack privacy; may be noisy; may not permit children and pets; and may lack adequate storage space.)*

Learning Activities

1. **Reading.** Have students find a magazine or newspaper article describing how a family used skills, time, and energy to stretch their housing dollars. Ask students to summarize their articles for the class and share any related pictures. (Key Skill: *Communication*)

Around the World

After reading the feature, have students investigate what different types of materials other countries use to build their homes. *(Answers might include concrete blocks, concrete, or clay.)*

Affordable housing is sometimes a challenge to find. How can using the telephone be a benefit when looking for affordable housing?

However, high housing costs in their area prevented this. A place that size would have required nearly all of her monthly paycheck. The family finally located a three-room apartment near her mother's job. Location, cost, and available choices played a major role in their selection.

Human resources, such as skills, time, and energy, can stretch housing dollars. For instance, An-Sook's foster parents bought an old house that needed repairs and used their skills to improve it. Without their skills, they would have had to settle for a much smaller house.

Types of Housing

Taking a look at your needs, wants, and resources is one step in making good housing decisions. Another is learning about the various types of housing available. Each type has advantages and disadvantages.

Single-Family Homes

Single-family homes are freestanding. That is, they do not share any walls with another housing unit. They may be small or large, one story or several stories high.

Single-family homes offer more privacy than other types of housing. They are also usually more expensive because they require more land.

One type of single-family home is a manufactured home (sometimes called a "mobile home"). Manufactured homes are houses that are built in a factory then moved to their final location. Most manufactured homes are less expensive than a traditional single-family house. They may come complete with furniture, carpeting, window coverings, and appliances.

Around the World

Housing choices are influenced by available building materials and other uses for land. For the Hopi (HO-pee), Navajo (NAH-vah-ho), and Pueblo (PWEB-lo) Indians of the American Southwest, this resulted in the construction of hogans. These homes were built of logs or stone with domed clay roofs. They were round or hexagonal (six-sided). Hogans were usually spaced far apart, since much of the land was needed to graze sheep. What materials are available for home-building today? How does land use continue to affect housing choices?

More About Mobile Homes

The term "mobile home" is often inaccurate. True, a mobile home is designed to be moveable. However, mobile homes are much less mobile than their name implies. Many cities limit their location to a specific area. The cost of moving a mobile home, the need for professional movers, and highway restrictions all reduce the mobility. As a result, mobile homes are seldom moved more than a few miles. Most of these homes are actually permanent structures.

What might be the advantages and disadvantages of living in this manufactured home?

▼ Multiple-Family Dwellings ▼

A **multiple-family dwelling** is a structure that contains several housing units under one roof. There are many variations.

- A **duplex** is one building that contains two separate units. The units may be side by side, sharing one wall, or they may be on separate floors.
- A **multiplex** is similar to a duplex, but three or more units share one building.
- **Townhomes** are houses built in rows and attached at the side walls.
- Apartment and condominium buildings range from a large older home divided into three or four apartments to a high-rise with hundreds of units. A number of separate buildings may be grouped together in a complex.

All of these types of multiple-family dwellings use less land than single-family houses. They are especially common in large cities where land is scarce and housing is expensive.

Individual units may be small or large. Residents may share the use of a laundry, swimming pool, or other special features.

As with all types of housing, multiple-family dwellings have their disadvantages. Some people are concerned about noise or lack of privacy. They may want more space for storage and outdoor activities. Children and pets may not be allowed.

However, multiple-family dwellings meet the needs of many people. They are often more affordable and more readily available than single-family houses.

More About *Renting*

If you have signed a lease, but decide to move out early, what are your options? You can continue paying the rent until the lease expires. You can assign or transfer the unexpired portion of the lease to someone else. You can sublet the property by turning it over to another person for a period of time. If you assign the property, you are no longer responsible for the lease. If you sublet, both you and the other person are responsible to the landlord for all terms of the lease.

Learning Activities (continued)

2. **Questioning.** Why might a person want to develop basic home repair and improvement skills? *(People can stretch their housing dollars by developing the skills for making needed repairs and improvements.)* (Key Skill: *Problem Solving*)
3. **Collage.** Have students collect pictures of different types of housing. Have students use the pictures to create a collage of housing choices. (Key Skill: *Creativity*)

Follow Up

1. **Reteaching.** Have students create a chart on large pieces of newsprint paper outlining the characteristics, advantages and disadvantages of different housing choices including single-family dwellings, renting, and owning housing. (Key Skill: *Critical Thinking*)
2. **Enrichment.** Have students work in groups to develop interview questions on reasons people chose a particular type of housing and what they like and dislike about their housing choice. Assign students to interview people who live in different types of housing. Compile the results and draw conclusions regarding housing choices and advantages and disadvantages of different types of housing. (Key Skills: *Communication, Critical Thinking*)

Life Management Skills

Home Repairs

Do-it-yourself home repairs can help save housing dollars. Simple repairs might include repairing a leaky faucet, stopping the toilet tank from leaking, caulking a window, repainting a room, or rewiring a lamp. Books on home repairs are available in public libraries and bookstores. Local stores carry the tools and supplies needed for making most home repairs. Have students prepare a display of books, tools, and supplies for home repairs.

Teaching. . .
Ways to Obtain Housing and Renting a Home
(pp. 256-257)

Comprehension Check

1. Explain how modular homes are built. *(Homes are built in sections at the factory. Then the sections are moved to the building site and assembled. Any type of housing can be built by modular construction.)*
2. Define the following terms associated with rented housing: landlords, tenants, lease. *(Landlords are the owners of rental housing. Tenants are the renters. A lease is a written rental agreement.)*
3. What are some advantages of renting? *(Renting is convenient for people who do not want to be responsible for household repairs, saves the time and cost of selling, and avoids unexpected costs for repairs.)*

Learning Activities

1. **Discussion.** Discuss with students reasons one might choose to rent housing. (Key Skill: *Decision Making*)
2. **Reading.** Provide copies of applications and lease agreements for rental housing. Discuss reasons specific information is required on the application. Have students read the lease carefully, then answer questions regarding specific terms in the lease. Have them answer questions about the general terms of the lease, about requirements regarding care of the rental housing, about moving out terms, etc. (Key Skills: *Communication, Decision Making*)
3. **Reasoning.** Why do landlords require a security deposit? *(To provide money for repairs if the unit is damaged by the tenant.)* (Key Skill: *Critical Thinking*)
4. **Interviews.** Have students develop questions to ask people who rent regarding the advantages and disadvantages of renting. Ask each student to interview one renter. Have students share their findings with the class. (Key Skills: *Cooperation, Decision Making*)

Multiple-family dwellings are often more affordable and meet the needs of many people.

Building Technology

New technology is making it possible to build homes more efficiently. One example is the use of *modular construction*. With this building technique, homes are built in sections at a factory. Then the sections are moved to the building site and assembled. Any type of housing, from apartments to single-family houses, can be built by modular construction.

The cost of modular construction varies widely. It depends on the size, number of rooms, and special features. In general, however, assembling sections inside a factory helps keep costs down and quality high.

More About Why Housing Differs

People build many different kinds of housing throughout the world. The types of construction depends chiefly on the climate and on what building materials are available. Have students identify differences in homes in northern and southern climates. Ask students to identify building materials used in forested areas, in areas with little rainfall, and in wet tropical areas. Tradition and special hazards also influence the homes people build. Ask students to consider influences on homes in Latin America, Japan, and Indonesia.

Ways to Obtain Housing

Some individuals and families own the housing unit they live in, while others rent it from the owner.

Renting a Home

Renting means paying money to live in a housing unit that is owned by someone else. Owners of rental housing are sometimes called **landlords**. Renters are sometimes called **tenants**. Rental housing is available either furnished or unfurnished and at a range of prices.

All the types of housing units described in this chapter may be rented. In addition, you might rent a room in a house or dormitory. A room just for sleeping, with no private kitchen or bath facilities, is a relatively inexpensive form of housing.

When you rent a housing unit, you may have to fill out an application and sign a **lease** — a written rental agreement. The lease states that you agree to pay rent for a certain number of months. It specifies the monthly fee and any rules you must follow. Always read a lease carefully before you sign it. Many landlords require a security deposit equal to one month's rent or more. The deposit is returned when you move out if the unit has not been damaged.

Many people enjoy the advantages of renting. They include:

- ***Convenience.*** Tasks such as painting and household repairs usually are done by the owner rather than the tenant.
- ***Flexibility.*** Renters don't have to sell their home when it is time to move. Selling a home can be a long and costly process.
- ***Financial advantages.*** Both renting and owning have month-to-month costs. However, tenants do not face unexpected costs for repairs.

What are the pros and cons of renting a home with another person?

Follow Up

1. **Reteaching.** Have students make a chart depicting the advantages and disadvantages of renting different types of housing units. (Key Skill: *Critical Thinking*)
2. **Enrichment.** Have students obtain information about the types of housing units that are for rent in your community. Information may be obtained from advertisements in your local newspaper or from a real estate agency involved in property management. Have students share their findings with the class. (Key Skill: *Communication*)

The World Around You

Housing in Other Countries

Many of the existing homes in Europe were built in the late 1800s. In addition, many homes were damaged or destroyed during World War II. As a result, many new homes have been needed since the mid 1940s. Governments have helped meet housing needs by building low-cost apartments and by providing loan and rent subsidies for large families and for old-age pensioners. Still, many families in these countries live in housing that is crowded by American standards.

More About *The History of Shelter*

Early people lived in caves. Others built dwellings of animal hides, stones, straw, vines, clay bricks, or wood. Some houses stood on stilts for protection against animals. As people became more civilized, they built strong, defensive structures and impressive palaces. These efforts resulted in a new art — architecture.

Photo Focus

Discuss the photo at the bottom of page 256 with the students. What are some of the advantages of using modular construction methods to build a housing unit? *(Costs can be kept down without sacrificing quality; housing units can be completed very quickly; and much of the work is done inside, so poor weather cannot slow down construction.)*

Teaching. . .
Owning and Sharing a Home and Choosing a Place to Live
(pp. 258-259)

Comprehension Check

1. Why do people choose to own a home? *(People buy homes because they value a feeling of permanence, because they are free to remodel or redecorate, and/or because they can use the home as an investment.)*
2. What is a mortgage? *(A long-term loan, typically for 15 to 30 years.)*
3. How may someone own space in a multiple-family dwelling? *(Condominiums are individually owned units. The owner of each unit pays a fee to help cover the cost of maintaining common areas. In a cooperative, or co-op, residents form an organization in which owners buy shares and contribute to monthly costs. In return, they receive use of one of the living units.)*
4. What are the advantages of condominiums and cooperatives? *(They provide the advantages of home ownership and apartment living while avoiding the responsibilities of yard work and outside maintenance.)*
5. Discuss ways that shared housing can be made more successful. *(People must be thoughtful of one another. Each person needs to have some degree of privacy or a place to call his or her own. Each person also needs a place to visit with friends and to store personal belongings.)*
6. Why may people live in several different types of housing during their lifetime? *(Their needs and resources change.)*
7. What are some important considerations when choosing a place to live? *(Important considerations when choosing a place to live include price range, current situation, needs, location, and specific features.)*

▼ Owning a Home ▼

Many people choose to buy a place to live because they value a feeling of permanence. Homeowners also are free to redecorate or remodel their home to meet their personal needs and tastes. Others consider a home as an investment and value the financial security it may give them.

Most people plan for years before buying their housing. Purchasing a place to live is not a decision to be made lightly. Buying a home costs more than any other purchase most families will ever make.

Most people take out a long-term loan, called a **mortgage**, to buy a home. The mortgage is typically for 15 to 30 years. Buying a home requires that part of the purchase price be paid in cash. This sum, called a *down payment*, can be quite large.

Other costs must also be considered. A homeowner usually must pay property taxes and insurance, as well as utility and repair costs.

Any type of housing may be owned. Units in a multiple-family dwelling, such as an apartment building, are sometimes owned individually. In that case, they are called **condominiums**. One person does not own the entire building. The owner of each unit pays a fee to help cover the cost of maintaining common areas, such as hallways, lawns, and parking lots.

Another form of ownership is a **cooperative**, or co-op. In a co-op, residents of a multiple-family dwelling form an organization that owns the building. Instead of buying or renting an individual unit, they buy shares in the organization and contribute to its monthly costs. In return, they receive use of one of the living units.

Condominiums and cooperatives combine the advantages of home ownership and apartment living. Many people want to invest in a home but don't want the responsibilities of yard work and outside maintenance.

Buying a home is often the largest purchase a family will make. What are some reasons why owning a home may not be for everyone?

▼ Sharing a Home ▼

Sharing a home is an option that works well for many people. They can combine their resources with those of other individuals or families to better meet their housing needs.

Almost any type of housing may be shared with others. Friends just out of school may share an apartment to save money. Adult children sometimes return to live with their parents for a time. An older person may move in with a child's family for care and companionship.

More About Shared Living

When singles share living space, they are smart to understand and agree on the rules of the arrangement. Be sure to know what your legal obligations are in such situations, especially those related to the rent or purchase of your living space. In order to make joint living go smoothly, establish how you will split food and other household costs. Decide in advance who will cook and clean, and when. A schedule may help. Regardless of age, shared living arrangements work best when all parties cooperate.

Considering the needs of others is a top priority when sharing a home.

Sharing a home only works if people are thoughtful of one another. It is important for people to have some degree of privacy in the home — a place to call their own. They also need a place to visit with friends and a storage area for personal belongings.

Choosing a Place to Live

People often live in several different types of housing during their lifetime, as their needs and resources change. Each time, the decision is an important one. Here are some important points to consider.

- What price range can you afford?
- Is renting or owning right for you at this time?
- What type of housing would best suit your needs?
- What area would you like to live in?
- What specific features are you looking for? Which ones are priorities? On which would you be willing to compromise?

Few people are lucky enough to live in their "dream home." However, the more information you have to make a housing decision, the more satisfied you're likely to be. Finding a place you will call home can be both challenging and rewarding.

Learning Activities

1. **Comparisons.** After researching differences in condominiums and cooperatives, have students make a chart comparing these two forms of ownership. (Key Skill: *Critical Thinking*)
2. **Debate.** Have students debate renting on a long-term basis versus owning a home. Discuss the responsibilities involved in each situation. (Key Skills: *Communication, Critical Thinking*)
3. **Writing.** Have students write descriptions of their own "dream homes." Ask several students to share their descriptions with the class. (Key Skills: *Communication, Creativity*)
4. **Case Situations.** Provide students with descriptions of hypothetical families (such as a single dad with two kids, an extended family, and/or a single mom with a handicapped child). Then, have students work in groups to study housing options available in your local community and select housing which would meet as many of the family's needs and wants as possible. Have each group present their situation and housing decisions to the class. (Key Skills: *Cooperation, Management*)

Follow Up

1. **Reteaching.** Ask students to summarize important points to consider when choosing a place to live. (Key Skill: *Decision Making*)
2. **Extension.** Use the extension information handout on pp. 34-35 of the *Extending the Text* booklet in the TCR.
3. **Enrichment.** Have students contact a local lending institution to find out the interest rate on home loans. Then, have the students report their findings to the class and discuss if it is a good time to buy a home. (Key Skills: *Communication, Decision Making*)

Completing the Chapter

For Review

1. Emphasize the main concepts using the summary.
2. Have students complete the "Facts to Recall." (Answers below.)

For Reteaching

1. **Reteaching.** Use the activity on p. 30 of the *Reteaching and Practical Skills* booklet in the TCR.

For Enrichment

1. **Enrichment.** Use the activity on p. 41 of the *Enrichment Activities* booklet in the TCR.

For Evaluation

1. Choose items from "Ideas to Explore" and "Activities to Try."
2. Use the chapter test on pp. 49-50 in the testing booklet of the TCR or use the testmaker software.

Facts to Recall Answers

1. Physical needs. **Any one:** shelter; air, sunlight; sleep; food. Emotional needs. **Any one:** privacy; comfort; a place for fun and relaxation. Social needs: the need for love and belonging.
2. **Any four:** family size, family life cycle, special needs of family members, location, and lifestyle.
3. Basic services — electricity, gas or oil, and water.
4. Manufactured homes are built at a factory and then moved to a permanent site. Traditional single-family homes are built on the site they will occupy.
5. A structure that contains several housing units under one roof.
6. A duplex is one building containing two separate dwellings. A multiplex is one building containing three or more dwellings.
7. **Advantages:** multiple-family dwellings are often more affordable and more available than single-family dwellings; they use land more efficiently. **Disadvantages:** they offer less privacy, storage space, and room

Comparing your needs and the many types of housing available is a real benefit when choosing a place to live.

TAKING ACTION
Weighing Housing Options

Scott, a friend of your family, has just graduated from college and landed a good job as an assistant mechanical engineer. Now he has an important decision to make about housing. He's undecided whether to rent an apartment, or to try to arrange a mortgage for a condominium or small house.

He likes the idea of his own yard. On the other hand, he wonders if he would meet more people in an apartment complex. He knows he wants to settle in the area and hopes to marry someday. Scott comes to you for advice and would like to hear your views.

Using Your Resourcefulness

- Given Scott's needs, wants, and resources, what is your advice?
- Make a list of the advantages and disadvantages of each choice.
- Do you think Scott would be able to arrange a bank loan easily? Why or why not?
- How should Scott go about his housing search? What steps should he take?

TAKING ACTION

After students have read this feature, you may want to have them respond to the *Using Your Resourcefulness* questions in small groups. Have students review the advantages and disadvantages of renting and buying housing. Which choice do you think provides the most advantages and fewest disadvantages to Scott as a single adult? In an uncertain economy, what would be the impact of each choice if Scott were laid off his job? If Scott decides to marry, would owning a condominium or small house be an advantage or disadvantage? Why? What other housing needs is Scott likely to have as a young adult?

Chapter 23 Review

Summary

In this chapter, you have read about:

- How a family's needs, wants, and resources influence its housing decisions.
- Different types of housing available and their advantages and disadvantages.
- How renting and buying housing compare.
- Ways existing housing can be adapted for family members with special needs.

Facts to Recall

1. What three types of basic needs can housing fulfill? Give at least one specific example of each type.
2. Name four factors to be considered when thinking about a family's housing needs and wants.
3. What are utilities?
4. What is the difference between a manufactured home and a traditional single-family house?
5. What is a multiple-family dwelling?
6. How does a multiplex differ from a duplex?
7. What are two advantages and two disadvantages of living in a multiple-family dwelling?
8. What are the advantages of renting a home rather than owning one?
9. What are the advantages of owning your own home?
10. How does a cooperative differ from a condominium?

Ideas to Explore

1. List ten features you would look for in a home. Of these, which three are the most important to you? Why?
2. How might a person who has lived all of his or her life in a single-family home have trouble adapting to living in an apartment?
3. Identify housing concerns common at each stage of the family life cycle.
4. Brainstorm a list of situations when sharing housing might be a good option.

Activities to Try

1. Compare the types of housing being built in your community today with that built 50 to 75 years ago. What changes in families are reflected in the changes in housing? Consider points such as housing choices, size and types of room, and kitchens.
2. Using the ad section of a newspaper, choose 15 apartments that might interest you. Calculate the average monthly rent for these apartments.
3. Imagine that you are in a wheelchair. What difficulties would you encounter trying to get around in your own home?

LINK TO *Communication*

HOUSING ISSUES

You and a friend are thinking about sharing housing together after graduating from high school. Choose one of the following topics and develop a skit showing how you and your friend will identify: needs and wants, determine how much to spend on housing, determine the type of housing needed, or identify household responsibilities. What other topics might enter into your conversation? Why should you work through these issues before moving in with another person? Share your skit with the class.

Facts to Recall Answers (continued)

for outdoor activities; they may not allow pets or children.

8. Renters are not responsible for household repairs or lawn work; they don't have to worry about selling their home when they move; they do not need to invest as much money in their dwellings as homeowners do.
9. Home ownership gives a feeling of stability; homeowners can adapt their homes to their own personal needs and tastes; a home can be a good financial investment.
10. Condominiums are units in a multiple-family dwelling that are individually owned. A cooperative is an organization formed by the residents of a multiple-family dwelling, who contribute to the monthly cost of the building's upkeep in exchange for living in one of its units. The units are owned by the organization, not the individuals.

Ideas to Explore

1. Answers will vary.
2. Answers will vary but may include: they must adjust to living in a smaller space; to paying rent every month; to not being allowed to keep a pet.
3. Answers will vary and may include: affordability in the couple stage; more space and good neighborhood in the child-rearing years; less space and easy maintenance in the empty nest stage; safety and special needs concerns in later life.
4. Answers will vary and may include: young adults in their first apartment; older people on fixed incomes.

LINK TO *Communication*

Answers

Skits will vary. Other topics they might discuss include how much they can afford for utilities and whether they need furnishings or not in their new place. These things need to be discussed before they move in so that problems do not arise that could jeopardize their friendship.

Using Your Resourcefulness Answers

- Answers will vary. Have students give reasons why they chose a certain type of housing for Scott.
- Answers will vary. Have the students reread the chapter for ideas on each type of housing.
- Answers will vary. Have students provide reasons why they said yes or no to this question.
- To help Scott make a housing decision, he should write down what his needs and wants are and what resources are available to him. Then he should learn as much as he can about the advantages and disadvantages of each type of housing. From this information, Scott should be able to come to a housing decision that is right for him.

Preparing to Teach

Chapter Outline

Chapter Resources

The following booklet materials may be found in the *Teacher's Classroom Resources* box:

- Lesson Plans, p. 29
- Student Workbook, *Study Guide,* pp. 105-106; *Design Match-Up,* pp. 107-108
- Color Transparencies, *The Color Wheel,* CTs 23-30; *Putting the Pieces Together,* CT-31
- Technology and Computers, pp. 27, 29, 31, 32
- Cooperative Learning, p. 36
- Extending the Text, *What Is Your Design IQ?,* p. 35
- Reteaching and Practical Skills, *Identifying Color Schemes,* p. 32
- Enrichment Activities, *Creating Color Schemes,* p. 39
- Chapter and Unit Tests, pp. 51-52
- Testmaker Software

Also see:

- Meeting the Special Needs of Students
- Linking Home, School, and Community

CHAPTER 24

Understanding the Art of Design

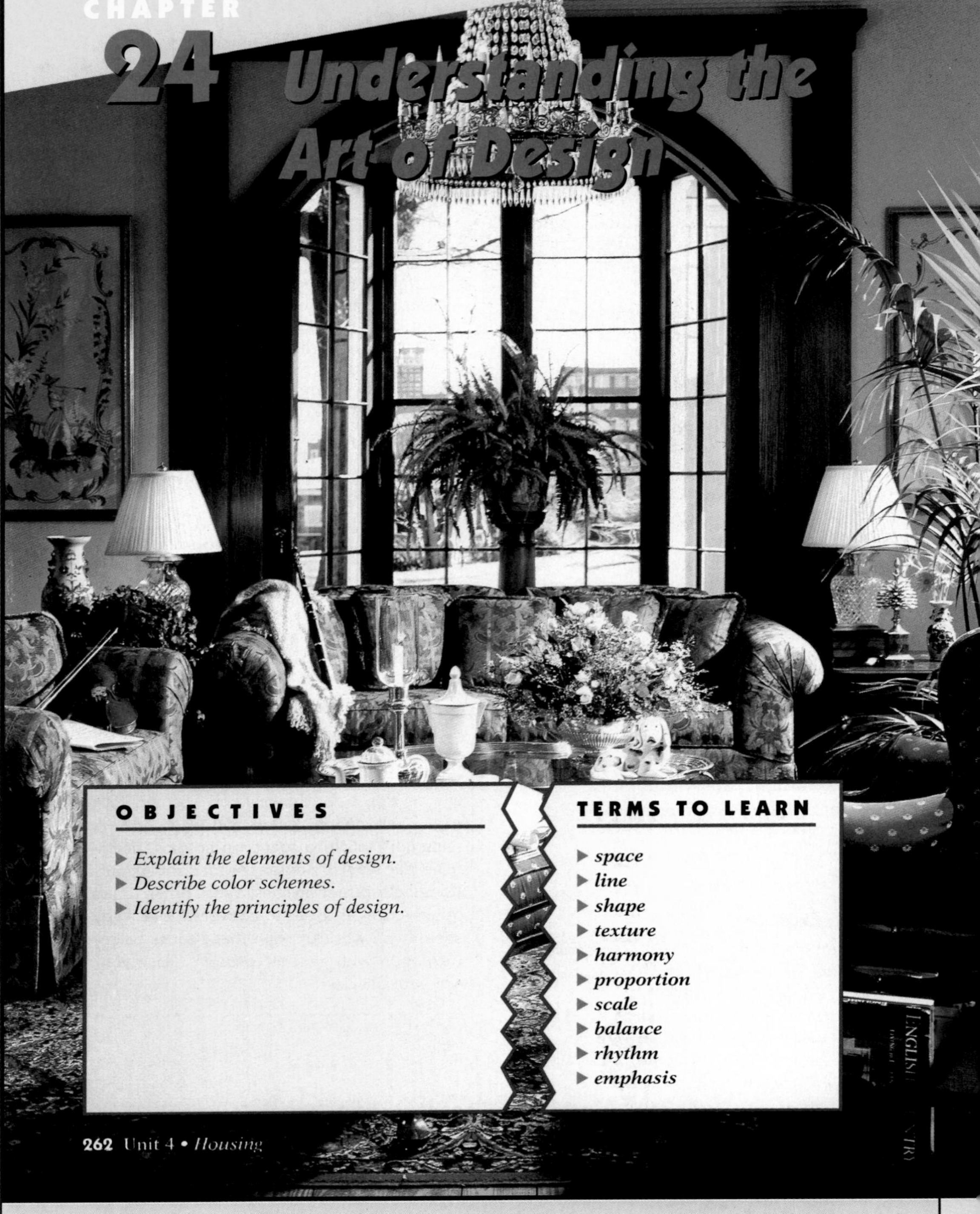

OBJECTIVES

- *Explain the elements of design.*
- *Describe color schemes.*
- *Identify the principles of design.*

TERMS TO LEARN

- ***space***
- ***line***
- ***shape***
- ***texture***
- ***harmony***
- ***proportion***
- ***scale***
- ***balance***
- ***rhythm***
- ***emphasis***

More About Do-It-Yourself Decorating

Do-it-yourself is becoming an increasingly important approach to home decorating. Obtaining professional results is easy when you take time to find out how to do each job properly and arm yourself with the correct equipment. The cardinal rules are to take your time and to work carefully. Do not cut corners or skimp on any part of the job. The materials used in decorating are often costly, but using quality materials saves money in the long run. The room will look good for far longer if you don't skimp.

Whenever you look at a car, a garden, a pair of running shoes, or a new sweater, you are seeing the results of others' designs. *Your* designs are around for people to see, too. For example, you create a design every time you decide which clothes to wear together, arrange food on a table, or decorate the space where you live. Design is everywhere!

Good design emphasizes the best features of a room or a person's appearance. At the same time, the design makes weaknesses less obvious. This ability to fool the eye is sometimes called *illusion*.

Some people seem to have a natural talent for design. Stephanie, for example, is considered a trend-setter in her choice of clothes. Most people don't realize she has fewer clothes and less expensive clothes than most of her friends.

Even without natural talent, you can learn to create pleasing designs. Understanding the parts — or elements — that make up designs is the first step. Then you will learn how to use these elements by following a set of guidelines called the principles of design.

Elements of Design

The elements of design are five basic building blocks of any design: space, line, shape, texture, and color. As you read about these elements, think about how each is used to make your favorite room comfortable and attractive.

Space

Space refers to the three-dimensional area that is to be designed — a room or a backyard, for example. Space can give different feelings depending on how it is used. For example, a room that contains many pieces of furniture may make some people feel cozy. Others may find the same room uncomfortably crowded. How would you feel in a large room with little furniture?

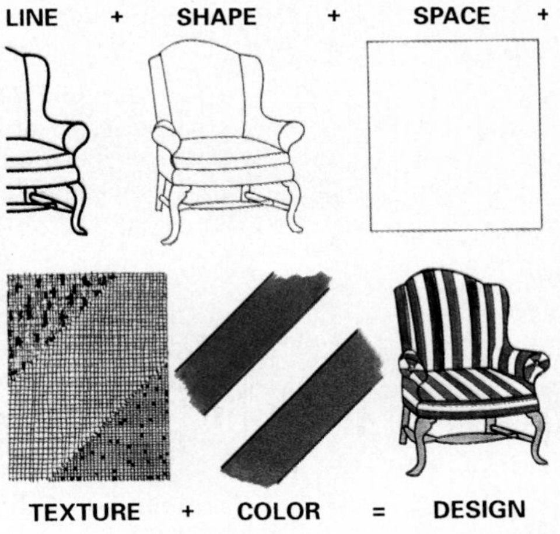

Introducing the Chapter

Motivators

1. **Ask the class.** Arrange an assortment of books with covers that are bright and eye-catching next to some duller colors with ordinary lettering. Ask students questions such as: Which books catch your eye? Why? Why didn't you notice the others as quickly? Discuss the fact that design is used in all areas of life. Point out that people can use design to make housing, clothing, and food more attractive. (Key Skill: *Creativity*)
2. **Discussion.** Use the analogy of a recipe to introduce the elements and principles of design. Explain that the elements of design — space, line, shape, texture, and color — are like the ingredients in a recipe. The same ingredients can be combined in different ways and in different amounts to yield different results. Explain that the principles of design — harmony, proportion, scale, balance, rhythm, and emphasis — are like the directions for combining the ingredients in a recipe. (Key Skill: *Critical Thinking*)

Chapter Objectives and Vocabulary

1. Have students read the chapter objectives and rephrase the objectives as questions.
2. Ask students to state, in their own words, the purpose of studying this chapter.
3. Pronounce the vocabulary terms listed on the previous page. Ask students whether they are familiar with any of these. Explain that the terms will be defined in the chapter.

Guided Reading

1. Have students read the chapter and use the Study Guide on pp. 105-106 of the *Student Workbook*.

More About *Environment-Friendly Decorating*

We need to do all that we can to help protect our environment and to conserve world resources. When planning home decorating projects, make use of recycled materials, such as old timber, whenever possible. When buying products, make certain that any aerosols you use are ozone-friendly and that wood preservatives are water-based. Also, make sure that you observe the latest water regulations to protect the quality of our water supply.

Teaching. . . Elements of Design (pp. 263-265)

Comprehension Check

1. What are the five basic elements of design? *(The elements of design are space, line, shape, texture, and color.)*
2. What are some things you should keep in mind when you work with space? *(The amount of space and its use affects the way people feel. Space use should make it easy to move from one area to another and from one room to another. Space must be allowed for furniture to be used.)*
3. What are some effects of different lines in a design? *(Lines can cause your eyes to move up and down or across an object. Lines can create different feelings or moods. The width of lines also makes a difference in the effect of a design.)*
4. What is value and how are differences in value distinguished? *(Value refers to the lightness or darkness of a color. Light values are sometimes called tints and dark values are called shades.)*

Learning Activities

1. **Optical Illusions.** On the overhead projector, show squares with different types of lines inside: vertical, horizontal, zigzag, and curved. Also show the effect of line width. What effect does each type of line have on the appearance of the shape that surrounds them? Point out that the shapes are all squares of the same size. (Key Skill: *Science*)
2. **Tracing Lines.** Have students select a picture of a room. Have them cover the picture with a piece of tracing paper and trace

TIPS:

Creating Feelings with Line
Have students read the feature. Then, have them look over the lines in your classroom. What types of lines are used and what's the purpose of them? *(Answers will vary.)*

TIPS: *Creating Feelings with Line*

Lines can be used to create any number of feelings in a room. Think about the purpose of each room. How can line be used to enhance the purpose? Here are some examples:

- Use horizontal lines in a room to create a feeling of restfulness. How might you use horizontal lines in a bedroom?
- Vertical lines suggest action. They might be especially helpful in a family room or play room.
- Using vertical and diagonal lines together suggests a feeling of excitement.

Whenever you arrange furniture, think about how it will be used. People must be able to move easily from one area to another and from one room to another.

Be sure to leave space for the furniture to be used. Can you open the drawers in your bedroom without sitting on the bed? If you pull out the chairs to sit down for a meal, is there still space to walk around the table? Keep the space needs of people and objects in mind for successful decorating.

▼ Line ▼

Line refers to the outline of an object or to obvious lines within it. Lines can cause your eyes to move up and down or across an object. For example, horizontal lines (those that go from side to side) can be used to draw attention to the length of a room. Long, low bookshelves do this. Vertical lines (those that go up and down), can create the illusion of height. Tall bookcases draw the eyes upward. Diagonal and zigzag lines add excitement and interest but should be used only in small amounts. Curved lines are softer and more graceful. The width of lines also makes a difference. Wide lines, especially in bright colors, catch the eye more than narrow lines.

▼ Shape ▼

Shape, or the form of a solid object, is created when lines are combined. Shapes take up some of the space in a room. The shapes of objects can make them seem to be heavy or light. For instance, compare an easy chair in a living room to a chair at a kitchen table. Both would look out of place if their locations were reversed.

▼ Texture ▼

Bumpy, soft, silky, shiny, rough. All these words could be used to describe the **texture** of objects — the way their surfaces look and feel.

A basic rule in combining textures is that they should seem to go together or to relate to each other. For example, dried grasses and berries, being rough in texture, would look appropriate in a piece of old pottery or in a basket. On the other hand, they would look out of place in a shiny plastic dish. Rough texture gives an informal feeling. Smooth, shiny textures seem more formal.

The texture of an item can affect its apparent color. Two fabrics with different textures may not look the same, even though they are of identical color. This is important to keep in mind when trying to match colors.

More About *Form*

The shape or form of an object should fit its function. For instance, reclining chairs have a form that allows people to sit comfortably and relax. Office chairs have a form that allows people to maintain good posture while they type or write. A chair that has a good form for watching television would be inappropriate for typing.

In England, one trend in home decorating is the use of handmade fabrics and handmade items such as quilts. Some designers believe this is due to an increased awareness of the environment. How might this trend express concern for the environment?

▼ Color ▼

Color is one of the most important design elements. It even has its own language. When you understand the basics of color, you can use it to give the look you want.

In the study of color, *value* refers to the lightness or darkness of a color. For instance, pink is the lightest value of red, and maroon is its darkest value. Light values are sometimes called *tints* and dark values are called *shades*.

Value affects how large a room or object looks. For example, Leah painted the walls of her small apartment pale blue and light peach to make the rooms appear larger and more open. Dark walls would have made the rooms seem smaller.

The term *intensity* describes how bright or dull a color appears. A color at full intensity, such as bright red, is very striking. It tends to stand out. Colors with lower intensity, such as dusty rose, are less obvious. In general, low-intensity or dull colors are better for large areas, such as walls and floors. Bright colors often are used for smaller accents, such as pillows and pictures.

When choosing colors, think about the way they make you feel. Yellow, yellow-orange, orange, red-orange, and red are associated with warmth. Warm colors also make objects appear larger and closer to you.

Green, blue, blue-green, blue-violet, and violet are called cool colors. They may remind you of water, trees, and sky. Cool colors tend to make objects look smaller and farther away. Using cool colors in a small, sunny room would give feelings of coolness and space.

Light Value
Dark Value

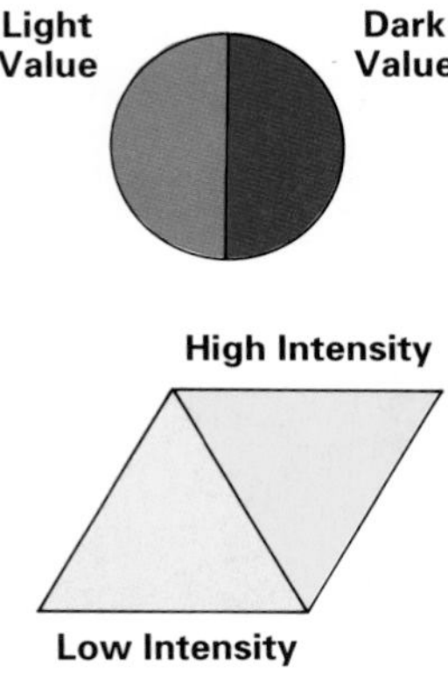

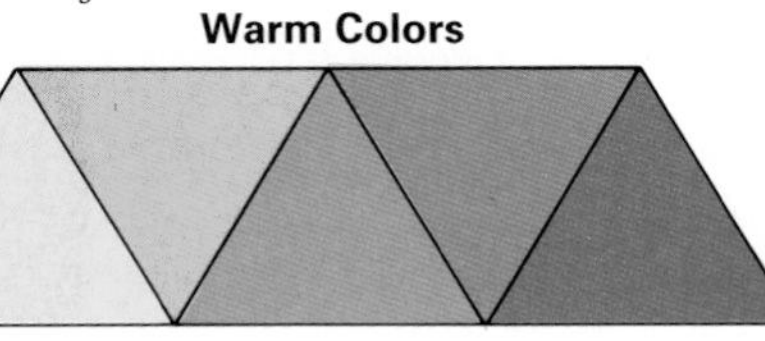

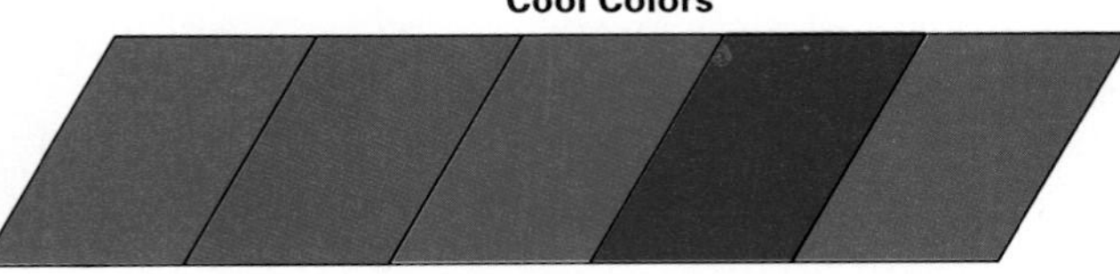

Learning Activities (continued)

the predominant lines in the room. What effect do the lines have on the apparent size and shape of the room? What feeling or mood do the lines create? (Key Skill: *Science*)

3. **Demonstration.** On the chalkboard, place two dots several inches apart. Connect the dots. Point out that the resulting line has only one dimension, length. Use four lines to create a square. Use additional lines to turn the square into the shape of a box. Ask students whether the shape appears heavy or light. Use chalk to color the box to make it appear solid. Ask again whether the box appears heavy or light. (Key Skill: *Science*)
4. **Observation.** Provide students with fabrics of the same color but different textures. Ask students to observe the effects of texture on the colors of the fabrics. (Key Skill: *Science*)
5. **Changing Color Values.** Have students use watercolors or tempera paints to create tints and shades of their favorite colors. Point out that tints and shades help to add interest and variety to designs. (Key Skills: *Science, Creativity*)

Follow Up

1. **Reteaching.** Have students locate and label illustrations depicting the elements of design. (Key Skill: *Critical Thinking*)
2. **Enrichment.** Have students develop a collage of materials to illustrate colors, patterns, and textures that might be used together effectively in decorating a room. Display the collages in the classroom. (Key Skill: *Creativity*)

More About Color and Light

Color and light are related. Dark-colored walls absorb most of the light falling on them, making the room seem dim. The same amount of light will appear brighter in a room with pale-colored walls because pale colors reflect light. People are most comfortable in rooms that have some variation in color and light. Uniform light is appropriate for a business setting, but it would be boring for relaxing or dining.

Around the World

After reading the feature, have students look at home for household items that are environmentally friendly. *(Answers will vary.)*

Teaching. . .
The Color Wheel and Color Schemes
(pp. 266-267)

Comprehension Check

1. What are the primary, secondary, and tertiary colors and how is each created? *(The primary colors are red, yellow, and blue. All the other colors on the color wheel can be made from them. The secondary colors are violet, green, and orange. They are formed by mixing equal amounts of two primary colors. The six tertiary colors are a mixture of a primary color and a secondary color. The six tertiary colors are yellow-green, blue-green, blue-violet, red-violet, yellow-orange, and red-orange.)*
2. What are the neutral colors? *(The neutral colors are black, gray, and white. Ivory, beige, and tan are also sometimes considered neutrals.)*
3. Name and describe the color schemes based on the color wheel. *(Monochromatic is a color scheme that uses tints and shades of only one color. An analogous color scheme is made up of two or more colors next to each other on the color wheel. A complementary color scheme is made up of two colors that are directly opposite each other on the color wheel. A split-complementary color scheme results when a color is combined with colors on either side of its complement. A triadic color scheme uses three colors the same distance from one another on the color wheel.)*

Learning Activities

1. **Creating Low-Intensity Colors.** Have students use watercolors or tempera paints to mix their favorite color with a small amount of its opposite on the color wheel. Add additional amounts of the color complement until a very dull color results. (Key Skills: *Science, Creativity*)
2. **Creating a Color Wheel.** Have students use watercolors or tempera paints to create a color wheel from the three primary colors. Have students paint the primary colors on a copy of a

The Color Wheel

The color wheel is a helpful tool for understanding and using color. It starts with a circle divided into twelve pie-shaped sections.

Red, yellow, and blue are called the *primary colors*. All the other colors on the color wheel can be made from them. The primary colors are placed an equal distance apart on the color wheel (every fourth section).

When two primary colors are mixed in equal amounts, a *secondary color* is formed. The three secondary colors are violet, green, and orange. Violet is made by mixing red and blue. Green is a mixture of yellow and blue, and orange is made from red and yellow. The secondary colors go on the color wheel halfway between the primary colors from which they are made.

When you mix a primary and a secondary color, a *tertiary color* (TUR-shee-air-ee) is formed. There are six tertiary colors: yellow-green, blue-green, blue-violet, red-violet, yellow-orange, and red-orange. These tertiary colors fill in the remaining spaces on the color wheel. (Note that the primary color comes first in the name of each tertiary color.)

Black, gray, and white are neutral colors. Sometimes ivory, beige, and tan are also considered neutrals. They are not found on the color wheel.

THE COLOR WHEEL

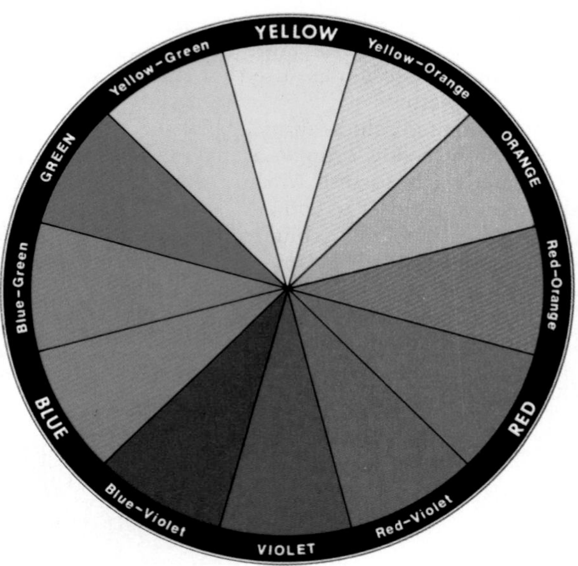

More About Colors' Symbolism

Colors have very different meanings in different cultures. While black is the symbol of mourning in this country, white is the color of mourning in many cultures. In the early twentieth century, white walls and kitchens signaled "sanitary awareness." White rugs and furniture often symbolize wealth, as only the rich can afford to keep them clean. White, as a symbol of purity, is the traditional color of bridal gowns in the United States, but other colors are acceptable in other parts of the world.

Mixing Secondary Colors

Materials
Red, yellow, and blue tempera paint; white paper

Equipment
Small paint brush; foam plate for mixing paint

Directions:
Mix equal parts (3 drops each) of the following primary colors to make the secondary colors:

- ✔ red + yellow = orange
- ✔ yellow + blue = green
- ✔ blue + red = violet

After mixing the secondary colors, compare them to the secondary colors on the color wheel on page 266 of the text. Are the colors the same as or different from those found in the text? Why or why not? What happens when primary colors are mixed in unequal proportions?

Color Schemes

There are a number of color schemes, or combinations, that are pleasing to the eye. Each one is based on the color wheel.

- ▶ ***Monochromatic.*** This color scheme uses tints and shades of only one color. For example, grass and trees form a monochromatic color scheme made of various values and intensities of green.
- ▶ ***Analogous*** (uh-NAL-uh-gus). This color scheme is made up of two or more colors next to each other on the color wheel. Blue-green, green, and blue, for example, form an analogous color scheme.
- ▶ ***Complementary.*** This color scheme is made up of two colors that are directly opposite each other on the color wheel. Examples are blue and orange, red and green, and yellow and violet.
- ▶ ***Split-complementary.*** This scheme results when a color is combined with colors on either side of its complement. Blue, red-orange, and yellow-orange form a split-complementary scheme.
- ▶ ***Triadic.*** This color scheme uses three colors the same distance from one another on the color wheel. For example, the primary colors — red, blue, and yellow — form a triadic scheme.

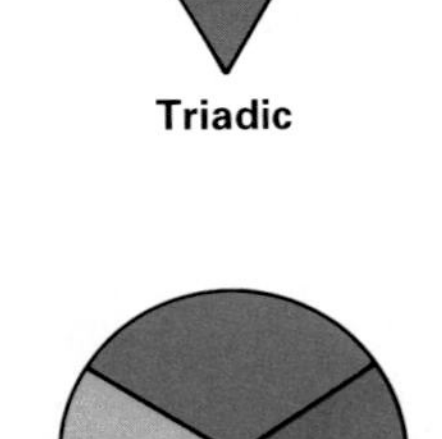

Triadic

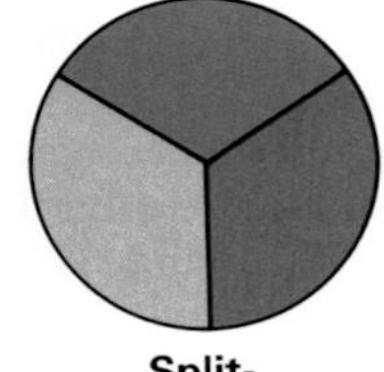

Split-complementary

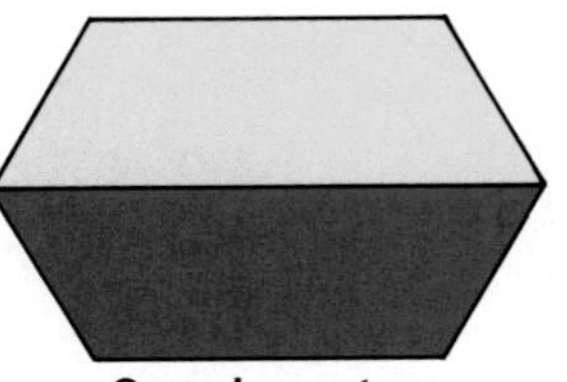

Complementary

Monochromatic

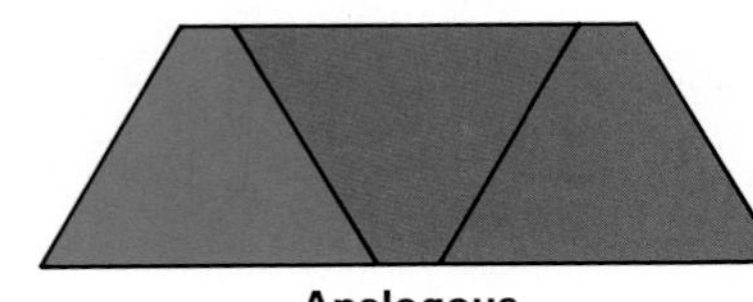

Analogous

Mixing Secondary Colors

Materials: Red, yellow, and blue tempera paint; white paper.

Equipment: Small paint brush; foam plate for mixing paint.

Purpose: To mix equal parts of primary colors in order to make secondary colors that match those shown on the color wheel.

Outcomes:
Students may not come up with secondary colors that exactly match those on the color wheel because their proportions of primary colors may not be perfect. Some students' proportions of primary colors may even be off enough that they will produce tertiary colors.

Learning Activities (continued)

color wheel first. Next, have them mix primary colors to create the secondary colors. Finally, have them mix primary and secondary colors to create the tertiary colors. (Key Skills: *Science, Creativity*)

3. **Finding Illustrations.** Have students select three pictures that illustrate the use of the elements of design. Have students write an analysis of each picture describing the use of each element of design. (Key Skill: *Critical Thinking*)

Follow Up

1. **Reteaching.** Have students create a word game using words associated with color. Reproduce the word games for students to use in class for review. (Key Skill: *Creativity*)
2. **Enrichment.** Challenge students to find a creative way to illustrate the color wheel or one of the color schemes. *Examples:* a flower arrangement, a mobile, a painting. (Key Skill: *Creativity*)

Making a Difference

Because color is the least expensive decorating element, organizations often choose painting as a way to make a difference in the lives of families living in low-income areas of their community. Interior design students may have the opportunity to help brighten the daily lives of others by getting involved in locally sponsored home improvement projects.

In Touch with Technology

Computers now available in paint stores can analyze the color in a sample brought in by a customer and create a paint formula which results in a perfect match. This takes much of the guesswork out of paint selection.

Teaching. . .
Principles of Design and Using Design Effectively (pp. 268-270)

Comprehension Check

1. What are the six principles of design? *(The principles of design are harmony, proportion, scale, balance, rhythm, and emphasis.)*
2. Define harmony. *(Harmony is the feeling that all parts of a design belong together.)*
3. Describe ways to create harmony in a room. *(Harmony is created by using the elements of design so that they relate well to one another. For example, by using furniture that matches in style, color, or shape, and by using textures that go well together.)*
4. How does proportion affect design? *(Proportion is the way one part of a design relates in size or shape to another or to the whole.)*
5. Define scale and give examples of items that are out of scale with each other. *(Scale refers to the overall size of an object or its size compared to other objects. A huge bed in a tiny room, a tiny sofa in a large room, a large lamp on a very small table, and a really small lamp on a large table are examples of objects that are out of scale with each other.)*
6. How do formal and informal balance differ? *(In formal balance, the objects on each side of an imaginary center line are the same — or at least the same in several elements. In informal balance, the objects on each side of the center are different in size, form, texture, and/or color.)*
7. What is the role of rhythm in design? *(Rhythm gives a feeling of movement by leading the eye from one point to another. This is done by repeating one or more elements of design.)*
8. What is the purpose of emphasis in design? *(The role of emphasis is to create a point of interest by attracting your eyes to one part of a design.)*

How to . . .
Bring Design into Everyday Life

Have you ever walked into a room and felt that something didn't look quite right? Perhaps a chair wasn't in the right place, or the carpeting seemed to be fighting with the wallpaper. You may have that same feeling as you put together an outfit or prepare a meal. As you will see, the elements and principles of design that are used to decorate a room also apply to clothing and food.

In drawing A, the teen girl is wearing a denim skirt and jacket with a tucked-in chambray shirt. Her accessories include black shoes, a simple black belt with a gold buckle, a gold pendant, and hoop earrings. Notice how line and color are used to create vertical movement. The point of emphasis draws your eye to the neckline.

In drawing B, the same girl changes the look of her outfit by wearing the shirt over the skirt and adding some bold jewelry. Horizontal lines are created at the waist and neckline. In both cases, all parts of the design are attractive and seem to go together.

Look at the food examples in drawings C and D. In drawing C, the plate contains a nutritious meal. However, baked white fish with mashed potatoes, cauliflower, and cottage cheese salad isn't very appealing to the eye. All of the foods are light in color and have a soft texture.

In drawing D, the same white fish is garnished with colorful vegetable strips and served with boiled new potatoes, broccoli spears, and a crisp tossed salad. Notice how paying a little attention to design brings real appeal to this meal.

By using the principles and elements of design when choosing what to wear, preparing food for you and your family, or decorating your room, you can bring beauty into every part of your life.

Drawing A

Drawing B

Drawing C

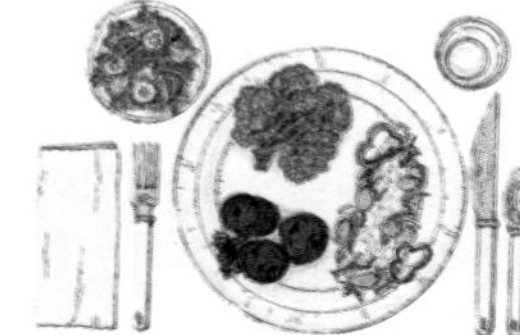

Drawing D

How to ... Bring Design into Everyday Life

Have students read the feature. Ask students to discuss the methods they use when putting together different outfits to wear to school. Could they design their outfits so that they are more appealing? Also, have students look at the design of their next meal. Were the principles and elements of design thought of when this meal was planned?

Using the principles of design effectively can increase your enjoyment of a room. In what ways can you identify the use of harmony, proportion, scale, balance, rhythm, and emphasis in this room?

Principles of Design

The recipe for your favorite cookies is based on principles of baking developed over the years. The same is true of design. The principles of design have been tested for centuries. They can help you combine the ingredients, or the elements, of design to fit *your* personality.

Harmony

Harmony is the feeling that all parts of a design belong together. That doesn't mean that everything has to match. Variety is interesting if the objects grouped together have something in common, such as style, shape, color, or size.

Proportion

Choosing a centerpiece for a table or placing furniture in a room involves **proportion**. It is the way one part of a design relates in size or shape to another or to the whole.

The ancient Greeks discovered that certain uneven proportions create the most pleasing effects. For example, a table that is 2 feet wide by 3 feet long is more pleasing to the eye than one 2 feet square. Proportions are usually expressed as ratios. The first table would have a ratio of 2:3 (2 to 3). Other pleasing proportions include 3:5 and 5:8.

Scale

Scale refers to the overall size of an object or its size compared to other objects. For example, a very small lamp seems even smaller when placed on a large table. Both are considered out of scale with each other.

Learning Activities

1. **Demonstrating Harmony.** Play a recording of a barber shop quartet that emphasizes the use of harmony in singing. Compare the use of harmony in singing with harmonious use of the elements of design in a room. (Key Skills: *Communication, Critical Thinking*)
2. **Demonstration.** Show students a series of rectangles divided into parts with lines. Ask students to select the ones they find most pleasing. Compare the results with the Greeks' findings that certain proportions are more pleasing than others. (Key Skill: *Critical Thinking*)
3. **Pictures.** Show students pictures to illustrate the design principles of scale. Examples: a small child sitting in a large chair, a small child walking with a tall adult, a parent sitting in a first-grader's desk. Discuss what would improve the scale in each situation. (Key Skill: *Critical Thinking*)
4. **Greeting Card Design.** Assign students to create greeting cards that demonstrate the use of as many elements and principles of design as possible. Display the cards and discuss the elements and principles of design that are illustrated. (Key Skill: *Creativity*)

Follow Up

1. **Reteaching.** Have students locate and label illustrations depicting the principles of design. (Key Skill: *Critical Thinking*)
2. **Extension.** Use the extension information handout on p. 35 of the *Extending the Text* booklet in the TCR.

More About Professional Interior Designers

The job of the professional interior designer involves creating interiors to meet the needs and desires of the client. On a large project, such as an office building, the designer may spend several months planning the interior. The designer must identify the special needs and uses of the area, the goals of the client, and the amount of money to budget on each item. The designer may then spend several more months developing the design plans, purchasing materials and furnishings, and making the plan a reality.

Photo Focus

Discuss the photo at the top of page 269 with the students. What effect does each principle of design have on the room shown in the photo? *(Answers will vary.)*

Completing the Chapter

For Review

1. Emphasize the main concepts using the summary.
2. Have students complete the "Facts to Recall." (Answers below.)

For Reteaching

1. **Reteaching.** Use the activity on p. 31 of the *Reteaching and Practical Skills* booklet in the TCR.

For Enrichment

1. **Enrichment.** Use the activity on p. 42 of the *Enrichment Activities* booklet in the TCR.

For Evaluation

1. Choose items from "Ideas to Explore" and "Activities to Try."
2. Use the chapter test on pp. 51-52 in the testing booklet of the TCR or use the testmaker software.

Facts to Recall Answers

1. Space, line, texture, shape, and color.
2. People must be able to move easily from one area to another and from one room to another; there must be enough space to use an object.
3. Vertical lines give the illusion of height. Horizontal lines draw attention to the length of a room.
4. Combine textures that are alike or somehow related to each other.
5. "Value" is a color's lightness or darkness.
6. Warm colors are those associated with warmth, such as yellow, yellow-orange, orange, red-orange, and red. They make objects appear larger and closer to you. Cool colors are those associated with coolness, such as green, blue, blue-green, blue-violet, and violet. They tend to make objects appear smaller and farther away.

▼ Balance ▼

A design that has **balance** gives a feeling of equal weight among all parts of a design. Balance can be formal or informal. In formal balance, the objects on each side of an imaginary center line are the same — or at least the same in several elements. One side seems like a reflection of the other. In informal balance, the objects on each side of the center are different in size, form, texture, and/or color.

▼ Rhythm ▼

Rhythm, or a feeling of movement, leads the eye from one point to another. This is done by repeating one or more elements of design. For instance, there is rhythm in the folds of a skirt or the increase in size of kitchen canisters.

▼ Emphasis ▼

In a design, your eyes are attracted to the point of greatest interest, or **emphasis**. A room's point of emphasis might be a poster. An outfit's might be a bright scarf.

Using Design Effectively

Whether you're designing an outfit, a table setting for a meal, or the space where you live, you can make it reflect your tastes and interests. By putting the elements and principles of design to work, you can increase your enjoyment and your family's, too.

TAKING ACTION
Putting Design Skills into Practice

Mr. Raible, your friend Jenine's father, plans to open a cafe. His idea is to offer inexpensive but nutritious foods such as salads, soups, and sandwiches. He hopes to attract teens, as well as adults.

Mr. Raible has asked you and Jenine what you would do if you were the interior designers on the project. The dining area is a narrow room with a low ceiling and one large window.

Using Your Resourcefulness

- Decide on an overall design theme that will appeal to both teens and adults.
- Choose a color scheme.
- Sketch your design suggestions. Keep the elements and principles of design in mind.
- Find out where you can learn about fire and safety regulations that may affect the design.

TAKING ACTION

Some students may find it difficult to sketch their ideas. These students may be more successful in describing their ideas with words on paper or on an audio tape, or they may be able to find pictures to illustrate their ideas on a poster. Encourage students to use the media or combination of media that allows them to most clearly express their decorating ideas. You may have students make a class presentation to present their ideas. Use students' posters to create a classroom display.

Using Your Resourcefulness Answers

- Answers will vary.
- Answers will vary.

Chapter 24 Review

Summary

In this chapter, you have read about:

- The ways design is used in many aspects of everyday life.
- How every design is made up of five elements.
- How understanding color can help you use it effectively.
- The ways color schemes are formed.
- How the principles of design can be used to create an attractive living space.

Facts to Recall

1. What are the five basic elements of design?
2. What are two practical things to remember when using space?
3. How do vertical lines affect an object or a room? Horizontal lines?
4. What is one basic rule of combining textures?
5. Define value as it relates to color.
6. Define warm and cool as they relate to color. Give two examples of each.
7. What are the three primary colors? Why are they called primary?
8. What is the difference between a secondary and a tertiary color?
9. What are the six principles of design?
10. What is the difference between formal and informal balance?

Ideas to Explore

1. Why might someone paint a room a dark color?
2. What textures might be appropriate for a two-year-old's playroom? How might they differ from those in a formal dining room?
3. Explain how rhythm is created by hanging three pictures on a wall, with the picture in the center higher than the ones on the side.

Activities to Try

1. Analyze your appearance today in terms of design elements and principles. For example, what type of color scheme do your clothes form? What is your point of emphasis?
2. Make a poster showing at least one example of each of the five types of color schemes. You may use rooms, clothes, or foods as examples.

LINK TO Art

VALUES OF COLOR

Value refers to the lightness or darkness of a color. Use the following guidelines to create a light value (a tint) and a dark value (a shade) of your favorite primary color:

1. On a sheet of white construction paper, use a ruler and a pencil to draw three, 2-inch (5-cm) squares. Number the squares 1, 2, and 3.
2. Using tempera paint in your favorite primary color, paint square number 1.
3. Mix equal parts (3 drops each) of primary color tempera paint with white tempera paint to create a *tint*. Paint square number 2.
4. Mix equal parts (2 to 3 drops each) of primary color tempera paint with black tempera paint to create a *shade*. Paint square number 3.

Which square of paint appears to look larger? Smaller? Why?

Facts to Recall Answers (continued)

7. The three primary colors are red, yellow, and blue. They are called primary because they are the colors from which all others on the color wheel can be made.
8. A secondary color is the mixture of equal parts of two primary colors. A tertiary color is a blend of a primary color and a secondary color.
9. Harmony, proportion, scale, balance, rhythm, and emphasis.
10. In formal balance, objects are arranged so that one side of the room appears to reflect the other in some noticeable element or elements of design. In informal balance, the objects on each side differ from those on the other in size, texture, and/or color.

Ideas to Explore

1. Answers will vary and may include: to make furnishings appear larger; to cover flaws such as cracks or repairs in the walls.
2. Answers will vary. The textures of a playroom should be inviting but not dangerous to a young child. They could be soft, furry, bumpy or wavy. They should not be pointed or sharp. Textures found in a dining room might be less noticeable and more practical: smooth, hard, square, or flat.
3. Answers will vary and may include: rhythm may use zigzag lines to make objects stand out; long vertical and/or horizontal lines to give the illusion of height and/or length.

- Answers will vary.
- Answers will vary. Some possibilities include OSHA, a building code book for restaurants, or an architect.

LINK TO Art

Answers

The square with a *tint* should look larger because light colors reflect light and make an area seem larger than it really is. The square with a *shade* should look smaller because dark colors absorb light and make an area seem smaller than it really is.

Preparing to Teach

Chapter Outline

Chapter Resources

The following booklet materials may be found in the *Teacher's Classroom Resources* box:

- Lesson Plans, p. 30
- Student Workbook, *Study Guide*, pp. 109-110; *Deciding About Design*, pp. 111-112
- Color Transparencies, *Arranging Accessories*, CT-32
- Technology and Computers, pp. 27, 29, 31, 32
- Cooperative Learning, p. 37
- Extending the Text, *Picture This*, p. 36
- Reteaching and Practical Skills, *Design Match-Ups!*, p. 33
- Enrichment Activities, *Arranging a Room to Share*, p. 40
- Chapter and Unit Tests, pp. 53-54
- Testmaker Software

Also see:

- Meeting the Special Needs of Students
- Linking Home, School, and Community

CHAPTER

25 Making Design Work for You

OBJECTIVES

- *Identify the backgrounds in a room.*
- *Select and arrange furniture and accessories.*
- *Describe ways to make sharing space easier.*

TERMS TO LEARN

- ***functional furniture***
- ***furniture joints***
- ***upholstery***
- ***traffic lanes***

Whether your home has a single room or many, you can use your knowledge of design to make it more comfortable. Remember that good design doesn't mean starting with an empty room and buying everything new. Even small changes can make a big difference. A few bright pillows, a can of paint, or simply rearranging furniture can add new appeal to a room.

Of course, a home is meant for people to live in. A good design must be both pleasing to the eye and comfortable and convenient for those who use it.

Designing Living Space

Whether you are a professional interior designer or simply someone trying to make a bedroom more appealing, the task is similar. Here's a step-by-step plan you can follow for improving any room.

- ***Step 1: Identify needs and wants.*** Planning a good design starts with identifying needs and wants of those who will use a room. Is there a major goal to be achieved? What activities will take place in the room? What type of storage is needed? The Sanchez family wants to make space in their kitchen for a table and chairs. Stephanie and Tim Rogy have a small apartment. Their decorating plan includes painting their living room to make it brighter and adding storage space. Carlos and Mike want more privacy in their shared bedroom.
- ***Step 2: Evaluate the current room using the elements and principles of design.*** What aspects work well and which need improvement? This analysis will help you make your design plan.

What elements and principles of design are used in this room? How might the way the elements are used be improved?

More About *How Interior Designers Work*

Whether planning a hotel lobby or a living room, an interior designer uses a problem-solving process. First, the designer must determine all the activities that may take place in the area. The designer must also consider who will use the area and what mood it should convey. Each interior poses special problems. For example, a bedroom must create a relaxing atmosphere. A child's room should have walls, floors, and furniture that create a happy mood and withstand hard wear. A kitchen must be cheerful and easy to clean.

Introducing the Chapter

Motivators

1. **Ask the class.** On the chalkboard, draw a two-column chart divided into eight sections. Ask students to name items found in a room (walls, chairs, lamps, closets, etc.). Group the items by their functions within the room (i.e. walls as backgrounds; lamps as accessories), and write the names of the items in the four sections on the right side of the chart. When these spaces are filled, ask students to guess the name of each group of items. Help them arrive at the correct listings to fill in the sections on the left side of the chart: backgrounds, furniture, accessories, and storage. Explain that Chapter 25 will show them how to use all four groups of items to make design work in their own surroundings. (Key Skill: *Critical Thinking*)
2. **Description.** Ask students to write a paragraph describing their personal space as it is now and as they would like it to be. Ask several volunteers to read their paragraphs to the class. (Key Skill: *Communication*)
3. **Ask the class.** Ask students to name as many styles of furniture as they can. List these styles on the board. Share a few interesting facts about the origin and popularity of each style of furniture to introduce the section on furnishings. (Key Skill: *Social Studies*)

Chapter Objectives and Vocabulary

1. Have students read the chapter objectives and rephrase the objectives as questions.
2. Ask students to state, in their own words, the purpose of studying this chapter.
3. Pronounce the vocabulary terms listed on the previous page. Ask students whether they are familiar with any of these. Explain that the terms will be defined in the chapter.

Guided Reading

1. Have students read the chapter and use the Study Guide on pp. 109-110 of the *Student Workbook*.

Teaching. . .
Designing Living Space
(pp. 273-275)

Comprehension Check

1. What steps can you take when designing living space? *(**Step 1:** Identify needs and wants. **Step 2:** Evaluate the current room using the elements and principles of design. **Step 3:** Consider your resources.)*
2. What provides the backgrounds for furnishings and accessories? *(Walls, windows, and floors serve as backgrounds for furnishings and accessories.)*
3. What advantages do the various types of floor covering materials offer? *(Wood, vinyl, and ceramic tile are durable and easy to clean. Carpets and rugs can provide extra comfort and color. Wall-to-wall carpet covers the entire floor in a room. Rugs come in many shapes and sizes.)*
4. Discuss ways in which furniture can be functional and/or decorative. *(Functional furniture meets specific needs. It may provide storage space or space for eating or doing homework. Furniture is decorative when it is used to make a room attractive. Furniture may be both functional and decorative.)*

Learning Activities

1. **Case Situations.** Divide the class into groups and assign each group one of the three situations described under Step 1 of the step-by-step plan for designing living space. Ask each group to use the three steps to identify possible solutions to the problem described. Ask a spokesperson for each group to summarize the

TIPS:

Decorating Walls
After students read the feature, have them check out the walls in their room at home. Are the items on their walls arranged in an attractive way? Could these items be arranged differently so that their room is more attractive? *(Answers will vary.)*

TIPS: *Decorating Walls*

Here are some tips for arranging wall decorations:

- Hang decorations at eye level.
- Place single wall decorations over a piece of furniture that is in proportion to the decoration.
- Choose frames that complement the artwork or needle work.
- Use an uneven number of items if you are creating a wall arrangement. Uneven numbers are more pleasing to the eye.
- When arranging a wall grouping, try tracing each item on paper and cutting them out. Practice arranging your paper "wall decorations" (using masking tape on the back) before fastening the hangers or nails to the wall.
- Avoid hanging items where they could be damaged by heating vents or dirt.

- ***Step 3: Consider your resources.*** Changing your room's look doesn't mean you have to start from scratch. Adding a few new touches to what you already have can make a big difference. So can reducing clutter by giving away things you no longer want or need. Remember that *resources* mean more than money. You also can put your skills to work. Perhaps a friend or relative can help you learn a new skill as you work.

Careful planning will help you meet your design goals. Backgrounds, furniture, accessories, and storage areas must all work together in a successful design.

▼ Backgrounds ▼

Walls, windows, and floors serve as backgrounds for furnishings and accessories. They help show off furniture and decorative objects to their best advantage.

Walls

Walls form the shape of a room and divide a large area, such as an apartment, into smaller areas. Walls also help give people privacy and cut down on noise.

The number of ways to make walls attractive is limited only by your imagination. The two most popular ways use paint or wallpaper. With paint, you can have your choice of colors or even paint a design. Wallpaper can add interesting patterns and textures to walls and ceilings.

You can combine wall treatments, or finishes, in a room. For example, you might wallpaper one wall and paint the other three. Another option is to paint the lower half of each wall and wallpaper the upper part.

In what ways do the walls, windows, and floors show off the best features of the furnishings in the photo? How do these backgrounds help create interest?

More About *Wall Coverings*

Other wall coverings include fabrics, tiles, wood paneling, mirrors and laminates. Most of these options are more expensive than paint or paper.

More About *Selecting Backgrounds*

In shopping for background elements, bring samples home so you can view them in natural light and with the room's other design elements. Colors often look different in the store than in your own room.

Windows

Window treatments (sometimes called window coverings) provide both privacy and decoration. There are many choices including curtains, drapes, shutters, blinds, or shades.

You can use one or more window treatments. For instance, you might use curtains or drapes along with fabric shades or mini-blinds. With basic sewing skills you might make simple curtains yourself. Window coverings can really change the look of a room. Think about the options and check their costs before making your choice.

Floors

Floor coverings can add both comfort and beauty to a room. Many people like flooring materials such as wood, vinyl, and ceramic tile. They are durable and easy to clean. Carpets and rugs can provide extra comfort and color. Wall-to-wall carpet covers the entire floor in a room. Rugs usually cover only part of the floor. Rugs come in many shapes and sizes.

▼ Furniture ▼

Furniture has many roles. It provides a place for all kinds of activities: visiting with your family and friends, watching television, relaxing, eating, and sleeping. Most furniture is **functional furniture**. That means it meets specific needs. Chests, for example, provide storage space. Tables give space for eating and, perhaps, doing your homework. Of course, functional furniture is usually decorative as well.

The use of wood lattice was brought to Mexico by Spanish explorers and is still popular there today. Lattice (LAT-iss) is a design created by criss-crossing strips of material, leaving space between them, or by cutting patterns in the material to achieve the same effect. These patterns can be intriguing and appealing. Lattice is also practical since it partially hides whatever is behind it. It is used in chest doors, bookcases, and over windows. How could you use lattice to improve your living space?

Learning Activities (continued)

group's discussion for the class. (Key Skill: *Problem Solving*)

2. **Room Analysis.** Show students pictures of problem rooms. Have students evaluate the room using the elements and principles of design. Discuss ways the room could be improved. Show pictures of how a designer improved the room. (Interior design magazines are a good source of before and after pictures illustrating ways rooms can be improved.) (Key Skill: *Critical Thinking*)
3. **Demonstration.** Demonstrate several painting techniques, such as combing, sponging, striating, dry brushing, or stenciling. Discuss possible uses of these techniques in decorating rooms. (Key Skill: *Creativity*)
4. **Catalog Selections.** Provide students with catalogs and have them select pictures of window treatments they would select for a kitchen, a bedroom, and a living room. (Key Skill: *Decision Making*)

Follow Up

1. **Reteaching.** Have students develop a collage of pictures illustrating various wall coverings, window treatments, and floor coverings. (Key Skill: *Creativity*)
2. **Enrichment.** Have students use the three steps for designing living space to plan ways to improve a room in their own home. Ask students to involve other family members in working through the three steps and developing a plan for improvement. (Key Skill: *Problem Solving*)

AROUND THE WORLD

After reading the feature, have students look at home for furniture or areas that make use of wood lattice. Is wood lattice used in chest doors, bookcases, or over windows? Have students report their findings to the class. *(Answers will vary.)*

More About *Changing Room Proportions*

Wall coverings are good disguisers. They can be used to change the apparent proportion of a room by visually enlarging or minimizing space. Dark and warm colors make walls seem closer, while light and cool colors visually move the walls farther away. Dark colors make ceilings seem lower, while light colors raise them. Small prints create a sense of space in small rooms. Large patterns make a room seem smaller. Vertical designs make the ceiling seem higher, while horizontal ones make the room seem wider.

Teaching. . .
How to . . . Paint a Room
(pp. 276-277)

How to ...
Paint a Room

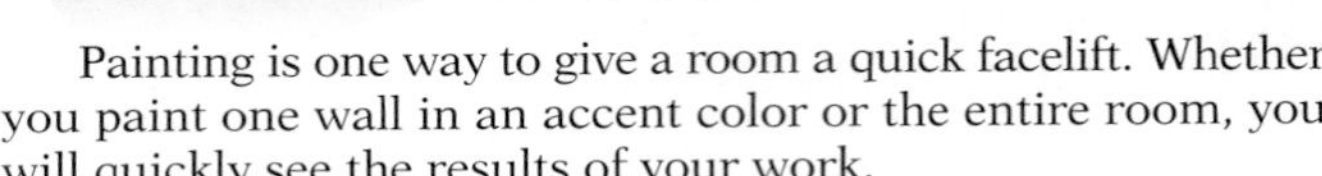

Painting is one way to give a room a quick facelift. Whether you paint one wall in an accent color or the entire room, you will quickly see the results of your work.

Painting isn't a difficult skill to learn. You do need a steady hand and a willingness to work carefully. Here are the steps to follow.

▶ ***Step 1: Choose the paint.*** Use what you have learned about color to choose paint that will highlight the room's features. Interior paint comes in latex and oil varieties. Walls and ceilings are usually painted with flat (not shiny) paint. Choose gloss or semi-gloss for the trim, such as window frames.

▶ ***Step 2: Get the room ready.*** Move everything possible from the room, including curtains and rugs. Cover the floor and any remaining items with plastic or canvas drop cloths. Next, clean the areas to be painted. Use spackle — a plasterlike material that comes in a can — to fill any cracks or holes. Scrape or sand away any loose paint.

▶ ***Step 3: Assemble your equipment.*** Walls and ceilings can be painted with a roller or brush. For window and door frames and other trim, use an angled trim brush. Use masking tape or special painting tape to protect areas (such as windowpanes) that will not be painted. Keep at least one rag handy to wipe up any paint spills or splatters.

▶ ***Step 4: Plan your job.*** The best order for painting a room is ceiling first, walls second, and trim last.

Wellness

Floor coverings can either be a safety factor or a hazard. Carpets and rugs deaden sound and provide safety from falls and breakage. However, unanchored throw rugs may cause a person to trip and fall. They are especially dangerous for elderly persons.

How to ... Paint a Room

After the students read the feature, have them go to a paint store and find out what the differences are between latex paint and oil paint. Then, have students practice putting strips of masking tape around windows so that they'd be protected if the areas around them were being painted. Finally, have students practice painting with a roller and/or brush on wood scraps in order to find out how much paint to apply on the surface.

▶ ***Step 5: Begin painting.*** Stir the paint thoroughly with a clean mixing paddle. If you are using a roller, pour paint into the roller tray. First use a trim brush to paint a strip on the ceiling where it meets the wall. Use the roller to paint the remainder. Repeat the procedure with the walls. Some rooms may need a second coat of paint to cover the existing color.

▶ ***Step 6: Paint trim.*** Carefully, paint any trim with the trim brush. This includes windows and doors and baseboards. Use pieces of cardboard to shield the nearby walls as you paint the trim.

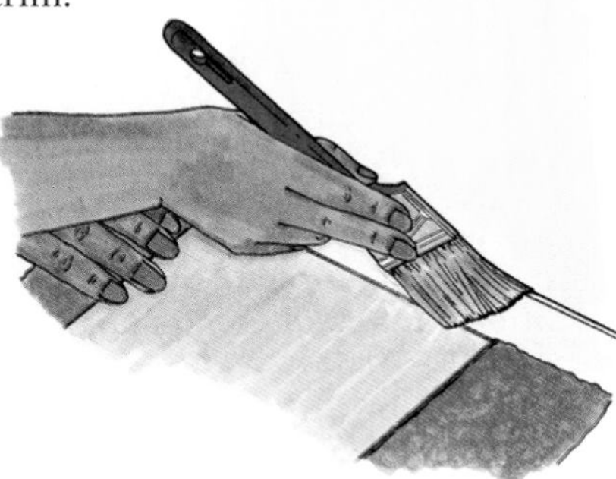

▶ ***Step 7: Clean up.*** When you are finished, clean your brushes, roller, and tray thoroughly. With latex paint, use water for cleanup. With oil paint, use turpentine or paint thinner. Keep any leftover paint tightly sealed in the can. Make a record of how much paint you used, what brand, and what color. That information will help if you need to touch up problem areas or decide to paint the room again.

In Touch with Technology

Paints are now available in an almost unlimited number of colors due to computerized mixing equipment. Many stores now have computers that can scan a color sample and tell the system operator exactly how to duplicate that color.

Teaching. . .
Looking at Furniture Styles and Choosing Furniture
(pp. 278-279)

Comprehension Check

1. What are the two basic types of furniture styles? *(Furniture styles can be divided into two basic types: traditional and contemporary.)*
2. What are traditional styles of furniture based on? *(Traditional styles are based on designs that have been used for hundreds of years.)*
3. Describe some traditional styles of furniture. *(Traditional styles include English and French furniture, Early American furniture, and Oriental furniture. French and English traditional furniture influenced much of the traditional furniture available today. Informal early American furniture is made of maple, pine, or oak and has a simple design. Oriental furniture generally has very simple lines and is made of dark or black wood with a shiny finish.)*
4. Describe contemporary furniture. *(Contemporary furniture is simple and reflects today's lifestyles. It has straight or smoothly curved lines with little or no decoration. It may be made of plastic, glass, metal, wood, and fabric.)*
5. What sources of furniture might you use if your money is limited? *(Garage sales, flea markets, and consignment or secondhand shops often have used furniture bargains.)*
6. What points should you check when selecting furniture, new or used? *(See the "Furniture Buying Checklist" on page 279.)*

Learning Activities

1. **Slides.** Show slides of different furniture styles. Point out whether the furniture styles are traditional or contemporary, formal or informal, and their country of origin. (Key Skill: *Social Studies*)

TRADITIONAL

EARLY AMERICAN

CONTEMPORARY

Looking at Furniture Styles

Because people's tastes differ, manufacturers make many styles of furniture. These styles can be divided into two basic types: traditional and contemporary.

Traditional styles are based on designs that have been used for hundreds of years. Wealthy people who lived in cities had fine furniture made of beautiful woods and elegant fabrics. This furniture often had carving or other decorations. Those who lived in the countryside made similar furniture but with simpler lines and less decoration. Thus traditional furniture can be formal or informal and fancy or plain. English and French furniture influenced much of the traditional furniture you see today.

Early American furniture is another traditional style. It was developed in the American colonies. It often is made of maple, pine, or oak and has a simple, informal design. Many people like the warm, relaxed feeling it gives.

Oriental furniture generally has very simple lines. The furniture is made of dark or black wood with a shiny finish. Oriental design also influenced traditional European furniture.

Contemporary furniture is simple and reflects today's lifestyles. It has straight or smoothly curved lines with little or no decoration. Although some pieces of contemporary furniture are made of plastic, glass, and metal, wood and fabric are often used, too.

Should you use only one furniture style in a room? Sometimes it is more interesting to combine furniture from several periods. For example, you might try using an Early American rocking chair in a contemporary bedroom. It's best to choose styles that have a similar feeling, such as simple country styles from different time periods. This can help give a room a special look.

Choosing Furniture

Before selecting furniture, determine what you have and what you need. Maybe your bed and chest of drawers are in good condition, but you would like a desk and chair. If money is limited, put your creativity to work. Garage sales, flea markets, and consignment or secondhand shops often have used furniture bargains just waiting for you. With a coat of paint or a new cushion these pieces may be just what you have in mind.

When selecting furniture, new or used, evaluate it carefully. See the "Furniture Buying Checklist" on page 279 for points to consider.

More About Choosing Furniture

Furnishing a home is an evolutionary process. Although you may dream of furnishing your home all at once, you probably will be buying things for it all of your life. You and your family are constantly changing, and your home should change with you. To meet the test of time, the furniture you choose should fit your family, your way of life, and your tastes. In addition, furniture should fit the space available, be affordable, and last.

When buying furnishings, whether new or used, evaluate them carefully. What characteristics should you look for before making a purchase?

Furniture Buying Checklist

Will the proportion and scale fit the room and other furnishings?

- ✓ Can the piece serve more than one purpose?
- ✓ Does the piece feel sturdy?
- ✓ Do drawers slide smoothly in and out?
- ✓ Are the **furniture joints**, (the points at which any two furniture parts connect) firm and tight?
- ✓ Do knobs and handles all match and are they firmly attached?
- ✓ Does upholstery have straight seams and well-fitted corners? (**Upholstery** refers to materials such as fabric, padding, and springs, that are used on covered sections on furniture.)
- ✓ What kind of upkeep does the furniture need?

Learning Activities (continued)

2. **Display.** Display different types of woods used to make furniture. Point out differences in the woods used for formal and informal furniture styles. (Key Skill: *Science*)
3. **Picture Analysis.** Have students work in groups to locate pictures of different furniture styles. Have them identify the style, the country of origin, tell whether the style is formal or informal, and identify the materials used to make the furniture. (Key Skill: *Cooperation*)
4. **Guest Speaker.** Invite the industrial arts/technology education teacher in to discuss and demonstrate the construction features of well-made furniture. (Key Skill: *Management*)

Follow Up

1. **Reteaching.** Create flash cards of various furniture styles. Have students use the flash cards to practice identifying traditional and contemporary, formal, and informal styles of furniture. (Key Skill: *Communication*)
2. **Enrichment.** Have students visit garage sales, flea markets, and consignment or secondhand shops to locate furniture bargains. Ask students to describe a piece that interests them and tell what could be done to improve the appearance of the piece. (Key Skill: *Problem Solving*)

The World Around You

Secondhand and Unfinished Furniture

Secondhand and unfinished furniture can help a family stretch its furniture budget. When you shop for such pieces, evaluate them just as you would any other furniture. On secondhand pieces, evaluate the time and effort it will take to restore the piece. Developing the skills for repairing, stripping, and refinishing furniture not only saves money, it's also a great way to recycle.

More About Working With Designers

A good designer can often help you get the most value from limited resources — and help you avoid costly mistakes. An interior designer can advise you on decorating treatments, room arrangements, furnishings, and wise use of space. Interior designers may charge an hourly fee, or they may include the cost of their services in the price of the furnishings.

Teaching. . .
Arranging Furniture, Accessories, Storage Areas, and Sharing Space
(pp. 280-282)

Comprehension Check

1. How can you plan successful furniture arrangements? *(Measure the size of the room and draw the outline of the room on graph paper. Mark the size and placement of windows, doors, and other features. On another piece of graph paper, draw the sizes and shape of each piece of furniture, cut them out, then try different arrangements.)*
2. What are traffic lanes? *(Traffic lanes are paths from one area or room to another.)*
3. What accessories can be used to make a room more interesting? *(Lamps, candles, plants, pictures, posters, wallhangings, books, baskets, and vases are just a few possibilities.)*
4. What should you keep in mind when selecting accessories? *(Keep in mind the elements and principles of design.)*
5. What can you do to improve storage space? *(First, organize existing storage space to improve its usefulness. Use boxes, plastic crates and containers, pegboards, and baskets to stretch storage. Make stored items part of your room design. Also see Chapter 26 for ideas.)*
6. What can you do to make sharing space easier? *(Agree on a few ground rules. If you have different needs and schedules, let furniture help solve the problem. Think of sharing space as a plus, not a minus.)*

Learning Activities

1. **Demonstration.** Demonstrate how to measure a room and draw its outline on graph paper. (Use a transparency of graph paper and a transparency pen.) Show how to measure a piece of furniture and make a cutout of it. Demonstrate how to try different furniture arrangements using furniture cutouts. (Key Skills: *Math, Creativity*)

Arranging Furniture

The smart way to arrange furniture is to use paper before muscles. All you need are graph paper and a measuring tape. Measure the size of the room. Use your measurements to draw the outline of the room on graph paper. Make each square represent 6 inches (15 cm) or 1 foot (30.5 cm). Be sure to mark the size and placement of windows, doors, and other features. On another piece of graph paper draw the sizes and shape of each piece of furniture. Cut them out. Then try different arrangements just by moving the paper "furniture."

You can also buy kits that contain precut furniture shapes. The shapes are made of plastic that clings to an outline of your room. The "furniture" is easy to move around.

There are also computer software programs that can help you try out various furniture arrangements. Some are simple, inexpensive programs that function much like the graph paper approach. Others (often called CAD programs for computer-aided design) can give lifelike views of how a finished room will look. Professional designers find these very useful.

Take time to think about your arrangement plan. Ask others for their ideas. Check to see if the **traffic lanes** — paths from one area or room to another — are uncluttered and fairly direct. Don't block them with furniture.

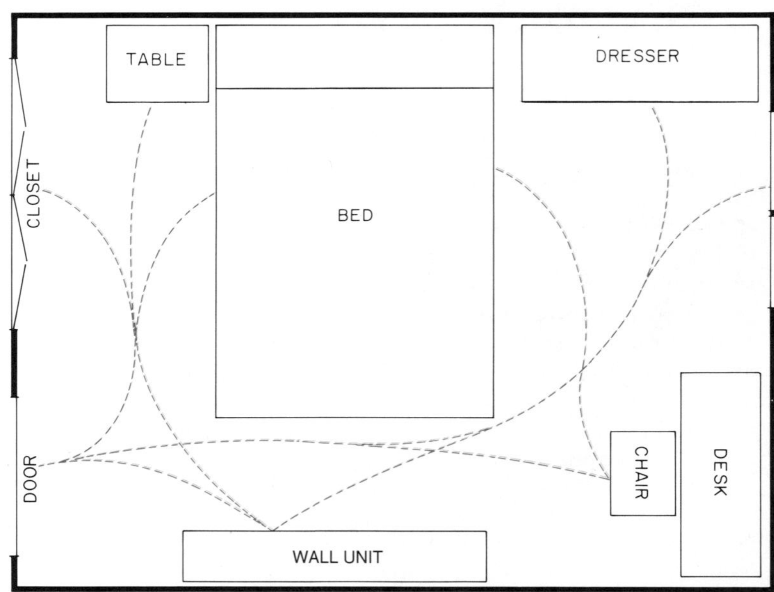

Planning effective traffic lanes makes a room more functional.

More About Furniture Arrangement

There is no such thing as a "perfect" arrangement of furniture in a room. Some arrangements, however, work better than others. To find a satisfactory arrangement for a room, follow the principles listed below.

- Keep the room's purpose in mind when arranging furniture.
- Look at the architectural and mechanical features of the room when arranging furniture. For example, heating and cooling vents should not be covered.
- Create a feeling of balance in the room.
- Consider the size of the room when arranging furniture.

How are accessories used to enhance the appearance of this room?

Accessories

Accessories can make the difference between an uninteresting room and an exciting one. Lamps, plants, posters, books, baskets, and pictures are just a few possibilities. What other low-cost ideas can you add?

When selecting accessories, keep in mind the elements and principles of design. A large lamp, for example, would overwhelm a small delicate table. Remember that a few carefully selected accessories can be far more effective than many less attractive ones.

Storage Areas

No matter how much storage space a family has, there never seems to be enough. A first step is to organize existing storage space to improve its usefulness. If more storage is needed there are many options.

Boxes, plastic crates and containers, pegboards, and baskets are just a few inexpensive storage stretchers.

Not all storage needs to be hidden. Think of ways to make stored items part of your room design. You might, for example, display your baseball cap collection or scarves on a pegboard on the wall. The next chapter gives additional storage tips.

Effective storage allows you to make the best use of space.

Sharing Space

Everyone must share space. It may be at home, at work, in a shopping mall, or even on the beach. In a family, everyone shares areas such as the kitchen and living room. Bathrooms usually are shared, too.

Learning Activities (continued)

2. **Room Arrangement.** Provide students with drawings of a room and paper furniture cutouts. Have students practice arranging furniture using the cutouts. When an arrangement is selected, have students glue the furniture in place and mark the traffic lanes. (Key Skill: *Creativity*)
3. **Display.** Create a display of a variety of home accessories. Include a variety of low-cost suggestions. Refer to the display as you lead a discussion on accessories you might choose for a room. Point out ways the elements and principles of design can aid in selecting accessories. (Key Skill: *Creativity*)
4. **Creating Storage Devices.** Assign each student to design and create an inexpensive storage device for personal use. (Key Skill: *Problem Solving*)
5. **Discussion.** Lead a discussion about activities in which family members engage. Have students identify those that require privacy and those that require shared space. (Key Skill: *Critical Thinking*)

Follow Up

1. **Reteaching.** Have students make a list of home accessories. Ask them to develop pointers for selecting home accessories. (Key Skill: *Communication*)
2. **Extension.** Use the extension information handout on p. 36 of the *Extending the Text* booklet in the TCR.
3. **Enrichment.** Have students design and create a home accessory. Ask students to describe or demonstrate how to make the accessory. Use the accessories to create a display. (Key Skill: *Creativity*)

- Do not overcrowd a room or leave it too stark.
- Place large pieces of furniture parallel to the walls.
- Create groupings of furniture. For example, tables and lamps need to be beside chairs or sofas.
- Consider the room's shape when arranging furniture.

Photo Focus

Discuss the photo on this page with the students. What types of accessories are in their rooms at home? What low-cost accessories could be added to enhance the appearance of these rooms? *(Answers will vary.)*

Completing the Chapter

For Review

1. Emphasize the main concepts using the summary.
2. Have students complete the "Facts to Recall." (Answers below.)

For Reteaching

1. **Reteaching.** Use the activity on p. 32 of the *Reteaching and Practical Skills* booklet in the TCR.

For Enrichment

1. **Enrichment.** Use the activity on pp. 43-44 of the *Enrichment Activities* booklet in the TCR.

For Evaluation

1. Choose items from "Ideas to Explore" and "Activities to Try."
2. Use the chapter test on pp. 53-54 in the testing booklet of the TCR or use the testmaker software.

Facts to Recall Answers

1. It must be both pleasing to the eye and comfortable and convenient for those who use it.
2. Identify needs and wants; evaluate the current room using the elements and principles of design; consider your resources.
3. Walls, windows, and floors.
4. Paint and wallpaper.
5. **Any four:** curtains, drapes, shutters, blinds, shades.
6. Traditional furniture has either simple or elaborate decorations and is made of wood and fabric. Contemporary furniture has little or no decoration and can be made of plastic, glass, and metal as well as wood and fabric.
7. **Any five:** Furniture is high quality if it can serve more than one purpose, if it feels sturdy, if the drawers slide smoothly in and out, if the furniture joints are firm and tight, if the knobs and handles all match and are firmly attached, if the upholstery has straight seams and well-fitted corners, and if it does not need a lot of upkeep.

Which ground rule do you think would be most helpful to these teenage roommates?

Many teens share a bedroom with one or more siblings. If you share a room, you've probably discovered that differences in age, interests, types of friends, and study habits can create problems.

Whenever people share the same space, it helps to agree on a few ground rules. You will enjoy each other more and have fewer conflicts. This also will help keep conflicts at a minimum. Respect and consideration for the other person are the keys. You might, for example, agree not to use each other's books or clothes without permission. Stick to the rules you make.

If you have different needs and schedules, let your furniture arrangement help solve the problem. For example, try separating the sleeping and activity areas of the room. In a shared bedroom divide the room so you each have a private area.

Think of sharing space as a plus, not a minus. Learning how to share space can teach you a lot about yourself and others. The cooperation and communication skills you learn will help you both now and in the future.

TAKING ACTION

Planning Shared Space

In a few months, Guy will have to begin sharing his bedroom with his ten-year-old brother Kirk. The new baby the family is expecting will go in Kirk's room. Guy isn't happy about the idea but knows there's no other choice. Mrs. Thompson has agreed to redecorate the room in order to make both sons as comfortable as possible.

Guy asks you for your ideas. The bedroom is 12 feet (3.7 m) square with one large closet. There are two twin beds, chests of drawers, and desks. Guy also wants to keep a big arm chair and a bookcase. He's concerned about overcrowding the room, and he knows his parents' budget is limited.

Using Your Resourcefulness

- Design a furniture plan that takes into account comfort, privacy, and traffic lanes.
- How can you involve Kirk in this process?
- What are inexpensive ways Guy and Kirk might accessorize the room?
- Where could you turn for more information or help in planning?

TAKING ACTION

Sociologists say it is normal for people to be territorial. In fact, the more territorial people are, the better they seem to get along. In isolation studies done for the U.S. Navy with two people sharing a small room for ten days, the pairs who *did not* make rules early on about who owned what space were unable to stick it out for the full length of the experiment. The pairs who decided on the first day how to divide the space and organize their time were able to remain in isolation to the end.

Using Your Resourcefulness Answers

- Answers will vary.
- Answers will vary. Possibilities include

Chapter 25 Review

Summary

In this chapter, you have read about:

- ▶ A three-step plan for designing or improving your living space.
- ▶ How a room's background elements can be used for the most pleasing effect.
- ▶ Furniture styles from different time periods and parts of the world.
- ▶ How to select and arrange furniture.
- ▶ How accessories can personalize a room.
- ▶ Creative use of space for storage.
- ▶ Tips on sharing space with others.

Facts to Recall

1. What two basic characteristics must a good design have?
2. List the three steps in planning improvements to living space.
3. What parts of a room are considered as the backgrounds for furniture?
4. What are the two most popular types of wall treatments?
5. Identify four types of window treatments.
6. Describe two ways in which traditional furniture differs from contemporary furniture.
7. List five signs of quality in furniture.
8. Explain how to test different furniture arrangements using paper.
9. What are traffic lanes and why are they important?
10. What are the keys to successfully sharing living space with another person?

Ideas to Explore

1. What pieces of furniture can you think of that serve more than one purpose?
2. Identify the accessories in your classroom. Are they functional, decorative, or both? How might you use accessories to make the room more appealing without making it distracting?
3. Develop a list of the ten rules you think would be most important if you shared a bedroom with a brother or sister.

Activities to Try

1. Decide what background materials and colors you would choose to make a cold room seem warmer. What would you choose to make a warm room seem cooler? (Refer to Chapter 24 for ideas.)
2. Examine two pieces of classroom furniture. Discuss both their good and poor construction features.
3. Draw sketches or write descriptions of at least three ways to use items as decorative accessories instead of storing them out of sight.

LINK TO *Social Studies*

FURNITURE STYLES AND HISTORY

At the library, research three traditional furniture styles. Furniture styles that you might choose to research include Colonial, William and Mary, Queen Anne, Chippendale, Federal, Shaker, or Victorian. Use the following questions to guide your research:

- ▶ Describe the unique design features of each style of furniture.
- ▶ What historical factors influenced each furniture style? Include the needs of people, era of time, tools available, etc.
- ▶ How did other cultures influence traditional furniture styles in America?

Facts to Recall Answers (continued)

8. Measure the room and draw its outline on graph paper. On another sheet of graph paper, draw the shapes and sizes of the furniture in proportion to the room outline. Cut out the furniture drawings and place them in different arrangements on the room outline.
9. Traffic lanes are paths from one area or room to another. They are important to a room's appearance and they need to be convenient, so they should be uncluttered and fairly direct.
10. Respect and consideration for the other person.

Ideas to Explore

1. Answers will vary.
2. Answers will vary.
3. Answers will vary.

asking Kirk what he wants in the room and letting him help decide where things will go in the room.

- Answers will vary. Possibilities include posters, pictures, and lamps.
- Answers will vary. Possibilities include magazines and books on home design.

LINK TO *Social Studies*

Answers

- Answers will vary.
- Answers will vary.
- Answers will vary. (Most students will find that furniture styles in France and England influenced traditional styles in America.)

Preparing to Teach

Chapter Outline

Chapter Resources

The following booklet materials may be found in the *Teacher's Classroom Resources* box:

- Lesson Plans, p. 31
- Student Workbook, *Study Guide,* pp. 113-114; *Safe at Home?,* pp. 115-116
- Personal Safety, *Be Prepared for Disaster,* pp. 28-29; *Preventing Fires,* pp. 30-31
- Technology and Computers, pp. 30, 31, 32, 33
- Cooperative Learning, p. 38
- Extending the Text, *Staying Safe From Fire,* pp. 37-38
- Reteaching and Practical Skills, *Organize Your Cleaning Schedule,* p. 34
- Enrichment Activities, *Cleaning Products: Are They Safe for the Environment?,* pp. 42-43
- Chapter and Unit Tests, pp. 55-56; pp. 118-120
- Testmaker Software

Also see:

- Meeting the Special Needs of Students
- Linking Home, School, and Community

CHAPTER

26 Keeping Your Home Clean and Safe

OBJECTIVES

- *Develop a maintenance plan for your home.*
- *Identify important home sanitation, safety, and security practices.*
- *Identify repairs best left to professionals.*

TERMS TO LEARN

- ***maintenance***
- ***sanitation***
- ***hazard***

More About
Starting a Cleaning Service

A cleaning service is easy to start when compared to many types of businesses. Only basic cleaning tools and supplies are necessary. Jobs may be obtained through word of mouth or by advertising in the local newspaper. The business may focus on cleaning homes or

It's not just people, pets, and plants that need regular care. Your home also needs care to keep it running smoothly. You and your family will find life much easier if you work together to keep your living space clean, safe, and organized.

Keeping belongings put away, disposing of garbage, and cleaning your home regularly are necessary for your family's comfort, health, and safety. Also important are caring for equipment and repairing or replacing broken or worn-out items.

Getting Organized

The first step in organizing for home maintenance is to develop a plan of work. Home **maintenance** includes cleaning, making repairs, and checking appliances and equipment regularly. A good maintenance plan can catch small problems before they become large expensive ones.

To develop a maintenance plan, list the jobs for each room or area of your home. Decide how often each should be done — daily, weekly, or occasionally. Then consider how much time each job will take and the order in which it needs to be done. The last step is deciding who will be responsible for each job. Even small children can be given simple tasks. Many families rotate job assignments.

When family members work together to keep a home clean and safe, the results are rewarding. How can families benefit by working together?

Introducing the Chapter

Motivators

1. **Brainstorming.** Lead students in brainstorming a list of household tasks. Write the list on the chalkboard and have students classify them as "daily," "weekly," "monthly," or "seasonal" tasks. Next, ask students to name reasons why home maintenance is important. Conclude by stating that a major reason for home maintenance is to save money in the long run for items and activities the family enjoys. (Key Skills: *Communication, Critical Thinking*)
2. **Discussion.** Ask students to share information about home accidents they or members of their family have experienced. Discuss common causes of home accidents. (Key Skill: *Communication*)

Chapter Objectives and Vocabulary

1. Have students read the chapter objectives and rephrase the objectives as questions.
2. Ask students to state, in their own words, the purpose of studying this chapter.
3. Pronounce the vocabulary terms listed on the previous page. Ask students whether they are familiar with any of these. Explain that the terms will be defined in the chapter.

Guided Reading

1. Have students read the chapter and use the Study Guide on pp. 113-114 of the *Student Workbook*.

Making a Difference

As students study this chapter, encourage them to think of ways they can assist poor, handicapped, or elderly people in their community in keeping their homes clean and safe. Community volunteers often provide their services to do housecleaning, lawn mowing, tree trimming, painting, and home repairs for needy families. Local businesses may provide the materials and supplies needed.

offices or both. Services may be provided part-time or become a full-time career. If you are interested, read everything you can find about small businesses and learn all you can about cleaning companies in your area. Poll relatives and friends to learn what they want in a cleaning service. Talk to people who use a cleaning service regularly to find out what improvements they would suggest. Print up flyers to post on community bulletin boards and to give to potential customers and you are in business.

Teaching. . .

Getting Organized and Daily, Regular, and Occasional Tasks

(pp. 285-287)

Comprehension Check

1. What is home maintenance? *(Home maintenance includes cleaning, making repairs, and checking appliances and equipment regularly.)*
2. What are some steps for organizing home maintenance? *(List the jobs for each room or area of your home and decide how often each should be done — daily, weekly, or occasionally. Then consider how much time each job will take and the order in which it needs to be done. Finally, decide who will be responsible for each job.)*
3. What are some home maintenance tasks that are usually done daily? *(Daily home maintenance tasks often include washing dishes, disposing of garbage, wiping up food spills as they occur, and putting away clothes and other belongings.)*
4. Why do kitchens and bathrooms need frequent and careful cleaning? *(Kitchens and bathrooms need frequent and careful cleaning to keep germs under control.)*
5. What are some occasional or seasonal maintenance tasks? *(Occasional tasks include cleaning the refrigerator, washing walls and windows, and cleaning out closets. Outdoor tasks may include raking leaves or cutting grass.)*

Learning Activities

1. **Brainstorming.** Have students brainstorm a list of home maintenance tasks. Have students divide the list into categories based on how often the task should be done — daily, weekly, or occasionally. (Key Skill: *Critical Thinking*)
2. **Discussion.** Discuss how much time various home maintenance jobs take, the order in which tasks should be done, and who might be responsible for each job. What are the advantages and disadvantages of rotating job responsibilities? (Key Skill: *Critical Thinking*)

THE VALDEZ FAMILY'S MAINTENANCE PLAN

	Task	MOM	DAD	HOLLY (15)	CALVIN (13)	BECKY (10)	ANDY (4)
DAILY	Make your bed. Put away clean clothes and place dirty clothes in the laundry.	■	■	■	■	■	■
	Wash and rinse dishes. Take out the garbage.				■		
	Dry and put away dishes. Sweep kitchen floor.			■			
	Clean table, countertops, and appliances.					■	
WEEKLY	Dust your room. Straighten closets and drawers.	■	■	■	■	■	■
	Vacuum carpeting.		■				
	Mop hard floors. Clean oven. Change linens.	■					
	Clean all bathtubs, showers, sinks, toilets, and mirrors.			■		■	
	Dust all the furniture in living, dining, and family rooms.				■		■
MONTHLY	Clean refrigerator. Dust upholstery and the draperies.	■					
	Clean medicine cabinets and lampshades. Check for burned out light bulbs and replace them.					■	
	Conduct fire drill.				■		
	Polish furniture in living, dining, and family rooms.				■		■
	Clean all throw rugs. Dust walls and ceilings for cobwebs.			■			
	Check smoke detectors and fire extinguishers. Change filters in heating/cooling system. Turn all bed mattresses.		■				
SEASONALLY	Clean basement, garage, and/or attic.	■	■	■	■	■	■
	Clean all woodwork (i.e. baseboards, doors, windowsills).				■		■
	Wash windows and screens.			■		■	
	Shampoo carpeting.		■				
	Air blankets and pillows. Clean out kitchen cabinets and hall closets.	■					

More About *Cleaning Tools*

To clean your home efficiently, you must have the proper tools and supplies. Here is a list of basic house-cleaning tools and supplies: a vacuum cleaner (upright or canister); a small, hand-held vacuum for light cleaning and spills; brooms (soft bristles for use indoors and hard bristles for use outdoors); a dustpan; brushes (soft for dusting and hard for scrubbing); a dust mop; a mop and mop bucket; sponges; dust cloths or a duster; cleaning solutions; polishes; and a stepladder.

3. **Debate.** Have students debate the topic, "Everyone in a family should agree on an acceptable standard of cleanliness." (Key Skill: *Problem Solving*)

Follow Up

1. **Reteaching.** Assist students in making a list of individual and family household chores to be done daily, weekly, and occasionally. (Key Skill: *Decision Making*)
2. **Enrichment.** Have each student interview an elderly person about ways household tasks were done when he or she was a teenager. Ask students to share their interviews with the class. (Key Skills: *Social Studies, Communication*)

Some maintenance tasks, such as cleaning the refrigerator, need only be done occasionally. What other tasks can you think of that need to be done seasonally or occasionally?

▼ Daily, Regular, and Occasional Tasks ▼

Look around, and you can see that people have different standards of cleanliness. For example, Kim's family likes to keep their home spotless, with everything in its place at all times. On the other hand, Eric's parents don't mind a certain amount of clutter. Although there is no right or wrong, you and your family need to agree on an acceptable standard of tidiness. This may take some compromise on everyone's part.

Many families consider these to be daily tasks:

- Washing dishes.
- Disposing of garbage.
- Wiping up food spills as they occur.
- Putting away clothes and other belongings.

When everyone is willing to help, these chores can be finished more quickly.

Each family decides how often other cleaning tasks must be done. Many schedule a general cleaning of their living space once a week. Others may do these tasks more or less often. The kitchen and bathroom need frequent and careful cleaning to keep germs under control.

Your list of maintenance tasks will also include some to be performed occasionally or seasonally. Occasional tasks include cleaning the refrigerator, washing walls and windows, and cleaning out closets. Check the instruction books that come with furnishings and equipment for proper maintenance. Add those tasks to your list. Many families also need to list outdoor tasks such as raking leaves or cutting grass.

More About Easy-to-Maintain Furnishings

Housecleaning can be made easier by selecting easy-to-clean furnishings. Many furnishings on the market today have stain-resistant finishes and are washable, colorfast, and durable. Their labels should provide information about these features. The furniture store may apply special stain-resistant finishes to the upholstered furniture purchases for an additional fee.

The World Around You

Household Cleaners and the Environment

Many household cleaners contain chemicals that may be threats to your health and to the environment if handled improperly. Before buying household chemicals, investigate less dangerous choices. Dispose of leftover household cleaners properly. Dumping chemicals into sinks or toilets can damage sewage treatment plants. Those thrown into the trash can injure refuse collectors and landfill tractor operators. These chemicals can also pollute water supplies, air, and soil. Before disposing of the containers, make certain they are empty. If you have questions about their disposal, call local public health or sanitation officials for advice.

Teaching...

Storage, Cleaning Products and Equipment, and Keeping Your Home Clean and Healthy

(pp. 288-289)

Comprehension Check

1. What two basic rules should be followed when organizing storage space? *(Store items near where they are used, and store items where they can be reached easily.)*
2. What points should you consider when choosing and using household cleaning products? *(Products come in a wide variety, although many of them do the same job; read labels carefully before selecting one; whenever possible, avoid dangerous products; read warning labels and follow product directions exactly.)*
3. What are some basic cleaning products that are both inexpensive and kind to the environment? *(Baking soda can be used for cleaning and to remove odors. Products that clean more than one type of surface often are a good buy.)*
4. What equipment do you need for cleaning? *(You need brooms, mops, buckets, brushes, sponges, dusting cloths, and vacuum cleaners.)*
5. What is sanitation? *(Sanitation includes cleaning, removing dust and dirt, disposing of garbage, and controlling pests.)*
6. How should you work when you dust? *(As you are dusting, work from the top to the bottom.)*
7. In what order should you work when you clean a room? *(Clean your way around the outside edges of a room, then clean the center, and finish with the floors.)*

Learning Activities

1. **Demonstration.** Demonstrate how to determine where items can be most easily reached. Point out that items that are stored near the floor, on a high shelf, or behind other items require extra effort to reach. (Key Skill: *Science*)

How can well-organized storage space make home maintenance easier and safer?

▼ Storage ▼

Clothes, toys, towels, dishes, cleaning supplies, and tools are found in every home. Where do they belong? Each room needs space for storing items that normally are used there. Having organized storage space available encourages family members to put things away after each use.

Two basic rules to follow when organizing storage space are:

- Store items near the area they are used.
- Store frequently used items where they can be reached easily.

Storage that is easy to use is especially important in kitchens, bathrooms, and children's rooms. One of the best ways to save time cleaning is to keep items picked up as you go along.

How does clutter affect family safety?

▼ Cleaning Products and Equipment ▼

Part of getting organized for cleaning your living space involves selecting appropriate products and equipment. Household cleaning products come in such a wide variety that you may find it hard to choose among them. Many products serve the same function, so read labels carefully before selecting the one you need. Whenever possible avoid dangerous products. Warning labels on the container mean a product requires special caution. Always follow product directions exactly.

More About Cleaning Products

Many common household cleaning products can be poisonous. Keep all cleaning products in their original containers. Keep all containers securely closed. Store household cleaners and other chemicals in a locked cabinet out of children's reach. Before you use any cleaning product, read the label for directions and warnings. Follow the directions carefully. *Never* mix two or more cleaning products together, such as bleaches, chlorine, ammonia, toilet bowl cleaners, rust removers, or oven cleaners. Do not even mix different brands of the same kind of product. Chemicals in mixtures may interact and explode or release poisonous gases. Use spray products only in well-ventilated areas. Be sure the spray nozzle is

Many basic cleaning products are both inexpensive and kind to the environment. Baking soda, for example, makes a good, gentle cleansing powder for sinks, refrigerators, and microwave ovens. It can also be used to remove odors. Products that clean more than one type of surface often are a good buy. However, remember that no matter what advertisements say, cleaning products cannot work without your help. You'll have to do some wiping or scrubbing to loosen dirt and grime. Fortunately, a thin layer of dust and dirt is easy to remove. Only when the dirt piles up do you need to spend extra time and energy on cleaning.

Using the proper equipment also makes cleaning easier. Brooms, mops, buckets, brushes, sponges, dusting cloths, and vacuum cleaners are the major pieces of cleaning equipment needed for home maintenance.

Using the proper equipment makes cleaning easier. What equipment do you find most useful in cleaning your home?

Keeping Your Home Clean and Healthy

Keeping your home neat and organized makes it a pleasant place to live. Proper care makes furnishings and equipment last longer. Actual cleaning is even more important. By removing dust and dirt, disposing of garbage, and controlling pests, you keep your home a healthy place to live. These tasks are sometimes called **sanitation**. Dirt and bacteria can lead to illness.

- ***Dust and dirt.*** To remove dust and dirt, you need to sweep, dust, vacuum, wash, and mop. Sweeping with a broom removes dirt from hard floors. Brooms also can be used for seasonal jobs such as cleaning window screens and dusting cobwebs from walls and ceilings.

  Use a clean cloth or a duster to wipe window sills and baseboards. Then dust all furnishings except upholstered pieces. Don't forget areas such as chair legs and lamp shades. Wood furniture needs occasional polishing to keep it in good condition.

  For cleaning jobs, it helps to know that certain tasks will just naturally come first. For example, as you are dusting work from the top to the bottom. That way dust doesn't fall on areas you have already dusted. It also helps to clean your way around the outside edges of a room. Then clean the center and finish with the floors. This way you won't forget any areas.

Learning Activities (continued)

2. **Label Reading.** Have students read the labels on various cleaning products. What uses does each product have? Do warning labels identify special cautions for using the products? What are the directions for using each product? Are the products hazardous to the environment? (Key Skill: *Science*)
3. **Brainstorming.** Have students brainstorm a list of housekeeping tasks they enjoy. Have them develop a similar list of housekeeping jobs they dislike. Discuss the reasons why some jobs are disliked and others are not. Conclude with a discussion of ways to deal with negative feelings when doing tasks that are important to the family's happiness, health, or safety. (Key Skill: *Critical Thinking*)
4. **Demonstration.** Select housekeeping tasks that students need to learn or improve upon. Demonstrate quick and efficient methods for each task. (Key Skill: *Management*)

Follow Up

1. **Reteaching.** Have students demonstrate the use of various cleaning products and tools. (Key Skill: *Management*)
2. **Enrichment.** Have students develop a household maintenance handbook. The handbook should identify household maintenance tasks, how often they should be performed, household maintenance equipment and supplies, and procedures for controlling dust and dirt, garbage, and pests. (Key Skill: *Communication*)

pointed away from your face and away from another person.

Teaching. . .
Keeping Your Home Safe, Falls, and Electrical Hazards
(pp. 290-291)

Comprehension Check

1. Why must vacuum cleaner bags and containers be removed or cleaned frequently? *(Vacuum bags and containers must be removed or cleaned frequently for the machine to operate properly.)*
2. Why should garbage be disposed of daily? *(Garbage not only looks bad, but it also can endanger your family's health. Garbage contains thousands of germs and gives off an unpleasant odor.)*
3. How can you keep pests under control? *(By keeping your housing clean, you can usually keep pests under control. If you use pest control products, read and follow the directions carefully. If a pest problem becomes severe, call a professional pest control service.)*
4. What is a hazard? *(A hazard is a source of danger.)*
5. How can falls be avoided? *(Avoid falls by wiping up spills promptly, securing throw rugs to the floor, using a ladder or stepstool to reach items in a high place, storing items properly, and using adequate lighting.)*
6. How can you avoid electrical hazards? *(You can avoid electrical hazards by not plugging too many cords into an outlet, not using electrical appliances near water, not running electrical cords underneath rugs or carpeting, not leaving outlets that small children can reach uncovered, and keeping appliances in good working order.)*

SAFETY CHECK✓

Have students read the safety check. Then, have them check at home to see if cleaning products are stored properly. If not, have them discuss this problem with their parents.

Regular vacuum cleaning removes dust and dirt from carpets, hard floors, upholstered furniture, and draperies. How often should vacuuming be performed?

SAFETY CHECK✓

Though you may not have thought about it, cleaning itself can be dangerous. Here are some guidelines to keep you safe and your home clean:

- Follow the directions on cleaning products exactly. Never mix products. The results could be poisonous, explosive, or fatal.
- Keep cleaning products in their original container. That way you will always know what they are and how they should be used.
- Never store cleaning products near food.
- Store cleaning products in a locked cabinet, out of the reach of small children.
- Some cleaners give off powerful fumes. Use a fan and open windows to bring in fresh air.
- Use a sturdy stepladder, not a chair, to reach items stored in high places.
- Be sure the braces on the ladder are fully extended. Never climb all the way to the top step. Follow the ladder manufacturer's directions carefully.

A vacuum cleaner can remove dust and dirt from carpeting, hard floors, upholstered furniture, and draperies. Through suction, it draws soil into the machine where it is trapped inside a bag or container. Vacuum bags and containers must be removed or cleaned frequently for the machine to operate properly.

Washable hard floors need regular washing to remove stubborn dirt. Use a mop, water, and a cleaner safe for the type of floor you have. Mopping generally is done weekly.

- ***Garbage.*** To be sanitary, you should dispose of garbage daily. It's a good habit to empty all the wastebaskets into a central container at the end of each day. Garbage not only looks bad, but also can endanger your family's health. Garbage contains thousands of germs and gives off an unpleasant odor.

  Leftover food on dishes in the kitchen sink is a form of garbage. Make sure food scraps are disposed of properly. Dishes should be washed after meals in hot, sudsy water to remove germs.
- ***Pests.*** Roaches, ants, mice, flies, and termites are all types of household pests. They carry germs that can make you and your family sick. Pests love dust, dirt, and garbage. By keeping your housing clean, you can usually keep pests under control. If you use pest control products, read and follow the directions carefully. If a pest problem becomes severe, call a professional pest control service.

Keeping Your Home Safe

A clean and well-maintained home usually is safe and secure. In fact, maintenance plays a big role in the safety and security of your home. On the other hand, when maintenance jobs are neglected, accidents and even illnesses can

More About Using a Ladder for Home Maintenance

Make sure the ladder you are using is sturdy. Be sure that the connections will not allow the ladder to slip when extended. Remember that a stepladder is firmly footed only when the spreader is fully opened and locked. Never stand above the second step from the top. Face the ladder as you climb and do not lean too far to either side while working.

occur. For example, toys on the floor can cause someone to fall. Electrical equipment that isn't used properly can become an electrical **hazard** (HAS-urd), or source of danger. Open garbage can lead to fires or illness. An open, improperly stored cleaning product could be poisonous if swallowed.

How might this fall have been avoided?

▼ Falls ▼

Good home maintenance cannot guarantee your family's safety. However, it can prevent unnecessary risks. For instance, many falls can be avoided by:

- ▶ Wiping up spills promptly.
- ▶ Securing throw rugs to the floor.
- ▶ Using a ladder or stepstool to reach items in high places.
- ▶ Storing items properly.
- ▶ Using adequate lighting.

▼ Electrical Hazards ▼

It's easy to forget the dangers of electricity. Electricity is powerful and should be treated with respect. To avoid electrical hazards:

- ▶ Never plug too many cords into an outlet.
- ▶ Never use electrical appliances near water.
- ▶ Never run electrical cords underneath rugs or carpeting.
- ▶ Never leave outlets that small children can reach uncovered.

Electrical hazards can also be avoided by keeping appliances in good working order. Items that are broken or don't work properly can be a safety hazard, and should be unplugged immediately, then repaired or replaced. Check appliances regularly.

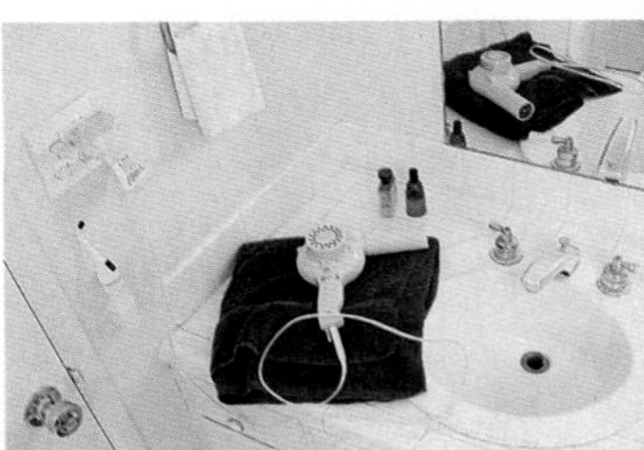

Never use electrical appliances near water. The risk of electrical shock greatly increases.

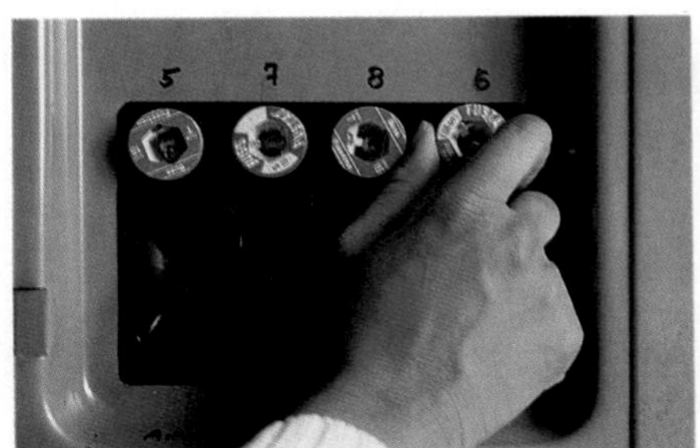

When circuits are overloaded, fuses melt and circuit breakers turn off to prevent damage to the electrical wiring in your home. Be sure to replace fuses with the correct sizes for your system. If you have a circuit breaker box, simply unplug appliances on the overloaded circuit and turn the breaker back on.

Learning Activities

1. **Guest Speaker.** Invite a pest control expert to discuss the importance of controlling household pests. Ask the speaker to identify ways to keep pests under control, how to use pest control products, and when to call a professional pest control service. (Key Skill: *Science*)
2. **Newspaper Clippings.** Have students clip newspaper articles on home accidents. What are some common causes of home accidents? (Key Skill: *Communication*)
3. **Brainstorming.** Have students brainstorm ways to avoid falls. Why does the risk of falls increase with age? What can young people do to help older family members avoid the risk of falling? (Key Skill: *Citizenship*)

Follow Up

1. **Reteaching.** Have students create posters on home safety and repair. Display the posters in the classroom. (Key Skill: *Communication*)
2. **Enrichment.** Have students interview their parents or teachers to identify the biggest problems in home management. Direct each student to write up the interview as a feature story for a newspaper or magazine. (Key Skill: *Communication*)

Family Perspective

Safety awareness is especially important when there are children or older family members in the home. Keeping children safe requires constant alertness. Have students identify ways to keep children safe in the home. Older people may not see as well or have as much energy and strength as they used to. Some have health problems and physical impairments. These changes make it easier for accidents to occur. Have students identify ways to help older family members avoid falls, burns, and other accidents.

Teaching. . .

Fires, Poisons, Keeping Your Home Secure, Making Repairs, and Keeping a Positive Attitude

(pp. 292-294)

Comprehension Check

1. What are the most common causes of fires? *(Matches, cigarettes, candles, grease, and electrical appliances are the most common causes of fires.)*
2. How can you and your family prepare for a possible fire in your home? *(Every home should have fire extinguishers and smoke alarms. Include a monthly fire drill, along with a smoke detector test, in your home maintenance plan.)*
3. Name some poisons found in the home. *(Soaps, bleach, shampoos, aspirin, paint, prescription drugs, most cleaning products, and even some house plants can be deadly.)*
4. What is the most basic need in keeping a home secure? *(The most basic need in home security is strong doors with good locks.)*
5. When should an expert be hired to make repairs? *(Always hire a licensed electrician to do wiring, a qualified heating technician to repair the furnace, and a licensed plumber to do major plumbing repairs.)*
6. What are some benefits of a well-maintained home? *(Instead of having to replace items that are neglected, the family can spend its resources on items and activities that everyone will enjoy. A well-maintained home is also better for the environment.)*

Around the World

After reading the feature, have students investigate other cultures to see if they have certain beliefs that influence how a house is constructed. *(Answers will vary.)*

Around the World

For many Chinese and Chinese-American people, a home is not hazard-free unless it possesses feng shui (feng-shway). This ancient Asian belief stresses the importance of harmony between people and their surroundings, both natural and manmade. For example, a house with feng shui will not have the front and back door in a straight line with each other. It is believed that this could result in poor health or financial trouble. Some home builders in areas with large Chinese-American populations consider feng shui when building houses.

How does testing all smoke detectors once per month help keep your family safe?

Fires

Matches, cigarettes, candles, grease, and electrical appliances are the most common causes of fires. Garbage cans, mattresses, and upholstered furniture are ideal places for a fire to start. Keep matches out of children's reach. Store flammable products away from all heat sources.

Every home should have fire extinguishers. Keep a chemical extinguisher near the kitchen range for grease and electrical fires. Be sure you know how to use it.

Smoke detectors can provide early warning in case of fire and smoke. Make sure your home has smoke detectors near bedroom areas and on each floor. Check all detectors once a month to see that they are functioning properly.

Saving your home isn't as important as saving your life. It is a good idea to include a monthly fire drill, along with a smoke detector test, in your home maintenance plan. You and your family need to know how to escape from every room. If you live in a building with an elevator, always use stairs instead if there is a fire. Plan for the family to meet in a specific place outside if there's a fire. That way, you will know everyone is safe.

Poisons

Poisons exist in nearly every room of your home. Soaps, bleach, shampoos, aspirin, paint, prescription drugs, most cleaning products, and even some house plants can be deadly. Small children are usually the victims of accidental poisoning. Therefore, poisonous products need to be stored out of children's reach in a locked cabinet. Never tell children that medicine is candy. Also, remove poisonous house plants if there are young children or pets in the home.

More About Fires

A fire goes through four stages. In the first stage, the fire smolders. Invisible toxic (poisonous) gases may be produced even though there is no flame, smoke, or noticeable heat. A fire may smolder for hours. In the second stage, some smoke and more toxic gases are produced. In the third stage, the flame begins to spread, but there is little heat. Finally, in the fourth stage, there is high, uncontrolled heat. In this stage, toxic gases expand rapidly. Three-quarters of the people who die in house fires die upstairs from fires that start downstairs. The majority of these people do not die from burns. Rather, they are asphyxiated in their sleep by the toxic gases produced during the early stages of the fire.

If someone swallows something poisonous, act quickly. Call your community's Poison Control Center or a hospital emergency room. Be ready to say what was swallowed and how much. You will also need to know the approximate age and weight of the victim. Carefully listen to the professionals' instructions, and follow them immediately. Quick action can save a life.

Keeping Your Home Secure

Everyone wants to feel safe and secure at home. That means keeping both your family and your belongings safe from harm.

In a home, strong doors with good locks are the most basic need. Deadbolt locks are the best choice. When you turn the key (from inside or outside the door), a strong metal bar slides into the door frame. Some other types of locks can easily be opened by someone trying to break in. Windows and sliding glass doors also need locks. Check with a lock shop for advice on the best types to use.

Make sure the area around outside doors is well lighted. This will help you get in and out of your home safely. One type turns the light on automatically whenever motion is detected. This provides safety yet saves energy. Experts also advise eliminating large bushes near entrances where intruders may hide.

Many other security devices are available. Some, like home alarm systems, are expensive. Others, such as forming a neighborhood watch system, are free. People in the neighborhood simply make it a point to look out for each other and report any suspicious activity. You must also watch out for your own personal safety. As you come and go from your home, especially at night, stay alert. Make it a point to avoid dangerous places.

Making Repairs

You and your family can do some repairs yourselves. For example, you should know what to do if the toilet overflows, the kitchen sink becomes clogged, or a fuse blows. You should know how to handle a hammer, screwdriver, wrench, caulking gun, and paintbrush. However, leave difficult repairs

Common household products can be very poisonous. Where do you store poisonous products for safety?

Simple household repairs, such as repairing bathroom caulking, can help save a family money. What types of simple repairs might you learn to help with?

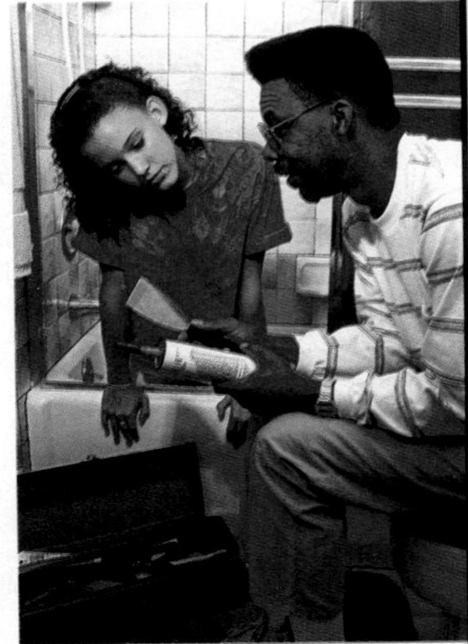

Learning Activities

1. **Guest Speaker.** Invite a fire fighter in to discuss home fires with the class. Ask the fire fighter to identify common causes of home fires and ways to avoid them. Have the fire fighter display and demonstrate the use of fire extinguishers and smoke detectors. Discuss procedures to follow in case a fire does occur. Why should a monthly fire drill be part of a home maintenance plan? (Key Skill: *Management*)
2. **Demonstration.** Demonstrate proper ways to store poisonous products. (Key Skill: *Management*)
3. **Display.** Create a display of basic tools for making household repairs. Discuss uses for each tool. (Key Skill: *Problem Solving*)
4. **Demonstration.** Invite the industrial arts/technology education teacher in to demonstrate procedures for making basic household repairs. (Key *Skill: Management*)
5. **Discussion.** Discuss the benefits of a well-maintained home. What are the benefits to the community? What are the benefits to the environment? (Key Skill: *Citizenship*)

Follow Up

1. **Reteaching.** Have students make a list of the poisonous items that are stored in their homes. Then, have them list what kind of warning label is on each poisonous item. (Key Skill: *Science*)
2. **Extension.** Use the extension information handout on pp. 37-38 of the *Extending the Text* booklet in the TCR.

Photo Focus

Discuss the photo at the bottom of page 293 with the students. Ask the students what types of home repairs are done by their parents and what types are done by professionals. Do their parents try to do some home repairs that they shouldn't? *(Answers will vary.)*

Completing the Chapter

For Review

1. Emphasize the main concepts using the summary.
2. Have students complete the "Facts to Recall." (Answers below.)

For Reteaching

1. **Reteaching.** Use the activity on p. 33 of the *Reteaching and Practical Skills* booklet in the TCR.

For Enrichment

1. **Enrichment.** Use the activity on pp. 45-46 of the *Enrichment Activities* booklet in the TCR.

For Evaluation

1. Choose items from "Ideas to Explore" and "Activities to Try."
2. Use the chapter test on pp. 55-56 in the testing booklet of the TCR or use the testmaker software.

Facts to Recall Answers

1. List the jobs for each room or area; put down how often they should be done; consider how much time each job will need and the order in which they should be done; decide who will be responsible for each job.
2. Store items where they are used; store them where they can be reached.
3. Choices will vary and may include **any five:** brooms; mops; buckets; brushes; sponges; dusting cloths; vacuum cleaners. Reasons may include: they are useful for many jobs; they do a few essential jobs very well.
4. Clean from top to bottom and from the outside edges toward the center.
5. They carry germs that can make you and your family sick.
6. A hazard is a source of danger. **Any three:** toys on the floor; improperly used electrical equipment; open garbage; an open, improperly stored, cleaning product.

A well-maintained home is good for the environment. How is this family helping to take care of the environment?

to the experts. Hire a licensed electrician to do wiring, a qualified heating technician to repair the furnace, and a licensed plumber to do major plumbing repairs.

In many communities, low-cost classes are available to teach repair skills. Learning these skills can save your family money.

Keeping a Positive Attitude

Attitude plays a major role in the level of maintenance within your home. If all members do their share, the family's maintenance plan will save a lot of time, money, and energy. Instead of having to replace items that are neglected, the family can spend its resources on items and activities that everyone will enjoy.

A well-maintained home is also better for the environment. The more regular cleaning and repairing you do, the less often you will need harsh chemical cleaners or poisonous substances that could pollute the air or water. When you take good care of your *own* environment, you are actually helping everyone else's.

TAKING ACTION

Devising a Work Plan

Your friend Kelly offers you a part-time job helping her clean Mrs. Ellinger's house twice a week. You need extra money and agree to give her a hand. Mrs. Ellinger is Kelly's 75-year-old neighbor who often bakes cookies for the two of you. While she's very kind, she is not very neat. Mrs. Ellinger is the first to admit her small house — with one bedroom, bathroom, living and dining area, and kitchen — often looks like it was "struck by a tornado."

To complicate things, Kelly isn't the most organized person you know. She has asked you to think of a fair way to split the cleaning and chores.

Using Your Resourcefulness

- Devise a general maintenance plan for Mrs. Ellinger's house, broken down into daily, weekly, and monthly chores.
- How will you and Kelly divide the chores? Will you repeat the same chores or rotate them?
- What are four ways to insure the house is sanitary and healthy?

TAKING ACTION

Discuss with students the steps in problem solving. Ask them to identify the problem. Then have them identify possible solutions to the problem. Discuss advantages and disadvantages of each alternative. Ask students to decide which alternative is best and have them support their choice. Have students assume that the alternative chosen is tried. Ask students what questions they would ask to evaluate the effectiveness of the choice.

Using Your Resourcefulness Answers

- Answers will vary. See the chart on page 286 of this text for a possible home maintenance plan that they could follow.

Chapter 26 Review

Summary

In this chapter, you have read about:

- Organizing your family's home maintenance plan, according to when tasks are done and who does them.
- Basic cleaning products and equipment and their use.
- Cleaning tasks and maintenance habits that help keep your home safe and attractive.
- Important safety practices to follow.

Facts to Recall

1. List four steps in organizing a home maintenance plan.
2. What are two basic rules to follow when organizing storage space?
3. Which five major pieces of cleaning equipment would you consider most important? Explain your choices.
4. When cleaning a room or area, in what order should the jobs be done?
5. How can garbage and pests endanger your family's health?
6. What is a hazard? Give three examples.
7. Name three ways falls can be avoided.
8. What two types of equipment should every home have to prevent the spread of fire?
9. Name three ways to prevent the accidental poisoning of children.
10. Name three household repairs that you and your family can do yourselves. Name three types of repairs that should be handled by qualified professionals.

Ideas to Explore

1. Which five qualities do you think are most important for a clean and safe environment?
2. At what age should children become involved in home maintenance and cleaning? What tasks might be appropriate for a three-year-old? For an eight-year-old?

Activities to Try

1. You are having a problem keeping your room neat. You know that one reason is lack of closet and drawer space. Devise at least three ways to improve storage using free or inexpensive materials.
2. Identify three cleaning or maintenance tasks you dislike doing. Come up with a plan for making each easier or more enjoyable.

LINK TO *Health and Safety*

PLANNING AN ESCAPE ROUTE

Having a plan of escape from your home in case of fire, can be the key to saving your life and the lives of your family members. Use the following guidelines to develop a fire escape plan for you and your family:

- Draw a floor plan of your home. Be sure to indicate the location of all windows and doors.
- On the floor plan, mark the location of smoke detectors.
- Draw two escape routes from your home. Include one escape route from the bedrooms and another from some other area of the home such as a basement or family room. If there is more than one floor in your home, plan a way to escape from additional floors, too.

After you have finished your plan, discuss it with your family. Some authorities suggest having a monthly fire drill to make sure all family members understand how to get out of the home safely.

Facts to Recall Answers (continued)

7. **Any three:** wiping up spills promptly; securing throw rugs to the floor; using a ladder or stepstool to reach items in high places; storing items properly; using adequate lighting.
8. Every home should have fire extinguishers and smoke detectors to prevent the spread of fire.
9. Store poisonous products out of children's reach in a locked cabinet; never tell children that medicine is candy; make sure they do not put plants, leaves, or berries in their mouths.
10. You can safely stop an overflowing toilet, unclog a sink, and change a blown fuse. You should leave wiring jobs, furnace repairs, and major plumbing work to licensed professionals.

Ideas to Explore

1. Answers will vary.
2. Answers will vary and may include: a three-year-old child could pick up his or her toys and help clear the table of nonbreakable utensils; an eight-year-old child could make the bed, take out the garbage, and dry and put away nonbreakable dishes.

- Answers will vary.
- Answers will vary. Possible answers include dusting the furniture regularly, vacuuming regularly, sweeping and mopping floors regularly, disposing of garbage daily, and keeping pests under control.

LINK TO *Health and Safety*

Answers

Students' floor plans will vary. Make sure that students mark the location of smoke detectors on their floor plans, and make sure that each floor plan has at least two escape routes drawn on it.

CAREER *Connections*

Get Ready for Your Future Through Volunteering

Brad

"I'd like to become an architect one day, though I've heard jobs may be hard to get in the future. I know I have to get a head start. I looked around for a part-time job or volunteer work in a related area. I asked everybody I knew, and finally Ruth Kendricks — a friend of my uncle's — suggested I help her out in her interior design firm.

"Although I had no actual knowledge, I had formed ideas about interior design and didn't know if the work would prove valuable for architecture. I started out answering phones and learning how to write purchase orders for furnishings that Mrs. Kendricks bought for clients. I also watched her deal with architects. After a time, I realized that architecture and interior design work to complement each other in a successful housing or commercial design project.

"Mrs. Kendricks is very tuned in to how clients will use their living or working space. She chooses furniture, fabrics, and wall treatments that are as practical as they are pleasing to the eye. As I watched her work, I learned that architects need to be extremely sensitive to their clients' needs. They need to understand the intended use of each room they design. I can't predict my career future, but I know this experience has been far more valuable than I ever imagined."

"Designing buildings was my dream. However, I knew it wouldn't be an easy dream to make come true. I worked hard to build a solid educational foundation by taking art, design, drafting, and math courses in high school and college.

"After four years of study in college and two years of working on a master's degree in architecture, I started looking for a job. There were some very discouraging moments. After many weeks of searching, I was hired by an architectural firm as a draftsperson.

"When I look back on school, I think of all the time I used to spend in the computer and drafting labs —

Career Connections

Volunteer Options

- Neighborhood Watch volunteer.
- Preparing meals and getting beds ready at homeless shelters.
- Neighborhood beautification volunteer.
- Cleaning houses for the sick and elderly.
- House painting volunteer.
- Carpentry work.
- Plumbing work.
- Interior design work.
- Architectural work.

Volunteer Organizations

Habitat For Humanity
121 Habitat Street
Americus, GA 31709

American Red Cross
1730 East Street, NW
Washington, DC 20006

The Salvation Army
799 Bloomfield Avenue
Verona, NJ 07044

National Coalition for the Homeless
1621 Connecticut Avenue, NW
Washington, DC 20009

Discussing *Career Connections*

Have students read the *Career Connections* feature. Ask students:

- What characteristics or qualities should be present in both volunteer jobs and a career job?
- In what ways can volunteering benefit you in the future?
- Should some type of volunteer work be a requirement for high school graduation? Why or why not?

sometimes 30 or 40 hours a week. It turns out that the self-discipline and the skills I developed were incredibly helpful when I took the state licensing exam.

"Now that I'm a licensed architect, I have a wide range of responsibilities. The part I like most about my job is working on my firm's design projects for apartment complexes in a local retirement community."

"I always loved the idea of designing buildings, but I also love computers. In college, I took both architectural and computer-software design courses. It's no accident that in my chosen career I help design computer-aided design software (CAD) for architects. The team I work with develops computer programs that help architects consider design variations at the touch of a few buttons. Other programs can quickly prepare materials lists and cost estimates. It's amazing how computers have streamlined work that would have taken hours or perhaps days to complete in years past."

Barry

MAKING THE CONNECTION

- What other related volunteer work would give Brad valuable experience to reach his goals?
- Amy freely admits that searching for a job was frustrating at times. What steps can someone looking for a job take to make the search go as smoothly as possible?
- If Barry were unable to find a job designing computer software for architects, what other jobs might he consider that would employ his professional skills?

Occupational Outlook

Listed below are some possible housing-related occupations. Some require little training while others require a 4-year degree.

- House cleaner
- Housekeeper
- Apartment house manager
- Title searcher
- Mortgage processing clerk
- Furniture salesperson
- House painter
- Carpenter
- Upholsterer
- Exterminator
- Bricklayer
- Plumber
- Rug and carpet weaver
- Housing project manager
- Real estate appraiser
- Furniture reproducer
- Real estate agent
- Surveyor
- Building inspector
- Interior designer
- Urban planner
- Landscape architect
- Architect

Housing-Related Organizations

National Society for Interior Designers
1430 Broadway
New York, NY 10018

Director, Education Programs
The American Institute of Architects
1735 New York Ave. NW
Washington, DC 20006

Making the Connection

Answers

- Answers will vary. Some possibilities may include volunteering at an architectural firm, at an architectural supplies business, at a landscape architecture business, or for a building contractor.
- Answers will vary. Possible steps may include checking classified ads in the newspaper frequently for possible jobs, going through an employment agency to find a job, having a well-written and attractive resume and cover letter, and preparing well for job interviews.
- Answers will vary. Possible jobs might be a draftsman for an architectural business, a computer programmer for any business, or a computer software salesman.

Planning the Unit

Ch. 27: Looking Your Best — Emphasizes proper care of skin, hair, teeth, and nails in addition to protecting skin in the sun.

Ch. 28: Selecting Clothing — Addresses wardrobe planning, evaluating clothing needs and wants, using the elements and principles of design, and shopping strategies.

Ch. 29: Fibers to Fabrics — Examines the characteristics of natural and manufactured fibers and fabric construction.

Ch. 30: Caring for Clothing — Discusses routine care and storage, sorting and pretreating clothes, choosing laundry products, and machine and hand washing, drying, and pressing clothing.

Ch. 31: Selecting a Pattern — Addresses choosing correct pattern sizes based on measurements, using a pattern catalog, choosing the pattern, and reading the pattern envelope.

Ch. 32: Fabric and Notions — Discusses choosing fabrics based on pattern, appearance, sewing skills, and fabric care. Also addresses buying interfacing and figuring the cost of a project.

Ch. 33: Sewing Equipment — Discusses cutting, measuring, marking, and pressing equipment, sewing machine and serger parts, threading and stitching, sewing machine care, and sewing with a serger.

Ch. 34: Preparing to Sew — Addresses pattern fitting and alterations, fabric grains and straightening the grain, and pattern layout, cutting and marking.

Ch. 35: Basic Sewing Essentials — Discusses fitting, directional and staystitching, darts, seams, seam finishes, applying interfacing, grading clipping, facings, understitching, gathering, patch pockets, and hems.

Ch. 36: Challenging Sewing Essentials — Addresses collars, zippers, set-in and kimono sleeves, attached waistbands, elastic waistbands, drawstring waistbands, and altering and recycling clothing.

UNIT 5 Clothing

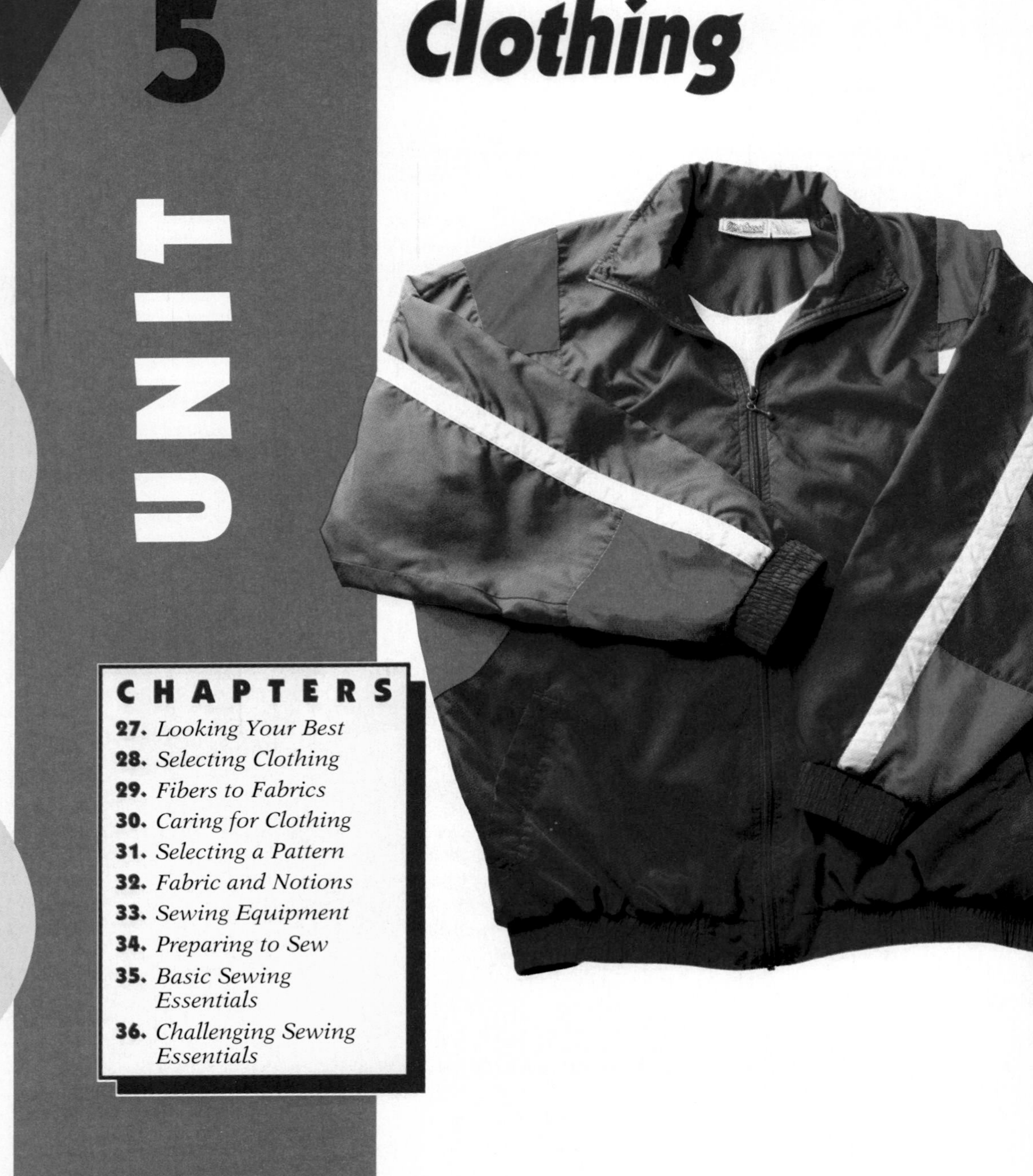

CHAPTERS

Cooperative Learning Tips

Time management is an essential component of cooperative learning. Students tend to use small portions of time more efficiently than larger portions. To help students stay on task and make optimal use of class time, start out by giving cooperative groups less time than it will take to complete a task. For example, if a task will take 20 minutes to complete, start out by giving students 10 minutes to complete the activity. As students are working, check for progress and completion. Then assign more time as needed in 5 to 10 minute increments.

See the *Cooperative Learning* booklet in the TCR for more information.

Introducing the Unit

Unit 5 Overview

Unit 5 gives students an understanding of how clothing helps a person express individuality. The elements and principles of design are presented as ways to help students highlight their best features. Fibers, fabrics, and finishes are discussed. Students learn to evaluate quality, fit, and garment construction. Along with basic sewing equipment and skills for sewing, the unit also discusses clothing care, repair, and recycling. The careers in the clothing and textile industry are also discussed.

Unit Motivators

1. **Product Analysis.** Display a variety of laundry products — detergents, bleaches, pretreatments, and fabric softeners. Ask students to explain how and where they might use each item. Explain that they will learn more about clothing care in this unit. (Key Skill: *Decision Making*)

Completing the Unit

Review

1. **Buy or Sew?** Have students examine catalogs to find a ready-to-wear garment they would like to own. Have them write down the price and description of the garment. Then have them find a pattern for a similar garment and figure the cost of making that garment (cost of pattern, fabric, and notions). They should compare the cost of the two garments. What factors other than price would students consider before deciding to buy or sew? (Key Skills: *Critical Thinking, Math*)

Evaluation

1. **Unit Test.** Have students complete the unit test on pp. 121-124 of the *Chapter and Unit Tests* booklet in the TCR.
2. **Testmaker Software.** Use the *Testmaker* software program to design your own unit test.

Implementing Cooperative Learning

In using the *Roundtable* technique, each team is given one sheet of paper and one pencil. The teams are give a question or problem by the teacher or from a textbook. Team members take turns writing an answer or solution and then pass the paper on to the next team member. The paper continues around until time is called. *Simultaneous roundtable* by Spencer Kagan, a key leader in the cooperative learning movement, allows each team member to have a sheet of paper and a pencil. This increases participation as several papers are passed around at the same time.

See the *Cooperative Learning* booklet in the TCR for more information.

Preparing to Teach

Chapter Outline

Chapter Resources

The following booklet materials may be found in the *Teacher's Classroom Resources* box:

- Lesson Plans, p. 32
- Student Workbook, *Study Guide,* pp. 117-118; *Good Grooming = Good Looks,* p. 119; *Schedule Your Good Grooming,* p. 120
- Personal Safety, *Protecting Your Skin,* p. 32
- Technology and Computers, p. 39
- Cooperative Learning, p. 39
- Extending the Text, *Ten Steps to Better Looking Nails,* p. 39
- Reteaching and Practical Skills, *Personal Grooming Standards,* p. 35
- Enrichment Activities, *Selecting a Shampoo,* pp. 44-45
- Chapter and Unit Tests, pp. 57-58
- Testmaker Software

Also see:

- Meeting the Special Needs of Students
- Linking Home, School, and Community
- Dealing with Sensitive Issues

CHAPTER

27 Looking Your Best

OBJECTIVES

- *Discuss how good grooming and hygiene contribute to health and success.*
- *Describe how to care for your skin, hair, teeth, hands, and nails.*

TERMS TO LEARN

- ***grooming***
- ***hygiene***
- ***dermatologist***
- ***dandruff***
- ***plaque***

"Hey, you look great today!" That kind of a compliment would brighten anyone's morning.

People make an impression on others within the first few minutes after meeting. You often base decisions about whether you want to get to know someone better on your first impression of them. At the same time, they are using their impression of you to decide whether they want to learn more about you. The way people look, as well as the way they act, affects first impressions.

What does it take to look great? If you put "the right clothes" on the top of the list, think again. Being beautiful or handsome isn't a requirement either. The first key to looking your best is actually good grooming. Even the latest clothes can't make up for dirty hair, grimy fingernails, or lack of a shower. This chapter includes helpful suggestions for looking your best.

Good Grooming

Good **grooming** means developing a personal-care routine to keep yourself clean, neat, and attractive. Not everyone is born with perfect looks, but everyone can be good-looking by paying attention to the details of his or her grooming.

Cleanliness is essential for both good health and attractiveness. Following some simple guidelines of proper **hygiene**, or cleanliness, can give you a head start on making yourself a more attractive person. How does your routine measure up? Do you take a bath or shower each day? Do you take care of your complexion? Do you keep your hair clean and neatly styled? Do you brush and floss your teeth regularly? Are your nails clean and neatly trimmed? Neglecting any of these areas can keep you from looking and feeling your best.

Taking the time to be well-groomed reflects a positive self-concept. In what ways do your grooming habits show how you feel about yourself?

More About Acne

Acne tends to be more severe among boys because their bodies begin increased production of male hormones, androgens, which, among other things, stimulate the activity of the sebaceous gland. Girls also produce these hormones, but only one-tenth as much. The exact role hormones play in acne is not known.

Introducing the Chapter

Motivators

1. **Ask the class.** Imagine that you and a few friends are stranded on a deserted island. There's plenty of food, but you have none of your belongings with you. What are some of the things you would miss? *(Lead them to consider personal care items: toothbrushes, comb, shampoo, curling iron, etc.)* How would you look to others when you were rescued? *(Unkempt)* What would you look for first when you were "back in civilization?" We use and depend on personal care products to feel and look our best. (Key Skill: *Critical Thinking*)
2. **Focus on familiar items.** Prepare a tray of personal care products such as soap, deodorant, toothpaste, shampoo, hair spray, lotion, sunscreen, nail clippers, and cologne. Ask class members to choose which item they could most easily do without. Continue to eliminate items until only one or two remain. Making the choices should provoke discussion and direct attention to personal care. (Key Skill: *Decision Making*)

Chapter Objectives and Vocabulary

1. Have students read the chapter objectives and rephrase the objectives as questions.
2. Ask students to state, in their own words, the purpose of studying this chapter.
3. Pronounce the vocabulary terms listed on the previous page. Ask students whether they are familiar with any of these. Explain that the terms will be defined in the chapter.

Guided Reading

1. Have students read the chapter and use the Study Guide on pp. 117-118 of the *Student Workbook.*

Teaching. . . Good Grooming and Your Skin (pp. 301-303)

Comprehension Check

1. What are the three functions of your skin? *(Protect your body; feel heat, cold, pain; rid body of wastes.)*
2. How does your skin stay soft? *(It gives off oils and moisture.)*
3. What do soap and water do for your skin? *(Wash away dirt; remove dried skin, oil, surface bacteria.)*
4. What is the difference between a deodorant and an antiperspirant? *(Deodorant controls odor; antiperspirant controls odor and checks perspiration where it is applied.)*
5. What are some factors that may lead to acne? *(Heredity, stress and strong emotions, some medications.)*
6. How do blackheads develop? *(Glands below pores become blocked, trapping oil in areas which may become irritated.)*

Learning Activities

1. **Skit.** Give students the following information: An android appears in your neighborhood and overhears a conversation between two teens who are discussing their skin problems. The android comments that it is happy not to have to worry about skin. This leads the teens to consider the positive aspects of having skin and they speak out in defense of skin. (Key Skill: *Creativity, Critical Thinking*)
2. **Informal Research.** Encourage students to interview friends or family members of older generations. Ask them about hygiene practices from their childhood.

AROUND THE WORLD

After reading the feature, have students discuss the pros and cons of conformity in dress and social unity. *(Answers will vary.)*

AROUND THE WORLD

The desire for social unity is a traditional Japanese value that influences modern dress. Many Japanese people strictly follow the latest fashion trends, choosing neutral colors and simple accessories to avoid drawing attention to themselves. Some people are critical of this, saying it puts too much pressure on individuals to conform. Is this true in the United States? How do you personalize your appearance? How do others?

▼ Your Skin ▼

Your skin is like a fabric that covers and protects your body. Skin has important functions. It protects your body. It can feel heat, cold, and pain. Skin helps rid your body of wastes. It gives off oils to keep itself soft and moisture to help regulate your body temperature.

You look your best when your skin is in good condition. Healthy skin starts with eating right. Chapter 39 gives more information on healthful eating habits. Keeping clean is the most important habit for both good looks and good health. Soap and water wash away dirt. They also remove dried skin, extra oil, and surface bacteria that can cause odors and infections.

Start with a daily bath or shower. Remember, just dipping in and out of water doesn't get you clean. You need to use soap. Start washing at the hairline and work down. If you are taking a shower, step from under the spray while you lather so the soap has a chance to work. If you can't take a bath or shower every day, wash well from head to toe.

Eating a variety of healthful foods and drinking plenty of water helps keep skin in good condition. How healthful are your eating habits?

A small brush can help you clean your hands, elbows, ankles, heels. For your back, use a long-handled brush. Rinse well with clean water so that no soap is left on the skin.

If you have dry skin, use lotion after your shower or bath. Many people have dry skin in some areas and oily skin in others. Tanya, for example, has dry skin on her legs and arms but an oily face. She treats each part differently.

Hygiene doesn't end with a shower or bath. Your face needs washing at least twice a day. Your hands need frequent washing. Throughout the day, they pick up dirt and germs. These can easily make you and others ill. Always wash your hands well before meals and snacks. Hands also need to be washed after you use the toilet, touch a pet, or complete cleaning chores. Put germs down the drain. Don't share them with your family and friends.

Antiperspirants and Deodorants

As part of your daily cleanliness schedule, remember to use an antiperspirant or deodorant. You can't count on a daily bath to prevent perspiration odor. Only regular use of a good deodorant or antiperspirant will do this. Many people who offend others with perspiration odor never suspect it. Their own sense of smell does not warn them.

A deodorant controls odor. It does not affect the flow of perspiration. An antiperspirant controls odor and also checks perspiration in the area to which it is applied. Both products come in several forms, such as solid, liquid, spray, or cream. Apply them to clean, dry skin.

Acne

About 80 percent of all teenagers develop acne. Many adults also have this problem.

No one knows exactly what causes acne. A number of factors can play a role. If one of your parents had acne, you are more likely to have it, too. Stress and strong emotions, such as anxiety and fear, can trigger acne. Some medicines can cause skin problems. There is no medical evidence that foods such as chocolate, cola drinks, or potato chips can cause acne or make it worse.

Acne develops when glands below the pores (tiny openings) in the skin become blocked. The oils that normally move through the pores to soften the skin are trapped beneath it. As more oil becomes trapped, blackheads and whiteheads develop. Often, these areas become irritated or infected and develop into pimples.

Acne is most common in teens. The body begins to produce more oily substances. Problems are most common on the face, upper chest, and the back.

Learning Activities (continued)

Discuss or report on the reasons for and results of the changes which have occurred. This could be an oral or written report. (Key Skill: *Communication*)

3. **Posters.** Have students create a poster about one of the following: create a drawing of the formation of a blackhead; compare the merits of deodorants and antiperspirants; give reminders about the importance of hand washing. (Key Skill: *Science*)

Follow Up

1. **Reteaching.** Present this scenario for class suggestions: "Your younger brother has not yet learned the value of regular bathing, shampooing, and/or teeth brushing. To prevent him from developing a health problem, you must give him some logical reasons and concrete suggestions for practicing good hygiene. What would they be?" (Key Skill: *Problem Solving*)
2. **Enrichment.** Suggest that a student or two contact a local dermatologist and ask for some additional information and prevention tips about acne, dandruff, and tanning. These students would then present this information to the class (or write a group report on it). (Key Skill: *Communication*)

More About *Hand Care*

By rubbing and scrubbing your soapy hands together as you wash them, you pull the dirt and oily soils free from your skin. These are suspended in the lather and rinsed away with warm running water. Washing hands during the cold and flu season is a good idea so germs are also washed away.

The World Around You

Packaging

Personal care products are usually packaged in plastic or metal containers which are often not recyclable. Many aerosol products are now available as pumps. Ask students to think of ways to improve packaging. If they do, have them, as a class, write the manufacturer.

Teaching. . .
Protecting Your Skin and Your Hair
(pp. 304-305)

Comprehension Check

1. How are sunscreens numbered? What is a good number to use? *(The higher the number, the greater the protection — use 15+ for skin that burns easily.)*
2. Why are ultraviolet rays so dangerous? *(They don't feel hot; are active on cloudy days; can penetrate light clothing; reflect; pass through wet shirts and underwater.)*
3. How does your hair reflect your general health? *(Poor diet, emotional upsets, or illness can affect appearance of hair.)*

Learning Activities

1. **Goal Setting.** Ask students to make a list of the hygiene practices they would like to make a part of their regular routine. Encourage them to keep track, for one week, of how well they are able to carry these out. At that time, they could evaluate their list and make a new, more realistic list to adopt for the rest of the school year. (Key Skill: *Management*)
2. **Reading.** Divide the class into five groups, assigning each to a topic: skin (perspiration and tanning), acne, nails, hair, teeth. Give each group materials containing in-depth information about their subject. Each group will make a short presentation to the class and/or contribute to a "Personal Care Newsletter." This newsletter could contain illustrations by artistic students and hygiene trivia to enhance the newsletter. (Key Skills: *Cooperation, Creativity*)

How to . . .
Enjoy the Sun and Protect Your Skin

Too much exposure to the sun's rays damages the skin and causes sagging and wrinkling. The major threat of too much sun is skin cancer (or melanoma).

Ultraviolet light doesn't feel hot, so it's easy to think you don't need extra protection from the sun's ultraviolet rays on cooler days. Clouds or even thin clothing offer little protection. Ultraviolet rays also pass through wet T-shirts and penetrate through several feet of water. The rays also reflect off beach sand and water, increasing your exposure.

What can you do to protect your skin from overexposure to the sun's ultraviolet rays? Doctors recommend using sunscreens for protection. Sunscreens work by absorbing or scattering the harmful rays of ultraviolet light.

Sunscreens are sold with an SPF (sun protection factor) number. The SPF number indicates the amount of protection you receive against the harmful rays of the sun and sunburn. An SPF of 10, for example, allows a person who would normally burn after 30 minutes exposure to the sun to safely be in the sun for five hours or 10 times longer than usual.

How do you select and use sunscreens?

- If you burn easily with minimum exposure, you would want to pick a sunscreen with a 15 SPF or higher, especially in a hot climate.
- As a rule of thumb, you'll get the best SPF protection by applying the sunscreen liberally over your entire body.
- It's best to apply a sunscreen approximately 30 minutes before exposure to sunlight. This allows it to be absorbed so it will be less likely to be washed off by perspiration.
- If you perspire heavily or go into the water often, reapply the sunscreen.

How to ... Enjoy the Sun and Protect Your Skin

Have students read the feature. Ask students to discuss the consequences of not protecting their skin in the sun. What might be the long term effects of overexposure to the sun? What cultural influences brought about the notion that tanned skin is healthy skin? What suggestions do students have for encouraging people to protect their skin from the harmful rays of the sun?

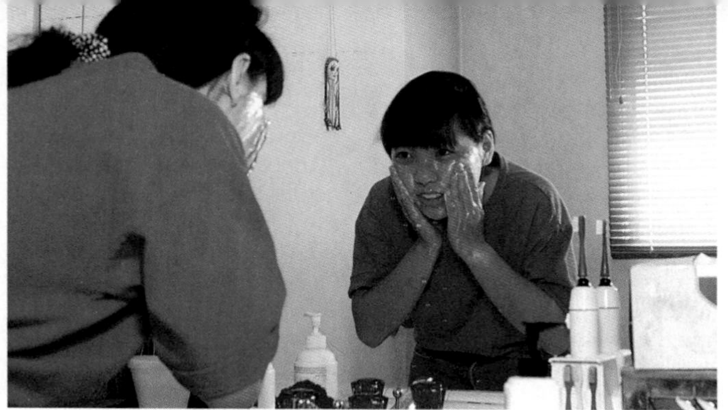

Cleansing your face several times per day can help you treat acne. Choose soaps and other cleansing products that are suited to your type of skin.

What can you do if you develop acne? Mild or slight cases of acne are best treated by washing your face twice daily. You can blot your face with a tissue between washings to remove the oil. Acne medicine that you can buy without a doctor's prescription may help. Avoid using oily makeup or other skin products on the problem areas. Avoid picking or squeezing the acne. This can injure the skin. It can also spread bacteria.

A serious case of acne needs treatment by a doctor. **Dermatologists** are doctors specializing in skin problems. They can usually help minimize acne.

▼ Your Hair ▼

Hairstyles change just as clothing styles change. Experiment to find a look that flatters your face. People often find that an easy-to-care-for style works best. A professional hairstylist can help you choose a good style for the shape of your face and type of hair.

Did you know that hair reflects your general health? Beautiful hair begins inside. A poor diet, emotional upsets, or a bad cold can change the appearance of your hair.

There are many products on the market to clean your hair and to keep it healthy. How can you choose the ones that are best for you? Consider the type and condition of your hair. Dry hair is harsh to the touch and has a strawlike texture. Hair is oily if it becomes stringy and sticky within a day or two after shampooing. Your hair is normal if you have none of the above problems. Choose products that match your hair type. High prices don't necessarily mean a shampoo or conditioner will work better for you. (Conditioners add shine and make hair more manageable.) Look for small sample-size bottles at first, so you can try out new varieties for a small price.

A flattering, easy-to-care-for hairstyle works best for most people.

Learning Activities (continued)

3. **Survey analysis.** Have students write a survey about the risks vs. beauty of tanning. Give the survey to as many students in the school as possible. The class members can then tabulate and analyze their answers, which could be published in the school newspaper or copied and distributed to survey participants. Discuss the findings in class. What concerns do students have or not have about tanning? (Key Skill: *Critical Thinking*)
4. **Speaker.** Ask a popular hair stylist in your town to give your class information about hair and hair care. This might include a "make-over" to a volunteer student. The hair stylist might also have some good nail care advice.

Follow Up

1. **Reteaching.** Ask students to list four rules for effective sunscreen use. *(Use 15+, apply one ounce, put lotion on 30 minutes early, reapply if in water.)* (Key Skill: *Communication*)
2. **Enrichment.** Compare the claims and directions listed on the sunscreens available at a local store. Chart similarities and differences. Give an oral or written report. (Key Skill: *Communication*)

More About *Water Conservation*

The average family uses from 255,000 to 365,000 gallons of water a year. Up to 50% of this water could be saved. Here are some tips:

1. Run hot water first, then turn on cold to adjust.
2. Block the drain before running bath water.
3. Limit showers to five minutes.
4. Fill the bathtub only ¼ full.
5. Install low-flow showerheads.
6. Displace water in the toilet tank with a plastic jug filled with marbles or stones.

Teaching. . .
Your Hair, Your Teeth, Your Nails
(pp. 306-307)

Comprehension Check

1. How can damage to wet hair be prevented? *(Avoid vigorous rubbing, do not yank or pull.)*
2. Name three ways to prevent tooth decay. *(Eat nutritious food, limit snacks, brush and floss, see dentist regularly.)*
3. How should you care for your nails as part of a good grooming routine? *(See bulleted list on the bottom of p. 307.)*

Learning Activities

1. **Bulletin Board.** Divide the class into small groups. Have each group create a bulletin board emphasizing good grooming habits for skin care, hair care, dental care, nail care, or good grooming in general. Bulletin boards may be used in class or throughout the school building. This could be an extra credit project. (Key Skills: *Creativity, Cooperation*)
2. **Demonstration.** Show students *Ten Uses for Dental Floss.* Begin with nine humorous uses (such as tying up a package of fresh fish, hanging balloons, making emergency repairs to shoes, sewing on buttons, slicing unbaked cinnamon rolls, stringing beads, pulling loose teeth, hanging objects on walls, and so forth) and end with a demonstration on flossing teeth. This could also be a student project. (Key Skills: *Creativity, Communication*)

Carefully read the labels on hair-care products to choose the product best for your hair.

TIPS: *Buying Shampoo*

Are you confused by the many different types and brands of shampoo on store shelves? These facts may help you choose:

- Shampoos do one thing only — clean hair — regardless of advertised promises.
- Shampoos containing protein can make your hair look and feel fuller and less limp temporarily. However, getting enough protein in your diet is the only way to get it in your hair.
- Dandruff can sometimes be controlled by washing hair 3 or 4 times a week. You may not need a special anti-dandruff shampoo.

Shampooing

How often you shampoo depends on your hair. Many teens have so much natural oil in their hair that they need to shampoo every day. Wash your hair often enough to keep it looking good.

While regular shampooing won't harm your hair, you do have to be careful about how you shampoo. Hair is weaker when it is wet. To prevent damage, avoid vigorous rubbing during washing or drying.

Washing your hair is so routine, you probably never think about how you do it. Do you skip any of these steps?

1. Gently brush your hair from the scalp to the ends.
2. Wet hair with warm water.
3. Work the shampoo into a lather with your fingertips. Massage both the hair and scalp.
4. Rinse thoroughly. Hair is clean when it squeaks between your fingers.
5. If you are using a separate conditioner, apply it according to the package directions.
6. After rinsing, squeeze extra water from your hair. Blot dry with a towel, but don't rub.
7. Comb your hair gently with a clean comb. If the hair is tangled, work the snarl out carefully with a wide-toothed comb. Take care not to yank or pull.

Dandruff

Dandruff, or scales and flakes on the scalp, is a problem for many people. There are many causes.

To help control dandruff, keep your hair clean. Special dandruff shampoos are often helpful. Keep combs, brushes, and other hair-care equipment clean. Change pillow cases often. Avoid scratching the scalp with sharp combs or fingernails. If dandruff is severe and does not improve, consult a dermatologist.

▼ Your Teeth ▼

If your teeth are to last a lifetime, they need regular care. What are the greatest enemies of healthy teeth? Until your mid-twenties, decay is the biggest cause of problems. After this age, gum disease becomes the biggest dental problem — causing more tooth loss in adults than any other dental disease.

The chief cause of tooth decay is **plaque** (plak). This is a sticky film of harmful bacteria that is constantly forming inside your mouth. Foods, especially those with a lot of sugar, cling to the teeth. The sugar and plaque form an acid that eats away at your tooth enamel and gums.

TIPS:

Buying Shampoo
Have students read the feature. Ask students how they think advertising affects consumer choices of hair care products. What characteristics do students look for in hair care products?

More About *Dandruff*

What causes occasional dandruff? Dermatologists suggest these possibilities: an increase in cell turnover; changes in the weather; shampooing too infrequently; inadequate rinsing. For relief try a shampoo with pyrithione zinc or selenium sulfide. Use as directed when needed.

You can help prevent decay by:

- Eating nutritious food.
- Limiting between-meal snacks.
- Brushing properly and flossing after meals and snacks.
- Seeing a dentist regularly.

If possible, brush your teeth right after eating. Brushing will take away plaque and food particles from easy-to-reach tooth surfaces. However, a toothbrush can't reach between teeth and the gumline. This is where most dental disease starts. Use dental floss, a string-like material, to reach these areas. Floss your teeth every day.

What if you're not always able to brush after eating? Rinse with water after you eat. Swish the water around to help remove small bits of food.

Every few months, replace your toothbrush. When the bristles begin to show signs of wear, the brush can't do a good job of cleaning.

At least once a year, have your teeth checked by a dentist. A cleaning will help your gums. Cavities can also be discovered and treated while they're still small.

Flossing your teeth daily helps remove plaque and food particles that you can't reach with your toothbrush.

▼ Your Nails ▼

Nail care should be part of your good grooming routine. Dirty, broken, or bitten nails hurt your appearance. Here are some tips:

- Clean your hands and nails at least once a day. Use a small brush to remove stubborn dirt.
- Cut toenails straight across.
- Fingernails look best in a slightly oval shape. Be careful, however, not to cut or file too close to the corners.
- Use an emery board or file to smooth nail edges.
- Wear gloves for cleaning, gardening, and other activities that are hard on the hands.
- Use lotion to keep dry hands smooth.
- Nail biting is a habit that can be broken. Gradually decrease the number of nails you bite until you eliminate the problem.

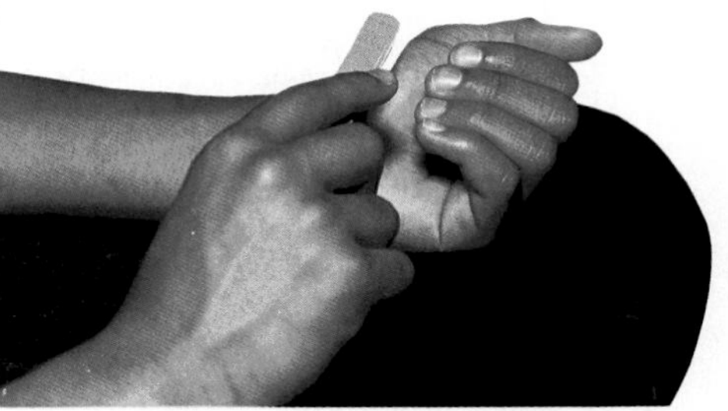

How does proper nail care lead to attractive hands?

Learning Activities (continued)

3. **Product analysis.** Ask each student to survey hair care products at a store in which they regularly shop. Students should examine at least five different brands. Ask them to analyze and compare the following information: price, ingredients, special claims, and directions. Have students report their comparisons to the class. How would students use this information in deciding which product to purchase? (Key Skill: *Critical Thinking*)

Follow Up

1. **Reteaching.** Have students write down three key points for each of the following: hair care, care of teeth, and nail care.
2. **Extension.** Use the extension information handout on p. 37 of the *Extending the Lesson* booklet in the TCR.
3. **Enrichment.** Have small groups of students create a radio public service announcement concerning one of the following: hair care, dental care, or nail/hand care. Students should emphasize the effective care procedures and benefits. Encourage students to create a jingle or other way to catch the listener's attention. May be used for extra credit. (Key Skills: *Communication, Cooperation*)

Photo Focus

Ask students to look at the photo in the upper right corner of p. 307. What are the benefits of flossing teeth regularly? What are the consequences of not flossing teeth? *(Benefits: removes plaque and food particles not reached by brushing, improves gumline health. Consequences: possible increased decay, gum disease.)*

Completing the Chapter

For Review

1. Emphasize the main concepts using the summary.
2. Have students complete the "Facts to Recall." (Answers below.)

For Reteaching

1. **Reteaching.** Use the activity on p. 35 of the *Reteaching and Practical Skills* booklet in the TCR.

For Enrichment

1. **Enrichment.** Use the activity on pp. 44-45 of the *Enrichment Activities* booklet in the TCR.

For Evaluation

1. Choose items from "Ideas to Explore" and "Activities to Try."
2. Use the chapter test on pp. 57-58 in the testing booklet of the TCR or use the testmaker software.

Facts to Recall Answers

1. **Any three:** skin acts as protective covering for body; feels heat, cold, and pain; rids your body of wastes; helps regulate body temperature.
2. Dried skin, extra oil, and surface bacteria that can cause odor and infection.
3. A deodorant controls odor, but does not affect the flow of perspiration; an antiperspirant controls odor and checks perspiration where applied.
4. Acne occurs when dirt and oil block the glands beneath skin pores. Daily washing helps rid the face of these oils and dirt.
5. Hair is clean when it squeaks between your fingers.
6. **Any three:** Keep your hair clean; keep combs, brushes, and other hair care equipment clean; change pillow cases often; avoid scratching the scalp with sharp combs or fingernails.
7. Bacteria in plaque combines with the sugar in foods, clings to the teeth, and forms an acid that eats away at tooth enamel and gums.

The Confident Look

Confidence in your appearance grows as you begin taking responsibility for your own cleanliness and personal grooming. The grooming habits you develop now will tend to stay with you for a lifetime. As you develop positive grooming habits, you will look and feel better all the time. This sends a positive message to others around you that you really care about looking your best.

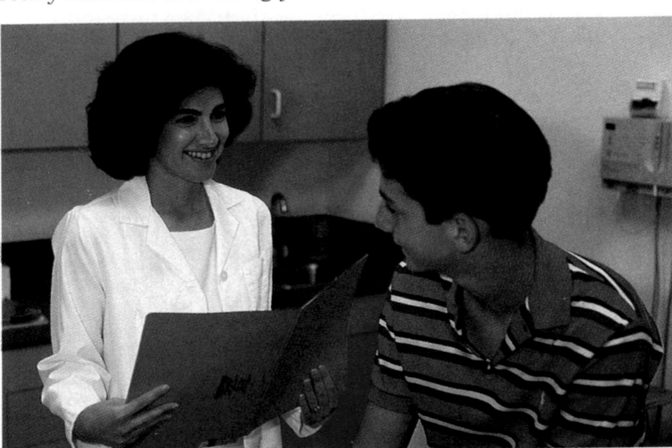

Good grooming habits help build confidence and last a lifetime. In what ways is this teen showing he feels confident about himself?

TAKING ACTION

Dressing for Confidence

Breanne's first thought is, "What can I wear?" Mr. Shanks, the principal, wants her to represent Irving High School at the city council meeting next month. A citation for the school's community service project will be presented, and he has asked Breanne to accept the award.

Having never done anything like this before, Breanne turns to you, her good friend, for advice. You know that new clothes will not be possible for her. Breanne's family does not have much money for extras. Breanne wants to feel good about herself when she stands before the council. She wants you to help her figure out how to put her best foot forward.

Using Your Resourcefulness

- What kinds of clothes would be appropriate? What would be inappropriate?
- What might Breanne do to present a good appearance by spending little or no money? What resources can she draw on other than money?
- Do you think appearance is related to self-esteem? Explain your answer.
- In what ways might healthy self-esteem be a resource?

TAKING ACTION

Have students read the feature. Ask students to think about situations in which they might have to wear special clothing. How might students adapt clothing in their current wardrobes to meet the needs of a special occasion?

Using Your Resourcefulness Answers

- Answers will vary, but may include: skirt and blouse; dress pants and shirt; a simple dress. Inappropriate dress would include jeans; T-shirts; tennis shoes, etc.
- Answers will vary, but may include: look for inexpensive accessories; borrow something from a friend; look for something at

Chapter 27 Review

Summary

In this chapter, you have read about:

- How to care for your skin by washing regularly and using lotion if needed.
- What causes acne and how you can treat it.
- Selecting and using the shampoo and other hair-care products that are right for you.
- How to prevent tooth decay.
- How to keep your nails clean and attractive.

Facts to Recall

1. Name three functions of your skin.
2. Besides dirt, what three things do soap and water wash away?
3. What is the difference between a deodorant and an antiperspirant?
4. How can washing your face daily help prevent acne?
5. How can you tell if hair is clean when you are washing it?
6. Name three things you can do to prevent dandruff.
7. How does plaque contribute to tooth decay?
8. What are four things you can do to help prevent tooth decay?
9. List five tips for keeping your nails clean and attractive.
10. Name two ways that you can protect your skin from the ultraviolet rays of the sun.

Ideas to Explore

1. In what ways can being well-groomed reflect a good self-image? How can good grooming reflect your attitude toward life? What message does poor grooming send to others?
2. Suppose your best friend believes that the way to look healthy is to have a deep suntan. What would you say to your friend? How would you encourage your friend to protect his or her skin?

Activities to Try

1. With a partner, brainstorm a list of characteristics you notice about a person the first time you see them. How do these characteristics influence the way you respond to a person?
2. Write a public service announcement about protecting skin from the sun's ultraviolet rays. The announcement should be geared toward teens. What message would you send to teens that would effectively convince teens to take better care of their skin?

LINK TO Math

THE COST OF GROOMING PRODUCTS

Identify three types of grooming products that you use regularly. Comparison shop for five different brands of each product. Write down the product name, manufacturer's name, a brief description of the container, weight, and cost. Use the following guidelines for a cost comparison:

1. Compute the unit price for each product by dividing the weight of the product into the cost.
2. Compute the average cost for each type of product by adding the costs of all five products together and dividing by five.
3. Suggest some factors that contribute to cost differences.

Facts to Recall Answers (continued)

8. Eat nutritious foods; limit between-meal snacks; brush properly and floss after meals and snacks; see a dentist regularly.
9. **Any five:** clean hands and nails at least once a day; cut toenails straight across; shape fingernails into a slightly oval shape; use an emery board or file to smooth nail edges; wear gloves for gardening, cleaning, and other activities that are hard on the hands; use lotion to keep dry hands smooth; avoid biting your nails.
10. **Any two:** if you burn easily, pick a sunscreen with a 15 SPF or higher; apply sunscreen liberally over your entire body; apply sunscreen approximately 30 minutes before exposure to sunlight; if you perspire heavily or go into the water often, reapply sunscreen.

Ideas to Explore

1. Answers will vary. Responses may include: good grooming habits can show that a person feels good about and respects himself or herself; poor habits can show low self-esteem, depression, or lack of organization and time management skills.
2. Answers will vary. Responses may include: too much exposure causes skin to age, sag, and possibly develop cancer; ways to protect skin from overexposure; affirm that friend looks healthy without a deep suntan.

a secondhand clothing shop. She might ask for help from family and friends.

- Answers will vary.
- Having healthy self-esteem helps you reach out to others and take positive risks.

LINK TO Math

Answers

1. Answers will vary.
2. Answers will vary.
3. Factors may include: cost of ingredients, cost of advertising if name brand, demand for supply, etc.

Preparing to Teach

Chapter Outline

Chapter Resources

The following booklet materials may be found in the *Teacher's Classroom Resources* box:

- Lesson Plans, p. 33
- Student Workbook, *Study Guide*, pp. 121-122; *Cue In on Fashion*, pp. 123-124
- Color Transparencies, *Checking Clothing for Quality*, CT-33
- Personal Safety, *Shopping Safety*, pp. 33-34
- Technology and Computers, pp. 36, 37, 38, 39
- Cooperative Learning, p. 40
- Extending the Text, *An Eye for Quality*, p. 40
- Reteaching and Practical Skills, *Analyzing Clothing Needs and Wants*, p. 36
- Enrichment Activities, *Who Cares About Clothing Labels?*, p. 46
- Chapter and Unit Tests, pp. 59-60
- Testmaker Software

Also see:

- Meeting the Special Needs of Students
- Linking Home, School, and Community
- Dealing with Sensitive Issues

CHAPTER 28 Selecting Clothing

OBJECTIVES

- *Develop a wardrobe plan.*
- *Select attractive clothes using the elements and principles of design.*
- *Give guidelines for shopping for clothes.*

TERMS TO LEARN

- ***clothing inventory***
- ***multipurpose clothes***
- ***fashions***
- ***classics***
- ***fads***
- ***separates***
- ***silhouette***

More About Line

- **Curved lines** are considered transitional lines. When softly curved they may give a vertical or horizontal effect. Tightly curved lines add to the apparent size of the wearer, such as ruffles.
- **Vertical lines** are dignified and usually carry the eye upward. **Horizontal lines** are restful and usually carry the eye across.

Look around the classroom. Are most people wearing similar clothes, or is there great variety? Some similarities might be explained by the weather or a school dress code.

If all your classmates were strangers, what clues might each one's choice of clothes give you about that person? Your clothes also send a message to others about how you want to be seen.

Being well-dressed does not necessarily require closets full of clothes. It's more important to have clothes you enjoy wearing and that mix and match well together. This chapter will help you choose flattering clothes that are both comfortable and well-made.

Planning Your Wardrobe

A wardrobe that works well for you doesn't just happen. It takes some thought. If you want to avoid having to say, "I don't have anything to wear," take some time to plan your wardrobe. You may discover ways to combine clothes you already have to make new outfits. An inventory can also help you decide which new clothes would make the biggest impact on your wardrobe.

Taking an Inventory

The best way to start planning your wardrobe is to take a look at what you already have. Making an organized list of your clothes is called taking a **clothing inventory**. An inventory can help you decide what you need and set priorities for shopping.

To take a clothing inventory, first sort your clothes into three groups:

- Clothes you like and wear regularly.
- Clothes you no longer wear and don't want.
- Clothes that you aren't certain about.

This "maybe" or "if" group is for items you might like to wear *if* they were repaired ... or *if* you had something to wear with them ... or *if* they were more in style.

Next, make a separate list for each different type of activity in which you participate. These might include school, sports, special occasions, relaxing, and possibly a job. List the items you put in your first pile — the clothes you wear and like — under the appropriate activities. Some items may

Classic designs in clothing stand the test of time. What are some ways the clothing worn by this teen will stand the test of time?

Introducing the Chapter

Motivators

1. **Ask the class.** You and a few friends are still stranded on a deserted island (See Ch. 27 Motivators). You've been there awhile and, although your food supply is fine, your clothes are beginning to fall apart. You need to decide whether or not to replace them, because it will take some effort and creativity to make new ones. What are some of the reasons for having clothes? *(Warmth; protection from sun, rain, sand, brush; modesty; support — comfort)* Which of these reasons are true for us? For what other reasons do we wear clothing? (Key Skill: *Critical Thinking*)
2. **Visual "aid."** Bring a dressmaker's mannequin to class and introduce it as a new student for this unit. (A helium balloon attached as a head might give it some character.) Dress it in clothes from the 1960s or 70s and ask the class to judge its "age." Change clothes on it several times during the unit and ask the students to "date" the model. How might they dress it to have it fit into their school now? (Key Skill: *Critical Thinking*)

Chapter Objectives and Vocabulary

1. Have students read the chapter objectives and rephrase the objectives as questions.
2. Ask students to state, in their own words, the purpose of studying this chapter.
3. Pronounce the vocabulary terms listed on the previous page. Ask students whether they are familiar with any of these. Explain that the terms will be defined in the chapter.

Guided Reading

1. Have students read the chapter and use the Study Guide on pp. 121-122 of the *Student Workbook*.

Diagonal lines slant and are read from left to right.

- The lines used in a garment become more dominant when they are accented by stitching, trim, or contrasting fabric.
- Details on a garment also create lines. Therefore, look carefully at size and placement of pockets, width of collar, width and kind of belt, length of skirt, and kind of buttons used.
- Even though vertical lines tend to add height and horizontal ones usually add width, the spacing of these lines can create a different effect. Widely-spaced lines are bolder and cause more attention to direction than narrowly-spaced lines.

Teaching. . .
Taking an Inventory and Planning Your Purchases
(pp. 311-313)

Comprehension Check

1. What is a clothing inventory and why would you make one? *(An organized list of clothes to help decide needs and priorities)*
2. What should you consider when you are planning to add to your wardrobe? *(Needs and wants, budget, fashion, versatility, mix and match possibilities, accessories)*
3. What is the difference between **classics** and **fads**? *(Classics are fashions that stay in style; fads last only a short time.)*

Learning Activities

1. **Discussion.** Divide the class into small groups. Give each group ten minutes to come up with a list of five classic and five fad clothing items. Compare the lists and make a composite list. Encourage students to discuss the merits of classics and fads. (Key Skill: *Communication*)
2. **Writing.** Ask each student to make a clothing inventory and summarize his or her findings. What have they learned about themselves from the lists? (Key Skill: *Critical Thinking*)
3. **Discussion.** Describe this scenario: "Your family cannot afford to buy expensive jeans and popular brand name shirts and sweaters for you. What are some ways to stretch your clothing budget?" (*Buy one brand name item and supplement with less expensive separates and*

Around the World

After reading the feature, ask students to discuss the advantages and disadvantages of simple clothing. *(Advantages include: easy care, eliminate self-esteem problems related to clothing. Disadvantages include: some loss of individuality, loss of creativity.)*

Around the World

For the Amish people of Lancaster County, Pennsylvania, clothing expresses important religious beliefs. These "plain people" dress conservatively. Attire for men and boys includes black broadfall (zipperless) pants without hip pockets, black vests and coats fastened with hooks and eyes, and broad-brimmed hats. Women and girls are often seen in simply designed, solid-color dresses, black aprons, and black or white bonnets. The Amish believe that plain dress emphasizes the virtues of simplicity, modesty, and humility by which they try to live.

be listed under several activities. Your favorite sweater, for example, might look good with both casual and dressier clothes. **Multipurpose clothes** — those suitable for a variety of situations — stretch your wardrobe.

Now look again at the clothing items in your "if" pile. Would repairing or updating some of the items make them more appealing? If so, add these garments to your inventory. Plan what you will do to make the items usable. In Chapter 36, you'll find directions for making minor repairs and ideas for updating garments.

What about the pile of clothes you don't want? Give them to someone else who can use them. You might offer them to a younger brother or sister or donate them to a charitable organization.

Also take time to check the basics in your wardrobe. To be well-dressed you need shoes, nightwear, undergarments, and other basic items.

▼ Planning New Purchases ▼

After you complete your clothing inventory, look over your lists. Do you see any gaps? You should have the most clothing for the activities you participate in most often. For activities that come up less often, one or two outfits may be enough.

By planning for additions to your wardrobe, you can make choices that will make a real difference. Some points to consider are:

- ▶ ***Needs and wants.*** Which items do you really need? Which do you want but could get along without? Needs are usually more important than what you want. You may also have to consider how your needs fit in with the needs of others in your family.

More About *Thrift-Shop Chic*

Fashions found in thrift or consignment shops can give you a unique, top-quality look if you know how to pick them. Here are some tips.

- Vintage clothing is often in style at any time.
- Don't be put off by the thought of buying clothes someone else has worn. Most shops accept only dry-cleaned or washed clothes.
- Females should scout the men's department for shirts, vests, slacks, jackets, and hats.
- Go often. You never know when something useful will turn up.
- Keep an open mind. Some garments may look awful on the hanger but great on you. Check the "junk" basket, too.

- ▶ ***Budget.*** How much money do you have to spend on clothes? If a family's clothing budget is limited, decisions must be made about whose needs are most important.
- ▶ ***Fashion.*** Be aware that advertising, fashion, and fads influence what you may want. **Fashions** are styles that are currently popular. Some fashions are considered **classics**. These styles never seem to disappear completely, although they may be changed a little from time to time. Fashions that last for only a short time are called **fads**. It's usually not wise to spend a lot of money on fads, because you can't wear them too long.
- ▶ ***Versatility.*** Choose multipurpose clothing items that can be used for several activities.
- ▶ ***Mix-and-match possibilities.*** You'll be more pleased with the new clothes you buy if they fit in with what you already own. Shop for **separates**, garments that can be combined with one another to make several different outfits. Shirts, pants, jeans, skirts, sweaters, and jackets are all separates. Choose colors that will go with the clothes you already own. If the colors of your clothes go together, you will have many more possible outfits to wear.
- ▶ ***Accessories.*** Using accessories — small items of clothing that complete an outfit — is an inexpensive way to update clothes in your wardrobe. Belts, ties, scarves, and jewelry can give new life to the clothes you already own.

Mix and Match Math

Materials
current fashion catalogs; advertisements

Equipment
pen; paper, 4" × 6" index cards; glue; scissors

Directions:
Select pictures of twelve separate items of clothing. Choose 2 jackets, 2 sweaters, 4 skirts/pants, and 4 shirts. Choose solids/prints in two colors that go well together such as black and white. Choose a third color, like red, for accent if you wish. Select shapes, patterns, and textures that go well together. Glue each picture on a separate card. Number the cards 1 to 12. Now see how many different outfits you can create by mixing and matching the separates. Record the numbers of the combinations you used:

- ✔ How many different outfits did you create? Did all of the different items go well together?
- ✔ What are the advantages of buying compatible separates?
- ✔ How could you mix and match six separates for a weekend trip?

Mix and Match Math

Materials: Current fashion catalogs and advertisements.

Equipment: Pen, paper, 4-inch × 6-inch index cards, glue.

Purpose: To allow students to observe the possibilities of mixing and matching separates.

Outcomes:

- Answers will vary. As many as 40 different combinations are possible.
- Coordinated separates give you more flexibility and save money.
- One jacket, one sweater, two skirts/pants, and two shirts would provide several different looks for a three-day trip.

Learning Activities (continued)

accessories; shop at garage sales; add home-sewn garments to your wardrobe) (Key Skill: *Decision Making*)

4. **Discussion.** As a class, compose a "Golden Rule for Used Clothing Etiquette" to remind students to treat someone who is wearing older clothing the way they would like to be treated in that situation. In other words, they should say nothing. What may be intended as a playful remark might embarrass someone else. (Key Skill: *Citizenship*)

Follow Up

1. **Reteaching.** Ask students to identify the benefits of having a wardrobe of mainly mix and match separates.
2. **Enrichment.** Have each student compile pictures for a wardrobe of 15 mix and match articles that they would wear. How many combinations can be made? Are there outfits for a variety of occasions? (Key Skill: *Creativity*)

The World Around You

Recycling

Organize a *recycling sale* for your class, grade, or school. Ask students to donate used clothing in good condition that they no longer wear. Donate proceeds to a predetermined source. Have a plan for leftover clothing such as donating them to a community used clothing center, shipping them to a third-world country or other needy place (perhaps using the proceeds from the sale for shipping costs), or bring them to a senior center that makes quilts or rugs out of old clothing.

Teaching. . . Elements of Design (pp. 314-315)

Comprehension Check

1. What are three of the most important elements in clothing? *(Line, color, texture)*
2. What creates "lines" in clothing? *(Fabric design, seams, pleats, trims, silhouette)*
3. How can you tell what is a good color for you? *(It flatters the colors of your hair, skin, and eyes)*
4. How does texture affect the way clothing looks? *(Bulk and shine can seem to add pounds; smooth, flat texture can seem to take pounds away)*

Learning Activities

1. **Independent Practice.** Bring pieces of fabric in a variety of colors and allow students to hold them up to their faces and choose those most flattering. This might be done in groups of three or four, with group members helping each other. You may want to set a three to five minute time limit per person to keep it fair. Each student should make a list of colors that are flattering to him or her. (Key Skill: *Critical Thinking*)
2. **Group Work.** Ask groups to find out all they can about clothing *texture*. They should put all their knowledge into posters, incorporating fabric swatches and magazine photos of textures illustrated. They might suggest when and where various textures are appropriate because of how a garment looks and how it feels. Don't overlook nightwear and holiday clothing. (Key Skill: *Critical Thinking*)

TIPS:

Dressing to Save Energy
Discuss with students the types of dress that would promote energy conservations in your geographic area. *(Answers will vary depending on geographic area.)*

TIPS: *Dressing to Save Energy*

You can actually dress with energy conservation in mind. Just remember these guidelines:

- Dark colors can help you stay warm by absorbing heat from the sun. Light colors help you feel cooler in sunlight.
- Close-fitting clothes trap body heat to keep you warmer. To feel cooler, wear clothes with large neck, arm, and leg openings, open-type shoes, and fewer accessories.
- Clean clothes keep you warmer in the winter. Dirt clogs open spaces and decreases a fabric's insulation quality. In the summer, clean clothes are more comfortable to wear.

Individualizing Your Clothes

The way you dress communicates messages you want to send to others. Why not select clothing that will highlight your best features and downplay problem areas? If you know something about design, you can use it to say, "Look at my best features. This is the person I want you to see."

Many of the illustrations in this chapter show you how to apply basic design elements and principles to the way you dress. Chapter 24 discusses the design elements and principles in more detail.

▼ Elements of Design ▼

In clothing, three of the most important elements of design are line, color, and texture. Understanding how they work will help you choose attractive styles. **Figure 28.1** shows you how these elements work.

Line

Lines in garments can be formed by fabric design, such as a striped pattern. They can also be formed by seams, pleats, and trims. The **silhouette** (sill-uh-WET), or outline of

Figure 28-1 Using the Elements of Design

You can use the elements of design shown below to make subtle changes in your appearance.

Vertical lines run lengthwise. These lines can make the body seem taller than what it is.

Horizontal lines run from side to side. These lines lead the eyes across the body making it seem broader.

Cool colors tend to pull back and give the illusion of reduced size.

More About *Using Color in Your Wardrobe*

When taking a clothing inventory and planning new purchases, take color into consideration. Observing color as it appears in nature can help you to make smart clothing decisions. In nature:

- There is no color matching. For example, there are thousands of greens.
- There is no color uniformly the same color. There are many shades and tints of a color.
- Texture is used everywhere to create color shading, such as tree bark.
- There is primarily a dull finish with tiny bits of brightness.
- Bright colors are used in small amounts, such as flowers and flowering bushes.

a garment, creates an important line. Think of the difference between narrow, straight pants and loose, baggy ones.

Lines guide eye movement up and down or across an area. Clever placement of lines can actually change what people see.

Color

What are the best colors for you? They may not be your favorites or the latest fads. Your best colors are the ones that flatter the colors of your hair, skin, and eyes.

One good clue is to decide which of your clothes bring you the most compliments. Those colors are probably good choices.

You can also experiment by holding up different colors to your face and looking in a mirror. Which colors are most flattering? Do you look better in bright or soft colors? Do certain colors seem to make your eyes and hair shine? Your best colors should make your face look healthy and glowing. This is a good way to discover which colors make you look and feel your best. You can also learn which you should avoid.

Texture

Texture is the surface characteristic that you can see or feel in a fabric. The texture of your clothing can also affect your appearance.

Warm colors tend to draw attention and can give the illusion of increased size.

Shiny textures in fabrics, such as these slacks are made from, tend to give the illusion of increased size.

Bulky textures in fabrics, such as the fluffy yarn used in this sweater and the corduroy used in the slacks, tend to add to apparent size. Smooth textures have the opposite effect.

Learning Activities (continued)

3. **Alternate Group Work.** Give each group several swatches of different colored and/or different textured fabric. Ask each group to come up with clothing and use suggestions. What color eyes, skin, hair or body type might a garment of this fabric flatter? You might include a flat knit, wide wale corduroy, flannel, a shiny swimsuit knit, oxford cloth, and a satin or lame. Groups should share their findings with the rest of the class. (Key Skill: *Cooperation*)

Follow Up

1. **Reteaching.** How should a flattering color make your face look? *(Healthy and glowing)* What accessories will add a splash of color near your face? *(Scarf, necktie, colorful jewelry)* (Key Skill: *Decision Making*)
2. **Enrichment.** Have students ask their parents and grandparents what colors were popular when they were in grade school and high school (ask for the approximate dates) or other times they can remember. Students can compare their information, and, if it is fairly consistent, they can make a time line of popular colors over the last 50 years. See if there is any pattern of repetition. Have students predict what colors will crop up in the next few years. Can they think of any social or historical events that affected the colors of clothing? (Key Skill: *Cooperation*)

- The dominant colors are undemanding and restful, such as the blue sky.
- Even though in nature we see a variety of colors, there is a look of unity within the variety. Think of unity of colors when planning your wardrobe.

You may want to build your wardrobe around a color or two that go well together and that each go well with other colors, too, to provide variety in your look and to keep you from getting tired of the colors.

Teaching. . .
Principles of Design and Shopping for Clothes
(pp. 316-317)

Comprehension Check

1. When it comes to clothing, what are two of the most important principles of design? *(Proportion and emphasis)*
2. What should you do before leaving home to go shopping for clothes? *(Know what you need to buy; discuss priorities with family members)*
3. What are two other tips for getting ready to shop? *(Allow time to make comparisons; wear comfortable clothing)*

Learning Activities

1. **Personal Evaluation.** Divide the class into pairs or trios, preferably of friends. Ask students to evaluate each others' points to emphasize — eyes, waist, or shoulders, for example. Each student should make a list of these positive attributes — possibly with their good color list — to carry in their wallets as a reminder when they are shopping. (Key Skill: *Cooperation*)
2. **Picture Analysis.** Ask students to bring in pictures from magazines that show celebrities dressed for special events. As a class, analyze the clothing. Determine what the eyes notice first and discuss the celebrities' efforts to emphasize their best features. How successful were they? (Key Skills: *Critical Thinking*)

▼ Principles of Design ▼

The principles of design discussed in Chapter 24 apply to clothing, as well as homes. Two of the most important are proportion and emphasis. They help you combine the elements of design you have just read about to compliment your personality. **Figure 28-2** shows you how to use the principles of design.

Figure 28-2 Using the Principles of Design

The principles of design act as guidelines for using the elements of design. The garments below show how proportion and emphasis are used to enhance clothing.

Proportion involves the relationship of one part to another and to the whole. If you make one section of your body look long, wide, or large, then another section will appear shorter, narrower, or smaller. Notice how the slacks on the left appear to lengthen the legs. When using a longer shirt, as with the garment to the right, the shirt length creates shorter looking legs.

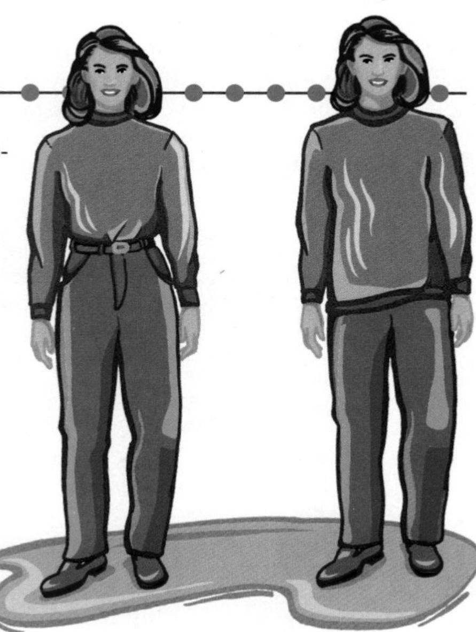

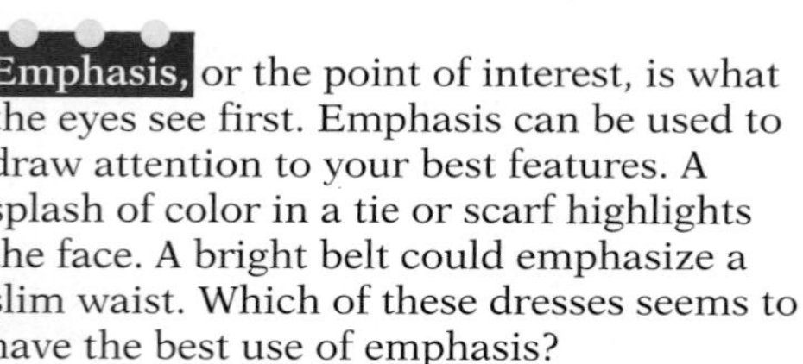

Emphasis, or the point of interest, is what the eyes see first. Emphasis can be used to draw attention to your best features. A splash of color in a tie or scarf highlights the face. A bright belt could emphasize a slim waist. Which of these dresses seems to have the best use of emphasis?

More About Texture

Texture is the surface appeal of an object. The way a fabric is constructed and the type of yarn used determine its texture. The "hand" of a fabric refers to the weight, thickness, and how the fabric drapes or falls. Some terms used to describe texture include:

- Coarse vs. fine
- Opaque vs. sheer
- Thin vs. bulky
- Soft vs. stiff/limp vs. crisp
- Cool vs. warm/light vs. heavy
- Shiny vs. dull
- Stretchy vs. firm/spongy vs. firm
- Smooth vs. rough

Labels on each garment list the care guidelines for that garment. How might reading the care guidelines affect your clothing purchases?

Shopping for Clothes

Have you ever shopped at dozens of stores to find the right shirt? Have you ever looked for a winter coat in January, only to find racks of bathing suits? Shopping is not always easy.

You can better meet the shopping challenge if you are an organized and well-informed consumer. You are not born with shopping savvy, or know-how. However, you can learn the "how-tos" of being a smart consumer. Chapter 20 has basic information that applies to all types of shopping. This chapter will help you sort through some of the decisions you have to make when buying clothes.

Getting Ready to Shop

Before you leave home to go shopping, have a good idea of what you need to buy. If you completed a clothing inventory, you should know what you need to fill the gaps in your wardrobe. You may also want to talk with family members about the needs of others in the family. Do others have some high-priority needs? Where do your needs fit in to the family budget? You may need to prioritize your "needs" list and buy the highest priority items first.

Allow enough time to shop and make comparisons. Avoid waiting until a week before a big event to find something new to wear. Remember to dress in comfortable clothing.

MEETING SPECIAL NEEDS

With Clothing

It's frustrating! Clothing is designed for the "average" person. It's often not suitable or comfortable for people with physical disabilities.

Jennifer Dalton uses a wheelchair to get around. Like most teens, she likes to look her best. She is active in the student council and the debate team. As she explains, clothing is a real problem for her.

"Most people don't realize what it's like for me to shop for clothes. When you are in a sitting position, most clothes pull in the back and bunch up in the front. It's very uncomfortable. Since my legs are paralyzed, it's hard for me to get in and out of clothes. My grandmother helps by sewing some of my clothes and altering others.

I wish more clothing manufacturers would realize that there's a real need for stylish clothes for people with physical limitations. I know they can't meet everyone's individual needs. But there are lots of people — even without disabilities — who would choose clothes that are easy to put on and take off. Maybe that's what I'll do after college — design my own clothing line!"

Follow Up

1. **Reteaching.** Ask the class: "You find a shirt at an outlet store that's a fabulous price. You're not quite sure it will fit and there's no fitting room. Also, all sales are final. The shirt is a great color for you, though, and last year you had a similar style that was very flattering. What are the pros and cons of buying this shirt?" *(Pros: color, price; Cons: can't check fit, can't return.)*
2. **Enrichment.** Have each student develop a shopping plan for his or her family. The plan should include wants and needs of family members, budget concerns, and priorities. (Key Skill: *Management*)

MEETING SPECIAL NEEDS

Through Clothing

Have students read the special needs feature. Ask them to brainstorm a list of ways clothing could be adapted for people with special needs.

Family Perspective

On holidays and special occasions you and your parents may disagree about how dressed up you should be. In fact, your parents may not be crazy about what you wear to school, either. To them, dressing up means showing respect. To you, it means being uncomfortable. Discuss this situation. Can compromise work?

More About *Planning Your Wardrobe Shopping*

Smart wardrobe planning begins with knowing the best times to shop. Some key months include: January — sale month, best buy on coats; February — spring lines begin to arrive; April — spring stock at peak; May — summer clothes begin arriving; July — sale time; August — fall and back-to-school lines arrive; October — best winter coat and boot selection; November — holiday clothes are features; December — the 26th is the best bargain day.

Teaching . . .
Shopping Strategies, Responsible Shopping, and Deciding to Buy
(pp. 318-319)

Comprehension Check

1. What four things should you check about a garment before buying it? *(Care, price, fit, workmanship)*
2. What do damaged garments and shoplifting eventually mean to the customer? *(Higher costs of every item to make up for damaged and stolen goods)*
3. What should you know about a store's exchange or return policy? *(Exchanges only/no returns? Sales slip necessary? Time period for returns?)*

Learning Activities

1. **Discussion.** Present this scenario: You have been looking for a black silky shirt. You find one that's perfect — well, almost. Would you buy this shirt if: • there is a small hole in the seam (the clerk will take 20% off the price and you know you can make the repair); • one of the three buttons is missing (the clerk offers 25% off but you will have to buy new buttons and sew them on); • there's a tear in the fabric near the bottom front of the blouse (the clerk offers 50% off but you know that the tear cannot be repaired without showing. This shirt is absolutely perfect otherwise — and this is the only way you can afford it.)? (Key Skill: *Problem Solving*)
2. **Display.** Collect yourself or assign students to supply a collection of similar garments (sweaters, shirts, slacks) of various quality and price. Show students how to compare the workmanship. Ask for suggestions about when and

SAFETY CHECK ✓

Have students read the safety check. Discuss with students reasons for considering safety when choosing children's clothing.

SAFETY CHECK ✓

Tips for buying safe children's clothing include:

- Buy children's sleepwear labeled "flame-retardant."
- Avoid garments with long strings and ties for infants. If they get wrapped around an infant's neck, they could cause strangulation.
- Avoid garments with buttons that could easily be pulled off and swallowed.
- Buy pants that are hemmed, not cuffed. They are less likely to catch and cause falls.
- Choose outdoor wear with separate hats or hoods. One-piece outfits may keep children from seeing well.

How does checking garment quality before you buy help save you money? What benefits does this have in the long run?

Carefully examine children's clothing for durability and safety.

▼ Shopping Strategies ▼

Try to stick with your shopping plan. At the same time, you have to be flexible. You may not be able to locate the exact item you want. If not, decide what would be the best substitute. You might use sewing skills to make the garment you want.

You may breathe a sigh of relief when you do find the right style, color, and size garment for which you are searching. Should you buy it? Not yet. You will want to look more closely at a few key areas first.

- ***Check the care label.*** Make sure you have the time, energy, and money needed to give the garment proper care.
- ***Check the price tag.*** Will the price of the garment fit in your budget? Don't buy something just because it is on sale. If an item is not the right color or style for you, it's not the bargain you may think it is.
- ***Check the fit.*** Try the garment on to be sure the garment doesn't pull or wrinkle when you walk, sit, bend, or move your arms. Waistbands should be comfortable, not too loose or too snug. Uncomfortable clothes are never a good buy.
- ***Check the quality of workmanship.*** If you plan to wear a garment often, buy the best quality you can afford. Remember, the garment will have to stand up to the strain of being worn and laundered frequently.

How to ...
Select Quality Clothing

Shoppers who know quality when they see it look for these points:

- Machine stitching is straight, even in length, and appears strong. Thread color should be close to the color of the fabric.
- Seams are smooth and straight, and stitches are even. They don't show any signs of puckering or pulling. Seam edges are finished to prevent raveling.
- The hem of the garment is even and parallel to the floor.
- Plaids, stripes, and large designs are matched at the seams.
- Points of strain are strengthened with double stitching or seam tape.
- Buttonholes are closely stitched and reinforced with extra stitching at the ends. Buttonhole openings fit the buttons and lie flat when closed.
- Zippers zip easily. When they are closed, zippers lie flat and are covered by the fabric.

▼ Responsible Shopping ▼

As you begin your shopping trip, think about the way you care for the clothing you look at and try on. You are responsible for keeping it clean and undamaged. Here are some tips for responsible shopping:

- Look at clothes carefully. Make sure your hands are clean.
- Avoid wearing jewelry that could snag or catch on clothing.
- Carefully remove clothes from hangers when you try them on. Unbutton buttons and unzip zippers.
- If you wear makeup, be careful not to get it on the clothing you try on.
- Alert a sales clerk if you find a damaged garment.

How to ... Select Quality Clothing

Have students read the feature. Then pass around ad or magazine photos or sketches of quality garments which illustrate the points listed. Otherwise, ask students to select the illustrations from fashion magazines or catalogs. Check the descriptions to see if these qualities appear. Other options include bringing a few garments to display on which you can point out these qualities. Or, take students (or assign them to go) to a store featuring well-made garments. Have them find garments which illustrate the points brought out in the feature. Have students write down the style number (and price) and ask a clerk to sign their paper.

Learning Activities (continued)

where a particular garment needs to be well made (strong seams for active wear, finished seams for fabrics that ravel, etc.). Remind students about the responsibilities for handling clothing when they check out your display. (Key Skill: *Citizenship*)

3. **Display or poster.** Ask students to display and report on the responsibilities of being a good shopper. Have them list and illustrate on fabric swatches the effects of make-up, snags, and so forth. (Key Skill: *Creativity*)

Follow Up

1. **Reteaching.** What are the advantages of saving sales receipts? How long should you keep them? Where might be a good place to store them? *(For returns; keep them several months to a year for garments; store them in an easily-accessible, well-organized place)*
2. **Extension.** Use the information on p. 40 of the *Extending the Lesson* booklet in the TCR.
3. **Enrichment.** Ask each student to bring a small box or old file box for 3 × 5 index cards. Make tabs for file cards and have students set up a box for keeping and organizing receipts. (Key Skill: *Management*)

Family Perspective

Being part of a family can affect clothing needs and wants, purchases, and responsibilities. The clothing needs of a growing child or a parent entering the workforce may take priority over the wants of other family members. Responsibility for selecting and caring for clothes may be given to one person or shared by family members.

Completing the Chapter

For Review

1. Emphasize the main concepts using the summary.
2. Have students complete the "Facts to Recall." (Answers below.)

For Reteaching

1. **Reteaching.** Use the activity on p. 36 of the *Reteaching and Practical Skills* booklet in the TCR.

For Enrichment

1. **Enrichment.** Use the activity on p. 46 of the *Enrichment Activities* booklet in the TCR.

For Evaluation

1. Choose items from "Ideas to Explore" and "Activities to Try."
2. Use the chapter test on pp. 59-60 in the testing booklet of the TCR or use the testmaker software.

Facts to Recall Answers

1. Sort clothes into three groups: clothes liked and worn; clothes no longer worn and wanted; questionable clothes. Make a list for each activity you participate in. Put clothing from first pile under the appropriate activities. Add clothing items in the "if" pile to your inventory if they can be repaired or updated. Give unwanted clothing to someone in need.
2. Clothing suitable for many situations.
3. **Any four:** needs and wants; budget; fashion; versatility; mix-and-match possibilities; accessories.
4. Answers will vary. Any one: vertical lines to add height; wearing colors that make eyes and hair shine; bulky clothing to add the appearance of size.
5. Proportion — change appearance of one section of body to another. Emphasis draws attention to best features.
6. The care label; price tag; fit; quality of workmanship.

- When you are through trying on a garment, return it to the rack or a sales clerk if you do not buy it.
- Shoplifting is illegal. Most stores turn shoplifters over to the police.

▼ Deciding to Buy ▼

WAREHOUSE POLICY
- NO CASH REFUNDS
- NO CHARGE CARD CREDITS

EXCHANGE WITHIN 7 DAYS WHEN ACCOMPANIED BY REGISTER RECEIPT AND PRICE TICKET
- LAY-A-WAYS ⅓ DEPOSIT — 14 DAYS TO PICK UP

THANK YOU!

Exchange policies vary from store to store.

After checking the care instructions, price, fit, and quality, you should have a good idea of whether this garment is right for you. Don't buy anything if you have serious doubts about it.

Check stores' exchange or return policies before you buy. Discount stores and factory outlets have stricter rules than most department stores. If the policy is "exchanges only, no returns," you know that you won't get your money back. Instead, you're able to exchange an item for one of equal value.

Keep the sales slip until you are absolutely certain you won't return the item. Many stores make exchanges only with the original sales slip. Some stores have a time period during which items may be returned. Usually this period is 30 days or less.

TAKING ACTION

Making a Wise Decision

Lionel takes one look at the classic leather jacket in the store window and says to you, "I've got to have it." The two of you walk into the store and Lionel tries on the jacket in his size. It not only looks great on him, but it is on sale for half-price. The salesman assures him, "You won't find a deal like this again."

Lionel is in a dilemma. He intended to go shopping for some badly needed fall clothes. Most of his pants are too short for him, and several shirts need repairs. The amount he planned to spend on new clothes equals the sale price of the leather jacket. If he buys the jacket, he'll have to wait at least three months before he can afford to buy anything else. Lionel wants your advice.

Using Your Resourcefulness

- What would you suggest Lionel do? Offer three reasons to support your answer.
- If Lionel decides to shop for pants and shirts, what choices does he have in terms of where to shop? What are the advantages and disadvantages of these choices?
- If Lionel decides to buy the jacket, what can he do about shirts and pants until he can save some more money?
- What options does Lionel have if he decides he would like to have the jacket and the shirts and pants?
- How is Lionel effectively using his resources? Explain your answer.

TAKING ACTION

After students have read the Taking Action feature, you may want to have them respond to the *Using Your Resourcefulness* questions in small groups. Ask the students to consider the implications concerning the responses they would give to Lionel.

Using Your Resourcefulness Answers
- Answers will vary.
- Lionel could shop at a department store, discount store, outlet store, or specialty store. Advantages: more choices and a variety of prices. Disadvantages: may have to shop at more than one place, quality may vary from store to store.

Chapter 28 Review

Summary

In this chapter, you have read about:
- ▶ How careful planning can help you build a wardrobe that will meet your needs.
- ▶ How to take a clothing inventory as the first step in wardrobe planning.
- ▶ How the elements and principles of design can help you choose flattering clothing.
- ▶ Strategies that can help you make wise decisions when you shop for clothing.
- ▶ How to evaluate the quality of a garment.

Facts to Recall

1. Describe how to take a clothing inventory.
2. Define multipurpose clothing and give an example.
3. Name four points to consider when planning what to add to your wardrobe.
4. Give an example of using design elements to highlight one's best features.
5. Describe how proportion and emphasis enter into clothing design.
6. Name four key areas to check before deciding whether to buy a garment.
7. List five signs of quality workmanship in a garment.
8. Name at least four guidelines to follow when buying clothing for people with special needs.

Ideas to Explore

1. What do you think is the most common mistake people make when shopping for clothing? Why is it a problem? How could the problem be prevented?
2. Why do fashions change?
3. Give three examples of classic fashions and three examples of fads. In general, how do classic fashions differ from fads?
4. Suppose you have enough money to buy a good-quality pair of slacks. Then you find another pair that is half the price of the first, but of poor quality. Which would you buy and why? What is the importance of quality when buying clothing?

Activities to Try

1. Using magazines and newspapers, find pictures of clothes that are examples of fads and classics. Cut out the pictures and label them. Write an explanation for your selections.
2. Create a clothing design that would minimize one of the following: wide shoulders; long, thin legs; short arms; large hips; small chest.

LINK TO *Communication*

MAKING CLOTHING CHOICES

Develop a skit showing the positive and negative aspects of peer pressure concerning clothing choices. Include some ways that you and your friends affect each other's clothing choices. In addition, act out situations in which teens and their parents may have conflicts over clothing choices (you may want to incorporate ways in which peer pressure affects the teen/parent conflict). Be sure that your skits *fairly* represent different points of view as well as express ways to resolve conflict over clothing choices.

Facts to Recall Answers (continued)

7. **Any five:** straight, even machine stitching; seams are smooth and straight; garment hem is even and parallel to the floor; plaids, stripes, and large designs are matched at seams; points of strain are reinforced; buttonholes stitched closely and reinforced with extra stitching at the end; zippers zip easily.

Ideas to Explore

1. Answers will vary.
2. Answers will vary and may include: to accommodate changes in lifestyles; in availability of clothing materials; in ideas of beauty.
3. Examples will vary. Classic fashions are enduring, while fads are short-lived. Classics are practical and useful, fads tend to be impractical.
4. Answers will vary.

- Answers will vary but may include repairing his shirts or lengthening his pants.
- Answers will vary but may include putting the jacket on lay-away, buying some shirts and pants now and waiting until later to buy others, or borrow money for the jacket from his parents.
- Answers will vary.

LINK TO *Math*

Answers

Skits will vary. Students should use communication and conflict resolution skills discussed in Chapters 8 and 9.

Preparing to Teach

Chapter Outline

Chapter Resources

The following booklet materials may be found in the *Teacher's Classroom Resources* box:

- Lesson Plans, p. 34
- Student Workbook, *Study Guide,* pp. 125-126; *Fiber Figures,* p. 127; *Fabric Magic Square,* p. 128
- Personal Safety, *Dressing for Safety,* pp. 35-36
- Technology and Computers, pp. 36, 37, 38
- Cooperative Learning, p. 41
- Extending the Text, *The Greening of Cotton,* p. 41
- Reteaching and Practical Skills, *Puzzling Over Fibers and Fabrics,* pp. 37-38
- Enrichment Activities, *Practicing Piece Dyeing,* pp. 47-48
- Chapter and Unit Tests, pp. 61-62
- Testmaker Software

Also see:

- Meeting the Special Needs of Students
- Linking Home, School, and Community

CHAPTER 29 Fibers to Fabrics

OBJECTIVES

- *Describe how natural and manufactured fibers differ.*
- *Identify the characteristics of common fibers.*
- *Explain three methods of making fabric.*
- *Describe how finishes change fabrics.*

TERMS TO LEARN

- ***fibers***
- ***natural fibers***
- ***manufactured fibers***
- ***luster***
- ***generic name***
- ***trade name***
- ***fabric blends***

More About Microdenier Fibers

One of the most recent fiber developments is Microdenier fiber. These fibers are finer than silk and are soft and smooth to the touch, creating rich fabric looks and textures. The fibers are so small that they require special care when they are dyed and finished. For example, because there are more fibers, it takes more dye to get a given color. Dupont is manufac-

Alicia's new shirt was made from a soft rayon fabric. She had several washable rayon shirts that were easy to care for. After wearing the shirt once, Alicia washed and dried it the same way she washed and dried her other rayon shirts. Alicia wondered what she had done wrong when the shirt came out of the dryer covered with little matted balls and sleeves that were several inches shorter than when it went into the dryer.

When you buy clothing, do you stop to think about the fabric from which it is made? Taking time to learn about fabrics will help you to:

- Become a smarter consumer.
- Take care of clothing correctly so it looks better and wears longer.
- Be happier with your clothing and fabric purchases.

Fibers

Fibers are hairlike substances that are twisted together to make yarns and fabric. There are two groups of fibers: natural and manufactured.

Natural fibers come from plants or animals. They include cotton, linen, wool, silk, and ramie, among others.

Fabrics are used in many things besides clothing that affect your life daily. How many products can you name in which fabrics are used?

turing Microdenier fibers as "Micromattique," and Fortrell as "MicroSpun." The fibers are so fine that, bundled into yarns, they are still finer than human hair and are four times finer than wool.

Manufacturers say that Microdenier can recreate any fabric — better than it was — with better performance, more flexibility, and greater functions. They mention such fabrics as silk, suede, velvet, wool crepe and satin. The fibers can be knitted or woven and used for clothing and home furnishings. It can also be blended with other manufactured and natural fibers. Many blends are also easy to care for and can be washed and dried at home with perfect results.

Introducing the Chapter

Motivators

1. **Visual "aide."** Display clothing of natural fibers: ramie blouse, wool jacket, silk scarf, linen skirt, cotton stockings, for example. Ask individuals to identify the fabrics. On another day use manufactured fabrics for the same exercise. Compare the characteristics and uses of particular fabrics, and compare their qualities. (Key Skill: *Critical Thinking*)
2. **Fabric Identification.** Ask a volunteer who is wearing a variety of clothing to stand. How many fabrics can the class recognize? Or, find the person wearing the widest variety of fabrics. (Key Skill: *Critical Thinking*)
3. **Fabric IQ.** Give students a list of fabrics. Ask them to tell where the fabric comes from, what it looks like, how it is used, and what its strengths and weaknesses are. (Key Skill: *Critical Thinking*)
4. **Silly Stories.** Give groups the name and traits of a synthetic fabric. Ask them to "create" an animal from which this fiber supposedly comes, relating the characteristics of the fiber to the habits and characteristics of the animal. (Key Skill: *Creativity*)

Chapter Objectives and Vocabulary

1. Have students read the chapter objectives and rephrase the objectives as questions.
2. Ask students to state, in their own words, the purpose of studying this chapter.
3. Pronounce the vocabulary terms listed on the previous page. Ask students whether they are familiar with any of these. Explain that the terms will be defined in the chapter.

Guided Reading

1. Have the students read the chapter and use the Study Guide on pp. 125-126 of the *Student Workbook*.

Teaching. . .
Fibers, Natural and Manufactured
(p. 323-325)

Comprehension Check

1. How are tiny fibers put together to make a fabric? *(They are twisted together.)*
2. What fibers come from plants? From animals? *(Plants: ramie, linen, cotton; Animals: wool, silk)*
3. What are characteristics of manufactured fabrics? *(Strong, spring back into shape, sensitive to heat, shed water quickly, are warm)*
4. What kind of fibers absorb moisture best? *(natural fibers)*

Learning Activities

1. **Display.** This chapter is perfect for displaying samples of a variety of fabrics or displaying clothes made from the fabrics. Or, display several articles made from different forms of the same fabric, such as wool. (Key Skill: *Creativity*)
2. **Posters.** Ask students to make posters about one particular natural fiber. Encourage them to collect and show fibers in their raw and finished states — and any steps in between. (Key Skills: *Creativity, Cooperation*)
3. **Group Presentations.** Ask students to look up and present information about animal fibers: Angora, alpaca, merino, cashmere, mohair, etc. Samples would be great. (Key Skill: *Science*)

Liquid nylon is forced through the spinnerette and hardens into fibers. How might nylon fibers be used?

Manufactured fibers, also called synthetic (sin-THET-ik) fibers, are made all or in part from chemicals. Some manufactured fibers are made from products such as coal and oil. To make the fibers, a syrupy substance is forced through a spinnerette — a metal plate full of very tiny holes that looks similar to a shower head. The liquid coming through the spinnerette is hardened to form stringlike fibers. The fibers are about the thickness of sewing thread. Some new fibers, called *microfibers*, are forced through a spinnerette with micro-sized holes. The microfiber yarns are twice as fine as the best silk yarn.

Cotton is the most widely used natural fiber.

Linen is made from the stems of the flax plant. It is used in clothing and home decorating products.

▼ Natural Fibers ▼

Natural fibers have been used for thousands of years. Cotton is the most widely used natural fiber. Both cotton and linen come from plants. These fibers absorb moisture well. This makes them comfortable to wear in warm weather. Cotton and linen also wrinkle, shrink, and mildew easily.

Wool comes from the fleece of sheep. It absorbs moisture and still feels dry. It resists wrinkling and is valued for its warmth. Wool fibers trap air and prevent the loss of body heat. Wool shrinks when washed in hot water. It also burns when exposed to very high heat.

Silk is the strongest of the natural fibers. It is spun by silkworms. It is comfortable to wear because it absorbs body moisture and resists wrinkles. Silk is a luxury fiber and is very expensive. However, there are many other less costly fibers that have the look and feel of silk.

Ramie comes from the stalks of China grass in Southeast Asia. It is a strong, durable fiber. It is often combined with other fibers, such as cotton, in making fabrics. Ramie absorbs moisture and dries quickly. It has a natural **luster**, or shine, and can be dyed easily.

AROUND THE WORLD

After reading the feature, ask students what advantages there might be in using raw silk. *(Less processing so it might be less expensive; Coarse, stiff fabric better for some uses)*

More About Cotton

Cotton is easy to launder. While able to withstand high temperatures, cotton tends to shrink when exposed to heat. Today, cotton is often treated with easy-care finishes or blended with polyester to limit its shrinkability.

Almost half of all clothing manufactured for children is made of cotton. The slightly wrinkled "status" look that natural fibers impart has increased cotton's popularity. T-shirts, shorts, socks, dresses, skirts, and jeans are all increasingly made of cotton.

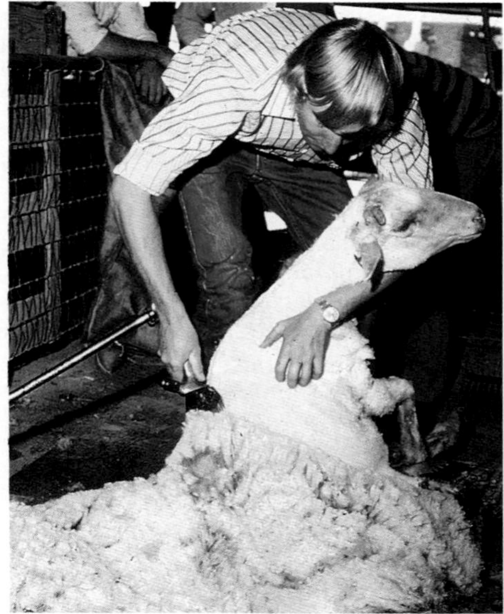

The fleece of sheep is fine and soft. Fabrics made from wool are good to wear in cold weather.

Luxurious silk fibers are being spun into yarn at this textile factory in Thailand.

AROUND THE WORLD

Americans are most familiar with the satiny smoothness of finished silk, but it is used raw in other countries, such as India. When first spun, silk is a stiff yarn that is woven into a coarse, crisp fabric called tussah (TUSS-ah). The silkworm's natural gum makes these fabrics dye-resistant; if the gum is removed, however, the yarns can be dyed and woven into bright, colorful patterns.

▼ Manufactured Fibers ▼

Manufactured fibers are generally strong. They have a natural ability to spring back to their original shape. Many manufactured fibers are sensitive to heat. They can be damaged by a hot iron.

Manufactured fibers are made to look, feel, and act like natural fibers. However, several qualities make manufactured fibers unique. Almost all of these fibers tend to shed

Learning Activities (continued)

4. **Guest Speaker.** Find someone to demonstrate a spinning wheel to show how fibers are twisted together. Check yarn stores, historical or craft groups to locate someone. (Key Skill: *Science*)
5. **Map.** Give groups a natural fiber to research. Have them tell where it is produced, and locate the area on a map. Try combining with Activity 4. (Key Skill: *Communication*)
6. **Demonstration.** Using an eye dropper, squeeze drops of water on squares of natural and manufactured fibers to see if the water beads up or is absorbed. Test this beforehand to avoid any surprises. (Key Skill: *Critical Thinking*)
7. **Display.** Ask students to bring in fabric content/care labels or tags and write the item it came from on it. Point out what information is on the tags. Compare fabric content. Refer to these labels later, in the fiber care unit. Ask students to locate and read the labels on their own clothing. (Key Skill: *Critical Thinking*)

Follow Up

1. **Reteaching.** Have students investigate what characteristics make natural fibers good choices for clothing. (Key Skill: *Critical Thinking*)
2. **Enrichment.** Investigate how it was discovered that plants and fur could be made into fiber and then woven into cloth. (Key Skills: *Problem Solving, Critical Thinking*)

More About *Rayon*

More and more clothes are either rayon or a blend containing rayon. Rayon used to be considered a cheap substitute for the more expensive silk. Today rayon is found in expensive clothes. Imported rayon is subject to large importation duties and often costs more than linen or cotton. It has become popular because it feels expensive, dyes beautifully, and drapes well.

Rayon presents care problems. It wrinkles and lacks what experts call "memory" — it doesn't spring back into shape. Some rayon clothes are washable, but many must be dry cleaned, which increases the cost of the garment.

Photo Focus

Discuss the top left photo on p. 325 with the students. What time of the year do you think they shear sheep? *(Spring, after winter coat of wool)* In what condition do you think the wool is? *(Probably dirty, needs cleaning)*

Teaching. . .
Blends and Fabric Construction
(p. 326-327)

Comprehension Check

1. Which fabrics are considered the strongest? *(Ramie, silk, nylon)*
2. Which fabrics wrinkle easily? *(Cotton, linen, ramie, rayon)* Are they of the same type? *(Mostly plant fibers)* Which fabrics resist wrinkling? *(Wool, acrylic, modacrylic, nylon, polyester)* Are they of the same type? *(Mostly manufactured fibers)*
3. Which fabrics are affected by chlorine bleach? *(Silk, spandex)*
4. Which fabrics are easily laundered? *(Cotton, linen, nylon, polyester)*
5. What are three common ways that yarn is made into fiber? *(Weaving, knitting, bonding)*

Learning Activities

1. **Discussion Topic.** You are going to Europe and can take only one small bag. Irons and washers will not be available although you can wash things out by hand. Which fabrics will you try to pack and why? (Key Skill: *Problem Solving*)
2. **Impromptu Skit.** Select students to play teens planning a camping trip. They will be canoeing (getting wet) and, although the days will be warm, the nights will be cool. One camper insists cotton sweaters are better; the other believes in wool sweaters. Allow time to come up with some good points for debate. (Key Skills: *Creativity, Communication*)

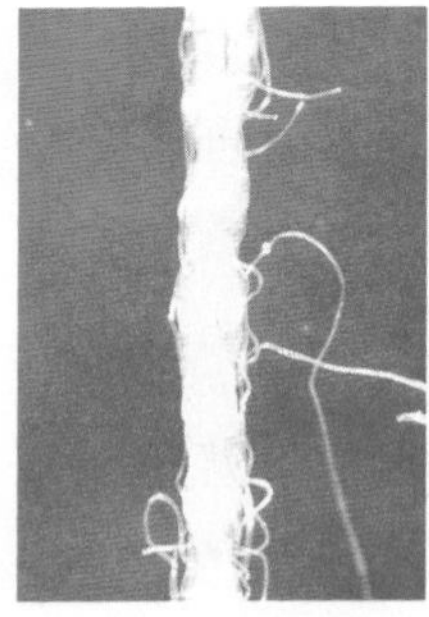

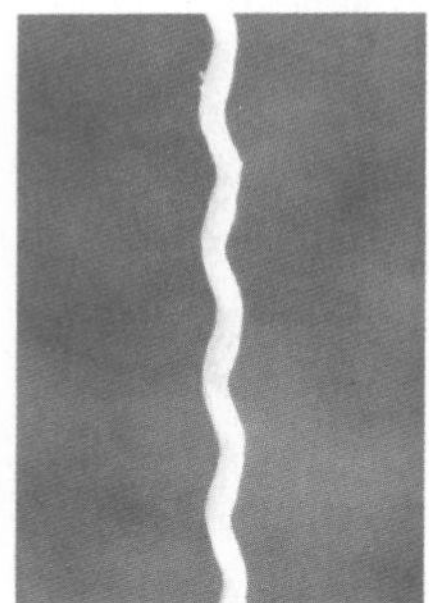

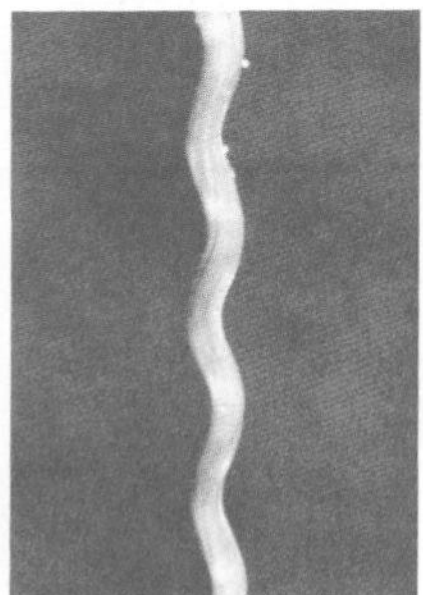

Above are three common manufactured fibers. The top photo is an example of nylon; the middle photo is an example of Dacron© polyester; the lower photo is an example of Orlon© acrylic. Many labels often provide the trade names and the generic names of fibers.

water rather than absorb it. As a result, they dry quickly and shrink very little. They also tend to be warm to wear. Some manufactured fibers have been improved to absorb moisture better. For example, fabrics can be made to have more volume or bulk. The added bulk allows more air to move through the fabric in order to absorb perspiration. This makes clothing made from manufactured fibers more comfortable to wear in warm weather.

Manufactured fibers, such as nylon, rayon, spandex, and polyester, add to your choices of fabrics. Each manufactured fiber has two names. It has a **generic name** — or the common name for a group of similar fibers, and a **trade name** — or the manufacturer's name for a specific fiber or fabric. Every manufactured fiber is put into a group depending on the materials from which it is made. For example, Dacron®, Fortrel®, and Kodel® are all trade names for polyester fibers. All members of the polyester family have similar characteristics and need the same type of care. Labels on garments and fabrics usually carry both names.

▼ Blends ▼

Every fiber has good qualities. However, no fiber is perfect. As a result, manufacturers have developed **fabric blends** — fabrics containing two or more fibers. Blends combine the best qualities of each fiber. As an example, mixing cotton and polyester offers the moisture absorbency of cotton and the quick drying and wrinkle resistance of polyester.

The percentage of each fiber needed in order to build in certain qualities varies. For example, a blend of 50 percent polyester and 50 percent cotton with a durable-press finish resists wrinkling. Without a durable-press finish, a blend of 65 percent polyester and 35 percent cotton is needed to resist wrinkling.

Fabric Construction

Fibers are twisted together to make yarns. These yarns are usually about the thickness of sewing thread. Yarns are then put together to form fabric. The final yarn arrangement affects the wear you can expect from the fabric. It also affects the care a fabric needs. Three common methods of making fabric from yarn are weaving, knitting, and bonding.

More About Fiber Blends

In a blended fabric, fibers are mixed before they are spun into yarns. Yarns are blended for economy, variety, strength, less shrinkage, more absorbency, and to provide warmth or coolness.

More About Fiber Facts

- Each fiber contributes its best qualities to a blend only when it is present in sufficient quantity.
- Acrylic or polyester decreases drying time when added to cotton or rayon.
- Cotton, linen, ramie, or rayon increase absorbency.
- Cotton, rayon, or acetate lowers cost.

Natural and Manufactured Fibers

Natural Fibers	Characteristics	Uses
Cotton	Dyes and prints easily. Absorbent and comfortable. Wrinkles. Easily laundered.	Jeans, shirts, sportswear, socks, undergarments and household textiles such as towels and sheets.
Linen	Very durable. Very absorbent. Wrinkles. Easily laundered.	Suits, jackets, dresses, tablecloths.
Ramie	Strong. Dyes well. Wrinkles easily.	Knit tops, scarves, sweaters, upholstery.
Silk	Strong. Lightweight. Weakened by perspiration. Damaged by chlorine bleach. Sometimes washable, usually dry-cleaned.	Shirts, dresses, ties, scarves.
Wool	Warm. Resists wrinkling. Absorbent. Attracts moths. Usually dry-cleaned, sometimes washable.	Coats, suits, slacks, sweaters, hats, gloves.
Manufactured Fibers	**Characteristics**	**Uses**
Acetate	Drapes well. Poor abrasion resistance. Usually dry-cleaned. Heat sensitive.	Sportswear, shirts, dresses, ties, scarves.
Acrylic	Resists wrinkling. Lightweight and soft. May pill or form small matted balls. Dry-cleaned or laundered.	Knitted garments, sportswear, blankets, upholstery.
Modacrylic	Soft. Resists wrinkling. Not absorbent. May pill. Dry-cleaned or laundered.	Sportswear, knitted garments, fake furs, blankets.
Nylon	Strong. Resists wrinkling. Poor absorption. Washable. Dries quickly.	Swimwear, hosiery, undergarments, sportswear.
Polyester	Resists wrinkling. Retains pleats and creases. Low absorption. Holds oil stains and soil. Washable. Dries quickly.	Shirts, dresses, slacks, sportswear, pillow stuffing.
Rayon	Highly absorbent. Easy to dye. Drapes well. Wrinkles. Usually dry-cleaned. Sometimes washable.	Dresses, shirts, ties, scarves, window coverings, undergarments.
Spandex	High degree of stretch. Lightweight. Weakened by chlorine bleach. Washable.	Swimwear, undergarments, skiwear, aerobicwear, bicycle shorts, support hosiery.

- Silk increases cost.
- Wool and acrylic both add warmth but wool is more expensive.
- Wool, silk, and polyester all provide crease resistance, but wool and silk are more expensive.
- Nylon and silk add strength and luster.
- Acetate contributes draping qualities.
- Wool needs 55% acrylic and polyester to retain washability, quick drying, wrinkle resistance.

Learning Activities (continued)

3. **Discussion.** Present students with the following situation: Several teens are stranded on a desert island. Altogether the stranded teens have a silk shirt, a cotton shirt, an acetate shirt, a ramie shirt and several cotton/polyester blends. What are the advantages and disadvantages of each under these conditions: hot days, cool nights, continual wear, no deodorant. Which shirt fabric would you prefer? (Key Skills: *Critical Thinking, Creativity*)
4. **Group Work.** Ask each group to invent a new fabric, give it a name, and create advertising materials telling what it is and what it does. Give the groups the same climate and activity conditions (cold days, warm nights, very active person, no dry cleaning nearby, for example) or different conditions. Groups may compete to find the most clever. (Key Skill: *Problem Solving*)
5. **Posters.** Distribute catalogs and sale flyers. Ask students to find pictures of clothes in assorted fabrics to paste onto tag board labeled "Wool," "Silk," "Cotton/Poly Blend," and so on. Hang the posters around the room. (Key Skill: *Creativity*)
6. **Exploration.** Give students each a short length of different spun yarns. Have them separate the yarn into strands; exchange all but one strand; recombine or retwist the strands together; and analyze the results. How have the characteristics of the twisted yarn changed? (Key Skill: *Critical Thinking*)

Follow Up

1. **Reteaching.** Ask students to check the chart on page 327 and give awards for the "Warmest," "Easiest to Launder," "Most Wrinkle Resistant," "Most Absorbent," "Strongest," and so forth. (Key Skill: *Critical Thinking*)
2. **Enrichment.** Ask students to list their favorite clothes; check the labels at home; list the fabric content; chart or write a paragraph about which fabrics appear most. Why do students choose the fabrics that they do? (Key Skill: *Critical Thinking*)

Teaching. . .
Weaving, Knitting, Bonding, Fabric Finishes, Dyeing and Printing, Other Finishes
(p. 328-330)

Comprehension Check

1. What are some advantages and disadvantages of knits over woven fabrics? *(Advantages: stretchy and comfortable; Disadvantages: easily snagged.)*
2. How are "bonded" fabrics made? What are their assets and drawbacks? *(Fibers are mechanically or chemically joined to give shape, flexibility, wrinkle resistance; may be unwashable.)*
3. What is the difference between a waterproof and a water-repellent fabric finish? *(Waterproof: helps fabric shed water; water-repellent: helps fabric resist water)*

Learning Activities

1. **Knit Survey.** To show how widely knit fabrics are used, point out the variety of knit articles worn by students each day (hosiery, T-shirts, double knits, sweatshirts, sweaters). Don't forget underwear! Ask students why knits are so popular. (Key Skill: *Critical Thinking*)
2. **Hands-on Project.** Give each student string or thread to weave in plain, twill, and satin weaves. Make simple looms from nails and boards, tacks and cardboard, or staples and paper. Add different yarns, dental floss, or even rubber bands to spark discussion on possibilities. (Key Skill: *Creativity*)
3. **Demonstration.** Invite a hand or machine "knitter" to demonstrate their skill. (Include a weaver or spinner and have an "Artisan Fair"!) Give students an opportunity to try these crafts or tie this activity into a career or hobby day. (Key Skill: *Creativity*)
4. **Display.** Collect samples of woolens (fine woolens, coat woolens, inexpensive blends) or knits to examine and compare. Arrange the samples on a poster, with an edge frayed to show fibers. (Key Skill: *Critical Thinking*)

FABRIC WEAVES

PLAIN

TWILL

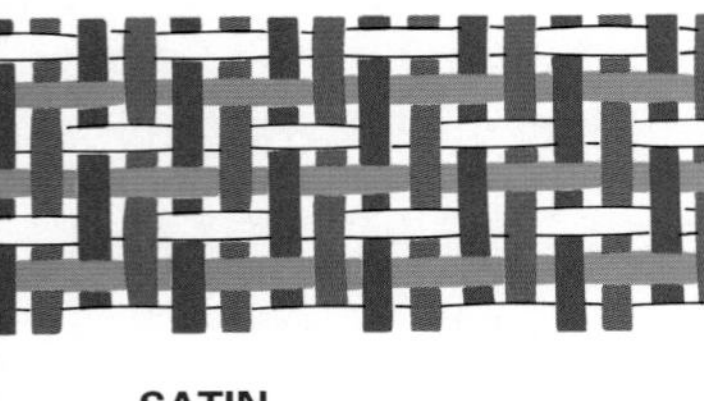

SATIN

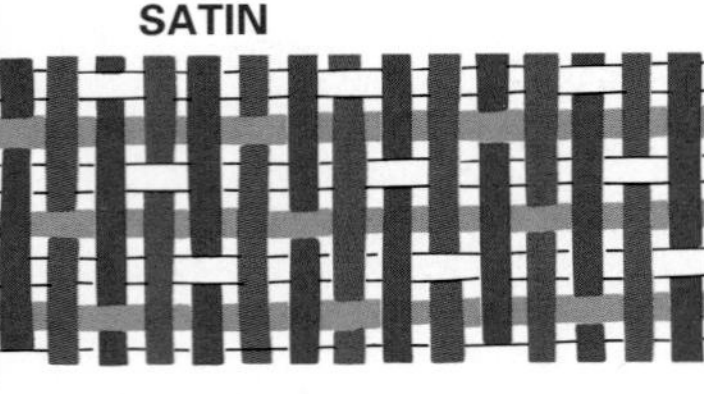

OXFORD CLOTH

DENIM

SATIN

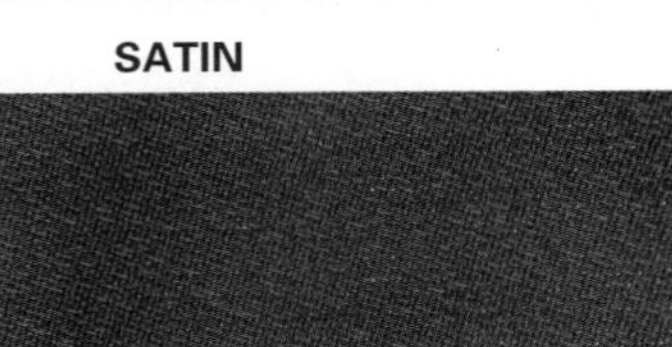

Weaving

In weaving, lengthwise and crosswise yarns are laced together at right angles. The tightness of the weave determines the firmness of the fabric and affects how it will wear. Generally, tightly woven fabrics wear better than those that are loosely woven.

Different types of weaves are used to make fabric. Plain, twill, satin, and pile weaves are the most common.

- ***Plain weave.*** In this simple weave, each crosswise yarn passes over and under each lengthwise yarn. Broadcloth and gingham are examples of plain weave fabric.
- ***Twill weave.*** The lengthwise yarns pass over two and then under two crosswise yarns. In twill weave fabrics, the diagonal ridges made by yarns can be seen on the surface of the fabric. The twill weave produces a stronger fabric than other weaves. Jeans are usually made of denim fabric, a hard-wearing twill weave.
- ***Satin weave.*** A satin weave produces a shiny fabric. The lengthwise yarns pass over four or more crosswise yarns and generally under one crosswise yarn. The satin weave is not as strong as the twill or plain weave.
- ***Pile weave.*** Three sets of yarn are used to make the pile weave. Pile fabrics such as velvet and corduroy are first woven in a plain, twill, or satin weave. Then an extra set of yarns is woven in to form a pile, or cut surface.

Knitting

Another way of making fabrics is by knitting. Knitted fabrics are stretchy and comfortable. They are made by interlocking loops of yarn together row after row. Yarns of various fibers, weights, and textures are knit by machine or hand. Knits are more easily snagged and pulled than woven fabrics.

Clothing made from knitted fabrics allows free movement. It generally holds its shape well. As with woven fabrics, knitted fabrics may be made by several different methods.

- ***Single knits.*** These are often used for T-shirts and simple dresses. Single knits have a flat, smooth appearance on the front side and horizontal loops on the back side.
- ***Double knits.*** These knits are made with two interlocking layers on the front and back that cannot be separated. Double knits are durable and wrinkle resistant. Interlocks, the simplest type of double knit fabrics, are often used for career clothing.

More About Knits

Not all knits are polyester! Today many fibers are used in knits: cotton, acetate, nylon, acrylic, wool, polyester, spandex, and blends of these which can include silk, ramie, and linen. Polyester and nylon are the most durable and have the easiest care. Acrylic is one of the most heat sensitive. Cotton is the coolest, but must be preshrunk and it does not hold its shape unless a special finish has been added. Wool is the most resilient. Spandex is used in action wear, inner wear, and swimwear. Acetate is more absorbent and less expensive than other synthetics; however, it is very heat sensitive and less durable.

- ***Tricot knits (TREE-coh).*** Narrow vertical ribs on the front and crosswise ribs on the back, characterize tricot knits. They have plenty of stretchability and are runproof, snag-resistant, and nonraveling. These qualities make tricot knits useful for undergarments, dresses, shirts, blouses, and swimwear.

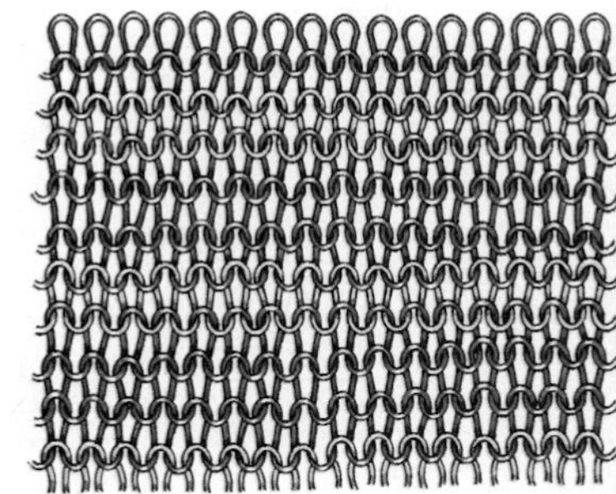
Knitted fabric.

Bonding

Bonding is a method used for making nonwoven fabrics. Fibers are mechanically or chemically joined together. Steam or heat, used with an adhesive, bonds nonwoven fabrics together. Bonding gives shape to nonwoven fabrics, helps make them flexible, and helps prevent wrinkling.

Long-lasting nonwoven fabrics may be used for blankets, carpet backing, and interfacing — a fabric used inside garments that gives hidden support and stability. Some nonwoven fabrics are disposable and may be used for items such as disposable diapers.

Fabric Finishes

Finishes are one of the final touches put on yarns or fabrics. Finishes change some of the natural characteristics of fabrics to make them more appealing and useful. Many different finishes can be added. These range from dyeing and printing, to waterproofing.

Dyeing and Printing

Adding color to fabric is an age-old art. It also is as new as the most complex computer. Some dyes come from nature and some are developed in the lab. The way dye is applied varies. Sometimes yarn is dyed before it is woven into fabric. The most common method of dyeing is called piece dyeing. The dye is applied after the yarn is made into fabric.

Fabrics are dyed in machines such as these.

Color can also be applied by using a printing process. Patterns, such as flowers, ducks, or polka dots, can be rolled onto fabric by using rollers or cylinders. Sometimes patterns are applied by screen printing, in which dyes are forced through a screen onto the fabric. This process is similar to stenciling.

Weaving patterns out of selected colors of pre-dyed yarn is another way to create a design in fabric. Patterns such as plaids can be formed this way.

More About Fabric Finishes

Finishes on fabrics play an important role in the satisfaction you receive from your fabric. Finishes improve a fabric's appearance and/or performance.

The biggest problem is that many finishes do not last. Ideally, a fabric finish would last the life of the fabric; however, many finishes are "finished" after the fabric is washed or dry cleaned. Presently, there is no law requiring the labels for fabric finishes. Many manufacturers provide this information, though so read labels!

5. **Demonstration.** Gather a variety of swatches of varying fiber content. Dip them in fabric dye or food coloring to see how different fabrics accept color. Have students write "lab reports." Check for relationships between fiber types and dye successes. (Key Skill: *Science*)
6. **Group Work.** Ask groups to report on how pioneers dyed fabric in a certain color. Have students make their own dyes. Try them on muslin. Beet juice and tea should work well. How have fabric dyeing processes changed over the years? (Key Skill: *Science*)

Follow Up

1. **Reteaching.** Ask students or groups to list the steps early settlers had to take to get fabric to make a shirt or dress. *(Pick the cotton or shear the sheep; spin it into yarn; dye the yarn; weave or knit the yarn into fabric)* (Key Skill: *Problem Solving*)
2. **Extension.** Use the extension information handout on p. 41 of the *Extending the Lesson* booklet in the TCR.
3. **Enrichment.** Have students look up information about dyes and dyeing cloth. (Key Skill: *Communication*)

Completing the Chapter

For Review

1. Emphasize the main concepts using the summary.
2. Have students complete the "Facts to Recall." (Answers below.)

For Reteaching

1. **Reteaching.** Use the activity on pp. 37-38 of the *Reteaching and Practical Skills* booklet in the TCR.

For Enrichment

1. **Enrichment.** Use the activity on pp. 47-48 of the *Enrichment Activities* booklet in the TCR.

For Evaluation

1. Choose items from "Ideas to Explore" and "Activities to Try."
2. Use the chapter test on pp. 61-62 in the testing booklet of the TCR or use the testmaker software.

Facts to Recall Answers

1. It can help you become a smarter shopper, take care of clothes correctly, and be happier with your clothing and fabric purchases.
2. **Any three:** cotton comes from the cotton plant; wool comes from the fleece of sheep; silk is spun by silkworms; ramie comes from stalks of China grass.
3. The advantage is that they dry quickly and shrink very little. The disadvantage is that they tend to be warm to wear.
4. Because fabric blends combine the best qualities of different fibers.
5. In a plain weave, each crosswise yarn passes over and under each lengthwise yarn; in a twill weave, the lengthwise yarns pass over two and then under two crosswise yarns.
6. By interlocking loops of yarn together row after row.
7. **Any three:** stretchability; runproof; snag-resistant; nonraveling. **Any three:** undergarments; dresses; shirts; blouses; swimwear.

This machine is used for screen printing fabric.

▼ Other Finishes ▼

A number of fabric characteristics can be changed by finishing processes. Some finishes are permanent, and some are not. It's best to check the label. Here are some finishes you will see when you read the labels on textile products.

- ***Flame-retardant.*** Helps fabric resist burning.
- ***Permanent or durable press.*** Requires little or no ironing of fabric after washing.
- ***Sanforized.*** Prevents fabric from shrinking more than 1 percent.
- ***Stain- and spot-resistant.*** Helps fabric resist stains and spots.
- ***Waterproof.*** Helps fabric shed water.
- ***Water-repellent.*** Helps fabric resist water but does not waterproof it.

Many fabric finishes can be destroyed if fabrics are not cared for properly. Check the care labels and follow the manufacturer's directions carefully. You will learn more about caring for clothing in Chapter 30 of the text.

TAKING ACTION

Choosing Performance Outfits

The "Pop Choir" at your school has been asked to perform at the opening ceremonies for the *Fourth of July* celebration in your community. The choir members would like to have new performance outfits for the occasion.

You are a choir member and part of the teacher-student committee that has been asked to choose the new outfits. The choir director has several concerns about the outfits and has shared them with the committee. They include: the outfits need to be easily and inexpensively cared for; the outfits need to be comfortable and allow for movement; the outfits must be durable enough to last several years; and the outfits need to be suitable for the celebration.

Using Your Resourcefulness

- What fibers and fabrics may meet the outfit needs of the "Pop Choir"? Discuss the advantages and disadvantages of each.
- What fabric finishes might be most suitable for the performance outfits?
- How can the committee best make use of community resources in locating outfits to meet the needs of the "Pop Choir"?

TAKING ACTION

Ask students to read "Taking Action" and direct them to respond to the questions in "Using Your Resourcefulness." They may wish to draw on their own experiences in choir or band when they design an outfit.

You may want your students to interview teens involved in performing groups in your school. What types of garments and fabrics would be best suited to their needs?

Using Your Resourcefulness Answers

- Answers may include: cotton, cotton/poly blend, polyester
- Answers may include: permanent press, sanforized, stain resistant

Chapter 29 Review

Summary

In this chapter, you have read about:

- ▶ The characteristics and uses of natural and synthetic fibers.
- ▶ How fabrics are formed by weaving, knitting, and bonding yarns.
- ▶ How colors and patterns are added to fabrics.
- ▶ Other fabric finishes and how they affect the fabric's characteristics.

Facts to Remember

1. List three benefits of learning about fabrics.
2. Name three natural fibers and their sources.
3. What advantage is there in the tendency of manufactured fibers to shed water rather than absorb it? Disadvantage?
4. Why have manufacturers developed fabric blends?
5. How does a plain weave differ from a twill weave?
6. How are knitted fabrics made?
7. Name three qualities of knit fabrics. Give three examples showing how knits are used.
8. Describe two ways that patterns can be applied to fabric.
9. Name four fabric finishes and a benefit of each.

Ideas to Explore

1. Why might articles made from natural fibers be more expensive than those made from manufactured fibers?
2. How can an increase in the use of manufactured fibers affect a region's or a nation's economy and way of life?
3. Using the chart "Natural and Manufactured Fibers" on page 327, identify the different fibers you would wear in the following situations: a safari in Kenya; a ski trip in Colorado; a formal dinner at the White House.

Activities to Try

1. Debate the use of natural and manufactured fibers. Defend your position stating the advantages and disadvantages of each.
2. Collect small samples of different natural and manufactured fabrics. Mount each sample on its own index card or in a pocket-size spiral notebook. On the back of each card or page, write the fabric characteristics and care suggestions. Use your fabric notebook as a shopping guide when you are buying clothing or fabric.
3. Using ½ inch (1.3 cm) by 12 inch (30.5 cm) strips of construction paper, make the following weaves: plain, twill, and satin. Use different colors for lengthwise and crosswise yarns. You will need about 20 strips for each weave. Mount your weaves on construction paper and label them.

LINK TO Art

DESIGNING A T-SHIRT

Draw the silhouette of a basic T-shirt on a piece of paper. Assume you are producing a decorative fabric design that will be stenciled or painted on the T-shirt. (Refer to Chapter 28, pages 314-316 on individualizing your clothes.)

Use markers or paint to develop the design on paper. Explain how you used the elements and/or principles of design in developing the decorative fabric design to be applied to the T-shirt.

Facts to Recall Answers (continued)

8. Patterns can be rolled onto fabric with rollers or cylinders, or applied by screen printing, in which dyes are forced through a screen onto the fabric.
9. **Any four:** flame-retardant, helps fabric resist burning; permanent or durable press, requires little or no ironing of fabric; sanforized, prevents fabric from shrinking more than 1 percent; stain- and spot-resistant, helps fabric resist stains and spots; waterproof, helps fabric shed water; water-repellent, helps fabric resist water but does not waterproof it.

Ideas to Explore

1. Answers will vary and may include: natural fiber production is more affected by uncontrollable factors, such as weather; it may also require more labor hours.
2. Answers will vary and may include: it could result in less farming or ranching and more manufacturing, leading to a growth in cities and a population drop in rural areas.
3. Answers will vary and may include: on a safari, cotton or linen because it is comfortable, absorbent, and launders well; on a ski trip, wool for warmth, nylon for strength and water resistance; at a formal dinner, polyester because it retains pleats, rayon because it drapes well.

- Answers may include: buying clothes or fabric locally; holding fund-raising service projects locally; borrowing uniforms from another group.

LINK TO Art

Answers

T-Shirts will vary. If you have time, have students paint the designs on T-shirts which they provide (or purchase from you).

Preparing to Teach

Chapter Outline

Chapter Resources

The following booklet materials may be found in the *Teacher's Classroom Resources* box:

- Lesson Plans, p. 35
- Student Workbook, *Study Guide,* pp. 129-130; *Clothing Care Crossword,* p. 131; *Storage Strategy,* p. 132
- Color Transparencies, *Clothing Care Close-Ups,* CT-34
- Technology and Computers, p. 40
- Sewing and Serging Handbook
- Cooperative Learning, p. 42
- Extending the Text, *Choosing Clothing Care Products,* p. 42
- Reteaching and Practical Skills, *Sorting Laundry Match,* p. 39
- Enrichment Activities, *Choosing Ironing Products,* pp. 49-50
- Chapter and Unit Tests, pp. 63-64
- Testmaker Software

Also see:

- Meeting the Special Needs of Students
- Linking Home, School, and Community

CHAPTER 30 Caring for Clothing

OBJECTIVES

- *Describe routine clothing care and storage.*
- *Describe how to launder and press clothes.*
- *Explain how to make simple clothing repairs.*

TERMS TO LEARN

- ***routine***
- ***pretreatment***
- ***pressing***
- ***ironing***
- ***dry clean***
- ***shank***

More About Drawers

If the bottoms of your storage drawers are rough, line them with paper or fabric to keep your clothes from snagging. Use shelf paper or self-sticking plastic, but avoid newspapers. The printing ink can transfer onto your clothing.

It's Wednesday morning. With eyes half open, you reach in the closet for a shirt. There isn't one. How could you have forgotten to do the laundry last night? Yesterday's shirt has been in the hamper with the other dirty clothes all night. That's not an option. Finally, at the back of the closet, you discover a clean one. It's your least favorite, but at least it's clean. Relief! Oh, no ... not one, but two buttons are missing. What a choice! A pullover sweater may be the answer. As you frantically search for something to wear, you realize the importance of taking good, daily care of your clothes.

When you change clothes, what do you do with the clothes you have taken off? Do they end up on the chair or the floor rather than in the drawer or closet? By looking after your clothes, putting them away, and making repairs when needed, you come out ahead. It takes a few extra minutes, but your clothes will be ready to go when you are.

Routine Care

The purpose of **routine**, or regular, care of your clothes is to avoid such disasters. You will have clean clothes ready to wear when you need them. If you want to save time caring for your clothes, look for easy-care fabrics. Check hangtags and labels on garments before you buy. Find out what type of care clothes will require. Do they have any special finishes?

You can prevent many problems by taking a little extra time in the routine. Then, when you get ready to put on your favorite shirt, you won't have to use a safety pin in place of a button or apply tape to keep up a hem. You can be sure you are looking your best.

When you dress or undress, open all the fasteners, such as buttons, zippers, and snaps. This helps to keep rips and tears to a minimum. Allow deodorant to dry before dressing, so you don't stain your clothes. Put cologne and perfumes on your body, not on your clothes. They can stain and weaken fabric. If possible, put clothes on and take them off over your head, rather than getting in and out of them feet first. This prevents picking up dirt and lint from the floor. For pants or shorts, taking your shoes off before getting in and out of these garments will help them stay cleaner.

Check for spots, ripped seams, and loose buttons right after taking off your clothes. Remove spots as soon as you

Carefully remove clothing when dressing and undressing.

More About Storage Containers

Different storage containers can help organize space in drawers, closets, and your room itself. Consider: albums, straw and plastic baskets, covered or painted cans, cardboard or shoe boxes, wooden and plastic crates, cutlery organizers, grids on the wall, hooks, ice cube trays or egg cartons, laundry baskets, lazy Susans, tie and belt racks, plastic garbage bags (well marked so they don't get tossed), shoe bags, fishing tackle boxes, and stacking plastic vegetable bins.

Introducing the Chapter

Motivators

1. **Laundry Race.** Give each group a basket of assorted unfolded clothing. Begin the race! The team finishing first *and folding and hanging correctly* wins! Include pants and hangers, unzipped items, and sweaters. This is a chance to highlight clothing care.
2. **Collage.** Distribute family-type magazines and ask students to glue ads relating to clothing care products to a poster board. Give points for variety. Ask students why there are so many products available. Do they believe the claims the ads make? Display the posters. A variation would be to distribute catalogs, magazines, and sale flyers and look for ideas on arranging closets — including purchased or home-made organizers. Ask about the proliferation of organizers. What does this indicate about our lifestyles and affluence? Can organizers really help a messy person?
3. **Display.** Gather a collection of irons, from flat irons to current models. This could be a permanent collection for your room. Research (or ask students to do it) information about their use and history. Type a label with the information and place it by each iron.

Chapter Objectives and Vocabulary

1. Have students read the chapter objectives and rephrase the objectives as questions.
2. Ask students to state, in their own words, the purpose of studying this chapter.
3. Pronounce the vocabulary terms listed on the previous page. Ask students whether they are familiar with any of these. Explain that the terms will be defined in the chapter.

Guided Reading

1. Have the students read the chapter and use the Study Guide on pp. 129-130 of the *Student Workbook.*

Teaching. . .
Routine Care and Storage
(pp. 333-335)

Comprehension Check

1. Give two reasons why regular care of your clothing is a good habit. *(You will have clean clothes ready when you need them; your clothes will last longer and look better.)*
2. What two ways of putting on clothes will help keep them from being soiled? *(Don't step into them; remove shoes.)*
3. What's a good way to organize closets and drawers? *(Group similar items together.)*

Learning Activities

1. **Impromptu Skit.** Choose students to be a teen and parent. Scenario: the teen's room is a mess; clothes are lying on the floor, drawers are open; the disgusted parent refuses to buy any new clothes until these are kept in better shape. The teen argues that there's no good storage. They must come to a solution that satisfies both. What options might be available to a teen with a large wardrobe and tiny closet? Ask the class for further solutions. (Key Skills: *Communication, Problem Solving*)
2. **Closet design.** Ask students to create a "dream closet," including any drawers and cupboards they plan to use. (Key Skills: *Creativity, Critical Thinking*)

Family Perspective

Refer to the cartoon on p. 334. Two brothers (or roommates) share a room. One is a neat freak; one is a slob. What conflicts might arise? How can they work out a peaceful co-existence?

Which one of these roommates displays a good example of clothing care?

can. The longer stains remain in clothing, the harder they are to remove. Repair clothes as soon as possible.

Wet clothes need special attention. Hang clothes in a cool, well-ventilated area away from direct heat. Heat may cause some garments to shrink. Stuff the toes of wet shoes with paper and also dry them away from heat.

Put clothes that need to be washed in a dirty clothes bag or basket. If you store dirty and clean clothes together, the clean clothes will take on the odor of the dirty ones.

By storing out-of-season clothes, you will gain more closet and drawer space.

Storage

If drawer space is limited, organization can again come to the rescue. Use drawer dividers or small boxes to keep items in place. Group similar items together. This makes them easier to find.

Avoid putting too many clothes into a drawer. Garments are less likely to be damaged or wrinkled when you allow enough storage space.

If you live in an area where the seasons change, you will probably store some clothes while you're using others. Before putting clothes away for a season, check to be sure they are repaired and clean. Dirty clothes invite textile-eating insects to have a banquet at your expense.

Before storing clothes, remove all belts and close all fastenings so that garments will keep their shape. Hang clothes carefully or fold and put them in boxes or drawers. Sweaters or loosely knitted garments should be stored flat. Tissue

More About Clothing Care

After wearing, air out clothes you plan to wear again before putting them away. Close zipper and buttons. Lay garments over a chair or place them on a hanger outside the closet.

More About Mending

Since less money is available to spend on clothing today, it has become necessary to think of ways to make clothes last longer. Mending is done to prolong the life of a garment. How do you decide whether or not to mend clothes? Mending is repairing or replacing a worn or ripped area in a garment. Preventive mending is reinforcing areas of strain paper or thin plastic bags placed between folds helps to prevent creases from forming. Be sure to store clothes in a place that's cool, dry, and out of direct sunlight. Garment bags are good to use for storage.

It's easy for a closet to become disorganized, especially when you are in a hurry. You can create more storage and become more organized with a closet organizer. You can buy or create your own. See **Figure 30-1**.

Figure 30-1 **An Organized Closet**

Here are a few ideas on how to use a closet organizer. Are there others that would be more suitable for your wardrobe and accessories?

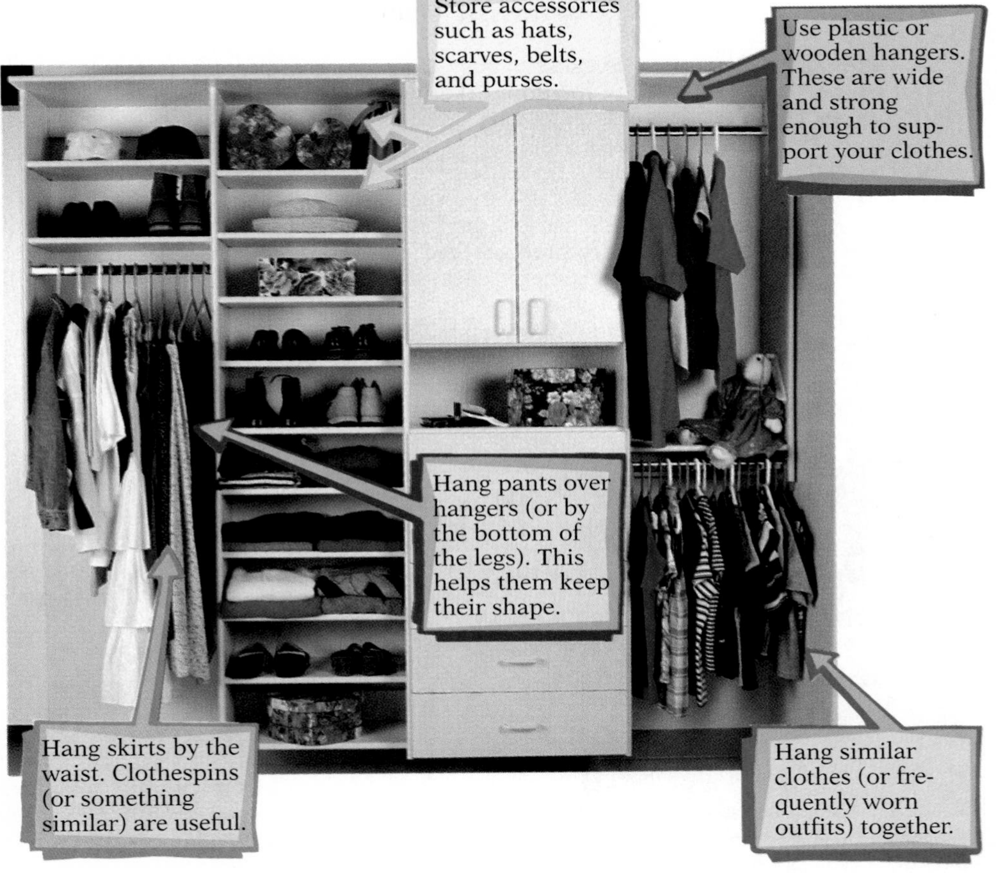

or restitching construction details before they are a problem. When deciding about mending, ask:

- How large is the damaged area?
- How difficult will it be to repair?
- Is the garment worth repairing?
- How long will it take to mend?
- Do I have the time?
- Can I afford to replace the garment?
- Is the garment part of an outfit?
- Does the garment have special meaning?
- Will I wear the garment after I mend it?

Learning Activities (continued)

3. **Closet planning.** Have students measure their closets and draw them *twice* on graph paper. On the first draw how closets are arranged now. On the second create a new storage system. Ask students where they will store all items. (Use clothing inventory from Ch. 28). Avoid direct comparisons between student wardrobes and closets. (Key Skills: *Critical Thinking, Creativity*)
4. **Demonstration.** Bring an assortment of hangers to class — wire, plastic, heavy plastic, wooden, clip-on, and pants hangers. Ask volunteers to choose the appropriate hanger for a variety of garments. Include a bent wire hanger and a broken plastic hanger to illustrate incorrect use. Ask which hangers to use for drip drying garments (plastic, heavy plastic, clips; wire will stain). To introduce or conclude the demonstration plan a clothes-hanging relay. (Key Skill: *Critical Thinking*)
5. **Student Poll.** Ask the class to poll their friends about laundry responsibilities. Who does the laundry in their house? Is it all done on one day or a load here and there? Are clothes ever line dried? Do they use a laundromat? What types of laundry products are used? Tabulate results and write a report or chart. (Key Skills: *Math, Communication*)

Follow Up

1. **Reteaching.** Have students list the stain prevention steps, on the first pages in the chapter. *(Allow deodorant to dry before dressing. Put perfume on body not clothes. Put clothes on over your head. Take shoes off when putting on pants or shorts. Remove spots as soon as possible.)* (Key Skill: *Communication*)
2. **Enrichment.** Have students investigate what insects attack natural fibers, wool especially. Hang pictures of the culprits so students will recognize dangerous insects. What can be done to prevent damage to fibers from insects? (Key Skill: *Problem Solving*)

Teaching. . . Washing Clothes (pp. 336-337)

Comprehension Check

1. What is *pretreatment* and why do it? *(Treat before washing to remove stains, soil)*
2. What happens to grease when it meets laundry detergent? *(It is broken down into fine particles which are held in the water until it is drained.)*
3. What happens when you put too many clothes in a load? *(Water doesn't circulate freely so dirt isn't forced out.)*

Learning Activities

1. **Discussion.** Present this dilemma. There are just enough red articles in the laundry for a small load: a new thick towel, a sweatshirt, a nylon nightgown, and a cotton shirt. Should you wash these items together? *(Probably)* Dry them together? *(No. Nightgown would dry quickly, towel would take forever; it would be hard on the other items.)* (Key Skill: *Critical Thinking*)
2. **Hands-on.** Test stain removal methods on swatches or old garments. Make lipstick, ketchup, blood, mustard, berries, ballpoint ink, and grease stains. Follow a stain removal chart, your advice, or their own ideas for pretreatment. Record procedures and results. Make a chart of successes. Test various kinds of fabrics for stain release. (Key Skill: *Science*)
3. **Experiment.** Make three sets of several stains—chocolate, mustard, spaghetti sauce, oil. Fill three buckets with water. Add a mild detergent to the first,

Around the World

Classics are garments that always seem to be in style. The people living in some parts of Mexico wear clothes that have been in fashion there for almost five hundred years. Researchers studying Indian groups in the mountains of Mexico have found strong similarities between their garments and those of the Aztecs, people who lived in Mexico in the 1500s. A man's fringed vest, for example, looks much like ones seen in Aztec statues. A shawl worn by present-day women villagers is also very similar to those seen in Aztec drawings. Why do you think these styles have remained popular for so long?

Washing Clothes

Because of busy schedules, many families share responsibility for doing the laundry. Laundry isn't a difficult job. However, it isn't quite as fast or effortless as commercials make it seem.

Jeff's first laundry experience wasn't the snap he expected. He tossed all the clothes into the washer. They didn't quite fit until he packed them down a bit. All the boxes and bottles of laundry products had him thoroughly confused. Finally, he added some of each, turned the washer on "soak," and left for a ballgame.

How many of Jeff's errors did you catch? What ending would you write for this story?

Laundry isn't difficult — if you know what you're doing. Here are some tips.

Care labels provide important information about how to clean garments.

▼ Check Care Labels ▼

When it comes to clothing care, your best source of information is the care labels sewn into the garment. If the garment is washable, the label will tell what steps to follow in washing and drying. Care labels also tell you what *not* to do, such as "Do not bleach."

▼ Sort Clothes ▼

Sorting is important in order to get clothes clean, to prevent colors from running together, and to keep garments in good condition. Not all clothes need the same water temperature, washing action, and washing time.

Around the World

After reading the feature, ask students to discuss the question. What other cultures have timeless styles? *(Arab, African garments, Indian saris, for example)* What influences these regional clothes? *(weather, religion, poverty)*

More About Stains

In general, if a washable fabric is stained, try sponging it with cool water. Hot water often sets a stain. If cool water doesn't remove the stain, rub liquid detergent or a stain remover into it from the back side of the stain and rinse with cool water.

More About Detergents

Here are some factors to consider when you are selecting a detergent for your general laundry needs:

- **Phosphate-powdered detergents.** These detergents perform well in hard or soft, hot or cold water. They are prohibited by local law in some places.

Using the care labels, sort the clothes to be machine washed into separate piles as follows:

- Delicate fabrics that require warm water and a gentle cycle.
- Sturdy white and light-colored clothing.
- Permanent press and knit fabrics.
- Dark-colored clothes.
- Heavily soiled garments that should be washed separately.

As you sort the clothes empty all pockets. Also close all zippers, snaps, hooks, and buttons.

Sorting clothes before you do laundry can keep you from damaging your clothes.

Pretreat Clothes

Pretreatment refers to any special attention you give a garment before laundering. Pretreatment helps remove heavy soil and stains. Necklines and the cuffs of long-sleeve shirts, for example, often need special attention. Washing alone may not be enough to get such areas clean. Rub undiluted liquid detergent on the soiled or stained area or use a special pretreatment product. Follow label directions.

Also check carefully for stains. Stains that are not removed in the wash cycle may become permanent when the garment is machine-dried. The longer any stain remains, the more difficult it is to remove. Different types of stains require different treatments. Stain removal charts are helpful in deciding the best method to use. For many stains, try sponging them with cool water.

Use laundry products according to the manufacturer's directions to get clothes clean.

Choose Laundry Products

Many different kinds of products are available for doing laundry. Detergents, bleaches, and fabric softeners each have special jobs to do.

- ***Detergents.*** The primary job of detergent is to remove the dirt from clothes. Detergents also aid in removing grease by breaking it into fine particles. These particles are held in the water until it is drained. Regardless of what brand of detergent you use, be sure to put in the recommended amount. If too little is used, clothes will not get clean. If too much is used in an automatic washer, it is difficult to rinse out all the suds.
- ***Bleach.*** Bleach helps to remove grayness, stains, and, in some cases, germs from clothes. Liquid chlorine bleach is so strong, it must be diluted before use. Be sure to read all the instructions carefully before you use a bleach product.

a regular detergent to the second, and a detergent with bleach to the third. Swish and soak the stained fabric, rinse, compare results. (Key Skill: *Science*)

4. **Experiment.** Soak light fabric in a plastic pail with unwashed red or dark fabric which will fade to show the importance of sorting clothes. Quickly rewash or use bleach to see if the color comes out. (Key Skill: *Science*)
5. **Demonstration.** Make a large, dark stain on an old white shirt. Show results using bleach full strength (a hole). Now dab diluted bleach on with a cotton swab. Rinse bleach so it won't affect other clothes in a load. (Key Skill: *Science*)
6. **Survey.** Have students make a chart about fabric softeners: name of product, how it is used, cost per load. Ask each student to fill out a copy at a grocery store. Compare results, discuss, and post them. Add or substitute any laundry product. (Key Skill: *Math*)

Follow Up

1. **Reteaching.** Ask students to list items that should be hand washed. What procedures should they follow? *(Use a large container so clothes can move freely; use appropriate soap; add water, soap, clothes in order; soak the clothes; drain the soapy water, rinse gently two times.)* (Key Skills: *Critical Thinking, Communication*)
2. **Enrichment.** Ask students who are able to line dry laundry outdoors to hang out sheets and towels and compare sun-dried and machine-dried clothes according to how they smell, how they feel, and the amount of time it takes to dry them. (Key Skill: *Problem Solving*)

- **Non-phosphate powdered detergents.** These detergents perform satisfactorily in soft or moderately hard water, but should not be used in cold or hard water.
- **Liquid detergents.** These detergents perform well in soft water and better in hard water than powdered non-phosphates. They clean synthetics and blends well and are excellent as concentrates for removing spots. They dissolve completely even in cold water.

The World Around You

Recycling

Ask students to discover if and how plastic laundry detergent bottles are recycled. Have them display the information on posters or write an article for the school newspaper.

Teaching. . .

Select Cleaning Action, Hand Washing, and Machine Drying

(pp. 338-339)

Comprehension Check

1. What do fabric softeners do? *(Soften, control static electricity, reduce wrinkling.)*
2. How is the permanent press drying cycle different than other cycles? *(It cools down to minimize wrinkles.)*
3. How should you dry loosely-woven or knit garments? *(On a flat surface.)*

Learning Activities

1. **Group Work.** Ask groups to compile an inventory of a typical family's garments and linens. Divide according to laundry and dry cleaning, and sort the laundry into loads. Don't forget to add drying care. Compare lists and discuss differences or plans which have pitfalls. (Key Skills: *Cooperation, Critical Thinking*)
2. **Demonstration.** If you have access to a washer and dryer, show what happens when stains are washed and dried without any treatment. Wash stained swatches or garments of different fabrics, compare the results, and draw conclusions. Or, assign particular stains to groups to speed things up. (Key Skills: *Science, Critical Thinking*)
3. **Recycling Survey.** Have students check local stores for improved laundry care products, including refills, pumps, cardboard instead of plastic containers, condensed products. (Key Skills: *Critical Thinking*)
4. **Conservation Survey.** Ask a student or group to call the electric and gas companies to find the cost of drying a load of clothes and how much energy it takes. Figure out how much it costs to dry laundry for a family for a year. How much energy is used? (Key Skills: *Math, Critical Thinking*)

If you don't follow directions, garments may be ruined. Putting chlorine bleach directly on fabrics can even make a hole in the fabric.

- ***Fabric softeners.*** These help to soften fabric, control static electricity, and reduce wrinkling. Some fabric softeners are added to the rinse cycle of the washer, some are contained in the detergent, and others are added to the dryer in sheet form. Follow the manufacturer's instructions for use.

Effects of Chlorine Bleach on Stains and Fabrics

Materials
6 stained fabric samples obtained from your teacher; chlorine bleach; water

Equipment
pan; tongs

Directions:
Observe the stains on the fabric samples. Try to identify the cause of each stain. Carefully, make a solution of 1 quart water and 2 tablespoons bleach. Place fabric samples in the pan for 5 to 10 minutes and observe the results.

✔ Which stains did the bleach remove?

✔ Which fabrics were damaged by the bleach?

▼ Select Cleaning Action ▼

Different types of clothing require different water temperatures, water levels, and wash cycles. Be sure to choose the right settings for each load of laundry. For example, use a cold temperature and a low water setting for a small load of brightly colored clothing.

Garments need to circulate freely while being washed and rinsed. The movement of water through clothes helps to force dirt out of the fabric. Avoid overloading the washer. A washer is fully loaded when garments placed loosely in the empty washer tub almost reach the top.

Use a cold-water rinse for every load to save energy. Rinse-water temperature has no effect on the cleaning process.

▼ Hand Washing ▼

Some clothes require the gentle handling of hand washing. Of course any machine-washable item can also be washed by hand. Here are a few tips:

Effects of Chlorine Bleach on Stains and Fabrics

Materials: 6 fabric samples with stained fruit juice, lipstick, ink, oil, paint, grass, coffee, chocolate, tea, or blood.

Equipment: pan; tongs.

Outcomes:

- Bleach is effective in removing fruit, berry, coffee, teas, chocolate, ink, grass, dye, and blood. It will not remove chewing gum, grease, nail polish, paint, pencil, perspiration, or cosmetics.
- Bleach damages some fabrics such as silk, wool, and spandex. It fades the colors or damages the finishes of other fabrics.

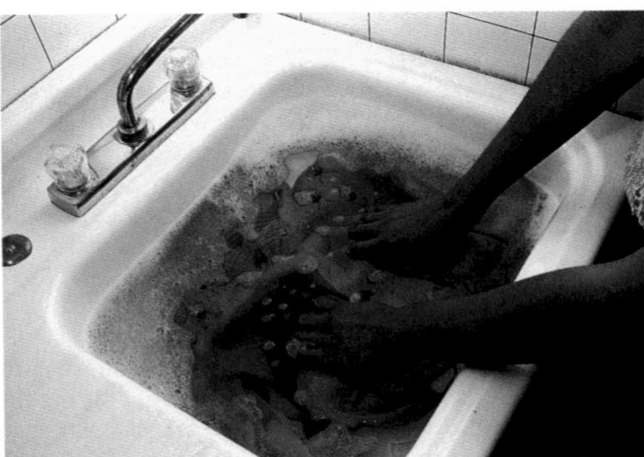

Gently squeeze sudsy water through delicate hand washables for the best results.

TIPS: *Getting Out Stains*

To get out some of the most common stains, follow these guidelines:

- **Blood.** First soak stain in cold water for 30 minutes, then in a presoak product. Wash in cool or warm water. (Hot water will set a protein stain, such as blood.)
- **Oil and grease.** Use a prewash stain remover, according to label directions. Wash in hottest water recommended on garment care label.
- **Soft drinks, tea, and coffee.** Sponge with cool water. Use prewash stain remover. Wash in hottest water recommended on garment care label.

- Use a sink or container large enough for the clothes to move freely. You may be able to wash only one or two items at a time.
- Choose a soap or detergent to match the clothes.
- Put water into the sink, add the detergent, mix, and then put in the clothes.
- Soak the clothes for 5 to 30 minutes, depending on the amount of soil and detergent directions. The detergent will do most of the work for you.
- Drain the sink and add fresh water. Gently squeeze sudsy water through the garments. You don't have to do a lot of hard rubbing. Be sure to have at least two clean rinses to remove both suds and soil.

Drying Clothes

Most clothes can be either air-dried or dried in a dryer. Generally, articles that can be washed together can be dried together. However, some need to be dried in a particular way. Check the information on the care label.

▼ Machine Drying ▼

Always shake out laundered clothes before tossing them into the dryer. This will help them dry faster. Avoid overloading the dryer. Overloading increases drying time and can cause uneven drying and wrinkles.

Learning Activities (continued)

5. **Group Work.** Ask students to find out the possibilities and methods for safely venting hot dryer air into the house during the winter. Are there any possible dangers (fire, for example)? Have each group contact a different source of information — appliance store, hardware store, gas and electric companies, home builder. (Key Skills: *Critical Thinking, Communication*)
6. **Demonstration.** If you have the facilities, let students observe and practice how to operate a washer and dryer. You might try drying similar items at the various settings. Dry two permanent press shirts. Hang one up as soon as the buzzer sounds. Allow the other one to sit in the dryer for a while. The difference in wrinkle content should be noticeable. (Key Skill: *Critical Thinking*)

Follow Up

1. **Reteaching.** Have students list five to ten kinds of clothing. Ask how each should be washed and dried. (Key Skills: *Communication, Problem Solving*)
2. **Enrichment.** Ask students to find out what chemical reaction takes place when bleach is applied to stains. (Key Skill: *Critical Thinking*)

TIPS:

Getting Out Stains
Have students read the feature. Ask them to try removing the stains listed in the feature according to the directions.

More About *Drying Down-Filled Garments*

Many down-filled garments can be successfully laundered. First, read the care label to determine the recommended cleaning method. For garments that can be machine washed, use the gentle cycle and do not overload the washer. Dry clothing thoroughly using a low setting on the dryer.

A clean tennis ball or tennis shoe added to the dryer with the garment should help to refluff the down.

Photo Focus

Direct the students to the photo on p. 339. Ask when they think hand washing comes in handy. *(trip, immediate stain treatment, fragile garments, emergencies)*

Teaching. . .

Air Drying; Pressing and Ironing; Dry Cleaning; Rips and Tears; and Buttons (pp. 340-341)

Comprehension Check

1. What is the difference between "pressing" and "ironing?" *(Pressing is lifting and lowering; ironing is moving back and forth.)*
2. What are three ways to mend a tear in a garment? *(Stitch, iron-on tape, patch.)*
3. How is dry cleaning different than regular clothes washing? *(Dry cleaning uses chemicals rather than soap and water.)*

Learning Activities

1. **Discussion.** Ask students why they think fashions have gone back and forth between ironed and wrinkled looks in the last 20 years. Is this related to fiber trends (Polyester vs. cotton, for example)? (Key Skill: *Critical Thinking*)
2. **Discussion.** Talk with your students about the realities of ironing — how many of their clothes need ironing, how often they need to do it, and the importance of knowing the basics even though they may not have many clothes that need ironing at the moment. Have them suggest easy times to tackle ironing — watching television, for example. If they like to iron they could "barter" — trade ironing for another household task. (Key Skill: *Critical Thinking*)

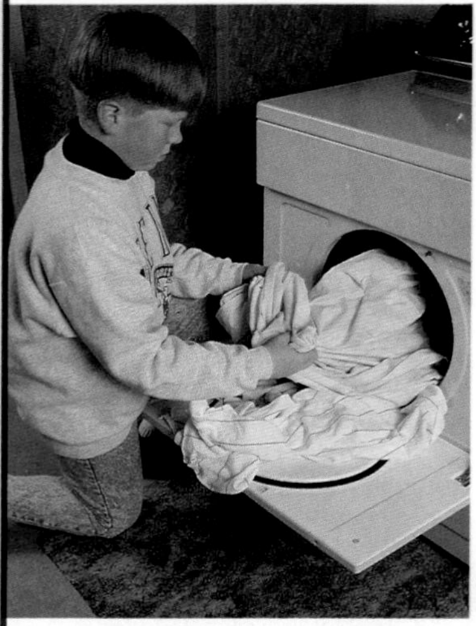

Avoid overloading the dryer. Clothes won't dry efficiently and are more likely to wrinkle.

SAFETY CHECK✓

To press and iron safely:

- Don't touch a hot iron.
- Keep your hands and face away from the steam.
- Position the cord so the iron doesn't get pulled off the ironing board.
- Keep the iron upright when not in use.
- Turn off and unplug the iron after each use. Steam irons should also be drained of water.
- Let the iron cool completely before storing it.

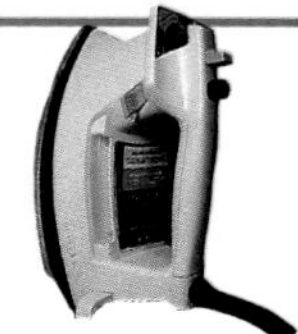

Select the dryer setting designed for the load you're drying. (The instruction book is your best source of information.) Most dryers have a permanent press cycle that cools down clothes after drying to minimize wrinkles. Avoid overdrying clothes. This can cause shrinkage. For best results, remove clothes from the dryer as soon as it stops. Remember to clean the lint filter each time after using the dryer to improve air circulation and dry clothes faster.

▼ Air Drying ▼

Air drying is an energy-saving alternative to machine drying. After washing, clothes are placed on a clothesline, rack, or on plastic hangers to dry. Loosely woven or knit garments should be laid on a flat surface to dry.

Pressing and Ironing

After washing and drying, some clothes need additional treatment to remove wrinkles. This is done with moisture, heat, and pressure. Pressing and ironing are the two techniques used. **Pressing** is the process of lifting and lowering the iron onto an area of fabric. **Ironing** involves moving the iron back and forth over the fabric to remove wrinkles.

The correct iron temperature depends on the garment's fiber content. Check the care label before pressing or ironing. If the fabric is a blend, set the iron for the fiber that requires the lowest setting. If you do not know the fiber content, test a hidden seam or hem.

Knits and wool should be pressed, not ironed, to avoid stretching. Most woven fabrics can be ironed.

Always press or iron articles that need the lowest setting first. Move to higher settings later. Begin with small areas, such as collars, sleeves, and cuffs. Then move on to the body of the garment. Remember to press dark and wool fabrics inside out. These fabrics will become shiny when heat and pressure are applied to their right side. Pile fabrics like velvet and corduroy need special care. They should be steamed to avoid flattening the pile.

Dry Cleaning

Some care labels tell you to dry-clean garments. To **dry-clean** means to clean with chemicals rather than with detergent and water. The cleaned garment is steamed to remove

SAFETY CHECK✓

Read the Safety Check with your students. Ask them why each rule is important. Or, choose a volunteer to mime the consequences of breaking the rules.

More About Removing Wrinkles

Here are some helpful ways to remove wrinkles.

- Retumble on permanent press setting.
- Rerinse and dry on permanent press setting.
- Retumble on high heat for 10-12 minutes and hang immediately.
- Iron carefully.

More About Irons

Many people use steam/dry irons, which combine moisture and heat. Some irons also have a power spray to spray water ahead of the iron. Other people use a spray bottle filled with water with their dry irons. This eliminates buying distilled water and corroding the interior of irons by minerals in the water.

wrinkles. Not all fabrics can be successfully dry cleaned. Check the care label.

There are two types of dry-cleaning services available. Professional dry cleaners are more expensive, yet they can remove most spots and stains from your garments. Coin-operated machines cost less, but do not always provide special treatment for spot or stain removal or pressing.

Clothing Repair

Clothes kept in good repair look better and last longer. Making simple repairs is easy. Here are some of the most common problems you will find.

▼ Rips and Tears ▼

Ripped seams are easily repaired. Use a color of thread that matches the fabric. By hand or with a sewing machine, make a new line of stitching. Begin and end the stitching just beyond the ripped section. (See Chapter 35 for more on machine stitching.)

Tears on your clothing can be straight, diagonal, or three-cornered. Iron-on mending tape can help you repair them. Choose a color that matches the garment. The tape is ironed on the inside of the garment, following package directions.

Tears can also be repaired with patches on the right side of the garment. Choose a fabric similar to the garment fabric. Use hand or machine stitching to attach the patch to the garment.

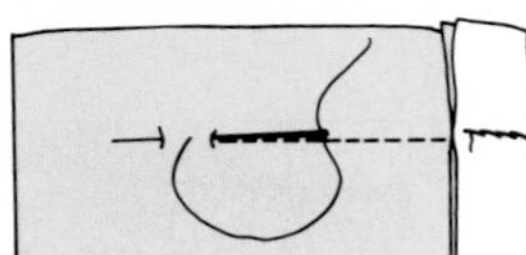

Learning how to make simple clothing repairs is a step you can take toward being well-groomed, and it can save you money, too. Ripped seams are easily repaired on the sewing machine or by hand sewing.

▼ Buttons ▼

Buttons should be securely attached to the garment. Continued buttoning and unbuttoning causes threads to weaken and break. Therefore, it's important to know how to replace buttons.

There are two types of buttons — sew-through and shank. With sew-through buttons, the thread comes up through the button and shows on the top side. Shank buttons have a **shank**, or stem, on the bottom to hold the thread. The shank gives you room to work the button through the buttonhole. Because sew-through buttons don't have shanks, you must make a thread shank for them. See page 342 to learn how to make a thread shank.

Learning Activities (continued)

3. **Comparison.** Ask for three volunteers to compare the merits of dry irons, steam irons, and spray bottles and irons. Give each a similar item (from shirt to dish towel) and have them iron simultaneously. Part way through, have them switch, and then later, switch again. Ask them for their evaluations. (Key Skill: *Critical Thinking*)
4. **Group Work.** Ask several groups to each present one part of the chapter to the rest of the class. One group could show ironing procedures for basic items such as jeans and shirts. One could show pressing and ironing techniques. Another might compare steam and dry ironing and spray starch. Another could sort clothes or tell how to take care of clothes that are air dried. (Key Skill: *Cooperation*)
5. **Interview.** Ask students to compile a list of questions for a dry cleaner (chemicals used, spot removal, basic procedures). Have one student per shop call local dry cleaners to find and compare answers. Ask for a written report or survey. (Key Skill: *Communication*)
6. **Field Trip.** Take the class to a local dry cleaning shop to see how clothes are treated. (Key Skill: *Science*)
7. **Survey.** Ask the class to set up criteria to compare irons (features, functions, cost) and/or starch products. Have individuals or groups look for the information at local stores. (Key Skill: *Critical Thinking*)

Follow Up

1. **Reteaching.** Ask students to write a step-by-step guide for ironing a dress shirt/blouse. (Key Skill: *Communication*)
2. **Enrichment.** Ask students to find out about flat irons and mangles and report to the class. What are the purposes and the uses for each? Pictures and samples (of irons, not mangles!) would be fun. (Key Skill: *Communication*)

More About Wrinkling

In addition to leaving clothes in the dryer too long after it stops, wrinkling in permanent press and "no-iron" garments may be due to:

- Drying more than one load at a time.
- Washing permanent press with regular laundry. Avoid mixing heavy and light garments.
- Overloading the washer — use medium loads with full load water level.
- Using the regular wash cycle instead of the permanent press cycle which has a cool down rinse to minimize wrinkles.
- Washing in hot water instead of warm or cool.

Teaching. . . Buttons, Hooks and Eyes, and Snaps

(pp. 342-344)

Comprehension Check

1. How is a shank button different from other buttons? *(No holes on top, stem on bottom to hold thread.)*
2. Where and why would you use a hook and eye? *(Point of strain — ends of collars, neck edges, waistbands.)*
3. What might you sew between buttons that gape in a light fabric? *(Silver hook and eye.)*

Learning Activities

1. **Hands-on.** Ask students to bring to school articles that need repair. Set aside a class period to demonstrate various repair techniques. Have students make the repairs. (Key Skill: *Management*)
2. **Relay.** Before class sew several sets of two pieces of fabric together, leaving a gap in the seam. Also cut a three-cornered tear. Distribute fabric, needles, thread, and iron-on-tape to each group to mend the seam and tear. (Key Skill: *Management*)
3. **Display.** Have students bring old or unusual buttons to school to display. Do they know stories about the original garments. Find information or speculate on the history of buttons and materials (bone, pearls, shells, metal, ivory, gems). (Key Skill: *Communication*)

How to ...

Replace Buttons

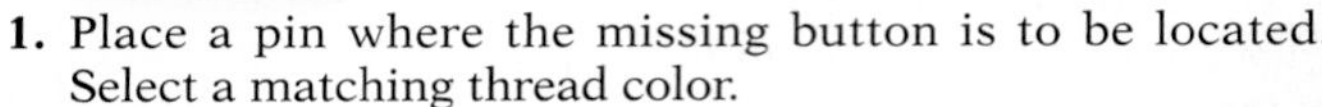

1. Place a pin where the missing button is to be located. Select a matching thread color.
2. Double the thread in the needle and knot both ends together. Bring the needle up from the wrong side to the right side of the garment.
3. Take a small stitch to secure the thread knot.
4. Remove the pin you used to locate the button.
5. Bring the needle through the button. Place a toothpick across the top of the button to allow for a thread shank.
6. Make several stitches through the fabric, the button, and over the toothpick.
7. Remove the toothpick. Bring the needle and thread between the button and the fabric. Wrap the thread around the threads under the button several times to make a thread shank.
8. Bring the needle back to the wrong side of the fabric and fasten the thread securely to the fabric. Clip the thread.
9. Your finished button.

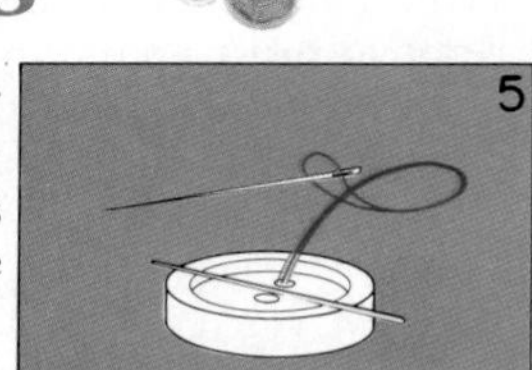

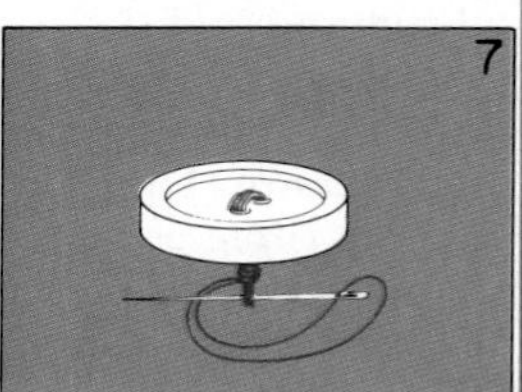

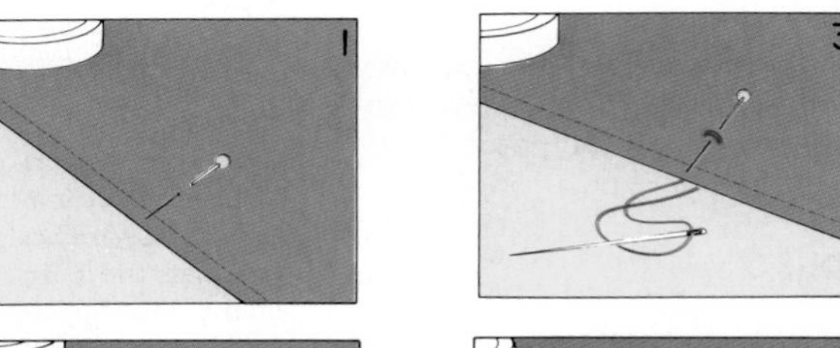

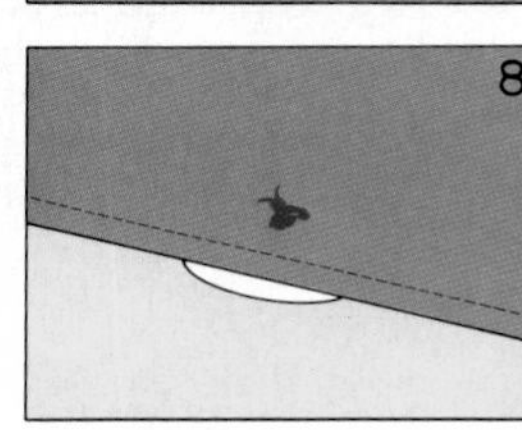

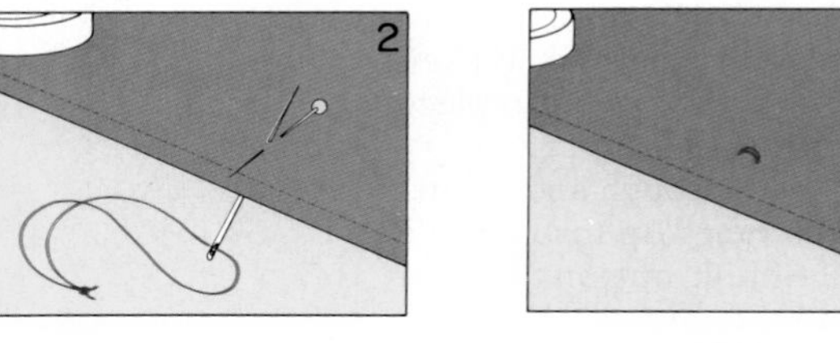

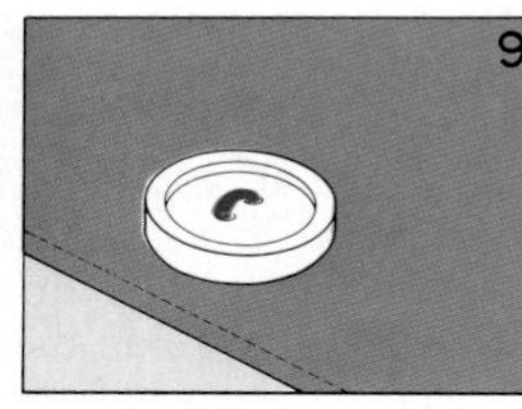

Making a Difference

Have students volunteer to sew on several buttons or iron two garments for family members. Ask students how they felt after the tasks were completed. Would they repeat it?

How to ... Replace Buttons

Ask students to bring to class a garment which needs a button. Be sure to also have them bring the missing button (or a reasonable facsimile!). You provide the needles, thread, and a few generic types of buttons. You might also provide extra shirts of your own that need buttons for students who forgot. Direct students to the "How To" feature for specific directions on sewing buttons on the right way.

▼ Hooks and Eyes ▼

Hooks and eyes are often used to fasten openings on which there is a strain. They are often found on the ends of collars, neck edges, and waistbands. Use black hooks and eyes for dark fabrics and silver ones for light-colored fabrics. On edges that overlap, as on a waistband, use a straight eye. On edges that meet, as on a neck edge, use a round eye. To sew on hooks and eyes:

- Place the hook on the underside of the overlap at least ⅛ inch (3 mm) from the edge. Using small stitches and a single thread in the needle, stitch around each loop or ring. Sew through one layer of fabric so that the stitches will not show on the right side. Bring the needle between the two thicknesses of fabric to the end of the hook. Take three to four stitches around the end of the hook so it is held down firmly. See pages 406-407 for more information on hand sewing stitches.
- Overlap the edge and mark the position of the straight eye on the left-hand side with a pin. Stitch the eye in place around both loops using small stitches. Fasten the thread securely and clip.
- For edges that meet, sew the hook ⅛ inch (3 mm) from the edge. Stitch around each loop. Match the garment edges. Position the eye so that the loop extends ⅛ inch (3 mm) beyond the edge. Stitch in place on the garment underside. When the hook and eye are attached the edges should meet exactly. Secure the thread, and clip close to the fabric.

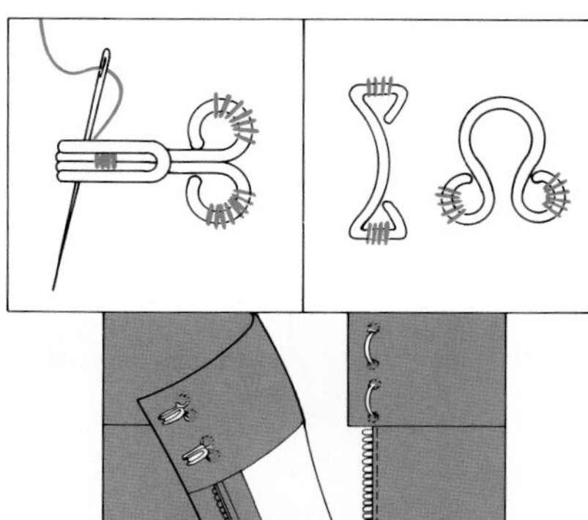

The hooks and eyes shown here are attached to the garment with a whipstitch. The straight eye might be used on a garment waistband while the round eye might be used at the neckline of a garment. See Chapter 35 for directions on how to sew a whipstitch.

Learning Activities (continued)

4. **Group Work.** Give groups a piece of felt, assorted buttons, hooks and eyes, and snaps to create a "work of art." Make sure each student sews on two or three items. Or, pass those materials around the room during class. Ask each student to sew on a certain number of items. (Key Skill: *Creativity*)
5. **Demonstration.** Find a garment with prominent buttons. Try out several kinds of buttons (metal, contrasting plastic buttons, self-fabric buttons, or several colored buttons of the same style) to illustrate the difference buttons can make. (Key Skill: *Creativity*)
6. **Survey.** Ask each student to check three ready-to-wear garments to see how securely fasteners are attached. Compare results. They can save money and time by adding stitches right away. (Key Skill: *Critical Thinking*)
7. **Demonstration.** Put a blouse that gapes at the neckline or between buttons on a mannequin or volunteer. Ask students where they would add fasteners and have them do it. Remind them that hooks and eyes or snaps on a garment are a sign of quality. (Key Skill: *Problem Solving*)
8. **Hands On.** Distribute a 3-inch by 12-inch strip of fabric, a button, snaps, and hook and eye to each student. Fold under ends for facings, and cut slits for buttons. Have students attach fasteners to each end, aligning them correctly, so that the strip will come together in a circle (similar to a belt). (Key Skill: *Creativity*)

Follow Up

1. **Reteaching.** Ask three groups each to demonstrate sewing either buttons, hooks and eyes, or snaps. (Key Skill: *Communication*)
2. **Extension.** Use the activity on p. 42 of the *Extending the Lesson* booklet in the TCR.
3. **Enrichment.** Invite students to think of creative ways to use buttons to decorate shirts, socks, sweatshirts. (Key Skill: *Creativity*)

More About *Clothing Repair*

Here are some helpful hints for clothing repair:

- Button size refers to diameter, not thickness. Minimum buttonhole length is diameter plus thickness plus ⅛ inch.
- Work with no more than 18 inches of thread to avoid knotting or twisting when sewing on buttons.
- Use beeswax to strengthen thread and use a double thread (four thicknesses for heavy fabric).
- Use a drop of glue stick to hold snaps in place for sewing. Let the glue dry first.
- Newer clear nylon snaps are available in addition to black and nickel finish. Nylon snaps are perfect for sheers or lightweight fabric.

Completing the Chapter

For Review

1. Emphasize the main concepts using the summary.
2. Have students complete the "Facts to Recall." (Answers below.)

For Reteaching

1. **Reteaching.** Use the activity on p. 39 of the *Reteaching and Practical Skills* booklet in the TCR.

For Enrichment

1. **Enrichment.** Use the activity on pp. 49-50 of the *Enrichment Activities* booklet in the TCR.

For Evaluation

1. Choose items from "Ideas to Explore" and "Activities to Try."
2. Use the chapter test on pp. 63-64 in the testing booklet of the TCR or use the testmaker software.

Facts to Recall Answers

1. Open all fasteners; allow deodorant to dry; put cologne on your body, not clothes; if possible, put clothes on and take them off over your head; take off your shoes before putting on pants.
2. Hang similar clothing together; use hangers wide and strong enough to support clothes; hang pants by the bottom of the legs or over hangers; hang skirts by the waist; store accessories on shelves, floor, or closet walls.
3. Check care label; sort clothes; pretreat if necessary; choose right laundry products; select right cleaning action.
4. Delicate fabrics; sturdy white and light-colored clothing; permanent press and knit; dark colored clothes; towels.
5. As soon as the stain is discovered, before laundering.
6. Shake out laundered clothes before putting them in the dryer; avoid overloading the dryer; select proper setting for each load; avoid overdrying; remove clothes from dryer as soon as it stops, clean lint filter after each use.

▼ Snaps ▼

An opening that doesn't have much strain, such as the top of a buttoned neckline, is often fastened with a snap. Use black snaps for dark fabrics and silver ones for light-colored fabrics.

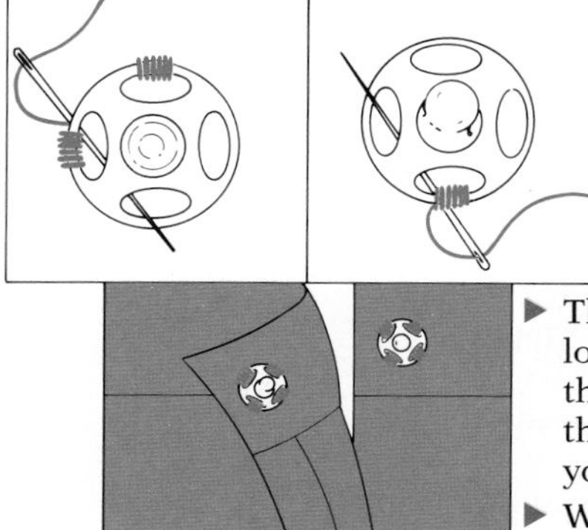

Snaps are used for openings that do not have much strain, such as the top of buttoned necklines. Snaps are sewn onto a garment with a whipstitch.

- The ball section of the snap is usually sewn to the underside of the overlap. Place the ball section of the snap about ⅛ inch (3 mm) from the edge of the overlap. Make several small stitches close together in each hole of the snap using a single thread in the needle. Sew through one layer of fabric so that stitches don't show on the right side.
- Then, pin the closing together and mark the socket location, or flat part of the snap. Mark the position of the socket by placing a pin through the center hole of the ball section. Sew the socket section in place as you did the ball section.
- When going from hole to hole, slide the needle through one hole and under the snap to the next hole. Fasten the thread when finished.

TAKING ACTION

Sorting Clothes

When his uncle asked him, Warren agreed to help out at the family business, "Garcia Cleaners." The business offers services such as dry cleaning, machine or hand washing and drying, and ironing. Warren has had no training because the place is usually so busy that none of the experienced employees have time to help him.

On his first day, the manager said to him, "Sort this bundle of clothes into three baskets. Put the clothes that need dry cleaning in the first basket, those that need machine washing in the second, and those that need hand washing in the third." Warren is left with the following items to sort: soiled denim pants, cotton slacks, stained rayon pants, a silk blouse, a linen sports jacket, a polyester bathrobe, a wool coat, lace handkerchiefs, and a satin dress.

Using Your Resourcefulness

- What resources might Warren draw upon to find out more about clothing care and fabrics?
- At the present time, how should Warren sort the clothes? Where might he find information that would help him right away?
- Should any articles be pretreated? How?
- Clothing care is one skill Warren needs on the job. What other skills will help him succeed at work?

TAKING ACTION

Have students read the feature and answer the questions in *Using Your Resourcefulness.* You might want to have each student bring an article of clothing to class. Be sure each garment is labeled with the student's name. Put the garments in a large bundle. Have the students demonstrate how to sort the clothing for laundering or dry cleaning.

Using Your Resourcefulness Answers

- Answers will vary, but may include garment manufacturers, home economics teachers, extension agents, etc.
- Answers will vary. He should check the garment labels.

Chapter 30 Review

Summary

In this chapter, you have read about:

- How routine care and proper storage of clothing can help make them last longer.
- How to sort and treat soiled garments for washing.
- Laundry products and how to use them.
- How to press and iron clothes when needed.
- Sewing on hooks and eyes and snaps.

Facts to Recall

1. Name four things to remember when dressing and undressing to help keep your clothes clean and in good repair.
2. Identify three ways to organize your closet.
3. What are five tips for machine washing clothing?
4. Identify five groups that clothes can be sorted into for machine washing.
5. When should clothes be pretreated?
6. List four things to remember when machine drying clothes.
7. In what three ways can rips and tears be mended?
8. Briefly explain how to make a thread shank for a sew-through button.
9. Briefly describe how to fasten overlapping fabric edges using a hook and eye.

Ideas to Explore

1. Discuss the benefits of properly taking care of clothes. Is wearing stained or torn clothing a fashion statement or a statement of neglect?
2. How can having garments professionally dry-cleaned when indicated save money over time?
3. What is your biggest clothing storage problem? What are some possible solutions to this problem?

Activities to Try

1. Using magazines, catalogs, or newspapers, cut out pictures of clothing you might typically find weekly in the laundry basket. Sort the pictures of clothes into appropriate loads using the guidelines found in this chapter. Mount each load onto a piece of paper and write a brief explanation about your sorting decisions.
2. Develop a care chart for your clothes. Use the care labels in your clothes as a guide. Make a column for each different type of care and label the top of each column on your chart. List each of your clothing items under the appropriate label.

LINK TO *Science*

How Detergents Work

Try the following experiment to see how detergent works.

- Fill a glass with water and then pour 2 tablespoons (30 mL) of vegetable oil on top.
- Stir the oil and water mixture with a spoon. Observe the results.
- Add 2 tablespoons (30 mL) of laundry detergent to the oil and water mixture. Stir briskly. Observe the results.

What happened after you stirred the oil and water mixture together? What happened when you added the detergent to the mixture and stirred it together? How could the results that you observed explain the cleaning action of a detergent?

Facts to Recall Answers (continued)

7. By hand or machine sewing; iron-on tape; patches.
8. Place a pin or toothpick on top of the button. Sew over the pin or toothpick when reattaching the button to the garment. Remove the pin or toothpick to create the extra thread needed for the shank.
9. Sew the hook ⅛ inch (3 mm) from the edge of the right-hand side of the fabric. Place the straight eye on the back of the left side, a little over the edge of the opening. Using a single thread, sew through one thickness of fabric with whip stitches or buttonhole stitches. Bring the needle between the two fabric thicknesses, take three or four stitches around the end of the hook, secure the thread. Snip it close to fabric.

Ideas to Explore

1. Answers may include: putting on and taking off clothes properly can prevent tears and soiling; washing items according to their care labels can prevent shrinkage and other damage; storing clothes properly can prevent stains, wrinkles, and damage by insects. Answers to second question will vary.
2. Answers may include: dry-cleaning will keep them clean, and make them last longer; machine or hand washing them leave stains or damage.
3. Answers will vary.

- The soiled denim pants and the rayon pants might be pretreated. Follow manufacturer's directions and stain removal guidelines.
- Answers will vary, but may include communication, math, and science skills.

LINK TO *Science*

Answers

Oil and water do not mix; oil stays on top of the water. Detergent breaks down oil, helping it mix better, so oil can be carried away in water in wash.

Preparing to Teach

Chapter Outline

Chapter Resources

The following booklet materials may be found in the *Teacher's Classroom Resources* box:

- Lesson Plans, p. 36
- Student Workbook, *Study Guide,* pp. 133-134; *Reading the Envelope Back,* pp. 135-136
- Color Transparencies, *Pattern Back Facts,* CT-35
- Technology and Computers, p. 41
- Sewing and Serging Handbook
- Cooperative Learning, p. 43
- Extending the Text, *Suitable Selections for Simple Sewing,* p. 43
- Reteaching and Practical Skills, *Misplaced Words,* p. 40
- Enrichment Activities, *Analyzing Patterns,* pp. 51-52
- Chapter and Unit Tests, pp. 65-66
- Testmaker Software

Also see:

- Meeting the Special Needs of Students
- Linking Home, School, and Community

CHAPTER 31 Selecting a Pattern

OBJECTIVES

- *Take measurements to determine pattern size.*
- *Select a pattern that matches your skill level.*
- *Interpret pattern envelope information.*

TERMS TO LEARN

- ***ease***
- ***yardage***
- ***view***
- ***notions***

More About Selecting the Right Pattern Size

If your measurements fall in between two pattern sizes, decide on the basis of your build and taste. If you prefer a closer fit, choose the smaller size. If you like looser fitting garments, choose the larger size.

If your figure seems to be one size on the top and another on the bottom, multi-sized

Have you ever struggled to find clothes that fit just right? Are shirt sleeves always too short? Are pant legs always too long?

If you have struggled with problems like these and others, then learning to sew can be a real benefit and a lot of fun, too. Practice and a little patience are all you need to sew clothing that fits well and does the most for you.

The Right Pattern Size

The success of any sewing project depends on choosing the right pattern. Making a pillow or tote bag does not require taking personal measurements. However, if you are making a garment for yourself or someone else, knowing how to take measurements will help you to select the best pattern size. Read on to learn how to determine pattern size for both females and males.

Ready-to-wear sizes are not always the same as pattern sizes. However, pattern sizes are similar among the major pattern companies. Pattern sizes will vary slightly, depending on the amount of **ease**, or room needed for comfort and movement, allowed for in the pattern.

You will need to take several body measurements. Accurate measurements can be taken over any garments that fit well. Bulky sweaters, jackets, and belts should be taken off before taking measurements.

In order to take accurate measurements, work with a partner and measure each other. Take each measurement twice. Check to be sure both measurements are within ½ inch (1.3 cm) of each other. If they are not, check again.

When taking measurements, hold the tape measure so it fits comfortably. It should not be too tight or too loose. If you are unsure about the correct size even after following these directions, check with your teacher.

As you and your partner take each other's measurements, write the measurements down. You will need them to select the correct pattern size. Measurements are also used to make any pattern adjustments that may be needed.

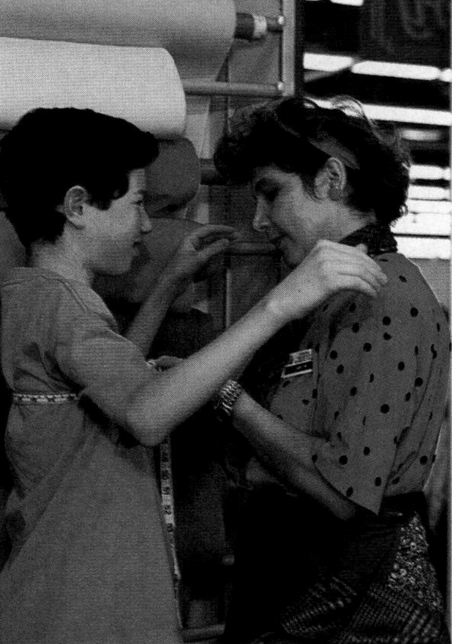

Taking accurate measurements will help you select the correct pattern size.

patterns will solve your fitting problems. Two or three sizes are printed on each pattern section, giving you the opportunity for instant adjustments. Each cutting line is labeled with a pattern size. Use these multi-sized patterns for fast pattern adjustment. For example, if you are a larger size below the waist, taper into the larger size's cutting line as you cut out the pattern section. Cut out adjoining pattern sections the say way — by tapering from one size to another — and your pattern will fit your figure!

Introducing the Chapter

Motivators

1. **Display.** Bring samples of patterns covering as many years as possible. Ask students to look for similarities, changes, and trends. Find old patterns in used book stores, antique shops, and garage sales. Ask students to bring in old patterns from their mothers and grandmothers. Arrange patterns on a bulletin board (or tag board to use year after year). Attach swatches of fabrics, if possible. (Key Skill: *Creativity*)
2. **Pattern Fitting.** Have students pin pattern pieces to a mannequin to show how any darts, tucks, round armholes and sleeves fit together. Or, give students muslin and ask them to fit it to the mannequin, cutting it where necessary. Compare their pieces of muslin to pattern pieces. (Key Skills: *Creativity, Critical Thinking*)
3. **Contest.** Show students the pattern illustration on the envelope of a simple garment. Ask them to draw their ideas of what pattern pieces might be required on graph paper. Give a prize to the student who comes the closest. This will indicate how familiar your class is with patterns. (Key Skills: *Problem Solving, Creativity*)

Chapter Objectives and Vocabulary

1. Have students read the chapter objectives and rephrase the objectives as questions.
2. Ask students to state, in their own words, the purpose of studying this chapter.
3. Pronounce the vocabulary terms listed on the previous page. Ask students whether they are familiar with any of these. Explain that the terms will be defined in the chapter.

Guided Reading

1. Have the students read the chapter and use the Study Guide on pp. 133-134 of the *Student Workbook.*

Teaching. . .
The Right Pattern Size
(pp. 347-349)

Comprehension Check

1. Why should you take measurements instead of just relying on pattern sizes? *(Pattern sizes are different.)*
2. Besides measurements, what is an important factor to consider when choosing a pattern size? *(The ease of the garment fit)*
3. Why shouldn't you measure your waist as tightly as you can pull the tape measure? *(Waistband would be too tight)*

Learning Activities

1. **Discussion.** List standard measurements. Ask students to name garments in which particular measurements are and are not crucial. *(Bust or chest measurement is more crucial in a fitted shirt than a sweatshirt. Shoulder measurement is more important in a dress shirt than a raglan-sleeve bathrobe.)* (Key Skill: *Critical Thinking*)
2. **Discussion.** Mandy, a teen who has been sewing for several years, takes pride in her ability to sew garments quickly. She sees a pattern she likes, buys it in her ready-to-wear size, and chooses a fabric that catches her eye (without checking its content and care). She cuts the pattern out and sews it without reading the pattern first. Because she has had good luck, Mandy believes this hurry-up method will always work. What are the advantages and disadvantages of her method? Can you predict any pitfalls that might come her way? (Key Skill: *Critical Thinking*)
3. **Small Group Work.** Ask groups to practice measuring on the mannequin. Reward any group whose measurements coincide exactly with yours. (Key Skill: *Math*)

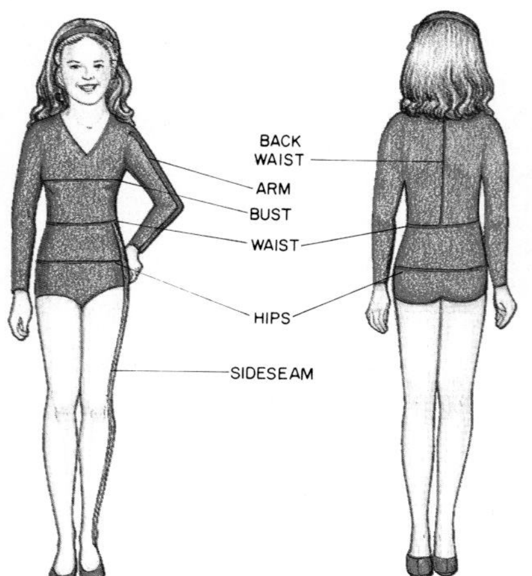

Female Measurement Record

	Your Measurement	Total	Pattern Measurement	Difference
Bust				
Waist				
Hips				
Back Waist Length				
Arm				
Height				

▼ Measurements for Females ▼

Before selecting a pattern size, you need to determine your measurements and figure type. Take the following measurements:

- ▶ ***Bust.*** Measure over the fullest part of the bust and straight across the back.
- ▶ ***Waist.*** Tie a string around your waist to identify the narrowest point. Measure around the natural waistline with a tape measure.
- ▶ ***Hips.*** Measure around the largest part of the hips, anywhere from 6-9 inches (15-23 cm) below the waist.
- ▶ ***Side seam.*** Measure from the waist along the side seam to the top of the foot or desired pant length.
- ▶ ***Back waist length.*** Measure from the bone at the base of the neck to the natural waistline.
- ▶ ***Arm length.*** Measure from the top of the shoulder and over the bent elbow down to the wrist.
- ▶ ***Height.*** Measure when standing tall, without shoes, against a wall.

Figure Types

Figure types are based on body proportion and two measurements — height and back waist length. Today, pattern companies divide female figure types into two main groups — girls' and misses'. Compare your body proportion, height, and back waist length with those on the chart on page 349 to determine your figure type.

After identifying your figure type, compare your body measurements with those on the chart. Your measurements may not exactly match those given. The following guidelines can help you in selecting the pattern size that most closely matches your measurements:

More About *Ease in Patterns*

After you have determined your proper size, the most critical thing to understand is "ease." Ease is the additional fullness built into a garment beyond the actual body measurements. The amount of ease built into a garment varies from pattern to pattern and is determined by the silhouette the designer wanted to create. For the best indication of how the pattern will fit, including ease, read the caption (garment description) on the back of the pattern envelope. The garment will always be described by one of the following five terms: close-fitting, fitted, semi-fitted, loose-fitting, very loose fitting. These terms are describing how much ease is in the garment. Determining the ease in a garment can

- Use the bust measurement for garments requiring fit in the top, such as blouses, dresses, suits, and coats.
- Use the hip measurement for garments that fit snugly over the hips and are not affected by bust measurement. This includes fitted skirts, pants, and shorts. The hip measurement is more important than the waist measurement because the waist is easier to alter.
- Use the waist measurement for skirts with pleats or fullness beginning at the waistline.
- If you fall between two sizes, pick the smaller size if you are small-boned. Select the larger size if you are large-boned. With loose-fitting patterns you might choose the smaller size; if the garment is fitted, choose the larger size. Pattern companies also have adjustable patterns that make it easier to cut the pattern to the right size.

GIRLS'

Girls' patterns are designed for the girl who has not yet begun to mature. See chart below for approximate heights without shoes.

Size	7	8	10	12	14
Breast	26	27	28½	30	32
Waist	23	23½	24½	25½	26½
Hip	27	28	30	32	34
Back Waist Length	11½	12	12¾	13½	14¼
Approx. Heights	50"	52"	56"	58½"	61"

MISSES'

Misses' patterns are designed for a well-proportioned and developed figure: about 5'5" to 5'6" without shoes.

Size	6	8	10	12	14	16	18	20	22	24
Bust	30½	31½	32½	34	36	38	40	42	44	46
Waist	23	24	25	26½	28	30	32	34	37	39
Hip	32½	33½	34½	36	38	40	42	44	46	48
Back Waist Length	15½	15¾	16	16¼	16½	16¾	17	17¼	17⅜	17½

▼ Measurements for Males ▼

Take the following body measurements to help you select your best pattern size:

- ***Chest.*** Measure around the fullest part of the chest.
- ***Waist.*** Measure over the shirt at the natural waistline.
- ***Hips.*** Measure around the fullest part of the hips anywhere from 6-8 inches (15-20 cm) below the waist.
- ***Neck.*** Measure around the base of the neck and add ½ inch (1.3 cm) for shirt neck size.
- ***Arm length.*** With the arm bent up at the elbow, measure from the bone at the base of the neck, around the elbow, and up to the wrist bone.
- ***Inseam.*** A simple way to take this measurement is to use a favorite pair of pants that are the correct length. Place the pants on a flat surface. Measure from the crotch seam to the bottom of the pant leg.
- ***Side seam.*** Measure from the waist down to the point where the pant leg breaks slightly on the shoe.
- ***Height.*** Measure when standing tall, without shoes, against a wall.

Body Type

To determine your body type, compare your body proportion, height, and back waist length with those on the chart on page 350.

4. **Charts.** Have partners take each other's complete measurements. Use a string for one measurement (measure the string later) so students will know how to use this method. Provide note cards for making a *Personal Measurement Chart* for students to keep in their wallets. Make sure each student has a complete, legible chart. (Key Skill: *Math*)
5. **Measurement Math.** Bring a shirt or top pattern to class. Ask students to find the *actual* shoulder, chest, and neck to waist measurement of the finished garment. Remind them to double most pattern pieces and subtract seam allowances. (Newer patterns have *actual* measurements on the pattern pieces.) Compare the measurements with the size chart. Why might there be differences? When might that affect the size pattern you select? (Key Skills: *Math, Critical Thinking*)

Follow Up

1. **Reteaching.** Ask students to compare the types of measurements for males and females. What are the similarities and differences? (Key Skills: *Communication, Critical Thinking*)
2. **Enrichment.** Have students compare the measurements of a basic shirt pattern to a ready-to-wear shirt of the same size and style. Are the measurements similar or different? What might account for variations? (Key Skills: *Critical Thinking, Math*)

Family Perspective

Lauren wants to make shorts and a top, but the pattern she picked is sold out in her size. Her friend Meredith told her to forget the hassle and buy expensive brand-name items. Lauren's mom is wary of altering patterns. What are the options? *(Change patterns, measure pattern pieces of another size, compare the cost of sewing and purchasing ready-to-wear items.)*

help eliminate some fitting adjustments later. Simple ease allowances in skirts, pants, and shorts:
- fitted: 2 inches to 3 inches
- 3 inches to 4 inches in semi-fitted
- 4 inches to 6 inches in loose, and
- over 6 inches in very loose fitting garments

More About *Keeping a Tape Measure Handy*

It's a good idea to carry a regular-sized tape measure with you. When you see an interesting feature or try on a garment that *fits* perfectly, measure the feature or the garment and jot the numbers down. Store the tape measure in a resealable bag or a 35mm film container.

Teaching...
Measurements for Males, Using a Pattern Catalog, and Choosing the Right Pattern
(pp. 350-351)

Comprehension Check

1. When selecting a pants pattern, do you use hip or waist measurement if they are different than the chart? *(Hip — waist is easier to alter)*
2. A friend gives you the number of a pattern to look at. How do you find it in the pattern book? *(Check the numerical list in the back which gives pages where patterns appear.)*
3. What pattern characteristics are good for a beginner? *(Few pieces and details, little fitting)*

Learning Activities

1. **Group Demonstrations.** Ask groups to demonstrate, first the wrong, and then the right way to: take measurements, select a pattern, choose a size, look through the pattern book. Or, choose two groups of four students. Tell the first group they are The Four Stooges at the Pattern Counter. Have them do all the wrong things mentioned above. Name the second group after people who are currently popular. Have them reenact the scenario, making all the right moves. Ask the class to suggest any blunders the Stooges or Super Stars missed. Students could write scripts instead of acting. (Key Skills: *Communication, Creativity*)
2. **Chart.** Have students figure out their body types and sizes according to the chart in the book. Add that info to their *Personal Measurement Chart* (Learning Activities, preceding page). (Key Skills: *Critical Thinking, Math*)
3. **Head Start.** Before students look at patterns, suggest that they check current styles in a clothing store, trying on a few to see what looks best, noting the fit at different points. (Key Skill: *Critical Thinking*)

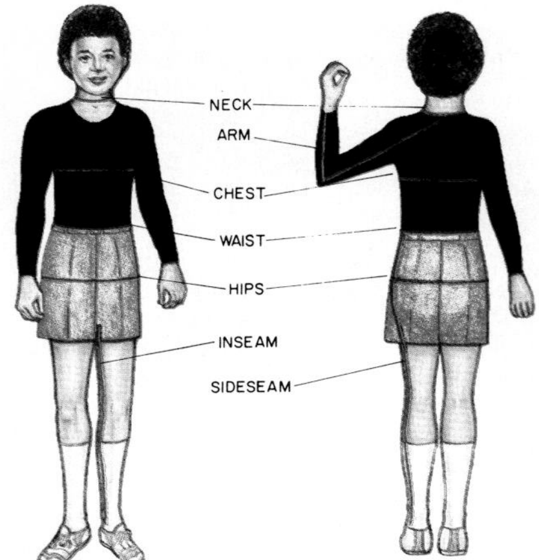

Male Measurement Record

	Your Measurement	Total	Pattern Measurement	Difference
Chest				
Waist				
Hips				
Neck				
Arm				
In-Seam				
Side Seam				
Height				

After determining your body type, compare your body measurements with those on the chart. Your measurements may not exactly match those given. Use the following guidelines to pick the correct pattern size:

- Use the chest measurement to select the pattern for a coat or jacket.
- Use the neck and chest measurements to select shirt patterns. If measurements vary, use the chest size and alter the neck.
- Use the waist measurement as a guide to select a pants pattern. If the hips are very large or small in comparison to the waist, buy the pattern by the hip measurement and alter the waist.
- Body measurements may fall between two sizes. Choose the larger size if you are husky or like a looser fit. Use the smaller size if you are slim or like a snug fit.

	BOYS'				TEEN BOYS'			
Size	**7**	**8**	**10**	**12**	**14**	**16**	**18**	**20**
Chest	26	27	28	30	32	33½	35	36½
Waist	23	24	25	26	27	28	29	30
Hip (Seat)	27	28	29½	31	32½	34	35½	37
Neckband	11¾	12	12½	13	13½	14	14½	.15
Height	48	50	54	58	61	64	66	68
Shirt Sleeve	22⅜	23¼	25	26¾	29	30	31	32
	MEN'S (height approximately 5'10")							
Size	**34**	**36**	**38**	**40**	**42**	**44**	**46**	**48**
Chest	34	36	38	40	42	44	46	48
Waist	28	30	32	34	36	39	42	44
Hip (Seat)	35	37	39	41	43	45	47	49
Neckband	14	14½	15	15½	16	16½	17	17½
Shirt Sleeve	32	32	33	33	34	34	35	35

More About Design Features

To make it easier for students to identify features on patterns — and different views on patterns — point out style details. For example, neckline and other collar styles include: boatneck, cowl-neck, crew-neck, stand-up collar, round collar, notched lapels, and so forth.

Sleeve styles include: raglan, puffed, gathered, dolman, and drop-shoulder.

Shirtwaist, chemise, princess, and coat dress would also be helpful to know as well as structured and unstructured jackets, fitted and full men's shirts.

Young sewers should also be encouraged to see which of these styles is flattering to their body style. They will save time and money before investing in fabric and a pattern if

Measurement charts can be found in the back of pattern catalogs. They also provide you with pattern illustrations and skill-level sections to help you develop sewing skills with success.

Using a Pattern Catalog

After you have determined your figure or body type and pattern size, you will be ready to look through a pattern catalog.

All pattern catalogs are divided into sections. Sections cover such topics as different figure/body types, size ranges, and garment and craft categories. Take a minute or two to look over the titles of the various sections. You will find the titles helpful in selecting sections that fit your skill level.

As you look through the catalog, you will see sketches and pictures of different garments or crafts. For each picture, there will be a description and the **yardage** — the amount of fabric needed for each project. Although the pictures and sketches don't tell it all, they can give you a clue as to how easy or difficult each pattern will be.

Body measurement charts, like those used to determine your pattern size, are at the back of the catalog. There is also a numerical listing of all the pattern numbers and the page numbers on which they can be found. This makes it easy to look for a specific pattern number.

Choosing the Right Pattern

Selecting a pattern that is right for your skill level generally leads to a more positive sewing experience. If you tackle a pattern that is too difficult at first, it is easy to become discouraged and unhappy with the finished product.

The three main parts of a pattern are the envelope, the instruction sheet, and the pattern pieces.

Learning Activities (continued)

4. **Pattern "Shopping."** Have students find several patterns of totally different styles, write down the numbers and a brief description, and two reasons why they like them. Use *Personal Measurement Charts* to find sizes. Or, have students choose three patterns: easy, medium, and difficult. What makes them easy, medium, or hard? (Key Skill: *Decision Making*)
5. **Group Work.** Have students select three patterns from which to build a basic wardrobe, using pattern and fabric variations. Groups can draw or list their choices. (Key Skill: *Creativity*)
6. **Demonstrate.** Compare a ready-to-wear garment and a home sewn garment of the same size and style. Measure both at several points, noting differences and similarities. (Key Skill: *Critical Thinking*)

Follow Up

1. **Reteaching.** Give students the measurements of several imaginary people. Have students determine the size patterns they would need for a dress, shirt/blouse, pants, bathrobe. (Key Skill: *Problem Solving*)
2. **Enrichment.** Ask students to find information about Ebenezer Butterick and James McCall and share it with the class. *(Butterick, a tailor from Massachusetts, developed the first paper pattern from patterns his wife used to make his shirts. They were selling patterns all over the world by 1865. McCall, also a tailor, came up with a system for drafting patterns and began to sell them in New York in 1870.)* (Key Skill: *Communication*)

they know whether or not a particular style will look good on them.

More About Designing a Pattern

Designing a pattern is a complicated task. From the designer's sketch a drawing of various views and suggested fabrics is made. Then the design is draped in muslin on a dress form and stitched into a garment that is modeled and checked for fit and appearance. A master pattern is made as a guide for making various sizes.

Photo Focus

Direct students to the top photo on page 351. Ask them where the size charts are located in a pattern book *(usually in the back)* and how often a sewer should check them *(often, or when weight changes)*.

Teaching...
Reading the Pattern Envelope Front and Back
(pp. 352-354)

Comprehension Check

1. What are the three main parts of a pattern? *(Envelope, guide sheet, pattern pieces)*
2. What do the sketches on the back of the envelope represent? *(The back views of all the front views)*
3. What information do you need to find the correct amount of fabric for your garment? *(View, size, width of fabric)*

Learning Activities

1. **Preplanning.** Remind students, before they buy, to add the cost of pattern, fabric, and notions. Compare the total with the cost of a similar ready-to-wear garment. Using a pattern and prices which you furnish, ask students to compute the cost of a garment. Compare answers. Ask what a comparable ready-to-wear garment might cost. Is it more or less than the home-sewn item? What is the biggest variable in the cost of sewing? *(Probably the fabric.)* (Key Skills: *Math, Critical Thinking*)
2. **Group Race.** Give each group a pattern envelope (or copy). The group which lists the most pieces of information first, wins. (Key Skill: *Critical Thinking*)

Around the World

After reading the feature, ask students what religious dress they can think of *(Amish wear plain, dark clothes and bonnets; Hasidic Jews dress differently)*. What would be the advantages or disadvantages of wearing uniforms to school? *(Answers will vary.)*

If you are a true beginner, look for the "easy to sew" section of the pattern catalog. Patterns in this section have several things in common:

- They have a small number of pattern pieces.
- They don't require a great deal of fitting.
- The designs are simple and have very few sewing details, such as darts, pleats, sleeves, collars, trim, and pockets.

After mastering some of the basic sewing skills, you'll be ready to take on the challenge of more complicated patterns. If you like sewing, try a new construction technique or fabric type when selecting each new pattern.

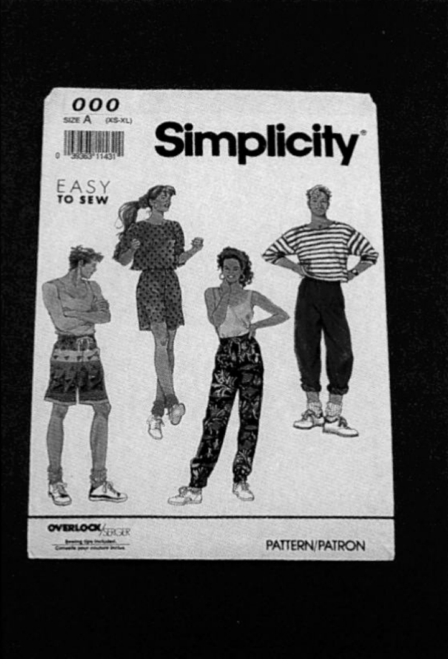

The front of the pattern envelope shows different views and details of each pattern.

Reading the Pattern Envelope

The three main parts of a pattern include the envelope, the guidesheet, and the pattern pieces. The pattern envelope contains the instruction sheet and pattern pieces. Both the front and back of the envelope contain important information.

The Envelope Front

The front of the envelope shows several colorful **views**, or garment styles that can be made from a pattern. Slightly different details, such as long or short sleeves, types of collars, and trims, make each view unique. Views are also shown in various fabrics, so you'll get an idea of how different one pattern can look. It also identifies the pattern number, size, figure/body type, and any special information such as "Suitable for Serger Sewing." (A serger stitches, trims, and finishes a seam all at the same time.)

Around the World

When a garment has religious meaning, it can cause conflict. In France, for example, school officials have been debating whether to allow female students of the Islamic faith to wear head scarves. The students' religious teaching requires them to wear the scarves in public, but French public schools, like those in the United States, may not show support or favoritism for any one religion. School officials find themselves caught between their duty to remain neutral and the students' right to practice their faith through dress. How would you resolve this conflict?

More About *Pattern Selection*

If you took a survey among all your friends who sew, each would probably have at least one construction detail she or he avoids at all costs. One never has pockets. Another only sews garments which can be pulled on without buttonholes or zippers. It is not uncommon to have certain sewing phobias; however, it is unnecessary. If you understand how and why a technique works and gather the tools to help you do the job you can sew anything!

PICK-A-KNIT® RULE | **FOR THIS PATTERN—4"(10cm) OF KNIT FABRIC MUST STRETCH CROSSWISE FROM HERE →** | **TO HERE →**

REGLE "CHOISISSEZ-UN-TRICOT" | **POUR CE PATRON—4"(10cm) DE TRICOT DOIVENT S'ETIRER EN TRAVERS D'ICI →** | **JUSQU'ICI**

000
10 PIECES

MISSES', MEN'S OR TEEN BOYS' PANTS OR SHORTS AND KNIT TOPS. . . TANK TOP SIZED FOR STRETCH KNITS ONLY: Tank top has racer back. Cropped loose-fitting top has extended shoulders and three-quarter length sleeves. Pull-on pants or shorts with side seam pockets have triple elastic waistline casing with optional purchased drawstring. Pants have double elastic ankle casings. Shorts can be made in border printed or plain fabrics.

Fabrics—Cotton interlock, cotton-lycra blends, jerseys. Top, pants and shorts also in sweatshirt knits. Pants and shorts also in broadcloth, challis, lightweight faille, supplex. Shorts also in border printed fabric. See Pick-A-Knit® Rule for tank top. Not suitable for obvious diagonals. Extra fabric needed to match plaids, stripes or one-way design fabrics. For pile, shaded or one-way design fabrics, use with nap yardages/layouts.

Notions: Thread. Look for Simplicity notions.

Multi-Sized Pattern

BODY MEASUREMENTS						
Chest/Bust	30-32	34-36	38-40	42-44	46-48	Ins.
Hip	31-32½	35-37	39-41	43-45	47-49	"
Sizes U.S.A. ONLY	(X-Small	Small	Medium	Large	X-Large)	
Sizes	(X-Small	Small	Medium	Large	X-Large)	
Tank-Top—Sized for stretch knits only						
60"**	1	1	1	1	1	Yd.
Top						
60"**	1¼	1¼	1¼	1¼	1⅜	Yds.
Interfacing—¼ yd. of 22" to 25" fusible						
Pants						
45"**	2¼	2⅝	2¾	2¾	2¾	Yds.
60"**	1¾	2	2¼	2¼	2¾	"
Elastic—5⅝ yds. of ½" wide						
Shorts—Plain Fabric—Cut lengthwise						
45"**	1½	1½	1½	1⅝	1¾	Yds.
60"**	1⅛	1⅛	1⅛	1⅝	1⅝	"
Shorts—Border Printed Fabric—Cut crosswise						
45"*	1¾	1⅞	2	2⅛	2¼	Yds.
Shorts Elastic—3¾ yds. of ½" wide						
Pants or Shorts Drawstring (opt.)—1¾ yds. of ¼" cord or one novelty shoe lace approx. 63" long						
Pants side length	40	40½	41	41½	42	Ins.
Shorts side length	19	19½	20	20½	21	"

*without nap **with nap ***with or without nap

PANTALON OU SHORT ET T-SHIRTS POUR JEUNE FEMME, HOMME OU ADOLESCENT . . . DEBARDEUR EN JERSEY EXTENSIBLE SEULEMENT: Débardeur avec dos cycliste. T-shirt court et ample avec emmanchures tombantes et manches trois-quarts. Pantalon ou short avec poches dans les coutures de côté, triple élastique coulissé à la taille et cordon acheté facultatif. Pantalon avec élastique double coulissé aux chevilles. Le short peut être réalisé dans du tissu imprimé à bordure ou en tissu uni.

Tissus–Coton interlock, coton Lycra mélangé, jersey. T-shirt, pantalon et short en jersey molletonné pour sweatshirt. Pantalon et short en popeline, étamine, faille légère, supplex. Short en tissu imprimé à bordure aussi. Voyez la Règle "Choisissez-Un-Jersey" pour le debardeur. Les tissus à diagonales apparentes ne conviennent pas à ce patron. Prévoyez davantage de tissu pour raccorder les écossais, rayures ou motifs unidirectionnels. Pour les tissus à long poil, de différents tons ou à motifs unidirectionnels, utilisez métrages et plans de coupe "avec sens".

Mercerie: Fil. Demandez la mercerie Simplicity.

Patron à tailles multiples

MESURES NORMALISEES						
Poitrine	76-81	87-92	97-102	107-112	117-122	cm
Hanches	79-83	89-94	99-104	109-114	119-124	"
Tailles/Sizes	(X-Petite	Petite	Moyenne	Grande	X-Grande)	
Tailles-Europe	(X-Petite	Petite	Moyenne	Grande	X-Grande)	
Débardeur-En jersey extensible seulement						
150cm**	0.90	0.90	0.90	0.90	0.90	m
T-shirt						
150cm**	1.10	1.10	1.10	1.10	1.30	m
Entoilage-thermocollant-0.30m de 55cm à 64cm						
Pantalon						
115cm**	2.10	2.40	2.50	2.50	2.60	m
150cm**	1.60	1.80	2.00	2.10	2.50	"
Elastique-5.10m de 1.3cm de large						
Short-Tissu uni-coupé dans la longueur						
115cm**	1.30	1.40	1.40	1.50	1.60	m
150cm**	1.00	1.10	1.10	1.40	1.50	"
Short—Tissu imprimé à bordure-coupé dans la largeur						
115cm*	1.60	1.70	1.80	1.90	2.10	m
Short Elastique—3.50m de 1.3cm de large						
Pantalon ou Short-cordon (facult.)-1.70m de 6mm ou un lacet de soulier fantaisie de 160cm de long						
Longueur côté du pantalon	102	103	104	106	107	cm
Longueur côté du short	48.5	49.5	51	52	53.5	"

*sans sens **avec sens ***avec ou sans sens

▼ The Envelope Back ▼

More detailed information is on the back of the envelope. Look for the following information:

- ▶ ***Views.*** The envelope back often includes sketches of a garment's back and front views. These show design lines and details that are not easily seen in sketches or photographs on the envelope front.
- ▶ ***Garment description.*** A detailed description of the garment will give you lots of information about how each view is constructed.
- ▶ ***Suggested fabrics.*** The pattern company lists the types of fabrics that will work well for every pattern. A wide choice is usually given for each view.
- ▶ ***Notions.*** **Notions** are the smaller items needed to make a garment. Thread, buttons, zippers, snaps, hooks and eyes, and any trims you will need are listed.
- ▶ ***Advice on special fabrics.*** For example, the advice for one pattern might read, "Extra fabric needed to match plaids, stripes, one-way designs. Not suitable for obvious diagonal fabrics."

Each type of notion has a different function. Check your pattern for what you need.

More About *Old Patterns*

There are many uses for old pattern pieces. Stores sometimes wrap fragile items in them. Others use them as packing filler when mailing breakable objects. How can you use them at your house? To wrap Christmas ornaments? To cushion items to mail? Share ideas. On the other hand, if you are looking for wrapping or packing materials, check out garage sales and buy old patterns to use for that purpose. They're inexpensive or free.

Learning Activities (continued)

3. **Discussion.** Show students pattern envelopes with photos of the garment. Ask what the advantages *(see how it really looks, get ideas)* and disadvantages *(lines and details don't always show in the pose)* of photos are. (Key Skill: *Critical Thinking*)
4. **Demonstration.** Show a multi-sized unisex pattern. Ask how to cut it for a person whose waist is smaller than hips. Would the sewer need more fabric? *(Probably not)* What alterations require more fabric? *(Lengthening)* (Key Skill: *Critical Thinking*)
5. **Demonstration.** Show an "off-brand" pattern which has many sizes on heavier paper. Point out similarities and differences. Ask what looks interesting or complicated about each kind of pattern. (Key Skill: *Critical Thinking*)
6. **Demonstration.** Show bolts of 36-inch, 45-inch, and 60-inch fabrics. Unroll enough so students can compare a yard of each. Point out the end of the bolt, where care, content, width, manufacturer, and price are found. (Key Skill: *Communication*)
7. **Style Show.** Ask volunteers to model clothes they have sewn and show their patterns, to help students who have difficulty visualizing a finished garment and to show who sews and how well. (Key Skill: *Creativity*)

Follow Up

1. **Reteaching.** Ask students to list the information on a pattern envelope without looking, numbering items of information in their order of importance. Discuss the results.(Key Skill: *Communication*)
2. **Extension.** Use the activity on p. 43 of the *Extending the Lesson* booklet in the TCR.
3. **Enrichment.** Have students find out how patterns are manufactured. If they are made nearby, arrange a tour. Or, ask students to imagine how patterns might be mass produced. (Key Skill: *Problem Solving*)

Completing the Chapter

For Review

1. Emphasize the main concepts using the summary.
2. Have students complete the "Facts to Recall." (Answers below.)

For Reteaching

1. **Reteaching.** Use the activity on p. 40 of the *Reteaching and Practical Skills* booklet in the TCR.

For Enrichment

1. **Enrichment.** Use the activity on pp. 51-52 of the *Enrichment Activities* booklet in the TCR.

For Evaluation

1. Choose items from "Ideas to Explore" and "Activities to Try."
2. Use the chapter test on pp. 65-66 in the testing booklet of the TCR or use the testmaker software.

Facts to Recall Answers

1. **Any four:** Remove bulky sweaters, jackets, or belts; take each measurement twice; hold the tape measure so it fits comfortably; write the measurements down.
2. Around the largest part, from 6-9 inches (15-23 cm) below the waist.
3. The hip measurement.
4. It equals the neck measurement plus ½ inch (1.3 cm).
5. They have a small number of pattern pieces; they don't require a great deal of fitting; the designs are simple and have very few sewing details.
6. **Any three:** View, pattern number, size, figure type, any special information.
7. **Any five:** views, garment description, suggested fabrics, notions, advice on special fabrics, body measurements, yardage charts, garment measurements.

Selecting the right pattern results in a well-fitting garment.

- ***Body measurements.*** To select the correct size, compare your measurements with those listed. The measurements and sizes are listed on the back of the pattern envelope as an easy reference.
- ***Yardage chart.*** Usually the largest amount of space on the back of the envelope is devoted to a chart that helps you determine the amount of fabric to buy. The pattern sizes, different views, and fabric widths are listed. Typically, you will see 45-inch and 60-inch (115- and 150-cm) fabric widths. The size and the view you are making will determine the amount of fabric you need to buy. Identify and circle the size, view, and fabric width you will be using on the chart. This will help you avoid making mistakes. Next, draw a line down the size column and another across from the fabric width until the lines intersect, or cross each other. At the point the lines cross, you will find the exact yardage needed to sew the garment.
- ***Garment measurements.*** These measurements may vary depending on what you are making. They may include finished back length or width of the lower edge.

Using the information on the pattern envelope can help you to begin your sewing project successfully.

TAKING ACTION

Selecting Pattern Sizes

Brenda wants to give special presents to her brother and sister, who are twins, for their tenth birthday. She can't afford to buy ready-to-wear clothes at this time. However, she owns a sewing machine and decides to make her presents for David and Cleo.

Brenda is a beginner and intends to choose an "easy to sew" pattern for tank-tops and shorts. In the summer, the twins are outside all day long — biking, swimming, or playing in a nearby park.

Brenda needs David's and Cleo's measurements in order to buy a pattern. David's measurements are: Chest 29", Waist 25", Hips 30", Height 55". Cleo's measurements are: Chest: 28", Waist 25", Hips 31", Back waist length 13", Height 56". Brenda wants the outfits to be fun, colorful, and comfortable. She turns to you for help.

Using Your Resourcefulness

- What pattern sizes should she choose for David and Cleo?
- Describe a pattern style that Brenda could use for David's and Cleo's outfits. Give examples of colors and fabrics that could be used for this pattern. Give a reason for each of your choices.
- In what ways is Brenda being resourceful?
- Would you consider making something special for a relative's birthday? Why or why not?

TAKING ACTION

Direct students to read the feature. Divide the class into groups to discuss, write, and share answers to the questions. Ask students to brainstorm a list of items that they might make for gifts.

Using Your Resourcefulness Answers

- Choose one pattern that will have the larger size, especially the hips. The twins will grow into them if they're too large.
- She could make them the same outfit in different solid colors, or use stripes, plaid, geometric or other colorful prints in fabrics that are cool, easy to launder, probably

Chapter 31 Review

Summary

In this chapter, you have read about:

- Taking body measurements for females and males.
- Determining the most important measurement for sewing different garments.
- Locating information on pattern envelopes.
- Using a yardage chart.

Facts to Recall

1. Name four things you should do to take accurate body measurements.
2. Where should the hips be measured on a female?
3. What is the most important measurement to consider when selecting a pattern for a fitted skirt, pants, or shorts?
4. How is the shirt neck size determined for males?
5. Name three characteristics of patterns found in the "easy to sew" section of a pattern catalog.
6. Identify three types of information found on the pattern envelope front.
7. List five types of information found on the pattern envelope back.

Ideas to Explore

1. What are some advantages to knowing how to sew your own clothing?
2. Suppose your waist and hip measurements fall between two sizes listed for a pants pattern in the catalog. Your waist is 1 inch (2.5 cm) smaller and your hips are 2 inches (5 cm) larger. Which measurement would you use to buy the pattern? Why?
3. How can simple sewing skills help improve or personalize ready-made garments?

Activities

1. Obtain two patterns, each from different companies. How are the patterns similar and different? Locate information such as body measurements, fabric suggestions, notions needed, and yardage needed for several sizes. Is the information easily found? Which pattern brand did you prefer? Why?
2. Using one or more pattern catalogs, select three patterns you think would be good for someone who is learning to sew. Why do you think these patterns would be good for beginners? What are the similarities and differences in the patterns?

LINK TO *Math*

TAKING MEASUREMENTS

With a partner, take your body measurements as described in this chapter. Measure your body in the following locations: bust or chest, waist, and hips. Use these measurements and a pattern chart (from the back of a pattern book or pages 349-350 in the text) to determine the pattern size that you need. Answer the following questions:

- How should you choose a pattern size if your measurements do not match the measurements on the pattern charts?
- If you wear a different size shirt than you do pants, how should you choose your pattern size? What alternatives do you have?

Ideas to Explore

1. Answers may include: some articles are less expensive to make than to buy; homemade clothing can be tailored to fit better than store-bought items; homemade garments can be personalized, more unique.
2. You would use the hip measurement and alter the waist when you made the pants. This would be more accurate and give a better fit.
3. Answers will vary and may include: buttons can be added to or changed on a garment; hems can be raised or lowered; decorations such as beads and sequins can be sewn on.

permanent press — perhaps a poly/cotton blend.

- She will save money using one pattern and one kind of fabric and her own time.
- Answers will vary.

LINK TO *Math*

Direct students to read the feature, do the activity, and answer the questions:

- Choose a size according to the most fitted or hardest to alter part of the garment (hips, bust/chest).
- Depends on the style. Choose the largest size or size of the most fitted garment. It might be better to purchase the pattern in two sizes, or look for a pattern that has multiple sizing.

Preparing to Teach

Chapter Outline

Chapter Resources

The following booklet materials may be found in the *Teacher's Classroom Resources* box:

- Lesson Plans, p. 37
- Student Workbook, *Study Guide,* pp. 137-138; *I've Got a Notion,* p. 139; *Shopping for Sewing,* p. 140
- Color Transparencies, *Inspect Before You Select,* CT-36
- Technology and Computers, p. 36
- Cooperative Learning, p. 44
- Extending the Text, *Are You Ready to Buy Fabric?,* p. 44
- Reteaching and Practical Skills, *Notion Know-How,* p. 41
- Enrichment Activities, *Choosing Fabrics,* p. 53
- Chapter and Unit Tests, pp. 67-68
- Testmaker Software

Also see:

- Meeting the Special Needs of Students
- Linking Home, School, and Community

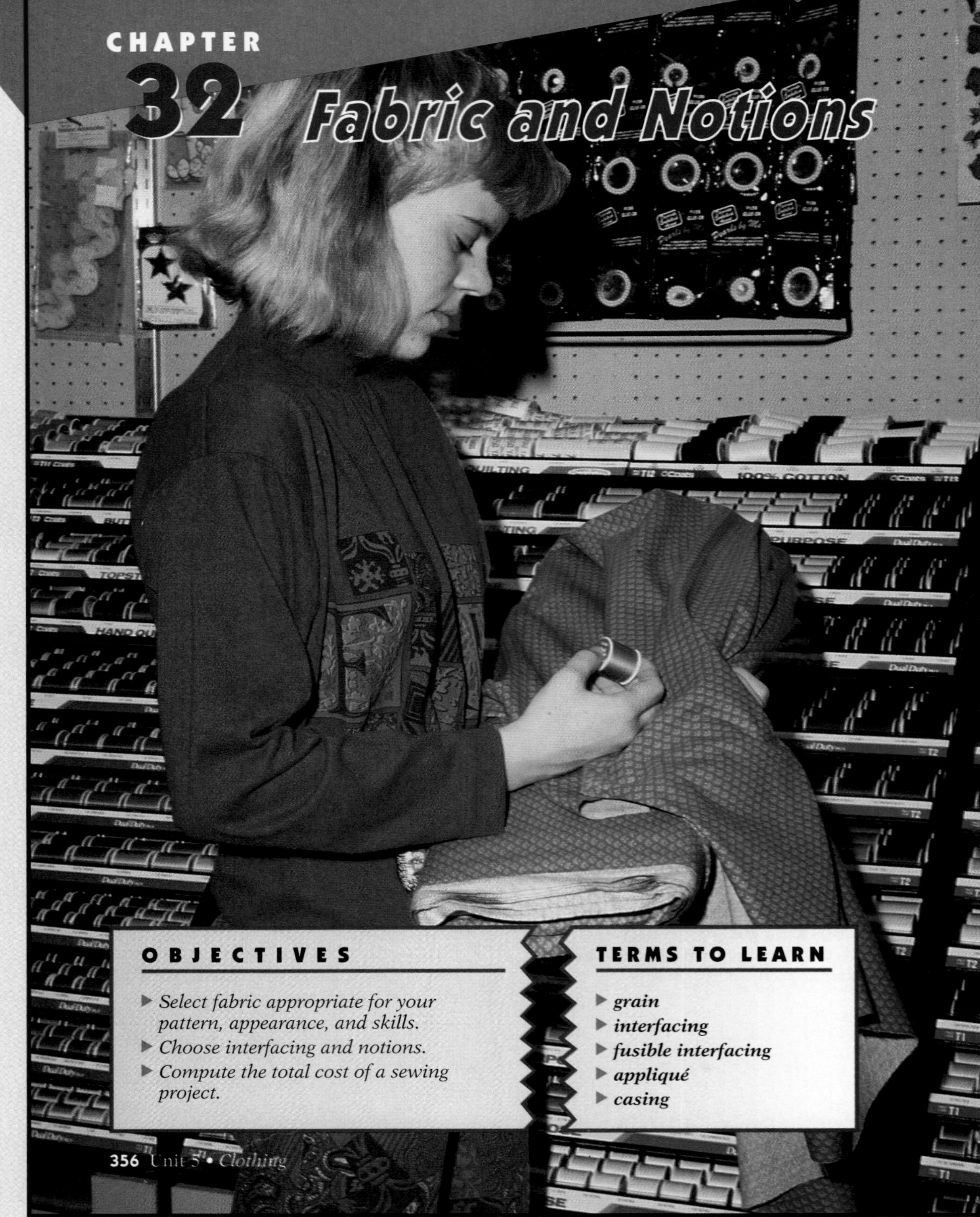

CHAPTER 32 Fabric and Notions

OBJECTIVES

- *Select fabric appropriate for your pattern, appearance, and skills.*
- *Choose interfacing and notions.*
- *Compute the total cost of a sewing project.*

TERMS TO LEARN

- ***grain***
- ***interfacing***
- ***fusible interfacing***
- ***appliqué***
- ***casing***

Have you ever been shopping for that perfect garment — something unique that expresses who you really are? Is it sometimes discouraging to see the same type of clothing in store after store?

By using your imagination and creativity when selecting fabric and notions, you can create clothing that is as original and unique as you are. Personal touches such as trims, interesting fabric combinations, or unusual buttons will help you create fashionable clothing.

Browsing through a fabric store will give you a good idea about the types of fabrics, patterns, and notions that are available. How will you know which fabrics and notions are right for your pattern? As you read this chapter, you will discover some helpful guidelines for making wise fabric and notion choices.

Selecting Fabric

Before you buy a piece of fabric, think about how appropriate the fabric is for your pattern, your appearance, and your sewing skills. What kind of care will the fabric need?

Buy fabric you like and will enjoy working with. After all, you are investing your time, money, and creativity. You will want to enjoy using the finished product.

Selecting fabric that is appropriate for your pattern, appearance, and sewing skills will result in a sewing project you can be proud of.

More About *Selecting Fabric*

When buying fabric, check the hangtag or bolt-end for information. Often manufacturers will list care instructions, fiber content, and type of fabric. Jot this down and slip it into the pattern envelope for easy reference as you sew. As you sew, you will need to know how to press your fabric and if you should preshrink it. Keep scraps of your fabric to test care properties and stain removal. Having scraps for testing is one of the advantages of home sewing. When your outfit is finished, take the time to add a special care label. This will be a handy reference when you are laundering the garment.

Introducing the Chapter

Motivators

1. **Bulletin Board.** Find black and white ads featuring current styles, especially the same kind of garment in a similar style. Mount all on a black or white back. In the center place a brightly-colored pattern envelope with an interesting garment and some variations. The headline: "In the middle of a world of sameness there is you." Point out that sewing is a great way to be an individual. (Key Skill: *Critical Thinking*)
2. **Discussion.** Ask students why they think people sew their own clothing. *(Save money, hard-to-fit body)* Emphasize the creativity and leisure-time aspects. (Key Skill: *Critical Thinking*)
3. **Poster/Essay.** Fill a poster with rows of black construction paper silhouettes of people. In the middle, place a large picture of a sewing machine with colorful "rays" extending from it. Title: "Set Free by Sewing." Ask individuals to write an essay on what the poster means. Have the class choose the best. Award a free pattern at a fabric store, a yard of fabric, or several spools of colorful thread. The fabric store might like to supply the prize or display the essays. (Key Skill: *Creativity*)

Chapter Objectives and Vocabulary

1. Have students read the chapter objectives and rephrase the objectives as questions.
2. Ask students to state, in their own words, the purpose of studying this chapter.
3. Pronounce the vocabulary terms listed on the previous page. Ask students whether they are familiar with any of these. Explain that the terms will be defined in the chapter.

Guided Reading

1. Have the students read the chapter and use the Study Guide on pp. 137-138 of the *Student Workbook.*

Teaching. . .
Selecting Fabric, Consider Your Pattern, Appearance, and Sewing Skills
(pp. 357-359)

Comprehension Check

1. If you are planning to make tennis shorts, what kind of fabric would you look for? *(Durable, hard-wearing, easy to launder, cool.)*
2. You are taller and thinner than many of your friends, and, want to choose a design to make you feel less conspicuous. What designs might you look for? *(Horizontal stripes, diagonal top, light colors.)*
3. Why is it a good idea to pick a color which goes with the main colors in your wardrobe? *(Coordinating colors means you can mix and match items, which makes your wardrobe seem larger.)*

Learning Activities

1. **Discussion.** Tell the class that many well-known public figures have some items of their wardrobe designed and sewn just for them. Ask students why they think that is? *(One-of-a kind items, perfect fit, distinctive styles)* Ask them if any of these characteristics appeal to them? Could they learn to sew clothing that would reflect these traits? What skills do professional designers or sewers need? (Key Skill: *Critical Thinking*)
2. **Preplanning.** (Do this after you select a project but before students go shopping.) Ask students to list old favorite garments of the type they will be making in class. Include color, style, and fabric. Encourage students to take the list with them when they shop for this project. (Key Skill: *Critical Thinking*)
3. **Demonstration.** Collect some samples of fabric that are badly off grain. A plaid design and a knit would be great. Show students how to tell if the grain is off. Then cut two pieces (follow the design of the plaid) of each. Wash and dry one of the pieces of each. Compare the results so

▼ Consider Your Pattern ▼

When you shop for fabric, bring your pattern and the money needed to buy the fabric and notions. Both your pattern and the money you have to spend will influence your decisions about fabric and notions.

Where do you begin? Your pattern envelope is a good place to start. As you learned in Chapter 31, both the front and back of the envelope provide important tips on selecting fabric. Give special attention to the advice about suitable fabrics.

Using your own good judgment is a key to wise fabric choices. If you are making an active sportswear garment, look at fabrics that are durable and hard-wearing. The fabric will also have to stand up to frequent washings. If you are making something for a special occasion, a dressier fabric might be just what you want.

▼ Consider Your Appearance ▼

When making a garment, think about how the fabric will look on you. Do the design elements of the fabric accent your best features? Use design to your advantage just as you would when buying clothes. Consider each of the following items:

- ***Color.*** In Chapter 28, you learned that everyone looks better in some colors than in others. When you find a fabric you like, locate a mirror and hold the fabric close to your face. Try a few different colors against your skin. Which ones bring out the best in your natural coloring? Also consider whether the color you choose will go with the main colors in your wardrobe. Coordinating colors is a good way to expand your wardrobe with fewer articles of clothing.
- ***Line.*** If you want to look taller, pick fabric with vertical (up-and-down) lines or design. Continuous vertical lines also have a slimming effect. If you want to look shorter, pick horizontal (side-to-side) lines or patterns. To emphasize curves or to appear more full-bodied, try a pattern with diagonal lines.
- ***Proportion.*** Keep fabric designs in proportion with your body. If you are short and have a small bone structure, choose smaller designs. If you are tall or have a large bone structure, a larger design may be the choice for you.

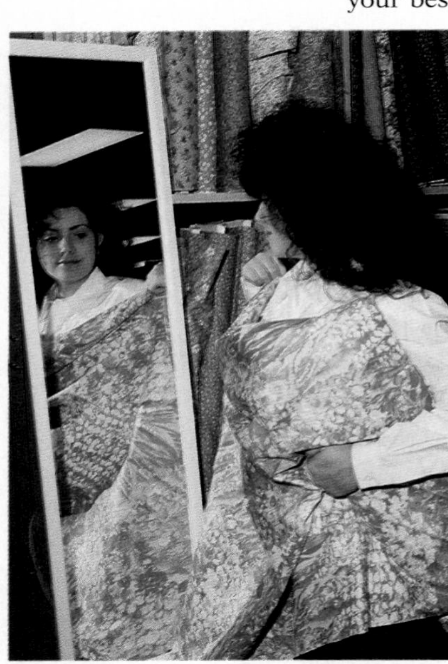

Fabric colors affect your appearance in many ways. What colors enhance your best features?

More About *Buttons*

Before you throw out an old worn garment, such as shirt, cut off the buttons. If there are quite a few that match, store them together in a small plastic bag. Be especially sure to save expensive and unusual buttons from garments that cannot be recycled. Keep odds and ends buttons in an attractive clear glass jar in your sewing room.

More About *Notion Remnants*

Keep leftover pieces of bias tape, seam binding, lace and trims together in a drawer or decorative tin. You'll know just where to find them when you are sewing a small project or need a small amount for a trim or craft project. There's no expiration date!

- ▶ ***Texture.*** Fabrics with a great deal of texture — bulky, heavy, rough, and coarse-looking — will make a body appear larger. In contrast, smooth-looking fabrics will minimize body size.

▼ Consider Your Sewing Skills ▼

Confidence in your ability is a real benefit for a successful sewing experience. If you are just learning to sew, choose a fabric with qualities that are easy for a beginner to handle. After learning the basics of sewing, you can move on to more challenging fabrics.

Here are some fabric qualities to consider:

- ▶ ***Construction.*** How is the fabric made? Is it woven, or is it knit? Firmly woven fabrics, in a plain weave, are easier to work with than loosely woven or knitted fabrics. They are less likely to stretch or unravel.
- ▶ ***Weight.*** Mediumweight fabrics are easier to work with than sheer, heavy-textured, or bulky fabrics.
- ▶ ***Grain.*** **Grain** refers to the direction in which yarns run in fabric. A fabric is *on-grain* when lengthwise and crosswise threads are at right angles to each other. It is *off-grain* when lengthwise and crosswise threads do not meet at right angles and are curved or slanted. Check fabric carefully before you buy it. Do not buy fabric that is badly off-grain, no matter how little it costs. Straightening fabric takes time, and sometimes it cannot be done at all. If fabric is printed, make sure the print matches the fabric grain. It's difficult to work with off-grain prints. You will learn more about grain in fabric in Chapter 34.
- ▶ ***Design.*** Solid-colored fabrics or those with a small design are easiest to work with.
- ▶ ***Challenging fabrics.*** If you are a beginner, avoid plaid or striped fabrics and those with one-way designs. These fabrics, along with corduroy and velvet-type fabrics, all require special handling and extra fabric. Lines in plaids and stripes need to be matched in order to have a quality look.
- ▶ ***Wrinkle resistance.*** Check for wrinkle resistance by squeezing a small amount of fabric in your hand. Hold it for 30 seconds and release it. If most of the wrinkles disappear quickly, the fabric's wrinkle resistance is good.
- ▶ ***Imperfections.*** Look at the large piece of fabric you want to buy. Check for snags, spots, defects, and faded colors.

More About Interfacing

Interfacing plays a key role in both the appearance and longevity of a garment. For example, interfacing helps create and maintain the smooth roll required in collars, cuffs, and lapels. It stabilizes and reinforces areas of strain — necklines, facings, pockets, plackets, waistbands, and buttonholes. It adds the required shape to detail areas. Although fusible interfacings seem easier to apply than woven, they take time at the ironing board instead of the machine. Once applied, however, both the fabric and interfacing are easily handled as one, which is a blessing to beginning sewers.

students can see what will happen if they sew on off-grain fabrics. You might do this at the same time you do the interfacing samples on the next page. (Key Skill: *Critical Thinking*)

Follow Up

1. **Reteaching.** Ask students to think about the clothes that make them look attractive and in which they receive the most compliments. Note the color, silhouette, and details of these garments and write them down. In small groups, have them ask for feedback about the things they've written down and for suggestions about what other colors and styles flatter them. (Key Skills: *Communication, Critical Thinking*)
2. **Enrichment.** When students shop for fabric for their projects ask them to check out five woven and five knit fabrics with stripes or plaids to see if they are printed on grain. Have students compare and compile their results. (Key Skill: *Decision Making*)

Life Management Skills

Consumerism

Susannah has been invited to the prom and is dying to go. Her parents cannot afford to buy an expensive dress; however, Susannah's mom has offered to sew a dress and spend $50. What styles should Susannah consider? *(Low yardage, no expensive trim).* She finds a washable, dressy fabric for $5 per yard (She needs eight yards.) and taffeta, which requires dry cleaning, for $3 per yard. Which is the better choice for a prom dress? *(A one-occasion dress won't need cleaning; there would be more money for notions, trims.)* (Key Skill: *Problem Solving*)

Teaching. . .

Consider Fabric Care, Buying Interfacing, Buying Notions, Thread, Zippers, and Trims

(pp. 360-361)

Comprehension Check

1. Why should notions and interfacing require the same care as your fabric? *(So it won't shrink, fall apart, or be ruined when it's cleaned.)*
2. Why buy matching thread when seams are on the wrong side of the fabric? *(Sometimes thread shows through or dangles.)*
3. Why choose a zipper in a background color? *(So it won't be noticeable.)*

Learning Activities

1. **Discussion.** Ask the class what they would do: Jason is making a lightweight jacket which zips down the front and has a stand-up collar on which the lining shows. He can't find a zipper to match his turquoise cotton/poly fabric. Would a dress zipper work for a jacket? *(No, it's closed at the bottom)* Can you think of any solutions or lessons? *(Use a contrasting lining at the collar and a zipper to match the lining. Lesson: Don't buy fabric unless all of the notions are available.)* (Key Skill: *Problem Solving*)
2. **Debate.** Choose volunteers to debate zippers vs. hook and loop fasteners. Ask each side to tell the merits of their fastener and when it works particularly well. They might tell the shortcomings of the opposing fastener. Have the class choose which side did the best job. (Key Skills: *Communication, Creativity*)
3. **Discussion.** Display several patterns which lend themselves to variations. Read (or copy) the list of notions. Ask students what notions they would choose. Encourage them to think of ways to personalize the garment. Point out variations that the designers have included. (Key Skill: *Creativity*)

▼ Consider Fabric Care ▼

The care needed by a fabric will depend on the fiber content and any special finishes applied to the fabric. If you don't want to spend time hand washing or pressing, choose washable fabrics with a permanent-press finish. If you don't want to spend money on cleaning bills, avoid fabrics that require dry-cleaning.

Ready-to-wear garments must have care instructions sewn into a seam. Fabric sold by the yard must also come with a care label that you can sew into the seam. Ask the salesperson for the care label. The label on the end of the bolt of fabric will list the fiber content and any special finishes that are used.

Interfacing must match the characteristics of your fabric.

Buying Interfacing

Interfacing is a special fabric that gives support and body to a garment. Although the interfacing isn't visible in finished garments, it makes them look better and last longer. Interfacing is often used at necklines, openings, and collars.

Interfacing can be classified into two groups — sew-on and fusible. Within these groups, you will find woven, nonwoven, and knit types of interfacing. **Fusible interfacing** has an adhesive coating that bonds it to the fabric when pressed with a hot iron. Fusible interfacing should be tested on a scrap of your fabric before using.

Here are some helpful tips for choosing interfacing:

- ▶ Choose an interfacing that has weight, body, and care requirements similar to those of your fabric.
- ▶ Drape your fabric over the interfacing before you buy it. The interfacing should not show through the fabric.
- ▶ Check to see that the interfacing has give, or stretch, that matches your fabric. Some interfacings have stretchability that is ideal for knit fabrics that need some stability.

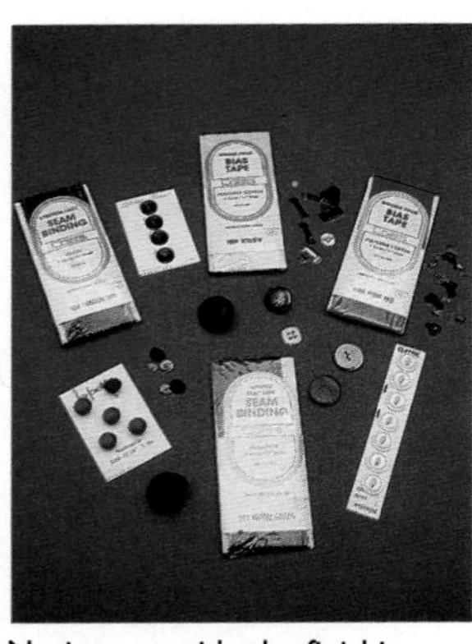

Notions provide the finishing touches to your garment.

Buying Notions

Notions are small items, such as thread, zippers, buttons, trim, seam binding, snaps, and hooks and eyes, that are needed to complete a garment. The back of the pattern envelope lists the notions needed to complete a sewing project.

More About *Appliqués*

Coloring books are good sources of traceable appliqué patterns. Cookie cutter shapes also make interesting patterns. To appliqué a sweatshirt, trace the pattern onto fusible interfacing, iron the interfacing to the wrong side of the appliqué fabric and cut out the shape. Backing will keep the material from wrinkling and pulling. Pin it down and sew it flat with a large zigzag stitch. You can also use double-sided fusible material. Trace and iron on as before, remove paper backing, fuse to front of sweatshirt. Then stitch.

Be sure the care requirements for notions are the same as those for the fabric. For example, if the fabric is washable, all notions should be washable.

▼ Thread ▼

Thread holds your seams together. Buy the best quality thread you can find. It will be stronger and easier to use in sewing. For solid-color fabrics, select thread that is slightly darker than the fabric. For prints, look for thread that matches the main color in the print.

For most projects, either cotton-covered polyester or 100 percent polyester thread would be a good choice.

Always select a good quality thread that matches the main color in printed fabrics. For plain-colored fabrics, thread should be the same color or slightly darker than the fabric.

▼ Zippers ▼

Zippers come in a variety of colors, lengths, and styles. Some open at the bottom, and some are closed at both ends. Check the pattern envelope for the zipper length and type suggested. Match the color of the zipper to the fabric as closely as possible. If the fabric has several colors, match the zipper with the background color.

AROUND THE WORLD

The little nut of the tagua (TAG-wah) tree is making a big difference for the environment. The tagua tree grows in the Ecuadoran rain forest. The nut, which looks like ivory, is gathered and sold by villagers to be made into buttons and jewelry. This has several benefits. First, it provides the villagers with an income. Secondly, it encourages the preservation of the rain forests, which are important to the global environment. Finally, it discourages the illegal hunting of elephants for their tusks. The tagua tree nut is one example of how helping the environment helps us all.

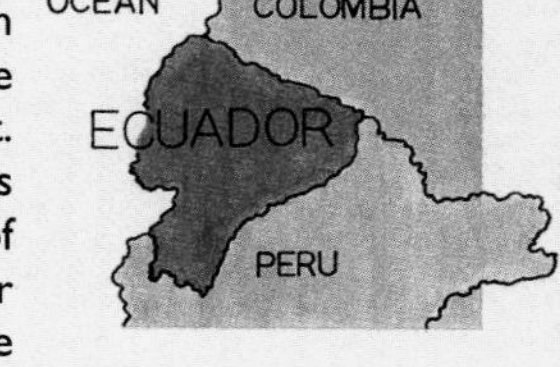

▼ Trims ▼

Trims are available in a wide variety of shapes, sizes, and colors. Ribbon, piping, lace, eyelet, and braid are all types of decorative trims. An **appliqué** (ap-pluh-KAY), a cut-out fabric decoration that is sewn onto a larger background, can also be used as a trim. Most trims can be purchased ready-made and are easily attached by hand or machine stitching.

Learning Activities (continued)

4. **Demonstration.** Show samples of threads — different qualities, weights, fibers, and purposes (*metallic, quilting, button and leather, elastic, serger spools*). What projects would be appropriate for each? (Key Skill: *Critical Thinking*)
5. **Group Work.** Assign three groups one notion: seam binding, bias tape, or elastic. Give samples and reference material on how and when to use them. Have groups present their information to the class. (Key Skills: *Communication, Creativity*)
6. **Experiment.** Apply fusible and non-fusible interfacing to the wrong sides of several fabrics. Wash and dry them several times and discuss the results. Which interfacing works best on which fabric? The fabric with interfacing should be in better shape than the other fabric. Apply wrong weight interfacing or apply it incorrectly so it won't hold up. Ask students to identify reasons why the fabrics or interfacing didn't hold up. (Key Skill: *Critical Thinking*)

Follow Up

1. **Reteaching.** Ask students to look at their clothes. What kind and color of thread was used? What trim or finishing notion was used? (Key Skill: *Critical Thinking*)
2. **Enrichment.** Ask students to find out what remnants are, where they are located in a popular fabric store, how they are priced, and how they might be used. (Key Skill: *Communication*)

More About *Irons and Fusible Web*

Sometimes fusible web sneaks under the backing and gets stuck to the iron. When that happens, put a dab of prewash solution on a cloth. Rub it over the hot sole plate. The web adhesive should come right off.

More About *Thread*

Sewing machines can be temperamental about the kind of thread they like. Most machines respond well to high quality thread. If you have trouble with thread continually breaking or getting jammed in the machine, try changing brands of thread.

AROUND THE WORLD

After students read the feature, ask: What other materials are used in buttons? *(plastic, metal, wood)*. What other natural products might be used? *(nut and fish shells, bone, etc.)*

Teaching. . .
Other Notions and Considering Costs
(pp. 362-364)

Comprehension Check

1. What types of fabrics should beginning sewers avoid? *(Loosely woven, knitted, sheer, bulky, plaid, striped, one-way design, napped.)*
2. How would you select the right zipper for your fabric? *(Check zipper type and length on the pattern envelope and match it to your fabric.)*
3. What are the main categories to consider when figuring the cost of a home-sewn garment? *(Pattern, fabric, interfacing, notions.)*
4. What is bias tape like? *(Has stretch or give, good for curved hems and casings.)*

Learning Activities

1. **Fabric Selection Game.** Gather a variety of fabric swatches. Place them in an attractive gift bag. Pass the bag to each student. As a student picks a fabric ask him or her what kind of fabric it is and what kind of garment it would be suited for. If you wish, ask students what kind of care the fabric requires. An alternate plan would be to display swatches of fabric and ask students to match them to a particular kind of garment. You might also ask (or assign) each student to choose a garment and then pick a swatch from which it could be made. See another variation in "Reteaching." (Key Skills: *Creativity, Critical Thinking*)
2. **Display.** Show the class sewing projects (or photos of them) completed by previous classes. Ask students what makes each project suitable for beginning sewers. Were projects individualized? If so, in what way? (Key Skill: *Critical Thinking*)

Sewing skills can be used for more than just garments. You can make items for your room, for gifts, or for your personal use. What are some other items you could make by using your sewing skills?

Trims give you an opportunity to personalize your project. They can add color or give an item a totally different look. Be sure to coordinate trims with your fabric and project design. The trims that you select should be able to be cleaned the same way as your fabric. Preshrink trims by placing them in hottest water the fiber content will allow for 30 minutes. Allow trims to air-dry.

▼ Other Notions ▼

Depending on the sewing project, you may need seam binding, bias tape, elastic, buttons, hooks and eyes, or snaps.

- ***Seam binding.*** A flat tape that is sometimes used for finishing hem edges. It is either a woven or a lace-type tape. Since the lace tape stretches, it is often used on knitted fabrics. When purchasing tape, try to match the fabric color as closely as possible.
- ***Bias tapes.*** Folded strips of fabric tape. The word "bias" tells you that the tape has give or stretch. It is used on curved hems and as a **casing** — a closed tunnel of fabric that holds a piece of elastic or a drawstring inside.
- ***Elastic.*** A stretchable fabric tape available in several different types and widths. The type of elastic you choose will depend on whether it will be used in a casing or stitched directly to a garment. Read the label when purchasing elastic to be sure it will serve the correct purpose.

- ▶ ***Buttons.*** Help to keep a garment closed. They are also decorative and can be the center of interest. You may want to match the color of your buttons with the fabric color or create interest by choosing a button that contrasts with your fabric.
- ▶ ***Snaps and hooks and eyes.*** Used for holding small openings, such as waistbands and neck openings, together. They come in black and silver. Black is good for dark-colored fabrics. Silver is better with light-colored fabrics. Clear plastic snaps are also available.

Considering Costs

The total cost of a sewing project will include the price of the pattern, fabric, and any notions or interfacing that are required to complete the project.

Remember, the amount of fabric needed is listed on the back of the pattern envelope. It is based on your size, the garment view you are using, and the fabric width.

To figure the cost of the fabric and interfacing, multiply the yardage you need by the cost per yard. For example: Lakisha needs 3 yards of fabric at a cost of $4.95 per yard. She will pay $14.85 for the fabric. In addition, she needs 1 yard of interfacing at $1.89 per yard for a total cost of $1.89. To these amounts, Lakisha must add the cost of the notions (one spool of thread at $1.25 and a zipper at $1.10), the pattern (which costs $4.95), and five percent sales tax. After she totals the costs of all these items, Lakisha will have a good idea about how much her project will cost by the time she reaches the cashier.

The amount and type of fabric your pattern requires often affect your choice of fabric.

Learning Activities (continued)

3. **Group Work.** Divide students into groups. Give each group several magazines, catalogs, or newspapers containing clothing photos or sketches. In addition, give each group a list of garment illustrations to find and list or to cut out. This list might include: a tailored dress or sport coat with inconspicuous buttons, a striped garment that would be slenderizing to the wearer, a garment with contrasting buttons or trim, a garment made with a small print or large print fabric, and a garment suitable for a beginner to sew. (Key Skills: *Creativity, Critical Thinking*)

Follow Up

1. **Reteaching.** Place a collection of small notions in a paper bag and pass it around the room as if you were playing a "Hot Potato" game. In order to pass the bag along, the student must pick an object, identify it, and tell its use. (Key Skill: *Communication*)
2. **Extension.** Use the activity on p. 44 of the *Extending the Lesson* booklet in the TCR.
3. **Enrichment.** Have students find some information in the dictionary or encyclopedia and report on the process and inventor of the zipper and hook and loop fasteners. (Key Skills: *Communication, Social Studies*)

More About Calculating Cost

It's tempting to calculate the cost of a garment based on an estimate of fabric alone. Encourage students to take a pocket calculator along when they shop and add the costs as they go. One way to help remember to include all the costs is to think of Fabric plus *PIN* (Pattern, Interfacing, Notions). You can also get a fairly good idea of the total cost by rounding off numbers and keeping track of them on a slip of paper. Encourage students to redo this problem, rounding off the numbers, and compare it to the actual cost. Also, you might want to have them see what percentage of the garment cost is fabric (fabric divided by total).

Photo Focus

Direct the students to the photograph on page 363. What are some things to consider when you are choosing fabric for a garment? *(Answers may include: drape, suitable weight for the season when the garment is worn, heavy enough to hang right, not too thick for any gathers, not too sheer, cost, care).*

Completing the Chapter

For Review

1. Emphasize the main concepts using the summary.
2. Have students complete the "Facts to Recall." (Answers below.)

For Reteaching

1. **Reteaching.** Use the activity on p. 41 of the *Reteaching and Practical Skills* booklet in the TCR.

For Enrichment

1. **Enrichment.** Use the activity on p. 53 of the *Enrichment Activities* booklet in the TCR.

For Evaluation

1. Choose items from "Ideas to Explore" and "Activities to Try."
2. Use the chapter test on pp. 67-68 in the testing booklet of the TCR or use the testmaker software.

Facts to Recall Answers

1. Your pattern, your appearance, your sewing skills, and fabric care.
2. They make a body appear larger.
3. Firmly woven fabrics can be handled a great deal and are easier to work with than loosely woven fabrics; loosely woven fabrics tend to unravel easily along cut edges and should be handled as little as possible.
4. Plaid or striped fabrics; fabrics with one-way designs; corduroy and velvet-type fabrics.
5. The interfacing should have similar weight, body, and care requirements as your fabric; it should be lighter in weight than your fabric; it should not show through the fabric; and it should have the same stretch or give as the fabric.
6. The zipper should match the background color.
7. A flat tape used for finishing hem edges.
8. The price of the pattern, of the fabric, and of any required notions or interfacing.

Figure the Cost of a Sewing Project

Here is the way Lakisha figured the cost of her sewing project:

Item	Cost
Fabric ($4.95 per yard × 3 yards)	$14.85
Interfacing ($1.89 per yard × 1 yard)	$ 1.89
Notions (Thread at $1.25 + zipper at $1.10)	$ 2.35
Pattern	$ 4.95
Subtotal	$24.04
+ **Tax (5 percent)**	$ 1.20
= **Total Cost**	$25.24

TAKING ACTION

Fabrics and Notions of the Past

Your school is celebrating its 50th anniversary this year. As part of the school celebration, the senior class historian has asked the FHA chapter to do some research about the types of clothing that students wore when the school first opened. The idea has been suggested that the FHA chapter sponsor a "Now and Then" style show sometime during the celebration.

As part of the FHA chapter, you have been assigned to find out about the fabrics and notions used in garments 50 years ago.

Using Your Resourcefulness

- Brainstorm a list of resources that you might use to find out about fabrics and notions used in garments 50 years ago.
- What are the similarities and differences between the fabrics and notions used 50 years ago and those used today? What has influenced some of the similarities and differences?
- How are the needs of people reflected in the types of fabrics and notions used in garments?
- What suggestions do you have for putting together a "Now and Then" fashion show? Where might you find the garments needed?

TAKING ACTION

Direct the students to read the feature and discuss the questions as a class or in small groups. In addition, you may want to have students contact a representative of your local historical society to find out if they have a historical clothing collection. Arrange a tour if possible. Some large theater companies and universities have good period costume collections as well.

Using Your Resourcefulness Answers

- Answers may include: library books on clothing; old newspaper and magazine files; conversations with older people.
- Answers may include: Natural fibers are the

Chapter 32 Review

Summary

In this chapter, you have read about:

- ▶ Factors to consider when selecting a fabric for a sewing project.
- ▶ How to select interfacing and notions that are right for your project.
- ▶ How to determine your project's total cost.

Facts to Recall

1. What four things should you consider before buying a piece of fabric?
2. What effect do heavy, bulky fabrics have on body appearance?
3. How can the weave of a fabric affect your ability to work with it?
4. Name two kinds of fabrics someone just learning to sew should avoid.
5. List four guidelines to selecting appropriate interfacing.
6. How do you match a zipper to a multicolored fabric?
7. What is seam binding?
8. What should be included in figuring the total cost of a sewing project?

Ideas to Explore

1. Determine what colors, lines, proportions, and/or textures would be appropriate in each of the following situations: a small woman with a light complexion who wants to look taller and slimmer; a tall, thin man who wants to add bulk to his frame; a woman with a dark complexion who wants to emphasize her face.
2. Suggest ways in which notions might be used to make a plain black shirt look brighter or more interesting.
3. Do you think there is a stigma, or negative feeling, attached to wearing homemade clothing? If so, how can this attitude be changed?
4. Sewing has traditionally been thought of as something only women should be interested in. How might young men get more involved in the activity?

Activities to Try

1. Collect five small pieces of different types of fabrics. Mount each fabric type on a separate sheet of paper. On each paper under the fabric, explain whether or not the fabric would be a good choice for someone who is just learning to sew.
2. Choose a pattern out of a pattern catalog that you would like to sew. Make a checklist of all the items you will need to sew this garment. Include types of fabrics and notions on your checklist. Take your checklist with you to the fabric store.

LINK TO *Math*

SEWING COSTS

Compute the cost of your sewing project. Identify the pattern view and size to determine the yardage needed and the notions such as thread, trim, elastic, or buttons. Use the actual cost of your fabric and notions to determine the total cost of your project. Remember to include the state sales tax. Answer the following questions:

- ▶ How would the cost of your project change if you received a 10 percent discount?
- ▶ How would the cost of your project change if you received a 25 percent discount?

(**Note:** To determine the discount, multiply the pre-taxed total by the percentage of discount and then figure the amount of tax.)

Ideas to Explore

1. Answers will vary and may include: the small woman might choose a fabric with medium-to-dark colors, vertical lines, small designs, and a smooth texture; the man, a fabric with horizontal lines, large designs, and a bulky, heavy texture; the dark-complected woman, a fabric with bright colors and diagonal lines.
2. Answers will vary and may include: sewing brightly colored buttons down the front; adding a white lace collar; trimming the hem or sleeves with black lace; accenting any part with sequins or beads.
3. Answers will vary.
4. Answers will vary.

same although blends and manufactured fibers may be different. Wider use of petroleum products have made manufactured fibers less expensive.

- Answers may include: more women work out of the home who want easier-to-care-for garments. Permanent press is new. There's also a trend toward natural fibers, though.
- Answers may include: finding old garments in antique and used clothing stores and in attics.

LINK TO *Math*

Direct students to read the feature and compute the cost of their class project. Answers will all be different, but may be calculated as follows:

- Multiply total by 0.10 and subtract that amount from the total.
- Multiply total by 0.25 and subtract that amount from the total.

Preparing to Teach

Chapter Outline

Chapter Resources

The following booklet materials may be found in the *Teacher's Classroom Resources* box:

- Lesson Plans, p. 38
- Student Workbook, *Study Guide,* pp. 141-142; *Equipment Identification,* p. 143; *Machine Parts Magic Square,* p. 144
- Color Transparencies, *Safe Sewing,* CT-37
- Cooperative Learning, p. 45
- Extending the Text, Special Serger Equipment, p. 45
- Reteaching and Practical Skills, *Get Ready, Set ... Sew!,* pp. 42-43
- Enrichment Activities, *Fine-Tuning the Serger,* pp. 54-55
- Chapter and Unit Tests, pp. 69-70
- Testmaker Software

Also see:

- Meeting the Special Needs of Students
- Linking Home, School, and Community

CHAPTER

33 Sewing Equipment

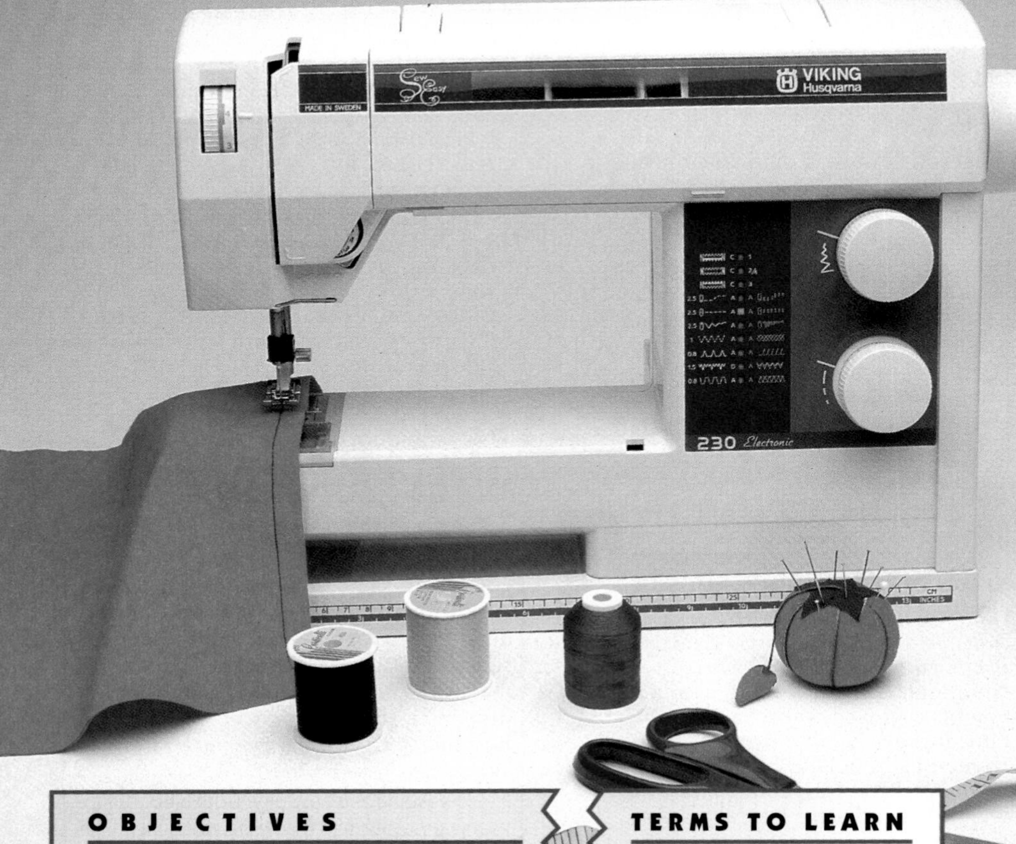

OBJECTIVES

- *Identify and explain the use of small sewing equipment.*
- *Demonstrate operation of a sewing machine.*
- *Explain the usefulness of sergers in sewing.*

TERMS TO LEARN

- ***trim***
- ***backstitching***
- ***tension***
- ***serger***

More About *Cutting Equipment*

Look for scissors and shears made from hot drop forged steel or stainless steel. To prevent rusting, they should have a nickel or chrome plating. The key to quality scissors and shears lies in the tension assembly. Better ones are joined together with a screw, not a rivet.

To keep scissors and shears in good working order, they should be periodically lubricated

The equipment section of a fabric store can seem a bit overwhelming for someone learning to sew. There are dozens of tools. Fortunately, you will need only a few basic items for most sewing projects. As you expand your sewing skills, you might find other equipment helpful for special techniques.

This chapter will introduce small equipment that is used for cutting, marking, measuring, and pressing. Your teacher will tell you which equipment is available in the clothing lab and which items you will need to buy.

In addition to small equipment, this chapter also explains the types and features of sewing machines and how to care for them. Learning to use a sewing machine takes some practice, but it is a skill you will have for life.

Small Sewing Equipment

Having the right tools can make sewing faster, easier, and more fun. The small articles of equipment you will be reading about are organized in groups according to their use.

Cutting Equipment

All the pieces of cutting equipment belong to the scissor family. Keep cutting equipment sharp by using it only for sewing. Never cut paper with a sewing scissors. Basic cutting equipment includes:

- ***Small scissors.*** Use small scissors to clip threads and **trim**, or cut off, extra fabric from seams.
- ***Shears.*** Shears are used for cutting out the fabric. They have long blades with either bent or straight handles. The finger holes on shears are a different shape than those on scissors. Bent-handled shears improve accuracy since the fabric is hardly lifted from the table when it is being cut. Both right- and left-handed shears are available.
- ***Pinking shears.*** Use pinking shears to finish the edge of a firmly woven fabric or a knit fabric. They help to prevent raveling by cutting a zigzag edge.
- ***Seam ripper.*** The seam ripper has a hooklike point. It is handy for cutting and removing stitches.

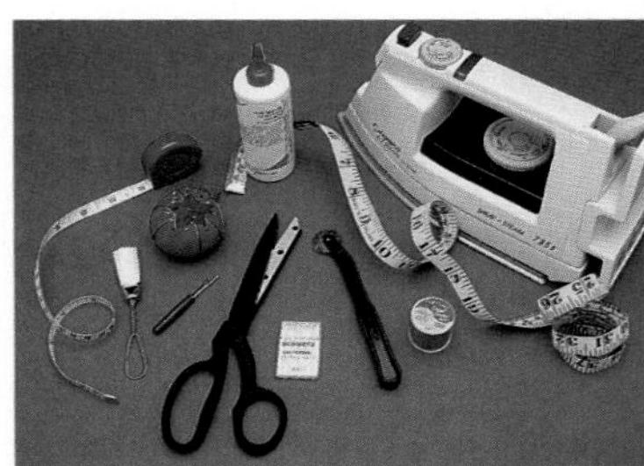

Every piece of sewing equipment has a purpose. You can save time and personal energy by using the right equipment for the job.

Pinking shears, shears, small scissors, and a seam ripper help make sewing easier. Keep safety in mind when working with sharp objects.

Measuring Equipment

To measure the pattern, fabric, and garment pieces accurately as you sew, the following measuring equipment will be helpful:

and sharpened. Oil the screw portion with sewing machine oil and wipe with a soft cloth. Don't use sewing scissors for anything but fabric and pattern tissue. Using them to cut paper can ruin the alignment of the blades.

Never try to adjust the tension screw yourself. It is too easy to strip the screw and, once that happens, the scissors can never be fixed. If sharpening or adjustment is needed, have it done by a professional. Look in the telephone book under "Sharpening Services" or inquire at a fabric store.

Introducing the Chapter

Motivators

1. **Bulletin Board.** On sturdy paper, place a two-foot wide picture of a sewing machine. Put a circle of self-stick hook and loop tape over the parts of the machine you want the students to know. Write the names of the parts on pieces of cardboard and fasten the other side of the tape to the backs. Put other halves of tape around the edge to provide resting places for the names. Have students race to place the rectangles correctly. Do the same for sergers. (Note: If you used the silhouette/sewing machine bulletin board in the last chapter, put part names on that machine.) (Key Skill: *Critical Thinking*)
2. **Discussion.** You need plain black slacks for school tomorrow. Now the electricity is off. The slacks are cut out and you have them mostly sewn together, but there are the long seam, the waistband, and hem to finish. What are your options? How does hand sewing compare to machine stitching? (Key Skill: *Problem Solving*)

Chapter Objectives and Vocabulary

1. Have students read the chapter objectives and rephrase the objectives as questions.
2. Ask students to state, in their own words, the purpose of studying this chapter.
3. Pronounce the vocabulary terms listed on the previous page. Ask students whether they are familiar with any of these. Explain that the terms will be defined in the chapter.

Guided Reading

1. Have the students read the chapter and use the Study Guide on pp. 141-142 of the *Student Workbook.*

Teaching. . .
Small Sewing Equipment for Cutting, Measuring, Marking, and Pressing
(pp. 367-369)

Comprehension Check

1. What tool is best for cutting out fabric? *(Shears with a bent handle.)*
2. On what kind of fabric do pinking shears work best? *(Firmly-woven or knit fabric.)*
3. When do you need to use a marking tool? *(Mark position of pockets, buttonholes, hems, collars, darts, trim.)*

Learning Activities

1. **Display.** Write "Types of Needles and Pins" on one side of a piece of poster board. On the other side write "Pin Containers." Ask students to list as many kinds as they can during the unit. Provide as many samples as possible. Discuss advantages and drawbacks of each. (Key Skill: *Critical Thinking*)
2. **Grab Bag.** Place small sewing tools in a bag. Pass the bag around the room, asking each student to choose and identify one tool and tell its uses. At the end of all the chapters mix all grab bag items together for review. (Key Skill: *Critical Thinking*)
3. **Group Work.** Assign small groups or pairs each a small sewing tool to learn to use and to demonstrate to the class. (Key Skill: *Communication*)
4. **Demonstration.** Gather several colors of fabric and a variety of marking tools. Show how fabric markers work. Point out which tools work best on which fabric. Allow students to practice. (Key Skill: *Critical Thinking*)

SAFETY CHECK✓

Have students read the feature and explain the reasons for the tips listed in the feature. Give each student a band-aid to put on a finger to remind them that careless sewing procedures can hurt!

SAFETY CHECK✓

To use equipment safely:

- Keep shears, scissors, and seam rippers closed when not in use.
- Pass sharp objects handle first.
- Keep pins in a pincushion — not in your mouth or clothing.

- ***Tape measure.*** A narrow strip of durable plastic or firm fabric, often marked with both inches and centimeters.
- ***Measuring stick.*** A measuring stick, or yardstick, is useful for measuring both the pattern and fabric on a flat surface. Choose one with smooth edges to prevent snagging the fabric.
- ***Seam gauge.*** This small ruler has a slide marker that can be set to measure specific lengths. It can be used for measuring small areas, such as hems, buttonholes, and seams.

▼ Marking Equipment ▼

Marking equipment will help you transfer important construction markings from your pattern pieces to your fabric. It can be used to mark the correct position of features such as pockets, buttonholes, hems, and collars. Here is some of the most common marking equipment:

- ***Tracing wheel and paper.*** A tracing wheel is used with special fabric tracing paper to transfer pattern markings to the wrong side of fabric.
- ***Tailor's chalk.*** Pencils, small squares, or chalk wheels made of chalk or wax are used to mark fabric. Wax is used for wool fabrics. Chalk can be used on all other fabrics.
- ***Fabric marker.*** This is a special pen that puts markings on fabrics temporarily. Some fabric pen marks can be removed with water. Others fade in a short period of time. It's best to test fabric markers on a scrap of fabric before using them. Never use markers meant for writing on fabric. The marks may be permanent.

Using measuring and marking equipment accurately leads to a better-fitting, professional-looking garment.

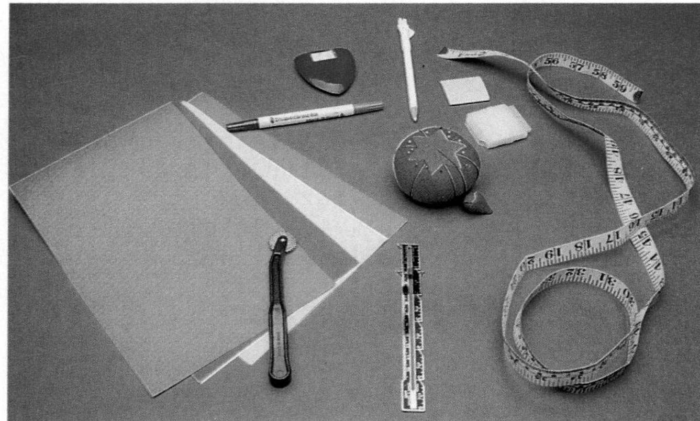

More About Basting Aids

The notions department has a number of basting aids which can be helpful:

- **Glue stick** can be used to hold seam, trims, pockets, appliqués, facings, and zippers in place before stitching. It works best on firmly woven or knitted fabrics. Apply along the sections to be basted. Press them together with your fingers and let them dry a few minutes before stitching.
- **Glue basting liquid** works like the glue stick but can be applied in a finer line.
- **Basting tape** is good for slippery or hard-to-match designs. Place the double-faced tape on the seam allowance, ¼ inch from

▼ Pressing Equipment ▼

In Chapter 30, you learned how pressing and ironing can give your clothing a crisp, neat appearance. In addition, pressing your project as you sew will give it a finished and professional look. Basic pressing equipment includes:

- ***Iron and ironing board.*** A steam iron and a well-padded ironing board are necessary for pressing as you sew.
- ***Press cloth.*** Using a press cloth between the fabric and iron when pressing helps to keep dark fabrics from developing a shine. You can buy ready-made press cloths, or you can make your own from lightweight muslin or cheesecloth.

Good pressing is done carefully and safely. Pressing equipment gets very hot and can easily cause injuries if not handled properly. Review the "Safety Check" box on page 340 for tips about safe pressing.

A *tailor's ham* is a very firm cushion that is used to press curved seams and darts.

A *sleeve board* is a small ironing board. It is helpful when you need to press sleeve seams or small pieces.

▼ Other Small Equipment ▼

You will use some additional equipment to complete sewing projects.

- ***Hand Sewing Needles.*** Needles are numbered from 1 (very thick) to 12 (very fine). A sharp point and medium length makes "sharps" best for general hand sewing. Try a size 7 or 8. Ballpoint needles are helpful for knit fabrics. They have rounded points, which separate the knit as you sew.
- ***Machine Needles.*** Machine needles come in both United States sizes and European sizes. The sizes range from very fine — U.S. size 10 (European size 70) for lightweight fabrics, to U.S. size 14 (European size 90) for mediumweight fabrics, to very coarse — U.S. size 18 (European size 110) for heavyweight fabrics. Select the size best suited to your fabric. Choose ballpoint needles for knit fabric.
- ***Straight pins.*** Straight pins are used to hold the pattern to the fabric and to hold pieces of fabric together for sewing. Most pins are made from stainless steel. There are sharp pins for woven fabrics and ballpoint pins for knit fabric.
- ***Pincushion.*** Use the cushion to keep needles and pins handy while you work. An emery bag, a strawberry-shaped bag, is attached to many pincushions. You can clean rusty or sticky needles and pins by pushing them into this bag a few times.
- ***Thimble.*** A thimble can be used to push a needle through the fabric while hand sewing. A thimble should fit snugly on the third finger of the hand that holds the needle.

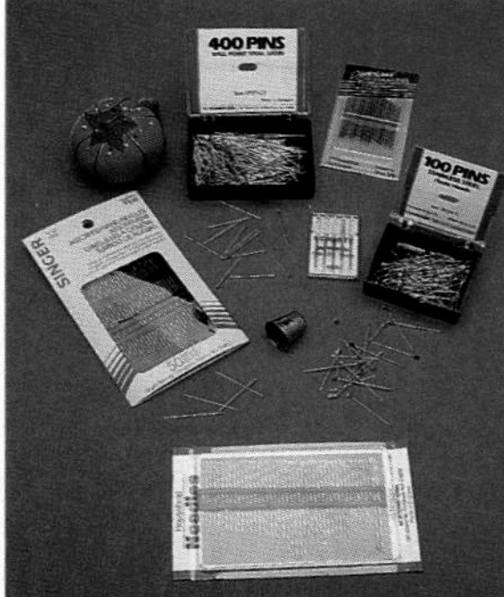

A variety of pins, needles, and other sewing equipment are very useful for sewing projects.

the stitching line. Do not stitch through it. Peel it off after stitching. The newer double-faced basting tape dissolves in water so it can be placed on the seam line.

- **Wash-away basting thread** is designed for temporary stitching on washable fabrics. To remove stitching before washing, press over a wet cloth with a steam iron.

Learning Activities (continued)

5. **Impromptu Skit.** Use the "Family Perspective" as a skit. Choose a student and friend as well as a mom and her friend. The friends can suggest solutions and compromises but the teen and mom have to work it out themselves. (Key Skill: *Communication*)
6. **Hands-On Activity.** Set up stations around the room with several kinds of fabric at each. At one station, have several scissors with which to practice (including one which has cut a lot of paper!). At another have a seam ripper and some seams to rip. Have marking tools and fabrics at one and measuring tools and instructions to measure a 2½ inch hem. Set up ironing boards with different irons and pressing tools. Include various needles to try on cloth. Have students spend three minutes at each station. (Key Skill: *Critical Thinking*)

Follow Up

1. **Reteaching.** Put all the tools on a tray in a visible place during the hour. At the end of class remove the tray and have students list all the items they can remember and their uses. (Key Skills: *Critical Thinking, Communication*)
2. **Enrichment.** Have students interview fabric store managers about new products and trends in home sewing tools. (Key Skills: *Communication, Cooperation*)

Family Perspective

You're eager to start your school sewing project and you'd like to practice at home. Your mother catches you looking for her sewing scissors and orders you to leave them alone. She remembers when you used her new shears to cut your hair and saw pins and earthworms in half. You remind her that you took care of the gardening tools last summer and that she wants you to learn to sew. Can you work out a compromise?

Teaching...
Sewing Machines and Parts of the Machine
(pp. 370-371)

Comprehension Check

1. What basic stitches should a sewing machine be able to do? *(Straight and zigzag.)*
2. What part of the sewing machine pushes the fabric past the needle? *(Feed dogs.)*
3. What holds the fabric in place as it goes past the needle? *(Presser foot.)*

Learning Activities

1. **Matching.** Hold up strips of paper, fan style, with a sewing machine part clearly written on each. Ask for volunteers to take a strip and show where that part is located on a sewing machine or picture. Give everyone a chance. A variation would be to divide the class into teams, call out a part name, and give a strip to the team which correctly identifies the part first. The team with the most strips wins. Do this several days in a row. (Key Skill: *Communication*)
2. **Comparison.** Set up a computer so that you are into a program and ready to go. Tell your students that working on the computer as you have set it up is like working on sewing machines that are threaded and ready to go. Why is it important to know how to get into the program? *(So they don't need to rely on you and to fix mistakes.)* How is this like a sewing machine? (You need to know how it runs.) (Key Skill: *Critical Thinking*)

Most highly automated sewing machines provide an assortment of decorative and functional stitches. Basic models stitch straight, zigzag, and often have a built-in buttonhole feature. What sewing machine features would be most useful to you?

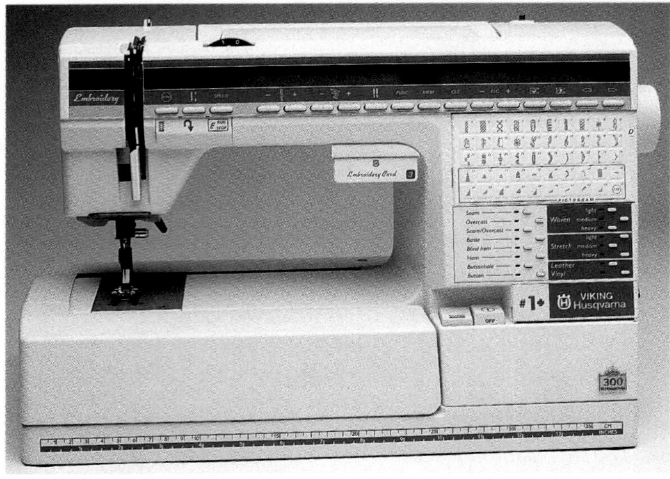

Sewing Machines

A sewing machine is one of the most important and most expensive pieces of sewing equipment you will need. Machines available today range from basic models to computerized machines that do a variety of jobs (like decorative stitches) at the touch of a button. Basic models can handle most general sewing. Look for one that can do both straight and zigzag stitching. Most machines today also have built-in button holers.

For successful sewing, take time to learn about the sewing machine you will use. Read the instruction booklet or have someone show you how to operate and care for the machine before you start to sew.

Around the World

The machines that make socks and hosiery must work very quickly and precisely. At a recent garment industry fair, some new machines from Italy were introduced. The wheels of some of these models are capable of 450 rpm (revolutions per minute), and some have over 200 needles. The action of these needles more closely resembles that of knitting needles or a crochet hook than of a regular sewing machine.

Around the World

Direct the students to read the feature. Ask why the machines must work so quickly. *(They must produce a lot of goods.)* Why are home machines much slower? *(Answers will vary.)*

More About *Machine Stitching*

Why does a sewing machine needle cause so much grief? The answer lies in the way the stitch is formed. As the needle penetrates the fabric, a loop forms in the area of the needle above the eye where it is thread (called the "scarf" area). When the hook with the bobbin thread passes between the thread and the needle, the stitch is locked. A dull needle or one that is the wrong type or size will take a fraction of a second longer to penetrate the fabric. This throws the timing off and results in skipped or uneven stitches. If your stitches are too long, the fabric may start to pucker. The best thing to do is shorten your stitch length. When doing this, you are adding more thread to the seam, which forces the fabric to lie flatter.

▼ Parts of the Machine ▼

All sewing machines function in a similar manner. Knowing the major parts will help you operate the machine easily and accurately. The parts that follow are found on most machines. Check the instruction booklet to see where they are located on your machine.

1. ***Hand wheel.*** This is the large wheel on the right side of the machine. It controls the up-and-down movement of the needle and thread take-up lever.
2. ***Thread take-up lever.*** This lever feeds thread from the spool to the needle.
3. ***Throat plate.*** This is the metal plate under the machine needle. On most machines, the throat plate also contains seam allowance markings for accurate sewing.
4. ***Bobbin.*** A small, flat spool that holds the bottom thread.
5. ***Bobbin case.*** This holds the bobbin and is found beneath the throat plate. Some bobbin cases are removable.
6. ***Bobbin winder spindle.*** This spindle holds the bobbin while thread is wound from the thread spool to the bobbin. The location of this spindle varies with each machine.

TIPS: ***Buying a Sewing Machine***

Look for these basic features when buying a sewing machine:

- The machine starts and stops smoothly.
- The bobbin is easily wound and inserted into the bobbin case.
- The foot pedal is comfortable to operate.
- The needle area is well-lighted.
- You can understand the instruction manual.

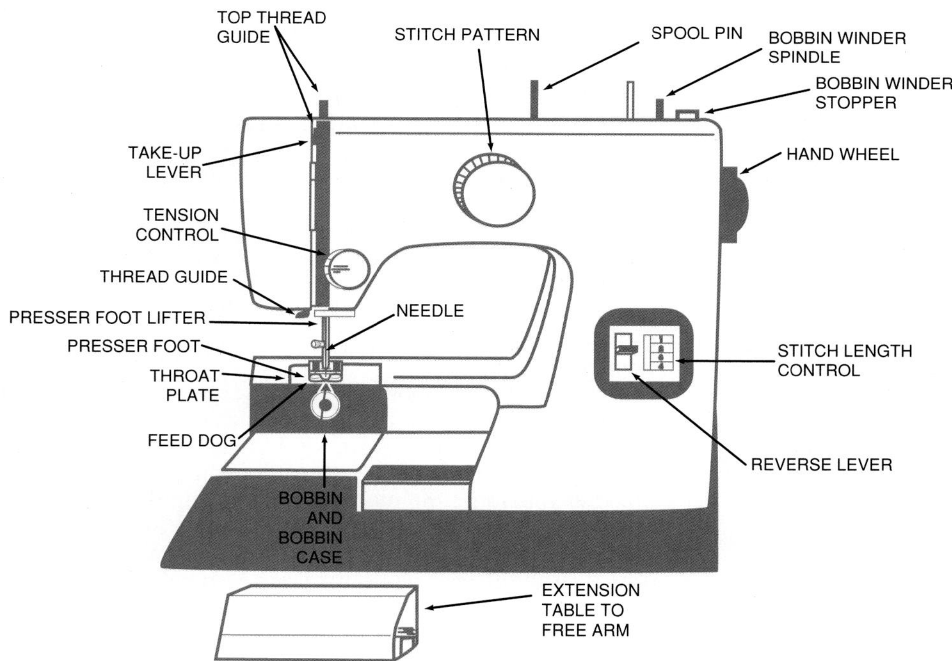

More About ***Technology***

Early sewing machines were operated by hand. The treadle then came into existence to free up hands. Electricity made machines even easier to operate. Computerization, while not necessarily making the operation easier, has added more capabilities to the sewing machine. The basic design, however, has changed very little.

3. **Group Work.** Assign each group names of several related sewing machine parts. Have each group write a silly poem or song about the part and what it does. Ask groups to perform for each other. (Key Skill: *Creativity*)
4. **Demonstration.** Ask students to help you find the parts you are learning on at least two different machines. Point out that important parts appear on each machine and similarities make each part recognizable. Review the general procedure for threading machines. (Key Skill: *Critical Thinking*)
5. **Dream Machine.** Ask students to draw their dream sewing machine of any style, antique to futuristic. They must include the necessary working parts. Place any spectacular designs in the school newspaper, fabric or sewing machine store. (Key Skill: *Creativity*)
6. **Skit.** Have students act out how a sewing machine works. Let students volunteer to be sewing machine parts, give them yarn for threading and the bobbin and, let them demonstrate how stitches happen. Give time to prepare and then perform. (Key Skill: *Creativity*)

Follow Up

1. **Reteaching.** Ask groups to draw or trace pictures of a sewing machine with all parts visible. Have them cut it apart as a puzzle, keeping each part intact as one piece. Have groups exchange puzzles and race to finish. (Key Skill: *Creativity*)
2. **Enrichment.** Have students go to a sewing store and compare features and prices of three different sewing machines (a basic model, another with a few attachments and extra stitches, and a deluxe model). Have them write several paragraphs comparing the machines. Have students make a recommendation based on the information they found. (Key Skills: *Critical Thinking, Communication*)

Teaching. . .
Threading the Machine, Machine Stitching, and Adjusting Stitch Length and Tension
(pp. 372-373)

Comprehension Check

1. In what position should the needle be when you begin to thread the machine? *(Raised to highest point.)*
2. What foot should you use for general sewing? *(Zigzag foot)*
3. Where are the guides located that help you keep your seams at a certain width? *(On the throat plate.)*

Learning Activities

1. **Demonstration.** Show students how to thread a machine, explaining as you go. Do it again. Then ask them to write the steps and reasons on a note card to keep with their sewing supplies. (Key Skill: *Critical Thinking*)
2. **Demonstration.** Show how to bring the bobbin thread up through the throat plate. Ask students to do it successfully three times so they don't forget. (Key Skill: *Critical Thinking*)
3. **Hands-On Activity.** Give each student a piece of cloth on which to practice stitching. Then give them a rectangle of woven fabric to fold in half. With a fabric marker draw a design of parallel and intersecting straight lines extending to the edge of the fabric. Use contrasting thread to sew the lines. Then ask students to practice zigzagging, and then finishing by zigzagging around the edges of the rectangle. (Key Skill: *Creativity*)
4. **Hands-On Activity.** Divide students into groups. Give each group fabric at least 24 inches by 24 inches. Fold fabric in half. Ask each student to sew a ⅝ inch seam along the longest side of the fabric, following the guides on the throat plate and trim the seam close to the seam line without cutting the stitches. The next student does the same thing. The object is to finish with a rectangle that is the same width at top and bottom. Do one for practice

7. ***Feed dogs.*** The feed dogs have a toothlike surface that moves the fabric during stitching.
8. ***Presser foot.*** The presser foot holds the fabric firmly in place against the feed dogs for sewing.
9. ***Presser foot lifter.*** This raises and lowers the presser foot.
10. ***Tension control.*** The tension control adjusts the tightness or looseness of the upper thread.
11. ***Stitch length control.*** This is used to adjust the length of stitches from short to long.
12. ***Stitch width control.*** This control is used to adjust the width of a stitch when using zigzag or decorative stitches.
13. ***Stitch pattern control.*** The stitch pattern control can be adjusted to make different decorative stitching patterns.
14. ***Reverse button or lever.*** Depending on the machine, this will be a button or a lever that allows you to stitch backward to secure the end of the seam.
15. ***Spool pin.*** This holds the spool of thread.
16. ***Thread guides.*** Thread guides hold the upper thread in place as it moves through the machine.
17. ***Foot control.*** The position of this depends on the machine. It regulates the starting, running, and stopping of the machine by the amount of pressure applied to the control.

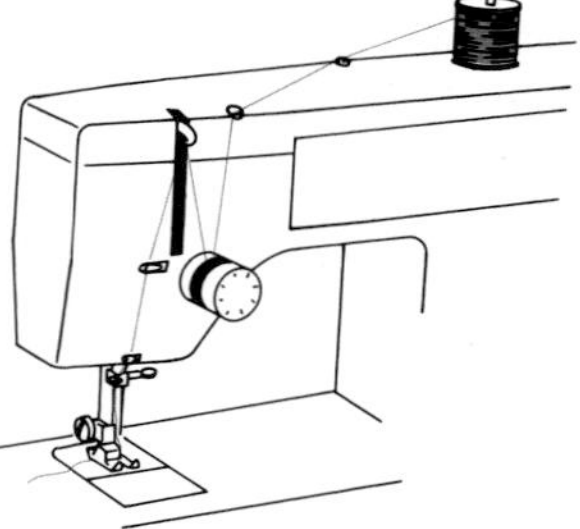

Correctly thread your sewing machine to prevent stitching problems.

Winding a bobbin.

▼ Threading the Machine ▼

Raise the needle and take-up lever to the highest position before threading the machine. The general order for threading all machines follows a similar pattern. The thread passes from the spool pin, through the tension control and thread take-up lever, and then through the hole in the needle. The thread guides help hold the thread in place and keep it from getting tangled. To make threading the needle easier, try cutting the thread on a slant.

The bottom or bobbin thread must also be wound onto a bobbin. The method will vary depending on the machine. Check your machine instruction booklet for specific directions for winding the bobbin thread of your machine.

After threading the machine and putting the bobbin into the bobbin case, bring the bobbin thread up through the hole in the throat plate before you begin to sew. Hold the end of the needle thread while turning the hand wheel one full turn toward your body. The upper thread will pull up a loop of bobbin thread. Pull up on the loop of bobbin thread until the thread end is out of the throat plate.

More About Sewing Machine Care

Sewing machine manufacturers claim that 80 percent of all expensive repairs could be avoided if those who used the machine followed a few simple guidelines: 1) Read the manual; 2) Change the needle often; 3) Keep the machine clean; 4) Keep the machine well oiled according to the manufacturer's instructions. Every sewing machine is different. Features vary from manufacturer to manufacturer and from model to model. The only way to learn about a machine's characteristics is by reading the manual and testing the techniques. If you can't find the manual, write to the manufacturer for a new one. To ensure that you get the right manual, include the model number of the machine. It is usually

▼ Machine Stitching ▼

All machines straight stitch the same way. If you haven't sewn before or will be using a different machine, take time to practice stitching. Here are the general directions:

- Use a sharp needle for woven fabrics and a ballpoint needle for knits. See page 369 about correct needle sizes to use.
- For general-purpose sewing, use the zigzag foot and zigzag throat plate on the machine. Other accessories, such as a zipper foot, can be put on the machine for specific sewing techniques.
- Raise the take-up lever and needle to the highest point by turning the hand wheel toward your body before starting to stitch. Do the same when stitching is finished. This keeps the thread from pulling out of the needle.
- Before starting to sew, pull both the upper thread and bobbin thread to the right side of the presser foot. The threads should also be underneath the presser foot. This keeps the threads from becoming tangled in the bobbin case.
- Place the fabric under the presser foot. The beginning of the stitching line should be just under the point of the needle. First, lower the needle into the fabric and then lower the presser foot. The bulk of the fabric should be to the left of the machine.
- Start the machine slowly. A smooth, steady speed is better than speed-ups and slow-downs.
- Use the throat plate markings to guide your fabric through the machine. This will help you keep an even seam width.
- Slow the machine speed down for the last few stitches. This will help prevent you from stitching beyond the edge of the fabric.
- Secure stitching at both ends of a seam. There are several ways to do this. **Backstitching**, or retracing your stitches about ½ inch (1.3 cm), is done by using the reverse button or lever on your sewing machine. Another way to secure stitching is to tie the thread ends after the fabric is removed from the machine. Cut the thread ends long enough for tying. Bring both threads to the wrong side, tie a knot, and clip off the ends.

▼ Adjusting Stitch Length and Tension ▼

Some fabrics require different stitch lengths and tension adjustments. **Tension** refers to the tightness or looseness of the thread. Check the machine stitching on a two-layer scrap

SAFETY CHECK ✓

To use a sewing machine safely:

- Stitch slowly when learning how to use the machine.
- Keep your fingers away from the needle.
- Don't lean too closely over the machine, in case the needle breaks. Safety glasses can help prevent eye injuries.
- Position the cord so that people won't trip over it.
- Disconnect the cord from the outlet before disconnecting it from the machine.

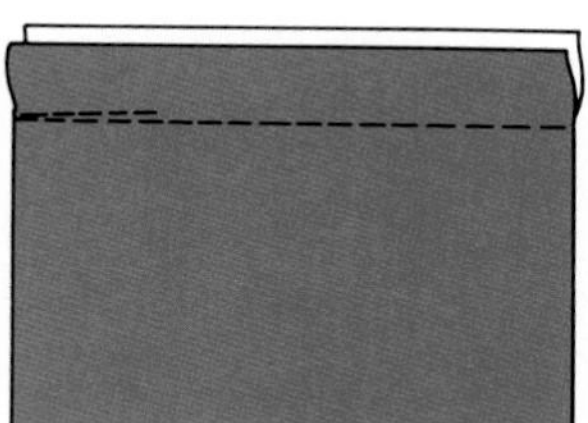

REVERSE STITCHING OR BACKSTITCHING

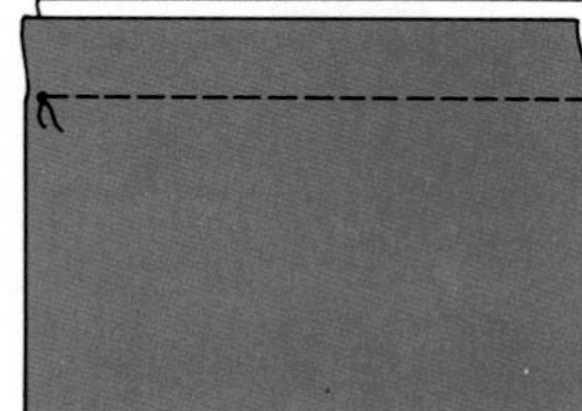

TIED THREADS

Learning Activities (continued)

and one for a group grade. (Key Skill: *Cooperation*)

5. **Sewing Math.** Ask the group in the previous activity to calculate how much fabric should remain after all the students have sewn and trimmed a piece away. Remind students that they are cutting off both ends of the fabric, so they need to double their numbers. (Key Skill: *Math*)
6. **Learning Centers.** After students have done some stitching on their own, set up several machines with different weight needles and fabrics. Ask them to take a turn at each one and jot down the differences. (Key Skill: *Critical Thinking*)

Follow Up

1. **Reteaching.** Divide the class into groups and have them make posters about threading the machine, threading the bobbin, choosing needles, and sewing and finishing seams. (Key Skills: *Communication, Creativity*)
2. **Enrichment.** Have students make a tissue holder. Give them a pocket-sized package of tissues. Ask them to measure around it. Add 3 inches to the length and 3 inches to the width. Cut a strip of colorful fabric. Hem the short edges with a 1½-inch hem. Fold the strip in half lengthwise to find the center. Make ¼-inch clips to mark it on either side. Refold the strip, right sides together, with the hemmed edges meeting in the center at the clips. Pin and sew a ⅝-inch seam along both unfinished sides. Zigzag edges. Turn. Press. Decorate with ribbon. Insert tissue package. (Key Skill: *Creativity*)

stamped on a small metal plate secured on the machine. On a free-arm machine, the plate is on the back of the machine. On a flatbed machine, it is on the front.

More About *Thread*

With the advent of sergers came large cones of thread. Depending on your particular machine, you may find that serger thread will work well on your regular sewing machine. Fabric stores often carry inexpensive adaptors. Using cones of thread may save you money and you can match the color on your serger.

SAFETY CHECK ✓

After students read the feature ask them why each rule is important. What might result if students are careless?

Teaching. . .
Adjusting Stitch Length and Tension
(pp. 374-375)

Comprehension Check

1. What is another word for "tension"? *(Tightness.)*
2. How can you tell if the tension is balanced? *(The stitching looks the same on both sides.)*
3. What often causes tension problems? *(Incorrect machine threading.)*

Learning Activities

1. **Demonstration.** On plain fabric with contrasting thread, sew samples: correct tension, loose upper tension, and tight upper tension. Pass the samples around as you explain tension and how to correct it. Then test the seams on the samples. Pull on them to show how the stitching shows through. Also show how easily the tighter thread pulls out — which is great for fixing mistakes but terrible if you pull a thread on your garment at a party! (Key Skill: *Critical Thinking*)
2. **Poster.** Begin a chart of sewing problems: "Sick Stitches." Entitle the columns: "Symptoms," "Diagnosis," and "Cure" or "Prescription." Encourage students to add to the list throughout the sewing unit. (Key Skill: *Problem Solving*)
3. **Checkup Chart.** Give students each a note card. Ask them to write "Checkup Chart" on the top and to make a list of simple cleaning procedures (probably not oiling) down the side. Have them draw vertical lines, ½ inch apart, across the rest of the page. Each time they do a cleaning task ask them to date and initial it on the card. Write how frequently tasks should be done on the reverse side. Punch a hole in the card, put a string through it, and attach it to the machine or sewing table. Collect the cards at the end of the unit and give points for diligent care. (Key Skill: *Cooperation*)

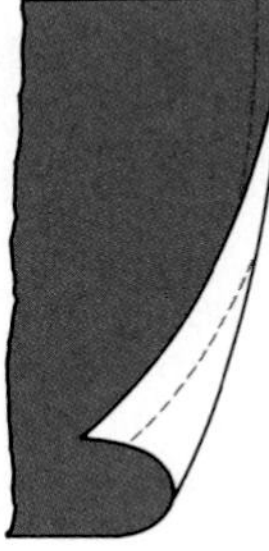

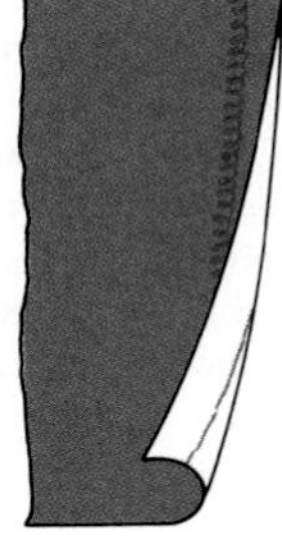

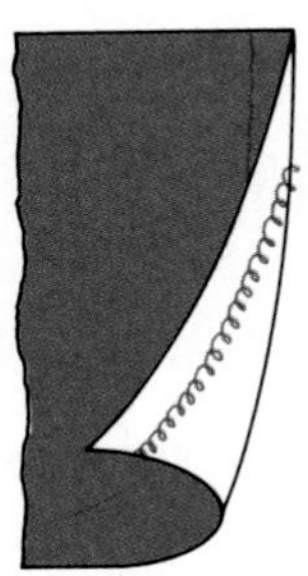

Before changing your tension settings, check the machine threading first.

of your fabric before beginning to sew. The correct stitch length and tension make a seam that is both attractive and strong. You can make changes in the stitch length by adjusting the stitch control.

The tension is balanced when the stitching looks the same on both sides. It is not in balance when the stitches are too tight on one side and too loose on the other. Here are some guidelines for correcting tension problems:

- Check the machine and bobbin threading first. Often times, tension problems are due to incorrect machine threading.
- If the upper tension is too tight, the upper thread puckers and loops form on the top of the seam. You can correct this problem by loosening the upper tension. Turn the tension control a little at a time while testing the stitch on a scrap of fabric. Look in the instruction booklet for the direction to turn the tension control.
- If the upper tension is too loose, the lower thread lies straight on the bottom of the seam and loops of the upper thread come through to the bottom. Correct this by tightening the upper tension a little at a time.

Choosing Stitch Length

Other Machine Settings	Uses and Fabrics
4	▶ Basting ▶ Sewing bulky, heavy fabrics
3	▶ Topstitching
2-2.5	▶ Staystitching ▶ Sewing mediumweight to lightweight fabrics
1-1.5	▶ Reinforcement stitching at points of strain

- Turn your stitch length control to set the desired stitch length.
- Zigzag stitches vary in width. Narrow zigzag stitches are used to make stretchable seams for knitted fabrics. Wider zigzag stitches are used for mending, decoration, or finishing seams.

More About Sergers

Sergers were originally developed in the early 1900s by manufacturers of military uniforms made of serge, a kind of cloth woven in a twill pattern from woolen fibers. Sergers enabled manufacturers to quickly provide a great many uniforms at a price the government could afford.

More About Stitching

A serger stitch interlocks exactly on the cut edge of the seam, in the middle of the fabric layers. A regular sewing machine stitch interlocks in the same place, but at some distance from the cut edges of the seam.

Common Causes of Sewing Machine Problems

In most cases, poor sewing results are due to an improperly threaded machine or a blunt or damaged needle. Always check the machine threading and the needle before taking any other action.

Problem	Possible Causes
Needle breaks	▶ The needle is dull or bent, the wrong size, or put in wrong. ▶ Pulling on fabric while sewing. (This bends the needle. It breaks when it hits the throat plate.)
Upper thread breaks	▶ Needle is blunt, bent, or put in wrong. ▶ Upper machine thread is not threaded correctly. ▶ Tension on the upper thread is too tight. ▶ The thread has knots.
Lower thread breaks	▶ Bobbin case is put in wrong. ▶ Bobbin thread is not threaded correctly. ▶ Lower thread tension is too tight. ▶ Bobbin is wound too full.
Unattractive stitches Unattractive seam	▶ Needle is blunt, bent, or put in wrong. ▶ Thread tension is not correct. ▶ Machine is not threaded correctly. ▶ The needle, thread, and fabric are not well-matched. ▶ Bobbin thread unevenly wound. ▶ Bobbin is not correctly inserted in the bobbin case.
Skipped stitches	▶ Heavy finish on fabric keeps stitches from forming. (Wash fabric before sewing.) ▶ The needle is dull, bent, or put in wrong. ▶ Machine is not threaded correctly.

▶ If you still have stitching problems after checking for possible causes, ask your teacher for help.

▶ Before adjusting the tension control on your classroom sewing machine, ask your teacher for help.

Learning Activities (continued)

4. **Demonstration.** In front of the class, sew around several sides of double fabric in a ⅝ inch seam. Then trim the seams ¼ inch. Zigzag around the edges of the trimmed seams. Now move to the serger, take another double cloth and serge several sides as you did on the first piece. Tell students that you have done virtually the same thing on both machines (to show that you can sew well without a serger). Then point out how much quicker the procedure went the second time with the same results. (Key Skill: *Critical Thinking*)
5. **Demonstration.** Show how to thread a serger and compare it to a regular machine. Point out that there are no bobbins to refill, and the spools are generally larger. You should not have to thread a serger as often as a regular machine. (Key Skill: *Critical Thinking*)

Follow Up

1. **Reteaching.** Pass samples of seams sewn with correct and incorrect tension around the room. Ask individuals or groups to describe the stitching and tell what, if anything, needs to be done to correct it. (Key Skill: *Problem Solving*)
2. **Enrichment.** Ask students to check a sewing machine store or catalog to compare features and prices of sergers. Look at a consumer magazine, too. Prepare a report of findings and recommendations. (Key Skill: *Critical Thinking*)

Family Perspective

Marcy's old sewing machine died. Since Marcy's mom and older sister and brother also like to sew, her parents have allotted $1200 to replace the machine. Marcy and her sister would like to buy both a sewing machine and a serger. Her mom and brother would like to buy a deluxe sewing machine. Discuss, debate, or write essays on the pros and cons.

More About *Pins*

Silk pins are designed for delicate fabrics and are very fine so that the fabric will not show puncture marks. Pins of any type or size should be brass or stainless steel dressmaker pins, because steel pins rust easily and can leave rust marks in fabric. Pins can damage sewing machine mechanisms and dull serger knives. This is a good reason for using a pincushion rather than placing pins on the machine base. Pincushions can be worn on the wrist. Magnetic pin holders are also popular since you can simply drop pins onto them. Be sure to remove pins before you sew over them whether you are using a sewing machine or a serger.

Teaching. . .
Machine Care and Serger Sewing
(pp. 376-378)

Comprehension Check

1. What are the steps in cleaning a sewing machine? *(Remove throat plate, clean teeth of feed dog with a small brush, brush bobbin case clean, oil according to instruction book.)*
2. What is a serger? *(A machine that stitches, trims, and finishes a seam in one step.)*
3. How do sergers differ from sewing machines in task? *(You can do the same jobs yourself using a sewing machine, but a serger does it faster because it combines steps.)*
4. What's the basic thing sergers do that sewing machines don't? *(They have knives to trim the fabric.)*
5. Do sergers use the same thread and needles that sewing machines do? *(No, sergers use several cones of thread, not small spools. They may use two needles instead of one.)*
6. Why must all pins be removed when sewing with a serger? *(To prevent the knives from becoming dull, which could lead to poor stitching.)*

Learning Activities

1. **Seam Check.** Ask students to (modestly!) check the seams on any ready-to-wear garments they are wearing. How many of them have serged edges? Have they ever wondered why purchased seams looked different? Did they realize that sergers were available for home sewing? (Key Skills: *Communication, Critical Thinking*)
2. **Discussion.** Chad is making a purple sweatshirt on his serger at home. He wants to sew an appliquéed logo on the front. He was able to locate serger thread in a perfect shade of purple, but he can't find the same color in a regular sewing machine spool of

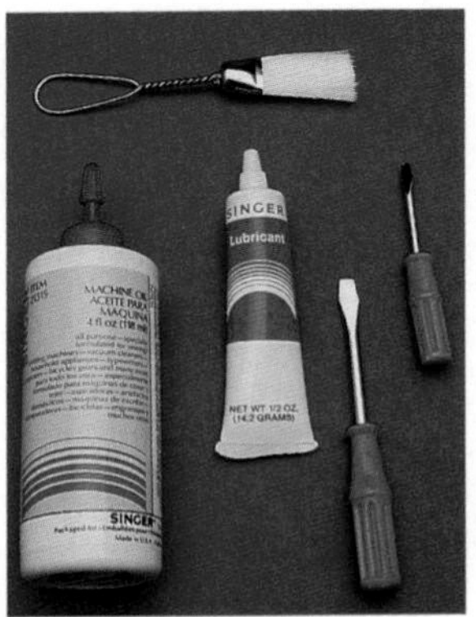

Use the proper equipment and materials to clean and lubricate your sewing machine properly.

▼ Machine Care ▼

To sew properly, the sewing machine needs to be cleaned regularly. Remove the throat plate and clean the teeth of the feed dogs with a small brush. Also brush the bobbin case clean. Most machines will need occasional oiling in order to keep all working parts lubricated. Check the instruction booklet for details.

If the machine jams because thread has become tangled in the bobbin or under the throat plate, the thread must be removed carefully. Turn off the machine. Remove your foot from the foot control and check the sewing machine instruction booklet for further directions.

Serger Sewing

Have you ever wondered why the seams in ready-to-wear clothing look so smooth and neat? Thanks to some new technology, people can now make garments at home that have the appearance of the finest ready-to-wear clothing.

A **serger** — or overlock sewing machine — is a machine that stitches, trims, and finishes a seam in one step. It sews the special stitches you have seen along the seam edges on the inside of most ready-to-wear clothing.

Some garments, such as sweatshirts, can be sewn entirely on the serger. However, many people combine the use of a conventional sewing machine and a serger.

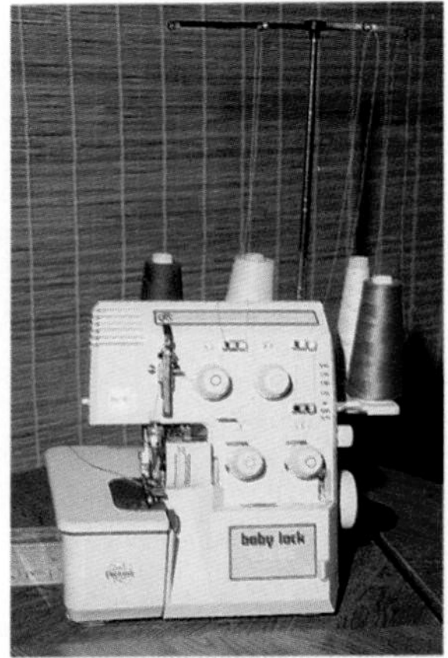

A serger conveniently decreases the amount of time that you spend sewing a garment. It completes many steps all at the same time.

Sergers are different from conventional sewing machines in the following ways:

- Sergers sew much faster than conventional sewing machines.
- Sergers have "knives" that trim the seam before it is stitched.
- Sergers use more thread. Most serger thread is on a cone that holds 1000 or more yards. Depending on the model, the serger uses two, three, four, or five cones of thread for stitching.
- Sergers may use one or two needles depending on the model.
- Sergers have no bobbins. Two loopers in the lower part of the serger take the place of bobbins.
- Lifting the presser foot is not necessary when starting to sew unless fabric is thick. The serger grabs the fabric as you begin to sew.

More About *Decorative Serger Stitching*

For an interesting, casual look, garments can be serged with the seams on the right side. A contrasting thread will highlight the seams. Raglan sleeves lend themselves to this style.

A metallic or shiny nylon thread can be used in one serger needle to give a dressy look to holiday napkins, tablecloths, or placemats. You can also use it to add glitz to doll clothes or other crafts.

Experiment with decorative or multicolored threads. This will add to your knowledge of which spool of thread does what on a serger stitch.

▶ All pins must be removed when sewing with a serger to prevent the knives from becoming dull. This could lead to poor stitching.

All brands of sergers basically sew the same way. As you feed the fabric into the machine, the feed dogs grab onto the fabric and pull it toward the knives. The knives trim the edges of the fabric before the fabric reaches the loopers and needles for stitching. After stitching, the fabric moves off the serger behind the needles. Instead of backstitching, you simply run the fabric off the serger and tie the loose ends. See page 416 for more information about securing serger seams.

Sewing with a serger has inspired many people to begin making their own clothing. Clothing items, such as sweatshirts, swimsuits, pants, shirts, and dresses, can be made quickly and easily with a professional look.

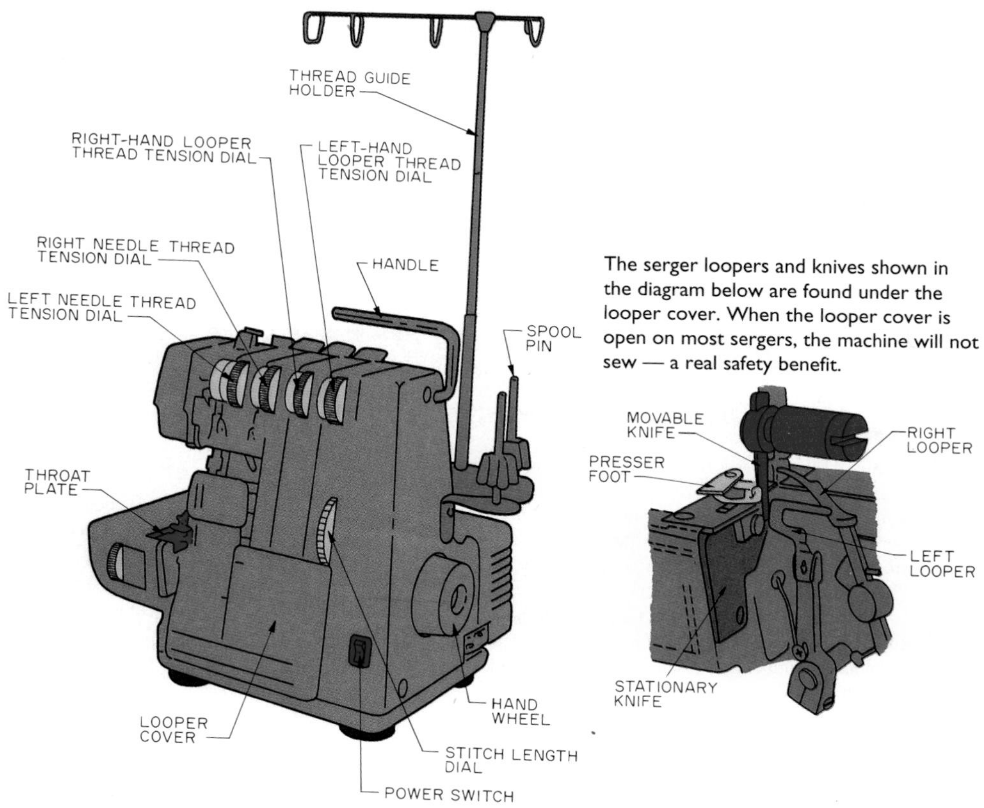

The serger loopers and knives shown in the diagram below are found under the looper cover. When the looper cover is open on most sergers, the machine will not sew — a real safety benefit.

Learning Activities (continued)

thread. What can he do? *(He can wind enough thread from the serger cone onto another small spool and bobbin to do the job, or he can buy an inexpensive adaptor and use the serger cone on his regular machine.)* (Key Skills: *Communication, Critical Thinking*)

Follow Up

1. **Reteaching.** Review with students the differences between conventional sewing machines and sergers by having them identify the main differences in their own words. List their responses on the board.
2. **Enrichment.** Write the names of the serger parts on small pieces of paper, place them in an envelope, and have students pick a piece. Students should then take turns to explain the function of the part of the serger they picked (without naming it). Encourage other students to identify the part that is being described.

Shortcut to Serger Threading

Materials: extra cones of serger thread

Equipment: threaded serger and scissors

Purpose: To teach students a fast method of threading a serger.

Outcomes: Answers may include:
- Tying on the thread was faster than threading the serger from scratch.
- If a thread breaks, you may have to thread the serger from scratch before you can continue sewing.
- The shortcut method saves time and energy.

Option: Use different colored thread on each spool to give a clearer picture of how the machine works and where the thread goes.

Photo Focus

Direct students to the top photo on p. 376. Ask students to identify each piece of equipment, tell its use, and explain what might happen that would require its use.

Completing the Chapter

For Review

1. Emphasize the main concepts using the summary.
2. Have students complete the "Facts to Recall." (Answers below.)

For Reteaching

1. **Reteaching.** Use the activity on pp. 42-43 of the *Reteaching and Practical Skills* booklet in the TCR.

For Enrichment

1. **Enrichment.** Use the activity on pp. 54-55 of the *Enrichment Activities* booklet in the TCR.

For Evaluation

1. Choose items from "Ideas to Explore" and "Activities to Try."
2. Use the chapter test on pp. 69-70 in the testing booklet of the TCR or use the testmaker software.

Facts to Recall Answers

1. Cutting scissors are used to clip thread and trim extra fabric from seams; shears are used to cut fabric; pinking shears are used to finish the edge of firmly woven or knit fabric; a seam ripper is used to cut and remove stitches between two pieces of fabric.
2. Marking equipment is used to identify important construction points on a sewing project, such as the location of pockets, buttonholes, hems, and collars. Tracing wheels, tracing paper, tailor's chalk, and fabric markers are all types of marking equipment.
3. By raising the take-up lever and needle to the highest point before and after stitching.
4. By backstitching, retracing the stitches about ½ inch (1.3 cm); by tying the thread ends on the wrong side of the fabric after removing it from the sewing machine.

Shortcut to Serger Threading

Materials
extra cones of serger thread

Equipment
threaded serger; scissors

Directions:
Observe a demonstration on how to thread an unthreaded serger, then try this shortcut method for changing threads. Cut the threads on the serger just above the thread cones. Remove the thread cones and replace them with the extra cones of serger thread. Tie the thread ends of the new cones to the clipped threads about two inches from the thread ends. Gently pull the thread ends coming from the needle(s) and loopers to pull the new thread color through the machine. Release the tension, if necessary, to allow the knots to pass through the tension disks. For the needle threads, continue pulling until the knot reaches the needle. Clip the thread, removing the knot, and rethread the needle. The knots in the looper threads should easily pass through the eye of the looper.

- ✔ Which method was faster?
- ✔ Why should you learn how to thread an unthreaded serger?
- ✔ Why would you want to use the shortcut method whenever possible?

TAKING ACTION

Making Equipment Substitutions

Aleatha was ready to start a sewing project at home when she discovered that she did not have some sewing equipment that might be necessary for her project. Some of the items Aleatha was missing included a sewing gauge, measuring stick, chalk, pincushion, and a press cloth.

The stores were about to close and there was no time for Aleatha to go buy the items she needed. Aleatha remembered a discussion that was held in a Social Studies class about reusing and recycling common household items for other purposes. She decided to think about that discussion as she started her project.

Using Your Resourcefulness

- Brainstorm a list of items Aleatha could use in place of (or use to make substitutes for) the sewing equipment she did not have.
- If Aleatha is unable to think of some alternatives on her own, where might she go for help?
- In what ways is Aleatha making wise use of all of her resources?

TAKING ACTION

Direct students to read the feature and discuss the options Aleatha has for finding makeshift equipment. Ask students to look around their own homes to find items they might substitute for certain articles of sewing equipment.

Using Your Resourcefulness Answers

- Answers might include: a ruler, a dowel rod, soap sliver (for chalk), small shallow bowl or magnet for pins, plain dish towel for press cloth.
- Answer might include: ask an experienced sewer, friends, or family members.
- She is reusing old resources instead of using up new ones.

Chapter 33 Review

Summary

In the chapter, you have read about:
- The different pieces of equipment used for cutting, measuring, marking, and pressing fabric.
- The parts of a sewing machine and the function of each part.
- Safety tips for hand and machine sewing.
- Sergers and how they can be helpful in sewing.

Facts to Recall

1. Identify four different pieces of cutting equipment. Explain the use of each.
2. Briefly explain the purpose of using marking equipment. Give four examples of different types of marking equipment.
3. When machine sewing, how can you keep the thread from coming out of the needle?
4. Describe two ways of securing stitches at the end of the seam.
5. List four safety tips for using a sewing machine.
6. What are three ways to keep a sewing machine clean and running smoothly?
7. Why should you remove the pins from the fabric when using a serger?
8. Briefly explain how a serger sews a seam.

Ideas to Explore

1. What personal traits do you think would help make a person good at sewing?
2. What might be some hazards of not knowing how to use a sewing machine properly?
3. Respond to the statement: "Sewing is its own reward. It is a skill that can be used throughout life." Do you agree or disagree with the statement? In what ways can sewing be a useful skill in life?

Activities to Try

1. Using your pattern or a pattern you have selected from a pattern catalog, predict how you might use the sewing equipment described in this chapter to sew the garment from this pattern.
2. Examine the seams and the hems on the clothing you are wearing. Which seams and hems do you think were sewn on a serger? Which do you think were sewn on a conventional sewing machine? Discuss your responses in class.
3. Using your machine instruction booklet, a spool of thread, and a bobbin, practice winding the bobbin and threading your machine. Be sure to check with your teacher if you have a problem.

LINK TO *Communication*

USING SMALL SEWING EQUIPMENT

Select an article of small sewing equipment from one of the following groups: cutting, measuring, marking, or pressing equipment. Organize a brief oral presentation to be given to your classmates concerning this article of equipment. Use the following guidelines in preparing your presentation:

- Describe the article of equipment and tell about how it can be used.
- Include information about buying a quality article of equipment. What should you look for? Are there important safety features?
- Demonstrate how to use this article of equipment correctly and safely.

Facts to Recall Answers (continued)

5. Stitch slowly when learning how to use the machine; keep your fingers away from the needle; don't lean too closely over the machine, in case the needle breaks; position the cord so that people won't trip over it; disconnect the cord from the outlet before disconnecting it from the machine; carefully close or cover the machine after use.
6. Remove the throat plate and brush; clean the teeth of the feed dog; brush clean the bobbin case; oil the machine occasionally.
7. To prevent the knives from becoming dull.
8. As you feed the fabric into the serger, the feed dogs grab onto the fabric and pull it toward the knives. The knives trim the edges of the fabric before it reaches the loopers and needles for stitching. After stitching, the fabric is fed off the serger behind the needles.

Ideas to Explore

1. Answers will vary and may include: patience, thoroughness; attention to detail; an eye for design.
2. Answers will vary and may include: injuring oneself; damaging the machine; ruining the fabric.
3. Answers will vary.

LINK TO *Communication*

Answer

Direct students to read the feature and assign the presentation to individuals or small groups. For fun you could suggest students make the presentation a television commercial for the product.

Preparing to Teach

Chapter Outline

Chapter Resources

The following booklet materials may be found in the *Teacher's Classroom Resources* box:

- Lesson Plans, p. 39
- Student Workbook, *Study Guide,* pp. 145-146; *The Magic Sewing Square,* p. 147; *Pattern Symbols,* p. 148
- Color Transparencies, *Marking Magic,* CT-38
- Sewing and Serging Handbook
- Technology and Computers, p. 41
- Cooperative Learning, p. 46
- Extending the Text, *Parts of Fabric,* p. 46
- Reteaching and Practical Skills, *Laying Out the Pattern,* pp. 44-45
- Enrichment Activities, *Evaluating Marking Methods,* p. 56
- Chapter and Unit Tests, pp. 71-72
- Testmaker Software

Also see:

- Meeting the Special Needs of Students
- Linking Home, School, and Community

CHAPTER 34 Preparing to Sew

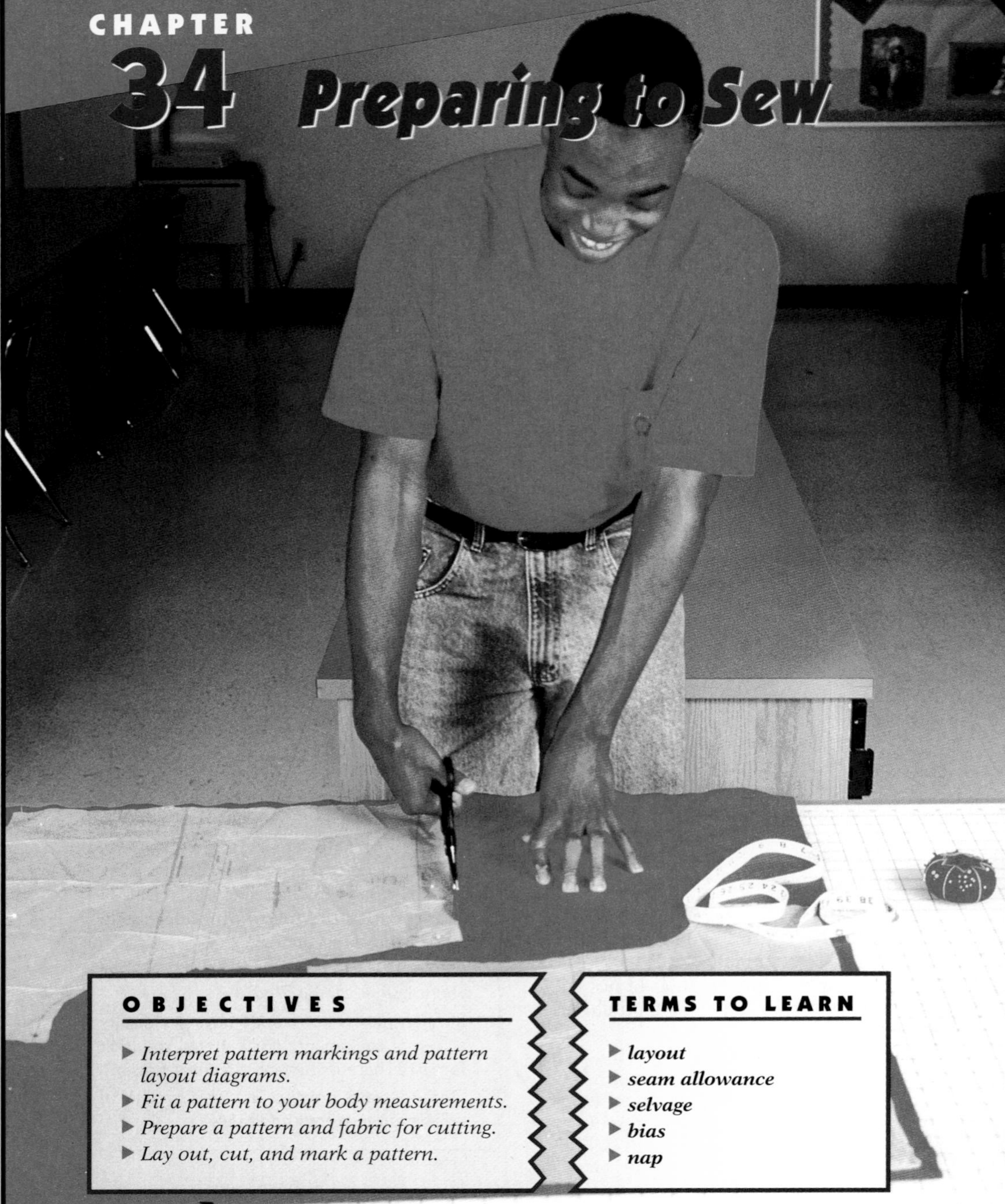

OBJECTIVES

- *Interpret pattern markings and pattern layout diagrams.*
- *Fit a pattern to your body measurements.*
- *Prepare a pattern and fabric for cutting.*
- *Lay out, cut, and mark a pattern.*

TERMS TO LEARN

- ***layout***
- ***seam allowance***
- ***selvage***
- ***bias***
- ***nap***

More About *Getting Organized to Sew*

You can do a number of things to make sewing easier and more pleasant:

- Set mini goals for yourself. Today you plan to stay stitch and sew darts. Tomorrow you will do something else. Even if you can only work half an hour several times a week, you'll get quite a bit accomplished.
- Save handwork, such as hems, buttons, snaps, etc. for the times when you are talking on the telephone, watching television, or waiting.
- Set up the iron and ironing board close to your sewing machine.
- Pin, tape, or clip the pattern instructions to a wall, curtain, or bulletin board directly

As Kendra looked at the fabric, pattern, notions, and equipment spread on the table in front of her, she wondered, "How will all of this turn into the shirt on the pattern envelope?" At this point, you may be feeling as confused as Kendra. However, beginning to sew is not as complicated as it may seem. Before starting to sew, you will need to lay out the pattern on the fabric, cut the pattern out of the fabric, and mark the construction points on the fabric. This chapter will help you complete those steps with ease and accuracy.

Using the Pattern

Inside the pattern envelope, you will find the guide sheet and pattern pieces. The guide sheet and the information printed on each pattern piece are your guides to successful sewing. The guide sheet contains:

- Sketches of different styles or views that can be made from the pattern.
- A list and diagram of pattern pieces.
- Cutting **layouts**, or diagrams, that show how to lay pattern pieces on the fabric for different sizes, fabric widths, and types of fabric.
- Step-by-step instructions for sewing the garment or project.

Each individual pattern piece has a number of pattern symbols or markings. Use the pattern symbols to guide layout of the pattern and to mark your sewing project. The most common symbols include:

1. ***Cutting line.*** The heavy line on the outside of the pattern should be followed when cutting out the fabric.
2. ***Grainline.*** This straight line with arrows on each end must be placed in the direction of the lengthwise grain, crosswise grain, or bias. Check the pattern layout on the instruction sheet.
3. ***Place on fold.*** This is a bracketed grainline that indicates that the pattern edge is to be placed exactly on the fold of the fabric.
4. ***Darts.*** The broken lines show the stitching line. The solid center line indicates where to fold the dart before stitching.
5. ***Solid line.*** A solid line is often used to show where pockets, trims, and other features will be located.

MARKING
CUTTING
LAYOUT
FABRIC
FITTING
PATTERN PIECES
INSTRUCTIONS

Carefully following these seven basic steps before you start sewing leads to a successful sewing experience.

Introducing the Chapter

Motivators

1. **Group Work.** Ask students about learning to cook. Did they rely on the directions? Have them compare patterns to recipes in an essay, poem, or song: "Sewing without a pattern is like cooking without a recipe." (Key Skill: *Creativity*)
2. **List.** Before reading this chapter, ask students to list the steps to sew their project. What information will they need? What will appear on the information sheet? (Key Skill: *Critical Thinking*)
3. **Bulletin Board.** Take three old pattern guides (so you have both sides) and cut two into: views, pieces — list and diagrams, layouts, instructions. Mount each on construction paper and title it. Place pieces in order on the board with a plus sign (+) between and an equal sign (=) next to the uncut pattern guide. (Key Skill: *Communication*)

Chapter Objectives and Vocabulary

1. Have students read the chapter objectives and rephrase the objectives as questions.
2. Ask students to state, in their own words, the purpose of studying this chapter.
3. Pronounce the vocabulary terms listed on the previous page. Ask students whether they are familiar with any of these. Explain that the terms will be defined in the chapter.

Guided Reading

1. Have the students read the chapter and use the Study Guide on pp. 145-146 of the *Student Workbook.*

above your sewing machine. This way you won't have to hunt for instructions, and you'll quickly know what the next step is.

- Tape a small paper bag to the edge of the table or sewing machine cabinet and the edge of the ironing board. Threads, fabric scraps, etc. can be quickly deposited here, saving clean-up time later.
- To keep track of your scissors, tie it to a long ribbon or string and wear it around your neck.
- If possible, have a full-length mirror close by to check fitting.

Teaching. . .
Using the Pattern and Fitting the Pattern
(pp. 381-383)

Comprehension Check

1. What information can you find on the information sheet? *(Views, diagram and list of pieces, layouts, instructions.)*
2. What are notches? *(Diamond-shaped symbols along the cutting line to align seams.)*
3. What is ease? *(The extra room allowed by the designer for comfort or style.)*

Learning Activities

1. **Discussion.** Ask students why they think pattern designers and manufacturers decided to use a ⅝ inch seam. Why isn't the seam allowance ¼ inch or 1 inch in garments? *(It allows for altering without being too bulky or getting into the next size.)* (Key Skill: *Critical Thinking*)
2. **Review.** Before you begin any altering, ask students to list the places where close fit is important in the patterns they will be using for their projects. Have them look up measurements on their Personal Measurement Chart. (Key Skill: *Communication*)
3. **Demonstration.** Use a volunteer or mannequin to help with altering length. Hold pattern (such as a sleeve) up and compare measurement between the person and the garment. Show students how you would go about deciding where and how much to increase or decrease. Also demonstrate how to measure the person and the pattern piece to get the best fit. (Key Skills: *Critical Thinking, Communication*)
4. **Small Groups.** In groups of two or three, have students help each other decide if, where, and how much to alter their patterns. When they have decided upon their recommendations, they can bring them to you to check before they mark or cut. Remind students to take seam allowances into account and to allow for double pieces. (Key Skills: *Cooperation, Critical Thinking*)

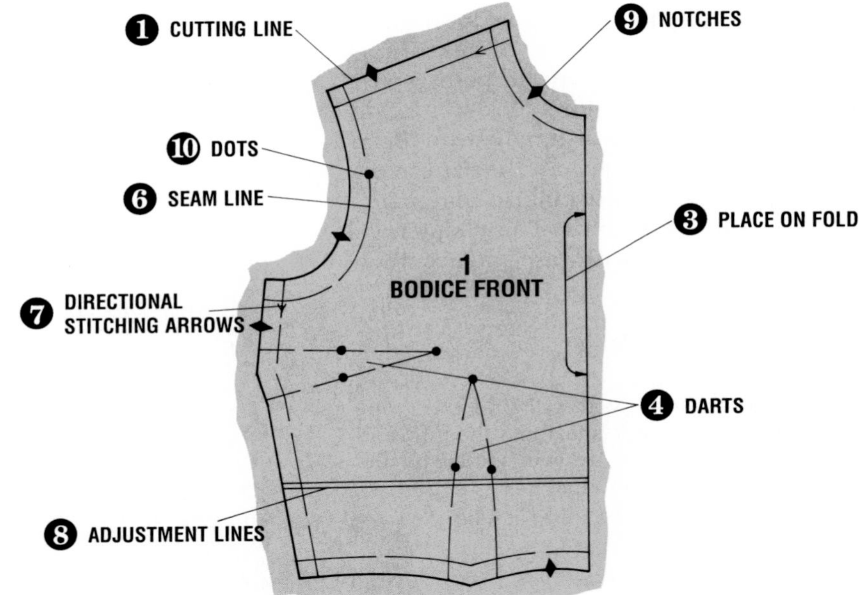

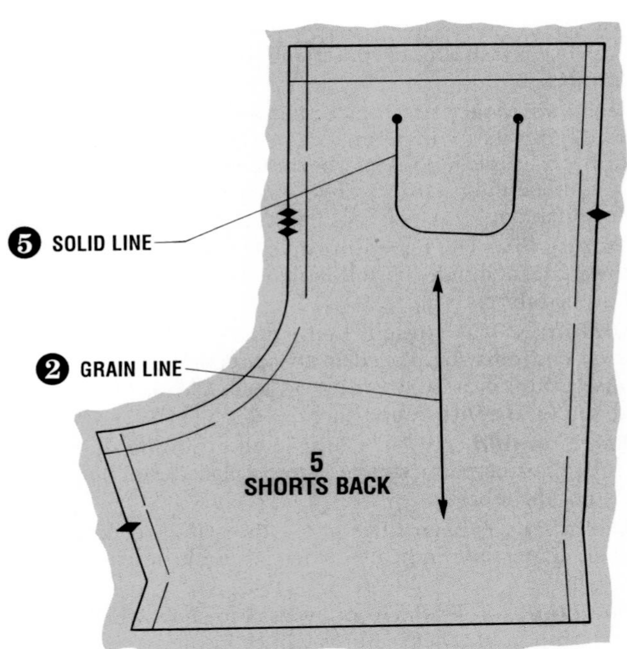

More About Woven Fabrics

Fabrics that are considerably off-grain and have been heat set are almost impossible to get really on grain. If you can't live without the fabric it probably would be best to wash a fairly large piece of it several times to see how much it actually changes. The heat set can be stronger than the grain line, especially in woven fabrics. Quilters, for example, will often align the lengthwise edges of their fabric after they wash it and square it off from the edge rather than pulling threads.

6. ***Seam line.*** This is a broken line, usually ⅝ inch (1.5 cm) inside of the cutting line. You stitch along the seam line.
7. ***Directional stitching arrows.*** These arrows indicate which way to sew seams.
8. ***Adjustment lines.*** Two parallel lines indicate where a pattern is cut or folded for lengthening or shortening.
9. ***Notches.*** These diamond-shaped symbols along the cutting line show where the pattern pieces are joined together.
10. ***Dots.*** Small dots are used for matching seams and construction details such as pocket placement.

Using Marking Equipment

Materials
tracing paper; tailor's chalk; fabric markers; fabric samples

Equipment
tracing wheel

Directions:
Experiment using different methods of marking each fabric sample.

- ✔ On what types of fabric did the tracing wheel and tracing paper work well?
- ✔ What factors influence the color of tracing paper that you choose?
- ✔ When would you choose tailor's chalk for marking? When did the pencil work best? When did the square of chalk work best?
- ✔ When did you prefer the fabric marker? Was the marker easy to remove from all fabric samples?

Fitting the Pattern

When checking how well a pattern will fit you, match your own measurements with those on the pattern envelope. By matching your measurements closely to the measurements on the pattern envelope, you can select a pattern with enough wearing ease for comfort. *Wearing ease* — the extra room needed in a garment for movement and comfort — allows you to sit, bend, and stretch without tearing your clothes. Wearing ease is built into patterns by the pattern companies.

Some garments also have built-in *design ease* which allows garment designers to create different styles. Design ease is additional ease built into a pattern beyond the wearing ease. It allows for details such as wider pant legs, fuller skirts, or over-sized shirts.

Learning Activities (continued)

5. **Demonstration.** Find and draw the grainline (with chalk) on several pieces of different fabric. Put arrows at the top and bottom of your lines so students will associate it with the pattern grainline. Pass around the samples as you discuss what grainline is and how to find and mark it. If possible, give individuals (or groups) a chance to find the grainlines on their own. (Key Skills: *Communication, Critical Thinking*)
6. **Group Work.** Bring a stuffed animal pattern to school. Crinkle up a few major pieces and give one to each group. Ask groups to cut the piece out of scrap fabric without ironing the pattern piece or the fabric. Then have the students iron both the pattern piece and the fabric and cut it out again. Ask them to compare the pieces with adjoining pieces cut out by other groups. Ask students to tell you what they have learned. Use the pieces for demonstrating seams, sleeves, and hems later on in the chapter. (Key Skills: *Cooperation, Critical Thinking*)

Follow Up

1. **Reteaching.** After reading the first part of the chapter, ask students to make any revisions on their brainstorming list of sewing steps. (See Motivators on page 381.) (Key Skill: *Critical Thinking*)
2. **Enrichment.** Ask students to compare the pattern guides from the major companies. You could also have them look at a information sheet from a smaller specialty company where there would be more difference. What are the similarities and differences? Why are they so much alike? (Key Skill: *Critical Thinking*)

Using Marking Equipment

Materials: tracing paper; tailor's chalk; fabric markers; fabric samples

Equipment: tracing wheel

Purpose: To give students the opportunity to try different methods of marking fabric.

Outcomes: Answers may include:

- Tracing wheel and tracing paper work best with hard-surfaced fabrics.
- White is best for white and light colors; red, yellow, or blue are better for dark colors.
- The chalk or chalk pencils are used on soft or hard-surfaced fabrics.
- Use marking pens wherever you would use a chalk pencil. The ink may not wash out of all fabrics, so test it first.

Teaching. . .
Preparing Fabric, Preshrinking Fabric, and Fabric Grains
(pp. 384-385)

Comprehension Check

1. What two things need to be done to prepare fabric? *(Preshrink and straighten.)*
2. Why do you straighten fabric? *(So it will hang correctly.)*
3. What is the selvage? *(The finished lengthwise edge.)*

Learning Activities

1. **Discussion.** Ask students if they have ever had a ready-to-wear garment shrink. Do any particular garments shrink more than others *(Knit tops and t-shirts.)*. Why? *(Both cottons and knits tend to shrink.)* (Key Skill: *Communication*)
2. **Discussion.** Bring a few articles of clothing that have shrunk to class and tell the sad story. Have students share similar experiences. Review information on fabric characteristics and care. Remind them to preshrink fabrics. (Key Skill: *Communication*)
3. **Demonstration.** Bring a piece of less expensive, loosely-knit cotton knit to class. Cut two 12-inch squares and trace them on the chalkboard. Cut one with the grain and one any direction. Wash both in hot water and dry them on a hot setting. Iron them and compare them to the original squares on the chalkboard. Both pieces should be smaller and the second one off grain. (Key Skill: *Critical Thinking*)

AROUND THE WORLD

Direct the students to read the feature and the questions. Answers might include: Pineapple industry might blossom. Other textile costs might drop because of more competition. What would happen to the price of pineapple? *(Might be less expensive if there were more trees and pineapples.)*

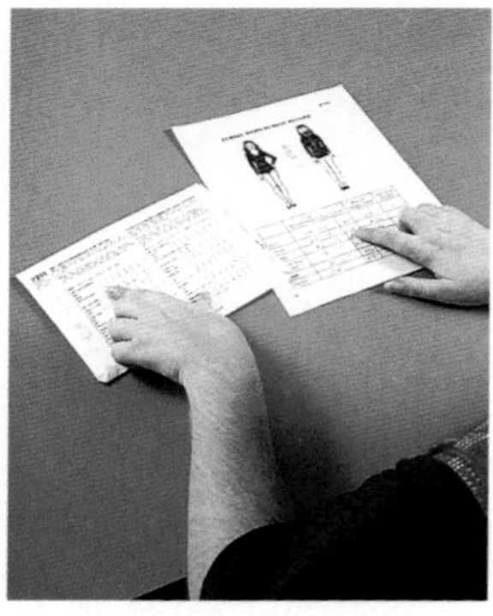

Compare your measurements with the measurements on the back of the pattern envelope to determine the best size to use.

Pattern pieces can be measured to help determine how a pattern will fit. When comparing your measurements, follow these simple guidelines:

- Press the pattern with a warm, dry iron, or smooth it out with your hands.
- Check measurements on the pattern at the same places where the body measurements were taken and write them down.
- Do not include **seam allowances** — the fabric between the cutting line and the stitching line — or darts when measuring the pattern pieces.

In most cases, you can expect your pattern pieces to be larger than your exact body measurements. Don't panic! Your pattern should be larger to account for wearing and design ease. How can you tell if there is enough room for wearing and design ease? Start by looking at the picture on the front of your pattern envelope. Also read the description of the garment on the back of the pattern envelope. Should the garment fit closely to your body or is it supposed to be loosely fitted? If the garment is loosely fitted and the pattern measurements are larger than your body measurements, any fitting problems can generally be taken care of in the sewing stage. However, if the garment is closely fitted and the pattern measurements are significantly larger (or smaller) than your body measurements, some adjustment in the pattern will be needed. It is easier to make changes before, rather than after, a pattern is cut.

Preparing Fabric

Both woven and knitted fabrics need to be preshrunk and straightened before you lay out the pattern and cut your fabric.

Fabric that is off-grain will not hang correctly when made into a garment. Straightening the grain makes sure the garment will hang properly on your body.

Preshrinking Fabric

Preshrinking makes sure that your fabric will not shrink once the fabric is made into a garment. Washable fabrics should be preshrunk according to the manufacturer's directions. Some fabrics, such as wool, need to be professionally dry-cleaned for preshrinking.

It is best to preshrink all fabrics. In addition to preventing further shrinkage, preshrinking removes fabric finishes

More About Grain

Today, more than ever, the grain of fabric is important. In the past, if a fabric was not grain perfect it was simple to restore the right-angle structure. This is no longer true. Why? Almost all fabrics are treated with some type of finish. During the finishing process the crosswise yarns are frequently pulled out of line. Also, many special finishes permanently lock the fibers in position. These make for easier care, but also make it impossible to restore grain perfection. Usually a one-inch variation is considered acceptable. If more, think carefully before buying the fabric, especially a plaid or design. Before buying, roll off a yard; match selvages carefully. Fold back one-half yard, matching selvages. Is it even?

that can leave a sticky substance on sewing machine needles that may cause skipped stitches. All woven interfacings, zippers, and trims should also be preshrunk.

To preshrink washable fabrics, follow the fabric care instructions for washing and drying listed on the bolt or care label. For fabrics that ravel easily, you may want to zigzag stitch or serge the cut edges before washing the fabric.

Washable knits should always be washed and dried before cutting. Knits are made up of loops that stretch as much as 10 to 35 percent during the knitting process. Knits will usually shrink more than woven fabrics.

Someday you may be wearing a dress or a shirt made from pineapple leaves. Scientists at a university in Colombia have discovered that material made from the leaf fibers is much like raw cotton and some synthetic materials. Each pineapple leaf produces about one pound of usable fiber. What effect might this discovery have on pineapple-growing regions? On producers of other textiles?

▼ Fabric Grains ▼

In Chapter 32, you learned that on-grain fabric is made of two sets of yarns that are at right angles to each other. The lengthwise grain is formed by the yarns that run the length of the fabric. Lengthwise grain has little or no stretch. The **selvage** is the finished lengthwise edge of the fabric. It will not ravel. The crosswise yarns run horizontally from selvage to selvage. This is called the crosswise grain. The crosswise grain has more stretch than lengthwise grain.

The true bias has the most stretch. True **bias** is the diagonal edge formed when the fabric is folded so that the crosswise grain is parallel to the selvage, or lengthwise grain.

Knits do not have a grain. However, knitted fabrics have a lengthwise chain of loops that correspond to the lengthwise grain. The crosswise row of loops corresponds to the crosswise grain. In most knits, the crosswise loops have more stretch.

SELVAGE
TRUE BIAS
CROSSWISE GRAIN
LENGTHWISE GRAIN
SELVAGE

Knowing the characteristics of fabric grains will help you lay your pattern on the fabric correctly.

Learning Activities (continued)

4. **Demonstration.** While you are washing your cotton squares add two pieces of woven fabric. Trim the selvage off one first. The laundered piece with the selvage should be drawn up at the edge while the trimmed piece should lie flat. A picture is worth a thousand words! Also sew a zipper in a piece of unshrunk cotton and wash it, too. The zipper should ripple. (Key Skill: *Critical Thinking*)
5. **Demonstration.** On several large knit pieces, show how to find the grain line, determine the amount of stretch, and tell which way stretches most. Pass out numbered samples and ask students to determine the grain line and the direction with the most stretch. (Key Skill: *Critical Thinking*)

Follow Up

1. **Reteaching.** Ask students to look at their brainstorming lists completed earlier (See Motivators) and make any further revisions after reading this part of the chapter. (Key Skill: *Problem Solving*)
2. **Enrichment.** Have students find out through research or experiments which fabrics are more susceptible to grain problems and why. (Key Skill: *Critical Thinking*)

Family Perspective

Kerry wants to make a knit shirt. His mom takes Kerry and his friend, Shawn, to the fabric store. Right away they spot an inexpensive, light-weight knit in a perfect shade of green. There is also a more expensive great teal. The salesclerk tells Kerry that the teal will be easier to work with because it has a straighter on the grain. Kerry's mom says she will pay the extra money because she knows nothing about sewing. Shawn thinks Kerry would be stupid not to buy the green knit. How much difference does grain really make? The clerk is just trying to sell the expensive material. What should Kerry do?

Teaching. . . Fabric Grain and How to Alter Your Pattern (pp. 386-387)

Comprehension Check

1. What's one good way to check the grain of a fabric? *(Pull a thread.)*
2. How do you straighten the edge of knitted fabrics? *(Cut across a crosswise row of loops from selvage to selvage.)*
3. What do you need to know to find the layout on your pattern information sheet? *(Pattern size, view, width of fabric.)*
4. How can you tell when you have stretched a fabric enough? What should you do then? *(When the selvage and cut — following a pulled thread — ends match up perfectly. Then, press with steam to set the yarns.)*

Learning Activities

1. **Demonstration.** Show students how to pull a thread in woven fabric. Let them see exactly what you are doing. Give students a chance to try it right away. Remind students to press the fabric with steam to set the yarns. (Key Skill: *Critical Thinking*)
2. **Demonstration.** If you have a long length of fabric, the heavier the better, place a yard or so on your cutting surface and the remainder on a chair or the floor. Make sure it keeps slipping down as you talk to the students. Put the fabric back up several times and then ask the students if they have noticed what's been going on. Tell them that if there is a constant pull on the fabric then the pieces may get pulled out of shape or the fabric off-grain. Now, arrange the fabric properly so there's no strain on it. (Key Skills: *Communication, Critical Thinking*)

How to ...
Alter Your Pattern

Successful pattern alterations result from using the following guidelines: make adjustments for length and width on both front and back pattern pieces; use a measuring stick to extend the grainline; make sure the grainline is straight; and redraw any design details or darts changed by the pattern alteration.

The following illustrations and directions tell about some common pattern adjustments.

Adjusting Width

An adjustment of 2 inches (5 cm) or less can be made along the side seams of a garment. Divide the adjustment needed by the number of seam allowances. If a garment has two side seams and four seam allowances, the amount to be adjusted on each pattern piece is one-fourth the total amount. For example, to increase the waistline by 1 inch (2.5 cm), you will add ¼ inch (6 mm) to the side seam of the front pattern piece and ¼ inch (6 mm) to the side seam of the back pattern piece. Both side seams will be increased by ½ inch (1.3 cm) and the total garment will be increased 1 inch (2.5 cm).

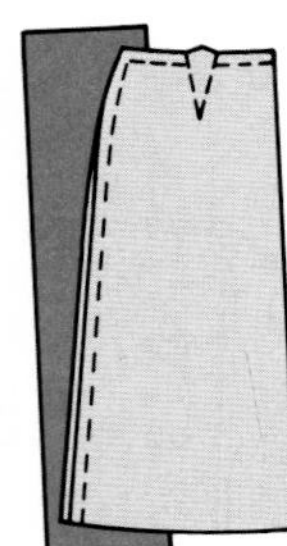

Increasing Pattern Width

Tape tissue paper along the pattern piece edge. Divide the total adjustment needed by the number of seam allowances. Measure out the amount needed from the cutting line. Carefully redraw the cutting lines and seam lines to blend in with areas of the pattern that did not need adjustment.

Decreasing Pattern Width

To decrease the width of a pattern, divide the total amount of adjustment needed by the number of seam allowances. Measure in the amount needed and redraw cutting lines and seam lines to blend in with the areas that did not need to be decreased.

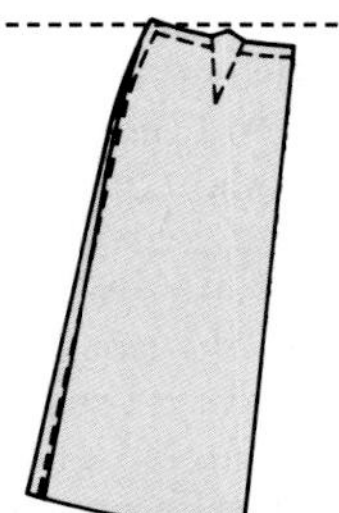

How to ... Alter Your Pattern

Use this exercise with the feature. Pin or tape three shirt pattern pieces to a board in this order, from left: back, front, front facing. They should be aligned, but not touching. Tell the class that this is a pattern for Nate, who needs the shirt to be 2 inches longer. On the shirt front, show how to lengthen the pattern on the adjustment line. Hang the piece back up, aligning the shoulders. It will be evident that the back and the facing will have to be adjusted also. Or, demonstrate how to make a skirt back narrower and waistband shorter. Encourage students to come up with the right directions themselves.

Lengthening a Pattern

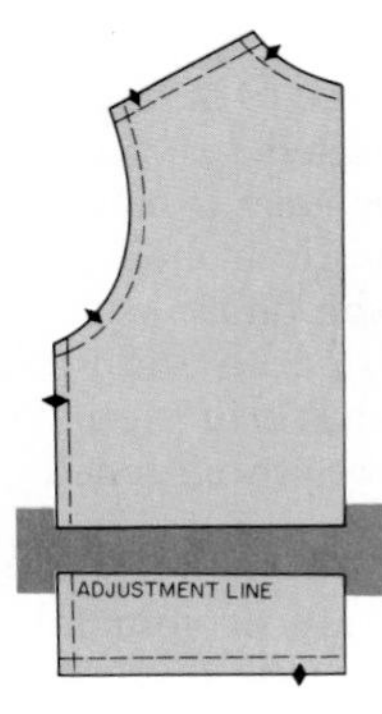

Cut the pattern apart on the adjustment lines. Tape one pattern piece to the tissue paper. Using a measuring stick, draw the grainline as one continuous straight line through the tissue paper. Measure down the amount needed for length and tape the second piece of the pattern to the tissue paper at that point. Make sure the grainlines match up. Connect the cutting lines. Use the same method to adjust the back pattern piece.

Shortening a Pattern

Measure the amount to be shortened upwards from the adjustment line on the front pattern piece. At that point, draw a second line that is parallel to the adjustment line. Fold the adjustment line and bring it up to the second line. Match the grainline markings. Tape the fold in place. Use the same method to adjust the back pattern piece.

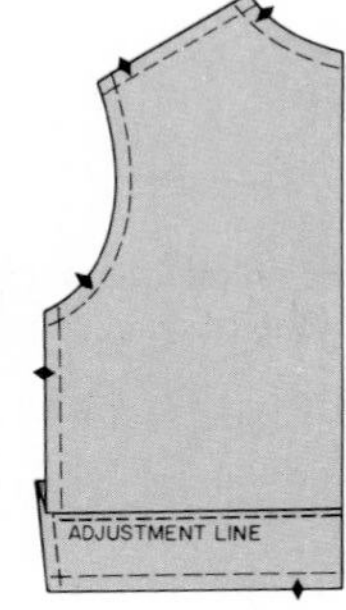

Checking the Grain

Fabric that is off-grain or is cut off-grain does not hang correctly when made into a garment. It is difficult to check the grain of the fabric if the cut edges are uneven.

If you can clearly see the individual crosswise yarns, cut along one yarn from selvage to selvage. If not, clip the selvage and pull one thread (yarn) across the fabric. Pull it gently with one hand while pushing the fabric back with the other hand. When the entire thread is pulled out, the empty space shows as a line. Cut along this line. If the thread breaks before it is completely pulled out, cut along the line where the thread was removed. Pick up the end of the broken thread and continue pulling it across the fabric. Cut off the remaining fabric along the line. Your fabric edge will be straight on the crosswise grain. Repeat on the other cut edge.

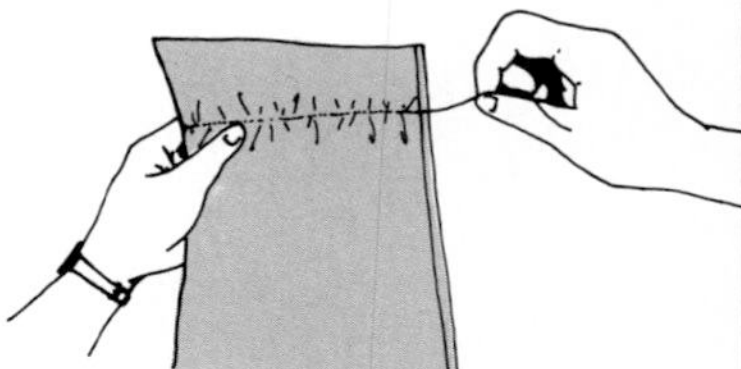

Pulling a thread on the crosswise grain determines whether or not a woven fabric is on-grain.

Learning Activities (continued)

3. **Group Work.** Have students take the pattern pieces out of the pattern envelope for their project. Ask them to measure the pattern pieces in the same places their body measurements were taken. Compare the body and pattern measurement. Is there enough room for ease? Have students identify areas that may need some alterations. (Key Skills: *Math, Critical Thinking*)

Follow Up

1. **Reteaching.** Have students examine the fabric they are using for their projects (or samples that you provide them with) and have them identify the grainline. Is the fabric on grain or off-grain? (Key Skill: *Problem Solving*)
2. **Enrichment.** Assign students to make the following pattern alterations on sample patterns: lengthen sleeve, shorten pant or skirt length, increase pant width at hip, decrease skirt width at waist. (Key Skill: *Problem Solving*)

More About *Cutting Pattern Tissue*

Many home sewers, who are extremely careful with their cutting shears, cut out tissue pattern pieces with paper scissors. They trim them to the cutting line so that they can cut with their good shears just off the edge of the tissue. Well-trimmed pattern pieces are easy to fit closely together on the fabric.

Teaching... Pattern Layout and Positioning the Pattern Pieces

(pp. 388-389)

Comprehension Check

1. When there is no grainline on a pattern piece, what should you look for to guide your placement? *("Place on Fold" line and arrows)*
2. What should you do when you can't tell which is the right side of your fabric? *(Choose one side and mark it.)*
3. How do you find the direction of nap? *(Brush your hand over it. The smooth direction is with the nap; the rough direction is against the nap.)*

Learning Activities

1. **List.** Ask students to list methods to help match plaids. *(Hand or machine basting, basting tape or glue, pins, machine basting)* (Key Skill: *Critical Thinking*)
2. **Demonstration.** Gather sets of plaid swatches. Sew a set or two together without pinning or basting, making sure they don't match! Use a basting stitch so you can reuse or fix samples. Have students practice matching plaids. (Key Skill: *Communication*)
3. **Demonstration.** Show how to lay out plaids so connecting pieces will match. Make sure notches and other markings correspond. (Key Skill: *Communication*)
4. **Display.** Gather a variety of plaids in different sizes (small ginghams to large wool plaids). Cut sets of 8-inch squares. Sew them together so the plaids are not matching. Iron and display. Which plaid mismatch shows the most? *(probably the largest)* The least? *(probably the smallest)* Therefore, matching plaids becomes more important as the plaid gets larger. Point out to students that plaids that are smaller than ¼ inch generally do not need to be matched. (Key Skills: *Communication, Problem Solving*)

To straighten the edge of knitted fabrics, simply cut across a crosswise row of loops from selvage to selvage. Knit fabrics do not have a thread that can be pulled.

After making the cut edges even, it is easy to check the grain. Work on a flat surface. Fold the fabric in half lengthwise with the selvages together. Smooth the fabric with your hands, but do not pull it. If the fabric is smooth and the selvages and raw edges are perfectly even, the fabric is on-grain. If the edges are not even, the fabric must be straightened.

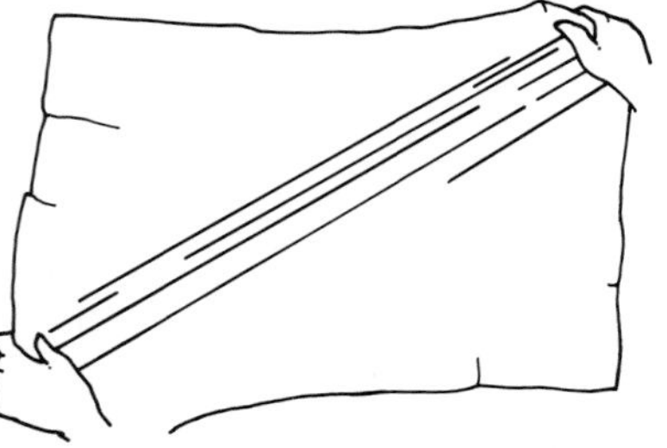

Pulling fabric on the bias will help straighten the grain of the fabric.

Straightening the Grain

In order to straighten the grain of your fabric, the fabric must be pulled on the true bias. Unfold the fabric and pull it in the opposite direction from the way the ends slant. Ask someone to help you pull the fabric — it is easier than straightening the fabric alone. After pulling the true bias, refold the fabric. If the selvages and cut edges match up perfectly at right angles, you have pulled enough. Press the fabric with steam to set the yarns in the on-grain position.

Pattern Layout

After you have prepared your fabric, the next step is to place the pattern pieces on the fabric. The pattern guide sheet lists the pattern pieces needed for each view. To prepare your pattern, follow these steps:

- Cut apart the pattern pieces you need. To avoid accidentally trimming away the cutting lines, leave some extra paper outside of the cutting lines on all pieces.
- Check off the pattern pieces needed as you find them. Place the extra ones back into the envelope.
- Press pattern pieces with a warm, dry iron.
- Write your name on the pattern pieces. When you are working in a clothing lab with other people, pattern pieces can easily get mixed up.

Positioning the Pattern Pieces

Placing the pattern pieces on the fabric correctly is an important step. Once the fabric has been cut, you may not be able to correct layout mistakes. To position the pattern pieces, follow these steps:

1. Find and circle the correct layout on your pattern guide sheet. This shows how to place the pattern pieces for the view, fabric width, and the pattern size you are making.

More About *Preshrinking Notions*

Although it may be preferable to preshrink all notions, avoid getting beginning sewers so bogged down that they are too discouraged to sew on their own. Zippers and trims on ready-to-wear garments are probably not prewashed, and, at this point, students are aiming no higher than meeting ready-to-wear standards. Point out the importance of reading the fabric content on zippers and trims. Encouraging them to prewash those that are all or mostly cotton may seem more realistic to them.

2. Check the layout instructions carefully. Note the following markings: the right and wrong sides of the fabric; the right and wrong sides of the pattern; and the pattern pieces to be cut a second time. Are any pieces to be cut from a single layer of fabric?
3. Fold the fabric as shown in the layout diagram. Generally, fabric is folded in half on the lengthwise grain with the right side on the inside. Because layouts can vary, however, check how the fabric should be folded. If your fabric is longer than your work table, keep extra fabric folded at the end of the table until it is needed.
4. Carefully place the pattern pieces on the fabric as shown. By following the layout diagram, all the pattern pieces you need should fit on the fabric you have. Remember that each pattern piece has the grainline indicated by an arrow or a "place on the fold" symbol. Use your eyes to line up those markings with the grain of the fabric. Use one or two pins to secure each piece. After you have pinned on a pattern piece, check it off on the guide sheet.
5. Pin each pattern piece securely to the fabric, checking grainlines. Start with large pattern pieces placed on the fold. Pin securely, inserting the pins perpendicular to the cutting line and smoothing out the pattern as you go.
6. Pin the remaining pattern pieces so the grainline symbol is straight on the fabric grain. Pin one end of the grainline symbol to the fabric. Measure the distance from both ends of the arrow to the selvage. If the measurements are not the same, move the pattern at the unpinned end until they are. Smooth the pattern and pin.

Be sure to read the layout instructions carefully and choose the correct layout for your view, size, and type of fabric.

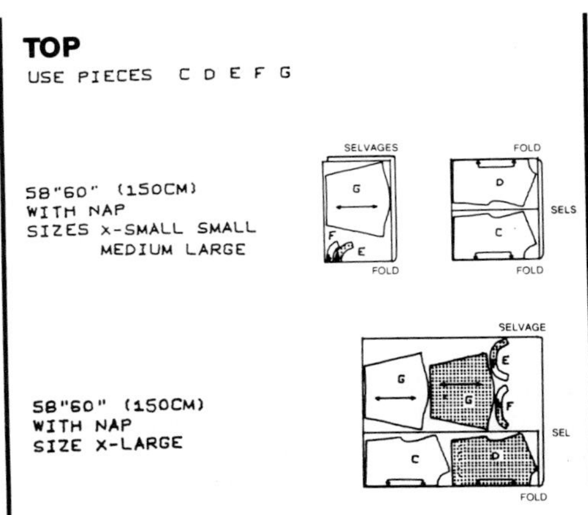

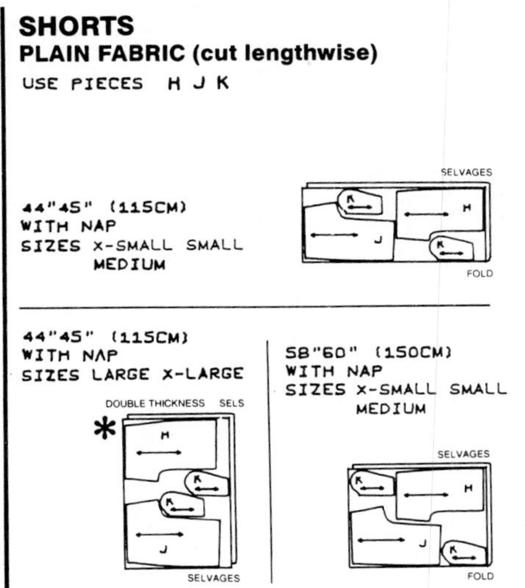

Learning Activities (continued)

5. **Layout Lab.** Have all students (if there is room) lay their pattern pieces out on their fabric and pin them in place. Before they begin laying out their pattern, have each student circle the correct layout diagram and check it with you. When all students are done pinning, have them check each other's layout diagram with the fabric layout. If it's okay, have them initial the diagram. This will expose them to several layout diagrams and give them some accountability. If space is limited, have group members help each other, one at a time, to lay out their patterns. (Key Skills: *Cooperation, Critical Thinking*)

Follow Up

1. **Reteaching.** Give individuals or groups several swatches of fabric and have them indicate which is the top and which is the bottom. Ask why, on fabrics with obvious directions, it is important to cut all pieces going in the same direction. (Key Skill: *Critical Thinking*)
2. **Enrichment.** Have students experiment with developing their own layout guide. They may or may not be able to come up with one which uses less fabric. Ask them to theorize why pattern companies often have all pieces facing one way and why many seem to allow some extra fabric. (Key Skills: *Problem Solving, Critical Thinking*)

In Touch with Technology

Even Feed presser feet are now available for many machines. These attachments feed the top and bottom layers of fabric through at the same rate and are useful for plaids, napped fabrics, and quilting. Although an *Even Feed* foot is expensive, it is a worthwhile investment for someone who often sews plaids.

Teaching. . .
Special Layouts, Cutting Out the Pattern, and Marking Fabric
(pp. 390-392)

Comprehension Check

1. Why is it important to transfer markings from the pattern to the fabric? *(For matching pieces, for sewing details, and for placing trims and pockets correctly.)*
2. List three completely different methods of marking fabric. *(Chalk, pins, fabric markers, tracing paper, thread.)*
3. On what side of the fabric should markings be made? *(Wrong side.)*

Learning Activities

1. **Chart.** Ask students to make a list of various marking methods and their pros and cons. Have them use the information in the text and any additional information you provide them. Ask students to put this information on poster board. (Key Skills: *Communication, Critical Thinking*)
2. **Discussion.** Relate this scenario: Aunt Tillie is eccentric — and she sews most of her own clothes, which are *very* original! Often her hems are wavy and the fabric looks pulled. Last summer Gina stayed with her for a week, and discovered that Aunt Tillie sewed and cooked the same way — without guidelines. When Aunt Tillie cut out a pattern she just placed pieces on the fabric in a random manner. Gina never saw an information sheet. Now Gina understands why Aunt Tillie's garments are so unusual. How would using a pattern guide help Aunt Tillie? (Key Skills: *Problem Solving, Critical Thinking*)

Right Side or Wrong Side

How can you tell which side of the fabric should be used for the outside of your garment? For many fabrics, it is easy to determine which side is the right side. However, some fabrics make it more difficult for you to decide. One clue is to fold back an edge and compare the two sides. The right side is often brighter and has a clearer print or a more obvious surface weave. However, some plain-weave fabrics are the same on both sides. Knitted fabrics can be stretched on a cut edge to determine the right side. The edge will usually roll toward the right side of a knitted fabric.

If you can't decide which side is the right side, then pick one. Mark the wrong side of the fabric with chalk so you'll use the same side as the right side throughout your project. Forgetting to mark the wrong side may leave you with a project of varying colors or degrees of shine.

▼ Special Layouts ▼

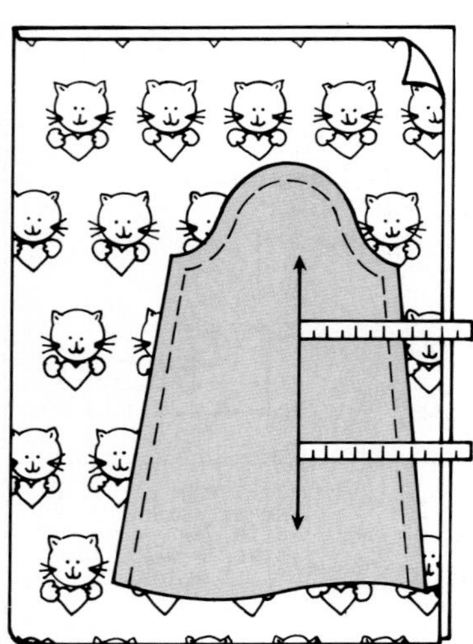

Check your pattern instructions for special fabric layouts to avoid problems. Place each pattern piece straight on the grain of fabric.

Checks, plaids, and stripes need special layouts. Each of these fabrics can present a problem unless pattern pieces are carefully placed. The lines of these designs should match along the seams. Check a sewing book for directions.

Some fabrics have a **nap**, or brushed surface. These include corduroy, suede cloth, and velveteen. To find the direction of the nap, stroke it with your hand. If it feels smooth, you are going in the direction of the nap. If it is rough, you are going against the nap. The nap must lie in the same direction on all pattern pieces. Otherwise, the garment may appear to be two different colors. You need to decide on the effect you want before placing pattern pieces on the fabric. Many napped fabrics are cut with the pile running up, so the color will be darker. However, corduroy is often cut with the pile running down for longer wear.

Look at one-way designs to determine if there is a logical top and bottom. Be sure the tops of all the pattern pieces and the top of the fabric design face in the same direction. Otherwise, the design will be upside down on the garment.

More About *Marking Fabric*

Marking should be done as soon as you have cut out the garment sections and before the pattern pieces have been removed. Consider the following:

- Remember no one method is suitable for all fabrics. Select the one most suitable for your fabric and skill.
- Pin marking is faster, but you must be accurate and careful not to lose pins. On some fabrics the pins will pull through or cause some damage.
- Tracing wheel and tracing paper are not a good choice for knits (they stretch) or sheers and light colors (marking can show).

▼ Cutting Out the Pattern ▼

Use a sharp shears with a long cutting blade to cut out your fabric. Follow the outside edges of the cutting lines carefully. Do not cut on the fold line. Hold the pattern and fabric flat with one hand as you cut with the other to prevent the pattern from moving under the fabric. Move around the table as you work instead of moving the fabric.

Cut the notches outward, not inward. Cutting inward can weaken the seam. You could also accidentally cut into the garment. If there are two or three notches together, cut them across the top as one long notch.

Keep pattern pieces pinned to the fabric for marking and identification. If you are using interfacing, cut out the interfacing when you finish cutting the fabric.

▼ Marking Fabric ▼

The lines and symbols on your pattern pieces serve as a guide for sewing accurately. These markings need to be transferred to the wrong side of your fabric before the pattern is unpinned. They must be visible as you sew, but should not show on the outside of the finished project.

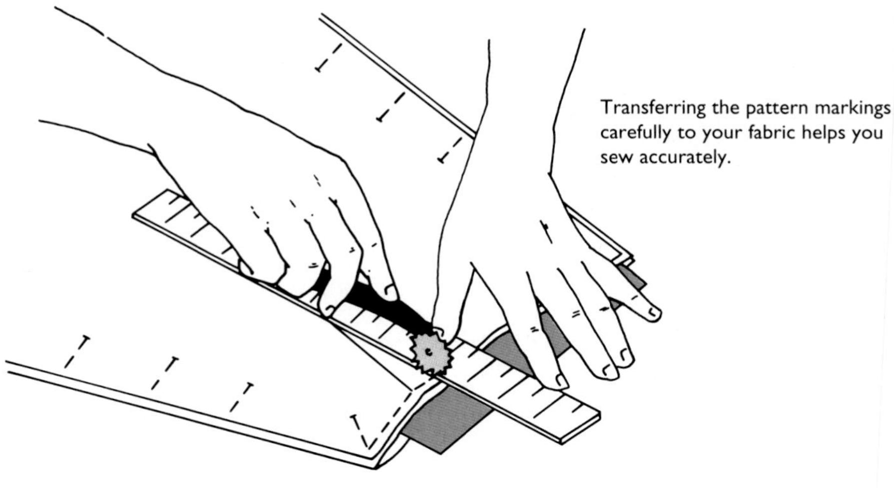

Transferring the pattern markings carefully to your fabric helps you sew accurately.

Learning Activities (continued)

3. **Panel Discussion.** Invite several home sewers or professionals to class to share their reasons for sewing, their greatest sewing satisfactions, any shortcuts they have devised or problems for which they have found creative solutions. You might ask them to bring samples of their greatest successes and worst failures. They may also have tips for making time to sew. Encourage students to ask questions — perhaps about their early sewing experiences. (Key Skills: *Communication, Problem Solving*)
4. **Hands-On Activity.** Gather an assortment of marking tools and fabrics. Allow students to try them all out. Encourage them to decide which methods work best on which fabrics. Perhaps they could jot their findings down in a lab report format — as individuals or as groups. (Key Skill: *Decision Making*)

Follow Up

1. **Reteaching.** Choose one student to act as a student who has never had a sewing class. Ask for a volunteer to tell the uninformed student how to begin to sew — as much as he knows so far. (Key Skills: *Communication, Critical Thinking*)
2. **Extension.** Use the activity on p. 46 of the *Extending the Lesson* booklet in the TCR.
3. **Enrichment.** Have students experiment with using several types of fabric markers on a variety of fabrics. They should keep track of how soon the disappearing markers disappear and how easily the water removable marks are removed. Include a pencil and pen so students can see how difficult they may be to remove. (Key Skill: *Problem Solving*)

- Tailor's tacks take a lot of time but are the best choice for delicate fabrics.
- Fabric marking pens may or may not wash out and are only as accurate as you are.
- Use a ruler for marking straight lines.
- Make a cross mark to indicate point of dart or where to stop stitching.

More About Fabric Markers

Some fabric markers which disappear after a certain amount of time will disappear faster when they are near strong lights — like your sewing machine light or sewing lamp. If you have a marker like that, keep marked fabric covered and watch to make sure your marks don't fade before you've sewn them. Remark if necessary.

Completing the Chapter

For Review

1. Emphasize the main concepts using the summary.
2. Have students complete the "Facts to Recall." (Answers below.)

For Reteaching

1. **Reteaching.** Use the activity on pp. 44-45 of the *Reteaching and Practical Skills* booklet in the TCR.

For Enrichment

1. **Enrichment.** Use the activity on p. 56 of the *Enrichment Activities* booklet in the TCR.

For Evaluation

1. Choose items from "Ideas to Explore" and "Activities to Try."
2. Use the chapter test on pp. 71-72 in the testing booklet of the TCR or use the testmaker software.

Facts to Recall Answers

1. Grainline: a straight line with arrows on each end to be placed in the direction of the specified grain; darts: two broken stitching lines with a solid fold line in the center; notches: diamond-shaped symbols that show where the pattern pieces are joined.
2. Extra room that allows movement. Design ease is part of the style.
3. Press the pattern; compare pattern and body measurements; do not include seam allowances or darts when measuring pattern pieces.
4. Divide the adjustment needed by the number of seam allowances in the garment.
5. The fabric will not shrink once it is made into a garment; fabric finishes are removed.
6. Clip the selvage and pull one yarn gently across the fabric with one hand while pushing the fabric back with the other. Cut along this line.

Markings can be transferred to fabric with a tracing wheel and tracing paper, tailor's chalk and pins, or fabric markers. Here are some guidelines for marking your fabric:

- ***Tracing paper and tracing wheel.*** Choose a color of tracing paper that can be easily seen, but is close to the color of your fabric. Slide the tracing paper under the pattern so that the colored side is against the wrong side of the fabric. If you need to mark two layers of fabric, use two sheets of tracing paper. Roll the tracing wheel along the necessary markings. Using a ruler will help keep the lines straight. Mark the dots with an "X."
- ***Chalk and pins.*** Put a pin through the pattern and fabric at the place to be marked. Make a chalk mark on the wrong side of both fabric layers at the pin marking.
- ***Fabric markers.*** Special liquid fabric markers can be used to make temporary markings on fabric. Some can be removed with water, and others will fade after several hours. Test markers on a scrap of fabric to be sure the markings will come out.

After carefully marking the fabric, you will be ready to start sewing your project together. You will learn about special sewing methods in the following chapters.

TAKING ACTION

Making Accurate Adjustments

Luther is having a problem and needs your help fast. His sewing project is due next week for Mrs. Burkett, the family and consumer sciences teacher, but Luther is having trouble getting past the pattern stage.

Luther decided to save money by borrowing a pants pattern from a friend. Luther's friend is shorter than Luther and wears one size smaller. Luther thinks he needs to add 1 inch (2.5 cm) to the width and 1 inch (2.5 cm) to the length.

Luther was in a hurry when he took his own measurements and thinks that he may not have been very accurate. He's also having a hard time figuring out where to make the needed adjustments. Luther hopes to finish his project on time.

Using Your Resourcefulness

- What were the advantages and disadvantages of borrowing a pattern?
- What are some ways that Luther can make the most of the time he has available to finish his project? Suggest a plan of action.
- Describe to Luther the benefits of having someone help him take his measurements.
- In what ways are accurate measurements a valuable resource for Luther?
- Where can Luther find help in learning how to adjust his pattern?

TAKING ACTION

After students have read the feature ask them if they have done something similar when measuring. Then have them discuss the questions. If students must borrow and alter a pattern, encourage them to retrace the pattern onto tracing fabric that is specially marked off in one-inch squares (it's similar to interfacing).

Using Your Resourcefulness Answers

- Saves money, but may waste time altering and risk having an unsatisfactory garment.
- Remeasure himself and the pattern, allowing for ease. Divide amount he must add by

Chapter 34 Review

Summary

In this chapter, you have read about:

- Pattern symbols that help you lay out, mark, and cut your sewing project.
- How to check your pattern for fit.
- How to alter pattern width and length.
- Preparing your fabric for sewing by preshrinking it and/or straightening its grain.
- Pattern layout, including pinning and cutting out your pattern, and marking your fabric.

Facts to Recall

1. Explain the meaning of each of the following pattern symbols: grainline, darts, notches. How can you recognize these symbols on a pattern piece?
2. What is wearing ease? How is it different from design ease?
3. Briefly explain how to check for fit by measuring pattern pieces.
4. When adjusting pattern width, how do you determine the amount to be adjusted on each pattern piece?
5. Give two reasons for preshrinking fabric before cutting and sewing it.
6. Explain how to straighten the crosswise ends of a piece of fabric when the crosswise yarns are not easily seen.
7. How can you straighten the grain of an off-grain fabric?
8. List the four steps to prepare your pattern for placement on the fabric.
9. What should you do if you can't decide which side of your fabric is the right side?
10. Briefly explain how to pin a large pattern piece to the fabric.
11. Name three methods you can use for transferring pattern markings to your fabric.

Ideas to Explore

1. What safety tips may be helpful when working with your pattern and fabric?
2. What might you do if you find that a garment is too small for you after you have started sewing it?
3. Predict what might happen if you don't preshrink your fabric.

Activities to Try

1. Lay out and pin a pattern on fabric following a pattern guide sheet. Do at least two things wrong. Have a partner see how quickly he or she can tell you what is wrong and how to correct the error.
2. With a partner, demonstrate how to straighten fabric that is off-grain.

LINK TO *Communication*

CREATING SEWING ENTHUSIASM

Write a one-page motivational article that is designed to encourage people just learning to sew. The article should be well organized and the main points should be clearly written. Address the following points as you write your article:

- Emphasize carefully following the major steps in preparing the pattern; layout and cutting the pattern out of the fabric; and transferring the pattern markings to the fabric.
- Create enthusiasm concerning the advantages of sewing your own clothing.

Facts to Recall Answers (continued)

7. Pull the fabric on the true bias. Open up the fabric and, with help, pull the opposite ends that are too short. Stop when the selvages and cut edges match up at right angles. Press with steam.
8. Cut apart the pattern pieces; check them off; press the pieces with a warm, dry iron; write your name on them.
9. Pick either side as the right one, mark the wrong side with chalk.
10. Place the pattern piece with its fold line exactly along the fabric fold; pin along the fold line with pins at right angles to the line every three to four inches (7.5 to 10 cm); smooth the pattern away from the fold and pin diagonally to the corners.
11. Tracing paper, chalk, tailor's marks, fabric marker.

Ideas to Explore

1. Answers may include: keep pins in a pin cushion, not in your mouth; pass scissors handle first; turn off and/or unplug irons when not in use.
2. Answers may include: give it as a gift; convert it to a different type of garment; lengthen or widen with cleverly contrasting fabric at seams or hems.
3. The fabric might shrink after the garment is made. There may be sticky substances on sewing machine needles that cause skipped stitches. Notions could cause puckering and damage to the garment.

number of seam allowances and mark on fabric or add to pattern piece. Make sure all necessary pieces are adjusted.

- Measurements more accurate when two are taking them.
- Save time and fabric to measure correctly the first time.
- Textbook, teacher, experienced sewers.

LINK TO *Communication*

Direct students to read the feature and write the articles. Submit articles to the school newspaper or a fabric store. Or, have each student write about one aspect and create your own newsletter.

- Articles should emphasize major steps in preparing pattern; layout and cutting; and marking.
- Articles should be enthusiastic.

Preparing to Teach

Chapter Outline

Chapter Resources

The following booklet materials may be found in the *Teacher's Classroom Resources* box:

- Lesson Plans, p. 40
- Student Workbook, *Study Guide,* pp. 149-150; *Everything 'Seams Finished',* p. 151; *Earning Your Hard Hat—With Construction,* p. 152
- Color Transparencies, *Step-by-Step Serging,* CT-35
- Sewing and Serging Handbook
- Cooperative Learning, p. 47
- Extending the Text, *Time-Saving Sewing,* p. 47
- Reteaching and Practical Skills, *Sewing Essentials Are a Must,* p. 46
- Enrichment Activities, *Assembly-Line Sewing,* pp. 57-59
- Chapter and Unit Tests, pp. 73-74
- Testmaker Software

Also see:

- Meeting the Special Needs of Students
- Linking Home, School, and Community

CHAPTER 35

Basic Sewing Essentials

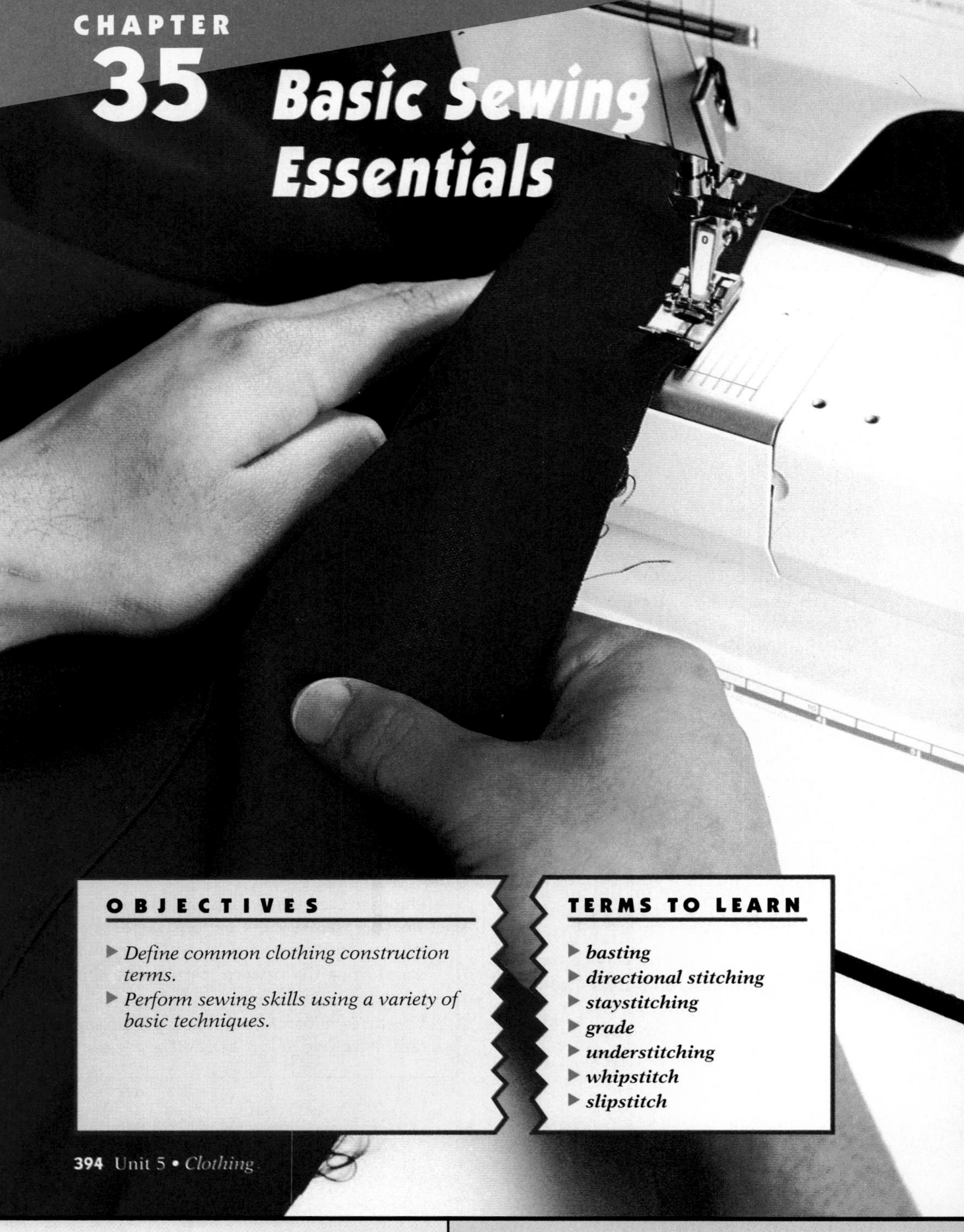

OBJECTIVES

- *Define common clothing construction terms.*
- *Perform sewing skills using a variety of basic techniques.*

TERMS TO LEARN

- ***basting***
- ***directional stitching***
- ***staystitching***
- ***grade***
- ***understitching***
- ***whipstitch***
- ***slipstitch***

More About *Hand Basting*

Although there is no doubt that machine basting is the fastest method, hand basting is often preferred in situations where accuracy is essential for several reasons.

1. Stitching control is much easier on curves or areas that require a great deal of easing, on sharp corners that require perfect

Spencer was ready to start sewing his project. As he started to read his pattern guide sheet, he discovered that there were a few things left that he had to learn. "How should a seam be sewn? What is understitching, grading, and clipping? How should I sew the pocket on my shirt?"

As you begin to sew your project, you may discover that you have as many questions as Spencer did. The directions and the pictures in this chapter will help you learn many new sewing skills.

Fitting a Garment

If you altered your pattern correctly before cutting it out, you will probably have few adjustments to make as you sew. However, it is best to check the fit of a garment while you are making it instead of waiting until it is finished. Changes can be made quickly and easily when they are done early.

- Fit the garment right side out.
- Fit at major construction seams, such as side seams, waistline seam, underarm seams, and major darts. It is easier to alter a garment at major construction seams.
- Make adjustments on both sides of a garment rather than on just one side.
- Check to be sure there is enough ease for movement and comfort. See if you can walk, sit, bend, and raise your arms without straining and pulling the garment.
- Be on the lookout for seams that do not hang straight. Watch out for wrinkles and sags. These are all signs of a poor fit.

To be certain about fit, you may need to baste parts of your garment together. **Basting** means holding fabric in place temporarily with pins or long stitches. There are several types of basting. Hand and machine basting use long stitches of thread. In pin basting, the pins substitute for stitching.

When basting, make sure the stitches or pins are next to, but not directly on, the seam line. This makes the basting easy to remove after the permanent seam is sewn.

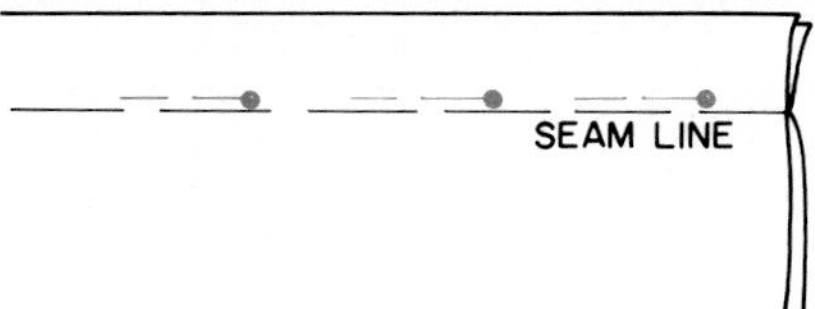

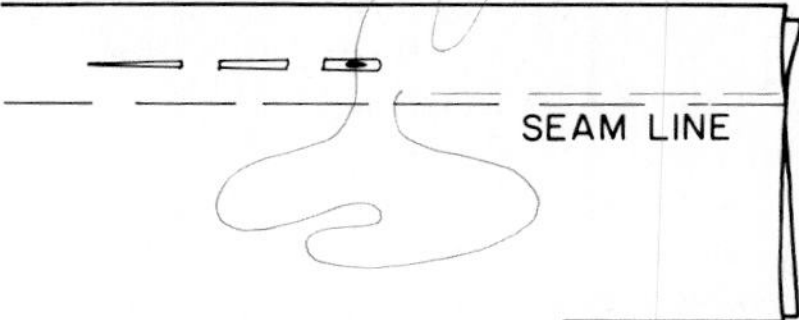

The figure on the left is an example of pin basting. The figure on the right demonstrates hand basting.

Introducing the Chapter

Motivators

1. **Demonstration.** Pour a jigsaw puzzle out on a table. Ask how its puzzle compares to sewing. Any differences? Remind students that sewing can be as fun and challenging as a puzzle. Or, make your own puzzle with a picture of a garment on a shallow box cover. Put pattern pieces in box and number of pieces on the outside.
2. **Bulletin Board.** Hang a long yellow rectangle which says, "Construction Zone." Down the sides of the board, hang yellow and red highway-type signs (Stop, Slow, Curves, One Way, Caution, Slippery). Add an appropriate reference to your sewing project. For example, after "Slow" write, "...your machine at the end of the seam."
3. **Discussion.** Point to the students' cut pattern pieces and pattern guides. Ask students to describe how they feel about their work up to this point. (Key Skill: *Critical Thinking*)

Chapter Objectives and Vocabulary

1. Have students read the chapter objectives and rephrase the objectives as questions.
2. Ask students to state, in their own words, the purpose of studying this chapter.
3. Pronounce the vocabulary terms listed on the previous page. Ask students whether they are familiar with any of these. Explain that the terms will be defined in the chapter.

Guided Reading

1. Have the students read the chapter and use the Study Guide on pp. 149-150 of the *Student Workbook.*

alignment, and on fabrics with designs that must be matched.
2. Certain design details, such as pleats and plackets, are easier to construct if the pieces are hand basted together first.

To make hand basting a more attractive option, keep an easy-to-thread needle handy. Thread it in a bright color that will show up on anything to be ready to sew at all times.

Teaching. . .
Machine Stitching, Directional Stitching, Staystitching, Sewing Techniques, Darts
(pp. 396-397)

Comprehension Check

1. What are three basting methods? *(Hand, machine, and pin basting.)*
2. How is staystitching different than regular stitching? *(Sew on one layer of fabric with a ½", not ⅝" seam.)*
3. How do you secure thread at the beginning and end of a dart? *(Backstitch at the beginning, tie off the pointed end.)*

Learning Activities

1. **Demonstration.** Demonstrate how to pin fabric pieces together. Have students list major construction seams (side, waist, underarm, major darts) and fitting procedures. Point out ease. (Key Skill: *Communication*)
2. **Discussion.** Present this scenario: Mike is making a knit polo-type shirt. He's a bit shortwaisted, but he also wants to be sure the shirt is long enough when he tucks it in. He made no alterations on his pattern. A friend helps him pin fit it. Bad news! The shirt front and back come almost to his knees. The shirt seems wide, too. Ask these questions. How should he make alterations at this point? *(Cut off the bottom front and back pieces the same amount. Measure the width and divide adjustments by number of seam allowances)* What lesson will he learn? *(Measure more carefully before he cuts.)* (Key Skill: *Problem Solving*)

AROUND THE WORLD

Direct the students to read the feature and discuss the questions. *(This probably boosts the Caribbean economy and lowers the U.S. economy. It also lowers prices for U.S. shoppers.)*

AROUND THE WORLD

Making and exporting clothing is a growing industry in Caribbean nations such as Jamaica, Haiti, Costa Rica, and the Dominican Republic. Wages are lower in these countries, so garments are less expensive to make. In addition, these countries are close to the United States, so shipping costs are lower. Since 1988, this industry has created over 100,000 new jobs for people in the Caribbean region. What impact do you think this has on the economy in the Caribbean and the United States?

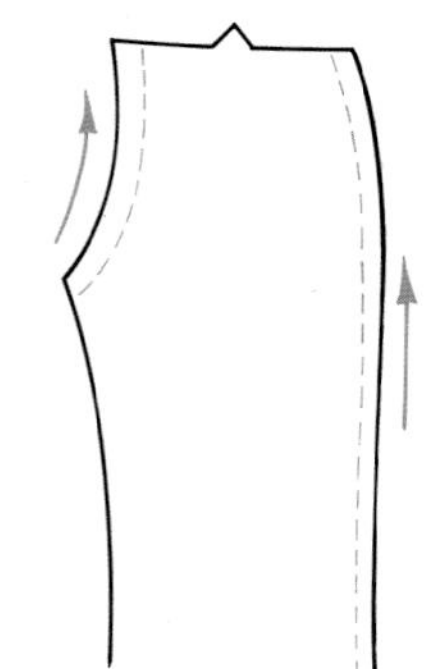

Directional stitching requires that you stitch in the direction of the arrows shown on the pattern. It helps keep the fabric from stretching as you sew.

Machine Stitching

Machine stitching is used for the major seams of the garment. It can be used for many different sewing techniques. Review the chart on page 374 in Chapter 33 to determine the stitch length to use for your fabric.

Pattern instructions generally use specific terms to describe each method of stitching. Two of the most common methods are directional stitching and staystitching.

Directional Stitching

All the stitching on a garment should be sewn with the grain of the fabric. Stitching in the direction of the grain is called **directional stitching**. If you sew with the grain, you are less likely to stretch the fabric.

There are several ways to determine the direction for stitching:

- Move your finger along the raw edge of the fabric. The direction that smooths the yarns against the fabric is with the grain. This is the direction you are going to stitch.
- Pattern tissues have arrows pointing to grain direction.
- As a general rule, stitch from the wide to the narrow part of the garment. For example, sew from the hem to the waist of a skirt.

Staystitching

Before you begin to put a garment together, it should be staystitched. **Staystitching** is a row of stitching on one layer of fabric that prevents fabric edges from stretching as you sew. To be effective:

- Staystitch in the direction of the grain.
- Use the same thread, tension, and stitch length you will use for the garment seams.
- Staystitch ½ inch (1.3 cm) from the raw edge. This is ⅛ inch (3 mm) inside the seam line. Staystitching should not show on the outside.
- Staystitch edges that are curved, on the bias, or cut off-grain (such as shoulder seams, necklines, armholes, waistlines, and the hiplines of garments). These areas are most likely to stretch.
- Staystitch armhole and neckline facings only along the curved edges to be attached to the garment.
- Do not staystitch vertical or straight seams.

SAFETY CHECK✔

As You Sew:

- Remove pins as you sew and put them into the pin cushion.
- Never put pins in your mouth.
- Keep your fingers away from the machine needle while sewing with the machine.
- When using a seam ripper to remove stitches, hold the point away from your body.

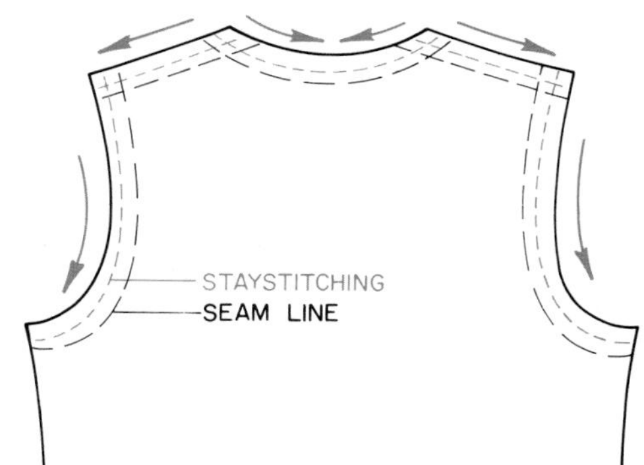

Staystitching is done on curved areas to keep the fabric from stretching.

Sewing Techniques

The sewing techniques described in this chapter are basic techniques you will use in many projects. Learning them is the next step on your sewing adventure.

Darts

Darts help a garment to fit more smoothly over curved areas of the body. They are most often used at the waistline and the front underarm seam.

A single-pointed dart has a point at only one end and is stitched before the seams are sewn. Follow these guidelines in making a dart:

1. Fold the fabric (right sides together) on the center line of the dart. Pin baste on the stitching line, carefully matching the lines accurately. Place the heads of the pins toward the point of the dart for easy removal as you stitch.

Learning Activities (continued)

3. **Impromptu Skit.** Use the previous scenario as a skit. Choose: Mike, his friend Tony, the home economics teacher, Kayla (a busybody who loves to point out other's mistakes), Sergio (a classmate who was able to fix the same problem successfully). (Key Skills: *Problem Solving, Creativity*)
4. **Demonstration.** Show students pattern pieces similar to those in their projects. Group pieces together in units and tell students the plan of attack for sewing their garments, echoing the plan in the guidesheet to avoid confusion. Hold up the pieces to lessen the chances of students joining the wrong ones! (Key Skill: *Management*)
5. **Display.** Show students samples of well-sewn and smooth darts and poorly-made, uneven darts which are coming apart at the point. What was responsible for the good as well as the bad parts? (Key Skill: *Critical Thinking*)

Follow Up

1. **Reteaching.** Ask students why "darts" are included at the beginning of this chapter. (Darts must be sewn before major seams can be joined.) Have students sew a practice dart, following the correct procedure. (Key Skill: *Cooperation*)
2. **Reteaching Lab.** Have students sew a sample of directional stitching and staystitching. (Key Skill: *Management*)
3. **Enrichment Lab.** Have students with advanced sewing skills make a sample of a double-pointed dart. (Key Skill: *Following Directions*)

More About Darts

Darts in the left and right sides of a garment should be the same distance apart and the same length and angle unless you have purposely altered them to accommodate a figure inconsistency. Also, be sure to press darts carefully so the fold doesn't make a line on the right side.

SAFETY CHECK✔

Divide the class into groups to act out what happens when a rule is not followed.

Teaching Seams and Seam Finishes (pp. 398-399)

Comprehension Check

1. What are three things to check before you sew a seam? *(Right sides together, edges aligned, notches matched.)*
2. Why are seam finishes used? *(Prevent raveling.)*
3. What are two different ways you can use a serger for seams? *(To sew the seam itself or to finish the edges.)*

Learning Activities

1. **Display.** Mount seams and seam finishing samples on a bulletin board. Refer to them during the chapter. Or, begin a collection using good examples of student work. This will reinforce and encourage others to do a good job. (Key Skills: *Creativity, Following Directions*)
2. **Demonstration.** Bring a garment (or make a sample and wash it several times) which has seams that are unfinished. Point out how the fabric has raveled. Ask students what will happen if the fabric continues to ravel. Have they had similar experiences? Then ask them to check the seams on the clothes they are wearing. Except for jeans, the seams are probably overlocked. Remind them that the garments they make should be at least the quality of ready-to-wear garments. (Key Skill: *Critical Thinking*)
3. **Seam Samples.** Ask groups to make a set of seam finishing samples following the directions in the chapter. Display the best on a poster. Use this as competition, graded project, or prerequisite to beginning the project. (Key Skills: *Following Directions, Creativity*)
4. **Sewing Practice.** Have students make simple patchwork pillows. Use the following measurements: cut two strips 2¾ inches wide by 13 inches long for the outer strips of pillow; cut five strips 2 inches wide by 13 inches long for the inner strips. Have students stitch the narrower strips with right sides together using a ¼-inch seam. Stitch the two wider strips, one on each

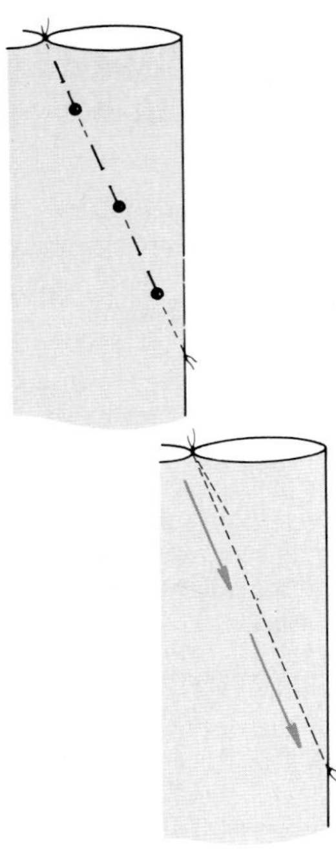

Pin baste and then stitch a single-pointed dart from the wide end to the point.

2. Stitch from the wide end to the point. Backstitch to secure the stitching at the wide end of the dart. Follow the stitching line, removing the pins as you sew. The last few stitches should be on the fold to give a smooth point. Secure the threads at the point of the dart by tying them together. Clip the thread ends to ¼ inch (6 mm) from the fabric.
3. Press the dart flat. Then press the dart to one side. Press underarm darts toward the waistline. Press all other darts toward the center of the garment.

Seams

Seams hold a garment together. They are formed by sewing two pieces of fabric together. A well-made seam affects the way a garment looks and wears. When stitched too tightly, the seam may pucker. If a seam is stitched too loosely, it may pull apart.

A plain seam is most commonly used in garments. In general, seams are ⅝ inch (1.5 cm) wide unless another width is given in the pattern directions. As you learned in Chapter 34, the fabric between the seam line and the cut edge is called the *seam allowance*.

SEAM ALLOWANCE

Secure the ends of a plain seam by backstitching on both ends.

Before you begin your project, sew a sample seam on a scrap of your fabric. Check the tension, stitch length, and general appearance. To make a plain seam follow these steps:

1. Put right sides of the fabric together. Match notches, cut edges, and both ends of the fabric. Place pins at right angles to the seam line at the ends and notches. Pin the rest of the seam, placing pins 2 to 3 inches (5 to 7.5 cm) apart.
2. Put the fabric under the presser foot with the cut edges of the seam allowance lined up with the proper seam guide on the throat plate. Turn the handwheel and insert the needle ½ inch (1.3 cm) from the top of the fabric. Lower the presser foot.
3. Backstitch to secure the top end of the seam.
4. Using a medium speed and an even pace, stitch to the other end of the seam.
5. Backstitch to secure the bottom end of the seam.
6. Press the seam open flat unless directed otherwise.

More About Stitching Seams

Intersecting seams require a certain amount of care. Seams in the crotch of pants are an example of this. They will, however, intersect perfectly when you stitch both seams separately. Press each seam open. Then pin the two seams with right sides together, using a pinpoint to match the crossed seams exactly (Stick the pin through the top seam and make sure it comes out in the correct place in the bottom seam.) Then pin and stitch. Trim corners diagonally to eliminate bulk. In addition to crossed seams, places of stress need extra attention. Special reinforcements strengthen a seam in areas where it may stretch, such as the waistline or shoulders. This is especially important if the seam is on the bias or if it

SUCCESSFUL SERGING

Serging a Seam

Serged seams work well on many garments. They are especially good on knits since the seams must stretch with the garment. You can also use serged seams with woven fabrics for loose fitting garments.

Planning ahead is important when using a serger. Sew a test seam first. Remember, the seam line is where the needle enters the fabric — not where the knives cut. If you begin with a ⅝ inch (1.6 cm) seam allowance, and your knives cut off ⅜ inch (1 cm), a ¼ inch (6 mm) seam allowance remains.

If your serger does not have a guide mark for sewing a ⅝ inch (1.6 cm) seam, simply measure ⅝ inch (1.6 cm) from the needle and mark the spot with a permanent marker or piece of tape.

Generally, pins are not needed for serger sewing. The serger feeds fabric evenly through the machine. If you do use pins, remove them before they hit the knives. If a pin hits the knives, the blades can be seriously damaged. In addition, pins that break and fly away from the machine, could cause injury.

Press serged seams to one side, front or back, depending on the garment you are making.

▼ Seam Finishes ▼

In many fabrics, the cut edge ravels as a garment is worn and laundered. Seam finishes are often used to prevent raveling on seams and facings.

The seam finish selected depends on the type of fabric and the amount of raveling. If you are unsure which to use, try different finishes on scraps of fabric. Use the one that appears to be the best for the fabric.

Here are the guidelines for several types of seam finishes:

- ***Stitched and pinked finish.*** Fabrics that ravel slightly can be stitched and cut with a pinking shears. Stitch ¼ inch (6 mm) from the cut edge. Pink the edge after stitching, being careful not to cut the stitching.

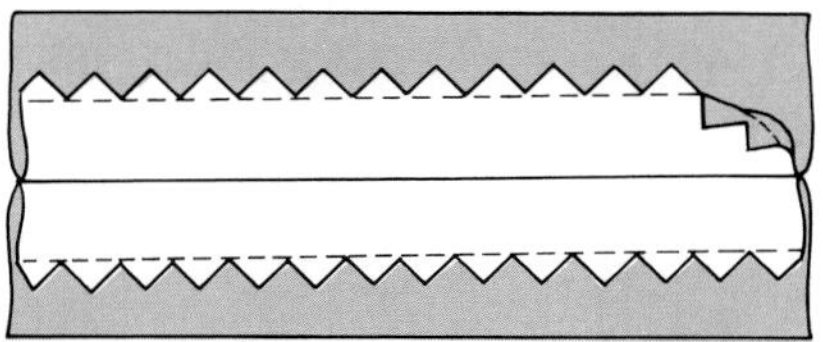

Stitched and pinked finish.

Learning Activities (continued)

side, to the strips already stitched using a ¼-inch seam. Press the seams one direction (zigzag them if students need practice). Sew the pieced front to a solid color back (13 inches by 13 inches), right sides together, using ½-inch seams around all sides, leaving a 4-inch opening on one side. Turn and stuff with a pillow form or fiberfill. (Key Skills: *Following Directions, Creativity*)

SUCCESSFUL SERGING

Serging a Seam

Have students read the feature. Then have them sew ⅝-inch seams: one set on a sewing machine, one on a serger (following the suggestions in the feature). Press seams and measure the strips at the beginning, middle, and end. Compare accuracy and ease of stitching in a lab report. Compare reports with the class.

Follow Up

1. **Reteaching.** Ask students to help you make a list of seams and seam finishes. After each tell when and where it should be used. (Key Skill: *Critical Thinking*)
2. **Enrichment.** Have students check out garment seam finishes at several stores. They should report their findings to the class. (Key Skill: *Decision Making*)

will have to support excess weight, such as in a full-gathered, or pleated skirt, or if the fabric is of a heavy weight. Center sheer stabilizing tape or woven seam binding over the seam line of the garment section. Baste, then stitch seam according to directions.

For lightweight or slippery fabrics that shift during sewing, place tissue paper on the machine bed under the seams. Stitch through the fabric and paper. Gently tear paper away.

Family Perspective

Margo is sewing a cotton shirt at home and asks her mom how she should finish her seams. Her mom laughs and says Margo shouldn't waste her time. What should Margo do?

Teaching. . .
Interfacing and Facings
(pp. 400-401)

Comprehension Check

1. What is the purpose of interfacing? *(Gives body and support to places that need it.)*
2. Why do you trim the corners off sew-in interfacing? *(To reduce the bulk)*
3. Why press as you sew? *(To be faster, be more accurate, have a professional look.)*
4. What can you use for pressing a curved area? *(A tailor's ham — an oblong cushion.)*

Learning Activities

1. **Survey.** Ask students wearing shirts with cuffs or collars or a stiff neckline to check their garments for interfacing. Did they realize it was there? Does it make a difference? Ask students to check other garments at home for interfacing, too. Point out that interfacing is common even though they may not know of it. (Key Skill: *Critical Thinking*)
2. **Demonstration.** Show various weights of both fusible and sew-in interfacing and the correct way to apply them. Trim the corners. Show what happens when you iron on the wrong side of fusible interfacing or scraps. There's a tip for cleaning the adhesive off irons in a previous sewing chapter. (Key Skill: *Following Directions*)
3. **Demonstration.** Cut several cuffs out of scrap fabric. Cut one facing from sew-on and two from fusible interfacing. Sew in the first interfacing without trimming it. Then sew the cuff front to the cuff back. Turn the seam without trimming. Note the bulk. Show how trimming makes a big difference. Now apply the fusible interfacing. Trim the seam. Then point out that the interfacing cannot be trimmed further than the fabric because they're fused together. Now, repeat the procedure and trim the points and edges before fusing. Sew a cuff back to the cuff front, trim, and turn. Compare the finished products. (Key Skill: *Communication*)

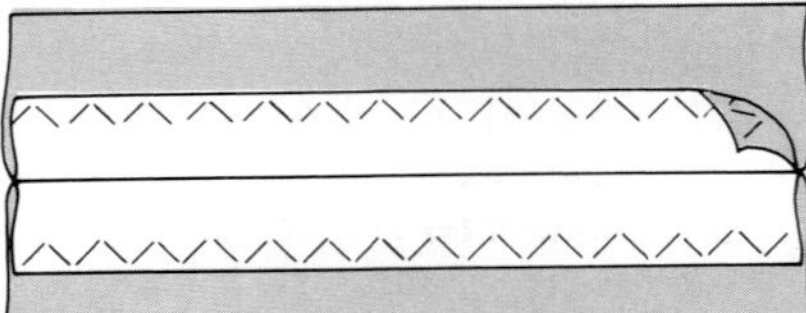
Zigzagged finish.

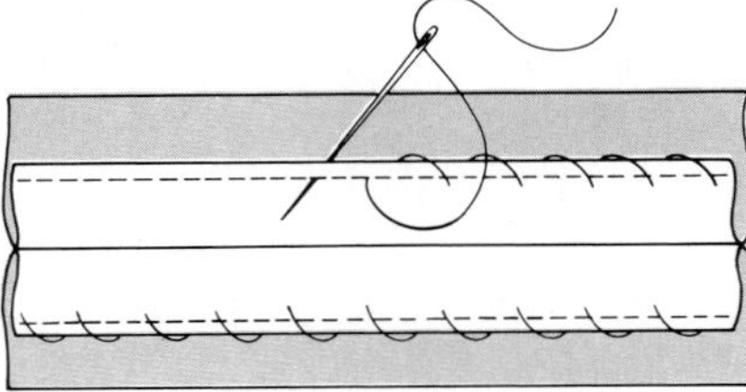
Overcast finish.

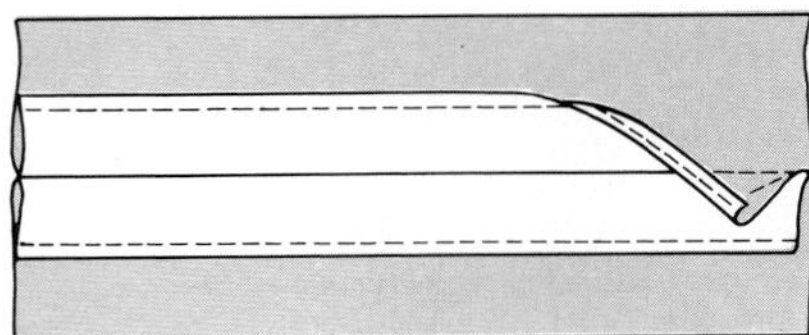
Clean finish.

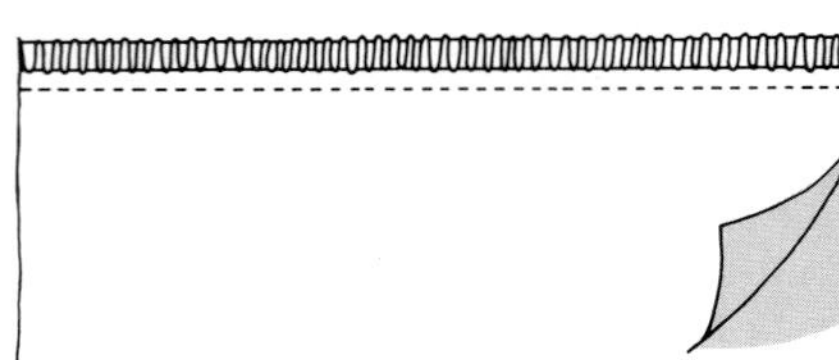
Serged finish.

- ***Zigzagged finish.*** For fabrics that ravel, zigzagging is a good seam finish. Use a medium-width machine zigzag stitch and sew along the edge of each seam allowance.
- ***Overcast finish.*** If your machine does not zigzag, you can overcast the edge of a fabric by hand. Stitch at a slant with large, even, closely-spaced stitches that go over and around the edge of the fabric.
- ***Clean finish.*** A clean finish is a turned and stitched finish used on lightweight and mediumweight fabrics. Machine stitch ¼ inch (6 mm) from the cut edge. Turn the cut edge toward the inside along the stitching line. Press. Machine stitch close to the folded edge. Facings, seams, and hems can be clean-finished.
- ***Serged finish.*** This may be used on any fabric. Serge along the cut edge of the seam, trimming ⅛ inch (3 mm) or less as you sew. A serged finish is especially helpful on heavy or bulky fabric and fabric that ravels easily.

▼ Interfacing ▼

Interfacing gives body and support to places where it is needed, such as necklines, buttonhole openings, and cuffs. Interfacing is applied before the facing is attached to the garment. Depending on the type used, it is either sewn or pressed onto the garment.

Applying Sew-on Interfacing

Here are some guidelines for applying sew-on interfacing:

1. Cut the pointed corners off the interfacing about ⅛ inch (3 mm) past the seam line to reduce bulk. This means ⅛ inch (3 mm) of the fabric corners will be without interfacing. Pin the interfacing to the wrong side of the fabric piece.
2. Machine baste the interfacing to the fabric ½ inch (1.3 cm) from the outer edges. Stitch with the direction of the grain.
3. Trim the interfacing as close to the stitching line as possible.
4. Handle the interfacing and the fabric as one piece when sewing the seams.

More About *Pleats*

One common way to construct a skirt is to add pleats. Their use and type vary with changing styles. Here are some kinds often used.

- **Accordion pleats** are thin, even pleats, one folded over another.
- **Knife pleats** are narrow and turned in the same direction.
- **Box pleats** are two knife pleats that are folded to face each other on the inside of the garment.
- **Kick pleats** — two knife pleats folded away from each other on the inside — are usually placed at the bottom of garments.

(See the *Sewing and Serging Handbook* for more information about pleats.)

Applying Fusible Interfacing

Follow these guidelines for applying fusible interfacing:

1. Trim fusible interfacing before it is pressed onto the fabric. Mark and trim ½ inch (1.3 cm) along the seam lines. Also, cut any pointed corners off the interfacing about ⅛ inch (3 mm) past the seam line to reduce bulk.
2. Place the coated side of the interfacing on the wrong side of the fabric. Be sure the cut edges are ½ inch (1.3 cm) from the fabric edges.
3. Follow the pressing instructions that come with the interfacing.

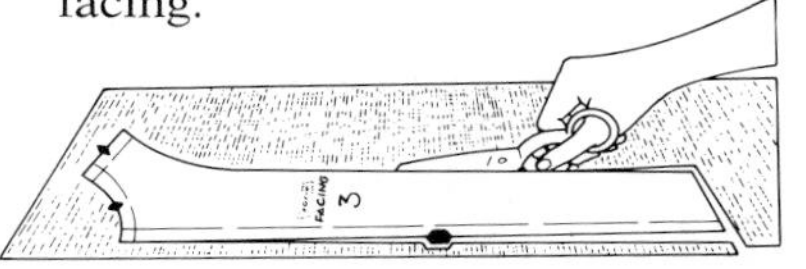

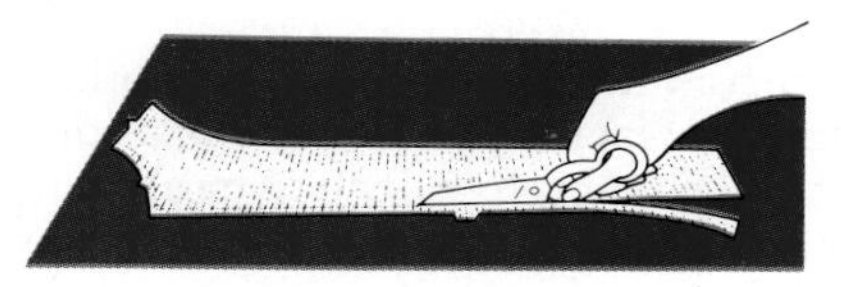

Cut out fusible interfacings using the correct pattern piece. Trim away the seam allowances and fuse to fabric.

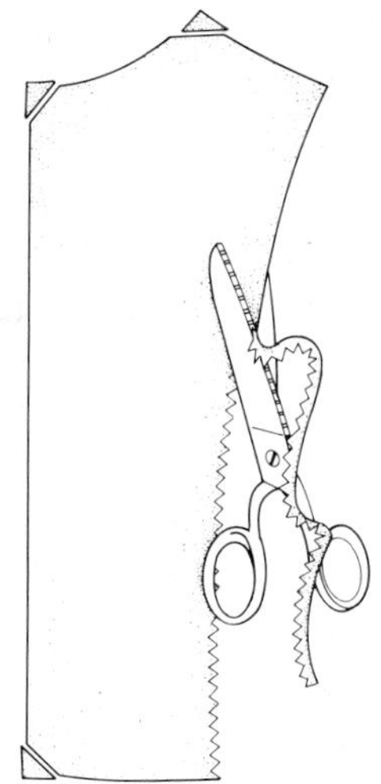

Trim sew-on interfacing before basting to fabric.

▼ Facings ▼

Facings are often used to finish the neckline, front opening, armholes, and collars of garments. There are several different types of facings. However, a shaped facing is used most frequently. It is cut the same shape as the edge onto which it is sewn.

Before learning to sew a facing to a garment, there are several techniques you will need to understand.

- ***Grading a seam allowance.*** After facings are joined to a garment, the seams are **graded**, or cut in layers to reduce bulk. To grade a seam: trim the interfacing as close as possible to the seam line; trim the facing seam to ¼ inch (6 mm); then trim the garment seam to ⅜ inch (1 cm). The wider seam on the outside cushions the narrower one and keeps it from showing when the seam is pressed. **Note:** Trim the seams together diagonally across sharp corners, such as collar points and neck facing edges, before continuing to grade the seam.

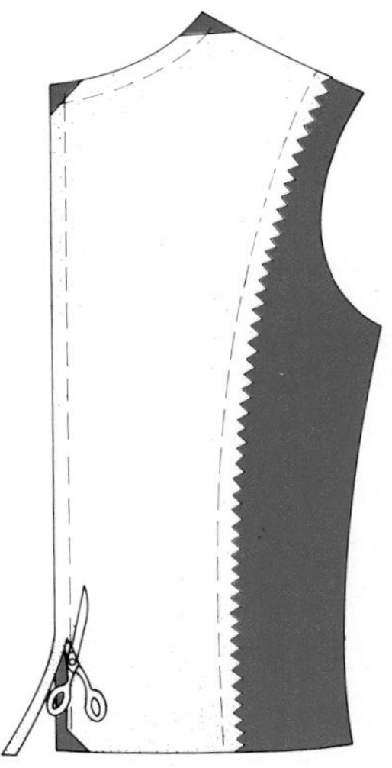

Baste sew-on interfacing to garment. Then trim the interfacing close to the basting.

Learning Activities (continued)

4. **Hands-On Activity.** Give students cuff sections and both fusible and sew-on interfacing. Instruct them to fuse one piece and sew one in. Have students compare and talk about which method seemed easiest. (Key Skill: *Critical Thinking*)
5. **Demonstration.** Show the stabilizing effect of interfacing by sewing buttons into it. Ask students to sew a button onto fabric that is interfaced and faced. Ask what the advantages are. (Key Skills: *Following Directions, Critical Thinking*)

Follow Up

1. **Reteaching.** Write on the board: "There's more to sewing than meets the eye." Ask students what that means. *(more steps and procedures that people don't see — facings, darts, seam finishing)* (Key Skill: *Communication*)
2. **Enrichment.** What happens if a sewer accidentally fuses interfacing to the wrong side or to the wrong piece? Give students fabric, interfacing, and an iron. Can they come up with remedies, such as reheating or pulling a corner? (Key Skill: *Problem Solving*)

More About *Seams*

The kind of seam commonly seen on jeans and other action wear is called a *flat-felled* seam. Both edges of the seam are enclosed and topstitched as part of the garment's design. Another kind of "double" seam, the *French* seam, makes the seams in sheer fabrics look neat and keeps them from raveling. These double seams often occur on woven garments that are laundered frequently.

Teaching. . .
Facings and Gathering
(pp. 402-403)

Comprehension Check

1. What is the purpose of facings? *(To have a finished look, to keep the edges from raveling, and to give shape.)*
2. Facing seams usually need to be graded, clipped, and understitched? Why? *(So facings lie smooth and flat.)*
3. Why secure one end of the basting thread when you are gathering fabric? *(It will probably pull it through the gathers and out the other end.)*

Learning Activities

1. **Discussion.** Hold a bodice front up to a student or mannequin. Darts and shoulder seams give it some shape. Tell students you will be adding sleeves, side seams, and a hem. Put a cardigan sweater on to cover the edges and tuck the bottom in. What still seems unfinished? *(the neck, front)* Ask how the edges are finished? This should help them to understand the need for facings. (Key Skill: *Critical Thinking*)
2. **Demonstration.** Sew a shaped facing to a plain round neckline. Don't trim, clip, or understitch it before you turn it. Try to get it to stay down and lie flat. Ask students for help. Then ask a student to read the directions in the text or pattern guide. Do one step at a time and ask students if it's enough. Continue until you have understitched and pressed the facing. (Key Skill: *Problem Solving*)
3. **Hands-On Activity.** Give students an opportunity to sew curved edges together before they tackle their own projects. Have them sew two neck facing pieces together out of their own scraps so they'll know how their fabric works. Make sure they grade, clip, and understitch so the facings lie flat. (Key Skill: *Problem Solving*)

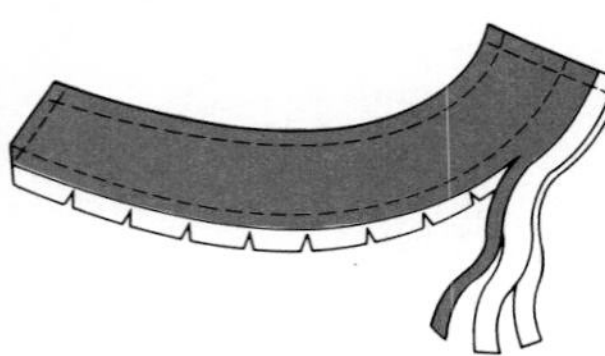
Grading and notching on an outward curved seam.

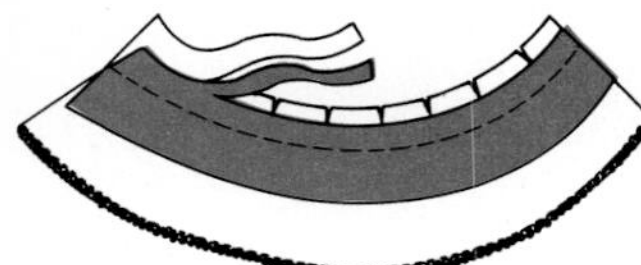
Grading and clipping on an inward curved seam.

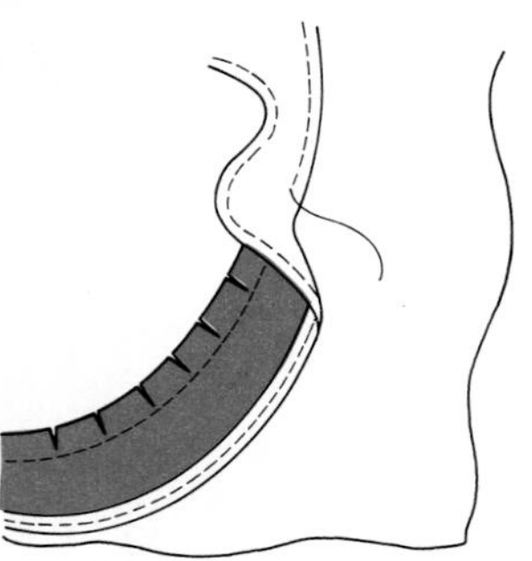
Understitch through all layers of the seam allowance and facing to keep the facing from rolling to the right side of the garment.

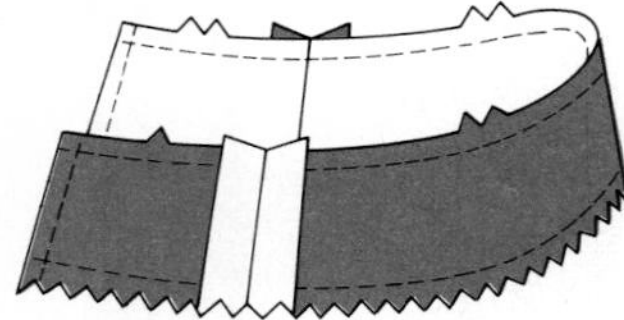
Join facing pieces together and finish the outer edges.

- ***Notching and clipping a seam allowance after grading.*** Outward-curved edges on collars and inward-curved edges on necklines need special treatment to lie flat. Cut V-shaped notches from the seam allowance on outer curves. Make small clips in the seam on an inner curve. Space the clips and notches around the edges so the curve will lie flat. Be careful not to clip through the stitching.
- ***Understitching.*** Understitching gives a smooth, flat edge to facings. It keeps the seams and facings from rolling to the right side of the garment. Before understitching, press seam allowances on both garment and facing toward the facing. Grade and clip the seams as needed. Work with the right side of the garment facing up. Sew, using a regular machine stitch, through the facing and the two seam allowances about ⅛ inch (3 mm) from the seam line. Press.

Now you are ready to learn how to sew on a facing. Follow these steps to attach a facing:

1. Staystitch curved facing edges that are to be attached to the garment. Sew facing pieces together as directed in the pattern. Trim the seams to ¼ inch (6 mm) and press open.
2. Finish the unnotched outer edges of the facing to prevent raveling. Use one of the finishing methods discussed earlier in this chapter. Press.

Press as You Go

"Press as you go" is a good rule to keep in mind. If you press each piece after it is sewn, your work will go faster and will be more accurate. Pressing as you sew gives your garment a professional look.

Here are some guidelines for pressing as you sew:

- Use pressing equipment correctly.
- Check the correct temperature setting on the iron by using a scrap of fabric.
- Press with the grain of the fabric.
- Press each seam and dart before joining that section to another one.
- Use the point of the iron to press seams open.
- Press flat garment areas on a flat surface. Use a tailor's ham — an oblong stuffed cushion that is shaped like a ham — for curved areas.
- Avoid pressing over pins. They can scratch the bottom of the iron and mark the fabric.

More About *Pressing as You Go*

Sometimes on wool or bulky garments (such as coats and blazers) it's hard to get a professional look with hand irons and steamers. Taking the garment to a professional dry cleaner for a good pressing may give it a more tailored look. It will be well worth the small cost.

More About *Ironing*

Fabric should be pressed or ironed in the direction of the grain to prevent stretching. Napped fabric, such as corduroy and velvet can be pressed on the outside with steam alone — without actually touching the iron to the fabric. When pressing on the inside, use very light pressure so as not to flatten the nap.

3. Place the right side of the facing against the right side of the garment. Match notches, seams, and pin together.
4. Stitch the facing to the garment at ⅝ inch (1.3 cm), sewing as evenly as possible.
5. Grade and clip the seams to reduce bulk.
6. Press the facing and seam allowance away from the garment.
7. Understitch the seam allowance. Press.
8. Fasten the facing to the inside of the garment by hand sewing it to the seam allowances or darts. Take a few tiny stitches over and over at the same place. Avoid sewing the entire facing edge to the inside of the garment. This will cause the garment to pull along the stitching line and look unattractive on the outside.

Sew facing to garment. Then grade and clip or notch the seam allowance.

Understitch the facing.

▼ Gathering ▼

Fullness on shirts, dresses, and skirts is often created by gathers. To make gathers, sew two evenly spaced rows of machine basting on the right side of the fabric, using a long machine stitch. Leave a 2 inch (5 cm) length of thread at the beginning and the end of each row. Stitch the first row on the seam line. Stitch the second row about ¼ inch (6 mm) from the seam line inside the seam allowance.

If a large amount of fabric is to be gathered, divide the amount to be gathered into four equal parts. Stitch and gather each part separately.

Pin the edge to be gathered to the corresponding straight edge (such as a sleeve to a cuff, a gathered skirt to a waistband, or a ruffle to a curtain edge) with the right sides together. Match all markings, notches and seams.

Adjust gathers to fit the straight edge. First, secure one end of the basting stitches by wrapping the thread ends around a pin in a figure eight. Working from the other end, gently pull the loose ends of the bobbin threads. Slide the fabric along with your fingers. After gathering the amount you think is needed, secure threads by wrapping them around a pin. Measure the exact width needed, and adjust the gathers. Pin about every ½ inch (1.3 cm).

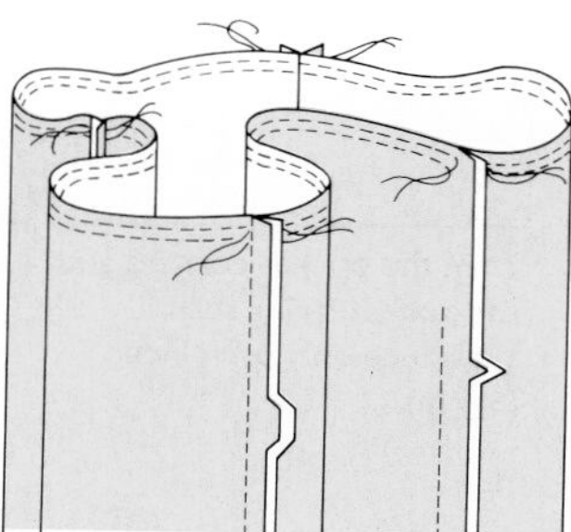

Gather each section using basting stitches.

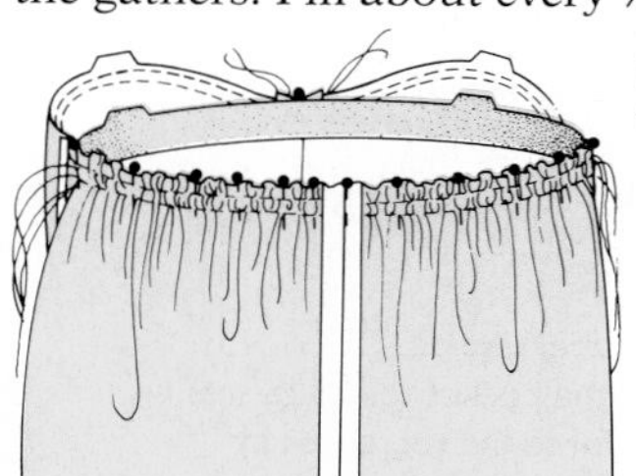

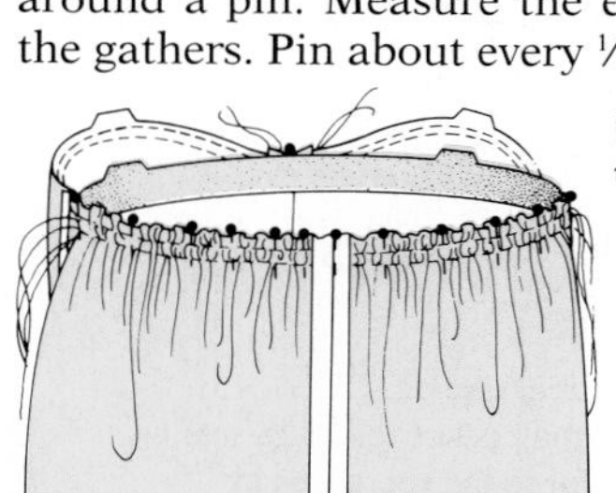

Pin the gathered edge evenly to the corresponding straight edge.

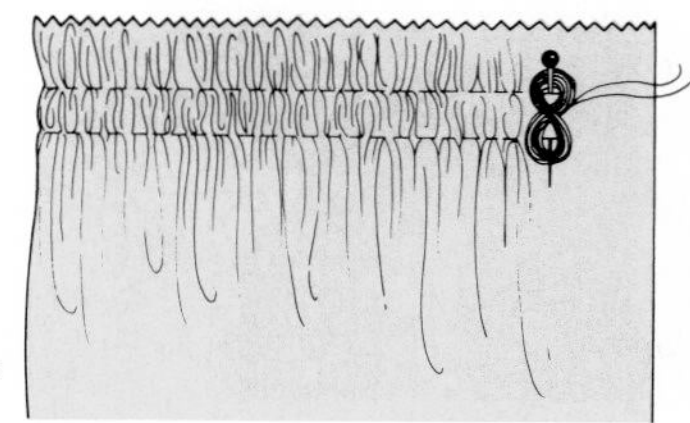

Secure the gathers around a pin, as shown.

Learning Activities (continued)

4. **Demonstration.** Using a wide, short strip of fabric — show students how to gather fabric using machine basting. Remind them to secure the basting at one end. Show what gathering looks like when you don't take time to divide the fabric into sections and even out gathers. (Key Skill: *Communication*)
5. **Hands-On Activity.** If your students have the ability, let them put a ruffle on their patchwork pillow top before stitching it to the back. Have them cut a piece of fabric twice the desired width of the ruffle plus seam allowances. The strip should be at least twice as long as the perimeter of the pillow. Sew the ends together, press the ruffle in half, right sides out, and sew two basting seams through both layers ¼ inch and ½ inch from the unfinished edge. Divide the ruffle into four quarters and mark them. Lay the raw edge of the ruffle over the raw edge of the pillow top. Pin the ruffle edge of the pillow top, placing the quartered marks at the center of each side of the pillow. Adjust gathers to fit. Stitch. Make sure no ruffles were caught in the seam. Sew the pillow back on over the ruffle, around all sides, leaving a 4-inch opening on one side. Turn. Press. (Key Skill: *Creativity*)

Follow Up

1. **Reteaching.** Have students help list of the steps in sewing on facing and gathering fabric. (Key Skill: *Following Directions*)
2. **Enrichment.** Sewing the pillow ruffle could be an enrichment project. Or, ask students to make two gathering samples, one with one row of basting stitches and the other with two rows. Compare procedure and product. (Key Skill: *Following Directions*)

More About Iron Care

The bottom, or sole plate, of a steam iron must be cleaned regularly to prevent the buildup of substances from fabrics, such as starches and finishes. Avoid pressing over pins as they can scratch the sole plate. Also take care when using fusible interfacings or webs so the adhesive does not touch the iron.

Teaching. . .
Patch Pockets and Hems
(pp. 404-405)

Comprehension Check

1. What is a patch pocket? *(A piece of fabric attached to the outside of a garment.)*
2. What decides how deep hems are? *(Fullness of garment.)*
3. What are some ways to finish the raw edges of hems? *(Clean finish, machine stitch under, zigzag or serge edge)*
4. How deep should a circular hem be? Why? *(No more than 1 inch to avoid bulk.)*

Learning Activities

1. **Demonstration.** Using contrasting fabric, show students how to cut a pocket, finish the raw edge, stitch the top hem, sew and turn the sides of the top edge. Show how to fold the bottom corners correctly, and then, using strips of fusible web, show how to anchor the pocket to the garment before sewing it. (Key Skills: *Communication, Following Directions*)
2. **Hands-On Activity.** Have students complete a patch pocket sample. Use the direction sheet found in the *Sewing and Serging Handbook.* As an alternative, have students recycle or update an old garment by adding colorful patch pockets. (Key Skills: *Creativity, Following Directions*)
3. **Demonstration.** Using a strip of fabric (or skirt or pants), show students how to measure and prepare a straight hem and a circular. (Key Skill: *Communication*)
4. **Hands-On Activity.** Give students enough 6-inch strips to prepare samples of each hem you demonstrate. Have students finish the hem edges by using a least three different finishing methods. Students should prepare the hems up to the point of hand sewing. (Key Skill: *Communication*)

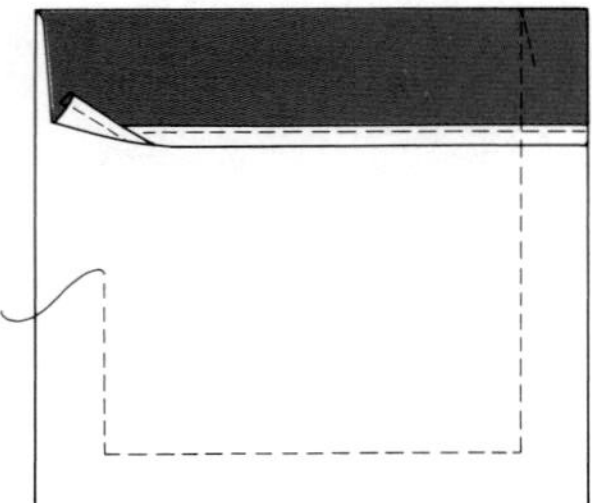

Finish and face the pocket edge. Stitch along the seam line.

When stitching a gathered seam, sew with the gathered edge on top. In this way, stitching is more accurate and the gathers will not be caught in the stitching. For safe sewing, remove the pins as you sew.

▼ Patch Pockets ▼

A patch pocket is made from a separate piece of fabric and is attached to the outside of the garment. Follow these directions for a square patch pocket:

1. Turn the top edge of the pocket under ¼ inch (6 mm) to the wrong side of fabric. Press. Stitch close to the edge.
2. Turn the top pocket edge to the outside (right sides of fabric together) along the fold line to form the pocket facing. Pin.
3. Stitch along the seam line from the top of the pocket on one side to the top on the other side. Backstitch at both ends.
4. Trim the corners and seam allowance on the pocket facing to about ¼ inch (6 mm). Turn pocket facing right side out and press.
5. Fold the seam allowances under along the stitching line. Press. This will give you a guideline to work with to form a square corner.
6. To form a square corner, open the seam allowances. Fold the corners under diagonally to the stitching line and press. Trim the diagonal seam allowance to ¼ inch (6 mm). Refold the seam allowances on both sides of the corner to form a square edge. Press again.
7. Place the pocket on the outside of the garment, with the wrong side down. Follow placement markings. Pin and baste.
8. Machine stitch close to the outer folded edge. Use the inside edge of the presser foot as a seam guide. Reinforce the top edges of the pocket by backstitching.

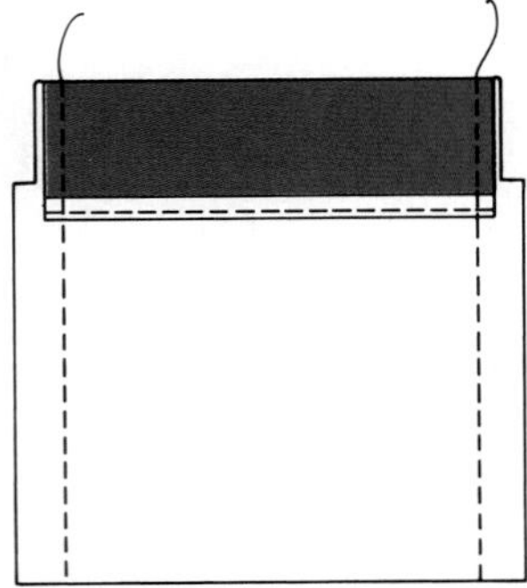

Trim the pocket corners and the pocket facing seam allowance only to ¼ inch (6 mm).

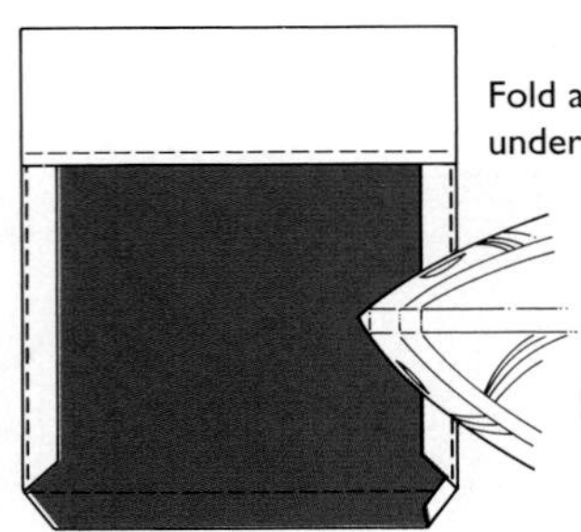

Fold and press seam allowances under along the stitching line.

Sew the pocket to the garment. Reinforce the top edges by backstitching.

More About Patch Pockets

Patch pockets, usually made from self-fabric and applied to the outside of the garment, can be either lined or unlined. When making a pair of patch pockets, check carefully to be sure both pockets are the same size and shape and are attached to the garment evenly. Some tips when working on pockets:

- Adding a lining actually saves sewing time. By lining the pocket to the edge, you can save time and skip mitering the corners on square pockets or eliminate the step of ease-stitching curves or rounded pockets. If you make a machine-stitched buttonhole in the lining, you can use it as an opening to turn the finished pocket right side out.

▾ Hems ▾

All hems are not the same. The type of hem you put in depends on the type of fabric and the amount of fullness to be handled. Some casual garments have a narrow, machine-stitched hem. However, most garments have hems that are finished by hand. This way the hem is almost invisible.

Marking the Hem

To mark the length of the hemline, put on shoes of the heel height you expect to wear with the finished garment. Decide on the most attractive length for the garment. Have another person measure the correct length up from the floor using a measuring stick. Place pins or chalk marks at the same distance all the way around the garment. Stand straight and still while the hem is being marked. Check to be sure the markings form an even line. Make any changes needed.

Using the marked line as a guide, turn the hem to the wrong side of the garment. Pin along the fold line. Place pins at a right angle to the folded edge.

Hem width varies depending on the fullness of the garment. Garments with less fullness can have deeper hems. Pants usually have a hem of 1½ to 2 inches (3.8 to 5 cm). Skirt hems vary from 1 to 3 inches (2.5 to 7.5 cm). For example, the hem in a straight or gathered skirt may be 2 to 3 inches (5 to 7.5 cm) deep. However, the hem of a circular skirt should be no more than 1 inch (2.5 cm) deep.

Measure the hem width needed plus ¼ inch (6 mm) for finishing. Use a sewing gauge, cardboard notched at the correct hem width, or a ruler to mark the correct width. Cut off extra fabric from the edge of the hem.

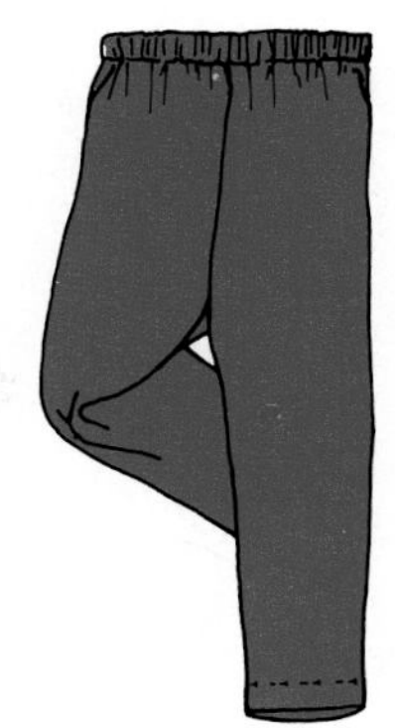

Mark the hemline accurately.

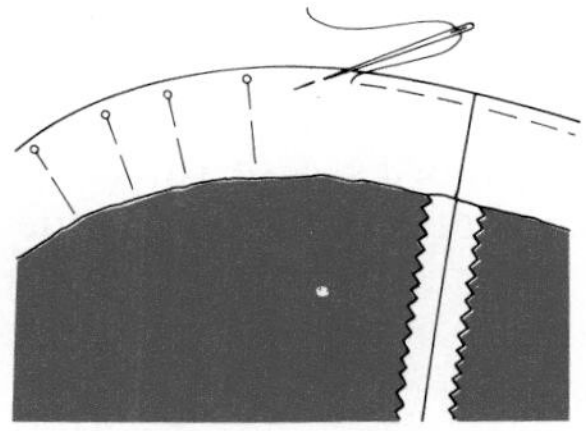

Pin and baste the hem along the fold.

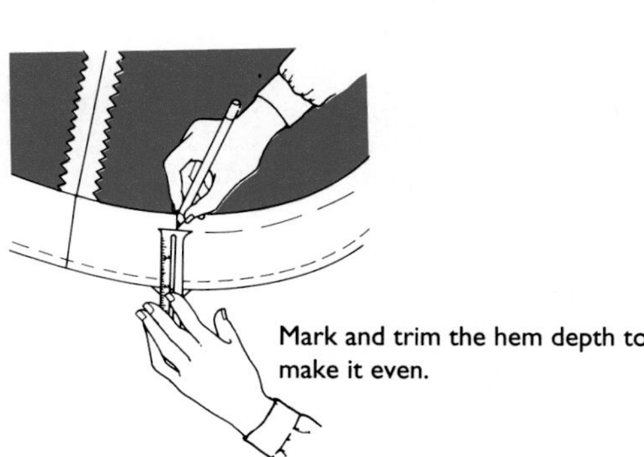

Mark and trim the hem depth to make it even.

Learning Activities (continued)

5. **Discussion.** Present this scenario. Micala has made a plaid skirt which is rather full at the bottom. She asks her friend Andrea to help her with the hem. Andrea suggests that Micala find the right length and hem the skirt along the same plaid line. (Her plaids meet at the seams.) Micala replies that she must measure the hem from the floor and ignore the plaid. What advice would you give Micala? (Key Skills: *Communication, Problem Solving*)
6. **Group Work.** Have students work in pairs to pin up hems. (Key Skill: *Cooperation*)

Follow Up

1. **Reteaching.** Ask students to survey the hems of garments hanging in their closets. How are the hems finished? Which appears to be the most durable? (Key Skills: *Critical Thinking, Communication*)
2. **Enrichment.** Have students survey ready-to-wear garments in local stores. Check to see how many hems are sewn by hand and how many by machine. Are there times when sewing a hem on the machine will make it look less "homemade" than if you sewed it by hand? Ask how they might use a serger to save time and bulk when hemming. (Key Skills: *Problem Solving, Critical Thinking*)

- Topstitch pockets before basting them into position on a garment for easier, neater results. Then simply edge stitch the pockets to the garment.
- Use glue stick or thin strips of fusible web to baste pockets quickly and securely into position on a garment.
- It is easier to apply patch pockets to flat garment sections than to apply after garment sections have been sewn together.

Teaching. . . Hems (pp. 406-408)

Comprehension Check

1. What should you use to finish the raw edge of a heavy fabric which ravels when you are putting up a hem? *(Woven tape.)*
2. What are two hand stitches that can be used to hem a garment? *(Whipstitch, slipstitch.)*
3. What is a quick, easy way to finish the bottom of a garment that will always be tucked into another garment? *(Serge it or zigzag it.)*

Learning Activities

1. **Speaker.** Invite an alterations person from a local department store or a tailor to give your students some tips for making professional-appearing hems. Which hems are sewn by hand? Which by machine? What special guidelines are there for hemming men's dress pants? You might ask specifically about jeans and knits. Allow time for students to ask questions, too. Ask the speaker to discuss the pros and cons of this career as well. (Key Skill: *Communication*)

SUCCESSFUL SERGING

Serge and Hem
Have the students read the feature. Discuss the benefits of using a serger to finish or complete a hem. Have students practice different serger methods for finishing hems such as: serge, turn under and topstitch; a plain serged edge; rolled hem edge.

Machine stitch ½ inch (1.3 cm) from the cut edge. Stitch only through the hem, not the outside of the garment.

If necessary, ease in extra fullness at the hemline so the hem will not be bulky and lumpy. Some fabrics shrink with steam. In this case, shrink the fullness along the hem by steam pressing in the direction of the grain. For fabrics that do not shrink, ease out the fullness by pulling up on the bobbin thread at different points along the stitching to take out fullness. Press with steam to flatten the eased material.

Shrink hem fullness in with steam on fabrics that shrink.

For fabrics that do not shrink with steam, machine baste close to cut edge. Pull up bobbin thread to ease in fullness.

SUCCESSFUL SERGING

Serge and Hem

Use the serger to give a smooth, finished edge to your hem. Simply mark and measure the hem as directed. Serge the hem allowance only to the desired width. Turn the hem under and press. Attach the hem to the garment with hand or machine stitching.

Some hems require only serger stitching. For example, serge off the bottom of a T-shirt or tuck-in shirt for a quick hem.

Check your serger directions for several decorative serger hem ideas.

Completing the Hem

Woven or lace seam tape can be used to finish raw edges of lightweight and mediumweight fabrics. Use woven tape for heavy fabrics that ravel. Pin tape or lace to the outside of the raw edge. Be sure ¼ inch (6 mm) of the seam tape overlaps the edge of the fabric. Machine stitch the tape to the fabric.

Attach the hem to the garment by using a **whipstitch**, a small diagonal handstitch. Using a single strand of thread in the needle, attach the thread to the hem at a seam. Take small, even stitches by catching both the garment and the edge of the tape or lace in each stitch. Pick up only one or two threads of fabric as you sew. The finished hem should have evenly-spaced diagonal stitches over the edge.

More About Hems

Many home sewers who are putting hems up that are not on the bias will, first of all, decide the length they want their skirts to be and then pin the hem up the same length all around without measuring it from the floor. They make adjustments after the hem is all pinned the same length.

Sometimes the raw edge of a hem is simply turned under and machine stitched before hemming. A **slipstitch** is used to attach the hem to the garment. Using a single thread in the needle, attach the thread to a seam at the hem. Slip the needle through the folded clean-finished edge. With the same stitch, catch one or two threads in the outer layer of fabric. Continue the stitches, always slipping the needle through the fold and then into the outer layer of fabric. Slipstitches should be spaced evenly along the hem about ½ inch (1.3 cm) apart. Be careful not to make the stitches too loose or too tight. The slipstitch is an almost invisible stitch when sewn correctly.

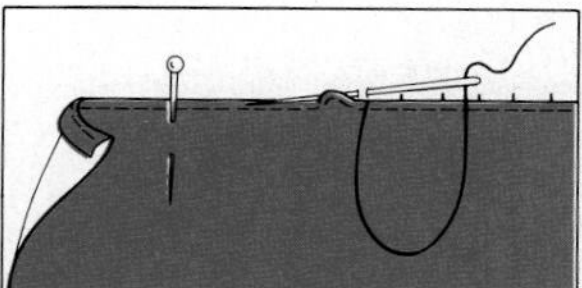
Slipstitch the hem edge to the garment.

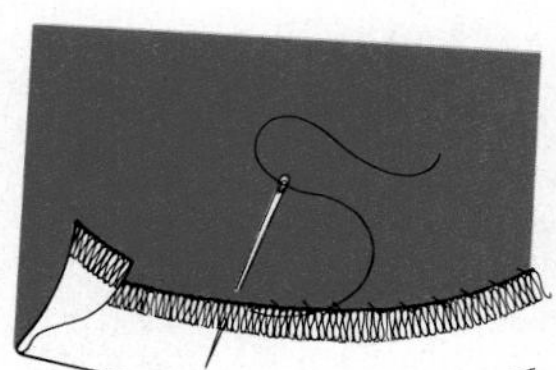
Hem edge finished by serging the fabric edge.

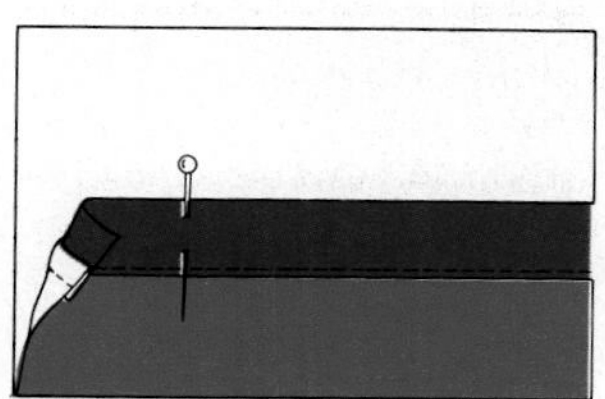
Hem edge finished with woven tape stitched to fabric edge.

Choosing Seam Finishes

Materials
Three 6-inch (15-cm) square scraps of heavyweight, medium-weight, and lightweight fabric

Equipment
sewing machine, serger, pinking shears

Directions:
On each side of each fabric sample, use a different type of seam finish: clean finish, stitched and pinked finish, machine zigzagged finish, serged finish.

- ✔ Which finish would you avoid using on a heavy-weight fabric? Why?
- ✔ Why would just pinking a seam edge be a poor seam finish? For what types of fabrics would you choose a stitched and pinked finish?
- ✔ When would you choose a machine zigzagged finish? Why?
- ✔ When would you use a serged finish? Why?

2. **Demonstration.** Show students how to complete the whipstitch and the slipstitch hems. Discuss the differences between the two types of stitches. (Key Skill: *Following Directions*)
3. **Hem Lab.** Have students complete their hem samples by stitching at least one with the whipstitch and another with the slipstitch. (Key Skill: *Following Directions*)

Follow Up

1. **Reteaching.** Hold up five different fabrics of varying weights, weaves, and knits. Ask students to suggest possible hem finishes for raw edges. What would be a good hem depth for a pair of pants made of this fabric? A full skirt? (Key Skills: *Critical Thinking, Problem Solving*)
2. **Extension.** Use the activity on p. 47 of the *Extending the Lesson* booklet in the TCR.
3. **Enrichment.** Have students with advanced sewing skills complete a hem for a knitted garment using the catch stitch. (Key Skill: *Following Directions*)

Choosing Seam Finishes

Materials: 6-inch squares of fabrics

Equipment: sewing machines, serger, pinking shears

Purpose: To help students learn how to select an appropriate seam or hem finish.

Outcomes:
- Avoid using a clean finish on bulky fabrics.
- Pinking alone will not prevent fabrics from raveling.
- A machine zigzagged or serged finish is a good choice for fabrics that ravel easily.
- A serged finish is an especially good choice for heavy or bulky fabrics and fabrics that ravel easily.

Photo Focus

Direct students to the photo on page 408. Ask students if they are accustomed to seeing males sew. What benefits are there for males learning a few repair techniques? Remind them that famous designers and tailors have usually been men.

Completing the Chapter

For Review

1. Emphasize the main concepts using the summary.
2. Have students complete the "Facts to Recall." (Answers below.)

For Reteaching

1. **Reteaching.** Use the activity on p. 46 of the *Reteaching and Practical Skills* booklet in the TCR.

For Enrichment

1. **Enrichment.** Use the activity on pp. 57-59 of the *Enrichment Activities* booklet in the TCR.

For Evaluation

1. Choose items from "Ideas to Explore" and "Activities to Try."
2. Use the chapter test on pp. 73-74 in the testing booklet of the TCR or use the testmaker software.

Facts to Recall Answers

1. **Any four:** Fit the garment right side out; fit a major construction seams; make adjustments on both sides of a garment; make sure there is enough ease for movement and comfort; watch for seams that do not hang straight, for wrinkles, and for sags.
2. Directional stitching is less likely to stretch the garment.
3. Darts help garments fit more smoothly over curved areas of the body; they are most often used at the waistline and the front underarm seam.
4. Fold the fabric (right sides together) on the center line of the dart and pin on the stitching line; stitch from the wide end to the point, removing the pins as you sew; secure the threads at the point by tying them together; press the dart flat.
5. With backstitching.
6. On woven fabrics for loose fitting garments; on lightweight fabrics that pucker easily.

Knowing how to hem garments is a good skill to have.

TAKING ACTION

Making a Child's Fabric Fastener Book

A new family, the Chans, recently moved into your apartment building. For the past six weeks you have been babysitting for their three-year-old son, Michael, every Thursday evening and Saturday morning. Although Michael knows most of his letters and colors, you have noticed that he has a hard time turning the pages of books and coloring pictures. He also gets very frustrated when it is time to get dressed in the morning or change into his pajamas at night. He can never seem to get his clothes on the right way.

Michael's birthday is next month. You have decided to make him a fabric book that will give him practice with various types of fasteners used on clothing.

Using Your Resourcefulness

- Make a list of the most common types of clothing fasteners you might include in the book. Which are commonly found on clothing for children?
- Which fasteners do you know how to sew? How could you learn others?
- Sketch out your plan for the book page by page. How can you use a story to make playing with the book fun?

TAKING ACTION

Direct students to read the feature. Ask students if they have or have seen books of this nature. Have students brainstorm a list of other types of gift ideas that they might sew themselves. Then have them answer the questions:

Using Your Resourcefulness Answers

- Answers may include: gripper and common snaps, hook and loop tape, zippers, buttons, hooks and eyes, ties — all of which may be found on children's clothing.
- Answers will vary. They can learn from books, teachers, or other sewers.
- Answers will vary.

Chapter 35 Review

Summary

In this chapter, you have read about:
- Fitting a garment as you work on it.
- Making darts.
- Stitching and finishing seams.
- Applying facings and interfacings.
- Sewing gathers, patch pockets, and hems.

Facts to Recall

1. List four tips for fitting a garment.
2. Why should all stitching on a garment be directional?
3. What is the purpose of darts? Where are darts most often used?
4. Briefly explain how to sew a dart.
5. How should the top and bottom ends of a seam be secured?
6. On what fabrics can serged seams be used?
7. Name three seam finishes. Give an example showing when each seam finish could be used.
8. How do you make the outward-curved edges of a collar lie flat?
9. Why is pressing as you go a benefit when sewing your project?
10. Briefly explain how to slipstitch a clean-finished hem to a garment.

Ideas to Explore

1. What are the advantages of having someone help you to measure and pin a hem?
2. How might you trim a patch pocket to make it more attractive?
3. What factors may influence your choice of interfacing? How would you choose interfacing for your fabric?

Activities to Try

1. Choose three seam finishes you think would work with the fabric for your project. Prepare a sample of each finish. Press. Compare the samples. Which appeared to work best? Why?
2. Assume you are a video script writer. You have just been assigned to write a script for a new video series called "Sewing Basics for Beginners." The producer indicated that you may choose one of the following topics for the script: applying interfacing (sew-on and fusible); seam finishes; or sewing darts and seams. The producer wants you to be as creative as possible. Share your script with the class.

LINK TO *Art*

ILLUSTRATING SEWING TECHNIQUES

Draw a colorful illustration for one or more of the following basic sewing techniques: stay-stitching, dart, plain seam, or serged seam. After your drawing is complete, make a fabric sample of the technique showing the correct way to do the technique. Use contrasting fabric and thread so the technique can be easily seen. Display the sample and illustration attractively on poster board.

Facts to Recall Answers (continued)

7. **Any three:** stitched and pinked finish, for fabrics that ravel slightly; zigzagged finish, for fabrics that ravel; overcast finish, if your machine does not zigzag; clean finish, for light and medium weight fabrics; serged finish, for any fabric.
8. By cutting V-shaped notches from the seam allowance on the curving, spacing them so that the curve lies flat.
9. Your work will go faster and be more accurate. It gives your garment a professional look.
10. Use a single thread and attach it to a seam at the hem. Slip the needle through the folded clean-finished edge, and with the same stitch, catch one or two threads in the other layer of fabric. Space the stitches about ½ inch (1.3 cm) apart.

Ideas to Explore

1. Answers may include: measuring and pinning can be done in one fitting; it will probably be more accurate; another person can offer suggestions for length looks.
2. Answers may include: with a band of contrasting fabric across the top; with buttons; with a scalloped upper edge.
3. Answers may include: degree of rigidity; color and sheerness of fabric; purpose of garment.

LINK TO *Art*

Answer

Procedures chosen will vary. Students should follow instructions as indicated in the text.

Preparing to Teach

Chapter Outline

Chapter Resources

The following booklet materials may be found in the *Teacher's Classroom Resources* box:

- Lesson Plans, p. 41
- Student Workbook, *Study Guide,* pp. 153-154; *Recycling to the Rescue,* pp. 155-156
- Sewing and Serging Handbook
- Cooperative Learning, p. 48
- Extending the Text, *How Big Should a Buttonhole Be?,* p. 48
- Reteaching and Practical Skills, *Sewing Skills,* p. 47
- Enrichment Activities, *Assembly-Line Sewing,* pp. 57-59
- Chapter and Unit Tests, pp. 75-76; pp. 121-124
- Testmaker Software

Also see:

- Meeting the Special Needs of Students
- Linking Home, School, and Community

CHAPTER 36

Challenging Sewing Essentials

OBJECTIVES

- *Practice challenging sewing techniques.*
- *Recycle and make basic garment alterations.*

TERMS TO LEARN

- ***lapped zipper***
- ***adjustable zipper foot***
- ***tapestry needle***

More About Sewing Videos

Sewing videos are the newest way to learn a wealth of sewing techniques. They are becoming a popular educational tool for people who sew. These videos have several advantages. First of all, you can view them at your convenience. Second, you can see the entire procedure or technique all the way through. Third, you can review the demonstration again

Now that you have started your sewing adventure, you may be beginning to realize that sewing can be very rewarding (and sometimes challenging). It is a creative way to personalize your clothes. Learning to sew also gives you a skill that you will be able to use throughout your lifetime.

Challenging Techniques

The techniques explained in this chapter will help you to further develop your sewing skills. You will learn how to make a collar, put in a zipper, sew a sleeve, and sew a waistband or elastic casing. Although these skills are still considered basic, you may find them more challenging than those in Chapter 35.

▼ Collars ▼

Collars come in many different shapes and sizes. Most collars have two parts — the *uppercollar* and the *undercollar*. The basic steps for making all collars are similar. Here are the guidelines for making a collar:

1. In general, pin the interfacing to the wrong side of the undercollar. (Check your directions to be sure which side of the collar you are to interface. There are some exceptions to the general rule.) Machine baste the interfacing to the undercollar ½ inch (1.3 cm) from the outer edge. If the collar is pointed, trim the corners off the interfacing before attaching it to the undercollar. If you are using fusible interfacing, trim off the interfacing ½ inch (1.3 cm) on all edges. Follow the manufacturer's directions for fusing.
2. With right sides together, pin the uppercollar and undercollar together.
3. Stitch the collar together on the seam line except at the neck edge. Use a short stitch length. Take one stitch diagonally across each corner of a pointed collar. This makes a neater point when the collar is turned.

Collar — Step 1

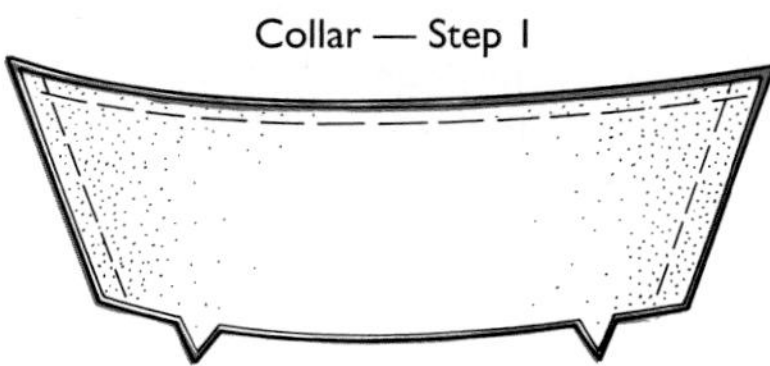

Collar — Step 3

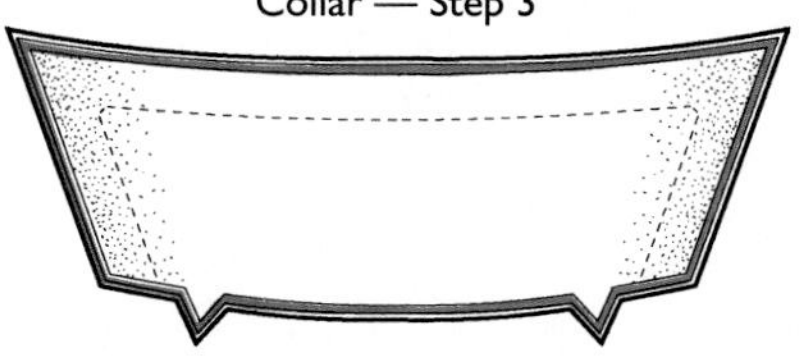

Introducing the Chapter

Motivators

1. **Discussion.** Dress a mannequin in a collarless shirt. Ask students what fashion details they could make (collar, zipper, waistband, sleeves) that would add interest to the shirt. (Key Skill: *Communication*)
2. **Identifying Details.** Have students look through their pattern guides and identify the fashion details they are making in their garments. Does the pattern offer any alternatives for design details? If so, what are they? What suggestions do they have for personalizing their garments? (Key Skill: *Critical Thinking*)

Chapter Objectives and Vocabulary

1. Have students read the chapter objectives and rephrase the objectives as questions.
2. Ask students to state, in their own words, the purpose of studying this chapter.
3. Pronounce the vocabulary terms listed on the previous page. Ask students whether they are familiar with any of these. Explain that the terms will be defined in the chapter.

Guided Reading

1. Have the students read the chapter and use the Study Guide on pp. 153-154 of the *Student Workbook.*

and again or select certain segments of special interest.

Video tapes are produced for beginner, intermediate, and advanced levels. Some topics include: sewing a wardrobe in a weekend; speed sewing tips; couture techniques; pants that fit; industrial shortcuts; special fabrics; serger techniques; and crafts.

There are also a number of regular television programs about garment sewing. You might record them with your VCR and watch and rewatch them at your convenience, saving the episodes you find particularly helpful.

Teaching. . .
Challenging Techniques, Collars, and Lapped Zippers
(pp. 411-413)

Comprehension Check

1. What three things make a collar? *(Upper collar, under collar, interfacing.)*
2. What helps make neat points on collars? *(One diagonal stitch.)*
3. How does a lapped zipper look? *(A single flap of fabric and one row of stitching.)*

Learning Activities

1. **Informal Survey.** Have students look at collars that their classmates are wearing. How many kinds are there? Would the basic directions for applying them work on each kind? (Key Skill: *Critical Thinking*)
2. **Posters.** Ask students to make two collar posters. On one, have students cut out (or draw) examples of different collars (shirt collars, Peter Pan, lace, shawl, square bib-type collars and so forth). On the other poster, ask volunteers to illustrate the steps in making and applying collars. Display the posters so sewers can see them. (Key Skill: *Creativity*)
3. **Demonstration.** Cut out two collar sets. Apply interfacing to the under collar on one and the upper collar on the other. Sew seams, turn, and press. Examine both collars. Which looks best? Students may choose the interfaced upper collar because the seam allowances don't show through as much when collar is pressed. (Key Skill: *Critical Thinking*)

Around the World

After reading the feature ask students to discuss what makes clothes comfortable and practical. Why would this appeal to American women?

4. Grade the seams. Trim the interfacing close to the stitching; trim the undercollar seam allowance to ¼ inch (6 mm); and trim the uppercollar seam allowance to ⅜ inch (1 cm). Trim both seam allowances diagonally across the collar points about ⅛ inch (3 mm) from the stitching line. Clip the seam as needed.
5. On a pointed collar, understitch to within 1 inch (2.5 cm) from each point. On a round collar, understitch all around the seam. Refer to page 402 for information about understitching.
6. Turn the collar right side out and gently push the points out. (Never use a scissors to do this. Use a point turn — a small piece of equipment you can buy at a fabric store.) Press the collar flat, being sure to roll the seam to the undercollar side so it will not show on the finished collar.
7. Baste the notched, raw neck edges together. Attach the collar to the garment as directed.

Collar — Step 4

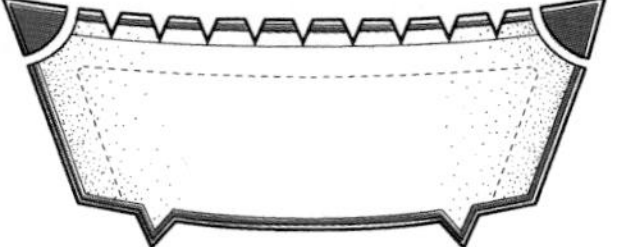

Collar — Step 5

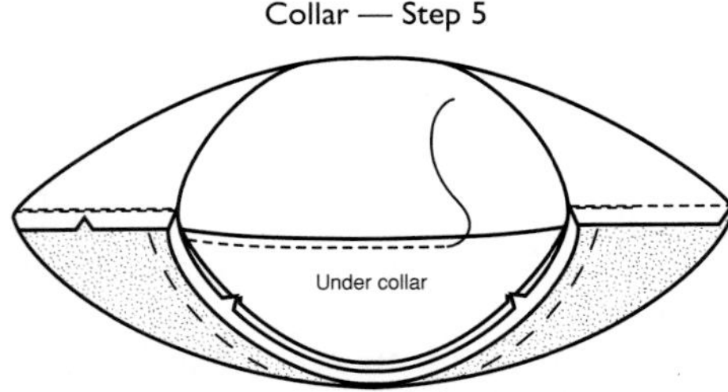

Around the World

For many years, European fashion designers set the trend in women's clothing in the United States. Often, the garments they created were beautiful but difficult to care for and not durable. Now American fashions, noted for comfort and practicality, are becoming very popular in Europe. Many designers believe this is because the lifestyles of the European women who buy these clothes are becoming more like those of American women. Busy with families, careers, and social activities, they need versatile clothes that are easy to care for.

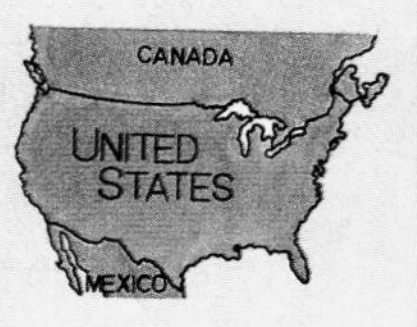

More About *Knit Collars*

Purchased knit collars can add a ready-to-wear look to a garment. Sometimes it is possible to make wrist cuffs to match a knit collar by purchasing a second collar, cutting it in half, and using each half to form a cuff. This is especially effective if the knit collar has a design or contrasting color in it.

▼ Lapped Zippers ▼

With a **lapped zipper**, a single flap of fabric and one row of stitching can be seen on the outside of the garment. This method of putting in a zipper can be used for lightweight or mediumweight fabrics. It totally hides the zipper and looks attractive on back, front, or side openings.

You will be using a **zipper foot**, a presser foot that can be positioned to the left or the right of the needle. This allows stitching to take place on either side of the zipper.

Follow these steps to insert a lapped zipper:

1. With the right sides together, pin the seam that will include the zipper. Make sure the top edges are even. With the wrong side up, place the zipper along the seam allowance. Position the top of the zipper teeth 1 inch (2.5 cm) from the top edge. Measure the length of the zipper opening. Use chalk to mark the bottom location of the zipper teeth on the seam allowance.
2. Using a standard presser foot and regular stitch length, sew the seam from the bottom of the garment up to the mark for the bottom of the zipper opening. Backstitch. Without removing the fabric from the machine, change the stitch length to basting. Continue sewing the seam to the top edge of the garment.
3. Press the seam open.
4. Attach the zipper foot to the machine. Position the foot to the right of the needle.
5. Open the zipper. With the top edge of the garment facing you, place the zipper — right side down — on the right-hand side of the seam allowance. The zipper teeth should be on the seam line. Match the bottom of the zipper teeth with the chalk mark made in Step 1. Pin the zipper in place.
6. Machine baste from the bottom to the top of the zipper, ⅛ inch (3 mm) from the zipper teeth. Stitch only through the zipper tape and seam allowance. Remove the pins as you reach them.
7. Close the zipper and turn it face up. Keep the garment to the left of the needle. Fold the seam allowance back from the zipper and pin in place. Move the zipper foot to the left side of the needle. Stitch through the folded edge of the seam allowance and the zipper tape from the bottom to the top of the zipper. This row of stitching should be close to the zipper teeth.

Zipper — Step 5

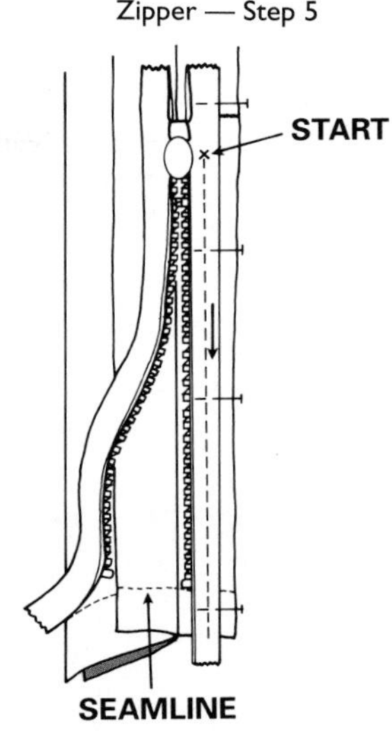

Zipper — Step 7

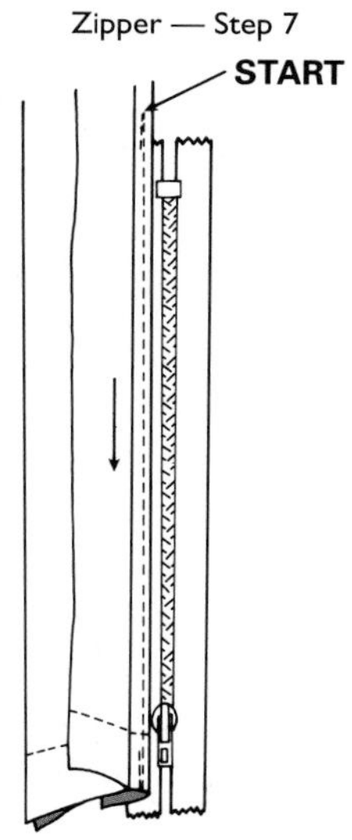

More About Zippers

Center back zippers, especially in close fitting garments, may be irritating to sensitive skin. Here is an easy remedy:

- Cut 1-inch wide grosgrain ribbon 1-inch longer than the zipper coil.
- Clean finish the top and bottom edges of the ribbon.
- Center the ribbon over the back of the zipper, with the top just above the zipper slider.
- Attach the left edge of the ribbon to the seam allowance and facing only, using a hand basting stitch. Tack the bottom of ribbon to the seam allowances.
- Secure the top right corner of the ribbon to the garment with a snap.

Learning Activities (continued)

4. **Poster.** Ask an artistic volunteer to create a poster illustrating the steps for putting in a zipper. Hang the poster in a prominent place so students can refer to it as they sew. (Key Skill: *Creativity*)
5. **Demonstration.** Insert a zipper into the back of a garment using the lapped method. Refer to the poster or the text as you demonstrate so students will associate the illustrations with the demonstration. (Key Skill: *Communication*)
6. **Collar Lab.** Have students complete a sample collar according to the directions in the text. Ask students to team up with a classmate and evaluate each other's collars. (Key Skills: *Following Directions, Critical Thinking*)
7. **Lapped Zipper Lab.** Have students complete a lapped zipper sample according to the direction in the text (or use the handout from the *Sewing and Serging Handbook*). Have each student team up with a classmate to evaluate each other's zipper samples. (Key Skills: *Following Directions, Critical Thinking*)

Follow Up

1. **Reteaching.** Type the directions for sewing collars and lapped zippers on separate sheets of paper. Do not number the steps. Make copies. Cut the direction steps into strips and put the strips into envelopes marked collars and zippers. Prepare a set for each student. Have students unscramble the steps and put them in correct order. The first student to completely unscramble the steps for collars or zippers wins. Offer a free zipper or interfacing for a collar for a prize. (Key Skill: *Following Directions*)
2. **Enrichment.** Ask students to create decorated collars (on paper or fabric) using lace, piping, appliqués, embroidery or double collars. (Key Skill: *Creativity*)

Teaching. . . Set-in Sleeves (pp. 414-415)

Comprehension Check

1. Why is the top of the sleeve larger than the armhole? *(To allow movement.)*
2. What can a sewer do to make the sleeve top fit onto the garment without puckers? *(Run two basting stitches and pull the ends to gather.)*
3. When you sew a sleeve to the garment should the sleeve be on the top or bottom under the presser foot? *(The top so the sewer can prevent puckers.)*
4. What are kimono sleeves? *(The sleeves are cut out as part of the garment.)*

Learning Activities

1. **Demonstration.** On a garment or small-scale sample, demonstrate the steps in setting in a sleeve. (Key Skill: *Communication*)
2. **Sleeve Lab.** Have students complete a set-in sleeve sample (either on a garment or small-scale sample) according to the directions in the text. (Key Skill: *Following Directions*)
3. **Comparison.** Show the difference between a sleeve that is gathered and one that is not. Show why a basting stitch is useful even on a sleeve that is not gathered. Try to insert it without a basting stitch and then with a basting stitch. (Key Skill: *Communication*)
4. **Clothing for Others.** For this project, students would make simple infant or small children's garments and ship them to an organization (such as the *Peace Corps*) that distributes them in underdeveloped countries. Students would use their sewing skills to construct garments such as a flannel kimono. Flannel is an ideal fabric for beginners as pieces cling. Students could do as much of the work in this project as you wish. You will need to: 1) contact a world relief, government, or mission organization to find an outlet for the project; 2) gather fabric, sewing supplies, and shipping funds. Encourage students to buy flannel themselves. A local service organization

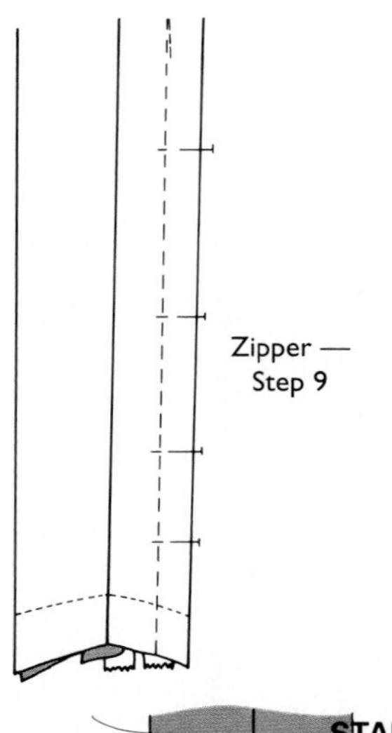

Zipper — Step 9

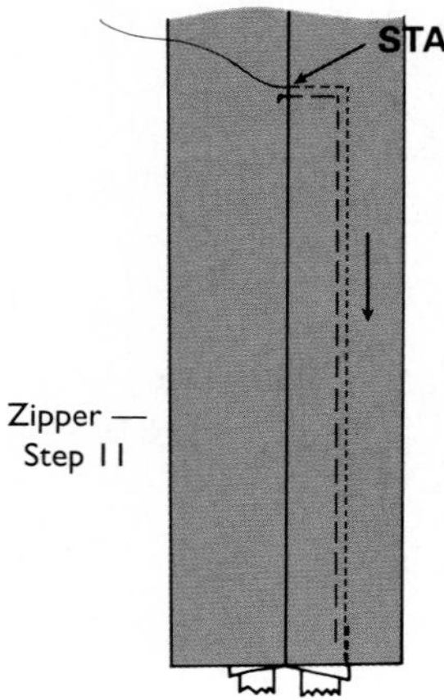

Zipper — Step 11

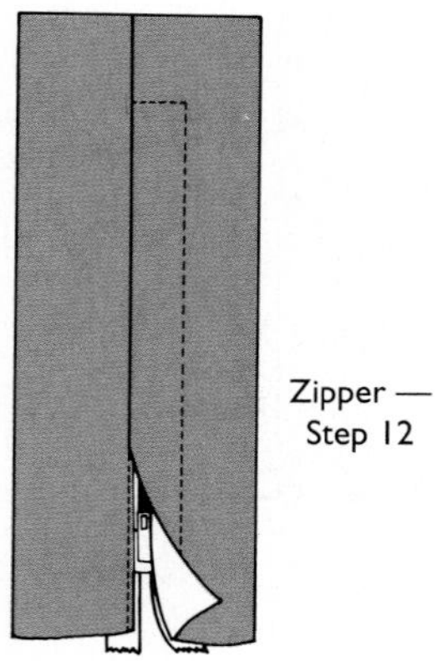

Zipper — Step 12

8. Fold the zipper over so the right side is flat against the other seam allowance. Turn the garment to the right. A tuck should form at the bottom of the zipper. Pin the zipper tape to the seam allowance only.
9. Machine baste the zipper to the seam allowance from the bottom to the top of the zipper. Stitch ⅛ inch (3 mm) from the zipper teeth.
10. Remove the garment from the machine and turn it right side out. Press lightly over the zipper area. Hand baste across the bottom of the zipper and up the side of the zipper, ⅜ inch (1 cm) from the seam.
11. Move the zipper foot to the right side of the needle, and begin stitching at the bottom of the zipper. Sew along the basting across the bottom of the zipper, stitching out from the seam ½ inch (1.3 cm). To pivot the corner: stop with the needle in the fabric; lift the presser foot and turn the fabric so the top edge of the garment is facing you; lower the presser foot. Continue stitching along the basting, ½ inch (1.3 cm) from the seam, to the top of the garment. Backstitch ¼ inch (6 mm) at the top of the zipper to secure the stitching.
12. Pull the upper thread at the bottom of the zipper to the wrong side of the garment by using a hand sewing needle. Tie the upper and bobbin threads together and clip the threads close to the garment. Remove all basting stitches. Press.

▼ Set-In Sleeves ▼

Set-in sleeves are sewn into the armholes of the garment after the side seams have been sewn. The top of the sleeve is larger than the armhole to allow room for movement. Although it may seem difficult to ease in the extra fullness, it helps to make the garment comfortable to wear. Here are the guidelines for sewing a set-in sleeve:

1. With the right side facing up, machine baste around the top of the sleeve on the seam line between the notches. Do not clip off the thread ends. Sew a second row of basting stitches ¼ inch (6 mm) from the first, inside the seam allowance.
2. To avoid making two sleeves to fit the same armhole, put both sleeves on a table with the right sides facing up. With right sides together, pin the underarm seam on each sleeve. Stitch the underarm seams. Finish the seam edges. Press the underarm seams open.

More About *Sleeves*

When you select patterns, check the descriptive caption on the back of the pattern envelope. Some types of sleeves will look better on you than others and can help solve some fitting problems without extensive adjustments.

Many set-in sleeves are joined either to extended or dropped shoulder seams which fall beyond the natural shoulders. The entire shoulder and sleeve cap area is higher and wider than on traditional set-in sleeves, often in order to make room for shoulder pads. The armhole seam also fits lower at the underarm than on traditional set-in sleeves.

Extended shoulders fall ⅞ inch to 1½ inches past your natural shoulders. Dropped shoulders

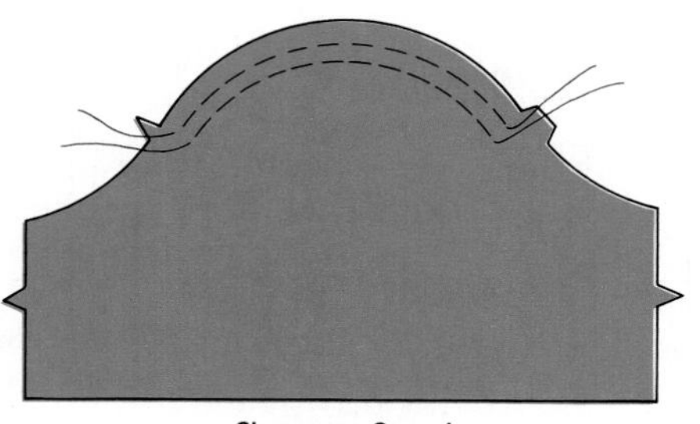

Sleeve — Step 1

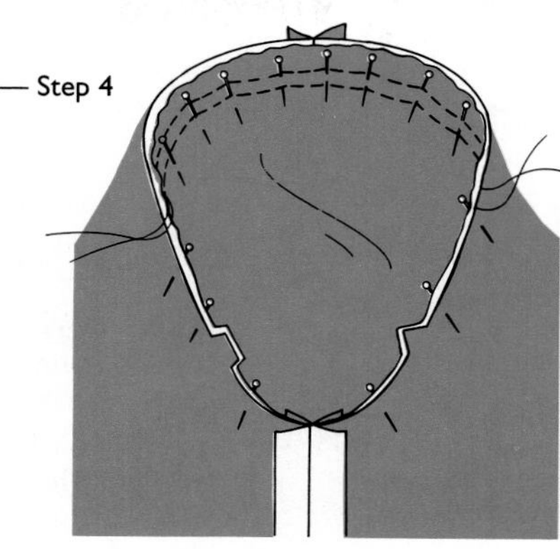

Sleeve — Step 4

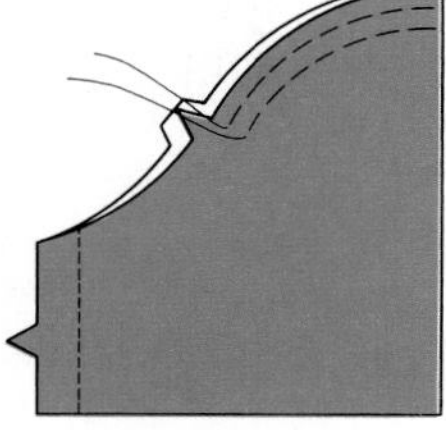

Sleeve — Step 2

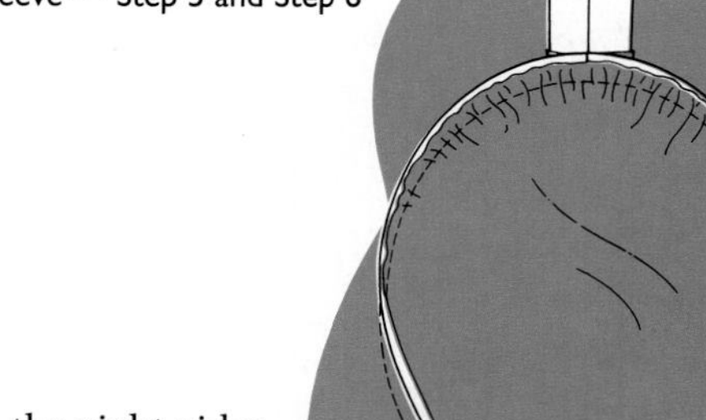

Sleeve — Step 5 and Step 6

3. Match each sleeve to the garment with the right sides together. Pin each sleeve on the garment at the underarm seams, shoulder seams, notches, and markings. Insert pins on the seam line to hold the seam securely. Use the following directions to finish pinning and sewing each sleeve.
4. Pull the bobbin thread ends, starting at each notch and ease the fabric toward the top until the sleeve fits the armhole. Secure threads around a pin in a figure eight. Distribute fullness evenly. Place pins ½ inch (1.3 cm) apart along the seam line. Keep the raw edges even. The sleeve should fit smoothly without puckers.
5. Machine stitch on the inside with the sleeve side facing up to be sure no puckers are caught in the seam. Begin and end the stitching at the underarm seam, backstitching to secure the seam. Then make a second row of stitching between the notches along the underarm area. Sew ⅛ inch (3 mm) from the first row of stitching, inside the seam allowance. This stitching gives extra strength to the area of strain.
6. Trim the seam between the notches at the underarm to ¼ inch (6 mm). Zigzag the seam allowances together to finish the seam. Press the armhole seam toward the sleeve.

SUCCESSFUL SERGING

Finishing the Armhole

After sewing the armhole seam on your conventional sewing machine, serge the seams together ⅛ inch (3 mm) away from the seam line. This provides a neat finish and saves time too!

Learning Activities (continued)

might donate shipping funds or fabric. To get positive publicity, tell the local newspaper or television station about your project. Talk to other teachers about coordinating the project with a unit in social studies. Be sure to have a specific project and outlet before you tell students. (Key Skills: *Cooperation, Social Studies*)

Follow Up

1. **Reteaching.** Measure the stitching line on the sleeve and then on the front and back sleeve openings. How do they compare? *(Sleeve will be longer.)* What does this mean? *(Excess must be eased in.)* (Key Skill: *Problem Solving*)
2. **Enrichment.** Ask students to look at the markings on their sleeve patterns. How do the markings for the front and back differ? *(One notch on front; two on back.)* Have students describe how these notches would be useful in matching plaids. (Key Skill: *Problem Solving*)

fall 1⅝ inches or more beyond your natural shoulders.

Such generously sized set-in sleeves broaden the top of the garment minimizing waist and hips for a trimmer head-to-toe appearance.

More About "Fake" Gathering

For easing the fullness of a sleeve cap without using two basting threads you may find this method helpful. Hold your left index finger behind the presser foot as you sew a regular stitch on the sleeve cap just inside the seam line. The fabric will not actually be gathered, but it will scrunch together enough to have that effect.

SUCCESSFUL SERGING

Finishing the Armhole

After reading the feature, have students practice finishing the armhole on their sleeve sample with the serger or use this method to finish the sleeves on their projects.

Teaching. . .
Kimono Sleeves and Attached Waistbands
(pp. 416-417)

Comprehension Check

1. Why are kimono sleeves the easiest to make? *(Because they are cut and sewn as part of the garment front and back.)*
2. Why should you interface a waistband? *(To prevent stretching.)*
3. Which side of the waistband should be pressed under? *(Unnotched.)*
4. Why is one end of the waistband longer than the skirt opening? *(To provide overlap room for the button.)*
5. How does the waistband line up with the zipper? *(Top edge of waistband is even with folded edge of zipper.)*

Learning Activities

1. **List.** Ask the class to list which styles of skirts and pants work best with set-in, elastic, or drawstring waistbands. Why? Write the list on the board. (Key Skill: *Critical Thinking*)
2. **Demonstration.** On a garment or small-scale sampler, show students how to complete the steps for an attached waistband. Where possible, have several students assist in the demonstration. Students might apply interfacing, assist with pinning, or assist with pressing. (Key Skill: *Following Directions*)

SUCCESSFUL SERGING

Sewing Kimono Sleeves
After reading the feature, have students make a sample of a kimono sleeve using a small-scale pattern. Ask them to end the seam by threading the chain of thread through a tapestry needle and pulling it through the looper threads.

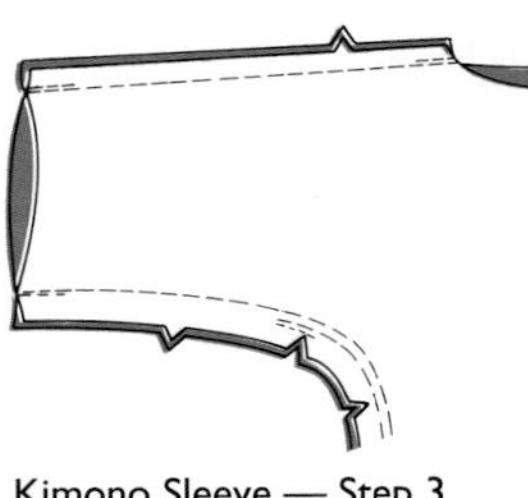

Kimono Sleeve — Step 3

▼ Kimono Sleeves ▼

Kimono sleeves are the easiest sleeve for a beginning sewer to make. They are cut as part of the of the garment front and back with a shoulder seam and underarm seam. Here are the guidelines for sewing a kimono sleeve:

1. With right sides together, pin the shoulder seam. Stitch on the seam line, backstitching at both ends of the seam. Press the seam open.
2. With right sides together, pin the underarm seam. Stitch the underarm seam on the seam line. Stitch again at the underarm curve, ¼ inch (6 mm) from the seam line.
3. Clip the underarm curve of the seam and press the seam open except at the underarm curve.

SUCCESSFUL SERGING

Sewing Kimono Sleeves

The seams for kimono sleeves can be sewn on the serger. This saves time in two ways. It eliminates the need for trimming and finishing the seams. The serger does this all in one step.

Because a serger does not backstitch, you will need a way to secure the seam ends. Using a **tapestry** (TAP-uh-stree) needle — a needle with a large eye and a blunt point — thread the chain of serger stitches through the needle eye and pull it under the looper threads of the seam about 1 inch (2.5 cm). Trim off any excess chain.

▼ Attached Waistbands ▼

Attached waistbands are usually interfaced to prevent stretching. Cut the interfacing the same length as the waistband and half of its width. Follow these steps for attaching a waistband:

1. With wrong sides of the fabric together, fold the waistband in half lengthwise matching the raw edges evenly. Press along the fold. This will mark the lengthwise fold.
2. Pin the interfacing to the wrong side of the waistband along the notched edge. The inside edge of the interfacing will be on the lengthwise fold.
3. Machine baste the interfacing to the waistband ½ inch (1.3 cm) from the notched edge. Stitch through the interfacing and one layer of fabric. Begin and end stitching ½ inch (1.3 cm) from each end of the band. Machine baste the remaining edges of the interfacing to the band ½ inch (1.3 cm) from the cut edge of the interfacing. Trim the interfacing to the stitching line. Refer to page 401 for instructions on using fusible interfacing.
4. Press the seam allowance on the unnotched edge to the wrong side along the seam line.
5. Pin the waistband to the garment, with the right sides together. Match the notches and ease the garment to the waistband between the markings. One end of the waistband will be longer than the other to give an underlap when the waistband is fastened. Check your pattern guide sheet to make sure the extension is on the correct side of the opening.

More About *Waistbands*

If you need some camouflage over the abdomen, choose a pattern with released pleats or tucks at the waist. Slight gathers for gentle fit also look attractive, and a waistband on the narrow side looks and feels better. Avoid darts, contoured midriffs, and wide waistbands unless you can afford to accent and reveal your shape through the middle.

If the waistband is fitted, baste it before the sewing is completed to evaluate the fit. Slip your thumb inside the waistband. There should be enough ease (about 1 inch) for comfort. If the waistband is wide, it may curl if you are a little full around the middle. You may decide to make the waistband narrower for a better fit.

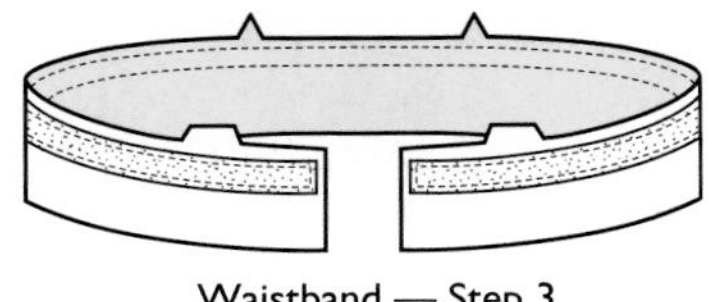

Waistband — Step 3

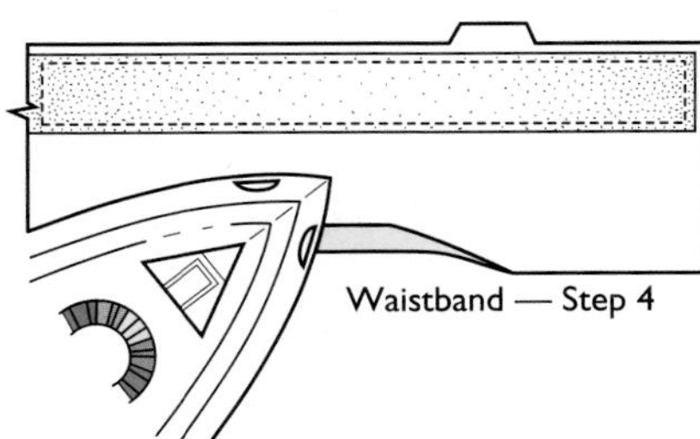

Waistband — Step 4

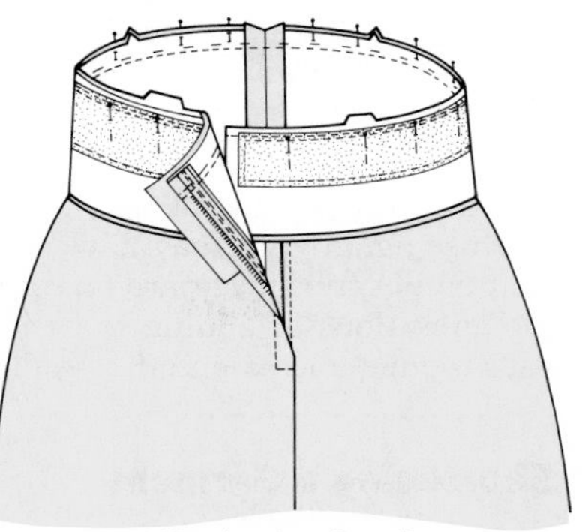

Waistband — Step 5

6. Stitch on the seam line from one end of the waistband to the other. Backstitch on both ends. Grade the seam. Trim the waistband seam allowance to ¼ inch (6 mm) and the garment seam allowance to ⅜ inch (1 cm). Press the seam flat and then up toward the waistband.
7. Fold the waistband in half lengthwise with right sides together. Pin and stitch the seam at each end of the waistband. The stitching will be even with the folded edge of the zipper on the overlap. The underlap will be longer. Trim the seams to ¼ inch (6 mm). Trim the corners diagonally being careful not to cut the stitching.
8. Turn the waistband right side out. Check to be sure the corners are square. Press along the fold line.
9. Pin the unnotched folded edge of the waistband to the seam allowance on the inside of the garment. Slipstitch the folded edge to the waistline seam.

SUCCESSFUL SERGING

Finishing a Waistband

Instead of pressing under the unnotched side of a waistband to finish it, try a serged finish. Simply serge off the seam allowance on the unnotched edge. This provides a smooth finish and takes more bulk out of the waistband seam.

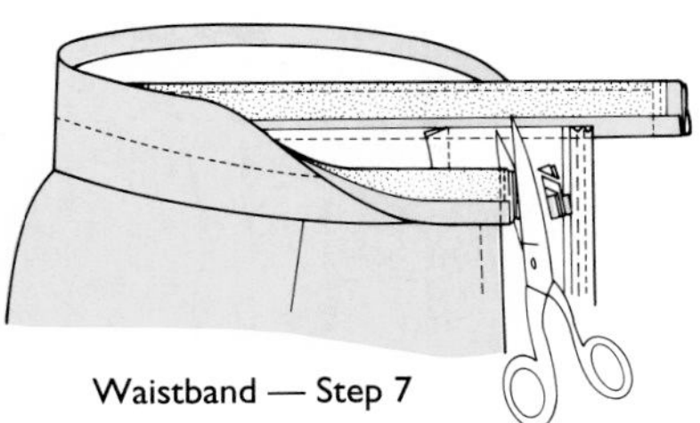

Waistband — Step 7

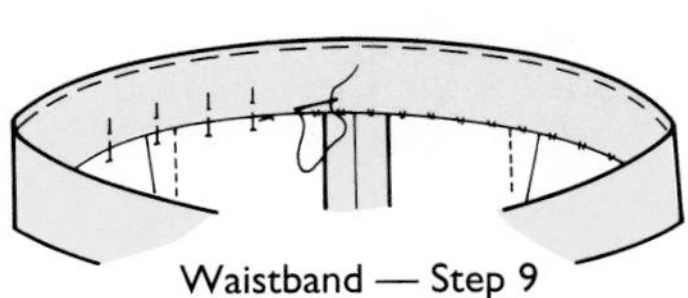

Waistband — Step 9

More About *Finishing Waistbands*

To avoid hand stitching and to give a finished look to a waistband, attach the waistband *first* to the wrong side of the garment. Then finish the ends, turn and pin the folded edge to the front, covering the first row of stitching. Top stitch the waistband to the front.

Learning Activities (continued)

3. **Hands-On Activity.** If students are not making a major garment, but you want to give them practice attaching a waistband, consider having them make "carpenter" aprons which, while not gathered, can have an attached waistband. If reversible fabric is used, the apron could simply be made from a rectangle, with the bottom hemmed, folded up and stitched vertically at intervals to form pockets, hemmed at the sides, and attached to a waistband which is long enough to tie around the waist. (Key Skill: *Creativity*)

Follow Up

1. **Reteaching.** Charity wants to make a black skirt with a few unpressed pleats in the front. What kind of waistband should she use? Why? (Key Skill: *Problem Solving*)
2. **Enrichment.** Hannah is making a pair of slacks. When she measured the waistband pattern she discovered that it was too snug. If she adds 1½ inches to the waistband, what should she do to the pants? What should she do if she is making pleated pants? (Key Skill: *Problem Solving*)

SUCCESSFUL SERGING

Finishing a Waistband

After reading the feature, have students complete a waistband sample. Ask students to prepare one waistband sample with a serged finish on the unnotched side and another sample finished with the traditional clean finish. Have students compare the two methods.

Teaching. . .
Alter and Recycle Clothing
(pp. 418-419)

Comprehension Check

1. What is the first step in shortening a garment? *(Removing the old hem stitching — not turning it up.)*
2. How can you hide the old hem line when lengthening a garment? *(Decorative trim or contrasting fabric.)*
3. What can you do if the new hem allowance is too narrow? *(Sew wide hem facing tape to the hem edge.)*
4. How can you make a garment a little bit larger in width? *(Sew new, shallower seams.)*

Learning Activities

1. **Discussion.** Ask students how many of them recycle aluminum soft drink cans. How about bottles, plastic, and newspaper? Now ask them if they routinely recycle clothing. What are some ways that clothing can be recycled? *(Hand-me-downs, rummage sales, use old clothes for rags, cut them up for quilts or rugs)* (Key Skill: *Critical Thinking*)
2. **Demonstration.** Show the class how to shorten the hem on a garment made of fairly bulky fabric. First, fold up the existing hem and stitch a few inches. Then shorten it the right way. Have students identify which method is better and why. (Key Skills: *Communication, Problem Solving*)
3. **Recycled Quilt.** Ask each student to bring in one mostly-cotton garment that is stained, worn, or no longer in style. Have students cut as many 6-inch squares on the straight grain as they can (have a template available to trace). Have students volunteer to sew squares together during free time at school, study halls, after school, or at home (or ask parents to help). Sew squares until you have enought for a twin or full-sized bed quilt. Obtain quilt batting and a sheet, sew it, turn it, and have students tie it. Donate

How to . . .
Alter and Recycle Clothing

Recycling means to change something into an item you can use again. You may have some garments in your closet that do not fit right or are out of style. By making some simple alterations or adding some trim, you can prevent waste, save money, and extend the usefulness of a garment.

Shortening a Garment

1. Remove the old hem stitching, and press out the crease.
2. Put on the garment and have someone mark the bottom of the hem.
3. Turn the hem to the inside along the new hemline. Pin the hem in place, matching the seams.
4. Baste the hem close to the folded edge. Try the garment on once more to make sure the hem length is correct.
5. Measure and mark the desired hem depth. Trim off the extra fabric.
6. Finish the raw edge of the hem.
7. Pin the top of the hem to the garment.
8. Machine or hand stitch the hem to the garment. Remove the basting. Press.

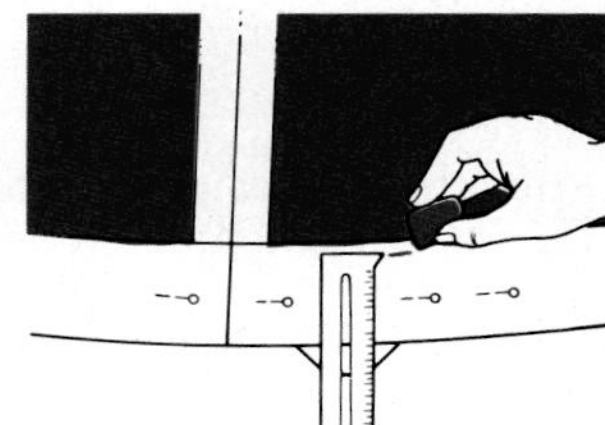

Lengthening a Garment

Follow the same steps for lengthening as you did for shortening hems. Creases from old hemlines may not always press out. A decorative trim or band of contrasting fabric may help cover the old hemline.

If the new hem allowance is too narrow, sew wide hem facing tape to the hem edge to create a new hem allowance.

Turn the hem facing tape to the inside and press. Hand or machine stitch the hem facing tape to the garment.

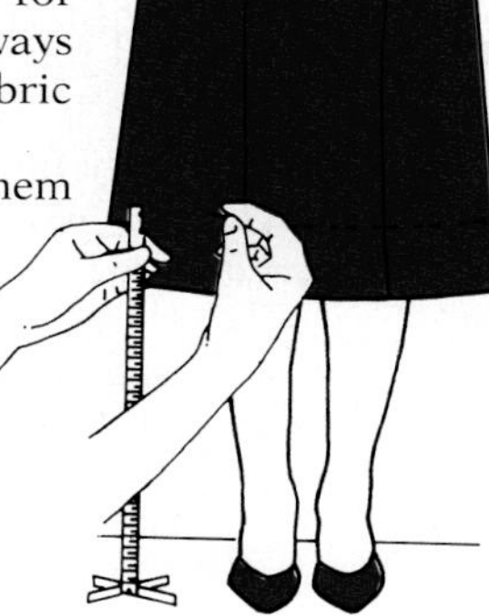

How to ... Alter and Recycle Clothing

Direct students to read the feature. Ask students to bring a garment that needs altering to class and spend a class period helping them make the alteration. Or, ask volunteers from all your classes to bring outgrown garments for an all-school rummage sale with proceeds for a class or community project. Make any necessary repairs before having the rummage sale.

Adjusting Width

Small width adjustments can be made at the side seams of a garment. Here are some guidelines for adjusting width.

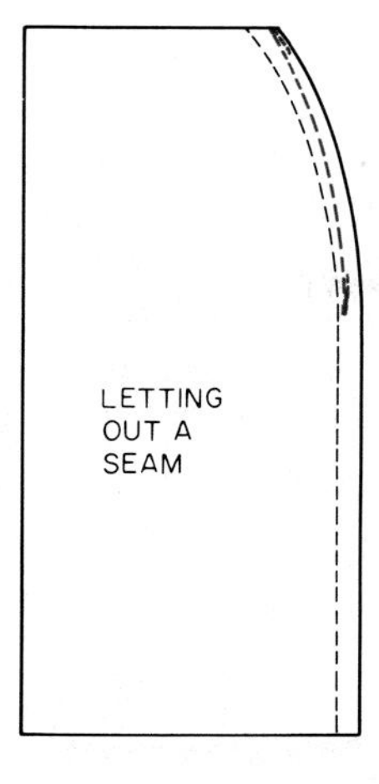

- **Making a garment larger.** Check the seam allowances to be sure there is enough fabric for new seams. Remove the old stitching in the seam section to which the width will be added. Try the garment on inside out and have someone pin the new seams. Machine baste the seams. Try the garment on to check fit. Stitch the new seams with a regular stitch length, carefully tapering the stitching into the old seam line. Backstitch at each end of the seam. Remove the basting. Press the seam open.
- **Making a garment smaller.** Put the garment on inside out and have someone pin the new seams on each side of the garment. Machine baste along the pin line, removing the pins as you stitch. Try the garment on to check fit. Stitch the new seams using a regular machine stitch, carefully tapering the new stitching into the old seam. Remove the basting stitches and old seam line. Press the seams open.

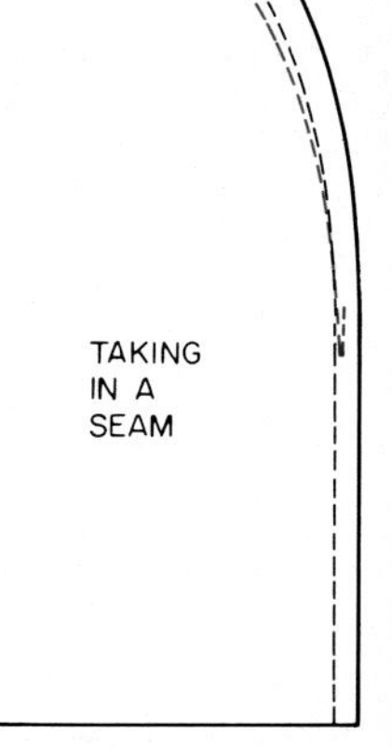

More Tips for Recycling Clothing

- Pass a garment on to another family member.
- Have a clothing swap with your friends.
- Sell used clothing at a garage sale, bazaar, flea market, or secondhand store.
- Recycle fabric from clothing that can no longer be worn. Make accessories, clothing for children, or craft projects. What accessories could you make from an old pair of jeans?

More About Hems

When lengthening or shortening a garment it is not always necessary to have someone repin the hem. First of all, check in the mirror or with a friend to see if the existing hem hangs straight when you have it on. If it does then you can be pretty sure that it will be all right if you just measure the new hem accurately from the old one. If it does not hang straight then you can indicate on the garment before you take out the old hem just where you think adjustments might be necessary and make them as you pin the new hem. Try the garment on before you rehem it to be sure your alterations are correct.

it to a local shelter or relief agency. The newspaper might be interested in your project, too. (Key Skills: *Cooperation, Creativity*)

4. **On-the-Job Recycling.** To emphasize the importance of recycling clothing, ask your students to volunteer to work at various jobs at a local used clothing depot for an hour or two during the quarter. Again, tell the school and local newspapers. Have students write a one-page paper concerning what they have learned from this experience. (Key Skills: *Communication, Social Studies*)

Follow Up

1. **Reteaching.** Have students explain, in their own words, how to shorten a garment. (Key Skill: *Communication*)
2. **Enrichment.** Ask students to check waistbands in garments at several stores. Did they find any skirts or pants without waistbands? If so, how were they finished? (Key Skill: *Communication*)

Family Perspective

It's spring and all three Blair children have grown since last year. Four-year-old Tara's little pants are an inch too short. Eleven-year old Marty's jeans are two inches short. Fifteen-year-old Lisa's favorite striped skirt (which she made last summer) is also too short. Unfortunately, Mr. Blair was laid off from his job, and money for new clothes is short, too. They have enough money from a garage sale to buy one good pair of pants. What options do the Blairs have? *(Lengthen Tara's pants and use decorative trims to cover the old hemline or just add ribbon and lace to make the pants longer. Cut off Marty's jeans and use them for shorts and buy him a new pair — or a used pair at a garage sale. Lengthen Lisa's skirt with leftover or contrasting fabric. Or, buy Lisa fabric for a new skirt if Marty can find recycled or cheap jeans.)*

Learning. . .
Elastic Waistbands and Drawstring Waistbands
(pp. 420-421)

Comprehension Check

1. What are the advantages of elastic waistbands? *(They are comfortable, allow movement, make a garment able to fit more sizes, can accommodate some weight gain or loss)*
2. What are the advantages of drawstring waistbands? *(They are adjustable and give garment size flexibility as well as a snug fit.)*

Learning Activities

1. **Discussion.** Ask the class whether a drawstring or elastic closure would be best in the following situations: casual skirt; dress pants; sweat pants; laundry bag; jewelry pouch. What reasons can they give to support their choices? Have them draw general conclusions about when to use drawstrings and when to use elastic. (Key Skills: *Critical Thinking, Communication*)
2. **Discussion.** Tell your students this story and ask for their help: Max wears his gray sweat pants at least once a week because they're so comfortable. The drawstring finally frayed to pieces and Max must repair the waist so the pants will stay on! He asked his mom if she had a piece of cording he could use. Max's mom suggested he replace the cording with elastic. What might Max and his mom need to take into consideration when they decide whether to use cording or elastic? How will they put in new cording or elastic? Are the procedures similar or different? (Key Skills: *Communication, Problem Solving*)

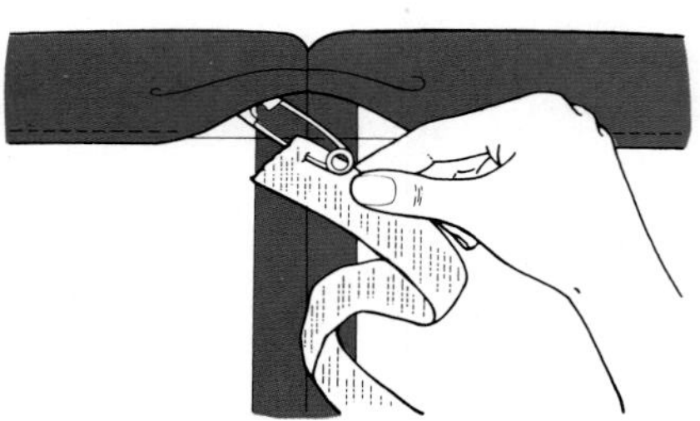
Elastic Waistband — Step 5

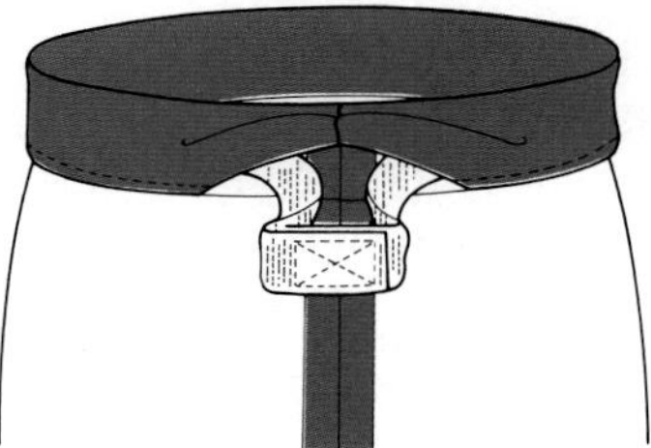
Elastic Waistband — Step 6

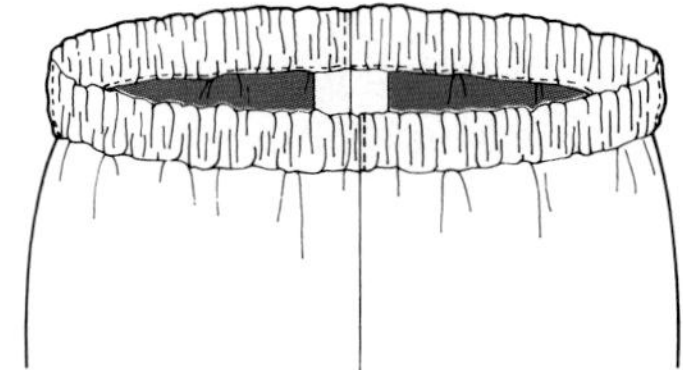
Elastic Waistband — Step 8

Elastic Waistbands

The elastic waistband is popular in both pants and skirts because it allows movement and is comfortable. The directions given here are for making a casing that is 1 inch (2.5 cm) wide, which will enclose ¾ inch (2 cm) wide elastic.

1. Use a zigzag stitch (or serge) around the top edge of the garment if the raw edges need to be finished.
2. Fold the waistline edge of the garment over 1¼ inches (3.2 cm), matching the wrong sides together to form a casing. Press the folded edge.
3. Stitch a seam 1 inch (2.5 cm) from the folded edge of the casing. Begin stitching at the center back or side seam. Leave a 1½ inch (3.8 cm) opening to insert elastic. Backstitch at each end of the seam.
4. Cut a piece of elastic to fit snugly around your waist. Remember, it must be able to slide over your hips. Add 2 inches (5 cm) to overlap and stitch the elastic together.
5. Put a safety pin in one end of the elastic. Insert the pin and elastic into the opening in the casing. Pull the pin and elastic through the casing, using the pin to guide the elastic. Hold onto the loose end of the elastic.
6. Overlap the elastic ends 1 inch (2.5 cm). Machine stitch the overlap securely in a square pattern.
7. Stitch the opening of the casing closed. Backstitch at each end of the opening.

More About Elastic

There are many varieties of elastic available, including specialty elastics for swimwear and lingerie. The proper width of elastic is generally listed on the pattern envelope and on the pattern guide. In general, the elastic should be ⅛ inch (3 mm) narrower than the casing so that it can be easily run through the casing. The elastic might twist inside the casing if the elastic is too narrow for the casing.

Many patterns include a special pattern piece for cutting the right length of elastic identified in the pattern guide. If the pattern or pattern guide does not give directions for elastic length, measure your body at the casing position and add 1 inch (2.5 cm) to overlap and secure the elastic ends.

8. Adjust the fabric evenly around the elastic waistband. Stitch through the casing and elastic at all seam lines, backstitching to secure all stitching. This will prevent the elastic from twisting in the casing.

Casings can be used at sleeve edges, necklines, and hemlines, as well as waistlines. The elastic makes the garment adjustable. It also helps to control fullness. Casings are much easier to make than attached waistbands or cuffs. You will find casings used in many beginner and easy-to-sew patterns.

▼ Drawstring Waistbands ▼

Drawstring closures are popular on many types of sport clothes. Drawstring openings that are in the seam are made as you sew the seam. Here are the guidelines for a drawstring casing:

1. At the seam where the drawstring is to be pulled through to the outside, stitch 1¼ inches (3.2 cm) of the seam starting at the top of the garment. Backstitch at both ends.
2. Leave a ¾ inch (2 cm) opening in the seam below the 1¼ inch (3.2 cm) stitched seam. Complete the seam below the ¾ (2 cm) opening. Backstitch at both ends of the seam.
3. Fold ¼ inch (6 mm) of the top edge of the garment to the inside. Press.
4. Fold the top edge of the garment over 1 inch (2.5 cm) to the inside, forming a casing. Press along the fold line. Stitch close to the lower edge of the casing. Backstitch at the beginning and end of the stitching.
5. Put a safety pin in one end of the drawstring. On the outside, insert the pinned drawstring through the casing opening and pull the drawstring through the opening. (Be sure to hold on to the loose end of the drawstring so it will not be pulled through). Tie a knot in each end of the drawstring. Distribute the fullness evenly.

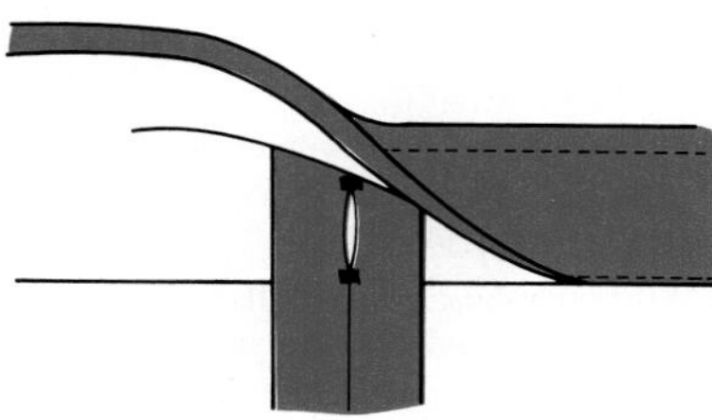

Drawstring Waistband — Step 2

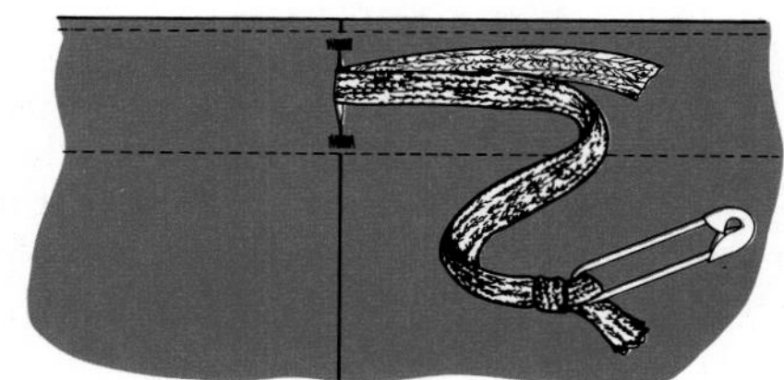

Drawstring Waistband — Step 5

More About
Personalizing Garments

One way to personalize your garments is with woven professional labels available by mail-order through various companies. A variety of styles, colors, and motifs are available. Labels are also a good way to identify camp and school clothing.

Follow Up

1. **Reteaching.** Have students describe the differences between elastic waistbands and drawstring waistbands. (Key Skill: *Communication*)
2. **Extension.** Use the activity on p. 48 of the *Extending the Lesson* booklet in the TCR.
3. **Enrichment.** Have students work with a partner to create illustrated annotations for either elastic waistbands or drawstring waistbands. (Key Skills: *Communication, Creativity*)

In Touch with Technology

To make an elastic casing for sleeves and waistlines on a serger, use a 3-thread overlock stitch and oval elastic ⅛ inch (3 mm) in diameter. Place the elastic between the serger knife and the needle (use a guide on a serger foot if you have one) and overlock stitch the elastic onto the seam allowance at the seam line. The serger threads form a casing over the elastic. Do not stretch the elastic as you sew. When you reach the place where the ends of the elastic meet, pull the beginning end of the elastic out of the thread casing. Hold it out of the way while you stitch off the seam and cut the elastic (bringing the elastic ends close together). Pull both elastic ends and draw up the elastic to the desired fit. Trim away excess elastic. Overlap elastic ends and stitch securely.

Photo Focus

Ask your students to look at the photo on page p. 422. What ways (besides finishing a new garment) can sewing boost self-esteem and a sense of accomplishment? *(Being able to hem and alter ready-to-wear or old garments for themselves; being able to recycle their garments to fit someone else — thereby saving money and resources.)*

Completing the Chapter

For Review

1. Emphasize the main concepts using the summary.
2. Have students complete the "Facts to Recall." (Answers below.)

For Reteaching

1. **Reteaching.** Use the activity on p. 47 of the *Reteaching and Practical Skills* booklet in the TCR.

For Enrichment

1. **Enrichment.** Use the activity on pp. 57-59 of the *Enrichment Activities* booklet in the TCR.

For Evaluation

1. Choose items from "Ideas to Explore" and "Activities to Try."
2. Use the chapter test on pp. 75-76 in the testing booklet of the TCR or use the testmaker software.
3. Use the unit test on pp. 121-124 in the testing booklet of the TCR or use the testmaker software.

Chapter 36 Review

Facts to Recall Answers

1. The interfacing is first pinned to the wrong side of the undercollar, then machine basted to the undercollar ½ inch (1.3 cm) from the outer edge. The interfacing corners are trimmed before it is attached to a pointed collar. Fusible interfacing is trimmed ½ inch (1.3 cm) on all edges and fused according to manufacturer's directions.
2. Roll the seam to the undercollar side as you press the collar.
3. You begin using a basting stitch at the point you have marked for the bottom of the zipper opening. The basting stitches hold the seam while you attach the zipper. You will replace them with regular stitches when you sew in the zipper.

Successfully finishing a sewing project builds your self-esteem and gives you a sense of accomplishment.

TAKING ACTION

Identifying Simple Sewing Projects

Mrs. Carlisle asks you to help her teach beginners in an adult education sewing class. The class includes people of all ages who are learning to sew for the first time.

Mrs. Carlisle has asked you to come up with an idea for a simple yet appealing project. What sewing project (other than an item of clothing) would appeal to people of various ages? The project should include one or more basic sewing techniques. You will be assisting with a small group of the students after Mrs. Carlisle gives some basic instructions. Remember to keep your own skill level in mind in choosing a project.

Using Your Resourcefulness

- Brainstorm a list of possible nonclothing sewing projects suitable for beginners. What skills will be needed to complete these projects?
- What interests and needs should you consider in selecting a project?
- What resources could you use to find out more about the interests and needs of people of different ages?
- What other qualities or skills in addition to sewing skills would make your efforts in Mrs. Carlisle's class a success?

TAKING ACTION

Direct students to read the feature. List possible project ideas on the board and discuss the questions in the feature in small groups.

Using Your Resourcefulness Answers

- Answers may include: plain or patchwork pillows and quilts or other easy craft ideas. Skills may include straight and zigzag seams.
- Gear projects to adult items or gift ideas which are inexpensive or use recycled garments or fabric.
- Answers may include: take a survey or hold a discussion about their interests.
- Answers may include: friendliness, communication skills, organization, time management.

Chapter 36 Review

Summary

In this chapter, you have read about:

- ▶ Using a zipper foot to attach lapped zippers to garments.
- ▶ Sewing set-in sleeves and kimono sleeves.
- ▶ Making attached, elastic, and drawstring waistbands.
- ▶ Recycling and updating your clothes.

Facts to Recall

1. Describe how interfacing is attached to a collar.
2. How do you keep the seam from showing on a finished collar?
3. When first sewing a seam that will include a lapped zipper, at what point do you change from a regular to a basting stitch and why?
4. Explain how set-in sleeves are attached and fitted to a garment before they are stitched in place.
5. How do you insert the elastic into the casing when making an elastic waistband?
6. Name three benefits of recycling clothing.
7. If you are lengthening a garment and find that the new hem allowance is too narrow, what can you do to make it wider?

Ideas to Explore

1. On what types of garments might kimono sleeves be more suitable than set-in sleeves?
2. What garments do you own that could be updated or recycled for another use? How would you do this?
3. How will accurately performing the sewing techniques discussed in this chapter increase your self-esteem?
4. Give three examples of ways the sewing techniques discussed in this chapter could be used in making clothing for people with special needs (such as someone in a wheelchair, someone with a broken arm, a teen with juvenile arthritis, etc.).

Activities to Try

1. If your project does not include a casing with elastic, make a sample casing to fit your wrist out of some scrap fabric. Practice putting in the elastic and securing it to fit your wrist.
2. Draw a cartoon to illustrate a variety of ways to recycle clothing or the fabric used in clothing.
3. Locate drawings or photographs of different collar shapes using a pattern catalog or sewing book. Trace and cut out at least six collars. Using an illustration of a person wearing a shirt, try the different collars around the neck. Which collars look best? What reasons can you give for some collars looking better than others? Write a brief summary of your findings.

LINK TO *Art*

SEWING TECHNIQUES AND CLOTHING DESIGN

Fashion designers use the principles of design to create unique and attractive clothing. Look in fashion magazines, catalogues, and newspapers to find examples of the following advanced construction techniques that creatively use the principles of design: collars, zipper closings, set-in sleeves, kimono sleeves, elastic waistbands, and drawstring waistbands.

Arrange an attractive display (such as on a bulletin board) that illustrates how these techniques create interest in clothing design. Create an appealing caption.

Facts to Recall Answers (continued)

4. The finished sleeves are matched to the garment with right sides together. Sleeves and garment are pinned together at the underarm seam, the shoulder seam, the notches and markings. The fabric is then eased toward the top of the armhole by pulling the bobbin thread ends until a smooth fit without puckers is attained. Fullness is evenly distributed, and the sleeve is pinned for stitching.
5. Put a safety pin in one end of the elastic and insert it into the casing opening. Use the safety pin as a guide as you pull both pin and elastic through the casing. Hold on to the opposite end of the elastic.
6. It prevents waste, saves money, and extends a garment's usefulness.
7. By sewing wide hem facing tape to the hem edge, creating a new hem allowance.

Ideas to Explore

1. Answers will vary.
2. Answers will vary.
3. Answers will vary.
4. Answers will vary.

LINK TO *Art*

Ask students to read the feature and complete the activity. Displays will vary.

Career Connections

Volunteer Options

- Community recycling center for used clothing.
- Salvation Army volunteer.
- Goodwill volunteer.
- Making clothing repairs at any of the above.
- Clothing resource person at a women's/children's shelter.
- Sewing clothing for any of the above organizations.
- Teaching clothing repair and care through an outreach program.
- Operating a secondhand clothing store at school.

Volunteer Organizations

Goodwill Industries of America
9200 Wisconsin Avenue
Bethesda, MD 20814

Salvation Army
615 Slaters Lane
P.O. Box 269
Alexandria, VA 22313

CAREER *Connections*

Get Ready for Your Future Through Volunteering

Meredith

"When I think about it, I've been working with clothing in some way since I was in fifth grade. My mom couldn't afford to buy the clothes that I wanted, but she gladly bought patterns and fabric and taught me how to sew. Now I use these skills in my volunteer work at the *Community Clothes Closet*.

"I started working at the *Community Clothes Closet* for my FHA volunteer project. We take in donated clothing and sell it at a minimal charge to people who can't afford new clothing prices. Several days each month are *free* days, when people can come and take the

"Some of my responsibilities are sorting through incoming clothing, looking for anything that needs minor repairs, and making the repairs before the clothing is offered for sale. This is a practical way to put my skills to use.

"I know that I'd like to have a clothing-related career in the future. The choices in this field are many, but I am seriously considering learning how to restore antique clothing and design clothing for people with disabilities. Whatever type of job I decide on, I feel confident that I will succeed, because I will be doing something that I love."

Nicholas

"My wife and I used to tease each other about working together one day, but I didn't take the idea seriously until Maureen came up with a brainstorm. She'd worked for a children's wear designer for several years and wanted to branch out on her own. She did some informal market research, which seemed to show that children's athletic clothing was a fast-growing market. I'd had some marketing and manufacturing experience. Maureen's idea seemed solid.

"We started small, working out of our home. Maureen had a few friends help out part-time making samples. I made contacts for supplies, sales, and kept our books. Maureen uses a computer program (CAD, for computer-aided design) to help develop her ideas and get them quickly on paper.

Discussing Career Connections

Have students read the *Career Connections* feature. Ask students:

- What characteristics or qualities should be present in both volunteer jobs and career jobs in clothing-related fields?
- How might volunteering benefit you in your future career?
- What opportunities for being an entrepreneur in the clothing field do you see as possibilities?

"Now after several years, we sell to stores around the country. We lease part of a small factory and have 25 full-time employees. The business has grown, and we've grown personally in these last few years."

"My official title is sales associate; however, some people call me a salesperson. This job involves so much more than showing customers to the size they need or ringing up a sale. Customers sometimes need help selecting an outfit for a special occasion, or they want to know the latest trend in colors. It's very rewarding to know you have helped someone find an outfit that enhances their best features and makes them feel good about their appearance.

"My experience here will also be valuable if I want to explore other careers in the fashion industry. For example, the information I'm learning about trend cycles and people's likes and dislikes in clothing will help me if I decide to become a merchandise buyer. Developing my ability to communicate with customers could lead to a job in public relations. My current job offers a lot of training, not only for my career but also for life."

MAKING THE CONNECTION

- In what ways does Meredith seem to have high self-esteem? How does Meredith's volunteer work contribute to her self-esteem? How will it help her succeed at work?
- In what other ways does Meredith benefit from her volunteer work?
- How can working as a volunteer be a benefit to a future entrepreneur?
- In what ways can you use the clothing skills that you have as a volunteer?

Occupational Outlook

Listed below are some possible clothing-related occupations. Some require little training while others require a 4-year degree.

- Sewing machine operator
- Fabric dyer
- Knitting machine operator
- Patternmaker
- Fashion designer
- Sheep shearer
- Stock clerk
- Fashion model
- Fashion writer
- Assistant clothing buyer
- Merchandise manager
- Dressmaker
- Milliner
- Garment inspector
- Fabric designer
- Fashion video producer
- Costume designer
- Dry-cleaning business manager
- Presser-dry-cleaning or garment industry
- Jeweler
- Sewing Instructor
- Fashion Photographer
- Apparel salesperson
- Dermatologist
- Chemist

Clothing-Related Organizations

American Apparel Manufacturers Association, Inc.
2500 Wilson Blvd.
Suite 301
Arlington, VA 22209

American Textile Manufacturers Institute, Inc.
1801 K Street N. W.
Suite 900
Washington, DC 20006

National Association of Schools of Art and Design
11250 Roger Bacon Dr.
Suite 21
Reston, VA 22090

Making the Connection

Answers

- Answers include: care and interest in people, willingness to serve others, an interest in making life happier for others. Helping others boosts her self-esteem. Volunteering provides Meredith with a number of skills useful in several clothing jobs.
- Answers include: developing friendships, developing work skills.
- Working as a volunteer can expose you to a variety of job skills and needs. Knowing what people need is a benefit to an entrepreneur.
- Answers will vary.

Planning the Unit

Ch. 37: Staying Healthy — Examines ways to promote health and wellness through good health habits, avoiding harmful substances, and understanding safety and healthcare concerns.

Ch. 38: Nutrients and Their Functions — Identifies the types, roles, and deficiencies of nutrients, digestion, and energy needs.

Ch. 39: Guidelines for Healthful Eating — Discusses the *Dietary Guidelines* and the *Food Guide Pyramid.*

Ch. 40: Managing Your Weight — Addresses ways to safely maintain a healthy weight and the characteristics and hazards of fad diets.

Ch. 41: Facts for Food Choices — Examines food choices, recognizing accurate information, how needs affect nutrition, and eating disorders.

Ch. 42: Planning Meals and Snacks — Discusses meal planning and ways to plan simple, nutritious, and appealing meals.

Ch. 43: Buying and Storing Food — Addresses factors affecting food prices, planning and shopping, and proper food storage.

Ch. 44: Kitchen Equipment — Describes basic types and uses of utensils and cookware and guidelines for selecting, using, and caring for appliances.

Ch. 45: Recipes and Measuring — Explains how to select and interpret recipes, measure ingredients, and alter the yield of a recipe.

Ch. 46: Preparation Terms and Techniques — Addresses cooking terms and methods, microwave safety, and nutrient conservation.

Ch. 47: Working in the Kitchen — Discusses safety and sanitation practices, working in foods lab, organizing workspace, and conserving kitchen resources.

Ch. 48: Milk and Milk Products — Examines the dietary role of dairy foods and how to buy, store and prepare dairy foods.

Ch. 49: Fruits and Vegetables — Explains the role of fruits and vegetables in the diet along with how to buy, store, and prepare fruits and vegetables.

Ch. 50: Protein Foods — Identifies the role of protein foods in the diet and how to buy, store, and prepare protein foods.

UNIT 6 Foods

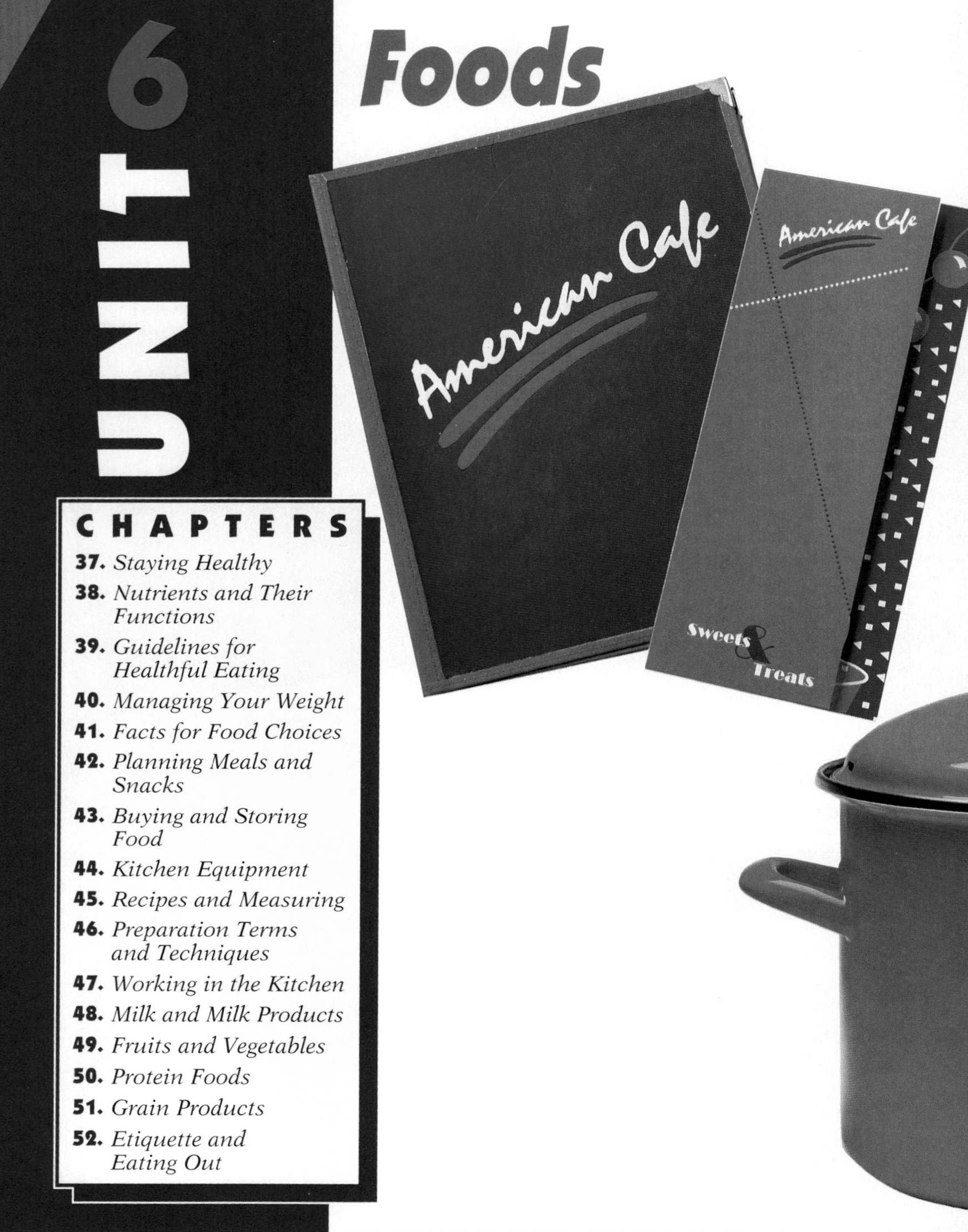

CHAPTERS

Cooperative Learning Tips

The most active part of cooperative learning for the teacher is *monitoring*. While moving around the classroom, the teacher monitors the teams at work building team relationships and developing social skills, in addition to providing feedback for the teams and answering questions. Using a clip board to make notes of overheard praises, shared ideas, and observations helps the teacher later during group processing and evaluation. As students observe the teacher monitoring the teams, they visibly attend to task better, use the desired skills, and collaborate more.

See the *Cooperative Learning* booklet in the TCR for more information.

Planning the Unit (continued)

Ch. 51: Grain Products — Explains the role of grains in the diet along with how to buy, store, and prepare grain products.

Ch. 52: Etiquette and Eating Out — Discusses setting a table, methods for serving food, and behavior guidelines while eating at home or in a restaurant.

Introducing the Unit

Unit 6 Overview

Unit 6 introduces students to wellness, nutrition, and food preparation. Students will explore factors affecting food choices, how to plan meals, shop for food, store food, keep food safe, and prepare food properly.

Motivators

1. **Brainstorming.** Write the word "wellness" on the chalkboard. Have students brainstorm a list of factors that affect wellness. Discuss ways in which nutrition and exercise, food choices, and food preparation affect wellness. (Key Skill: *Critical Thinking*)
2. **Taste Test.** Have students taste a variety of nutritious, but often unfamiliar foods. Use this activity as a springboard to introduce the concepts of nutrition and food choices. (Key Skill: *Communication*)

Completing the Unit

Review

1. **Food Mobiles.** Have each student select a nutrient and make a mobile explaining the importance of the nutrient, food sources, and benefits to the body. (Key Skills: *Critical Thinking, Creativity*)

Evaluation

1. **Unit Test.** Have students complete the unit test on pp. 125-128 of the *Chapter and Unit Tests* booklet in the TCR.
2. **Testmaker Software.** Use the *Testmaker* software program to design your own unit test.

Implementing Cooperative Learning

An excellent cooperative method for review is called *Send a Problem*. When using this method, cooperative team members act out the role of the teacher as they develop a problem or question and send it to another team. The problem may be broken into four parts (one for each team member). Each part should be written on an index card. When the cards are sent to another team, the answers are written on separate answer cards and shared upon the request of the originating team or the classroom teacher. The problems continue to move around the room from team to team until time is called.

See the *Cooperative Learning* booklet in the TCR for more information.

Preparing to Teach

Chapter Outline

Chapter Resources

The following booklet materials may be found in the *Teacher's Classroom Resources* box:
- Lesson Plans, p. 42
- Student Workbook, *Study Guide,* pp. 157-158; *Wellness Survey,* p. 159; *Managing Stress Effectively,* p. 160
- Color Transparencies, *Wellness,* CT-40
- Personal Safety, *Dealing with Emergency Situations,* pp. 37-38
- Technology and Computers, pp. 42, 44, 47
- Cooperative Learning, p. 49
- Extending the Text, *Wellness Today ...For Health Tomorrow,* p. 49
- Reteaching and Practical Skills, *Puzzling Over Health and Wellness,* p. 48
- Enrichment Activities, *Exercise for Peak Performance,* p. 60
- Chapter and Unit Tests, pp. 77-78
- Testmaker Software

Also see:
- Meeting the Special Needs of Students
- Linking Home, School, and Community
- Dealing with Sensitive Issues

ABCNews InterActive™ Videodiscs
- *Tobacco*
- *Drugs and Substance Abuse*
- *Alcohol*
- *Food and Nutrition*
- *Violence Prevention*

See the ABCNews InterActive™ Bar Code Correlation booklet for applicable segments.

CHAPTER 37 Staying Healthy

OBJECTIVES

- *Describe ways to promote physical, mental, emotional, and social health.*
- *Explain the dangers of tobacco, alcohol, and other drugs and how to avoid them.*
- *Identify safety and family health care concerns.*

TERMS TO LEARN

- ***health***
- ***wellness***
- ***aerobic exercise***
- ***immunizations***

More About *Wellness and Stress*

There is a direct relationship between wellness and stress, as the following facts indicate:
- 80% of all illness is related to stress or not being able to manage stress.
- People who can't handle stress spend billions of dollars every year for drugs, alcohol, tobacco, and/or other illnesses.
- Stress-related problems can stem from poor relationships, work-related issues, and/or family dysfunction.

How would you define good health? Some people might answer "Not being sick" or "Being in good physical shape." There is more to it than that, however.

Health refers to the total state of your well-being. It includes:

- Physical health — the condition of your body.
- Mental and emotional health — as reflected in your thoughts, attitudes, and feelings.
- Social health — as reflected in your relationships with others.

Physical, mental, emotional, and social health are interrelated. All are affected by your day-to-day actions and decisions. For instance, one night Gary didn't get very much sleep. The next day he felt grouchy and irritable. He didn't do as well on the math test or run as fast at track practice as he could have. He even snapped at his best friend Roger, who avoided him the rest of the afternoon. How would you rate Gary's overall health that day?

Sharing time with and getting support from friends is essential for wellness. In what ways do you get support from others?

Some Signs of Good Health

Physical
- Having enough energy for all your daily activities
- Looking and feeling your best

Mental and Emotional
- Feeling good about yourself
- Expressing your emotions in a mature way
- Being able to handle problems and manage stress

Social
- Getting along with others
- Giving and getting support when needed

Wellness

Fortunately, you can do something about your health. **Wellness** is a way of living based on healthful attitudes and actions. It means taking an active role in improving and maintaining your health.

Introducing the Chapter

Motivators

1. **Discussion.** Ask students what it means to be emotionally healthy. (Key Skill: *Communication*)
2. **Recall.** Ask students if they can remember immunization shots they received as children. Have them tell about the experience. (Key Skill: *Communication*)
3. **Visual "aid."** Display pictures of current Olympic athletes. Ask students to consider what they must do to stay healthy and fit. (Key Skill: *Critical Thinking*)

Chapter Objectives and Vocabulary

1. Have students read the chapter objectives and rephrase the objectives as questions.
2. Ask students to state, in their own words, the purpose of studying this chapter.
3. Pronounce the vocabulary terms listed on the previous page. Ask students whether they are familiar with any of these. Explain that the terms will be defined in the chapter.

Guided Reading

1. Have students read the chapter and use the Study Guide on pp. 157-158 of the *Student Workbook*.

More About *Handling Stress*

A sound and sensible prescription for handling stress includes the following:
- Learn how to accept what you cannot change.
- Learn how to change what you can.
- Know the difference between the two.

Teaching. . .
Wellness and Good Habits for Physical Health
(pp. 429-431)

Comprehension Check

1. Why is it important to make sound, healthy choices? (*Healthy choices will make your life happier.)*
2. What does a daily exercise program do for your body? *(It helps your body work effectively and adds firmness and tone to your muscles.)*
3. A total exercise program will benefit your body in four different areas. Name them. *(Heart and lung area, muscular endurance, muscular strength, and flexibility.)*
4. Name some examples of good aerobic exercises. *(Jumping rope, swimming, running, bicycling, and walking.)*
5. Name some guidelines for planning an exercise program. *(Include aerobic exercise three to five times a week, include a strength-building session two times a week, and perform stretching exercises several times a week.)*

Learning Activities

1. **Group Activity.** Use class time to take students on a brisk walk two or three times around the school building. (Key Skill: *Cooperation*)
2. **Community Resource**. Ask students to visit health care facilities in their community to see what services are offered for their age group (i.e., babysitting courses, AIDS information seminars). (Key Skills: *Communication, Decision Making*)
3. **Questionnaire.** Have students develop a questionnaire on health and wellness. Questions should apply to their age group. (Key Skill: *Communication*)

Choosing healthful foods helps you maintain your physical health.

Practicing wellness can have a positive effect on your life right now. It can help you look, feel, and perform your best. In addition, the choices you make today will influence the quality of your life in the future. Taking care of your health can help you reach your future goals.

Good Habits for Physical Health

Your body is the only one you will ever have. How well do you take care of it? Everyday habits such as eating, exercising, and sleep influence your physical health.

▼ Eating Right ▼

The food choices you make have a direct effect on your health. Every section of your body — skin, hair, teeth, nails, and blood — was once food! Your body uses food for energy, for growth, and to keep all its systems working properly.

Experts advise eating a variety of foods including lots of grains, fruits, and vegetables. In later chapters, you will learn more about making wise food choices.

▼ Exercise ▼

A regular exercise program helps to keep you physically fit. Exercise helps your body work more efficiently and adds firmness and tone to your muscles. It can also help you get rid of tension, sleep better, and feel more alert and energetic.

You need a variety of activities to benefit your body in different ways. A total exercise program works on all four of these elements:

- ***Heart and lungs.*** Your heart, lungs, and blood vessels deliver oxygen to your body tissues. You can train them to work more efficiently with regular aerobic exercise. **Aerobic exercise** (uh-ROE-bik) is any vigorous activity that causes your heart to beat faster for a sustained amount of time. Jumping rope, running, cycling, swimming, and walking are good aerobic exercises.
- ***Muscular endurance.*** This is the ability of your muscles to work for a long time without stopping. Most aerobic activities also improve muscular endurance.

More About Physical Health

You probably know that your physical health can affect your thoughts and feelings. Conversely, your thoughts and feelings can affect your physical health. The mind and body are connected in ways scientists are just beginning to understand. Emotional, mental, and social health are important parts of a healthy person.

- ***Muscular strength.*** Strength is what enables your muscles to push or pull with force. Having strong muscles can also improve posture and help prevent injury. Strengthening exercises work specific muscles of the body. For example, sit-ups strengthen the stomach muscles.
- ***Flexibility.*** This means the ability to move easily. You should be able to move muscles and joints through their normal range of motion without pain or stiffness. Slow, gentle stretching exercises help improve flexibility.

Getting regular exercise helps keep you physically fit. What activities do you participate in that benefit your heart and lungs, muscular endurance, muscular strength, and your flexibility?

An Exercise Program for You

In order to get the most benefit from exercise, you should make it a regular habit. Remember to include all four elements of fitness in your program. However, you don't have to work on all four every day. Here are some guidelines for planning your exercise program.

- Include aerobic exercise three to five times a week. Each session should consist of at least 20 minutes of brisk, nonstop activity.
- Include a strength-building session two times a week. Be sure to work all the major muscle groups: chest, stomach, back, legs, and arms. Allowing at least 48 hours between strength workouts lets the muscles rest and build new tissue.
- Perform stretching exercises several times a week. You might do them before and after your workouts or before going to bed.

Learning Activities (continued)

4. **Interview.** In order to determine the health habits of their peers, have each student interview three classmates using the questionnaire on health and wellness. (Key Skill: *Communication*)
5. **Program Design.** Have each student plan a daily, fifteen-minute, self-exercise program for one week. At the end of the week, survey the class to see if they notice any difference in the way they feel. Are they in favor of or against physical exercise? (Key Skill: *Management*)

Follow Up

1. **Reteaching.** Have students review a vitamin-and-nutrient chart to see which vitamins and nutrients aid in the maintenance of healthy skin, hair, teeth, nails, and blood. (Key Skill: *Decision Making*)
2. **Enrichment.** Have students plan a school-wide athletic event. Select students from each grade level to represent their class. The event can include such events as a tug-of-war, relay races, sack races, and/or any others the students can come up with. Have your students keep track of the results to see which grade level wins the competition. (Key Skills: *Cooperation, Creativity*)

Wellness

Engage your class in a discussion about healthy eating habits during pregnancy. Discuss how healthy eating habits impact the development of the fetus. Turn the discussion to drugs and alcohol and explain the effects of continued alcohol and/or drug use during a pregnancy and how their use might affect the fetus. Have students find magazine or newspaper articles on the subjects of Fetal Alcohol Syndrome and Crack Babies.

More About Exercise

Regular exercise is a critical factor in building and maintaining strong bones. Spending too much time in front of the television instead of being involved in some kind of physical activity puts young people at risk of poor bone development.

Teaching. . . Sleep and Rest, Other Health Habits, and Mental, Emotional, and Social Health (pp. 432-433)

Comprehension Check

1. Why is sleep important for good health? *(Sleep is important for good health because while you sleep, your body repairs itself, removes waste products from cells, and builds a supply of energy for the next day's activities.)*
2. What does "preventive health maintenance" mean? *(Taking healthy steps now to avoid major health problems later on in life.)*
3. Why is it important to practice good posture? *(It improves your appearance; it allows you to stand, sit and move without becoming tired; and it allows your internal organs, bones, and muscles to function better.)*
4. Besides eating right, exercising, and getting enough sleep, what are some other ways to manage stress? *(Other ways to manage stress include setting aside time for enjoyable activities, spending a few minutes each day just relaxing, trying not to get upset over little things, looking on the bright side of things, and finding someone to talk to when a problem arises.)*

Learning Activities

1. **Student Poll.** Survey each student in the class to see what time he or she goes to bed on school nights and what time he or she awakens each morning to get ready for school. Have each student calculate the average number of hours he or she

SAFETY CHECK✔

Have students read the safety check. Then, have them analyze their own workout programs to see if they are doing them safely. If they aren't, have students list what they could do to make their workouts safer.

SAFETY CHECK✔

To keep your workouts safe:

- Find out how to perform each exercise or activity correctly. Ask an instructor to show you, or read a reliable exercise guide.
- Drink plenty of water before, during, and after vigorous exercise.
- Begin each exercise session with a warm-up period. A warm-up prepares your body for the activity to come and helps prevent injury. You might march in place for a few minutes to warm your muscles, then do some stretching exercises. Finally, begin a "light and easy" version of the activity you are preparing for. After about ten minutes, you should be ready to exercise at your normal pace.
- End each exercise session with a cool-down period. Otherwise, you may feel lightheaded and muscles may cramp or tighten up. Gradually reduce the level of your activity to let your body slow down. Then stretch again to help prevent soreness.
- Don't overdo. If you feel any dizziness, nausea, or sharp pain while exercising, stop. If you feel exhausted after a workout, have trouble sleeping, or are not making progress in your exercise program, you may be trying to do too much.

It's easier to stick with an exercise program if you select activities that you enjoy. To keep from getting bored, vary your activities from time to time.

Lack of time or money should not keep you from exercising. Running, walking, and jumping rope are inexpensive and can be done almost anytime.

Think of ways to change your lifestyle to include exercise. You might walk or ride a bike to school instead of taking a car or bus. Plan social activities that include exercise, such as basketball, roller skating, or bowling. Exercise with a friend or participate in an organized team sport. Make exercise a lifelong habit and you will reap the rewards for many years.

▼ Sleep and Rest ▼

Sleep is important for good health. While you sleep, your body repairs itself, removes waste products from cells, and builds a supply of energy for the next day's activities.

You may think that you can do more if you sleep less. Actually, when you don't get enough sleep, it becomes harder to concentrate. It takes you longer to get things done.

Most people need seven to nine hours of sleep a night. Teens often need more because of rapid growth. If you have trouble getting up in the morning or feel tired during the day, try going to bed earlier. It may make a big difference in the way you feel.

Adequate sleep and rest play an important role in wellness. Is the amount of sleep you get each night adequate?

More About *Hygiene*

Two common culprits of bad breath are garlic and onion. Particles from foods can become lodged between teeth and cause bad breath because they start to ferment or rot. Because the mouth is dark, warm, and moist, it provides the perfect environment for odor-causing bacteria to thrive, particularly at night when there is little movement. Regular brushing and flossing is essential because they both reduce the mouth's bacterial population. The tongue, which harvests millions of bacteria, should be brushed as well.

▼ Other Health Habits ▼

There are many other ways to promote your physical health. Most of these are a matter of "preventive maintenance" — taking simple steps now to avoid big problems later on. Here are some examples.

- Use adequate lighting for reading and other activities. Rest your eyes periodically by looking away from close work.
- Use a sunscreen to protect your skin.
- Protect your hearing by avoiding loud sounds. Turn down the volume when listening to the radio, stereo, or television.
- Make hygiene a habit. Follow the suggestions for good grooming in Chapter 27.
- Practice good posture. It will improve your appearance and allow you to stand, sit, or move without getting tired. Your organs, bones, and muscles will develop and function better.

Good posture improves your appearance and helps your body function better.

Mental, Emotional, and Social Health

Many of the skills discussed in other units of this book can help you improve your mental, emotional, and social well-being. For example, having a positive attitude can help you face challenges. Communicating and resolving conflicts can help you build strong relationships.

Learning how to manage stress is essential for a balanced, healthful life. As you learned in Chapter 4, you cannot avoid stress. You can, however, learn to deal with stress before it causes physical and emotional problems. Following the healthful habits already mentioned — such as eating right, exercising, and getting enough sleep — will help. Keep in mind these other ways to manage stress:

- Set aside time for the activities you enjoy and the people you enjoy being with.
- Spend a few minutes each day just relaxing.
- Try not to get upset over little things.
- Look on the bright side. Don't lose your sense of humor.
- When you have a problem, find someone to talk to. You might try going to a close friend, a family member, a member of the clergy, or a community counseling center.

Talking about a problem with someone you trust is a healthful way to cope.

Learning Activities (continued)

sleeps on a school night. (Key Skill: *Math*)

2. **Consumer Awareness.** Bring to class a variety of numbered sunscreens. Have students read the labels to see the level of protection each sunscreen provides. (Key Skill: *Communication*)
3. **Listening Activity.** Teach students how to listen to one another. Direct students to make a statement about anything (i.e., "My boyfriend broke up with me when he found out my parents did not approve of my dating him."). Ask another student to repeat what was said by saying, "I heard you say ..." (Key Skill: *Communication*)

Follow Up

1. **Reteaching.** Use a phone book to show students how to locate community health and wellness resource people. Show them how to find the number of a doctor, a dentist, a social worker, a kid's talk hotline, an aerobics instructor, and a psychologist. (Key Skill: *Communication*)
2. **Enrichment.** Have students develop a flyer or pamphlet that lists the names of people in your school who can help if somebody has a particular problem. Have them list the names and room numbers of the school counselor(s), the school nurse(s), the school social worker(s), the substance abuse counselor(s), and the school psychologist(s). Then have students distribute the flyer or pamphlet to the student body. (Key Skills: *Communication, Cooperation*)

Making a Difference

Emotional wellness depends on how well you treat yourself. Try doing one nice thing for yourself every day and acknowledge the fact that you've been good to yourself.

Teaching. . . Avoiding Harmful Substances (pp. 434-435)

Comprehension Check

1. Name four diseases that smokers have an increased risk of contracting. *(Cancer, heart disease, bronchitis, and emphysema.)*
2. What risk is there for people who chew tobacco? *(People who chew tobacco increase their risk of getting cancer of the mouth.)*
3. Medical science has proven there is a strong link between alcohol abuse and four diseases. Name them. *(Heart disease, cancer, liver disease, and birth defects.)*
4. What percentage of traffic deaths are directly related to alcohol consumption? *(Nearly fifty percent of all traffic deaths are alcohol related.)*
5. What are some of the effects of drug use? *(People may become confused or violent. Physically, drug abuse can damage the body and lead to death.)*

Learning Activities

1. **Discussion.** Ask students to examine their own smoking habits and encourage them to share with the class when and why they picked up the habit. (Hopefully, none of them have picked up this habit.) (Key Skill: *Communication*)
2. **Discussion.** Ask your students to imagine themselves at an unchaperoned party where both alcohol (beer, wine, and mixed drinks) and soda are being served. Given the choice of alcohol or soda, which one would they choose and why? (Key Skill: *Decision Making*)
3. **Panel.** Invite a group of recovering alcoholics to class for an informational session about alcohol and how it affected their lives. Your local Alcoholics Anonymous Central Service Office will assist you in putting together a panel of recovering alcoholics. (Key Skill: *Communication*)
4. **Survey.** Explain to your students that alcoholism is a disease. Ask each of your students to survey ten people. Have the students ask this question: "Is alcoholism a disease or a moral problem?" Determine the percentage of

Avoiding Harmful Substances

Tobacco, alcohol, and other drugs are health abusers. They can cause serious problems for individuals, families, and society.

Tobacco

The use of tobacco products can shorten your life. Smokers have an increased risk of cancer, heart disease, and lung diseases. People who use chewing tobacco are increasing their risk of cancer of the mouth.

It is best never to begin smoking or chewing tobacco. However, once the habit is developed, it can be stopped with determination and effort.

Alcohol

It is illegal to sell alcohol to minors. Why? Alcohol has a number of negative effects that even many adults find hard to handle.

Alcohol is a depressant drug, a chemical that slows down the body's processes. The more people drink, the more they lose their sense of judgment. They cannot think clearly. Normal actions, such as hand movements, walking, and talking, become very clumsy.

Alcohol has a reputation as a killer. Medical science has proven there is a strong link between heavy drinking and heart disease, cancer, liver disease, and birth defects.

Drinking large amounts of alcohol can cut off the supply of oxygen to the brain, killing brain cells. Once brain cells are destroyed, they can't be replaced.

Drinking and driving is often a deadly combination. Alcohol is the nation's primary cause of traffic accidents, resulting in nearly half of all traffic deaths. Heavy drinking is also the cause of more than half of all home accidents.

For many people, it's easy to drink too much. Even though they aren't old enough to drink legally, some teens are alcoholics. They often deny they have a problem. Not only do they try to deceive others, but they often deceive themselves as well. Many drop out of school and, as a result, limit their future chances.

If you know someone who has an alcohol problem, encourage him or her to get help. See Chapter 14 for suggestions of where to find help for alcohol problems.

Avoiding harmful substances is a positive approach to maintaining wellness.

More About Alcohol

Alcohol abuse ranks as the number one drug problem among young people. About two-thirds of teenagers drink alcoholic beverages on a regular basis, and some twenty to forty percent of the fourteen- to seventeen-year-old group are estimated to be problem drinkers.

How to ...
Say "Yes" to Life and "No" to Drugs

You may face pressure to use harmful substances. What can you do?

- Learn the facts about tobacco, alcohol, and other drugs. The more you know about the harm these substances can do to you, the easier it will be to say "no" to them.
- Be alert to the signs of drug and alcohol use by friends. Try to persuade them to get help.
- Combat boredom. Take up a hobby, get a job, do volunteer work, or become active in school clubs.
- Learn how to have a good time with friends without using alcohol or other drugs.
- Decide ahead of time how you will handle the pressure to use harmful substances. Practice what you will say. NO is a powerful word. People won't like you more if you drink or take drugs. They will, however, respect you for not doing so.

▼ Other Drugs ▼

Alcohol is not the only drug that can cause problems. Drug abuse occurs whenever a person:

- Uses an illegal drug, such as marijuana or cocaine.
- Misuses medicines by taking more than directed or a drug prescribed for someone else.
- Uses substances not intended to be taken into the body. Inhaling the spray from an aerosol can is an example.

People who abuse drugs are hoping for a pleasant effect. However, the effects of drugs can be most unexpected and unpleasant. The person may become confused or violent. Physically, drug abuse can damage the body and lead to death.

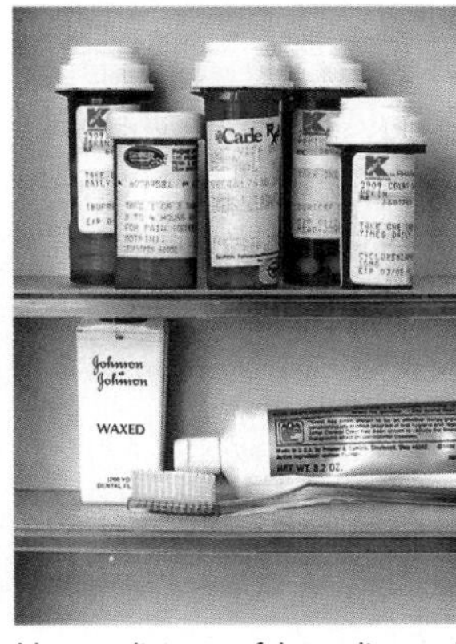

Use medicines safely as directed by your physician.

How to ... Say "Yes" to Life and "No" to Drugs

Have students read the feature. Discuss peer pressure with them regarding the use of drugs and alcohol. Are there times when the students have trouble saying "no" to friends that want them to use drugs and/or alcohol? Present hypothetical situations in which students can practice saying "no" to drugs and/or alcohol.

Learning Activities (continued)

people that see alcoholism as a disease and the percentage that see it as a moral problem. (Key Skills: *Communication, Math*)

5. **Community Research.** Have students investigate the number of rehabilitation hospitals that are available locally for people who wish to seek treatment for drug and/or alcohol addiction. Have students report their findings to the class. (Key Skill: *Communication*)

Follow Up

1. **Reteaching.** Bring samples of medicines to class, such as cough syrup and aspirin. Have the students read the directions on each type of medicine. Make sure they look at the recommended dosage on each one and how often each one can be taken. (Key Skill: *Communication*)
2. **Enrichment.** Have students visit a pharmacy or grocery store to examine cough syrups for children. Have them read the labels of five known cough syrups to determine which brands contain alcohol and which do not. Then have the students report their findings to the class. (Key Skill: *Communication*)

Photo Focus

Discuss the photo at the bottom of p. 435 with the students. Have them brainstorm how medicine should be safely stored in the home. *(Answers should include such things as storing medicine high enough so that it is out of children's reach, storing it in a locked cabinet, and storing it in a cool and dry place.)*

Teaching...
Safety, Preparing for Emergencies, and Family Health Care
(pp. 436-438)

Comprehension Check

1. Drug and alcohol use affects more people than just the individual using the drug. Give examples of those people who may be affected. *(Family members, friends, employers, and other innocent people.)*
2. What type of protective gear can be worn when bicycling or boating to protect yourself in the event of an accident? *(Helmets when bicycling and life jackets when boating.)*
3. When calling to report an emergency, there are two very important things to remember. What are they? *(Stay calm and state the facts.)*
4. What are immunizations? *(Immunizations are shots to protect against disease.)*
5. How can families ease the financial burden of health care costs? *(They can set aside savings for unexpected medical costs, learn about health care resources in their area,and obtain health insurance.)*

Learning Activities

1. **Discussion.** Talk to your students about the types of accidents that could occur while baby-sitting young children. The discussion could include such things as climbing and jumping off furniture, running in the house, and playing with sharp objects. (Key Skill: *Critical Thinking*)

TIPS:

Stocking a First Aid Kit
Have students read the feature. Then have them see if there is a first aid kit somewhere in their home. If there is, does it include all the basic items? If there isn't, have them talk to their parents about getting one. *(Answers will vary.)*

Many drugs are habit-forming. Over time, the body develops a physical and emotional need for the drug. Without it the person becomes ill. As the body becomes used to the drug, it may require more and more to produce the same effect.

Some people think that using drugs will help them escape their problems. In fact, drug use only causes new problems. At the same time, it reduces the person's ability to cope with life.

People who misuse or abuse drugs are not just hurting themselves. They are hurting the family members and friends who care about them. They hurt their employers because they cannot perform their jobs effectively. If the drug problem leads to an accident or crime, innocent people may be hurt or even killed. The cost of drug abuse to society is measured both in money and in human lives.

Overcoming a drug problem is not easy, but it can be done. See Chapter 14 for information on sources of help.

What steps are you taking to keep yourself safe?

TIPS: *Stocking a First Aid Kit*

Every first aid kit should include these basic items:

- Adhesive strip bandages, in a variety of shapes and sizes.
- Sterile gauze pads.
- Gauze rolls.
- Adhesive tape.
- Medicated soap.
- Antibiotic ointment.
- First aid manual.
- List of emergency telephone numbers.

Safety

It's easy to think, "Nothing could ever happen to me." However, accidents can and do occur. It's also true that most accidents can be prevented.

You have to take the lead in watching out for your safety. Safety is important 24 hours a day, in every situation. For example:

- ***At home.*** You are more likely to have an accident at home than anywhere else. Chapters 26 and 47 include important information on safety in the home. Many of these guidelines apply to other situations, too.
- ***At school or work.*** Schools and workplaces have rules for everyone's protection. Following the rules will help you avoid hurting yourself or others.
- ***In recreational activities.*** When you're having fun, it's easy to forget about safety. It can also be easy for accidents or injuries to occur. Always wear the proper protective gear, such as a helmet for bicycling or a life jacket for boating. Learn and follow the rules of your activity.
- ***On the road.*** Always wear a seat belt when driving or riding in a car. Obey traffic laws, whether you are driving, bicycling, or walking.

Safety also means protecting yourself against crime. When you are out, be aware of your surroundings. Notice where you are, who is around you, and what they are doing. Avoid unsafe areas, such as a poorly lit street, if at all possible.

▼ Preparing for Emergencies ▼

Prepare for an emergency before it occurs. Keep a list of emergency telephone numbers at your phone. In many areas, you can call 9-1-1 for fire, police, or medical emergencies. The telephone book has a listing of other hotline and crisis numbers.

If you call for help, the person answering your call will ask you important questions. Try to stay calm and state the facts.

You should also learn simple first aid for minor injuries. You can contact the local chapter of the American Red Cross. They can help you with basic information.

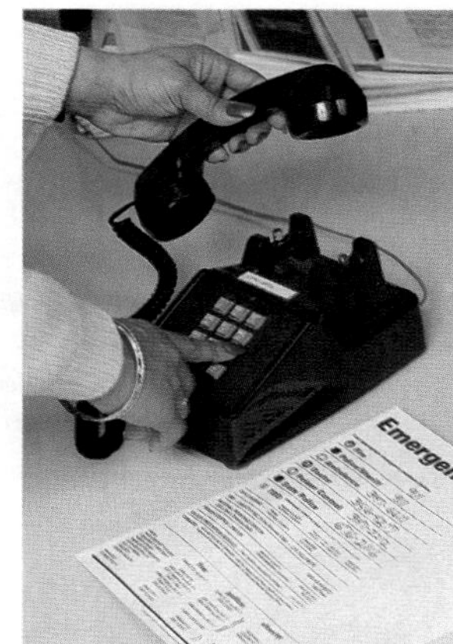

Having a list of emergency numbers next to the telephone is essential in crisis situations.

Family Health Care

Health care is an important consideration for families. An accident or illness may strike at any time. Children need **immunizations**, shots to protect against disease. Even if family members stay well, they should have regular medical and dental checkups and eye examinations. Planning and decision-making can help families meet their health care needs.

Depending on where you live, a number of different health care resources may be available. These might include hospitals, clinics, government and private agencies, and physicians. In addition, there may be ambulance and paramedic services that respond to emergencies. Families should be aware of the resources in their community, the services provided by each, and the relative costs.

Many people choose a family doctor or join a health maintenance orgnization (HMO) to handle most of their health care needs. That way, one physician or group of physicians has information about each family member's medical history and special needs. If additional treatment is necessary, referrals can be made to other health care providers.

Families should also keep their own health care records. These might include information about doctor visits, immunizations, allergies, and major illnesses.

Health care can be costly. Families can ease the financial burden by:

- Setting aside savings for unexpected medical costs.
- Learning about health care resources in their area.
- Obtaining health insurance. Although the insurance itself may be costly, it can be far less expensive than paying hospital bills. Many employers offer health insurance at low or no cost as a benefit to their workers.

What health care resources might you and your family need?

Learning Activities (continued)

2. **Display.** Post a list of safety rules that must be followed in the family and consumer sciences lab. Explain the necessity for each safety rule and possible accidents that could occur if the rule is not followed. (Key Skill: *Communication*)
3. **Discussion.** Ask students to share stories of accidents that have happened to them at home, school, or outdoors. Discuss ways in which the accidents might have been avoided. (Key Skill: *Communication*)
4. **Skit.** Bring an old telephone to class. Have students plan out hypothetical situations in which they must make a 9-1-1 emergency phone call for help. Make sure they focus on staying calm and stating the facts. (Key Skill: *Problem Solving*)
5. **Discussion.** Talk about the cost of health care in our country. Describe what things are and are not covered by the health insurance policy that you have through your school. (Key Skill: *Communication*)

Follow Up

1. **Reteaching.** Have students map out the most direct route from their house to a local hospital in case there is a medical emergency. (Key Skill: *Problem Solving*)
2. **Extension.** Use the extension information handout on p. 49 of the *Extending the Text* booklet in the TCR.
3. **Enrichment.** Invite a representative from the local Red Cross to school to demonstrate methods of applying simple first aid to someone injured at home or while baby-sitting. (Key Skill: *Communication*)

More About *Home Safety*

Homes need to be childproofed when little children are around. Electrical outlets need to be covered, electrical cords need to be taped down, safety gates should be placed at the top and bottom of stairs, and medicines and cleaning supplies need to be locked in cabinets where children cannot reach them.

Making a Difference

Have students develop and design a pamphlet called *Safety in the Kitchen for Latch Key Kids.* Focus on safety guidelines to be followed while working in the kitchen after school to prepare snacks and the safe use of kitchen tools.

Completing the Chapter

For Review

1. Emphasize the main concepts using the summary.
2. Have students complete the "Facts to Recall." (Answers below.)

For Reteaching

1. **Reteaching.** Use the activity on p. 48 of the *Reteaching and Practical Skills* booklet in the TCR.

For Enrichment

1. **Enrichment.** Use the activity on p. 60 of the *Enrichment Activities* booklet in the TCR.

For Evaluation

1. Choose items from "Ideas to Explore" and "Activities to Try."
2. Use the chapter test on pp. 77-78 in the testing booklet of the TCR or use the testmaker software.

Facts to Recall Answers

1. Health refers to the total state of your well-being. It includes physical, mental, and social well-being. Wellness is a way of living based on healthful attitudes and actions. It means taking an active role in improving and maintaining your health.
2. Eating, exercise, and sleep.
3. It trains the heart, lungs, and blood vessels to work more efficiently.
4. **Any three:** walk or ride a bike to school; plan social activities that include exercise; exercise with a friend; participate in an organized team sport.
5. During sleep, the body repairs itself, removes waste products from cells, and builds an energy supply for the next day's activities.

Around the World

After reading the feature, have students investigate other medical practices that have changed throughout the years in other cultures. *(Answers will vary.)*

For over 100 years, people in Egypt have had an unusual source of health care — their barbers. A symbol of this practice was the white pole with a spiraling red stripe — a symbol still used by many barbers today. Since the 1880s, barbers have been licensed to practice basic medical care. They were given training to treat simple ailments such as coughs, stomach aches, and abscesses. Today, because of the rapid advancements in medicine, doctors must be more specialized. The one-stop service of the barber-surgeon of long ago has become a lost profession.

Long-Term Health Care Needs

Some family members may have long-term health care needs. For example, Ray's father takes medication for high blood pressure. Sonya has cerebral palsy and walks with crutches. Ladonna's grandmother has arthritis.

The impact of a long-term health problem on the family may be small or large. A family that works together to talk about their needs, examine their resources, and make the necessary adjustments is likely to meet the challenge successfully.

TAKING ACTION

Recognizing Warning Signals

Lately Gary seems different. You've known him since fifth grade. His family life has had its share of problems, but in the past he seemed able to handle it. Now he often seems depressed and moody.

The other day before school, you asked Gary how his weekend was. He told about going to a party and getting drunk. You've heard similar stories about Gary from others. This is happening more and more often.

It's obvious to you that Gary has a problem. As a friend, you want to help — but how? You're not sure how Gary will react if you try to talk with him. He usually listens to you and respects your advice, but he's not comfortable talking openly about his feelings. You don't want to put him off. Still, you feel you need to do something.

Using Your Resourcefulness

- What might happen if you talk to Gary about his problem? If you do nothing?
- What other possible courses of action can you think of?
- To whom might you go for help and advice?
- Your community may have resources that can help teens who abuse alcohol or have other problems. How could you find out about those resources?
- List the resources in your community that might be able to help in this situation. Include how a person could get in touch with them.
- After thinking about possible courses of action, what is the first step you would take in this situation?

TAKING ACTION

Have the students read the feature. Then have them discuss similar situations that they know about or have heard about from other people. Make sure that students do not use the real names of the people they bring up during this discussion.

Using Your Resourcefulness Answers

- Answers will vary. Possible answers for the first question include: Gary might listen and seek help, Gary might get angry and not want to be friends anymore, Gary might say that there is no problem, or Gary might not even be willing to talk about the problem. Possible answers for the second question include: Gary might keep drinking

Chapter 37 Review

Summary

In this chapter, you have read about:

- The meaning of health and wellness.
- Habits that help you maintain your physical health.
- Ways to promote mental, emotional, and social health.
- The dangers of tobacco, alcohol, and other drugs.
- How to prevent accidents and handle emergencies.
- Ways for families to meet their health care needs.

Facts to Recall

1. What is health? What is wellness?
2. Name three everyday habits that affect physical health.
3. How does aerobic exercise improve fitness?
4. Suggest three ways to incorporate exercise into daily routines.
5. How is sleep important to good health?
6. Name three ways of managing stress.
7. Name four negative effects of alcohol use or abuse.
8. Identify four ways alcohol and drug abuse is harmful to the user and to others.
9. Give an example of a guideline for personal safety.
10. Name two ways you and your family can prepare for emergencies.
11. Identify three health care resources available to families.

Ideas to Explore

1. In what ways do you think mental, emotional, and social health can affect physical health? Explain.
2. What motivates a person to choose a wellness lifestyle? Why do you think some people neglect their health?
3. Discuss this statement from the text: "Taking care of your health can help you reach your future goals."

Activities to Try

1. Design a cartoon or poster promoting wellness. It may encourage people to practice health habits, such as exercising and eating right, or discourage them from developing poor habits, like smoking and alcohol abuse.
2. In small groups, brainstorm a list of activities or events that add stress to your lives. Then make another list of healthful ways to relieve stress.
3. Write an exercise plan that fits the recommendations made in this chapter.

LINK TO Math

FIGURING YOUR TARGET PULSE RATE

The best way to figure out if you are exercising hard enough to benefit your heart and lungs is to check your pulse rate. Immediately after exercising, your pulse should fall within a range called your *target pulse rate*. This tells you your exercise is giving you a good aerobic workout. Here's how to figure your target pulse rate:

1. Subtract your age from 220.
2. Multiply the result of Step 1 by 70 percent (.70). This gives you the *lower* number for your target pulse rate.
3. Multiply the answer from Step 1 by 85 percent (.85) to find the *upper* number for your target pulse rate.

For the most benefit from exercise, try to keep your pulse rate within this range.

Facts to Recall Answers (continued)

6. **Any three:** set aside time for activities and people you enjoy; don't get upset over little things; look on the bright side and keep a sense of humor; when you have a problem, find someone to talk to.
7. It slows down the body's mental processes; it has been linked to heart disease, cancer, liver disease, and birth defects; it can cut off the oxygen supply to the brain; it is a leading cause of traffic and home accidents.
8. **Any two:** it can cause the user to become confused or violent; it can damage the body and lead to death; it can be habit-forming and cause illness; it can reduce the person's ability to cope with life. **Any two:** it hurts family members and friends who care about the user; it hurts employers because users cannot perform their jobs effectively; it can lead to accidents and crime, possibly killing innocent people.
9. Safety is important to wellness because it can prevent accidents and injury that can harm your health. **Any one:** always wear protective gear for recreational activities; learn and follow the rules of your activity; always wear a seat belt when driving or riding in a car; obey traffic laws; when you are out, be aware of your surroundings; avoid unsafe areas.
10. Keep a list of emergency telephone numbers at your phone; learn simple first aid for minor injuries.
11. **Any three:** hospitals; clinics; government and private agencies; physicians; ambulance and paramedic services.

Ideas to Explore

1. Answers will vary.
2. Answers will vary.
3. Answers will vary.

LINK TO Math

Answers

1. Answers will vary.
2. Answers will vary.
3. Answers will vary.

more and more, and/or Gary might drink and drive and kill himself or someone else.

- Answers will vary. Possible answers might include talking to Gary's parents, getting a closer friend to talk to Gary, or talking to a professional about what to do to help Gary.
- Answers will vary. Possibilities include other friends, the student's own parents, or a professional.
- Answers will vary. Possibilities include the phone book, the school counselor, or the school may have pamphlets.
- Answers will vary.
- Answers will vary.

Preparing to Teach

Chapter Outline

Chapter Resources

The following booklet materials may be found in the *Teacher's Classroom Resources* box:

- Lesson Plans, p. 43
- Student Workbook, *Study Guide,* pp. 161-162; *Calcium—No Bones About It!,* p. 163; *It's No Secret—Vitamins and Minerals Do Count!,* p. 164
- Color Transparencies, *It's Your Choice,* CT-41
- Cooperative Learning, p. 50
- Extending the Text, *From Food to You...The Process of Digestion,* p. 50
- Reteaching and Practical Skills, *Nutrition on Your Plate,* p. 49
- Enrichment Activities, *Why Limit Fats and Cholesterol?,* p. 61
- Chapter and Unit Tests, pp. 79-80
- Testmaker Software

Also see:

- Meeting the Special Needs of Students
- Linking Home, School, and Community

ABCNews InterActive™ Videodiscs

- *Food and Nutrition*

See the ABCNews InterActive™ Bar Code Correlation booklet for applicable segments.

CHAPTER 38

Nutrients and Their Functions

OBJECTIVES

- *Identify six types of nutrients and their roles.*
- *Explain nutrient deficiencies.*
- *Describe digestion.*
- *Explain how to meet energy needs nutritiously.*

TERMS TO LEARN

- ***nutrients***
- ***carbohydrate***
- ***fiber***
- ***protein***
- ***legumes***
- ***cholesterol***
- ***deficiency***
- ***calorie***
- ***nutrient density***

"Wait a minute," Luis said as he stopped in front of the snack shop in the mall. His friends, Alex and Carolyn, waited patiently while Luis bought a pretzel with cheese sauce and a large soft drink. "That's the third time you've stopped for food," Carolyn said as Luis rejoined them. "Have you got a bottomless pit for a stomach?"

"I just didn't have time for breakfast or lunch today," Luis said. "But I figured I'd find plenty of food in this mall to fill me up — and I was right!"

Snacks can be fine, but Luis is forgetting something. Food is more than something that tastes good and fills you up when you're empty. It is your body's source of nutrients. **Nutrients** are substances that are found in foods and that the body needs in order to work properly. That's why choosing the right foods is so important.

The Nutrient Team

Your body needs nutrients for a number of jobs — energy, growth, repair, and basic processes. The six basic types of nutrients work together as a team. They are carbohydrates, proteins, fats, vitamins, minerals, and water. Each type of nutrient has a special role in keeping your body healthy.

Carbohydrates

Carbohydrates are the body's main source of energy. They consist of the starches and sugars in foods.

Sugars are also called *simple carbohydrates*. You don't need much sugar in your diet. Fruits, vegetables, and milk naturally contain a small amount of sugar plus other nutrients. Sugar is also added to some foods. Candy, soft drinks, and other sweets are high in added sugar and often lack more important nutrients.

Starches are also called *complex carbohydrates*. They should make up a large part of your diet. Good sources include breads, cereals, rice, pasta, dry beans and peas, and starchy vegetables such as potatoes and corn.

Many foods high in complex carbohydrates also contain fiber. **Fiber** consists of plant materials that do not break down completely when food is digested. Fiber is an important part of a healthy diet. It helps the body get rid of waste products and may have other health benefits as well. Whole-grain products, beans, fruits, and vegetables are good sources of fiber.

Carbohydrate foods are the main source of energy. They also contain fiber — an essential component in the digestive process.

Introducing the Chapter

Motivators

1. **Discussion.** Involve students in a discussion about food places at the local mall. Have them list all the different food places in the mall, their favorite places in the mall to snack, and their favorite snacks in general. Point out those snacks that are healthy versus those that are not healthy and explain why. (Key Skill: *Communication*)
2. **Consumerism.** Bring to class the empty packages of four popular brands of chocolate chip cookies. Have the students read the nutrient information on each package to determine the fat content of each brand. Ask the students which brand is the healthiest based on fat content. (Key Skill: *Decision Making*)
3. **Charts.** Divide your class into four groups. Have one group make a chart listing various foods from animal sources, have another group list foods from plant sources, have a third group make up a nutrient chart, and have the last group develop a chart on the nine essential amino acids. (Key Skill: *Cooperation*)

Chapter Objectives and Vocabulary

1. Have students read the chapter objectives and rephrase the objectives as questions.
2. Ask students to state, in their own words, the purpose of studying this chapter.
3. Pronounce the vocabulary terms listed on the previous page. Ask students whether they are familiar with any of these. Explain that the terms will be defined in the chapter.

Guided Reading

1. Have students read the chapter and use the Study Guide on pp. 161-162 of the *Student Workbook*.

More About Fiber

Technically, dietary fiber is not an essential nutrient. It is not broken down and absorbed by the body, and no specific deficiency symptoms develop in its absence. Fiber is essential for regularity in removing waste materials from the body and in relieving constipation. Studies have shown that fiber from fruits and vegetables alone is not as effective as combining this fiber with fiber from bran. It is wise to add fiber gradually to the diet. The digestive system needs time to adapt. Otherwise people may experience some unnecessary bloating and intestinal gas.

Teaching. . . The Nutrient Team (pp. 441-443)

Comprehension Check

1. What are nutrients? *(Nutrients are substances that are found in foods and that the body needs to work properly.)*
2. Name the six nutrients that give your body energy and help you grow. *(Carbohydrates, proteins, fats, vitamins, minerals, and water.)*
3. Give three examples of foods that are good sources of fiber. *(**Any three:** whole-grain products, beans, fruits, and vegetables.)*
4. Why is it important for you to get enough protein in your diet? *(Protein is a nutrient that helps build and repair body tissues. It also helps regulate a number of body functions and provides energy if your diet doesn't include enough carbohydrates.)*
5. What is the difference between saturated fats and unsaturated fats? *(Saturated fats are solid at room temperature and are found in foods like meats, poultry, fish, egg yolks, and dairy products. Unsaturated fats are usually liquid at room temperature and are found mainly in vegetable oils.)*
6. What is cholesterol? *(Cholesterol is a fat-like substance which the body uses to make necessary chemicals and to help in digestion.)*

Learning Activities

1. **Lab Activity.** Find a cookie recipe that uses fruit or fruit juice as a sweetener rather than sugar. Prepare the recipe for your students so they can sample something sweet that's made without sugar. (Key Skill: *Science*)
2. **Meal Planning.** Ask students to plan a week's menu of after-school snacks using nuts, seeds, vegetables, and grains. Explain that these are incomplete protein foods and make sure students combine them so that they are complete protein.

Sugar Sleuth

Materials
food labels

Equipment
none

Directions:
Find the food(s) listing the largest number of sugars and sweeteners such as corn syrup and dextrose. Write down the food's name and ingredient list. Circle each form of sugar listed. Ingredients are listed on the label in order by weight — from greatest to least. Note which foods list sugars as one of the first three ingredients or include several sugars.

- ✔ What kinds of sugars and sweeteners did you find?
- ✔ What did this activity tell you about sugars in food?
- ✔ Which products appear to be high in sugar?

Every part of your body contains protein — your hair, your skin, and your internal organs such as your heart and lungs. Eating a variety of protein foods is essential to good health.

▼ Proteins ▼

Protein is a nutrient used to build and repair body tissues. It is important for other reasons, too. It helps regulate a number of body functions. Protein can also provide energy if your diet doesn't include enough carbohydrates.

Protein is made up of chemicals called *amino acids*. Different kinds of protein are made up of different combinations of amino acids.

There are about 22 known amino acids. The body manufactures all but nine of them. Those nine are called *essential amino acids*. It is essential you get them from the food you eat because your body can't make them.

Foods from animal sources — meat, fish, poultry, milk and milk products, and eggs — contain all of the essential amino acids. That is why these foods are called *complete proteins*.

Plant foods, such as grains, dry beans and peas, nuts, seeds, and vegetables, also contain proteins. However, these proteins are lacking one or more of the essential amino acids. Therefore, they are called *incomplete proteins*.

To understand incomplete proteins, think of a safe with a combination lock. If you know only one or two of the numbers in the combination, you're locked out. If you have all three numbers, you can use them together to open the safe.

In the same way, amino acids must work together. Here's how to make use of the incomplete proteins in plant foods:

- Eat a wide variety of plant foods throughout the day. Even if you eat no complete protein foods, you can still get all the amino acids you need — some from dry beans or peas, others from grains, others from vegetables, and so on.

Sugar Sleuth

Materials: Food labels.
Equipment: None.

Purpose: To help students learn to identify the kinds of sugars in foods.

Outcomes:

- The sugars in food include white sugar, brown sugar, raw sugar, corn syrup, high-fructose corn syrup, honey, molasses, and maple syrup. Other names for sugars in food include sucrose, glucose, dextrose, sorbitol, fructose, maltose, lactose, and mannitol.
- Sugars are in many foods; foods differ in sugar content.
- Foods that list sugar as one of the first three ingredients or include several kinds of sugars are probably high in sugars.

▶ If you do eat complete protein foods, they, too, can help your body use the incomplete proteins in plant foods.

To find out more about proteins, read "How to Mix and Match Proteins" on pages 444-445.

▼ Fats ▼

Fats are the most concentrated form of food energy. They also carry the fat-soluble vitamins (A, D, E, and K) in the body. In addition, fats provide substances that your body needs for normal growth, reproduction, and healthy skin.

Foods such as butter, margarine, salad dressing, and sour cream add fats to the diet. Fats are also hidden in foods such as meat, fish, poultry, egg yolks, whole milk, cheese, pastry, and nuts. For most people, getting enough fat in the diet is easy. The challenge is to avoid getting too much.

There are two main types of fats:

▶ ***Saturated fats*** are solid at room temperature. They are found in animal foods such as meat, poultry, fish, egg yolks, and dairy products. Saturated fats are also found in tropical oils — coconut, palm, and palm kernel.

▶ ***Unsaturated fats*** are usually liquid at room temperature. They are found mainly in vegetable oils, with the exception of tropical oils.

While dietary fat is essential to a healthy diet, we need only one tablespoon (30 grams) per day. Yet many of the foods we eat are high in fat. How might you alter your food choices to include foods that are lower in fat?

Cholesterol and Saturated Fats

Cholesterol is a fat-like substance which the body uses to make necessary chemicals and to help in digestion. Your body manufactures all the cholesterol it needs.

Physicians can measure the amount of cholesterol in the bloodstream. When the level of certain types of cholesterol is high, there is a greater risk for heart disease. Therefore, health professionals advise people to reduce their cholesterol levels.

One way to reduce cholesterol in the bloodstream is to eat less cholesterol in foods. Cholesterol is found in foods from animal sources. Foods from plant sources are naturally cholesterol-free.

Another way to reduce cholesterol in the bloodstream is to cut down on fats, especially saturated fats. Researchers have discovered that saturated fats seem to raise the level of cholesterol in the blood.

▼ Vitamins ▼

In the early part of this century, researchers found that unknown substances seemed to be needed by the human body in very small amounts. These substances are now called vitamins.

Learning Activities (continued)

3. **Listing.** Help your students develop a list of foods high in fat. Include foods that are popular foods in their daily meal plan, such as butter, ice cream, cheese, and whole milk. Ask them to make substitutions that would have a lower fat content, such as skim milk, frozen yogurt, and low-fat cheeses. (Key Skill: *Critical Thinking*)
4. **Lab Activity.** Have half the class prepare a recipe using eggs and have the other half use egg whites or egg substitute in place of the eggs. Then have a taste test with your next class to see if your students can tell the difference between the recipe with the real eggs and the recipe with the artificial eggs. Focus on the fat and cholesterol levels of both recipes. (Key Skills: *Cooperation, Science*)

Follow Up

1. **Reteaching.** Select a recipe and have students list all the ingredients in one column. Next to each ingredient, have students determine which food group each ingredient belongs with. (Key Skill: *Critical Thinking*)
2. **Enrichment.** Divide students into groups. Give each group the task of inventing a mall-type snack place that serves only nutritious, healthy foods. Encourage students to name the snack place and to create names for the various foods served. For example, they could name the place "The Juice Bar" and serve things such as "Awesome Apple Juice" and "Outrageous Orange Shakes." (Key Skill: *Creativity*)

More About *Proteins and Fats*

Foods high in proteins and fats remain in the stomach longer than carbohydrate-rich foods. They satisfy hunger for a longer period of time. Perhaps you can remember how quickly you became hungry after having a piece of toast and a glass of orange juice for breakfast. It would have taken longer to become hungry if you would have had orange juice, an egg, toast, and milk.

Teaching. . .
Vitamins
(pp. 444-445)

Comprehension Check

1. What are vitamins? *(Vitamins are chemicals that regulate body processes.)*
2. How can you get all the vitamins you need? *(You can get all the vitamins you need by eating a variety of foods.)*
3. Explain the difference between fat-soluble vitamins and water-soluble vitamins. *(Fat-soluble vitamins, vitamins A, D, E, and K, are taken into the body with foods containing fat. They can be stored in the body. Water-soluble vitamins, vitamin C and the B-complex vitamins, are not stored in the body. We need to eat foods containing water-soluable vitamins every day.)*

Learning Activities

1. **Journal Writing.** Ask students to keep a food journal for two weeks. Have them record every food item they have consumed at the end of each day. The following day in class, have them refer to food composition charts to determine the amounts of vitamins and minerals consumed each day. Compare that number to the recommended daily allowance for vitamins and minerals that teens need each day. (Key Skills: *Communication, Math*)
2. **Group Activity.** Divide your class into groups. Give each group a vitamin to research. Students will need to investigate what foods contain their vitamin and how the vitamin works in our bodies. Students will then be responsible for introducing their vitamin to the class using any medium they choose, such as a skit, a visual display, or a video presentation. (Key Skill: *Creativity*)

How to . . .
Mix and Match Proteins

You can mix and match different proteins to round out those that are incomplete by themselves. Here's how.

Plant Protein Plus Plant Protein

Even though plant proteins are incomplete, they can supply all the protein your body needs. Just eat a wide variety of foods from plant sources each day, including plenty of grains and legumes. **Legumes** include dry beans, such as kidney beans; dry peas, such as split peas; peanuts, and lentils.

Grains and legumes are *complementary proteins*. That means each supplies amino acids that the other lacks. When you eat both grains and legumes during the day, they work together to give your body complete protein. The chart below can help you mix and match legumes and grains. For complete protein, include foods from each column in your daily choices.

Complementary Plant Proteins

Legumes:	Grains:
Peanuts	Whole-grain bread
Peanut butter	Enriched bread
Soybeans	Pita bread
Tofu	Bagels
Lentils	Tortillas
Black-eyed peas	Cornbread
Split peas	Other breads
Kidney beans	Pasta
Navy beans	Noodles
Pinto beans	Rice
Other dry beans and peas	Cereals

Plant Protein Plus Animal Protein

Another way to make use of plant proteins is by supplementing them with animal proteins. The proteins can be eaten together or at another meal the same day. For example, when you eat cereal and milk, the complete protein in the milk helps your body use the incomplete protein in the cereal.

How to ... Mix and Match Proteins

Have students read the feature. Then have each student write down everything they ate on the previous day. Did they mix and match proteins so that they were complete? If not, have students write down how they could have added proteins (plant and/or animal) to make them complete. Did they have any problems finding foods that they like that would have made the proteins complete? Have students keep this information about proteins in mind as they plan future meals.

Making the Match

Making good use of plant proteins is economical and adds variety to meals. Remember, you don't have to combine different kinds of protein in the same meal. Still, doing so is a good way to be sure you get all the amino acids you need.

Several food combinations are listed below. Which ones make use of the complementary proteins in grains and legumes? Which ones supplement incomplete proteins with small amounts of complete proteins?

- Peanut butter sandwich
- Macaroni and cheese
- Split-pea soup and bagel
- Chicken rice soup
- Spanish rice and diced ham
- Baked beans and cornbread

What other combinations can you think of?

Vitamins are chemicals that regulate body processes. Unlike carbohydrates, proteins, and fats, vitamins do not provide energy or become part of the body. However, a lack of vitamins can result in poor health. Generally, you get all the vitamins you need if you eat a variety of foods.

Vitamins can be grouped into two categories:

- ***Fat-soluble.*** Vitamins A, D, E, and K are taken into the body with foods containing fat. The body can store fat-soluble vitamins, so it does not have to depend on a day-to-day supply. If you get too much of vitamins A and D, the excess builds up in the body and can be harmful. This can happen if a person takes large doses of vitamin pills.
- ***Water-soluble.*** Vitamin C and the B-complex vitamins are water-soluble. Water-soluble vitamins are not stored in the body as fat-soluble vitamins are. Therefore, try to eat foods containing them every day. If you get too much of a water-soluble vitamin, the extra generally is passed out of the body in urine. Even so, very large doses may be harmful.

The charts on page 446 give more details about vitamins.

Choose a variety of foods daily to meet your need for vitamins.

Follow Up

1. **Reteaching.** Using the charts on plant proteins and vitamins, show your students how you can put together one meal that would include items from each chart. An example might be: Rice and kidney beans (legumes and grains) with a spinach walnut salad (vitamin A and vitamin E), a glass of milk (vitamin D) and fresh strawberries (vitamin C). (Key Skill: *Decision Making*)
2. **Enrichment.** Have students discuss the idea that many people think that they can take a vitamin pill and then eat anything they want. They say they are taking vitamin pills as *nutrition insurance.* You might have to talk with students about why this is wrong thinking. (Key Skill: *Communication*)

More About Vitamin A

Carotene gives green and orange fruits and vegetables their color. The body can use carotene to make vitamin A. However, too much vitamin A can be harmful. It can cause drying of the skin, loss of hair, irritability, and headaches.

Wellness

Milk is a source of carbohydrates, fat, and protein. It is rich in riboflavin, one of the B vitamins, as well as vitamin A, and it is often fortified with vitamin D. The milk group is the only one for which recommended servings change as a person grows older. Children need two or three daily servings of the milk group. Teenagers need four servings each day to supply themselves with enough milk nutrients. Most adults require only two servings. A serving could be an 8-ounce (250 mL) glass of milk, 1½ cups (375 mL) of cottage cheese, 1 cup (250 mL) of yogurt, or an ounce (30g) of cheddar cheese.

Teaching. . . Minerals (pp. 446-447)

Comprehension Check

1. Name three functions of vitamin A. *(It helps keep skin and hair healthy, it aids night vision , and it helps build strong bones and teeth.)*
2. Name three functions of the B-complex vitamins. *(They help the body use carbohydrates, fats, and proteins; they help produce energy in cells; and they help maintain a healthy nervous system, muscles, and tissues.)*
3. What are the two important jobs of minerals? *(Minerals make up part of the hard and soft body tissue, and they assist in body functions.)*
4. Why is it important for you to get enough calcium at this point in your development? *(Calcium is an important part of the structure of bones and teeth. Developing a good bone structure as a teen is essential to having strong bones later in life.)*

Learning Activities

1. **Writing.** Teens need 1,200 milligrams of calcium each day. Ask your students to compose a list of all the foods and beverages

AROUND THE WORLD

After reading the feature, have students investigate why people in some areas of the world are dying from malnutrition and what is being done to stop this tragedy. *(This may be because of poor farming practices, climate problems, or lack of money for local farmers to purchase seeds for crops. Government and private organizations can provide technological assistance to help farmers. Other assistance might include supplying nourishing foods, vitamin supplements, and medicines. Relief workers might also provide instruction about nutrition and healthy sanitation practices.*

AROUND THE WORLD

When you are eating a nutritious diet, it is easy to forget its importance. In some parts of India, however, many children die of malnutrition. Their families simply cannot afford to feed them properly. When these children were given a daily supplement of vitamin A, though, their death rate dropped by over 50% after just one year. To them, this one nutrient was literally the difference between life and death.

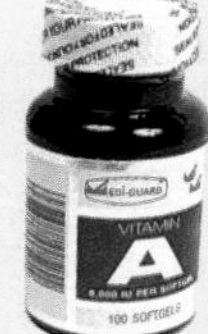

Fat-Soluble Vitamins

Vitamin	Sources	Functions
Vitamin A	▶ Dark green, leafy vegetables, such as spinach ▶ Deep yellow and orange fruits and vegetables, such as carrots, sweet potatoes, and apricots ▶ Liver ▶ Milk, cheese ▶ Eggs	▶ Helps keep skin and hair healthy ▶ Aids night vision ▶ Helps build strong bones and teeth
Vitamin D	▶ Milk with vitamin D added	▶ Helps build strong bones and teeth
Vitamin E	▶ Vegetable oils, margarine ▶ Whole-grain breads and cereals ▶ Dark green, leafy vegetables ▶ Dry beans and peas ▶ Nuts and seeds ▶ Liver	▶ Helps form red blood cells, muscles, and other tissues
Vitamin K	▶ Dark green, leafy vegetables ▶ Cabbage	▶ Helps blood to clot

Water-Soluble Vitamins

Vitamin	Sources	Functions
B-complex vitamins (including riboflavin, niacin, thiamine, B_6, and B_{12})	▶ Whole-grain and enriched breads and cereals ▶ Dry beans and peas, peanut butter, nuts ▶ Meat, poultry, fish ▶ Eggs ▶ Milk	▶ Help body use carbohydrates, fats, and proteins ▶ Help produce energy in cells ▶ Help maintain healthy nervous system, muscles, and tissues
Vitamin C	▶ Citrus fruits ▶ Many other fruits and vegetables, such as strawberries, broccoli, tomatoes, potatoes	▶ Helps maintain bones, teeth, blood vessels ▶ Helps heal wounds

More About *Vitamins and Minerals*

Vitamins known to be essential are A, C, D, E, K, thiamin, riboflavin, niacin, biotin, pyridoxine, pantothenic acid, folacin, and B_{12}. Minerals now considered to be required are sodium, potassium, chlorine, calcium, magnesium, phosphorus, sulfur, iron, zinc, copper, manganese, selenium, cobalt, molybdenum, chromium, fluorine, and iodine. Minerals that scientists also believe are probably needed are nickel, tin, vanadium, and silicon.

▼ Minerals ▼

Your body needs a large number of minerals, but only in small amounts. If you look at the chart, "Some Important Minerals," you can see that minerals have two important jobs. They make up part of the hard and soft body tissue, and they assist in body functions.

If you eat a variety of foods every day, you will generally meet your mineral needs. Getting enough calcium is especially important to you at this point in your development. Calcium is an important part of the structure of your bones and teeth. Developing a good bone structure now is essential to having strong bones when you are older. If you do not drink milk or or eat milk products every day, it can be difficult to get enough calcium.

Some Important Minerals

Mineral	Sources	Functions
Calcium	▶ Milk and milk products ▶ Sardines, salmon (eaten with bones) ▶ Dark green, leafy vegetables ▶ Dry beans and peas	▶ Helps build and maintain strong bones and teeth ▶ Helps heart, muscles, and nerves work properly ▶ Helps blood to clot
Phosphorus	▶ Meat, poultry, fish ▶ Eggs ▶ Dry beans and peas, nuts ▶ Milk and milk products	▶ Helps build and maintain strong bones and teeth ▶ Helps body use carbohydrates, fats, and proteins
Iron	▶ Liver ▶ Red meats ▶ Egg yolks ▶ Dark green, leafy vegetables ▶ Dry beans and peas, nuts ▶ Whole-grain and enriched breads and cereals ▶ Dried fruits, such as raisins	▶ Helps enable red blood cells to carry oxygen to all parts of the body
Potassium	▶ Oranges and orange juice ▶ Bananas ▶ Dried fruits ▶ Dry beans and peas, peanut butter ▶ Meats	▶ Helps heart and muscles work properly ▶ Works with sodium, another mineral, to keep fluid balance in cells ▶ Helps regulate blood pressure

they consumed the day before. Using a calcium chart, have students record the amounts of calcium in each food. Total the calcium amounts to see if they met their daily recommended allowance. Check over their lists to point out reasons why they did or did not meet their daily recommended allowance of calcium. (Key Skill: *Communication*)

2. **Identification.** Write each mineral on its own piece of 12-inch × 5-inch poster board. Use these pieces of poster board as flash cards. Review the types of foods that are high in each mineral. Then divide the class into two teams and create a game using the flash cards. Hold up a certain card and have a student name a food that's high in that mineral. If the student is correct, the team gets a point. If the student is wrong, the other team gets a chance to answer correctly. The team with the most points wins. (Key Skill: *Communication*)

Follow Up

1. **Reteaching.** Plan a menu with your students that will show them what foods they need to eat in order to acquire the recommended daily allowances of vitamins and minerals. (Key Skill: *Decision Making*)
2. **Enrichment.** Ask students to get permission from their favorite restaurant to bring a sample menu to class. Looking at the menu in class, have them select foods from the menu as though they were ordering a meal at the restaurant. Have them write down their selections. Refer them to the protein, vitamin, and mineral charts, and instruct them to list next to each food selection those vitamins, proteins (complete or incomplete), and minerals they would get from eating that meal. (Key Skills: *Communication, Management*)

Teaching. . .
Water, Deficiencies, Digestion, and Energy and Calories
(pp. 448-450)

Comprehension Check

1. Why is it important to drink water every day? *(Water is needed for digestion and to carry nutrients throughout the body. It also helps remove body waste and controls body temperature.)*
2. What is the key to avoiding nutrient deficiencies? *(The key to avoiding nutrient deficiencies is to eat a variety of foods daily. Each food has a different mix of the nutrients people need for good health.)*
3. Briefly explain the digestive process. *(The digestive process begins when the thought, sight, aroma, and taste of food stimulates the flow of saliva. The chemicals in saliva, along with chewing, begin to break the food down. Then the food moves from the mouth through the esophagus to the stomach. There digestive juices break the food down further. From the stomach, the food moves to the small intestine. From there, the nutrients are absorbed into the bloodstream. Unneeded nutrients and any undigested food are eliminated as body waste.)*
4. What is a calorie? *(A calorie is a unit used to measure energy supplied by food or used by the body.)*
5. Define nutrient density. *(Nutrient density is a comparison of the nutrients in a food to the number of calories.)*

Learning Activities

1. **Research.** Divide your class into two groups. Have one group research information on anemia and the other group research information on osteoporosis. Students should focus on what causes the illness they're researching, how it can be prevented, and if it is an inherited condition. Have each group report their findings to the class. (Key Skill: *Communication*)

Drinking six to eight glasses of water a day is essential to good health. What beverages do you choose when you are thirsty? Why might water be a better choice?

▼ Water ▼

You can live longer without food than without water. Water is needed for digestion and to carry nutrients throughout the body. It also helps remove body waste and controls body temperature.

Foods with a high water content, such as soups, provide some of the water you need. The rest must come from the liquids you drink, such as milk, juice, and water. Do you drink the recommended six to eight glasses of liquid daily?

Deficiencies

When nutrients are not eaten in large enough amounts, a **deficiency**, or shortage, results. The symptoms, or effects, depend on the seriousness of the deficiency.

At first, the symptoms may not seem very serious. They may include tiredness or difficulty sleeping or concentrating. Colds or other illnesses may be more frequent. Nutrient deficiencies can also cause weight gain or weight loss.

If a deficiency becomes more serious, specific parts of the body can be affected, such as the skin, eyes, tongue, or bones. It depends on which nutrient is lacking.

The key to avoiding nutrient deficiencies is to eat a variety of foods daily. Each food has a different mix of the nutrients you need for good health.

Frequent illness may be a sign of a nutrient deficiency. Are you eating a variety of foods necessary for good health?

Digestion

In order to use the nutrients in food, your body must first digest the food. The digestive process begins when the thought, sight, aroma, and taste of food stimulates the flow of saliva. The chemicals in saliva, along with chewing, begin to break the food down.

Food moves from the mouth through the esophagus to the stomach. There digestive juices break the food down further. Food remains in the stomach an average of three to five hours, but that depends on the type of food. Carbohydrates are digested more quickly than proteins and fats.

From the stomach, the food moves to the small intestine. From there, the nutrients are absorbed into the bloodstream. Some nutrients are used as building materials, some for energy, and some are stored. Unneeded nutrients and any undigested food are eliminated as body waste.

Energy and Calories

Food supplies the body with energy. Some energy is needed for normal processes, such as breathing and pumping blood. You also need energy for all your activities.

Calories are units for measuring energy, just as inches measure length. Calories are used to measure both the energy you take in from food and the energy you use up.

How many calories you need daily depends on factors such as your age and activity level. Taking in more calories than needed causes weight gain, while taking in fewer calories than needed causes weight loss. Chapter 40 discusses weight management in more detail.

The number of calories you need depends on your age and activity level.

▼ Meeting Your Energy Needs ▼

The source of the calories you take in is also important. The energy in foods comes from fats, carbohydrates, and proteins. Vitamins, minerals, water, and fiber do not provide energy. Fat is the most concentrated source of energy with 9 calories per gram. Carbohydrates and proteins have 4 calories per gram. (A gram is a metric unit of weight.)

For good health, experts recommend that:

- At least 55 percent of the calories you take in should come from carbohydrates (mainly complex carbohydrates).
- About 15 percent of your calories should come from protein.
- No more than 30 percent of your calories should come from fat (mainly unsaturated fat).

Learning Activities (continued)

2. **Calorie Counting.** Have students use a calorie chart to count the calories they consumed yesterday. Then have students compare their calories with those of others in the class. (Key Skills: *Communication, Math*)
3. **Poster.** Have students make a poster that explains why a popular snack food is not nutritious. (Key Skill: *Creativity*)

Follow Up

1. **Reteaching.** Have each student make a diagram of the digestive process. Make sure that students include every step of this process on their diagrams. (Key Skills: *Science, Creativity*)
2. **Extension.** Use the extension information handout on p. 50 of the *Extending the Text* booklet in the TCR.
3. **Enrichment.** Ask students to make a list of ten nutrient-dense snacks and post it on their refrigerators to see if it influences the kind of snacks they and their families eat. (Key Skills: *Communication, Decision Making*)

More About Calories

Fast-food restaurant fare is often very high in calories. You would have to bicycle for over an hour to work off the calories in one popular brand of hamburger. Just think how long you would have to work out to get rid of a chocolate shake (383 calories) and fries (220 calories)!

Photo Focus

Discuss the photo at the bottom of page 448 with the students. What are some of the illnesses caused by severe nutrient deficiencies? What are some of the effects of these illnesses and how can they be avoided? *(Answers might include descriptions of kwashiorkor, scurvy, rickets, beriberi, and pellagra.)*

Completing the Chapter

For Review

1. Emphasize the main concepts using the summary.
2. Have students complete the "Facts to Recall." (Answers below.)

For Reteaching

1. **Reteaching.** Use the activity on p. 49 of the *Reteaching and Practical Skills* booklet in the TCR.

For Enrichment

1. **Enrichment.** Use the activity on p. 61 of the *Enrichment Activities* booklet in the TCR.

For Evaluation

1. Choose items from "Ideas to Explore" and "Activities to Try."
2. Use the chapter test on pp. 79-80 in the testing booklet of the TCR or use the testmaker software.

Facts to Recall Answers

1. Carbohydrates, proteins, fats, vitamins, minerals, and water.
2. Simple carbohydrates are sugars; complex carbohydrates are starches. Complex carbohydrates.
3. Fiber is found in foods that are high in complex carbohydrates, such as whole-grain products, beans, fruits, and vegetables. Fiber helps rid the body of waste products and may have other health benefits as well.
4. Complete proteins are found in foods from animal sources, such as meat, fish, poultry, milk and milk products, and eggs. Incomplete proteins can be found in grains, dry beans and peas, nuts, seeds, and some vegetables.
5. It could lead to a high cholesterol level in the bloodstream, which increases the risk for heart disease.
6. Vitamins are chemicals that regulate body processes. They do not provide energy or become part of the body.
7. Calcium is important for the development of bones and teeth. Developing a good bone structure in the teen years is

Foods such as chips and soft drinks have low nutrient density. How might you change your food choices to increase the number of nutrient-dense foods?

▼ Nutrient Density ▼

When you choose foods, consider nutrient density. **Nutrient density** is a comparison of the nutrients in a food to the number of calories.

Foods such as candy, potato chips, and sugary soft drinks have low nutrient density. They add to your calorie intake, but contribute few important nutrients. Most of the nutrients they do supply are ones you probably don't need more of: fat and sugar.

Foods such as fruits, vegetables, whole grains, lean meats, and low-fat milk have high nutrient density. They do more than just help meet your energy needs. They also supply important nutrients such as proteins, vitamins, minerals, and fiber.

The way a food is prepared or served can make a difference in nutrient density. A plain baked potato, for instance, has higher nutrient density than french fries. Because they are cooked in oil, the french fries have more fat and calories.

Most of the foods you eat should be high in nutrient density. If you fill up on foods with low nutrient density, you may get too many calories and not enough of some nutrients. The next chapter will help you learn more about making wise food choices.

TAKING ACTION

Planning Healthful Menus

The school cafeteria menu has been pretty much the same for as long as you can remember — sloppy joes, pizza, french fries, chocolate cake, and other traditional, popular items. Now the school board has decided some changes may be needed. In particular, the board members are concerned about foods that are high in fat and sugar. However, they also know that these foods are among the most popular. They want to be sure the revised menu will appeal to students.

The school board has asked the FHA/HERO (Future Homemakers of America/Home Economics Related Occupations) club to help with this project. You have been chosen to lead the committee that will work with Mrs. Ragusa, head of the school food service. Where do you begin?

Using Your Resourcefulness

- How can you identify the nutritional pros and cons of each menu item?
- Where can you find suggestions on how to prepare food with less fat and sugar?
- How can you find out students' feelings about specific foods?
- List the different resources, both material and human, that can help you get the information you need to offer useful suggestions.

TAKING ACTION

Have the students read the feature. To get started, students can investigate federal requirements for school lunch programs, they can interview food service personnel, and they can talk to school board members about their philosophy with regard to the nutritional value of school lunches. Also, you could have your students plan meals for the school for a month.

Using Your Resourcefulness Answers

- Answers will vary. Possible answers might include analyzing menus with a computer program or using RDA charts to check menus.

Chapter 38 Review

Summary

In this chapter, you have read about:

- Sources and functions of important nutrients.
- How incomplete proteins can be combined to help meet your protein needs.
- What can happen if your diet lacks nutrients.
- How your body digests food to obtain nutrients.
- Recommendations for meeting your body's energy needs.

Facts to Recall

1. Name the six basic types of nutrients.
2. What are simple carbohydrates? Complex carbohydrates? Which is the most important part of a healthful diet?
3. What foods contain fiber? Why is fiber important to good health?
4. What foods are sources of complete proteins? Incomplete proteins?
5. What are the dangers of getting too much saturated fat?
6. What are vitamins? How do they differ from other nutrients such as proteins?
7. What mineral is especially important to teens for growth and development? Why?
8. Identify three early symptoms of a nutritional deficiency.
9. How does saliva help in digestion?
10. What do calories measure?
11. What percentage of calorie intake should come from carbohydrates? From proteins? From fats?
12. Explain the importance of nutrient density.

Ideas to Explore

1. What are some advantages of mixing and matching incomplete proteins to meet your protein needs?
2. Health experts recommend getting vitamins and minerals from foods rather than from pills. Why do you think this is so?

Activities to Try

1. In the chapter, find examples of how nutrients work together to perform related functions. Use your examples to write a paragraph on nutrient teamwork.
2. Carmen's food choices one day had a total of 85 grams of fat. How many calories does that equal? (Remember, one gram of fat has 9 calories.) If Carmen's total calorie intake that day was 2250 calories, what percentage of those calories came from fat? How does this compare with recommended guidelines?

LINK TO *Science*

IDENTIFYING FAT IN FOODS

Here's a simple experiment to check for the fat content in foods. Choose several different types of food (such as meat, french fries, potato chips, carrots, apple juice) to test. Cut as many 3-inch (7.5 cm) squares from a paper bag as you have foods. Rub each food on a paper square labelled with the food's name. Let the squares dry. Then hold each square up to a high-intensity lamp and observe the results.

- What effect did the different foods have on the paper?
- Can you determine the amount of fat in the different foods using this test? Explain.
- How may this information affect your food choices?

Facts to Recall Answers (continued)

essential to having strong bones in the future.

8. Tiredness or difficulty sleeping or concentrating; colds or other illnesses becoming more frequent; weight loss or gain.
9. It contains chemicals that help break food down.
10. Calories measure the energy you take in from food and the energy you use up.
11. At least 55% of calories should come from carbohydrates; about 15% should come from protein; no more than 30% should come from fat.
12. Nutrient density is a comparison of the nutrients in a food to the number of calories. For good health, it is important to eat foods with high nutrient density to get enough nutrients without getting too many calories.

Ideas to Explore

1. Answers will vary and may include: incomplete protein foods are often less expensive; they contain no cholesterol.
2. Answers will vary and may include: large doses of vitamin and mineral pills can be harmful to a person's health; foods may contain nutrients that have not yet been discovered.

LINK TO *Science*

Answers

- Answers will vary.
- Students cannot determine the specific amount of fat in the different foods using this test. However, they will be able to see which foods have the most fat content by looking at the amount of absorption in each piece of paper bag. To get specific amounts of fat in different foods, students need to look at an RDA chart.
- This experiment should show students what types of food need to be avoided or cut out of their diet because of high fat content.

- Answers will vary. Possible answers include cookbooks and government publications.
- Answers will vary. One way to find out students' feelings about specific foods would be to do a survey.
- Answers will vary. Possible resources might include dietitians and information from the American Heart Association.

Preparing to Teach

Chapter Outline

Chapter Resources

The following booklet materials may be found in the *Teacher's Classroom Resources* box:
- Lesson Plans, p. 44
- Student Workbook, *Study Guide,* pp. 165-166; *Help Yourself,* pp. 167-168; *Dining at the Tastee Burger,* p. 169; *The Secret of the Pyramid!,* p. 170
- Color Transparencies, *Dietary Guidelines,* CT-42; *The Food Guide Pyramid,* CT-43
- Personal Safety, *How to Help a Choking Victim,* pp. 39-40
- Cooperative Learning, p. 51
- Extending the Text, *Cholesterol Counts for Teens, Too!,* p. 51
- Reteaching and Practical Skills, *Mealtime Scorecard,* p. 50
- Enrichment Activities, *Salt...You Won't Miss It!,* pp. 62-63
- Chapter and Unit Tests, pp. 81-82
- Testmaker Software

Also see:
- Meeting the Special Needs of Students
- Linking Home, School, and Community
- Dealing with Sensitive Issues

ABCNews InterActive™ Videodiscs
- *Food and Nutrition*

See the ABCNews InterActive™ Bar Code Correlation booklet for applicable segments.

CHAPTER 39

Guidelines for Healthful Eating

OBJECTIVES

- *Identify and explain the Dietary Guidelines for Americans.*
- *Name the food groups in the Food Guide Pyramid and give recommended servings for each.*

TERMS TO LEARN

- ***Dietary Guidelines for Americans***
- ***obesity***
- ***Food Guide Pyramid***

You may not have control over all of the factors that influence your health. However, you do make choices about the foods you eat.

How can you make healthful food choices? Not all of the guidelines you read or hear about are reliable. Two simple sets of guidelines, based on scientific evidence, come from the U.S. government. They are known as the Dietary Guidelines for Americans and the Food Guide Pyramid.

Dietary Guidelines for Americans

Health experts are continually studying the relationship between eating habits and health. They have found that poor eating habits contribute to many serious health problems, such as heart disease, high blood pressure, stroke, diabetes, and some forms of cancer. Fortunately, good eating habits can reduce the risk of these diseases.

The **Dietary Guidelines for Americans** were developed to help you make healthful food choices. They include these six simple suggestions:

- Eat a variety of foods.
- Balance the food you eat with physical activity — maintain or improve your weight.
- Choose a diet with plenty of grain products, vegetables, and fruits.
- Choose a diet low in fat, saturated fat, and cholesterol.
- Choose a diet moderate in sugars.
- Choose a diet moderate in salt and sodium.

These guidelines are suggested for healthy people ages two years and over. They are not for younger children and infants, since their food needs are different.

Eat a Variety of Foods

You need more than forty different nutrients for good health. (Some of them were discussed in Chapter 38.) No one food can supply all the nutrients in the amounts you need. For example, milk supplies calcium but no fiber. Whole-grain breads supply fiber but little calcium.

Eating a variety of foods is the best way to insure that you get all the nutrients you need. Later in this chapter, you will learn how to use the Food Guide Pyramid to plan varied food choices.

Which is the better snack choice, the apple or slice of apple pie? Why?

More About Pizza

At least 53,000 pizza restaurants operate around the country. Americans eat about $15 billion worth of pizza annually. Can pizza be part of a healthy diet? The basics of a pizza, including the crust, tomato sauce, and cheese (if not added too liberally and low in fat), actually result in a dish that is a good source of complex carbohydrates. For a high-nutrition pizza, consider lean meats (such as Canadian bacon and ham) and vegetable toppings (such as green peppers, mushrooms, and onions). Thick crusts and French bread tend to make lower-fat pizza.

Introducing the Chapter

Motivators

1. **Sample Menus.** Ask each student or small groups of students to write healthful sample menus for two days. Have students share their ideas. Encourage them to give reasons for their choices and to discuss any differences. Ask them if their menus are realistic according to their tastes and budgets. Collect the menus and hand them back when you get to the Food Guide Pyramid. Ask students to compare their menus to the Pyramid, and then have them make any necessary alterations to these menus. (Key Skills: *Communication, Decision Making*)
2. **Bulletin Board.** Put a bare-bones outline of the Food Guide Pyramid on a large bulletin board. Place lines where titles and descriptions should go. Tell students the general idea of the Pyramid and ask them how they think it might be filled in. After students have read this chapter, have them help you fill it in correctly. You might want to give them magazines from which they can cut out pictures of foods to illustrate each group. Put the names of the groups on cardboard strips that can be removed for drills and tests. Pin the pictures up so that they can be removed easily. (Key Skill: *Decision Making*)

Chapter Objectives and Vocabulary

1. Have students read the chapter objectives and rephrase the objectives as questions.
2. Ask students to state, in their own words, the purpose of studying this chapter.
3. Pronounce the vocabulary terms listed on the previous page. Ask students whether they are familiar with any of these. Explain that the terms will be defined in the chapter.

Guided Reading

1. Have students read the chapter and use the Study Guide on pp. 165-166 of the *Student Workbook.*

Teaching. . .
Dietary Guidelines for Americans
(pp. 453-455)

Comprehension Check

1. Poor eating habits can contribute to some serious health problems. What are some of these problems? *(Heart disease, high blood pressure, stroke, diabetes, and some forms of cancer.)*
2. Why is it important to eat a variety of foods? *(Eating a variety of foods is the best way to insure that you get all the nutrients you need.)*
3. What factors influence whether your weight is a healthy one for you? *(The following are all factors: your age, height, and gender; how much of your weight comes from body fat compared to muscle, bone, and other lean tissue; and whether you or others in your family have high blood pressure or other weight-related medical problems.)*
4. What foods increase carbohydrates and decrease fats in your diet? *(Eating vegetables, fruits, and grain products increases carbohydrates and decreases fats in your diet.)*
5. What are some dangers of eating too much saturated fat and cholesterol in your diet? *(Too much saturated fat and cholesterol in the diet increases the risk for heart disease and can contribute to obesity.)*
6. What are some dangers of eating too much sugar? *(It may limit the number of other, more nutritious, foods you eat; it may cause you to gain weight; it may contribute to tooth decay.)*

Learning Activities

1. **Discussion.** Ask students what choices they are enjoying making as they get older — clothes, dates, recreation, friends, etc. Encourage them to include choosing what they eat. Ask how that has changed since they were babies. What are some of the food choices they make every day? What or who influences their choices? Which of these influences do they have control over? What influences have their

The right balance of food and exercise can help you maintain a healthy weight.

▼ Maintain or Improve Your Weight ▼

If you are too heavy or too thin, your chances of developing health problems increase. Somewhere between those two extremes there is a healthy weight for you.

Researchers are still trying to define "healthy weight" more exactly. They do know there is no magic number that is right for everyone. Whether your weight is a healthy one for you depends on factors such as:

- Your age, height, and gender (male or female).
- How much of your weight comes from body fat compared to muscle, bone, and other lean tissue. Having too much body fat is called **obesity**. It is linked to a number of health problems.
- Whether you or others in your family have high blood pressure or other weight-related medical problems.

Many people who think they have a weight problem actually do not. However, someone who is truly overweight, obese, or underweight is taking serious chances with his or her health. If you feel concerned about your weight, check with your doctor. Chapter 40 gives more information and suggestions for managing your weight.

▼ Choose a Diet with Plenty of Grain Products, Vegetables, and Fruits ▼

Do you know why this guideline was included? Grain products, vegetables, and fruits have so many benefits that it would be hard to eat too many of these foods.

In addition to great taste, grain products, vegetables, and fruits supply your body with many important nutrients.

More About *Calculating Fat in a Diet*

You can figure out exactly how many grams of fat you should be eating a day by going through the following steps. 1) Determine how many calories you eat a day. Let's say it's 2,000. 2) Multiply the number of calories by the percentage of fat you would like to eat. Let's say you want 30% of your diet to be fat. That means on a 2,000-calorie diet, you can eat 600 fat calories a day. 3) Each gram of fat has 9 calories. To determine how many grams you should be eating, divide 600 by 9. The total would be 67 grams of fat each day. There is a simpler formula for following a 30%-fat guideline. Eat no more than 3 grams of fat per 100 calories.

- They are high in complex carbohydrates and usually low in fats. By eating grain products, vegetables, and fruits more often, you can increase carbohydrates and decrease fats in your diet.
- They are good sources of fiber, which you need for good health.
- They are high in vitamins and minerals.

Choose low-fat foods for health.

Choose a Diet Low in Fat, Saturated Fat, and Cholesterol

Although fat is an essential nutrient, most Americans eat more than they need. Too much saturated fat and cholesterol in the diet increases the risk for heart disease. High-fat diets also contribute to obesity. Therefore, the Dietary Guidelines recommend cutting down on fat — especially saturated fat — and cholesterol.

Fortunately, eating the low-fat way can be not only healthful, but easy and good-tasting. For suggestions, read "How to Lower the Fat" on page 456.

AROUND THE WORLD

In Canada, people are ordering fewer hamburgers when dining out. A recent survey has shown that in 1990, 13.5% of all meals ordered in restaurants included a hamburger, compared to 17.1% in 1985. In that same period, the percentage of meals including chicken rose from 11.2% to 16.1%. How might this be related to a growing concern about eating more healthfully?

Choose a Diet Moderate in Sugars

Sugar is added to many foods, such as ice cream, candy, cakes, pastries, and sweetened cereals. Although sugar is a nutrient, it is not needed in large amounts. It's more important to get plenty of complex carbohydrates and enough vitamins, minerals, and protein. Eating foods with a high amount of sugar added may limit the number of other, more nutritious foods you eat. It might also cause you to gain too much weight.

Eating too many sweet foods can also contribute to tooth decay. The longer sugary or starchy foods stay in the mouth before teeth are brushed, the greater the chance that cavities will develop.

Learning Activities (continued)

best interests at heart? (Key Skills: *Communication, Critical Thinking*)

2. **List.** Ask students to quickly say some of the things that our bodies are able to do as you write them on the board (such as see, hear, run, heal, grow hair, reproduce, sweat, digest, breathe, etc.). Now ask students how many nutrients are necessary for good health. Ask students to compile a list of these forty nutrients in the next few days, or have groups compete to see which one can come up with all forty first. (Key Skills: *Critical Thinking, Cooperation*)
3. **Demonstration.** Display a collection of food packages having varying amounts of sugar. Have students rank the products from highest to lowest in sugar content. Then ask students to examine the labels to see how accurately they guessed. Ask students if they were surprised by any labels. (Key Skills: *Communication, Decision Making*)

Follow Up

1. **Reteaching.** Ask students to think of a slogan that encourages people to restrict their use of sugar, salt, and saturated fats. (Key Skills: *Creativity, Cooperation*)
2. **Enrichment.** Ask each student to report on the way one nutrient works in the body. On a piece of construction paper, have them write the name of the nutrient, its function, how much of it is needed daily, and in which foods it can be found. Display these pieces of construction paper around the room. (Key Skill: *Communication*)

AROUND THE WORLD

After reading the feature, have students investigate another country's most popular choice when dining out. Is this country's top choice different from what it was five years ago? If so, have students discuss why it's different. *(Answers will vary depending on what country each student chooses.)*

Teaching. . . Dietary Guidelines and Sodium (pp. 456-457)

Comprehension Check

1. What risk is associated with eating too much sodium? *(Too much sodium seems to increase the risk of high blood pressure.)*
2. Name some ways in which you could cut down on sodium. *(In order to cut down on sodium, you could flavor foods with herbs or spices instead of salt, you could eat salty foods less often and in smaller amounts, and you could read labels and choose foods lower in sodium.)*

Learning Activities

1. **Research.** Have students check out lower-fat alternatives the next time they are at a grocery store. Have them compare the number of fat grams in regular and low-fat mayonnaise, cheese, milk, salad dressing, pizza, and soda pop. Then have students summarize their findings in a couple of paragraphs. (Key Skills: *Communication, Math*)
2. **Discussion.** Ask students to name any low-fat products that they use at home. How do they like the products? Which do they recommend? Encourage students to get their parents to try low-fat alternatives. (Key Skill: *Communication*)
3. **Dessert Contest.** Have students work in groups of three to come up with a fruity dessert that has little or no sugar. They may make up a dessert or use one from a cookbook. You may want to give an award for the dessert that has the least sugar, for the most elaborate dessert, for the least expensive dessert, for the dessert that's easiest to make, and for the most glamorous dessert. To make these awards, you could hang ribbons from fruit shapes cut out of construction paper. (Key Skills: *Creativity, Problem Solving*)

How to . . . Lower the Fat

Health experts recommend that you get no more than 30% of your calories from fat. This guideline applies to your eating habits as a whole, not individual foods or meals. Eating less fat doesn't mean you have to give up favorite foods. Here are some suggestions you may want to try.

- Choose skim or low-fat milk instead of whole milk.
- Eat meat in moderation. One serving is just 2 to 3 ounces (55 to 85 grams) of cooked meat. Vary your protein sources, making sure to include dry beans and peas, poultry, and fish as well as meat.
- When buying meat, choose lean cuts. Some examples are beef round steak or ground round, pork tenderloin, and veal. Also look for "Select" or "Lean" on the meat label. Cut down on luncheon meats, bacon, and sausage.
- Trim the fat off meat before cooking or eating.
- Take the skin off chicken or turkey before eating. White meat has less fat than dark meat.
- Eat light-colored fish. Darker fish usually has a higher fat content.
- Buy tuna packed in water. If you buy oil-packed tuna, rinse off the oil.
- Try broiled, baked, or steamed foods. Avoid those that are fried.
- Add less butter, margarine, mayonnaise, and gravy to foods.
- Use plain low-fat yogurt or low-fat sour cream in dips and on potatoes.
- Look for low-fat or nonfat products when buying foods such as salad dressings.
- Go easy on foods such as hard cheese, nuts, and peanut butter. They are nutritious, but high in fat.

How to . . . Lower the Fat

Have students read the feature. Then ask them if their families have taken any steps to reduce the amount of fat in meals served at home. If students' families are not doing enough to reduce fat in meals, have them make a list of ways that this could be done, and then have them show this list to their parents. After students have done this, have them report back to the class any changes made in their eating habits at home.

Most regular soft drinks contain one teaspoon of sugar per ounce. What other beverages would be better choices on a regular basis?

TIPS: *Flavoring Foods for Lower Sodium*

If you automatically reach for the salt shaker to season foods, consider these low-sodium or no-sodium alternatives:

- Buy or make your own salt-free seasoning blends, for example, a combination of lemon pepper, garlic powder, basil, and thyme.
- Flavor vegetables with lemon or lime juice, or with flavored vinegars.
- Baste meats with fruit purées or preserves to enhance flavor. Try cranberry sauce on pork or poultry.
- Use bottled teriyaki sauce instead of soy sauce for a savings of 260 milligrams of sodium per tablespoon.

Choose a Diet Moderate in Salt and Sodium

Most Americans eat more salt and sodium than they need. In addition to table salt sprinkled on food, sodium is added during the processing and manufacturing of food.

Eating too much sodium seems to increase the risk of high blood pressure in some people. You can cut down on sodium by:

- Flavoring foods with herbs or spices instead of salt.
- Eating salty foods less often and in smaller amounts.
- Reading labels and choosing foods lower in sodium.

Shaking the Habit

Materials
plate covered with waxed paper; salt shaker; ingredient and nutrition labels

Equipment
none

Directions:
About one-third of the average person's daily intake of sodium comes from salt added to food in cooking or at the table. Try this test: Salt the covered plate as you would if it contained food. Collect the salt and measure it. If you used about ⅛ teaspoon, that amounts to 250 milligrams of sodium. Much of the sodium we consume is found in processed foods. Sodium is also naturally present in many foods such as oatmeal. Check the ingredient and nutrition labels for a variety of foods and specifically look for the words salt and sodium.

- ✔ Did you use more salt than you expected?
- ✔ Which foods have added salt?
- ✔ Which foods are high in sodium?
- ✔ How could you cut back on sodium in your diet?

Learning Activities (continued)

4. **Group Panel.** Divide the class into several groups. Give each group a profession related to eating a balanced diet, such as a physician, a dentist, a nutritionist, and an athletic trainer. Have each group get information about their area by doing research or by talking to a professional. Then have each group choose one person to represent them and *become* that professional in a panel discussion. Each "professional" will make a general statement about the importance of a balanced diet in their field and then will answer questions from you and others in the class. (Key Skills: *Cooperation, Communication*)

Follow Up

1. **Reteaching.** Ask students to make a list of some low-fat foods they enjoy eating. Remind them to consider these foods when choosing snacks or planning meals. (Key Skill: *Communication*)
2. **Enrichment.** Have students write down their favorite evening meal. Then ask them to rewrite the same menu using less sugar, salt, and fats. Encourage them to try the alternative menu and report on the results. If the meals were unsatisfactory, ask students to revise the menu more realistically. (Key Skills: *Communication, Decision Making*)

Shaking the Habit

Materials: Plate covered with wax paper or foil, salt shaker.

Equipment: None.

Purpose: To help students learn the sources of sodium in their diets and how to avoid getting too much.

Outcomes:

- Many people add more salt than they realize at the table.
- Many processed foods have added salt.
- Foods that are high in sodium include canned vegetables, commercially prepared meals, and snack foods.
- Avoid salting food at the table; season with spices and herbs.

TIPS:

Flavoring Foods for Lower Sodium
Have students read the feature. Then have the class brainstorm ways that they could cut down on sodium in the food they eat. After they're done brainstorming, have each student discuss these ideas with their parents. *(Answers will vary.)*

Teaching. . . The Food Guide Pyramid (pp. 458-460)

Comprehension Check

1. How many categories of food should be included in a diet every day? *(Five categories of food should be included in a diet every day.)*
2. Which age and gender group probably needs the most food per day? *(An active teen male probably needs the most food per day.)*
3. What is a mixed food and what is an advantage of including mixed foods in your menu? *(A mixed food consists of elements from more than one group. An advantage of including mixed foods in your menu is that you get a variety of nutrients in one dish.)*
4. What types of foods should be used sparingly? *(Foods high in fat and sugar should not be a major or frequent part of a person's eating plan.)*

Learning Activities

1. **Menu Planning.** Using the Food Guide Pyramid, ask students to plan meals for three to five days. Tell them to use a variety of foods (no repeats except milk). Encourage students to show these menus to their parents, and have them ask their parents if they can try them at home. Also, make sure students have included low-fat, low-sugar, low-sodium alternatives. (Key Skills: *Decision Making, Management*)
2. **Menu Evaluation.** Distribute copies of the school lunch menu. Ask students to evaluate lunches for a week according to the Food Guide Pyramid. How do they rate? Can students think of *feasible* changes or additions? After discussing this with your students, make a list of realistic suggestions that you might want to give to the school menu planner. (Key Skills: *Communication, Critical Thinking*)

Food Guide Pyramid
A Guide to Daily Food Choices

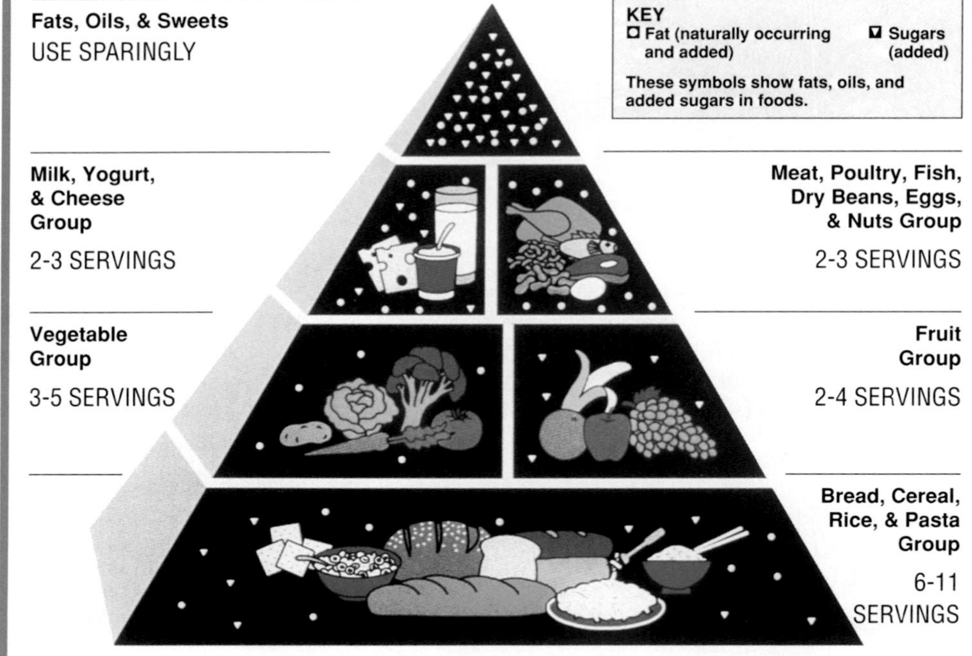

Food Examples for One Serving

Milk, Yogurt, and Cheese Group
- 1 cup milk or yogurt
- 1½ ounces ripened cheese
- 2 ounces processed cheese

Meats, Poultry, Fish, Dry Beans, Eggs, and Nuts Group
- 2 to 3 ounces of cooked lean meat, poultry or fish
- 1 cup cooked dry beans
- 2 Tbsp. peanut butter — ½ serving

Vegetable Group
- 1 cup leafy raw vegetables (lettuce, spinach)
- ½ cup other vegetables, cooked or raw
- ¾ cup vegetable juice

Fruit Group
- 1 orange, apple, banana, pear
- ½ cup chopped, cooked, or canned fruit
- ¾ cup fruit juice

Bread, Cereal, Rice, and Pasta Group
- 1 slice bread
- ½ cup cooked cereal, rice, or pasta
- 1 ounce ready to eat cereal

More About Grains and Vegetables

Since the beginning of the 20th century, Americans have been consuming less fiber, and the type of fiber eaten has changed. Today, we eat less whole-grain breads and cereals but more fruits and vegetables than our grandparents did fifty years ago. These figures can be misleading. Canned fruit juice (with only a trace of fiber) now accounts for about one-third of the processed fruit consumed. Although more vegetables are eaten, we have decreased our consumption of potatoes by some 50%, which results in a significant loss of fiber. Many of the potato products eaten are highly refined, such as potato chips. In the early days, most of the flour and cereals were whole-grain products. Throughout the

The Food Guide Pyramid

The **Food Guide Pyramid** is a simple method of diet planning based on food groups. Foods are organized into five major groups based on the nutrients they contain. If you eat the recommended number of servings from each of these five groups every day, you will probably get all the nutrients you need.

The Food Guide Pyramid can help you and your family put the Dietary Guidelines for Americans into practice. The guide is shown on page 458.

How Many Servings?

Notice that the Food Guide Pyramid gives the recommended number of servings from each food group as a range. Most people should have at least the lowest number of servings in the range. Some people may need more, depending on their age, body size, and activity level. For example, most teens need more because of rapid growth. A male teen who is very active would probably need the highest number of servings.

Some people wonder how they could possibly eat as many servings as the Food Guide Pyramid recommends. However, note that the serving sizes are not large. If you have cereal and toast at breakfast, a sandwich at lunch, and spaghetti and a roll at dinner, you've had six servings from the breads, cereals, rice, and pasta group.

Some foods, such as pizza or a salad, are mixtures of foods from more than one group. When you are figuring up your total number of servings, think of the individual items in each food mixture. A pizza, for instance, includes crust (a grain product), cheese, vegetables, and perhaps meat.

Limit your choices of sugary products to an occasional treat. What other food choices offer a sweet flavor, but are packed with nutrients?

years, more white flour and breads and more refined cereals have been used. In addition, many sugary foods now replace the starchy foods (many of which are good fiber sources) that once were the major source of energy for the body.

Learning Activities (continued)

3. **Personal Choices.** Ask each student to make a column for each of the five food groups. Under each column, have the student fill in all the choices in that group that he or she likes to eat. Hopefully, students will have fairly long lists of choices in each group. Have students share suggestions of mixed foods (pizza, salads, etc.) for those students who think they hate all vegetables and fruits. (Key Skills: *Communication, Management*)

Follow Up

1. **Reteaching.** Ask groups of students to reconstruct the Food Guide Pyramid from memory. Then have them consult the text to fill in whatever they missed. (Key Skills: *Communication, Cooperation*)
2. **Extension.** Use the extension information handout on p. 51 of the *Extending the Text* booklet in the TCR.
3. **Enrichment.** Divide students into five groups and assign each one of the food groups. Ask each group to pick two or three representative foods from their group, and then have them look up each food's nutritional content. (You will have to provide resource material, such as *Food Values of Portions Commonly Used:* Pennington and Church, Harper and Row.) How many nutrients are included when the groups combine their choices? Are similar nutrients found in choices within a group (such as vegetables)? (Key Skills: *Communication, Cooperation*)

Photo Focus

Discuss the photo at the bottom of page 459 with the students. What types of food have the students' parents bought for them to snack on when they get home from school? Do these snacks have lots of sugar, or have their parents tried to buy more nutritious snacks? *(Answers will vary.)*

Completing the Chapter

For Review

1. Emphasize the main concepts using the summary.
2. Have students complete the "Facts to Recall." (Answers below.)

For Reteaching

1. **Reteaching.** Use the activity on p. 50 of the *Reteaching and Practical Skills* booklet in the TCR.

For Enrichment

1. **Enrichment.** Use the activity on pp. 62-63 of the *Enrichment Activities* booklet in the TCR.

For Evaluation

1. Choose items from "Ideas to Explore" and "Activities to Try."
2. Use the chapter test on pp. 81-82 in the testing booklet of the TCR or use the testmaker software.

Facts to Recall Answers

1. Because no one food can supply all the nutrients in the amounts you need.
2. Your age, height, and gender; how much of your weight comes from body fat; and whether you or others in your family have weight-related medical problems.
3. They are high in complex carbohydrates and usually low in fats, they are good sources of fiber, and they are high in vitamins and minerals.
4. **Any three:** choose lean cuts; trim the fat off meat before cooking or eating; take the skin off poultry before eating; and eat white meat instead of dark meat.
5. No more than 30% of your calories should come from fat.
6. Eating foods that are high in sugar may limit the number of other, more nutritious, foods you eat; it can cause you to gain too much weight; and it can contribute to tooth decay.

▼ Choosing Foods from the Food Groups ▼

Be sure to choose a variety of foods from each food group. Although foods within a group are similar, they do not contain exactly the same nutrients. If you limit yourself to only a few choices, you may come up short.

The Food Guide Pyramid includes a reminder to use fats, oils, and sweets sparingly. It's fine to have small amounts once in a while, as long as your overall food choices are healthful ones. However, foods high in fat and sugar should not be a major or frequent part of your eating plan.

Keep the Dietary Guidelines in mind when you use the Food Guide Pyramid. Choose foods from each group that are low in fat, cholesterol, sugar, and sodium. By following the Dietary Guidelines and the Food Guide Pyramid, you will help yourself stay healthy, fit, and active for years to come.

TAKING ACTION

Promoting Healthy Habits

Your school is preparing for National Wellness Week. Each class has been asked to create a campaign promoting some aspect of wellness. Your class has been given the task of informing the community about the Dietary Guidelines for Americans. For this project, you and your classmates will rely not only on your knowledge of the Guidelines, but also on your understanding of people's active lifestyles and attitudes toward health. Your job is to convince them that practicing healthful habits can fit into their busy schedules. How will you find the information you need to get your message across?

Using Your Resourcefulness

- What ways can you use to encourage people to eat a wide variety of foods? Where will you find specific examples of the basic food groups and the nutritional benefits of each?
- How will you find out about the price and availability of different food items, to convince people that the products are inexpensive and easy to find?
- Where will you find more information on maintaining a healthy weight, including facts on body fat, weight-related medical disorders, and factors affecting healthy weight levels?
- Where will you find suggestions on ways to cut down on sodium, sugar, and fats?
- Where will you find different ways of preparing vegetables, fruits, and grain products, to encourage people to include more of these in their diets?
- Identify ways to learn more about Americans' present health habits, to know which guidelines need special emphasis.
- List all the resources that you think would help you to put your knowledge of nutrition to use in everyday life.

TAKING ACTION

After students have read this feature, you may want to have them answer the *Using Your Resourcefulness* questions as a class. Also, have the class discuss what kind of promotional campaign they would put together and how they would divide the different jobs that would need to be done.

Using Your Resourcefulness Answers

- Answers will vary but may include: Dietary Guidelines, Food Guide Pyramids, nutrient charts, etc.
- Answers include: survey supermarkets or possibly food coops.
- Answers include: physicians' offices, nutritionists, dietitians, library resources.
- Answers include: Dietary Guidelines,

Chapter 39 Review

Summary

In this chapter, you have read about:

- The Dietary Guidelines for Americans and the reasons for following each.
- How to lower the fat in your diet without giving up your favorite foods.
- How to use the Food Guide Pyramid to plan a healthful diet.

Facts to Recall

1. Why is eating a variety of foods important to maintaining good health?
2. Identify three factors that help determine whether your weight is a healthy one for you.
3. Name three reasons for eating plenty of grain products, vegetables, and fruits.
4. Name three ways to reduce fat when buying and preparing meat and poultry.
5. According to health experts, what percentage of your calories should come from fat?
6. Why should you choose a diet moderate in sugars?
7. What are three ways of cutting down on sodium in your diet?
8. Name the five major food groups and give the recommended number of servings for each.

Ideas to Explore

1. Many food labels or advertisements include phrases such as "no cholesterol," "light," "less fat," "low in sodium," or "good source of fiber." What examples have you seen or heard? How might these statements be helpful to consumers? How might they be misleading?
2. Why do government agencies play a role in developing nutrition guidelines and bringing them to the public? What might happen if this source of information was not available?

Activities to Try

1. Using the Food Guide Pyramid, create a three-day menu that includes at least the minimum number of servings from all five major food groups.
2. Imagine you are a writer or artist working for an advertising agency. Your client is a vegetable growers' association that wants your help in promoting its product. Use your creativity to design an advertisement or ad campaign to improve the image of a specific vegetable, such as broccoli, cauliflower, or brussels sprouts.

LINK TO *Math*

Figuring Percentage of Calories from Fat

For good health, no more than 30% of your daily calories should come from fat. Have you ever wondered how some of your favorite foods measure up? Using food labels from two foods and the formula below, determine the percentage of calories from fat for these foods:

1. Multiply the number of grams of fat by 9 (the number of calories in 1 gram of fat). This gives you the total calories from fat.
2. Divide the total calories from fat by the number of calories per serving.
3. Multiply the answer from Step 2 by 100.

Example: 1 serving corned beef hash has 490 calories and 34 grams of fat.

1. $34\text{ g} \times 9 = 306$ calories from fat.
2. $306 \div 490$ calories per serving $= 0.63$
3. $0.63 \times 100 = 63\%$ of the calories in corned beef hash come from fat.

nutritionists, dietitians, cookbooks, government publications.

- Answers include: cookbooks, hospitals, clinics, dietitians.
- Answers will vary but may include: magazines, government publications, nutrition books, etc.
- Answers will vary.

Facts to Recall Answers (continued)

7. You can cut down on sodium by flavoring foods with herbs or spices instead of salt, by eating salty foods less often and in smaller amounts, and by reading labels and choosing foods lower in sodium.
8. Bread, Cereal, Rice, and Pasta Group — 6 to 11 servings; Vegetable Group — 3 to 5 servings; Fruit Group — 2 to 4 servings; Meats, Poultry, Fish, Dry Beans, Eggs, and Nuts Group — 2 to 3 servings; and Milk, Yogurt, and Cheese Group — 2 to 3 servings.

Ideas to Explore

1. Answers will vary.
2. Answers will vary.

LINK TO *Math*

Answers

1. Answers will vary depending on what foods the students choose.
2. Answers will vary depending on what foods the students choose.
3. Answers will vary depending on what foods the students choose.

Preparing to Teach

Chapter Outline

Chapter Resources

The following booklet materials may be found in the *Teacher's Classroom Resources* box:

- Lesson Plans, p. 45
- Student Workbook, *Study Guide,* pp. 171-172; *Managing Weight Crossword,* pp. 173-174
- Color Transparencies, *Factors Affecting Weight,* CT-44
- Technology and Computers, pp. 42, 48
- Cooperative Learning, p. 52
- Extending the Text, *Fitness Formula,* p. 52
- Reteaching and Practical Skills, *Investigating Fad Diets,* p. 51
- Enrichment Activities, *Calorie Density,* p. 64
- Chapter and Unit Tests, pp. 83-84
- Testmaker Software

Also see:

- Meeting the Special Needs of Students
- Linking Home, School, and Community
- Dealing with Sensitive Issues

ABCNews InterActive™ Videodiscs

- *Food and Nutrition*

See the ABCNews InterActive™ Bar Code Correlation booklet for applicable segments.

CHAPTER 40 Managing Your Weight

OBJECTIVES

- *Discuss how to safely reach and maintain a healthy weight.*
- *Identify characteristics and hazards of fad diets.*

TERMS TO LEARN

- ***body image***
- ***basal metabolism***

Question: What is the perfect weight or the perfect body build?

Answer: When it comes to people's sizes and shapes, there's no such thing as "perfect." After all, everyone is an individual.

However, there is a weight range and fitness level that is right for you — one that helps you stay healthy and feel your best. Finding and reaching that level is what weight management is all about.

What Weight Is Right for You?

Weight management is a matter of good health, not just appearance. If you have read Chapter 39, you know that one of the Dietary Guidelines is "Maintain a healthy weight." Weight management can help you avoid the health risks of being overweight or underweight.

If you are a teen who is still growing, it is natural for you to be gaining weight. How can you find out whether your weight is within a healthful range? The best way is to consult a physician or other health professional.

Keep in mind that weight is only part of the story. How much of your weight comes from body fat may actually be a better clue to health. Extra pounds are not a problem if they come from muscle or bone. On the other hand, even a person who is underweight may have too much body fat.

If you need to gain or lose weight, or get rid of extra fat, this chapter can help you learn how to do it successfully and safely. If your current weight is about right, learning about weight management can help you keep it that way.

Your activity level is one factor that affects your weight.

What Affects Your Weight?

Your weight depends on a number of factors. Some of these cannot be changed. You inherited your basic body type: short or tall, large-boned or small-boned. You may have inherited a tendency to gain weight more or less easily than others.

However, you *can* change your activity level and eating habits. Together, these factors have a great effect on your weight and percentage of body fat. Recall the discussion of energy and calories from Chapter 38. Whether you gain, lose, or maintain weight is largely a matter of balancing energy.

More About Healthy Weight

The 1990 nutritional guidelines talk about *healthy* weight rather than *desirable* weight, shifting the emphasis from appearance to health. These guidelines suggest that if people lose weight, they should do so more slowly than previously recommended. Previously, a rate of one to two pounds a week was recommended as safe. The new guidelines say a weight loss of one-half to one pound a week is recommended. Reducing calories enough to maintain a faster loss could result in inadequate nutrition. Long-term studies show that people who lose weight quickly do not keep it off.

Introducing the Chapter

Motivators

1. **Discussion.** Ask students if they know anyone who has lost a lot of weight. How did they do it? Did they keep the weight off? Have the students ever dieted or tried to gain weight? What did they do? Did it work? What would make them want to lose or gain weight now? How would they go about doing it? What are some good reasons for gaining or losing weight? Who determines these reasons? What influence does society have on our shapes? (Key Skills: *Communication, Critical Thinking*)
2. **Bulletin Board.** Distribute current newspapers and magazines to students and tell them to cut out ads or articles relating to weight management. Divide a bulletin board into three parts — one red, one yellow, and one green. Have students place their ads on the green if they think the idea is a "Go," on the yellow if it's a "So-So," and on the red if it's a "No." Ask students to explain why they placed the ads where they did. When you've finished the chapter, go back over the bulletin board and ask students if they have changed their minds about any of the ads or articles. (Key Skills: *Communication, Critical Thinking*)

Chapter Objectives and Vocabulary

1. Have students read the chapter objectives and rephrase the objectives as questions.
2. Ask students to state, in their own words, the purpose of studying this chapter.
3. Pronounce the vocabulary terms listed on the previous page. Ask students whether they are familiar with any of these. Explain that the terms will be defined in the chapter.

Guided Reading

1. Have students read the chapter and use the Study Guide on pp. 171-172 of the *Student Workbook.*

Teaching. . .
What Weight Is Right for You?, What Affects Your Weight?, and A Weight Management Plan for You
(pp. 463-465)

Comprehension Check

1. How can you find out whether your weight is within a healthful range? *(The best way is to consult a physician or other health professional.)*
2. What are two things you can't change about your body? *(Your height and your bone size.)*
3. What two things can you change that affect your body? *(You can change your activity level and eating habits.)*
4. What two things must remain equal in order for you to maintain the same weight? *(The energy you take in from food must equal the energy you use.)*
5. What has research shown about losing weight? *(Research has shown that when it comes to losing weight, the combination of exercise and healthful eating habits is more effective than any diet.)*

Learning Activities

1. **Personal Inventory.** Ask each student to make a list of all the activities they enjoy doing that involve exercise (e.g., biking, swimming, hiking). Then ask students to make seven columns on another sheet of paper — one for each day of the week. Have them fill in the types of exercise that they do on each day of an average week. What exercise do students usually do each day or only on certain days? Are they satisfied with the amount of exercise they are getting? Is there any exercising activity they would like to be doing more often? If students want to be more active, have them work on a realistic plan to fit more enjoyable exercise into their lifestyle. (Key Skills: *Communication, Management*)

Body Image and Self-Esteem

Your **body image** is a mental picture of how you think your body looks. This mental picture may or may not be accurate.

It's difficult to see yourself objectively, or as you really are. Often people dwell on what they consider their flaws. They compare themselves to models or athletes with "ideal" body builds. When they look in the mirror, all they may see is their weight, the shape of their thighs, or the size of their arm muscles.

However, being critical of yourself will not help you make positive changes. It will only make you feel worse. Instead, learn to feel good about the person you are. Remember that you are more than just a number on a scale or a clothing size. You are a whole person with many good qualities, inside and out.

When you have high self-esteem — when you feel good about yourself — it's easier to see yourself objectively. You may still decide that you want to make changes in the outer you. However, it will be because you care about yourself, not because you are trying to fit some image of perfection.

- If the energy you take in from food *equals* the energy you use, your weight stays the same.
- If the energy you take in from food is *more* than the energy you use, you gain weight. Why? Your body converts the extra energy to body fat and stores it.
- If the energy you take in from food is *less* than the energy you use, you lose weight. Why? To get the extra energy it needs, your body converts body fat back to energy.

A Weight Management Plan for You

Good choices in eating and exercising can help you reach and maintain a healthy weight. Start by setting a goal and planning how to reach it. A good plan would include evaluating your exercise and eating habits and finding specific changes to focus on. Then carry out your plan. Evaluate your progress regularly to see how well your plan is working.

How Much Is a Serving?

Materials
mashed potatoes; grape jelly

Equipment
plate; serving spoons; measuring cups and spoons

Directions:
On your plate, serve the amount of mashed potatoes you would normally eat at a meal and the amount of jelly you would use on one piece of toast. Using measuring cups and spoons, measure the amounts of potatoes and jelly you took as a serving and record the amounts. Using a Nutritive Values of Foods table and the serving size listed on the jelly jar, compare your serving size with a standard serving size.

- ✔ Were your servings larger or smaller than the standard serving sizes?
- ✔ Why is it important to compare serving sizes when checking the number of calories you consume?
- ✔ Why is serving size an important consideration in maintaining your weight?

▼ Losing Weight ▼

Health experts recommend that if you want to lose weight, try to lose about a pound a week. Losing weight at a slow, steady rate is safer than trying to lose more rapidly. It's also more likely to be successful in the long run.

People often think of losing weight as "going on a diet." Instead, think of combining exercise with healthful, lifelong eating habits. Research has shown that when it comes to losing weight, the combination of exercise and healthful eating habits is more effective than any diet.

Why do so many weight-loss diets fail? People who try to follow a too-strict diet will often feel hungry and deprived. Eventually they go back to their old eating habits. In fact, they often eat more than ever and end up weighing more than when they started. This pattern of weight loss and gain is very dangerous. So is any strict diet that does not provide your body with enough energy and nutrients. See the box on page 466 for more information about dangerous diets.

If you need to lose or gain a large amount of weight, talk with a physician to get sound advice. Extreme changes can affect your health.

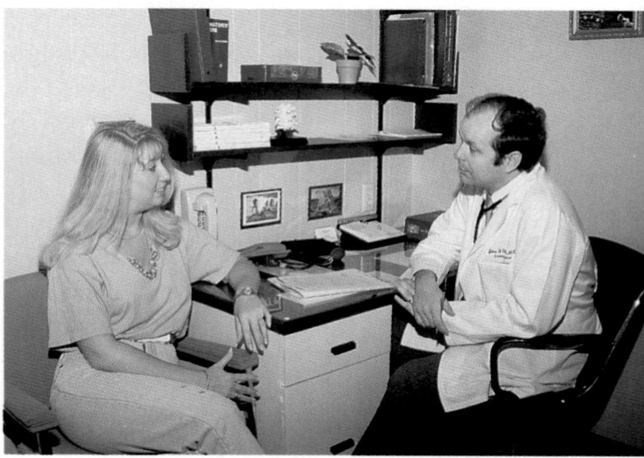

Learning Activities (continued)

2. **Survey.** Ask your students to construct a survey about weight management to give to their friends at school. Have them find out if kids are happy with their weight. If they aren't, why aren't they? Do they plan to do anything about their weight? What? When students come up with a form, make copies of it so the surveyees can remain anonymous. Tabulate the results and discuss how they relate to self-esteem and healthy weight management. If the results are interesting, submit them to the school newspaper. (Key Skills: *Communication, Critical Thinking*)

Follow Up

1. **Reteaching.** Divide students into groups. Give each group a piece of paper and have them come up with an illustrated slogan that has to do with balancing the amount of energy taken in with the amount used. (Key Skill: *Creativity*)
2. **Enrichment.** Have students record their energy intake and energy output for a day or two. How do they balance? (Key Skill: *Critical Thinking*)

How Much Is a Serving?

Materials: Mashed potatoes; grape jelly.

Equipment: Plate; serving spoons; measuring cups and spoons.

Purpose: To help students recognize the role of serving size in maintaining weight.

Outcomes:

- Many people do not realize that the serving sizes they consume are much larger than standard serving sizes.
- If your serving size differs from the standard serving size, the calories must be adjusted accordingly.
- Large serving sizes may lead to excess weight. They may also reduce the desire for other foods needed for variety in the diet.

Photo Focus

Discuss the photo at the bottom of page 465 with the students. What other sources can provide you with information about intelligent weight loss or gain? *(Answers will vary. Some possible answers include nutrition centers, weight loss centers, hospitals, metabolism clinics, and health and fitness centers.)*

Teaching. . .
Fad Diets, Exercise, and Eating Habits
(pp. 466-467)

Comprehension Check

1. What are some dangerous side effects of taking diet pills? *(People taking diet pills have been reported to have very high blood pressure, kidney failure, and strokes. Diet pills can also lead to drug abuse.)*
2. What makes a safe weight-loss plan? *(A safe weight-loss plan is based on real foods; it has enough calories per day to maintain energy; it includes a variety of foods from all five major food groups; it emphasizes whole grains, fruits, vegetables, and other low-fat foods; it does not promise weight loss without exercise; and it does not promise weight loss of more than one or two pounds per week.)*
3. What is basal metabolism? *(Basal metabolism is the number of calories needed for normal body processes.)*
4. What kinds of foods make it easier to meet your nutrition needs without exceeding your calorie needs? *(Low-fat, nutrient-dense foods make it easier to meet your nutrient needs without exceeding your calorie needs.)*

Learning Activities

1. **Impromptu Skit.** Choose students to create an ending to this situation. Tina wants to lose fifteen pounds for a big celebration coming up in two months. Carol has just read about a diet in a teen magazine that claims you can lose ten pounds in a week by eating only ice cream and drinking coffee. She thinks Tina should wait a month or so and try that diet. Julie thinks Tina should eat what she wants and exercise four or five hours a day. Cindy thinks that your body weight is a given. She has tried fad diets and exercise overkill, and they didn't work or last. Brenda has just been studying weight management in home economics class. She's eager to share her findings with Tina. She'd like to lose a few pounds

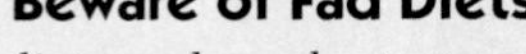

Beware of Fad Diets

Weight-loss diets and products are everywhere these days. They are discussed in books and magazines, advertised in print and on radio and television, and passed around among friends. Many of these diets are costly. Many don't work. Some are even health hazards. How can you tell? Here are some warning signs.

- ***Very few calories.*** No one should take in fewer than 1200 calories a day unless he or she is under a physician's care. Most people need more than that, even to lose weight.
- ***Unrealistic promises.*** Some advertisements promise that fat will "melt away" without exercise. They may tell stories of people who lost dozens of pounds in just a few weeks. However, there is no fast, easy way to lose weight.
- ***Limited food choices.*** Some diets require you to eat one food or just a few foods day after day. This type of diet does not take into account the nutritional needs of your body. Variety is the only way to be sure you are getting all the nutrients you need.
- ***Special products.*** Some diets are based on using special milkshake mixes, candy bars, or other products. You can't be sure of getting complete nutrition, but you can be sure that you have spent a lot of money. These weight-loss plans don't help you learn healthful eating habits.
- ***Diet pills.*** So-called "diet pills" are drugs that are supposed to cut down your appetite. They can have dangerous side effects. People taking these pills have been reported to have very high blood pressure, kidney failure, and strokes. Pills can also lead to drug abuse.

A safe weight-loss plan:

- Is based on real foods, not powders, pills, or special diet liquids.
- Has enough calories per day to maintain energy.
- Includes a variety of foods from all five major food groups in the Food Guide Pyramid.
- Emphasizes whole grains, fruits, vegetables, and other low-fat foods.
- Does not promise weight loss without exercise.
- Does not promise weight loss of more than one to two pounds per week.

More About Body Fat

One pound of body fat is equivalent to 3500 calories. Therefore, in order to lose one pound in a week, you would need to take in about 500 fewer calories each day than the amount required to maintain your weight. You must also take into account your activity level. For example, say you weigh 150 pounds and you are moderately active. You need 3000 calories per day to maintain your current weight (multiply your weight by 20). To lose one pound per week, you should take in 2500 calories per day.

Exercise

Being more active can help you lose weight. One reason is the extra calories you burn while exercising. However, exercise has other weight-loss benefits as well.

Up to 12 hours after vigorous exercise, your body burns calories at a higher rate than it would have otherwise. If you exercise in the morning and later in the day, you will burn bonus calories all day long. The extra exercise will even be working for you while you sleep.

If you become more physically active, you will probably look trimmer even if you don't lose weight. The reason is that you are likely to lose body fat and replace it with lean muscle tissue. A pound of muscle tissue takes up less space than a pound of body fat.

Muscle also requires more energy to maintain itself than body fat. Adding muscle can increase your **basal metabolism** — the number of calories needed for normal body processes. Raising your basal metabolism means you'll lose weight a little more easily, or can eat a little more without gaining weight.

Many people find that when they exercise regularly, they are more motivated to eat healthfully. And of course, exercise has many other health benefits, as you learned in Chapter 37.

Regular exercise helps you burn calories.

Eating Habits

The first step in improving your eating habits is to understand what your current habits are. Try keeping a food diary for one week. Each time you eat something, write down what it was and the amount. Also describe the situation — the time of day, where you were and with whom, and how you felt.

At the end of the week, look for patterns. Try to see when you're most likely to overeat or make poor choices. Is it when you're bored? When you're away from home? While you watch TV? Then think of a way to solve the problem. The next time you're bored, for example, try calling a friend or going for a bike ride.

Remember, healthful eating habits are based on the Dietary Guidelines and the Food Guide Pyramid. Many people find that they lose weight just by following these basic guidelines.

In particular, choose foods low in fat. Low-fat, nutrient-dense foods make it easier to meet your nutrient needs without exceeding your calorie needs. For a low-fat eating plan, follow the suggestions in Chapter 39. Be sure to eat plenty of whole grains and fresh fruits and vegetables.

When are you most likely to make poor food choices?

More About *Burning Calories*

Any physical activity, such as standing, walking, or cleaning your room, burns extra calories in addition to your basal metabolism. The more active you are, the more calories you use. Writing a letter, turning book pages, or playing a video game takes little energy. Strenuous activities — jogging, dancing, playing basketball — use lots of energy.

Learning Activities (continued)

herself and proposes that she and Tina try to develop some good habits. (Key Skills: *Communication, Creativity*)

2. **Posters.** Ask groups of students to create posters that explain *basal metabolism*. After studying what it is and how it works, have each group make their poster. This poster can explain what basal metabolism is or illustrate what it is. Have a representative from each group talk about their finished poster. Then, display the posters so students will have more exposure to the concept. You might have the class vote on a "People's Choice" award for the best job. (Key Skills: *Communication, Creativity*)
3. **Demonstration.** Bring a collection of items generally found on a salad bar. Borrow from the school cafeteria if possible. As a last resort, ask students to list common salad bar ingredients. Then rate the items according to calories, nutritional value, and fat content. Ask students to come up with the best possible combination and the worst possible combination. Then ask them to write out two possible combinations that they personally would eat. Have them figure out the calories, nutrients, and fat content of these combinations. (Key Skills: *Math, Decision Making*)

Follow Up

1. **Reteaching.** Have students list the pros and cons of fad diets on the board. What conclusions can they draw? (Key Skills: *Communication, Critical Thinking*)
2. **Enrichment.** Ask students to find out how many grams of fat a person should eat each day. How many should a person trying to lose weight consume? (Key Skill: *Decision Making*)

Teaching. . .
Tips for Losing Weight, Gaining Weight, and Maintaining Your Weight
(pp. 468-470)

Comprehension Check

1. What are two tools to help you keep track of calories? *(Food labels and a calorie chart can help you keep track of calories.)*
2. What is the formula for losing weight? *(The formula for losing weight is fairly simple: get plenty of exercise and make sensible, nutritious food choices.)*
3. Name four ways in which you can gain weight. *(To gain weight, you can split up the usual three meals a day into six small ones, you can eat nutritious snacks between meals, you can pass up water in favor of milk and juice, and you can include nutritious but calorie-dense foods in your diet.)*
4. How can you maintain your weight? *(To maintain your weight, you should eat right and stay active.)*

Learning Activities

1. **Lists.** Write "Good Eating Habits" on one side of the board and "Poor Eating Habits" on the other side. Ask students to give examples of each that they have observed. Discuss what makes habits good or poor. Also ask students to suggest ways to improve poor habits. (Key Skills: *Communication, Critical Thinking*)

AROUND THE WORLD

After reading the feature, have students investigate what other types of food products are being developed that would compete with food on the market now. What are the ingredients of these new products? Would they have fewer calories and be more nutritious than the existing products? *(Answers will vary.)*

Notice the serving sizes given in the Food Guide Pyramid (see page 458). In the beginning it may be helpful to measure the servings out so you'll know exactly what the portions look like.

If you want to keep track of calories, use food labels and a good calorie chart. Remember, calories are not bad for you. They are a measurement of the energy your body needs. Your physician can give you advice on the number of calories you need each day.

AROUND THE WORLD

A new product called Oatrim, developed at a U.S. Department of Agriculture research lab in Peoria, Illinois, could be good news for weight-conscious people and oat farmers alike. Oatrim is an oat bran-based fat substitute. In taste tests, ice milk and a frozen dessert made with Oatrim compared well against ice cream in taste and texture, while containing far fewer calories and much less fat and cholesterol. If Oatrim becomes popular, it could also open up a new market for oat farmers, who often have trouble getting good prices for their crop.

Making sensible food choices and varying your exercise routine are essential for successful weight loss.

Tips for Losing Weight

The formula for losing weight is fairly simple: get plenty of exercise and make sensible, nutritious food choices. The challenging part is sticking to your plan. Here are some tips from people who have been successful.

- Vary your exercise routine to keep from getting bored.
- Exercise with a friend. You'll be less likely to skip a session.
- Don't skip meals. People who do usually end up eating more food, and less nutritious food, than if they had eaten the meal.
- Sit down at a table and eat slowly. It's more relaxing and you will enjoy the food more. You'll also be less likely to overeat.
- Plan for snacks in advance. Choose nutritious snacks such as fresh fruit, whole-grain crackers, or raw vegetables.
- When eating away from home, look for healthful choices. Many restaurants offer grilled chicken, baked potatoes, salads, and low-fat milk. Ask for food to be served without high-fat condiments such as mayonnaise, sour cream, and regular salad dressing.

More About Calories

You don't always need a calorie chart to tell you whether foods are high or low in calories. Here are some guidelines to keep in mind:

- Low-calorie foods are often juicy or watery, bulky but without fat, coarse with lots of fiber, watery-crisp, or puffy and airy.
- High-calorie foods are often oily or greasy-crisp, thick and smooth, sweet and sticky, or concentrated and compact.

- Avoid thinking of certain foods as "bad." Your overall food choices are what counts. If you love ice cream or potato chips, eat a small amount once in a while to satisfy your craving. Just don't make a habit of eating these foods frequently or in large amounts.
- Avoid weighing yourself every day. Normal ups and downs can be discouraging. Instead, check every week or two weeks. You'll see more of a change.
- If you still don't see progress when you weigh yourself, try keeping track of your measurements instead. You may be losing inches, not pounds, as you replace fat with muscle.
- Remember that one slip doesn't mean you've failed. If you eat too much or miss an exercise session, don't punish yourself or give up. Just go back to your plan the next day.
- Have patience. The extra weight wasn't gained all in one day, so you can't expect to lose it overnight.

Gaining Weight

If you want to gain weight, you should still follow the Dietary Guidelines and Food Guide Pyramid. Just add extra servings or make servings slightly larger. Here are some suggestions:

- Split up the usual three meals a day into six small ones. This reduces the chances of feeling full before you have eaten enough food.
- Eat nutritious snacks between meals.
- Pass up water in favor of milk and juice. Milk and juice are more nutritious and add calories.
- Include nutritious but calorie-dense foods, such as nuts, cheese, peanut butter, or dried fruits, in meals and snacks. Avoid filling up on low-calorie foods, such as lettuce.

If you are trying to gain weight, snack on nutritious foods between meals.

Exercise is just as important for gaining weight as for losing it. If you eat more but don't exercise, you will gain fat. Too much body fat is not healthful no matter what you weigh. Exercise is essential for building muscles. Moderate exercise can also help stimulate your appetite for healthful foods.

A look at your day-to-day habits may help you see a reason for being underweight. For example, Yolanda often felt she was too busy to eat. Her active, growing body needed more calories than she was giving it. Once she slowed down and ate regular meals, her weight reached a healthy level and stayed there.

More About Sweet Treats

When you're yearning for a high-calorie, high-fat candy bar and nothing else will do, try buying a snack-size (trick-or-treat type packages) bar. You will get the whole taste with fewer calories and fat grams. A small taste of the "real thing" can be almost as satisfying as a large quantity!

2. **Advertising Campaign.** Have students take a look at ads for fad diets and popular weight-loss gimmicks. Then have small groups create their own advertising campaigns for healthful eating. Encourage them to give the ads crazy and catchy names, but make sure they are based on the Food Guide Pyramid and exercise. Display ads that are especially good in a school showcase or submit them to your school newspaper. (Key Skills: *Communication, Creativity*)
3. **Challenge.** Have each student pick *one* weight-loss or weight-gain tip that they would like to adapt. Suggest that one or more students challenge each other to do this activity for a specified period of time. Try to get each member of the class involved. Remind students to encourage each other and to think of these changes as lasting for a lifetime. (Key Skills: *Communication, Management*)

Follow Up

1. **Reteaching.** Ask students to outline the basic information about weight management by going through the chapter or by answering the following questions. What determines your desired weight? What causes weight gain or loss? What is basal metabolism and how does it work? Why is it more important to be physically fit than just thin? What are some good tips for weight management? (Key Skill: *Critical Thinking*)
2. **Extension.** Use the extension information handout on p. 52 of the *Extending the Text* booklet in the TCR.
3. **Enrichment.** Ask students to tell you what they know about eating disorders — what they are, symptoms, causes, what to do if they or a friend have an eating disorder. (Key Skills: *Communication, Critical Thinking*)

Completing the Chapter

For Review

1. Emphasize the main concepts using the summary.
2. Have students complete the "Facts to Recall." (Answers below.)

For Reteaching

1. **Reteaching.** Use the activity on p. 51 of the *Reteaching and Practical Skills* booklet in the TCR.

For Enrichment

1. **Enrichment.** Use the activity on p. 64 of the *Enrichment Activities* booklet in the TCR.

For Evaluation

1. Choose items from "Ideas to Explore" and "Activities to Try."
2. Use the chapter test on pp. 83-84 in the testing booklet of the TCR or use the testmaker software.

Facts to Recall Answers

1. Weight management is important to good health. It can help you avoid the risks of being overweight or underweight.
2. Body image is the mental picture of how you think your body looks. Having high self-esteem allows you to see yourself more objectively and to have a more accurate body image.
3. Your activity level and eating habits.
4. Health experts recommend that if you want to lose weight, try to lose about a pound a week.
5. Diets usually do not work because people tend to feel hungry or deprived and go back to their old eating habits. Also, diets can be dangerous if they restrict food choices or calorie intake too severely. It is better to lose weight slowly and steadily through a lifetime of exercise and healthful eating.

Making wise food choices leads to a healthful way of life.

Stress and tension can cause you to lose your appetite. Before sitting down to a meal, you might relax for a few minutes or take a short walk. Learning how to manage the stress in your life can help you maintain a healthy weight.

Some people are underweight because of an eating disorder. (See page 481 in Chapter 41.) Because they see themselves as fat, they work hard at losing weight. In reality, they may be dangerously thin. A person with an eating disorder needs professional help to overcome it.

▼ Maintaining Your Weight ▼

After losing or gaining weight, keep the good habits you've developed. Just remember to adjust your calorie intake and activity level to stay at your target weight.

If your weight is fine now, try to keep it that way by eating right and staying active. This will be especially important as you grow older and your lifestyle and energy needs change.

When you are at a weight that's a good one for you, and you are sensible about the way you keep your weight, you'll have gone a long way toward healthful living.

TAKING ACTION
Maintaining a Healthy Weight

Robin is quite a bit overweight. She doesn't exercise often and is the first to admit her favorite food is french fries. Though she has a sense of humor and laughs at herself, you know weight management is a real and difficult issue for her.

One day Robin is unusually frank with you. "I suppose I'll never be slim. Maybe I'm just meant to be this way." There is an awkward silence. You think Robin might want your help, but you're not sure.

Using Your Resourcefulness

- Do you think you should offer advice to Robin about her weight problem? Why or why not? If so, how would you bring up the subject? If not, what would you do instead?
- Suppose Robin asks for your help. List some things you could offer to do.
- What personal or material resources do you have that might be helpful to Robin?
- What questions could you ask Robin to help her take stock of her own resources?
- What types of community resources might be helpful in this situation? How could you find out about them?
- Suppose Robin comes to you one day, very excited and happy. "I just read about these amazing diet pills! I can't wait to try them." What would you do?
- How can you encourage Robin and help her feel successful on the way to her goal?

TAKING ACTION

Have the students read the feature. Then you may want to have a class discussion about Robin's problem and how she could be helped. To guide this discussion, have the students respond to the *Using Your Resourcefulness* questions at the end of this feature.

Using Your Resourcefulness Answers

- Answers will vary. Students may want to offer words of encouragement to Robin.
- Answers will vary. Possible answers might include helping Robin find a dietitian or encouraging her to cut back on certain foods.
- Answers will vary.
- Answers will vary.

Chapter 40 Review

Summary

In this chapter, you have read about:

- The best way to determine whether your weight is within a healthful range.
- Factors that affect your weight.
- The relationship between self-esteem and body image.
- How to lose weight through exercise and healthful eating habits.
- How to recognize dangerous fad diets.
- How to gain weight safely and sensibly.
- The importance of maintaining a healthy weight.

Facts to Recall

1. Why is weight management important?
2. What is a person's body image? How is it affected by self-esteem?
3. Name two factors affecting your weight that you can control.
4. A weight loss of how many pounds per week is considered safe?
5. Why is it unwise to try to lose weight by "going on a diet"? What is a better alternative?
6. Explain three ways in which exercise is of benefit in a weight-loss program.
7. List six tips for sticking with a weight-loss plan.
8. List four characteristics of a dangerous fad diet.
9. Why is exercise important for someone who wants to gain weight? Give two reasons.

Ideas to Explore

1. What do you think most people base their ideas of the "right" weight on? Why? What can happen as a result?
2. Recent studies have shown that many young people are overweight and in poor physical condition. What are some possible reasons?
3. Why should special care be taken when designing a weight loss program for young people?
4. What fad diets do you know of? What are the health hazards of each?

Activities to Try

1. Keep a food diary for two days. Identify at least one good habit and one poor habit based on your food diary. Make a plan for improving your food choices.
2. Evaluate a diet or diet aid using the guidelines listed in "Beware of Fad Diets" on page 466. Write a newspaper article explaining why you do or do not recommend this diet or product.

LINK TO Math

FIGURING CALORIE INTAKE

Balancing the calories that you eat with the calories you burn up is essential in maintaining a healthy weight. Use the following guidelines to figure the average number of calories you eat in a day:

1. Keep a food diary for three days. Write down everything that you eat and the amount that you eat.
2. Use a calorie chart to identify the calories per serving for each serving of food that you ate.
3. Add up the total number of calories that you ate for the three days.
4. Divide the total from Step 3 by 3 to figure the average number of calories you ate per day.

(**Note:** If you are maintaining your weight, the calories you burn in daily activities are balancing with the calories you eat.)

Facts to Recall Answers (continued)

6. You burn extra calories while you are exercising; your body burns calories at a higher rate after exercising; exercise increases muscle size and basal metabolism, so you burn more calories from normal body processes.
7. **Any six:** vary your exercise routine; exercise with a friend; don't skip meals; sit down at a table and eat slowly; plan for snacks in advance; look for healthful choices when eating away from home; avoid thinking of certain foods as "bad"; avoid weighing yourself every day; try keeping track of your measurements instead of your weight; remember that one slip doesn't mean failure; have patience.
8. **Any four:** very few calories; unrealistic promises; limited food choices; special products; diet pills.
9. **Any two:** If you eat more and don't exercise, you'll gain fat; exercise is essential for building muscles; moderate exercise can also help stimulate your appetite for healthful foods.

Ideas to Explore

1. Answers will vary.
2. Answers will vary and may include: urbanization and technology have eliminated many physical activities and chores; electronic entertainment discourages physical activities.
3. Young people are still growing and must be especially sure to get enough nutrients and calories. Also, their bones and muscles may not be strong enough for an exercise program designed for adults.
4. Answers will vary.

Answers will vary. Possible answers might include clinics, hospitals, nutritionists, and home economics teachers. To find out about these community resources, students could call them to get information, they could go there and get information, or they could ask somebody else about these resources.

- Answers will vary. Possible answers might include explaining the dangers of diet pills to Robin or having her talk to a doctor or nutritionist before trying them.
- Answers will vary.

LINK TO Math

Answers

1. Answers will vary.
2. Answers will vary depending on what foods the students ate.
3. Answers will vary.
4. Answers will vary.

Preparing to Teach

Chapter Outline

Chapter Resources

The following booklet materials may be found in the *Teacher's Classroom Resources* box:

- Lesson Plans, p. 46
- Student Workbook, *Study Guide,* pp. 175-176; *Food Additives—It All Adds Up,* p. 177; *Advice for a Champion,* p. 178
- Color Transparencies, *Factors Affecting Food Choices,* CT-45
- Cooperative Learning, p. 53
- Extending the Text, *Caffeine and Teens,* p. 53
- Reteaching and Practical Skills, *Food Facts or Fiction?,* p. 52
- Enrichment Activities, *Food—Fact or Fiction?,* p. 65
- Chapter and Unit Tests, pp. 85-86
- Testmaker Software

Also see:

- Meeting the Special Needs of Students
- Linking Home, School, and Community

ABCNews InterActive™ Videodiscs

- *Food and Nutrition*

See the ABCNews InterActive™ Bar Code Correlation booklet for applicable segments.

CHAPTER 41 Facts for Food Choices

OBJECTIVES

- *Identify influences on food choices.*
- *Recognize accurate information about food.*
- *Explain how individual needs affect nutrition.*
- *Describe common eating disorders.*

TERMS TO LEARN

- ***myth***
- ***megadoses***
- ***organically grown***
- ***additive***
- ***vegetarian***

More About
Nutritional Information

Nutrition scientists try to advance our knowledge of the body's need for nutrients and how they are used by careful studies with laboratory animals and with human subjects. Findings are published in over thirty medical and scientific journals. Practical nutritional advice we use on a day-to-day basis is made

When Hannah was a girl, a typical family dinner included foods like fried chicken, dumplings, and corn fritters. For dessert, there was often chocolate cake or ice cream.

Today, Hannah's fourteen-year-old son helps prepare the family meals. Brandon is an athlete who wants to be sure he gives his body the right fuel. They fix meals like broiled chicken, pasta with fresh tomatoes and green peppers, and broccoli with lemon juice. Sometimes they have a vegetarian meal. For dessert, they enjoy fresh fruit served over angel food cake. Their meals are planned with nutrition as well as taste in mind.

Hannah likes this new attitude toward food. Still, she sometimes misses the favorite dishes she grew up on.

Influences on Food Choices

Have you ever thought about why you choose the foods you do? When it comes to food, your likes, dislikes, and habits are influenced by:

- ***Family and culture.*** Most people tend to like the dishes and food customs they grew up with. Dislikes, too, may be learned from family members.
- ***Religious beliefs.*** Many of the world's religions include beliefs and practices relating to food.
- ***Friends.*** Eating is often a social event. You might have lunch at a fast-food restaurant just because your friends are going there.
- ***Emotions.*** People often associate certain foods with feelings of comfort or love.
- ***Trends.*** When certain foods are popular and readily available, you are more likely to choose them. How many pizza restaurants do you think there are today?
- ***Geographical area.*** Different regions or countries often have their own food traditions.
- ***Advertising.*** Food companies and restaurants spend millions of dollars each year to convince you to buy their products.
- ***Lifestyle and values.*** How much time do you have for meals? How important is your good health? Your answers to questions like these can make a difference in the foods you choose.

up as much from centuries of human experience with different foods as it is from scientific research. Research may turn up such things as the identification of dietary risk factors involved in cardiovascular (heart and blood vessel) disease, which may lead to recommendations for changing eating habits.

Translating research findings so that they are useful for people is not easy. Experimental evidence gained through laboratory research must be tested to see how it applies in real-life human situations. This requires many years of careful observation.

Introducing the Chapter

Motivators

1. **Bulletin Board.** Design a bulletin board with a healthy food/gas station theme. Put "Refuel Here" across the top and draw three large gas pumps to fill the rest of the space. Label them "High Octane for Moderate Energy," "Higher Octane for More Energy," and "Highest Octane for the Most Energy." Place drawings or cut out pictures of low-fat, nutritious foods in each pump. There should be increasingly larger amounts of food as the octane increases. The highest octane pump should contain an athlete's diet with lots of carbohydrates, etc. You might want to put the outline up and let your students fill in the food pictures. They may want to add more gas station language, too. (Key Skill: *Creativity*)
2. **Discussion.** Ask students, "If I told you that eating carrots could improve your complexion, what would you think? What questions would you ask yourself? How would you check this information to find out whether or not it was true?" Inform the class that many claims made about foods are not true and that this chapter will help determine which are and are not true. (Key Skills: *Communication, Critical Thinking*)

Chapter Objectives and Vocabulary

1. Have students read the chapter objectives and rephrase the objectives as questions.
2. Ask students to state, in their own words, the purpose of studying this chapter.
3. Pronounce the vocabulary terms listed on the previous page. Ask students whether they are familiar with any of these. Explain that the terms will be defined in the chapter.

Guided Reading

1. Have students read the chapter and use the Study Guide on pp. 85-86 of the *Student Workbook*.

Teaching. . .
Influences on Food Choices and Getting the Facts
(pp. 473-475)

Comprehension Check

1. What are eight influences on your food choices? *(Eight influences on food choices include family and culture, religious beliefs, friends, emotions, trends, geographical area, advertising, and lifestyle and values.)*
2. Where do people often get their information about nutrition? *(From television and radio, hearsay, newspapers, magazines, and advertisements.)*
3. What is a myth? *(A myth is an untrue statement that some people believe.)*

Learning Activities

1. **Personal Inventory.** Have each student write a summary of the influences on his/her diet. Give the students one topic at a time and ask them to write about it for two or three minutes. At the end of the time, have them check the categories they feel are the most influential. Then have students write a concluding paragraph that tells which influences they'd like to increase and which they'd like to decrease and how they would go about doing it. (Key Skills: *Communication, Critical Thinking*)
2. **Demonstration.** Bring a variety of cereal boxes (or have students bring in their favorites) or some other product that has lots of nutritional claims. Be sure you know the price of each kind. Look over the nutritional content of each and compare them.

AROUND THE WORLD

Have the students read the feature. Then have each student investigate the different types of food eaten in another country. When the students do their research, have them try to find out why these different foods are eaten. *(Answers will vary.)*

Many of your food preferences have been influenced by your family.

AROUND THE WORLD

Culture and tradition influence our food choices. In the United States, for example many people enjoy eating turkey on Thanksgiving Day. In China, many people enjoy dishes such as stir-fried snake, deep-fried scorpion, and peppered rat. While some may find these foods unusual, in the Chinese culture they are thought to be quite special and delicious.

Getting the Facts

Information about food and nutrition comes to you from many sources. For example:

- Your best friend tells you, "My brother heard someone say that bee pollen makes you stronger." Should you believe it?
- You see a television commercial for a breakfast cereal. The ad says, "Look at all the vitamins and minerals you get in one bowl." Should you buy the cereal?
- You see a newspaper headline: "Study shows chicken livers prevent cancer." Should you eat chicken livers every day from now on?

The information on food and nutrition in this book is based on scientific evidence. However, not all sources of information are reliable. The advice about bee pollen is a **myth**, an untrue statement that some people believe. The box on page 475 gives other examples of myths and compares them with the facts.

More About *Food Advertising*

Advertising is one of the greatest influences on food choices today. Commercials often try to convince people that a product will fill their needs and wants. Many food advertisements praise the product's flavor and don't even get into whether it is nutritious or not. Many food experts feel that television advertisements aimed at children have an undesirable influence. In many cases, children cannot resist the messages they see and hear on television. You need to learn how to evaluate advertising. Make sure that claims made in an advertisement are true before you buy a certain product.

In the second example, the television commercial is trying to sell a product. The cereal may indeed be nutritious, but so are many other cereals. You can get all the vitamins and minerals you need by eating a variety of foods throughout the day. There's no need to get them all in one bowl of cereal. You'd be wise to compare the price of this cereal with others before you buy.

Even information based on scientific research may be misleading. The newspaper report mentioned above is just a made-up example, but it is typical of reports you might see.

Food Myths

There's a lot of gossip circulating about certain foods, nutrients, and diets. Stories get passed along and changed. Sometimes, there is no factual basis for what you hear. Here are some examples of food myths and the real facts.

Myth:	Fact:
"Honey is more wholesome than sugar."	Honey is a mixture of several different sugars. Your body uses all sugars the same way, whether they come in liquid or granular form.
"Eating carrots will help you see better."	Carrots do help supply your body with vitamin A, and vitamin A is needed for healthy eye tissues. However, no vitamin can correct conditions like nearsightedness and farsightedness.
"An apple a day keeps the doctor away."	Apples are a low-calorie, high-fiber snack food. Eating one every day isn't a bad idea, but it won't prevent illness.
"Starchy foods are fattening."	Naturally starchy foods, such as potatoes, are usually low in fat. The real culprits are high-fat spreads and sauces. For instance, a small baked potato, a slice of bread, and a third of a cup of noodles all have fewer than 100 calories. However, a single tablespoon of butter adds *over* 100 calories.
"Margarine has fewer calories than butter."	Margarine and butter have exactly the same number of calories. They differ in the type of fat they contain. Butter is a highly saturated fat, while most margarines are made from unsaturated vegetable oils.

Do they contain similar amounts of the minimum daily requirements? Is their nutritional value related to the cost per ounce? List all the possible reasons why someone would buy a particular brand of cereal (cost, nutritional content, packaging, prizes, contests, taste, advertising, etc.). (Key Skills: *Communication, Critical Thinking*)

3. **Discussion.** Ask students what food claims they have heard or what their parents have heard. Ask them where they would go to check on the information. Show students copies of reliable sources of information. Get copies of material put out by special interests groups such as dairy, meat, or vegetable groups. Point out that the information may be true, but that they should always consider the group putting out the material because they have a vested interest and will put the best possible emphasis on the positive aspects of their products. (Key Skills: *Communication, Critical Thinking*)

Follow Up

1. **Reteaching.** Show students two or three examples of food claims and ask them what they would do if they came across them in a newspaper or magazine. (Key Skill: *Communication*)
2. **Enrichment.** Give students some magazines and have them look for ads or articles put out by a food industry. Then have them discuss what they find. (Key Skill: *Communication*)

Teaching. . .

Nutritional Supplements, "Natural" and "Health" Foods, and Organic Foods

(pp. 476-477)

Comprehension Check

1. What are two good strategies for making certain your information about food and nutrition is accurate? *(You should think critically and make sure your source is reliable.)*
2. What's the best way to make sure you eat a balanced diet? *(Make sure that you eat foods from each of the five groups in the Food Guide Pyramid.)*
3. What should you do before you buy a "natural" or "health" food? *(You should read the label carefully. Compare it with regular products. Then decide whether the product is worth the extra cost.)*
4. What does "organically grown" mean? *("Organically grown" describes food produced without manufactured chemicals.)*

Learning Activities

1. **Group Work.** Ask small groups to write a paragraph or compile a list of reasons why *natural foods* and *health foods* appeal to consumers. What impressions about products do these labels give? Why do people feel good about using these products? What are the positive and the negative effects of foods using these descriptions? Have groups share their results with the class. Encourage discussion and debate between groups to promote awareness. (Key Skills: *Communication, Critical Thinking*)
2. **Speakers.** Invite an area farmer and a produce manager from a local supermarket to class to speak to your students about organically grown food. Ask them about the percentage of food that's produced organically, how the marketing is controlled, how pests and weeds are controlled without herbicides and pesticides, how the cost to the consumer is affected, and what the trends in farming seem to be. (Key Skills: *Communication, Science*)

These reports are often based on the early results of just one study. Many other studies would have to confirm the results before scientists accept them as fact. Even then, you shouldn't jump to conclusions based on that information alone.

How can you be sure you are getting the facts? Here are two strategies to use.

- ***Think critically.*** Question what you read or hear. Is the person telling or writing about the information an authority? What is his or her training or education in nutrition? Is this person being paid to make certain claims or statements?
- ***Get reliable information.*** Some people who know the facts about nutrition are registered dietitians, family and consumer sciences teachers, family doctors, and school nurses. The library has magazines and books about health and nutrition. Be cautious about publications put out by organizations trying to sell their products.

Following is some information about topics that many people are concerned with today. These include nutritional supplements, "natural" and "health" foods, organically grown foods, and food additives. Knowing the facts about these topics can help you make better decisions.

▼ Nutritional Supplements ▼

Pills, liquids, and powders that are supposed to supplement, or give a boost, to your diet are expensive. Do you need them? The answer is "probably not." If you eat foods from the five food groups, you will have a balanced diet. The only exception is if a physician recommends taking a supplement.

Some products claim to provide complete nutrition. However, there is no way to guarantee that a product provides all the nutrients you need. Foods may contain vital nutrients that science has not discovered yet.

Some people think that taking **megadoses**, or very large amounts, of a vitamin or mineral will cure disease. This is not only untrue, it is dangerous. Taking too much of any nutrient can be harmful.

Eating a balanced diet eliminates the need for nutritional supplements.

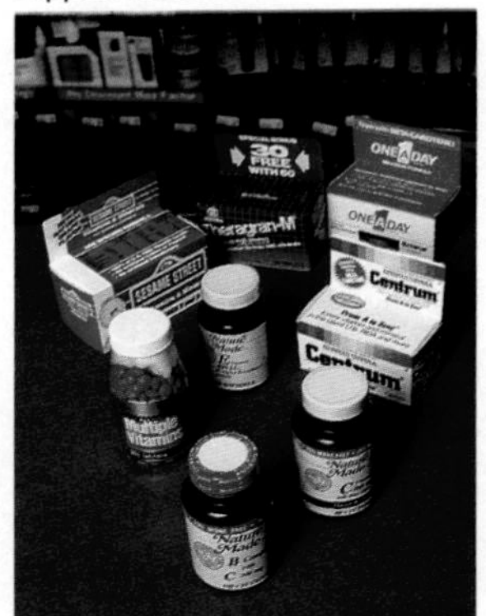

▼ "Natural" and "Health" Foods ▼

Companies that make and sell food products know that many people today are concerned about their health. That is why you often see terms like "natural" and "health" on food labels. These terms may mean different things to different people.

For example, Jana wanted to buy some fruit juice. She chose a bottle labeled "100% natural." When she looked more closely at the label, she was surprised to find that the

More About *Megadoses of Vitamins*

Megadoses of vitamins can cause loss of coordination, nausea, rashes, diarrhea, and fatigue. When excesses of vitamin A or vitamin E are stored in the body, they can be toxic.

beverage was mostly added sugar and water. Jana thought "natural" meant pure fruit juice. To the food manufacturer, however, "natural" simply meant that sugar and water come from nature.

You will notice that claims for many health food products do not explain exactly what the product will do. If this was done, government agencies could investigate and take legal action about the false statements. Instead, indirect claims are made. For example, an ad may have quotes from people who say the product helped them.

Many so-called "health" foods are neither more nor less nutritious than regular food products. There is one difference, however. Health foods almost always cost more. On the whole, these foods can cost from two to three times as much as regular food.

Before you buy a "natural" or "health" food, read the label carefully. Compare it with regular products. Then decide whether the product is worth the extra cost.

The nutritional value of organically grown foods and those grown with chemical fertilizer is the same.

▼ Organic Foods ▼

"Organic" is another popular word today. The term **organically grown** describes food produced without manufactured chemicals.

There is no nutritional difference between a food grown with organic fertilizers and the same food grown with chemical fertilizers. However, some people prefer to buy organic fruits and vegetables. They are concerned about the long-term effects of chemicals on people's health and the environment.

One problem is that people who sell organically grown food can't be certain it was organically grown. Foods fertilized with chemicals could be passed off as being organically grown. It is difficult to be sure about growing conditions unless you actually see how the plants are cultivated or you buy from a person you know.

Learning Activities (continued)

3. **Oral Reports.** Have groups of students do research and reports on various types of food production (e.g., tree fruit, vineyards, truck farming, large vegetable farming, and grain farming). An alternative would be to have the groups report on food production in different parts of the country. Have groups report their findings to the class. (Key Skills: *Communication, Science*)

Follow Up

1. **Reteaching.** Tell students that you read that if they take a megadose of vitamin C every day from September to March, they will not get a cold. Now ask students what they think of that piece of information. How would they go about checking its validity? (Key Skills: *Communication, Critical Thinking*)
2. **Enrichment.** Ask students to talk to a pharmacist or check at a vitamin counter to see what differences there are in *regular* vitamins and *natural* vitamins. Have students check the nutrient information, the claims, and the cost. (Key Skill: *Communication*)

Photo Focus

Discuss the photo at the bottom of page 476 with the students. What types of nutritional supplements do they take? Are any students taking nutritional supplements in place of having a well-balanced diet? *(Answers will vary.)*

Teaching. . .
Food Additives and Nutrition for Individual Needs
(pp. 478-479)

Comprehension Check

1. What do *additives* do to food? *(Additives prevent spoilage of food, add nutrients to food, add flavor to food, and add color to food.)*
2. How would our food supply change without *additives*? *(Without additives, our food supply would be more limited in quantity and quality.)*
3. What special dietary needs do pregnant women have? *(Pregnant women need extra calories and nutrients. They should be especially sure to get enough calcium.)*
4. Where do infants get their first nutrients? *(Infants get their first nutrients from breast milk or formula.)*

Learning Activities

1. **Survey.** Ask students to take a survey of some of the foods they have in their cupboards at home. Have them check ten items on their shelves for additives. How many contain a preservative? How many contain added nutrients? Flavorings? Color? Have students figure out percentages based on their random survey. Remind them that they are only considering products that are made to sit on the shelf. Fresh produce, for example, is not included in the survey. (Key Skills: *Communication, Math*)
2. **Panel Discussion.** Invite a few mothers with young children (and perhaps a pediatrician) to visit the class. Ask them questions such as: 1) How did you alter your diet when you were pregnant or breast feeding? 2) What did you feed your child when it was an infant, and how did the child react to it? 3) What food does your child like and dislike now? 4) What precautions did you take regarding food allergies in small children? Encourage students to ask questions of their own. (Key Skill: *Communication*)

Analyzing the Effects of Additives

Materials
one slice store-bought bread; one slice homemade bread

Equipment
plate; labels; plastic wrap

Directions:
Place one slice of store-bought bread and one slice of homemade bread each on a plate. Label and date each plate. Cover each plate with plastic wrap and leave them out at room temperature. Observe the bread slices daily. Record the date that mold appears on each slice of bread. After the mold appears, answer the following questions:

- ✔ How many days did it take for mold to appear on each slice of bread?
- ✔ What additives are listed on the store-bought bread label?
- ✔ Draw some conclusions about the importance of food additives.
- ✔ What might happen to our food supply if all additives were banned?

▼ Food Additives ▼

An **additive** is a substance added to food for a particular purpose. Additives may be used to:

- ▶ ***Prevent spoilage.*** BHT is a chemical often added to foods to keep them from spoiling. Vitamin C may be added to foods to keep them from turning brown.
- ▶ ***Add nutrients.*** For example, vitamin D is added to milk to help prevent deficiencies. Often, some nutrients are lost in the process of turning raw food into the food products you buy. Nutrients are then added to replace those lost.
- ▶ ***Add flavor.*** Vanilla, salt, sugar, and various seasonings are added to many foods for flavor.
- ▶ ***Add color.*** Food coloring is added to many foods to make them more attractive.

Many food additives help preserve the quality of food. Without their use, the food supply would be more limited in quantity and quality.

Before any new food additive can be used, it must be tested for safety and approved by the federal government. Some additives, originally thought to be safe, have been banned or withdrawn if there was any evidence they could be harmful.

Analyzing the Effects of Additives

Materials: One slice store-bought bread; one slice homemade bread.

Equipment: Plate; labels; plastic wrap.

Purpose: To find out what effects additives have on food.

Outcomes:

- Answers will vary.
- Answers will vary.
- Answers will vary. Possible answers might include that additives are important because they allow food to be transported without spoiling and because they allow food to have a longer shelf life.

Nutrition for Individual Needs

Did you know that good food choices for you may not be the best choices for someone else? Basic nutrition guidelines, such as the Dietary Guidelines, apply to almost everyone. However, people also have individual differences that can affect their nutritional needs.

Nutrition Through the Life Cycle

Everyone goes through different stages of life. At each stage, the need for calories and nutrients is slightly different.

- ***Pregnancy*** is the start of the life cycle. The food choices made by an expectant mother affect not only her own health, but that of the unborn baby. Women who are pregnant or breastfeeding need extra calories and nutrients. They should be especially sure to get enough calcium.
- ***Infants*** first get their nutrients from breast milk or formula. As babies grow, they can be introduced to other foods, such as cereal, fruits, vegetables, and meats. Foods for infants are specially prepared so that they are safe and easy to digest.

An expectant mother should follow her health professional's advice for the kind and amount of food to be eaten.

Older adults have the same nutrient needs as younger people, but may need fewer calories.

- Although banning food additives might reduce cancer risks, consumers would be limited to local food sources or to transported and stored foods that might lack quality and appeal. In some cases, foods without additives could prove dangerous.

Learning Activities (continued)

3. **Discussion.** Invite a mom or dad who has a one-year-old child to bring the baby to class at mealtime. Ask the parent to explain what he or she is feeding the child. How much does the child normally eat? What foods are the child's favorites? Least favorites? How is the food prepared? Is it purchased specially or ground up at home? Is it warm, cool, or room temperature? (Key Skill: *Communication*)
4. **Group Work.** As a class, talk about the life cycle and its variations in regard to nutrition. Divide the life cycle into segments and then ask a small group to illustrate one segment on a piece of construction paper. Combine the papers when each group has finished and you will have an illustrated life cycle to hang around the room or on a bulletin board. Encourage students to look up additional information to make their segment accurate. They might illustrate their segment with drawings, cartoons, or cut-out pictures from magazines. (Key Skills: *Communication, Creativity*)

Follow Up

1. **Reteaching.** Have students work individually or in groups to make an outline of the life cycle and the special needs that each stage requires. (Key Skill: *Communication*)
2. **Enrichment.** Have students look at baby-food labels at the store and make some comparisons between juices, fruits, vegetables, and combination foods. How would costs compare to buying fresh fruits and vegetables and preparing them yourself? Are there any additives? You might even ask students to prepare some themselves and compare the taste and preparation time to canned food from the store. (Key Skill: *Critical Thinking*)

Teaching. . .

Illness and Medical Conditions, and Nutrition for Vegetarians

(pp. 480-481)

Comprehension Check

1. When can children eat normal serving sizes of foods? *(Children can eat normal serving sizes of food by the time they're in school.)*
2. What chronic medical conditions can affect food needs? *(Diabetes, food allergies, or high blood pressure can affect food needs.)*
3. Name two eating disorders. *(Anorexia nervosa and bulimia.)*
4. What are some reasons why people choose to be vegetarians? *(People choose to be vegetarians because of religious beliefs, because they object to using animals for food, because they want to conserve natural resources, because they want to eat less fat and cholesterol and more fiber, and/or because it is more economical.)*

Learning Activities

1. **Group Work.** Give groups a food allergy on which they can do research and present a report to the class. Be sure to include allergies from grain products, milk products, and nuts, because these allergies can have serious consequences. Point out to students that all bodies do not work the same way. Also point out that as they grow older, certain foods may not cause allergic reactions, but they may be more difficult to digest. (Key Skill: *Communication*)
2. **Group Work.** Ask small groups to plan a week's worth of vegetarian menus. Make sure they include a variety of foods. You will want to remind them about balancing legumes and grains to get complete proteins. When they have finished their menus, ask groups to share their menus with the rest of the class. Challenge students to try a vegetarian meal at home. Remind them of the good reasons for eating vegetarian meals occasionally. (Key Skills: *Communication, Creativity*)

- ***Children*** need good nutrition for growth and health. Toddlers and young children should have a variety of foods from the five major food groups. Because their bodies are small, they need smaller servings. By the time children are in school, the normal serving sizes can be used.
- ***Teens*** need a lot of energy for rapid growth. During this time, you need the best nutrition you can get. In particular, be sure to get enough calcium for strong, healthy bones now and in later life.
- ***Young, middle, and older adults*** should continue to follow the Dietary Guidelines and the Food Guide Pyramid. Adults are no longer growing, and some may not be as physically active as they were when they were younger. Therefore, they usually need fewer calories.

Illness and Medical Conditions

Nutrition is a particular concern when someone is ill. Good nutrition, along with rest and proper care, can help the body get back to normal and regain strength. However, a person who is ill may not want to or be able to eat normally. It is best to follow a physician's advice about what the patient should eat.

Chronic, or long-term, medical conditions can also affect food needs. Some examples of chronic conditions are diabetes (dy-uh-BEE-tis), food allergies, or high blood pressure. A physician may prescribe a special diet to help control the condition.

Good nutrition and rest are needed during an illness. When you or someone you know is ill, it is best to follow a physician's advice about what to eat.

More About Diet Disorders

A significant number of adolescents suffer from eating disorders. It has been estimated that as many as five percent of high school girls are victims of either anorexia nervosa or bulimia nervosa. Many more teenagers suffer from a number of eating disorder symptoms, including obsession with weight, frequent dieting, and overly rigid adherence to an exercise program for the sake of burning calories. Twenty percent of adolescents are estimated to engage in bulimic behavior.

Some signs indicating an eating disorder problem include avoidance of meals, exercising obsessively, talking about food all of the time, stashing food, suffering from low self-esteem, and using drugs to control weight.

Eating Disorders

Another concern related to nutrition is the topic of eating disorders. The causes of eating disorders are not well understood. However, the effects are all too clear.

One such disorder is *anorexia nervosa* (an-uh-REX-ee-uh ner-VOH-suh). It basically means self-starvation. People with this disorder have a strong fear of being overweight. They eat very little and can become extremely thin, yet still think they weigh enough or too much. They become obsessed with thoughts of food, their weight, and dieting.

Another eating disorder is *bulimia* (buh-LIM-ee-uh). It is similar to anorexia in that the person is overly concerned with weight. People with bulimia will eat large quantities of food in a short period of time. This is sometimes referred to as binge eating. After eating, the individual will try to rid the body of the food to avoid weight gain. They may induce vomiting, abuse laxatives, go on a very strict diet, or over-exercise.

Anyone can have an eating disorder. Usually, however, the affected person is a teen or young adult. Females are affected more often than males.

Both anorexia and bulimia can cause serious medical problems. If left untreated, either one can become severe enough to cause death.

People with anorexia or bulimia need qualified professional help. If you recognize the signs of an eating disorder in yourself or someone you know, check with your school nurse or family doctor.

▼ Nutrition for Vegetarians ▼

A **vegetarian** is a person who does not eat meat, fish, or poultry. Some vegetarians also avoid other foods derived from animals, such as eggs or milk.

People who become vegetarians do so for a variety of reasons. It may be for religious reasons or because they are opposed to the use of animals for food. Some are concerned with conserving natural resources. (It takes more resources to produce animals for food than to raise crops.) Others see a vegetarian diet as a way to eat less fat and cholesterol and more fiber. It is also economical.

Trained personnel will provide information to callers on the Bulimia Anorexia Self-Help line (1-800-227-4785), 8:30 a.m. to 5 p.m. CDT. A Bulimia Anorexia Self-Help Crisis line (1-800-762-3334) is always open.

Learning Activities (continued)

3. **Discussion.** Bring a collection of vegetarian cookbooks or recipes to class. Allow time for students to look through the recipes. Ask them to find any that particularly appeal to them and have them vote on one to try when they have a foods lab. (Key Skill: *Communication*)
4. **Debate.** Have class members hold a debate on vegetarianism vs. eating meat. Allow time for both sides to do some research on the subject and then set up a formal or informal debate for the rest of your class or for another class. At the end of the debate, vote on which side was most convincing. (Key Skill: *Communication*)

Follow Up

1. **Reteaching.** Ask your students if any of them have food allergies. What foods are they allergic to? How do they react to these foods? How has the reaction altered their desire to eat that food? (Key Skill: *Communication*)
2. **Enrichment.** Have students interview vegetarians to find out why they chose to give up meat, what kind of vegetarian they are, and how they make sure their diet is balanced. (Key Skill: *Communication*)

Hands-on Activity

Prepare a vegetarian meal in class. The meal could be as simple as tacos with refried beans instead of hamburger. Some other easy (and probably likable) meals might include veggie pizza, spaghetti with meatless sauce, macaroni and cheese, or grilled cheese sandwiches. All of these selections include cheese, and cheese would not be acceptable in a strict vegetarian diet. Also, you might want to discuss the pros and cons of cheese as an alternative to meat.

Teaching... *Nutrition for Vegetarians and Nutrition for Athletes* *(pp. 482-484)*

Comprehension Check

1. What diseases are vegetarians less likely to get? *(Heart disease, high blood pressure, cancer, and obesity.)*
2. What nutrient is apt to be missing from a vegetarian diet? *(Vitamin B_{12}.)*
3. What are four things that athletes don't need to perform well? *(Athletes don't need salt tablets, extra protein, vitamin and mineral supplements, or "quick energy" drinks that are high in sugar.)*
4. What are some examples of nutritious complex carbohydrates? *(Breads, pasta, potatoes, rice, and fruit.)*

Learning Activities

1. **Survey and Interviews.** Plan a survey to give to all the athletic coaches in your school. Ask them for their opinions about special athletic diets, exercise, and other tips. Then assign individuals or pairs to talk to the coaches and ask them the survey questions. Be sure the kids tell the coaches they are studying weight management in home economics class. Have students compare the results and take note of where the coaches agree and disagree. Then have them write up their findings and give the coaches a copy. (Key Skill: *Communication*)
2. **Personalized Menus.** Assume that all your students are athletes at some time. Have them plan several meals that are high in complex carbohydrates and low in fat and sweets. These would be good meals to eat before athletic activity. Have students write their menus down on recipe cards and take them home. They might want to ask the cook in the family to keep this menu in mind for them or they might want to prepare it themselves. This exercise will help students recognize complex carbohydrates. (Key Skills: *Communication, Decision Making*)

Vegetarians need to carefully balance the types of foods they eat to get all the necessary nutrients. Many people who are not vegetarians enjoy adding vegetarian dishes to their meals for variety.

Evidence shows that a well-selected vegetarian diet is a healthy one. In fact, vegetarians are less likely to develop some of the common health problems related to diet, such as heart disease, high blood pressure, cancer, and obesity. This does not mean vegetarians will never have these health problems. It does mean that their diets are less likely to contribute to these conditions.

Since vegetarians limit their selection of foods, they must be careful to balance their diets nutritionally. The need for protein can be met by eating complementary plant proteins, such as legumes and grains. (You may want to review the discussion of complete and incomplete proteins in Chapter 38.)

If there is any nutrient lacking in a vegetarian diet, it is likely to be vitamin B_{12}. This B vitamin is found only in foods of animal origin. Vegetarians who do not eat dairy or egg products may need to take vitamin B_{12} tablets.

If milk is not included in the diet, it can be difficult to get enough calcium. Vegetables high in calcium include broccoli, kale, collard greens, and mustard greens. Tofu, a soybean product, is also a good source of calcium.

There are many good vegetarian cookbooks with lots of recipes and ideas. Looking through them can help you see that a vegetarian diet can have a lot of variety. Many people who are not vegetarians often use vegetarian dishes to add variety to the foods they eat.

▼ Nutrition for Athletes ▼

Everyone wants to be a winner or play on a winning team. It's a reward for the training and effort put into getting ready for an event. However, wanting to win can also present problems for athletes and their coaches. They become perfect targets for misinformation about nutrition.

More About *Nutrition for Vegetarians*

Strict vegetarians, especially women, should be sure to get enough iron. Plant sources of iron include dry beans, potatoes, dried fruits, fortified breads, and cereals. This iron, however, is not as well absorbed as iron from meat and dairy products. Foods high in vitamin C help the body absorb iron.

If you want to get your body in top form physically, you must practice good nutrition. Even if you are an occasional athlete who bicycles, hikes, jogs, or plays tennis, nutrition is important. The fuel you feed your body affects your performance, your enjoyment, and the physical benefits you obtain from the activity.

What Athletes *Don't* Need

A great deal of incorrect information is passed along to athletes. Here is a sample of poor advice that you would be better off without.

- ***Salt tablets.*** Some people advise taking salt tablets to replace the salt lost when sweating. This can be dangerous. When you take extra salt, water is pulled out of muscles to dilute the amount of salt in your system. As a result, your muscles cannot work efficiently and your performance is lowered. You can replace the salt lost during heavy exercise by eating regular foods with normal seasonings.
- ***Extra protein.*** Will eating a huge steak or taking protein powder make you stronger? No. Only exercise can strengthen and build muscles. A normal diet supplies all the protein your body needs. Extra amounts are usually converted to fat and stored. Breaking down the protein puts a heavy workload on the liver and kidneys and can create a water shortage in body tissues.
- ***Vitamin and mineral supplements.*** You do not need supplements to stay in top form or to give you energy. The extra fat-soluble vitamins are stored in your body fat. When the vitamins stored reach high levels, they can be toxic, or poisonous. If you are eating a variety of foods, why spend money for pills you don't need?
- ***"Quick energy" drinks that are high in sugar.*** Fluids with too much sugar draw water into the stomach so that the sugar will be diluted. The tissues and cells in the rest of your body won't have enough water. Sometimes this can cause an upset stomach or diarrhea. It's better to drink plain water or beverages low in sugar.
- ***Rapid weight loss.*** Athletes in some sports are often encouraged to "make weight" just before a competition. They may try crash diets, diet pills, or "sweating off" pounds. Such rapid weight loss programs are dangerous. They hurt your performance and can permanently damage your health. To make safe, long-term changes in your weight, follow the guidelines in Chapter 40.

More About *An Athlete's Diet*

Digestion requires 3 to 4 hours, and muscle glycogen formation in the liver and muscles takes at least 46 hours. Therefore, what you eat before any physical activity is not used to fuel that activity. Your exercise fuel comes mainly from nutrients in foods you ate about two days before the exercise that were stored as glycogen.

A meal high in protein and fat could cause indigestion, especially if you are tense. Aim for a meal with about 500 calories. Include plenty of fluids. Some good pregame meals include tortillas, pasta, cereals, pancakes, and toast. Combine these with fruits, fruit juices, and vegetables. Try to avoid gas-forming foods such as beans, peas, and vegetables of the cabbage family.

3. **Impromptu Skit.** Assign the following roles to volunteers: Raoul, a new kid in school who wants to go out for track but has never been in athletics before; Rafer, a hot-shot athlete who is into salt tablets and quick-energy drinks in a big way; Grant, a superstitious athlete who tries every fad that comes along (pick someone with a good imagination to make up some fun fads); Chip, who claims his mild athletic success is due to eating a huge steak before football games; Max, who is studying weight management in home economics class and has switched to eating carbohydrates several hours before an athletic event and has given up salt tablets and supplements; and Coach Snyder, whose plan for track athletes agrees with the text. The guys are talking in the locker room after school, giving advice to Raoul and arguing among themselves. Raoul gets more and more confused and the arguing becomes louder until the coach appears and talks to them about sensible eating habits. (Key Skills: *Communication, Creativity*)

Follow Up

1. **Reteaching.** Have students make a list of foods that would be good for any athletes to eat several hours before they compete. (Key Skill: *Decision Making*)
2. **Extension.** Use the extension information handout on p. 53 of the *Extending the Text* booklet in the TCR.
3. **Enrichment.** Ask students to find out what vitamin B_{12} does for the body. Why is it necessary? What are food sources of this vitamin for vegetarians and non-vegetarians? (Key Skill: *Science*)

Completing the Chapter

For Review

1. Emphasize the main concepts using the summary.
2. Have students complete the "Facts to Recall." (Answers below.)

For Reteaching

1. **Reteaching.** Use the activity on p. 52 of the *Reteaching and Practical Skills* booklet in the TCR.

For Enrichment

1. **Enrichment.** Use the activity on p. 65 of the *Enrichment Activities* booklet in the TCR.

For Evaluation

1. Choose items from "Ideas to Explore" and "Activities to Try."
2. Use the chapter test on pp. 85-86 in the testing booklet of the TCR or use the testmaker software.

Chapter 41 Review

Facts to Recall Answers

1. **Any four:** family and culture; friends; emotions; trends; advertising; lifestyle and values; religious beliefs; geographical area.
2. The school dietitian is more likely correct. Dietitians are educated in nutrition and food facts, and they get their information from books, articles in health and nutrition magazines, and other experts. Your friend probably has no more specialized training than you, and you don't know the source of his or her information.
3. If you eat from the five food groups, you probably don't need a nutritional supplement, unless your physician recommends taking one. Taking too much of any nutrient, in fact, can be harmful.
4. These terms make it sound as though the product is better for you than other foods. In reality, some "natural" foods, like sugar, can be harmful if taken in excess. Many so-called "health" foods are no more or less nutritious than regular food products. However, they are usually more expensive.

A balanced diet is a key to better athletic performance.

What Athletes Need

Good training and a balanced diet are the keys to peak performance. Because of the heavy energy demands on their bodies, most athletes need extra calories. A male teen athlete, for instance, would probably need the highest number of servings suggested in the Food Guide Pyramid.

Carbohydrates are the most efficient fuel your body can get. Athletes, like everyone else, should eat plenty of nutritious complex carbohydrates, such as breads, pasta, potatoes, rice, and fruit. Candy bars and sweet drinks are too sweet and don't carry the nutrients your body needs. If you eat a high-protein, high-fat, and low-carbohydrate diet, you'll be tired and perform poorly.

Timing is important, too. Smart trainers have their athletes eat three to four hours before an athletic event. This time lapse allows the athletes to digest their food before heavy exercise. A pre-event meal should be high in carbohydrates and low in fats and proteins.

If you are involved in athletics, follow this sound advice. You'll feel better and see a difference in your performance.

TAKING ACTION

Planning Special Diets

Your mother has just returned from a medical checkup. Her doctor is concerned about her high blood pressure and cholesterol levels. In addition to prescribing medication, she has told your mother to follow a low-sodium, low-fat, low-cholesterol diet and to avoid stress.

You want to help your mother by preparing meals that are both good for her and enjoyable to eat. You also want to do what you can to reduce the stress in her life.

Using Your Resourcefulness

- Where can you find information about the food sodium, fat, and cholesterol content in foods?
- Where can you look for recipes that would fit your mother's special nutritional needs?
- You and your mother would like to learn more about high blood pressure and how to manage it. Where do you start?
- How will you find time to prepare meals while still keeping up with your studies?
- Suppose other members of the family still want to eat their traditional favorite foods that your mother should not eat. What problems might this cause? What are some possible solutions?
- What could you do to help reduce the stress in your mother's life?

TAKING ACTION

Have students read the feature. Then you may want to have a class discussion about the different ways in which students could help their mother eat right and reduce her stress level. To guide this discussion, have students respond to the *Using Your Resourcefulness* questions in this feature.

Using Your Resourcefulness Answers

- Answers will vary. Possible answers might include food labels, nutrition books, and nutrition magazines.
- Answers will vary and may include cookbooks and nutrition magazines.
- Answers will vary. Possible answers might include getting pamphlets about high blood pressure or going to the library and

Chapter 41 Review

Summary

In this chapter, you have read about:

- Factors that influence eating habits.
- How to distinguish food facts from myths and misleading statements.
- Facts about nutritional supplements, "natural" and "health" foods, organic foods, and food additives.
- How nutritional needs vary throughout the life cycle.
- How nutritional needs can be affected by illness and medical conditions.
- How a vegetarian diet can meet nutritional needs.
- Good and poor nutritional practices for athletes.
- Symptoms of anorexia nervosa and bulimia.

Facts to Recall

1. List four influences on food choices.
2. A friend tells you that eating chocolate causes acne. The school dietitian says it does not. Whom do you believe and why?
3. Are nutritional supplements necessary to a balanced diet? Explain.
4. How can terms like "all natural" and "health food" be misleading? Give an example.
5. Identify four purposes for food additives.
6. Why are food choices especially important to pregnant women? To teens? To people who are ill?
7. Identify two possible nutritional deficiencies in a vegetarian diet and explain how they can be avoided.
8. List three nutrition guidelines for athletes.

Ideas to Explore

1. Which of the influences on food choices do you think has the strongest effect on most people? Why?
2. According to the chapter, news reports about nutrition research can sometimes be misleading. Would it be better not to publish the results of scientific studies until they are confirmed? Explain.

Activities to Try

1. Find a news report about scientific studies on food, drugs, or nutrition. Be prepared to explain what claim is being made, who is making it, and the facts or research behind it.
2. Plan a day's meals for one of the following: Sondra, a 25-year-old pregnant woman; Harold, a 60-year-old executive; Luisa, a 10-year-old who is allergic to milk; Darlene, a 16-year-old soccer player; Jim, a 34-year-old vegetarian. Explain how your plan suits the person's individual needs.

LINK TO *Geography*

GEOGRAPHIC INFLUENCES ON FOOD CHOICES

The availability of food choices around the world are often linked to geographic conditions. Select an area other than where you live (such as North Africa, the Middle East, Asia, Southeast Asia, South America, Europe, etc.). Locate information about this area. Use the following questions to guide your research:

- How do the climate and soil conditions affect the available food choices?
- What kinds of crops (foods) are generally grown in this area?
- How do the available foods fulfill nutritional needs? Is there a need to import some foods to fulfill nutritional requirements?
- How do economic conditions affect the availability of food in this area?

Facts to Recall Answers (continued)

5. Additives prevent spoilage; add nutrients; add flavor; and add color.
6. Food choices are important to pregnant women because they affect both their own health and the unborn baby's; to teens because they need a lot of energy for rapid growth, and they need good nutrition now for good health in the future; and to people who are ill because good nutrition can help the body regain strength.
7. **Any two:** a protein deficiency, which can be avoided by eating complementary plant proteins; a vitamin B_{12} deficiency, which can be avoided by taking vitamin B_{12} tablets; and a calcium deficiency, which can be avoided by eating tofu and vegetables such as broccoli, kale, collard greens, and mustard greens.
8. **Any three:** do not use salt tablets; avoid eating extra protein; do not use vitamin and mineral supplements; avoid drinking sugary, "quick energy" drinks; do not lose weight rapidly; get extra calories; eat plenty of nutritious complex carbohydrates; eat a high-carbohydrate, low-fat, low-protein meal three to four hours before an athletic event.

Ideas to Explore

1. Answers will vary.
2. Answers will vary.

researching blood pressure.

- Answers will vary.
- Answers will vary. This problem could cause the student's mother to revert back to her old eating habits, it could cause food bills to increase, or it could cause resentment between the student's mother and other family members. Possible solutions might include cooking the same food one way for the mother and another way for the rest of the family or cooking one meal for the mother and another for the rest of the family.
- Answers will vary. Possible answers might include helping mother with the housework, doing the cooking, doing the family's grocery shopping, and taking care of younger siblings.

LINK TO *Geography*

Answers

- Answers will vary.
- Answers will vary.
- Answers will vary.
- Answers will vary.

Preparing to Teach

Chapter Outline

Chapter Resources

The following booklet materials may be found in the *Teacher's Classroom Resources* box:

- Lesson Plans, p. 47
- Student Workbook, *Study Guide,* pp. 179-180; *Calling for Meal Planning Success,* p. 181; *What the Sumida Family Ate,* p. 182
- Color Transparencies, *Giving Meals Appeal,* CT-46
- Personal Safety, *Pack a Safe Lunch,* pp. 41-42
- Food Lab Management and Recipes, R-21, pp. 55-56; R-22, pp. 57-58; R-23, pp. 59-60; R-24, pp. 61-62
- Cooperative Learning, p. 54
- Extending the Text, *What to Choose When Choosing Fast Foods,* p. 54
- Reteaching and Practical Skills, *Meal Planning Savvy,* pp. 53-54
- Enrichment Activities, *Minimizing Cavities,* p. 66
- Chapter and Unit Tests, pp. 87-88
- Testmaker Software

Also see:

- Meeting the Special Needs of Students
- Linking Home, School, and Community

ABCNews InterActive™ Videodiscs

- *Food and Nutrition*

See the ABCNews InterActive™ Bar Code Correlation booklet for applicable segments.

CHAPTER 42 Planning Meals and Snacks

OBJECTIVES

- *Explain how meal patterns and resources affect meal planning.*
- *Give suggestions for simple and nutritious meals.*
- *List the elements of meal appeal.*

TERMS TO LEARN

- ***meal pattern***
- ***convenience foods***

More About Sandwiches

Thank the Earl of Sandwich, who ordered his servants to bring him two pieces of bread with meat in between so he could eat quickly, for inventing the sandwich.

Today, sandwiches can be anything you want to make them. Use the following choices to create a variety of great sandwiches by combining one or more of the proteins, vegetables,

"I know I should eat better," Melanie sighed. "Take today, for instance. A doughnut was all I had for breakfast. The only vegetables I've had were the ones on that slice of pizza. But I don't have time to think about nutrition! I just have to grab whatever's handy."

By now, you have learned a lot about nutrition and how it affects your health. Will you be like Melanie, who has trouble following through? Or will you apply what you've learned in your day-to-day life? This chapter will help you use your resources to plan meals and snacks that are nutritious and appealing.

Putting Nutrition to Work for You

Over a period of time, you develop a set of eating habits. Some of your habits may be good, and some may be less desirable. What are your habits? Do you nibble when studying or watching TV? Do you eat plenty of fresh fruits and vegetables? Do you snack on foods high in fat and salt? Think of ways to replace poor habits with better ones.

Keep the Dietary Guidelines and the Food Guide Pyramid in mind. As you learned in Chapter 39, they are valuable tools for planning nutritious meals and snacks.

The best way to be sure you get good nutrition is to plan for the whole day. That doesn't mean you need to carry around a list of everything you plan to eat. It simply means that all the food you eat — whether it comes from meals or snacks, early or late in the day — is part of your total nutrition picture. Good planning helps you make sure that all those individual food choices add up to good nutrition.

Using Meal Patterns

A **meal pattern** is the way your daily food choices are grouped into meals and snacks. Over a period of time, people establish meal patterns that work for them. Some people eat three meals a day and one or two snacks. Others prefer to have four, five, or even six smaller meals.

Having a meal pattern in mind can make it easier to plan how you will get your daily servings from the five major food groups. For instance, you need six or more servings of breads and cereals a day. You might plan to have two servings at each meal and get the rest from snacks.

Breakfast is an important part of any meal pattern.

Introducing the Chapter

Motivators

1. **Bulletin Board.** Cut letters out of different plaid fabrics to say "Meal Patterns." Arrange the letters across the top or down the center of the bulletin board. On one side of the board make divisions for three meals and one snack. On the other side, make divisions for five meals. Under each division, write the names and/or cut out photos of foods for that meal. Arrange the meals however you wish as long as the daily total equals the required number of servings from the Food Guide Pyramid. If you wish, you could make the food easy to move and change the menus and number of meals throughout the chapter to show the flexibility there is in planning meals. (Key Skills: *Communication, Creativity*)
2. **List.** Ask students to tell you what they think are influences on their eating patterns and meal planning. Write these things on the board. They might include money, convenience foods, time, personal taste, skill of preparer, etc. Encourage students to be aware of the endless variety of meal plans available and what factors influence their current patterns. (Key Skill: *Communication*)

Chapter Objectives and Vocabulary

1. Have students read the chapter objectives and rephrase the objectives as questions.
2. Ask students to state, in their own words, the purpose of studying this chapter.
3. Pronounce the vocabulary terms listed on the previous page. Ask students whether they are familiar with any of these. Explain that the terms will be defined in the chapter.

Guided Reading

1. Have students read the chapter and use the Study Guide on pp. 179-180 of the *Student Workbook.*

and seasoning with your favorite bread.

Alternative bread ideas: tortillas, pita bread, rice cake, bagels, sourdough bread, kaiser rolls, breadsticks, baking powder biscuits, cold pancakes.

Out-of-the-ordinary proteins: cooked beans, cottage cheese, cream cheese, falafel, seeds/nuts, tofu, cooked leftover meat, shaved deli meat and cheese, cooked fish, cheese, almond or cashew butter.

Vegetables to consider: sprouts, avocado, cucumber, grated raw veggies, cooked leftover veggies, olives, pickles, sauerkraut, tomato, onion.

Sizzling seasonings: mayonnaise, garlic, herbs, hot sauce, horseradish, mustard, salad dressings, yogurt, chutney.

Teaching. . .
Putting Nutrition to Work for You and Resources for Meal Planning

(pp. 487-489)

Comprehension Check

1. What's the advantage in having a meal pattern in mind? *(You can plan how to get your daily servings from the five food groups.)*
2. What two kinds of people can especially benefit from convenience foods? *(Beginning cooks and busy people.)*
3. What are "planned-overs"? *("Planned-overs" are when you make more than needed for a meal and plan to use the remainder at another time.)*

Learning Activities

1. **Bulletin Board Shuffle.** Direct attention to the "Meal Planning" bulletin board. Ask students to cut out food pictures to pin under the meal headings (or you could supply names of foods on strips of paper to pin on board). Take turns having groups plan meals, checking to make sure the Food Guide Pyramid is used, and rearranging the foods for other meal patterns. (Key Skill: *Problem Solving*)
2. **Discussion.** After completing a meal-pattern activity, ask students if they have learned or noticed anything new about food. Ask which foods were easier or more difficult to change from pattern to pattern. (Fruits or breads would be easy to fit into meals and snacks. Cooked vegetables might be harder.) What can they learn from this? (Keep plenty of fruit and breads on

Around the World

After reading the feature, have students investigate what a sandwich is called in another country and what ingredients are included in it. Have students report their findings to the class. *(Answers will vary.)*

Around the World

Do you think of sandwiches only as peanut butter or ham salad? In Denmark, a sandwich is a smorrebrod (smer-er-BREWTH). It is made with a wide variety of fillings and served open-faced. The ingredients include traditional Scandanavian staples: dark breads, fish, and milk products. Try making your own smorrebrod. Start with a nutritious multi-grain bread like rye or pumpernickel, fill it with tuna, lettuce, cheese, or onion, top it with a dollop of mayonnaise and a sprinkle of parsley. What other interesting combinations can you think of?

A typical meal includes a main dish, several side dishes, a beverage, and sometimes dessert. The main dish often supplies protein. Grain products, vegetables, and fruits can be included as side dishes or in other parts of the meal. You might use milk as the beverage or include another milk product, such as yogurt or cheese. Look at the sample food choices on page 489. You will find a good representation of foods from the five major food groups.

Meal planning becomes easier once you get in the habit. Eventually you may want to plan meals and snacks for several days or even a week at a time.

Resources for Meal Planning

Meal planning involves many decisions. What to eat is only one of them. You must also choose how to make the best use of your resources.

Available Choices

Years ago, pioneer families ate food that they had raised or hunted themselves and prepared at home. Today you have many more choices. Your next meal might come from a restaurant or be delivered to your door. At the supermarket, you can find fruits and vegetables from all around the world and complete dinners that microwave in minutes.

Convenience Foods

Convenience foods, those purchased partially or completely prepared, are a big help to beginning cooks and busy people. Convenience foods range from ready-to-serve canned soups to entire frozen meals. They can be a good choice when time and skills are limited.

Choose convenience foods carefully for good nutrition.

More About *Smart Meal Planning*

About a fourth of Americans in recent food industry surveys said speed and ease of preparation were their most important considerations when planning meals and buying food. More than a third said they rarely had more than 30 minutes to fix a meal.

Many time-saving options are available. The Association of Home Appliance Manufacturers (AHAM) estimates that 75% of American households now have a microwave oven. Today's supermarkets offer a variety of heat-and-serve items. Unfortunately, many convenience foods are also high in calories, fat, sugar, and sodium. Many are also more expensive than foods that require more preparation by the cook.

SAMPLE FOOD CHOICES FOR A DAY

	B	V	F	ME	MI
Breakfast:					
Cereal with milk	x				x
Toast	x				
Orange juice			x		
Snack:					
Apple			x		
Lunch:					
Turkey sandwich	xx			x	
Carrot sticks		x			
Milk					x
Snack:					
Whole-wheat crackers	x				
Peanut butter				x	
Milk					x
Dinner:					
Beans and rice	x			x	
Broccoli		x			
Corn		x			
Wheat roll	x				
Fruit cocktail			x		

B = Bread, Cereal, Rice and Pasta Group
V = Vegetable Group
F = Fruit Group
ME = Meat, Poultry, Fish, Dry Beans, Eggs, and Nuts Group
MI = Milk, Yogurt, and Cheese Group

However, convenience foods also have some disadvantages. Most are high in sodium. Many have significant amounts of fat and sugar. Look for nutrition information on the label and compare products before you buy.

Convenience foods can also be more expensive than ingredients you put together yourself. However, some convenience foods actually cost less than those you prepare. Check it out.

▼ Money ▼

Food costs can take up a large part of the family budget. Fortunately, nutritious food is not necessarily expensive. By making wise choices, you can have tasty, nutritious meals without spending a lot of money.

Another way to save money on food is to plan for the use of leftovers. Sometimes people call them "planned-overs." You can make more than needed for a meal and plan to use the remainder at another time. For example, leftover meat loaf can be used for sandwiches at lunch. Extra rice can be made into fried rice. Planned-overs can save time and cut down on food waste.

There are, however, due to heightened awareness of good nutrition and consumer demand, an increasing number of low-sodium, low-fat items on the market. A wise cook on a time budget can put together a quick salad, microwave a frozen vegetable, or cut up fruit and raw vegetables while a convenience-food entree is cooking.

hand. It takes more preplanning to include dishes that require some preparation.) Does junk food fit well into meal planning and the Food Guide Pyramid? (Key Skill: *Communication*)

3. **Demonstration.** Purchase a package of convenience food (such as "Hamburger Helper") as well as the ingredients to make a very similar dish from scratch. Ask one student to prepare the convenience food and one the "from scratch" food. Compare preparation times, amount of work, cost, and, of course, taste. Arrange this exercise in one of two ways. Have two students "compete" in front of the class or plan several similar exercises to go on simultaneously in your labs. Use rice- or potato-packaged dishes if you wish. If you use more than one, you might make sure that the times and taste comparisons will vary to get a true picture of convenience foods. Also, suggest using some convenience foods in preparing a "from scratch" dish. (Key Skills: *Cooperation, Creativity*)

Follow Up

1. **Reteaching.** Ask students to create three imaginary people — one who eats three meals a day plus two snacks, one who eats two meals a day plus three snacks, and one who eats four meals a day and no snacks. What kind of schedules makes these meal patterns appropriate for the three people? If there's time, ask students to arrange the same balanced diet of foods into these three plans. (Key Skill: *Critical Thinking*)
2. **Enrichment.** Ask students to track their meals at home for two days to see how many convenience foods they use and in what ways — as the primary meal or in combination with other foods — they are used. When they have finished, have them compile the results and draw conclusions. (Key Skill: *Critical Thinking*)

Teaching. . .
Other Resources and Planning Your Own Meals
(pp. 490-491)

Comprehension Check

1. Name some other resources for meal planning. *(Time, energy, skills, and equipment.)*
2. Why is it important to eat breakfast? *(Your body needs a new energy supply to function well, and you feel and work better.)*
3. Name two ways to keep a packed lunch safe. *(You can include something cold in your lunch container, and you can use an insulated lunch bag.)*

Learning Activities

1. **Resource Inventory.** Draw a circle on the board and divide it roughly into eight wedges. Using your own life (or making one up), evaluate the balance of resources available — time, energy, skills, equipment, and money — for meal planning. For example: 1/8=time; 1/8=energy; 2/8=skills; 2/8=equipment; 2/8=money. Now ask each student to make a similar inventory of his/her family. This might be done in class or given as an assignment to be completed at home as a family. When students have finished the circle, ask them what they have learned about their families. Does this explain some of their meal patterns? Follow it up by asking students individually or in groups to make recommendations for their family based on the chart. (Key Skills: *Communication, Critical Thinking*)
2. **Group Work.** Tell students that they have just inherited a small restaurant called the "Breakfast Cafe." They're only open for breakfast. They must compete with all the fast-food chains in the area and the menu definitely needs revising. Ask groups to come up with breakfast ideas using a bread/cereal, a fruit, a dairy product, and another ingredient, if desired. The group with the most creative and varied menu wins. Encourage students to try these breakfast

When family members help to get a meal on the table, it can be ready in just a few minutes.

▼ Other Resources ▼

Time, energy, skills, and equipment are also resources for meal planning. Remember, if some resources are in short supply, you may be able to make a tradeoff. For instance, if family members get home from work and school late in the day, there may not be very much time or energy to prepare the evening meal. What are some possible solutions? The family might decide to spend more money on convenience foods to save time. They might use a microwave oven to speed meal preparation. They might cook on the weekend when there is more time and freeze the meals for use during the week.

Personal skills are a valuable resource to consider. The rest of the chapters in this unit will help you learn how to use recipes and prepare many kinds of foods. People who know the basics of food preparation have more options. They can use their skills to prepare a meal that is more nutritious and less expensive than eating out. Can you think of other advantages of preparing food at home?

Planning Your Own Meals

If you are like most teens, you are on your own for at least some of your meals and snacks each week. Whether you prepare food at home, eat out, or "grab-and-go," your food choices deserve thought. The following suggestions will help you plan quick and easy meals and snacks.

More About *Breakfast*

Ideally, breakfast should be one of the most important meals of the day. Studies show that breakfast eaters compared to breakfast skippers benefit by showing faster reaction time, higher productivity during the late morning hours, and less muscle fatigue. People who skip breakfast are likely to be listless and to have trouble concentrating. These reactions are due to a low level of blood sugar after an all-night fast.

Breakfast skippers are likely to shortchange their bodies in essential nutrients. Many nutrients in a typical breakfast are not eaten in significant amounts during the rest of the day's meals. Nutrients, including protein and calcium, are absorbed better by the body if

▼ Breakfast ▼

Breakfast is often called the most important meal of the day, and with good reason. If you skip breakfast, your body goes for up to 18 hours without a new energy supply. It can't function well. Even a small nutritious breakfast can help you feel better and work better each day.

Some people dislike breakfast foods or say they don't have time to eat breakfast. Breakfast doesn't have to be boring or time-consuming. Any food is fine for breakfast as long as it's nutritious. You might try:

- A sandwich of peanut butter and sunflower seeds on whole-wheat bread.
- A container of yogurt with chopped nuts and raisins.
- A bean tostada.
- Leftover pizza.
- Milk, fresh or canned fruit, and wheat germ whirled in a blender.

There are many other fast and tasty possibilities. Use your creativity to think of interesting combinations.

▼ Packing a Lunch ▼

Many people take a packed lunch to school or to work. Use the Food Guide Pyramid to help you plan a nutritious packed lunch.

Dairy products, cooked meats, and some other foods can spoil if not kept cool. An easy way to keep your lunch safe is to include something cold in your lunch container. You might use a frozen gel pack or freeze some water or juice in a sealed container. Using an insulated lunch bag will also help keep foods safe.

What can you pack in your lunch? Sandwiches are popular because they are easy to pack and eat. Try different combinations of breads and fillings for variety. A tossed green salad is also a good choice. So are fresh fruits and crunchy vegetables, such as carrot or celery sticks, cauliflower chunks, cherry tomatoes, red bell pepper rings, or zucchini sticks. If you have a wide-mouth vacuum bottle, you can pack soup or other hot foods, such as spaghetti. You might round out the meal with milk, yogurt, or cottage cheese.

To save time, you can prepare part or all of the lunch ahead of time. Refrigerate or freeze the foods in their containers. In the morning, just pop them in your lunch bag and you're on your way. See page 492 for more tips on packing a lunch.

What food choices do you enjoy in a packed lunch?

Learning Activities (continued)

ideas out at home. (Key Skills: *Cooperation, Creativity*)

3. **Discussion.** Give students the following lunch menus, and have them suggest foods that could be added to each of these packed lunches to make them more nutritious: 1) a meat sandwich and oatmeal cookies; 2) hard-cooked eggs and crackers; 3) an apple and milk; and 4) a banana and peanut butter cookies. (Key Skills: *Communication, Critical Thinking*)

Follow Up

1. **Reteaching.** Across the board, make columns for time, energy, skill, money, and equipment. Down the side, list a small variety of popular dishes (order-out pizza, fast food, grilled chicken, frozen dinner, etc.). Ask students to indicate which resources are necessary for each kind of meal. Make checks in those columns. (Key Skills: *Communication, Decision Making*)
2. **Enrichment.** Ask students to figure out cost-per-serving of several meals or menus you have discussed so far in this chapter. Have students compare menus. Remind them that although money is important in meal planning, it is not the only resource to consider. (Key Skill: *Math*)

taken in small amounts throughout the day rather than in large amounts put into the digestive tract all at once. Calcium, riboflavin, and vitamin C are among the nutrients likely to be short-changed among breakfast skippers.

Some people say they are not hungry in the morning. This is more likely a matter of habit than a biological cause.

Hands-on Activity

In labs, have students prepare a variety of breakfast items. Encourage each group to be innovative. Make sure each group prepares enough so there are lots of samples. Print up recipes. You may even wish to have a "People's Choice Award" for the most popular entree.

Teaching . . .
Snacks, Quick and Easy Dinners, and Choosing from a Fast-Food Menu
(pp. 492-493)

Comprehension Check

1. What's the problem with snacking? *(Many popular snack foods are high in fat and sugar and have low nutrient density.)*
2. How can you make a simple and nutritious meal? *(A simple and nutritious meal can be made using a combination of fresh and convenience foods.)*
3. When you eat at a fast-food restaurant, what should you keep in mind? *(You should keep the Dietary Guidelines in mind.)*

Learning Activities

1. **Demonstration.** Using a variety of sandwich fillings (cheese, sliced or ground meat, lettuce, tomato, onion, and/or peppers) and breads, show students how to assemble and store sandwiches for lunches. Ask for suggestions from the class. Tell how to prepare sandwiches for freezing. Add fruit, soup, or vegetables to complete the lunch. Have a variety of food containers and lunch bags/boxes handy and show the advantages and disadvantages of each. (Key Skill: *Communication*)
2. **Show and Tell Lunches.** Ask students to prepare a packed lunch. During class, have students tell what's in their lunch, how nutritious it is, and what resources it requires or doesn't require. Then have students eat their lunches. If you wish, you could have students pick the most innovative, the least expensive, the most attractive, and the tastiest lunches. (Key Skills: *Communication, Management*)
3. **Dinner for One.** Have students plan a dinner for themselves that would be quick and easy, nutritious, and tasty. After their plans have been finalized, have students make and eat these dinners at home. Then have them report on how these dinners turned out. (Key Skills: *Communication, Decision Making*)

How to . . .
Pack a Lunch

Here are some suggestions to help you keep packed lunch foods safe and fresh.

- ***Sandwiches.*** Wrap the sandwich well or use an airtight container to keep it fresh. You might want to try making sandwiches ahead of time and freezing them. (Avoid freezing sandwiches with raw vegetables, mayonnaise, or hard-cooked eggs.) Pack the still-frozen sandwich in your lunch to help keep the other foods cold. By lunchtime it will be thawed and ready to eat.
- ***Sandwich additions.*** You can add flavor and texture to sandwiches with tomato slices, sprouts, green pepper rings, or other additions. Pack them separately and add them to the sandwich just before eating. Otherwise they might get soggy.
- ***Salads and vegetables.*** Pack in an airtight container. Pack dressings or dips separately.
- ***Hot foods.*** Preheat a vacuum bottle by filling it with hot water. When the food is steaming hot, pour the water out of the vacuum bottle and fill it with the food. Seal the bottle tightly.
- ***Milk.*** If you can't buy milk at lunchtime, bring your own in a vacuum bottle. Make sure the vacuum bottle and the milk are both cold when you pack your lunch.
- ***Other dairy foods.*** Pack chilled cottage cheese or yogurt in tightly sealed containers. Use an insulated lunch bag or include a frozen item to help keep them cold.
- ***Utensils.*** Don't forget to pack a napkin and a spoon or fork, if needed.

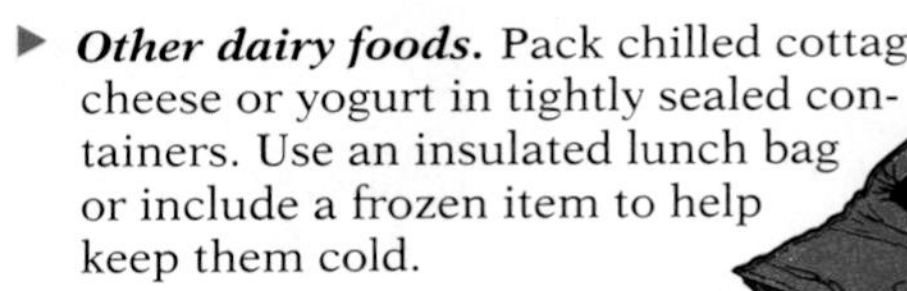

How to . . . Pack a Lunch

Have students read the feature. Ask students why it is important for foods to stay hot or cold (food safety, personal taste, flavor). Does their family use any good "tricks" for keeping foods cold or hot (e.g., frozen juice boxes)? What kind of containers do they use for carrying lunches? Ask students what kind of lunch they would prepare if they had nothing to keep the lunch cold (e.g., peanut butter and jelly sandwich). Make three lists on the board of lunch ideas. The first list should be lunches in which no temperature control would be required, the second list should be lunches that would need to be kept hot, and the third list should be lunches that would need to be kept cold.

▼ Snacks ▼

Would it surprise you to learn that snacking isn't bad for you? In fact, most growing, active teens need snacks. They would have a hard time getting the nutrients they need from meals alone.

The real problem is poor snack choices. Many popular snack foods, such as potato chips, candy bars, and cookies, have low nutrient density. They are high in fat and sugar and supply few of the nutrients you need. Filling up on these foods can lead to real problems.

Instead, snack on low-fat foods from the five major food groups. You might choose fresh fruit, raw vegetables, fruit juice, plain popcorn, or crackers with a little peanut butter.

Some foods that you might normally think of as part of a meal also make good snacks. Try a small sandwich, a cup of soup, or a glass of skim milk.

Nutritious snacks can help active, growing teens to meet their nutrient needs.

▼ Quick and Easy Dinners ▼

Sometimes you may want to prepare a quick evening meal for one. Many simple and nutritious dinners can be made using a combination of fresh and convenience foods. Following are some ideas for main dishes. To complete the meal, add simple side dishes such as a cooked frozen vegetable, a green salad, fresh fruit, or bread.

- Cook leftover chicken with frozen stir-fry vegetables. Serve over instant rice.
- Bake a potato in the microwave. Top with a scrambled egg or cottage cheese.
- Top bagel or English muffin halves with bottled pizza sauce and the toppings of your choice. Heat in a microwave or toaster oven.
- Combine canned kidney or pinto beans (mashed) with seasonings and chopped vegetables. Roll up in a tortilla.

A baked potato can be part of a quick, nutritious meal when topped with a protein food.

▼ Choosing from a Fast-Food Menu ▼

When you eat at a fast-food restaurant, keep the Dietary Guidelines in mind. Many fast-food menu items are high in fat, sodium, or sugar. For instance, a large cheeseburger, an order of fries, and a shake can easily provide about half the calories a typical teenager needs each day, along with about 60 grams of fat. (That's probably about two-thirds of a typical teenager's daily "fat budget.")

Fortunately, fast-food menus are changing in response to the needs and wants of customers. Many restaurants now

Follow Up

1. **Reteaching.** Ask groups or individuals to compile lists of tasty, nutritious snacks that they might actually consider eating. Share highlights from each list. (Key Skills: *Communication, Decision Making*)
2. **Enrichment.** Give groups of students an imaginary amount of money to spend on nutritious, realistic snacks for the week. Have at least one group check for exact prices in a local store. Evaluate the snacks in terms of cost, creativity, and nutrition. Have the students make a list of the best deals. (Key Skills: *Communication, Decision Making*)

Hands-on Activity

Have (or ask students to bring) a variety of sandwich fillings and breads in class. Allow students to experiment with combinations to broaden their "sandwich horizons." Have them cut their sandwiches in fourths and exchange three of them with other students.

Hands-on Activity

Ask students to prepare (or prepare yourself) a variety of sandwiches to freeze. Be sure to include some with mayonnaise and fresh vegetables. Then freeze the sandwiches. The next day check out the results. You might wrap up a sandwich or two in a lunch box to see how long they will stay cold.

More About Dinner

Due to people's work schedules today, dinner is sometimes the only meal when people can get together. People are better off with a light evening meal if they are concerned about maintaining healthy weight and getting a good night's sleep. It is best to limit protein and eat a generous serving of carbohydrates at night. Carbohydrate foods promote entry of tryptophan into the brain, which in turn produces serotonin, a natural sleep-inducing chemical. This effect can be diminished if you eat too much protein. (Protein foods contain tryptophan, but other substances in protein block its entry into the brain.)

Teaching. . .

Choosing from a Fast-Food Menu and Planning Family Meals

(pp. 494-496)

Comprehension Check

1. What are some high-fat, high-sodium toppings to avoid when eating fast-food? *(Cheese, bacon, mayonnaise, tartar sauce, special sauces, regular salad dressings, and butter.)*
2. What do you need to consider when planning meals in your home? *(Nutrition, meal timing, skills and equipment, personal tastes, special needs, meal appeal, money, time, and energy.)*
3. What appliances are especially useful for serving meals in shifts? *(A microwave oven, a slow cooker, and a refrigerator.)*
4. What five elements have nothing to do with nutritional content but are still important to a meal? *(Color, shape, texture, flavor, and temperature.)*

Learning Activities

1. **Survey.** Ask students to check out the fast-food restaurants in your area for low-fat menu items. These may be listed separately on the menu or students may have to check nutritional information (generally available at the counter). Compare students' findings and encourage them to try the lower-fat offerings. Check back every few weeks to see if they have tried these items. (Key Skills: *Communication, Citizenship*)
2. **Demonstration.** Prepare a "salad bar" to keep in the refrigerator for serving regular meals, for eating in shifts, and for packing lunches. Gather as many vegetables and greens as you can and an air-tight container (stackable, if possible) for each. Use a food processor or a chopping board to slice, dice, chop, and shred the vegetables. Don't forget carrots (sliced or grated), celery, onions, ripe olives, frozen peas, and sprouts. Grate some cheese and dice deli or leftover meat for main-dish salads. Wash and dry lettuce or other greens as well. Put all the ingredients in

You can choose nutritious, low-fat foods at many fast food restaurants.

offer items lower in fat, calories, and sodium. Look for signs or brochures that give information about the nutrition of menu items. Here are some examples of good choices:

- Sandwiches: lean roast beef or turkey, small hamburger, grilled chicken.
- Side dishes: plain baked potato, mashed potatoes, salad with low-fat dressing, fresh fruit from salad bar.
- Beverages: low-fat milk, water.
- Breakfast items: pancakes, cereal with low-fat milk.

Ask for food to be served without high-fat, high-sodium toppings, such as cheese, bacon, mayonnaise, and tartar sauce or special sauce. Go easy on salt, butter, and other toppings you add yourself.

Try to choose a good balance of foods from the five major food groups. If the meal is short on fruits, vegetables, grains, or dairy products, be sure you get enough of these foods at other meals that day. By following these guidelines, you can enjoy fast foods and still have a healthful diet.

Planning Family Meals

How is meal planning handled in your home? Is it the responsibility of one person or do several people share ideas? No matter how it's handled, planning family meals takes management skills.

If you are planning a meal for the whole family, what do you need to think about? Nutrition is an important consideration, just as it is when you are planning your own food choices. In addition, you need to think about questions such as:

- When will the meal be served? Will everyone eat at the same time or is everyone's schedule different? The box on page 495 gives some suggestions for busy families.
- Who will prepare the meal? If resources such as time, equipment, or cooking skills are limited, try to keep the menu simple.
- What foods do family members like and dislike? Even the best meal plan won't work if people don't eat the foods. Fortunately, each of the five major food groups has enough choices to satisfy even the pickiest eaters.
- Do any family members have special needs? Someone may be on a special diet or be allergic to certain foods, for instance. You may need to adapt the menu for that person.
- How can I make the meal appetizing? A successful menu is more than just nutritious and practical. It has something extra called "meal appeal."

More About *Meal Planning*

Don't overlook weekly grocery ads as an aid to planning meals. Often just looking over the specials will bring to mind ideas for meals that week. Ads remind you about what fruits and vegetables are in season and are at their optimum eating time. You can also be sure that certain ingredients are available. Also, there are often seasonal menu ideas in the food section of the newspaper. A side benefit is, of course, that by buying food at sale prices you cut down on the cost of eating.

Planning family meals can be a real challenge. How do you and your family handle meal planning?

Eating in Shifts

Meals, especially dinner, are a good time for the family to get together. Unfortunately, in real life it doesn't always work out that way. Families often have to plan meals around work hours, school activities, meetings, and other events. The whole family may not sit down at one time to eat.

Busy schedules don't have to mean another night of takeout pizza or frozen dinners. Here are a few ideas you and your family might want to try.

- Keep individual servings of leftovers or "planned-overs" in the refrigerator or freezer.
- Prepare a food that will keep for several hours. For instance, you might put a main-dish salad in the refrigerator. Family members can serve themselves whenever they are ready.
- Use a slow cooker to prepare a stew, soup, or other dish. The food can cook all day until it is done, then safely continue cooking a few more hours until everyone has had a chance to eat.
- Plan a casserole that can be reheated without losing flavor. Some food mixtures actually taste better after flavors have had time to mingle.
- Set aside a shelf in the refrigerator for do-it-yourself meals. For instance, prepare containers of lettuce, tomatoes, shredded cheese, meat sauce, beans, and other fixings for tacos or salads.

Learning Activities (continued)

containers. Then, start with the greens and make a great-looking, nutritious salad. Non-refrigerated salad ingredients can also be used: croutons, seeds, Chinese noodles, etc. Point out the following benefits: you don't have to chop each time you make a salad; you have to clean the food processor only once; you eat only the ingredients you choose; and the ease of preparation will make salads more tempting. After several days, use the appropriate leftovers in a casserole or tacos. This might also be a good time to demonstrate preparing some low-fat salad dressings. (Key Skills: *Management, Creativity*)

Follow Up

1. **Reteaching.** Ask students to list all the fast-food items they can think of and put them under the following categories: great nutritional choice, good choice, so-so choice, poor nutritional choice. (Key Skill: *Decision Making*)
2. **Extension.** Use the extension information handout on p. 54 of the *Extending the Text* booklet in the TCR.
3. **Enrichment.** Have students look through magazines with pictures of foods and evaluate them in terms of color, shape, texture, flavor, and temperature. (Key Skill: *Decision Making*)

Photo Focus

Discuss the photo at the top of page 495 with the students. Ask students if family meal planning in their home could use some helpful suggestions to make meals more nutritious and simpler to make. *(Answers will vary.)*

Completing the Chapter

For Review

1. Emphasize the main concepts using the summary.
2. Have students complete the "Facts to Recall." (Answers below.)

For Reteaching

1. **Reteaching.** Use the activity on pp. 53-54 of the *Reteaching and Practical Skills* booklet in the TCR.

For Enrichment

1. **Enrichment.** Use the activity on p. 66 of the *Enrichment Activities* booklet in the TCR.

For Evaluation

1. Choose items from "Ideas to Explore" and "Activities to Try."
2. Use the chapter test on pp. 87-88 in the testing booklet of the TCR or use the testmaker software.

Facts to Recall Answers

1. By planning your meals and snacks, you make sure that your individual choices add up to a day's worth of good nutrition. Each meal or snack becomes part of a total nutrition picture.
2. By knowing your meal pattern, you will be able to plan on when and from what source you will get your daily servings from the five food groups.
3. **Any four:** available choices; money; time; energy; skills; equipment.
4. Convenience foods can be a good choice when time and skills are limited. However, because many are high in sodium, fat and/or sugar, and more expensive than homemade meals, you should read the labels and compare products before you buy.
5. This saves money because one item is stretched into several meals; it saves time and energy because fewer meals must be prepared "from scratch"; it reduces food waste because the extra food is not thrown away.

Making meals look appealing is part of good planning and an enjoyable dining experience.

▼ Meal Appeal ▼

Close your eyes and think about your favorite meal. Does it look as good as it tastes? You can perk up appetites by paying attention to:

- ***Color.*** The colors of food come right from an artist's palette — green, yellow, red, purple, orange, and creamy white. Use this wide variety to avoid monotonous one-color meals.
- ***Shape.*** Different shapes make a meal more attractive. For instance, meatballs, peas, and boiled, small potatoes are all round. For variety, try hamburger, slivered beans, and a baked potato.
- ***Texture.*** Contrasting textures also add variety. If you are having mashed potatoes, you might plan on a crisp green salad rather than applesauce. Crispy stir-fried vegetables are a good contrast to rice.
- ***Flavor.*** Vary flavors to add interest to a meal. Plan flavors that go well together. If there are too many spicy or strongly flavored foods in one meal, they will fight with each other for your attention.
- ***Temperature.*** You might want a contrast of temperatures, such as a cold salad with steaming soup. Cold foods are appealing on hot days and hot foods on cold days.

TAKING ACTION

Encouraging Healthy Habits

Keith is working as a supervisor in a summer day-care program for nine- and ten-year-olds. The service does not include meals or snacks, so the children are required to bring their own. Keith has noticed many children bringing foods that seem like poor choices — cookies and potato chips, for example. He would like to encourage better nutrition among the youngsters, but knows they may not want to part with their sweets. He also realizes he must sell their parents on good nutrition if his plan is to have a lasting effect. He asks for your help in getting the children to eat more nutritiously.

Using Your Resourcefulness

- Where can Keith learn about any special nutritional needs of children in this age group?
- Where can Keith find out what foods can meet these nutritional needs?
- Where can Keith find suggestions on making nutritious snacks appealing to children?
- Where can Keith get information on the kinds of foods that can be safely packed in lunches?
- How can Keith make price comparisons, to convince parents that simple, healthful foods are also inexpensive?
- What suggestions can you offer Keith for talking with the parents about good nutrition?

TAKING ACTION

Have students read the feature. Then you may want to have a class discussion about how students could help Keith get the children to eat more nutritiously. To guide this discussion, have students respond to the *Using Your Resourcefulness* questions at the end of this feature.

Using Your Resourcefulness Answers

- Answers will vary. Possible answers might include nutrition books, nutrition magazines, the USDA, a nutritionist, and a dietitian.
- Answers will vary and might include nutrition books, the USDA, a nutritionist, a dietitian, or Keith could go to the supermarket and read the labels on different foods.

Chapter 42 Review

Summary

In this chapter, you have read about:

- Applying the Dietary Guidelines and the Food Guide Pyramid to your meal pattern.
- Resources to consider when planning meals.
- How convenience foods fit into meal planning.
- Ideas for easy, nutritious meals and snacks.
- How to pack a lunch.
- Making healthful choices from a fast-food menu.
- Hints for fitting nutritious meals into a busy family schedule.
- Ways to make meals appealing.

Facts to Recall

1. How can planning meals and snacks help ensure nutritious eating?
2. Why does knowing your meal pattern in advance help you eat healthfully?
3. Identify four resources to consider when planning meals.
4. Name two advantages and two disadvantages of convenience foods.
5. Explain how "planned-overs" can save a family money, time, and energy and cut down on food waste.
6. What are two ways of keeping foods from spoiling in a packed lunch?
7. Name two examples of a healthful sandwich choice and side dish at a fast-food restaurant.
8. List four questions to think about when planning a meal for the whole family.
9. Give three ideas for planning meals for a family that does not eat at one time.
10. Name five factors affecting meal appeal.

Ideas to Explore

1. Describe a meal pattern you might follow on a typical weekday. How has this pattern developed to suit your lifestyle? Does it present any problems in getting all your required daily nutrients? How might you change it to help you eat more healthfully?
2. How are current trends and technology influencing the way families plan, prepare, and eat meals? What are some positive results? What are some negative results and how can families respond?

Activities to Try

1. Bring a menu from a fast-food restaurant (or make a list of menu items) to class. Identify those items you would and would not choose as part of a nutritious meal. Explain your selections.
2. Brainstorm a list of snacks that are easy to prepare and eat, yet also nutritious.

LINK TO Communication

TEACHING CHILDREN ABOUT BREAKFAST

Learning to make healthful food choices starts in childhood. Plan a five- to ten-minute puppet show designed to teach young children about eating a nutritious breakfast. Emphasize the food groups from the Food Guide Pyramid. (Note: You can make interesting puppets out of socks, paper lunch bags, or other recyclable materials.) Present your puppet show to younger children.

As a follow-up activity, make some nutrition "flash cards" that show different foods from the food groups that can be eaten for breakfast. Involve the children by asking them to identify which food groups the foods come from.

Facts to Recall Answers (continued)

6. Include something cold in your lunch container; use an insulated lunch bag.
7. **Any two:** lean roast beef or turkey; small hamburger; grilled chicken. **Any two:** plain baked potato; mashed potatoes; salad with low-fat dressing; fresh fruit from salad bar.
8. **Any four:** When will the meal be served? Who will prepare the meal? What foods do family members like and dislike? Do any family members have special needs? How can I make the meal appetizing?
9. **Any three:** Keep individual servings of leftovers or "planned-overs" in the refrigerator or freezer; prepare a food that will keep for several hours; use a slow cooker to prepare a stew, soup, or other dish; plan a casserole that can be reheated without losing flavor; set aside a shelf in the refrigerator for do-it-yourself meals.
10. The color, shape, texture, flavor, and temperature of food.

Ideas to Explore

1. Answers will vary.
2. Answers will vary.

- Answers will vary and might include nutrition books, nutrition magazines, the USDA, a nutritionist, and a dietitian.
- Answers will vary and might include family and consumer sciences books and the USDA.
- Answers will vary. Keith could go to a supermarket and write down the prices of these foods and the prices of other types of food.
- Answers will vary. Keith should make sure that he has all his facts researched and written down before he goes to talk to the parents.

LINK TO Communication

Answers

The puppet shows designed by students will vary. Make sure that the puppet shows express positive food choices. Also, make sure that students' flash cards show healthful food choices.

Preparing to Teach

Chapter Outline

Chapter Resources

The following booklet materials may be found in the *Teacher's Classroom Resources* box:

- Lesson Plans, p. 48
- Student Workbook, *Study Guide,* pp. 183-184; *Organized Shopping,* p. 185; *Choosing the Best Price,* p. 186
- Color Transparencies, *What's on the Label,* CT-47
- Personal Safety, *Travel Safety,* pp. 43-44
- Technology and Computers, pp. 43, 45
- Cooperative Learning, p. 55
- Extending the Text, *Using Unit Pricing,* p. 55
- Reteaching and Practical Skills, *Shopping Sense Word Search,* p. 55
- Enrichment Activities, *Smart Storing,* p. 67
- Chapter and Unit Tests, pp. 89-90
- Testmaker Software

Also see:

- Meeting the Special Needs of Students
- Linking Home, School, and Community

ABCNews InterActive™ Videodiscs

- *Food and Nutrition*

See the ABCNews InterActive™ Bar Code Correlation booklet for applicable segments.

CHAPTER

43 Buying and Storing Food

OBJECTIVES

- *Name factors affecting food prices.*
- *Discuss how to prepare and shop for food.*
- *Explain how to store food.*

TERMS TO LEARN

- ***processing***
- ***cents-off coupons***
- ***unit price***
- ***open dating***
- ***perishable foods***

Have you ever shopped for food for your family? Everyone at some time has probably had to shop for a container of milk, a head of lettuce, or a loaf of bread. If you shop for a few items, your task is fairly easy.

Shopping for food becomes a more challenging task when the weekly shopping list is involved. Will you be able to get the best value for your dollar? Will you be able to resist many of the tempting treats along the supermarket aisles and buy only what you need?

In this chapter, you will learn more about the food you buy and techniques for buying it. Developing shopping savvy will help you get the most value for your food dollar.

Food Costs and Your Budget

As you learned in Chapter 42, money spent on food can use up a large part of the family budget. Before you start out for the supermarket, you need to figure out how much money you have to spend on food. Talking with family members about the food budget will help you carefully plan food choices.

Planning your food choices helps you stay within your food budget.

The price of food reflects the many steps food goes through before it reaches the marketplace:

- ***Production.*** The food on your plate began with farming or fishing. Factors such as weather and the time of year affect the supply of food, and therefore the cost. If supplies are limited — for instance, after a drought or freeze — prices go up. Foods are generally least expensive and taste best during the peak of their growing season. For example, tomatoes are usually tastier and less expensive in summer.
- ***Processing.*** Part of the cost of food is due to **processing,** or the steps that are taken to prepare and package food for sale. Foods may be processed to increase their safety and storage life, to add convenience, or to make them into specific products (such as flour made from wheat).
- ***Distribution.*** Transportation costs are also figured into the price of food. In most stores, foods have been shipped in from all over the United States and even some foreign countries.

More About *Who Shops for Food*

Recent surveys have shown that six out of ten teenagers do a considerable amount of their family's food shopping. Nearly as many boys do the shopping as girls. Why are teenagers increasingly involved in family food shopping? In more and more families, both parents work. The number of single-parent families are also increasing. As a result, responsibilities for food shopping are being shared by more family members than in the past.

Introducing the Chapter

Motivators

1. **Display.** Display a variety of processed and unprocessed foods. Ask students to identify factors that affect the availability and costs of food. Students should point out weather, season of the year, transportation, processing, packaging, government regulations, etc. (Key Skill: *Critical Thinking*)
2. **Discussion.** Ask students to identify places where their families shop for groceries. Categorize these as supermarkets, warehouse stores, convenience stores, specialty stores, farmers' markets, or food co-ops. Have students who are familiar with each source of food describe the features that are helpful to consumers. How might the choices of places to shop for food be different if you lived in a more or less populated area? (Key Skill: *Critical Thinking*)
3. **Writing.** Have students write a paragraph describing how the person in their family who shops for food gets ready to shop. Have several volunteers share their paragraphs with the class. How does preparation for food shopping save time, energy, and money? (Key Skills: *Communication, Management*)

Chapter Objectives and Vocabulary

1. Have students read the chapter objectives and rephrase the objectives as questions.
2. Ask students to state, in their own words, the purpose of studying this chapter.
3. Pronounce the vocabulary terms listed on the previous page. Ask students whether they are familiar with any of these. Explain that the terms will be defined in the chapter.

Guided Reading

1. Have students read the chapter and use the Study Guide on pp. 183-184 of the *Student Workbook.*

Teaching. . .

Food Costs and Your Budget and Getting Ready to Shop

(pp. 499-501)

Comprehension Check

1. What affects the cost of food? *(Weather, season of the year, processing, transportation, and marketing.)*
2. Where do people shop for food? *(Supermarkets, warehouse stores, convenience stores, specialty stores, farmers' markets, and/or food co-ops.)*
3. When should you shop for food? *(When you have time for one major shopping trip, when you are not hungry, and when stores are less crowded.)*

Learning Activities

1. **Family Food Budget.** Have students find out how much their families spend on food each month. Discuss factors that influence how much money a family budgets for food. (Key Skills: *Communication, Critical Thinking*)
2. **Where Food Comes From.** Have students research different foods to learn where the foods available in local stores are grown. Using a world map, attach pictures of foods to show where the foods available locally are grown. (Key Skills: *Communication, Social Studies*)
3. **Food Sources.** Using local newspapers and telephone directories, make a list of local sources of food. Categorize these sources by type as outlined in the text. Discuss reasons why people might use each source. What limitations does each source have? (Key Skills: *Communication, Problem Solving*)
4. **Group Presentations.** Have students work in groups to research different sources of food. Make sure they research the characteristics and advantages and disadvantages of each. Have each group present their findings to the class in a creative manner. (Key Skills: *Cooperation, Creativity*)

- ***Marketing.*** Food companies spend money to advertise their goods, design attractive packaging, and research new products. These costs are passed on to consumers.

Getting Ready to Shop

Shopping for food involves more than just a trip to the store. It involves using your planning and management skills before you leave home. Taking time to plan ahead can save time and money when you shop.

Deciding Where to Shop

If you live in a populated area, you will probably have a greater variety of stores to choose from than if you live in a small town or rural area.

- **Supermarkets** are large stores that sell a full line of food products and nonfood items. Many supermarkets include a bakery, a cheese shop, a deli, a fish market, a salad bar, or other specialty departments.

When shopping for food, choose a store that sells a variety of good quality foods.

More About *Food Packaging*

Food packaging? You mean bottles, jars, cans, and boxes, right? Not necessarily. Today's technology has created surprising new options for food packaging. Plastic containers are replacing glass bottles and jars for many products. Salad dressings and ketchup now come in squeezable containers that make it easy to get just the right amount. Instead of a can, the food you buy may come in a retort pouch. This lightweight container is made of aluminum foil and plastic and keeps food fresh without refrigeration. It's even boilable. Aseptic packaging is another alternative to the can. These containers are a single sheet formed of plastic, paperboard, aluminum foil, and adhesive. Like retort

- **Warehouse stores** take a "no-frills" approach to selling food. They carry a limited line of basic items, which are often displayed in cartons. Prices are lower than in a supermarket, but fewer services are offered. For example, you may have to bring your own bags and fill them yourself.
- **Convenience stores** carry a limited line of food and nonfood items. They are designed to attract shoppers who want to make a quick stop for a few items. Prices are usually higher than at a supermarket.
- **Specialty stores** concentrate on one type of food item, such as meat, fish, or baked goods. Often the prices are higher than at other stores. Specialty stores offer personal service and may prepare special items for you.
- **Farmers' markets** are places where local growers bring their harvest to sell. During the growing season, you can find low-cost fresh fruits and vegetables here.
- **Food co-ops** are owned and operated by members of the co-op (cooperative). The co-op buys food in quantity and distributes it among the members. Since members do the work, costs are kept down.

Wherever you shop, choose a store that has a good selection of quality foods. In addition, a store should be clean and neat.

Avoid shopping when you are hungry. You may find yourself buying more food because everything looks good to eat.

Planning Your Shopping Trip

Your schedule will help determine when and how often you shop for food. In most cases, you can make the best use of your time by going on one major shopping trip instead of several small ones.

If you shop when stores are less crowded, you'll spend less time waiting in line. Try not to shop on an empty stomach. Hungry shoppers often spend more than expected because everything looks "good enough to eat."

Make it a practice to check newspaper ads before you shop. By looking at different store ads, you can compare prices and find out what is on sale. Take advantage of sale items and seasonal foods as you plan menus.

Look through magazines, newspapers, and advertising fliers for cents-off coupons. **Cents-off coupons** are certificates that allow customers to buy products at reduced prices. Manufacturers print these coupons to encourage you to use their products. Some stores offer double or triple discounts on coupons.

When available, use coupons for items on your shopping list.

pouches, aseptic packages need no refrigeration until opened. Frozen dinners are also packaged differently these days. They come in dual-ovenable packaging made of paperboard, aluminum, or plastic. You can simply remove the package from the freezer and pop it into the microwave or conventional oven.

Follow Up

1. **Reteaching.** Have students make a list of things to consider before you shop for food. (Key Skill: *Communication*)
2. **Enrichment.** Have students research a method of food processing and write a report about their findings. How has food processing changed in the 20th century? (Key Skill: *Communication*)

The World Around You

World Food Supply

The food supply is the total amount of food available worldwide. It depends mainly on the world's farmers. They raise the crops and livestock that supply most of our food. The supply of food is affected by the weather and by natural disasters. Food shortages and famine occur when the food supply falls short of the amount needed. Population growth increases the demand for food. To increase the food supply, greater farm output is needed. This means developing new farmland and making existing farmland more productive. Other ways to increase the food supply involve reducing the demand for grain to feed livestock and developing new food sources.

Photo Focus

Discuss the photo at the bottom of page 500 with the students. Have students name the main store in which their family shops for food. Do they know the reasons why the shopping is done at that particular store? If not, have students discuss this with their parents and report their findings back to the class. *(Answers will vary.)*

Teaching. . .
Planning Your Shopping Trip and Shopping for Food
(pp. 502-503)

Comprehension Check

1. Why should you group similar foods together on your shopping list and arrange your list the way foods are organized in the store? *(To avoid skipping an item and to save time shopping.)*
2. How can you avoid making impulse purchases when shopping for food? *(By following your shopping list and by being aware of impulse buying tactics.)*
3. What does a typical food label contain? *(The name of the product; a description of the product; the net weight of the contents; the name and address of the manufacturer, packer, or distributor; and a list of ingredients.)*

Learning Activities

1. **Staple Foods.** Have students name foods that are normally kept on hand in the kitchen. List these foods on the chalkboard. Why is it a good idea to keep a supply of these foods on hand? (Key Skill: *Communication*)
2. **Shopping List.** Provide students with menus for a week, recipe books, and a diagram of the layout of a local supermarket. Have students work in groups to make a weekly shopping list. Which foods might you have on hand? Which foods would you probably need to purchase? Why is it important to note amounts needed when you make your shopping list? (Key Skills: *Cooperation, Problem Solving*)
3. **Shopping Order.** Provide students with a diagram of the layout of a local grocery store. Have students use lines and arrows to show the route they would take through the store. Would the route chosen make it easy to place heavier items on the bottom of the cart? Would the route allow students to select refrigerated or frozen foods last? (Key Skills: *Critical Thinking, Problem Solving*)

Have you ever returned from the store with bags full of items you didn't intend to buy — and none of the items you really needed? A shopping list can help you avoid this problem. Keep a list posted in the kitchen. When you are planning menus, write down the ingredients you'll need for recipes. Before shopping, check the cabinets, refrigerator, and freezer for items that are running low.

To make your list easier to use, group similar foods together — all the dairy products, all the canned goods, and so on. You can also save time by arranging your shopping list to match the way foods are organized in the store. Remember to take your list and your coupons to the store with you.

Shopping for Food

When you get to the store, keep your shopping list handy. As you select items, cross them off the list. A small calculator can help you keep track of how much you are spending.

Food stores use a number of techniques to encourage impulse buying — making purchases on the spur of the moment.

- Bright, colorful packaging and displays are designed to catch your eye.
- Special displays are often placed in the middle of the traffic lane or at the end of an aisle. You have to slow down to go around them. The items on display are sometimes sale priced, but not always.

Be aware of tactics that encourage impulse buying. The sight, aroma, and taste of food may tempt you to spend more than your budget allows.

More About Grocery Shopping

Use these tips to save time and money when you shop for groceries.

- Don't rush shopping. Give yourself time to consider the best buys. If rushed, you might not get the most for your money. "Grabbers" are usually losers when shopping.
- Keep your priorities in mind when shopping. Wheel your cart past "empty-calorie" foods and look for nutritional foods.
- Stock up on staples if items are on sale and you have storage. If space is limited, be creative. There's no reason you can't store canned goods under the bed.
- Stores use pricing to attract customers. They may offer "specials" (items at reduced prices) and "loss leaders" (items sold at or

- ▶ Popular items are often placed at eye level so you will be more likely to see and buy them.
- ▶ Slow, relaxing music encourages shoppers to take their time and buy more.
- ▶ Some stores offer food samples to encourage consumers to try new products. The sight, aroma, and taste of food can be very tempting.

By following your shopping list and being aware of these tactics, you'll be less likely to make impulse purchases.

▼ Comparison Shopping ▼

As you walk through the store, you will find many choices. Your shopping list may say "green beans," but do you want fresh, frozen, or canned? What brand and size should you choose?

Instead of grabbing a package at random, take the time to comparison shop. By comparing different items, you can be sure you are getting good nutrition and quality at a good price. Comparison shopping is easier if you have an understanding of labels, brands, prices, forms and sizes of food, and signs of quality.

Reading Labels

Are you a label reader? Reading labels is an important part of comparison shopping. The label tells you what is inside the package. A typical label includes:

- ▶ The name of the product.
- ▶ A description of the product, such as whole, halves, or diced.
- ▶ The net weight of the contents. (Net weight does not include the weight of the package.)
- ▶ The name and address of the manufacturer, packer, or distributor.
- ▶ A list of ingredients. They are listed in order of weight, beginning with the largest amount. For example, if a soup lists noodles before chicken, it has more noodles than chicken in the can.

In addition, you will often see brand names, pictures of the contents, and suggestions for preparation.

Nutrition information is often given on the label or on a sign posted near the item. This information can help you to select more nutritious foods.

Nutrition Facts

Serving Size 1/2 cup (114 g)
Servings Per Container 4

Amount Per Serving	
Calories 90	Calories from Fat 30
	% Daily Value*
Total Fat 3 g	5%
Saturated Fat 0 g	0%
Cholesterol 0 mg	0%
Sodium 300 mg	13%
Total Carbohydrate 13 g	4%
Dietary Fiber 3 g	12%
Sugars 3 g	
Protein 3 g	

Vitamin A	80%	Vitamin C	60%
Calcium	4%	Iron	4%

* Percent Daily Values are based on a 2,000 calorie diet. Your daily values may be higher or lower depending on your calorie needs:

	Calories	2,000	2,500
Total Fat	Less than	65 g	80 g
Sat Fat	Less than	20 g	25g
Cholesterol	Less than	300 mg	300 mg
Sodium	Less than	2,400 mg	2,400 mg
Total Carbohydrate		300 g	375 g
Fiber		25 g	30 g

Calories per gram:
Fat 9 • Carbohydrates 4 • Protein 4

By reading labels, you can choose foods that provide the best nutritional value for your money.

below cost). Not all advertised items are on sale or are bargains.

- "Reduced for quick sale" items can represent significant savings. Products with expired shelf removal dates are often greatly reduced in price. Take advantage of these savings if you can use the items quickly.

Learning Activities (continued)

4. **Field Trip.** Take students on a field trip to a local supermarket. Have students make a diagram of the store layout. Also have students identify examples of techniques the manager uses to encourage consumers to buy more. (Key Skill: *Critical Thinking*)
5. **Reading.** Provide students with several food labels. Have them identify the required and optional information provided on the labels. (Key Skill: *Communication*)

Follow Up

1. **Reteaching.** Have students list steps to take in getting ready to shop and shopping for food. Combine individual lists to create a class list. (Key Skill: *Communication*)
2. **Enrichment.** Have students interview a marketing teacher or supermarket manager to learn about selling techniques used in supermarkets. Have students share their findings with the class. (Key Skill: *Communication*)

Life Management Skills

Consumerism

Food shopping involves more than pushing a shopping cart around the grocery store and picking up whatever appeals to you. You can save both time and money by planning before you shop. A shopping list helps you avoid extra trips to the store. These extra trips are when you are most likely to purchase eye-catching extras. If the items on the shopping list are in the same order as they are found in the store, you save time while shopping as well. Planning also helps prevent waste. Some experts estimate that you can save as much as 20% by carefully planning your shopping.

Teaching. . . Comparison Shopping and Shopping for Convenience Foods (pp. 504-505)

Comprehension Check

1. What nutrient information is usually given on food labels? *(The amount of food that is considered a serving and the number of servings in the package, the number of calories in one serving, the amounts of several nutrients per serving, and percentages that show how the amounts of nutrients supplied by the product fit into an overall daily diet.)*
2. What is the unit price of an item? *(The unit price of an item is the price per ounce, pound, or other convenient unit of measure. Unit prices are often posted on the shelf near the item.)*
3. What is open dating? *(Open dating is a system used on food labels to help you determine the freshness of a product.)*
4. How should convenience foods be used? *(Convenience foods should be used in moderation and in combination with fresh foods.)*

Learning Activities

1. **Assignment.** Have students obtain and bring to class nutrition labels for raw fruits and vegetables and fresh fish, meat, and poultry. Discuss the information provided by these labels. (Key Skill: *Communication*)
2. **Survey.** Have students survey the food shoppers in their families regarding their brand preferences. Find out how many compare unit prices when making purchasing decisions. How do people's beliefs about brands and prices affect their shopping habits? (Key Skill: *Communication*)

By law, almost all foods must have "Nutrition Facts" labels. These labels include:

- Serving size and number of servings.
- Calories per serving and calories from fat.
- Grams of total fat, saturated fat, cholesterol, sodium, carbohydrates, and protein per serving and (for most of these) their percentage of daily value.
- Key vitamins and minerals and their percentage of daily value.

Comparing Brands

When you shop, compare national brands, private labels, and generic products.

- **National brands** are produced by major food companies. They are sold across the country and advertised nationally.
- **Private label**, or store brand, products are packaged for a particular chain of stores. Prices are usually lower than for nationally advertised brands. There may be or may not be differences in the quality. The nutritional value is the same as for the national brands.
- **Generic products** can be identified by their plain, simple packaging. They are less expensive than other brands. The nutritional value is the same as for other products, but the quality and appearance may not be as good.

G
WHOL KERNL GLDN CORN
03 27043 31 28 12OZ.
UNIT PRICE 5.67¢ PER OUNCE
68¢

The unit price allows you to compare the cost of different-sized packages of foods.

Using Unit Prices

Many stores offer a unit pricing system to help consumers comparison shop. The **unit price** is the price per ounce, pound, or other convenient unit of measure. Unit pricing makes it easy to compare the cost of products in different-size packages.

Unit prices are often posted on the shelf near the item. The total price for the package is also given. For example, a 15-ounce can of tomatoes may have a unit price of 3 cents per ounce. The total price for the can is 45 cents (3×15).

If unit prices are not given, you can calculate them yourself. Divide the total cost of the package by the number of units (such as ounces or pounds) to get the cost per unit. Repeat this process for other sizes and brands to determine the best buy.

Comparing Forms and Sizes

Compare the price of foods in different forms whenever you can. Foods may be purchased fresh, frozen, canned, or dried. They may be whole, sliced, diced, or chopped. How you plan to use the food will help you to decide what to buy. There's no point in paying the higher price for whole or extra fancy items if they are going to be used in a casserole.

More About Labels

Why is nutrient information given in amounts for some nutrients and percentages for others? The number of grams of protein, carbohydrates, and fats can help you determine the number of calories from each source. Protein and carbohydrates furnish four calories per gram, while fats contribute a whopping nine calories per gram. Other nutrients given in amounts are sodium and cholesterol. People on special diets often need to know how much of these substances are in foods. Recommended daily allowances have been established for all of the nutrients listed by percentage. Use of nutrient percentages makes it easier to determine how well a serving of the food meets your body's daily needs. Only

Buying in quantity or buying larger sizes often costs less, but not always. Compare the unit prices to be sure. If the extra food will be wasted, buying the larger size is not a bargain.

Some stores offer bulk foods that you can select and package yourself. Products are in large containers, and you scoop out the amount you want. Because food is not packaged, prices may be lower than individually wrapped products. Compare unit prices to make sure you are getting the best buy.

Judging Quality

Low-priced food is not a bargain if the quality is poor. It takes careful shopping to select food that is fresh and nutritious.

Open dating is a system used on food labels to help you determine the freshness of a product. Several different methods of dating are used. A "sell by" or "pull" date is often found on bakery goods, dairy products, meats, and other items that lose freshness quickly. This date tells the last day the product can be sold in the store. The product is still safe for home use after this date if stored properly and used quickly.

A "use by" date can be found on refrigerated doughs and packaged cold cuts. This shows the date after which the food will no longer be at its peak of freshness.

Other tools for judging quality include the grade labels, such as "grade A," that are found on some foods. You will learn more about specific grades and signs of quality in Chapters 47 to 51.

▼ Shopping for Convenience Foods ▼

Many foods are available in a wide variety of convenience forms. You can buy main dishes, side dishes, snacks, and entire meals already prepared. Some are frozen, while others can be stored at room temperature. Many can be heated in the microwave oven for quick meals.

Convenience foods can be part of a healthful diet. However, read labels carefully. Many convenience foods are high in fat, sugar, and sodium. They should be used in moderation and in combination with fresh foods. For instance, you might round out a frozen dinner by adding skim milk, whole-wheat bread, and an apple. Come to think of it, many fresh foods are convenient, too!

TIPS: ***Recognizing Signs of Food Spoilage***

How can you tell when food is unsafe to eat? Learn these "danger signs":

- ▶ The food has an unusual odor or color.
- ▶ The food has an unusual softness or mushy spots.
- ▶ The food looks or feels "slimy."
- ▶ Raw meat changes to a dull, gray-brown color.
- ▶ Cans of food have dents or bulges.

Open dating helps you determine the freshness of products that you buy.

protein, which provides calories and builds and repairs body cells, is listed both ways.

Learning Activities (continued)

3. **Comparisons.** Provide students with a national brand, a private brand, and a generic brand of several food products. Have students work in groups to compare the product labels, contents, and prices of these products. What conclusions can they draw based on their findings? How might their intended use of the product affect their buying decision? (Key Skills: *Cooperation, Critical Thinking*)
4. **Price Comparisons.** Provide students with information on the total price of several different sizes and brands of food products. Have students figure the unit price of each product and determine which is the best buy. Discuss the results. (Key Skills: *Math, Management*)
5. **Interpreting Label Information.** Provide students with the empty packages or wrappers from food items that have open dating. Differentiate between "sell by" or "pull" dates and "use by" dates. Discuss how open dating aids consumers in determining the freshness of the foods they buy. (Key Skills: *Communication, Management*)

Follow Up

1. **Reteaching.** Have students write "how to" articles describing procedures for comparison shopping. (Key Skill: *Communication*)
2. **Enrichment.** Have students read and summarize recent newspaper or magazine articles about food labeling. (Key Skill: *Communication*)

TIPS:

Recognizing Signs of Food Spoilage
Have students read the feature. Then have them investigate at home for signs of food spoilage. Was there any food at home that clearly had spoiled? If so, approximately how long had it been spoiled? *(Answers will vary.)*

Teaching. . .
Filling Your Cart and Checking Out and Storing Food
(pp. 506-508)

Comprehension Check

1. How can the consumer prevent errors at the checkout counter? *(By grouping similar items together, by placing groceries on the counter with prices or bar codes visible, by being familiar with prices and checking prices as they are rung up on the register, by making sure you receive the correct change, and by making sure all items you paid for are put into bags.)*
2. How should groceries be put away at home? *(Put frozen foods away first to prevent them from thawing. Next, put away foods that belong in the refrigerator. Then put your other items away last.)*
3. How should foods be prepared for the freezer? *(Foods to be frozen should be sealed in airtight, moisture-proof packaging. Plastic containers, freezer paper, heavy foil, and special freezer bags are good to use. Foods that you buy frozen can be stored in the original packaging.)*
4. What types of foods should be kept in dry storage? *(Canned and boxed foods that do not require freezing or refrigeration.)*

Learning Activities

1. **Observation.** Provide students with the UPC code for several food products. Have them observe the differences in the codes. Discuss how the lines are read by a computer. Why do students think the bar code does not include the price? Discuss ways the UPC is used by the store to keep an up-to-date inventory. (Key Skills: *Science, Critical Thinking*)

How to . . .
Be a Courteous Shopper

As you shop, practice courtesy toward other customers. Here are some tips for courteous shopping:

- Handle foods carefully to avoid damaging them. When careless shoppers damage products, store owners have to increase prices to cover the losses.
- Avoid blocking traffic in the store aisles.
- Have your coupons ready to hand to the checkout clerk.
- If you are paying with a check, write it out (except for the amount) while waiting in the checkout line.

Many supermarkets use a scanner to speed up checkout and maintain an accurate inventory.

▼ Filling Your Cart and Checking Out ▼

As you load your cart, put heavier items at the bottom. Put easily damaged items, such as tomatoes, bread, and eggs, where they will not be crushed.

Select refrigerated or frozen foods last so they don't thaw before you get them home. Many stores are arranged so that the frozen food aisle is your last stop.

In many supermarket checkout lanes, an electronic scanner reads prices automatically. The clerk passes each grocery item over the scanner. The scanner uses a laser to read a bar code — called a universal product code, or UPC — that is found on the package. The bar code identifies the product, size, and manufacturer. When the UPC is read by the scanner, the price of the item is automatically rung up on the cash register. The UPC not only speeds up checkout, it also helps the store keep an up-to-date inventory.

As you place your items on the checkout counter, make sure the prices or UPC symbols are visible. You can also help the checkout clerk by grouping together items that are all the same price, such as several cans of tomato soup.

Familiarize yourself with the grocery prices and check them as they are rung up on the register.

After you pay the bill, make sure you receive the correct change. Make sure all items you paid for are put into bags.

How to ... Be a Courteous Shopper

Have students read the feature. Ask students to list ways consumers damage products when they shop. The list might include squeezing products, dropping or throwing produce, sampling products, opening packages, leaving frozen or refrigerated foods on regular shelves, and not returning unwanted items to their proper location.

Storing Food

After you have finished shopping, take the food home immediately and store it. Put frozen foods away first to prevent them from thawing. Next, put away foods that belong in the refrigerator. (Any food that was kept cold at the store should be refrigerated or frozen at home.) Put your other items away last.

As you store your purchases, place them behind similar foods that are already in storage. That way, food that has been stored the longest is at the front of the storage area so that it will be used first. This is especially important for fresh and frozen products.

Putting food away after shopping is a quick and easy task when family members work together.

By storing food wisely, you will be able to enjoy fresh and nutritious food. Here are some guidelines for the three basic types of storage areas: refrigerator, freezer, and dry storage.

AROUND THE WORLD

In desert regions such as Morocco and Ethiopia, dairy products do not keep long without refrigeration. The people of these countries have solved part of the problem, however, by using *clarified* butter. Clarified butter is made by melting the butter and skimming off the milk solids as they rise to the top. The oily portion that remains keeps well at room temperature for about a month. It also burns less easily when used in cooking.

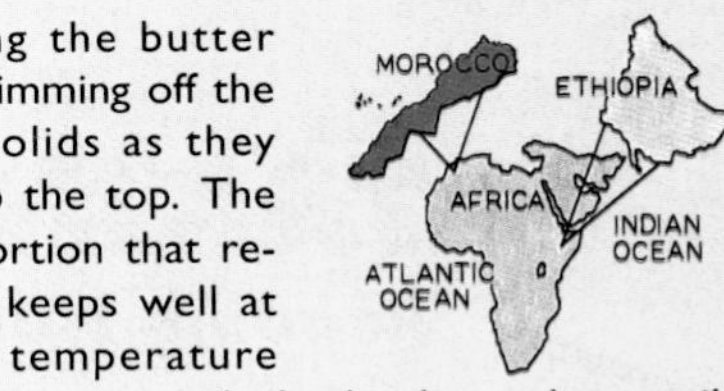

Refrigerator Storage

The refrigerator provides safe storage for **perishable foods**. These are foods that spoil easily, such as milk and other dairy products, eggs, meat, fish, poultry, and many fruits and vegetables. Storing perishable foods in the refrigerator helps prevent the growth of bacteria and keeps foods fresh and flavorful.

Inside the refrigerator, the temperature should be between 32°F and 40°F (0°C and 5°C). Cold air needs to be able to circulate in the refrigerator to keep food at proper temperatures.

Learning Activities (continued)

2. **Experiment.** Have students conduct an experiment to discover the importance of keeping foods tightly covered. Have them leave half an onion, a glass of milk, and a piece of cheese uncovered in the refrigerator overnight. Observe any changes in appearance. Ask volunteers to smell and taste the milk and cheese and note any changes in taste or odor. (Key Skill: *Science*)
3. **Display.** Display canned and boxed foods that do not require freezing or refrigeration. Point out foods that should be refrigerated after opening. Discuss the importance of keeping dry foods tightly covered to keep insects out. (Key Skills: *Communication, Creativity*)

Follow Up

1. **Reteaching.** Have two students act out the parts of the checkout clerk and the customer checking out groceries in the supermarket. Have other students evaluate their performances. How did the shopper aid or hinder the checkout clerk? (Key Skills: *Communication, Creativity*)
2. **Extension.** Use the extension information handout on p. 55 of the *Extending the Text* booklet in the TCR.
3. **Enrichment.** Have students study catalogs, visit a kitchen center, visit an appliance store, visit a container store, or visit a local supermarket to obtain information about devices available for improving food storage. Have students develop posters showing creative solutions to food storage problems. (Key Skills: *Problem Solving, Creativity*)

AROUND THE WORLD

After reading the feature, have students investigate what other countries have done to solve storage problems for food. Have students report their findings to the class. *(Answers will vary.)*

Completing the Chapter

For Review

1. Emphasize the main concepts using the summary.
2. Have students complete the "Facts to Recall." (Answers below.)

For Reteaching

1. **Reteaching.** Use the activity on p. 55 of the *Reteaching and Practical Skills* booklet in the TCR.

For Enrichment

1. **Enrichment.** Use the activity on p. 67 of the *Enrichment Activities* booklet in the TCR.

For Evaluation

1. Choose items from "Ideas to Explore" and "Activities to Try."
2. Use the chapter test on pp. 89-90 in the testing booklet of the TCR or use the testmaker software.

Facts to Recall Answers

1. A drought or freeze can limit supplies of some foods and cause prices to go up.
2. To increase its safety and storage life; to add convenience; to make it into specific products. It increases the price of food.
3. Supermarkets sell a full line of food and nonfood products. Many have specialty departments, such as a bakery. Warehouse stores carry a limited line of basic items and offer fewer services. Their prices are usually lower.
4. A food co-op is owned and operated by its members. They buy food in quantity and distribute it among themselves. Since members do the work, costs are kept down.
5. This allows you to compare different stores' prices; it helps you find out what foods are on sale; and it supplies you with cents-off coupons to use the next time you go grocery shopping.
6. Group similar foods together on your list; arrange your list to match the way foods are organized in the store.

Make use of the compartments and racks in your refrigerator. The meat keeper is extra cold to keep meat fresher. Vegetable bins help fruits and vegetables retain moisture. The door shelves can hold large bottles and cartons, but are not as cold as those inside the refrigerator.

Keep foods covered in the refrigerator to keep them from drying out and absorbing flavors and odors from other foods.

Put frozen foods away immediately after you arrive home from shopping.

▼ Freezer Storage ▼

Using the freezer allows you to store foods for longer periods of time. Freezer storage slows down the growth of harmful bacteria. The inside temperature of the freezer should be 0°F (−18°C) or below.

Foods to be frozen should be sealed in airtight, moisture-proof packaging. Plastic containers, freezer paper, heavy foil, and special freezer bags are good to use. Foods that you buy frozen can be stored in the original packaging.

▼ Dry Storage ▼

Canned and boxed foods that do not require freezing or refrigeration should be stored in a cool, dry place. Once they are opened, cover them tightly to keep out insects.

TAKING ACTION

Reading Nutrition Labels

Zach is on vacation with his best friend's family, the Wilders. One morning he volunteers to walk to the nearest market and buy food for breakfast. "Pick up some good healthy cereal," Mrs. Wilder tells Zach.

Now Zach is perplexed as he faces the cereal shelf. With so many brands to choose from, he doesn't know which to buy. Zach reads the following labels, listing nutritional information for a 1-ounce serving:

- *Knott's Natural Bran* has 4 grams of sugar, 2 grams of fat, and 4 grams of fiber.
- *Short's Shredded Wheat* has 0 grams of sugar, 0 grams of fat, and 6 grams of fiber.
- *Green's All-Natural Granola* has 6 grams of sugar, 4 grams of fat, and no listing for fiber.

Using Your Resourcefulness

- Which cereal appears to be the most nutritious from the label? Why?
- Both *Knott's* and *Green's* say "Cholesterol free" and "Low-fat" on the box. Are the claims misleading? Why or why not?
- Do you read food labels when you shop? Why or why not?
- How could reading food labels benefit you now in your life? In the future?

TAKING ACTION

Have students read the feature. Then have a class discussion about Zach's problem and which cereal he should buy for their breakfast. To guide this discussion, you may want to have students answer the *Using Your Resourcefulness* questions at the end of this feature.

Using Your Resourcefulness Answers

- *Short's Shredded Wheat* is the most nutritious. It has no sugar, no fat, and a good amount of fiber.
- In order to answer this question, students would need to compare the ratio of calories from fat to total calories.
- Answers will vary.
- Answers will vary. A possible answer might be that reading food labels will help

Chapter 43 Review

Summary

In this chapter, you have read about:

- How production, processing, distribution, and marketing affect food prices.
- Different types of food stores and the items and services found in each.
- How to save time and money when shopping by being prepared and organized.
- The techniques used by stores to encourage you to buy.
- How to get the most for your money by comparison shopping.
- Guidelines to help you be an efficient, courteous shopper.
- How to preserve the quality of food by proper storage.

Facts to Recall

1. Explain how weather can affect the price of food.
2. Name three reasons why food is processed. How does processing affect food prices?
3. What is the difference between a supermarket and a warehouse store?
4. Explain how a food co-op operates.
5. Identify three ways that looking at newspaper ads and magazines before going shopping can save you money.
6. Give two hints for organizing your shopping list for more efficient shopping.
7. List four types of information that you can find on packaged food labels.
8. How do generic products compare with national brands in price, nutritional value, and quality?
9. How is unit price calculated?
10. When is buying in quantity not a bargain?
11. What is the difference between a "sell by" date and a "use by" date?
12. What is the proper temperature range for inside the refrigerator? The freezer?

Ideas to Explore

1. What types of food stores are found in your community? What are the advantages and disadvantages of each?
2. In your experience, what is the biggest mistake people make when grocery shopping, in terms of spending time and money? Why?

Activities to Try

1. Write a sample grocery shopping list of items your family uses regularly. Use the tips found in the chapter to organize your list efficiently.
2. Write a radio public service announcement describing consumer tips for saving money when shopping for food.

LINK TO Math

FIGURING UNIT PRICE

Locate canned, boxed, and bottled food items (such as a canned vegetable, boxed cereal, and bottled juice) at the supermarket. For each food item, list a national brand, private label or store brand, and a generic brand. Write the price and the amount the package contains next to each food item. Compute the unit price for each food item using the formula found on page 504 of the text.

- Which brands appeared to be the best buy for each food item?
- Why is buying the lower-priced food items a benefit for the shopper?
- When might the lower-priced items not be the best buy? Why?

Facts to Recall Answers (continued)

7. **Any four:** the name of the product; a description of the product; the net weight of the contents; the name and address of the manufacturer, packers, or distributor; a list of ingredients.
8. Generic brands are less expensive than national brands. They are equal in nutritional value but may be lower in quality.
9. By dividing the package's total cost by the number of units.
10. When the extra food is wasted.
11. A "sell by" date tells the last day the product can be sold in the store. A "use by" date shows the date after which the food will no longer be at its peak of freshness.
12. Between 32°F and 40°F (0°C and 5°C); 0°F (-18°C) or below.

Ideas to Explore

1. Answers will vary.
2. Answers will vary.

LINK TO Math

Answers

- Answers will vary depending on which food items are chosen.
- Buying the lower-priced food items will keep total costs for groceries down.
- Answers will vary. Possible answers might include when the lower-priced items do not contain as much as the other brands, or when the lower-priced items are a lot lower quality than the other brands.

students eat more nutritiously and thus be healthier and feel better overall. Reading food labels now may help students remain healthy as they grow older.

Preparing to Teach

Chapter Outline

Chapter Resources

The following booklet materials may be found in the *Teacher's Classroom Resources* box:

- Lesson Plans, p. 49
- Student Workbook, *Study Guide,* pp. 187-188; *Equipment Is No Puzzle!,* p. 189; *Equipment Match,* p. 190
- Color Transparencies, *Know Your Knives,* CT-48
- Personal Safety, *Equipment Safety,* p. 45
- Technology and Computers, pp. 43, 45
- Cooperative Learning, p. 56
- Extending the Text, *Oven Options,* p. 56
- Reteaching and Practical Skills, *Small Kitchen Tools Scramble,* p. 56
- Enrichment Activities, *Appliance and Equipment Alternatives,* p. 68
- Chapter and Unit Tests, pp. 91-92
- Testmaker Software

Also see:

- Meeting the Special Needs of Students
- Linking Home, School, and Community

CHAPTER

44 Kitchen Equipment

OBJECTIVES

- *Identify basic utensils and cookware and describe their uses.*
- *Give guidelines for selection, use, and care of small and large appliances.*

TERMS TO LEARN

- ***utensils***
- ***cookware***
- ***kitchen appliance***
- ***immersible***
- ***microwaves***
- ***convection oven***

More About Measuring Ingredients

Standard measuring utensils should be used when following recipe measurements. Using anything other than a standard measuring utensil can alter the end results, especially in baked products. For example, a standard one-cup measure holds 8 fluid ounces. A coffee/tea cup can hold from 6 to 10 ounces.

Can you play basketball without a ball or baseball without a bat? You can't. You can ask the same type of question about the kitchen. Can you heat soup without a pan or make stew without a knife? The answer is "no."

However, it's not necessary to own every piece of kitchen equipment sold. If you did, you would run out of storage room! A better approach is to choose wisely and get the most out of each piece of kitchen equipment you have. You'll find some items are more useful than others.

You can often substitute one piece of kitchen equipment for another if you have limited space or the cost is too high. Mixing bowls can be used as serving dishes. A wire whisk could be used instead of an electric mixer.

Safety is an important consideration when using kitchen equipment. You can read about kitchen safety in Chapter 47.

Utensils

Small kitchen tools are called **utensils**. If you have already done some cooking, you know how helpful utensils can be. They save you time and enable you to prepare products you would not otherwise be able to make.

Sturdy, well-made utensils will last a long time. Careful use and storage also extend their life. If you have a dishwasher or microwave oven, buy utensils that are dishwasher-safe or can be used in the microwave.

▼ Measuring Utensils ▼

Measuring utensils help you to accurately measure ingredients for recipes. Some popular measuring utensils are shown here.

Dry measuring cups, used to measure dry ingredients such as flour and sugar, are usually in sets. The most common sizes in the U.S. are ¼ cup, ⅓ cup, ½ cup, and 1 cup. If you use recipes that give amounts in the metric system, you will need metric measuring utensils. Sizes found in a set of metric dry measures include 50 mL (milliliters), 125 mL, and 250 mL.

Dry measuring cups

Introducing the Chapter

Motivators

1. **Demonstration.** Explain to students that not all kitchens are equipped with every piece of kitchen equipment sold. Demonstrate how one could use two knives or a fork in place of a pastry blender to cut shortening into flour. (Key Skills: *Communication, Management*)
2. **Display.** Set up a display of every piece of kitchen equipment available to students in the foods lab. Distribute a worksheet that pictures each piece of equipment. Invite your students to follow you around the classroom as you point out each piece and explain what it does. Have students write the name next to each piece of equipment on their list and write a short description of what it does. (Key Skill: *Communication*)
3. **Homework Assignment.** Have students take this same worksheet home to see how many pieces of equipment from their list they can find in their own kitchens. (Key Skill: *Communication*)

Chapter Objectives and Vocabulary

1. Have students read the chapter objectives and rephrase the objectives as questions.
2. Ask students to state, in their own words, the purpose of studying this chapter.
3. Pronounce the vocabulary terms listed on the previous page. Ask students whether they are familiar with any of these. Explain that the terms will be defined in the chapter.

Guided Reading

1. Have students read the chapter and use the Study Guide on pp. 187-188 of the *Student Workbook.*

Terms such as "add a dash of" and "put a pinch" allow cooks to use their own judgment. Usually, these amounts are too small to measure with a measuring spoon. However, it is best to err with too little than too much. A "dash" usually means the amount that comes out of the shaker when shaken once. A "pinch" refers to the amount of ingredient that can be held between the thumb and another finger.

Teaching . . . Utensils

(pp. 511-513)

Comprehension Check

1. Name three types of popular measuring utensils. *(Dry measuring cups, liquid measuring cups, and measuring spoons.)*
2. How are sifters used? *(Sifters are used to sift and mix dry ingredients together as they pass through a mesh screen.)*
3. How is a rotary beater used? *(A rotary beater is used to beat eggs and mix thin batters, such as pancake batter.)*
4. Why should you use a cutting board for your cutting work? *(Cutting boards help keep knives sharp and keep counters in good shape.)*

Learning Activities

1. **Lab Activity.** Write a variety of measurements on index cards, such as ¼ c. sugar, ½ c. milk, and ¾ c. flour. Have all measuring utensils out on the demonstration table along with sugar, flour, and liquids. Pass out an index card to each student and invite each of them to the front of the class to demonstrate how to measure the amount of whatever is listed on his or her index card. (Key Skills: *Communication, Decision Making*)
2. **Research.** As a homework assignment, have students price the following pieces of kitchen equipment at the supermarket: a peeler, a strainer, a wire whisk, a metal mixing spoon, a wooden mixing spoon, a rubber scraper, a set of measuring spoons, a set of dry measuring cups, a liquid measuring cup, and a colander. Have students total the prices of all the equipment to get an understanding of how much it can cost to set up a kitchen. (Key Skills: *Management, Math*)
3. **Demonstration.** Use a chef's knife and vegetables such as onions, carrots, and potatoes to show the difference between cutting, mincing, and dicing. (Key Skill: *Communication*)

Liquid measuring cup

Measuring spoons

Sifter

Liquid measuring cups have a spout for pouring. They have measurements marked on the side in cups, ounces, and milliliters. Common sizes are 4 cups, 2 cups, and 1 cup (1000, 500 and 250 mL).

Measuring spoons are used for measuring smaller amounts of liquid and dry ingredients. The most common sizes are ¼ teaspoon, ½ teaspoon, 1 teaspoon, and 1 tablespoon. A set of small metric measures includes 1 mL, 2 mL, 5 mL, 15 mL, and 25 mL sizes.

▼ Mixing Utensils ▼

Mixing utensils help to blend ingredients together. Some mixing utensils can be used for a variety of tasks. Others are used only for one specific task.

Mixing bowls come in graduated sizes. They are used to hold the ingredients you are mixing.

Mixing spoons have long handles and are used for combining ingredients. You see them in wood, metal, and plastic.

Rubber or plastic scrapers are used to scrape bowls and fold ingredients together. They have a wide, flexible blade.

Sifters sift and mix dry ingredients together as they pass through a mesh screen. They come in various sizes.

A *pastry blender* cuts shortening into flour for piecrusts and biscuits. Sometimes people use two knives or a fork in place of a pastry blender.

Wire whisks are used for beating and blending. Whisks are especially good to use in beating egg white mixtures and stirring sauces.

A *rotary beater* is also known as a hand beater or eggbeater. It is used to beat eggs and mix thin batters, such as pancake batter.

Mixing spoon

Rubber scraper

Pastry blender

Wire whisk

Mixing bowls

Rotary beater

More About
Special Measuring Techniques

Before measuring honey, oil the cup or spoon with cooking oil, then rinse in hot water. The honey will not stick to the spoon. Dipping the spoon in hot water also works when measuring shortening or butter.

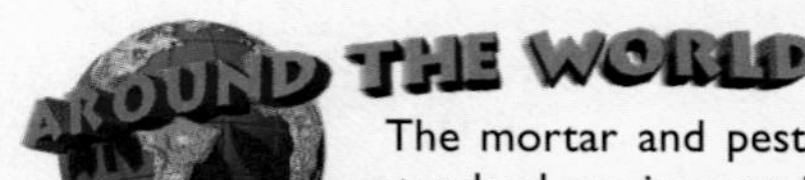

The mortar and pestle are standard equipment in the Vietnamese kitchen. Ingredients to be ground or crushed are placed in a small wooden or ceramic bowl, the mortar, and broken up with a pestle, which looks much like a very small baseball bat. Many cooks have two sets: a smaller one for nuts and spices, and a larger one for seafood and meat. For preparing small amounts of foods, the mortar and pestle are more convenient than an electric food processor.

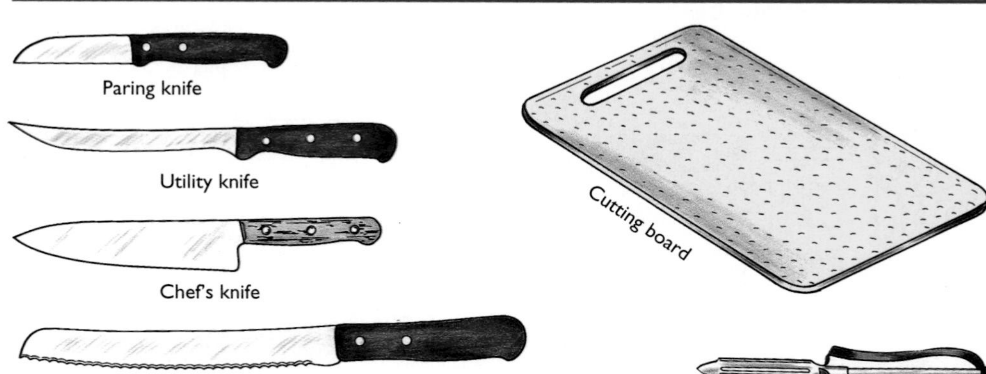

▼ Cutting and Chopping Utensils ▼

Cutting and chopping tools cut food into smaller pieces. Keep safety in mind as you use cutting tools.

Knives come in a variety of sizes. *Paring knives* are good for peeling fruits and vegetables. *Utility knives* are all-purpose knives for cutting and slicing many foods. *Chef's knives* are used for cutting, mincing, and dicing. *Bread knives* come in handy for slicing bread or baked goods.

Cutting boards are used as a base for your cutting work. They help to keep knife blades sharp and counters in good shape.

Peelers are used to peel vegetables and fruits. The blade swivels.

Kitchen shears are sturdy scissors. They are used to cut vegetables, pastry, poultry, and meat.

Graters are used to shred and grate vegetables and cheeses. Some graters shred both finely and coarsely.

Learning Activities (continued)

4. **Practice.** Demonstrate the proper way to hold knives when cutting. Focus on hand safety. Then have students practice the proper way to use cutting knives. (Key Skill: *Management*)

Follow Up

1. **Reteaching.** Familiarize students with the whereabouts of each utensil in their particular laboratory kitchen. Hold up a utensil and instruct a student from each kitchen to go and find that utensil in their kitchen unit. Make a game of it by giving points to the team that finds each utensil first. (Key Skills: *Communication, Decision Making*)
2. **Enrichment.** Explore how technology has made advances in the American kitchen. Then divide the class into four kitchen groups. The job of each group will be to beat egg whites. Have each group use a different utensil, and have each group time themselves to determine how long it takes to complete the job. Group one will use a hand beater. Group two will use an electric hand mixer. Group three will use a wire whisk. Group four will use a food processor. Encourage students to compare finished products to see if there is any significant difference in texture or consistency. (Key Skills: *Management, Cooperation*)

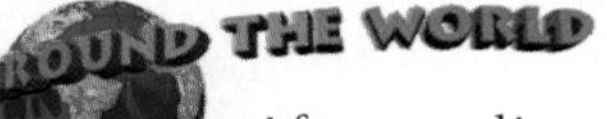

After reading the feature, have students investigate what different types of utensils are used in other countries to mix food ingredients. *(Answers will vary.)*

Teaching. . . Other Kitchen Utensils and Cookware

(pp. 514-515)

Comprehension Check

1. What is the difference between a colander and a strainer? *(A colander is a bowl with holes that is used for draining foods like cooked pasta. A strainer is a wire mesh basket that is used to strain solid particles from liquids or to drain food.)*
2. What type of spatula should you use to pick up small cookies from a baking sheet? *(A narrow metal spatula.)*
3. What does the term cookware refer to? *(Cookware is a term that includes pots, pans, and other containers that can be used on top of the range, in the oven, or in the microwave.)*
4. Give examples of four different types of pans. *(Cake, pie, muffin, and loaf pans.)*

Learning Activities

1. **Ad Design.** Ask students to design an ad for a cooking utensil. The ad should tell what job this tool is used for and how it makes cooking tasks easier. The ad should make the utensil seem indispensable. After students have completed their ads and turned them in, show them to the class. Discuss the positive and negative things about each ad, then let the students pick their favorite one. (Key Skills: *Communication, Creativity*)
2. **Discussion.** Have each student go to the store and write down the price of each of the kitchen utensils listed on page 514. Afterwards, have a class discussion about what the students found out. Were there many varieties of each utensil? Were the prices of any of these items a surprise to the students? Ask students which of these utensils they've used at home. Could they get along without any of these utensils? (Key Skill: *Communication*)

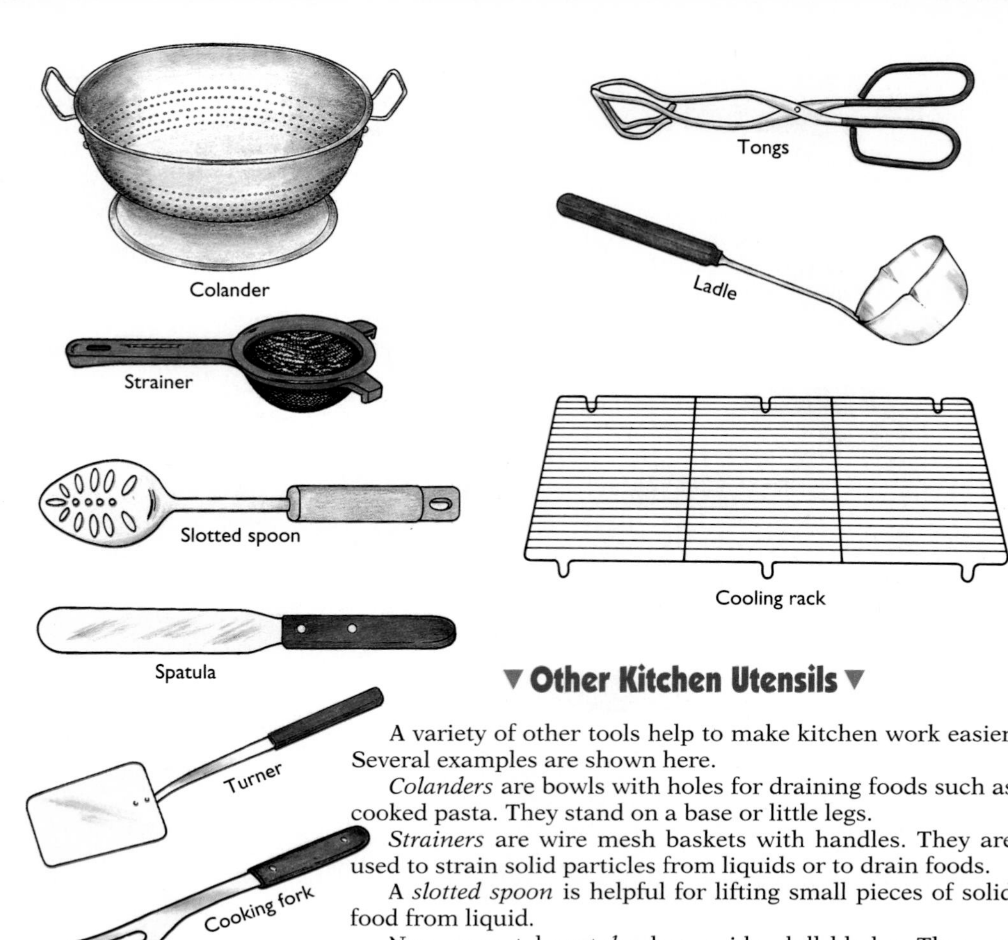

Other Kitchen Utensils

A variety of other tools help to make kitchen work easier. Several examples are shown here.

Colanders are bowls with holes for draining foods such as cooked pasta. They stand on a base or little legs.

Strainers are wire mesh baskets with handles. They are used to strain solid particles from liquids or to drain foods.

A *slotted spoon* is helpful for lifting small pieces of solid food from liquid.

Narrow metal *spatulas* have wide, dull blades. They are useful in leveling dry ingredients in measuring cups, picking up small cookies from baking sheets, and loosening baked products from the sides of baking pans.

Wide spatulas, or *turners*, are useful. They can lift and turn foods such as pancakes or hamburgers.

Tongs are grasping instruments. They help you lift large pieces of food, such as a chicken drumstick or a corncob.

Cooking forks are also used for lifting and turning foods.

Ladles are helpful when serving foods such as hot soup and stews.

Timers can remind you about cooking times. They usually can be set for periods of time up to 60 minutes.

Cooling racks are also known as cake racks. They are made of wire and allow air to circulate around hot baked products.

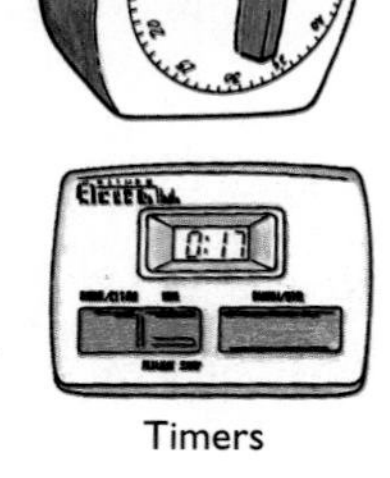

Timers

More About Small Appliances and Cookware

Purchasing appliances and cookware represents an investment of money. Some general points to look for include the following:

- Materials should be strong enough to withstand daily use, should be smooth without sharp edges, and should be easy to clean.
- The appliance or piece of cookware should have good balance and not tip over easily.
- Handles should be heat resistant and comfortable.
- If the appliance or piece of cookware has a lid, make sure it fits securely. The knob should be easy to grasp.
- The appliance or piece of cookware should be light enough to lift and carry easily.

Cookware

Cookware includes pots, pans, and other containers for use on top of the range, in the oven, or in the microwave. They are made of various materials. Some of the differences in these materials affect the way you use and care for them. The chart on page 516 explains the different types of materials.

Frying pans, or *skillets*, are shallow and have a long handle. They come in assorted sizes and sometimes have covers.

Saucepans and *pots* are deeper than frying pans. They come in a variety of sizes, usually measured in quarts or liters. Some have covers. Saucepans have one handle, while pots have two — one on each side.

Casseroles, or baking dishes, come in a variety of shapes and sizes. They are deep enough to hold a main-dish mixture and often have covers.

Cake pans are round, square, or rectangular. They can be used for baking many things in addition to cakes.

Baking sheets are rectangular, low-sided pans. They are most often used for baking cookies.

Pie pans are round with sloping sides. They come in different sizes.

Muffin pans have from six to twelve individual cups to hold muffins and cupcakes.

Loaf pans are used for breads and meat loaves. They come in different sizes.

Custard cups are made out of heatproof glass. You might use them to bake custard or microwave eggs.

Frying pan or skillet

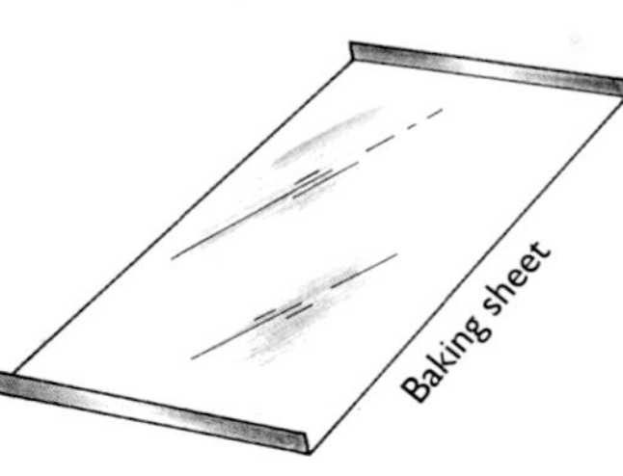

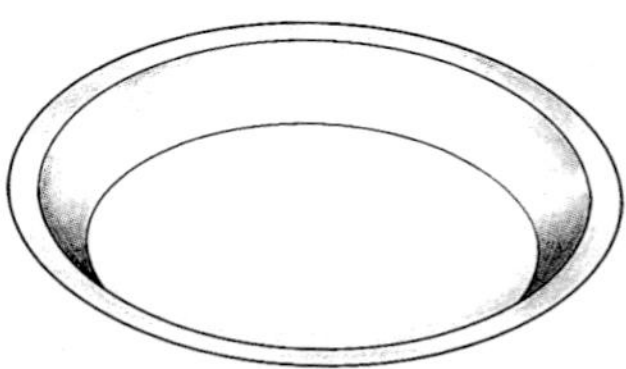
Pie pan

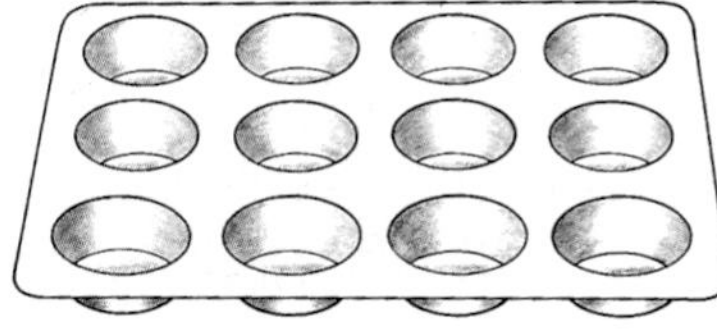
Muffin pan

Custard cups

Learning Activities (continued)

3. **Cookware Costs.** Using a mail-order catalog or newspaper ads, have students compare the costs of similar pots (1-qt., frying pan) made of different materials. Features such as nonstick surfaces or decorative designs should be taken into account. (Key Skill: *Math*)

Follow Up

1. **Reteaching.** Ask volunteers to name different kitchen utensils as you hold them up. If students have trouble identifying any of these utensils, have them reread this part of the chapter and then write a paragraph about what these utensils look like and how they are used. (Key Skills: *Communication, Decision Making*)
2. **Enrichment.** Ask students to list as many special cookware and bakeware items as they can think of (bundt pan, roasting pan). Gourmet shops, catalogs, and cookbooks are good sources for ideas. (Key Skill: *Communication*)

Photo Focus

Discuss the photo at the bottom of page 515 with the students. How many different types of pots and pans do students have in their kitchen at home? Are there some pots and pans that they wish they had? Would having these pots and pans make cooking easier? *(Answers will vary.)*

Teaching... Cookware Materials and Appliances (pp. 516-517)

Comprehension Check

1. What are the advantages and disadvantages of using aluminum cookware? *(**Advantages:** lightweight, durable, good conductor of heat. **Disadvantages:** minerals in food and water cause darkening, dishwater detergent stains and darkens.)*
2. What are the advantages and disadvantages of using cookware that has a nonstick finish? *(**Advantages:** allows fat-free cooking and easy cleaning, durable if used properly. **Disadvantages:** will scratch unless used with nylon or plastic utensils, overheating will cause staining and reduce the nonstick effectiveness.)*
3. What does the term "immersible" mean when written on an appliance? *(It means that the entire appliance can safely be put into water to be washed.)*
4. How can a hand-held mixer be used? *(For whipping cream, making cake batter, mixing pudding, and mashing potatoes.)*

Learning Activities

1. **Display.** Set up a classroom display of cookware made from metals such as copper, aluminum, stainless steel, and cast iron. Point out the price of each piece of cookware. (Key Skill: *Communication*)
2. **Lab Experiment.** Divide the class into groups. Give each kitchen group a saucepan made from a different metal: aluminum, copper, cast iron, and stainless steel. Have each group measure two cups of water and pour it into their saucepan. Then have them record the time it takes for the water to boil in their particular saucepan. As a class, compare the differences in time it takes to boil water in a variety of metal saucepans. (Key Skill: *Science*)

Cookware Materials

Material	Advantages	Disadvantages	Care
Aluminum	Lightweight, durable, good conductor of heat.	Minerals in food and water cause darkening. Dishwasher detergent stains and darkens. (Acid foods remove darkening.)	Soak, if needed. Clean in hot detergent water. Do not put in dishwasher.
Cast iron	Good conductor of heat.	Rusts unless dried thoroughly. Heavy.	Soak, if needed. Clean in hot detergent water. Dry well. Do not scour.
Porcelain enamel (glass on metal)	Spreads heat well.	Chips and stains easily.	Soak, if needed. Clean in hot detergent water. Remove stains with household bleach.
Stainless steel	Strong. Resists stains and rust. Keeps brightness under normal care. Durable.	Does not spread heat evenly. (Aluminum and copper, good conductors of heat, are often used on the bottom or as a core.) Will darken if overheated.	Soak, if needed. Clean in hot detergent water. Scour.
Glass	Transparent — you can see food in container.	Chips and breaks easily. Conducts heat unevenly. Most require wire trivet for use on electric range. Cannot hold up under extreme temperature changes.	Soak, if needed. Clean in hot detergent water. Do not scour.
Glass ceramic	Withstands sharp temperature changes — can go from freezer to oven. Resists scratching and cracking. Some are transparent.	Breaks when dropped. May develop hot spots that cause food to stick.	Soak, if needed. Clean in hot detergent water. Scour.
Plastic	Durable. Lightweight. Some can be used in conventional ovens as well as microwave.	Conducts heat unevenly. Cannot be used at temperatures higher than 350°-400°F (170°-200°C).	Soak, if needed. Clean in hot detergent water.
Nonstick finishes	Allow fat-free cooking and easy cleaning. Durable if used properly.	Will scratch unless used with nylon or plastic utensils. Overheating will cause staining and reduce the nonstick effectiveness.	Soak, if needed. Clean in hot detergent water. Do not scour with metal pads or abrasive powders.

More About Nonstick Finishes

Is it safe to use pans on which the nonstick surface is scratched or damaged? Some people think that scratched pans deposit dangerous substances into foods during cooking. Tests conducted by the Food and Drug Administration (FDA) and by manufacturers of cookware have shown the pans to be safe even when surfaces were marred. It is possible for flakes of substances, such as Teflon™, to get into food if the pan is scraped vigorously. If the flakes were to be swallowed, they would not be digested and would pass out of the body.

Appliances

Kitchen appliances are pieces of equipment for the kitchen powered by either gas or electricity. Using both small appliances and large appliances makes your cooking time more productive.

Small Kitchen Appliances

Small electric appliances can sit on a table or counter and be moved from place to place easily. There are hundreds of small kitchen appliances available today.

If you use an appliance frequently, it is a good investment. However, people often buy appliances, store them in a cabinet, and forget about them. If you keep appliances handy, you are more likely to use them.

Before buying a small appliance, ask yourself how often you will use it. Is it worth the cost? Consider the size of the appliance. Do you have enough space to store and use it?

Comparison shop to gather information about various appliance brands you're considering. What safety features are included? What is covered by the warranty? Sometimes a warranty covers parts, labor, and shipping costs. Other times, only certain parts are covered and nothing else. Refer to Chapter 20 for additional information on comparison shopping.

Look for the Underwriters Laboratories (UL) seal on the appliance. This seal certifies that an electrical appliance is safe to use.

Some appliances will have the term **immersible** (ih-MUHR-suh-buhl) on them. This means that the entire appliance can safely be put into the water to be washed. On such appliances, the electric unit has been sealed so no water can enter. If you do not see the term "immersible," never put the appliance in water. You could receive a bad shock.

Here are some common small appliances:

- ***Toaster.*** Holds at least two slices of bread for toasting — sometimes more. Some can adjust for thicker breads such as muffins.
- ***Toaster oven/broiler.*** Good for toasting breads, warming foods, and doing small cooking chores, such as broiling hamburgers.
- ***Hand-held mixer.*** Can be used for whipping cream, making cake batter, mixing pudding, and mashing potatoes. It's lightweight and fairly compact, so it's easy to manage and convenient to store.

TIPS:
Buying a Toaster

Look for these features when buying a toaster:

- Bread wells that are large enough for thicker foods, such as English muffins or frozen toaster foods.
- A snap-down crumb tray for easier cleaning.
- Heat-resistant handles, temperature control, and a well-insulated base.
- Energy-saving features.

Toaster

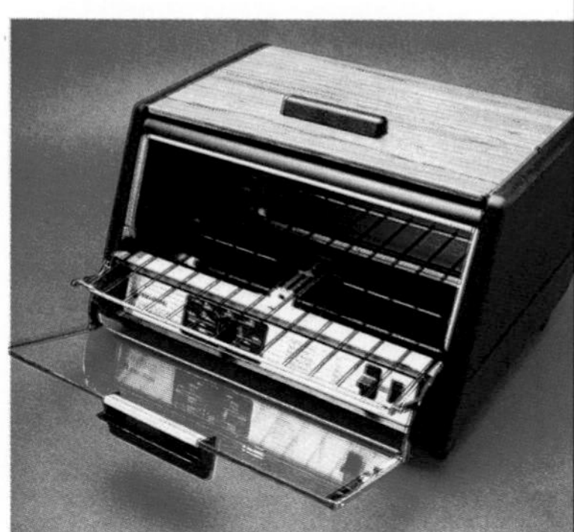

Toaster oven/broiler

Learning Activities (continued)

3. **Demonstration.** Use a toaster to demonstrate to your students the correct and safe method of cleaning a toaster. Focus on safety, such as unplugging the toaster before cleaning it. Be sure to mention never to stick sharp objects, such as knives, into toasters when they are in use or plugged in. (Key Skill: *Communication*)
4. **Survey.** Have students ask their parents what types of small appliances they received as shower or wedding gifts. Ask students to find out if their parents still use any of the appliances they received as wedding gifts, and if so, how old they are and what brand they are. (Key Skill: *Communication*)

Follow Up

1. **Reteaching.** Distribute copies of warranties from various small appliances to your students. Ask students to tell the class what is covered on their particular warranty, such as parts, labor, and shipping. (Key Skill: *Communication*)
2. **Enrichment.** Have students read newspaper pullout sections advertising special sales on small kitchen appliances. Select a specific appliance and have students find the best appliance for the price. (Key Skills: *Critical Thinking, Decision Making*)

More About *Small Kitchen Appliances*

An innovative kitchen item that adds freshness to anyone's breakfast menu is an automatic juice extractor. This small kitchen appliance makes it possible to extract fresh juice from almost any fruit or vegetable. Some models feature an automatic pulp ejection and a fruit tray.

TIPS:

Buying a Toaster
Have students read the feature. Then have them find out what kind of toaster their family uses at home. Does their toaster have the features mentioned here? If not, they may want to ask their parents if they can buy a new toaster. *(Answers will vary.)*

Teaching. . .
Small Kitchen Appliances and Large Kitchen Appliances
(pp. 518-519)

Comprehension Check

1. What is a blender used for? *(A blender has push-button speed controls for a variety of mixing and chopping tasks. Good for beverages, such as fruit drinks and milk shakes.)*
2. How is an electric frying pan used? *(An electric frying pan is used to fry, roast, simmer, or bake. It can also serve as a buffet server or hot tray.)*
3. When cleaning the inside and outside of your refrigerator, what is a good cleaning agent to use? *(Water mixed with a little baking soda.)*
4. How are ranges used? *(Ranges are used for baking, cooking, and broiling.)*

Learning Activities

1. **Contest.** Divide students into groups. Give each group magazines and challenge them to create a poster of as many small kitchen appliances as they can find. You may want to offer a reward of extra credit points or a homework-free night to the group that finds the most appliances. (Key Skills: *Cooperation, Creativity*)
2. **Discussion.** Talk to students about kitchen appliance safety. Discuss the age at which a child should be able to use kitchen appliances such as a toaster, a toaster oven, a blender, and a food processor. (Key Skill: *Communication*)
3. **Safety Awareness.** Explain the hazard of plugging too many kitchen appliances into an electrical outlet. Alert students to the possibilities of fuses blowing and electrical fires when too many appliances are run off one circuit. (Key Skills: *Management, Science*)

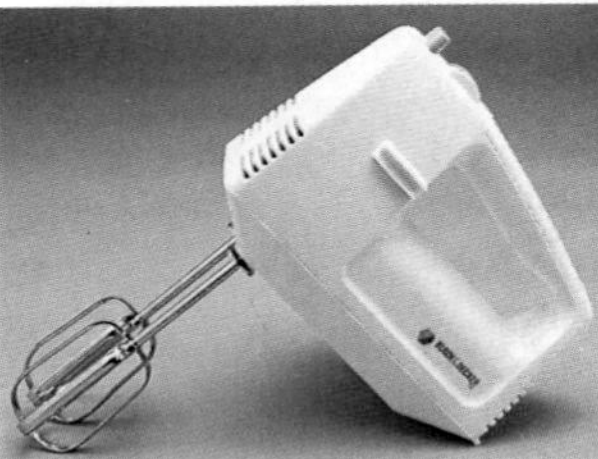

Hand-held mixer

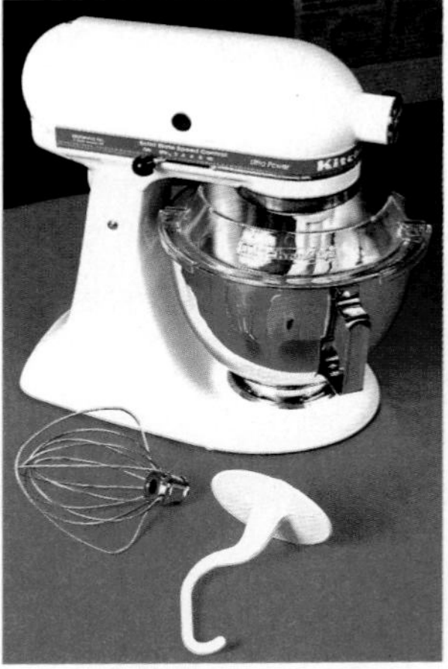

Stand mixer

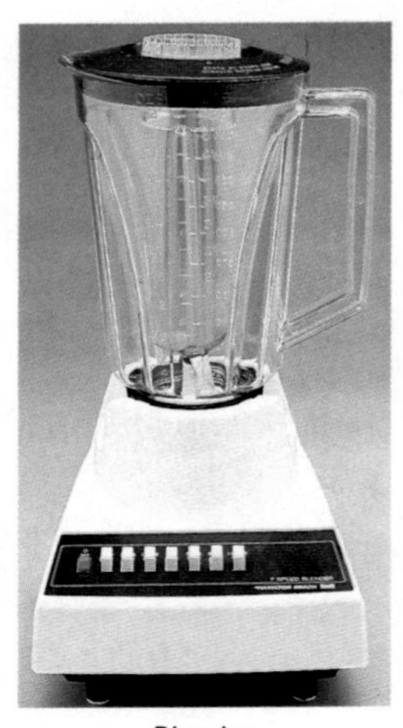

Blender

- ***Stand mixer.*** Has a bowl that rotates on a turntable in the base of the stand. Depending on the power of the motor, the mixer is either light-duty or heavy-duty. Heavy-duty mixers are better able to handle heavy cookie doughs and bread batters.
- ***Blender.*** Has push-button speed controls for a variety of mixing and chopping tasks. Good for beverages, such as fruit drinks and milk shakes.
- ***Food processor.*** Different blades and disks allow it to perform a variety of cutting and mixing tasks. Good for slicing or shredding vegetables, for example.
- ***Electric frying pan.*** A control on the handle regulates the cooking temperature. Use to fry, roast, simmer, or bake. Can also serve as a buffet server or hot tray.

Food processor

Electric frying pan

▼ Large Kitchen Appliances ▼

A large appliance, such as a range or refrigerator, is a major purchase. The cost depends on the style, size, and special features and on whether you buy a new or used appliance.

If you have a new appliance, read and save the owner's manual. It has a lot of valuable information about using and caring for the appliance.

If your family is shopping for a large kitchen appliance, follow the shopping principles outlined in Chapter 20. During your comparison shopping, be sure to compare the EnergyGuide labels for an estimate of the energy use of the appliance.

Another way to judge the quality of appliances is to look for safety and performance seals. You have already read about the Underwriters Laboratories (UL) seal placed on electrical appliances that have been tested for safety. The American Gas Association (AGA) certified seal is placed on tested gas appliances.

UL seal

Dishwasher
Capacity: Standard

(Name of Corporation)
Model(s) MR328, XL12, NA83

ENERGYGUIDE

Estimates on the scale are based on a national average electric rate of 4.97¢ per kilowatt hour and a natural gas rate of 36.7¢ per therm

Only standard size dishwashers are used in the scale

Electric Water Heater

Model with lowest energy cost $62 — $73 THIS MODEL — Model with highest energy cost $92

Estimated yearly energy cost

Gas Water Heater

Model with lowest energy cost $26 — $31 THIS MODEL — Model with highest energy cost $40

Estimated yearly energy cost

Your cost will vary depending on your local energy rate and how you use the product. This energy cost is based on U.S. Government standard tests.

How much will this model cost you to run yearly?

with an electric water heater

Loads of dishes per week		2	4	6	8	12
		Estimated yearly $ cost shown below				
Cost per kilowatt hour	2¢	$7	$15	$22	$29	$44
	4¢	$15	$29	$44	$59	$88
	6¢	$22	$44	$66	$88	$132
	8¢	$29	$59	$88	$117	$176
	10¢	$37	$73	$110	$146	$220
	12¢	$44	$88	$132	$176	$264

with a gas water heater

Loads of dishes per week		2	4	6	8	12
		Estimated yearly $ cost shown below				
Cost per therm (100 cubic feet)	10¢	$4	$8	$12	$16	$24
	20¢	$5	$11	$16	$22	$33
	30¢	$7	$14	$21	$28	$41
	40¢	$8	$17	$25	$33	$50
	50¢	$10	$19	$29	$39	$58
	60¢	$11	$22	$34	$45	$67

Ask your salesperson or local utility for the energy rate (cost per kilowatt hour or therm) in your area, and for estimated costs if you have a propane or oil water heater.

Important Removal of this label before consumer purchase is a violation of federal law (42 U.S.C. 6302)

(Part No. 73906)

An EnergyGuide label estimates the cost of operating an appliance for one year.

Refrigerators

The design of the refrigerator affects how long frozen food can be stored. Some refrigerators have only one outside door with a small freezer compartment inside. This type of freezer compartment does not stay cold enough for long-term storage of frozen foods. Generally, frozen foods should be stored for less than a week in this type of freezing compartment.

Combination refrigerator-freezers have two separate outside doors. One part is for storing fresh foods. The other one is for freezing fresh food and for long-term storage of frozen food. The freezer section may be located above, below, or alongside the refrigerator section. If the temperature in the freezer is at or below 0°F (−18°C), frozen foods can be stored for a long time.

Combination refrigerator-freezers have an outside door for each compartment.

Clean the outside and inside of the refrigerator often. You can use water mixed with a little baking soda. Wipe up spills right away to prevent odors and germs.

Check the owner's manual for other care instructions. You may need to defrost the freezer, clean coils at the bottom or back of the refrigerator, or empty a drip tray, for example.

Ranges

Ranges are used for baking, cooking, and broiling. You can choose from gas or electric models. The features available on ranges vary with the manufacturer and model.

A basic range includes a cooktop, one or more ovens, and a broiler.

Learning Activities (continued)

4. **Advertising.** Invite students to view the classroom refrigerator in its entirety. Point out all the features that make up the design of the refrigerator. Ask students to compare newspaper refrigerator ads, and then assign them the task of writing an advertisement that would promote the features of your classroom refrigerator. (Key Skill: *Communication*)
5. **Life Skills.** Discuss the steps involved in cleaning a refrigerator with the class. Then assign each kitchen team the job of cleaning the inside and outside of the refrigerator in their kitchen. (Key Skills: *Communication, Cooperation*)

Follow Up

1. **Reteaching.** Make up index cards with parts of the range written on each one, such as cooktop, oven, burner, heating element, and broiler. Place the cards face down on each student's table. Then have him or her pick any card and walk over to the range and identify the part listed on the index card. (Key Skill: *Decision Making*)
2. **Enrichment.** Do a foods lab on fish preparation. Discuss the variety of ways in which fish can be prepared. Give each foods team a simple fish recipe to prepare. Instruct one group to broil the fish, a second group to fry the fish, and a third group to bake the fish. Have students sample a portion of each recipe to determine the difference in taste and appearance. Then have students rate each fish recipe to see which is the most popular recipe. (Key Skills: *Communication, Cooperation*)

More About *Power Outages and Frozen Foods*

Prolonged power outages are a cause of concern for the safety of frozen foods. If power is out for 48 hours and a freezer is fully stocked, no special steps are required. Each frozen package acts like a block of ice that chills the items around it. A half-filled freezer will maintain food's frozen state for 24 hours as long as you don't keep looking inside. Each time the door is opened, warm air enters and raises the temperature.

After power is restored, check the food that's in freezer. Meat or poultry containing ice crystals can remain frozen. If protein foods are thawed, cook them immediately.

The World Around You

Environmental Awareness

Discuss the environmental advantages of cleaning large appliances, such as ranges, with hot water and vinegar as opposed to aerosol spray oven cleaners.

Teaching. . .
Ranges, Microwave Ovens, and Convection Ovens
(pp. 520-522)

Comprehension Check

1. What is a cooktop? *(The four cooking surfaces of a range.)*
2. What is the difference between a range and an oven? *(A range is a large appliance that includes a cooktop, one or more ovens, and a broiler. An oven is a closed compartment that is part of the range.)*
3. How does a magnetron tube work in a microwave oven? *(It changes electrical energy into tiny waves of energy called "microwaves." Some microwaves hit the food directly. Others bounce around the oven and off the metal walls until they hit the food.)*
4. What are the advantages of cooking in a microwave oven? *(Microwave cooking saves times and energy, it requires less cleanup, and it allows you to cook foods in individual serving dishes.)*
5. What is a convection oven? *(A convection oven is an oven with fans to help circulate the hot air. This speeds up the cooking process, although not as much as with the microwave oven. The circulating hot air also cooks and browns foods more evenly.)*

Learning Activities

1. **Lab Activity.** Do a foods lab on cooking hamburgers using the broiler method. Focus on the nutritional value of broiling as compared to frying hamburgers. (Key Skills: *Communication, Management*)
2. **Demonstration.** Explore the many different parts of a range with your students. Remove drip pans and drip trays, oven racks, and broiler pans. Examine how different parts can be removed in order to clean the range. Mention to students that they should avoid using harsh, gritty cleansers when cleaning the inside and outside of ranges. (Key Skills: *Communication, Management*)

- ***Cooktop.*** A range usually has four cooking surfaces. If it is a gas range, they are called burners. When you turn a gas burner on, you have an instant source of heat. With an electric range, the cooking surfaces are called heating elements. Usually these are coils that take a few minutes to heat up or cool off. When you turn the heating element off, the food will continue to cook unless you remove it from the heating element.
- ***Oven.*** Conventional ovens use gas or electricity to heat air in a closed compartment. The hot air flows around the food and cooks it. When putting items in the oven, allow enough space for the air to circulate. (Two other types of ovens — microwave and convection — will be discussed shortly.)
- ***Broiler.*** A broiler is used to cook foods under direct heat. In gas ranges, the oven and the broiler are often separate compartments. The broiler door is kept closed while broiling. In an electric range, the broiler is usually found in the oven compartment. The oven door should be left slightly open when you broil.

The different parts of a range can also be purchased as separate appliances. A cooktop can be built into a kitchen cabinet with storage space underneath. An oven and broiler can be built into a wall. Smaller countertop ovens are also available.

The inside and outside finishes on most ranges are made of stainless steel or porcelain enamel, which is glass on metal. When you clean them, avoid using harsh, gritty cleansers. While the surface is slightly warm, wipe up spills and spattered grease with a warm, sudsy cloth or sponge. Then wipe with a damp cloth rinsed in clear water. If food boils over, wipe off the burner or heating element, drip pan, and drip tray as soon as the unit is cool enough to touch. Hot water and detergent do a good cleaning job.

The broiler compartment in a gas range may be in the oven compartment or underneath the oven.

More About Purchasing Large Appliances

When purchasing large appliances, it is very important to consider the following things before making your purchase: the size, the quality, the brand name, the price, the color, and the warranty. A conscientious consumer will take the time to examine these things before making a final decision about a purchase. It is also wise to ask about warranties and service agreements when purchasing a reconditioned appliance. Reconditioned appliances can save you money, but they may cause you financial problems down the road if parts and labor are not guaranteed by a warranty.

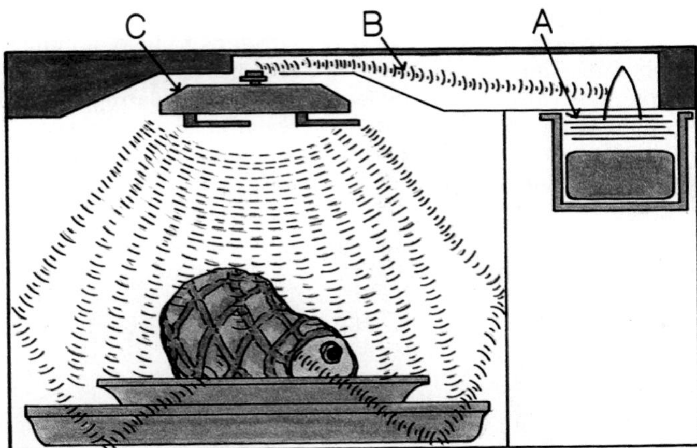

The magnetron tube creates microwave energy. The microwaves are distributed by a slowly rotating fan which causes the microwaves to bounce off the walls, ceiling, and bottom of the oven. Microwave energy causes food molecules to vibrate, producing friction. The friction produces heat and cooks the food.

Microwave Ovens

Some microwave ovens are part of a range or built into a wall. Most, however, are countertop models.

The most important part of a microwave oven is the magnetron tube. It changes electrical energy into tiny waves of energy called **microwaves**. Some of the microwaves hit the food directly. Others bounce around the oven and off the metal walls until they hit the food.

Microwave ovens don't get hot. Instead, the energy passes through the cookware into the food. It causes the water molecules in the food to vibrate, or rub against each other. This friction then produces heat that cooks or warms the food.

There are many advantages to cooking in a microwave oven. Microwave cooking can save time and energy. Baking one potato in a microwave oven takes a fraction of the time it would take to cook in a conventional oven. There is less cleanup with a microwave oven because spills do not bake on the surface. You can cook or heat foods in individual serving dishes, such as plates or bowls, as long as the dishes are made of microwave-safe materials. One disadvantage is that foods don't brown.

Metal reflects microwaves. This is why manufacturers tell you not to use metal cookware in the microwave oven. It could damage the magnetron tube, an expensive item to replace.

You can learn more about microwave cooking, as well as other cooking methods, by reading Chapter 46.

Learning Activities (continued)

3. **Display.** Create a display of cookware that is microwave safe. Also display cookware that is not microwave safe and explain why. (Key Skills: *Communication, Science*)
4. **Lab Activity.** Have each cooking team prepare a burrito recipe in class. Instruct one team to cook the burrito in a conventional oven, another team to cook their burrito in a toaster oven, and a third team to microwave their burrito. Discuss the energy-saving advantages of these types of cooking. (Key Skills: *Communication, Cooperation*)
5. **Meal Preparation.** Have students prepare a fun and simple recipe, such as Smores®. Have them cook the Smores® in a microwave oven. Review the correct buttons to push and proper cooking time to allow. Emphasize that not all microwave ovens operate in the same way. (Key Skill: *Communication*)

Follow Up

1. **Reteaching.** Demonstrate how to set cooking time on a microwave oven. Show how to set cooking times for minutes, seconds, or a combination of both. Explain the use of the cancel or stop button. (Key Skill: *Communication*)
2. **Extension.** Use the extension information handout on p. 56 of the *Extending the Text* booklet in the TCR.
3. **Enrichment.** Focus on safety measures to follow when using microwave ovens. Discuss things such as removing lids and using paper products as opposed to aluminum foil, which will cause sparking. Have students give examples of safety measures they must follow at home when using a microwave oven. (Key Skill: *Communication*)

Completing the Chapter

For Review

1. Emphasize the main concepts using the summary.
2. Have students complete the "Facts to Recall." (Answers below.)

For Reteaching

1. **Reteaching.** Use the activity on p. 56 of the *Reteaching and Practical Skills* booklet in the TCR.

For Enrichment

1. **Enrichment.** Use the activity on p. 68 of the *Enrichment Activities* booklet in the TCR.

For Evaluation

1. Choose items from "Ideas to Explore" and "Activities to Try."
2. Use the chapter test on pp. 91-92 in the testing booklet of the TCR or use the testmaker software.

Facts to Recall Answers

1. **Any four:** mixing bowls hold the ingredients you are mixing; mixing spoons combine ingredients; scrapers scrape bowls and fold ingredients together; sifters sift and mix dry ingredients; pastry blenders cut shortening into flour; wire whisks beat and blend; rotary beaters beat eggs and mix thin batters.
2. Because there is less chance of spreading harmful bacteria.
3. Tongs and cooking forks.
4. Frying pans and saucepans both may have lids and come in assorted sizes, but saucepans are deeper than frying pans.
5. **Any four:** cake pans; baking sheets; pie pans; muffin pans; loaf pans; custard cups.
6. **Any four:** use; cost; size; energy usage; safety features; warranty.
7. The entire appliance can safely be put into water. If a nonimmersible appliance is put into water, you could receive a bad shock.
8. Clean the outside and inside often with water mixed with a little baking soda; wipe up spills right away.

Convection Ovens

A **convection oven** is an oven with fans to help circulate the hot air. This speeds up the cooking process, although not as much as with the microwave oven. The circulating hot air also cooks and browns foods more evenly. Like other ovens, convection ovens may be built into a range or the wall, or they may stand on the kitchen counter.

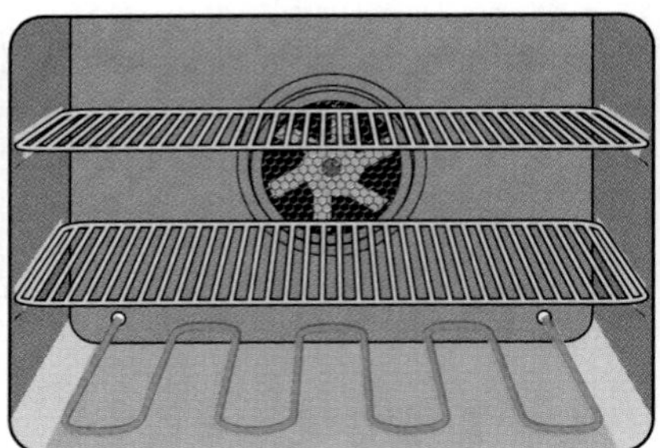

In a convection oven, a fan circulates heated air continuously throughout the oven. Temperatures are usually more even than in a conventional oven. This helps foods cook more evenly.

TAKING ACTION

Buying for the Kitchen

Your friend Clay has a problem. His older brother Andrew just moved into his first apartment, and Clay wants to get him a housewarming gift. Knowing Andrew has few kitchen utensils or appliances, he has decided to buy him some. "He needs almost everything, but he doesn't have much space," Clay explains. "I'd like to get him some things he can really use. However, I don't have too much to spend, so I want to be sure I'm getting the best buy for my money. What do you think I should do?"

Using Your Resourcefulness

- Identify resources Clay can use to find out about different kitchen appliances and utensils and their uses.
- What advice can you give Clay about selecting some essential kitchen equipment that might be useful to his brother?
- Suggest ways that Clay can compare the quality and reliability of different brands of the same item.
- How can he determine whether he is getting the most for his money?

TAKING ACTION

Have students read the feature. Then have a class discussion about what kitchen utensils or appliances Clay could get for Andrew without spending too much money. To guide this discussion, you may want to have students answer the *Using Your Resourcefulness* questions at the end of this feature.

Using Your Resourcefulness Answers

- Answers will vary. Possible resources might include *Consumer Reports* or other consumer information, or family and consumer sciences books.
- Answers will vary. One possible answer would be to tell Clay to get Andrew basic tools or equipment, such as a spatula, saucepans, a frying pan, and/or one or two glass baking dishes for microwaving.

Chapter 44 Review

Summary

In this chapter, you have read about:

- Kitchen utensils and their uses.
- Different types of cookware and cookware materials.
- Factors to consider when buying small and large kitchen appliances.
- Types of small appliances often found in the kitchen.
- How to care for refrigerators and ranges.
- How microwave and convection ovens cook food.

Facts to Recall

1. Name four mixing utensils. List the uses of each.
2. Why should plastic cutting boards be used instead of wooden ones for cutting raw meat, poultry, or fish?
3. What two types of utensils might be used for turning slices of bacon in a frying pan?
4. Name two similarities between frying pans and saucepans. Name one difference.
5. List four different types of baking pans.
6. Name four factors to consider when buying a small kitchen appliance.
7. What does "immersible" mean? Why is it important to know whether a small appliance is immersible?
8. List two tips for keeping a refrigerator clean.
9. How do microwave ovens cook food? Convection ovens?
10. What are three advantages of cooking with a microwave oven?

Ideas to Explore

1. Name some instances in which you could substitute one piece of kitchen equipment for another.
2. In what ways are microwave ovens easy for children to use? What are some risks involved in allowing young children (ten years and under) to use a microwave?

Activities to Try

1. Use your imagination to design a new type of utensil or appliance. If you prefer, design an improved version of an already existing article of kitchen equipment. Use words, pictures, or both to describe your invention, its use, and how it works.
2. Find studies or surveys in consumer magazines comparing different brands and models of one type of kitchen appliance. Decide which model you would buy, based on the magazine's findings.

LINK TO *Communication*

PROMOTING KITCHEN EQUIPMENT AND APPLIANCES

Many people rely on the knowledge of a salesperson when buying kitchen equipment or small appliances. Choose an item of kitchen equipment or a small appliance you find particularly useful (such as a food processor or type of bakeware). Locate as much information as possible about the item (such as how it works, usage, care, etc.). Assume the role of a salesperson who is convincing a customer to purchase this item. In your "sales pitch," talk about the safety features, use and care, the versatility, and advantages of owning this item. Keep your sales pitch to three minutes or less.

Facts to Recall Answers (continued)

9. The magnetron tube in the oven changes electrical energy into waves of energy called "microwaves." The microwaves pass through the cookware into the food, causing water molecules in the food to vibrate. This friction produces heat that cooks or warms the food. A convection oven is an oven with fans to circulate hot air around the food, which cooks or warms it. This speeds up the cooking process, although not as much as with the microwave oven.
10. It can save time and energy; there is less cleanup; you can cook or heat foods in individual serving dishes.

Ideas to Explore

1. Answers will vary. One possible answer might be that cakes can be baked in pie pans instead of round cake pans.
2. Answers will vary and may include: they have no open source of heat; built in timers remind children when food is ready; however, children may not realize that utensils get hot even though the oven is cool; they may use utensils not intended for use in microwave ovens.

- Answers will vary and might include looking in *Consumer Reports* and/or visually examining different brands.
- By comparing the prices and quality of different brands.

LINK TO *Communication*

Answers

Students' sales pitches will vary. Make sure that each student's sales pitch includes information about the item's features, safety, and warranty.

Preparing to Teach

Chapter Outline

Chapter Resources

The following booklet materials may be found in the *Teacher's Classroom Resources* box:
- Lesson Plans, p. 50
- Student Workbook, *Study Guide,* pp. 191-192; *Changing the Yield of a Recipe,* p. 193; *Equivalents and Substitutions,* p. 194
- Color Transparencies, *Utensils for Mixing and Measuring,* CT-49
- Cooperative Learning, p. 57
- Extending the Text, *How Does Metric Measure Up?,* p. 57
- Reteaching and Practical Skills, *How Do You Measure...?,* p. 57
- Enrichment Activities, *What's Wrong with This Recipe?,* p. 69
- Chapter and Unit Tests, pp. 93-94
- Testmaker Software

Also see:
- Meeting the Special Needs of Students
- Linking Home, School, and Community

CHAPTER 45

Recipes and Measuring

OBJECTIVES

- *Explain how to select and interpret a recipe.*
- *Demonstrate how to measure ingredients.*
- *Alter a recipe's yield and substitute ingredients.*

TERMS TO LEARN

- ***recipe***
- ***abbreviation***
- ***equivalents***
- ***yield***

How do you combine tomatoes, onions, garlic, basil, oregano, parsley, olive oil, salt, and pepper into a great pasta sauce? You can use your imagination and blend the ingredients until the mixture tastes just right. You could also look for a recipe that tells you how to make pasta sauce.

In this chapter, you will learn about choosing recipes and measuring ingredients. The next chapter will help you learn how to follow recipe directions for successful results.

Choosing a Recipe

A **recipe** is a set of directions used in cooking. Recipes list the amounts of ingredients needed and then tell you what to do with those ingredients. Look at the sample recipe on page 526.

Recipes can be found in cookbooks, magazines, and newspapers. Friends and family members often share favorite recipes with one another.

Before you choose, look over several recipes for the type of food you want to prepare. Compare them by asking yourself these questions:

- Is this recipe appealing? If you will be sharing the food with others, consider their preferences and special needs as well as your own.
- How long will the recipe take to prepare? Do I have enough time?
- Do I understand all the steps? Do I have the skills needed?
- Do I have all the necessary equipment? Will I be able to find all the ingredients?

If you haven't had very much cooking experience, look for recipes with fewer ingredients and steps. They are usually easy to prepare.

Measuring

Much of your success in preparing food depends on the way you measure ingredients. Knowing abbreviations, equivalents, and measuring techniques will get you off to a good start.

More About *Recipes*

Recipes in cookbooks and magazines can be arranged in several different *formats*, or ways to present information. The *standard format* lists all the ingredients first in the order in which they will be used. Then the directions are given in paragraphs or steps. This format is the most widely used in cookbooks. In the *action format*, directions for a step are given followed by the ingredients used in that step. This format is easy to follow but usually takes up more space. In the *narrative format*, the amounts of the ingredients are stated along with directions in paragraph form. This format is hard to follow unless the recipe is short and few ingredients are used.

Introducing the Chapter

Motivators

1. **Demonstration.** Choose a simple recipe and demonstrate how to prepare the recipe. Focus on measuring and give an explanation of what each ingredient does for the recipe. (Key Skill: *Communication*)
2. **Lab Activity.** Give students a copy of the recipe you used in your demonstration. Have them prepare the recipe in class. Observe their ability to recall the information given to them during the demonstration. (Key Skill: *Management*)
3. **Experiment.** Invite students to the demonstration table one by one and have them measure the following items: a speck of cinnamon, a pinch of salt, a dash of pepper, and a pat of butter. Observe how each student performs these measurements. Explain that some recipes call for a pinch or a dash. (Key Skills: *Communication, Management*)

Chapter Objectives and Vocabulary

1. Have students read the chapter objectives and rephrase the objectives as questions.
2. Ask students to state, in their own words, the purpose of studying this chapter.
3. Pronounce the vocabulary terms listed on the previous page. Ask students whether they are familiar with any of these. Explain that the terms will be defined in the chapter.

Guided Reading

1. Have students read the chapter and use the Study Guide on pp. 191-192 of the *Student Workbook*.

Teaching. . .
Choosing a Recipe and Measurement Abbreviations and Equivalents
(pp. 525-527)

Comprehension Check

1. What is a recipe? *(A recipe is a set of directions used in cooking. They list the amounts of ingredients needed and then tell you what to do with those ingredients.)*
2. Where can recipes be found? *(Recipes can be found in cookbooks, magazines, and newspapers. Friends and family members can also be sources of new recipes to try.)*
3. What is an abbreviation and why are they used in recipes? *(An abbreviation is a shortened form of a word. Recipes often use abbreviations or symbols to save space.)*
4. What are equivalents and when are they used? *(Equivalents are amounts that are equal, such as twelve inches and one foot. Equivalents come in handy when you don't have the right measuring equipment or want to change a recipe.)*

Learning Activities

1. **Recipe Hunt.** Have students look in cookbooks, magazines, and newspapers for recipes that they think they would like. Then have them bring these recipes to class to share with their classmates. (Key Skills: *Communication, Decision Making*)
2. **Abbreviation Flash Cards.** Make up flash cards for each abbreviation of the units of measure commonly used in recipes. Include abbreviations of customary units and metric units. Have volunteers state the full name of each abbreviation as you show the class these flash cards. Keep showing these cards until you feel that the whole class can identify the full name of all of these abbreviations. (Key Skills: *Communication, Decision Making*)

Homemade Granola

3 cups	rolled oats
1 cup	mixed seeds or grains (such as sunflower seeds, sesame seeds, wheat germ, or shredded wheat)
1 cup	coarsely chopped walnuts
½ cup	vegetable oil
½ cup	honey
1 cup	raisins
1 cup	diced dried fruits

Mix all ingredients except raisins and dried fruit in a large bowl. Spread in a single layer on a jelly roll pan. Bake at 300°F, stirring often, for 30 minutes or until golden brown. Remove from oven. Stir in raisins and dried fruit. Cool. Makes 8 cups granola.

Recipes may be written in different ways, but they all should include the information shown here.

Abbreviations and Equivalents

The chart below shows units of measure commonly used in recipes. Some recipes are written using customary measurements, such as cups and tablespoons. Others use metric measurements, such as milliliters. It's best to use the correct measuring equipment, metric or customary, for the recipe you're using.

Units of Measure

Type of Measurement	Customary Units and Abbreviations	Metric Units and Symbols
Volume	teaspoon (tsp.) tablespoon (Tbsp.) fluid ounce (oz.) cup (c.) pint (pt.) quart (qt.) gallon (gal.)	milliliter (mL) liter (L)
Weight	ounce (oz.) pound (lb.)	gram (g) kilogram (kg)
Temperature	degrees Fahrenheit (°F)	degrees Celsius (°C)

More About *The Metric System*

The metric system is a logical, easy-to-use system of measurement for length, area, volume, and mass. Since it is a decimal system, converting from one unit to another involves simply multiplying or dividing by a multiple of 10. The same prefixes for units of measure are used in measuring length, area, volume, and mass. On the contrary, the customary system can be confusing and, at times, an arbitrary system of measure. Converting from one unit to another cannot be done with only one method. In addition, there are 80 separate standards for measuring length, area, volume, and mass. The metric system has been legal for use in the United States since

An **abbreviation** is a shortened form of a word. Recipes often use abbreviations or symbols to save space. Be sure to look at the abbreviations and symbols shown on the chart and become familiar with them.

You'll also find it helpful to know some basic equivalents. **Equivalents** are amounts that are equal, such as twelve inches and one foot. Equivalents come in handy when you don't have the right measuring equipment or want to change a recipe. The chart below will help you learn basic equivalents.

Equivalents

Customary Unit	Customary Equivalent	Approximate Metric Equivalent
Dash	Less than ⅛ tsp.	Less than 0.5 mL
¼ tsp.		1 mL
½ tsp.		2 or 3 mL
1 tsp.		5 mL
1 Tbsp.	3 tsp.	15 mL
1 fluid oz.	2 Tbsp.	30 mL
¼ cup	4 Tbsp. OR 2 fluid oz.	50 mL
⅓ cup	5 Tbsp. + 1 tsp.	75 mL
½ cup	8 Tbsp. OR 4 fluid oz.	125 mL
⅔ cup	10 Tbsp. + 2 tsp. OR ⅓ cup + ⅓ cup	150 mL
¾ cup	12 Tbsp. OR ½ cup + ¼ cup OR 6 fluid oz.	175 mL
1 cup	8 fluid oz. OR 16 Tbsp.	250 mL
1 pt.	2 cups OR 16 fluid oz.	500 mL
1 qt.	2 pt. OR 4 cups OR 32 fluid oz.	1 L (1000 mL)
1 gal.	4 qt.	4 L
1 oz. (weight)		30 g
1 lb.	16 oz. (weight)	500 g
2 lb.	32 oz. (weight)	1 kg (1000 g)

1866. Ask students to list places where the metric measurements are used.

Learning Activities (continued)

3. **Identification.** Have students look over the chart on page 527 for a few minutes, and then have them shut their books. Ask students to identify the customary equivalent measurements of the following list of ingredients: 1 tablespoon of brown sugar *(3 teaspoons)*; 1 cup of milk *(8 fluid ounces)*; ⅔ teaspoon of sugar *(¼ teaspoon)*; and ¾ cup of lemon juice *(12 tablespoons)*. You might also want to have students identify the approximate metric equivalents of these same measurements. (Key Skills: *Math, Decision Making*)

Follow Up

1. **Reteaching.** Write a variety of measurements on index cards, such as cup, teaspoon, tablespoon, etc. Then write the abbreviations of these measurements on another set of index cards. Put all of these index cards on a table and have students match each abbreviation card with the card that has the measurement's full name on it. Students also could do this activity at home to become more familiar with these abbreviations. (Key Skill: *Decision Making*)
2. **Enrichment.** Discuss ethnic foods in class. Ask students to give examples of foods related to their ethnic backgrounds. Have students get a parent, grandparent, or other relative to help them prepare one of these foods. Then have students bring their prepared food to class for an "International Food Buffet." Invite school administrators and/or the social studies department to the event. (Key Skills: *Communication, Social Studies*)

Teaching. . .
Measuring Dry Ingredients, Liquid Ingredients, and Fats; Altering Recipes
(pp. 528-529)

Comprehension Check

1. When measuring dry ingredients, what should you use to level off the ingredient? *(Use the straight edge of a spatula to level off ingredients.)*
2. When leveling flour, why is it important not to tap the cup of flour to level it off? *(Tapping packs down the flour and gives you more than you need.)*
3. How do you measure liquid ingredients? (You place the cup on a flat surface, pour the liquid into the cup, and read the measurement at eye level.)
4. How do you measure solid fat in a dry measuring cup? *(To measure solid fat in a dry measuring cup, pack it into the cup and then level it off.)*
5. What is the most common reason for altering a recipe? *(To change the number of servings.)*

Learning Activities

1. **Experiment.** Place two canisters of flour on your demonstration table. Have two students come to the demonstration table. Instruct one student to sift the flour and then measure the flour by spooning it into a measuring cup and leveling it off. Ask the other student to spoon flour directly into the cup and then tap the cup on the counter to level it off. Once this is done, have two more students come to the demonstration table. Have them pour each cup of flour onto waxed paper and weigh each one separately to see if there is a difference in weight. (Key Skill: *Science*)
2. **Lab Activity.** Divide your class into groups. Each group will be required to demonstrate measuring to the class. Group one will demonstrate measuring dry ingredients, such as flour, brown sugar, oatmeal, and sugar. Group two will demonstrate measuring liquid ingredients, such as water, vegetable oil, milk, and juice. Group three will demonstrate

Read your recipe thoroughly to become familiar with symbols and abbreviations.

Level off dry ingredients with the straight edge of a spatula.

▼ Measuring Dry Ingredients ▼

Dry ingredients include sugar, flour, salt, and baking powder. To measure ¼ cup (50 mL) or more, use a dry measuring cup. Hold the cup over waxed paper or the ingredient's container. Spoon the ingredient into the cup, heaping it a little over the top. Then level off the ingredient with the straight edge of a spatula. For smaller amounts, use a measuring spoon in the same way.

Some dry ingredients call for special techniques:

- Flour has tiny granules that pack together. If the recipe calls for sifted flour, sift it first, then measure in the usual way. Otherwise, stir the flour before spooning it into the measuring cup. Don't tap the cup to level the flour. Tapping packs down the flour and gives you too much. Whatever you were making would turn out too thick or dry.
- To measure brown sugar, pack it firmly into a measuring cup and level off. It should keep the shape of the cup when turned out of the cup. (Other types of sugar are not packed, but measured in the usual way.)

Read liquid measurements at eye level.

▼ Measuring Liquid Ingredients ▼

Liquid ingredients, such as milk, water, or oil, are measured in liquid measuring cups. These measuring cups are clear so you can see the liquid as it fills the cup. They have extra space at the top to prevent spilling and a spout for pouring. For an accurate measurement, place the cup on a flat surface and read the measurement at eye level.

More About *Measuring Cups*

Measuring cups can be made of glass, metal, or plastic. Different cups are used for measuring liquids than are used for dry ingredients. Cups for measuring liquid have a lip so that you can pour the liquid out. Dry ingredient measuring cups have no lip. The rim of the cup is level all the way around. The measuring cups you use at home may range from ⅛ cup to 2 cups in size. Professional cooks use much larger containers which measure pints and gallons as well.

Small amounts of liquids are measured in measuring spoons. Just fill the spoon to the brim. You don't need to level off liquids.

▼ Measuring Fats ▼

Solid fats, such as shortening, can be measured in a dry measuring cup. Pack the fat into the cup and level off. Use a rubber or plastic scraper to remove the fat from the cup.

Sticks of margarine or butter have measurements marked on the wrapper. One stick equals ½ cup (125 mL). If you need just part of a stick, cut through the wrapper on the appropriate marking.

Solid fats can also be measured in a liquid measuring cup using the water displacement method. Here's an example. To measure ¼ cup of solid fat, use a 1 cup liquid measuring cup. Fill it with cold water to the ¾ cup mark (because 1 cup minus ¼ cup equals ¾ cup). Now add the fat, a little at a time, making sure it is covered by the water. When the water reaches the 1 cup mark, you have measured ¼ cup of fat. Pour off the water and scrape the fat out of the cup.

For most cooks, especially beginners, carefully measuring ingredients is a good idea. For the Cajuns (KAY-jenz) of southwest Louisiana, however, experimenting and substituting are valued in preparing meals. This has historical roots. When the first Cajuns settled in Louisiana in the mid 1700s, they lived off the land — and wasted nothing. Leftovers did not keep well in the humid climate, so they were often added to whatever dish was on the menu that day. Also, bartering, the trading of goods and services, brought different foods and spices to Cajun cooking. This spirit of adventure, born of necessity, makes Cajun cooking popular in all parts of America.

Altering Recipes

Very few recipes have to be followed exactly as written. The most common reason for altering a recipe is to change the number of servings. Other times you may need to substitute an ingredient for one that is missing. Some people like to experiment with recipes by adding their own touches. The following guidelines will help you alter recipes successfully.

how to measure baking soda, baking powder, and salt using measuring spoons. Group four will demonstrate measuring solid fat in a liquid measuring cup using the water displacement method. (Key Skills: *Cooperation, Following Directions*)

3. **Activity Sheets.** Distribute two recipes to your class. Instruct your students to double the first recipe and to cut the second recipe in half. Check the accuracy of their answers. (Key Skill: *Math*)

Follow Up

1. **Reteaching.** Write the following list of ingredients on the board: 1 c. milk, ½ t. vanilla, 2 c. flour, 1 T. butter, ⅛ t. nutmeg, ½ c. brown sugar, and ¼ c. corn syrup. Then have the students explain how each should be measured. (Key Skill: *Communication*)
2. **Enrichment.** Have students measure different ingredients (butter, salt, sour cream, bread crumbs, etc.) and share with the class the difficulties they encountered and how they handled them. (Key Skill: *Communication*)

AROUND THE WORLD

After reading the feature, have students discuss ways in which their leftovers could be used in other meals. Also, have students talk about any Cajun meals that they have tried. Did they like them? *(Answers will vary.)*

Making a Difference

Children often learn best from other young people. Invite preschoolers to your class and have your students teach them the art of measuring. Use sand and water for dry and liquid ingredients.

Teaching. . . Changing the Yield of a Recipe, Making Emergency Substitutions, and Making Creative Changes

(pp. 530-532)

Comprehension Check

1. The word *yield* is found at the end of a recipe. What does it mean? *(The amount of food or servings a recipe makes, such as eight servings or four cups.)*
2. When you double a recipe, do you need to alter the baking or cooking time? *(You need to alter the baking or cooking time if you put the mixture in a larger pan than the recipe calls for. The heat will have to pass through a larger amount of food.)*
3. Why is it important to read your list of ingredients before preparing a recipe. *(It is important to read over the list of ingredients so you can check to see if you have all of the items on hand.)*
4. What types of recipes allow you to make creative changes? *(Recipes for foods such as casseroles and stews are more flexible than recipes for most baked goods.)*

Learning Activities

1. **Lab Activity.** Choose a quick bread recipe and instruct your students to double the recipe. Have students select the right-sized baking pan or pans in which to bake the bread. Discuss what they could do at home if they did not have the right-sized baking pan. (Key Skill: *Problem Solving*)
2. **Discussion.** Talk about situations in which students may need to make substitutions in a recipe. Use baked goods, casseroles, and soups as examples. Encourage students to brainstorm possible substitutions for various recipes. (Key Skill: *Problem Solving*)

Use your knowledge of equivalent measurements to alter the yield of a recipe.

▼ Changing the Yield of a Recipe ▼

The amount of food or number of servings a recipe makes is called the **yield**. If you want more or fewer servings, you will have to alter the recipe. Your math skills and knowledge of equivalent measurements will come in handy as you make the changes.

Suppose you are going to prepare a favorite casserole recipe. You want to make four servings, but the recipe yields eight. First, divide the number of servings you want by the original yield. The answer is the number you will use to calculate the new amount for each ingredient. In this example, $4 \div 8 = \frac{1}{2}$. You will multiply the amount of each ingredient by ½.

Here's how it works. If the recipe calls for 2 pounds of ground beef, you would use 1 pound ($2 \times \frac{1}{2} = 1$). Instead of ½ cup milk, you would use ¼ cup ($\frac{1}{2} \times \frac{1}{2} = \frac{1}{4}$).

As you multiply, you may need to convert from one unit of measurement to another. Suppose the recipe calls for ¼ cup grated cheese. The new amount would be ⅛ cup ($\frac{1}{4} \times \frac{1}{2} = \frac{1}{8}$). Since you don't have a utensil that will measure ⅛ cup, use the chart on page 527 to help you figure out an equivalent measure. Can you see that if ¼ cup is equivalent to 4 tablespoons, ⅛ cup must equal 2 tablespoons?

Calculate the new amount for each ingredient in the recipe. Write the new amounts down on a piece of paper. It's easy to forget to change the amounts unless you write them down.

You need to think about some other points as well. Container sizes may have to be changed. For example, if you double a recipe, you will need to use either a pan that is twice as large or two pans of the original size.

The baking or cooking time may also have to be adjusted. If you put the mixture in a larger pan than the recipe called for, the heat will have to pass through a larger amount of food. The mixture will need to bake a little longer.

Be sure to change the size of the cooking container when you alter the yield of a recipe.

▼ Making Emergency Substitutions ▼

It's no fun to be in the middle of preparing a recipe and suddenly discover you are missing one of the ingredients. Before you begin, read through the ingredients list and make sure you have all the items on hand.

More About Seasoning Food

Seasoning food is an art. Try to avoid being heavy handed. However, cold foods require more intense seasoning that hot foods. Pasta salads are usually best when they are seasoned just before serving. If seasoned ahead of time, be prepared to add half the amount of dressing again just before serving. Do not add salt to dried peas and beans until they are cooked. Salt toughens these items. Do not add salt to meat and chicken until they are well browned on both sides. Salt draws the liquid out of these items. You need less salt in soup if you add it at the end of cooking. This seasons the broth and not the other ingredients. When increasing a recipe, do not increase the seasonings as drastically as the

If you do find yourself without an ingredient, you may be able to make a substitution. Experience has shown that some ingredients can be used in place of others with fairly good results. Some of these substitutions are listed below. You may find others listed in cookbooks. Substitutions are more successful in some products than others.

Another possible solution is to change your plans slightly. If there's no canned tuna, perhaps you can make an egg salad instead. If you don't have all the ingredients for icing a cake, you can sprinkle confectioner's sugar on top.

Substitutions That Work

- 2 Tbsp. (30 mL) flour = 1 Tbsp. (15 mL) cornstarch (for thickening)
- 1 cup (250 mL) sifted cake flour = 1 cup minus 2 Tbsp. (220 mL) sifted all-purpose flour
- 1 cup (250 mL) whole milk = ½ cup (125 mL) evaporated milk plus ½ cup (125 mL) water
- 1 cup (250 mL) sour milk or buttermilk = 1 cup (250 mL) fresh milk plus 1 Tbsp. (15 mL) vinegar or lemon juice
- 1 square (1 oz. or 28 g) unsweetened chocolate = 3 Tbsp. (45 mL) unsweetened cocoa powder plus 1 Tbsp. (15 mL) butter or margarine
- 1 cup (250 mL) granulated sugar = 1 cup (250 mL) packed brown sugar OR 2 cups (500 mL) sifted powdered sugar

For best results, check your supplies and make any needed substitutions before you begin to cook.

Learning Activities (continued)

3. **Personal Stories.** Have students tell stories relating to their own kitchen experiences. What types of foods do they prepare at home, and in what ways do they create unusual foods, snacks, or beverages for themselves. Students will enjoy hearing one another's inventions and creations. (Key Skill: *Communication*)

Follow Up

1. **Reteaching.** Give your students a copy of a simple muffin recipe that yields twelve muffins. Explain to them that you would like to serve muffins at your faculty meeting and you will need thirty-six (three dozen) muffins. Ask them to help you increase the recipe to yield thirty-six muffins. (Key Skill: *Math*)
2. **Extension.** Use the extension information handout on p. 57 of the *Extending the Text* booklet in the TCR.
3. **Enrichment.** Examine the boxed recipe for homemade granola. Ask your students to consider possible substitutions for the walnuts and raisins that might work. Also, have them consider combinations of mixed seeds or grains that might work in place of those that are suggested. Invite your students to create their own recipe for homemade granola. Encourage them to consider food items that are common in their own homes, such as bran cereals, wheat cereals, carob bits, or yogurt-covered fruit bits. Have your students give names to their granola creations. (Key Skills: *Communication, Decision Making*)

main ingredients. Make small changes and then taste the food.

Completing the Chapter

For Review

1. Emphasize the main concepts using the summary.
2. Have students complete the "Facts to Recall." (Answers below.)

For Reteaching

1. **Reteaching.** Use the activity on p. 57 of the *Reteaching and Practical Skills* booklet in the TCR.

For Enrichment

1. **Enrichment.** Use the activity on p. 69 of the *Enrichment Activities* booklet in the TCR.

For Evaluation

1. Choose items from "Ideas to Explore" and "Activities to Try."
2. Use the chapter test on pp. 93-94 in the testing booklet of the TCR or use the testmaker software.

Facts to Recall Answers

1. **Any three:** Is this recipe appealing? How long will it take to prepare? Do I understand all the steps? Do I have the skills required? Do I have all the necessary equipment? Can I find all the ingredients?
2. Ounce; teaspoon; gram; tablespoon; pint; milliliter; degrees Celsius; pound.
3. 8; 16; 3; 250.
4. Spoon the flour into a ½-cup measuring cup, heaping it a little over the top, then level it off with the straight edge of a spatula.
5. Brown sugar should be packed firmly so it keeps the shape of the cup when it is turned out of the cup. Granulated sugar is measured the usual way for dry ingredients.
6. Place the measuring cup on a flat surface and read the measurement at eye level.
7. Fill the cup with ½ cup of cold water and gradually add the fat until the water level reaches the 1-cup mark. Then pour off the water and you will be left with ½ cup of fat.
8. **Any two:** flour; milk; chocolate; sugar.

▼ Making Creative Changes ▼

A recipe is your guide to success. At first, it's a good idea to do exactly what the recipe tells you to do. However, after you have used a recipe several times, you may want to try some variations.

Seasonings can often be changed to suit your tastes. For example, some people like their chili to be extra spicy. They might add more chili powder or hot peppers. If someone in your family doesn't like nuts, you might substitute raisins in a cookie recipe. Trial and error will lead you to the perfect combinations for your tastes.

Some recipes are more difficult to alter successfully than others. Most baked goods, such as breads or cakes, require an exact balance of ingredients. Recipes for foods such as casseroles and stews are more flexible.

Adding your own touches to recipes can bring you special satisfaction. You may even develop recipes of your own someday.

TAKING ACTION
Using Equivalents and Making Substitutions

Every year you and your friends in the Washington Junior High French Club have an informal dinner for members and their guests. Each member is asked to bring an authentic French dish to share. This year you have found a recipe for croissants — French crescent rolls — in an authentic French cookbook. You have translated the directions correctly, but realize the ingredient amounts are given only in metric. Your customary measuring utensils are not marked with metric equivalents. You want to use this recipe, but you will need to convert the metric measurements into customary ones. In addition, as a health-conscious person, you are concerned that this traditional recipe calls for butter and whole milk. You are afraid this will make the croissants too high in fat and cholesterol. As you are working on the conversions, you wonder what substitutions could be made to reduce the fat and cholesterol without changing the taste or texture of the croissants.

Using Your Resourcefulness

- What sources can you use to find the customary equivalents for metric measurements?
- Where can you get information about the fats and cholesterol found in butter and whole milk?
- How can you learn about ingredient substitutions?
- In what way can you determine how these substitutions will affect taste and texture?
- List all the resources that can help you find the facts you need to solve this problem.

TAKING ACTION

Have students read the feature. Then have a class discussion about how to easily get the metric measurements for this croissant recipe converted into customary measurements. Also discuss what substitutions could be made in the recipe to make it lower in fat and cholesterol. To guide this discussion, you might want to have students answer the *Using Your Resourcefulness* questions at the end of this feature.

Using Your Resourcefulness Answers

- Answers will vary and may include textbooks and cookbooks.

Chapter 45 Review

Summary

In this chapter, you have read about:

- What to consider when choosing a recipe.
- Customary and metric abbreviations commonly used in recipes.
- Techniques for measuring dry ingredients, liquid ingredients, and fats.
- How to alter a recipe to increase or decrease its yield.
- Substitutions to try in case you are missing an ingredient.
- Ideas for adding your own touches to recipes.

Facts to Recall

1. List three questions to ask yourself when selecting or comparing recipes.
2. Write the terms the following abbreviations or symbols stand for: oz., tsp., g, Tbsp., pt., mL, °C, lb.
3. How many fluid ounces are in one cup? How many tablespoons are in one cup? How may teaspoons are in a tablespoon? How many milliliters are in one cup?
4. Briefly explain how to measure ½ cup of sifted flour.
5. Explain how the technique for measuring brown sugar differs from that for measuring granulated white sugar.
6. What two things should you do to measure liquid ingredients accurately?
7. Explain how you would measure ½ cup of solid fat in a 1-cup liquid measuring cup.
8. Name two types of ingredients that might be easiest to vary in a recipe.

Ideas to Explore

1. What do you think is the most common mistake made by beginning cooks when choosing a new recipe to try?
2. Why might it be easier to substitute ingredients in a vegetable stew than in a chocolate layer cake?
3. How might a cookie recipe that calls for butter, sugar, eggs, and a frosting be altered to make it lower in fat, sugar, and calories?

Activities to Try

1. Find examples of confusing or poorly written recipe directions. Explain how you would rewrite them to make them clearer.
2. Choose a recipe from this textbook or another source. For each ingredient listed, tell exactly what measuring equipment you would use to measure the required amount.

LINK TO Math

ALTERING A RECIPE

Learning to alter recipes can be a real benefit in making recipes meet the needs of you and your family. Find a new recipe or use an old family favorite that includes at least eight ingredients. Alter the recipe to make three times as many servings as the original yield. Use the method described on page 530. Then answer the following questions:

- Which ingredients need to be converted to another unit of measurement for ease in measuring? For example: if an altered recipe called for ⅝ cup flour, the equivalent measure you would need is ½ cup (4/8 cup) plus 2 tablespoons (⅛ cup).
- How does altering the recipes affect the size cooking container needed?
- If cooking time is required, how will it be affected by altering the recipes?

Ideas to Explore

1. Answers will vary.
2. Because recipes for stews are more flexible than recipes for cakes. Most recipes for cakes require an exact balance of ingredients.
3. Answers will vary and may include: margarine may be substituted for the butter; fruit juice for part of the sugar.

LINK TO Math

Answers

- Answers will vary depending on what recipe each student chooses.
- Answers will vary. In most cases, students should have to use a larger container to accommodate the larger yield.
- Answers will vary. In most cases, the cooking time for these recipes should have to increase because of the higher yield.

- Answers will vary. Possible answers may include food labels, USDA pamphlets, the American Dairy Council, magazine and newspaper articles, and nutrition books.
- Answers will vary and may include textbooks, cookbooks, and County Extension Offices.
- Answers will vary. One possible answer would be to have taste tests.
- Answers will vary. Possible answers may include textbooks, cookbooks, nutritionists, and home ec teachers.

Preparing to Teach

Chapter Outline

Chapter Resources

The following booklet materials may be found in the *Teacher's Classroom Resources* box:

- Lesson Plans, p. 51
- Student Workbook, *Study Guide,* pp. 195-196; *Cooking Terms Crossword,* pp. 197-198
- Color Transparencies, *Creative Cuts,* CT-50
- Technology and Computers, p. 45
- Cooperative Learning, p. 58
- Extending the Text, *What Goes In Must Go Out,* p. 58
- Reteaching and Practical Skills, *Preparation Terms to Know,* p. 58
- Enrichment Activities, *More About Microwaving,* p. 70
- Chapter and Unit Tests, pp. 95-96
- Testmaker Software

Also see:

- Meeting the Special Needs of Students
- Linking Home, School, and Community

CHAPTER

46 Preparation Terms and Techniques

OBJECTIVES

- *Interpret recipe terms.*
- *Describe basic cooking methods.*
- *Give safety guidelines for microwave cooking.*
- *Conserve nutrients during preparation.*

TERMS TO LEARN

- ***broiling***
- ***baking or roasting***
- ***boiling***
- ***simmering***
- ***frying***

More About *Microwave Ovens*

Microwave oven output can vary from 200 watts to around 750 watts. Some microwave-packaged foods are labeled with heating directions by wattage. To determine wattage in a microwave oven, do the following:

- Fill a glass measuring cup with exactly 1 cup of water.

Today everyone needs to learn how to prepare food. Many families share kitchen responsibilities. It may mean getting a fast meal together or helping to prepare a meal for a special occasion. Even if you prepare only convenience foods, you still need to know the meaning of basic terms so that you can follow directions correctly.

This chapter explains basic techniques and cooking methods. Once you master them, food preparation won't be a mystery to you.

Recipe Terms

Some words have special meanings when used in food preparation. At each step in a recipe, pay attention to the exact term used. It is your clue to the tool you need and the technique to follow.

Mixing Terms

A number of recipe techniques are used to combine ingredients or bring about a change in texture.

- ***Stir.*** Use a spoon and a circular or figure-eight motion.
- ***Blend, mix, combine.*** Stir two or more ingredients together thoroughly.
- ***Beat.*** Use this technique to make mixtures smooth or to beat egg whites. Use a quick, over-and-over motion with a spoon or wire whisk. You can also use a rotary beater or electric mixer.
- ***Whip.*** Beat the ingredient (such as cream) very rapidly to bring in air and increase volume. Use a wire whisk, rotary beater, or electric mixer.
- ***Cream.*** Using a spoon, beater, or mixer, combine ingredients until soft and creamy. This technique is often used to combine fat and sugar.
- ***Cut in.*** This is a way to mix a solid fat with dry ingredients. Use a pastry blender, fork, or two knives and a cutting motion.
- ***Fold.*** Use this technique to gently combine a delicate mixture, such as beaten egg whites, with other ingredients. Use a rubber or plastic scraper. See "How to Fold in Egg Whites" on page 536.

Stir

Blend, mix, combine

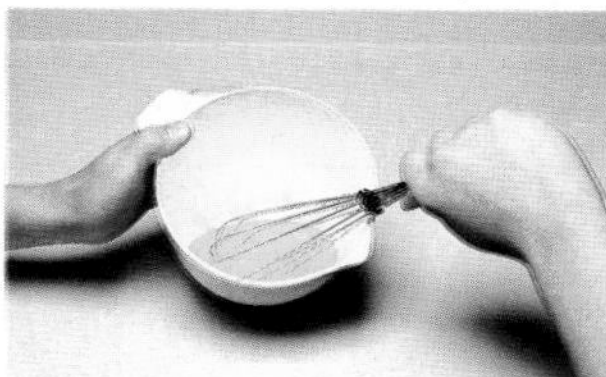
Beat

Whip

- Microwave the water uncovered on "high" until it begins to boil. If boiling occurs in less than three minutes, wattage is 600-700; in three to four minutes, wattage is 500-600; in more than four minutes, wattage is less than 500 watts.

Most microwave recipes are tested for 600-700-watt microwave ovens. If you have a 400- to 500-watt unit, add 20 seconds to each minute of cooking time. If you have a 500- to 600-watt unit, add 10 seconds to each minute of cooking time.

Introducing the Chapter

Motivators

1. **Cooking "Bee."** Collect a number of cooking items that suggest a certain way of preparing food (e.g., pie plate — baking, frying pan — frying, meat thermometer — roasting, broiler pan — broiling, etc.). Line up small groups around the room. The first group to call out the correct term when you hold up a cooking item gets a point. You might also do this as a class opener and ask the class to name the cooking method. Include a wok, deep-fat fryer, and a long spatula or mitt for grilling. (Key Skills: *Communication, Decision Making*)
2. **Bulletin Board.** On a bulletin board that runs across the top of a chalkboard, pin pictures or drawings of the following cooking utensils: a spatula, a parer, a chopping knife, a whisk, a grater, a pastry blender, etc. Print the name of the tool near the illustration (perhaps on a removable piece of paper). (Key Skill: *Creativity*)
3. **Recall.** Ask students how many cooking utensils they can name from their cupboards at home. Do they know how they're used? (Key Skill: *Communication*)

Chapter Objectives and Vocabulary

1. Have students read the chapter objectives and rephrase the objectives as questions.
2. Ask students to state, in their own words, the purpose of studying this chapter.
3. Pronounce the vocabulary terms listed on the previous page. Ask students whether they are familiar with any of these. Explain that the terms will be defined in the chapter.

Guided Reading

1. Have students read the chapter and use the Study Guide on pp. 195-196 of the *Student Workbook*.

Teaching. . .
Mixing Terms and Cutting Terms (pp. 535-537)

Comprehension Check

1. What motion should you use for stirring? *(A circular or figure-eight motion.)*
2. What does using a whisk, beater, or mixer do to an ingredient? *(It brings in air and increases volume.)*
3. What is the difference between chopped, minced, cubed, and diced foods? *(Chopped — small, irregular pieces; minced — pieces as small as possible; cubed — evenly shaped ½-inch pieces; diced — evenly shaped ¼-inch pieces.)*

Learning Activities

1. **Demonstration.** Find a recipe for cookies or bar cookies that includes several techniques in this chapter (e.g., beating, folding, creaming, and cutting in). While preparing the recipe, demonstrate these different methods and explain why they are used. Bake the cookies or bars and share them with the class or freeze them for later use. (Key Skill: *Communication*)
2. **Skill Contest.** Practice paring and shredding by holding contests between pairs or groups. See who can make the longest apple peel (not a speed race) or who can shred a carrot the quickest. Use the carrots to make a carrot cake or carrot bread. Demonstrate mixing methods at the same time. Have students slice and eat the pared apples or have them chop them for an apple cake, bread, or pie. (Key Skills: *Communication, Cooperation*)

Follow Up

1. **Reteaching.** Have small groups make flash cards for each recipe term or procedure. Give groups a few minutes a day to quiz each other with the cards. (Key Skill: *Cooperation*)

How to . . .
Fold in Egg Whites

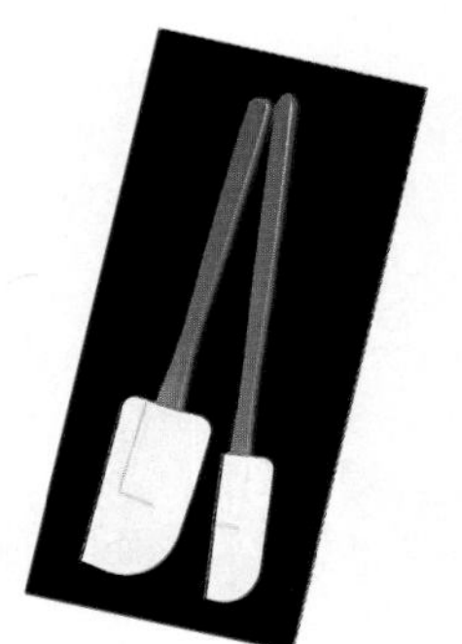

1. Add some of the egg whites to the bowl with the other ingredients.
2. Cut the scraper down through the center of the mixture.
3. Turn the scraper at the bottom of the bowl and gently bring it up along the side. You are bringing some of the mixture from the bottom of the bowl to the top.
4. Give the bowl a quarter turn. Fold again. Repeat several times.
5. Add the rest of the egg whites. Fold until the mixture is uniform.

Cream

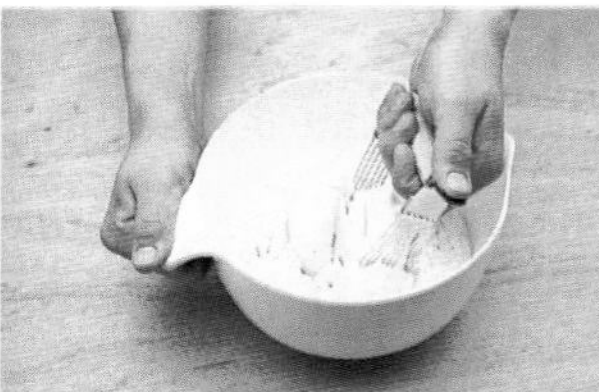

Cut in

Fold

How to ... Fold in Egg Whites

Have students read the feature. Then use the egg white lesson with other mixing methods. Make an angel food cake from scratch or a fluffy tapioca pudding using the recipe on a package of quick tapioca. This includes cooking egg yolks.

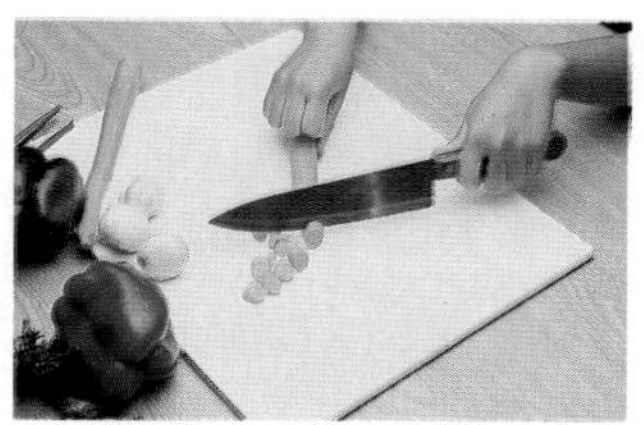

Chop

Mince

Cube

Dice

Pare

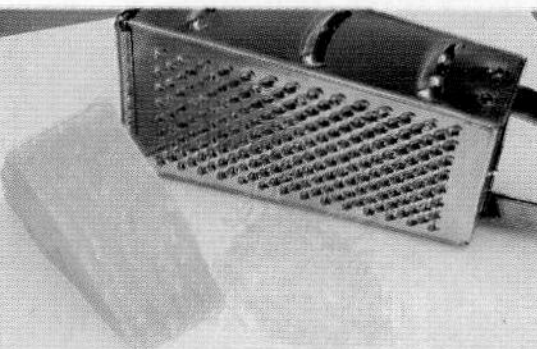

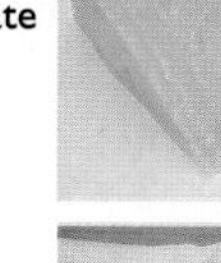

Grate

Shred

▼ Cutting Terms ▼

Do you know the difference between mincing and chopping, or between cubing and dicing? Becoming familiar with these terms will add to your success in the kitchen.

- ***Chop.*** Cut food into small, irregular pieces.
- ***Mince.*** Chop food into pieces that are as small as possible.
- ***Cube.*** Cut into evenly shaped pieces about ½ inch (13 mm) on each side.
- ***Dice.*** Cut into evenly shaped pieces about ¼ inch (6 mm) on each side.
- ***Pare.*** Cut off the outside covering of a fruit or vegetable. Use a peeler or a paring knife.
- ***Grate.*** Rub food over a grater (the side with small holes) to get fine particles.
- ***Shred.*** Cut or tear food into long, thin pieces. When using a grater, rub the food over the large holes. Depending on the food, you might use a knife, two forks, or a food processor instead.

SAFETY CHECK✓

To safely use knives:

- Use sharp knives. They are less likely to slip and cause an accident.
- Always use a cutting board. Never hold the food in your hand while cutting or cut toward yourself.
- When using one hand to hold the food steady, tuck your fingers under. That way your knuckles, not your fingertips, are closest to the knife.

Follow Up (continued)

2. **Enrichment.** Ask students to do some baking or cutting at home. Have them write down the recipe they used and the procedures involved. Parents should indicate whether the student did the activities alone or with the parent. Perhaps students could bring a sample to show to the class as they describe what they did. (Key Skills: *Communication, Following Directions*)

Hands-on Activity

Demonstrate or explain various mixing methods using the proper utensils and ingredients. Toward the end, demonstrate cutting in and rolling out pie crust dough. Cut the rolled dough into strips. Have students sprinkle strips with poppy seeds, Parmesan cheese, and/or cinnamon and sugar. Bake and share samples with the students. Students can clean up while the pie crust is baking.

Hands-on Activity

Gather (or ask students to bring) an assortment of salad vegetables and toppings. Demonstrate and then ask students to carry out cutting methods. Examples might include chopping a tomato, dicing an onion, slicing mushrooms, shredding carrots, slicing or cubing a green pepper, grating Parmesan cheese, etc. You might also demonstrate cutting and baking bread cubes for croutons. Make or bring low-fat salad dressings and share a salad with the class.

SAFETY CHECK✓

After students have read this safety check, discuss these tips with them. Re-emphasize how important it is that students follow these safety tips when using knives. Following these tips could help avoid a nasty accident.

Teaching. . .
Other Recipe Terms and Basic Cooking Methods
(pp. 538-539)

Comprehension Check

1. What's the difference between coating and greasing? *(Coat — cover food with a dry ingredient; grease — rub lightly with a fat.)*
2. What's the difference between draining and straining? *(Drain — remove excess liquid; strain — remove solid particles from a liquid.)*
3. Define broiling and give two advantages of using this cooking method. *(Broiling is cooking directly under or over the source of heat. One advantage of broiling is that cooking is quick because the food is tender and usually in small pieces. Another advantage is that if the food contains fat, the fat drains away from the food while it's broiling.)*
4. What do baking and roasting mean? *(Baking and roasting both mean cooking in an oven or oven-type appliance with dry heat.)*

Learning Activities

1. **Impromptu Charades.** Write the name of each recipe term on a slip of paper. (Write the definition, too, if you wish.) Ask each student to draw a slip of paper and then mime the activity that's written on it. Have the rest of the class try to guess the correct answer. Time each student if you wish. These charades could also be acted out within small groups as a review activity. (Key Skills: *Communication, Creativity*)
2. **Cookbook Race.** Just for fun or to start a discussion, give small groups a cookbook or two. Ask them to see how many different cooking methods they can discover. These groups should jot down the name of the recipe and the page number. The team with the most methods wins. An alternate way to do this activity would be to give the students a list of cooking methods along with the cookbook and ask them to find a recipe for each method. (Key Skills: *Communication, Cooperation*)

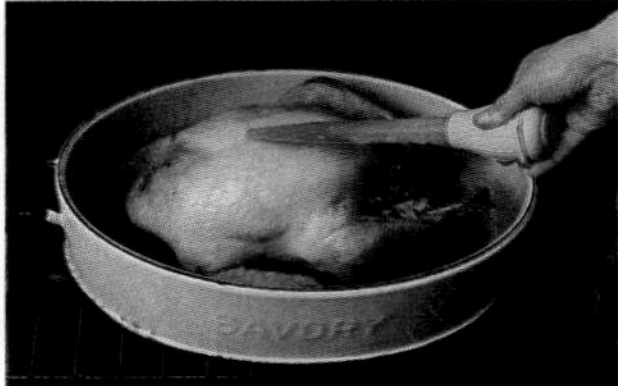

Baste

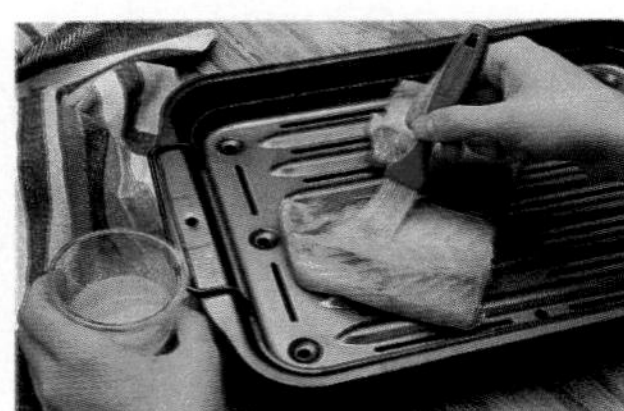
Brush

▼ Other Terms ▼

Here are some additional terms you might find in a recipe.

- ▶ ***Baste.*** Moisten foods, such as meat, while cooking. Basting adds flavor and helps keep the food from drying out. You might baste with meat drippings, a sauce or marinade, or melted butter. Use a brush or a baster.
- ▶ ***Brush.*** Use a brush to lightly cover the surface of a food with another food, such as egg white.
- ▶ ***Coat.*** Cover the surface of a food with a dry ingredient, such as flour, cornmeal, dry bread crumbs, or sugar.
- ▶ ***Garnish.*** Decorate a finished dish with a small food item, such as a sprig of parsley, a carrot curl, or a sprinkling of paprika.
- ▶ ***Grease.*** Rub lightly with a fat, such as butter, margarine, oil, or shortening.
- ▶ ***Season.*** Add seasonings, such as salt, pepper, herbs, or spices, to improve the flavor of a food.
- ▶ ***Strain.*** Remove solid particles from a liquid by pouring the liquid through a sieve or strainer.
- ▶ ***Drain.*** Remove excess liquid by placing food in a strainer or colander.

Coat

Grease

Strain

Garnish

Season

Drain

More About *Recipe Terms*

Additional recipe terms are:

- *Bread* — to coat a food (such as chicken) with bread, cracker, or cereal crumbs.
- *Dilute* — to add water to another liquid.
- *Dissolve* — to mix a solid, such as a bouillon cube, with a liquid until they form a solution.
- *Julienne* — to cut food, such as vegetables, meat, or cheese, into narrow, long strips.
- *Marinate* — to soak in a liquid, usually an acid-oil mixture or dressing.
- *Melt* — to change a solid food to liquid by heating it.

Broiling is a quick, nutritious way of cooking food.

Basic Cooking Methods

If you leaf through cookbooks and recipes in magazines, you can get lots of ideas about different ways to cook foods. Most recipes that involve cooking are based on a few basic methods. These include broiling, baking or roasting, boiling, simmering, frying, and microwave cooking.

Broiling

Broiling is cooking directly under or over the source of heat. If you broil in a range, countertop broiler, or toaster oven, the heat is above the food. If you broil on an outside grill, the food is on top and the heat comes from below. To control how fast the food broils, you adjust the distance the food is placed from the source of heat.

Foods that can be broiled include tender cuts of meat and poultry, fish, and some vegetables and fruits. Perhaps you have had broiled tomatoes or broiled eggplant.

Broiling has several advantages. Cooking is quick because the food is tender and usually in small pieces. If the food contains fat, the fat drains away from the food.

Baking or Roasting

Baking and **roasting** both mean cooking in an oven or oven-type appliance with dry heat. You control the heat by setting the temperature control.

Foods commonly baked or roasted include tender cuts of meat and poultry, fish, some fruits and vegetables, breads, pies, cakes, and cookies. Cooking time depends on the size of the food to be cooked. Larger pieces of food take longer than smaller size foods.

- *Puree* — to make a food smooth or semi-liquid by using a food processor or pressing it through a strainer or food mill.
- *Reconstitute* — to add water to a concentrated food, such as orange juice, to return it to its original state.
- *Reduce* — to cook a liquid until some moisture evaporates and the liquid is more concentrated.

Learning Activities (continued)

3. **Discussion.** Use a variation of the previous activity as a discussion starter. Ask the class to tell you recipes they know that require the various cooking methods. Can they think of recipes requiring more than one method? Frying ground beef and boiling macaroni to bake in a casserole would be an example. (Key Skills: *Communication, Critical Thinking*)
4. **Demonstration.** Show students which cooking utensils are used for each cooking method. Be sure to show which part of the stove is used also. Since *broiling* is sometimes unfamiliar to students, you might demonstrate a quick food preparation using this method. For example, cover a slice of bread with grated or sliced Cheddar cheese and broil it until the cheese bubbles. A nutritious lunch variation would be to put plain canned tuna on top of the bread and under the cheese. (Key Skill: *Communication*)

Follow Up

1. **Reteaching.** Direct students to make a small poster illustrating each cooking method, including the procedure, advantages, and disadvantages of each. (Key Skill: *Creativity*)
2. **Enrichment.** Ask students to plan menus for two or three days using a variety of cooking methods, keeping in mind the Food Guide Pyramid and available time. (Key Skills: *Problem Solving, Decision Making*)

Teaching. . . Boiling and Simmering (pp. 540-541)

Comprehension Check

1. How can you tell if water is boiling? *(Bubbles rise and break on the surface.)*
2. What is steaming? *(Steaming is a method of cooking food over boiling water rather in it.)*
3. How can you tell if water is simmering? *(Bubbles form slowly and break below the surface.)*
4. What is braising? *(Braising involves browning food in a little fat and then simmering it in very little added liquid.)*

Learning Activities

1. **Discussion.** Ask students why steaming is a good way to cook vegetables. *(Steaming helps retain nutrients, especially water-soluble vitamins.)* Then have volunteers talk about different vegetables they've eaten that were steamed. Did they like their taste? How was their texture? (Key Skill: *Communication*)
2. **Demonstration.** Illustrate the merits of simmering or slow boiling by conducting this experiment. Peel (or have students practice doing it) six or eight similarly sized potatoes. Place half of the potatoes in a pan of cold water and the rest in another pan of cold water. Bring both pans of water to a boil. Turn the temperature of one pan down significantly and let the other boil like crazy. When the potatoes in both pans have cooked, drain them separately. Now have students compare the results. The potatoes cooked slowly should be firmer and more intact than those boiled at a high temperature. Point out that more nutrients are lost when food is boiled furiously. With any luck, the highly boiled potatoes will have fallen apart and you can also note that they are less appetizing and harder to cut up. (Key Skills: *Communication, Critical Thinking*)

Baked foods are cooked uncovered by dry heat in an oven.

Except for occasional basting of poultry and fish, roasting or baking allows you to do other things while the food is in the oven. Check food for doneness at the shortest suggested cooking time.

▼ Boiling ▼

A liquid is **boiling** when bubbles rise and break on the surface. Boiling is usually done on the rangetop. For example, noodles and pasta are cooked in boiling water. The rolling boil helps to keep the noodles from sticking together. However, few other foods are boiled.

Steaming is a method of cooking food over boiling water rather than in it. The food is held out of the water by a metal basket or other utensil. Holes in the basket allow the hot steam to rise up and cook the food. The pan is tightly covered to keep the steam inside. This cooking method is most often used for vegetables.

Boiling water is used for cooking foods such as pasta and corn-on-the-cob.

More About Boiling

Water boils at 212°F (100°C) at sea level. One mile above sea level (as in Denver, Colorado), water boils at 198°F (90°C). At higher altitudes, there is lower atmospheric pressure that causes a change in boiling point. Instructions for cooking at high altitudes are often included in recipes.

▼ Simmering ▼

Simmering means keeping the temperature of a liquid or mixture just under the boiling point. Bubbles form slowly and break below the surface. Like boiling, simmering is often done on the rangetop. However, food can also be cooked at a simmer in the oven or using other appliances, such as a slow cooker.

Simmering is usually preferable to boiling. Foods keep their shape better and fewer nutrients are lost. Cooking is sometimes begun by bringing the water or other cooking liquid to the boiling point. Then the heat is turned down and cooking continues at a simmer.

Foods that can be simmered include fresh or frozen vegetables, some fresh or dried fruits, meat, poultry, and fish. Simmering is a good way to tenderize less tender cuts of meat and poultry. Mixtures of food can be simmered together to make a soup or stew.

Braising involves browning food in a small amount of fat, then simmering in very little added liquid. Less tender cuts of meat are sometimes braised.

Simmering cooks foods just below the boiling point. Simmering helps foods such as vegetables retain their shapes and nutrients.

The Viking range allows cooks to prepare a number of foods in a variety of ways at the same time. With two gas ovens, six grates, and a grill, it can be used to roast, broil, grill, sauté, and simmer all at once. It also has special insulation to reduce the risk of kitchen fires from an overheated range. The Viking is an all-American creation, designed by a Mississippi contractor and his wife in 1980.

Follow Up

1. **Reteaching.** Ask students to explain the difference between boiling and simmering. Then have them list different foods that are cooked using these two methods. (Key Skill: *Communication*)
2. **Enrichment.** Have each student develop a collage of different foods that can be simmered. Have the students get the pictures for their collages out of magazines at home. After you collect the finished collages, show each one to the class and have them pick their favorite. (Key Skill: *Creativity*)

Hands-on Activity

Prepare a pasta salad in class using several techniques from this chapter. The main objective is to demonstrate boiling pasta. You might boil small amounts of several kinds of pasta to give students a chance to do the boiling and to show a variety of pasta to use in a warm or cold salad. Good salad pasta choices include rotini, macaroni, spaghetti, and shells.

While students are waiting for the water to boil and then timing the cooking pasta, have them chop, dice, slice, and shred raw vegetables for the salad.

Demonstrate proper draining methods when the pasta is cooked. Then show students how to rinse the pasta with cold water. Point out that is done for a cold salad only.

At the end of the class period (or the next day), sample the salads. Encourage students to create a similar salad at home with ingredients they have on hand.

Around the World

After reading the feature, have students look at home to see what kind of range or stove they have. Is it gas or electric? How many grates does it have? *(Answers will vary.)*

Teaching. . . Frying and Microwave Cooking (pp. 542-543)

Comprehension Check

1. What are the differences between deep-fat frying, pan frying, and stir frying? *(Foods are immersed in fat during deep-fat frying. Pan frying is done in a skillet with less fat. Stir-fried food is cooked and stirred quickly in a small amount of fat.)*
2. Why is microwave cooking so popular today? *(The main reason is that it saves time. Many convenience foods can be prepared even more quickly in the microwave oven. You can also reheat leftover foods, defrost frozen foods, and cook many fresh foods faster than with a conventional range.)*
3. What materials are safe to use in the microwave oven? *(Heatproof glass containers, plastic containers labeled "microwave-safe," paper plates labeled "microwave-safe," paper towels that do not contain plastic fibers or recycled paper, microwave-safe plastic wrap, waxed paper, and metal cookware labeled "microwave-safe.")*
4. What materials should not be used in the microwave oven? *(Brown paper bags, paper towels made of recycled paper, metal pans made for conventional ovens, large pieces of aluminum foil, and plastics that are not microwave-safe.)*

Learning Activities

1. **List.** Ask students to name foods that are commonly deep-fat fried as you write them on the board. In another column, ask them to tell you another way that these foods can be prepared. Compare the food items. What does deep-fat frying do to foods? (It adds fat.) Which food preparation methods listed are more healthful? Are there some realistic changes they can make in their eating habits? Since teens are probably not going to eliminate all deep-fat fried foods from their diets, encourage them to

SAFETY CHECK✓

To safely fry foods:

- Be sure food is dry before putting it in the fat or oil. Moisture can cause hot fat to spatter and burn you.
- Put food into the fat slowly and carefully so it won't splash. Use a spoon or tongs, not your fingers.
- If a grease fire starts, smother the flame with the cover of the pan or with salt. DO NOT put water on the fire.

Frying

Frying means cooking foods in fat. Frying can be done on the rangetop or with small appliances, such as an electric skillet or electric fryer.

If the food is immersed (completely covered) in fat, the method is called *deep-fat frying*. Chicken, sliced potatoes, and some other vegetables can be deep-fat fried. Deep-fat frying browns the food and makes it crisp. However, because this cooking method adds a considerable amount of fat to foods, it should not be used frequently.

Pan frying is done in a skillet with a smaller amount of fat. Pan frying is used for tender cuts of meat, fish, eggs, and some vegetables. When thinly sliced vegetables are cooked in a very small amount of fat, it is called *sautéing* (saw-TAY-ing).

Stir-frying is another variation. Foods such as vegetables, meat, poultry, or fish are cut into small pieces, then quickly cooked and stirred in a small amount of hot oil. Stir-frying is considered a fairly healthy way to prepare foods because little fat is used.

Pan frying

Stir-frying

Microwave Cooking

Why is microwave cooking so popular today? The main reason is that it saves time. Many convenience foods can be prepared even more quickly in the microwave oven. You can also reheat leftover foods, defrost frozen foods, and cook many fresh foods faster than with a conventional range. (Check page 521 for a discussion of the way microwave ovens work.)

Microwave cooking requires different materials and techniques than you would use in a conventional oven. Be sure to read the instruction book that came with the microwave oven you use.

More About Deep-Fat Frying

When fats and oils are heated at too high a temperature, they reach their smoking point or break down and develop an off-flavor and odor. For deep-fat frying, use a deep-fat frying thermometer to check the temperature. If the temperature is too low, food will soak up fat. If it's too high, food will burn on the outside.

For a tasty treat, try dipping sliced zucchini, mushroom, cauliflowerettes, onion chunks, and clumps of shredded carrots in a light batter and deep frying them briefly to make tempura.

Carefully choose cookware that is safe to use in the microwave oven.

SAFETY CHECK ✓

To safely use a microwave oven:

- Read the owner's manual and follow its instructions for use and care of the oven.
- Do not let young children use the microwave without supervision.
- In case of sparks or fire, leave the oven door closed. Turn off or unplug the oven.

Microwaves pass through some cookware materials and are reflected by others. During cooking, microwave energy is not evenly distributed. Food in some spots gets hotter than the rest. Trapped steam can cause food to "pop" or explode. For these reasons, it is important to follow the recipe or package directions and the guidelines that follow. They will help you cook food evenly and safely.

Materials to Use

Materials that are safe to use in the microwave oven include:

- Heatproof glass containers.
- Plastic containers labeled "microwave-safe."
- Paper plates labeled "microwave-safe."
- Paper towels that do not contain plastic fibers or recycled paper.
- Microwave-safe plastic wrap.
- Waxed paper.
- Metal cookware specifically designed for use in microwave ovens and labeled "microwave-safe."

Other materials are not safe to use in the microwave oven. Brown paper bags or paper towels made of recycled paper may burn when heated. Plastics that are not microwave-safe can melt from the heat of the food or cause chemicals to get into the food. Metal pans made for conventional ovens and large pieces of aluminum foil reflect microwaves. They can cause uneven cooking and damage the oven.

SAFETY CHECK ✓

When microwaving foods:

- Pierce foods with skins, like potatoes, in several places with a fork before placing them in the microwave. Otherwise they may explode in the oven.
- Do not microwave in tightly sealed containers. When using plastic wrap, fold back one corner or pierce the wrap in several places with a fork.
- Do not microwave eggs in the shell. They may explode during or after cooking.

Learning Activities (continued)

find ways to cut down on this type of food and to be aware of the disadvantages of consuming too much fat. (Key Skills: *Communication, Critical Thinking*)

2. **Posters.** Ask students to create posters regarding microwave safety. These posters should include things such as safe containers, unsafe containers, safe procedures, and unsafe procedures. Display the posters near microwave ovens. (Key Skills: *Cooperation, Creativity*)

Follow Up

1. **Reteaching.** Ask students to list the advantages and disadvantages of using a microwave oven. How has it changed meal preparation in their homes? In restaurants? In schools? (Key Skill: *Communication*)
2. **Enrichment.** Have students research how microwave ovens work. What safety precautions must manufacturers take to ensure that microwave ovens are contained? How safe are they? Who invented the microwave oven and when and where did it happen? (Key Skill: *Communication*)

SAFETY CHECK ✓

Have students read the feature. Discuss with students why it is important to follow safety rules when using a microwave oven.

SAFETY CHECK ✓

Have students read the feature. Make sure students understand what kind of mess will be made in the microwave oven if they don't follow these guidelines.

Teaching. . . Microwave Cooking and Conserving Nutrients (pp. 544-546)

Comprehension Check

1. Why is it a good idea to use round or ring-shaped containers to cook in a microwave oven? *(They help food cook more evenly.)*
2. What can happen to food that is overcooked in the microwave? *(It becomes too tough to eat.)*
3. Which cooking methods tend to rob food of the most nutrients? *(Boiling and frying.)*

Learning Activities

1. **Demonstration.** Prepare a head of broccoli or cauliflower for microwave cooking. Cut it apart and arrange it in a spoke pattern on a round container. Check it every minute or so as you cook it to see which part of it cooks first. You might include some large and some small pieces to compare cooking times for them, too. Small and inner pieces should cook more quickly than large or outer pieces. Ask students for suggestions on how to cook these vegetables efficiently. (Key Skill: *Communication*)
2. **Demonstration.** Bring several packages of microwave convenience food. Try to find some that have several cooking steps and have special containers. Show how to lift cellophane coverings from steaming hot foods. Ask students to think of ways they could duplicate purchased convenience foods using leftovers or common ingredients and containers at home. (Key Skill: *Communication*)

TIPS:

Buying a Microwave Oven
Have students read the feature. Then have them check newspaper and magazine ads to see how much different microwave ovens cost. Which one has the most features for the money? *(Answers will vary.)*

Use a ring or spoke pattern to insure that foods cook evenly in the microwave.

TIPS: *Buying a Microwave Oven*

These are some of the most popular microwave oven features. Consider your family's needs when deciding which features are most important:

- Temperature probes help prevent overcooking by taking the temperature of cooking food and shutting off the oven when it reaches a predetermined temperature.
- Automatic programs determine the right cooking time and power level based on the food, its weight, and how it is to be prepared.
- Multistage cooking allows the oven to automatically change power levels according to preset controls.

Preparing Food for Microwaving

The recipe or instruction book should tell you what type of container to use. Be sure the container fits into the microwave comfortably without touching the walls, door, or top of the oven. Round or ring-shaped containers are often recommended because they help food cook more evenly.

When heating liquids such as soups or sauces, use a container two to three times larger than the amount of food you are putting into it. Otherwise the liquid may spill over as it cooks or as you stir it.

Keep food pieces as uniform as possible. If they are different sizes and shapes, some will cook faster than others.

Arranging foods as specified in the recipe will also help ensure even cooking. Individual items are often arranged in a ring or a spoke pattern. The parts of the food that will take longest to cook should be placed toward the outside of the container, where they will receive the most microwave energy. These are usually the parts that are thicker, denser, or tougher, such as the thick part of a chicken leg or the tough stems of broccoli spears.

Covering food helps prevent drying out and spattering. If the dish does not have its own cover, use microwave-safe plastic wrap, waxed paper, or paper toweling.

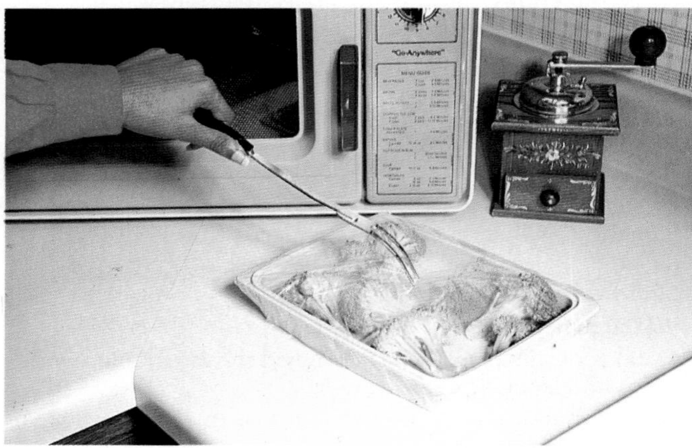

Pierce plastic wraps to release steam during microwave cooking. This helps eliminate steam burns.

More About Microwave Cooking

A common mistake when using the microwave oven to cook vegetables is that people often overcook the food. Tell students that it is best to shut off the oven before the food is done because the food continues to cook after the food has been removed from the oven. For example, the center of a potato that has been microwaved for five minutes will be too hard at first but will be cooked thoroughly after five minutes of standing at room temperature. Have students cook various types of vegetables in the microwave and compare the cooking and standing times.

Many convenience foods are packaged in microwavable containers. You may need to remove part of the package or follow other special instructions. Check the package directions for what to do.

Follow recipe directions for accurate microwave cooking.

Setting the Controls

Set the power level and cooking time as instructed in the recipe or package directions. Be accurate. A few extra seconds or minutes of cooking can make the food too tough to eat.

Cooking time depends partly on the particular microwave oven you use. The cooking power of a microwave oven is measured in watts. Most microwave recipes are written for 600- to 700-watt ovens. If your oven has a lower wattage, the cooking time will be a little longer. If your oven has a higher wattage, food will cook faster. Check the owner's manual to find the wattage of the oven you are using.

Some recipes give a range of time, such as 6 to 8 minutes. It's a good idea to use the shortest time suggested or to set the timer for a few seconds or minutes before you think the food will be done. You can always add more cooking time if needed.

During Cooking

For more even cooking, the directions may tell you to do one or more of the following partway through cooking.

- ***Rotate.*** Turn the dish around. If the directions say "¼ turn," the part of the dish that was facing front should now face the side of the oven. If the directions say "½ turn," the front of the dish should now face the back of the oven.
- ***Stir.*** Stir food from the outsides of the dish toward the center.
- ***Rearrange.*** Move the food around in the dish. Move pieces from the outside to the center and from the bottom to the top.
- ***Invert.*** Turn the food over in the dish.

Standing Time

After the cooking time is up, the directions may tell you to let the food stand. During the standing time, the food continues to cook even though the oven is shut off. Leave the food covered and in the oven for the amount of time specified. Then check the food for doneness. Add more cooking time if needed.

SAFETY CHECK✓

After microwaving:

- Use potholders when removing dishes from the oven. Hot food heats up the container.
- Be careful when removing covers or opening bags of popcorn. To avoid steam burns, keep the cover or bag tilted so the steam flows away from you.
- Watch out for hot spots that could burn your mouth. Stir to distribute the heat evenly, or let the food cool before eating.

Learning Activities (continued)

3. **Magazine Race.** Give each group a pile of magazines and a time limit. See how many references to microwave ovens they can find and cut out. These might include microwave products, special microwave cooking instructions, feature stories or columns, or ads for microwave ovens themselves. When the groups have finished, ask them if they were surprised by the number of references to microwave ovens. What does the popularity of microwaves tell us about lifestyles? (Key Skills: *Communication, Cooperation*)

Follow Up

1. **Reteaching.** Ask students how they would make popcorn in the microwave oven. Would they use a brown paper bag? Would any microwave-safe container work? How should they open hot bags of prepackaged microwave popcorn? (Key Skill: *Communication*)
2. **Extension.** Use the extension information handout on p. 58 of the *Extending the Text* booklet in the TCR.
3. **Enrichment.** Ask students to check out several cookbooks to find recipes for soups or stews in which they could use liquids from vegetables that have been cooked. Ask them how they would store the liquids until they used them. (Key Skill: *Decision Making*)

SAFETY CHECK✓

Have students read the safety check. Emphasize how badly students could be burned if they do not follow the safety guidelines listed in this feature.

Photo Focus

Discuss the photo at the bottom of page 544 with the students. Ask students if they have had any accidents while microwaving food. What happened? Were they injured? *(Answers will vary.)*

Completing the Chapter

For Review

1. Emphasize the main concepts using the summary.
2. Have students complete the "Facts to Recall." (Answers below.)

For Reteaching

1. **Reteaching.** Use the activity on p. 58 of the *Reteaching and Practical Skills* booklet in the TCR.

For Enrichment

1. **Enrichment.** Use the activity on p. 70 of the *Enrichment Activities* booklet in the TCR.

For Evaluation

1. Choose items from "Ideas to Explore" and "Activities to Try."
2. Use the chapter test on pp. 95-96 in the testing booklet of the TCR or use the testmaker software.

Facts to Recall Answers

1. It is your clue to the tool you need and the technique to follow.
2. Cutting in is a way of mixing a solid fat with dry ingredients. You use a pastry blender, a fork, or two knives and a cutting motion. Folding involves combining a delicate mixture with other ingredients. You use a rubber or plastic scraper and a gentle, up-and-down motion.
3. To shred means to cut or tear food into long, thin strips. To grate food is to rub it over a grater into fine particles.
4. Foods are basted to add flavor and to keep them from drying out. Meat drippings, sauces or marinades, and melted butter are often used for basting.
5. **Any two:** use sharp knives; always use a cutting board; when using one hand to hold food steady, tuck your fingers under.

Conserving Nutrients

During preparation, foods can lose some of their nutrients. By taking care when you handle and prepare foods, you can help keep as many nutrients as possible. Here are some guidelines.

- Leave the skins on fruits and vegetables if possible. The skin contains vitamins, minerals, and fiber.
- Consider nutrition when choosing cooking methods. Boiling and frying tend to rob food of the most nutrients. Baking or roasting, broiling, microwaving, and simmering in a small amount of water generally conserve more nutrients.
- Avoid overcooking food. Carefully follow the directions for cooking temperature and time.
- Save the liquid in which food is cooked. It contains valuable nutrients. If the liquid will not be eaten with the food, you might use it for making soup.

Learning to prepare food is like any other skill you acquire. A good beginning is to start with the basics and then practice. Some attempts will be more successful than others, but you will always learn.

Now that you know the meaning of many cooking terms and techniques, you are off to a good start. You may find, like many people have, that preparing food is enjoyable and rewarding.

TAKING ACTION

Learning Terms and Techniques

Jason has an ambitious plan. To celebrate his mother's promotion at work, he is going to cook her a special dinner this weekend with some of her favorite foods — roasted Cornish hen, mixed vegetables, and chocolate cake. "I know it's a lot of work," he admits, "but with all our kitchen gadgets, a good cookbook, and the help of a good friend like you, I know I can pull it off."

You know Jason has more enthusiasm than experience. If he is to create a masterpiece — and not a mess — he will need a crash course in cooking terms and techniques. And, if you are to help him, so will you.

Using Your Resourcefulness

- Where can you and Jason find recipes for the dishes he wants to make?
- Where can you find explanations for the cooking terms you don't understand?
- How can you decide which utensil to use for each technique?
- Where can you learn suggestions for preparing the different recipes, for example, ideas on seasoning the hens and vegetables or garnishing the cake?
- Who might you contact if you have questions as you cook, or if a recipe doesn't turn out as you think it should?

TAKING ACTION

Have students read the feature. Then have a class discussion about the different cooking terms and techniques they would have to be familiar with in order to help Jason prepare this special dinner for his mother. To guide this discussion, you may want to have students answer the *Using Your Resourcefulness* questions at the end of this feature.

Using Your Resourcefulness Answers

- Answers will vary. Possible answers might include Jason's mother's recipe box, a cookbook, and magazines.
- Answers will vary and might include family and consumer sciences books and magazines.

Chapter 46 Review

Summary

In this chapter, you have read about:

- Recipe terms for mixing, cutting, and other ways of preparing foods.
- Different cooking methods and their uses, advantages, and disadvantages.
- Tips on using a microwave oven for safe, even cooking.
- How to save nutrients in the foods you prepare.

Facts to Recall

1. When reading a recipe, why should you pay attention to the exact term used?
2. What is the difference between cutting in and folding ingredients? Explain in terms of ingredients, tools, and motion used.
3. What is the difference between shredding and grating food?
4. Why is food basted? Name three types of food products used for basting.
5. Give two guidelines for using a knife safely.
6. What is the difference between boiling and simmering food? Which technique is preferred and why?
7. List three variations of frying.
8. Identify four materials that are safe to use in a microwave oven.
9. When cooking with a microwave oven, what parts of the food should you place toward the outside of the container? Why?
10. When preparing food in a microwave oven, why is it a good idea to use the shortest suggested cooking time?
11. Give three guidelines for conserving nutrients when preparing food.

Ideas to Explore

1. Discuss examples of how using the wrong cooking techniques or tools could affect the way a recipe turns out.
2. Discuss some advantages and some disadvantages of microwave cooking.
3. Think about a problem you have had in using a kitchen tool. What do you think caused the problem? How could this problem have been prevented or solved?

Activities to Try

1. Find a recipe in a cookbook or other source. Identify and explain the different terms used.
2. Find recipes that give directions for both microwave and conventional preparation. What are the differences in tools, ingredients, amounts of ingredients used, and techniques? What do you think are the reasons for these changes?

LINK TO *Science*

CONTAINER SHAPES AND MICROWAVE COOKING

The shape of the cooking container often effects how evenly food cooks in the microwave. Using a canned convenience pasta product, compare how evenly the products cooks in a rectangular, round, and doughnut-shaped container. Microwave each container for 3 minutes at 100 % power. Answer the following:

- Describe how evenly the pasta product cooked in each container. Include the similarities and differences.
- How did the appearance of the pasta product compare in each container? Explain.
- Did any of the pasta products have an overcooked or burnt flavor due to uneven cooking? Explain.

Facts to Recall Answers (continued)

6. Food is boiled when it is cooked in a liquid in which bubbles rise and break on the surface. It is simmered when it is cooked in a liquid in which bubbles form slowly and break below the surface. Simmering is usually preferred because foods keep their shape better and lose fewer nutrients.
7. **Any three:** deep-fat frying, pan frying, sautéing, stir-frying.
8. **Any four:** heatproof glass containers; plastic containers labeled "microwave-safe"; paper plates labeled "microwave-safe"; paper towels that do not contain plastic fibers or recycled paper; microwave-safe plastic wrap; waxed paper; metal cookware specifically designed and labeled for use in microwave ovens.
9. The parts that will take longest to cook, because in this way they will receive the most microwave energy.
10. A few extra seconds or minutes of cooking can make the food too tough to eat, and you can always add more cooking time if needed.
11. **Any three:** leave the skins on fruits and vegetables if possible; consider nutrition when choosing cooking methods; avoid overcooking food; save the liquid in which food is cooked.

Ideas to Explore

1. Answers will vary.
2. Answers will vary.
3. Answers will vary.

- Answers will vary and might include looking in a family and consumer sciences book for guidance or asking a family and consumer sciences teacher for help.
- Answers will vary. Possible answers might include family and consumer sciences books, a family and consumer sciences teacher, cookbooks, magazines, and a nutritionist.
- Answers will vary and might include a professional cook, a family and consumer sciences teacher, or the cook in the family.

LINK TO *Science*

Answers

- Answers will vary.
- Answers will vary, but food in rectangular dish should show evidence of uneven cooking.
- Answers will vary.

Preparing to Teach

Chapter Outline

Chapter Resources

The following booklet materials may be found in the *Teacher's Classroom Resources* box:

- Lesson Plans, p. 52
- Student Workbook, *Study Guide,* pp. 199-200; *Juanita's Problem,* p. 201; *Kitchen Scramble,* p. 202
- Color Transparencies, *Teamwork in the Kitchen,* CT-51
- Personal Safety, *Kitchen Safety,* p. 46
- Technology and Computers, pp. 43, 45
- Cooperative Learning, p. 59
- Extending the Text, *Don't Be Poisoned by the Foods You Prepare!,* p. 59
- Reteaching and Practical Skills, *Packing Your Lunch,* p. 59
- Enrichment Activities, *Conservation Begins at Home,* p. 71
- Chapter and Unit Tests, pp. 97-98
- Testmaker Software

Also see:

- Leadership and Citizenship
- Meeting the Special Needs of Students
- Linking Home, School, and Community

ABCNews InterActive™ Videodiscs

- *Food and Nutrition*

See the ABCNews InterActive™ Bar Code Correlation booklet for applicable segments.

CHAPTER 47 Working in the Kitchen

OBJECTIVES

- *Demonstrate safety and sanitation procedures for working with food.*
- *Work cooperatively in the foods laboratory.*
- *Organize workspace, plan time schedules, and conserve resources in the kitchen.*

TERMS TO LEARN

- ***food-borne illness***
- ***bacteria***
- ***pre-preparation tasks***
- ***kitchen work center***

Working in the kitchen can be an enjoyable experience. To keep it that way, make the kitchen a safe and sanitary place to work and use good management skills.

Kitchen Safety

More accidents take place in the kitchen than any other room in the home. The same accidents can occur in the foods lab, too. To prepare yourself for accidents that do happen, become familiar with basic first aid techniques. Know where first aid supplies are kept.

You can help prevent accidents by thinking ahead and working safely. Following are some guidelines that can help you to make the kitchen or foods lab a safe place to work. Think of other safety rules to add to the list.

How many hazards can you find in this kitchen?

Preventing Cuts and Bruises

It is very easy to cut yourself in the kitchen because of the sharp utensils used. Falls are another common cause of injury. To prevent cuts and bruises:

- Wash knives and other sharp objects separately. Never put a sharp knife in a sink of sudsy water to soak.
- Store sharp knives separately from other utensils.
- Keep knives sharp so they will be less likely to slip while cutting.

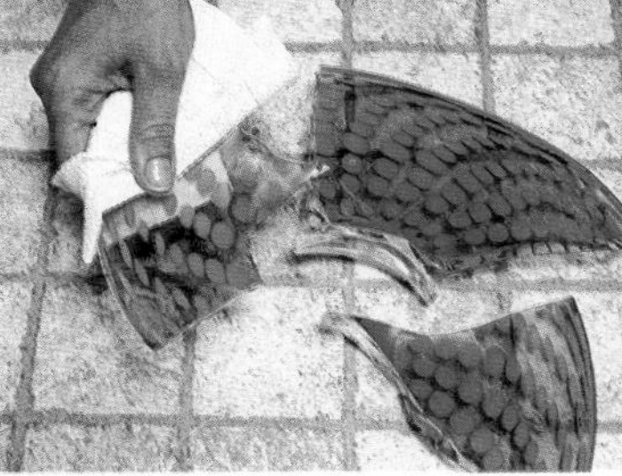

To prevent cuts, use a damp paper towel to pick up broken glass.

More About Safety

Across the United States, 20,000 deaths and nearly 25 million injuries occur in homes each year. Many are kitchen related. Falls are the most common home accident. Fires and burns occur with the second-most frequency.

Introducing the Chapter

Motivators

1. **Bulletin Board.** Make a 12-inch stop sign out of red paper. Cut out a matching green sign that says "Go" on it and glue it to the back of the stop sign. Punch a hole in the top and hang it in the middle of the bulletin board by a short piece of string. Have the red side showing. Draw pictures of unsafe situations and hang them in a similar fashion around the stop sign. Draw pictures of the situation corrected and glue them to the back of the unsafe picture. Have students identify the situation. Then flip to the go sign and go back over the situations, flipping each picture so that the corrected picture is showing. You might have students participate by drawing the situations and/or drawing the corrections. (Key Skills: *Communication, Creativity*)
2. **Discussion.** Ask your students if they have ever pulled out a plug by the cord, used a knife in a toaster, used a dish towel as a pot holder, eaten a piece of pizza left on the counter all night, stood on a rickety chair to change a light bulb, etc. Then tell the class that many accidents in the home occur in the kitchen, and that they might be an accident waiting to happen. Direct them to the chapter to see why. (Key Skill: *Communication*)

Chapter Objectives and Vocabulary

1. Have students read the chapter objectives and rephrase the objectives as questions.
2. Ask students to state, in their own words, the purpose of studying this chapter.
3. Pronounce the vocabulary terms listed on the previous page. Ask students whether they are familiar with any of these. Explain that the terms will be defined in the chapter.

Guided Reading

1. Have students read the chapter and use the Study Guide on pp. 199-200 of the *Student Workbook*.

Teaching. . . Kitchen Safety (pp. 549-551)

Comprehension Check

1. What should you do before trying to retrieve an object from a garbage disposal? *(Unplug the unit.)*
2. Why should you dry food thoroughly before putting it into hot fat? *(Water causes fat to spatter.)*
3. How should you deal with a grease fire in the kitchen? *(Smother it with a pan cover or with salt.)*
4. Why should you not connect an electrical appliance while you are standing on a wet floor? *(You could get a shock.)*

Learning Activities

2. **Group Work.** Divide the safety tips in this chapter among groups of students. Ask each group to demonstrate their safety procedures and precautions for the rest of the class. Encourage them to be creative in their presentations. Give students class time to work together, depending on how long you want the presentation to be, and grade them for creativity, clarity, and staying on task. (Key Skills: *Creativity, Cooperation*)

- ▶ Use a cutting board. Keep your fingertips out of the way of the knife.
- ▶ Before trying to retrieve an object from a garbage disposal, unplug the unit.
- ▶ Close cabinet doors and drawers when not in use. Otherwise, someone could walk into them and be injured.
- ▶ Use a safe ladder or step stool for reaching high or hard-to-get items.
- ▶ Wipe up spills from the floor right away. Do not walk on a wet floor.

▼ Preventing Burns ▼

You can't be too careful when working around gas and electric appliances. Here are some ways to prevent burns.

- ▶ Teach young children not to touch the heating units on a range.
- ▶ Use flat-bottomed and well-balanced cooking utensils on the range so they will not tip over easily.
- ▶ Turn handles of cooking utensils inward on the range so they will not be knocked off the burner. Be sure handles do not extend over another burner or surface unit that is hot.
- ▶ Use thick, dry potholders when handling hot utensils.
- ▶ Remove the cover from a pan by lifting the far side of the cover first. That way the steam flows away from you.
- ▶ Dry food thoroughly before putting it into hot fat in a pan. Water causes fat to spatter.
- ▶ Use kitchen tongs to remove food from hot water and to turn food that is frying. The tongs will help to keep your hand away from the hot fat or water.

Using thick, dry potholders helps prevent injury from burns.

More About *Safety Tips*

The most effective way to prevent accidents is to eliminate the hazards that are a part of daily living. Here are some additional tips:

- Are all hard-surfaced floors clean? Are spills wiped up immediately?
- Is non-skid wax used on all polished floors?
- Do you know how to shut off the electrical, water, and gas sources to your home?
- Does your home have adequate electrical power in all areas to safely operate all your electrical appliances?
- Is the ground prong still on all electrical plugs that came equipped with one?
- Are small electrical appliances (electric knives, coffee pots, blenders, etc.) unplugged when they are not in use?

Preventing Fires

Fires can start very easily at the range. If a grease fire starts, do not throw water on the flames — they will spread. Instead, smother the fire with the cover of the pan or with salt. Keep a working fire extinguisher in the kitchen and learn how to use it. Here are some ways to prevent a fire from starting.

- Avoid wearing dangling jewelry or loose-fitting clothes. They can get caught in appliances or catch fire over heating units.
- Keep paper towels, dish towels, and electric cords away from the range.
- Do not use the range as a source of heat to warm the kitchen.
- Avoid using a dish towel to handle hot utensils. Its drooping ends could catch on fire.
- Be sure no more than two appliances are plugged into an electrical outlet at one time. Overloading circuits may result in a fire.

An *electrical octopus* overloads a circuit and may cause a fire.

Preventing Electrical Shock

Electrical equipment should be in good working order and used properly. Remember that water and metal are good conductors of electricity. You could be, too, if you're not careful. To prevent electrical shock:

- Dry hands thoroughly before touching electrical equipment.
- Never connect an electrical appliance while you are standing on a wet surface.
- Do not put the heating unit, motor, or cord of an electrical appliance in water unless it is marked "immersible."
- Always unplug a cord from the wall outlet before removing it from the appliance. Otherwise electricity continues going through the cord, and you can receive a shock.
- Disconnect an appliance by pulling on the plug. If you pull on the cord, it can become damaged and cause a shock.
- Keep forks and knives out of electric toasters. If food gets stuck in a toaster, disconnect the appliance, turn it over, and try to shake the food loose.

Preventing Poisoning

Household chemicals, such as cleaning products, are often kept in the kitchen. Many contain dangerous substances that can be poisonous if swallowed, inhaled, or splashed on the

- Is the hot-water temperature 120°F or less to prevent burns?
- Do you keep matches where young children cannot reach them?
- Are small children kept out of the kitchen while you are cooking, baking, and handling hot objects?

Learning Activities (continued)

3. **Discussion.** Ask students to tell about accidents they have had (or known of) in the kitchen. Discuss how they might have been averted. Have a few back-up incidents of your own to get the ball rolling. (Key Skill: *Communication*)
4. **Speaker.** Ask a science teacher to visit your classroom and give a short presentation on electrical current in outlets and plugs, grease fires, and/or mixing household chemicals. Make sure the teacher directs the information toward safety in the kitchen. Encourage students to ask questions. (Key Skill: *Communication*)
5. **Demonstration.** If you have a deep sink or another good place to start a fire safely, pour some grease in the bottom and set it on fire. First, try dousing it with water. Then try salt or a pan cover. Practice this beforehand so you will know exactly what will happen. Keep a fire extinguisher handy. You might pretend to get a little rattled to see if the students can keep their heads in an emergency — which a real fire would be. Tell them later that was part of the demonstration. (Key Skills: *Communication, Problem Solving*)

Follow Up

1. **Reteaching.** Ask students to close their books and put their notes away. Then have them make a list of kitchen safety procedures and precautions for you to write on the board or on a poster to keep for reviewing. (Key Skill: *Communication*)
2. **Enrichment.** Ask students to find out why appliances should not be pulled out by their cords, why non-immersibles should not be wet, and why they should not use flatware in toasters. This could be done by individuals or groups and reported to the class. (Key Skill: *Communication*)

Teaching. . .

Preventing Poisoning; Food Safety and Sanitation (pp. 552-553)

Comprehension Check

1. Why should you keep the number of the nearest poison control center by your telephone? *(Because many household chemicals and cleaning products can be poisonous if swallowed, inhaled, or splashed on the skin.)*
2. What three things are needed for bacteria to grow? *(Food, moisture, and the right temperature.)*
3. When should you wash your hands if you are going to handle food? Why? *(Wash your hands before you handle food, after you cough or sneeze, after you use the toilet, and after you touch pets. Otherwise bacteria on your hands can be transferred to the food.)*
4. What four foods may contain harmful bacteria? What should you do to destroy the bacteria? *(Raw meat, poultry, fish, and eggs. These foods should always be cooked thoroughly so that the bacteria are destroyed.)*

Learning Activities

1. **Epidemic Research.** Impress your students with the reality and danger of bacteria by "exposing" them to information about well-known local or national bacteria epidemics. This can be done in one of several ways. You can check the *Reader's Guide to Periodical Literature* or your local newspaper for information on outbreaks of hepatitis, salmonella, etc. You might also include encephalitis. You can present the information yourself or give it to groups of students to present to the class. If you have lots of time, ask the students to do the research themselves. Be sure the origin of the epidemic, the manner in which it was spread, the remedy, and the consequences are clear. (Key Skills: *Communication, Cooperation*)

Store hazardous cleaning agents and chemicals away from food and children.

skin. Keep the number of the nearest poison control center by the telephone and call it in an emergency. To prevent poisoning:

- Keep drain openers, household cleaners, and poisons in their original containers. Read the warnings and directions on the label. Follow directions exactly.
- Keep household chemicals where children cannot reach them. Store them away from food items.
- Avoid mixing household chemicals together. Some mixtures cause dangerous chemical reactions.

Food Safety and Sanitation

Many people get an upset stomach and think they have the flu. Sometimes they do. Other times they may have a **food-borne illness**, often called food poisoning. It is caused by eating spoiled food or food containing harmful bacteria. **Bacteria** are one-celled living things so small they can be seen only with a microscope. Many people call harmful bacteria germs. Food containing harmful bacteria does not always smell or taste spoiled. For that reason, many people aren't aware of the real cause of their illness.

Bacteria require three things to grow: food, moisture, and the right temperature. With just a little carelessness, you can create these ideal growing conditions in your kitchen at home or in the foods lab at school.

You can prevent food-borne illness by practicing sanitation. Sanitation is keeping bacteria down to as small a number as possible through cleanliness and proper food handling. Follow these guidelines to prevent food-borne illness.

Cleanliness

Bacteria are present everywhere. Practicing cleanliness helps keep harmful bacteria out of food.

- Keep the kitchen clean and free of pests.
- Wear clean clothes when you work with food.
- Wash your hands before you handle food, after you cough or sneeze, after you use the toilet, and after you touch pets. Otherwise bacteria on your hands can be transferred to the food.
- If you have a cut or break in the skin on your hands, wear rubber or plastic gloves.
- If you taste food during cooking, use a clean spoon each time.

Always wash your hands before handling food.

More About Salmonella

New forms of salmonella bacteria are appearing, increasing the possibility of food-borne illness. In 1988, it was estimated that one out of every three chickens leaving processing plants was contaminated. Salmonella in eggs is becoming an increasingly serious problem. A few states are banning the shipment of eggs from highly contaminated areas. Proper sanitation and cooking can prevent illness due to salmonella.

How Clean Are You?

Materials
growing medium

Equipment
4 petri dishes

Directions:
Using the petri dishes with growing medium your teacher has obtained from the science department, contaminate the growing medium with the following samples from your body: scrapings from under fingernails, a hair, and scrapings from your face. As a control, wash your hands thoroughly using soap and warm water, then rub your clean fingers across the growing medium in another petri dish. Be sure to label each of the petri dishes with the contaminant each contains. Allow the bacteria to grow at room temperature. Check the results after 24 hours.

- ✔ Which samples did the bacteria grow on?
- ✔ Did any bacteria grow on the control dish?
- ✔ Draw some conclusions about the importance of cleanliness in the kitchen.

- ▶ When handling dishes and other eating utensils, avoid touching surfaces that come in contact with food. For instance, hold forks by the handle, not by the tines.
- ▶ Change dishcloths and dish towels often. Have separate towels for wiping hands and wiping dishes.

▼ Handling Meat, Poultry, Fish, and Eggs ▼

Raw meat, poultry, fish, and eggs may contain harmful bacteria. These foods should always be cooked thoroughly so that the bacteria are destroyed. Never eat these foods when raw or only partly cooked. Do not cook the food partway and finish cooking another time — it will not be safe to eat.

When you touch raw meat, poultry, fish, or eggs, the bacteria can get on your hands. They can also get on any utensils or dishes, such as a cutting board, knife, or plate, that came in contact with the raw food. Immediately after handling the raw food, wash your hands and the utensils with hot, soapy water. Otherwise the bacteria could be transferred to other foods, such as a salad or cooked meat, and cause illness.

INVESTIGATE!

How Clean Are You?

Materials: Growing medium.

Equipment: Four petri dishes.

Purpose: To help students understand the importance of cleanliness when preparing food.

Outcomes:

- Most of the samples should have grown bacteria, some more than others.
- Little, if any, bacteria should have grown in the control dish.
- Cleanliness is essential for avoiding contamination of food during preparation.

Learning Activities (continued)

2. **Demonstration.** Prepare a piece or two of chicken to bake. Use a plastic cutting board and wash your hands and all the utensils and sink in hot, soapy water. As you prepare the chicken, tell the class what you are doing and why you are doing it. At the same time, you might demonstrate how to remove the skin from chicken and how to bake it for use in another dish, such as chicken salad. Instead of just doing all the correct things, you could ask the students to give you directions. For example, you could pretend to not know whether to use a plastic cutting board or a wooden bread board. Be sure to ask students the reasons behind their directions to you. (Key Skills: *Communication, Decision Making*)
3. **Video.** Show the class a video on bacteria in food preparation. There are some excellent productions available, and, since bacteria cannot be seen by the naked eye, cameras are especially helpful for this subject. (Key Skill: *Communication*)

Follow Up

1. **Reteaching.** Ask students to pretend they are bacteria. As individuals, as groups, or as a class, have them talk about places they like to live, climates they like, and other conditions they like. (Key Skill: *Communication*)
2. **Enrichment.** Have students contact the health department and/or local food establishments to find out what precautions are taken to prevent any outbreaks of bacteria. Have them prepare oral or written reports of their findings. (Key Skill: *Communication*)

Teaching. . .
Proper Temperatures, Kitchen Management, and Working in the School Foods Lab
(pp. 554-555)

Comprehension Check

1. At what temperatures do bacteria multiply quickly? *(Between 60°F and 125°F [15°C and 50°C].)*
2. What does working with others teach you? *(It teaches you how to be a team member and to handle responsibility.)*
3. What is the purpose of having a plan for working in the foods lab? *(So everyone will be successful.)*
4. What should you do to prepare your person for working in the foods lab? *(Tie back long hair, roll up dangling sleeves, and wash your hands.)*

Learning Activities

1. **Demonstration.** Choose a favorite recipe that involves quite a few pre-preparation tasks. Make the recipe in front of the class, explaining what you are doing and why you are doing it. If there is time, tell the students why you like to make the recipe and some memorable occasions on which you have served it. (Key Skill: *Communication*)
2. **Demonstration with Directions.** A variation on the previous activity would be to distribute copies of the recipe to students at the beginning of class. Let them suggest an order of preparation for you. If your usual method varies in some way that is better, explain why you do it that way. Then prepare the recipe. In order to keep their attention, you might falter along the way so that students can catch you. (Key Skills: *Communication, Critical Thinking*)

Store foods at proper temperatures to prevent bacterial growth.

▼ Proper Temperatures ▼

Bacteria multiply quickly between 60°F and 125°F (15°C and 50°C). To make sure food stays out of this danger zone, keep it hot or cold.

- Serve hot foods steaming hot, above 140°F (60°C). If you prepared a large quantity, keep the extra portions hot during the meal rather than bringing all the food to the table.
- Keep cold foods cold until you are ready to use them. Be sure the refrigerator temperature is 40°F (5°C) or below.
- To thaw frozen food, place it in the refrigerator overnight (longer if needed) or use a microwave oven. Never let frozen food sit out at room temperature to thaw.
- After a meal, refrigerate or freeze leftovers right away. Don't let them sit on a counter or table for long. Put hot foods into shallow containers so they will cool more quickly.
- Take special care when packing food for a lunch or picnic. Use ice packs and an insulated container to keep cold foods cold. Use vacuum bottles to keep hot foods hot. (See page 492 for more information.)

Kitchen Management

When you plan and prepare meals, you use resources such as money, food, fuel, water, time, and energy. Good management helps you make the best use of your resources. This is true whether you are working in the foods lab at school or in the kitchen at home.

▼ Working in the School Foods Lab ▼

Most of your work in the school foods lab will be done in groups. Learning how to work with others is as important as any other skill you practice in the lab.

Working with others gives you an opportunity to learn to be a team member and to handle responsibility. Each person in the group is important. You are each responsible for certain jobs. When one member of the team doesn't do a job correctly or on time, it affects everyone else. When all members pitch in and do their share, the group is a winner. They're successful.

In every phase of the lab — planning, working, and evaluating — you'll need to cooperate with others. Cooperation makes the work pleasant for everyone.

More About Microwave Ovens and Food Safety

Do not refreeze meat or poultry thawed in a microwave oven. Some areas of meat thawed in a microwave actually begin to cook because defrosting exposes food to very low cooking temperatures. The warm temperatures increase the chance that bacteria present will multiply to dangerously high levels. Refreezing will halt further growth of bacteria but won't kill what is already there. If you thaw food in a microwave, cook it immediately.

Working cooperatively in a group allows all group members to achieve success and have a pleasant experience.

AROUND THE WORLD

In some remote African villages, bread baking is not done in the home. Instead, the bread dough is mixed daily by each family, then taken to a community oven in the village to be baked. In this way, bread baking is as much a social activity as a dietary necessity. As African nations become more developed, however, this practice is growing less common. What do you think might be some consequences of the loss of this custom?

Planning Your Work

To work in the foods lab your group will need a plan, just as a coach has a game plan for a team. Plans are made so that everyone will be successful.

Each part of the plan is important. For example, your teacher may ask you to list the ingredients you need and the amounts. Your supplies will be added to the total grocery list for the lab. If your list isn't accurate, then your group or another group may not have the ingredients needed.

When you are in a foods lab, you'll often be working against the clock. Lab times are usually short, so you'll have to plan to use the time wisely. Work out a schedule by listing the major jobs in the order they need to be done. Estimate how long it will take to do each job.

Be sure your schedule allows time for getting ready to cook. Before you actually begin following the steps in the recipe, you will need to:

- Put on a clean apron, tie back long hair, roll up dangling sleeves, and wash your hands.
- Get out all the ingredients and equipment you'll need. This will save time and steps later and prevent mix-ups.

Following a work plan and time schedule keeps you organized.

Learning Activities (continued)

3. **Group Work.** Give groups copies of several recipes, each containing pre-preparation tasks. Ask students to make a plan for preparing each recipe. Have groups go over each other's plans and make corrections or suggestions. (Key Skills: *Communication, Cooperation*)

Follow Up

1. **Reteaching.** Ask individuals or groups to make posters illustrating each pre-preparation task, including personal readiness. (Key Skill: *Creativity*)
2. **Enrichment.** Have students copy their favorite recipe from their family collection and explain the recipe briefly. Have classmates determine if the recipe could be made in the foods lab, considering skills, budget, and time to prepare the recipe. (Key Skills: *Communication, Decision Making*)

AROUND THE WORLD

After students have read the feature, have them investigate another country's customs when it comes to preparing food. Do any of them involve group preparation? *(Answers will vary.)*

Photo Focus

Discuss the photo at the top of page 555 with the students. Ask them if they would rather work in a group or individually. Have the students explain their answers. *(Answers will vary.)*

Teaching. . .
Planning Your Work, Carrying Out Your Plan, and Cleaning Up
(pp. 556-557)

Comprehension Check

1. What are some pre-preparation tasks that you can do? *(Preheat the oven, grease pans, measure ingredients, peel or chop foods, heat water, and/or melt fat.)*
2. What clean-up method can you use as you go along to make the final cleaning job easier? *(Have warm, sudsy water available to wash dishes as you use them.)*
3. How do you take care of a cooking utensil that is very dirty or greasy? *(Scrape or wipe it and then soak it.)*
4. Which dishes do you wash first when you are doing the dishes by hand? *(The cleanest — usually the glassware and then flatware.)*

Learning Activities

1. **Demonstration.** Draw a rough floor plan of a foods lab on the board. Indicate each team member with an X and line up the team "players" in the lab. As each team member moves to do a preparation task, circle the X and draw an arrow to the spot where he or she will be — as if you are a football coach describing a complicated play. Emphasize the importance of each team member doing his or her job correctly and at the right time. Also remind students that *each* job is important. In contrast, you might draw another "play" diagram with each team member wandering all over the lab

MEETING SPECIAL NEEDS

. . . In Kitchen Design

After reading the feature, have students discuss other ways in which a kitchen could be modified to accommodate physically disabled people. *(Answers will vary.)*

MEETING SPECIAL NEEDS

In Kitchen Design

People who are physically disabled are often at a greater risk for home accidents. With careful thought and planning, home design and furnishings can be modified to meet special safety needs. The following modifications in a kitchen will make it easier to maneuver in a wheelchair:

- Providing complete work centers with lower-than-normal counters and sinks with space beneath to accomodate a wheelchair.
- Providing space beneath a built-in cooktop instead of base cabinets to accommodate a wheelchair.
- Including base cabinets with pullout storage trays.
- Placing range controls to the side of the burners to avoid reaching across hot burners.
- Installing a built-in oven at counter level to prevent leg burns from hot oven doors.

For safety, wipe up spills immediately.

- Complete tasks that you need to do before you combine ingredients. For instance, you may need to preheat the oven, grease baking pans, measure ingredients, peel or chop foods, heat water, or melt fat. These are called **pre-preparation tasks**.

After you have listed all the tasks, decide who will do each job. Divide the work fairly so that everyone shares responsibility.

The advantage of teamwork is that several tasks can be dovetailed, or done at the same time. If a casserole calls for several different items to be chopped, more than one person can do the chopping. Someone can wash utensils or set the table while others are finishing the food preparation.

Carrying Out Your Plan

When you go into the lab, be sure you know what your assigned jobs are. Post your time plan where everyone in the group can see it.

Follow the rules about dress, behavior, and lab procedures. The rules are set for your safety and to help you work within the time limits of your class period.

When you complete your work, volunteer to help someone else who is behind. If you see something that needs to be done, pitch in and do it.

Cleaning Up

Cleaning up as you go along will help the final cleanup go faster. If food spills on the counter or floor, wipe it up right away. Have a sink or dishpan of warm, sudsy water ready. When you finish using a utensil, put it in the water to soak (except for sharp knives). Whenever you have a few minutes while waiting for something to cook, wash and rinse the utensils.

When you have finished preparing the recipe, transfer the food to a serving dish or plate. If the cooking utensil is very dirty or greasy, scrape it or wipe with a paper towel. Then put the utensil in warm, sudsy water to soak. If food is stuck to a pan, simmer a detergent-and-water solution in it for about 10 minutes.

After you have enjoyed the food you made, it's time for the final cleanup. Clear the dishes from the table and store any leftovers properly. Scrape food scraps into the garbage container or disposal. If you left pots and pans soaking, empty the sink, rinse the pots and pans, and place them with the other dishes to be washed. Follow the suggestions on page 557 for washing dishes.

Remember to wipe off tables and counters and sweep the floor. Leave the foods lab clean and ready for the next group.

How to ...
Wash Dishes by Hand

- After scraping, stack dishes carefully at one side of the sink. Fill the sink with hot water and liquid detergent.
- Use a clean dishcloth. For stuck-on food, use a scrubber or scouring pad. (Nylon scrubbers can be used on most dishes and cookware without scratching.)
- Start with the cleanest items and work your way to the dirtiest ones. Usually this means you wash glassware first, then flatware and dishes, and finally pots and pans.
- Handle dishes carefully so they don't break or chip.
- Change the wash water if it becomes cold, greasy, or dirty.
- Rinse dishes with hot water. Place them in a rack or on a towel so water can drain.
- Dry with a clean dish towel or leave the dishes in the rack to air dry.
- Put dishes away carefully as soon as they are dry.

Automatic Dishwasher

- Be sure you have read the instructions in the owner's manual.
- Scrape dishes. Rinse them if the owner's manual recommends it.
- Load the dishwasher as instructed in the owner's manual.
- Add detergent to detergent dispenser. (Rinse agents can be used to prevent spotting.)
- Select correct cycle and start dishwasher. (Note: A cycle will go through several rinses and one or two washes.)
- Use dishwasher dry cycle, or air dry.
- Put dishes away carefully as soon as they are dry.

Learning Activities (continued)

trying to find something to do or looking for a piece of equipment. You might show several students colliding and "dropping the ball." (Key Skills: *Communication, Management*)

2. **Group Work.** Before the next foods lab, ask groups to make a plan just for cleaning up. Make sure each area is specifically covered by at least one person and that each person has some clean-up responsibilities. Have groups circulate their plans among the other groups so that they can see other ways of doing the job. After the lab is over, ask students to review their plan. How did it work? Did everyone do his or her job? Did any jobs involve more (or less) work than the group had originally thought? What changes would they make in their plan the next time? (Key Skills: *Cooperation, Management*)
3. **Discussion.** Ask students to share how they do dishes at home. Do they take turns? How do they decide whose turn it is? Do family arguments result? How could doing dishes be a more positive experience? (Key Skills: *Communication, Problem Solving*)

Follow Up

1. **Reteaching.** Ask students to list clean-up procedures while you write them on the board. You could also ask each group to make a clean-up poster to hang in their foods lab. (Key Skills: *Communication, Creativity*)
2. **Enrichment.** Ask individuals or groups to come up with a plan for a group of students interested in preparing an entire meal in the foods lab. (Key Skill: *Critical Thinking*)

How to ... Wash Dishes by Hand

Ask a good-natured volunteer to come to the front of the class to be your "scullery maid," "restaurant dish washer," or "robot." Tie an apron on your dishwasher and make it a fun time. While you go through the dish washing steps listed, your volunteer will carry out the steps. You might want to emphasize washing the rims of glassware and the tines and bowls of flatware because that's where people put their mouths.

If you have an automatic dishwasher in your lab, choose another volunteer to demonstrate exactly how to use it. Remind students that arranging dishes in dishwashers varies according to where the arms are located.

Teaching. . .
Working in the Home Kitchen and Conserving Natural Resources
(pp. 558-560)

Comprehension Check

1. What is a kitchen work center? *(An area of the kitchen designed to fill a particular purpose.)*
2. What three work centers do most kitchens have? *(A mixing center, a cooking center, and a clean-up center.)*
3. What are two ways to save water during meal preparation and clean up? *(Turn off faucets when not in use; reuse water that would otherwise go down the drain.)*
4. How can you reduce trash? *(Choose reusable rather than disposable items; avoid products with wasteful packaging; buy recycled items; recycle what you use; run a recycling program.)*

Learning Activities

1. **Discussion.** Ask students to share how their family works together to prepare meals at home. Does each person prepare one dish alone or do family members collaborate on most dishes? Can students think of any meals or dishes that lend themselves to group work? Individual work? (Key Skill: *Communication*)
2. **Kitchen Evaluation.** Ask students to draw a diagram of their kitchens at home. Have them indicate mixing centers in red, cooking centers in blue, and cleaning centers in green. Are all components of the various centers located together? Are different parts spread all over the kitchen? Would possible changes make working in the kitchen easier? You might have students write three paragraphs to accompany the diagrams. First of all, have them describe their existing work centers. Second, ask students to recommend possible changes. Finally, ask them to describe the work centers in their dream kitchens. Have students take their papers home

Evaluating the Lab

Evaluation is an important part of the lab experience. When you evaluate your work, you judge the quality of it. Your teacher may have you use a rating sheet to evaluate the way your recipe turned out. You should also evaluate your teamwork by asking yourself some very important questions: Did everything work as planned? What did we do well? How could we have improved? The answers to these and similar questions will be the key to your success in future labs.

▼ Working in the Home Kitchen ▼

In many ways, preparing food in a home kitchen is similar to working in the foods lab. In both situations, time and energy are often limited. Organizing the kitchen and planning your time will help you work efficiently.

Organizing Your Work Space

An efficient kitchen is organized into several work centers. A **kitchen work center** is an area of the kitchen designed to fill a particular purpose. The work center includes all of the appliances and equipment you need for that task. By storing items near the place they will be used, you save time and energy.

Most kitchens include a a mixing center, a cooking center, and a cleanup center. The chart on page 559 shows examples of the items that might be stored in each of these areas. What other work centers might a kitchen include? What items would be found there?

Organizing your work space allows you to prepare delicious meals efficiently.

Examples of Kitchen Work Centers

Work Center	Location	Items to Store Nearby
Mixing center	A counter or other workspace where recipe ingredients can be assembled	▶ Measuring utensils ▶ Mixing bowls and utensils ▶ Ingredients such as flour and spices
Cooking center	Near the range and/or microwave oven	▶ Saucepans, pots, and other cookware ▶ Cooking utensils such as spatulas, tongs, and cooling racks ▶ Potholders and oven mitts
Cleanup center	Near the sink	▶ Dishwashing and cleaning supplies ▶ Everyday dishes, glasses, and flatware ▶ Containers for leftover foods

Managing Your Time

At home as well as at school, it helps to write out a time plan or schedule. Allow a little extra time in your schedule for unexpected delays.

Often two or more family members work as a team. Decide together how you will divide tasks.

When you work alone, you can still be efficient. Look for ways to dovetail tasks. For instance, during the time that it takes for water to start boiling or for noodles to cook, you can be working on another part of the meal.

Planning a schedule is especially important when you are preparing an entire meal. You want all the food to be ready at the same time. Begin your schedule with the foods that take the longest to prepare and cook. For example, it may take 20 minutes to put a casserole together and another 45 minutes for it to bake. If you were also having a canned vegetable and a tossed green salad, you can see that you would need to begin the casserole first.

With more experience, you may not need to write out a schedule every time. Experienced cooks can think through their preparation plans mentally.

▼ Conserving Natural Resources ▼

Conservation and the environment are important issues today. Everyone needs to do his or her part to conserve natural resources. Here are some simple everyday habits you can put to use in the kitchen. Can you think of other ways to conserve?

You can conserve water by:

- ▶ Turning off faucets when not in use. For example, don't leave water running constantly while you do dishes.
- ▶ Reusing water that would otherwise go down the drain. For instance, when you wash vegetables, catch the water in a container and use it to water your plants.

and share them with their families. The next day, you might ask them to tell how their families responded. (Key Skills: *Communication, Creativity*)

3. **Group Work.** Assign each group to present a skit, mime, or report on one area of recycling. Encourage groups to be creative and to use props. (Key Skills: *Communication, Critical Thinking*)
4. **Posters.** Ask individuals or groups to make creative recycling posters to hang in the hallways. If your school doesn't have containers for recycling aluminum cans or paper, have students ask for or arrange for them to be put in the lunchroom, hallways, or classrooms. They might also write articles on kitchen recycling for the school newspaper. (Key Skills: *Creativity, Leadership*)

Follow Up

1. **Reteaching.** Run off copies of a diagram of a kitchen (not your foods lab). Be sure the stove and sink are indicated. Ask students to find the areas where the work centers might or must be located. You could also use an overhead or draw a diagram on the board and have the class as a whole find the work centers. (Key Skill: *Decision Making*)
2. **Extension.** Use the extension information handout on p. 59 of the *Extending the Text* booklet in the TCR.
3. **Enrichment.** Ask students to call the city hall or a local waste management office to see what items can be recycled in your community. Where are these items taken and what are they used for? Have any new developments in recycling been made? (Students might have to check magazines or newspapers for current information.) (Key Skills: *Communication, Citizenship*)

More About *Conserving Energy*

Cooking all or most of a meal in a crock pot can save heating up the whole oven or cooking on the range top. These slow cookers can be especially handy in the summer because you don't have to use the oven, which usually heats up the whole kitchen. This may also save fuel for air-conditioning. In fact, because a slow cooker is portable, you can plug it in the basement so it won't heat up the kitchen at all.

Completing the Chapter

For Review

1. Emphasize the main concepts using the summary.
2. Have students complete the "Facts to Recall." (Answers below.)

For Reteaching

1. **Reteaching.** Use the activity on p. 59 of the *Reteaching and Practical Skills* booklet in the TCR.

For Enrichment

1. **Enrichment.** Use the activity on p. 71 of the *Enrichment Activities* booklet in the TCR.

For Evaluation

1. Choose items from "Ideas to Explore" and "Activities to Try."
2. Use the chapter test on pp. 97-98 in the testing booklet of the TCR or use the testmaker software.

Facts to Recall Answers

1. **Any five:** wash and store knives and other sharp objects separately; keep knives sharp; use a cutting board; close cabinet doors and drawers; use a safe ladder or step stool for reach or hard-to-get items; wipe up spills right away.
2. Turn handles inward to avoid spills; do not allow handles to extend over other burners.
3. **Any four:** avoid wearing dangling jewelry or loose-fitting clothes; keep paper towels, dish towels, and electric cords away from the range; do not use range as a source of heat; avoid using a dish towel to handle hot utensils; plug no more than two appliances into an electrical outlet at one time.
4. **Any two:** dry hands thoroughly before touching electrical equipment; always unplug the cord before removing it from the appliance; disconnect the appliance by pulling on the plug only.
5. Store away from food items and children's reach, in original containers.

Recycling as many products as possible saves landfill space. What products do you recycle?

You can conserve electricity and fuel by:

- Cooking an entire meal in the oven at one time.
- Matching the size of the heating element on an electric range to the size of the pot or pan.
- Using hot water only when necessary.

You can conserve food by:

- Buying only as much food as you will use.
- Following recipes carefully.
- Taking a helping that you are sure you will eat. You can always ask for seconds if you want more.
- Using leftovers instead of throwing them away.

You can reduce the amount of trash by:

- Choosing reusable items rather than disposable items.
- Avoiding products with wasteful packaging.
- Buying items that can be recycled or are made from recycled materials.
- Making sure that materials such as glass, newspapers, aluminum cans, and plastic milk jugs are collected for recycling.

See Chapter 22 for more information about conserving and managing natural resources.

TAKING ACTION

Preventing Kitchen Accidents

"They could have lost everything." Sasha's eyes are wide, her voice somber, as she tells you of her neighbor's calamity. "They were making french fries and forgot to turn off the burner under the oil. It caught on fire and set fire to the curtains — it was a good thing they had a fire extinguisher nearby."

Sasha's friends escaped disaster, but you wonder if your own family would fare as well. You don't have a fire extinguisher — you're not sure you would even know how to use one. You decide right then and there to accident-proof your kitchen. What happened to Sasha's neighbors won't happen to your family. You are not sure, though, where to start.

Using Your Resourcefulness

- What resources can you use to learn how to safely operate your kitchen appliances?
- Who can tell you if your utensils or appliances need repair or replacement to avoid a dangerous accident?
- Where can you find information on using, storing, and disposing of cleaning products safely?
- Where can you learn basic first aid for treating minor cuts and burns?
- How do you decide whom to contact if a serious accident does occur?
- Where can you find tips on teaching young children about kitchen safety?

TAKING ACTION

Have students read the feature. Then have a class discussion about the things that students would need to do to accident-proof their kitchens at home. To guide this discussion, you may want to have your students answer the *Using Your Resourcefulness* questions at the end of this feature.

Using Your Resourcefulness Answers

- Answers will vary and might include a kitchen appliance store, an owner's manual, and an appliance repairer.

Chapter 47 Review

Summary

In this chapter, you have read about:

- ▶ Preventing accidents and injury when working in the kitchen.
- ▶ Preventing food-borne illness through good sanitation.
- ▶ Working efficiently in the foods lab and the home kitchen.
- ▶ Helping the environment by conserving resources and reducing trash.

Facts to Recall

1. Give five guidelines for preventing cuts and bruises.
2. How should cooking utensils be positioned on the range? Why?
3. List four safety rules for fire prevention.
4. Give two guidelines for safely unplugging an electrical appliance.
5. Where and how should household chemicals be stored to prevent poisoning?
6. Give four guidelines for practicing cleanliness in the kitchen.
7. Explain how to safely thaw meat, poultry, and fish.
8. At what temperature should hot food be served to avoid food-borne illness?
9. List two ways to store leftovers safely.
10. How is dovetailing helpful in planning to prepare food?
11. What is the benefit of organizing a kitchen into several work centers?
12. List four ways to conserve food.

Ideas to Explore

1. Explain how good time management can help reduce the chances of accident or injury in the kitchen.
2. How can you help prevent injury and conserve resources by keeping appliances in good working order?
3. Do you think a kitchen needs to be large to be well-organized? Explain.

Activities to Try

1. Draw a picture of a kitchen with at least three safety hazards. Have the rest of the class identify the hazards.
2. Make posters promoting safe kitchen work habits. Place them in the school foods lab.
3. Find pictures of a kitchen in a magazine. What work centers are included? Which of the basic floor plans is used? Evaluate the storage, work space, and traffic patterns. How might the kitchen be made more efficient?
4. Write a paragraph describing your role as a "team player" in the foods lab. How can working as a team benefit you, your lab group, and the foods class?

LINK TO *Health*

SANITATION SAVVY

Health experts agree that to prevent the spread of bacteria to food, certain sanitation practices should be followed. With a partner, develop a demonstration showing correct procedures for the following:

- ▶ **Handwashing.** Show how to thoroughly wash hands and exposed areas of the arms — scrubbing hands and between fingers for 20-30 seconds. Use a brush to clean fingernails.
- ▶ **Proper Food Temperatures.** Use a chart or other visual to emphasize the proper temperatures to keep hot and cold foods safe. Include some effective ways to store foods properly in the refrigerator.

Facts to Recall Answers (continued)

6. **Any four:** keep kitchen clean and free of pests; wear clean clothes to work with food; wash hands before handling food, after you cough or sneeze, after using the toilet, and after touching pets; wear rubber or plastic gloves if you have a cut; use a clean spoon to taste food during cooking; avoid touching the food contact surfaces; change dishcloths and dish-towels often.
7. Thaw meat, poultry, and fish in refrigerator or microwave. Never thaw at room temperature.
8. Above 140°F (60°C).
9. Refrigerate or freeze them.
10. It helps you use your time efficiently by planning tasks that can be done at the same time.
11. Saves time and energy because items are stored near the place they will be used.
12. Buy only as much food as you will use; follow recipes carefully; take only what you will eat; use leftovers instead of throwing them away.

Ideas to Explore

1. Many accidents and injuries occur when people are in a hurry and become careless. By planning your work, you can allow enough time to accomplish your task.
2. Appliances in good condition are less likely to malfunction or to expose you to the hazards of gas or electrical fires, thus preventing injury. Also, appliances work more quickly and efficiently when they are in good condition, saving time, energy, and money.
3. Answers will vary.

LINK TO *Health*

Answers

- Make sure that each group demonstrates this procedure correctly. If not, you may want to explain what they did wrong and have them do it again.
- Charts or other visuals will vary. Make sure groups follow guidelines listed in this chapter.

- Answers will vary. Possible answers might include an appliance repairer and a kitchen appliance store.
- Answers will vary and may include labels on the back of cleaning products, magazines, and the EPA.
- Answers will vary. Possible answers might include first aid books, first aid pamphlets, and by taking a first aid class.
- Answers will vary and might include talking it over with family members, getting pamphlets that will give information about what to do, and looking in the phone book for emergency numbers.
- Answers will vary. Possible answers might include family and consumer sciences books, magazines, and pamphlets.

Preparing to Teach

Chapter Outline

Chapter Resources

The following booklet materials may be found in the *Teacher's Classroom Resources* box:

- Lesson Plans, p. 53
- Student Workbook, *Study Guide,* pp. 203-204; *A Fairy Tale,* p. 205; *Milk—Simply A-"maze"-ing,* pp. 206-207; *Using Milk and Milk Products,* p. 208
- Color Transparencies, *The Milk, Yogurt, and Cheese Group,* CT-52
- Technology and Computers, p. 47
- Foods Lab Management and Recipes, R-1, pp. 15-16; R-2, pp. 17-18; R-3, pp. 19-20; R-4, pp. 21-22
- Cooperative Learning, p. 60
- Extending the Text, *Making Milk Decisions,* p. 60
- Reteaching and Practical Skills, *Milk Madness,* pp. 60-61
- Enrichment Activities, *Choosing Cheese Selectively,* pp. 72-73
- Chapter and Unit Tests, pp. 99-100
- Testmaker Software

Also see:

- Meeting the Special Needs of Students
- Linking Home, School, and Community

ABCNews InterActive™ Videodiscs

- *Food and Nutrition*

See the ABCNews InterActive™ Bar Code Correlation booklet for applicable segments.

CHAPTER 48 Milk and Milk Products

OBJECTIVES

- *Explain the role of milk and milk products in the diet.*
- *Describe how to buy, store, and prepare dairy products.*

TERMS TO LEARN

- ***pasteurized***
- ***homogenized***
- ***reconstitute***

When you were younger, were you often told "Drink your milk"? That's good advice, even now that you are a teenager. Milk is one of the most nutritious and refreshing beverages you can drink. Milk and milk products, such as yogurt and cheese, fit well into meals and snacks. How many of your favorite foods contain dairy products?

Nutrients in Dairy Products

Milk and milk products are good sources of important nutrients. They are high in protein, which you need for growth and repair of the body. The calcium, phosphorus, and vitamin D in dairy products help build strong bones and teeth. Dairy products also supply vitamin A and B vitamins for health and growth. The nutrients dairy products provide are needed throughout life.

Health guidelines recommend two to three servings of milk or milk products each day. They also recommend choosing low-fat versions of dairy products. These have fewer calories and less fat, but the same important nutrients. Milk provides a good example. Compare a 1-cup (250-mL) serving of these three types:

	Calories	Fat (grams)	Calories from fat
Whole milk	150	8	48%
Low-fat (2%) milk	120	5	38%
Skim milk	80	almost none	5%

Milk is a healthy beverage because it contains many nutrients.

Regardless of age, everyone needs the nutrients found in milk and milk products.

More About *Calcium*

If you don't like milk or are a strict vegetarian, you can meet your calcium needs by eating the right fruits and vegetables. Choose any of these: asparagus, beet greens, bok choy (an Oriental vegetable), raw broccoli, cauliflower, dandelion greens, curly endive (chicory), escarole, dried figs, kohlrabi, leaf or romaine lettuce, lima beans (fresh or dried), mustard greens, okra, parsley, rhubarb, spinach, or watercress. A 3½-ounce serving would provide you with 100 or more milligrams of calcium.

Introducing the Chapter

Motivators

1. **Survey.** Survey students to find out what forms of milk and milk products they include in their diets. Which are most popular? Least popular? Why is milk an important part of a healthy diet throughout life? (Key Skill: *Communication*)
2. **Taste Test.** Have students taste samples of whole milk, low-fat milk, and skim milk. Have them note observable differences in taste. Ask students how they would go about switching to milk with less fat. (Key Skills: *Communication, Science*)
3. **Discussion.** Ask students to describe ways people who do not like milk as a beverage can include milk and milk products in their diets. (Key Skill: *Problem Solving*)

Chapter Objectives and Vocabulary

1. Have students read the chapter objectives and rephrase the objectives as questions.
2. Ask students to state, in their own words, the purpose of studying this chapter.
3. Pronounce the vocabulary terms listed on the previous page. Ask students whether they are familiar with any of these. Explain that the terms will be defined in the chapter.

Guided Reading

1. Have students read the chapter and use the Study Guide on pp. 203-204 of the *Student Workbook*.

Teaching. . .
Nutrients in Dairy Products and Buying Dairy Products
(pp. 563-565)

Comprehension Check

1. Why are dairy products important in your diet? *(They are good sources of important nutrients — protein, calcium, phosphorus, vitamin A, B vitamins, and vitamin D.)*
2. Why should you choose low-fat dairy products? *(They have fewer calories and less fat, but the same important nutrients.)*
3. How is cheese made from milk? *(The milk is first thickened. Then the solid part, or curd, is separated from the liquid, called whey, and made into cheese.)*
4. What should you compare when you buy yogurt products? *(The fat content and calories.)*

Learning Activities

1. **Reading Labels.** Provide students with empty containers for several forms of milk. Have them compare the nutrient contents of the different forms of milk. Discuss reasons for fortification. (Key Skills: *Communication, Science*)
2. **Display.** Display single servings of milk, cheese, and yogurt. Discuss reasons for variations in serving size. (Key Skill: *Science*)

AROUND THE WORLD

After reading the feature, have students investigate the origin of another type of cheese. Where was it invented? Who invented it? How was it invented? *(Answers will vary.)*

TIPS:

Choosing Cheese
After students read the feature, have them discuss their favorite types of cheeses. Do they eat these types of cheeses as is or do they like them in some type of cooked food? *(Answers will vary.)*

AROUND THE WORLD

Blue (sometimes spelled bleu) cheese gets it name from the blue or green veins of mold that run through it. This harmless mold gives the cheese its unusual flavor. Blue cheese is believed to have originated near Roquefort (ROKE-fert), France many years ago. According to legend, a shepherd forgot his lunch in a cave, and returned weeks later to find the cheese, though molded, was still edible and highly flavorful. Roquefort cheese is still made entirely of sheep's milk. Two other types of blue cheese are Stilton, from England, and Gorgonzola (gore-gon-ZOE-la), from Italy.

Almost all dairy products have low-fat versions. You can also buy substitute products, such as nondairy whipped topping to use in place of whipped cream.

Buying Dairy Products

Be a wise consumer when purchasing and storing milk and milk products. Read the labels to be sure you get the product you want. Check the date on the package. This is the last date the product should be sold.

- ***Milk.*** When you shop for fresh milk, you will see the words "pasteurized" and "homogenized." **Pasteurized** (PASS-tyoor-ized) means that the milk has been heated to destroy harmful bacteria. This process increases the length of time you can store milk. **Homogenized** (huh-MAH-juh-nized) means that the fat particles in the milk have been broken up and distributed throughout the milk. If milk is not homogenized, the fat would rise to the top, forming a layer of cream.
- ***Cheese.*** Cheese is another popular milk product. To make cheese, milk is first thickened. The solid part, or *curd*, is then separated from the liquid (called *whey*). The curd is made into cheese. There are dozens of varieties available. Some cheese is aged or ripened. Examples are cheddar and Swiss cheese. Cottage cheese and cream cheese are not aged. Process cheese is made by combining different aged cheeses. Check cheese labels carefully and choose low-fat varieties whenever possible.
- ***Yogurt.*** Yogurt is a milk product with a smooth, thick texture and a tangy flavor. It is available plain or flavored. Frozen yogurt is a popular substitute for ice cream because it is lower in fat. When you buy yogurt, check the labels to compare the fat content and calories in products.

TIPS:
Choosing Cheese

The type of cheese you use in a dish depends on the flavor you want. Here are some of the most popular varieties and how they are used:

- **Cheddar.** Mild to sharp taste; eaten as is or shredded in cooked foods.
- **Mozzarella.** Very mild flavor; usually used in cooking.
- **Romano.** Very sharp taste, especially if aged; eaten as is or grated to season cooked foods.
- **Swiss.** Mild, slightly sweet and nutty taste; eaten as is or used in cooked foods, salads, and fondues.

More About Yogurt

In the United States, yogurt is a trendy food. More than a billion pounds a year are sold, not including frozen yogurt items. However, Asians and Middle Easterners have been eating yogurt for centuries. Yogurt is high in calcium, often higher than milk. People who have trouble digesting lactose, the sugar in milk, can eat yogurt made with "active cultures." The active cultures digest the lactose for them. The best nutritional selections are low in fat and sugar. Choose low-fat yogurts and yogurt made without so-called fruit fillings. The fillings are usually jam, not fruit. Buy plain or vanilla nonfat or low-fat yogurt and add your own fruit instead.

Many varieties of cheese are available. When possible, choose varieties that are low in fat.

Other Milk Products

- ***Nonfat dry milk.*** Powdered product made by removing the water from milk. When mixed with water, can be used as fresh milk.
- ***UHT milk.*** Milk processed at very high temperatures to kill all bacteria. It needs no refrigeration until the carton is opened.
- ***Buttermilk.*** A tart, thick product made by adding a safe bacteria culture to milk (usually skim or low-fat).
- ***Evaporated milk.*** Canned milk from which 60% of the water has been removed.
- ***Sweetened condensed milk.*** Canned, concentrated milk with added sugar.
- ***Half-and-half.*** A mixture of milk and light cream. Used in coffee.
- ***Heavy whipping cream.*** Higher in fat than half-and-half or other creams. The high fat content aids whipping.
- ***Sour cream.*** Cream cultured with safe bacteria to give it a tangy flavor.

Learning Activities (continued)

3. **Tasting.** Have students taste aged and unaged cheeses. Discuss differences in characteristics. Compare cheese labels. Which varieties are low in fat? (Key Skill: *Science*)
4. **Laboratory Experience.** Have students prepare several flavors of yogurt using plain or vanilla yogurt. Add fresh fruits, wheat germs, and flavorings. Compare the number of calories in the homemade and commercial versions. (Key Skill: *Decision Making*)
5. **Discussion.** Have students study the chart on page 565 that describes forms of milk available. Discuss possible uses for each form. (Key Skill: *Decision Making*)

Follow Up

1. **Reteaching.** Have students prepare a chart showing the different forms of milk, their nutrient values, and possible uses. (Key Skills: *Communication, Science*)
2. **Enrichment.** Arrange for students to take a field trip to a milk processing plant. Afterwards, ask students to prepare a diagram showing the steps in milk production and processing. (Key Skill: *Science*)

Wellness

Milk that is not pasteurized is called "raw milk." Some people believe that raw milk is more nutritious because it has not been processed. However, it may contain harmful bacteria that cause disease.

More About
Nutrients in Milk Products

Cheese is high in calcium, phosphorus, protein, and fat-soluble vitamins. However, it is also high in fat. Unlike milk, cheese contains only a trace of B vitamins because most are left behind in the *whey*. A 1 in. (2.5 cm) cube of Cheddar cheese equals ½ cup (125 mL) of milk.

More About
Including Milk in Your Diet

If you don't like to drink milk, you can find ways to include it in your diet. Eat soups, casseroles, and puddings made with milk. Add a little extra dry milk to recipes that call for milk to increase the milk in your diet.

Photo Focus

Discuss the photo at the top of page 565 with the students. Then have them go to the supermarket and compare the prices of different types of cheese. Have students report their findings back to the class. *(Answers will vary.)*

Teaching. . .
Storing Dairy Products and Preparing Dairy Products
(pp. 566-568)

Comprehension Check

1. How should milk be stored? *(Keep fresh milk refrigerated in its original container. Store canned, nonfat dry, or UHT milk in dry storage until opened or mixed with water.)*
2. At what temperature should you cook or heat milk products? *(Low heat.)*
3. What precautions should you take when heating milk in the microwave? *(Be sure to follow directions for the cooking time and temperature. Turn off the power as soon as the milk starts to foam. Stir the milk after heating to distribute the heat evenly.)*
4. How do you reconstitute dry milk? *(This means that you replace the water which was removed from it originally. Follow the directions given on the package.)*
5. Why might you want to add dry milk granules directly to recipes? *(To improve foods' nutritional value.)*

Learning Activities

1. **Discussion.** Have students work in groups to develop guidelines to ensure that milk is kept cold and spends as little time as possible outside the refrigerator. Have groups share their guidelines with the class. (Key Skills: *Cooperation, Problem Solving*)
2. **Posters.** Have students work in groups to research one of these aspects of cooking with dairy products: effects of heat, scalding milk, preventing scum formation. Have each group prepare a poster explaining the principles and procedures involved. (Key Skill: *Science*)
3. **Application.** Have students work in lab groups to prepare pudding on the range and in the microwave oven. Compare the time required to prepare each. What precautions should be observed when using each method? (Key Skills: *Cooperation, Management*)

Milk you buy in UHT packaging is safe and convenient for packed lunches.

Storing Dairy Products

Fresh milk spoils easily. Keep it refrigerated in its original container. Store unopened canned, nonfat dry, or UHT milk in a dry, cool area. Once opened, canned and UHT milk must be refrigerated. When a box of nonfat dry milk is opened, transfer the dry milk to an airtight container. Refrigerate nonfat dry milk when it is mixed with water.

Preparing Dairy Products

Milk, yogurt, and cheese can be eaten as is or combined with other foods. Try blending milk and fresh fruit for a nutritious milkshake. Plain yogurt mixed with seasonings makes a delicious dip to eat with fresh vegetables.

Some recipes, such as puddings and sauces, call for cooking or heating milk products. Since dairy foods are high in protein, they must be cooked over low heat. High heat can cause the protein to scorch or burn easily. It also causes cheese to become rubbery.

Sometimes you will see a recipe that calls for scalded milk. To scald milk, heat it to just below the boiling point.

A film, known as scum, can form on the top of heated milk. The film contains proteins, minerals, and fat. It forms because of the evaporation of liquid from the surface of the heated milk. You can prevent the formation of scum by covering the pan as the milk is being heated. Stirring often during cooking also helps prevent the skin from forming.

Cover or stir heating milk to prevent skin formation.

More About
Preparing Dairy Products

Like milk, cheese is high in protein and fat and must be cooked with care. Avoid using too high a temperature or cooking it for too long a time. If you overcook cheese, it becomes tough and rubbery. Also, the fat separates into globules of grease. This makes the food look unappetizing.

Effect of Acid on Milk

Materials
1 cup milk; 1 tablespoon vinegar

Equipment
glass measuring cup

Directions:
Measure 1 cup milk and add 1 tablespoon vinegar. Try different ways of adding acid to milk (such as pouring the milk into the acid, adding 1 tablespoon of milk to the acid and then adding it to the remainder of the milk, etc.) Observe the results.

✔ Describe what happened to the milk.

✔ What other products would curdle milk?

✔ How might you add acid to milk without causing it to curdle?

Hot Cocoa

Customary	Ingredients	Metric
6 Tbsp.	Cocoa	90 mL
6 Tbsp.	Sugar	90 mL
⅛ tsp.	Salt	.5 mL
4 c.	Skim milk	1 L
1 stick	Cinnamon (optional)	1 stick

Yield: 4 servings

Nutrition Information
Per serving (approximate): 180 calories, 10 g protein, 34 g carbohydrate, 2 g fat, 4 mg cholesterol, 250 mg sodium
Good source of: calcium, riboflavin, and phosphorus

Conventional Directions
Pan: 2-quart (2-liter) saucepan
Temperature: Medium-low

1. **Stir** together cocoa, sugar, and salt in a 2-quart (2-liter) saucepan.
2. **Stir** in about one-fourth of the milk slowly to form a smooth paste.
3. **Stir** in the remaining milk gradually. If desired, add the cinnamon stick.
4. **Heat** milk mixture over medium-low heat, stirring occasionally, until bubbles form around the edge of the pan.
5. **Remove** from heat and stir vigorously with a wire whisk until cocoa is smooth and foamy.
6. **Pour** cocoa mixture into 4 mugs.
7. **Serve.**

Microwave Directions
Pan: 4-cup (1-liter) glass measuring cup
Power Level: 100 percent power

1. **Stir** together cocoa, sugar, and salt in a 4-cup (1-liter) glass measuring cup.
2. **Microwave** the cocoa and sugar mixture at 100 percent power for 30 seconds or until cocoa and sugar dissolve.
3. **Stir** in the milk gradually. If desired, add the cinnamon stick.
4. **Microwave** at 100 percent power for 8 to 10 minutes or until heated thoroughly. Stir after 4 or 5 minutes and again at the end of the cooking time.
5. **Pour** cocoa into 4 mugs.
6. **Serve.**

Effect of Acid on Milk

Materials: 1 cup milk; 1 tablespoon vinegar.
Equipment: Glass measuring cup.
Purpose: To show students the effect of acids on milk.

Outcomes:
- The milk curdled.
- Any acid would have the same effect.
- Add some of the acid to the milk, stirring constantly to raise the acid level of the milk so there is less chance of curdling.

Learning Activities (continued)

4. **Demonstration.** Demonstrate how to reconstitute dry milk. Have students taste the reconstituted milk just after it is mixed, then again after it has been refrigerated overnight. Discuss possible uses for dry milk. (Key Skill: *Science*)
5. **Group Work.** Have students work in lab groups using nonfat dry milk to prepare foods such as baked products, cream soups, mashed potatoes, and meat loaf. Compare the cost of using nonfat dry milk with the cost of using other forms of milk to prepare these products. How does the type of milk used affect the number of calories in the food? (Key Skill: *Cooperation*)

Follow Up

1. **Reteaching.** Have students write guidelines for scalding milk, avoiding formation of scum, and preventing scorching. (Key Skills: *Communication, Science*)
2. **Extension.** Use the extension information handout on p. 60 of the *Extending the Text* booklet in the TCR.
3. **Enrichment.** Have students prepare cheese sauce using natural shredded cheese and processed cheese. What are the advantages and disadvantages of using each type of cheese? What guidelines should be followed when cooking with cheese? (Key Skills: *Science, Critical Thinking*)

Using the Recipe

Have students read the feature. Then divide students into two groups. Have one group make cocoa using the conventional directions and the other make cocoa using the microwave directions. Which group finished first? Does one type of cocoa taste any better than the other type? *(The group following the microwave directions should finish first. Students' cocoa preferences will vary.)*

Completing the Chapter

For Review

1. Emphasize the main concepts using the summary.
2. Have students complete the "Facts to Recall." (Answers below.)

For Reteaching

1. **Reteaching.** Use the activity on pp. 60-61 of the *Reteaching and Practical Skills* booklet in the TCR.

For Enrichment

1. **Enrichment.** Use the activity on pp. 72-73 of the *Enrichment Activities* booklet in the TCR.

For Evaluation

1. Choose items from "Ideas to Explore" and "Activities to Try."
2. Use the chapter test on pp. 99-100 in the testing booklet of the TCR or use the testmaker software.

Facts to Recall Answers

1. They are high in protein, needed for growth and repair of the body; they contain calcium, phosphorus, and vitamin D to build strong bones and teeth; and they contain A and B vitamins, which are important to health and growth.
2. Whole milk has the most calories and is highest in fat, with 150 calories and 8 grams of fat per 1-cup serving; low-fat milk has 120 calories and 5 grams of fat per 1-cup serving; and skim milk is lowest in both categories, with 80 calories and almost no fat per 1-cup serving.
3. It is the last date the product should be sold.
4. To increase the length of time you can store it.
5. Milk is thickened, and then the solid part, called curd, is separated from the liquid, called whey. The curd is then made into cheese.
6. It is milk processed at very high temperatures to kill all bacteria.

▼ Microwaving Dairy Products ▼

When heating milk in the microwave oven, keep in mind that microwaves cook rapidly and that milk is sensitive to heat. Be sure to follow directions for the cooking time and temperature. Since milk boils over easily, turn off the power as soon as the milk starts to foam. Stir the milk after heating to distribute the heat evenly.

When microwaving cheese, use care to avoid overcooking. Cheese is less likely to overcook if you grate it or use process cheese. Stop cooking as soon as the cheese starts to melt.

Nonfat dry milk is a nutritious addition to many baked and cooked foods.

▼ Using Nonfat Dry Milk ▼

Nonfat dry milk can be used in both dry and liquid form. When you **reconstitute** (ree-KAHN-stih-toot) dry milk, it means you replace the water which was removed from it originally. Follow the directions given on the package. You can drink the reconstituted milk or use it for cooking. You can also add dry milk granules directly to some recipes to improve foods' nutritional value. Try adding a small amount to baked products, cream soups, mashed potatoes, and meat loaf.

TAKING ACTION

Meeting Calcium Needs

Your friend Carmen has recently become very concerned about calcium. She explains that she has been reading that women, especially teens, need a lot of calcium. She also wants to make sure her four-year-old sister Regina gets enough calcium for her growing bones and teeth. Also, her seventy-five-year-old grandmother will soon be moving in with the family, and Carmen has heard that older people can face special problems with brittle, easily broken bones. Her grandmother has always been very active, and Carmen wants to help her stay strong and healthy.

Carmen has decided that including more milk and milk products in the family's diet will help everyone's nutritional needs, but she is unsure about many things. How much do they need? What products should they buy? How will this affect other aspects of their health? She asks you for advice.

Using Your Resourcefulness

- What resources do you suggest Carmen use to find out about her own, her sister's, and her grandmother's calcium requirements and the role of milk products in a healthful diet?
- Where can she learn about the role milk products play in the physical development of young children and teens, and in the health maintenance of older people?
- Where can she get suggestions for including more milk products in her family's diet? How can she find out which of these products are also best for them in terms of fat, calories, and cholesterol?

TAKING ACTION

Have students read the feature. Then have a class discussion about what recommendations students could give Carmen to get more milk products into her family's diet. To guide this discussion, you may want to have students answer the *Using Your Resourcefulness* questions at the end of this feature.

Using Your Resourcefulness Answers

- Answers will vary. Possible answers might include a doctor's office, Dietary Guidelines, a nutritionist, and a dietitian.
- Answers will vary and might include family and consumer sciences textbooks, a family and consumer sciences teacher, and Dietary Guidelines.
- Answers will vary. Possible answers might include a doctor's office, Dietary Guidelines,

Chapter 48 Review

Summary

In this chapter, you have read about:

- Why milk and milk products are an important part of a healthful diet.
- The many different milk products that are available.
- How to store milk products to preserve freshness and nutrients.
- How to prevent common problems when cooking milk products.
- Ways to use nonfat dry milk.

Facts to Recall

1. What important nutrients do milk and milk products contain? How do these nutrients contribute to good health?
2. How does whole milk compare to low-fat and skim milk in fat and calories?
3. What does the date on packages of milk products indicate?
4. Why is milk pasteurized?
5. How is cheese made?
6. What is UHT milk?
7. Explain how nonfat dry milk should be stored, both before and after it has been mixed with water.
8. Describe two ways of preventing scum from forming when heating milk.
9. How can you avoid overcooking cheese in the microwave oven?
10. Why might you add dry milk granules to baked products or meat loaf?

Ideas to Explore

1. Discuss ways in which you could replace one milk product with another one that is lower in fat and calories.
2. In some parts of the world, and for some families, milk products are difficult to obtain and store. Of those milk products that you have read about in this chapter, which might be used to solve this problem? Explain.
3. What might be some ways to incorporate milk and milk products into the diet for someone who doesn't like to drink milk?

Activities to Try

1. Research and write a short report on different sources of milk products around the world. Share your findings with the class.
2. Bring a favorite recipe to class. Be prepared to explain how milk products could be added or substituted for other ingredients to increase the nutritional value of the recipe.
3. Work with a partner to develop a public service announcement (for radio) that encourages people to include milk products as part of a healthful diet.

LINK TO *Art*

FAT IN MILK PRODUCTS

Create a mobile or a collage showing milk products that are higher in fat content and milk products that are lower in fat content. List the percentage of fat in each product. Indicate the benefits of choosing low-fat milk products. Use at least one element of design (see Chapter 24, pages 263-268) and one principle of design in the display.

Facts to Recall Answers (continued)

7. The dry milk powder should be kept in an airtight container after the box is opened. After it is mixed with water, it should be refrigerated.
8. Put a lid on the pan as the milk is being heated; stir the milk often during cooking.
9. Grate it or use process cheese; stop cooking as soon as the cheese starts to melt.
10. To improve foods' nutritional value.

Ideas to Explore

1. Answers will vary and may include: low-fat or skim milk can be used instead of whole milk for drinking; baked potatoes can be served with cottage cheese instead of sour cream; buttermilk can replace sour cream in some baked products; cottage cheese can be used instead of cream cheese in cheese cakes.
2. Nonfat dry milk, UHT milk, and evaporated milk might all be used. They require less or no refrigeration, so they can be shipped long distances and stored for long periods of time. They are also usually less expensive than fresh milk.
3. Answers will vary.

a nutritionist, a dietitian, family and consumer sciences textbooks, a family and consumer sciences teacher, the Dairy Council, and reading labels on milk products.

LINK TO *Art*

Answer

Students' mobiles or collages will vary. Allow them to be creative, but make sure that they use the correct fat amounts for the different milk products. Also, make sure students include all the benefits of choosing low-fat milk products.

Preparing to Teach

Chapter Outline

Chapter Resources

The following booklet materials may be found in the *Teacher's Classroom Resources* box:

- Lesson Plans, pp. 54-55
- Student Workbook, *Study Guide,* pp. 209-210; *The Search for Nutrients,* p. 211; *Vegetables Will Grow on You!,* p. 212
- Color Transparencies, *The Fruit Group,* CT-53; *The Vegetable Group,* CT-54
- Technology and Computers, pp. 46, 47
- Foods Lab Management and Recipes, R-5, pp. 23-24; R-6, pp. 25-26; R-7, pp. 27-28; R-8, pp. 29-30; R-9, pp. 31-32; R-10, pp. 33-34; R-11, pp. 35-36; R-12, pp. 37-38
- Cooperative Learning, p. 61
- Extending the Text, *Getting Vegetables to the Table,* p. 61
- Reteaching and Practical Skills, *My Favorite Vegetables,* p. 62
- Enrichment Activities, *Cooking Vegetables,* p. 74
- Chapter and Unit Tests, pp. 101-102
- Testmaker Software

Also see:

- Meeting the Special Needs of Students
- Linking Home, School, and Community

ABCNews InterActive™ Videodiscs

- *Food and Nutrition*

See the ABCNews InterActive™ Bar Code Correlation booklet for applicable segments.

CHAPTER 49 Fruits and Vegetables

OBJECTIVES

- *Explain the role of fruits and vegetables in the diet.*
- *Describe how to buy, store, and prepare fruits and vegetables.*

TERMS TO LEARN

- ***produce***

More About Nutrients in Fruits and Vegetables

Fruits and vegetables have long been associated with good health. In the 18th century, citrus fruits were found to cure scurvy, a disease that plagued sailors during long voyages. Today, nutritionists tell us that the fiber in fruits and vegetables helps prevent colon problems. Diets low in fiber may increase the risk of developing colon cancer.

Vegetables and fruits are nutritional bargains. They are rich storehouses of nutrients, yet they are low in calories.

Today, fresh fruits and vegetables from around the world are available in many supermarkets. Try new varieties. You may find some new favorites.

Nutrients in Fruits and Vegetables

Fruits and vegetables have high nutrient density. For the number of calories they supply, most pack large amounts of vitamins and minerals. They make the calories you take in count toward good nutrition.

Calories in Fruits and Vegetables

Most fruits and vegetables are naturally low in fat and calories. However, the way they are prepared and seasoned can make a big difference. Take a look at a popular vegetable, the potato:

1 baked potato, plain	145 calories
20 potato chips	230 calories
1 baked potato with butter and sour cream	240 calories
1 cup (250 mL) potato salad	250 calories
20 french fries	270 calories

Fruits are naturally sweet. When extra sugar is added in processing or preparation, calories add up. For example, take a look at these values for ½ cup (125 mL) of peaches:

Fresh, unsweetened peaches	36 calories
Peaches canned in heavy syrup	95 calories
Frozen, sweetened peaches	118 calories

Although specific fruits and vegetables differ in the amounts and types of nutrients they offer, there are some similarities. Fruits and vegetables are good sources of:

- Carbohydrates (sugars and starches) for energy.
- Vitamin A for good vision, healthy skin, and strong bones and teeth.
- Vitamin C for fighting infections.
- Fiber to aid digestion.
- Minerals such as potassium and calcium.

More About *Fruits and Vegetables*

Anyone can grow fruits and vegetables at home. All you need is a small area, a few simple tools, and a little spare time. Especially nutritious garden vegetables include greens, green peas, broccoli, sweet potatoes, lima beans, winter squash, carrots, and brussels sprouts. Many other popular, but less nutritious, choices can be grown as well. You can plant fruit trees (dwarf varieties require little space) or strawberries. You can even garden in containers if you lack space.

Introducing the Chapter

Motivators

1. **Identification.** Have students identify their favorite junk food snacks and their favorite raw fruits and vegetables. Have students compare the nutrient values and calories of the foods identified. Which are the healthiest food choices? Why? (Key Skill: *Science*)
2. **Display.** Display several fruits and vegetables that are unlikely to be familiar to students. Describe each product, where it is grown, its nutrient value, and how it is used. Provide samples for students to taste. (Key Skills: *Science, Social Studies*)
3. **Discussion.** Have students describe their favorite fruit and vegetable dishes. Discuss which are high in calories and why. (Key Skills: *Communication, Science*)

Chapter Objectives and Vocabulary

1. Have students read the chapter objectives and rephrase the objectives as questions.
2. Ask students to state, in their own words, the purpose of studying this chapter.
3. Pronounce the vocabulary terms listed on the previous page. Ask students whether they are familiar with any of these. Explain that the terms will be defined in the chapter.

Guided Reading

1. Have students read the chapter and use the Study Guide on pp. 209-210 of the *Student Workbook*.

Wellness

Fruits are tasty and satisfying because of the sugar they contain naturally. The sugar in fruit is called fructose. Processed fruits may contain unwanted added sugar.

- ½ cup frozen = ½ cup fruit sweetened fruit + 6 tsp. sugar
- ½ cup fruit = ½ cup fruit canned in heavy + 4 tsp. sugar syrup
- ½ cup fruit = ½ cup fruit canned in light + 2 tsp. sugar syrup

Teaching. . .
Nutrients in Fruits and Vegetables; Buying Fruits and Vegetables
(pp. 571-573)

Comprehension Check

1. Why are vegetables and fruits important in our diets? *(They are rich sources of nutrients, yet are low in calories.)*
2. How is color a clue to the nutritional value of fruits and vegetables? *(Yellow and dark green vegetables and fruits are better sources of vitamin A than those with a pale color.)*
3. In what forms are fruits and vegetables available? *(Fresh, frozen, canned, and dried.)*
4. What are some signs of quality in fruits and vegetables? *(Solid feel, heavy for size, crisp, and uniform size.)*

Learning Activities

1. **Reading Nutrient Value Chart.** Have students work in groups to identify the nutrients in which fruits and vegetables are usually high and low using a nutrient value chart. Have students categorize vegetables according to those that are high in carbohydrates, vitamin A, vitamin C, fiber, and minerals. (Key Skills: *Science, Critical Thinking*)
2. **Listing.** Have students make a list of fruits and vegetables that are yellow, orange, or dark green. Are all of the fruits and vegetables listed high in vitamin A? (Key Skill: *Science*)
3. **Comparisons.** Have students compare the amounts of iron provided by iron-rich fruits and vegetables with recommended dietary allowances. Identify those that students eat frequently. (Key Skill: *Science*)
4. **Self-Evaluation.** Have students make a list of the fruits and vegetables they have eaten in the past 24 hours. Have students evaluate calories, vitamin A, vitamin C, calcium, and iron in their selections. What changes are needed in their diets? (Key Skill: *Problem Solving*)

Choose a variety of fruits to help meet your nutritional needs. What are some of your favorites?

One clue to the nutritional value of fruits and vegetables is color. For example, deep yellow and dark green vegetables and fruits are better sources of vitamin A than those with a pale color. When you buy salad greens, choose varieties that are dark green rather than pale green. Choose dark yams instead of lighter yellow sweet potatoes. Other good sources of vitamin A are apricots, cantaloupes, carrots, collards, kale, broccoli, green peppers, spinach, and turnip greens.

Citrus fruits, such as oranges, grapefruit, and lemons, are outstanding sources of vitamin C. Other good sources are tomatoes, cantaloupes, and strawberries. Vegetables such as broccoli, green cabbage, green peppers, white potatoes, turnip greens, and collards are also good sources of vitamin C.

Green leafy vegetables, such as turnip greens, kale, and collards, provide calcium for your bones and teeth. Spinach, kale, collards, and turnip greens are iron-rich vegetables.

Dried fruits, such as raisins and prunes, are also excellent sources of iron, important for your blood.

For good health, you need two to four servings of fruits each day and three to five servings of vegetables. How do your current eating habits measure up?

Nutrient-rich vegetables are available every season of the year either fresh, frozen, canned, or dried. Many provide calcium, vitamins A and C, and iron.

More About *The Color of Vegetables*

Carotene is what gives the yellow color to apricots, carrots, and other yellow and orange fruits and vegetables. Your body uses carotene to make vitamin A. In some vegetables, the yellow is camouflaged by chlorophyll and becomes a deep green. Examples include turnip greens and broccoli. As a rule, the deeper the yellow, orange, or green color, the more vitamin A the food contains.

On the outside, the breadfruit looks like a big, bumpy, green orange. Inside, though, the fruit's pale color, smooth texture, and starchy flavor do remind you of fresh bread. It is a staple in diets on Caribbean and South Pacific islands, where it is grown. There it is prepared much as potatoes are in the United States. It may be baked or boiled, fried, or roasted. It is often mixed with fish, cheese, or meat.

Buying Fruits and Vegetables

Your family's preferences, the cost, and your need for convenience will determine what fruits and vegetables you buy. You can select from fresh, frozen, canned, or dried fruits and vegetables.

Fresh fruits and vegetables are also called **produce** (PRO-doos). Produce is generally least expensive at the peak of its growing season. For the best value, compare the cost of fresh, canned, frozen, and dried fruits and vegetables.

▼ Buying Fresh Produce ▼

Choose fresh fruits and vegetables carefully. Avoid produce that is wilted, is discolored, or has soft spots. These are signs of age and poor quality. They also mean loss of nutrients.

Most produce loses quality quickly. It's best to shop for produce often and use what you buy within a few days. If packages of produce are too large for your needs, ask a clerk to package a smaller amount for you.

What signs of quality should you look for? Head lettuce and cabbage should feel solid. Citrus fruit, squash, cucumbers, and tomatoes should feel heavy for their size. Celery, asparagus, and snap beans (green beans) are best when crisp. Root and tuber vegetables, such as potatoes and onions, should not have sprouts.

Size is not a sign of flavor or nutritional value. Very large fruits and vegetables can have poor texture and taste.

If produce looks good on the outside, it is probably good on the inside. Examine fresh produce carefully before you buy.

Learning Activities (continued)

5. **Guest Speaker.** Invite the produce manager from a local supermarket in to discuss which fruits and vegetables are most plentiful each season, how fruits and vegetables are priced, how the store avoids spoilage, and how the customer can help keep prices down. (Key Skills: *Communication, Management*)

Follow Up

1. **Reteaching.** Have students create posters showing fruits and vegetables that are high in carbohydrates, vitamin A, vitamin C, fiber, and minerals. (Key Skills: *Science, Creativity*)
2. **Enrichment.** Have students compare unit prices of various forms of the same fruit or vegetable. Have them summarize the factors that influence the price of the various forms of the same fruit or vegetable. (Key Skill: *Management*)

AROUND THE WORLD

After reading the feature, have students investigate another out-of-the-ordinary fruit that is grown and eaten in a foreign country or on an island. How is it prepared? Is it eaten by itself, or is it mixed with another type of food? *(Answers will vary.)*

Photo Focus

Discuss the illustration at the bottom of page 573 with the students. Then have each student examine the fresh produce that's in their kitchen at home. Is all of this produce still fresh, or does some of it need to be thrown away? How can they tell? Have students report their findings to the class. *(Answers will vary.)*

Teaching. . .
Buying Processed Fruits and Vegetables; Storing Fruits and Vegetables; Preparing Fruits and Vegetables
(pp. 574-575)

Comprehension Check

1. What precautions should you observe when purchasing canned and frozen fruits and vegetables? *(Be sure cans and packages are in good condition. Avoid buying dented cans. Avoid frozen foods with ice crystals on the packages.)*
2. How should fresh fruits and vegetables be stored? *(Store ripe fruits, unwashed, in the refrigerator in a plastic bag or in the crisper. Allow unripe fruits to ripen at room temperature. Refrigerate most fresh vegetables promptly. Store potatoes and dry onions in a cool, dry, dark area.)*
3. How can you avoid nutritional loss from fresh vegetables and fruits? *(Prepare just before cooking; avoid soaking in water.)*
4. How can you avoid darkening of fruits such as apples? *(Prepare just before serving. If prepared ahead, coat with citrus juice.)*

Learning Activities

1. **Discussion.** Have students identify situations in which they would choose fresh, frozen, canned, and dried fruits and vegetables. (Key Skill: *Decision Making*)
2. **Posters.** Have students work in groups to develop guidelines for purchasing fresh, canned, frozen, and dried fruits and vegetables. Have students use the guidelines to create posters to share with the class. (Key Skills: *Critical Thinking, Cooperation*)
3. **Demonstrations.** Have students work in groups to plan demonstrations on how to store various fruits and vegetables. Have students present their demonstrations to the class. Discuss when fruits and vegetables should be washed. (Key Skills: *Cooperation, Communication*)

Buying Processed Fruits and Vegetables

Read the labels on frozen, canned, and dried fruits and vegetables. Labels tell whether the item is whole or in halves, slices, or pieces. The label also lists any seasonings, preservatives, or other ingredients that have been added. For example, some frozen vegetables are packaged in sauces that are often high in fat and salt. Would vegetables frozen without sauce provide better nutrition at a lower cost?

Carefully examine beverage labels. Only those labeled *juice* contain 100 percent juice.

Many fruit and vegetable juices are available. Only products labeled "juice" are 100 percent juice. Products with a different name, such as "fruit beverage," may contain added water or sugar.

Be sure cans and packages are in good condition. Avoid buying dented cans. Frozen foods with ice crystals on the packages are a sign that the packages have not been stored under the best conditions.

Storing Fruits and Vegetables

Fresh fruits and vegetables need careful handling after purchase. Store ripe fruits, unwashed, in the refrigerator. Place them in a plastic bag or in the crisper section. Allow unripe fruits to ripen at room temperature before refrigerating them.

Most fresh vegetables need prompt refrigeration. Potatoes and dry onions are the exception. Store them in a cool, dry, dark area.

Keep canned foods in a cool, dry location, if possible at 65°F (20°C). Keep frozen foods at 0°F (−18°C) or below. Long freezer storage is not recommended. Try to use frozen fruits and vegetables within a few months.

Store potatoes in a cool, dry, dark area.

Preparing Fruits and Vegetables

Fruits and vegetables add flavor, texture, appearance, and nutritional value to meals. Preparing them carefully will help maintain the quality in each fruit and vegetable you serve.

Oxidation of Fruit

Materials: Apple, water, lemon, labels.

Equipment: Peeler, paring knife, cutting board, 3 saucers, 2 small bowls, glass measuring cup.

Purpose: To help students understand how fruit oxidizes and how to prevent oxidation.

Outcomes:

- The fruit contains substances which oxidize when exposed to oxygen.
- Ascorbic acid protects the fruit from oxidation.
- Holding the apple slices under water will prevent oxygen from reaching the surface of the fruit, but it also will allow valuable

▼ Handling Produce ▼

Fresh fruits and vegetables should be washed under cold running water before use. Use a brush to clean hard vegetables, such as potatoes and carrots.

To save nutrients, pare fresh vegetables and fruits as little as possible. In general, most of the nutrients are found just under the skin. If you want to pare, slice, or cut fruits and vegetables, wait until just before you use them. Water-soluble nutrients (the B vitamins and vitamin C) are destroyed by exposure to air. Soaking produce in water also causes water-soluble nutrients to be lost.

Some fresh fruits, such as bananas, apples, peaches, and pears, darken when cut and exposed to the air. If you need to cut them before serving, squeeze lemon, orange, or grapefruit juice on them to prevent browning.

Most fresh fruits and many fresh vegetables can be served raw. For easier eating, cut vegetables into sticks or bite-size pieces.

Oxidation of Fruit

Materials
apple, water, lemon, labels

Equipment
peeler, paring knife, cutting board, 3 saucers, 2 small bowls, glass measuring cup

Directions:
Set out 3 saucers labeled "lemon juice," "water," and "control." Squeeze the juice from the lemon into a small bowl. Pour 1/4 cup cold water into another small bowl. Peel and slice the apple. Dip one-third of the apple slices in lemon juice. Spread them on the saucer labeled "lemon juice." Dip one-third of the apple slices in water. Spread them on the saucer labeled "water." Place the rest of the apple slices on the saucer labeled "control." Look at the apple slices on each saucer after 30 minutes and compare what has happened to them.

- ✔ Why does fruit turn brown (oxidation) after it is cut?
- ✔ What substance prevents oxidation (fruits from turning brown)?
- ✔ What other factors might speed up or slow down the oxidation process?

nutrients to diffuse into the water. Putting the cut fruit into the refrigerator will allow oxidation to occur more slowly than at room temperature because molecular activity slows down with a decrease in temperature. Coating the cut fruit with lemon juice and refrigerating it is the best method of inhibiting oxidation. The best way to preserve the most nutrients is to cut the fruit at the last possible minute before serving it.

Learning Activities (continued)

4. **Discussion.** Discuss reasons why potatoes and onions should be stored in a cool, dry, dark place. Why would under the kitchen sink be a poor place to store potatoes and onions? (Key Skills: *Communication, Critical Thinking*)
5. **Demonstrations.** Have students work in groups to demonstrate how to handle fresh fruits and vegetables. (Key Skills: *Cooperation, Communication*)

Follow Up

1. **Reteaching.** Have students write a "how to" article on preparing fruits and vegetables. (Key Skill: *Communication*)
2. **Enrichment.** Ask students to take the temperature of the various places where fruits and vegetables are stored in their kitchens at home to see if they conform to the guidelines suggested in the text. (Key Skill: *Decision Making*)

The World Around You

Recycling

Don't feed the wastes from fruits and vegetables to the garbage disposal. Instead, use these and other kitchen wastes, like coffee grounds and egg shells, along with grass clippings and garden waste materials, to make compost. Compost is a black, crumbly residue made when organic waste materials are broken down over time.

Wellness

Avoid buying green or sprouted potatoes. The green parts of potatoes contain *solanine*, which is a bitter, poisonous chemical. It develops in potatoes when they are stored improperly or too long.

Teaching. . .
Making Salads; Cooking Fruits and Vegetables
(pp. 576-578)

Comprehension Check

1. How should greens be prepared for salad? *(Rinse in cold water, then allow to dry; tear, don't cut.)*
2. How can you save water-soluble nutrients when cooking fresh fruits and vegetables? *(Whenever possible, leave the skins on fruits and vegetables; cook them whole or in large pieces; and cook them in a small amount of water.)*
3. How can you save nutrients when preparing canned vegetables? *(Drain the liquid into a saucepan and gently boil until it is half the original amount; add vegetables to the liquid, cover, and heat to serving temperature. You can also drain and save the liquid for future use.)*
4. What guidelines should you follow when cooking frozen vegetables? *(Place frozen food in small amount of boiling water; separate frozen pieces with a fork after cooking begins; cook for as short a time as possible.)*

Learning Activities

1. **Lab Experience.** Have students prepare salads using fresh fruits and vegetables. What guidelines should be followed? (Key Skills: *Cooperation, Management*)
2. **Comparison.** Have students compare the nutrient values of the same fruit or vegetable prepared different ways. Ask students to generalize their observations to other fruits and vegetables. (Key Skills: *Science, Critical Thinking*)
3. **Demonstration.** Demonstrate how to bake, steam, and stir-fry fruits and vegetables. (Key Skills: *Science, Management*)
4. **Brainstorming.** Have students think of as many possible uses for fruit and vegetable juices as they can. How does utilizing the liquids from canned and cooked fruits and vegetables save nutrients? (Key Skill: *Problem Solving*)
5. **Comparison.** Have students compare procedures for cooking frozen vegetables with those for cooking fresh vegetables. How

Making Salads

Tossed green salads are popular. Crisp greens are the key. For added appeal, combine several types in the salad. Greens must be cared for properly if the salad is to be crisp and fresh. Before storing, remove discolored leaves, rinse the greens in cold water, and drain them thoroughly.

Some greens, such as spinach, escarole, and curly endive, tend to hold dirt. Put them in a sink or pan of cold water, stir slightly, and lift them out of the water. The dirt settles on the bottom. Greens that are very dirty may need more than one rinsing.

Allow greens to dry before putting them in a salad. This helps the dressing cling to the leaves. If you are making a tossed salad, tear the greens into bite-size pieces. Cutting them with a knife will cause the cut edges to turn brown.

Many other fresh vegetables can be added to a tossed salad. Carrots, onions, broccoli, cauliflower, radishes, tomatoes, cucumbers, and mushrooms are popular choices. Clean the vegetables well and cut them into small pieces for easy eating.

When you add salad dressing, put it on just before serving to keep the greens from wilting. Add just enough to coat the leaves lightly. Many low-fat salad dressings are available.

To save nutrients, cook fruits and vegetables in a small amount of water until just crispy tender.

Cooking Fresh Fruits and Vegetables

When fruits and vegetables are cooked, the starch and fiber in them softens. As a result, fruits and vegetables become less crisp. In addition, some of the nutrients are lost during cooking. Water-soluble vitamins tend to move from the food to the cooking water. The vitamins can also be destroyed by heat. When foods are cooked in a large amount of water for a long time, many nutrients are lost.

More About Frozen Fruits and Vegetables

In the United States, food companies freeze over 10 billion pounds (4.5 billion kilograms) of food each year. Almost all frozen foods are quick-frozen and stored at temperatures of 0°F (–18°C) or below. Clarence Birdseye, a Massachusetts inventor, is generally credited with developing the modern quick-freezing process. While on a trip to Labrador in about 1915, Birdseye observed that quickly frozen fish were flavorful and fresh when thawed. He first marketed quick-frozen fish in 1925. Large-scale quick-freezing of foods did not begin until 1929 when General Foods Corporation acquired the process. Today, a wide variety of frozen fruits and vegetables is available. You can choose fruit juice or fruits

Dilled Green Beans with Almonds

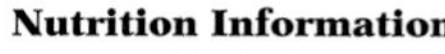

Customary	Ingredients	Metric
2 c.	Frozen Green Beans	500 mL
1½ tsp.	Margarine	7.5 mL
1 tsp.	Dill Weed	5 mL
¼ cup	Slivered Almonds	50 mL

Yield: 4 servings

Nutrition Information
Per serving (approximate): 90 calories, 3 g protein, 6 g carbohydrate, 3.5 g fat, 0 mg. cholesterol, 35 mg sodium
Good source of: vitamin A, riboflavin

Conventional Directions
Pan: 2-quart (2-liter) saucepan
Temperature: Medium-low

1. **Simmer** green beans according to package directions until tender-crisp.
2. **Drain** liquid from green beans. (Reserve the liquid for another use, if desired.)
3. **Stir** in margarine and dill weed until well blended.
4. **Add** the slivered almonds and stir.
5. **Serve** hot.

Microwave Directions
Pan: 1-quart (1-liter) microwave-safe covered casserole dish
Power Level: 100 percent

1. **Place** green beans in casserole dish. Add 2 tablespoons (30 mL) of water. Cover.
2. **Microwave** at 100 percent power for 10 minutes or until tender-crisp. Stir after 4 minutes.
3. **Stir** in margarine and dill weed until well blended.
4. **Add** the slivered almonds and stir.
5. **Serve** hot.

Proper cooking can help save nutrients. Whenever possible, leave the skins on fruits and vegetables. Cook them whole or in large pieces. When cooking on the range, simmer or steam the fruits or vegetables using a small amount of water. Stop cooking as soon as the food is tender, but still slightly crisp. To get all the nutritional value you can, eat the cooking liquid along with the fruits or vegetables, or save the liquid to use in soup.

▼ Cooking Canned Vegetables ▼

Actually, canned vegetables are already cooked. They need only be heated. Drain the liquid from the can into the saucepan and bring it to a simmer. Add the vegetables to the liquid, cover, and heat to serving temperature.

frozen whole or in pieces. You can purchase frozen vegetables, boil-in-bag vegetables, vegetable soups, vegetables in butter or a special sauce, and gourmet vegetable specialties. Frozen potato products include ready-to-fry hash browns, precooked french fries, and baked stuffed potatoes that require only heating.

Learning Activities (continued)

are the procedures similar? How are they different? (Key Skill: *Critical Thinking*)

Follow Up

1. **Reteaching.** Have students develop a creative saying, rhyme, or rap to describe the effects of method of preparation and seasoning on the number of calories in fruits and vegetables. (Key Skill: *Creativity*)
2. **Extension.** Use the extension information handout on p. 61 of the *Extending the Text* booklet in the TCR.
3. **Enrichment.** Have students visit a local restaurant that features a salad bar. Ask students to make a list of the salads and salad fixings included on the salad bar. Which are the most and least nutritious choices? (Key Skill: *Decision Making*)

Using the Recipe

Have students read the recipe. Then divide the class into two groups. Have one group prepare this dish using the conventional directions, and have the other group prepare this dish using the microwave directions. When the dishes are ready, let each student taste both of them. Do the students think one tastes better than the other? Have a representative from each group discuss any problems they encountered while preparing this dish. *(Answers will vary.)*

Life Management Skills

Resource Management

You can save time and fuel by using good management techniques when cooking fruits and vegetables. Cook potatoes and carrots in the same pot with a pot roast. Bake apples or potatoes in the oven while baking a chicken. Save fuel by stir-frying vegetables quickly until just done.

Completing the Chapter

For Review

1. Emphasize the main concepts using the summary.
2. Have students complete the "Facts to Recall." (Answers below.)

For Reteaching

1. **Reteaching.** Use the activity on p. 61 of the *Reteaching and Practical Skills* booklet in the TCR.

For Enrichment

1. **Enrichment.** Use the activity on p. 74 of the *Enrichment Activities* booklet in the TCR.

For Evaluation

1. Choose items from "Ideas to Explore" and "Activities to Try."
2. Use the chapter test on pp. 101-102 in the testing booklet of the TCR or use the testmaker software.

Facts to Recall Answers

1. They are high in nutrients, yet low in calories. They make the calories you take in count toward good nutrition.
2. Vegetables and fruits with deeper or darker colors are better sources of vitamin A than those with pale colors.
3. **Any three:** oranges, grapefruit, lemons, tomatoes, cantaloupes, strawberries. **Any three:** broccoli, green cabbage, green peppers, white potatoes, turnip greens, collards.
4. Produce is most nutritious when it is freshest; it loses nutrients as it ages. Crispness is a sign of freshness in celery and asparagus; fresh potatoes and onions do not have sprouts.
5. Labels give important information about serving size and added ingredients. This directly affects the number of calories and amount of fat and sodium in the product.
6. Unripened fruit should be allowed to ripen at room temperature, then refrigerated.

Cooking Frozen Vegetables

When cooking commercially frozen vegetables, follow the directions on the package. Cook vegetables in a small amount of water and for as short a time as possible to preserve nutrients.

Nutrients and flavor are kept if the food is still frozen when put in boiling water. Separate frozen pieces with a fork after cooking begins so they can cook more evenly.

Cooking fruits and vegetables in the microwave helps save nutrients.

Microwaving Fruits and Vegetables

Microwaving is an excellent way to cook fruits and vegetables. Since little water is needed and the food cooks quickly, nutrients are saved.

To microwave fresh fruits and vegetables, follow the directions in the owner's manual or a microwave cookbook. Usually the food is placed in a dish with a small amount of water and covered. For canned and frozen vegetables, check the label for microwave directions.

TAKING ACTION
Using Fruits and Vegetables in Recipes

A classmate, Christine, greets you Monday morning with exciting news. Several statewide produce growers' organizations are sponsoring a cooking competition for teens. Contestants are to submit menus using fruits and vegetables in as many courses as possible — appetizers, main courses, and desserts. Each group of recipes will be judged on creativity, flavor, ease of preparation, and overall nutritional value. First prize is a two-week summer course at a prestigious food preparation school in France with all expenses paid.

Christine is a talented cook, and would like to become a professional chef. She sees this as an excellent opportunity to advance in her career. She asks you for suggestions on what recipes she should enter.

Using Your Resourcefulness

- Where can Christine find new ideas for using vegetables and fruits?
- Where can she learn about unusual fruits and vegetables?
- How can Christine determine the nutritional advantages and disadvantages of each recipe?
- How can she calculate the time and effort needed to prepare each recipe?
- How might Christine evaluate the recipes for flavor and other meal appeal factors?
- Identify all the resources, human and material, that Christine can use to help her make her decision.

TAKING ACTION

After students have read the feature, have them discuss what menu suggestions they could make to Christine to help her win the competition. To guide this discussion, you may want to have students answer the *Using Your Resourcefulness* questions at the end of this feature.

Using Your Resourcefulness Answers

- Answers will vary and might include cookbooks, magazines, and family and consumer sciences textbooks.
- Answers will vary. Possible answers might include family and consumer sciences textbooks, a professional cook, and cookbooks.
- Answers will vary and might include talking to a nutritionist about the recipes, talking

Chapter 49 Review

Summary

In this chapter, you have read about:

- The variety of nutrients found in different fruits and vegetables.
- How to select quality produce.
- What to look for when buying processed fruits and vegetables.
- How to store fruits and vegetables to preserve nutrients and freshness.
- How to prepare fresh, canned, and frozen fruits and vegetables to preserve their nutrients.

Facts to Recall

1. What makes vegetables and fruits "nutritional bargains"?
2. What does color tell you about a vegetable or fruit as a source of vitamin A?
3. Name three fruits and three vegetables that are good sources of vitamin C.
4. How does freshness affect the nutritional value of produce? What are signs of freshness in celery and asparagus? In potatoes and onions?
5. Why should you read the labels on packages of processed fruits and vegetables?
6. Explain how to store unripe fruit.
7. What is the advantage of the leaving skins on fruits and vegetables?
8. Briefly describe the steps in preparing a tossed green salad.
9. How do air, heat, and water affect the nutritional value of fruits and vegetables?

Ideas to Explore

1. Discuss the advantages and disadvantages of buying processed vegetables and fruits instead of fresh produce.
2. One of the appealing features of vegetables and fruits is the many different varieties. What new or unusual types of produce have appeared in supermarkets in the last few years? How might they be used in meals?

Activities to Try

1. Write a short, imaginative essay in which you "invent" a new produce item. The item should combine the best traits of existing fruits and vegetables, such as taste, appearance, availability, and versatility. Explain what characteristics you selected from each fruit or vegetable. Offer preparation and recipe suggestions, and don't forget to name your new creation.
2. Bring to class labels or packages from processed fruits and vegetables. Using the ingredients list and nutrition information, analyze the nutritional value of the product. Use reference books to find the nutrient content of the same food without processing. How does the processed version compare with the fresh version?

LINK TO Math

COMPARING COST PER SERVING

Complete a cost comparison study for fruits and vegetables. List three types of fruits and three types of vegetables. Compare the costs per serving for as many forms of these fruits and vegetables as possible (fresh, frozen, canned, and dried). Be sure to compare equal size portions for each form. Answer the following questions about your study:

- Which fruits and vegetables (type and form) have the highest cost per serving?
- Which fruits and vegetables (type and form) have the lowest cost per serving?
- What factors do you think contribute to the differences in cost per serving?

Facts to Recall Answers (continued)

7. It saves nutrients, because most of the nutrients are found under the skin.
8. Rinse the greens until clean and allow them to dry. Tear them into bite-size pieces. If you add other vegetables, clean them well and cut them into small pieces. Put on salad dressing just before serving, using just enough to coat the leaves lightly.
9. Air, heat, and water cause fruits and vegetables to lose nutrients, especially water-soluble vitamins and vitamins B and C. They should therefore be cooked in as little water and for as short a time as possible.

Ideas to Explore

1. Answers will vary. Advantages may include: processed vegetables and fruits are more conveniently stored and prepared; they may be cheaper when the fresh produce is out of season. Disadvantages may include: they may be more expensive than fresh produce when the produce is in season; they may contain unwanted added ingredients.
2. Answers will vary.

to a dietitian about them, and talking to a family and consumer sciences teacher about them.

- Answers will vary. Christine could study the ingredients needed and the procedure required for each recipe. She also could ask someone who has prepared each recipe how long it took and how difficult the procedure was.
- Answers will vary. Christine could make each recipe and taste and evaluate them herself, have her family and friends taste and evaluate them, and have a family and consumer sciences teacher taste and evaluate them.
- Answers will vary and might include a family and consumer sciences teacher, a nutritionist, a dietitian, a professional cook, cookbooks, magazines, and family and consumer sciences textbooks.

LINK TO Math

Answers

- Answers will vary depending on which fruits and vegetables students choose.
- Answers will vary depending on which fruits and vegetables students choose.
- Answers will vary depending on which fruits and vegetables students choose.

Preparing to Teach

Chapter Outline

Chapter Resources

The following booklet materials may be found in the *Teacher's Classroom Resources* box:

- Lesson Plans, p. 56
- Student Workbook, *Study Guide,* pp. 213-214; *Getting Around Protein Foods,* p. 215; *Comparing Protein Prices,* p. 216
- Color Transparencies, *The Meat, Poultry, Fish, Dry Beans, Eggs, and Nuts Group,* CT-55
- Technology and Computers, pp. 46, 47
- Foods Lab Management and Recipes, R-13, pp. 39-40; R-14, pp. 41-42; R-15, pp. 43-44; R-16, pp. 45-46
- Cooperative Learning, p. 62
- Extending the Text, *How to Cut Up a Chicken,* p. 62
- Reteaching and Practical Skills, *Protein Food Match,* p. 63
- Enrichment Activities, *Your Protein Needs,* pp. 75-76
- Chapter and Unit Tests, pp. 103-104
- Testmaker Software

Also see:

- Meeting the Special Needs of Students
- Linking Home, School, and Community

ABCNews InterActive™ Videodiscs

- *Food and Nutrition*

See the ABCNews InterActive™ Bar Code Correlation booklet for applicable segments.

CHAPTER 50 Protein Foods

OBJECTIVES

- *Identify the role of protein foods in the diet.*
- *Describe how to buy, store, and prepare protein foods.*

TERMS TO LEARN

- ***marbling***
- ***tofu***

More About *Nutrients in Meat*

Meats are important sources of the minerals iron and copper. Your body needs these minerals to build red blood cells. Iron gives the blood its red color and is needed to make hemoglobin. The hemoglobin in red blood cells transports oxygen from the lungs to all body cells. It also removes waste from cells. When the body's supply of iron is low, there will be too

People often plan meals around a protein food. There are many protein foods to choose from, including meat (beef, pork, veal, and lamb), poultry, fish, eggs, and legumes (dry beans and peas). With so many choices, it's possible to plan an almost endless variety of main dishes. What are some of your favorites?

Nutrients in Protein Foods

What do foods in the Meat, Poultry, Fish, Dry Beans, Eggs, and Nuts Group have in common? All are good sources of protein. Meat, poultry, fish, and eggs have *complete* proteins. As you learned in Chapter 38, that means they have all the essential amino acids your body needs to build and repair its cells. Legumes and nuts contain *incomplete* proteins. When combined with other plant or animal proteins, they too can meet your body's protein needs.

Besides protein, each of the foods in this group provides additional nutrients.

- Meat supplies B vitamins and iron.
- Poultry has iron, B vitamins, and phosphorus for strong bones.
- Fish and shellfish are often good sources of iron and vitamins A and D. Most saltwater fish and shellfish supply iodine.
- Eggs have vitamins A and D, as well as riboflavin and iron.
- Legumes are rich in carbohydrates and fiber. They are also good sources of iron, calcium, phosphorus, B vitamins, and vitamin E.

What types of protein foods do you generally eat? Remember to choose protein foods that are low in fat.

Although all protein sources are nutritious, they differ in fat content. The Dietary Guidelines recommend a diet low in fat, especially saturated fat. Here are some tips to help you follow the Dietary Guidelines when choosing protein foods:

- Eat a variety of protein foods, including lower-fat ones. Skinless, light-meat poultry has less fat than most red meats. Fish is generally low in fat. In addition, the fat found in poultry and fish is less saturated than that in meat. Most legumes have almost no fat at all.
- To reduce the fat in meat, choose lean cuts. You can sometimes tell which cuts have less fat just by looking. Trim away the fat you can see.

few red blood cells. This results in a condition known as *anemia*. Anemia causes fatigue and may result in lowered resistance to infection. Girls and women are more likely to be anemic than boys and men because of the loss of blood, and therefore, iron, during the menstrual period. Iron is not widely available in common foods. Liver is the best food source. Heart and kidney are also high in iron. Lean meats and egg yolks are other protein foods that are good sources of iron. Iron from animal sources is absorbed more efficiently than iron from vegetable sources.

Introducing the Chapter

Motivators

1. **List.** Have students compile a list of foods used as main dishes. If the dish is a combination of foods, what is the main ingredient? Categorize the foods used as main dishes as meat, poultry, fish, legumes, and eggs. Ask students what nutrient these foods have in common. (Key Skill: *Critical Thinking*)
2. **Posters.** Have students work in groups to create posters of the different kinds of protein foods. Each poster should include pictures of the protein foods in the group, the amount eaten in the United States each year, the nutrients provided, and guidelines for selection. Display the posters in the classroom. (Key Skills: *Cooperation, Creativity*)
3. **List.** Have students make a list of popular protein dishes. Which do they think are high in fat and calories? Which do they think are low in fat and calories? (Key Skill: *Critical Thinking*)

Chapter Objectives and Vocabulary

1. Have students read the chapter objectives and rephrase the objectives as questions.
2. Ask students to state, in their own words, the purpose of studying this chapter.
3. Pronounce the vocabulary terms listed on the previous page. Ask students whether they are familiar with any of these. Explain that the terms will be defined in the chapter.

Guided Reading

1. Have students read the chapter and use the Study Guide on pp. 213-214 of the *Student Workbook*.

Teaching. . .
Nutrients in Protein Foods; Buying Protein Foods; Shopping for Meat
(pp. 581-583)

Comprehension Check

1. How can incomplete protein foods be used to provide good nutrition? *(Combine incomplete protein foods or combine small amounts of a complete protein food with an incomplete protein food.)*
2. How can you reduce the fat content of meat and poultry? *(Choose foods low in fat content and trim any visible fat.)*
3. Why must shoppers be careful when planning and selecting protein foods? *(Because protein foods are more expensive than many other foods.)*
4. How are cuts of meat labeled? *(The label lists the source of meat, the name of larger wholesale cut, and the name of retail cut.)*
5. How can the tenderness of meat be judged? *(By the amount of connective tissue in the meat.)*

Learning Activities

1. **Review.** Review the complete and incomplete proteins. Have students categorize protein foods as complete or incomplete proteins. (Key Skill: *Critical Thinking*)
2. **Listing.** Have students name combinations of protein foods that are traditionally eaten together. Examples include beans and rice, and a peanut butter sandwich. Discuss how complete protein is formed. (Key Skill: *Science*)

AROUND THE WORLD

After reading the feature, have students investigate the main dishes of other cultures. Which dishes are made from combinations of incomplete proteins or complete and incomplete proteins? Why do students think these combinations are popular? *(Answers will vary.)*

- Choose low-fat cooking methods, such as baking or broiling instead of frying.
- Remove skin from poultry before eating. Most of the fat is just underneath the skin.
- Eat moderate portions. Many people eat more protein foods than they really need. Two servings of meat, poultry, or fish — each about the size of a deck of cards (3 oz. or 85 g) — supply all the protein you need for an entire day.
- Limit egg yolks, which contain saturated fat, to three per week. In many recipes, you can replace whole eggs with egg whites or egg substitutes.

AROUND THE WORLD

Many people of India are vegetarians for religious and economic reasons. They get their complete proteins by combining incomplete ones. One common way is by eating a meal of chapatis (chah-PAH-tee) and dal. A chapati is a small flat bread made with whole wheat flour. Dal is a soup or stew named for the Indian legume (similar to split peas) that is its main ingredient. What food groups provide the protein in this meal? What combinations do people in the United States eat that might be similar to chapati and dal?

Buying Protein Foods

Skillful shopping is important with protein foods. Fish, poultry, and meat are expensive. By considering nutrition, quality, and money-saving options, you can make good choices.

Some of the suggestions given for lowering fat can also help you save money. For instance, legumes are a low-cost, as well as low-fat, source of protein. You can also save by combining a small amount of meat with other foods, as in a soup or stew.

Shopping for Meat

Most meat comes from cattle (beef and veal), hogs (pork and ham), and sheep (lamb). Federal laws require that all animals used for food be inspected and found healthy.

Meat is made up of the lean portion (muscle), connective tissue, fat, and bone. The thick white connective tissue holds muscle fibers together.

More About Amount of Meat to Buy

Remember, you only need a total of about 6 ounces of meat, poultry, fish, dry beans, eggs, and nuts each day. Three ounces of cooked lean beef or chicken without skin — about the size of a deck of cards — is a serving. One egg, not two, is a serving. Three fish sticks provide 1.5 servings of protein plus 1 bread serving. (Also don't forget that 40 percent of fish sticks' calories come from fat.) One-half cup cooked beans can be counted as one ounce of meat or as a serving of vegetables.

Smaller pieces of meat, called retail cuts, are what you find in the supermarket. Read the labels carefully to determine the source of the meat and the retail cut.

Cuts and Labeling

Meat is first divided into large pieces called *wholesale cuts*. These wholesale cuts are divided into the smaller pieces called *retail cuts*. Retail cuts are the ones you find in the supermarket. The chart on page 584 shows the wholesale and retail cuts of beef.

Generally, you'll find retail cuts wrapped and labeled. The label identifies the cut with a name such as "Beef Flank Steak." This name tells you the source of the meat (beef), the wholesale cut it comes from (flank), and the specific retail cut (steak).

What to Look For in Meat

You will find many choices in the meat case. Here are some guidelines to help you find quality meat at a good price.

- ***Grading.*** Meat is often graded according to overall quality. The three top grades of beef are *Prime*, *Choice*, and *Select*. (For veal and lamb, "Good" replaces "Select.") All three grades are nutritious. Meat graded "Prime" is the most expensive and highest in fat. It usually goes to restaurants. The "Select" or "Good" grade generally is the least expensive and has the least fat.
- ***Tenderness.*** Meat with less connective tissue is usually more tender. Connective tissue builds up most in body areas which are exercised the most. For example, chuck from the shoulder is less tender than tenderloin from the short loin. Tender cuts usually cost more. Less tender cuts are just as nutritious and can be made tender by long, slow cooking in moist heat.

Cuts labeled "Choice" are generally higher in fat and cost than similar cuts labeled "Select."

Learning Activities (continued)

3. **Label Reading.** Provide students with labels from several retail cuts of meat. Have students identify the source of meat, names of wholesale and retail cuts, and grade. (Key Skill: *Management*)
4. **Demonstration.** Point out the muscle, connective tissue, fat, and bone on a cut of meat. Show students examples of fat and lean cuts of meat. Demonstrate how to remove the fat from meat. Demonstrate how to remove fat from cooked hamburger meat by rinsing it in hot water. (Key Skills: *Science, Management*)

Follow Up

1. **Reteaching.** Have students practice matching pictures of retail cuts of meat with their names and sorting the cuts of meat into tender and less tender categories. (Key Skill: *Decision Making*)
2. **Enrichment.** Ask students to write a news bulletin about protein and amino acids, including foods that contain complete and incomplete proteins. Have them include the effects of not getting enough protein in the diet. (Key Skills: *Communication, Creativity*)

Wellness

Some nutrition experts advise limited use of processed meats. Most processed meats, such as wieners, bacon, and bologna, are high in sodium. Therefore, people who need to restrict their sodium intake should not eat much processed meat. Cured meats, such as ham and bacon, are treated with sodium nitrite to prevent botulism and to give the meat a pinkish color. Some studies have shown that under certain conditions, nitrites can cause cancer. These concerns help to show why it is important to eat a variety of foods.

Teaching. . .
What to Look For in Meat and Shopping for Poultry
(pp. 584-585)

Comprehension Check

1. What is marbling? *(Marbling refers to small veins of fat scattered throughout the muscle of meat. Marbling adds flavor and juiciness to meat.)*
2. Why should you consider the cost per serving when buying meat? *(Because with some cuts, you are paying for a large amount of bone or fat that will be wasted. Another cut the same size, but with less bone and fat, will give you more servings. Even if the cost per pound is higher for the second package, the cost per serving may be less.)*
3. What are the two most common types of poultry? *(Chicken and turkey.)*

Learning Activities

1. **Chart.** Display a meat chart showing wholesale and retail cuts of beef, pork, veal, and lamb. Have students identify characteristics of each. Ask students to generalize about the part of the animal that produces the most tender cuts of meat. (Key Skills: *Science, Critical Thinking*)
2. **Comparisons.** Have students study the chart on page 586 to learn how to determine the amount of meat to buy. Have students compare the costs per serving of different cuts of meat. How does the cost per serving compare with the cost per pound? Have students draw conclusions. (Key Skill: *Management*)
3. **Supermarket Visit.** Have students visit the meat department in a supermarket to observe the kinds and cuts of meat available. Ask them to find examples of several retail cuts of meat. For each cut, have them record the weight, price, and description of cut from the label. (Key Skill: *Management*)

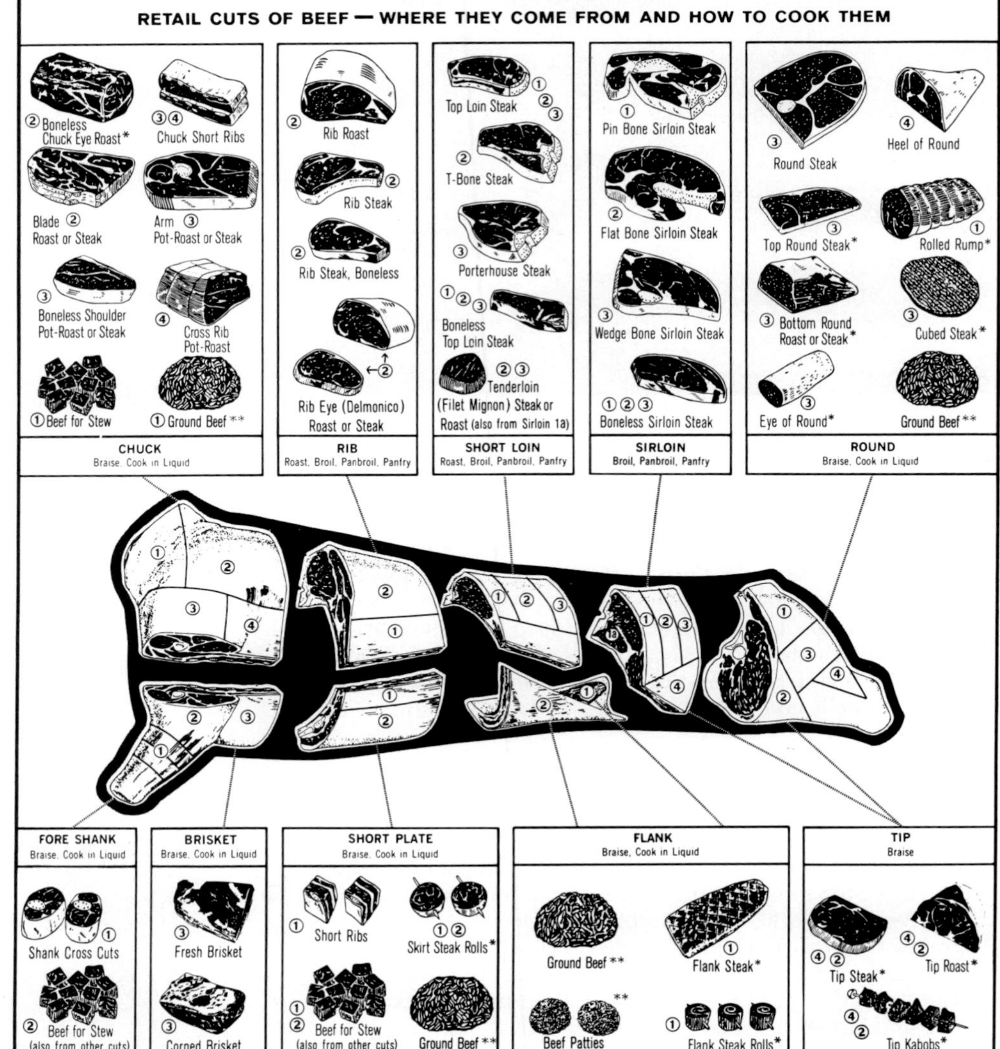

More About Meat and Poultry

Livestock and poultry breeders are responding to Americans' demands for less fat and cholesterol. Livestock breeders are producing cattle and hogs with meat that is lower in fat without sacrificing tenderness. A new, leaner grade of beef, "select," was introduced in 1987. Poultry breeders have developed breeds of birds that produce more meat or eggs than other types. For example, turkeys raised in the United States have an extremely broad breast that provides large amounts of white meat. Researchers are also working to develop chickens that lay eggs with less cholesterol.

- ▶ ***Leanness.*** Fat in meat is found in two forms. The large sections of fat found around the edges of meat can be trimmed away before cooking. **Marbling** refers to small veins of fat scattered throughout the muscle. Marbling adds flavor and juiciness to meat. However, lean meat can also be flavorful and juicy if cooked properly.
- ▶ ***Cost per serving.*** Meat labels tell you the cost per pound, the number of pounds, and the price you pay for the package. To find the best buys, you should also consider the cost per serving. With some cuts, you are paying for a large amount of bone or fat that will be wasted. Another cut the same size, but with less bone and fat, will give you more servings. Even if the cost per pound is higher for the second package, the cost per serving may be less.

▼ Shopping for Poultry ▼

The two most common types of poultry are chicken and turkey. Grading for quality is voluntary. You'll usually see Grade A in the store. You can buy poultry fresh, hard chilled, or frozen. "Hard chilled" means chilled between 0°F (–18°C) and 26°F (–4°C), while "frozen" means below 0°F (–18°C).

When you shop for poultry, compare the prices of different forms. Larger turkeys and chickens usually cost less per pound than smaller ones, and you get more meat per pound. Whole poultry generally costs less per pound than cut-up poultry. You can also buy packages with only specific pieces, such as legs or breast portions, and boneless, skinless pieces. As when buying meat, consider the cost per serving.

You can buy poultry in different forms ranging from whole to cut-up. Whole poultry usually costs the least per pound, but has more waste. Boneless, skinless chicken breasts may be the most costly, but have no waste. Check the cost per serving to determine the best buy for you and your family.

Learning Activities (continued)

4. **Demonstration.** Demonstrate how to cut up a chicken. Show how fat can be removed by removing skin and visible fat. (Key Skill: *Management*)
5. **Supermarket Visit.** Have students visit the meat department of a local supermarket to observe the kinds and forms of poultry available. Have students obtain prices for whole and cut-up poultry, for individual pieces, and for boneless and skinless pieces. In class, determine which are the best buys. (Key Skill: *Math*)

Follow Up

1. **Reteaching.** Write the following sentence on the board: "When shopping for protein sources, there are several things to consider." Then write the following words on the board: *cuts, labels, grades, marbling, and poultry.* Then ask students to write a two-paragraph essay starting with the topic sentence and using all the words in their appropriate contexts. (Key Skill: *Communication*)
2. **Enrichment.** Have students write a recipe or serving suggestion for the various cuts of chicken (or turkey) — legs, wings, thighs, breasts. They might consider how white and dark meat differ and when each is appropriate. (Key Skill: *Communication*)

Wellness

Cholesterol is a fatty substance found only in animals. It is present in every cell in the human body. The body needs cholesterol for digestion and to make certain body chemicals. However, we do not need extra cholesterol from the foods we eat. We can limit both fat and cholesterol by limiting butter, eggs, fatty meats, and organ meats. We can also reduce fat and cholesterol by choosing lean cuts of meat, eating more fish and poultry, removing the skin from chicken and turkey, trimming off and draining off fat, and avoiding fried foods.

Teaching. . .

Shopping for Fish; Shopping for Eggs; Shopping for Legumes

(pp. 586-587)

Comprehension Check

1. How can you tell if fish is spoiled? *(By its odor.)*
2. What are some advantages of using eggs? *(They provide important nutrients at a fairly low cost, and there are a variety of uses for eggs.)*
3. What should you look for when buying legumes? *(Firm, clean legumes of uniform size and color.)*
4. What is tofu? *(Tofu is a product made from soybeans, a type of legume. Tofu is white in color with a texture somewhat like custard or soft cheese.)*

Learning Activities

1. **Display.** Display examples of the forms of fish and shellfish available in the supermarket. Discuss pointers for buying fresh and frozen fish. (Key Skills: *Communication, Management*)
2. **Price Comparisons.** Provide students with price information on different forms of fish: whole, dressed, steaks, fillets, portions, sticks, and canned. Have students figure the cost per serving of each. Discuss reasons why prices for fresh fish change frequently. (Key Skills: *Math, Management*)
3. **Observation.** Have students break Grade AA, Grade A, and Grade B eggs on small plates. Ask students to note differences in size, shape, and appearance. Have students compare differences in cost per ounce. (Key Skills: *Critical Thinking, Management*)
4. **Display.** Display a variety of common legumes. Ask students to identify the legumes and their uses. Discuss characteristics to look for when buying legumes. (Key Skill: *Management*)

Servings per Pound

Meat, poultry, or fish that contains...	Such as...	Will give you...
Little fat and no bone	▶ Ground beef ▶ Boneless chicken breasts ▶ Tuna steaks	3 to 4 servings per pound (500 g)
Moderate amounts of fat and/or bone	▶ Pork chops ▶ Chicken or turkey parts	2 to 3 servings per pound (500 g)
Large amounts of fat, bone, or other waste	▶ Pork spareribs ▶ Whole fish	1 to 2 servings per pound (500 g)

To figure the cost per serving...
Find the cost per pound on the package. Divide it by the number of servings per pound.
Example: Ground beef — $1.99 per pound. Round off to $2. If you get 4 servings per pound, the cost per serving is $2.00 ÷ 4, or 50 cents.

Because they are concerned about saturated fat in the diet, many Americans are enjoying more fish in their diets.

▼ Shopping for Fish ▼

Fish and shellfish are usually bought fresh, frozen, or canned. The cost and supply of fresh fish varies with the season of the year. Frozen and canned fish are available all year.

Fish spoils easily. Fresh or frozen fish should have a fresh fish smell, not an unpleasant odor. You'll know the difference immediately.

As with meat and poultry, consider the cost per serving. The chart on this page shows how many servings you can get from a quantity of meat, poultry, or fish. This will also help you decide how much to buy.

▼ Shopping for Eggs ▼

Eggs provide important nutrients at fairly low cost. An omelet made from eggs might be the main dish for a meal. Eggs are also used as ingredients in other foods ranging from meat loaf to cake.

More About Shopping for Fish

The fat content of most fish is low. However, some fish are naturally leaner than others. Fish that are low in fat are easily recognized by their white flesh. Lean fish include halibut, cod, flounder, haddock, pollock, mullet, ocean perch, turbot, carp, and whiting. Tuna, salmon, mackerel, herring, catfish, and lake trout have more fat. The fish oil from these fatty cold-water species is highly polyunsaturated. This means that, unlike saturated fats, it is beneficial in reducing blood cholesterol levels. Fish with a high fat content have yellow, pink, or grayish-colored flesh. Most shellfish contain little fat and are lean. Processing also affects the amount of fat in fish. Tuna, which is naturally low in fat, is only 5% fat when canned

When buying eggs, you will probably have a choice of size and perhaps of grade. Grade is based on the quality of the egg. Stores most often sell grades AA and A eggs in medium, large, and extra large sizes.

Generally, higher-grade and larger-size eggs are more expensive. However, prices vary depending on the supply of different sizes. Recipes are usually tested using large eggs.

Some stores sell eggs with brown shells. Brown and white eggs have the same nutrients and taste.

Eggs should be refrigerated both before and after purchase. They lose their freshness quickly at room temperature. Open the egg carton before buying to check that the eggs are not cracked or broken.

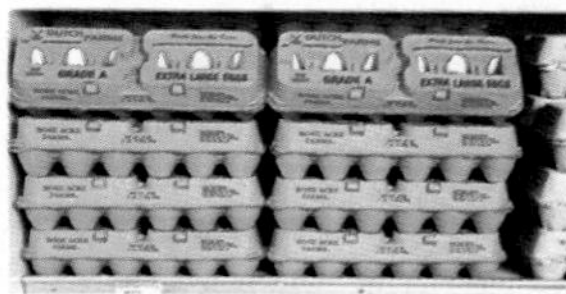

Eggs provide good nutrition at a lower cost. However, many health experts recommend limiting the number of eggs you eat because they are high in cholesterol.

▼ Shopping for Legumes ▼

Most legumes are packaged in boxes or plastic bags. Some are sold from large sacks or bins by the pound. Beans are also available canned and ready to use.

Allow about ¼ cup (50 mL) of uncooked legumes per serving. Although the amount may seem small, legumes expand greatly when cooked.

Look for firm, clean legumes of uniform size and color. If sizes are uneven, they will not cook evenly.

Tofu (TOE-fu) is a product made from soybeans, a type of legume. Tofu is white in color with a texture somewhat like custard or soft cheese. Its mild flavor is ideal for blending with other foods in soups, casseroles, and stir-fried dishes. It is low in fat and sodium, high in protein and calcium.

Some tofu comes in a special package that can safely be kept at room temperature. Otherwise, it should be found in the refrigerated case. Choose from firm or soft tofu depending on how you want to use it. Make sure the package is tightly sealed, and check the freshness date.

Legumes are an excellent, low-cost source of protein and other nutrients. Combine them with corn muffins and other whole grains for complete protein.

Follow Up

1. **Reteaching.** Provide students with a drawing of a traffic signal. On each light, have students summarize guidelines for shopping for protein foods using these categories: "Go," "Caution," and "Stop." (Key Skill: *Communication*)
2. **Reteaching.** Write the following list on the board: fish, eggs, and legumes. Then have students copy down the words and write next to each what form(s) it is usually sold in, whether it is a complete or an incomplete protein, and what vitamins and minerals it contains. (Fish: fresh, frozen, or canned; complete; vitamins A and D and iron. Eggs: fresh brown and white; complete; vitamins A and D, riboflavin, and iron. Legumes: packaged in boxes or plastic bags, or sold from large sacks or bins by the pound; incomplete; B vitamins, vitamin E, iron, calcium, and phosphorus.) (Key Skills: *Communication, Decision Making*)
3. **Enrichment.** Have students research one of the following industries: livestock, poultry, fishing, or farming. What challenges does the industry face in providing people with safe, nutritious, reasonably priced protein while addressing world environmental concerns? (Key Skills: *Communication, Science*)

in water, but it contains 38% fat when canned in oil. Frying and the addition of sauces also increase the fat content of fish.

Photo Focus

Discuss the photo at the bottom of page 586 with the students. Ask them if their families include a lot of fish in their meals at home. Are students' parents aware of the advantages of replacing red meat with fish? Ask students if they like fish. If they do, what are some of their favorite types of fish? *(Answers will vary.)*

Teaching. . .
Storing Protein Foods; Preparing Protein Foods; Cooking Meat, Poultry, and Fish
(pp. 588-589)

Comprehension Check

1. How should you store protein foods? *(All, except legumes, should be stored in the refrigerator or freezer and used within a reasonable period of time.)*
2. Why should protein foods be cooked at low to moderate cooking temperatures? *(To allow the protein to become firm without being tough, dry, or rubbery. The protein cooks evenly and is less likely to shrink.)*
3. Why shouldn't you thaw frozen meat, poultry, or fish at room temperature? How should you thaw these items? *(If you thaw frozen meat, poultry, or fish at room temperature, they could spoil and cause illness. Instead, place the frozen package in the refrigerator the day before you will need it. To save time, you can use a microwave oven to defrost food.)*
4. How do methods for cooking young and tender poultry differ from those used for mature poultry? *(Young and tender poultry — broil, fry, roast, or microwave; mature poultry — braise, steam, or stew.)*
5. Why is the cooking time for fish usually short? *(Because fish is tender.)*
6. What time guideline should be observed when cooking fish? *(A good time guideline to use is 10 minutes for every inch of thickness.)*

TIPS:

Flavoring Meats
Have students read the feature. Then discuss the students' favorite ways to add flavor to different types of meat. Are these methods of flavoring meat unhealthy choices? Could students pick a healthier method of flavoring meat without changing the taste too much? *(Answers will vary.)*

TIPS: *Flavoring Meats*

Meat dishes may be flavored in a variety of ways. Here are some examples.

- **Seasoning.** Sprinkled with salt, pepper, herbs and/or spices while cooking.
- **Marinating.** Soaked in, and sometimes basted with, a seasoned, usually acidic liquid (a marinade). Also tenderizes the meat.
- **Sauce or gravy.** Served with a seasoned mixture of meat juices thickened with flour or cornstarch. The sauce is often passed at table.
- **Coating.** Covered with seasoned bread or cracker crumbs or cornmeal, and baked.

Storing Protein Foods

All protein foods, except legumes, should be refrigerated or frozen. The length of time they will stay fresh in the refrigerator varies:

- Most fresh meat and poultry — 2 to 3 days.
- Ground meat — 1 to 2 days.
- Fresh fish — up to 2 days. Cover tightly to keep odors from transferring to other foods.
- Eggs — 5 weeks. Keep them in the store carton. Do not wash them.

Meat, poultry, and fish can be frozen for longer storage. Use freezer-safe wrap.

Store legumes in a tightly covered container in a cool, dry place. To store tofu, follow package directions.

Preparing Protein Foods

It's best to use low to moderate cooking temperatures for protein foods. Lower temperatures allow the protein to become firm without being tough, dry, or rubbery. The protein cooks evenly and is less likely to shrink.

Cooking Meat, Poultry, and Fish

Cookbooks can give you many ideas for preparing meat, poultry, and fish. You may want to review the basic cooking methods discussed in Chapter 46.

Effects of Heat on Protein

Materials
2 cups of milk

Equipment
2 small saucepans

Directions:
Place 1 cup of milk in each of two small saucepans. Heat the milk in one saucepan over low heat (below 140°F or 60°C). Heat the milk in the other saucepan over high heat (above 175°F or 80°C). Observe the appearance of the milk in the two saucepans. Carefully taste the milk from each saucepan. Answer the following:

- ✔ What results did low heat have on the appearance and flavor of the milk?
- ✔ What results did high heat have on the appearance and flavor of the milk?
- ✔ How might these results apply to heating other protein foods?

Effects of Heat on Protein

Materials: 2 cups of milk.
Equipment: 2 small saucepans.

Purpose: To help students understand the effects of heat on protein.

Outcomes:

- The milk heated over low heat did not scorch or stick to the pan. No change in flavor occurred.
- The milk heated over high heat scorched and stuck to the pan. A tough, rubbery skin or "scum" may have developed. The milk may have curdled. The milk developed an off taste.
- Protein foods should be cooked over low heat.

Thawing Safely

Never thaw frozen meat, poultry, or fish at room temperature. It could spoil and cause illness. Instead, place the frozen package in the refrigerator the day before you will need it. (A whole turkey takes 2 to 5 days to thaw.) To save time, you can use a microwave oven to defrost food. Follow the directions in the owner's manual. Food defrosted in the microwave oven must be cooked right away.

Small pieces, such as hamburger patties or fish fillets, can often be cooked while still frozen. Allow extra cooking time.

Most frozen convenience foods are cooked without thawing. Check package directions.

Plan ahead — allow enough time to thaw a frozen turkey safely before cooking it.

Choosing a Cooking Method

When deciding how to cook meat, the most important factor is tenderness. Tender cuts of meat usually are cooked by a dry-heat method, such as roasting, broiling, or pan frying. Less tender cuts of meat are cooked with a moist-heat method, such as braising or stewing.

Poultry labeled "broiler-fryer" or "roaster" is young and tender. It can be cooked just as the name states or by other methods, such as microwaving. Mature poultry (a hen or stewing chicken) is the most tender and juicy when braised, steamed, or stewed.

Fish is tender because there is very little connective tissue. Broiling or baking works well with fish.

When Is It Done?

Meat and poultry should be cooked until there is no pink inside and juices run clear. When roasting a large cut of meat or whole poultry, use a meat thermometer. Before cooking, insert the thermometer in the center of the roast or bird. Be sure it does not rest on bone or fat. Cook meat to at least 160°F (71°C) and whole poultry to 180°F (82°C).

Because fish is tender, the cooking time is usually short. A good time guideline to use is 10 minutes for every inch of thickness. Overcooking dries out fish and causes it to break apart. Fish is finished cooking when the flesh flakes, or separates easily, when tested with a fork.

Perfectly cooked fish separates, or flakes, easily with a fork.

Learning Activities

1. **Storage Recall.** Place several examples of each type of protein food in a grocery bag. Hold the protein foods up one at a time. Have students give instructions for proper storage of each type of food. Keep pulling these protein foods out of the grocery bag until everyone is sure how they should be stored. (Key Skills: *Communication, Critical Thinking*)
2. **Lab Experience.** Have students cook small amounts of an inexpensive cut of meat using different dry-heat and moist-heat methods. Ask students to compare the appearance and taste of the meat cooked by different methods. (Key Skills: *Science, Management*)
3. **Lab Experience.** Have students prepare the same kind of fish using different cooking methods. Have students taste the fish and determine which methods they prefer. (Key Skills: *Cooperation, Management*)
4. **Demonstration.** Demonstrate how to tell when fish is done cooking. Intentionally overcook a small sample of fish. Have students compare the properly cooked and overcooked fish. Identify characteristics of each. (Key Skills: *Science, Critical Thinking*)

Follow Up

1. **Reteaching.** Ask students what cooking methods could be used to prepare pot roast, steak, turkey, shrimp, and less tender cuts of meat. (Key Skill: *Communication*)
2. **Enrichment.** Ask students to write a cooking column for a local newspaper. Tell them that this week's feature highlights the ways of cooking protein foods. Have students choose one food for the column's feature and describe the correct cooking methods. The column should include three recipes. (Key Skill: *Communication*)

More About *Cooking Fish*

Match the cooking method with the amount of fat in the fish. Fish with a lot of fat are best broiled or baked. Their fat content keeps them from drying out during cooking. Lean fish are usually fried, poached, or steamed. They may be broiled or baked, however, if they are brushed with fat or cooked in a sauce to prevent drying.

Teaching. . . Cooking Eggs; Cooking Legumes; Microwaving Protein Foods

(pp. 590-592)

Comprehension Check

1. Why should eggs be cooked thoroughly? *(Undercooking may fail to destroy salmonella bacteria found in some eggs.)*
2. Explain how to make hard-cooked eggs. *(Place the eggs in a saucepan and cover them completely with cold water. Bring the water to a boil. Remove the pan from the heat and cover it. After about 15 to 20 minutes, take the eggs out of the hot water and put them into cold water. If you do this, the shell will be easier to remove.)*
3. What is the advantage of soaking dry beans before cooking them? *(It softens them and shortens cooking time.)*
4. Why shouldn't you ever microwave eggs in the shell? *(They could explode during or after cooking.)*

Learning Activities

1. **Lab Experience.** Have students hard-cook eggs. Discuss how piercing the large end of the shell prevents the shell from cracking. Emphasize the importance of thoroughly cooking eggs. Point out reasons why the yolk may discolor or the white

Using the Recipe

Have students read the recipe. Then divide the class into two groups. Have one group prepare this dish using the conventional directions, and have the other group prepare this dish using the microwave directions. When the dishes are ready, let each student taste both of them. Do the students think one tastes better than the other? Have a representative from each group discuss any problems they encountered while preparing this dish. *(Answers will vary.)*

Hot Bean Tortilla Pizza

Customary	Ingredients	Metric
4	Flour Tortillas, 10-inch size	4
4 tsp.	Oil	20 mL
2 16 oz. cans	Red Kidney Beans, drained and mashed	2 453-g cans
5	Green Onions (minced)	5
¼ c.	Salsa	50 mL
1½ c.	Shredded, Low-fat Cheddar Cheese	375 mL

Yield: 4 servings

Nutrition Information

Per serving (approximate):
195 calories, 29 g protein, 69 g carbohydrate, 18 g fat, 0 mg cholesterol, 700 mg sodium

Good source of:
phosphorus, folic acid, iron, calcium, and thiamine

Conventional Directions

Pan: Cookie sheet
Temperature: Broil

1. **Preheat** the broiler.
2. **Sprinkle** each tortilla with 1 teaspoon of oil on one side and place them on the cookie sheet oil-side down.
3. **Combine** mashed red kidney beans, green onions, and salsa in a bowl.
4. **Spread** one-fourth of the bean mixture on each tortilla.
5. **Sprinkle** one-fourth of the shredded, low-fat cheddar cheese on each tortilla.
6. **Place** tortillas under the broiler on the lower rack (about 10 inches from the broiler) to prevent tortillas from burning.
7. **Cook** for 8 to 10 minutes or until the beans are heated through and the cheese has melted.
8. **Serve** hot.

Microwave Directions

Pan: Microwave-safe plate
Power Level: 100 percent power
Note: Omit oil for microwaved tortillas.

1. **Place** each tortilla on a microwave-safe plate.
2. **Follow** steps 3 through 5 of the conventional directions.
3. **Microwave** each tortilla at 100 percent power for 45 seconds to 1 minute or until cheese melts and beans are heated through.
4. **Serve** hot.

Cooking Eggs

Eggs can be cooked in a variety of ways. Whatever method is used, be sure to cook eggs thoroughly — until the yolks are firm or hard. Undercooking may fail to destroy salmonella bacteria found in some eggs. Salmonella can cause food poisoning.

More About Cholesterol

When extra cholesterol is a health concern for someone in your family, try these tricks. Substitute two egg whites for each whole egg needed in recipes. Discard half of the yolks when preparing scrambled eggs or omelets. You could also investigate egg substitutes. These products have lower fat, cholesterol, and calorie counts than eggs. Several are available in liquid, frozen, or dried forms. Egg substitutes can be used to prepare omelets or scrambled eggs. They may be substituted for eggs in recipes that call for whole eggs. However, those made of milk proteins do not have the thickening power of eggs and are not suitable for recipes that use eggs as a thickener (such as custards).

How to ...
Separate Eggs

1. Place a clean egg separator over a small bowl.
2. Crack the egg; open the shell.
3. Allow the yolk to fall into the center of the separator. The white will slip through the slots of the separator into the bowl.
4. If a piece of shell falls into the egg white, remove it with a clean spoon.

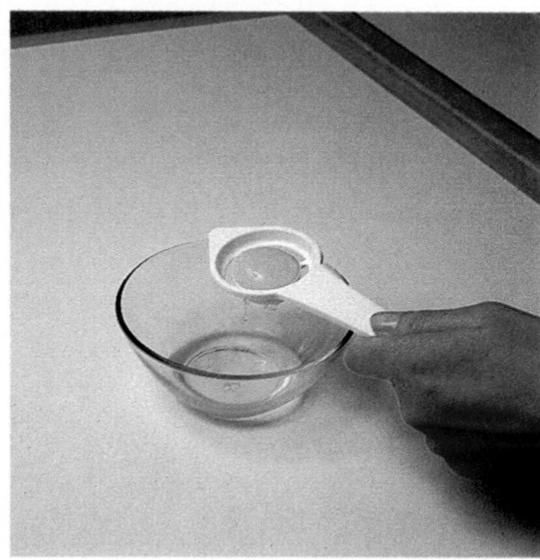

NOTE: Do not pass the yolk back and forth between shell halves. There might be bacteria present in the shell that could contaminate the yolk or the white.

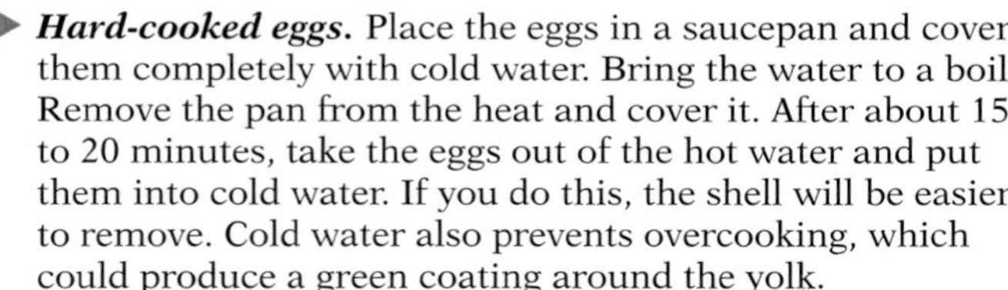

- ***Hard-cooked eggs.*** Place the eggs in a saucepan and cover them completely with cold water. Bring the water to a boil. Remove the pan from the heat and cover it. After about 15 to 20 minutes, take the eggs out of the hot water and put them into cold water. If you do this, the shell will be easier to remove. Cold water also prevents overcooking, which could produce a green coating around the yolk.
- ***Separating eggs.*** Some recipes call for egg whites or egg yolks as ingredients. It's not difficult to separate eggs. Follow the steps shown above.

Eggs can be cooked in a variety of ways.

How to ... Separate Eggs

Have students read the feature. Then have each student practice separating eggs. Observe the students as they practice this process to make sure that they are following the steps given in this feature. If there's time, have students prepare a recipe that calls for either egg whites or egg yolks as ingredients.

may become tough and rubbery. (Key Skills: *Cooperation, Management*)

2. **Demonstration.** Demonstrate how to separate eggs following the steps shown on page 591. Point out the parts of the egg. Discuss uses for separated eggs. (Key Skills: *Science, Management*)
3. **Demonstration.** Demonstrate how to prepare and cook legumes. Explain why legumes should be checked for foreign materials and washed thoroughly before using. Discuss reasons and methods for soaking beans and peas. Note the expansion of legumes as they cook. (Key Skills: *Science, Management*)
4. **Demonstration.** Demonstrate how to make scrambled eggs in the microwave oven. After the eggs are done, let the students taste them. Ask students if these scrambled eggs are as good as scrambled eggs made the conventional way. (Key Skills: *Communication, Decision Making*)

Follow Up

1. **Reteaching.** Distribute slips of paper on which you have written guidelines for cooking protein foods. Have students tell to which protein food(s) each rule applies. (Key Skills: *Communication, Management*)
2. **Extension.** Use the extension information handout on p. 62 of the *Extending the Text* booklet in the TCR.
3. **Enrichment.** Have students survey cookbooks to find recipes for protein foods. Ask students to select one recipe each for meat, poultry, fish, eggs, and legumes. Ask students to identify the form of protein food to use, to identify the method of cooking used, and to determine whether the food is a complete, incomplete, or combination protein food. (Key Skill: *Management*)

Completing the Chapter

For Review

1. Emphasize the main concepts using the summary.
2. Have students complete the "Facts to Recall." (Answers below.)

For Reteaching

1. **Reteaching.** Use the activity on p. 63 of the *Reteaching and Practical Skills* booklet in the TCR.

For Enrichment

1. **Enrichment.** Use the activity on pp. 75-76 of the *Enrichment Activities* booklet in the TCR.

For Evaluation

1. Choose items from "Ideas to Explore" and "Activities to Try."
2. Use the chapter test on pp. 103-104 in the testing booklet of the TCR or use the testmaker software.

Facts to Recall Answers

1. **Any three:** meat supplies B vitamins and iron; poultry has iron, B vitamins, and phosphorus; fish and shellfish are often good sources of iron, vitamins A and D, and iodine; eggs have vitamins A and D, riboflavin, and iron; legumes are good sources of carbohydrates, fiber, iron, calcium, phosphorus, B vitamins, and vitamin E.
2. **Any four:** eat a variety of low-fat protein foods; choose lean cuts of meat; low-fat cooking methods; eat moderate portions; remove skin from poultry; limit egg yolks to three per week.
3. Tender cuts have less connective tissue.
4. It may be the better buy if it contains less bone or fat. It costs more per pound, but you may get more servings from it.
5. Tofu is a protein product made from soybeans. White in color with a texture like custard or soft cheese. Low in fat and sodium, high in protein and calcium. Used in soups, casseroles, and stir-fried dishes.

▼ Cooking Legumes ▼

Dry beans may be soaked before cooking. This softens them and shortens the cooking time.

To soak, cover the beans with water and simmer for two minutes. Take the pot off the heat, cover, and let the beans stand for one hour. Drain and rinse the beans. Then follow the recipe directions.

▼ Microwaving Protein Foods ▼

Microwave cookbooks include many recipes for protein foods. Legumes take about as long to simmer in the microwave as they do on the range. However, meat, poultry, and fish can be microwaved quickly.

You can microwave eggs by breaking each one into a custard cup. Pierce the yolk to prevent bursting. Cover and microwave according to the directions in the owner's manual or cookbook. Scrambled eggs are also easy to make in the microwave.

Never microwave eggs in the shell. The egg could explode during or after cooking.

TAKING ACTION

Investigating Proteins

The track team at your school is having its first meet in one month and you have been preparing all winter. You've been jogging in the gym and doing flexibility exercises every morning and night. You feel fit and healthy and ready for your first competition.

In your third hour foods class, however, you were discussing the need for protein in developing and maintaining a healthy body. You've heard that athletes need extra protein for muscle growth, but you're not sure if that's true — or if it is, how much you need. You want to be in the best possible shape for track season. This sounds like something you should investigate.

Using Your Resourcefulness

- Where can you get correct information about the protein needs of athletes?
- Where can you learn about the different sources of protein?
- What are the advantages and disadvantages of each source of protein?
- Where can you find information about the possible hazards of getting too much protein?
- In what ways can you find tips on preparing protein foods for good nutrition and taste?

TAKING ACTION

Have students read the feature. Then have a class discussion about the types and amounts of protein athletes need to develop and maintain a healthy body. To guide this discussion, you may want to have students answer the *Using Your Resourcefulness* questions at the end of this feature.

Using Your Resourcefulness Answers

- Answers will vary and might include a nutritionist, a dietitian, an athletic trainer, a family and consumer sciences teacher, and magazines.
- Answers will vary. Possible answers might include family and consumer sciences

Chapter 50 Review

Summary

In this chapter, you have read about:

- How protein foods contribute to a healthful diet.
- Identifying and selecting cuts of meat.
- Buying the best quality poultry, fish, eggs, and legumes.
- Properly refrigerating, freezing, and thawing protein foods.
- Safely and nutritiously preparing protein foods.

Facts to Recall

1. Identify three types of protein foods and the nutrients each supplies.
2. List four ways of limiting fat when choosing and preparing protein foods.
3. Explain why some cuts of meat are more tender than others.
4. Explain how one package of meat, with a higher cost per pound than another, may still be the better buy.
5. What is tofu? Describe its texture, appearance, nutritional value, and uses.
6. Identify one advantage and one disadvantage of convenience foods.
7. Explain the difference in cooking methods used for tender and less tender cuts of meat and types of poultry. Give three examples of each method.
8. Identify a good time guideline for cooking fish, and a sign of doneness.
9. Give two reasons for putting eggs in cold water immediately after they are finished cooking.
10. Describe how to soak dry beans.

Ideas to Explore

1. Discuss ways of choosing and preparing protein foods economically, to get the greatest nutritional value for the least amount of money.
2. Everett is buying chicken for dinner for his family of four people. He is trying to choose between a package of boneless, skinless chicken breasts that weighs 1.25 pounds and sells for $2.49 a pound, and a package of chicken parts that weighs 2.25 pounds and sells for 69¢ a pound. According to the chart on page 586, which is the better buy? What factors in addition to price should Everett consider when making a decision?

Activities to Try

1. Bring to school recipes featuring protein foods. Be ready to identify the sources of protein in each recipe, and if possible, to suggest ways of modifying the recipe to make it lower in fat or sodium.
2. Research a short report on protein foods popular in other regions of the world. Present your findings to the class.

LINK TO *Social Studies*

PROTEIN FOODS AROUND THE WORLD

People around the world eat a variety of foods to meet their protein needs. Using cookbooks or other resources, investigate major protein sources used in different countries around the world. Then answer the following questions:

- How does a country's economy (industrial or under developed) influence the types of protein foods available?
- In what ways do the land and climate of a country influence available protein foods?
- How might culture and religion influence the choice of protein foods?

Facts to Recall Answers (continued)

6. Advantage — can be quickly heated in a microwave oven. Processing lowers their nutritional value and often adds fat, sugar, and sodium.
7. Tender cuts are cooked by dry-heat methods, such as roasting, broiling, or pan frying. Less tender are cooked by moist-heat methods, such as braising, steaming, or stewing.
8. Cook 10 minutes for every inch of thickness. Fish is done when it flakes when tested with a fork.
9. Shells are easier to remove; prevents overcooking.
10. Cover the beans with water and simmer for two minutes, then remove from the heat, cover, and let stand for one hour.

Ideas to Explore

1. Answers will vary and may include: compare the price per pound and price per serving; combine complete proteins with those supplying incomplete proteins; eat no more protein foods than needed.
2. Price per serving for chicken breasts is $.77 to $1.04. Chicken parts cost $.52 to $.77 per serving. Other factors: chicken parts have more waste; what time and skills are needed for extra preparation; can the recipe be modified for parts or breasts, and are leftovers desired.

textbooks, a family and consumer sciences teacher, magazines, a nutritionist, and a dietitian.

- Have students refer back to this chapter for advantages and disadvantages of each source of protein.
- Answers will vary and might include family and consumer sciences textbooks, a family and consumer sciences teacher, Dietary Guidelines, a nutritionist, and a dietitian.
- Answers will vary. Possible answers might include talking to a nutritionist, talking to a dietitian, looking in cookbooks, and talking to a family and consumer sciences teacher.

LINK TO *Social Studies*

Answers

- Answers will vary. In general, wealthy countries may have more protein sources from animals, and underdeveloped countries get much of their protein from plant foods.
- Answers will vary. Available farmland, water, and length of growing season all affect what types of protein food are available to a country.
- Answers will vary. Some cultures and religions forbid the consumption of certain types of or all animal foods.

Preparing to Teach

Chapter Outline

Chapter Resources

The following booklet materials may be found in the *Teacher's Classroom Resources* box:

- Lesson Plans, p. 57
- Student Workbook, *Study Guide,* pp. 217-218; *Grain Product Magic Square,* p. 219; *Coded Messages About Grains,* p. 220
- Color Transparencies, *The Bread, Cereal, Rice, and Pasta Group,* CT-56
- Technology and Computers, pp. 46, 47
- Foods Lab Management and Recipes, R-17, pp. 47-48; R-18, pp. 49-50; R-19, pp. 51-52; R-20, pp. 53-54
- Cooperative Learning, p. 63
- Extending the Text, *Breakfast Cereals—What's in the Box?,* p. 63
- Reteaching and Practical Skills, *All About Grain,* p. 64
- Enrichment Activities, *More About Rice,* p. 77
- Chapter and Unit Tests, pp. 105-106
- Testmaker Software

Also see:

- Meeting the Special Needs of Students
- Linking Home, School, and Community

ABCNews InterActive™ Videodiscs

- *Food and Nutrition*

See the ABCNews InterActive™ Bar Code Correlation booklet for applicable segments.

CHAPTER 51 Grain Products

OBJECTIVES

- *Explain the role of grain products in the diet.*
- *Describe how to buy, store, and prepare grain products.*

TERMS TO LEARN

- ***bran***
- ***endosperm***
- ***germ***
- ***enriched***
- ***leavening agent***

More About Nutrients in Grain Products

Diseases associated with diets high in certain grain products led to the discovery of the B vitamins known as thiamin and niacin. For centuries, people whose diet consisted mainly of polished rice died of beriberi, a disease that affects the nervous system. A Japanese physician discovered that a diet of polished rice must be supplemented with meat, fish, and vegetables to prevent the disease. Likewise, a Dutch physician learned that birds fed white rice developed beriberi, while those fed brown rice did not. These findings led to the discovery of Vitamin B1, or thiamin. In the early 1900s, the disease pellagra was common in the southern United States. It occurred among poor people who ate only

Grains are the primary source of food for most of the people in the world. Why? They are inexpensive and can be stored without refrigeration. Grains can be combined with small amounts of other ingredients to be made more nutritious. People from all cultures have found ways to use grains in their diets.

Nutrients in Grain Products

Why are more and more people in the United States finding ways to include grains in their daily diets? Grains, especially whole grains, represent an investment in good health. They are high in complex carbohydrates, especially fiber. They contain iron and B vitamins. When combined with legumes or animal proteins, they also provide high-quality protein. Most importantly, they do not contain saturated fat or cholesterol.

Structure of Grains

Grains are the seeds or fruits of cereal grasses. Though different in size and shape, the structure of grains, such as wheat, corn, and oats, is similar. Each part of the kernel contributes different nutrients. The grain kernels contain the following parts:

- ***Bran.*** The **bran** is the outside covering of the grain kernel. It has six thin layers of protective skin and contains mostly fiber. Bran contains many B vitamins and about 20 percent of the protein in grains.
- ***Endosperm.*** The **endosperm**, the largest part of the grain, is located inside the kernel. The endosperm is made up mostly of carbohydrate, but also contains about 75 percent of the grain's protein.
- ***Germ.*** The **germ** is the sprouting section of the kernel. It contains vegetable oil and is a rich source of vitamins. The germ is often removed during processing because its fat content limits how long grains can be stored.

Some grains, such as stone-ground whole wheat, rolled oats, and brown rice, are left practically whole. They contain almost all the nutrients originally found in the grain.

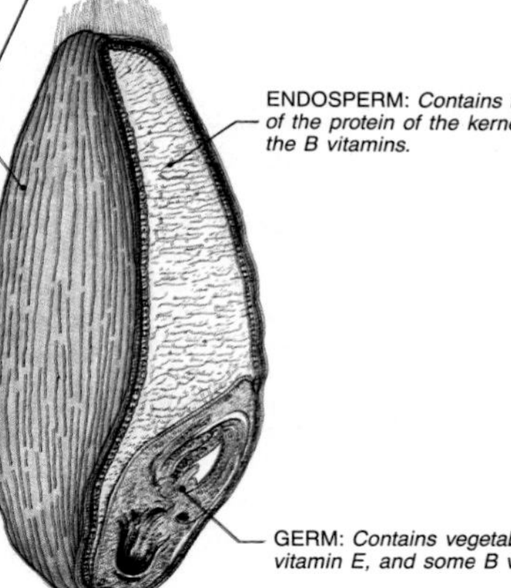

A kernel of grain has three parts — the bran, the endosperm, and the germ. The bran and the germ are the best sources of nutrients. Whole grain products use these parts.

corn and fat meat. The victims became depressed and suffered from signs of mental illness. In 1937, researchers discovered that niacin, a B vitamin, cured pellagra. Corn is a poor source of niacin. These diseases occur when people limit themselves to a small variety of foods lacking in B vitamins.

Introducing the Chapter

Motivators

1. **Discussion.** Bread has been called the "staff of life." Ask students what they think this means. What does this say about the importance of grain in the human diet throughout much of history? (Key Skill: *Critical Thinking*)
2. **Display.** Display various types of grain and grain products. Include refined, enriched, and whole-grain products. Discuss ways grains are used in the diets of people in various parts of the world. (Key Skills: *Social Studies, Science*)
3. **Bulletin Board.** Have students collect pictures of grain products as they are prepared in various cultures. Use the pictures to create a bulletin board. (Key Skills: *Social Studies, Creativity*)

Chapter Objectives and Vocabulary

1. Have students read the chapter objectives and rephrase the objectives as questions.
2. Ask students to state, in their own words, the purpose of studying this chapter.
3. Pronounce the vocabulary terms listed on the previous page. Ask students whether they are familiar with any of these. Explain that the terms will be defined in the chapter.

Guided Reading

1. Have students read the chapter and use the Study Guide on pp. 217-218 of the *Student Workbook*.

Wellness

Two forms of fiber — insoluble and soluble — are important in our diets. Insoluble fibers add bulk and softness to our body wastes and speed elimination. Whole-grain cereals and bran are good sources of insoluble fiber. Soluble fibers help reduce blood cholesterol levels. Grains such as oatmeal are good sources of soluble fibers. Health experts recommend eating a variety of fiber-rich foods every day.

Teaching. . .

Nutrients in Grain Products and Buying Grain Products

(pp. 595-597)

Comprehension Check

1. Why are grains the primary source of food for most of the people in the world? *(They are inexpensive, they can be stored without refrigeration, and they can be combined with small amounts of other ingredients to be made more nutritious.)*
2. Why is the germ removed during the processing of grain? *(Because its fat content limits how long grains can be stored.)*
3. Why are processed grains enriched? *(To add back nutrients lost when the bran and germ are removed.)*
4. What should you avoid when selecting cereals? *(Those that are heavily enriched and those in which sugars are the main ingredient.)*
5. Name four types of rice that are on the market. *(Brown rice, enriched rice, precooked rice, and converted rice.)*

Learning Activities

1. **Label Reading.** Provide students with the nutrition labels from a variety of grain products. Have students work in groups to determine the main nutrients provided by grains and grain products. Do grains contain saturated fat or cholesterol? (Key Skill: *Critical Thinking*)
2. **Microscope Observation.** Provide students with cross sections of several common grains (wheat, corn, rice, oats, barley). Have students view the cross sections under a microscope. Discuss the three parts of the grain kernels (bran, endosperm, and germ) and the functions of

AROUND THE WORLD

After reading the feature, have students investigate how corn is used by some other cultures. *(Answers will vary.)*

AROUND THE WORLD

Corn is the world traveler of the grain family. Introduced to Europe from Central America in the 1500s, it is now found in many diverse cultures. It appears as a cornmeal mush called *polenta* (poe-LEN-tuh) in Italy; in a spicy stew known as *curry* in India; and as a thickener in coconut-milk ice cream in Thailand.

Some cereals are ready-to-eat and others need cooking.

When grains are processed to turn them into flour or cereals, the bran and the germ are often removed. The nutrients found in the bran and the germ are lost. The carbohydrate and protein in the endosperm remain. Federal law requires that processed grains be enriched. The term **enriched** describes foods that have had nutrients added back after processing.

Buying Grain Products

Since there is such a wide variety of grain products on the market, read the labels carefully to buy the type best suited to your needs. Select products that contain whole grain or bran for a more healthful diet.

Shopping for Cereals

When sugar appears near the top of an ingredient list, you receive few nutrients for the calories.

INGREDIENTS: CORN, SUGAR, SALT, MALT FLAVORING, CORN SYRUP,
VITAMINS AND IRON: VITAMIN C (SODIUM ASCORBATE AND ASCORBIC ACID), NIACINAMIDE, IRON, VITAMIN B_6 (PYRIDOXINE HYDROCHLORIDE), VITAMIN B_2 (RIBOFLAVIN), VITAMIN A (PALMITATE; PROTECTED WITH BHT), VITAMIN B_1 (THIAMIN HYDROCHLORIDE), FOLIC ACID, AND VITAMIN D.

As you shop for cereals, you will find some types that are ready-to-eat and others that need cooking. They may be made from whole or enriched grains or a combination of both.

Ready-to-eat cereals may be flaked, puffed, granulated, or shredded. Simply add milk to the cereal and it is ready to eat. Cereals that need cooking generally come in three forms: instant, quick-cooking, and regular. Follow the package directions to prepare the cereal.

Cereals that are heavily enriched with "a day's supply of vitamins and minerals" or have added dried fruit and nuts are costly. In addition, it is impossible to get all of your nutrients from one bowl of cereal. Eating a variety of foods at regular intervals is the best way to insure a healthy diet. There are no shortcuts to good nutrition.

Read nutrition labels to compare the amount of sugar in different cereals. In some cereals, sugars are the main ingredients. For good nutrition, choose cereals with less sugar.

More About Grains

A variety of grains, in addition to wheat, are finding their way into the American diet.

- Rye is used mainly for bread flour.
- Barley is used for the flour in baby foods and in the production of malt.
- Buckwheat grew in China in prehistoric times and is a staple food for many people in Eastern Europe. In the United States, buckwheat is most often used for pancake flour. Some buckwheat grains are used as a breakfast cereal or instead of wild rice.
- Millet is gaining popularity in the United States. It is a staple grain in West Africa. The tiny yellow grains are high in protein and fiber and have a mild flavor. Millet cooks into a thick, heavy mixture that can

▼ Shopping for Rice ▼

You will find several types of rice on the market. They include:

- ***Brown rice.*** Whole-grain rice is known as brown rice. It retains its natural nutrients and fiber and has a nut-like flavor.
- ***Enriched rice.*** This type, also called regular white rice, is enriched to replace nutrients lost in processing. It takes less time to cook than brown rice.
- ***Precooked rice.*** Precooked rice is known as instant or quick-cooking rice. It is made from either brown or enriched rice that has been cooked and dehydrated. Your cooking time at home is shorter.
- ***Converted rice.*** Converted rice is partially cooked before the bran is removed. This allows the nutrients in the bran to enter into the endosperm. Converted rice takes longer to cook than regular white rice.

In addition, rice comes in either long-grain or short-grain varieties. Long-grain rice tends to cook up fluffy, while short-grain rice tends to stick together.

▼ Shopping for Pasta ▼

Pasta, or macaroni and noodle products, is an excellent source of carbohydrates. Macaroni is made from a paste of flour and water and contains no fat. Many noodle products have eggs added for tenderness. How may this affect your choice in which product to buy?

Pastas come in a variety of shapes — elbows, shells, long spaghetti strands, spiral pasta or rotini, and flat lasagna noodles. Most pasta is dried and sold in boxes or bags. Fresh pasta is often available in the refrigerated section of the supermarket.

▼ Shopping for Flour ▼

As you look at the supermarket shelves, you will find an assortment of flours. Here are just some of the types available.

- **All-purpose flour** is also called white flour. It is the most commonly used type. If a recipe simply says "flour," use all-purpose flour.
- **Cake flour** is very fine. It is used in cakes to provide a light, velvety-smooth texture.

Pasta is an excellent source of complex carbohydrates. It comes in a variety of shapes and sizes.

Learning Activities (continued)

each. Which nutrients are provided by each part? (Key Skill: *Science*)

3. **Product Comparison.** Have students work in groups to compare a variety of uncooked and ready-to-eat cereals. Have students compare amount of preparation required, serving sizes, calories, nutrients supplied, ingredients, and additives. Have each group report their findings to the class. (Key Skills: *Cooperation, Management*)
4. **Display.** Display the following types of rice: precooked rice, long- and short-grain rice, brown rice, and converted rice. Have students study the directions for preparing each and the nutrition labels. Have students taste cooked samples of each type of rice. Have them draw conclusions about nutrition, preparation time, flavor, and appropriate uses. (Key Skills: *Science, Management*)
5. **Display.** Display a variety of pasta products. Discuss the differences between macaroni and noodles. Discuss similarities in the nutritional value of different pastas. What is the main disadvantage of egg noodles? Point out uses for different shapes of pasta. (Key Skill: *Management*)

Follow Up

1. **Reteaching.** Have students develop guidelines for buying grain products. (Key Skills: *Critical Thinking, Management*)
2. **Enrichment.** Have students make homemade pasta using a pasta machine or by hand. Compare the appearance, texture, taste, and cost of the homemade pasta with a similar commercial product. (Key Skill: *Science*)

be used as a side dish or as a hot breakfast cereal. It can also be used to thicken casseroles or main dishes.

- Bulgar, or bulgar wheat, originally came from the Near East. It is made from whole wheat that is cooked, then dried and cracked.
- Triticale is a cross between rye and wheat. It is more nutritious than wheat and has a mild flavor and a grainy texture. Triticale is available as flour, flakes, and berries.

Wellness

Health experts recommend that carbohydrates from foods high in complex carbohydrates should make up half of our daily calorie intake. Whole-grains are a good source of complex carbohydrates.

Teaching. . .
Shopping for Flour; Storing Grain Products; Preparing Grain Products
(pp. 598-599)

Comprehension Check

1. What is self-rising flour? *(All-purpose flour that has a leavening agent and salt added.)*
2. What may happen if you substitute a different type of flour in a recipe for a baked product? *(Undesirable results.)*
3. How can you keep bread from molding when it is hot and humid? *(Refrigerate it.)*
4. What happens to starch granules when you cook pasta, rice, and other cereal grains? *(They absorb water, become soft, and grow in size.)*
5. How should you check grain products for doneness? *(Sample them. In general, grain products should be tender but firm, not mushy.)*

Learning Activities

1. **Display.** Have students work in groups to study packages of all-purpose flour, cake flour, and self-rising flour. Ask students to identify the similarities and differences between these products. Have students compare the texture and taste of the three types of flour. Define leavening agent. (Key Skills: *Cooperation, Critical Thinking*)
2. **Discussion.** Discuss with students the effects of substituting one type of flour for another when preparing baked products. Ask them if they have ever substituted one type of flour for another when baking. If they have, what were the results? (Key Skill: *Communication*)
3. **Recall.** Ask students to make a list of the grain products used by their families and note where each is stored. Have students share their lists. What differences, if any, are there in where the grain products are stored? (Key Skill: *Management*)

- **Self-rising flour** is all-purpose flour that has a leavening agent and salt added. The **leavening agent** (LEV-uh-ning) causes baked products to rise. If you are not sure whether the flour you have is self-rising, taste it. Self-rising flour will have a salty flavor.
- **Whole-wheat flour** is made from the whole grain. It has a coarser texture and stronger flavor than all-purpose flour.

Check your recipe and use the type of flour called for. Substituting a different type of flour without making other adjustments can give poor results in baked products.

Storing Grain Products

Store grain products in a cool, dry place. Tightly seal packages or containers of grain products to keep them fresh and free from insect contamination.

Most bread can be left at room temperature. However, if it is hot and humid, you may want to refrigerate bread to keep it from getting moldy. Freeze bread for long-term storage.

Preparing Grain Products

Ready-to-eat grain products do not require cooking. You can easily combine them with your favorite ingredients. Other grain products require different preparation techniques.

Cooking Pasta, Rice, and Cereals

Pasta, rice, and other cereal grains are cooked in water. The starch granules absorb water, become soft, and grow in size. For example, pasta generally doubles in size and rice expands up to three times its original volume. Choose a pan large enough to allow room for the expanding grain products as they cook. Rice will absorb all the cooking water. In contrast, cooking water must be drained from pasta.

Follow the package directions for cooking grain products. They list the amount of grain product and water to use per serving and the length of cooking time. The cooking times listed are only approximate. Sample the grain you are cooking close to the end of the cooking time to determine doneness. In general, grain products should be tender but firm, not mushy.

Pasta expands up to three times its original volume during cooking. Be sure to use a pan size that will accommodate the pasta as it cooks.

How to ...

Cook Pasta

1. Put 2 qt. (2 L) water into a large saucepan. Add 1 tsp. (5 mL) oil to keep the pasta from sticking together. Bring to a boil.
2. Slowly add the pasta to rapidly boiling water. The water should keep boiling as you add the pasta.
3. Follow the package directions for the length of cooking time. Pasta is done if it is tender but firm in the center.
4. Drain the pasta immediately, but do not rinse — valuable nutrients could be lost.

Step 1

Step 3

Step 2

Step 4

How to ... Cook Pasta

Have students read the feature. Ask students to discuss any problems they have had in the past while cooking pasta. Did they skip one or more of the steps listed in this feature? Then divide students into groups and have them practice cooking pasta. Oversee these groups as they work to make sure that they follow the steps correctly.

Learning Activities (continued)

4. **Reading Directions.** Have students read and compare the directions for preparing pasta, rice, and other cereal grains. What conclusions can be drawn? (Key Skills: *Communication, Management*)
5. **Demonstration.** Demonstrate how to cook pasta. Have students taste the pasta when it is undercooked, tender and firm in the center (al dente), and again after it is overcooked. Point out the importance of following package directions and sampling to determine doneness. (Key Skills: *Science, Management*)

Follow Up

1. **Reteaching.** Have students write instructions for preparing various grain products. (Key Skill: *Communication*)
2. **Enrichment.** Have students find recipes for grain products from other cultures. Have students compare these recipes with recipes for grain products popular in the United States. (Key Skills: *Communication, Social Studies*)

Wellness

Most grain products will keep for about a year. Whole-grain products do not keep as well as processed grains. Because whole grains retain the germ that contains fat, they are more likely to become rancid if kept too long. If this is a problem, store whole grains and wheat germ in the refrigerator or freezer. In warm weather, flour and other grain products may become infested with weevils. A bay leaf in each container will deter weevils. Check grain products regularly and discard those that develop an off taste or become infested.

Teaching. . . Making Quick Breads (pp. 600-601)

Comprehension Check

1. How do the two categories of breads — quick breads and yeast breads — differ? *(Leavening, time required to rise.)*
2. What are two methods used for mixing quick breads? *(Muffin method and biscuit method.)*
3. What happens if you overmix muffins? *(Toughness, peaks on top, tunnels or long holes inside.)*
4. What does the term "cutting in" mean? *("Cutting in" breaks the solid fat into pea-size pieces and mixes it with the dry ingredients. A pastry blender or a criss-cross motion with two knives is used to do this.)*

Learning Activities

1. **Definitions.** Define quick bread and yeast bread. Point out the differences in leavening and preparation. Based on the definitions, ask students to name breads in each category. (Key Skills: *Science, Critical Thinking*)
2. **Posters.** Have students collect pictures of breads. As a class, categorize the breads as quick breads or yeast breads. Identify the culture with which each is associated. Use the pictures to create posters about breads around the world. (Key Skills: *Science, Social Studies*)
3. **Recipe Reading.** Have students study recipes for muffins and biscuits and note the differences in mixing. Provide other recipes and have students determine which method is used for mixing. (Key Skills: *Communication, Critical Thinking*)
4. **Demonstration.** Demonstrate the muffin method used for all types of muffins and loaf-type quick breads. Stress the importance of not overmixing. Place half of the batter in muffin tins. Overmix the other half of the batter and fill the remaining muffin tins. Bake and have students compare the muffins in terms of appearance and texture. (Key Skills: *Science, Management*)

Steps 1 and 2

Step 3

Step 4

Step 5

Fill muffin pans two-thirds full.

▼ Making Quick Breads ▼

There are two categories of breads:

- **Yeast breads** use yeast as a leavening agent. After the dough is mixed, it requires time to rise before it can be baked. White or whole wheat bread, hamburger buns, and dinner rolls are yeast breads.
- **Quick breads** can be baked shortly after mixing. The leavening agent is usually baking powder or baking soda. Quick breads include muffins, pancakes, biscuits, and waffles.

Ingredients for quick breads usually include flour, sugar, salt, a leavening agent, a liquid, fat, and eggs. These ingredients are mixed using one of two basic methods. The *muffin method* is used not only for muffins, but also for loaf-type quick breads, pancakes, and waffles. In contrast, biscuits are mixed using the *biscuit method*.

Mixing Muffins

To mix muffins, or another quick bread that uses the muffin method, follow these basic steps.

1. Measure the dry ingredients (flour, sugar, baking powder, and salt) into a bowl and mix them together.
2. Make a well with the back of a spoon in the center of the dry ingredients.
3. Measure the liquid ingredients (milk, oil or melted shortening, and eggs) into another bowl and mix them together.
4. Add the liquid ingredients to the dry ingredients.
5. Stir the ingredients together just enough to moisten the dry ingredients. The batter should be lumpy.

Mixing is the key to success in making muffins. Overmixing generally results in muffins that are somewhat tough. In addition, peaks will form on top, and tunnels or long holes will appear inside the muffins.

After mixing, fill muffin pans according to the recipe and bake in a preheated oven. Remove the muffins from the pan and serve them warm.

Remove from pan and serve warm.

More About Pancakes

Pancakes have been popular for centuries. The ancient Egyptians cooked a wheat flour gruel on a flat hot stone. Later they added leavening to the gruel and cooked the "pancakes" in an oven. Pancakes became part of Lenten shriving observances. In these observances, the flour symbolized the staff of life, the milk symbolized innocence, and the egg symbolized rebirth. The Pilgrims made pancakes from cornmeal. In the 1700s, pancakes were known as "hoe cakes" because they were cooked on a garden hoe blade. The French introduced thin filled pancakes called "crepes." Jewish people serve "blintzes," another type of filled pancake.

Cinnamon Oatmeal Muffins

Customary	Ingredients	Metric
¾ cup	Whole-wheat flour	175 mL
¾ cup	White flour	175 mL
1 cup	Uncooked rolled oats	250 mL
1 Tbsp.	Baking powder	15 mL
3 Tbsp.	Sugar	45 mL
½ tsp.	Cinnamon	3 mL
¼ tsp.	Salt	1 mL
1	Egg	1
1 cup	Milk	250 mL
¼ cup	Oil	50 mL

Yield: 12 muffins

Nutrition Information
Per serving (approximate):
150 calories, 4 g protein, 20 g carbohydrate, 6 g fat, 19 mg cholesterol, 135 mg sodium
Good source of:
thiamine, calcium, phosphorus

Conventional Directions

Pan: Muffin pan
Temperature: 400°F (200°C)

1. **Grease** and flour muffin pan.
2. **Combine** flours, rolled oats, baking powder, sugar, cinnamon, and salt. Mix well.
3. **Beat** egg in a separate bowl.
4. **Add** milk and oil to egg. Stir well.
5. **Add** liquid mixture to flour mixture.
6. **Stir** until just blended. Batter should be lumpy.
7. **Fill** muffin cups ⅔ full.
8. **Bake** 15 to 20 minutes or until muffins spring back when touched.

Microwave Directions

Pan: Microwave-safe muffin pan
Power Level: 100 percent power

1. **Line** microwave-safe muffin pan with paper muffin liners.
2. **Follow** steps 2 through 6 of the conventional directions.
3. **Fill** muffin cups half full.
4. **Microwave** at 100 percent power. For 4 to 6 muffins, microwave 2 minutes or until batter is no longer doughy and springs back when touched lightly.

Making Biscuits

Here are the steps for making biscuits. Notice how the mixing method differs from the one used for muffins.

1. Measure the dry ingredients into a bowl and mix them together.
2. Measure the shortening — a solid fat — and add it to the dry ingredients.
3. Cut the shortening into the dry ingredients. Use a pastry blender or a criss-cross motion with two knives. "Cutting in" breaks the solid fat into pea-size pieces and mixes it with the dry ingredients.

Step 3

Learning Activities (continued)

5. **Demonstration.** Demonstrate how to prepare biscuits. Point out differences between the muffin method and the biscuit method of mixing. Define "cutting in." Demonstrate how to knead the biscuits. Intentionally overknead half of the dough. Bake the biscuits and have students compare the differences in texture and appearance of the overkneaded biscuits. (Key Skills: *Communication, Science*)

Follow Up

1. **Reteaching.** Have students prepare posters outlining the steps in mixing muffins properly. (Key Skill: *Communication*)
2. **Enrichment.** Have students compare the costs of different forms of a baked product, such as blueberry muffins. Compare making the baked product from scratch with the cost of the same product made from a mix, a purchased frozen baked product, and a ready-to-eat bakery product. (Key Skills: *Critical Thinking, Management*)

Using the Recipe

Have students read the feature. Then divide the class into two groups. Have one group prepare the muffins using the conventional directions, and have the other group prepare the muffins using the microwave directions. When the muffins are done, let students taste one of each. Do students think one tastes and/or looks better than the other? Did the group that followed the microwave directions finish baking the muffins much faster than the other group? Have a representative from each group discuss any problems they encountered while preparing the muffins. *(Answers will vary.)*

Teaching. . .
Making Biscuits; Making Cookies; Making Cakes
(pp. 602-603)

Comprehension Check

1. What are the characteristics of good quality biscuits? *(Double in size when baked, and have lightly browned tops with cream-colored, straight sides.)*
2. What qualities should cookies have? *(All cookies should be the same size and thickness, and they should be delicately browned.)*
3. What ingredients do most cakes contain? *(Aside from flavoring ingredients such as chocolate and vanilla, most cakes contain flour, sugar, and eggs.)*
4. How should cake pans be prepared to prevent the cake from sticking to the pan? *(Grease the pan, grease and flour the pan, or put wax paper on the bottom of the pan.)*

Learning Activities

1. **Recipe Search.** Have students find recipes for cookies that sound appealing. Have them categorize the recipes by type: drop, rolled, refrigerator, molded, or bar. What differences can they observe in these types of cookies? (Key Skill: Critical *Thinking*)
2. **Lab Experience.** Have students work in groups to prepare drop, rolled, refrigerator, molded, and bar cookies. Have them display and taste the cookies. (Key Skills: *Management, Cooperation*)
3. **Reasoning.** Have students identify the ingredients found in most cakes. What types of cakes have no fat? What other ingredients may be added? (Key Skill: *Critical Thinking*)
4. **Recipe Reading.** Have students study cake recipes to identify cakes made with and without fat. Ask students to note the differences in the type of leavening used. Discuss how eggs can be used as a leavening agent. (Key Skill: *Communication*)

Step 4

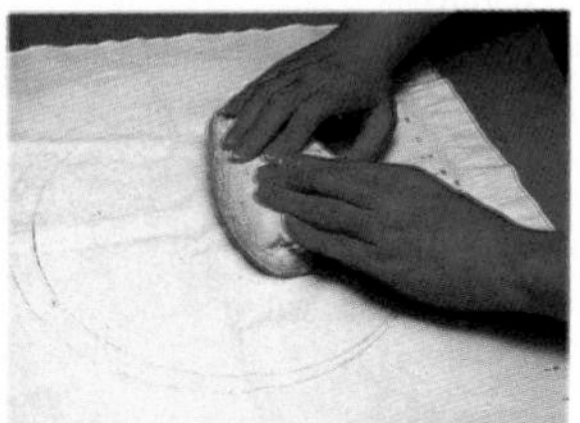
Step 5

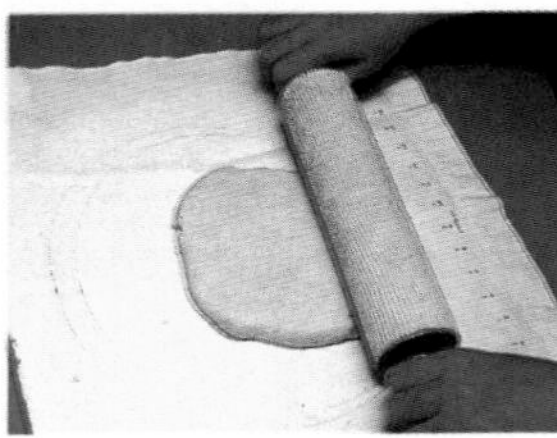
Step 6

Step 7

4. Add the liquid ingredients and mix until a ball of dough forms.
5. Put the dough on a lightly floured board. Knead the dough, using the heels of your hands to press down and away from you. Rotate the dough a quarter turn and fold it toward you. Repeat, kneading about 10 times in all. Kneading the dough makes a flaky biscuit with a fine texture. Overkneading makes a compact and tough product.
6. Use a rolling pin to roll out the biscuit dough until it is about ½ inch (1 cm) thick.
7. Cut out the biscuits using a biscuit cutter or a floured glass.
8. Place the biscuits on a cookie sheet and bake as directed in the recipe.

Rolled biscuits should double in size when baked. They should have lightly browned tops with cream-colored, straight sides.

When done, remove biscuits from pan and serve warm.

▼ Making Cookies ▼

The word "cookie" actually means "little cake." Crisp cookies usually have more fat, sugar, or both than soft cookies or cakes.

There are many types of cookies, including drop, rolled, refrigerator, molded, and bar cookies. They differ in how stiff the dough is and in the way it is handled for shaping.

To bake evenly, all cookies should be the same size and thickness. As a general rule, cookies should be spaced at least 1 inch (2.5 cm) apart on a cookie sheet to allow the cookies to expand during baking.

Arrange the racks in the oven before preheating it. Put the lower rack in the middle of the oven and the upper rack about three inches higher. Place one cookie sheet on the upper shelf and another one on the lower shelf for baking.

More About *Baking*

When selecting recipes for baked products, choose carefully or adapt the recipe to make it more nutritious.

- For the most nutrition, select recipes that use whole-grain flour. You can also replace half of the all-purpose flour in a recipe with whole-grain flour. Look for cookie and muffin recipes that use bran cereals to increase fiber.
- To reduce fat and cholesterol, substitute two egg whites for one whole egg or use a commercial egg substitute.
- Select recipes that call for liquid vegetable oil when possible. Substitute all-vegetable

Allow cookies to cool on a wire cooling rack before storing.

Occasionally enjoy cookies for desserts or snacks. What are some of your favorites?

Put the cookie sheets in the middle of each rack away from the walls of the oven. This allows the hot air to circulate around the cookies and bake them evenly.

Check the cookies a few minutes before the end of the baking time listed in the recipe. When cookies are done baking, they will be delicately browned. Remove the cookies from the sheet immediately using a spatula. Place them in a single layer on a wire cooling rack. When they are cool, put them in a storage container.

▼ Making Cakes ▼

Have you ever thought about what ingredients go into your favorite cake? Aside from flavoring ingredients such as chocolate and vanilla, most cakes contain flour, sugar, and eggs. Depending on the type of cake, fat may or may not be used. Cakes made with fat, such as butter or pound cakes, are leavened with baking powder or baking soda. Cakes made without fat, such as angel food cakes, use a large number of egg whites. The air beaten into the egg whites is the main leavening agent in these cakes.

Before you mix the batter for a cake, check the recipe to see how to prepare the cake pans. You may need to grease the inside of the pans to prevent the cake from sticking. You can use a paper towel or wax paper to spread a thin layer of solid shortening in the pans. If you prefer, you can use a cooking spray. The recipe may tell you to grease the pans on the sides and bottom or the bottom only. With some recipes, you grease the pans and lightly dust them with flour.

shortening or all-vegetable margarine for butter. Grease the pan with a vegetable cooking spray instead of shortening.

- In some recipes, you can reduce the amount of sugar by one-third without losing tenderness or browning. You can also look for recipes that use sugar substitutes.
- Use more nutritious liquids in recipes whenever possible. Substitute skim milk for whole milk or fruit juice for water.
- You can reduce or eliminate the salt in most baked products (but not yeast breads).

Learning Activities (continued)

5. **Student Demonstrations.** Have groups of students draw a slip of paper describing one of the methods for preparing cake pans to prevent the cake from sticking to the pan. Have each group obtain the necessary supplies and demonstrate the method to the class. (Key Skills: *Cooperation, Management*)

Follow Up

1. **Reteaching.** Have students summarize the methods for preparing muffins, biscuits, cookies, and cakes. Have students list appearance qualities for each. (Key Skill: *Critical Thinking*)
2. **Enrichment.** Have students go to a local bakery and find out the names of all the different types of cookies and cakes that are sold there. Have them report their findings to the class. (Key Skill: *Communication*)

Life Management Skills

Time Management

The quickest method of making cakes that contain shortening is the one-bowl method. Time is saved by mixing all the ingredients in one bowl. The dry ingredients are first sifted into a large bowl. Then, softened shortening and part of the liquid are added. The remaining liquid is then added along with unbeaten eggs. This quick method produces a cake with a coarser texture than one made by the conventional method.

Photo Focus

Discuss the photos at the top of page 603 with the students. What happens to cookies if they are not stored in a container shortly after they've cooled? *(If cookies are allowed to sit out too long, they will become hard and stale.)*

Teaching. . .
Cakes Continued; Using Thickening Mixtures; Microwaving Grain Products
(pp. 604-606)

Comprehension Check

1. How should you test a cake for doneness? *(Lightly touch the center of the cake. If no imprint remains, the cake is done. You can also insert a toothpick or cake tester in the center of the cake. If it comes out clean, the cake has finished baking.)*
2. How should you determine when to remove the cake from the pan? *(Follow the recipe directions.)*
3. Why should you stir constantly when thickening liquids? *(Stirring helps keep starch from forming lumps in the liquid.)*
4. How can you eliminate lumps from thickened liquids? *(Mix with a beater or blend in a blender.)*
5. What are the disadvantages of preparing grain products in a microwave oven? *(Products baked in the microwave do not brown and may have a higher volume.)*

Learning Activities

1. **Demonstration.** Demonstrate how to mix a cake using the conventional method. Show how to cream the fat and sugar. Explain why dry and liquid ingredients should be added alternately. Emphasize the importance of following directions. Bake the cake and demonstrate how to test for doneness and how to cool the cake. (Key Skill: *Science*)

TIPS:

Making Cakes
Have students read the feature. Then have them think about the last cake that they baked. Did they follow these guidelines? If not, how was their cake affected? *(Answers will vary.)*

Instead of greasing and flouring cake pans, you can line the bottom of the cake pan with waxed paper. Simply trace the bottom of the cake pan onto the waxed paper, cut along the line you traced, and place the waxed paper into the cake pan.

TIPS: *Making Cakes*

Whether you use a mix or bake from scratch, follow these tips for a successful cake.

- Preheat the oven.
- Use the size of pan specified in the recipe.
- Prepare pans exactly as directed.
- Follow mixing instructions exactly. For the best volume and texture, stir for the length of time suggested.
- When placing pans in the oven, make sure they do not touch the oven walls or each other. Leave room for air to circulate.

Some people prefer to cut pieces of wax paper to fit on the bottom of the pan. This makes it easier to remove the cake from the pan without the use of added fat.

There are several methods for mixing cakes with fat. The following method, called the *conventional method,* is used most often.

1. Cream the fat and sugar together until the mixture is light and fluffy.
2. Add the eggs. Beat the mixture again until it is light and fluffy.
3. Measure and combine the dry ingredients in a separate bowl.
4. Measure and combine the liquid ingredients in a separate bowl.
5. Add the dry and liquid ingredients alternately to the creamed mixture. Begin and end with dry ingredients to keep the mixture from separating. After each addition, stir until well blended.

A few minutes before the baking time is up, test the cake for doneness. Lightly touch the center of the cake. If no imprint remains, the cake is done. You can also insert a toothpick or cake tester in the center of the cake. If it comes out clean, the cake has finished baking.

Follow the recipe directions for removing the cake from the pan. Some cakes should be taken out of the pan right away. Others need to cool a short time in the pan. Before removing the cake from the pan, loosen the sides of the cake with a table knife. In most instances, allow a cake to cool completely before applying frosting or other toppings.

More About Baking Cakes

Be sure to use the pan size specified in the recipe. If you use a different size, fill the pan only a little more than half full. Also remember that changing pan size might change the baking time.

Properties of Starch

Materials
⅓ cup (80 mL) rolled oats,
1 potato, flour, water

Equipment
bowl, saucepan, wooden spoon

Directions:
Soak ⅓ cup (80 mL) of rolled oats in cold water overnight. Soak thinly sliced potatoes in water overnight. Cook a spoonful of flour in a cup of water. Observe the results.

✔ How did soaking affect the rolled oats?

✔ What did you observe in the potato water?

✔ What effect did heat have on flour?

✔ What characteristics of starch make it useful as a thickening agent?

▼ Using Thickening Mixtures ▼

Have you ever wondered what gives thickness to a rich gravy or a creamy soup? Gravies, cream sauces, soups, and puddings are often thickened with flour. As the mixture is heated, starch granules in the flour absorb liquid and thicken the mixture. The thickness depends on the amount of flour used.

Thickening liquid mixtures is a basic cooking technique that can be used with many recipes. Follow these steps to thicken a liquid:

1. Melt the solid fat, usually butter or margarine, in a saucepan.
2. Add the desired amount of flour to the melted fat. Stir to make a paste.
3. Cook the paste a minute or two over medium heat to avoid a "starchy" or flour-like flavor.
4. Add the liquid all at once. Stir constantly until the mixture is thick.

Why should you stir constantly? Stirring helps keep the starch from forming lumps in the liquid. Starch particles next to the bottom and sides of the pan heat quickly and

Step 1

Step 2

Step 3

Step 4

Properties of Starch

Materials: ⅓ cup (80 mL) rolled oats, 1 potato, flour, water.

Equipment: Bowl, saucepan, wooden spoon.

Purpose: To help students understand the characteristics of starch.

Outcomes:
- The oats swelled but did not dissolve.
- A fine white sediment settled from the potatoes.
- A thick, sticky mass resulted.
- Water softens the tough outer layers of the starch granule. Heat causes the tough outer layers of the starch granule to open and absorb water. When the center of the starch granule absorbs water, it becomes sticky, resulting in a thickening effect.

Learning Activities (continued)

2. **Tasting.** Provide students with samples of cakes made with and without fat. Ask them to taste the cakes and note differences in appearance, taste, and texture. Which cakes are more nutritious? (Key Skill: *Critical Thinking*)
3. **Listing.** Have students think of a variety of alternatives to high-calorie cake frostings. Which types of cakes use less frosting? How can the cake be made more attractive if you choose not to use a frosting? (Key Skill: *Creativity*)
4. **Lab Experience.** Divide students into groups to make thin, medium, and thick white sauce following the steps described on page 605. Why is it important to stir constantly when thickening liquids? Have students compare the three sauces. Discuss possible uses for each sauce. (Key Skills: *Science, Management*)
5. **Recipe Reading.** Have students find recipes for sauces. Ask students to determine whether the recipe is a thin, medium, or thick sauce. (Key Skill: *Critical Thinking*)
6. **Microwave Use.** Have students work in groups to prepare the same grain product by both conventional and microwave methods. Note differences in preparation and time required. (Key Skills: *Science, Critical Thinking*)

Follow Up

1. **Reteaching.** Have students develop guidelines for using thickening mixtures and for cooking grain products. (Key Skill: *Critical Thinking*)
2. **Extension.** Use the extension information handout on p. 63 of the *Extending the Text* booklet in the TCR.
3. **Enrichment.** Have students learn to make basic sauces: white sauce, brown sauce, and Hollandaise sauce. Discuss ways these basic sauces can be varied. Challenge students to create a dish of their own using one of these sauces or a variation. (Key Skill: *Science*)

Completing the Chapter

For Review

1. Emphasize the main concepts using the summary.
2. Have students complete the "Facts to Recall." (Answers below.)

For Reteaching

1. **Reteaching.** Use the activity on p. 64 of the *Reteaching and Practical Skills* booklet in the TCR.

For Enrichment

1. **Enrichment.** Use the activity on p. 77 of the *Enrichment Activities* booklet in the TCR.

For Evaluation

1. Choose items from "Ideas to Explore" and "Activities to Try."
2. Use the chapter test on pp. 105-106 in the testing booklet of the TCR or use the testmaker software.

Facts to Recall Answers

1. They are inexpensive and can be stored without refrigeration, and they can be combined with small amounts of other ingredients to be made more nutritious.
2. The bran contains many B vitamins and about 20 percent of the protein in grains. The endosperm contains carbohydrates and about 75 percent of the protein in grains.
3. Costly; impossible to get all nutrients from one bowl of cereal.
4. Brown rice retains natural nutrients and fiber while white rice is enriched to replace nutrients lost in processing; brown rice has a longer cooking time; brown rice is made with whole grains.
5. Self-rising flour has a leavening agent and salt added which causes baked products to rise; all-purpose flour does not.
6. Pasta and rice grow as the starch granules in each absorb water. Pasta generally doubles in size, rice triples in size. Pasta must be drained of excess water,

A smooth sauce results from stirring constantly.

absorb liquid faster than particles in the center. When some starch particles get larger faster than others, you have lumps. Lumps also occur if you add the starch directly to the liquids without first making the fat-starch paste. You can eliminate lumps by mixing with a beater or blending in a blender.

▼ Microwaving Grain Products ▼

In general, it takes almost as long to cook grain products in the microwave oven as it does using conventional cooking methods. Grains such as pasta and rice need time to absorb liquid. Although microwaves speed up cooking time, they cannot speed up the time it takes grains to absorb liquid. Some exceptions to this may be instant or quick-cooking cereals, precooked rice, and precooked pasta.

A variety of baked products, such as muffins and cakes, can be prepared in a microwave oven. However, products baked in the microwave do not brown. They often have a higher volume because there is no crust to stop the product from further rising. The leavening process stops shortly after the microwave oven stops. Recipes developed for microwave cooking usually provide the best results.

To save preparation time, look for convenience grain products that are made for the microwave oven. Some examples are microwave cake mixes and microwave pastas.

TAKING ACTION

Adding Nutrition with Grains

Laurel has volunteered to make baked goods for her neighborhood rummage and bake sale. The money raised will be used to buy trees to plant on Laurel's street. She wants to bake breads and cookies that are appealing, but nutritious as well.

She knows that adding or substituting ingredients can make foods more nutritious. Since flour is a major ingredient in all her recipes, she will begin there. She would also like to add other grain products, such as wheat germ and oats, to increase the fiber and vitamins in her baked goods. She asks for your suggestions.

Using Your Resourcefulness

- Suggest ways that Laurel can find out about different types of flour and the nutritional value of each type.
- In what ways can Laurel determine how flour substitutions will affect her recipes?
- Where can Laurel find recipes designed with good nutrition in mind?
- How can she decide whether wheat germ would be an appealing addition to chocolate chip cookies?
- What other resources might be helpful for Laurel?

TAKING ACTION

Have students read the feature. Then have a class discussion about possible suggestions that students could give Laurel to help make her baked goods for the rummage and bake sale appealing and nutritious. To guide this discussion, you may want to have students answer the *Using Your Resourcefulness* questions at the end of this feature.

Using Your Resourcefulness Answers

- Answers will vary. Possible answers might include family and consumer sciences textbooks, a family and consumer sciences teacher, a nutritionist, and a dietitian.

Chapter 51 Review

Summary

In this chapter, you have read about:

- ▶ The different parts of grain kernels and the nutrients found in each part.
- ▶ Shopping for grain products to best meet your nutritional needs.
- ▶ Preparing grain products, both conventionally and in a microwave oven.
- ▶ Baking foods made with grain products, in a conventional oven and in a microwave oven.

Facts to Recall

1. Identify three ways that grains represent an investment in good health.
2. What nutrients are found in the bran? In the endosperm? What percentage of the kernel's protein is found in each part?
3. Give two reasons why it is not an advantage to buy heavily enriched cereals.
4. Identify three differences between brown rice and enriched white rice.
5. How does self-rising flour differ from all-purpose flour?
6. How are rice and pasta similar in cooking? How are they different?
7. Briefly explain the five steps in the muffin method for mixing quick breads.
8. How and why is biscuit dough kneaded?
9. List three ways to prepare cake pans to prevent the cake from sticking.
10. Explain two ways to test a cake for doneness.
11. Why do baked products prepared in a microwave oven often have a higher volume than those baked in a conventional oven?

Ideas to Explore

1. Besides the reasons given in the chapter, why do you think grains are so popular around the world?
2. Discuss some possible hazards of relying on heavily enriched cereals for your daily nutritional needs.

Activities to Try

1. Obtain three kinds of ready-to-eat cereal. Compare the nutrition labels and the prices. Which cereal is the best nutritional value for the money?

LINK TO Social Studies

GRAINS AROUND THE WORLD

Most Americans are familiar with corn, wheat, and rice as nutritious grain foods. However, many other nutritious grain foods are used around the world — and many are gaining popularity in the United States. Select one of the following grains or grain foods to investigate: kasha, couscous, amaranth, millet, or quinoa (KEEN-wa). In your research, find the following information:

- ▶ How is this grain food most often prepared?
- ▶ What area of the world is this grain food most commonly found in? Why?
- ▶ What are the characteristics of this grain food (flavor, texture, etc.)?
- ▶ How does the nutritional value of this grain food compare to other grains such as wheat?

- Answers will vary and might include asking a family and consumer sciences teacher or the cook in her family.
- Answers will vary and might include family and consumer sciences textbooks, cookbooks, and magazines.
- Answers will vary. Laurel could ask a family and consumer sciences teacher or the cook in her family about it.
- Answers will vary.

Facts to Recall Answers (continued)

while rice absorbs the water it is cooked in.

7. Measure dry ingredients into bowl and mix; make a well in center of dry ingredients; measure liquid ingredients into another bowl and mix; add liquid ingredients to dry ingredients; stir ingredients together just enough to moisten dry ingredients.
8. On a lightly floured board, knead by using heels of hands to press down and away, rotate ¼ turn and fold toward you, repeating process about 10 times. Kneading makes flaky biscuits with a fine texture.
9. Put cookie sheets in middle of each rack away from walls of oven; this allows them to bake evenly.
10. **Any three:** grease inside of pan using a paper towel or waxed paper to spread a thin layer of solid shortening in the pan; cooking spray; grease the pan and lightly dust with flour; cut pieces of waxed paper to fit the bottom of the pan.
11. Lightly touch the center of the cake and if no imprint remains, the cake is done; insert a toothpick or cake tester in the center, and if it comes out clean, the cake is done.
12. Because there is no crust to stop the product from further rising.

Ideas to Explore

1. Answers will vary and may include: they come in many varieties, making them adaptable to a number of different climates; they can be used to make many kinds of products; they are economically grown, making them valuable where land and money are scarce.
2. Answers will vary.

LINK TO Social Studies

Answers

- Answers will vary.
- Answers will vary.
- Answers will vary.
- Answers will vary.

Preparing to Teach

Chapter Outline

Chapter Resources

The following booklet materials may be found in the *Teacher's Classroom Resources* box:

- Lesson Plans, p. 58
- Student Workbook, *Study Guide,* pp. 221-222; *Etiquette—The Clue to Success,* pp. 223-224
- Cooperative Learning, p. 64
- Extending the Text, *Special Flatware for Special Foods,* p. 64
- Reteaching and Practical Skills, *How Good Are Your Manners?,* p. 65
- Enrichment Activities, *Etiquette Around the World,* p. 78
- Chapter and Unit Tests, pp. 107-108; pp. 125-128
- Testmaker Software

Also see:

- Meeting the Special Needs of Students
- Linking Home, School, and Community
- Dealing with Sensitive Issues

ABCNews InterActive™ Videodiscs

- *Food and Nutrition*

See the ABCNews InterActive™ Bar Code Correlation booklet for applicable segments.

CHAPTER 52 Etiquette and Eating Out

OBJECTIVES

- *Set a table correctly.*
- *Describe different methods of serving food.*
- *Give guidelines for appropriate manners and behavior when eating at home or in a restaurant.*

TERMS TO LEARN

- ***etiquette***
- ***tableware***
- ***flatware***
- ***place setting***
- ***course***
- ***appetizer***
- ***entree***
- ***a la carte***

More About Tableware

Attractive tableware is available in a wide range of prices. For your first apartment, you might choose inexpensive plastic dinnerware, plastic tumblers, and stainless steel flatware. Later, you might add stoneware dishes and glass tumblers. These dishwasher-safe choices are practical for everyday use. If your lifestyle includes formal entertaining, you may need china dinnerware, crystal glassware, and sterling silver or silver-plated flatware. These more expensive choices require hand washing.

When you eat out or have guests for dinner, you want to know the right things to do so that you and your companions will feel comfortable. Through the years, certain mealtime customs, or ways of doing things, have become common practice. Customs regarded as the "correct" way to do things in social situations are referred to as **etiquette** (ET-ih-ket). By becoming familiar with the customs and etiquette to follow when eating with others and going to restaurants, you will feel much more comfortable. You can be at ease and enjoy the occasion.

Setting the Table

An attractively set table will help make the meal more enjoyable. Customs for setting the table make the table more attractive and the meal more convenient to eat.

The first step in setting a table is to decide what tableware is needed. **Tableware** includes dishes, glasses, and **flatware** (eating utensils). Each person will need at least one plate, glass, fork, knife, and spoon. Depending on what food is being served, other tableware may be needed. For example, a separate, smaller plate and fork are needed for salad, a bowl and soup spoon for soup, and a cup and saucer for a hot beverage. Other essential items include a napkin for each person and a tablecloth or place mats to protect the table.

A **place setting** is the arrangement of tableware for each person who will be eating a meal. To find out how to arrange the items, read "How to Set a Table" on page 610.

Serving Food

Families usually have their own habits and preferences when it comes to serving meals. Your family may serve everyday meals one way and special occasion meals another. The way you serve food often depends on what food you're having, the amount of time and space you have, the number of people eating, and who is helping. The common styles of serving food include:

- ***Family-style service.*** Dinner plates are at each person's place. The foods are in serving dishes on the table and are passed around from person to person to help themselves.

Food is passed from person to person when family-style service is used.

More About *Flatware*

The cost of flatware depends largely on the amount of silver used to make it. The sterling tableware treasured in many homes is mostly silver. Sterling silver contains a high percent of silver mixed with copper to form an alloy. Silver plate, which is less expensive, is made by coating base metals with pure silver on silver alloy by electrolysis. Silver plate does not wear as well as sterling silver. Stainless steel flatware, which contains no silver, is made from alloy steels that resist corrosion and are polished to resemble silver.

Introducing the Chapter

Motivators

1. **Place Setting.** Write a menu on the chalkboard. Make available a place mat, napkin, flatware, dinnerware, and glasses for a place setting. Ask a student to set up one place setting for the menu on the board. Have students critique the place setting and correct any errors. Discuss the importance of knowing how to set a table correctly. (Key Skill: *Management*)
2. **Bulletin Board.** Have students collect pictures of attractively set tables. Have students point out similarities and differences in the place settings. Use the pictures to create a bulletin board titled, "Creative Table Setting." (Key Skills: *Critical Thinking, Creativity*)
3. **Discussion.** Ask students to describe times when they've felt uncomfortable because they were unsure of correct etiquette. Discuss how etiquette helps to put people at ease in social situations. (Key Skills: *Social Studies, Problem Solving*)

Chapter Objectives and Vocabulary

1. Have students read the chapter objectives and rephrase the objectives as questions.
2. Ask students to state, in their own words, the purpose of studying this chapter.
3. Pronounce the vocabulary terms listed on the previous page. Ask students whether they are familiar with any of these. Explain that the terms will be defined in the chapter.

Guided Reading

1. Have students read the chapter and use the Study Guide on pp. 221-222 of the *Student Workbook*.

Teaching. . .
Setting the Table; Serving Food; Table Manners
(pp. 609-611)

Comprehension Check

1. What is included in a place setting? *(Dinnerware, flatware, glasses, and napkin for one person's meal.)*
2. What are the common styles of serving food? *(Family-style service, plate service, head-of-table service, and buffets.)*
3. Should you reach for food when you are at the table? *(Reach for food only if you do not have to lean across the table or reach in front of anyone. Otherwise, ask the person nearest the food to pass it to you.)*

Learning Activities

1. **Reading.** Have students read about the origins of etiquette. Discuss reasons why prehistoric people may have developed rules for behavior. Why did much of today's formal etiquette originate in the French royal court? (Key Skill: *Social Studies*)
2. **Discussion.** Discuss reasons why etiquette is not limited just to royalty and the rich these days. Why has etiquette become less concerned with rigid rules established for formal occasions? What is the most important function of etiquette today? (Key Skill: *Critical Thinking*)
3. **Demonstration.** Demonstrate how to correctly set a place setting. Point out the correct position of the dinner plate, flatware, salad plate, glassware, cup and saucer, and napkin. (Key Skill: *Management*)
4. **Drawing.** Provide students with several menus. Have students draw an appropriate place setting for each menu. (Key Skill: *Decision Making*)

How to . . .
Set a Table

1. Arrange a tablecloth or place mats on the table.
2. Place the dinner plate in the center of the place setting one inch from the edge of the table.
3. Arrange the flatware around the dinner plate, following these guidelines:
   - The knife goes to the right of the plate, with the cutting edge facing the plate.
   - Spoons go to the right of the knife, with the bowl of the spoon face up.
   - Forks go to the left of the plate, with the tines or prongs curving upward.
   - If more than one spoon or fork will be used, place the one that will be used first (such as the soup spoon or salad fork) farthest from the plate.
   - The bottom of the handle of each piece of flatware should line up with the lower edge of the plate.
4. If a salad is to be served with the meal, place the salad plate above the forks. If the salad is to be the first course, the salad plate can be placed on the dinner plate and removed after the salad is eaten.
5. Put the water glass just above the tip of the knife. If there is another beverage glass, place it to the right and slightly in front of the water glass.
6. If a hot beverage is to be served, place the cup and saucer to the right of the spoons. Sometimes the cup and saucer are not placed on the table until the hot beverage is served.
7. Place the napkin to the left of the forks. The folded edge should be placed to the outside.

How to ... Set a Table

Have students read the feature. Then have each student practice setting a table properly. Oversee students as they practice to make sure that the items are being arranged correctly. Point out any incorrect arrangements and explain why they are incorrect.

On special occasions, you may use head-of-table service in serving food.

- ***Plate service.*** The food is placed on each person's plate in the kitchen, and then the filled plates are brought to the table.
- ***Head-of-table service.*** This service is often used for special occasion meals. The person at the head of the table puts food on the plates and passes the plates down the table. People wait to eat until everyone has been served.
- ***Buffets.*** This is a good way to serve food when there are too many people to seat around the table. Dishes, flatware, napkins, and serving dishes with food are put on the table or counter. People take what they want and find a place to sit while they eat.

Table Manners

Have you ever felt confused about "what to do when" at mealtime? Here a few guidelines to help you feel more comfortable when eating:

- Place the napkin on your lap.
- Reach for food only if you do not have to lean across the table or reach in front of anyone. Otherwise, ask the person nearest the food to please pass it to you.
- When serving forks and spoons are provided, use them to serve yourself food. Be sure to put them back into the serving dish after you have used them. Try not to use your own flatware when serving yourself.

Learning Activities (continued)

5. **Practice.** Have students work in groups to practice serving food using the four common styles of serving food. (Key Skill: *Management*)
6. **Discussion.** Discuss advantages and disadvantages of each style of serving food. Which style would be most likely to encourage overeating? Which style would be most likely to result in food waste? Which style would be best for a family with young children? Which style would be best for casual entertaining? For formal entertaining? (Key Skill: *Critical Thinking*)

Follow Up

1. **Reteaching.** Have students work in groups to plan a creative way to teach table setting to young children. Arrange for students to teach table setting to a preschool or elementary school class. (Key Skills: *Cooperation, Leadership*)
2. **Enrichment.** Have students learn to make several creative napkin folds. Ask students to demonstrate one of the napkin folds to the class. (Key Skill: *Creativity*)
3. **Enrichment.** Have students plan attractive table settings, including centerpieces, to fit a theme for a special-occasion meal. Have students create a display using their ideas. (Key Skill: *Creativity*)

More About Glassware

Glassware is made chiefly from sand, soda, and lime. The first glass vessels were produced about 1500 B.C. in Egypt and Mesopotamia. Glass blowing, a method of forming glass using a blowpipe, was invented about 30 B.C. Lead glass, prized for its high quality, was first produced in England in 1674. When tapped, lead crystal has a clear, bell-like ring. It is the finest, most expensive glassware. Crystal must be carefully washed by hand to prevent chipping.

Photo Focus

Discuss the illustration at the top of page 611 with the students. Ask students which style of serving food is normally used in their home. Is a different style used for special occasions? If so, which style is used for these occasions? *(Answers will vary.)*

Teaching. . .

Table Manners Continued; Eating Out

(pp. 612-614)

Comprehension Check

1. Where should you put the knife and fork when you have finished eating? *(Next to each other across the center of the plate.)*
2. What are the two ways of pricing food on a menu? *("A la carte" means each item is listed separately on a menu at an individual price. The menu may also list a complete meal for a certain price.)*
3. When eating out, what should you do if you need something? *(You should politely ask the waiter or waitress for it.)*
4. What should you do if you are invited out and it's not clear who is paying? *(Bring enough money so you can pay your own bill.)*
5. What is the customary tip for the person who served you at a restaurant? *(10 to 15 percent of the bill.)*

Learning Activities

1. **Student Demonstrations.** Have students draw slips of paper listing guidelines for table manners. Ask each student to demonstrate and explain the guideline drawn. (Key Skill: *Communication*)
2. **Menu Reading.** Provide students with menus from several restaurants. Discuss whether the restaurant is a fast-food or table-service restaurant. Have students locate appetizers, soups, entrees, salads, vegetables, desserts, and beverages on each menu. Determine whether each menu is priced "a la carte" or "prix fixe." Define any unfamiliar terms on each menu. (Key Skills: *Communication, Management*)

Around the World

After reading the feature, have students investigate the dining etiquette followed by other cultures. How do their dining rules differ from ours in the United States? *(Answers will vary.)*

Around the World

For the Hindus of India, dining etiquette goes far beyond table manners. This belief system teaches respect for all things connected to life, including preparing and eating meals. The cook must bathe before entering the kitchen to prepare a meal. Knives are not used because they are associated with violence and destruction. Food is eaten with the right hand only — the left hand is thought unclean.

- If you're not sure which piece of flatware to use, follow the lead of the person at the head of the table.
- Cut one bite at a time; then eat it. Do not cut all your food into pieces all at once.
- Break, rather than cut, bread and rolls into small pieces.
- Eat as quietly as you can by chewing with your mouth closed. Do not talk with food in your mouth.
- Try to keep your arms and elbows off the top of the table.
- Push foods such as peas and corn onto the fork with a piece of bread or a knife.
- It is usually acceptable to eat certain foods with your fingers. Some examples are sandwiches, bread, pickles, carrot sticks, celery, pizza, and corn-on-the-cob.
- When food is too hot to eat, wait until it cools.
- When you are not using a knife or fork, put it across your plate.
- When you have finished eating, put the knife and fork next to each other across the center of the plate. Leave the dishes where they have been during the meal, and put your napkin on the table to the left of your plate.

Eating out can be a pleasant, relaxing experience.

Eating Out

Going out to eat can mean going to a fast-food restaurant, a cafeteria, or a restaurant with table service. You are probably familiar with fast-food restaurants. You select what you want from the menu above the counter, place your order, and then take it out or find your own table. In cafeterias, you take a tray, select your food as you walk through the serving line, and find a table. At a restaurant that offers table service, someone takes your order at the table and brings the food.

More About Eating Out

Remember these pointers to make eating out a more pleasant experience:

- At formal restaurants, wait to be seated by the host or hostess. At many coffee shops and other casual restaurants, you may seat yourself. If you are unsure, look for a sign or ask the cashier or server.
- To signal that you are ready to order, simply close the menu. If pressed for a decision before you are ready, politely ask the server to return in a few minutes.
- Servers usually follow a pattern for taking orders. Women's orders may be taken first, or the server may simply progress around the table.

Some restaurants require that you telephone ahead and reserve a table. Even if a reservation isn't required, it can help you avoid a long wait if the restaurant is crowded. If you haven't been to the restaurant before, it's also a good idea to find out the price range and what type of dress is appropriate. If you have a reservation, arrive at the restaurant by the appointed time or telephone to cancel the reservation.

At many restaurants, someone will greet you when you come in. This person will probably ask how many are in your party and what type of seating you prefer. If you have a reservation, give the name to the person who greets you. When your table is ready, someone will lead you to it.

If you are eating at a restaurant where no one greets you, seat yourself. Find a table that is agreeable to everyone.

▼ Ordering from the Menu ▼

The menu is often divided into sections for different types of food or different **courses** (parts of the meal). For example, the menu might include appetizers, soups, salads, entrees, desserts, and beverages. An **appetizer** is an optional first course. The **entree** (AHN-tray) is the main course.

The food on a menu may be listed and priced in one of two ways:

- Items may be listed separately, or **a la carte** (ah-la-CART). Each item has an individual price.
- The menu may list a complete meal for a certain price. Be sure to notice what is included in the meal. For instance, the price of a dinner may include your entree, salad, potato, and bread. Other items would cost extra.

▼ Behavior at the Restaurant ▼

When eating out, be considerate of other people. Most people want to eat and talk quietly to their companions. Loud, noisy conversation can bother other diners and interfere with the enjoyment of their meal.

If you need anything during the meal, politely ask the waiter or waitress. Usually he or she will stop by your table several times during the meal. If the problem can't wait until then, get the server's attention by raising your hand and saying "waiter" or "waitress" quietly. If the person waiting on your table is far away, ask a waiter or waitress who is nearby to get the person for you.

Taking ashtrays, glassware, or utensils as souvenirs is theft. The manager could take legal action against you.

TIPS: *Understanding Menu Item Terms*

Avoid confusion — and surprises — when ordering from a menu by learning these frequently used terms:

- **Cacciatore.** Italian for "hunter style." Chicken cooked in a spicy tomato sauce.
- **Alfredo.** Pasta served in a white sauce made with cream, butter, and cheese.
- **Au gratin.** A browned topping of buttered bread crumbs and sometimes cheese. Primarily used for vegetables.
- **Au jus.** French for "in juice." Meat served in its own juices.

At many restaurants, you may request to take any leftovers home with you.

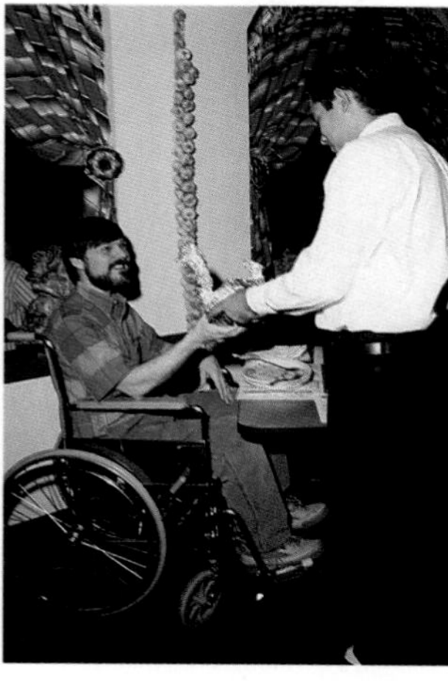

Learning Activities (continued)

3. **Group Problem Solving.** Divide students into groups and ask them to draw a slip of paper that describes a situation in a restaurant. Examples: noisy guests at the next table; loud, unruly children nearby; person in your party takes ashtray; companion wants a bite of your dessert; you can't finish your meal. Have each group identify possible solutions and decide which solution would be best. (Key Skills: *Cooperation, Problem Solving*)
4. **Guest Checks.** Provide students with sample guest checks. Have students identify the menu items and charges, the sales tax, and the tip on the check. Determine where each check should be paid. (Key Skills: *Communication, Management*)

Follow Up

1. **Reteaching.** Have students demonstrate procedures for paying the bill and tipping at a restaurant. (Key Skills: *Cooperation, Management*)
2. **Extension.** Use the extension information handout on p. 64 of the *Extending the Text* booklet in the TCR.
3. **Enrichment.** Take students on a field trip to a restaurant with table service. Have students observe table settings and food service. Ask the restaurant manager to answer questions about the menu, place settings, and service. (Key Skills: *Social Studies, Citizenship*)

- Unacceptable food may always be sent back. Simply call over the server and explain the problem and what you want done.
- To signal that you have finished with a course, place your knife and fork parallel to one another on the side of your plate. Crossing your knife and fork over one another shows that you are resting, but not finished eating.
- Remember to say "Please" and "Thank you" when making requests of servers.

TIPS:

Understanding Menu Item Terms
After reading the feature, have students discuss other menu terms that they've seen and don't understand. Have they ever ordered something off a menu without knowing what it was? If so, what was it and how did they like it? *(Answers will vary.)*

Completing the Chapter

For Review

1. Emphasize the main concepts using the summary.
2. Have students complete the "Facts to Recall." (Answers below.)

For Reteaching

1. **Reteaching.** Use the activity on p. 65 of the *Reteaching and Practical Skills* booklet in the TCR.

For Enrichment

1. **Enrichment.** Use the activity on p. 78 of the *Enrichment Activities* booklet in the TCR.

For Evaluation

1. Choose items from "Ideas to Explore" and "Activities to Try."
2. Use the chapter test on pp. 107-108 in the testing booklet of the TCR or use the testmaker software.
3. Use the unit test on pp. 125-128 in the testing booklet of the TCR or use the testmaker software.

Facts to Recall Answers

1. Knowing etiquette will make you and your companions feel more comfortable and at ease, so you can enjoy the occasion.
2. The knife is placed to the right of the plate, with the cutting edge of the blade facing the plate. The spoon is placed to the right of the knife, bowl facing up. The fork is placed to the left of the plate, with tines curving upward. If more than one spoon or fork is to be used, those that will be used first are placed farthest from the plate. The bottom of the handle of each piece of flatware should line up with the lower edge of the plate.

When you are dining out with a group, individual meals may be put together on one bill or on separate bills. Be sure to let your server know before ordering a meal.

Paying the Bill and Tipping

At the end of the meal, it's time to pay. If the check is not given to you, say "Check, please."

Who pays? This can often be settled before you get to the restaurant. If you invite someone out, be clear about who is paying. You may say, "It's on me. I'll pay." You may say, "Let's go Dutch," which means each person pays for his or her own meal.

If you are invited out and it's not clear who is paying, bring enough money so you can pay your own bill just in case.

Before paying, check the bill to be sure it is accurate. Remember, many states add a sales tax to restaurant bills.

It's customary to leave a tip for the person who served you. The amount is usually 10 to 15 percent of the bill. A tip is for service, not for food. If the food was bad but the service was good, leave a tip. When no tip is left, the message is clear that the service was poor.

Some checks say at the bottom, "Pay the cashier." In that case, leave a tip at the table and pay on the way out. Sometimes you pay the person serving you, and he or she takes your money and the check to the cashier. You then get the change from the waiter or waitress and leave a tip.

Knowing what to expect in different kinds of restaurants will help you feel more comfortable in a variety of situations.

TAKING ACTION

Understanding Proper Etiquette

Kameel is elated and scared. He is thrilled that Jeanette has accepted his invitation to the Garfield Junior High Spring Dance, but he is concerned about the other part of their date — the dinner at a nice restaurant that he has also promised. Kameel doesn't eat out much, certainly not at a restaurant as nice as the one he would like to take Jeanette to. He's worried that he won't be able to afford it, or that he will say or do something terribly inappropriate. He asks for your help in making this an evening that they both will want to remember — and not one they wish they could forget.

Using Your Resourcefulness

- How can Kameel find out which restaurants are within his budget?
- Where can he learn what behavior is appropriate when on a date?
- How can Kameel prepare himself so he will feel comfortable ordering from a menu?
- Where can he find out about different dining utensils and their proper use?
- In what way should Kameel decide how much to tip the waiter or waitress? How should the tip be left?
- List all the sources Kameel might use to help him find the information he needs.

TAKING ACTION

Have students read the feature. Then have a class discussion about what dining guidelines could be given to Kameel to make sure that his dinner with Jeanette goes smoothly. To guide this discussion, you may want to have students answer the *Using Your Resourcefulness* questions at the end of this feature.

Using Your Resourcefulness Answers

- Answers will vary and might include asking his parents about it, asking his friends about it, and calling restaurants to find out their prices.
- Answers will vary. Possible answers might include talking to his parents about it and reading about it in a family and consumer sciences textbook.

Chapter 52 Review

Summary

In this chapter, you have read about:

- How to arrange the dinnerware, flatware, glasses, and napkins for a meal.
- Different ways of serving food.
- Mealtime etiquette for dining out or at home.
- Proper restaurant behavior, including ordering from a menu, paying the bill, and tipping the waiter or waitress.

Facts to Recall

1. How can knowing mealtime etiquette increase your enjoyment of a meal?
2. Describe the arrangement of flatware around the dinner plate.
3. Identify three factors affecting how food is served.
4. Explain how food is served in *family-style* service.
5. What is a good rule to follow if you're not sure which piece of flatware to use?
6. Give five examples of foods that can be eaten with the fingers.
7. What is meant by "going Dutch"?
8. Is a tip for the food or for the service? Explain your answer.

Ideas to Explore

1. What do you think is the most common mistake people make in mealtime etiquette?
2. What practical benefits can you find in the rules of etiquette discussed in this chapter?
3. How might you tactfully correct a member of your dining party who was showing poor table manners?

Activities to Try

1. With two or three other students, practice proper restaurant behavior in front of the class. Include arriving at the restaurant, being seated, ordering the meal, and paying the bill.
2. Practice and demonstrate eating with different types of utensils, such as chopsticks, fondue forks, or seafood forks.
3. Write a paragraph describing a humorous experience you have had while dining at home or out.

LINK TO *Communication*

CREATING A TABLE SETTING

Write a menu that you would like to prepare for several friends. Create a demonstration showing how you will properly set the table for this meal. Be sure to include all items of tableware necessary to serve this meal. When setting the table, take into consideration the attractiveness of the table setting. Use the elements and principles of design (see Chapter 24) when deciding about placemats or a tablecloth and centerpiece for the table.

Facts to Recall Answers (continued)

3. **Any three:** what food you're having; the amount of time and space you have; the number of people eating; who is helping.
4. Foods are in serving dishes on the table and are passed around from person to person to help themselves.
5. Follow the lead of the person at the head of the table.
6. **Any five:** sandwiches, bread, pickles, carrot sticks, celery, pizza, corn-on-the-cob.
7. Each person pays for his or her own meal.
8. A tip is for service. It should reflect the quality of the service, regardless of the quality of the food.

Ideas to Explore

1. Answers will vary.
2. Answers will vary.
3. Answers will vary.

- Answers will vary and might include going to a restaurant and looking over the menu before his date.
- Answers will vary. Possible answers might include family and consumer sciences textbooks, a family and consumer sciences teacher, and his parents.
- Kameel should evaluate the service before deciding on a tip. If the service was decent, the amount should be 10 to 15 percent of the bill. If the service was poor, no tip should be left. Generally, the tip should be left on the table.
- Answers will vary.

LINK TO *Communication*

Answer

Demonstrations will vary depending on what menus students write. Let students use some creativity in their demonstrations, but make sure that they still follow the guidelines for setting a table.

Career Connections

Volunteer Options

- Food coop volunteer.
- Community garden volunteer.
- Soup kitchen volunteer.
- Agricultural volunteer.
- Food pantry volunteer.
- Hospital volunteer.

Volunteer Organizations

Share U.S.A.
3350 E Street
San Diego, CA 92102

Salvation Army
615 Slaters Lane
P. O. Box 269
Alexandria, VA 22313

CAREER *Connections*

Get Ready for Your Future Through Volunteering

Will

"After listening to a speaker in my foods class talk about hunger, I started to wonder about people in my own community. I found that there are many hungry people here. There are also groups of people working to help them, like the food pantry not far from my home.

"I started volunteering at the food pantry two evenings a week about six months ago. My job involves stocking and organizing shelves in a small warehouse area. I take careful inventory of the foods on hand and what foods are needed. In this way, those in the community that donate food (and sometimes money) can provide items that are really necessary. Since I've had some computer experience, I was able to create a data base to keep track of our inventory.

"In the future, I'm considering a career in food technology. I would like to find ways to improve the quantity and quality of safe foods."

Pearl

"My degree in Family and Consumer Sciences and my experience as a volunteer photographer for the college newspaper helped pave the way to my career in advertising. I work in a fast-paced world and create ideas that sell food products. For example, to make a new pasta product a hit, I served a spaghetti dinner to a thousand runners the night before a marathon!

"As an account executive, I supervise magazine ads, work with copywriters, designers, and photographers. I often work with food scientists — mostly home economists — and test new recipes in a test kitchen located in our building. I'm on the scene to supervise when ads are shot for magazines or TV. I love my job and look forward to work every day. What more can you ask?"

Discussing Career Connections

Have students read the *Career Connections* feature. Ask students:

- What personal qualities and skills might be necessary to work in a food-related career or job?
- What skills or aptitudes do you have that might be beneficial in a food-related career?

Have students investigate the approximate wages and schooling necessary for a variety of food-related careers and jobs.

"My experience as a hospital volunteer first sparked my interest in dietetics. I saw firsthand how important nutrition is to a healthy way of life.

"You might think a dietitian is someone who is only concerned with other people losing weight. But that's not true. A dietitian promotes better health through better nutrition — whether people are healthy or ill, overweight, or underweight.

"To become a dietitian, I had to earn a college degree plus a one-year master's degree and six months of work experience. Then I took a registration examination so that more career choices would be open to me.

"Generally there are two types of dietitians, clinical and administrative. Clinical dietitians help people learn about food so they can change their eating habits. These dietitians often work in a health care setting such as a hospital.

"As an administrative dietitian, I'm a specialist in food systems. I coordinate buying, budgeting, and serving food for a large company cafeteria. If you like working with people and nutrition, have reasonable math skills and a feel for science, you may want to choose a career as a registered dietitian just as I did."

Julie

MAKING THE CONNECTION

- Make a list of as many food-related careers as you can think of. Are any appealing to you?
- What skills can you learn through other types of volunteer experiences that you can apply to any career?
- What volunteer experiences in your area could lead to a food-related career? What steps can you take to find out?
- What resources in your school library can help you find out more about food-related careers?

Occupational Outlook

Listed below are some possible food-related occupations. Some require little training while others require a 4-year degree.

- Detassler
- Fast-food worker
- Hospital food service worker
- Dairy farm worker
- Fruit or vegetable farm worker
- Domestic cook
- School cafeteria cook
- Fishing vessel deckhand
- Aerobics instructor
- Short order cook
- Baker
- Caterer
- Hotel or restaurant chef
- Beekeeper
- Corn, soybean, or wheat grower
- Food inspector
- County Extension Service worker
- Nutritionist
- Family and consumer scientist
- Dietitian
- Athletic trainer
- Food products tester
- Food chemist

Food-Related Organizations

The Education Foundation of the National Restaurant Association
250 South Wacker Drive
Chicago, IL 60606

The American Dietetic Association
216 West Jackson Blvd.
Suite 800
Chicago, IL 60606

Making the Connection

Answers

- Answers will vary, but may include those careers and others listed on this page.
- Answers will vary, but may include management skills, skills in working with people, organizational skills, etc.
- Answers will vary.
- Answers will vary, but may include book, magazines, college and technical school catalogs, *The Dictionary of Occupational Titles*, newspapers, etc.

Glossary

A

a la carte: having food items listed and priced individually on the menu. (52)

abbreviation: a shortened form of a word. (45)

acquaintances: people whom you know, but who are not your friends. (10)

addicted: physically or psychologically dependent on something. (14)

additive: a substance added to food for a specific purpose. (41)

adolescence: the stage of growth between childhood and adulthood. (4)

aerobic exercise: vigorous activity that causes your heart to beat faster for a sustained amount of time. (37)

age span: the number of years between children. (13)

alcoholics: people who are addicted to alcohol. (14)

alcoholism: a disease involving an addiction to alcohol. (14)

alternatives: the different choices you can make to deal with a situation. (3)

apathy: not caring and not trying; the opposite of involvement. (6)

appetizer: an optional first course in a meal. (52)

applique: a cut-out fabric decoration that is sewn onto a larger fabric background. (32)

apprenticeship: on-the-job training with pay. (7)

aptitudes: natural abilities or talents for learning certain skills. (7)

assertive: standing up for yourself in a determined or confident way without bullying others with words or actions. (8)

ATMs (automatic teller machines): computers that customers can use to make their banking transactions when tellers are busy or the bank is closed. (21)

B

backstitching: a reverse stitch used to secure the ends of a seam. (33)

bacteria: one-celled living things so small they can be seen only with a microscope. (47)

baking or **roasting:** cooking in an oven or oven-type appliance with dry heat. (46)

balance: the remaining amount of money you have in your account. (19)

balance: a feeling of equal weight among all parts of a design. (24)

basal metabolism: the number of calories needed for normal body processes. (40)

basting: holding fabric in place temporarily with pins or long stitches. (35)

Better Business Bureau: a private agency that works to improve local business practices. (20)

bias: diagonal line formed when the crosswise grain is parallel to the selvage. (34)

blended families: nuclear families in which one or both adults have been married before and one or both have children from a previous marriage. (12)

body image: a mental picture of how you think your body looks. (40)

body language: nonverbal communication; communication without words. (8)

boiling: cooking at a temperature at which bubbles rise and break on the surface of a liquid. (46)

bran: the outside covering of the grain kernel. (51)

broiling: cooking directly under or over the source of heat. (46)

budget: a plan for how you want and intend to use your money. (19)

C

calorie: unit used to measure energy supplied by food or used by the body. (38)

carbohydrate: a nutrient that is the body's main source of energy. (38)

career: chosen occupation. (7)

casing: a closed tunnel of fabric that holds a piece of elastic or a drawstring inside. (32)

cents-off coupons: certificates that allow customers to buy items at a reduced price. (43)

character: a quality of a person who acts according to a set of high moral principles. (4)

check register: a place in your checkbook where you keep a record of the checks you write and the deposits you make. (19)

cholesterol: a fat-like substance used by the body. (38)

citizen: someone who is a member of a group, such as a city or town, state, or country. (6)

citizenship: the way that you handle your responsibilities as a citizen. (6)

classics: fashions that remain popular year after year. (28)

clique: a group of people who exclude others from their circle. (10)

clothing inventory: an organized list of the clothing you have. (28)

communication: the exchange of information, including facts, opinions, and feelings; sending and receiving messages. (8)

comparison shopping: taking the time to shop around and compare products, prices, and services. (20)

compromise: the result of each person's giving up something to reach a satisfactory solution; give-and-take. (9)

condominium: units in a multiple-family dwelling that are individually owned. (23)

conflict: a disagreement or struggle between two or more people or groups who have opposing points of view. (9)

conservation: protecting natural resources against waste and harm. (22)

conscience: an inner sense of right or wrong. (15)

consumer: a person who purchases and uses goods and services. (20)

convection oven: an oven with fans to help circulate the hot air. (44)

convenience foods: foods that are purchased partially or completed prepared. (42)

cookware: pots, pans, and other containers for use on top of the range or in the oven or microwave. (44)

cooperation: working together for the good of all; teamwork. (9)

cooperative: a form of ownership in which residents of a multiple-family dwelling form an organization that owns the building. (23)

course: part of a meal made up of foods served at one time. (52)

credit: an arrangement by which you purchase things now and are allowed to pay for them later. (19)

credit rating: a record that shows your ability and willingness to pay your debts. (14)

crush: a strong attraction to a member of the opposite gender. (11)

custody: court awarded care of a child or children following separation or divorce. (12)

D

dandruff: scales and flakes on the scalp. (27)

decision making: the act of making a choice or coming to a solution. (3)

deficiency: a shortage of nutrients. (38)

deposit slip: a slip of paper on which you record the amount of money being deposited into your account. (19)

dermatologist: a doctor who treats skin problems. (27)

Dietary Guidelines for Americans: suggestions developed by health experts and the U.S. government to help people make healthful food choices. (39)

directional stitching: stitching in the direction of the grain of the fabric. (35)

discipline: training given by parents and caregivers that helps children become responsible and cooperative. (17)

dry clean: cleaning with chemicals rather than with detergent and water. (30)

duplex: a building that contains two separate housing units. (23)

E

ease: amount of room needed in a garment for comfort and movement. (31)

equivalents: two or more amounts that are equal to each other. (45)

empathy: the ability to understand what someone else is experiencing. (9)

emphasis: the point of interest in a design. (24)

endorse: to sign over your rights to a check by writing your name on the back. (19)

endosperm: the largest part of the grain, located inside the kernel. (51)

enriched: describes foods that have had nutrients added back after processing. (51)

entree: the main course. (52)

entrepreneur: a person who owns and manages a business. (7)

environment: everything around you, including people, places, and events. (1)

ethics: a set of high moral principles. (4)

etiquette: customs regarded as the correct way to do things in social situations. (52)

expenses: the things on which you spend your money. (19)

extended family: a family that includes one or more relatives in addition to the basic family unit. (12)

F

fabric blends: combinations of two or more different fibers. (29)

fads: fashions that last only a short time. (28)

fashions: styles that are currently popular. (28)

fetus: an unborn child. (15)

fiber: plant materials that do not break down completely when food is digested. (38)

fibers: hairlike substances twisted together to make yarns and fabric. (29)

financial: relating to money. (14)

first aid course: instruction on basic emergency care for injuries; provided by the Red Cross and other community agencies. (16)

flatware: eating utensils such as knives, forks, and spoons. (52)

food-borne illness: sickness caused by eating spoiled food; often called food poisoning. (47)

Food Guide Pyramid: a simple method of diet planning based on food groups. (39)

frying: cooking in fat. (46)

functional furniture: furniture that is useful as well as decorative. (25)

furniture joints: points at which any two furniture parts connect, such as a leg to the seat of chair. (25)

fusible interfacing: interfacing with an adhesive coating that bonds to the fabric when pressed with a hot iron. (32)

G

generic name: the common name for a group of similar fibers. (29)

germ: the sprouting section of the grain kernel. (51)

goal: something you plan to be, do, or have, and for which you are willing to work. (2)

grade: to cut seams in layers to reduce bulk. (35)

graffiti: unwanted drawings and writing on walls and other property. (6)

grain: the direction in which yarns run in fabric. (32)

grooming: what you do to make yourself both neat and attractive. (27)

group dating: going places and doing things with a group of both males and females. (11)

growth spurt: a time when your body makes a rapid increase in height. (4)

H

harmony: the feeling that all parts of a design belong together. (24)

hazard: source of danger. (26)

health: the total state of your physical, mental, emotional, and social well-being. (37)

heredity: the qualities and traits passed along from parents to children through the genes. (1)

homogenized: processed to break up the fat particles in milk so they won't separate out. (48)

hormones: chemical substances in your body. (4)

human resources: resources that have to do with people. (1)

hygiene: cleanliness. (27)

I

immersible: capable of being put entirely into water safely. (44)

immunizations: shots to protect against disease. (37)

impulse buying: making unplanned purchases on the spur of the moment. (20)

income: the amount of money that you have coming in. (19)

independence: the ability to take care of yourself. (5)

infancy: the stage of development from birth to one year of age. (15)

interest: on savings — the amount of money the bank pays you for allowing it to use your money; on loans — the money that you pay the lender for the privilege of using credit. (19)

interests: what you like to do. (7)

interfacing: special fabric that gives hidden support and body to a garment. (32)

interpreting: understanding what the speaker actually says and means. (8)

interview: a meeting between a potential employer and a job-seeker. (7)

ironing: the process of moving the iron back and forth over fabric to remove wrinkles. (30)

K

kitchen appliance: a piece of equipment for the kitchen powered by gas or electricity. (44)

kitchen work center: an area of the kitchen designed to fill a particular purpose. (47)

L

landlord: the owner of housing that is rented to someone else. (23)

lapped zipper: zipper style in which a single flap of fabric and one row of stitching show on the outside of the garment after the zipper is sewn into the garment. (36)

layout: a diagram included on the pattern guide sheet that shows how to place the pattern pieces on the fabric. (34)

leader: a person who has influence over a group. (6)

leadership: the ability to lead. (6)

leavening agent: ingredient that causes baked products to rise. (51)

lease: a written rental agreement. (23)

legumes: a class of vegetable that is high in protein, including dry beans, dry peas, and peanuts. (38)

line: the outline of an object or the major lines within it. (24)

luster: shine. (29)

M

maintenance: regular cleaning, repairs and inspections that keep a home in good condition. (26)

management: using your resources to achieve your goals; using what you have to get what you want. (3)

manufactured fibers: fibers made all, or part, by chemicals. (29)

marbling: the small deposits of fat scattered throughout the muscle of meat. (50)

material resources: resources, usually objects, that are not human. (1)

maturity: a process of reaching full development. (5)

meal pattern: the way daily food choices are grouped into meals and snacks. (42)

mediator: someone from outside who helps resolve a conflict. (9)

megadoses: very large amounts, as of a vitamin or mineral supplement. (41)

microwaves: tiny waves of energy produced by a microwave oven to heat or cook food. (44)

modeling: watching and imitating the behavior of others. (5)

modem: a special piece of equipment that connects a computer to a telephone line, linking that computer to other computers. (21)

mortgage: a long-term loan used to buy a home. (23)

multiple-family dwelling: a structure that contains several housing units under one roof. (23)

multiplex: a building similar to a duplex, but with three or more housing units. (23)

multipurpose clothes: clothes suitable for a variety of situations. (28)

myth: an untrue statement that some people believe. (41)

N

nap: brushed surface. (34)

natural fibers: fibers made from plant or animal products. (29)

natural resources: resources which occur in nature. (22)

needs: things that are essential to one's health or well-being. (3)

nonrenewable resources: natural resources that can't replace themselves and, therefore, are limited in supply. (22)

nonverbal communication: communication without words. (8)

notions: the smaller items, such as thread, zippers, and buttons, needed to construct a garment. (31)

nuclear families: families in which two parents share a household with their children. (12)

nurturing: providing love, affection, attention, and encouragement. (17)

nutrient density: a comparison of the nutrients in a food to the number of calories. (38)

nutrients: substances in food that the body must have in order to work properly. (38)

O

obesity: having too much body fat in comparison to the amount of muscle, bone, and other lean tissue. (39)

obligations: things that you must do or have promised to do. (18)

open dating: a date stamped on food packages to help the customer determine the freshness of a product. (43)

organically grown: produced without manufactured chemicals. (41)

P

paraprofessionals: people trained to assist professionals. (7)

parenting: the process of caring for children and helping them grow and develop. (17)

parliamentary procedure: rules used by a leader to keep order while allowing the group to reach a majority decision. (6)

pasteurized: heated to destroy harmful bacteria. (48)

peer pressure: the stress or pressure you feel to do what others your age are doing. (10)

peers: people of similar age. (10)

perishable foods: foods that spoil easily. (43)

personality: a combination of the feelings, character traits, attitudes, and habits that you display to others. (1)

place setting: the arrangement of tableware for each person who will be eating a meal. (52)

plaque: a sticky film of harmful bacteria that forms on the teeth. (27)

poison control centers: a staff of trained people who advise and treat poison victims; often located in a hospital. (16)

potential: the possibility of becoming more than you are right now — all that you can be. (1)

prejudice: an unfair or biased opinion formed without knowing the facts or ignoring the facts. (9)

pre-preparation tasks: tasks that you need to do before you combine ingredients. (47)

preschooler: a child from three to five years of age. (15)

pressing: the process of lifting and lowering the iron onto an area of fabric. (30)

pretreatment: giving special treatment to a garment before laundering it. (30)

prioritize: to rank items according to their importance. (18)

processing: the steps that are taken to prepare and package food for sale. (43)

procrastination: the act of postponing something, or putting it off until later. (18)

produce: fresh fruits and vegetables. (49)

proportion: the way one part of a design relates in size and shape to another part or to the whole. (24)

protein: a nutrient that helps build and repair body tissues. (38)

puberty: the time when boys and girls start to develop the physical characteristics of adult men and women. (4)

R

rapport: harmony or understanding between two people. (8)

recipe: a set of directions used in cooking. (45)

reconstitute: replace water taken out. (48)

recycling: using used, discarded products or scrap or waste materials to make new products. (22)

relationship: a bond between people. (8)

renewable resources: natural resources that can renew, or replace, themselves over time. (22)

resourceful: having the ability to identify and use resources in order to accomplish something or solve a problem. (1)

resource: anything used to help accomplish something. (1)

responding: your reaction, in words and actions, to a communicated message. (8)

rhythm: a feeling of movement caused by repeating one or more elements of design. (24)

role model: someone who, through behavior and attitudes, serves as an example for others. (5)

roles: the parts that people play in life; for example, athlete, student council president, father, or daughter. (5)

routine: taking place regularly. (30)

S

sanitation: the act of keeping your living environment clean and healthy. (26)

scale: the overall size of an object, or its size compared to other objects. (24)

seam allowance: the fabric between the cutting line and the stitching line. (34)

self-concept: the picture you have of yourself and the way you believe others see you. (1)

self-esteem: the way you feel about yourself — the confidence and happiness you have in yourself. (1)

selvage: the finished lengthwise edge of the fabric. (34)

separates: garments that can be combined with one another to make several different outfits. (28)

serger: an overlock sewing machine that stitches, finishes, and trims a seam in one step. (33)

shank: the stem on the bottom of some buttons. (30)

shape: the solid form of an object. (24)

sibling rivalry: competitive feelings between brothers and sisters. (13)

siblings: brothers and sisters. (13)

silhouette: the outline of a garment. (28)

simmering: keeping the temperature of a liquid or mixture just under the boiling point. (46)

single-parent family: a family that has only one parent living in the household. (12)

skills: abilities that come from training and practice. (7)

slipstitch: an almost invisible hand stitch used on a folded edge. (35)

space: the three-dimensional area to be designed. (24)

spouse: a husband or wife. (14)

staystitching: a row of stitching on just one layer of fabric that prevents fabric edges from stretching as you sew. (35)

stereotype: a belief that an entire group of people fit a fixed, common pattern — that they are alike in certain ways. (9)

stress: physical or emotional strain or tension that is caused by changes in your life. (4)

T

tableware: items used to serve and eat a meal, such as dishes, glasses, and flatware. (52)

tapestry needle: a needle with a large eye and a blunt point. (36)

technology: the way in which science and inventions are put to practical use in everyday life. (21)

tenants: people who rent, rather than purchase, their housing. (23)

tension: tightness or looseness of the thread. (33)

texture: the way the surface of an object looks and feels. (24)

time management: planning the use of your time so that you can get the most out of the time you have. (18)

time out: a disciplinary technique in which a misbehaving child is removed from the activity for a short period of time. (17)

toddler: a child from one to three years of age. (15)

tofu: a protein food made from soybeans. (50)

townhomes: houses built in rows and attached at the side walls. (23)

trade name: the manufacturer's name for a specific fiber or fabric. (29)

traffic lanes: the paths people take from one room or area to another. (25)

trim: to cut off extra fabric. (33)

U

understitching: to stitch the seam allowance to the facing to prevent the seam from rolling to the outside. (35)

unit price: the price per ounce, pound, or other unit of measure. (43)

UPC (universal product code): a bar code (or pattern of stripes) that identifies a product and gives the product's price. (21)

upholstery: materials such as fabric, padding, and springs, that are used on covered sections of furniture. (25)

utensils: small kitchen tools. (44)

V

values: the beliefs, ideas, and feelings that are important to you. (2)

vandalism: destruction of property. (6)

vegetarian: one who does not eat meat, fish, or poultry. (41)

verbal communication: communication with spoken words. (8)

view: a garment style that can be made from a particular pattern. (31)

volunteers: people who offer their services free of charge. (6)

W

wants: things that are not essential that make life more enjoyable. (3)

warranty: states that a product will work as it should for a specific time; usually includes the manufacturer's promise to repair or replace the item if the problem was caused by defective parts, materials, or workmanship. (20)

wellness: a way of living based on healthful attitudes and actions. (37)

whipstitch: small diagonal hand stitch. (35)

work simplification: finding the easiest and quickest way to do each job well. (18)

Y/Z

yardage: the amount of fabric needed to sew a garment. (31)

yield: the amount of food or number of servings a recipe makes. (45)

zipper foot: a sewing machine attachment that allows stitching to take place on either side of the zipper. (36)

Credits

Interior Design: Morgan Cain & Associates

Cover Photography: Mark Romine

American Egg Board, 591
American Plywood Association, 260, 288
Arnold & Brown, 61, 78, 452, 474, 560
Art MacDillo's, Gary Skillestad, 505
Jim Ballard, 8
Roger B. Bean, 69, 151, 294
Boatel-Page Division, 260
Uzi Broshi, 437
Burlington Industries, Inc., 330
Angela Burns, 610
Cannon Mills, 329
Todd Carroll, 357
CBI Industries, Inc., 260
Closet Works, 281
H. Wesley Coulter, 163
Howard Davis, 377, 511, 512, 513, 514
Drexel Heritage Furnishings, 262
Laima Druskis, 252, 253, 274, 279, 281, 285, 287, 289, 290, 291, 292, 293
David Falconer, David R. Frazier Photolibrary, 58
Fotosmith, Jeff Smith, 199, 335
David R. Frazier Photolibrary, 103, 130, 183, 237, 312, 325, 336, 580
Ann Garvin, 12, 15, 129, 141, 152, 162, 166, 175, 179, 182, 187, 205, 256, 302, 318, 323, 336, 351, 352, 353, 354, 356, 358, 360, 361, 363, 367, 368, 369, 370, 376, 380, 384, 394, 408, 410, 429, 433, 437, 440, 449, 450, 454, 456, 462, 465, 478, 479, 482, 486, 488, 491, 493, 495, 496, 508, 517, 518, 534, 535, 536, 537, 538, 539, 540, 541, 542, 543, 544, 545, 548, 550, 554, 555, 556, 562, 565, 567, 568, 570, 572, 577, 587, 589, 590, 594, 599, 601, 603, 605, 606, 609, 612, 613, 614
Grand Illusions, 467
Linda K. Henson, 46, 65, 79, 92, 113, 121, 142, 146, 157, 164, 167, 175, 178, 187, 198, 207, 208, 211, 212, 221, 230, 232, 250, 258, 265, 268, 275, 277, 291, 317, 335, 435, 438, 441, 442, 445, 446, 448, 455, 456, 463, 480, 487, 488, 492, 499, 500, 501, 506, 507, 513, 520, 536, 555, 557, 564, 566, 591, 596, 599, 610
Chuck Hofer, 328
Llyn Hunter, 217, 220, 221, 238, 239, 240, 381, 528, 558, 611
Impact Communications, 549
Mike Jenkins, 504
Bob McElwee, 288, 291, 552
Jon McIntosh, 21, 37, 44, 53, 56, 195, 201, 220, 259, 334, 337, 464, 490, 531, 549, 563, 573, 576, 581, 589, 598
Ted Mishima, 100, 101, 366, 370, 583, 591
Monsanto Textiles Co., 324
Morgan Cain & Associates, 48-49, 102, 103, 105, 196-197, 199, 314-315, 316, 335
NASTA Pasta Assn., 597
National Pork Producers Council, 606
North Wind Pictures Archives, 254
Pacific Homes Inc., 256
Pennsylvania House, 278
N. A. Peterson, 339
Brent Phelps, 13, 333, 430, 443, 444, 457, 459, 494, 502, 530, 552, 578, 585
Liz Purcell, 197, 198, 280, 327, 328, 329, 341, 342, 343, 344, 348, 350, 371, 373, 395, 396, 397, 398, 399, 400, 401, 402, 403, 404, 405, 406, 407, 412, 415, 416, 417, 418, 419, 484, 496, 595
Mark Romine, 16, 17, 98, 99, 192, 193, 248, 249, 298, 299, 426, 427
Rubbermaid, 574
Jill Seiler, 28, 38, 50, 62, 72, 82, 86, 94, 106, 110, 114, 119, 122, 126, 130, 134, 138, 144, 148, 154, 160, 168, 176, 180,

184, 188, 200, 202, 214, 219, 224, 228, 234, 244, 260, 263, 265, 267, 268, 270, 276, 277, 282, 294, 302, 308, 311, 316, 320, 325, 330, 341, 344, 354, 361, 362, 364, 370, 372, 373, 374, 377, 378, 382, 385, 386, 387, 388, 390, 391, 392, 396, 399, 400, 401, 403, 404, 405, 408, 412, 413, 414, 415, 417, 418, 420, 421, 422, 433, 438, 450, 460, 469, 470, 474, 484, 492, 496, 507, 508, 512, 513, 514, 521, 522, 529, 532, 536, 546, 557, 560, 563, 568, 578, 582, 592, 606, 612, 614

Simplicity Pattern, 351, 352, 353, 364, 382, 386, 389

Jeff Stoecker, 522

Rick Sullivan, 69, 278, 340, 600, 601, 602

Kevin Syms, David R. Frazier Photolibrary, 32

Texas Highways, 324, 325

Thomasville Furnishings, 269

Ken Trevarthan, 254, 524

Unisys, Inc. 233

Unity Systems, 229

USA Rice Council, 445

USDA, 458, 468, 584

Viking Range Corp., 541

Steve Wertz, 124, 126

Dana C. White, Dana White Productions Inc., 6, 7, 9, 10, 18, 22, 23, 24, 25, 26, 27, 28, 30, 31, 32, 33, 34, 35, 38, 40, 41, 42, 43, 45, 52, 54, 55, 59, 60, 62, 64, 66, 68, 70, 71, 74, 75, 76, 78, 80, 81, 82, 84, 85, 86, 87, 88, 89, 90, 91, 92, 94, 96, 97, 108, 109, 114, 116, 117, 119, 120, 122, 125, 127, 128, 134, 135, 136, 143, 145, 147, 151, 170, 184, 185, 186, 190, 191, 194, 199, 200, 204, 206, 213, 214, 216, 219, 226, 227, 230, 234, 236, 241, 242, 243, 244, 246, 257, 272, 282, 284, 296, 300, 305, 307, 308, 310, 315, 318, 322, 332, 334, 346, 347, 422, 424, 425, 428, 432, 454, 456, 467, 468, 472, 477, 498, 506, 510, 566, 586, 608, 616, 617

Nancy Wood, 102, 103, 104, 105, 106, 110, 111, 137, 138, 164, 165, 166, 172, 173, 177, 454, 470, 484

Duane R. Zehr, 8, 9, 10, 11, 13, 14, 57, 112, 118, 132, 133, 140, 153, 154, 155, 156, 158, 159, 167, 174, 247, 255, 297, 301, 304, 306, 319, 337, 340, 342, 364, 385, 386, 418, 419, 434, 435, 437, 448, 453, 466, 476, 503, 518, 519, 530, 538, 551, 574, 587, 604, 616

Special thanks to the following individuals, schools, businesses, and organizations for their assistance with photographs in this book. **In Peoria, Illinois:** Adams Furniture; Hotel Père Marquette; Peoria Notre Dame High School; Peoria Police Department, Officers Craig W. Ganda, Mike Doyle, and Robin Turner; Woodruff High School. Limestone Community High School, Bartonville, Illinois. Morton High School, Morton, Illinois. **In Chicago, Illinois:** Harlem Avenue Sewing Center; Vogue Fabrics, Evanston, Illinois. **In Denton, Texas:** Albertson's, Denton County Independent Hamburger Company, El Matador Restaurant, Good Samaritan Village, Piggly Wiggly Market. **In Southern California:** Bank of America, Bobi Leonard Interior Design, Berkley Convalescent Hospital, Elizabeth Casillas, Marie Everett, House of Fabrics, H.U.D.D.L.E., Hughes Markets, John Adams Middle School, Conrad Johnson, Kjersti—Cotton Rainbow, Rosemead Asian Youth Center, The Manuel & Charlotte Myers Family, Mt. Olive PreSchool, Martin Minkardo, Sheriff & Associates Architects, Josea Kramer, Windward School, Sandor Rosenfield, Santa Monica Museum of Art, Santa Monica High School, Santa Monica YMCA, The Wesley and Vicki Tanaka Family, Westside Food Bank.

Models and fictional names have been used to portray characters in stories and examples in this text.

Index

E

F

T